H A

D0171660

PANAMA

WILLIAM FRIAR

Puerto Limón

Caribbean Sea

Uatsi

Sixaola

Changuinola

Bocas

Parque Nacional
Bastimentos

Almirante

Parque
Internacional
La Amistad

BOCAS
DEL TORO

Laguna de
Chiriquí

Golfo de los
Mosquitos

COLÓN

Chiriquí Grande

COSTA
RICA

PN
Volcán Barú

Bosque
Protector de
Palo Seco

Parque Nacional
Omar Torrijos H
(El Copé)

Río
Sereno

Volcán

Boquete

El Copé

COCLÉ

CHIRIQUÍ

VERAGUAS

La Concepcion

COMARCA
NGÖBE-BUGLÉ

Santa Fé

Penonomé

1

David

1

Antón

Puerto
Armuelles

Las
Lajas

Tolé

San Francisco

Aguadulce

Bahía de
Parita

PN
Sariga

Bahía de
Charco Azul

Parque Nacional
Golfo de Chiriquí

1

Divisa

Chitré

Golfo de Chiriquí

Santiago

HERRERA

2

Ocú

Las
Minas

Las Tablas

LOS
SANTOS

Isla de
Coiba

Parque
Nacional
Coiba

Refugio de Vida
Silvestre Isla de Cañas

Arenas

Tonosí

Parque Nacional
Cerro Hoya

PACIFIC   OCEAN

PANAMA

Parque Nacional
Portobelo

El Porvenir

Portobelo

Parque Nacional
Chagres

Cartí

COMARCA
KUNA YALA

Lago
Alajuela

Sabanitas

Colón

Lago
Bayano

COMARCA
KUNA DE
MADUGANDÍ

Chepo

Panama Canal

1

PANAMA CITY

PANAMA

COMARCA
KUNA DE
WARGANDÍ

Lago
Gatún

Puerto
Obaldía

PN Altos de
Campana

COMARCA
EMBERÁ

Santa Fé

El Valle
de Antón

Chame

San Carlos

Archipiélago
de las Perlas

San Miguel

La Palma

Isla del
Rey

Río Tuira

Yaziva

El Real de
Santa María

Golfo de Panamá

COMARCA
EMBERÁ

DARIÉN

Parque Nacional Darién

Pocrí

Pedasí

Jaqué

COLOMBIA

Juradó

Cupica

Golfo de
Cupica

0   25 mi

0   25 km

Contents

Discover Panama

A word of warning: Panama is hard to shake. It has incredible natural beauty, a modern infrastructure, good roads, clean water, a booming economy, year-round warm weather, a peaceful atmosphere, a rich history, and excellent health conditions.

Travelers are beginning to discover all the country has to offer. It's not yet overrun with hordes of tourists, unlike some of its neighbors, but people have come to realize that Panama is more than just a canal.

Democracy and prosperity haven't squeezed all the intrigue out of this intriguing country, which has been the plaything of empires for half a millennium. To its boosters, Panama is still "the crossroads of the world"; to jaded locals, "a racket with a flag." To a Panamanian poet, it's the "heart of the universe"; to a spy novelist, "Casablanca without heroes." But there's one thing nobody calls it: boring.

Panama City alone can keep travelers plenty busy. It is by far the most sophisticated and vibrant city in Central America. You can literally see it grow: As I write this, nearly 200 new high-rise buildings are going up in Panama City.

The natural wonders of Panama are just as overwhelming. A quarter of the country is protected wilderness, much of which has never seen a road. Even in Panama's busiest towns, the tropical night air vibrates with the calls of a thousand frogs, and you wake to the songs of hundreds of

brilliant birds. Where else can you find a national park so close to the capital you can pop over to watch wild kinkajous, capybaras, and coatimundis, then be back in time for lunch at a fancy French restaurant?

There's always something new to learn about a country with more biodiversity per square meter than the Amazon, not to mention a diverse mix of indigenous people and immigrants. Panama attracts adventurers and misfits, entrepreneurs and schemers, dreamers and full-on nutcases. If you don't encounter a colorful character during your stay, you aren't getting out enough.

And then there's that famous canal, which is in the middle of a multibillion-dollar expansion program that should make it as much an engineering marvel for the 21st century as it was of the 20th.

There's an old saying that visitors who drink water from the Chagres, the powerful river that feeds the canal, are bound to return. Two things to remember: 1) The Chagres is Panama's primary source of drinking water, and 2) in Panama, it's safe to drink the water.

Planning Your Trip

▶ WHERE TO GO

Panama City

Panama City is by far the most cosmopolitan city in Central America, yet it is rich in history. The heart of this burgeoning metropolis of soaring skyscrapers, sophisticated restaurants, and international banks and businesses is Casco Viejo, a charming and well-preserved neighborhood that dates from the 16th century.

The Panama Canal and Central Isthmus

In addition to seeing and transiting the Panama Canal, visitors can explore the historic townsites and tropical forests of the Pacific side of the canal, as well as the

raptor migration, Panama City

IF YOU HAVE...

- **ONE WEEK:** Visit Panama City, the Panama Canal, and either a nearby Pacific beach or El Valle.

- **TWO WEEKS:** Skip El Valle and nearby beaches and add the western highlands and either Bocas del Toro or an island group in the Golfo de Chiriquí.

- **THREE WEEKS:** Add the Darién or Kuna Yala.

- **FOUR WEEKS:** Add the Azuero Peninsula.

Spanish ruins and tranquil waters of the Caribbean side.

Bocas del Toro

The Bocas archipelago is a bohemian playground of white-sand beaches, big surf, pristine coral reefs, and interesting creatures. The humans are pretty fascinating, too, with a rich mix of diverse peoples that includes indigenous and Afro-Caribbean inhabitants who've called Bocas home for hundreds of years.

Central Panama

The central provinces contain Panama's most accessible highlands and popular beaches. From any of the beaches it's easy to head for the hills and escape the heat in the town of El Valle de Antón, nestled at the bottom of an extinct volcano and known for its waterfalls, square trees, golden frogs, and a popular Sunday crafts market.

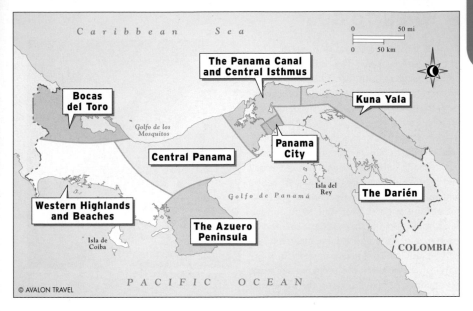

Western Highlands and Beaches

The cool highlands of western Panama are home to the country's highest mountain, Volcán Barú. The dormant volcano's fertile volcanic soil produces gourmet coffee, gorgeous flowers, and delicious oranges and strawberries. But its sprawling protected areas, most notably the gigantic Parque Internacional La Amistad, are what really set the region apart.

The Azuero Peninsula

The Azuero Peninsula, Panama's heartland, is the most culturally rich region of the country, with Spanish colonial towns that time has forgotten. The Azuero, known for its festivals, hosts the country's most important Carnaval celebration. The peninsula also has a ribbon of barely visited beaches that offer good surfing, snorkeling, and fishing.

Kuna Yala

Only about 40 of the nearly 400 islands in Kuna Yala, commonly known as the San Blas Archipelago, are inhabited. On these live the Kuna, the most fascinating and intact indigenous culture in the Americas. The uninhabited islands are palm-covered paradises of white sand and clear blue water straight out of *Robinson Crusoe*.

The Darién

The legendary Darién jungle has long attracted adventurers. Parque Nacional Darién is one of the largest and most vital tropical forests in the western hemisphere. The forested coast offers a completely different experience, including astonishingly abundant sea life just offshore. The Darién is also home to three nations of indigenous people who cling to the rugged ways of life they've sustained for centuries.

▶ WHEN TO GO

Panama has two seasons, rainy and dry. The dry season lasts mid-December–mid-April and is Panama's "summer." This is the high season for tourism. The weather can be especially lovely at the beginning of the dry season.

The rainy season lasts mid-April–mid-December. During most of the rainy season, storms pass through quickly, leaving much of the day and evening clear. Storms tend to start earlier and last longer in the final months of the rainy season; this is not a great time to go on long hikes or drive on rough roads, as the countryside turns to mud and routes can be impassable.

The rain never stops completely in some parts of the country. Be prepared for some precipitation year-round along the Caribbean coast, in the western highlands, and on the islands of Bocas del Toro. September–October and February–March are the driest times in Bocas. Late February–March is considered the best time to visit the islands of Kuna Yala.

Temperatures in Panama don't change much during the year. In the lowlands, expect a high of about 32°C (90°F) in the day, down to 21°C (70°F) in the evening. It never gets cold in the lowlands, and the dry-season

red-legged honeycreeper at the Coffee Estate Inn, Boquete

breezes in the evening are pleasant. It gets considerably cooler in the highlands. Panama can be quite humid year-round, but especially so in the rainy season.

Panama's biggest holiday is Carnaval, held each year in the four days leading up to Ash Wednesday. The country comes to a complete halt during those days. November is filled with fiestas patrias (national-independence holidays).

▶ BEFORE YOU GO

Passports, Tourist Cards, and Visas

Citizens of the United States, Canada, most of western Europe, much of Latin America, and a few other countries do not need a visa to enter Panama, but their passport must be valid for at least six months beyond their date of entry. Tourists from these countries are normally allowed to stay in Panama for up to 90 days. Nationals of other countries must apply for a stamped visa or authorized visa, which

birders at Canopy Lodge, El Valle

Eclypse de Mar Acqua Lodge, Bocas del Toro

are available through a Panamanian consulate or embassy.

Vaccinations

All visitors should make sure their routine immunizations are up to date. The CDC (Centers for Disease Control, www.cdc.gov/travel) recommends that travelers to Central America be vaccinated against hepatitis A and, in some cases, hepatitis B. A typhoid fever vaccination is also recommended, though the chance of contracting the disease in Panama is slim. A rabies vaccination is recommended for those who expect to spend a lot of time outdoors, particularly in rural areas.

Those planning to travel to rural parts of Panama should probably be vaccinated against yellow fever and may want to consider antimalarial medication. Yellow-fever vaccinations are recommended, but no longer required, for those arriving in Panama from a country where yellow fever is endemic. This includes much of South America.

Getting There and Around

Panama's main international airport is the newly renovated Tocumen International Airport, about 25 kilometers from downtown Panama City. Rental cars are available at the airport, but only those planning road

trips outside Panama City should consider this option. The better way to get to Panama City from the airport is by taxi or bus.

Those traveling on to other major destinations within Panama can fly out of Albrook Airport, just a few kilometers from Panama City. Long-distance regional buses are also available at the Gran Terminal de Transportes in Panama City.

Bocas del Toro has great beaches and surf breaks.

Explore Panama

▶ THE 14-DAY BEST OF PANAMA

Two weeks is just about enough time to see the highlights of Panama, including the Panama Canal, Panama City, the western highlands and both Pacific and Atlantic tropical beaches.

To truly touch on every part of Panama worth visiting, including the Caribbean forts, the Darién, and the Azuero Peninsula, requires at least three weeks, and even then only if one has the cash and inclination to do a fair amount of flying. Four weeks is a more reasonable estimate.

Day 1
Arrive at Tocumen International Airport and transfer to a hotel in Panama City.

Day 2
Visit the ruins of Panamá la Vieja, go for a walking tour of Casco Viejo, and have dinner in one of Panama City's elegant international restaurants.

Day 3
Begin your visit to the Panama Canal by exploring the townsites of Balboa and Ancón, where a hint of the well-ordered life of the former Canal Zone lives on. Tour Miraflores Locks, perhaps stopping for lunch on the balcony of the visitors center, where one can watch ships transit while dining. Be sure to pass by the impressive Gaillard Cut, where canal builders cleaved the mountains of the Continental Divide in two. Make at least a brief stop to see the wildlife at Gamboa and Parque Nacional Soberanía, a true tropical rainforest just a short drive from downtown Panama City. End the day with a ramble along the Amador Causeway, a good place to stop for a drink as the Panama City skyline lights up across the bay.

Days 4-7
Fly off for a few days of Caribbean sun and sea. Choose between one of two stunning tropical archipelagos: the booming bohemia of Bocas del Toro or the more rustic but culturally fascinating attractions of Kuna Yala; those with a few more days can visit both. The best way to explore Kuna Yala is from the deck of a hired yacht; those on a

Miraflores Locks

THE PANAMA CANAL IN A DAY (OR TWO)

Panama Canal's Gaillard Cut

Some save for years to afford a Panama Canal cruise. But those already in Panama can make a day transit of the canal for a tiny fraction of what the luxury liners charge. Two companies on the Pacific-side of the isthmus offer passenger service. (The adventurous, especially those short of cash, can sometimes get a free transit by working as a line-handler on a yacht.)

From January to March, day transits are offered only on Thursday, Friday, and Saturday. They're offered only on Saturday the rest of the year. Most are partial transits, although even these take nearly a full day. Plan accordingly. The partial transit takes 4–5 hours and costs US$115 for adults, US$60-65 for children, including transfers. Full transits are offered one Saturday a month (US$165 for adults, US$75 for children).

One of the companies also offers a partial Friday-night transit, which gives a very different perspective on the canal. The locks are brightly lit by high-mast lighting, turning night into day.

Nearly as storied as the Panama Canal is the Panama Railroad, which ferried Forty-Niners across the isthmus during the California gold rush. Its descendent is the **Panama Railway,** which offers passengers an incredibly scenic early-morning ride from the Pacific to the Atlantic along the banks of the canal. The coast-to-coast ride lasts only an hour, but creates memories that will last a lifetime.

Once on the Caribbean side, you can hire a taxi to explore the Spanish ruins. **Portobelo** and **Fuerte San Lorenzo** transport visitors back to the days of pirates and conquistadors, and the mile-long **Gatún Locks** bring them back to the high-tech present. If time allows, squeeze in a wildlife-viewing tour, by boat or kayak, down the lower reaches of the **Río Chagres,** a storied river where one can spot the occasional caiman or crocodile. Finish up in time to catch the train back to Panama City, or take one of the frequent buses.

PANAMA HISTORY 101

If you're fascinated by Panama's role as a crossroads of the world, you can cover 500 years of history in less than a week. Concentrating on the human efforts to conquer the isthmus by trail, railway, and canal, most sights are within 100 kilometers from the capital, making this an especially economical and speedy introduction to the country.

- **Colonial Panama City:** Panamá la Vieja, Casco Viejo, Avenida Central, and Plaza Santa Ana.

- **Conquistadors, Pirates, and Forty-Niners:** Portobelo, Fuerte San Lorenzo, Río Chagres, and the Camino de Cruces.

- **The Path Between the Seas:** Miraflores Locks, Gaillard Cut, Panama Railway, Ancón, and Balboa.

limited budget can stay in simple Kuna hotels and get around by motorboat. This is a place for snorkeling off remote cays, walks through traditional island villages, and forest hikes to powerful waterfalls and sacred cemeteries on the mainland.

Days 8-10

Head for the highlands of western Panama. Visit the garden town of Boquete, famous throughout Panama for its flowers, oranges, and rainbows. Go on a hike up Panama's tallest peak, Volcan Barú, or just admire it from a distance.

Days 11-12

To see how the Pacific side of the isthmus compares with the Caribbean, head back down the mountain to the Golfo de Chiriquí. The area around the fishing village of Boca Brava is a gateway to the islands of two national parks, Parque Nacional Marino Golfo de Chiriquí and Parque Nacional Coiba, which offer world-class diving. Cool little hotels for every budget are springing up around Boca Brava.

Day 13

Head back to Panama City by land or air for last-minute shopping, sightseeing, and a farewell dinner.

Day 14

Transfer to Tocumen International Airport for the flight home.

kayaking in Bocas del Toro

▶ PANAMA'S MILD WILD SIDE

Some are drawn to Panama's rich wildlife but would rather see it from a safe, comfortable distance. It's quite possible for travelers to get a taste of nature without the worry that nature will try to get a taste of them. This itinerary is suitable for families, including those with small children.

Day 1

Arrive at Tocumen International Airport and transfer to a hotel in Panama City or in the less-hectic former Canal Zone. The Gamboa Rainforest Resort and InterContinental Playa Bonita Resort and Spa are particularly promising possibilities for families.

Day 2

Spend the morning visiting Casco Viejo and the ruins of Panamá la Vieja. After lunch, head over to the breezy Amador Causeway, with its great views of the canal entrance and Panama City skyline, and explore the aquariums at the Smithsonian's Centro de Exhibiciones Marinas. Have dinner in one of the causeway's open-air restaurants.

Day 3

Take a tour of Miraflores Locks and its museum, then head to Gamboa for a ride up the Gamboa Rainforest Resort's aerial tram through tropical forest. Visit the flora and fauna exhibits: Be sure not to miss the serpentarium and the butterfly pavilion. Another option is a boat trip on Lago Gatún to visit the islands of a primate sanctuary that is home to five species of monkeys. Keep an eye out for caimans and the occasional crocodile. Have lunch at the resort's lakeside Restaurante Los Lagartos, where there's an excellent chance of spotting freshwater

three-toed sloth and baby

PANAMA FOR THE BIRDS

Panama doesn't just attract bird-watchers: It creates them.

It's smaller than South Carolina, but has more bird species than the United States and Canada put together. That means beautiful birds are everywhere all the time, and impossible to ignore. There's always something singing, crying, croaking, flitting, flapping, or soaring overhead. More than likely it's something you've never seen before, flashing colors you thought only existed in a box of Crayolas.

Birders have counted 972 species in Panama so far. Migrants visit from North and South America, and more than 100 species are endemic. Twelve are found nowhere else on earth. Hundreds of species are easy to find without much effort.

Important areas for endemics are the **Caribbean and Pacific lowlands and islands,** the **Darién,** and, especially the **western highlands,** the last of which also happen to be among the most accessible, lovely, and comfortable areas for visitors.

Panama offers good birding year-round, though the isthmus is hopping September–April, as that's when North American migrants (avian and human) arrive to escape the cold. A special event during this time is the spectacular raptor migration of millions of **broadwinged hawks, Swainson's hawks,** and **turkey vultures,** which takes place October–mid-November and March–early April. They pass overhead in flocks that can number in the many thousands. The former Canal Zone is the best place to witness this extraordinary phenomenon. June and July are the toughest times to spot birds.

Long-established lodges and inns are dotted around the top birding areas, with knowledgeable owners who can supply expert naturalist guides and detailed birding information. Some of these are world famous, ranging from the upscale Canopy Tower (in the former **Canal Zone,** close to Panama City) to the rustic lodge at Cana (on the remote **Cerro Pirre,** in the Darién), which has been called one of the world's top-10 birding destinations.

Many lodges are simply great places to stay, even for those with no interest in anything with wings. They are listed throughout this guidebook, as are recommended naturalist guides and birding areas. For detailed birding itineraries and tips, the up-to-date *A Bird-Finding Guide to Panama,* by George R. Angehr, Dodge Engleman, and Lorna Engleman, is an indispensable resource. The classic *A Guide to the Birds of Panama,* by Robert S. Ridgely and John A. Gwynne, is an encyclopedic, beautifully illustrated list of species found in Panama.

The resplendent quetzal has been called the world's most beautiful bird.

green iguana at the Portobelo Ruins

boat trip down the lower Río Chagres, which ends right below the fort at San Lorenzo. Take the train back to Panama City.

Days 5-6

Transfer to one of the resorts or smaller hotels at Coronado, Farallón, or Santa Clara. Spend a couple of days playing in the surf and splashing in the pool. It's generally easy to arrange other activities, from horseback rides on the beach to banana-boat rides in the ocean.

Days 7-8

Transfer to El Valle de Antón for cooler weather and a taste of the highland forests of Panama. Those feeling brave can consider the Canopy Adventure zipline tour. Other possibilities include horseback riding, a visit to a spooky serpentarium, a walk through a small zoo with golden frogs and other exotic creatures, easy bike rides, walks to petroglyphs and waterfalls, and shopping at a bustling crafts market.

Day 9

Return to Panama City for shopping and additional sightseeing.

Day 10

Transfer to Tocumen International Airport for the trip home.

turtles as well as caimans. Stop by Summit Botanical Gardens and Zoo on the way back to Panama City. The highlight will probably be the harpy eagle exhibit.

Day 4

Book a tour that includes an early-morning train across the isthmus and a car trip to explore the Spanish ruins of Portobelo and Fuerte San Lorenzo. Stop by the mile-long Gatún Locks and, if possible, take a jungle

▶ OCEAN TO OCEAN ON FOOT

The ultimate Panama destination for hardcore outdoor adventurers is the Darién, and the ultimate Darién adventure is a trek through the jungle between the Atlantic and Pacific oceans. But Trans-Darién expeditions are grueling, expensive, and not always available, depending on the security situation near the Colombian border.

But there is a safer, easier and far cheaper way to hike from (close to) the Pacific Ocean to the Atlantic. This suggested itinerary crosses the isthmus on the west side of the Darién. Note that this itinerary is intended only for the highly energetic and fit.

For those who truly want to immerse themselves in the Darién, Ancon Expeditions offers an intense two-week trek that takes in the rivers, rainforests, and highlands of

GO GREEN

Although all tourism affects the environment, it's getting easier to travel around Panama in reasonable comfort and with a moderately clear conscience. Here are some tips for those who want to stray from the beaten path without beating down a new one.

VISIT THE AZUERO PENINSULA

The Azuero Peninsula sees relatively few foreign visitors and was deforested generations ago. It's unlikely visiting will do much harm, and it's a way to get to know what Panamanians consider the "real" Panama.

VOLUNTEER

It's increasingly easy for foreigners to volunteer with community and environmental projects in Panama. Hostels and language schools can often arrange volunteer work, sometimes offering discounts as incentives. Local non-profits and eco-lodges also sometimes accept volunteers. All these are listed throughout the book.

THINK SMALL

Every day seems to bring a new luxury hotel tower or beach mega-resort to the isthmus. But every time I tour the country, what impresses me most are the little places, many of which add more to their natural surroundings and local community than they take. For the first time, it's possible to go from one end of Panama to the other and stay only at these charming little places, with hosts that go out of their way to make you feel at home.

- **Azuero Peninsula:** Casa de Campo Pedasí
- **Bocas del Toro:** Al Natural Resort, Bluff Beach Lodge, Eclypse de Mar, La Coralina, La Loma Jungle Lodge, Soposo Rainforest Adventures, Tesoro Escondido
- **Boquete:** La Montaña y El Valle, The Coffee Estate Inn, Tinamou Cottage
- **Cerro Punta and Vicinity:** Hostal Cielito Sur Bed and Breakfast
- **El Valle:** Park Eden
- **Former Canal Zone:** Dos Palmitos
- **Fortuna Road:** Finca la Suiza, Lost and Found Eco-Resort
- **Pacific Beaches:** Tógo B&B
- **Playa Santa Catalina:** La Buena Vida
- **Santa Fé:** Hostal La Qhia

the region. Custom-designed trips are also possible.

Day 1

Arrive at Tocumen International Airport and transfer to a hotel in Panama City.

Day 2

Transfer in the early morning to the Bayano area. If time allows, take a boat across Lago Bayano, a large artificial lake, to explore the caves on the far side. This will probably only be possible if the tour includes transportation up to Burbayar. Otherwise, begin hiking up to the Continental Divide from El Llano. Spend the night in Burbayar Lodge, in lush tropical forest about 15 kilometers north of the Interamerican Highway.

Day 3

Explore the forest around Burbayar, then head over the Continental Divide, through Kuna territory, toward the ramshackle coastal town of Cartí on the Caribbean coast, 22 kilometers from Burbayar. Camp in the forest.

Days 4-5

Arrive in Cartí early in the morning and hire a boat to one of the nearby inhabited islands. Snorkel around the crystal-clear waters of Achutupu, an uninhabited islet with its own little shipwreck. Spend a night or two in a rustic Kuna hotel.

Day 6
Fly back to Panama City. Spend the day sightseeing and resting.

Day 7
Transfer to Tocumen International Airport for the flight home.

Plaza de la Independencia, Panama City

► BOCAS, BOQUETE, AND THE BIG DITCH

Time-pressed travelers will be forced to focus on the "must-see" destinations, which for most people means the Panama Canal, the Caribbean islands of Bocas del Toro, and the cool highlands of Boquete. It's possible to visit all three in about 10 days, but that leaves little time for lazing, and lazing is a top draw of the highlands and islands. Decide if you're more of a mountain or a beach person and, if possible, consider adding an extra day or two there. Those with only a week should cut out either Bocas or Boquete.

Day 1
Arrive at Tocumen International Airport and transfer to a hotel in Panama City or the former Canal Zone.

Days 2-3
Tour the canal, spending enough time at Miraflores Locks to see a transit or two and explore the visitors center. Cross the canal at the Puente Centenario (Centennial Bridge) for views of Gaillard Cut. If time

Boquete is known for its rainbows, flowers, and coffee.

EMBERÁ-WOUNAAN ART

The Emberá-Wounaan of the Darién are renowned for their artistic abilities. This is especially true of the Wounaan, who are generally thought to produce the finest works. Three crafts are popular with travelers, and are a major source of income for the Emberá-Wounaan. These can be bought directly from their makers in the **Darién** or one of the villages up the **Río Chagres** close to the canal. But some of the best examples can be found at the handicrafts market near the YMCA in the townsite of **Balboa.**

DECORATIVE BASKETS

A variety of baskets are painstakingly crafted from the fine leaf fibers of the *chunga* (black palm). Traditional baskets are plain or contain black-and-white geometrical patterns. But brightly colored ones depicting detailed scenes of butterflies, macaws, and forest animals have become popular, and the artisans are always experimenting with new ideas. The most sought-after baskets use natural dyes for the vivid colors.

The finest baskets are so tightly woven it's been said they can hold water, although there's no indication the baskets were ever actually used for that purpose. You won't want to spoil yours by testing the theory.

CARVED TAGUA NUTS

The tagua nut, also known as "ivory nut" or "vegetable ivory," is the seed of a variety of palm tree that grows throughout the tropics. The Emberá-Wounaan learned to carve beautiful and delicate miniature sculptures of forest animals out of the nut, depicting everything from ants to jaguars. These can be remarkably detailed and lifelike. They are made by the men, who primarily use the particularly hard nut of *Phytelephas seemannii,* often leaving the bottom half of the nut intact as a base. Because a good crop of tagua nuts requires healthy tagua trees, this is a particularly sustainable, environmentally friendly source of income for the Emberá-Wounaan.

COCOBOLO STATUES

Cocobolo (*Dalbergia retusa*) is a kind of rosewood that Emberá-Wounaan men carve into sculptures. As with the tagua nuts, these usually depict forest animals. When polished, the wood is a deep, lustrous red.

allows, visit the former Canal Zone townsites of Balboa and Balboa Heights. Try to squeeze in visits to Panamá la Vieja and Casco Viejo to get a sense of Panama City's rich, colorful history. Stay on for dinner in Casco Viejo.

Days 4-5 or 6

Transfer to Boquete. Explore the town, hike or bird-watch along Sendero Los Quetzales, take a coffee tour, go river rafting, or just enjoy the gardens and the changing face of Volcan Barú throughout the day. The truly fit can plan a night ascent of Barú, arriving in time to catch the dawn and a view of both oceans.

Days 6 or 7-8

Transfer to Bocas. Take a boat tour around Isla Colón and snorkel the clear waters of Cayo Crawl or Cayos Zapatillas. Surf, splash, or lounge around Playa Bluff or the north-shore beaches of Isla Bastimentos. Enjoy the nightlife of Bocas town or simply a tropical evening breeze blowing across the sea.

Day 9

Transfer to Panama City and see any remaining sights or do some last-minute shopping.

Day 10

Transfer to Tocumen International Airport for the trip home.

PANAMA CITY

Panama City surprises newcomers. It is by far the most cosmopolitan city in Central America, which becomes obvious as soon as one sees its densely packed towers. But its vibrant modernity really shouldn't be surprising, given the capital's status as an international banking center and its location next to the Pacific entrance of the Panama Canal, the "crossroads of the world." Panama City has been important to world commerce since its founding nearly 500 years ago.

It's also an international city. The shops of Indian and Chinese merchants have been city institutions for generations. Any given day might find Colombian émigrés having a drink in a British pub, Japanese businesspeople making a deal in an Argentine steakhouse, and North American retirees looking for their place in the tropical sun.

The city's rich diversity can be seen in its houses of worship: Along with its Roman Catholic churches are synagogues, mosques, one of the world's seven Baha'i Houses of Worship, the Greek Orthodox Metropolitanate of Central America, a prominent Hindu temple, and gathering houses for every conceivable Protestant congregation.

The one faith that draws all these people together is business. Deals are being made everywhere at all times, from kids hawking cellphone accessories at congested intersections to developers determined to build on every square centimeter of open space. Life is fast-paced compared with the rest of Panama, and the city's residents are comparatively assertive, street-savvy, and no-nonsense. Panama City is to, say, the Azuero Peninsula as New York

© WILLIAM FRIAR

HIGHLIGHTS

◖ Panamá la Vieja: Founded nearly 500 years ago, this original Panama City was the first Spanish city on the Pacific coast of the Americas. Its stone ruins transport you back to the time of gold-hungry conquistadors and pillaging buccaneers (page 30).

◖ Casco Viejo: This charming colonial neighborhood is the cornerstone of modern Panama City. It was founded in 1673 after the sacking of Panamá la Vieja, and an ambitious renovation project has brought restaurants, theaters, and clubs to its historic buildings, sidewalk cafés to its quaint plazas, and new life to its crumbling churches. It's the most colorful part of Panama City (page 31).

◖ Avenida Central: The walking street that extends from Plaza Cinco de Mayo to Parque Santa Ana is one of the most vibrant parts of town. A bustling commercial center that draws a cross-section of Panamanian society, it takes visitors back to an older Panama City that is still very much alive (page 40).

◖ Parque Natural Metropolitano: More than a city park, this 265-hectare tropical forest within the city limits offers a glimpse of Panama's flora and fauna for those who can't make it to the country's enormous national parks (page 46).

◖ Bella Vista and Marbella: Panama City's most dynamic nightlife destination lies along Calle Uruguay, where trendy new restaurants and clubs open and close constantly (page 52).

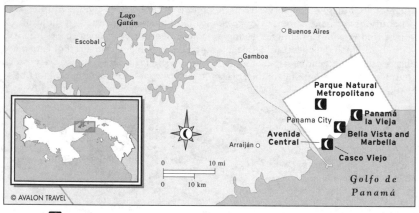

LOOK FOR ◖ TO FIND RECOMMENDED SIGHTS, ACTIVITIES, DINING, AND LODGING.

City is to rural Nebraska. Everyone on the road is in a great hurry, and skyscrapers pop up overnight.

Still, by the standards of many other countries' capitals, Panama City is a mellow, fun-loving place. Any excuse for a party will do, and big celebrations, especially Carnaval, shut down the whole city.

Those who come to Panama solely for its natural treasures will be tempted to blast right through the capital on their way to the country's forests, mountains, islands, and beaches. But it'd be a shame not to spend some time in the capital. Hundreds of years of history live on in its streets, and its more modern attractions are especially appealing after roughing it in the wilderness for a while. Besides, it has its very own tropical forest. Even city streets aren't far removed from nature; an entire book has been written on the birds of Panama City.

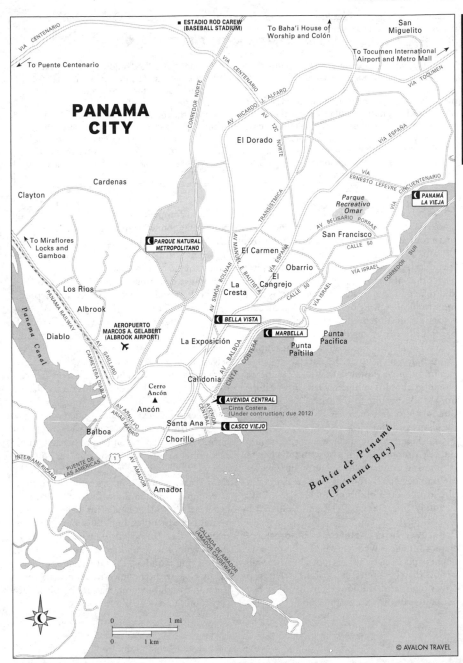

PANAMA CITY

■ ESTADIO ROD CAREW (BASEBALL STADIUM)
To Baha'i House of Worship and Colón
San Miguelito
To Tocumen International Airport and Metro Mall

VÍA CENTENARIO
To Puente Centenario
VÍA CENTENARIO
VÍA TOCUMEN

CORREDOR NORTE
AV. RICARDO J. ALFARO
AV. 12C NORTE
El Dorado
VÍA ESPAÑA

Cardenas
VÍA ERNESTO LEFEVRE CINCUENTENARIO
Clayton
🌙 PANAMÁ LA VIEJA

Parque Recreativo Omar

To Miraflores Locks and Gamboa
🌙 PARQUE NATURAL METROPOLITANO
AV. BELISARIO PORRAS
San Francisco
CALLE 50

TRANSÍSTMICA
El Carmen
VÍA ESPAÑA
Obarrio

Los Ríos
AV. SIMÓN BOLÍVAR
AV. MANUEL E. BAUTISTA
La Cresta
El Cangrejo
CALLE 50
VÍA ISRAEL
CORREDOR SUR

Albrook
🌙 BELLA VISTA

AEROPUERTO MARCOS A. GELABERT (ALBROOK AIRPORT) ✈
La Exposición
🌙 MARBELLA
Punta Pacífica

Diablo
PANAMA RAILWAY
CARRETERA DIABLO
AV. GALLARD
AV. BALBOA
CINTA COSTERA
Punta Paitilla

Panama Canal

Cerro Ancón ▲
Calidonia
AVENIDA CENTRAL
🌙 AVENIDA CENTRAL
Ancón
Cinta Costera (Under contruction; due 2012)

Balboa
AV. ARNULFO ARIAS MADRID
Santa Ana
🌙 CASCO VIEJO
Chorillo

INTER-AMERICANA
PUENTE DE LAS AMÉRICAS
1
AV. AMADOR

Amador

Bahía de Panamá (Panama Bay)

CALZADA DE AMADOR (AMADOR CAUSEWAY)

0   1 mi
0   1 km

© AVALON TRAVEL

"PANAMA": AN ABUNDANCE OF THEORIES

The country of Panama gets its name from the city of Panama, but what does "Panama" mean? No one knows for sure.

The Spanish first used the name in conjunction with a native fishing village they soon claimed as the cornerstone of their new capital. It's little wonder, then, that the most common explanation is that Panama (or, to be proper, Panamá) is a forgotten indigenous word for "abundance of fishes." Another theory is that the word means "abundance of butterflies." Yet another posits that the striking (and abundant) Panama tree lent its name to the city and then the republic. Some say the word just meant "abundance," hence the odd variety of plentiful things associated with it. A personal favorite is that it means "to rock in a hammock." Take your pick: All definitions still fit.

PLANNING YOUR TIME

Those in a big hurry can see Panama City's main tourist attractions, from Casco Viejo to Panamá la Vieja, in a single day. But try to spend at least a couple of days in the capital. That's the only way to get a sense of its rhythms and to experience its less-showy charms: feeling a tropical evening breeze at a sidewalk café, splurging on dinner at an elegant restaurant, bargaining for *molas* (handcrafted blouses) with a Kuna, dancing at an all-night club, or just people-watching on the streets.

The ruins of **Panamá la Vieja** can be explored in about two hours. Plan on a half day for a walking tour of the historic quarter of **Casco Viejo** that includes visits to its major museums and churches.

Consider spending a day wandering around the city's more colorful **shopping districts.** If time and budget allow, plan on at least one evening out on the town. Good areas to combine dinner and clubbing include the **Calle Uruguay** area, **Casco Viejo,** and **Calle 53 in Marbella.**

Parque Natural Metropolitano offers a chance for those who can't make it to the national parks to enjoy a true tropical nature walk within the city limits. It's a short drive from downtown, and the longest trail takes two hours to walk.

Those compelled to see and do it all should count on about four full days in Panama City, after which they'll be ready for a rest. Most, however, will be content to hit the highlights over the course of two or three days.

Because downtown Panama City is so close to the Panama Canal, many visitors prefer to extend their stay in the city and make day trips to explore the canal area rather than shift their home base to lodging in the former Canal Zone. (Some do just the opposite—base themselves in a canal-area hotel and explore Panama City from there.) In that case, plan on an extra day or two to see the major sights on the Pacific side of the canal, and at least another day or two to explore the Caribbean side.

The climate in Panama City is hot and humid in the dry season (approximately mid-December to mid-April) and hot, very humid, and wet in the rainy season. But for most of the rainy season storms don't sweep in until mid-afternoon and generally come down in short, powerful bursts that race on as quickly as they arrive. Because of the high ratio of concrete to trees, midday can be wiltingly hot. Explore in the early mornings and reserve the afternoons for relaxing. Sunday is by far the quietest time in the city, with the fewest cars on the road. Keep in mind, however, that many places are closed on Sunday.

Sights

ORIENTATION

Panama City is a growing metropolis of 813,000 people, or more than 1.2 million if you include the greater metropolitan area. All of them seem to be on the road 24 hours a day. Streets and public transportation have not kept pace with the city's growth, and the roads are choked during morning and evening rush hours. In recent years the city has grown east toward Tocumen International Airport, and with the city's absorption of the former U.S. Canal Zone, urban sprawl has been creeping north and west as well.

Note that Panamanians typically drop the "city" when referring to the capital and just call it "Panama." As with the country, the accent is on the last syllable—Panamá (pah-nah-MA)—when speaking Spanish. Formally, it's La Ciudad de Panamá.

The city is bounded by the Bahía de Panamá (Panama Bay) and the Pacific Ocean to the south and the Panama Canal to the west. The terrain is fairly flat—the United States dug the canal nearby because the Continental Divide is particularly low-lying here—though a few isolated hills, most notably Cerro Ancón, jut up near the canal's Pacific entrance.

The section of the city of most interest to visitors runs along the coast from Casco Viejo, the cornerstone of modern Panama City, east to the ruins of Panamá la Vieja, eight kilometers away. Most of the cosmopolitan parts of the capital lie between these two boundaries.

An exception to this rule is **Costa del Este,** a new city within (or, more accurately, on the outskirts of) Panama City. It's a rapidly growing mini-metropolis of upscale homes and condos whose skyline is beginning to rival downtown's in its concentration of skyscrapers. It's a new frontier for privileged Panamanians escaping the city's congestion and noise and for international jet-setters adding to their portfolio of vacation homes. But it doesn't yet hold enough interest to the average visitor to justify making the long trip from the center of the city.

Getting one's bearings can be tricky in Panama City, given its confusing mass of winding streets and its topsy-turvy geography (some never get used to seeing the Pacific Ocean lying to the south, for instance).

The city is organized into a series of loosely defined neighborhoods. The only ones most travelers will be concerned with are **Punta Pacífica, Punta Paitilla, Marbella, Bella Vista, El Cangrejo, Calidonia/La Exposición, Santa Ana,** and **San Felipe/Casco Viejo.** There are also a few places of note a bit farther east, in **Obarrio** and **San Francisco.**

Vía España, a busy commercial street, has long been the heart of modern Panama City. In recent years, though, the action has spread just north to El Cangrejo and south to Bella Vista and Marbella. Most of Panama's upscale hotels, restaurants, and shops are in these areas.

An area of about three square blocks between Bella Vista and Marbella, centered on **Calle Uruguay,** is a booming nightlife destination of restaurants and clubs, as is, to a lesser degree, the main strip through Marbella, **Calle 53.**

An older commercial center is found along **Avenida Central** in the Calidonia and the Santa Ana districts. Bordering it is the district of **San Felipe,** which contains the historic neighborhood of **Casco Viejo,** tucked away on a small peninsula.

Avenida de los Mártires, formerly known as **Fourth of July Avenue,** used to mark the boundary between Panama City and the former Canal Zone.

A new major artery is the **Cinta Costera** (Coastal Belt), a multilane highway built on landfill at the edge of Panama Bay. It runs roughly parallel to **Avenida Balboa,** which extends from Casco Viejo to the posh condo towers of Punta Paitilla and Punta Pacífica. The bustling commercial street of **Calle 50** runs between and parallel to Vía España and Avenida Balboa.

North of all of these is the **Transístmica**

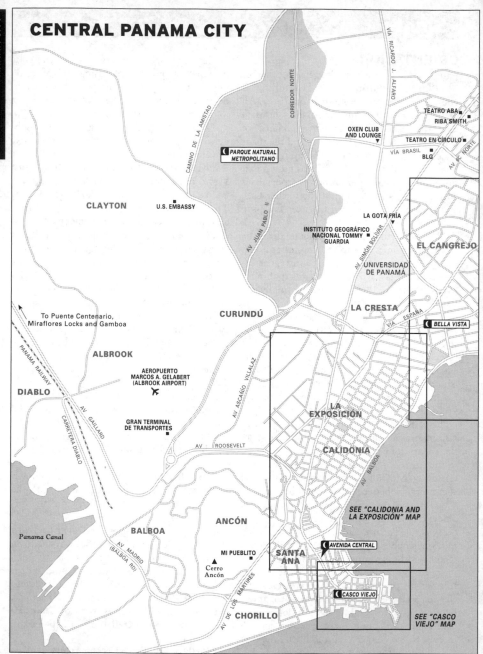

CENTRAL PANAMA CITY

TEATRO ABA ■
RIBA SMITH ■

OXEN CLUB
AND LOUNGE
▼

TEATRO EN CÍRCULO ■

VÍA BRASIL ■
BLG ■

CORREDOR NORTE

VÍA RICARDO J. ALFARO

AV. 6C NORTE

CAMINO DE LA AMISTAD

☾ *PARQUE NATURAL METROPOLITANO*

CLAYTON

U.S. EMBASSY ■

AV. JUAN PABLO II

LA GOTA FRÍA
▼

INSTITUTO GEOGRÁFICO
NACIONAL TOMMY ■
GUARDIA

AV. SIMÓN BOLÍVAR

EL CANGREJO

UNIVERSIDAD
DE PANAMÁ

To Puente Centenario,
Miraflores Locks and Gamboa

CURUNDÚ

LA CRESTA

VÍA ESPAÑA

☾ *BELLA VISTA*

PANAMA RAILWAY

ALBROOK

AV. ASCANIO VILLALAZ

DIABLO

AEROPUERTO
MARCOS A. GELABERT
(ALBROOK AIRPORT)
✈

AV. GAILLARD

CARRETERA DIABLO

GRAN TERMINAL
DE TRANSPORTES ■

AV. ROOSEVELT

LA
EXPOSICIÓN

CALIDONIA

AV. BALBOA

Panama Canal

BALBOA

AV. MADRID
(BALBOA RD)

ANCÓN

MI PUEBLITO ■

▲
Cerro
Ancón

SANTA
ANA

SEE "CALIDONIA AND
LA EXPOSICIÓN" MAP

☾ *AVENIDA CENTRAL*

☾ *CASCO VIEJO*

AV. DE LOS MÁRTIRES

CHORILLO

SEE "CASCO
VIEJO" MAP

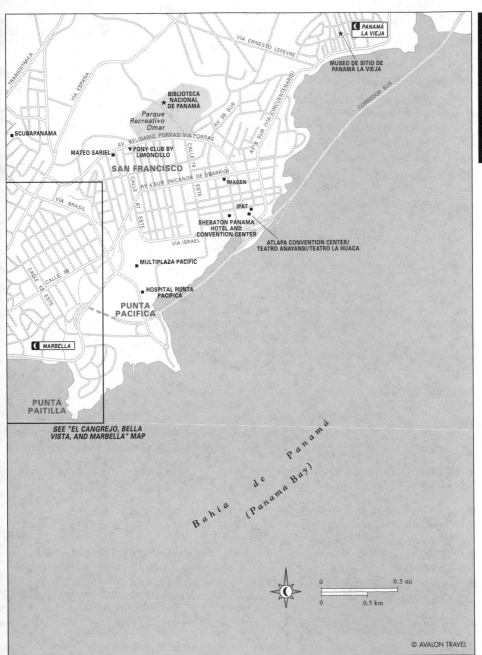

VÍA ERNESTO LEFEVRE

★ PANAMÁ LA VIEJA

MUSEO DE SITIO DE PANAMÁ LA VIEJA

CORREDOR SUR

★ BIBLIOTECA NACIONAL DE PANAMÁ

Parque Recreativo Omar

VÍA ESPAÑA

TRANSÍSTMICA

AV 3B SUR

AV 8 SUR (VÍA CINCUENTENARIO)

■ SCUBAPANAMA

AV. BELISARIO PORRAS/VÍA PORRAS

MATEO SARIEL ■ ▼PONY CLUB BY LIMONCILLO

SAN FRANCISCO

CALLE 74 ESTE

AV 4 SUR (NICANOR DE OBARRIO)

■ IMAGEN

CALLE 67 ESTE

VÍA BRASIL

IPAT ■
● SHERATON PANAMA HOTEL AND CONVENTION CENTER

ATLAPA CONVENTION CENTER/ TEATRO ANAYANSI/TEATRO LA HUACA

VÍA ISRAEL

■ MULTIPLAZA PACIFIC

CALLE 54 ESTE

CALLE 50

■ HOSPITAL PUNTA PACIFICA

PUNTA PACIFICA

◖ MARBELLA

PUNTA PAITILLA

SEE "EL CANGREJO, BELLA VISTA, AND MARBELLA" MAP

B a h í a   d e   P a n a m á
(Panama Bay)

0 _____ 0.5 mi

0 _____ 0.5 km

© AVALON TRAVEL

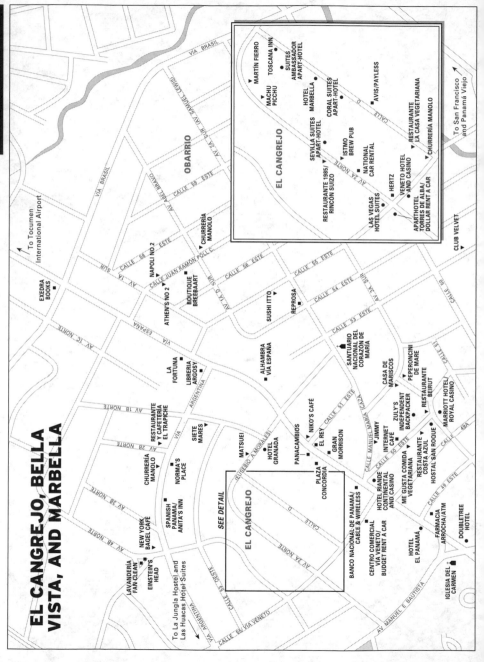

EL CANGREJO, BELLA VISTA, AND MARBELLA

OBARRIO

EL CANGREJO

SEE DETAIL

To Tocumen International Airport

To San Francisco and Panamá Viejo

To La Jungla Hostel and Las Huacas Hotel Suites

CLUB VELVET

MARTÍN FIERRO
TOSCANA INN
SUITES AMBASSADOR APART-HOTEL
MACHU PICCHU
CORAL SUITES APART-HOTEL
HOTEL MARBELLA
AVIS/PAYLESS
RESTAURANTE LA CASA VEGETARIANA
CHURRERÍA MANOLO
SEVILLA SUITES APART-HOTEL
ISTMO BREW PUB
RESTAURANTE 1985/ RINCÓN SUIZO
NATIONAL CAR RENTAL
VENETO HOTEL AND CASINO
HERTZ
LAS VEGAS HOTEL SUITES
APARTHOTEL TORRES DE ALBA/ DOLLAR RENT A CAR

CHURRERÍA MANOLO
NAPOLI NO 2
ATHEN'S NO 2
BOUTIQUE BREEBAART
SUSHI ITTO
REPROSA
EXEDRA BOOKS
LA FORTUNA
LIBRERÍA ARGOSY
ALHAMBRA VÍA ESPAÑA
SANTUARIO NACIONAL DEL CORAZÓN DE MARIA
CHURRERÍA MANOLO
NORMA'S PLACE
SIETE MARES
RESTAURANTE CAFETERÍA EL TRAPICHE
MATSUEI
HOTEL GRANADA
NIKO'S CAFÉ
PANACAMBIOS
EL REY
GRAN MORRISON
CASA DE MARISCOS
PEPERONCINI DE MARE
RESTAURANTE BEIRUT
ZULY'S
JIMMY
INDEPENDENT BACKPACKER
MARRIOTT HOTEL ROYAL CASINO
SPANISH PANAMA/ ANITA'S INN
NEW YORK BAGEL CAFÉ
EINSTEIN'S HEAD
LAVANDERÍA FAN CLEAN
PLAZA CONCORDIA
HOTEL RIANDE CONTINENTAL AND CASINO
INTERNET CAFÉ
ME GUSTA COMIDA VEGETARIANA
RESTAURANTE COSTA AZUL
HOSTAL SAN ROQUE
BANCO NACIONAL DE PANAMÁ/ CABLE & WIRELESS
CENTRO COMERCIAL VÍA VENETO/ BUDGET RENT A CAR
HOTEL EL PANAMÁ
FARMACIA ARROCHA/ATM
DOUBLETREE HOTEL
IGLESIA DEL CARMEN

VIA BRASIL
AV SAMUEL LEWIS
VÍA BRASIL
AV ABEL BRAVO
CALLE 59 ESTE
CALLE 58 ESTE
CALLE JUAN RAMÓN POLL C.
CALLE 56 ESTE
CALLE 55 ESTE
CALLE 54 ESTE
CALLE 53 ESTE
CALLE 51 ESTE
CALLE 50 ESTE
CALLE 49 ESTE
CALLE 49A
AV 1A SUR
AV 1A D SUR
AV 2A NORTE
AV 1C NORTE
VÍA ESPAÑA
VÍA ARGENTINA
AV 1B NORTE
AV 2B NORTE
AV 3B NORTE
AV 4B NORTE
CALLE EUSEBIO A MORALES
CALLE MANUEL MARÍA ICAZA
CALLE D
AV 2A NORTE
CALLE E
AV MANUEL E BAUTISTA
CALLE 55 VÍA VENETO
AV ARGENTINA
CALLE 33 OESTE

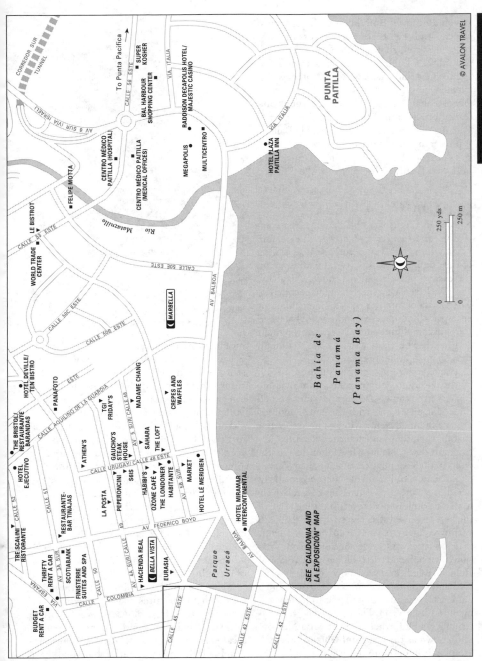

© AVALON TRAVEL

(**Avenida Simón Bolívar),** which cuts across the city and then heads north across the isthmus. However, those planning to head north toward the Caribbean are much better off taking the new toll road, **Corredor Norte,** which extends across the isthmus and ends close to the city of Colón. Another toll road, **Corredor Sur,** leads from Tucumen International Airport to Panama City, where it meets Avenida Balboa. A project to extend the Corredor Norte to meet the Corredor Sur, near the international airport, may finally be completed by the time you read this.

◖ PANAMÁ LA VIEJA

Known in English as Old Panama, these extensive ruins (8:30 A.M.–6:30 P.M. Tues.–Sun., US$4 adults, US$2 students) are all that's left of the original Panama City. The ruins are on the eastern outskirts of the modern-day city, an easy drive east along Vía Cincuentenario. The Corredor Sur arcs right by it, making for an especially impressive sight at night, when the ruins are illuminated. Note that the site is commonly known as Panamá Viejo, though that's not its proper name.

The city was founded on August 15, 1519, by the notorious conquistador Pedro Arias de Ávila, better known as Pedrarias, and burned down during a battle with the equally notorious Welsh pirate Henry Morgan in 1671. After that disaster, the Spanish moved Panama City to a more defensible site a few kilometers southwest, in the area now known as Casco Viejo.

Since most of Panamá la Vieja was made of wood, only the partial remains of a relatively few stone buildings were left standing. Two of the best-preserved structures are near the main entrance. The first is the **cathedral tower,** which is largely intact. It's one of Panama's national symbols and was built between 1619 and 1626. The cathedral was known officially as La Catedral de Nuestra Señora de la Asunción, a name that was later transferred to its replacement in Casco Viejo. The other well-preserved structure, a bit farther in, is the Casa Alarcón, also known as the **Casa del Obispo** (Bishop's House). Built in the 1640s, it was a three-story

the cathedral tower of the original Panama City, sacked by Henry Morgan in 1671

building with a wooden top floor. It's the largest and most intact house on the site, but it's still just fragments of walls. There are other ruins worth exploring, but try not to wander too far—the more distant ruins border a neighborhood plagued by crime and gangs.

For that same reason, I also recommend visitors come only during regular opening hours, even though parts of the site can be explored anytime. It's also the only time visitors can climb to the top of the cathedral tower, something that has only recently become possible.

A restoration project is buttressing the crumbling, rough-hewn stone walls with red bricks completely out of keeping with the original architecture. There are now signs in English and Spanish that explain the history of some of the ruins.

There are lots of souvenir kiosks in the buildings next to the ruins that sell devil masks, *molas* (handcrafted blouses), Ngöbe-Buglé necklaces, and various other trinkets. There's a cafeteria inside as well. An ATP information booth is on the premises, but you'll have a better chance turning up lost pieces of eight than finding anyone actually working there.

Museo de Sitio de Panamá la Vieja

During the restoration archaeologists found Spanish pots, plates, and utensils dating from the 16th and 17th centuries, as well as a much older cemetery with bones dating from 50 B.C. These and other relics are kept in the Museo de Sitio de Panamá la Vieja (tel. 226-9815 or 224-6031, www.panamaviejo.org, 9 A.M.–5 P.M. Tues.–Sun., US$3 adults, US$0.50 students), about a kilometer before the ruins themselves. It's one of Panama's best museums, a modern, two-story place with attractively presented displays. If you stop here first, be sure to buy a ticket that includes entry to the ruins; it's cheaper than buying them separately.

Start on the top floor and work your way down. Displays include indigenous artifacts from the hundreds of years before the Spanish conquest, when the site was a fishing village. One of the more haunting exhibits is the skeleton of a woman believed to have died at about age 40; she was apparently an important figure, whose grave also included the skulls of nine males. Other displays include items from the early Spanish colonial days, such as shards of cooking pots, coins, lead musket balls, trinkets, and so on. There's also a model of the city as it looked before Morgan's incendiary visit. The ground floor has details on the restoration of the site. There is limited information in English, and no English-speaking guides.

◀ CASCO VIEJO

Casco Viejo has always had a romantic look, but for decades the romance has been of the tropical-decadence, paint-peeling-from-rotting-walls variety. For more than a decade, though, it's been undergoing a tasteful and large-scale restoration that's giving the old buildings new luster and has turned the area into one of the city's most fashionable destinations for a night out. Elegant bars, restaurants, and sidewalk cafés have opened. Hotels and hostels are arriving. Little tourist shops are popping up.

Amazingly, this is being done with careful attention to keeping the old charm of the place alive. In some places the district now resembles the French Quarter of New Orleans. It also looks very much like a smaller, much-less-touristy Cartagena. Unfortunately, the renovation is squeezing out the poorer residents who've lived here for ages.

The "Old Part," also known as Casco Antiguo or the San Felipe district, was the second site of Panama City, and it continued to be the heart of the city during the first decades of the 20th century. UNESCO declared it a World Heritage Site in 1997. It's a city within the city—940 buildings, 747 of which are houses—and one from a different age. It's a great place for a walking tour. You can wander down narrow brick streets, sip an espresso at an outdoor café, visit old churches, and gaze up at wrought-iron balconies spilling over with bright tropical plants. Its buildings feature an unusual blend of architectural styles, most notably rows of ornate Spanish- and French-colonial houses but also a smattering of art deco and neoclassical buildings.

In some respects Sunday is a good day for exploring Casco Viejo. For one thing, it's the likeliest time to find the churches open and in use. However, though more bars and restaurants are now staying open on Sunday, many others aren't, and even some of the museums are closed. Several places are also closed on Monday. Getting a look inside historic buildings and museums is easiest during the week, especially since some are in government offices open only during normal business hours. Churches open and close rather erratically. Friday and Saturday nights are the best bets for dining and partying.

Safety Considerations

Even with the makeover, Casco Viejo is not the safest part of Panama City. I've long urged visitors (and locals) to explore the area, and I've never felt threatened myself, but it's become less safe in the last few years. Ironically, the area's renaissance seems to be driving it: With more tourists and affluent residents in Casco

PANAMA CITY

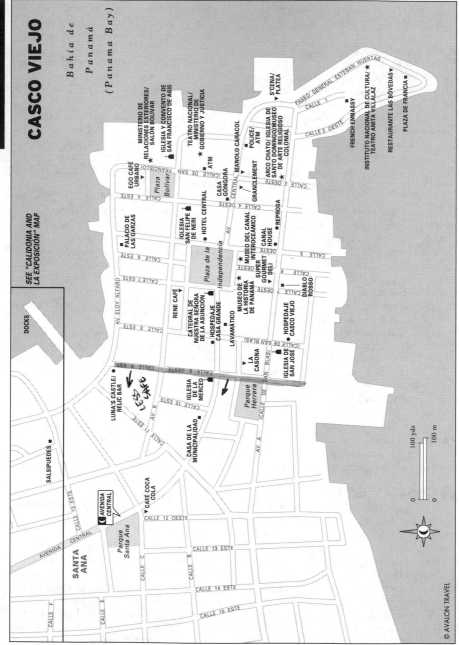

CASCO VIEJO

Bahía de Panamá (Panama Bay)

SEE "CALIDONIA AND LA EXPOSICIÓN" MAP

DOCKS

© AVALON TRAVEL

0   100 yds
0   100 m

Viejo, there's just more to steal. On my most recent visits, I heard a few stories of backpackers getting mugged in the middle of the day. And a street-wise Panamanian I know had to shut down his fledgling tourist information office after it was twice robbed at gunpoint.

There's no reason to be overly concerned, but use common sense in exploring Casco Viejo. I cringe when I see obvious tourists wandering around there. If you're pale and gringo, you're going to stand out, but try to look as though you're a resident foreigner. Don't wear shorts, fanny packs, Hawaiian shirts, or the like, and be discreet with the cameras and maps. Don't come dripping jewelry and dressed in expensive clothes. Don't wander around at night, and be cautious on deserted side streets or when venturing beyond the major activity hubs (Plaza Bolívar, Plaza de la Independencia, and Plaza de Francia). Look at the map of Casco Viejo and mentally draw a line from Luna's Castle to Parque Herrera: At night, do not venture west of this area on foot. Also avoid the block of Calle 4 between Avenida Central and Avenida B at night. Parque Herrera is beginning to gentrify, but it's still on the edge of a sketchy area.

All that said, the neighborhood is well patrolled by the *policía de turismo* (tourism police), who cruise around on bicycles and are easy to spot in their short-pants uniforms. They've been trained specifically to serve tourists, and they're doing an impressive job. It's not unusual for them to greet foreign tourists with a handshake and a smile and offer them an insider's tour of the area or help with whatever they need. Visitors have reported many pleasant encounters with them. Don't hesitate to ask them for help or directions. Their station is next to Manolo Caracol and across the street from the Ministerio de Gobierno y Justicia (Avenida Central between Calle 2 Oeste and Calle 3 Este, tel. 211-2410 or 211-1929). It's open 24 hours, and the officers will safely guide you to your destination night or day.

There's a heavy police presence around the presidential palace, but those police are stern and no-nonsense. Their job is to protect the president, not help tourists.

The decay and the renovation work present the most serious potential hazards: Several people were killed or injured by masonry falling from crumbling buildings in 2006 and 2007. Also watch out for foot-eating potholes, missing drain covers, and so on.

Plaza de la Independencia

In the center of Casco Viejo is the Plaza de la Independencia, where Panama declared its independence from Colombia in 1903. This area was the center of Panama City until the early 20th century. The buildings represent a real riot of architectural styles, from neo-Renaissance to art deco.

Construction began on the cathedral, the **Catedral de Nuestra Señora de la Asunción,** in 1688, but it took more than 100 years to complete. Some of the stones used in its construction come from the ruins of Panamá la Vieja. It has an attractive marble altar and a few well-crafted stained-glass windows, though

Panama City's cathedral, on Plaza de la Independencia, is a good place to start touring Casco Viejo.

otherwise the interior is rather plain. The towers are inlaid with mother of pearl from the Perlas Islands. Little-known factoid: The bones of a saint, Santo Aurelio, are contained in a reliquary hidden behind a painting of Jesus near the front of the church, on the left as one faces the altar. Visitors have been known to nudge the painting aside to take a peek when no one's looking.

Opposite the cathedral is the historic **Hotel Central,** a grand 19th-century hotel that over the decades deteriorated into a flophouse. It's being "renovated" by a Spanish consortium that aims to turn it into a five-star hotel. In reality, the hotel has been entirely gutted except for its facade, which has outraged preservationists. A large apartment building that looms over the entire plaza is being built right next to its north side. The construction of the hotel has been much delayed because as soon as work started in the fall of 2007, archaeologists uncovered many layers of artifacts and evidence of public works that date back at least to the 17th century.

Museo del Canal Interoceánico

The Museo del Canal Interoceánico (Avenida Central between Calle 5 Oeste and Calle 6 Oeste, tel. 211-1995 or 211-1649, www.museodelcanal.com, 9 A.M.–5 P.M. Tues.–Sun, US$2 adults, US$0.75 students) is dedicated to the history of the Panama Canal. The museum is housed in what started life as the Grand Hotel in 1874, then became the headquarters of the French canal-building effort, and later spent the early part of the 20th century as the capital's central post office. It's worth a visit, but be prepared for some frustration if you don't speak Spanish. Everything is Spanish only, which is a problem for those who don't speak the language since the "exhibits" often consist more of text than anything else. However, an audio guide in English, Spanish, and French is available. The displays tell the story of both the French and American efforts to build the canal, and throw in a little bit of pre-Colombian and Spanish colonial history at the beginning. There's some anti-American

propaganda, and most of what's written about the canal from the 1960s on should be taken with a big chunk of salt. Sadly, history here gives way to polemics, distortions, and pure myth. There's a good coin collection upstairs, as well as a few Panamanian and Canal Zone stamps. There's also a copy of the 1977 Torrijos-Carter Treaties that turned the canal over to Panama. You can tour the whole place in about an hour.

Museo de la Historia de Panamá

The Museo de la Historia de Panamá (Avenida Central between Calle 7 Oeste and Calle 8 Oeste, tel. 228-6231, 8 A.M.–4 P.M. Mon.–Fri., US$1 general admission, US$0.25 children) is a small museum containing artifacts from Panama's history from the colonial period to the modern era. It's in the Palacio Municipal, a neoclassical building from 1910 that is now home to government offices. At first glance it seems like just another one of Panama's woefully underfunded museums housing a few obscure bits of bric-a-brac. But anyone with some knowledge of Panama's history—which is essential, since the Spanish-only displays are poorly explained—will find some of the displays fascinating.

Among these are a crudely stitched Panama flag, said to have been made by María Ossa de Amador in 1903. She was the wife of Manuel Amador Guerrero, a leader of the revolutionaries who conspired with the Americans to wrest independence from Colombia. The flag was hastily designed by the Amadors' son, and the women in the family sewed several of them for the rebels; the sewing machine they used is included in the display. If the revolution had failed, this quaint sewing circle might have meant death by hanging for all of them. Instead, Manuel Amador became the first president of Panama.

On a desk by the far wall is the handwritten draft of a telegram the revolutionaries sent to the superintendent of the Panama Railroad in Colón, pleading with him not to allow Colombian troops from the steamship *Cartagena* to cross the isthmus and put down the revolution. This was one of the tensest moments in the birth of Panama. In the end, they didn't cross over, and the revolution was nearly bloodless. The telegram is dated November 3, 1903, the day Panama became independent, and those who sent it are now considered Panama's founding fathers.

Other displays include a stirrup found on the storied Camino de Cruces, a plan for the fortifications built at Portobelo in 1597, 17th-century maps of the "new" Panama City at Casco Viejo (note the walls that originally ringed the city, now all but gone), and the sword of Victoriano Lorenzo, a revered hero of the War of a Thousand Days.

Western Fringes of Casco Viejo

The church with the crumbling brown facade and white-washed sides near the corner of Avenida Central and Calle 9 Oeste is **Iglesia de la Merced,** which was built in the 17th century from rubble salvaged from the ruins of Panamá la Vieja. It's worth a quick stop for a look at its wooden altars and pretty tile floor. The neoclassical building next to it, the **Casa de la Municipalidad,** is a former mansion now used by the city government.

The little park, **Parque Herrera,** was dedicated in 1976. The statue of the man on horseback is General Tomás Herrera, an early hero of Panama's complex independence movements. Some of the historic buildings ringing the park are under renovation; rumor has it that eventually at least one of them will house a hotel.

Church of the Golden Altar

The massive golden altar *(altar de oro)* is a prime tourist attraction at **Iglesia de San José** (Avenida A between Calle 8 and Calle 9, 7 A.M.–noon and 2–8 P.M. Mon.–Sat., 5 A.M.–noon and 5–8 P.M. Sun.). Legend has it that the altar was saved from the rapacious Welsh pirate Henry Morgan during the sacking of the original Panama City when a quick-thinking priest ordered it painted black, hiding its true value.

The Flat Arch

The original **Iglesia de Santo Domingo**

(Avenida A and Calle 3 Oeste) was built in the 17th century, but it burned twice and was not rebuilt after the fire of 1756. But it remains famous for one thing that survived, seemingly miraculously: the nearly flat arch *(Arco Chato).* Since it was built without a keystone and had almost no curve to it, it should have been a very precarious structure, yet it remained intact even as everything around it fell into ruins. One of the reasons a transoceanic canal was built in Panama was that engineers concluded from the intact arch that Panama was not subject to the kinds of devastating earthquakes that afflict its Central American neighbors.

On the evening of November 7, 2003, just four days after Panama celebrated its first centennial as a country, the arch finally collapsed into rubble. Predictably, attempts to find someone to blame for its neglect—it had been left exposed to the sun, rain, and rumbling traffic of Panama for ages—began almost before the dust settled. It has since been rebuilt, but its main appeal, its gravity-defying properties through the centuries, can never be restored. The church itself is undergoing a slow restoration.

Plaza de Francia

The Plaza de Francia (French Plaza) has seen a great deal of history and was among the first parts of Casco Viejo to be renovated, back in 1982.

The obelisk and the marble plaques along the wall commemorate the failed French effort to build a sea-level canal in Panama. The area housed a fort until the beginning of the 20th century, and the *bóvedas* (vaults) in the seawall were used through the years as storehouses, barracks, offices, and jails. You'll still hear gruesome stories about dungeons in the seawall, where prisoners were left at low tide to drown when the tide rose. Whether this actually happened is still a subject of lively debate among amateur historians. True or not, what you will find there now is one of Panama's more colorful restaurants, Restaurante Las Bóvedas. Also in the plaza are the French Embassy, the headquarters of the **Instituto Nacional de**

Cultura (INAC, the National Institute of Culture) in what had been Panama's supreme court building, and a small theater, **Teatro Anita Villalaz.** Tourists are not allowed into the grand old building that houses INAC, but it's worth peeking into from the top of the steps or the lobby, if you can get that far. Note the colorful, if not particularly accomplished, mural depicting idealized versions of Panama's history. (Movie trivia: The building was used as a movie set for the 2008 James Bond film *Quantum of Solace,* as were the ruins of the old Union Club.) Next to the restaurant is an **art gallery** (tel. 211-4034, 9:30 A.M.–5:30 P.M. Tues.–Sat.) run by INAC that displays works by Panamanian and other Latin American artists. It was closed for renovation in mid-2010.

Walk up the staircase that leads to the top of the vaults. This is part of the old seawall that protected the city from the Pacific Ocean's dramatic tides. There's a good view of the Panama City skyline, the Bridge of the Americas, and the Bay of Panama, and the breeze is great on a hot day. The walkway, **Paseo General Esteban Huertas,** is shaded in part by a bougainvillea-covered trellis and is a popular spot with smooching lovers. Along the walkway leading down to Avenida Central, notice the building on the waterfront to the right. For years this has been a ruin, but progress on turning it into a long-promised hotel is finally being made. This was once the officers' club of the Panamanian Defense Forces; it was largely destroyed during the 1989 U.S. invasion. Before that, it was the home of the Union Club, a hangout for Panama's oligarchy that's now on Punta Paitilla.

Casa Góngora

Built in 1756, the stone house of Casa Góngora (corner of Avenida Central and Calle 4, tel. 212-0338, 8 A.M.–4 P.M. Mon.–Fri., free) is the oldest house in Casco Viejo and one of the oldest in Panama. It was originally the home of a Spanish pearl merchant. It then became a church and has now been turned into a small, bare-bones museum. It's had a rough history— it has been through three fires and the current

wooden roof is new. A 20th-century restoration attempt was botched, causing more damage. There isn't much here, but the staff can give free tours (in Spanish) and there have been noises about making it more of a real museum in the future. There's an interesting, comprehensive book on the history of the house and neighborhood (again, in Spanish) that visitors are welcome to thumb through while visiting. It contains rare maps, photos, and illustrations. Ask for it at the office. The museum hosts jazz and folkloric concerts and other cultural events in the tiny main hall on some Friday and Saturday nights, and occasionally hosts art shows.

Iglesia San Felipe de Neri (corner of Avenida B and Calle 4) dates from 1688 and, though it has also been damaged by fires, is one of the oldest standing structures from the Spanish colonial days. It was recently renovated but wasn't open when I last tried to check it out.

The National Theater

The intimate Teatro Nacional (National Theater, between Calle 2 and Calle 3 on Avenida B, 9:30 A.M.–5:30 P.M. Mon.–Fri.) holds classical concerts and other posh events. It was built in 1908 on the site of an 18th-century monastery. It's housed in the same building as the **Ministerio de Gobierno y Justicia** (Ministry of Government and Justice), which has its entrance on Avenida Central, across the street from Manolo Caracol, a fun restaurant.

Inaugurated on October 1, 1908, the neo-baroque theater is worth a brief visit between concerts to get a glimpse of its Old World elegance. The public can explore it during the week but not on weekends. The first performance here was a production of the opera *Aida,* and for about 20 years the theater was a glamorous destination for the city's elite. (Note the bust of the ballerina Margot Fonteyn in the lobby; she married a Panamanian in 1955 and lived out the last part of her life in Panama.) But after that it gradually deteriorated.

A 1974 restoration brought it back to life until the rainy season of 2000 wrought serious damage. The ceiling is covered with faded but still colorful frescos of cavorting naked ladies, painted by Roberto Lewis, a well-known Panamanian artist. Leaks in the roof destroyed about a quarter of these frescos, and the roof partially collapsed. The roof was restored and the theater reopened in 2004. Be sure to walk upstairs to take a look at the opulent reception rooms.

A bit of local color: Old-timers remember the days before air-conditioning, when performances were sometimes drowned out by traffic noise and heavy rains wafting through the open doors. Occasionally a bat would zoom into the gallery, adding a bit of unplanned excitement.

Plaza Bolívar

Plaza Bolívar (on Avenida B between Calle 3 and Calle 4) has been undergoing a charming restoration, and several cafés and restaurants have sprung up (and folded) here. It's especially pleasant to hang out on the plaza in the evening, when tables are set up under the stars. It's a good rest stop for a drink or a bite. Cafés don't tend to last long on the plaza, but as soon as one closes another one opens. A long-term survivor that's likely to be there when you arrive is Restaurante Casablanca.

The plaza was named for Simón Bolívar, a legendary figure who is considered the father of Latin America's independence from Spain. In 1826 Bolívar called a congress here to discuss forming a union of Latin American states. Bolívar himself did not attend and the congress didn't succeed, but the park and the statue of Bolívar commemorate the effort.

The congress itself was held in a small, two-story building that has been preserved as a museum, now known as the **Salón Bolívar** (Plaza Bolívar, tel. 228-9594, 9 A.M.–4 P.M. Tues.–Sat., 1–5 P.M. Sun., US$1 adults, US$0.25 students).

While the museum is designed attractively, there's not much in it. The room upstairs contains the text of the protocols of different congresses called during the independence movement. There's also a replica of Bolívar's jewel-encrusted sword, a gift from Venezuela (the original is now back in Venezuela). The actual room where the congress took place is on the ground floor.

The little museum is entirely enclosed by glass to protect it and is actually in the courtyard of another building, the massive **Palacio Bolívar,** which was built on the site of a Franciscan convent that dates from the 18th century. The little building that houses the Salón Bolívar was originally the *sala capitula* (chapter house) of that convent, and is the only part of it that is still intact. The *palacio* dates from the 1920s and was a school for many years. Now it's home to the Ministerio de Relaciones Exteriores (Foreign Ministry). During regular business hours (about 8 A.M.–3 P.M. Mon.–Fri., 9 A.M.–1 P.M. Sat.) it's possible, and well worthwhile, to explore the huge inner courtyard, which has been outfitted with a clear roof that's out of keeping with the architecture, but protects it from the elements. The courtyard is open to the surf in the back, where part of the original foundation can be seen. Be sure to notice the beautiful tile work, and the posh chandelier at the entrance.

Next door but still on the plaza is a church and former monastery, **Iglesia y Convento de San Francisco de Asís.** The church dates from the early days of Casco Viejo, but was burned during two 18th-century fires, then restored in 1761 and again in 1998. It's been closed for renovation for ages.

The Presidential Palace

The presidential palace, **El Palacio de las Garzas** (Palace of the Herons), is on the left at Calle 5 Este, overlooking Panama Bay. It's an attractive place that houses the presidential office and residence. The president lives here and visitors are not permitted. The place and the neighboring streets are surrounded by guards who may ask for your passport, but more likely will just wave you by. Be polite and deferential—they should let you walk by the palace. Walk slowly and take a quick peek inside at the courtyard, visible from the street, and try to spot the herons around the fountain.

COURTESY OF JIM GUY

The presidential palace, El Palacio de las Garzas, is named for the herons wandering its courtyard.

Near Casco Viejo

The area that leads into Casco Viejo from the northeast, centered around the waterfront strip of Avenida Eloy Alfaro, is one of the most colorful, lively, squalid, and—especially at night—intimidating parts of Panama City. The municipal government is determined to clean up this bustling area of commerce—legal and otherwise—since it is the main entrance into the rapidly gentrifying Casco Viejo, but it's happening slowly.

For ages small fishing boats have pulled up to the deteriorating docks, but now seafood is sold through the clean, modern fish market, the **Mercado de Mariscos** (5 A.M.–5 P.M. daily), nearby at the west end of Avenida Balboa. This is an eternally popular place to sample ceviche made from an amazing array of seafood, sold at stalls around the market. There's usually a line at Ceviches #2 (4:30 A.M.–5 P.M. daily), though whether it's because the ceviche is truly better or because it's simply closer to the entrance and open later than the other

stalls is something I'll leave to ceviche connoisseurs. The large jars of pickled fish, flies buzzing above them, don't make for an appetizing scene, but I've never heard of anyone getting sick from ceviche, which is "cooked" in a pretty intense bath of onions, limes, and chili peppers. Prices for a Styrofoam cup of fishy goodness range from US$1 for *corvine* up to $3 for *langostinos.*

The other merchants and tiny repair kiosks in the waterfront area, known as the **Terraplén,** were supposed to have been moved years ago, but they are proving as hard to pry off as barnacles, I'm happy to say.

Up Calle 13 is the crowded shopping area of **Salsipuedes** (a contraction of "get out if you can"). The area is crammed with little stalls selling clothes, lottery tickets, and bric-a-brac. Just north of this street is a small **Chinatown,** called Barrio Chino in Spanish, which frankly has little to interest tourists. Most of the Chinese character of the place has been lost through the years; the ornate Chinese archway over the street is one of the few remaining signs of a less-assimilated time.

Meat and produce are sold at Panama City's **Mercado Público** (public market). For nearly 100 years it was in the same building at the intersection of Avenida Eloy Alfaro and Calle 13, and it looked like it hadn't been cleaned since it opened. It has completed its move to a less charismatic but more hygienic new building on nearby Avenida B, just off Avenida Eloy Alfaro near the Chinese gate of the Barrio Chino. The new market is still plenty colorful, and worth a visit. It's gated and has a guard at the entrance, which may reassure those nervous about its sketchy surroundings.

The meat section, though cleaner, is still not fully air-conditioned, and the humid, cloying stench of blood in the Panama heat may convert some to vegetarianism. The *abarrotería* (grocer's section) is less overwhelming and more interesting. Shelves are stacked with all kinds of homemade *chichas* (fruit juices), hot sauce, and honey, as well as spices, freshly ground coconut, duck eggs, and so on. The produce section is surprisingly small.

Panama City's Mercado de Mariscos (fish market) is just outside Casco Viejo.

© WILLIAM FRIAR

There's a **food hall** (4 A.M.–3 or 4 P.M. daily) in the middle of the market. The perimeter is ringed with *fondas* (basic restaurants) each marked with the proprietor's name. A heaping plateful costs a buck or two.

Lottery vendors line the walls by the entrance, and across the gated parking lot is a line of shops selling goods similar to and no doubt intended to replace those on the Terraplén. These include hammocks, army-surplus and Wellington boots, machetes, camping gear, and souvenirs such as Ecuadorian-style "Panama" hats. Each store keeps different hours, but most are open 8 A.M.–4 P.M. Monday–Saturday, and some are open Sunday mornings.

The market is staffed with friendly, uniformed attendants who can explain what's going on, especially if you speak a bit of Spanish. There's a Banco Nacional de Panamá ATM near the entrance.

The traditional time to hit the market is around 5 A.M. on Sunday, though early Saturday morning is also busy. The market is open 2 A.M.–3 or 4 P.M. daily and is good for sightseeing anytime. Bring a camera, but as always, be respectful about taking photos, and tuck the camera away before leaving the market.

Practicalities

There are two places in Casco Viejo proper to withdraw cash. The first, and safest, is next to the tourism police station on Avenida Central near Calle 2. The other is a Banco Nacional de Panamá ATM on Calle 3 Oeste between Avenida Central and Avenida A. It's behind the large outer doors of an office at the side of the Teatro Nacional, and because of that it's only accessible during regular business hours during the week. There's a guard by the door. Ideally, though, come to Casco Viejo with sufficient cash.

Getting Around

A good way to explore the area is to come with a knowledgeable guide or taxi driver who can drop you in different areas to explore on foot. Safety aside, you'll probably save time this way, as the streets are confusing and it's easy to get lost. Do major exploring only during the daytime; those who come at night should taxi in and out to specific destinations. Restaurant and bar owners can call a cab for the trip back.

Those who prefer to drive should note that even locals get lost here. Watch out for narrow one-way streets and blind intersections. Street parking is hard to find in the day and on weekend nights. There's a paid lot with an attendant on the side of the Teatro Nacional that faces Panama Bay. It's open 24 hours a day and costs US$0.50/hour.

AVENIDA CENTRAL

The west end of Avenida Central, from Plaza Cinco de Mayo to Parque Santa Ana, is a busy walking street lined with shops. Except for the handicraft stalls on Plaza Cinco de Mayo, the shops won't interest foreign visitors much, as they deal mainly in cheap clothes and jewelry, electronics, and photo-development services. But the people-watching on the street is fun. The area provides a real sense of daily life in an older, humbler section of Panama City. The walk along Avenida Central goes through the heart of the Santa Ana district to the outskirts of San Felipe/Casco Viejo.

To take a walking tour, start at the highly congested **Plaza Cinco de Mayo.** Note the massive building. It was inaugurated in 1912 as the terminus of the Panama Railroad and had an on-again, off-again life as Panama's anthropology museum until the museum was finally moved to the Curundu area. To the east is the rather unattractive Palacio Legislativo, which houses the Asamblea Legislativa (Panama's national legislature).

Now head down Central. Visitors are often warned to beware of pickpockets in this area, which is probably a good idea, but this place is well patrolled by police and you're unlikely to have an unpleasant encounter, at least during the day. The area is a photographer's dream. On a typical stroll one can spot Kuna women going about their business in traditional clothing, juice vendors squeezing tropical fruit or crushing sugarcane in hand-cranked presses

(try some!), and hawkers luring customers into stores by clapping their hands. The crumbling old buildings reflect a real mish-mash of architectural styles, including neoclassical, neobaroque, and art deco. Some are quite striking. When you come to the major intersection, note the art deco building on the corner, the one housing the **Banco Nacional de Panamá.** Also check out the facade of the old building right next to it on the walking street. Its tiles are covered with pretty murals depicting the history of Panama from the conquest to the building of the Panama Canal.

Be sure to walk all the way to **Parque Santa Ana.** The twice weekly lottery drawings were held here for many years, and it's like a place from another, very Spanish era. It's very pleasant to get here before 8 A.M., when it's still cool under the ancient shade trees, and eavesdrop on the old men sitting around reading newspapers or arguing politics while getting a spectacularly vigorous shoeshine. The dilapidated old church on the plaza was getting a much-needed facelift in 2010. Consider a visit to **Café Coca Cola** across the street. Walk down the opposite side of Central on the way back.

Slip into the maze of side streets if you want to do some more exploring. A likely spot is the major intersection with Calle I; head uphill to Calle Estudiante, where you'll find Pizzeria Napoli and the **Instituto Nacional.** The latter was built in 1911 and has a rather heroic, neoclassical yellow facade. Students here are known for frequent participation in demonstrations, most notably the Flag Riots of 1964, which had as its main battleground the nearby Avenida de los Mártires (Martyrs' Avenue, which until the riots was called Fourth of July Avenue). This area was once quite vibrant, with everything from fine jewelry shops to brothels (ask old-timers about the notorious Ancon Inn, now closed), but is virtually abandoned these days. Don't wander around here at night.

MUSEUMS

You'd never get a sense of the rich history of Panama if all you had to go on were the museums of its capital city. They are all neglected and underfunded, and what few exhibits they contain are generally poorly presented and contain almost no explanation of their significance.

That said, Panama has paid more attention to its cultural treasures in recent years. The city's anthropology museum, Museo Antropológico Reina Torres de Araúz, has a new home. The modern art museum, Museo de Arte Contemporáneo, once an art gallery more than anything else, has emerged as a respectable repository of Panama's better-known and emerging contemporary artists. And one day the ambitious new Museum of Biodiversity, designed by Frank O. Gehry, may actually be completed. The latest estimate is that it will finally open at the end of 2011.

Most of the museums are in Casco Viejo. This section covers notable museums outside of Casco Viejo.

El Museo Antropológico Reina Torres de Araúz

Panama's anthropology museum (Avenida Juan Pablo II and Calle Curundu, tel. 232-7644, 9 A.M.–4 P.M. Tues.–Fri., 10 A.M.–5 P.M. Sat. and Sun., US$2 adults, US$0.25 students) has a troubled history, including a dramatic robbery in 2003 and funding shortages that forced it into a moribund existence for years. Sometimes known by the acronym MARTA, it was taken in 2006 from its longtime home in what had originally been the terminus of the Panama Railroad, on Plaza Cinco de Mayo.

The new Museo Antropológico Reina Torres de Araúz is a cement monolith from the exposed-duct school of modern design. It's hard to predict what will actually be on view when you visit, but described here are some of the highlights of the museum's permanent collection of 15,000 pieces.

Most intriguing to me are the pieces from the **Barriles culture,** believed to be Panama's earliest major civilization. The figures on display came from a ceremonial center that dates from around 60 B.C. and consist of about a dozen and a half carvings of stone figures and fragments.

The museum's **gold collection** includes figures of animals, armor plates, ceramics, jewelry, breast plates, a crown, and other items made by ancient indigenous peoples and recovered from archaeological sites around the country.

Most of the items are *huacas,* ceremonial treasures buried with prominent indigenous people. The oldest item, a copper and gold nose ring found on Cerro Juan Díaz on the Azuero Peninsula, dates from 180 B.C. As part of Panama's centennial celebration in 2003, the Reprosa jewelry store, well known for its replicas of *huacas,* made reproductions of some of the prized ones in this collection. One especially impressive piece is a large spider made of gold and copper.

El Museo de Arte Contemporáneo

The Contemporary Art Museum (Avenida San Blas, tel. 262-3380 or 262-8012, www.macpanama.org, 9 A.M.–5 P.M. Tues.–Sun., US$3 adult, US$1 children) is one of Panama's best and best-maintained museums. Bear in mind, though, that it doesn't take much to reach that level in Panama. This one still more resembles an art gallery than a museum (many of the pieces are for sale). But it does present a reasonable cross-section of Panama's best-known and emerging modern artists as well as some work from other parts of Latin America. It sometimes presents film series. The museum is housed in a two-story building on the edge of the former Canal Zone in Ancón, next to the old Ancón Elementary School and not far from the headquarters of the Smithsonian Tropical Research Institute (Instituto Smithsonian de Investigaciones Tropicales).

El Museo de Ciencias Naturales

Panama City's Natural Sciences Museum (Avenida Cuba and Calle 29 Este, tel. 225-0645, 9 A.M.–3:30 P.M. Tues.–Sat., US$1 adults, US$0.25 students) is a modest place consisting of four rooms mainly containing some stuffed and mounted animals and geological specimens. It's worth a quick visit, at least if you're in the neighborhood, to get a

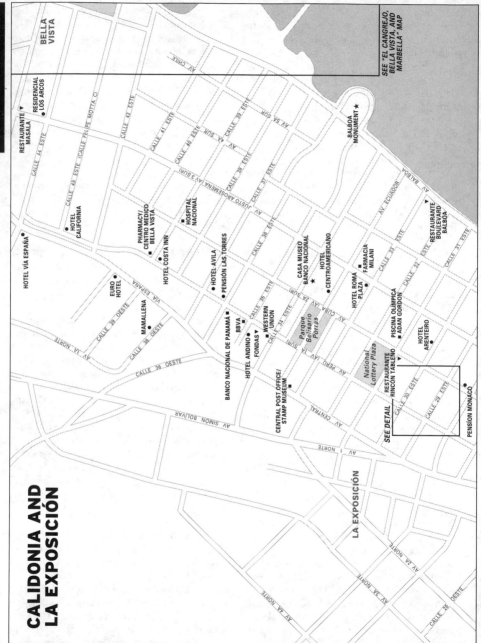

CALIDONIA AND LA EXPOSICIÓN

BELLA VISTA

SEE "EL CANGREJO, BELLA VISTA, AND MARBELLA" MAP

LA EXPOSICIÓN

RESTAURANTE MASALA
RESIDENCIAL LOS ARCOS
CALLE 44 ESTE
CALLE 43 ESTE (CALLE FELIPE MOTTA C)
HOTEL CALIFORNIA
HOTEL VÍA ESPAÑA
CALLE 42 ESTE
CALLE 41 ESTE
AV CHILE
PHARMACY/ CENTRO MÉDICO BELLA VISTA
HOTEL COSTA INN
HOSPITAL NACIONAL
CALLE 40 ESTE
CALLE 39 ESTE
JUSTO AROSEMENA (AV 3 SUR)
AV 5A SUR
CALLE 38 ESTE
CALLE 37 ESTE
BALBOA MONUMENT ★
EURO HOTEL
VÍA ESPAÑA
HOTEL ÁVILA
PENSIÓN LAS TORRES
CASA MUSEO BANCO NACIONAL ★
HOTEL CENTROAMERICANO
AV ECUADOR
AV BALBOA
RESTAURANTE BOULEVARD BALBOA
CALLE 33 ESTE
CALLE 32 ESTE
CALLE 31 ESTE
MAMALLENA
CALLE 39 OESTE
CALLE 38 OESTE
BBVA
CALLE 35 ESTE
CALLE 34 ESTE
CUBA (AV 4A SUR)
HOTEL ROMA PLAZA
FARMACIA MILANI
PISCINA OLÍMPICA ADÁN GORDÓN
AV 1A NORTE
BANCO NACIONAL DE PANAMÁ
HOTEL ANDINO
FONDAS
WESTERN UNION
Parque Belisario Porras
HOTEL ARENTEIRO
CALLE 36 OESTE
CENTRAL POST OFFICE/ STAMP MUSEUM
PERÚ (AV 7A SUR)
AV CENTRAL
National Lottery Plaza
RESTAURANTE RINCÓN TABLEÑO
CALLE 30 ESTE
CALLE 29 ESTE
PENSIÓN MÓNACO
SEE DETAIL
AV SIMÓN BOLÍVAR
AV 1 NORTE
AV 2A NORTE
AV 3A NORTE
AV 4A NORTE
CALLE 26
CALLE OESTE

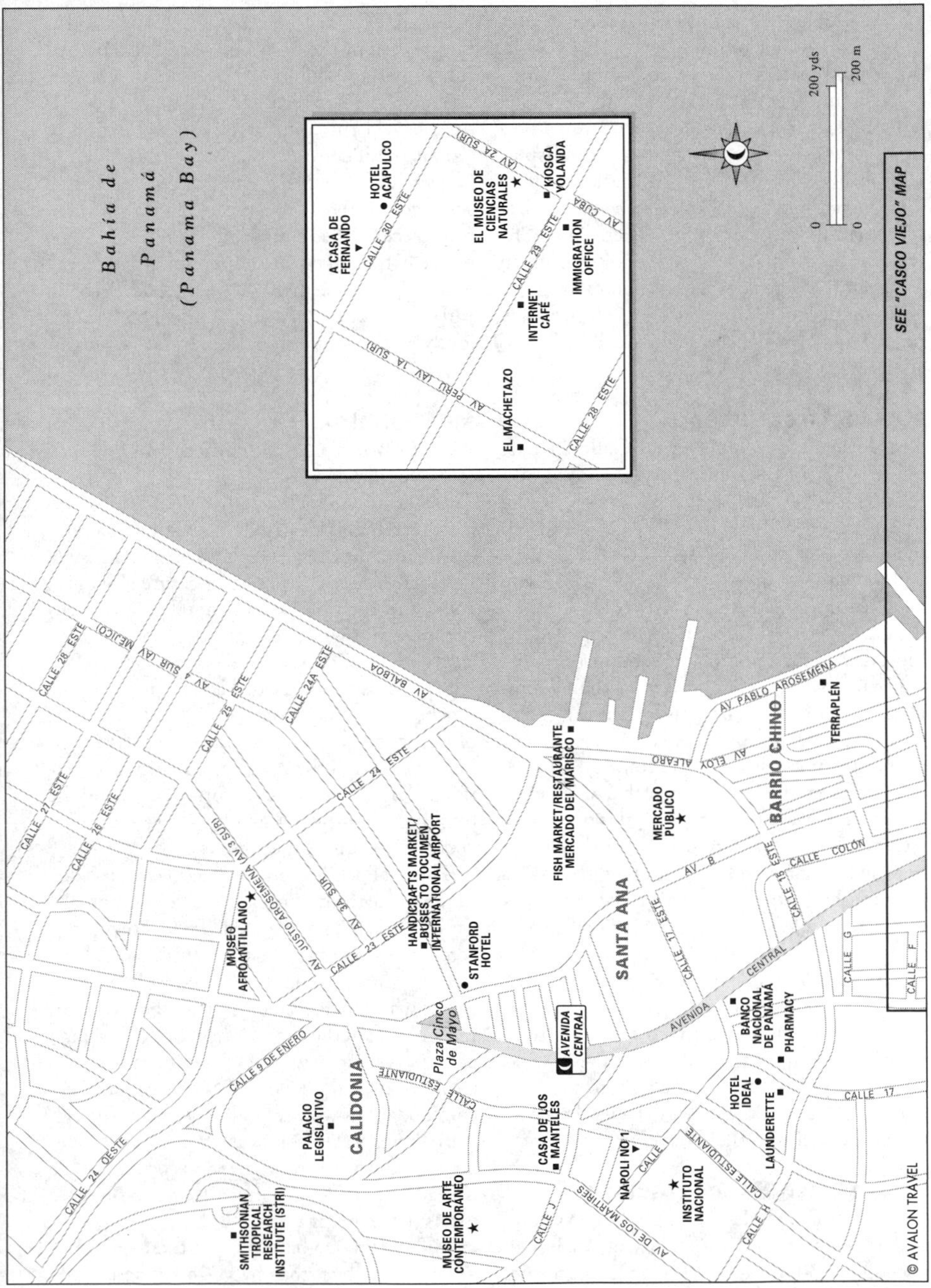

Bahía de Panamá
(Panama Bay)
A CASA DE FERNANDO
HOTEL ACAPULCO
CALLE 30 ESTE
(AV 2A SUR)
EL MUSEO DE CIENCIAS NATURALES
KIOSCA YOLANDA
AV CUBA
CALLE 29 ESTE
IMMIGRATION OFFICE
INTERNET CAFÉ
AV PERU (AV 1A SUR)
EL MACHETAZO
CALLE 28 ESTE
0
200 yds
200 m
SEE "CASCO VIEJO" MAP
CALLE 27 ESTE
CALLE 26 ESTE
CALLE 25 ESTE
CALLE 24A ESTE
CALLE 24 ESTE
CALLE 23 ESTE
AV BALBOA
AV 4 SUR (AV MEXICO)
AV JUSTO AROSEMENA (AV 3 SUR)
AV 3A SUR
MUSEO AFROANTILLANO
HANDICRAFTS MARKET/ BUSES TO TOCUMEN INTERNATIONAL AIRPORT
STANFORD HOTEL
FISH MARKET/RESTAURANTE MERCADO DEL MARISCO
MERCADO PÚBLICO
AV PABLO AROSEMENA
AV ELOY ALFARO
TERRAPLÉN
BARRIO CHINO
SANTA ANA
AV B
CALLE 17 ESTE
CALLE 15 ESTE
CALLE COLÓN
CALLE G
CALLE F
AVENIDA CENTRAL
Plaza Cinco de Mayo
CALLE 9 DE ENERO
CALLE 24 OESTE
CALIDONIA
PALACIO LEGISLATIVO
SMITHSONIAN TROPICAL RESEARCH INSTITUTE (STRI)
MUSEO DE ARTE CONTEMPORÁNEO
CALLE ESTUDIANTE
CASA DE LOS MANTELES
CALLE J
CALLE I
CALLE H
NAPOLI NO 1
INSTITUTO NACIONAL
AV DE LOS MÁRTIRES
HOTEL IDEAL
LAUNDERETTE
BANCO NACIONAL DE PANAMÁ
PHARMACY
CALLE 17
© AVALON TRAVEL

close-up look at some of Panama's more interesting animals, including a jaguar, harpy eagle, howler and spider monkeys, and a huge iguana. It's also fun to get a close look at the amazing hanging nest of an oropendola (a common bird in Panama). But the most interesting display is probably a handful of fossilized bones of a 50,000-year-old sloth *(Eremotherium rusconi)*, estimated to have been four meters long. The remains were found on the Azuero Peninsula in 1991. Only the geology and paleontology room is air-conditioned, ensuring that the rocks stay nice and cool while the snake exhibit, for instance, is hot and humid.

Museo Afroantillano

The Afro-Antillean Museum (Calle 24 Este off Avenida Justo Arosemena/Avenida 3 Sur, tel. 262-5348 or 501-4130, 8:30 A.M.–3:30 P.M. Tues.–Sat., US$1 adults, US$0.25 children) preserves the memory of the thousands of West Indian workers, mostly from Barbados, who supplied most of the labor for the building of the Panama Canal. These workers, who had the most dangerous and grueling jobs during canal construction, are often little more than a footnote in accounts of the building of the canal. Their descendants today make up a significant part of the population of the country.

The museum is tiny and worth a quick visit. However, beware that its location is on a dicey street and not the sort of place a tourist should be wandering around. If you do come, take a taxi and have the driver wait outside the entrance for you; you can see everything the museum has to offer in about a half hour.

The museum is installed in an old wooden house stocked with canal construction-era furnishings and photos meant to give a sense of what life might have been like for these workers, though it is certainly much more comfortable than the shacks many of the workers had to make do with in those days.

Casa Museo Banco Nacional

This elegant little house (Calle 34 Este and Avenida Cuba, tel. 225-0640, 8 A.M.–12:30 P.M. and 1:30–4:30 P.M. Mon.–Fri., free), the former

residence of a doctor, dates from 1925 and is now owned by the Banco Nacional de Panamá. It has rotating exhibits of arts and crafts for sale, though those I've seen have been quite poor. It does have a tiny but interesting collection of Panamanian commemorative coins, including a silver 20 balboa piece about the size of a fist, a small gold 100 balboa piece, and a tiny 2.5 centavo piece. Other coins date from 1904, some of the earliest days of the republic. It's worth visiting just to see how the well-heeled lived in early-20th-century Panama City. The house is lovely, with marble staircases, ornate wrought-iron fixtures, and several types of tile floors.

Mi Pueblito

Also known as Los Pueblitos, Mi Pueblito (off Avenida de Los Mártires, 9 A.M.–9 P.M. Tues.–Sun., US$1), literally, "my little town," is a charming, if idealized, re-creation of a typical Panamanian town on the Azuero Peninsula, Panama's heartland. The architecture is Spanish colonial, which is especially notable in the red-tile roofs and whitewashed walls, the mission-style church, and the central plaza and fountain. The builders have included lots of small, loving touches, from the lesson plan on the blackboard of the schoolhouse to the telegraph office that looks as though the operator has just left for a siesta. There's even a rustic outhouse behind the buildings. Nearby is a small *pollera* (traditional embroidered dress) museum.

The Mi Pueblito complex has been expanded to recognize the traditional dwellings of some of the other peoples of Panama. These are directly across the street from the Spanish colonial village. The first site honors the West Indian immigrants who provided most of the labor force for the building of the Panama Canal. The brightly painted two-story wooden buildings are an extremely fanciful take on what the laborers' accommodations were really like. A walk through a little forest takes you to more accurate re-creations of the way three indigenous peoples—the Kuna, Emberá-Wounaan, and Ngöbe-Buglé—lived, and in many cases still do.

Mi Pueblito is a bit neglected these days, and unless a tour bus stops by you may be its only visitor. There was once a cute little restaurant on the site, but it recently closed. Admission ostensibly is US$1, but there was no one there to collect it the last I visited. Souvenirs are on sale at shops throughout the complex, and the proprietors are likely to be desperate to make a sale, any sale.

Mi Pueblito is near the base of Cerro Ancón (also known as Ancon Hill), just off the westbound side of Avenida de Los Mártires. It's a quick right turn off this busy road that's easy to miss. Taxi drivers should know where it is.

CHURCHES AND SHRINES

Panama City's cathedral and most of its historically significant Catholic churches are in Casco Viejo. A couple of other prominent churches are scattered around modern Panama City.

Despite being an overwhelmingly Catholic country, Panama has a live-and-let-live attitude toward the many minority faiths brought by immigrants from around the world or still practiced by its indigenous peoples. The Baha'i House of Worship and Hindu Temple are especially prominent and draw curious visitors.

Santuario Nacional del Corazón de María

The National Sanctuary (tel. 263-9833), on Calle Manuel María Icaza near Calle 53 Este, was dedicated on August 22, 1949. It's a relatively simple church with pretty stained-glass windows and a modern interior, but atmosphere is provided by a riot of peacocks. Other domesticated birds wander around a fountain near the crypts. The crypts themselves are a bit creepy but worth a look; they're out the side entrance to the right as one faces the altar. Masses are held several times daily. The church's facade is attractive at night, when it's illuminated and provides a striking contrast to the glittery modern buildings that surround it. It's not worth making a special trip for, but given its central location it might be convenient to pop in briefly.

Iglesia del Carmen

The Iglesia del Carmen (tel. 223-0360), at Vía España and Avenida Federico Boyd, across the street from the Hotel El Panamá, is the most conspicuous church in modern Panama City. A cream-colored, neogothic confection with tall twin towers, it was built in 1947. It's a Panamanian landmark and worth a quick peek for those in the neighborhood

Baha'i House of Worship

Panama's Baha'i House of Worship (tel. 231-1191, 9 A.M.–6 P.M. daily, free), the only one in Latin America and one of only seven in the world, is an impressive structure that resembles an egg, with huge, open arched entrances that let the breezes blow through but keep the rain out. The temple interior is entirely unadorned. It has an unusual panoramic view of the city, the Pacific Ocean, and the surrounding countryside.

The temple is northeast of Panama City, near Las Cumbres. To get there, head east and then north on the Transístmica (Vía Simón Bolívar) from downtown Panama City. After about 15 kilometers there's a big intersection with Tumba Muerto (Avenida Ricardo J. Alfaro). Continue north on the Transístmica. About four kilometers past the intersection there should be a Bacardi rum factory on the left. Turn left here and head uphill for 1.5 kilometers to the temple.

Hindu Temple

The Hindu Temple (7:30 A.M.–noon and 4–8 P.M. daily, free) is less impressive than the Baha'i House of Worship, but easier to get to. It's a rather modern, spartan place that looks more imposing from a distance than it does close up. The most interesting thing about it, at least when worshipers are around, is the sense it gives you of how extensive and well-established Panama's South Asian community is.

The temple is off Tumba Muerto (Avenida Ricardo J. Alfaro). Head east a couple of kilometers past Calle de la Amistad (Friendship Highway) and make a left turn. Visitors must sign in at the gate. The temple is a short drive uphill.

PARKS

Other than Parque Natural Metropolitano, Panama City isn't blessed with much in the way of impressive or well-tended open spaces. Even little plazas are hard to find outside of Casco Viejo and the walking section of Avenida Central—they're one bit of the city's Spanish heritage that, sadly, is slipping away.

The Cinta Costera and Avenida Balboa

Panama City's newest and grandest avenue also offers some of its most dramatic views. Built on landfill, the Cinta Costera (coastal belt) sweeps along the edge of Panama Bay from Casco Viejo to ritzy Punta Paitilla and Punta Pacífica. It offers good views of the modern skyline of Panama City, Panama Bay, and the old seawall, churches, and historic buildings of Casco Viejo. The original concept for the promenade called for huge expanses of parkland and lovely facilities to attract families and tourists down to the sea edge. The reality is far more pedestrian and far less pedestrian-friendly. While there are some playing fields and such, most of the common spaces are simply large fields of grass that turn brown in the dry season. Getting to these spaces isn't that easy, either. The few pedestrian overpasses are spaced widely apart. (Do not attempt to cross the Cinta Costera itself; it's a multi-lane highway.)

These caveats aside, it's still a pleasant place for a morning or evening stroll. Try to time that stroll to coincide with high tide, when the view is nicer and the smell less potent. (Panama City dumps its untreated sewage into the bay. The government says it's going to build an incredibly expensive sewage treatment system, but don't hold your breath—or rather, do.)

The Cinta Costera runs parallel to Avenida Balboa, which for decades was the city's bayside promenade, lined with high-rises that hugged the edge of the sea. But with the advent of the Cinta Costera, Avenida Balboa is no longer on the waterfront much, no doubt, to the consternation of those who own property along it. About midway along Avenida Balboa is a little park that contains an enormous statue of Balboa "discovering" the Pacific, though these days he's far enough from the water that it looks more like he's trying to hail a cab.

Parque Belisario Porras

Though it's not worth a special trip, those staying in Calidonia who need a little open space can visit Parque Belisario Porras, between Calle 33 Este and Calle 34 Este and Avenida Perú and Avenida Cuba. It's an austere, formal plaza with a monument to Porras, thrice president of Panama and one of its founding fathers, looking rather dapper and jaunty. The plaza is surrounded by attractive old buildings, housing various government offices and the Spanish embassy. A line of kiosks serve greasy fast food to office workers on Avenida Perú near Calle 35, next to the Ministerio de Economía y Finanzas.

Parque Urracá

This is just a small city park off Avenida Balboa and Avenida Federico Boyd, but it's often filled with people, and it's fun to wander from here north and west through the hilly backstreets of Bella Vista. This is the edge of the *area bancaria* (banking area), so-called because of its many banks, often built into old houses. They're fast disappearing thanks to the construction boom, but it's still possible to walk down tree-lined streets and see beautiful Spanish-colonial mansions with red-tiled roofs and stone walls.

Parque Natural Metropolitano

Amazingly enough, you don't even have to leave the limits of Panama City to find a tropical forest. This 265-hectare park (entrance on Avenida Juan Pablo II, tel. 232-6713 or 232-5516, 5 A.M.–6 P.M. daily, free, donations encouraged) is just minutes from downtown, and it's a lovely little place with a surprising amount of wildlife given its location and size. Only brief day hikes are available here. Give it a miss if you plan to visit any of Panama's national parks.

Most of the park is dry lowland Pacific forest, now rare in Central America because of deforestation, and it's home to about 45 species of mammals, 36 species of reptiles, and 14 species of amphibians. These include such colorful creatures as two- and three-toed sloths, *monos tití* (Geoffroy's tamarin), and boa constrictors. As usual, however, don't be surprised if you see only birds during a hike. The park has recorded 227 bird species.

Having an urban center this close to a nature park has its drawbacks: A highway, Corredor Norte, cuts right through the park's eastern edge, and other busy streets run by its borders. You're never far from the roar of the road. Sadly, there have also been reports of occasional muggings. Don't wander on a trail alone.

There are about four kilometers of trails spread among three main loops. Not surprisingly, the most strenuous one, **La Cienaguita,** also offers the best chance of seeing animals. It takes about two hours to walk. It's an interpretive trail; the visitors center sells an informative booklet about it for US$2. The **Mono Tití Road** is, as the name suggests, a rocky road. Mountain biking is allowed on it, which would be great if there was a place to rent mountain bikes. The easiest trail is **Los Momótides,** across an extremely busy road—be careful crossing the street. It's short and level, designed for people in a hurry or who have difficulty walking, and it is a nice little walk.

The entrance to the park is on Avenida Juan Pablo II in the Curundu district of Panama City. Trails are open 5 A.M.–6 P.M. every day. The visitors center (tel. 232-6713 or 232-5516, 8 A.M.–4 P.M. Mon.–Fri., 8 A.M.–1 P.M. Sat.) offers a free brochure, but ask for the glossy color trail guide, which has a much-needed map. Guided tours in English and Spanish are sometimes available, but you have to arrange this at least a day or two in advance.

Cerro Azul

This hilly area about an hour east of Panama City has long been popular with more affluent city dwellers looking to escape the hot lowlands—the elevation reaches 950 meters, high enough to cool things off significantly.

Attempts have been made to attract tourists to the area, but only serious birders are likely to find it of great interest. They come for the foothill species, including some that are otherwise found only in the Darién. There are some stretches of elfin forest, but getting to the less-developed areas requires a four-wheel drive with high clearance, and some places can only be approached on foot. Birders should go with a knowledgeable naturalist guide. Other than that, this is mostly an area of suburban homes and little else.

To get to Cerro Azul, take the Corredor Sur toll road toward the international airport. When the road ends at the Riande Aeropuerto Hotel and Resort, turn left onto the Interamerican Highway. Make another left at the Super Xtra supermarket and follow the Cerro Azul signs. Casa de Campo is about a 20-minute drive up the hill. Turn left at Urbanización Las Nubes and follow the signs. To get to Cerro Azul by public transportation, take any bus going to 24 de Diciembre. Get off at the Super Xtra supermarket and transfer to a Cerro Azul bus.

There is one nice place to stay on Cerro Azul. **Hostal Casa de Campo Country Inn and Spa** (39 Avenida Los Cumulos, Panama City tel. 226-0274, Cerro Azul tel. 297-0067, cell 6677-8993, www.panamacasadecampo. com, starts at US$74.40 s/d) is a large, upscale country home that's been turned into a pleasant, well-maintained inn with lots of character and extensive grounds. All rooms are different, and some are considerably nicer than others. Note: Despite the connotations of the name, this is not a hostel. There's a small swimming pool, a full-service spa, and good views of the surrounding forested hills and Lago Alajuela. The inn offers a variety of spa and outdoor-adventure packages, including bird-watching trips. Meals are available for an extra charge. Round-trip transportation from Panama City, about an hour away, can be arranged for US$60 per couple. The staff speaks English, Spanish, and Italian.

Entertainment

NIGHTLIFE

Panama City has experienced a nightlife boom in recent years, concentrated in a handful of streets and neighborhoods around the city.

The most popular area is a densely packed grid of restaurants, clubs, cafés, and bars bounded by the **Bella Vista** district to the west and **Marbella** to the east. The center of this area is **Calle Uruguay.** Businesses come and go overnight, but there's always someplace worth visiting. At least for now, that is: Skyscraper construction is putting the future of the clubs, bars, and restaurants in this area in doubt. There is some evidence more and more action may move north to **Vía Argentina,** an older and traditionally more sedate area for an evening out. If the long-awaited Buddha Bar franchise ever opens an outlet in Panama, it will instantly be the hottest nightspot in the city. It's allegedly going up on Vía Brasil, but though it was originally supposed to open in 2010 the latest estimate is end of 2011.

Calle 53 Este, the main street through the upscale business district of Marbella, draws young singles and couples to its music clubs. The names of the clubs change, but the venues themselves have stayed pretty much intact for some years now.

The renovation of **Casco Viejo** has made it an ideal place for clubs, sidewalk cafés, bars, and seafood restaurants, at least on the weekends.

The newest entertainment area in Panama City is not actually in the city proper, but along the Calzada de Amador (Amador Causeway) in the old Canal Zone.

Clubs start late in Panama City. Very late. Most don't really get going until midnight and others don't reach their stride until 2 A.M. The partying often lasts all night. There has recently been an attempt to legislate a bar and disco closing time of 2 A.M. It's hard to imagine Panamanians standing for that, though.

Cover charges at prominent clubs on a big night can be US$10–20, though there are all kinds of promotions to offset this. Many clubs don't charge a cover during the week or early in the evening, usually before 11 P.M. Often women are admitted and/or drink free at least once a week, and some clubs have all-you-can-drink "open bar" specials before 11 P.M. Less-trendy spots typically charge US$5 or less.

Oddly, in a country where kids learn to dance to salsa and merengue as soon as they can walk and where partying is virtually a civil right, it's not unusual to see little or no dancing at a Panama City club these days. Even if the place is packed and the music deafening, most people may just be talking, flirting, and drinking. Music is generally played at ear-shattering volumes; bring earplugs.

Note: Don't ask a taxi driver to take you to a good "nightclub" unless what you're looking for is a strip club or brothel. What gringos call "nightclubs" or "clubs" are still usually known as "discos" in Panama.

A popular place for salsa lessons is **Bohío Florencia** (Vía España near ULACIT and Hospital San Fernando, tel. 221-7582), but it's in a busy industrial area that's a bit of a haul from downtown. Lessons are given Thursday 6–10 P.M. and cost US$3, but call ahead of time to make sure the schedule hasn't changed. The place can also sometimes arrange private lessons at a place of the students' choosing. Friday and Saturday are the hottest nights for actual dancing. The area can be intimidating at night, and you may be the only foreign visitor. But it's certainly an off-the-beaten-path option for those who want an urban adventure away from the touristy parts of Panama City. Be alert, dress neatly, and leave the bling behind.

Clubs and bars come and go fast in Panama City, and what's popular one week can be dead or out of business the next. That's why it's best to aim for a neighborhood rather than a specific bar or club. If all you want is a nice quiet bar, five-star hotels are a good option.

STRIP CLUBS, BROTHELS, AND BATHHOUSES

Prostitution is legal and regulated by the Panamanian government, but it's hardly free from exploitation. And AIDS and other sexually transmitted diseases are serious risks for those who engage in casual or commercial sex.

Those considering to partake should be aware of the following: An estimated 20,000 people in Panama are living with HIV, and epidemiologists believe the true number could be twice that. Given the country's small population, that gives Panama one of the highest rates in Central America. Perhaps surprisingly, more people die of AIDS in Panama than in any other Central American country; it is the country's seventh leading cause of death. And the rate of HIV infection is on the rise.

The prevalence of HIV/AIDS is especially high in Panama City and other metropolitan areas, but the United Nations' AIDS agency reports a high concentration of cases among poor indigenous peoples, especially the Kuna.

While Panama has made some progress with its HIV/AIDS programs, much more needs to be done. The UN estimates that fewer than half the prostitutes in Panama have been reached

by an AIDS-prevention program. It also has found that more than 10 percent of men who have sex with men are now HIV-positive. Many of these men also have sex with women. And there are plenty of other nasty sexually transmitted diseases out there as well.

Panama has several "gentlemen's clubs" or "nightclubs" with strip shows and the like. These usually have fancy names with words such as "elite" or "palace" in them. Those interested will have no trouble finding advertisements in tourist-oriented publications.

At last count, there were two gay bathhouses in Panama City, one of which is quite upscale. Again, those who are determined will likely find them, most likely through contacts at gay bars or the Internet.

The area around the public market in San Felipe and the back streets near Avenida Central have lots of rough and seedy bars, including some gay bars and places that are more or less brothels. This area can be quite dangerous, though, and one of the toughest Panamanians I know thinks it's a dumb move for a gringo to bar-hop around here – there's an excellent chance of getting mugged on the way home. You've been warned.

The **Sparkles Bar,** on the fifth floor of the InterContinental Miramar, has a terrific view of the skyline and Panama Bay.

Internet entertainment listings in Panama are getting a bit better, but including addresses, hours, and phone numbers is still an alien concept and listing sites are constantly abandoned without warning. Try cocoas.net, www.deal-ante.com, www.buscapanama.net, or www.elcuara.com.

Casco Viejo

Many of the first nightspots that followed the start of renovation work in Casco Viejo failed, most likely because affluent city dwellers are still sometimes leery of going to Casco Viejo at night. But a more interesting kind of nightlife has been emerging in the last few years.

Something of a bohemian, international art scene has begun to bubble up from the underground, fueled by the arrival of young backpackers and, especially, European and South American expats. The last time I was in Plaza Bolívar at night, I saw plenty of Europeans (especially Spaniards), South Americans, and young gringos dining al fresco on the plaza while a fire dancer vied for their attention. But I encountered almost no Panamanians, oddly enough.

The art scene is kept alive through a loose network of friends, artists, musicians and artist-friendly establishments, especially La Casona, Relic Bar, the Diablo Rosso café/art gallery, and the Super Gourmet store.

Most of the more mainstream action is concentrated around Plaza Bolívar, though nightspots pop up from time to time on the streets leading up to Plaza de Francia. The Parque Herrera and Plaza de la Independencia areas look poised to take off in the next couple of years.

Be careful in this area at night, particularly around Parque Herrera. It's best to come and go by taxi; ask the bar or club to call one for you.

Relic Bar (at Luna's Castle: Calle 9 Este and Avenida Eloy Alfaro, tel. 262-1540, www. relicbar.com, Tues.–Sat. nights) is a funky bar with an underground vibe. It's on the lowest level of the Luna's Castle hostel, so patrons must be buzzed in through the security gate. The bar opens onto a huge patio that looks up into the homes of the poorer residents of Casco Viejo, who no doubt find the shenanigans of the generally far-more scruffy tourists below at least as interesting as the tourists do the "Rear Window" peek into their lives. The bar itself is cavelike and contains part of the old wall that used to ring Casco Viejo.

The week before my most recent visit, the bar's most prominent neighbor stopped by: Panama's president, Ricardo Martinelli, and assorted ministers showed up unexpectedly to an event at the bar, much to the surprise of everyone there. Luna's Castle's staff report that Señor Presidente and his entourage were very cordial and encouraging of what the hostel and its bar were bringing to Casco Viejo. The only moment of consternation came when Martinelli ordered Johnny Walker Blue, a premium scotch that costs more per bottle than most backpackers spend in a fortnight. Naturally, the bar didn't have it in stock. ("But we do now," a Luna's Castle manager assured me. You never know when the unpredictable president might pay a second visit.)

La Casona (just east of Parque Herrera, behind the old Hotel Herrera at Calle 9 Oeste, tel. 211-0740, www.enlacasona.com, hours vary Wed.–Sat.) is a combination bar/ dance club/cultural center. It has inspired more affection and excitement since it opened in 2005 than any new place I can remember; it's filled a major gap in the nightlife scene.

People love its informal vibe—it's one of the few hot spots in Panama that doesn't have a dress code—as well as the mixture of people it attracts, from backpackers to the hipster art crowd to overdressed yuppies. They also love the ambience: The heart of the place is a large interior courtyard that preserves the crumbling colonial charm of the dilapidated mansion it's housed in. There's an art gallery, and La Casona occasionally hosts films, artists' talks, live concerts, and traveling exhibitions.

Platea (near the intersection of Avenida Central and Avenida A, tel. 228-4011, www. scenaplatea.com, 6 P.M.–2 A.M. daily) is a cozy cave of a bar on the ground floor of the same building that houses S'Cena, a Mediterranean restaurant, across from the ruins of the old Union Club. There's live jazz and salsa Thursday–Saturday.

The bar at **Restaurante Las Bóvedas** (Plaza de Francia, tel. 228-808 or 228-8068, 5:30 P.M.–late Mon.–Sat.) hosts live jazz Friday and Saturday after about 9:30 P.M.

Man, I hope this new place makes it: **Habana Panama** (Calle Eloy Alfaro and Calle 12 Este, tel. 212-0040 or 212-0152, cell 6780-2183 or 6678-1415, www.habanapanama.com, Thurs.–Sat. nights) is an attempt to bring actual dancing back to Panama City clubs, and to play something other than the same old típico, salsa, and reggaeton. It's a Cuban music hall that quite accurately bills itself as *el bunker de la música cubana*. Bunker indeed: It's right across from the ruins of the old public market, just down from the entrance to Casco Viejo, in an area that's supremely dangerous to wander around at night. Huge spotlights beam down onto the street from the entrance to the surprisingly upscale club, keeping the vampires at bay. This is definitely a place to take a cab door-to-door. The proprietors are going for old-Havana romance. This place was still getting on its (dancing) feet as this book went to press, but it looked likely it might be able to attract touring Cuban musicians and serve real Cuban food. Fingers crossed.

GAY BARS AND CLUBS

Panama City is still a place where gay bars have to keep a low profile, but you don't hear horror stories of police raids, gay bashings outside of clubs, and so on – not, at least, among the relatively affluent. It's more a matter of people wanting to be cautious and discreet. Gay bars and clubs are either in remote locations or hidden in plain sight – it's possible to walk right past one and not know anything's there at all.

Like other clubs, they come and go quickly. A mega-club on the outskirts of Panama City, known variously over the years as Boy Bar, Box, Glam, etc., has closed down, seemingly permanently, as have other shorter-lived places. That leaves BLG as the stalwart among the prominent gay clubs, though a newer one, Lips Dance Club, has the busiest events calendar. The Internet is the best source for current gay bar information; start with www.farraurbana.com.

The three clubs listed here are the most prominent and popular spots. They draw mostly a gay male clientele (the one lesbian bar closed years ago), but lesbians and straight singles or couples are welcome. Visitors will likely find the vibe at these places friendlier, more low-key, more inclusive, and less macho than at many of the city's straight bars and clubs.

There are also so-called "camouflage" bars – ostensibly straight bars that draw closeted gays – and rough dives. Neither kind is included here, for reasons of privacy and safety.

BLG (Transítmica and Avenida Brasil, tel. 265-1624, 10 P.M.-late Wed.-Sun., US$5 cover most nights), also known as Balagan's, recently moved from the Calle Uruguay area to a much-less-convenient spot for visitors along the Trasnsístmica near the Colpan Ford dealership. I haven't been to the new place yet, but BLG has always been relatively upscale, and, from the outside, the new home looks positively posh. Look for the "BLG" out front. It draws men, women, and some straight couples. The music is mostly electronica. It has *transformista* (drag) shows, comedians, and other special events on some nights.

La Gota Fría/Lips Dance Club (Avenida Manuel Espinosa Batista near the intersection of Avenida Simón Bolívar/Transístmica and Avenida Ricardo J. Alfaro/Tumba Muerto, no phone, www.lipspanama.net, 10 P.M.-late Wed. and Fri.-Sun., US$3–5 cover) has the most organized club schedule. It has a stage and frequently hosts *transformista* (drag) shows and other events. It hosts special shows throughout Carnaval. The club manages the neat trick of being in one of the most visible spots in the city but staying well hidden. It's on the 2nd floor of a building behind the Splash carwash, which is next to the large roundabout at the intersection of the Transístmica and Tumba Muerto. It's taken the place of the old Runway Bar. Everyone in the city knows this area, even if they don't know the club.

Oxen Club and Lounge (Tumba Muerto and Avenida Juan Pablo II, no phone, www.oxenpanama.com, check website for hours) is the massive warehouse club of choice now that Box and Boy Bar are no more. Like them, it can be bloody hard to find the first time. To get there from Tumba Muerto, first look for Plaza Edison, the distinctive cone-shaped office building. The cross street is Avenida Juan Pablo II; turn west onto it. The club is in the commercial complex on the right side of the road. Look for the "Oxen" sign. Oxen reopened in 2008 after a major renovation. The club hosts elaborate *transformista* (drag) shows from time to time. These can be entertaining even (or especially) when they're not particularly skilled.

⟨ Bella Vista and Marbella

Most of the popular clubs and bars in this area are on or near Calle Uruguay, Panama City's major nightlife destination. Places fold and new ones pop up at lightning speed, so it's impossible to say what will be there when you visit. The best bet is just to stroll around late on a Thursday, Friday, or Saturday night and follow the crowds. Monster venues that were closed down when I was last there, but will most likely have a new incarnation by the time you visit, are located across the street from Crepes & Waffles (Avenida 5B between Calle Uruguay and Calle Aquilino de la Guardia) and—sad but true—next to the Panama City Hooters (Calle 49 and Calle Uruguay).

How much longer this dynamic nightlife zone will stay intact is uncertain. This area is seeing more skyscraper construction than any other part of central Panama City.

Note: Street names are confusing around here. Calle Uruguay is also sometimes known as Calle 48 Este, and the cross streets have all kinds of names. Fortunately, "Calle Uruguay" is winning the battle. The cross streets are often called simply Calle 45, 46, 47, and so on, even though they are officially low-numbered avenues. In any case, the area is too small to get lost for long.

A few other nightlife mainstays are a short cab ride from Calle Uruguay, primarily on Calle 53 in Marbella.

S6is (Calle Uruguay between Avenida 4A and 5A, tel. 264-5237, Tues.–Sun. nights until late), pronounced *seis* (the number six), is a DJ bar/cocktail lounge in an old house that projects the air of a party in a pleasant, minimalist apartment. It attracts a mid-twenty-something and older crowd.

Sahara (Calle Uruguay and Calle 48, tel. 214-8284, 9 P.M.–late Tues.–Sat.) has been around for a few years. It's popular with gringos who like reggae and classic rock, and probably should be avoided by those who don't. However, it has outdoor seating in front, which can be appealing. The club next to it changes identities constantly but tends to attract a somewhat hipper crowd. Across the street is

Moods (tel. 263-4925, Wed.–Sat. nights), which attracts significantly fewer gringos.

Uruguay, at the north end of Calle Uruguay, and **The Loft,** at the south end, were popular when I was last in the area.

T.G.I. Friday's (Avenida 4A Sur near Calle Aquilino de la Guardia/49 Este, tel. 269-4199), ghastly though it may be, is mentioned here just because it's a perennially popular destination for young singles on the prowl or just hanging with their friends. There's another one attached to the Country Inns and Suites on the Calzada de Amador (Amador Causeway).

As a Panama kid who now lives in London, there was no way I'd skip a Panama pub called **The Londoner** (Calle Uruguay between Avenida 5A Sur and Avenida 5B Sur, tel. 214-4883, 5 P.M.–late daily). I found it's actually owned by a South African, it doesn't have beer on tap, and the Panamanian bartenders were puzzled by the concept of a gin and tonic, in any language. On the other hand, they were gracious and eager to learn—noticing my dismay at their ice-filled concoction, they actually tossed it and started from scratch, asking me for pointers. That's service you rarely find in Panama. Bottled imports include Guinness, Newcastle Brown Ale, and Strongbow cider. The Londoner is a homey place with a pool table and a less gringo-heavy crowd than other expat magnets: It's a good place to encounter Brits and Commonwealth types. It's where I'd head to watch a football (that is, soccer) game on a big screen, rather than resort to a sports bar. The English pub grub (US$5–11.50) includes shepherd's pie, bangers and mash, and fish and chips. But US$11.50 for fish and chips? I thought only London itself had the audacity to charge that.

Club Velvet (Plaza New York, Calle 53 Este at Calle 50, tel. 265-3284, schedule varies) is another club that morphs constantly. But whatever it's called, for several years now the venue has tended to attract the best electronic music in the city (granted, there's not much competition) and occasionally hosts international DJs and music festivals. Because of that, it's worth venturing over to the venue, which is in a large shopping plaza. The main promoter for the space is an outfit called Level Club: http://levelclub.blogspot.com/.

In and Around El Cangrejo (Includes Vía Argentina)

Nightlife in El Cangrejo centers around the big hotels and casinos and a handful of venerable old restaurants. When I was in high school, this was one of my favorite places for a night out, and I still go back for the occasional meal or drink.

But though it's still popular with some Panamanians and resident expats, today many of its nightspots strike me as overrated and/or overpriced. For instance, I've never understood the appeal of Caffé Pomodoro and Wine Bar, both of which are on the ground floor of the building that houses the Las Vegas Hotel Suites, but they've been popular for years so you may want to judge for yourself. More recently, the Vía Veneto hotel strip has become notorious as a place for prostitutes to meet customers.

One place I do like in the area is the **Istmo Brew Pub** (Avenida Eusebio A. Morales, tel. 265-5077, noon–late daily in the dry season). It's an open-air venue, right across the street from Wine Bar and Las Vegas Hotel Suites, with a friendly atmosphere, a pool table, and a big-screen TV showing whatever game happens to be on. This is the only place in Panama I know of that makes its own beer. It only makes three kinds, and on any given day only one may be in stock. The beer definitely tastes homemade rather than "artisanal," and at nearly $5 a pint is steep for Panama, where a local bottle is easy to find for a tenth of that price. Still, the home brew is light and refreshing and this is a comfortable spot to hang out and people watch. The only real misstep at this place is the disdain for Panama's own perfectly respectable German-style lagers. They serve no domestic beers, only "imported" beers along the lines of Amstel Light, Corona, and Budweiser. As these cost nearly $4 a bottle, the pints are a far better value. There's a daily happy hour until 8 P.M. The pub also serves bar food.

Some predict **Vía Argentina** may become more of a nightlife destination as high-rise construction puts the squeeze on the area. For now, though, it remains primarily what it's been for decades: a place to have a quiet meal, coffee, or late-night snack. The bar and club options thus far will appeal mainly to those who think karaoke or a bar band doing Journey covers makes for a fine night out.

CASINOS

Gambling is legal in Panama and casinos are scattered throughout the city, primarily in the better hotels around Vía España. Centrally located ones include the **Royal Casino,** next to the Marriott (tel. 210-9100, Calle 52 at Calle Ricardo Arias); the **Majestic Casino** (tel. 215-5151) in the Multicentro Mall on Avenida Balboa; and the **Fiesta Casino** (tel. 208-7250) behind the Hotel El Panamá. The newish **Veneto Hotel and Casino** is the glitziest (tel. 340-8888, Vía Veneto between Avenida 2 Norte/Eusebio A. Morales and Calle D). The hotel itself is a 17-story, 300-room Vegas knock-off with decor that's an odd mix of the garish and the generic—more Atlantic City than Panama City.

CINEMAS

There are plenty of movie theaters in Panama City. Mostly these are multiplexes showing recent Hollywood spectacles and are generally in English with Spanish subtitles rather than dubbed. Most ticket prices for adults are US$4 or less. Tickets are generally about half price on Tuesday or Wednesday.

The daily newspapers carry a list of current movies, locations, and show times. A good online list is located at www.cine.com.pa/, or try the La Prensa newspaper's online listings: www.prensa.com.

Popular, centrally located multiplexes include **Alhambra Vía España** (Vía España, tel. 264-6585), **Extreme Planet** (Vía España, tel. 214-7022) and **Cinemark Albrook** (Albrook Mall, tel. 314-6001). A new Cinemark multiplex in the **Multicentro** mall should be open by the end of 2010; see www.cinemarkca.com for updates.

The fancy Mexican-owned cinema chain **Cinépolis** (Multiplaza Pacific Mall, tel. 302-2463) has arrived in Panama, with its first beachhead in the upscale Multiplaza Pacific Mall. It offers two kinds of movie experiences: the usual multiplex theater at usual multiplex prices, or Cinépolis VIP, which allows patrons to choose their (overstuffed, reclining) seat in advance. Moviegoers can order food and drink to be delivered to their seats. It's pretty posh. Tickets for this cost US$10.50, which strikes the average Panamanian as extortionate, but is of course an unexpected bargain for many first-world visitors.

The **Diablo Rosso café/art gallery** (#11, Avenida A and Calle 7, tel. 228-4833 or 228-4837, www.diablorosso.com) in Casco Viejo hosts an indie film night on Tuesdays, a welcome addition to the movie scene for culture-starved residents who don't relish seeing the umpteenth retread of *The Fast and the Furious*.

CONCERTS AND THEATER

Panama City has an active theater scene, with regular productions featuring plays by Panamanian playwrights as well as classic and contemporary plays from other countries.

The easiest music performance to find on any given night is a *típico* combo, though salsa, Latin pop/rock, and other high-energy music forms are also popular. Most of these are local acts that perform in clubs, but with the opening of more modern, high-capacity venues such as the **Figali Convention Center** at the Panama Canal Village, the city is beginning to attract more big-name international pop acts. Big concerts are sometimes held in the baseball stadium, **Estadio Nacional Rod Carew,** as well. Classical music and dance groups come through less often. Tickets for major concerts and other events are usually available through Blockbuster outlets or online at www.blockbusterpanama.com or through Ticket Plus outlets, which are located in Farmacias Metro stores, at Extreme Planet, and in a few other spots around the city. Note: Official ticket outlets are constantly in flux in Panama and may

change by the time you arrive. The confusion is taken advantage of by ticket brokers and the occasional scammer. Make sure you're buying from a legitimate source. Also, official online outlets restrict sales by region, so you probably won't be able to buy tickets for a hot show until you're actually in Panama, unless you go through a local, trustworthy contact who can buy them for you.

Panama's elegant old **Teatro Nacional** (Avenida B between Calle 3 and Calle 4 in Casco Viejo, tel. 262-3525 or 262-3582) hosts visiting classical music ensembles and other arts events.

Teatro en Círculo (Avenida 6C Norte near Vía Brasil, tel. 261-5375), near Scubapanama, in a quiet residential area east of downtown, presents many of the city's highest-profile plays, from Spanish-language renditions of Shakespeare to well-received original productions by Panamanian playwrights. The small **Teatro Anita Villalaz** (tel. 211-4017 or 211-2040), in Plaza de Francia in Casco Viejo, is another prominent playhouse. Performance groups often rent out the **Teatro ABA** (Avenida Simón Bolívar/Transístmica near Avenida de los Periodistas, tel. 260-6316) for their productions. It's near the Chinese restaurant Palacio Lung Fung and not far from Teatro en Círculo.

The **Atlapa Convention Center** (tel. 526-7200), next to the Sheraton Panama Hotel and Convention Center off Vía Israel, has two theaters, the 3,000-seat **Anayansi** and the 600-seat **La Huaca.**

THE LOTTERY

The Lotería Nacional de Beneficencia, or national lottery, is a tenacious carryover from a time when Panamanians had fewer entertainment options. The first lottery was held in 1882, and the current system dates from 1919. It's still hugely popular.

Every Sunday and Wednesday at 1 P.M., a crowd gathers for the drawing, broadcast live throughout the country on TV and radio. Drawings are held in Plaza Víctor Julio Gutiérrez, which is covered by an open-sided

© WILLIAM FRIAR

There are nearly 10,000 lottery vendors in Calidonia alone.

shed that takes up an entire block between Avenida Perú and Avenida Cuba and Calle 31 and Calle 32. Anyone can drop by to watch.

The ritual is as solemn and unwavering as a church service. First, the lottery balls are turned incessantly back and forth in a shiny steel cage by a designated official. This seems to last for hours. At last, the cage is stopped and a ball is extracted by a child dressed in his or her very best. The ball is twisted apart to reveal a number printed inside, which is held up for all to see, read aloud by the emcee, and then carefully recorded on a board behind the stage. Three sets of four numbers are chosen, corresponding to the first, second, and third prize. A ticket holder must have all four numbers in the correct order to win one of the three prizes, though there are small prizes (US$1–50) for getting some of the numbers right.

Often, the ball must be loosened with a special contraption, heightening the suspense.

(In 1991 lottery officials tried to update the system with a fancy new pneumatic machine, but a suspicious and tradition-minded public rebelled.) Going through this process 12 times turns the drawing into an event long enough to allow for all kinds of side shows: beauty queens in *polleras,* folkloric dances, musical performances, visiting dignitaries, and so on.

All this for a first prize of...US$2,000. Second prize is US$600 and third US$300. That's still a lot of money for the average hard-working Panamanian. And people often buy multiple tickets with the same numbers; theoretically, the maximum prize is US$540,000—if one has bought 270 winning tickets.

There are also special drawings that pay more. *Gorditos del Zodíaco* (little fat ones of the Zodiac) are held on the last Friday of each month, for instance. First prize is US$4,000 (for a maximum of US$700,000 with multiple tickets). A new gimmick, the *sorteo de oro* (the gold drawing), increases the payout if a winning ticket has certain letters printed on it. To purists like me, though, adding this alphabet soup to the mix ruins the charming purity of those three rows of numbers, which are posted diligently around the country on bus station chalkboards and other public spots twice a week, year in and year out.

Four-number tickets cost US$1. If that's too expensive, two-number *chances* go for US$0.25. These pay out if the numbers correspond to the last two numbers of any of the winning combinations. First prize for these is US$14, second prize is US$3, and third prize is US$2. The maximum for multiple tickets is US$280.

Tickets are sold by freelance vendors around the country. Those interested in playing should have little trouble finding a vendor on any street with lots of foot traffic. A whole battalion has stalls set up on the Avenida Perú side of the plaza, between Calle 31 and Calle 32. There are nearly 10,000 vendors in Panama.

Shopping

Panama certainly has no shortage of shopping malls and commercial centers—at last count there were more than two dozen of various sizes. Many of these, however, look better-stocked from the outside than they do on closer inspection, and the city is not the best place to look for the latest fashions (many better-off Panamanians fly up to Miami for their shopping). However, those in the market for cosmetics and perfumes can find better deals than they would in the United States at the nicer department stores, such as the **Stevens, Collins, Felix B. Maduro,** and **Dante** chains. There are branches of these on Vía España, on Tumba Muerto (Avenida Ricardo J. Alfaro) in El Dorado, and in some of the malls.

One of the newer and glitzier malls is the upscale **Multiplaza Pacific,** in Punta Pacífica. The youth-oriented **Multicentro** is on the west end of Avenida Balboa near Punta Paitilla. There's a gringo-style food court on the top floor that has a great view of the city and the bay. Another new and growing complex is the **Albrook Mall,** sometimes also called Los Pueblos II, next to the Gran Terminal de Transportes, the main bus terminal, which is near the domestic airport in Albrook, a former U.S. Air Force base. It's many locals' favorite.

The newest ritzy shopping center is **Metro Mall,** about halfway between downtown and the international airport on Vía Tocumen, the old road (not the highway) to the airport. However, it's too far from town to be of much interest to visitors. Other upscale shopping destinations include the **Bal Harbour** mini-mall (mainly for food, especially kosher food) in the Punta Paitilla area, the designer-name shops along **Calle 53 in Marbella** (especially in the **World Trade Center**), and the tony jewelry stores and galleries on **Avenida 2 Sur/ Samuel Lewis** in Obarrio. More bargain-oriented stores are on **Vía España** and in the

street artist, Plaza Bolívar

malls and strip malls of the **El Dorado** neighborhood, though both places have higher-end shops as well.

ART GALLERIES

Panama's best high-end art gallery is **Imagen** (Calle 50 and Calle 77, tel. 226-8989, 9 A.M.–1 P.M. and 2–6 P.M. Mon.–Sat.). It's in a lovely old building and the staff is gracious. It's small, but it's a good place to go just to get a sense of what's happening in the local art scene. **Habitante** (Calle Uruguay, tel. 264-6470, 9 A.M.–6 P.M. Mon.–Sat.), in the Calle Uruguay nightlife area, is also small, but less interesting, though it's certainly more central. **Mateo Sariel** (Vía Porras and Calle 66 Este, tel. 270-2404, 9 A.M.–6 P.M. Mon.–Fri.), though also well known, often feels more like a framing shop than an art gallery, though those willing to rummage around the piles of paintings sometimes unearth a find.

The hippest of the new art galleries sprouting up in Casco Viejo is the **Diablo Rosso café/art gallery** (#11, Avenida A and Calle 7, tel. 228-4833 or 228-4837, www.diablorosso.com). It frequently hosts after-hours art shows and events.

BOOKSTORES

Panama City is not a great town for readers, but the bookstore offerings have gotten somewhat better in recent years. Don't expect bargains, though—shipping heavy books to Panama is expensive, and that's reflected in the prices. Both the Gran Morrison department store and the Farmacia Arrocha drugstore chains carry books and magazines. Offerings are hit-or-miss, though occasionally a rare find surfaces. The Gran Morrison on Vía España is particularly promising.

Librería Argosy (Vía Argentina near Vía España, tel. 223-5344, 10 A.M.–6 P.M. Mon.–Sat.), run by a friendly Greek émigré named Gerasimos (Gerry) Kanelopulos, has been a Panama City institution for more than three decades. It's a small, crowded place. Be sure to dig below the piles—a lot of books are buried under each other. The shop carries a substantial collection of works about Panama or written by Panamanian authors. Note Gerry's extensive collection of autographed photos. Pride of place belongs to Dame Margot Fonteyn, who spent her twilight years in Panama.

There are several outlets of **El Hombre de la Mancha,** a local bookstore/café chain, mostly in shopping malls. They typically have a small English-language book selection with a few bestsellers and a lot of bulk discount books, as well as a reasonable selection of Spanish-language books by Panamanian authors. The branch near the Country Inns and Suites in El Dorado (Central Comercial Camino de Cruces, tel. 360-2063, 10 A.M.–10 P.M. Mon.–Sat., 11 A.M.–8 P.M. Sun.) has the best selection, at least in Spanish, but it's also the least conveniently located for most tourists. There are branches in the Multiplaza Pacific, Multicentro, and Albrook shopping malls, the domestic airport at Albrook, and the Sheraton Panama Hotel and Convention Center. See www.bookshombredelamancha.com for a current list of all the branches.

Exedra Books (Vía España and Vía Brasil, tel. 264-4252, noon–7 P.M. Mon.–Sat.) is modeled after U.S. chains, such as Borders, minus the books. For such a large, attractive store, most of its offerings are odd and very limited. The English-language books in particular seem to consist of by-the-pound leftovers. It does have a decent selection of Spanish-language fiction, though, and it seems to be making a genuine effort to become a real bookstore. It also carries some used books at better prices. Upstairs there's an Internet café that actually has a café. It's also a ticket outlet for local concerts and other events. Literary talks, in Spanish, are given on Monday night at 7 P.M.

CRAFT SHOPS AND BOUTIQUES

The **Reprosa** jewelry store (Avenida 2 Sur/Samuel Lewis and Calle 54 Este, tel. 271-0033, www.reprosa.com, 9 A.M.–6 P.M. daily) is a Panama institution. It's a great place to go for unique presents or souvenirs. There's a second Reprosa store (9 A.M.–5 P.M. daily) in

BOUTIQUE BREEBAART: A DASH OF PARIS IN PANAMA

The small fashion house **Boutique Breebaart** (Calle Abel Bravo, Casa #5, Obarrio, tel. 264-5937, 9 A.M.–6 P.M. Mon.–Fri., open weekends by appointment), until a few years ago located on Calle 50, is now in the home of its owner and designer, the warm and utterly charming Helèné Breebaart, an artist who first came to Panama as the local representative for Christian Dior perfumes. Try to chat with her, in any of her several languages, if she's around: She is a relentlessly creative and upbeat person, and she has some great stories of her years in Panama, ranging from life as a clothing designer during the military dictatorship to dressing Rosalynn Carter for a gala evening of former and current U.S. first ladies. (Ms. Carter was by far the most beautifully dressed; I've seen the photos.) This may not be easy, though, as Helèné is a human dynamo and very busy; she's never still for long.

The boutique offers unusual dresses, bathing suits, cushions, place settings, tablecloths, handbags, napkins, and other items. Recurring motifs include butterflies, hibiscuses, hummingbirds, pineapples, coral, and other tropical-Panama flora and fauna, usually appliquéd onto the dresses and other items. But most of all, her signature work is inspired by the colorful *molas* of the Kunas, who are the ones who actually stitch the clothing and other pieces she designs. Those staying in high-end hotels may recognize her work (or in some cases poorer-quality rip-offs) from the pillows and other furnishings in their rooms. Her collections appear from time to time in upscale department stores in the United States.

Much of the work is quite lovely and elegant; some is rather kitschy and works best on the beach. Each piece is handmade and can cost anywhere from US$10 to thousands of dollars. Tablecloths alone start at around US$300, or US$1,000 and up for custom-made ones.

Women of considerable means who'd like a one-of-a-kind dress or jacket can meet with Helèné and brainstorm a colorful creation. Simple shifts start at about US$400. Producing the final article can take weeks and the boutique would like to do at least one fitting, but these can be created with extra material and shipped to the purchaser for final adjustments back home if time is short. Those on a more modest budget can pick up one of her butterfly, hibiscus, or hummingbird patches, starting at around US$8, and later pin or sew them onto an article of clothing, or even use them as drink coasters. The patches come in attractive wrapping and make nice little gifts.

A few items are on display, as are some jewelry, hats, and other accessories made by other designers. If you visit, peek in the back to see the dozen Kuna women (and perhaps a gay Kuna man – gay men in Kuna society take on traditional women's roles) at work.

Casco Viejo. Reprosa is most famous for its reproductions of gold and silver *huacas,* figures recovered from pre-Colombian graves. The figures are created by using molds made through the so-called "lost wax" process, which creates exact replicas, including the imperfections in the original. This process is virtually the same as that used to produce the ancient original pieces.

Prices at Reprosa are very reasonable—some start at less than US$10, though the cost goes straight up from there depending on the purity of the gold or silver. Pieces include replicas of some of the finest and oldest *huacas* in the collection of Panama's anthropology museum. The store carries other jewelry as well, including replicas of pieces of eight and the pearl-encrusted brooches known as *mosquetas,* the latter were traditionally worn with the *pollera.*

Reprosa offers tours of its factory near Panamá la Vieja; send an email to tours@reprosa.com for details. Its website also offers a thorough virtual tour of the factory, plus a map of how to get there. (Local trivia: The blonde model in Reprosa's fanciful ads is the owners' daughter.)

Linen House, **Casa de los Manteles** (Avenida de los Mártires near Calle J, tel. 262-0822, 9 A.M.–6 P.M. Mon.–Sat.), is known for its lovely embroidered tablecloths, napkins, and other linens. It also carries good-quality guayaberas (the semiformal traditional Latin American shirt). This area is not the safest these days, though it should be fine in the daytime and the store has a parking lot behind the building.

There is a **handicrafts market** in Plaza Cinco de Mayo, behind the anthropology museum, that offers hats, *mola* blouses, hammocks, sandals, and the like. Hats are especially well-represented. A place here takes passport photos for US$1 per half dozen. Most stalls open by 9 A.M. daily and stay open until sundown. If you have trouble finding this market, ask for the *artesanía* near Plaza Cinco de Mayo. Better handicrafts markets are in Balboa, in the old Canal Zone.

DISCOUNT DEPARTMENT STORES

The **Gran Morrison** department store chain is a bit like a Kmart in the United States. The Vía España branch (Vía España near Calle 51, tel. 269-2211, 9 A.M.–6 P.M. Mon.–Sat., 9 A.M.–6 P.M. Sun.) is close to many of the city's more popular hotels. In addition to a wide assortment of low-end household goods and such, the store has a music department with a decent selection of *típico, rock en español,* salsa, merengue, and a bit of gringo music. It also carries some souvenirs, local books, and an extensive collection of magazines in English and Spanish.

There's a huge, five-story outlet of the **El Machetazo** discount department-store chain in the Calidonia area (Avenida Perú between Calle 28 Este and Calle 29 Este, tel. 227-3014, 8:30 A.M.–7:30 P.M. daily). There's a grocery store on the ground floor. It also has a pharmacy, cheap clothing, and lots of assorted junk.

ELECTRONICS AND PHOTO SUPPLIES

Panafoto (Calle 50 and Calle 49A Este, tel. 263-3000, 9 A.M.–7:30 P.M. Mon.–Sat., noon–6 P.M. Sun.) is a modern, glass-enclosed consumer electronics store and the first stop for camera buffs. There's an espresso bar upstairs.

TAILORED SUITS

La Fortuna (Vía España at Calle 55 Este near Vía Argentina, tel. 302-7890 or 263-6434, 9 A.M.–6 P.M. Mon.–Sat.) is Panama's best-known destination for tailored men's suits. It's been around since 1925 and has dressed ambassadors and presidents. A custom-made suit or tuxedo made from high-quality imported fabric is sold for around US$500; knock US$100–200 off that estimate for less-expensive material. One of the nifty things about having a suit made here is that the tailors sew a panel inside the suit with the buyer's name and the statement that it was made *exclusivo* for him. Another cool thing is that if you don't care for any of their styles, you can bring in a photo of what you like and they'll create it for you. I've had jackets and suits made here based on ads from fashion magazines and photos downloaded from the Internet, and I've been pleased with the results. (And no, I didn't get a price break for writing that.) They carry a range of fabric from famous European and North American designers.

The late dictator Omar Torrijos reportedly once declared that the owner, José Abadí, was the only man who could make him drop his trousers. There are autographs on display from Geoffrey Rush, Jamie Lee Curtis, and Pierce Brosnan, who were in Panama to make the dreadful movie adaptation of John Le Carré's *The Tailor of Panama*—inevitably, Brosnan's note dubbed Abadí the "real tailor of Panama." Since this is the tailor of choice for many high-ranking Panamanian politicians, it's said he was one of the inspirations for Le Carré's book, about a tailor to powerful Panamanian officials who is forced by a British agent to spy on his customers. Fittingly enough, the first time I was there the head of the Asamblea Legislativa (the national legislature) was in the store buying suits for his five bodyguards. Every time I come a power player seems to be shopping.

Visitors should place an order at the start of their travels, as the process requires two fittings, and the shop normally needs at least 10 days to make a suit, more during peak seasons, such as before the independence holidays in November, when they're busy making uniforms for bands and such. Those pressed for time can sometimes have a suit made in 24 hours, but don't expect a perfect fit. Try to give it at least a week.

Sports and Recreation

Panama City is really not the best spot for either spectator or participant sports. Generally only the most expensive hotels have tennis courts, pools big enough to swim laps in, or decent gyms. Most sports clubs are upscale places open to members and their guests.

The best options for those interested in golf are Summit Golf, Hotel and Spa in the former Canal Zone or, for those going to the Pacific beaches, the course at the Coronado Hotel and Resort or the newer El Mantarraya Golf Club at the Royal Decameron Resort. They are well-maintained, championship courses with good facilities.

PISCINA OLÍMPICA ADAN GORDON

Piscina Olímpica Adan Gordon (between Calle 31 and Calle 32 and Avenida Cuba and Avenida Perú, 8:30–11:45 A.M. and 1–3:45 P.M. Tues.–Sat., 8:30–11:45 A.M. and 12:30–2:45 P.M. Sat. and Sun.) is a decent, Olympic-sized swimming pool across from the national lottery plaza in the heart of the budget hotel district. Tourists are welcome to go for a splash for US$0.50, but passports must be left with the attendant. Don't leave valuables unattended.

ESTADIO NACIONAL ROD CAREW

Panama produces a disproportionate number of U.S. Major League baseball players given its small size. *Fútbol* (soccer) is beginning to nudge *beisbol* from its pedestal as the country's favorite team sport, but it is still Panama's national pastime, has a passionate following, and produces some of the best players in the world.

The national baseball stadium (tel. 230-4255, www.estadionacional.com.pa), named after native son and Hall of Famer Rod Carew, is in the Cerro Patacón area on the northwest outskirts of Panama City. The stadium is bounded by three major arteries—the Corredor Norte, the Camino de la Amistad, and the Transístmica—which makes it easy to get to. The stadium seats 26,000, but during a routine game between provincial teams, it may be nearly empty, making it easy to get close to the action and possibly see a major-leaguer in the making. Tickets typically cost US$5 or less. Note that baseball is played only during Panama's summer (e.g., the dry season, the baseball off-season in the U.S.). The baseball season ends in May. More information is available at www.estadionacional.com.pa and www.fedebeis.com.

Big concerts featuring international stars are sometimes held at the stadium.

HIPÓDROMO PRESIDENTE REMÓN

Panama has a well-established horse-racing industry. The national racetrack, Hipódromo Presidente Remón (tel. 217-6060, www.hipodromo.com) is on the outskirts of the city. It's about eight kilometers east of Punta Paitilla in the Juan Díaz area, on the way to the international airport. It holds races Thursday, Saturday, Sunday, and holidays. The quickest way to get there is via the Corredor Sur. It's also accessible from Vía España, which becomes Vía José Agustín Arango east of the city. The racecourse is just past the 45,000-seat national football (i.e., soccer) stadium, Estadio Rommel Fernández.

SCUBAPANAMA

Scubapanama (Avenida 6C Norte, tel. 261-3841 or 261-4064, www.scubapanama.com), Panama's largest dive operator, also rents and sells snorkeling and diving gear. Those who plan to do a fair amount of snorkeling should know that most of the equipment available on Panama's beaches and islands is mediocre at best. This is a decent place to buy some if you didn't bring your own.

Accommodations

Panama City offers good lodging options for almost any budget. But finding an available room has gotten harder and harder in the last several years. The city just doesn't have enough rooms yet to accommodate the boom in tourism and business.

Developers are scrambling to build major new hotels. Advance reservations are essential, especially for midrange and luxury hotels. Try to book as far ahead of time as possible if visiting during holidays and the dry season. Some travelers have found themselves in the odd position of having to aim for a cheaper hotel than they'd like because the pricier places were packed. Panama City hotels tend to be terrible about answering email and responding to reservation-request forms on their websites. This is especially but not exclusively true of the lower-end lodgings. If you don't hear back in a few days, your best bet is to call.

WHAT TO EXPECT

Hotels often charge the same for one or two guests, so those traveling solo can save money by buddying up with fellow travelers. A third or fourth guest often costs just a fraction more, so small groups can get deals even at the higher end of the scale.

The midrange and high-end hotels often offer corporate rates and promotional deals that can be significantly cheaper than their standard rates. It never hurts to ask for the discount, which one can often get without so much as a business card.

The biggest problem with Panama City's cheaper hotels, as with those throughout the country, is management's belief that mattresses last forever. Given that they tend to be poor quality to begin with, it's not unusual to find thin, squishy, or plank-hard mattresses in otherwise decent-looking hotels. Try the beds in a few rooms before deciding to stay.

Prices quoted here are generally for standard rooms. Luxury hotels all have more expensive options for those who can't burn through their money fast enough. All prices listed include Panama's 10-percent room tax.

Hostels

Panama City is seeing a welcome surge in hostels, and these tend to be the safest of the bare-bones accommodations. The best can be surprisingly pleasant, but dispel any notion of European- or even American-style youth hostels: Panama City hostels tend to be grungy, makeshift affairs installed in converted apartments. Still, there's no better place to meet fellow backpackers and get insider tips on budget travel. Many hostels are now serving as de facto travel agencies, helping guests with area tours and travel throughout Panama and to Colombia and Costa Rica. Wi-Fi access and use of Internet-enabled computers, luggage storage, and a modest breakfast are now standard free extras at the city's hostels. Some have air-conditioning, at least at night. They also increasingly have private rooms that can be pretty decent, especially for the price; these are popular and tend to fill up fast. Note that Panama City hostels are often on the move. Real-estate is so expensive in the city that hostels often take up residence in an old apartment building that's waiting to be bought up, torn down, and replaced with a skyscraper. When that happens, the hostel owner packs up and moves on to the next skyscraper-in-waiting.

ROOMS DURING THE BOOM

Panama City has the fullest hotels in Central or South America, despite adding new hotel rooms at a faster pace than any of its neighbors. In 2007, the city had the second highest hotel occupancy rate in the world. Nearly 85 percent of hotel rooms were full on any given day that year, according to Deloitte's Global Ranking Index, the industry standard for room occupancy statistics. It was the first time a Central American country had even cracked the list.

Not surprisingly, high demand drove prices up: Room rates at midrange and high-end hotels nearly doubled between the first and second editions of this guidebook, in 2005 and 2008.

By 2010 the worldwide recession was slowing the arrival of foreign visitors, but not the hotel-building spree. So by the time you visit, it may be a bit easier to get a reasonably priced room.

Fortunately, prices for the lower-end options go up much more slowly than the posher places, and there are more decent options in this category than ever.

Two last things to bear in mind: The explosion in high-rise construction means the gorgeous sea or city view shown on the website may be gone by the time you arrive: A skyscraper can shoot up virtually overnight right outside your window. Try to get the hotel to confirm that your room has a view, if that's important to you, but be prepared to pay a bit more for it. Also, in 2010 I encountered more construction in every direction than ever before. It was nearly impossible to find a spot entirely free from the chatter, whine, and bang of construction anywhere in the city, though the plate-glass windows and air-conditioning of the fancier hotels muffle the noise.

This can, and has, happened suddenly. Make sure you know where your hostel really is before you show up!

Under US$25

At the low end of the scale, every US$5 extra can mean dramatically better digs. For US$10, single or double (s/d), a night, don't expect much more than a bare room with a cold-water bathroom and a fan, though occasionally even these places offer air-conditioning for a couple of bucks more.

US$25-50

Air-conditioning is universally available once the price gets up to around US$25–30 s/d per night; hot water kicks in at less than that. For US$40–50, it's possible to find some quite pleasant, clean hotels with modern furnishings, reliable air-conditioning, clean hot-water bathrooms, and sometimes free wireless Internet access and cable TV.

US$50-150

For around US$70–100, you're getting into two-and-a-half- and three-star hotel territory. At that price, it's possible to find lodgings with lots of character, attractive rooms with good beds, and amenities such as cable TV, in-room telephones, free wireless Internet, in-room safes, a decent restaurant/bar, a small swimming pool (often on the rooftop), and so on. Some of these places are in high demand and should be booked several days or even weeks in advance if possible.

Many of the options for US$100–150 a night are so-called *aparthotels,* which offer furnished, usually large studio and one-bedroom apartments with a full kitchen and utensils, telephone, and washer and dryer either in the apartment or in a laundry facility on the premises. These also sometimes have a business center and small pool. They typically offer price breaks for long stays. These have proved popular and prices have climbed accordingly, but they still get booked solid with long-term visitors doing business in or moving to Panama.

Over US$150

Rack rates for most four- and five-star hotels

are US$200–300 a night per couple. Guests may find these rates a good-value splurge at the very best places and excessive at others. Prices can vary wildly from day to day, and deals are often available. Booking far enough in advance—a good idea since these places are in great demand—can knock about US$100 off the rack rate. Luxury hotels universally offer high-speed wired or wireless Internet, but expect to pay at least US$15 a day or more for the privilege. Given that free Wi-Fi has become standard at hotels that charge a tenth as much as these supposedly "service-oriented" luxury places, this just seems petty. If all goes as planned, many new brand-name hotels in these categories are expected to open during the life of this book, ranging from Doubletree and Westin to Hilton and, perhaps, a Buddha Bar Hotel and Spa.

Panama City is gearing up to introduce a couple of closely related kinds of hotels: high-end apartment-style suites and condo hotels. The first are basically *aparthotels* for the luxury market. The second are timeshare-style condos that can be rented out as hotel rooms when the owner is out of town. Both ideas are new to Panama, at least at this level. No doubt developers who have seen demand for apartment and condominiums turn flat while hotel demand soars will be watching this experiment with great interest, prepared to retool if it succeeds.

CASCO VIEJO

Safe and pleasant places to stay have been slow to come to Casco Viejo, but it's finally happening. A couple of hostels, a gorgeous boutique hotel, and luxury apartments have arrived, and more options are coming. Lovely apartments can often be rented by the night. The websites www.loscuatrotulipanes.com and www.arco-properties.com (enter "San Felipe" in the search engine) are good places to start looking.

Under US$10

Hospedaje Casa Grande (Avenida Central and Calle 8 Este in Casco Viejo, tel. 211-3316, US$6 s/d, US$7 s/d with balcony) is in a historic yellow building, Aspinwall House, that now has the feel of a dicey squat. The thin walls are made of plywood and reach only two-thirds of the way to the very high ceilings. Rooms have foam mattresses and fans and little else. Bathrooms are shared. This is a bottom-of-the-barrel place and is only for those with the tightest of budgets and a sense of adventure. Guests should keep a firm grasp on their belongings and pray no one smokes in bed. But you can't beat the price, because of which this place is always full. It's on well-trafficked Avenida Central. It has a gated entrance.

US$10-25

⟨ Luna's Castle (Calle 9 Este and Avenida Eloy Alfaro, tel. 262-1540, http://lunascastle.com, US$12 in dorms, US$28 s/d in private rooms, breakfast included) opened in 2008 and has quickly become the Hilton of Panama's hostels. It's owned by the same guys who made Mondo Taitu (now under new ownership) and Hostel Heike in Bocas popular.

Luna's Castle is in a lovely three-story colonial house with high ceilings and ornate balconies. French doors on the 2nd and 3rd floor open onto million-dollar views of Casco Viejo, Panama Bay, and the downtown skyline. Original fixtures include tile floors and a handsome wooden staircase. On the ground floor is Relic Bar, a Casco Viejo hotspot that is open to all. (For security in the evening, only hostel guests with wristbands are allowed upstairs into the hostel itself. The wristbands also entitle guests to discounts at some area restaurants.) In the back, the hostel faces dilapidated buildings that are still very much occupied by the poorer families of Casco Viejo; a friendly greeting will almost certainly be warmly returned.

The hostel has both dorms and private rooms. One dorm has four beds. The rest have 6–12 beds. All are mixed sex. Dorm rooms 7, 10, and 12 have ocean views. Number 10 is the most spacious. There are seven private rooms. A movie theater (!) downstairs shows current releases to hostel guests, who can recline on three tiers of mattresses that serve as stadium-style seats. There's a lounge area, table tennis, and computers with free Internet access, as well as free Wi-Fi for those with their own electronic gizmos. The included breakfast consists of (make-your-own) pancakes, bananas, coffee, and tea. The hostel also occasionally hosts art exhibitions and other cultural events.

Luna's Castle has a fat binder that contains up-to-date information for budget travelers on where to go and how to get around in Panama City and other backpacker destinations. The hostel also has maps of Casco Viejo and the rest of Panama City. They can help make arrangements for stays in other parts of Panama, including land transits to Kuna Yala. Guests have access to lockers, free luggage storage, a book exchange, a communal kitchen, and local and international calling. One of the managers is a massage therapist who offers on-site massages. She even gives haircuts.

In short, this place is frickin' impressive. It's my first choice for budget travelers who want to spend time exploring Casco Viejo, meet other travelers, and get help with onward travel. On the other hand, it's a big, self-contained backpacker enclave and it's not terribly convenient to other parts of the city. Travelers who want to meet locals and see other parts of the city on the cheap may find it easier to stay in more centrally located places such as Mamallena, La Jungla, or Pension Las Torres.

Note: Guests need to be especially careful in this part of Casco Viejo. The hostel is at the entrance to the old town, at the top of a ramp leading up from the rough streets of the Terraplén, which is deserted at night since the old public market was torn down. Please do not walk through this area at night; splurge on a taxi. However, the area around the hostel should be safer than most parts of Casco Viejo because it's directly across from a house patrolled by guards and just down the street from the presidential palace, which bristles with armed police. There is a security gate and a night security guard. There's one especially nice touch for prospective guests who arrive in the middle of the night: The security guard will admit you and let you crash on the movie-theater mattresses. You can check

into the hostel in the morning when the staff arrives.

Opened in 2005, **Hospedaje Casco Viejo** (Calle 8 and Avenida A, tel. 211-2027, www.hospedajecascoviejo.com, starts at US$10) offers 16 rooms in an old three-story house behind the Iglesia de San José (Church of the Golden Altar). All the rooms have ceiling fans only. Rates are US$10 per person in dorm rooms, US$18 s/d in a private room with shared bathroom. None of the bathrooms have hot water. Some of the bedrooms have balconies. There's a tiny interior patio and a TV room for hanging out, a shared kitchen, a gated entrance with 24-hour reception, free wireless Internet, and lockers. With just a little bit of work this place could be great, but as of now it tends to the grungy side. In any case, the location can't be beat. The hostel can arrange airport pickup for US$20.

Over US$150

A truly boutique hotel, **▐ Canal House** (Avenida A and Calle 5 Oeste, tel. 228-1907 or 228-8683, toll-free U.S./Canada tel. 888/593-5023, www.canalhousepanama.com, starts at US$231 s/d including breakfast) is by far the best place to stay in Casco Viejo. In fact, it offers some of the handsomest accommodations in the country. A four-story, 4,000-square-foot house built in 1893 and beautifully restored in 2005, it has just two suites and one guest room. The opulent furnishings manage to be both contemporary and in keeping with the colonial feel of the building. As its name suggests, the Canal House pays homage to the Panama Canal, down to the books in the library and the photos on the walls.

The master suite is the Miraflores (US$373), which features a huge bedroom with a king-size bed and walk-in closet, a sitting/dining area, a wraparound balcony, and a spiral staircase that leads to a loft study with a daybed, desk, and library. The Gatun Suite (US$297), on the top floor, has a king-size bed and a separate sitting room. The Pedro Miguel Room (US$231) is dramatically smaller, little bigger than its queen-size bed, but guests have access to the same common areas and services as other guests.

All three accommodations feature high-gloss hardwood floors, plasma-screen TVs with cable TV, free wireless Internet, iPod docking stations, a loaner cell phone, and French doors that open onto wrought-iron balconies with fascinating views of the surrounding neighborhood. (Be sure to check out the view from the roof.) The management promises round-the-clock attentive service. The entire house can be rented for US$880 and accommodate up to 10 people, which can be a good deal for families or groups of friends. This place books up well in advance, especially the least-expensive room (Pedro Miguel).

CALIDONIA, LA EXPOSICIÓN, AND SANTA ANA

Most of the budget hotels are in and around the Calidonia/La Exposición district. This is a busy, older neighborhood near Panama Bay, with a high concentration of cheaper hotels, most of them in a 10-block area between Avenida Perú and Avenida Cuba. Note that Avenida 3 Sur is quieter than these two major avenues, something to consider when choosing a place to stay; it's just two blocks from the bay. This area is not exactly overrun with good restaurants, but there are plenty of cheap places and some deliver.

Note: Some of the cheaper options, especially those with the word "pension" or "residencial" in their names, often are used by local couples needing, shall we say, a little quality alone time. This isn't necessarily as tawdry as it sounds. While some twosomes are engaging in a financial transaction or adulterous liaison, others simply live in small houses with large families and never get any privacy at home. In any case, these assignations happen in hotels around the world at every price level; they just tend to be more blatant at el cheapo places. If this sort of thing makes you uncomfortable, consider paying more money for a hotel that's more discreet about guests that are not looking for a good night's sleep.

Though a somewhat poor neighborhood,

© WILLIAM FRIAR

The people-watching on Avenida Central is always fascinating and lots of fun.

Calidonia is a bustling area and travelers generally feel safe enough here. Still, as always it pays to stay alert, especially at night, when it's probably a good idea to get around by taxi. The neighborhood deteriorates as the street numbers go down and one approaches the Santa Ana district. I have found just a few places below Calle 28 Este I consider safe or decent enough to recommend. Adventurous types can try one of the rock-bottom pensions along the pedestrian section of Avenida Central, but these are known hangouts for prostitutes and their customers. I don't recommend them. That area is busy day and night, which can add a sense of safety but makes for a noisy night's sleep. It's unquestionably a colorful place to stay, though.

US$10-25

The well-established **(Mamallena** (Casa 7-62, Calle 38 Oeste just off Avenida Central, cell 6676-6163, www.mamallena.com, starts at US$12 pp) has moved to a cool, old, two-story house with a terrace. It's in a relatively quiet residential area of Calidonia, which, though close to Bella Vista, has not yet been discovered by developers. The hostel, which is partnered with the newer, instantly popular hostel of the same name in Boquete, is better looking than most: The ceilings are high, the tile floors are lovely, and there's art on the walls. Movies are shown on a big-screen TV in the front living area. Facilities include two 8-bed dorms and one 12-bed dorm (the 12-bedder is actually less crowded). Mattresses are thin but decent, and management told me they were planning to upgrade them soon. Stays include the ubiquitous pancake breakfast. There are also a dozen small private rooms with shared bathrooms (US$27.50 s/d) that are dark and a bit cell-like but basically okay, with semi-orthopedic mattresses, in a separate building set in a "rock garden" (i.e., gravel backyard), which also has attractive, custom-made wooden picnic tables and hammocks and serves as a common area for the hostel. The private rooms are popular and fill up fast. Both private and dorm rooms have air-conditioning 9 P.M.–8 A.M. There's good security and the hostel offers good-value tours, including a full-day sampling of the Caribbean-side attractions (Fuerte San Lorenzo, Portobelo, Gatun Locks, plus a visit to the zipline ride if people want to pay extra for that) for US$45. There are also tours of Lago Bayano. There's a book exchange and shared kitchen. Airport transfers are available for US$17 per person (US$4 more if traveling alone).

Pensión Las Torres (Calle 36 and Calle Perú, tel. 225-0172, starts at US$15 s/d) is a very friendly place. It consists of 24 rooms in a converted house, built in 1931, that retains its original Spanish tile and other old touches that give the place character and an almost Moroccan air. A tiny fan-cooled room with shared bathroom goes for US$15 s/d. Large rooms with air-conditioning, cable TV, and private hot-water bathroom are also available starting at US$18 s/d. Rooms are spartan but funky and the beds are decent. If you think of it as a hostel that has only private rooms, you'll probably be pleasantly surprised. This

is a good budget place away from the normal tourist haunts—the one weird thing about it is that the rooms with private baths don't have bathroom doors, which can be awkward if you're sharing a room. Note that the entrance to the place is hidden behind bushes and a bit hard to find.

The five-story **Hotel Ideal** (Calle 17 near Calle I, tel. 262-2400, $22/25.60 s/d) is one of the last remnants of a certain strain of wackiness that used to flourish in Panama City (ask a local about the bizarre and sadly missed Restaurante La Cascada, for instance). The hotel lost a lot of customers when the Tica bus terminal moved from here to Albrook a few years back, but it remains a popular, if ramshackle, budget-lodging option. It's hard to do justice to this place in words, but let's just say pink flamingos and garden gnomes would fit in nicely. The ceiling and walls of the lobby are covered with mirrored discs, for instance. The rooms are old and a bit shabby (ask to see several), but they have good air-conditioning, private bathrooms with hot water, and TVs. Lockers in the lobby are US$0.25. Be sure to check out the sailfish fountains by the pool. There's a basic cafeteria and, next door, a self-service launderette (US$0.50–US$1 wash, US$1–1.50 dry, 7:30 A.M.–7:30 P.M. daily). The hotel is right across the street from a large public clinic, Policlínica President Remón, which contains a pharmacy (7 A.M.–7 P.M. Mon.–Fri.).

The nine-story **(Pensión Monaco** (Avenida Cuba between Calle 28 Este and Calle 29 Este, tel. 225-2573, marting@cwpanama.net, US$18 s/d) is one of the best budget hotels in Panama City. Opened in late 2002, it offers large modern rooms with a breakfast table, spacious bathrooms, air-conditioning, and cable TV. Mattresses are thin but okay. Rooms are unadorned, but feature attractive wooden furniture.

Hotel Andino (Calle 35 Este between Avenida Perú and Vía España, tel. 225-1162 or 225-0702, www.hotelandino.net, US$24.20 s/d) has 40 large, spartan air-conditioned rooms with cable TV and beds that have seen better years. Rooms with two beds are US$3 more. The word "functional" comes to mind at this worn but okay place. It's a decent value. There's a bar/restaurant on the premises.

US$25-50

Hotel Santana (Calle 17 Oeste and Calle C, tel. 228-2828, www.hotelsantana.com.pa, US$43 s/d) is a simple but clean, modern, attractive, well-run, and surprisingly sizable hotel in a fascinating part of town that has never had anything comparable. I do not normally recommend visitors spend the night in the barrio of Santa Ana, both because it can be sketchy at night and because safe, comfortable lodgings haven't existed there in many decades. But this place takes security seriously. The hotel, which opened in November 2009, is located a few blocks west of Parque Santa Ana and a short walk from the beginning of Casco Viejo (which, though close, should be reached by cab at night). Rooms are air-conditioned and have cable TV, free Wi-Fi, and hot-water private bathrooms. The reception is open 24 hours. The whole operation is reminiscent of an efficient, minimalist northern European pension. The room price is an exceptional value for what this place appears to offer; that's the benefit of staying in an area that still makes some people nervous. The hotel looks to be a good option for pioneering souls with a spirit of adventure, common sense, and street smarts. They speak English and Spanish at the hotel. Airport transfers are available for US$30 (international airport) and US$10 (the domestic airport at Albrook).

The three-story **Residencial Los Arcos** (Avenida 3 Sur and Calle 44 Este, tel. 225-0569, 225-0570, or 225-0571, US$44 s/d) offers simple but immaculate and tasteful modern rooms with air-conditioning in a quiet neighborhood close to the action. Rooms can also be rented by the hour, but the place does not have a tawdry atmosphere at all.

The six-story **Hotel San Remo** (Calle 31 Este near Avenida Perú, tel. 227-0958 or 227-2840, www.hotelsanremopanama.com, US$33 s, US$36 d), across the street from Plaza Víctor Julio Gutiérrez (the national lottery plaza),

opened in early 2003 and offers 60 simple but clean, modern rooms with air-conditioning and good beds. Some of the rooms are quite small and look out on brick walls. The hotel also has a restaurant/bar, secure parking, and Internet and laundry service. This place is a good value.

Hotel Centroamericano (Avenida Ecuador between Avenida Cuba and Avenida Perú, tel. 227-4555, www.hotelcentroamericano.com, US$44 s/d) is overdue for a makeover. It has 61 old but reasonably maintained, fairly clean, and rather bare air-conditioned rooms. Some beds are better than others. They're proud here, for some reason, of having ice machines on every floor. There's a restaurant/bar on the premises.

The **Hotel Acapulco** (Calle 30 Este between Avenida Cuba and Avenida Perú, tel. 225-3832, US$38.50 s/d) is an older but very well-maintained six-story place with 55 clean, pleasant rooms tastefully decorated with wooden furniture, tile floors, and new wallpaper. The beds are on the soft side but acceptable. This place is efficiently run by a proud, friendly staff. All rooms have air-conditioning and cable TV, and some have little balconies. There's a 24-hour restaurant. This is a good option in its price range.

Euro Hotel (Vía España next to Hotel Bella Vista, tel. 263-0802 or 263-0927, http://euro-hotelpanama.com, US$55 s/d), the successor to the old Hotel Europa, opened at the end of 2004. It was spruced up by a renovation but is not terribly different-looking from its older self. It offers 103 rooms, a small pool, a bar, and a roomy cafeteria. Rooms are simple, plain, and dark but otherwise perfectly okay. The furnishings are older but in good shape, and the beds are firm. Don't waste money on the suites, which are just connecting rooms featuring bedrooms barely big enough to contain the bed. The Euro is near the Hotel California, with the same advantages and disadvantages of location.

The 60-room, five-story ◖ **Hotel California** (Vía España and Calle 43, tel. 263-7736, starts at US$44) has been known for many years as a place to get a decent room at a great price. Beds are somewhat hard, but rooms are nicely maintained, clean, and cheerful and have air-conditioning, hot-water bathrooms, free wireless Internet access, safes, telephones, and cable TV. Some have a bay view partly obstructed by high-rises. Rooms are somewhat small. The hotel is on loud, crowded Vía España and is not conveniently close to much, at least for pedestrians. Try to get a room at the back of the building, away from the road. A small gym and whirlpool tub were recently installed on the roof. There's also laundry service and a bar/restaurant.

US$50-100

Hotel Roma Plaza (Calle 33 Este and Avenida 3 Sur, www.hotelromaplaza.com, tel. 227-3844, US$55–60 s/d including breakfast) would be considered a decent two- or (on a good day) three- star hotel, if Panama used such ratings. Its rooms are light and airy and have dressing tables, larger-than-normal TVs with cable, and phones. Some of the rooms smell of smoke, and a few are windowless; try to arrive early enough so you can switch rooms if you don't like the one you're shown. There's a pleasant 24-hour cafeteria, restaurant, bar, safe-deposit boxes, an attractive rooftop pool with a good view, a small gym, and free Wi-Fi. This place fills up. The hotel offers airport transfers for US$31.50 for two people, which is a few dollars higher than the average taxi fare.

The only real problem with the **Hotel Arenteiro** (Calle 30 Este between Avenida Cuba and Avenida Perú, tel. 227-5883 or 225-3175, www.hotelarenteiropanama.com, US$49.50 s, US$60.50 d) is that it's five stories high but has no elevator. If you have a lot of luggage, ask for a lower floor. It offers 58 small, minimalist rooms with thin mattresses. It may remind you of a European pension. All rooms have air-conditioning, cable TV, and phones. There's a restaurant/bar and a protected parking lot.

Hotel Vía España (Vía España at Avenida Martín Sossa/Calle 44, tel. 264-0800 or 264-2873, www.hotel-viaespana.com, US$66 s/d),

which opened in 2002, is on one of the busiest intersections in the city. Buses rocket by day and night, but the rooms are surprisingly quiet, especially with the air-conditioning on. Still, try to get a room at the back of the building. This place is not the bargain it once was and it's aging fast, but it's centrally located and still a decent fall-back option. The fact that it accepts euros and yen, almost certainly the only hotel in Panama that does so, suggests it's popular with international travelers. Rooms have cable TV, safes, telephones, but not wireless Internet (though the common areas do). The hotel isn't in the nicest location by any means and this is not a place to wander around at night, but the security is pretty tight—guests must be buzzed in and there's a walled parking lot. The hotel has a cafeteria.

Hotel Costa Inn (Avenida Perú and Calle 39 Este, tel. 227-1522, www.hotelcostainn.com, US$66 s, US$77 d, including airport pickup and breakfast) is a seven-story hotel offering 87 air-conditioned rooms, a 24-hour bar/restaurant, a parking lot, room service, and a small rooftop pool with a good view of the city and the Bay of Panama. It was remodeled a few years back, and the rooms are now cheerful, with good beds and modern furnishings, cable TV, and free wireless Internet. This place often has promotional deals, and the standard rates have not gone up in two years. It's popular with Latin American businesspeople. Free airport pickup at either the international or domestic airport is included. The hotel also runs a free shuttle that drops guests off at the airport at 5 A.M., 8 A.M., and 2 P.M. Both are unusual pluses for a hotel in this category.

Well, I never thought I'd see the day: The **Stanford Hotel** (off Plaza Cinco de Mayo, tel. 262-4933 or 262-4948, www.hotelstanford-panama.com, US$44 s, US$55 d) now occupies what for many, many years had been the Hotel Internacional. You'd have sworn the old hotel hosted Balboa when he first came scouting. (For a couple of historic photos, see the hotel's website, which isn't quite sure if it wants to spell the new name "Stanford" or "Standford").

The change agrees with the old girl. It's been renovated and, though still a rather spartan place, it's spruced up and more comfortable than it's been in years. The beds are cheap, but new and firm, and the rooms are fairly clean except for the smudged walls, which could use a lick of paint. Service is a bit disorganized, but friendly. The hotel's main appeal is its location right on Plaza Cinco de Mayo, at the entrance to the pedestrian section of Avenida Central. This should appeal to those who want to be in the thick of an older, commerce-driven section of Panama City and away from the more touristy areas. In the past, this was one of the noisiest parts of the city to stay, but with so much construction everywhere else this may well end up being a comparatively calm, if hardly quiet, section of the city in which to base oneself. The view of Panama Bay and the city is also less likely to be blocked by new skyscrapers, at least on the higher floors. There's a restaurant, a rooftop terrace, Internet-enabled computers in the lobby, and a neighboring casino.

A key to getting a good-value hotel room in Panama City is to stumble upon a shiny new business hotel before it gets discovered and the prices rise or entropy sets in. As this edition went to press, **⟨ Hotel Avila** (Avenida Perú between Calle 36 Este and Calle 37 Este, tel. 394-1155 or 225-2499, www.hotelavila. com.pa, US$76 s, US$87 d, including buffet breakfast) fit that description perfectly. It's a clean, friendly, modern place in a new six-story building. It's on the edge of Calidonia, close to Bella Vista, and a couple of blocks down from Hospital Nacional. Rooms are simple but attractive, with flat-screen TVs, in-room safes, and free Wi-Fi. There's basement parking and a restaurant (7:30 A.M.–10 P.M. daily). Email ahead of time to get a corporate discount.

IN AND AROUND EL CANGREJO (INCLUDES VÍA ARGENTINA)

Most of the midrange hotels, including nearly all the *aparthotels,* are in or around El Cangrejo, in the center of Panama City. They are mainly clustered together on busy Avenida Eusebio A. Morales/2 Norte or the rather quieter Calle D. Many of the city's tourist services and better restaurants are in the area as well. More recently, hostels have been trying to establish a beachhead in the area.

Note: Panama City's pioneering hostel, the **Voyager International Hostel,** changes location more often than the backpackers who stay there. On my most recent visit it was in a residential neighborhood in El Dorado, which is not a convenient spot for backpackers. Keep an eye on their website (but be sure to call or email ahead of time to double-check, since Voyager's website and fliers are not kept very current): www.voyagerhostelpanama.net. The uncertainty of location, plus past complaints about service and accommodations, make this a backup hostel option, not a first choice.

US$10-25

La Jungla Hostel (Calle 49 Oeste near the corner of Vía Argentina, cell 668-5076, 6620-2275, or 6920-4170, www.miradoradventures. com, starts at $12 pp) is one of the city's more appealing hostels, not to mention one of the cleanest. Run by the same folks who have Nomba Hostel in Boquete, it occupies the top two floors of a six-story apartment building in a relatively quiet residential section of El Cangrejo, three buildings up from Hotel Las Huacas (which is more familiar to taxi drivers). It sleeps up to 56 people in 6–10 person mixed-sex dorms with thin mattresses and four private rooms. Beds are US$12 in a fan-cooled room, US$3 more for air-conditioning. Women who'd like a single-sex dorm pay US$13. Private rooms start at US$30 s and US$39 d for a decent bedroom with shared bath; they cost a bit more with air-conditioning. Room #10, a curved room with lots of windows, is particularly popular. The nicest dorms and private rooms are downstairs, in the more chic part of the hostel. Baggage storage and towel rental are available for a buck a day. Internet computers are US$1 per hour (though Wi-Fi access is free). The hostel also has snorkel equipment to rent and an in-house washer/drier. Students with international ID get a

10 percent discount, as do those who do local volunteer work (which the hostel can arrange). This is a laidback, friendly place. There's a security gate, closed-circuit video cameras, 24-hour staffing, a shared kitchen, and a large terrace to hang out on. Lavandería Fan Clean is about a block away. Vía Argentina has lots of inexpensive cafés as well as Internet places, pharmacies, the Argosy bookstore, and other things of interest to travelers.

US$50-100

Hotel Marbella (Calle D near Avenida Eusebio A. Morales, tel. 263-2220, www.hmarbella. com, US$55, US$60 d s/d), near the Hotel Granada, is generally considered one of the better economy hotels. It's a clean, modern, five-story place on a pleasant residential street but close to a lot of urban action. However, I find the rooms dark and austere, and most look out on blank walls. There's a restaurant on site.

Las Huacas Hotel and Suites (Calle 49 Oeste, a half block from the corner of Vía Veneto and Vía Argentina, tel. 213-2222, www.lashuacashotel.com, starts at US$88 s, US$94.50 d, including breakfast) is a pleasant, reasonably priced surprise tucked away on the back streets of El Cangrejo. A renovation in mid-2010 replaced most of its rather kitschy safari trappings, and its 33 rooms now have a sleek, modern look. The rooms vary in size but all feature a minibar, free Wi-Fi, and safe. Most have a small balcony.

US$100-150

Aparthotel Torres de Alba (Avenida Eusebio A. Morales, tel. 300-7130, www.torresdealba. com.pa, US$97.90 s/d,) offers what are essentially small modern apartments, each of which has a bedroom, sitting room, fax machine, full kitchen, safe, and washer and dryer. The place consists of twin 13-story towers and is mainly aimed at short-term residents. But even tourists who don't need all that stuff might consider staying here; it's simple but quite nice. There's a small gym, a pool that's borderline big enough for lap swimmers, and a parking garage in the building.

Rooms at **Sevilla Suites Apart-Hotel** (Avenida Eusebio A. Morales, tel. 213-0016 or 213-1312, fax 223-6344, www.sevilla-suites.com, US$132 s/d), built in 2000, are smaller and darker than those at the Torres de Alba, but the furnishings are quite nice. Accommodations lie closer to the hotel end of the apartment-hotel spectrum, but all the suites have mini-kitchens and wireless Internet access, and some have terraces. There's a small gym and pool. Two of Panama's best restaurants, Restaurante 1985 and Rincón Suiza, are right across the street, and several others are very close.

Coral Suites Apart-Hotel (Calle D, tel. 269-2727, fax 269-0083, www.coralsuites. net, US$132 s, US$154 d including continental breakfast) is a modern, nicely maintained place built in 2001. It features 63 rooms with very firm beds, full kitchenette, 125-channel cable TV, in-room safe, ironing board, and a sitting area with table. There's room service, but no restaurant. There's a decent-sized rooftop pool without much of a view and a small but reasonably equipped gym. Service is rather disorganized, but this is otherwise a good place.

The **Suites Ambassador Apart-Hotel** (Calle D, tel. 263-7274 or 263-6068, starts at US$121 s/d, including continental breakfast) is right next door to Hotel Marbella and has some of the same pluses and minuses (e.g., on a pleasant and centrally located street, but in the shadow of neighboring buildings). The 31 suites (US$132 s/d) and eight studios (US$121 s/d) are well maintained and have kitchens, but the beds need replacing. The suites are good-sized apartments with sitting room, bedroom, and kitchenette with fridge, oven, and microwave. There's a small rooftop pool without much of a view, coin-operated washers and dryers, and a cafeteria. Rack rates have doubled here in the last few years: Ask for the corporate rate to get a discount.

The newest addition to the row of business hotels on Calle D is the six-story █ **Toscana Inn** (Calle D, tel. 265-0018 or 265-0019, www. toscanainnhotel.com, US$121 s/d, including breakfast). The rooms are decorated simply with a rather old-fashioned aesthetic, but the furnishings are new and each room is equipped with a flat-screen TV, a mini-fridge, a safe, and firm beds. The corporate rate is about 10 percent cheaper; be sure to ask. Service is friendly and attentive. The Toscana opened in late 2009 and it still has that pleasant "new hotel" look and feel that makes it a top choice, at least until the next new kid on the block comes around. There's a small restaurant and bar, but no pool.

BELLA VISTA AND MARBELLA

Most of Panama's luxury hotels and a few hostels are found on or south of Vía España in the *area bancaria* (banking area) and the surrounding districts of Bella Vista and Marbella. These were originally upscale residential neighborhoods that have now given way to restaurants, bars, clubs, and, especially, high-rise towers. Streets here are alive 24 hours a day.

Being conveniently close to both Vía España and the Calle Uruguay nightlife area makes this a popular location for travelers, who will definitely feel they're in the throbbing heart of Panama City.

US$10-25

Zuly's Independent Backpackers (Calle Ricardo Arias near Avenida 3 Sur, tel. 269-2665, cell 6605-4742, www.zulysbackpackers.com, starts at US$8.50 pp) recently moved from its old home to a new spot across the street, though given its central location it's quite likely skyscraper construction will uproot it again before too long. To get there, stand with your back to Restaurante Costa Azul and walk straight for 30 meters, crossing Calle Ricardo Arias and heading up the alley; Zuly's will be on the right.

It hardly seemed possible, but the "new" Zuly's is even more grungy and decrepit than the old one. This is definitely not one of the city's cleaner hostels. On the other hand, it occupies the entire four-story apartment building, and it has a strong gate out front and a walled garden behind, which makes for a relatively

secure and (at least during the day) peaceful setting for a hostel in the heart of the city. It's run by Panamanian Zuly Gutierrez and her German partner, Richard Hoehe, who are this place's secret weapon. They are friendly, helpful, and stuffed full of useful information for budget travelers.

The hostel consists of 43 beds scattered among 12 rooms. Rates are US$8.50–9 for a bed in a fan-cooled dorm and US$10 for an air-conditioned dorm. Per-person rates are US$0.50 (fan) or US$1 (a/c) lower for couples who share a double bed in the dorms. Per-person rates for private rooms are US$11 (fan) and US$12.50 (a/c). If all the beds are taken, guests can camp in the garden for US$6. Guests can check in as early as 5 A.M. and as late as 1 A.M. The hostel offers free Wi-Fi and coffee. Breakfast is not included, but there's a shared kitchen. Guests can use the washer (US$2) and dryer (US$2).

The owners will help arrange overland trips to Kuna Yala or passage on a sailboat to Cartagena, Colombia. (The latest departures for Cartagena are listed on Zuly's website; they'll help even if you aren't a guest.)

Across the street from Zuly's, next to Restaurante Costa Azul, is **Hostal San Roque** (Calle Ricardo Arias and Avenida 3 Sur, tel. 264-3566, starts at US$15 pp), one of a growing number of local converted apartments trying to get in on the hostel craze. This one has a few things going for it, including a small inside courtyard and thick walls that make it a relatively quiet oasis in the middle of a busy part of town—as long as fellow guests keep it down, which they did when I visited; this is not a party place. There is a single eight-bed dorm. It's plain and windowless, but air-conditioned and pretty clean, with a shared bath. Private rooms are also air-conditioned and start at US$40 s/d. This place has a very Panamanian vibe and has yet to be discovered by the gringo backpacker crowd.

US$100-150

The corncob-shaped **Hotel Plaza Paitilla Inn** (Vía Italia in Punta Paitilla, tel. 208-0600, www.plazapaitillainn.com, US$127 s/d) was originally a rather upscale Holiday Inn. It's now at the upper end of the midrange hotels, and though it has aged considerably, it was renovated a few years back and rooms look rather spiffy, with new floor-to-ceiling windows that replaced fragile balconies. Many of the 272 rooms have dramatic views of Panama Bay and the city skyline, though skyscraper construction is eating away at these. The hotel has a casino and pool. The (excessive) rack rates are nearly double the price listed here, but good-value promotional discounts are the norm. Historical note: This hotel was one of the tallest buildings in Panama City well into the 1990s. Now it's lost in a forest of giant towers.

(Hotel Ejecutivo (Avenida Aquilino de la Guardia between Calle 51 and Calle 52, tel. 265-8011 or 264-3989, toll-free U.S./Canada tel. 866/876-0915, www.executivehotel-panama.com, rack rates US$138 s/d) has been a favorite with Latin American businesspeople for more than 30 years, and it's easy to see why. The Ejecutivo (roughly eh-HEC-oo-TEE-voh), known as the Executive in English, is a solid value. (It's unusual to pay the rack rates listed here; several kinds of promotional discounts are routinely available—corporate, weekend, booking by Internet—that lower the cost by about 25 percent.) Rooms are similar to what you'd expect at a Best Western–style hotel: clean, pleasant enough, but nothing fancy. All come equipped with a refrigerator, TV, coffeepot, telephone, desk, and balcony. Wi-Fi is free in the common areas, and for US$0.95 guests can get wireless Internet access in the room and use of a local mobile phone during their stay. The hotel is centrally located just down from Vía España, and some rooms have terrific views of the lights of the city and Panama Bay. These are disappearing thanks to the skyscraper-construction epidemic. The 24-hour coffee shop offers big portions at low prices. It's a popular place for breakfast (which is served day or night); in the morning there's a breakfast buffet. There's also a free daily happy hour. Guests are allowed to use some of the business center's

facilities for free. Amenities include a tiny pool and fitness center.

Over US$150

The 363-room **Hotel Riande Continental and Casino** (Vía España and Calle Ricardo Arias, tel. 263-9999, www.hotelesriande.com, US$176 s/d), right on busy Vía España, is another old Panama City landmark, but it's benefited from a tasteful remodeling that transformed it to an upscale business hotel. It's part of the Riande chain, which also owns the Hotel Granada and the Riande Aeropuerto Hotel and Resort near the international airport. Everyone refers to it simply as the Hotel Continental. All the rooms are nice, but some are bigger and more elegantly appointed than others; ask to see several. The hotel has a restaurant, cafeteria, small pool, and casino. There are often promotional deals of various kinds here. Check to see if the "Riande Club of Coronado" packages are available; they include day beach/golf passes and transfers to Coronado. One tower of the hotel is exclusively for "female executives."

The **(Panama Marriott Hotel** (Calle 52 at Calle Ricardo Arias, tel. 210-9100, fax 210-9110, www.marriott.com, US$197 s/d) is quite an elegant place, with 295 rooms (and dozens more on the way), a small pool, a fitness center, a spa, and a pleasant, upscale cafeteria, but no formal restaurant. There's also a deli with sandwiches and salads. Ask for a corner room; they're the largest of the standard rooms, which come with the usual business-hotel amenities. Corporate and other special rates are often available. There are six wheelchair-accessible rooms on the lower floors. This place is one of the most popular of the higher-end hotels. It's an attractive place in a central location, with lots of dining, shopping, and entertainment options an easy walk away. Be alert wandering near the hotel at night.

Hotel Lé Meridien (Avenida Balboa and Calle Uruguay, tel. 297-3200, www.starwoodhotels.com, US$250 s/d) is a new member of the ever-expanding hotel portfolio of local-developer Empresas Bern that also includes the InterContinental Miramar next door and the Gamboa Rainforest Resort. This one goes for a hipster-chic ambiance reminiscent of a W Hotel, down to the electronic-lounge beats pulsating through the shiny lobby. Its 111 rooms feature modern, minimalist furnishings that suggest a nicely appointed frequent-fliers lounge. There's a restaurant, a spa, and a small pool that, at least until the surrounding buildings are completed, may not be the most comfortable spot for female sunbathers, as it draws unwelcome attention from construction workers next door. The location is convenient for those with business in the financial district or who want to explore the Calle Uruguay nightspots, but it's a bit isolated otherwise, especially at night. Note that if you ask the reception to call you a cab, you'll get a tourist taxi that is authorized to charge several times the street-taxi rate. It should be easy to catch a cab on Avenida Balboa or up Calle Uruguay if you prefer. (Note: Shortly after Lé Meridien opened, Google searches were confusing it with Hotel El Panamá.)

Built in 1951, the **Hotel El Panamá** (Vía España next to Iglesia del Carmen, tel. 215-9000 or 215-9181, www.elpanama.com, US$238 s/d) was for many years Panama's premier hotel. It has 330 rooms, including some cabañas by the large, attractive pool. The hotel has changed hands and been renovated repeatedly over the years, but one thing remains constant: The service is lousy. Because of its international name recognition (the only reason it's listed here), it still draws a lot of guests, many of whom are on package holidays and determined to see who can be louder and more obnoxious. For the money, you can do better elsewhere without the potential hassle. However, frequent promotional offers can slash the rates, and it is centrally located.

(**Hotel DeVille** (Calle Beatriz M. de Cabal near Calle 50, tel. 206-3100 or 263-0303, www.devillehotel.com.pa, starts at US$286) is an elegant, rather formal boutique hotel with four types of rooms: deluxe rooms, junior suites, two-bedroom duplex suites, and grand luxury suites. The "deluxe" is a spacious room with the simplest furnishings. It features a marble-tiled bathroom, high ceilings, a high-speed Internet connection, sitting area, and in-room safe. The junior suite is quite opulent, with highly polished dark woods, antique Vietnamese furniture inlaid with mother of pearl, a large bathroom with two sinks, a fax machine, and so on. The duplex suite resembles the junior suite but has an upper level with a bedroom and second bath. The grand luxury suite, oddly, isn't quite as luxurious as the duplex suites. Amusingly enough, given the (at best) ambivalent feelings towards Teddy Roosevelt in Panama, one of the suites is named for him. Even the fanciest suites, though more luxurious than the average overnight guest would need during a short stay, can be a decent value for families or groups. Art from local galleries is displayed in the lobby.

The ultramodern (**Radisson Decapolis Hotel** (behind the Multicentro Mall on Avenida Balboa, tel. 215-5000, toll-free U.S./Canada tel. 800/395-7046, www.radisson.com, rack rates start at US$270 s/d) is "inspired by the avant-garde hip hotels" of Europe and North America. It's quite an impressive place that will appeal to those who prefer the sleek and streamlined over Old World elegance. Note: Try to book as far in advance as possible. Sufficiently advance bookings can knock about US$100 off the rack rate. Many other promotional offers are typically available. Opened in 2004, it's a 29-story concoction of brushed stainless steel and glass, including a glass elevator that goes to the 14th floor and is worth the ride just for the view. Traditional Panamanian elements—*mola* patterns, devil masks, ships—inform the modern decor. The standard rooms are quite large, sleek, attractive, and minimalist, with photo blowups of Panama's indigenous peoples over the beds and large windows looking out on the view. The view is spectacular on the ocean side, particularly on the higher floors, offering a panorama that encompasses Panama Bay, the towers of Paitilla, and, in some rooms, Casco Viejo. (Note, however, that the same hotel group is building the absolutely massive Megapolis "condo hotel" towers, sometimes known as the Meagalopolis, right next door, so those on the west side of the Decapolis may lose much or all of their view.)

Each room at the Decapolis has a safe, ironing board, hair dryer, coffeemaker, Internet connection, cable TV, and so forth, and English- and Spanish-language newspapers are delivered daily. Other features include the equally striking Fusion restaurant, a martini/sushi lobby bar, a tiny pool on the 4th floor with a hot tub and bar, and several executive floors, including two exclusively for business-women. The hotel's spa, Aqua, has some exercise machines and offers a full range of spa services, including facials, sauna, and steam baths. The hotel connects through a walkway with the glitzy Majestic Casino and the Multicentro Mall.

From the outside, the **Bristol** (Calle Aquilino de la Guardia between Calle 51 and Calle 52, just down from the Hotel Ejecutivo, tel. 264-0000 or 265-7844, www.thebristol.com, rack rates start at US$390 s/d) is a nondescript, salmon-colored building that's easy to overlook, especially now that bigger buildings are going up all around it. (This includes a Bristol-owned apartment complex going up right next to the hotel. Find out if construction is finished before booking here because the noise detracts from the stay.) Inside, however, the Bristol is a lovely boutique hotel. It's quite a luxurious place. Standard rooms are "deluxe," and they truly are. All the rooms are lovely and tastefully done. The furnishings are elegant, with local touches such as *mola* pillows and lamp bases made from Ngöbe-Buglé sandstone figurines. The attached Restaurante Barandas is attractive and one of Panama City's most ambitious. Note that this isn't a huge resort. If you want a pool and several restaurants to choose from, try the Sheraton Panama Hotel and Convention Center or InterContinental Miramar; this place is more low-key.

The **Hotel InterContinental Miramar Panama** (Avenida Balboa, tel. 206-8888, fax 223-4891, www.miramarpanama.com, rack rates US$330 s/d) is on the middle of Avenida Balboa and has great views of the Pacific and the Panama City skyline. With the building of the Cinta Costera, however, it's no longer on the edge of the bay but rather on a landfill island between these two major traffic arteries. It's a 185-room luxury hotel that's part of the InterContinental chain and comes with the works: two restaurants, a largish pool, a health spa, tennis court, several bars, and so on. It's about due for an upgrade but is still a comfortable place to stay. All rooms have an "executive desk," three phones, broadband access, minibar, safe, and other amenities. The best things about the hotel are its views and attractive pool.

The new **Finisterre Suites and Spa** (Avenida 3A Sur and Calle Colombia, tel. 214-9200, www.fspty.com, starts at US$280 s/d for a master suite) is shaping up to be a handsome-looking place. It consists of 126 suites in a new tower just off Vía España across from the Iglesia del Carmen. The smallest and least expensive of these is the 600-square-meter executive suite, which features a king or two double beds, a couple of sofa beds, a 32-inch LCD TV, a dining area, fully equipped kitchen, etc., etc., all decorated in understated modern taste. Check for promotional packages.

EAST PANAMA CITY
Over US$150

Sheraton Panama Hotel and Convention Center (Vía Israel and Calle 77 across the street from the Atlapa Convention Center, tel. 305-5100, www.starwoodhotels.com, rack rate US$340 s/d) has the most loyal clientele of the Panama five-star hotels. It's a huge complex with 362 rooms, three restaurants, a shopping gallery, an appealing casino that has expanded in recent years, an athletic club, a pool, a spa, and so on. This is the second-oldest luxury hotel in the city, after Hotel El Panamá, and it's changed hands several times through the years; it used to be called the Caesar Park, and its incarnation as a Sheraton is fairly recent. This is definitely a place to book well in advance, as it's possible to get a room for around US$200 with enough warning. Expect to pay more than twice that if you plan to visit with less than a month's notice. (Do not confuse it with the more business-traveler-oriented Four Points Sheraton in Marbella.) Note that the hotel is on the eastern outskirts of town, quite a hike from everything but the convention center, the ruins of Old Panama, and the international airport.

Food

WHAT TO EXPECT

The restaurants are among the best things about Panama City. It's easy to find good food, pleasant surroundings, and a surprisingly wide variety of cuisine. Overall, Panama City is still waiting for a truly great restaurant, but there are quite a few good ones.

The dining scene in Panama was for many decades dominated by sophisticated restaurants catering to well-heeled locals and business-people on expense accounts, many of which offered a far better dining experience for considerably less money than a visitor could find back home. However, a rising middle class with a fondness for American junk food, and the recent influx of likeminded tourists, seem to be driving down the average quality of the capital's food.

All that said, there are still plenty of solid options in every price range to keep short-term visitors happy.

Look out for the trend toward including a 10 percent service charge on the bill; it's easy to double tip. Fortunately, the fad of placing bottled water on the table appears to be on the wane. These bottles are neither free nor necessary: Tap water in Panama is clean. If you're offered bottled water and don't want it, smile, shake your head, and ask for "Chagres" (pronounced "CHA-gress") instead. It'll probably make the wait staff chuckle. (The Río Chagres is the source of Panama City's drinking water.)

For the higher-end restaurants, expect to pay about what you would for a similar place in the United States. But it's also quite possible to stuff yourself on tasty, simple food for about US$2–3, if ambience means nothing to you. Panamanian *comida corriente* (literally "current food," meaning typical dishes of the day served cafeteria style) venues are scattered around the city, as are all kinds of American fast-food franchises.

Many of the upscale restaurants are found in two general areas on either side of Vía España: El Cangrejo to the northeast of the Hotel El Panamá, and the booming nightlife area around Calle Uruguay (also known as Calle 48 Este).

Service is not as good as it once was at the better restaurants. As more restaurants pop up, there just aren't enough trained waitstaff to go around, and the best ones get poached by rivals with bigger budgets. But at the higher end, service at least tends to be friendly.

Consistency is also a problem: A restaurant can be great one night and disappointing the next. Again, the best chefs get headhunted, and their departure—or even day off—can cause the quality of a restaurant's fare to plummet overnight.

Make reservations at the fancier places, if only to be sure the restaurant is actually open. However, even the best restaurants can be surprisingly empty, especially in the early evening. Things tend to get busier at lunchtime, when the upscale establishments draw a schmoozing business clientele. Many restaurants are closed for lunch on Saturday and all day on Sunday or Monday.

Vegetarians may have to rely on the limited vegetarian options at meat-eaters' restaurants. The safest bets are usually Asian or Italian places. But veggie havens are at last beginning to pop up around the city, usually in the shape of basic cafeterias serving hippie food. Some of these mystery meals can be surprisingly palatable, and even cheaper than the offerings at meat-oriented *comida corriente* places.

CASCO VIEJO

Places to eat come and go especially quickly in Casco Viejo. Included here are some of the longer-term survivors. Note that it can be hard to find a decent place to eat on Sunday and Monday, and breakfast is tough any day. The **Super Gourmet Deli** (Avenida A between Calle 5 Oeste and Calle 6 Oeste, 8 A.M.–6 P.M. Mon.–Sat., 9 A.M.–5 P.M. Sun.) is a good option for breakfast or to grab a sandwich for lunch. Guests can sit outside or in.

Cafés

◖ **René Café** (Calle 7 Este on the north side of the cathedral, tel. 228-3487, www.renecafe. com, 10 A.M.–3 P.M. and 6–10 P.M. Mon.–Sat.) has survived for a few years now in a spot that has seen many cafés come and go. It's a pleasant little air-conditioned oasis with just six table-clothed tables and a gracious and attentive staff. Lunch here is a great deal: two starters (e.g., a large salad and crepes), a choice of main course (chicken, fish, pork, or veggies) and dessert (e.g., coconut flan) for just US$8.50.

Everything I've had here has been pretty good, especially for the price. The set dinner menu consists of more than double the number of items—at more than double the price.

Diablo Rosso café/art gallery (#11, Avenida A and Calle 7, tel. 228-4833 or 228-4837, www. diablorosso.com, café 9 A.M.–7 P.M. Tues.–Sat.) is a café, but more important it has quickly turned into an arts and culture hub for Casco Viejo. Owned by the popular Panamanian rock band Señor Loop, it displays modern works by local artists, hosts after-hours art openings and events, and holds a Tuesday night dinner-and-a-movie evening, showing independent films and documentaries. It's part of an emerging arts scenes that includes Relic Bar/Luna's Castle, Super Gourmet, and La Casona.

Granclement (Avenida Central between Calle 3 Oeste and Calle 4 Oeste, tel. 223-6277, 11:30 A.M.–8 P.M. Mon.–Thurs., 11:30 A.M.–9:30 P.M. Fri.–Sat., 12:30–8 P.M. Sun.) serves gourmet ice cream and sorbet by the scoop or the tub in flavors that range from the tropical (mango, *guanábana,* passion fruit) to the exotic

© WILLIAM FRIAR

lunchtime at Luna's Castle, a popular hostel in Casco Viejo

(basil, lavender, spearmint), as well as more conventional choices. It's pricey for Panama, but hard to resist on a hot day (i.e., every day).

International

Ego y Narciso (Plaza Simón Bolívar, tel. 262-2045, noon–3 P.M. and 6 P.M.–11 P.M. Mon.–Fri., 6–11 P.M. Sat. and Sun.) is a stylish café and bar with two non-connecting dining areas as well as outdoor tables set along a corner of Plaza Simón Bolívar. It offers a small menu of pastas, meats, and fish for about US$10–15, as well as a bar menu of brochettes, salads, and such. It's been a popular place for several years. Some really enjoy the food here, but I've had mixed experiences. The safest bets are the appetizers and desserts. In any case, it's a pleasant spot for an evening drink. Service can be sluggish, particularly if you're seated in the more formal dining room, which is sort of an annex to the main café. The bar stays open after the kitchen closes so long as there are customers.

◖ **Manolo Caracol** (Calle 3 and Avenida Central, tel. 228-4640, 228-9479, or 228-0109, www.manolocaracol.net, noon–3 P.M. and 6:30–10 P.M. Mon.–Fri., 6:30–10 P.M. Sat.) is the namesake restaurant of Manolo Maduño. Manolo promises *cocina con amor* (food made with love) and he delivers. There is one menu each night (if you talk to Manolo ahead of time he'll try to accommodate vegetarians), and food starts arriving as soon as you sit down. The menu changes with the season, but a typical offering might include seafood salad, portobello mushrooms, grilled shrimp, mussels, marinated tomatoes, red snapper, tuna, and something exotic for dessert. Price for the whole thing? US$25 (plus a 15 percent service charge). The lunch menu is US$20, plus the service charge. You definitely have to be in a receptive mood for this kind of food bombardment, but if you're willing to surrender to the experience, it offers one of the more entertaining dining options in Panama City.

Manolo's open kitchen sits right in the dining room, under a copper smoke hood and behind mounds of fresh produce set on a counter. In front of this is a dugout canoe filled with

bottles of Spanish wine (the only kind served). Modern art hangs on the walls. The only real problem with this place is the acoustics—the restaurant is a stone and concrete box, so when it's crowded, it's loud. Manolo himself, a Spaniard by way of Colombia, is a kinetic character likely to be the loudest person there. He presides over everything unless he's away on a special assignment (he's been known to cook for Mick Jagger on his yacht when he's in the area). He'll likely greet you as a long-lost friend with a crushing hug, and slip you a glass of wine on the house if he sees your cup is empty—just because you're such a terrific person.

Restaurante Las Bóvedas (Plaza de Francia, tel. 228-808 or 228-8068, 5:30 P.M.–late Mon.–Sat.) is built right into the historic stone vaults *(bóvedas)* of the old city's seawall, so you're dining in what was once a dungeon. It's not a cheap place; expect to pay around US$20 for French-inspired main dishes. The food has always been a secondary reason to visit, though it seems to have been on an upswing lately. The second room in the place is a bar called Los Piratas. The house drink is the caipirinha, a potent Brazilian concoction. There's live jazz in the bar on Friday and Saturday nights after about 9:30 P.M.

Mediterranean

S'Cena (near the intersection of Avenida A and Avenida Central, tel. 228-4011, www.scena-platea.com, noon–4 P.M. and 7–10:30 P.M. Mon.–Sat., noon–4 P.M. Sun., US$15–22) is on the 2nd floor of an old two-story house just across the street from the ruins of the old Union Club. It's a small place with a great location, though the view of the ocean a few steps away is severely limited. A couple of narrow French doors lead out onto a balcony; be sure to take a look. The food is pricey and the decor is simple, but the service is friendly, and I've had delicious seafood here. Try the *mero a la brasa con fondo de romesco* (grilled grouper with romesco sauce). Note the exposed ancient wall made of bits of brick and stone. The restaurant is affiliated with the Platea Bar downstairs, which means you'll be hearing live jazz Thursday–Saturday, like it or not.

CALIDONIA, LA EXPOSICIÓN, AND SANTA ANA
Cafeterias and Diners

Restaurante Boulevard Balboa (Avenida Balboa and Calle 33, tel. 225-0914, 6:30 A.M.–1 A.M. Mon.–Sat.) was a Panama institution that opened in 1958 and attracted a mix of power-breakfasting politicians and regular josés, waited on by servers who'd been there almost since the beginning. Its most notorious moment came in July of 2001, when a prominent lawyer, Roque Alberto Pérez Carrera, was assassinated there. He was shot twice in the face by a man who then escaped by taxi.

The original diner finally fell victim to Panama's construction boom just shy of its 50th birthday, but it has reopened two blocks away with the same staff and clientele, but a significantly spiffier modern look. It'll never have the same crummy-but-cozy coffee-shop vibe, but it does have free wireless Internet and a terrace overlooking Avenida Balboa. This is the place to come for breakfast Panama City style, such as eggs with beefsteak. Breakfast can be had for less than US$5. It's known for its grilled sandwiches and its *batidas* (milkshakes).

Café Coca Cola (Calle C and Calle 12 Oeste, tel. 228-7687, 7:30 A.M.–11 P.M. daily), across the street from Parque Santa Ana, is a slightly grungy air-conditioned diner and a Panama City institution. This place has been here forever—the building it's housed in was erected in 1907, just four years after Panama became a country—and is a good spot for people-watching and soaking up the atmosphere of a slower, quainter Panama City from an earlier era. Food ranges from sandwiches to chop suey to pasta. You can fill up here for less than US$5. The espresso drinks are palatable.

A Casa de Fernando (Calle 30 Este between Avenida Perú and Avenida Cuba, tel. 225-2378, 24 hours daily, under US$10) is a pleasant tavern likely to be of interest to those staying in the Calidonia/La Exposición area, mainly because it's got a central location and

produce market on wheels, Calidonia

© WILLIAM FRIAR

is open 24 hours. It serves an absurdly ambitious variety of food, including salads, soups, sandwiches, and all the usual meats, seafood, and pasta. It's not air-conditioned, but there are ceiling fans. This is a good find.

Indian

Indian restaurants have been slow to catch on in Panama City, despite a significant South Asian population. Why eat out when no Panama restaurant can compete with grandma's home cooking? There are usually only one or two places in the entire city, and they don't tend to stick around long. They also tend to lay off the chilies in deference to the Panamanian palate, so ask for food to be prepared *"picante"* if you want it with a bit of a bite and *"muy picante"* if you prefer it moderately hot. Those who like it fiery are probably out of luck.

Restaurante Masala (Avenida 3 Sur and Calle 45, tel. 225-0105, 11:30 A.M.–3 P.M. and 6–10:30 P.M. Mon.–Sat., under US$15) offers the usual North Indian dishes, including ample vegetarian offerings. Food here is similar to an average takeout place in the United States or the United Kingdom. The kitchen must lack a proper tandoori oven, however, as the naan is more like fried bread. Its old home, a charming Bella Vista house, was bulldozed for yet another skyscraper and its new digs are small and dark, but pleasant enough and decorated with the expected Indian flourishes. Both table and floor seating is available. It's right next to Residencial Los Arcos.

Panamanian

Fast-food stands on Avenida Perú and Calle 35, near the Ministerio de Economía y Finanzas, cater to office workers who want cheap deep-fried goodies. They're convenient to those staying in Calidonia.

Restaurante Rincón Tableño #5 (Avenida Cuba near Calle 31 Este, tel. 227-5649, 5:30 A.M.–4:30 P.M. Mon.–Sat., 5:30 A.M.–2:30 P.M. Sun., US$3–4) is a basic *comida corriente* cafeteria except that the waitresses wear pretty *pollera*-style blouses. The menu changes daily.

coconut water vendor waiting for customers, Avenida Central, Calidonia

Pizzerias

Panama City has two branches of the beloved Napoli pizzeria. Napoli is famous for its clam pizza, but I've always been partial to its wonderfully charred, greasy pepperoni pies. I consider it some of the best pizza in Panama, but it's impossible to be objective about it since I practically grew up on this stuff. There are plenty of pastas and such on the menu, but people come here for the wood-oven–baked pizza. Plate-sized individual pizzas are available for about five bucks.

The older and much plainer **Napoli** (Calle Estudiante and Calle I, one block from Avenida de los Mártires, tel. 262-2446 or 262-2448, 11:30 A.M.–11:30 P.M. Wed.–Mon.) is a good place to grab lunch during a walking tour of Avenida Central. It's a short walk up from the heart of Central. This branch has been around since 1962 and is an institution. It has an air-conditioned interior and an outdoor seating area where you can look out on what's left of the street life in this once bustling, now declining, area. (This is not a safe place to wander around at night.) The second branch is in Obarrio.

Seafood

Restaurante Mercado del Marisco (Avenida Balboa, tel. 377-0379, 11 A.M.–6 P.M. daily, closed the first Monday of each month, US$8–11) is just upstairs from the city fish market, which is at the west end of Avenida Balboa. It boasts that it has the "best and freshest fish and seafood in Panama," and one would hope so, given its downstairs neighbor. (The fish market is modern and fairly clean, so you shouldn't have to worry too much about a fishy smell wafting upstairs, at least if you come for an early lunch.) It's reasonably priced and offerings include ceviche, seafood soup, corvina, jumbo shrimp, and octopus in garlic sauce. The ceviche is particularly popular. If you don't see anything on the menu you like, buy your own fish downstairs and have it cooked here. The restaurant is a spartan place with little atmosphere, but there's a partial view of the bay and the Panama City skyline. The

buying ceviche at the Mercado de Mariscos

© WILLIAM FRIAR

waitstaff is friendly and speaks a little English. Since the area is a bit rough, it's best to come here at lunch. Come early or late, as this place fills up.

IN AND AROUND EL CANGREJO (INCLUDES VÍA ARGENTINA)

Some of the city's most established restaurants are in El Cangrejo, particularly along Avenida Eusebio A. Morales. Vía Argentina is mostly known as a relatively quiet place to go for breakfast, a cup of coffee and a snack, or typical Panamanian food.

Cafés

It's about time Panama City got a place like the ◖ **New York Bagel Café** (off Vía Argentina, next to Einstein's Head, tel. 390-6051, 7 A.M.–8 P.M. Mon.–Fri., 9 A.M.–8 P.M. Sat., 8 A.M.–4 P.M. Sun.). It serves half a dozen decent coffees by the cup in a coffee-house atmosphere that's more San Francisco than New York, with thrift-store furniture and art on the walls. I even spotted a beret-wearing beardo who must have taken a wrong turn in the 1950s and just kept walking. Full breakfasts are served all day for around US$5.50. The bagels actually taste like bagels, they try their hand at Tex-Mex, and there's free Wi-Fi.

Cafeterias and Diners

If you're just looking for a simple place for breakfast or a snack, try **Churrería Manolo** (Vía Argentina 12 at Avenida 2B Norte, tel. 264-3965, 7 A.M.–1 A.M. daily, under US$5). Though it's been given a rather austere remodeling, it still has an unpretentious coffee-shop atmosphere that has attracted both locals and resident foreigners for years. (It was one of my haunts in high school.) It's hard to explain our fondness for this place. The food quality goes up and down; the only things you can really count on are the churros (a sugary fried pastry shaped like a hot dog). The yummiest churro is the *manjar blanco*—the filling is similar to condensed milk and looks disgusting, but it's so tasty it'll curl your toes. For a real sugar

buzz, order the churros along with Spanish hot chocolate *(chocolate a la española)*, which is thick and delicious. Mainly, though, Manolo is just a relaxing place to hang out on one of the few streets in the city that strike a nice balance between bustle and mellowness. A full breakfast costs less than US$5. After breakfast, sandwiches are the best bet. Other offerings include pasta, meat, and seafood.

East Asian

Panama City's most established Japanese restaurant is **Matsuei** (Avenida Eusebio A. Morales, tel. 264-9562 or 264-9547, www.matsueipanama.com, 11 A.M.–11 P.M. Mon.–Sat., 4:30–10:30 P.M. Sun., US$20), a small, simple place with a sushi bar that's been around since 1978. It has an extensive menu of sushi and sashimi, as well as tempura, but far from budget prices. Cooked options include corvina prepared "Japanese style," tempura, and so on. The sushi's okay, but nothing special. This place is pretty consistent for Panama, where sushi places come and go. The *ebi* (shrimp) is tasty, but I don't recommend the California rolls. Imported fish is more expensive. The ravenous can opt for an odd all-you-can-eat "open sushi" deal noon–8 P.M. Monday–Saturday. The catch is you have to pay extra for anything you leave on your plate, to discourage waste.

International

Restaurante 1985 (Avenida Eusebio A. Morales near Vía Veneto, tel. 263-8571 or 263-8541, www.1985.com, 11:30 A.M.–11:30 P.M. Mon.–Fri., 5–11:30 P.M. Sat.–Sun.) is one of Panama's best restaurants, and one of its most expensive. It's under the command of Chef Willy Diggelmann, who also oversees Rincón Suizo, Caffé Pomodoro, and a rather pedestrian wine bar called the Wine Bar. It specializes in French cuisine and seafood but also offers German, Swiss, Spanish, and gourmet vegetarian dishes. The atmosphere is kind of floral country French, and not at all stuffy. This is a nice place for a splurge, as most dishes are in the double digits. If you're going by taxi, tell the driver you want to go to *restaurante* *mil noveciento ochenta y cinco,* or just point to this entry.

Rincón Suizo (Avenida Eusebio A. Morales near Vía Veneto, tel. 263-8310, www.1985.com, 11:30 A.M.–11:30 P.M. Mon.–Fri., 5–11:30 P.M. Sat.–Sun.) is upstairs from Restaurante 1985, in the same building, and serves good Swiss and German food in a darker, cozier atmosphere. Offerings include raclette, *berner rösti* (fried potatoes), and cheese fondue. The food tends to be a bit cheaper here than at 1985.

Panamanian

Restaurante y Cafetería El Trapiche (Vía Argentina, tel. 269-2063, tel. 269-4353 for takeout orders, 7 A.M.–11 P.M. daily, US$4–9) has long been a local favorite for traditional Panamanian fare such as *mondongo* (tripe), *hojaldres* (frybread), tortillas, tamales, and *ropa vieja* (shredded beef with rice). Those who want to sample a variety of things can go for the *"típico* platter" (US$11). Breakfast is served until 11:30 A.M. and includes such hearty fare as scrambled eggs, steak, white cheese, and *carimañola* (a fried, meat-stuffed roll) for around US$5. There's an air-conditioned interior as well as seating outside on Vía Argentina.

Peruvian

Machu Picchu (Calle Eusebio A. Morales, tel. 264-9308, noon–3 P.M. and 6–11 P.M. Mon.–Sat., noon–9 P.M. Sun.) is a pleasant, cozy, and moderately priced Peruvian restaurant with friendly service and decent seafood, which is its specialty. A good value here is to share a number of appetizers, which average around US$5. Try the Peruvian ceviche, which is prepared quite differently from Panamanian ceviche. The house wine is good, but consider sampling a pisco sour if you've never had one and are willing to risk a drink made with raw egg. Machu Picchu has a sister restaurant of the same name in Boquete. Interestingly, the food is actually better in Boquete.

Seafood

My favorite place for seafood is **◖ Siete Mares** (Calle Guatemala near Vía Argentina,

tel. 264-0144 or 264-32032, 11:30 A.M.–11:30 P.M. daily, under US$15). One of the most consistent and consistently popular restaurants in the city, it's a cozy, tranquil place and the service is good. An unusual house specialty is fried ceviche, a light and tangy appetizer. The fish is so tasty you won't need to order anything fancier than *corvina a la plancha* (grilled corvina). The restaurant has a modern look reminiscent of an upscale hotel lobby, including an artificial waterfall near the entrance. It does have one peculiar touch: chairs on rollers, like those you might find in a plush conference room. A pianist performs in the evening.

Steakhouses

Martín Fierro (Avenida Eusebio A. Morales, tel. 264-1927 or 223-1333, noon–3 P.M. and 6–11 P.M. daily) is a brightly lit place where decor runs a distant second to simply serving slabs of meat—grilled beef, chicken, and pork, either domestic or imported from Omaha, Nebraska. Expect to pay upwards of US$25 for imported beef. The restaurant also serves pasta, seafood, and fish, but that's not why anyone comes here. Meals include access to a meager salad bar, but who's kidding whom? If you really feel like punishing your heart, try the tasty *mozzarella frita* (fried mozzarella— oh, go ahead, you're on vacation). Then try the quite good *tres leches* (three-milk) cake. Book your angioplasty ahead of time.

Vegetarian

Restaurante La Casa Vegetariana (Calle D near Vía Veneto, tel. 391-4410, 7 A.M.–11 P.M. Mon.–Fri., 7 A.M.–9 P.M. Sat.–Sun.), in the El Cangrejo *aparthotel* quarter, is so utilitarian it makes a post office look cozy—and this is its new location. The owners are earnest and friendly, the place is certainly roomy, and the food ranges from flavorful to at least virtuous-tasting. Dishes are Asian-oriented and focus on soy and other beans prepared numerous ways. Each portion on the sizable cafeteria line costs less than a dollar. Try one of the homemade (nonalcoholic) *chichas* (fruit juices).

BELLA VISTA AND MARBELLA

Cafés

Crepes and Waffles (Avenida 5B between Calle Uruguay and Calle Aquilino de la Guardia, tel. 269-1574 or 305-6536, www.crepesandwaffles.com, noon–11 P.M. Mon.–Sat., 9 A.M.–11 P.M. Sun.) is a popular Latin American chain that serves—guess what?—in a sunny, modern, brick-and-glass building with an air-conditioned interior, outdoor terrace, and yuppie vibe. Only the 1970s soft rock mars the pleasant atmosphere. Its large selection of savory and sweet crepes include some vegetarian options. Other offerings include lots of coffee drinks, a salad bar, pita sandwiches, and other café goodies. It'd be hard to spend more than US$10 here without getting sugar poisoning. There are newer branches in the Multiplaza Pacific and Albrook malls.

A newer creation by the chef behind Tre Scalini, **Peperoncini** (Calle 49 and Calle Uruguay, tel. 265-1312, www.peperoncinipanama.com, noon–4 P.M. and 6–11 P.M. daily, US$10–15) is a trendy, overly bright new place that attracts the nouveau riche. The food is fairly tasty if over-salted, and the mod, orange-and-white decor is sleek and cheerful. A sitting area outside is pleasant on dry season evenings. A similar-looking sister restaurant, Peperoncini de Mare, is near the Marriott on Calle Manuel María Icaza. As the name suggests, it specializes in seafood.

The menu at **Ozone Café** (Calle Uruguay near Calle 48, tel. 214-9616, 11 A.M.–3 P.M. and 6–10 P.M. or so daily, US$5–15) is almost comically eclectic: Among other things it features Indian, Iraqi, Indonesian, German, Lebanese, Senegalese, Italian, Tunisian, and Alabaman(!) cuisine. Of these, the Middle Eastern fare is probably the safest bet, and you'd probably also do okay with the pastas, salads, and grilled meats. The food is tasty but the chef has a fondness for oil. This is a cozy, popular little place with a low slanting ceiling and little lamps that hang above the tables. The servers are gracious and attentive.

Cafeterias and Diners

The small Vía España branch (Vía España to the side of the El Rey supermarket, tel. 223-0111, 24 hours daily) of the **Niko's Café** chain is centrally located. These cafeterias have proven to be quite popular because of their wide selection of simple and tasty food, fast service, cleanliness, long hours, and cheap prices. A few dollars buy heaps of meat, starches, and some veggies from long rows of steam tables. Niko's also offers fresh sandwiches, soups, individual pizzas, and desserts. Most breakfast items are US$2–3 or less.

There are several cafeterias within a five-minute walk of the Hotel Continental, some of which are open 24 hours a day. The best known of these, though no longer open 24 hours, is **Restaurante Jimmy** (Calle Manuel María Icaza, tel. 223-1523, 7 A.M.–11 P.M. Mon.–Sat., US$5–7), just down from the hotel. It's a neighborhood institution that moved to new digs across the street in 2003. It has a spartan but clean and modern diner atmosphere that's several steps up from its old greasy-spoon ambience. It serves a wide range of items, including its own take on Greek food (pita, tzatziki, fried eggplant, *keftedakia,* and so on), which can be odd but rather tasty. Other possibilities include *sancocho* (a local stew), pasta, sandwiches, seafood, pizza, and various meats.

The coffee shop of the **Hotel Ejecutivo** serves breakfast 24 hours a day in a cozy, friendly atmosphere. Offerings range from a full Panamanian-style breakfast with lots of fried things bad for your health to an all-you-can-eat breakfast buffet.

East Asian

◖ **Madame Chang** (Calle 48 near Calle Uruguay, tel. 269-1313 or 269-9654, noon–3 P.M. and 6–11 P.M. daily, US$15) is Panama's best and most upscale Chinese restaurant. The seafood here is excellent. Try the clams in black bean sauce to start. The *guabina* (a mild-flavored fish) steamed in soy sauce and Chinese vegetables is light and delicious. The atmosphere is pleasantly upscale, with tile floors and peach walls and tablecloths, but it's not particularly dressy. More recently the restaurant has taken a stab at Thai food, including salads, soups, and curries.

Guatemalan

Hacienda Real (Calle 49 and Calle Colombia, tel. 264-0311, www.hacienda-real. com, noon–midnight daily), which opened in January 2010, is a bright new star on the Panama City dining scene. Though part of a Guatemala-based group of restaurants with branches around Central America, it doesn't feel like a chain restaurant at all. Decorating the place reportedly cost millions, and it shows. Great care has been taken with this place. One of the waiters told me the parent company even has a kind of exchange program: waiters from Guatemala were sent down to help get the Panama City branch off the ground, and the Panamanian staff was sent to Guatemala City to learn a bit about Guatemalan food and culture.

The food is tasty rather than outstanding, but the restaurant alone is lovely enough to justify a visit. It takes up three floors and has the feel of a Guatemalan coffee baron's opulent home. It specializes in grilled meats, with main dishes starting at around US$17, but a plate of soft tacos or fajitas go for half as much. Be sure to try the typically Guatemalan black beans with thick tortillas. The *choricero* starter includes these along with (delicious) French fries, a heap of chorizo sausage, and guacamole. It can easily feed two people with no need for a main course. The house flan is exceptional.

The colorful basement dining room shares its space with an open-plan kitchen, but the vaulted brick ceiling makes this room noisy, especially when filled with the business crowd holding power lunches. The glassed-in terrace two floors up is a quieter option, and it has a view of the leafy neighborhood and a sliver of sea. There are many other nooks and private rooms to choose from, as well as an attractive front patio with ceiling fans for those who'd prefer to dine al fresco.

International

Eurasia (Calle 48 between Avenida Federico

© WILLIAM FRIAR

The new Hacienda Real serves Guatemalan food in a handsome former home in Bella Vista.

Boyd and Parque Urracá in Bella Vista, tel. 264-7859, noon–3 P.M. and 7–10:30 P.M. Mon.–Fri., 7–11 P.M. Sat., US$30) opened in 2002 and quickly emerged as one of Panama City's better restaurants. It lost its original chef but is still going strong. It's an elegant place in a lovely house built in 1936, with wrought-iron grillwork, tile floors, high ceilings, and antique mirrors and chairs. It's one of Panama's more expensive places, but it's a good place for a splurge and is worth visiting for a glimpse of what posh Panama City houses used to look like.

The food is a fusion of French and various Asian cuisines. There are about a dozen and a half first courses. Try the lobster and seafood bisque with tamarind, lemongrass, and basil. The more than two dozen second courses include unusual combinations such as the Japanese glazed salmon with tender spinach and water-chestnut fricassee.

La Posta (Calle 49 just west of Calle Uruguay, tel. 269-1076, www.lapostapanama.com, noon–2:30 P.M. and 7–10:30 P.M. Mon.–Sat., US$13–24) has become one of Panama City's favorite restaurants in the last few years. It serves imported and local seafood and meats along with a number of pastas. Some of us find the food uneven, but that's no reason not to visit it. It's located in a sprawling old Bella Vista home, and it's been restored and decorated in a style very different from Eurasia and Hacienda Real, which had a similar idea. La Posta is going for tropical elegance, with bamboo and wicker chairs, ceiling fans, old tile floors, and a long, elegant bar. Somerset Maugham and Hemingway would have felt right at home.

As its name suggests, **Fusion** (Radisson Decapolis Hotel, tel. 215-5000, 6:30–10:30 A.M., noon–3 P.M., and 6–10:45 P.M. daily, US$10–25) offers a fusion of different cuisine, especially Asian and Peruvian. The best bet for food is the buffet lunch, which consists of an attractive array of salads, sushi, and cold cuts, plus your choice of hot entree and dessert for less than US$20. It's offered noon–3 P.M. daily. This is easily the most striking-looking restaurant in Panama City. At least

stop by for a drink. Be sure to sit inside the cone-shaped room, which shoots up for three floors and is dominated by a seven-meter bust that vaguely resembles an Easter Island statue and supposedly is meant to represent the fusion of the world's different races. The hotel's swimming pool is on the floor above it. The pool has a partial glass bottom, which allows light to stream through and gives the feel of dining in an underwater temple in Atlantis. Avoid the house wine. The passion fruit dessert is delicious.

Le Bistrot (Calle 53 Este, tel. 264-5587 or 269-4025, 11:30 A.M.–11:30 P.M. daily), tucked away in a nondescript office building across from the World Trade Center in Marbella, is a Panama institution that's been around for nearly 30 years. Year after year it's been one of the city's more consistent spots for fine dining, especially compared to some of its trendier (and more expensive) rivals. The chairs on rollers may remind you of Siete Mares, which makes sense since they're both owned by the same folks. It's a good place for a romantic dinner, as the banquettes and mood lighting offer lots of privacy. Food tends toward the usual array of seafood, fish, and meats, but it's quite well prepared. The *calamari a la plancha* (grilled squid) is a bit oily but delicious. Also try the *langostinos a la thermidor* (prawns thermidor), or the very tender *filete a la pimienta* (pepper steak). I've also heard good things about the paella. The *flan de queso* (cheesecake flan) is good if you still have room.

Italian

Tre Scalini Ristorante (Calle 52 in Bella Vista, tel. 269-9951 or 269-9952, www.trescalini-panama.com, noon–3:30 P.M. and 6–11 P.M. daily, US$12–15) offers decent Italian food and friendly service in a cozy faux-Italian atmosphere. It's been around for more than two decades and is an old standby for many a Panama City dweller. There's a second Tre Scalini in the El Dorado district (Boulevard El Dorado and Calle Miguel Brostella, tel. 260-0052 or 236-5303), if you happen to find yourself out that way. Avoid the house wine at either place.

Mediterranean

❖ Restaurante Beirut (Calle Ricardo Arias and Avenida 3 Sur, tel. 214-3815, noon–3 A.M. daily) has quickly become one of Panama City's favorite restaurants. What's not to like? Huge amounts of yummy, reasonably priced Lebanese food is whisked to your table by a friendly waitstaff, whether you sit in the air-conditioned interior or outside on the breezy covered terrace, which has fake stalactites dripping from its ceiling, creating a cave-like effect. The latter is the louder option, since the restaurant sits on a busy street across from the Marriott, but, especially in the evening—and especially on a Friday evening—that's where the action is, and the people-watching is fun. Go for one of the combination platters for around US$14; it consists of eight tasty items that can feed two reasonably hungry people. Even the pita is fresh and piping hot. Oddly enough, the only thing I haven't been crazy about here is the hummus, which is a bit bland. The reasonable prices attract a younger crowd than one normally finds at this kind of restaurant, but everyone loves this place.

Habibi's (Calle Uruguay and Calle 48, tel. 264-3647, 10 A.M.–12:30 A.M. daily, US$10 or less) is a Lebanese café in a lovely old home that's been given an attractive modern makeover. It offers tasty Middle Eastern food, complete with hot pita bread. It's a popular place with a large front terrace for those who'd rather dine al fresco—a good option on dry-season evenings. This is also a good place for drinks and appetizers before a meal elsewhere.

The inexpensive **Athen's** (Calle 50 and Calle Uruguay, tel. 265-4637, www.athenspizzapanama.com, 11 A.M.–11:30 P.M. Thurs.–Tues., US$5–10) is a popular place for pizzas (about US$5 for a nine-inch pie), and for Greek salads, gyros, souvlaki, and other Greek dishes. It's a casual, fast-food kind of place with an air-conditioned interior and an outdoor terrace overlooking Calle 50 and Calle Uruguay. (And yes, sadly, it really is spelled "Athen's.") Each table has a phone customers can use to place an order, a gimmick undercut by the fact that the servers come around unprompted. The pizzas are just so-so. The pita sandwiches are huge and drowned in yogurt sauce but otherwise tasty. There's a second Athen's in the Obarrio neighborhood (Calle 57, tel. 223-1464) that's open on Wednesday when this branch is closed; its night off is Tuesday. A third one recently opened up in El Dorado, far away from the usual tourist haunts.

Panamanian

Restaurante-Bar Las Tinajas (Calle 51 near Avenida Federico Boyd, tel. 263-7890 or 269-3840, 11 A.M.–11 P.M. daily, US$10–15) is an unabashed tourist restaurant. It's worth checking out for its folkloric dance performances at 9 P.M. Tuesday through Saturday. The cover for the show is US$5 per person, and reservations are required. The cuisine is Panamanian and the restaurant is decorated to suggest a traditional town on the Azuero Peninsula.

The upscale **❖ Restaurante Barandas** (Calle Aquilino de la Guardia between Calle 51 and Calle 52, tel. 264-0000 or 265-7844, 6:30 A.M.–11 P.M. daily) in the Bristol hotel is noted for its nouvelle Panamanian cuisine. Traditional Panamanian fixtures such as *carimañolas* (fried, meat-stuffed rolls), corvina, and yuca are given the fusion treatment, with unusual sauces and generally lighter, healthier recipes. The executive chef is Coquita Arias de Calvo, who has her own local cooking show, books, and magazine. She is sort of Panama's answer to Martha Stewart. The dining room is formal and quite pleasant. Food is not always consistent here, but I've had no complaints on my last few visits. Tip: Barandas offers a delicious three-course Sunday brunch (11:30 A.M.–1 P.M.) with all-you-can-drink Chandon champagne. It costs US$30 but is a good-value splurge.

Seafood

One of Panama City's old standbys has once again become a destination restaurant thanks to a recent move to flashy new digs. **❖ Casa de Mariscos** (Calle Manuel María Icaza, tel. 223-7755 or 264-2644, www.lacasadelmariscoacha.com, noon–11 P.M. daily, US$20–30) is an impressive-looking place with a polished stone facade, two-story ceilings, a plate-glass wall overlooking a small illuminated garden, and big, colorful paintings on its walls. The restaurant is still affectionately known to regulars as Acha in honor of its Spanish owner, Ramón Martínez Acha, who founded the original Casa de Mariscos in 1965 with his wife, Claudia Vásquez de Martínez. The seafood is well-prepared and delicious. For such a stylish and modern place, the restaurant holds on to some old ways it should have ditched by now, such as a pedestrian wine list and hairnets for some of its waitstaff. But it's still a good bet for a fancy night out.

Steakhouses

Market (Calle Uruguay and Calle 47, tel. 264-9401, noon–2:30 P.M. and 6:30–11 P.M. Mon.–Wed., 11 A.M.– 11 P.M. Thurs.–Sat., 10:30 A.M.–9 P.M. Sun.), by the owner of the popular Restaurante La Posta, is a new favorite among Panamanian, gringo, and European meat lovers. Note: There's a chance the restaurant will change locations; be sure to check before visiting. Market is known for its steaks (around US$30 for imported U.S. beef; about half that for tougher local beef from Chiriquí) and burgers (about US$7 for most, or more than double that for a "colossal Angus beef burger"). The imported beef is tender but not necessarily cooked evenly, and the wine is what you'd expect to find in your average California supermarket. Burgers and beer are the best value. Market also does a pretty tasty Cobb salad and maracuya (passion fruit) pavlova. This is a fairly casual place with a large, high-roofed bar area, separated by walls of wine bottles from a slightly more formal dining area. The sound can be deafening when it's busy, such as a Sunday night, which is the traditional family night out for Panamanians who can afford it. Market also serves brunch on Saturday and Sunday.

An old standby, **Gaucho's Steak House** (Calle Uruguay and Calle 48, tel. 263-4469 or 263-1406, noon–3 P.M. and 6–10:30 P.M. daily) serves decent steaks for those who don't expect much more in a dining experience. Both the atmosphere (brightly lit, chain-steakhouse vibe) and the food (this is a place for *meat;* you won't find much green outside the potted plants) are unadorned. The service tends to be fast and perfunctory. Though ostensibly an Argentine steakhouse, Gaucho's imports its meat from the United States. Expect to pay upwards of US$25 for imported beef. Chicken and seafood are also on the menu, but that's not why people come here. For starters, try the *picado de chorizo* (a plate of sliced sausages). It's delicious.

Vegetarian

Me Gusta Comida Vegetariana (Calle Ricardo Arias, no phone, 7:30 A.M.–8 P.M. Mon.–Sat.) is very similar to La Casa Vegetariana, in both (lack of) ambience and food. Portions here are US$0.60/each. Other goodies include soy milk and veggie burgers. Its name, by the way, translates to the suitably plain "I like vegetarian food." It's near Restaurante Costa Azul.

Supermarkets and Specialty Foods

Supermarkets are everywhere in Panama City, and in recent years their selections have vastly improved. They now more closely resemble mega-markets in the United States, with an array of imported and local goods, including a better choice of fresh produce (difficult growing conditions make much beyond tropical fruit hard to come by in the tropics).

Panama's biggest grocery-store chain is **El Rey.** It has a half-dozen stores in Panama City alone. The one on Vía España (tel. 223-7850, 24 hours daily) is centrally located and has a pharmacy and many other services. The more upscale **Riba Smith** supermarket has four locations in Panama City. The most convenient for visitors are in Bella Vista (Calle 45, tel. 225-6247, 7:30 A.M.–9 P.M. Mon.–Sat., 8 A.M.–8 P.M. Sun.), on the Transístmica (tel. 299-3999, 7:30 A.M.–9 P.M. Mon.–Sat., 8 A.M.–8 P.M. Sun.), and in the Multiplaza Pacific shopping center (tel. 302-3793, 7:30 A.M.–9 P.M. Mon.–Sat., 8 A.M.–8 P.M.

Sun.). The stores have buffet-style cafeterias as well. Riba Smith also does home (and presumably hotel!) deliveries with 24 hours notice and a minimum US$7 purchase.

Some of Panama's best coffee is at **Café Ruiz** (World Trade Center on Calle 53, tel. 265-0779, www.caferuiz.com, 7 A.M.–6 P.M. Mon., Tues., Wed., and Fri., 7 A.M.–5 P.M. Thurs.). It's a café and shop that carries all kinds of roasts and flavors of coffee, both whole bean and ground. Attractive gift packages and mugs are available. Café Ruiz coffee is also available at some supermarkets, but the gourmet roast is available only at the Café Ruiz shops.

Felipe Motta in Marbella (Calle 53, tel. 269-6633, 9 A.M.–7 P.M. Mon.–Fri., 9 A.M.–6 P.M. Sat.) has a good selection of wines at prices comparable to what you'd find in the United States. It also has some gourmet foods and fresh bread and pastries.

EAST PANAMA CITY
Cafeterias and Diners

There's a newer, rather sleek outlet of Churrería Manolo in Obarrio (Avenida 1D Sur and Calle Juan Ramón Poll C., tel. 214-3986, 7 A.M.–1 A.M. daily). Check out this well-loved chain for its great churros, Spanish hot chocolate *(chocolate a la española),* breakfast, and sandwiches.

East Asian

Sushi Itto (Calle 55 Este near Avenida 2 Sur/Samuel Lewis, tel. 265-1222 or 265-1136, noon–10 P.M. Mon.–Thurs., noon–11 P.M. Fri. and Sat., 12:30–10:30 P.M. Sun.), right next to the Reprosa jewelry store, is part of a Mexican sushi chain (yep, Mexican). It's a modern place with an extensive sushi menu as well as tempura, rice dishes, pastas, soups, and even a few Thai dishes. The sushi's okay. There's a second outlet in the Multiplaza Pacific Mall.

International

The ◖ **Pony Club by Limoncillo** (Calle 69 Este just south of Vía Porras, tel. 270-0807, www.limoncillo.com, noon–2:30 P.M. and

7–10:30 P.M. Mon.–Thurs., noon–2:30 P.M. and 7–11 P.M. Fri. and Sat., US$14–25) is the successor to the late, lamented Limoncillo, one of Panama's best restaurants, which fell victim to the construction boom. The new place has a more casual café feel and is quite small (seats about 40), but the food is still delicious. In the kitchen is Clara Icaza, one of Panama's most celebrated chefs. The restaurant specializes in "contemporary American" cuisine, but my favorites here are nouvelle twists on traditional Panamanian fare. Beef and yuca, for instance, become a marinated *entraña* (skirt steak) with an unusual yuca cake. It's almost sweet, but it's tender and delicious (US$23). The salads are also good. The manager, Jennifer Spector, understands the importance of decor, lighting, and music in creating a mood that complements fine food. This is not a place for a cheap meal on the run, but when it all comes together it's worth the taxi ride to its location near Parque Recreativo Omar, not far from the Sheraton Panama Hotel and Convention Center. (Print or jot down the map on the restaurant's website, as not all taxi drivers will know where it is.)

Pizzerias

Napoli No. 2 (Calle 57 and Avenida 1D Sur, tel. 263-8799 or 263-8800, noon–midnight Tues.–Sat.) is the somewhat more upscale younger sister of the original Napoli in the much more upscale neighborhood of Obarrio. It's air-conditioned and pleasant. The service is not-so-hot, but the food comes fast once you finally get to order.

PUNTA PAITILLA
Supermarkets and Specialty Foods

There's a kosher cafeteria/bakery, a kosher restaurant, and even a kosher supermarket clustered together in Punta Paitilla. These have good, unusual (for Panama) offerings that may be of interest even to those who don't keep kosher. They are great options on Sunday, when many other places are closed, but expect crowds. **Pita-Pan Kosher** (Vía Italia, tel.

264-2786 or 265-1369, 7 A.M.–9 P.M. Mon.–Thurs., 7 A.M.–5 P.M. Fri., 9 A.M.–9 P.M. Sun., US$3.50–6) is an air-conditioned kosher cafeteria in the upscale Bal Harbour shopping center just off Avenida Balboa. It serves fish, salads, pasta, sandwiches, pizza, quiche, hummus with falafel, and so on. It even has kosher sushi. The food here is tasty. Another plus is that it serves pita and other fresh bread by the loaf. It's closed Friday evening through Sunday morning for the Sabbath.

Next to Pita-Pan Kosher is **Foodie Market** (Bal Harbour shopping center, 7:30 A.M.–8:30 P.M. Mon.–Fri., 8 A.M.–7 P.M. Sat., 9 A.M.–8 P.M. Sun.), a small market that has good veggies and fruit.

Super Kosher (Calle 56 Este, tel. 263-5253, 8:30 A.M.–8:30 P.M. Sun.–Thurs., 8:30 A.M.–4:30 P.M. Fri.) is an upscale kosher supermarket one street north of the Bal Harbour shopping center. It has good veggies and products from the United States. There's a cafeteria inside that serves breakfast items, sandwiches, and other goodies, all kosher.

Information

Panama's government tourism ministry, the Autoridad de Turismo Panamá (ATP), has its administrative headquarters at the Atlapa Convention Center next to the Sheraton Panama Hotel and Convention Center off Vía Israel, but it's not set up to deal with actual visitors. If you're eternally optimistic, you can try calling the office at 226-3544 or 226-7000. Until recently it was known as IPAT (Instituto Panameño de Turismo).

You will occasional see ATP information booths around town, including ones at the ruins of Old Panama. However, I've never seen anyone actually working in them. There's also an information booth between Immigration and Customs at Tocumen International Airport that's sometimes staffed, though don't expect much more than a handful of hotel fliers. (Grab the business cards, if there are any—these offer 10 percent off at restaurants and businesses you might actually want to visit.)

Tour operators, guides, and hostels are the best bet for information about Panama City. Most of Panama's tour operators have their headquarters in Panama City, and nearly all offer city tours of different kinds.

Taxi drivers often double as tour guides. Don't expect a scholarly lecture on the sights, but it can be a reasonable way to cover a lot of ground. Agree on a price ahead of time.

Check out *Focus Magazine, The Visitor* (www.thevisitorpanama.com), or *Rumbos* for bilingual coverage geared toward tourists.

MAPS

Tourist maps of Panama City are still a halfhearted affair. They tend not to be widely available, user-friendly, or terribly accurate or up-to-date, and they often seem little more than a guide to advertisers who paid to be put on the map, literally. Other than (I hope) the maps in this book, your best bets are the foldouts that come with the free *Focus Magazine,* copies of which are easy to find in hotels and tourist-oriented sights around the city. City maps are sometimes for sale at bookstores, pharmacies, and Gran Morrison department stores. The stores also may carry one of several pictorial maps of Casco Viejo that have popped up in the last few years; these can make navigating around its maze of streets a bit easier.

HOSPITALS, POLICE, AND EMERGENCIES

The emergency number for the police *(policía nacional)* is 104. The emergency number for the fire department *(bomberos)* is 103. Directory assistance *(asistencia al directorio)* is 102. The national operator can be reached at 101. To reach the international operator, dial 106.

The fire department *(bomberos)* has a reputation for arriving on the scene of an emergency before the police. Panama City finally has an official emergency medical response service. Dial 911 to call an ambulance (note that this is only for medical help; dial 104 for the police). This service, *Sistema Único de Manejo de Emergencias* (translation: Unified System for the Management of Emergencies, www. sume911.pa/) is slowly being rolled out around the country. This is a new service and how well it works will take time to ascertain. If an ambulance doesn't come quickly, your best bet may be to grab a taxi and get to the closest hospital. Hospital Punta Pacifica and Hospital Nacional would be my first choices in an emergency, and both are central. There are private-ambulance services in Panama City, though these are really aimed at already-existing subscribers. One to try is **SEMM** (tel. 366-0122 for emergencies, tel. 366-0100 for office, www.semmemergencias.com).

Panama City has first-world medical facilities and excellent doctors, many of whom were trained in the United States and speak English. Even those without medical insurance can receive good care for far less than in the United States.

Please note: I'm hearing more reports of foreign tourists and expats using the government-funded *seguro social* (social security) hospitals and clinics, such as Hospital Santo Tomás, for their medical complaints. These public hospitals are certainly the cheapest options, but they are intended for Panama's poor and working classes who can't afford other treatment. The small amount patients pay does not begin to cover the real cost of care, which is subsidized by the taxes of Panamanians who have worked hard all their lives (much like Social Security in the United States, or the National Health Service in the United Kingdom). This subsidized care is one of the only safety nets the Panamanian government provides for hundreds of thousands of Panamanians who live hand to mouth and barely scrape by. These hospitals are crowded and underfunded, and foreigners using them increase the drain on their resources. It is also illegal for foreigners to use them (unless they work in Panama and

have an employer who pays into the *seguro social* system).

Centro Médico Paitilla (Calle 53 and Avenida Balboa, tel. 265-8800 or 269-0333, www.centromedicopaitilla.com) has long been considered Panama's best medical center. The **Hospital Nacional** (Avenida Cuba between Calle 38 and Calle 39, tel. 207-8100 or 207-8102, emergency room tel. 207-8110, 207-8136, or 306-3310, ambulance tel. 207-8119, www.hospitalnacional.com) opened a modern facility in 1998 and has been positioning itself as catering to the expatriate and foreign tourist market. The glittery new kid in town is **Hospital Punta Pacífica** (Punta Pacífica, tel. 204-8000, emergencies tel. 204-8184 or 204-8185, www.hospitalpuntapacifica.com). The hospital is affiliated with Johns Hopkins Medicine International, which provides advice and training from the acclaimed medical center in Baltimore, Maryland.

The pharmacy at the centrally located **El Rey supermarket** (tel. 223-1243) on Vía España is open 24 hours a day. **Farmacia Milani** (Calle 33 and Avenida Justo Arosemena/Avenida 3 Sur, tel. 225-0065), across the street from Hotel Roma Plaza in Calidonia, is also open 24 hours a day. The pharmacy at **Centro Medico Bella Vista** (Avenida Perú and Calle 39, tel. 227-4022, 7:30 A.M.–10 P.M. Mon.–Fri., 7:30 A.M.–8 P.M. Sat., 7:30 A.M.–4 P.M. Sun.) is across the street from the Hotel Costa Inn, in the Bella Vista/Calidonia area. **Farmacia Arrocha** is a large drugstore chain. Centrally located branches include one just off Vía España (Calle 49 Este, tel. 223-4505, 7 A.M.–9:45 P.M. daily), about midway between the Hotel Ejecutivo and the Hotel El Panamá, and one in the Albrook Mall (tel. 315-1728).

PUBLICATIONS
Newspapers and Periodicals
All of Panama's daily newspapers are published in Panama City and are widely available at newsstands and in shops. Most are in Spanish (there are also long-established Chinese-language papers for the Chinese immigrant population). There are currently no

standalone English-language daily newspapers, though some of the Spanish-language dailies are flirting with running stories in English, both in print and online.

Focus Magazine, a free magazine published twice yearly in English and Spanish, contains brief, enthusiastic articles on various attractions around the country, as well as maps, hotel and restaurant listings, and general tourist information. The same folks put out *The Visitor* (www.thevisitorpanama.com), a free, twice-monthly, bilingual tourist newspaper. Both are widely available at hotels and other locations that cater to travelers. A newer publication called **Rumbos** is printed bi-weekly and distributed with the *Panamá América* daily newspaper. Each (bilingual) issue focuses on a different region or aspect of Panama, and it does a surprisingly thorough job of covering nooks and crannies of Panama that traditionally have been overlooked by local tourism publications.

National Library

Panama's national library, the four-story **Biblioteca Nacional de Panamá** (Parque Omar off Vía Porras, tel. 224-9466 or 221-8360, 9 A.M.–6 P.M. Mon.–Fri., 9 A.M.–5 P.M. Sat.) may be of interest to those who want in-depth information on Panama. It's off Vía Porras in the middle of Parque Recreativo Omar. The collections include books by Panamanian authors or about Panama, and newspaper morgues dating from the 19th century. A wall of filing cabinets contains biographical information on prominent Panamanians and expatriates. The library is open to the public, but the stacks can't be browsed: Visitors search the electronic catalog on the 3rd floor and then request their selection from a librarian. All books must be perused on the premises; borrowing privileges have been "suspended" because too many people did not return books. There are several quiet, comfortable areas to read inside the library.

NAUTICAL CHARTS

Islamorada Internacional (Bldg. 808, Avenida Arnulfo Arias Madrid/Balboa Road, tel. 228-4348 or 228-6069, Skype: Islamoradacharts, www.islamorada.com, 8 A.M.–5 P.M. Mon.–Fri.) is the place to go in Panama for nautical charts, books, software, instruments, flags, and pendants. It's actually in Balboa, in the former Canal Zone, across the street from the huge fountain of Arnulfo Arias. It lays claim to being the largest nautical bookstore in Panama. It also has general guidebooks to the Caribbean and elsewhere. Yachties can reach it in Balboa harbor at VHF channels 12 and 16; in Cristóbal try VHF 65 and 85, "Radio Balboa." The staff speaks fluent English here.

Services

Any business that visitors need to transact, from visa extensions to flight changes, is best done in Panama City. It has far better facilities and options than are generally available in the hinterland.

CHANGING, RECEIVING, AND SENDING MONEY

Strangely enough for an international banking capital, until recently there were only two places in and around Panama City where visitors could exchange currencies. New places have begun to pop up around Plaza Concordia on Vía España and Vía Veneto next to Hotel El Panamá. But these deal mainly in Euros and Colombian pesos, and they tend to be a bit casual and borderline shady, the kind of places where you can also cash checks and buy cheap watches.

Those who must exchange currency are much better off going to **Panacambios** (Vía España, tel. 223-1800, 8 A.M.–5 P.M. Mon.–Fri.), toward the back of the Plaza Regency next to Plaza Concordia. It's a Panama institution that's been in the same place since 1990.

It's set back from the street, away from prying eyes, and comes equipped with an armed guard and security gate.

Panacambios carries every currency you can think of. (When I last stopped by, I tried unsuccessfully to stump the friendly guy at the counter. He had everything from Russian rubles to Malagasy ariarys, and just that week had exchanged some Jersey pounds.) How good the exchange rate will be depends on the currency: There's not much of a market to buy Colombian pesos, for instance, so you're probably better off spending them in Colombia than selling them here. The guys I've met here are good-natured pros, and if you ask they'll probably tell you if they can offer a good rate for whatever currency you have or want. Rates for euros and colones are more competitive, but in general they will be no better than those at a U.S. airport exchange counter—in other words, not a steal. Panama is dollar country.

Be sure to check out the small but impressive proof sets of rare Panamanian coins. Some of the commemorative coins and stamps are for sale.

I've heard good reports about **Italtransfer** (Avenida Manuel E. Bautista, tel. 265-7270, 265-7271, or 265-6243, info@italtransfer. com, 8 A.M.–5 P.M. Mon.–Fri., 8:30 A.M.–noon Sat.), in the same complex as the Hotel Crowne Plaza, but they were closed when I tried to visit during their alleged opening hours. They cash travelers checks and transfer money as well, but expect to pay a 2–4 percent commission.

The **Banco Nacional de Panamá** branch (7 A.M.–11 P.M. daily) in Tocumen International Airport exchanges most major currencies.

The centrally located **Scotiabank** (Avenida Federico Boyd and Calle 51, 8 A.M.–3:30 P.M. Mon.–Fri., 9 A.M.–12:30 P.M. Sat.) in Bella Vista cashes travelers checks, something that can be quite a hassle in Panama.

Banks with ATMs are all over Panama City. For those staying in the Calidonia area, branches of **Banco Nacional de Panamá** (BNP) and **BBVA** (hours for both: 8 A.M.–3 P.M. Mon.–Fri., 9 A.M.–noon Sat.) are centrally located on a busy street. They both have 24-hour ATMs.

The **HSBC** (10:30 A.M.–6 P.M. Mon.–Fri., 9 A.M.–3 P.M. Sat.) at the Multicentro Mall has unusually long hours during the week. Avoid the main BNP branch on Vía España; it gets absolutely packed.

Those who need to send or receive money the old-fashioned way can find **Western Union** outlets just about anywhere in Panama City. The main office is in the Plaza Concordia shopping complex (Vía España, tel. 800-2224, 8 A.M.–7 P.M. Mon.–Fri., 8 A.M.–5 P.M. Sat.). Other centrally located offices include a large center in the Albrook Mall (tel. 269-1055, 10 A.M.–7 P.M. daily), as well as an outlet next door in the Gran Terminal de Transporte. There's an outlet in the Super Empeñas San Ramón store in Calidonia (Calle 34 near Avenida Perú, tel. 225-1952, 7:30 A.M.–5:30 P.M. Mon.–Sat.). For other locations, visit www.westernunion.com. **MoneyGram** has about three dozen outlets in Panama City. The one at the Plaza Concordia is in the Bambi Empeños stores (Vía España, tel. 263-4293, 8 A.M.–6 P.M. Mon.–Fri., 8 A.M.–3 P.M. Sat.).

POST OFFICE

Panama's main post office is in Calidonia (Avenida Central between Calle 33 and Avenida Perú, 7 A.M.–5:45 P.M. Mon.–Fri., 7 A.M.–5 P.M. Sat.), across from the Basílica Don Bosco church. There's a small "stamp museum" (tel. 512-0601, 8:30 A.M.–4:30 P.M.) in the complex that consists of a few recent first-day covers stuck on the wall of an office. Other post office branches include ones in the Plaza Concordia shopping center on Vía España and next to Restaurante Boulevard Balboa (Avenida Balboa near Calle 31). All are open the same hours as the main post office.

COMMUNICATIONS

Free Wi-Fi has sprung up everywhere in Panama—in hotels, hostels, restaurants, cafés, you name it—and nowhere is this more true than in the capital. Often, for better and worse, there's no password protection and it's just a matter of firing up your computer or phone and logging on. Even if you find a place that isn't yet Wi-Fi equipped, chances are you'll have a half dozen other signals from neighboring establishments to choose from, with proprietors who don't care if you piggyback.

Internet cafés open and close constantly in Panama City. Most are just bare-bones air-conditioned rooms with terminals, but the rates are good—usually around US$0.50–0.75 an hour. It's often possible to pay for just a half hour or 15 minutes. Some offer international calling at competitive rates (about US$0.20 a minute to Costa Rica or the United States, for instance). A few also send and receive faxes; domestic faxes tend to be reasonable, but sending an international fax can cost US$5 a page or more. Be sure to ask for rates ahead of time.

There are plenty of Internet cafés in the Calidonia area, where most of the budget hotels are. Many of these hotels also have Internet computers, often dollar-fed ones. A convenient Internet café is between the immigration office and Restaurante Pizzeria Romanaccio (Calle 29 Este between Avenida Perú and Avenida Cuba, no phone, 8 A.M.–midnight daily).

The Plaza Concordia shopping complex on Vía España has several places to access the Internet, the nicest of which is next to Western Union in the Cable and Wireless international call center (8 A.M.–9:30 P.M. Mon.–Sat., 9:30 A.M.–8 P.M. Sun.), which also charges standard rates for international phone calls. The Multicentro Mall also has call centers and Internet cafés. There are also passport-photo shops in the same complex. There are plenty of other Internet places in the heart of Vía España. Centro Comercial Vía Veneto, the shopping center to the side of the Hotel El Panamá on Vía Veneto, has several 24-hour Internet cafés/international call centers. Names and ownership change seemingly overnight. Other Internet cafés in the Vía España area include a couple on Calle Ricardo Arias off Vía España, just south of the Hotel Continental.

Norma's Place (Vía Argentina, no phone, 9 A.M.–10 P.M. daily) is across the street from and just north of the Vía Argentina branch of Churrería Manolo. It also places international calls.

Enterprising street vendors are now offering use of their cell phones to make local calls for around US$0.20, which can be more convenient than hunting for a pay phone. These are easiest to find in working-class commercial areas such as Calidonia, La Exposición, and Santa Ana.

However, those expecting to make lots of local calls are better off buying a local mobile phone that can be "recharged" with prepaid phone cards. Surprisingly good ones with clear sound and long battery life are widely available in shops throughout Panama for about $15–20, including a local SIM card, immediate activation, and US$2 in phone credit.

Internet cafés have been slow to come to Casco Viejo. But free Wi-Fi is increasingly common in the area's lodgings and restaurants.

IMMIGRATION OFFICE

Panama City's main **Migración y Naturalización** (Immigration and Naturalization, Avenida Cuba and Calle 29 Este, tel. 207-1800, 777-7777, or 227-1077, tel./fax 227-1227, 8 A.M.–3 P.M. Mon.–Fri.) office is in Calidonia, close to most of the budget hotels. Visitors who need to change or extend their visa should come here (and be prepared for a long day).

LAUNDERETTES

Lavamáticos (launderettes) are harder and harder to find in central Panama City (as opposed to *lavanderías,* which are comparable to dry-cleaning places in the United States). Hostels and both budget and business-oriented hotels often provide laundry service at quite reasonable rates; be sure to ask for prices ahead of time. Some hotels, especially *aparthotels,* have self-service washers and dryers. *Lavamáticos* generally charge around US$3–4 total to wash and dry a load. Washing in cold water is often US$0.25 cheaper.

A nameless *lavamático* (Avenida 2 Norte/ Eusebio A. Morales, 7:30 A.M.–7 P.M. Mon.–Fri., 8 A.M.–7 P.M. Sat.) near the Aparthotel Torres de Alba and the Las Huacas Hotel and Suites in El Cangrejo may possibly still be there when you visit. **Lavandería Fan Clean** (tel. 399-2108, 7 A.M.–8:30 P.M. Mon.–Sat., 7:30 A.M.–5 P.M. Sun.) is across the street from Einstein's Head, about a block north of Vía Argentina in El Cangrejo.

Launderettes are scarce in Calidonia/La Exposición, but the midrange hotels often have laundry service. There's a *lavamático* in Casco Viejo (Avenida Central near Calle 8 Este, 7 A.M.–7 P.M. Mon.–Sat., 7 A.M.–3 P.M. Sun.) next to the cathedral. It charges US$0.50–0.75 to wash, US$0.75 to dry.

SPANISH COURSES

The Canadian-run **Spanish Panama** (Vía Argentina and Avenida 3B, tel. 213-3121, www.spanishpanama.com) is a well-established school in El Cangrejo that offers a range of private and group classes. In April 2010 it moved to new digs a few blocks away from its old home, which had been plagued by construction noise. Group classes that include airport pickup, lodging, breakfast and (optional) salsa dance classes start at US$400/week. A one-week crash course (language instruction only) is US$180. Free weekly cultural and orientation activities are also available.

To get to Spanish Panama, turn north off Vía Argentina on the street between Churrería Manolo and Restaurante y Cafetería El Trapiche. The school will be on the right.

Getting There and Away

Panama City, not surprisingly, is the country's transportation hub. It has its major international and domestic airports, its biggest bus terminal, its main ship ports, and plenty of rental car companies.

Most travelers come to and leave the country through Tocumen International Airport, 25 kilometers east of Panama City. The nearest cruise-ship port is at the end of the Calzada de Amador, which is near the Pacific entrance to the Panama Canal a few kilometers from downtown. The national bus terminal, for both international, regional, and local buses, is the Gran Terminal de Transportes in Albrook. It's quite close to Panama City's domestic airport, Aeropuerto Marcos A. Gelabert, also in Albrook.

Note that no roads or ferry service currently link Panama and Colombia; only airlines provide regular passenger service between the two countries.

DOMESTIC FLIGHTS

Panama City's small domestic airport, officially called **Aeropuerto Marcos A. Gelabert,** is near the Gran Terminal de Transportes in Albrook, a former U.S. Air Force base. It's just a couple of kilometers northwest of the heart of Panama City. Flights generally leave Panama City early in the morning, though some popular destinations have multiple daily departures scattered throughout the day.

Most taxi drivers won't know the airport by name: Ask to go to the "Aeropuerto de Albrook." Emphasize that you want to go to Albrook to avoid being taken to Tocumen, the international airport. The fare from most parts of Panama City should be only a few dollars. It will generally make more sense, and even be more economical overall, to take a taxi directly to the airport than fool with making the short ride from downtown to Albrook by bus.

Panama's two domestic carriers fly out of the airport, the country's major domestic air hub. They fly to Bocas del Toro, Kuna Yala, the Darién, David, the Islas Perlas, and a few other mainland destinations. Prices are the same for both airlines.

Aeroperlas (tel. 315-7500, fax 315-7580, www.aeroperlas.com) is the dominant carrier, with more routes and business. The newer **Air Panama** (tel. 316-9000, www.flyairpanama.com) flies to most of the same destinations as Aeroperlas.

At the airport, good Boquete-grown coffee is available at Café Kotowa (5 A.M.–6 P.M. Mon.–Fri., 6 A.M.–6 P.M. Sat., 7 A.M.–6 P.M. Sun.). A branch of El Hombre de La Mancha bookstores recently opened. There's also a greasy-spoon cafeteria that opens before dawn. Branches of the major rental-car companies are at the airport, but whether they'll be staffed is a different question. There's an ATM near the airport entrance.

REGIONAL BUSES

Most long-distance buses leave from the capital's impressive **Gran Terminal de Transportes** (www.grantnt.com). It's pretty *gran,* all right—huge and two stories high. Buses arrive on the top floor and leave from street level, which is where all the ticket booths are. Destinations are posted on each booth, and a schedule of hours and intermediate destinations is sometimes posted behind the ticket seller. The Gran Terminal now has a website listing details and prices for all destinations, which would be super swell if the list wasn't two years out of date, which it was the last time I checked. It also gets the prices for some destinations wrong by a factor of ten, which doesn't inspire confidence.

There may be more than one bus headed to your destination at any given time. If a bus that has your destination as a final stop isn't convenient, look for one that has it as an interim stop. Those heading to Santiago, for instance, can buy a ticket at the Santiago booth or, say, the David booth (Santiago is on the way to David). There's a US$0.05 departure fee for long-distance bus service, payable at the turnstiles on the way to the buses; change machines are nearby. Using the bathrooms in the terminal costs US$0.25.

Panama City and local area buses also operate from the terminal, including buses to Tocumen International Airport (look for the "Tocumen, Corredor Sur" bus). They leave from the ground floor, on the side facing the shopping mall. Destinations are signposted.

The ground floor has shops, pharmacies, a half-dozen banks and ATMs, a branch of the low-cost Niko's Café cafeteria, two U.S.-style food courts, pharmacies, places to take passport-size photos and laminate ID cards, places selling cheap mobile phone and phone cards, and other businesses likely to be of interest to travelers. However, the last Internet café disappeared and there is no indication of a new one arriving. The terminal is next to a shopping mall, Los Pueblos Albrook Mall, and a movie multiplex, Cinemark. A few notable services include:

Farmacia Albrook (10 A.M.–11 P.M. Mon.–Sat., 8 A.M.–10 P.M. Sun.), one of two pharmacies more or less next door to each other.

HSBC bank (10:30 A.M.–5:30 P.M. Mon.–Fri., 9 A.M.–2 P.M. Sat.), which has a 24-hour ATM. There are now lots of ATMs, but if there are crowds or you'd rather not withdraw money at a bus terminal, use one of the ATMs in the shopping mall next door.

Telxpress (tel. 269-1055, 8 A.M.–8 P.M. daily), which offers international phone-call service at prices that tend to be excessive.

The bus terminal's information desk downstairs is useless.

Schedule

Here are some bus destinations likely to be of interest to visitors:

Almirante (port for Bocas del Toro archipelago) and Changuinola: One daily bus, at 8 P.M. The bus sells out so get to the station and buy tickets early. The ride takes about 10 hours. Note that the company that runs this route has been adding and dropping a second departure, in the morning, for years now. If it's available and scheduled to leave later than about 7 A.M., any delay will mean you stand an excellent chance of missing the last water taxi to the islands and have to spend the night in either Almirante or Changuinola, neither of which is appealing, or at a more appealing, but more remote and expensive hotel called La Escapada. The last water taxi leaves at 6:30 P.M., and it sometimes fills up. It's safer to overnight on the bus and get to the islands during the day. It arrives at about 6 A.M. the next morning at the Almirante crossroads (US$23) and 7 A.M. at Changuinola (US$24). Note: There's a two-suitcase maximum included in the fare.

Bayano: Every 40 minutes or so 3:20 A.M.–6 P.M. (US$3 to Lago Bayano, 2.5 hours).

Chitré: About once an hour 6 A.M.–11 P.M. (US$7.50, 3.5 hours).

Colón: Every 20 minutes or less 4:40 A.M.–10:10 P.M. for air-conditioned bus (US$2.50 for express, about 1.5 hours; regular bus is US$1.80 but can be far slower). Look for the names ULTRACOLPA or EPACOC, the two companies that run the fancy air-conditioned buses. Non-air-conditioned buses leave constantly day and night and cost US$0.50 for the route that uses the Corredor Norte toll road. Note: Be very careful at the Colón bus station. Those who want to go to Portobelo or Isla Grande by public transportation should take a Colón-bound bus and transfer at Sabanitas, on the Boyd-Roosevelt Highway (Transístmica), well before reaching Colón.

Coronado: Every 15 minutes 6 A.M.–9 P.M. (US$2.40, 1.5 hours).

Darién: 4 A.M. and 4:15 P.M. Because of road conditions, Metetí (US$9, 6 hours) is usually the last stop. In dry season, early morning buses sometimes make it all the way to Yaviza (US$14, about 7 hours). Add at least an hour to these estimates if the road is bad.

David: Two well-established companies run large, long-haul, air-conditioned buses between Panama City and David. The fare is US$12.60 one-way, or US$15 for a one-way "express" bus. The trip theoretically takes about 6.5 hours, but buses frequently run late; express buses can shave up to an hour off that time. Buses generally stop at provincial towns along the Interamerican Highway, most notably Aguadulce, Penonomé, and Santiago. Other stops are made by request. In Santiago, buses usually take a half-hour break at the Pyramidal or Los Tucanes complex, which have a cafeteria, restaurant, bathrooms, pharmacy, ATM, and other services. Seats are assigned, and passengers can request seat assignments. For safety's sake, avoid seats at the front of the bus.

The bathroom is in the back, so avoid sitting near there as well. Note that the companies frequently tinker with their schedules, so don't count on precise timing. However, buses leave virtually around the clock, and there is usually more than one option per hour during daylight hours. (A third company, PANAFROM, was running this route in 2010. They have eight daily departures.)

The largest of the companies, with the most frequent trips, is **Terminales David-Panama** (tel. 314-6228, tel. 314-6395 for cargo, terminal@cwpanama.net). Buses leave every 60–90 minutes 5 A.M.–midnight. The last two buses, at 10:45 P.M. and midnight, are expresses. **Padafront** (tel. 314-6264) has departures to David about every 1–2 hours approximately 6:30 A.M.–midnight. The last two buses, at 10:45 P.M. and midnight, are expresses.

El Copé and La Pintada: Once an hour 6 A.M.–7 P.M. (US$4.90 to La Pintada, 2.5 hours; US$5.50 to El Copé, 3 hours).

El Valle: Every 30 minutes 7 A.M.–7 P.M. (US$3.50, 2.5 hours).

Farallón and Santa Clara: Every 20 minutes 5:30 A.M.–8 P.M. (US$3.25 to Santa Clara, US$4 to Farallón, 2 hours).

Las Tablas: About once an hour 6 A.M.–7 P.M. (US$8, 4 hours).

Paso Canoa (border crossing with Costa Rica): One of the companies that makes the Panama City–David run, Padafront, continues west to Paso Canoa, the main border crossing with Costa Rica. The trip takes 8–9 hours, slightly less for an express. Most travelers will be better off taking one of the international buses that continue to Costa Rica and beyond. But if you just needs to make it to the border, these companies make more frequent trips. Another possibility is to take any bus to David and switch to one of the small regional buses that run constantly between that city and the border.

Penonomé: Every 20–30 minutes 4:45 A.M.–10:45 P.M. (US$4.35, 2 hours).

Santiago: About every 30 minutes 3 A.M.–1 A.M. (US$7.50, about 4 hours). Note: Two companies, Expreso Veraguense and

Sanpasa, work this route and compete aggressively with each other. Be prepared for *boleteros* (ticket touts) trying to get your business as you approach their counters.

Soná (for those going to Playa Santa Catalina): 8:20 A.M., 10:20 A.M., 12:45 P.M., 2:20 P.M., 4:20 P.M., and 5:45 P.M. (US$8, about 4.5 hours). Get a Santa Catalina bus or taxi in Soná. Note that the last bus for Santa Catalina leaves Soná at 4 P.M.

BY CAR

New highways that crisscross Panama City are making it easier to bypass heavy traffic on the way out of town.

The **Corredor Norte,** a toll highway with several entrances on the north and west outskirts of the city, leads north across the isthmus, ending at Sabanitas, not far from the outskirts of Colón, on the Caribbean coast. This is a far better option than taking the old, slow potholed Transístmica (also known as the transisthmian highway, officially it's the Boyd-Roosevelt Highway, though no one calls it that).

The **Corredor Sur,** another toll highway that begins just east of Punta Paitilla, leads to Tocumen International Airport, where it links with the Interamerican Highway. There, at a clover-leaf intersection next to Hotel Riande Aeropuerto Hotel and Resort, the Interamerican "Highway" (really just a two-lane road) continues east toward Cerro Azul and the Darién. This road passes through the Darién and finally ends at Yaviza, the beginning of the Darién Gap, through which no road has ever been built.

To all points west of Panama City—the beaches, mountains, Azuero Peninsula, Bocas del Toro, Costa Rican border, and the rest— there are only two ways to begin the journey by land: by crossing the **Puente de las Américas** (Bridge of the Americas) near the Pacific entrance to the Panama Canal or by taking the newer **Puente Centenario** (Centennial Bridge) across the canal near Pedro Miguel.

West of either bridge, the road eventually connects with another toll highway, the **Autopista Arraiján-La Chorrera.** This is now a divided highway for much of the way to the western frontier, though most of the stretch between Santiago and David is still a two-lane road. Nevertheless, this entire ribbon of road is officially part of the Interamerican Highway.

Most Pacific-side destinations in the former Canal Zone are accessible from Panama City by taking **Gaillard Highway** (now officially known as Avenida Omar Torrijos Herrera), which borders the east bank of the canal and runs past the domestic airport at Albrook, the Panama Railway terminal at Corozal, Clayton, Miraflores and Pedro Miguel Locks, and so on. The road forks outside Gamboa. Left leads to the attractions around Gamboa before Gaillard Highway dead-ends in Gamboa itself. Right leads through part of Parque Nacional Soberanía, including part of the historic Las Cruces Trail, before intersecting the Transístmica, the old road linking Panama City with Colón.

One canal-area attraction, the booming Calzada de Amador (Amador Causeway), is now easier to get to from Panama City thanks to highway ramps that lead onto and off Avenida de los Mártires near the foot of the Bridge of the Americas.

Getting Around

Traffic in Panama City is bad and getting worse all the time. If possible, avoid car trips during morning and evening rush hours, especially 8–9 A.M. and 4:30–6:30 P.M. A couple of toll roads that cut through the city—Corredor Norte and Corredor Sur—are a quick escape from some of the congestion, since they're priced out of reach of the average Panama City driver. Most tolls are less than US$1, so you'll save a lot of time and aggravation by taking them.

Taxis are inexpensive and easy to find at all hours, making them the transportation of choice even for Panamanians of modest means. Buses are frequent and even cheaper, but they are a far slower and less convenient way to get around most parts of the city. Flag them down as you would a cab.

I don't recommend that those unfamiliar with Panama City, especially those unaccustomed to Latin American roads, attempt to drive in the city. It's a good way to spoil your day, if not your whole trip. Drivers are aggressive, streets are confusing and poorly marked, and there's a severe shortage of traffic signals, which most drivers treat merely as friendly suggestions in any case. Streets have been known to change from two-way to one-way literally overnight, without anyone bothering to change the signs. It's no fun to turn a corner of what you thought was a two-way street and see a battalion of SUVs barreling down on you. Other nuisances include the occasional stolen manhole cover.

Traffic in the former Canal Zone remains more orderly, but it too is increasingly showing the effects of chaotic road expansion and urban sprawl. Taxis, and in some cases buses, are cheap and convenient options for trips into the canal area, particularly for Pacific-side destinations such as the Calzada de Amador (Amador Causeway), Albrook, Miraflores Locks, and Balboa.

Adding to the confusion of getting around is the fact that many streets have multiple names.

The names used in this chapter are generally those most likely to be recognized by taxi drivers and other locals. Some destinations, especially in the former Canal Zone, are much more likely to be known by proximity to landmarks than by any street name.

BY TAXI

Taxis offer by far the easiest way to get around the city. There are about 20,000 of them in Panama City, all jockeying for your business. Most are small Japanese cars that will take an individual just about anywhere in town for US$2 or less. Don't be put off by taxi drivers beeping their horns at you; it can be annoying, but it's just their way of finding out if you want a ride. All legal taxis in Panama, except "tourist taxis," must be painted yellow.

Taxis are not metered in Panama City or anywhere else in the country. In Panama City, taxis charge according to a government-mandated zone system. The city is carved up into six zones; fares are based on the number of zones crossed. The current rate chart and a fare calculator are available online here: http://bit.ly/PTYTaxiZones. (If the link is broken, check www.panamaguidebooks.com for updates.) The minimum fare is US$1, and each zone crossed is another US$0.35. Each additional passenger adds US$0.40 to the fare, regardless of the distance. There's also a US$0.25 surcharge on Sunday, holidays, and at night (10 P.M.–5 A.M.). How taxi drivers manage to make any money at all at these rates is a mystery.

Most taxi drivers are honest and decent, even if their driving is a little nuts. They might kill you in a crash, but they'll rarely cheat you. However, I'm beginning to hear more stories of tourists being overcharged, usually by just a few bucks.

Asking the fare ahead of time is one way to know what you're in for, but it also betrays your ignorance of the going rate to your destination. Another common strategy for trips within the city limits is just to hand the driver US$2 at the end of the ride; if the legitimate fare is more than that, they'll most definitely let you know, but they're less likely to think they can scam you. Taxi drivers are required to present the zone chart on demand.

A bigger concern recently has been taxi drivers who refuse to take a fare because the destination is not convenient or profitable. Such a tactic is understandable, but it's illegal. The government was cracking down on the so-called *"no voy"* ("I'm not going that way") problem as this book went to press. If this happens to you, you can report the culprit at tel. 502-0591.

Don't be alarmed if your driver stops to pick up another fare heading the same way. It's a normal practice, but tell the driver not to do it if it makes you uncomfortable (though expect to pay extra for the privilege of a private ride).

The bashed-up bodies of the average cab will give you some sense of how these Mad Maxes drive. Pulse-pounding near misses are common; think of it as local color. Fortunately, traffic congestion and moderate speeds mean most actual mishaps end up as fender benders.

Fares for rides outside the central city, for instance into the former Canal Zone, go up according to distance, but not as quickly as one might think. A ride as far as Gamboa, on the Panama Canal about halfway across the entire isthmus, costs around US$20. Taxis can also be hired for day tours, but bear in mind that few taxi drivers speak much English or are particularly knowledgeable tour guides, though all know the city well. There are no standard rates—it depends on the distance, the mood of the driver, and your bargaining skills, but about US$7–8 an hour is a decent rule of thumb.

A few larger, air-conditioned cabs lurk around the more upscale hotels and are allowed to charge several times what the smaller guys do. They are "tourist taxis," recognizable by the "SET" license plates. You can always just walk down the street to find a cheaper ride if you can do without air-conditioning and the sense of safety that comes from riding in a bigger hunk of metal.

Taxis are almost always easy to find, but "radio taxis" can be called as well. Hotels and restaurants will usually be happy to make the call for you.

BY RENTAL CAR

The major U.S. car rental agencies have outlets scattered around Panama City as well as at the international and domestic airports. Several outlets are within a few blocks of the Hotel Continental and Hotel El Panamá on or near Vía España.

Again, for most visitors, taking taxis will be a better option than driving around Panama City. But driving is likely to be the best way of getting to the beaches within a couple hours of the city. And for exploring both the nearby canal area and distant locations it's a reasonable alternative to taxis, buses, and organized tours.

A few of the more centrally located offices are listed here. Most of these are within easy walking distance of each other near the Hotel El Panamá. Which one to go with is a hard call. I've had good experiences with customer service and cars at Thrifty in recent years, but all it takes is a change of management for that to change overnight and one of the other chains to be at the top of the heap. Your mileage, as they say, may vary.

Avis Rent A Car (Calle D, tel. 278-9444, www.avis.com, 7 A.M.–9 P.M. daily) is near the El Cangrejo branch of Churrería Manolo, not far from the Hotel El Panamá. At last count it had five other branches in the Panama City and Panama Canal areas.

Budget Rent A Car (central reservations tel. 263-8777, www.budgetpanama.com) has two branches in the Vía España area. The larger one is on the western end of Vía España itself (tel. 263-9190, 7 A.M.–10 P.M. daily), just before Calle Gabrielle Mistral in Bella Vista. The other is at the entrance to the Hotel El Panamá (tel. 214-6806, 8 A.M.–5 P.M. daily).

Hertz (Vía Veneto and Avenida Eusebio A. Morales, tel. 264-1111, www.hertz.com, 8 A.M.–9 P.M. daily) has an office around the corner from Avis, next to the El Cangrejo branch of Churrería Manolo. There's another branch at the Marriott Hotel (tel. 210-9213, 8 A.M.–5 P.M. Mon.–Fri., 8 A.M.–4 P.M. Sat.). Including the international airport, Hertz at last count had five outlets in Panama City. For other locations, check their website.

National Car Rental (Vía Veneto and Avenida Eusebio A. Morales, tel. 265-5092, www.nationalcar.com, 8 A.M.–5 P.M. Mon.–Sat.) is right across the street from the Hertz office in El Cangrejo, but the main office is some distance away on Calle 50 (tel. 265-3333, 7 A.M.–10 P.M. daily). For other locations, check their website.

There's a **Thrifty Car Rental** (Vía España, tel. 214-7677) near the southern end of Vía España, opposite Budget Rent a Car.

ORGANIZED TOURS

All of Panama's major tour operators have their headquarters in Panama City, and they all offer Panama City tours. They're more of an after-thought for the ecotourism outfits, though, so those looking for a group tour might consider going with a more traditional tour company that offers city tours as a more or less daily business, or simply book through your hotel. However, those planning an adventure outside Panama City with an ecotourism operator may want to add on a city tour with the same group for simplicity's sake.

Because Panama City is a relatively compact place, half-day and full-day tours typically give an overview of the entire city, including the ruins of Panamá la Vieja (Panamá Viejo), parts of the reviving colonial district of Casco Viejo, and at least a drive through the major sections of modern, central Panama City. The full-day tours in particular usually find time for a visit to the area of the Panama Canal close to the city. This part of the tour inevitably includes a visit to Miraflores Locks and sometimes throws in stops at the handicrafts market next to the YMCA in Balboa and the Panama Canal Authority's Administration Building, a historic structure perched on a hill that has impressive murals depicting canal construction days in its rotunda and offers dramatic views of the former Canal Zone. All three canal stops are worthwhile, so look for tours that include more than just Miraflores Locks.

Pesantez Tours (tel. 223-5374, 263-7577, or 366-9100, www.pesantez-tours.com) is a long-established tour operator with a reputation for dependable service. Other possibilities include **Panoramic Panama** (tel. 314-1581 or 314-1604, wwww.bedandbreakfastpanama.com), which is affiliated with La Estancia, a popular bed and breakfast in the former Canal Zone; **Ecocircuitos** (tel. 324-0068, fax 314-1586, www.ecocircuitos.com); and **Gray Line Panama** (tel. 323-2333 or 323-3328, www.grayline-panama.com).

Whoever you go with, expect to pay US$80–100 per person for a half-day tour and US$110–165 for a full day tour. Larger groups pay less per person. Lunch is sometimes included. The exception is Panoramic Panama, which charges the same rate, US$110, for half-day city and canal tours for either one or two people, which is more reasonable. The company also offers a half-day tour for those just passing through Panama with a layover of at least seven hours. The rate for one or two people is US$180, including pickup and drop-off at the international airport.

Average rates for city tours have nearly doubled in the last couple of years. Given that some tour guides are often no more knowledgeable than the average taxi driver, you may be inclined just to negotiate an all-day rate with a cabbie that suits your personality instead.

Revelers may be interested in the *chiva parrandera,* a party bus that roams some of the city's scenic spots at night with a *murga,* a traditional Panamanian band that plays Panamanian folk music and salsa. The trip includes local booze, and the bus is thoughtfully outfitted with cup holders so your drinks don't tip over even if you yourself do. *Parranda,* by the way, means both "strolling band of musicians" and "to go on a binge." Whether this all sounds like heaven or hell is obviously a matter of taste. Most tour operators who offer city tours can arrange for seats for about US$40 per person. Bring earplugs and a spare liver.

BY BUS

There are several bus hubs around Panama City, but the main two are in **Albrook** and **Calidonia**. Long-distance buses leave from the **Gran Terminal de Transportes** in Albrook.

Many city and regional buses also pass by the Albrook terminal, on the side opposite the long-distance buses. **Plaza Cinco de Mayo** in Calidonia, next to the walking section of Avenida Central, is the terminus for many routes within the city and greater metropolitan area. Most buses stop in front of the handicraft kiosks on the plaza.

Taking buses within Panama City is an exercise in frustration, especially when travelers can zip around in a cab for very little. Buses make constant stops and are often crowded and hot. And they're not exactly safe. They're known by locals as *diablos rojos* (red devils) because of the way they so often barrel recklessly through traffic—whoever's biggest wins on the roads of Panama. (Few of them are red, incidentally. In fact, they're typically painted over with all kinds of bright-colored murals, especially at the rear of the bus, which makes for great photo possibilities.)

Note: The days of the *diablos rojos* may be numbered. Under the current government there is a push to create an official, orderly city bus network to supplement a proposed subway system called the Metro that would criss-cross the city. It's an ambitious and hugely expensive project, but given how determined the current president, Ricardo Martinelli, has been to drag Panama into the 21st century, this may actually happen faster than anyone quite expects.

Buses are frequent and dirt cheap, so those with a lot more time than money might want to give them a try. Destinations are painted on the front windshield. The fare anywhere within the city limits is US$0.25.

Passengers flag down a passing bus as they would a cab, and once on board indicate their desired stop by shouting out *parada* (pah-RAH-da; "stop"). For destinations outside the city center, look for buses that have *corredor* painted on the windshield or side. That means the bus uses the toll roads, which means fewer stops and much faster transportation.

Buses are a more reasonable option for destinations outside the central city, especially into the former Canal Zone. Buses to various points in the canal area now leave from the Gran Terminal in Albrook. It's easy to miss these buses because they're hidden away in a little nook of the Albrook terminal. As you face Niko's Café, the entrance to this little sub-terminal will be on the right. Look for a sign that says SACA or COOP SACA.

Note that the following schedules are more ideal than exact.

Clayton: Every half hour 5:30–10 A.M., noon, every half hour 1:30–5 P.M., 6:30 P.M., and 8 P.M. Monday–Friday. On weekends the bus leaves at 6:45 A.M., 8 A.M., 10 A.M., noon, 2 P.M., 6:30 P.M., 9 P.M., and 10:45 P.M. The price is US$0.35.

Amador: Every half hour from about 6 A.M.–8 P.M. The price is US$0.25; US$0.50 in the evenings or on weekends and holidays.

Gamboa: Roughly every 1–2 hours 5 A.M.–10:45 P.M. Monday–Friday and 6:45 A.M.–10:45 P.M. Saturday and Sunday. The price is US$0.65. This bus can drop passengers off at Pedro Miguel Locks, Paraíso, Parque Nacional Soberanía, Summit Botanical Gardens, and other destinations en route to Gamboa for US$0.25–0.65.

Miraflores Locks (take the Paraíso, Gamboa, or Clayton bus): Buses run on the same schedule as the Albrook and Clayton bus. Note: Most buses do not go all the way to the locks—they only do so at shift changes for canal workers, which when I last checked meant the 5:30 A.M., 6:30 A.M., and 2:30 P.M. buses. All other buses stop along the main road, and passengers must walk about one kilometer to get to and from the locks. The schedule is inconvenient for visitors since they are not allowed into Miraflores until 9 A.M. and the visitors center closes at 5 P.M. In other words, plan to hoof it. Fortunately, it's a scenic walk.

THE PANAMA CANAL AND CENTRAL ISTHMUS

The Panama Canal is one of the most awe-inspiring of all human endeavors. Built across the isthmus of Panama at one of its narrowest and lowest points, it is 50 miles (80 kilometers) long, extending from Panama City on the Pacific Ocean to the city of Colón on the Caribbean Sea. To the bafflement of many a visitor, the Caribbean entrance is northwest of the Pacific entrance.

What was once the Canal Zone ran the length of the canal, extending five miles (eight kilometers) on either side of it. The U.S. civilian townsites and military bases are now abandoned or being engulfed by the surrounding urban centers, though some of the forested lands in the former Canal Zone have been set aside as protected areas.

The canal itself is so impressive it's easy to overlook nature's equally astonishing handiwork on its banks and in its waters. Parque Nacional Soberanía is one of the most accessible tropical forests in the world. It and the surrounding forests have some of the best bird-watching in the country. There's also a surprisingly decent chance of coming across largish mammals, including three species of monkeys (white-faced capuchins, Geoffroy's tamarins, and howlers), sloths, kinkajous, coatimundis, and capybaras (the largest rodent in the world) in the extensive moist tropical forests still standing here. Even jaguars and harpy eagles are not unheard of, but the chances of spotting either are extremely slim. You may also see a green iguana or two.

Though less visited than the Pacific side, the Caribbean side of the Panama Canal and the

HIGHLIGHTS

◖ **Miraflores Locks:** The most accessible set of locks at the Panama Canal offer a close-up look at one of the world's great engineering feats (page 105).

◖ **Balboa:** This historic townsite offers a glimpse of what life in the former Canal Zone was like (page 109).

◖ **Amador Causeway:** This beautiful breakwater has spectacular views of Panama City and the Pacific entrance of the Panama Canal (page 111).

◖ **Panama Canal Transit:** One of the world's top cruising destinations is also an affordable day trip (page 113).

◖ **Panama Railway:** Travel from ocean to ocean in an hour on this historic and highly scenic rail line (page 113).

◖ **Parque Nacional Soberanía:** This species-rich tropical forest is just a few minutes' drive from downtown Panama City (page 124).

◖ **Portobelo Ruins:** It's fascinating to wander around the battered remains of one of the most important, pirate-pestered ports in the Spanish empire (page 146).

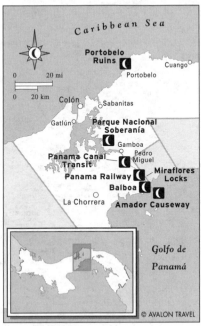

LOOK FOR ◖ TO FIND RECOMMENDED SIGHTS, ACTIVITIES, DINING, AND LODGING.

THE PANAMA CANAL

nearby coastline are rich in history and even richer in natural beauty. Evidence of the former includes the well-preserved ruins of Spanish forts, built to protect looted Inca treasure, and some of the most awe-inspiring structures of the canal. The area's natural attractions can be found among the mangroves, coral reefs, beaches, and forests that still abound with wildlife. Scuba diving and snorkeling are popular and easily accessible in the warm Caribbean waters, home to brilliant tropical fish and ancient shipwrecks. All this begins within a two-hour drive of Panama City.

PLANNING YOUR TIME

It's possible to visit **Miraflores Locks, Pedro Miguel Locks, Gaillard Cut,** and the townsites of **Balboa** and **Ancón** in a single day. A good way to end that day is with an evening walk and a meal or a drink on the **Amador Causeway (Calzada de Amador).** A quick visit to **Gamboa** can be tacked on, but really exploring that area takes a second day. A **Panama Canal transit** is an all-day event; taking the **train** across the isthmus requires a half day to a full day, depending on the return trip. **Isla Taboga** is better for a day trip than an overnight visit, and those planning to visit other islands can skip it altogether.

Most visitors to the Caribbean side go just for the day and return to Panama City at night. It's possible to take in **Portobelo,** the attractions near the Caribbean entrance to the Panama Canal (most notably **Gatún Locks** and **Gatún**

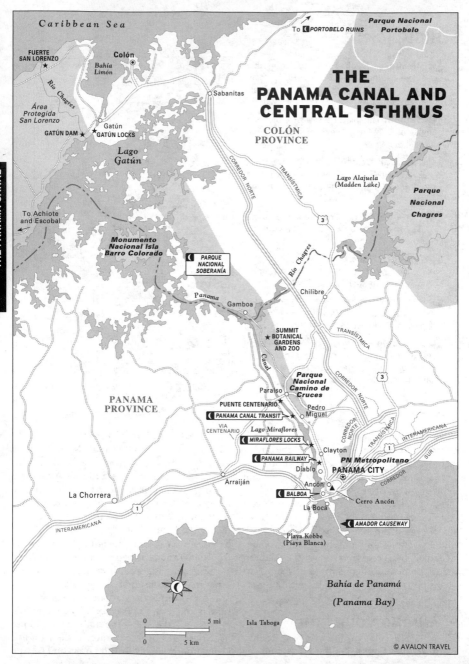

Caribbean Sea

To ⊏ PORTOBELO RUINS

Parque Nacional
Portobelo

FUERTE
SAN LORENZO
★

Colón
⊙

Bahía
Limón

Río Chagres

○ Sabanitas

THE
PANAMA CANAL AND
CENTRAL ISTHMUS

COLÓN
PROVINCE

Área
Protegida
San Lorenzo

Gatún
GATÚN DAM ★   ★ GATÚN LOCKS

Lago
Gatún

CORREDOR NORTE

TRANSISTMICA

Lago Alajuela
(Madden Lake)

Parque
Nacional
Chagres

To Achiote
and Escobal

3

Monumento
Nacional Isla
Barro Colorado

⊏ PARQUE
NACIONAL
SOBERANÍA

Río Chagres

Panama   Gamboa
                    ○

Chilibre
○

SUMMIT
★ BOTANICAL
GARDENS
AND ZOO

TRANSISTMICA

Canal

Parque
Nacional
Camino de
Cruces

CORREDOR NORTE

3

PANAMA
PROVINCE

Paraíso
○

PUENTE CENTENARIO ★
⊏ PANAMA CANAL TRANSIT

Pedro
Miguel
○

VIA
CENTENARIO   Lago Miraflores
⊏ MIRAFLORES LOCKS

CORREDOR NORTE

TRANSISTMICA

INTERAMERICANA

1

⊏ PANAMA RAILWAY ★

Clayton
○

Diablo
○

PN Metropolitano
⊕
PANAMA CITY

CORREDOR
SUR

Arraiján
○

Ancón ○
⊏ BALBOA ▲

Cerro Ancón

La Chorrera
○

La Boca
○

1

INTERAMERICANA

Playa Kobbe
(Playa Blanca)

⊏ AMADOR CAUSEWAY

Bahía de Panamá

(Panama Bay)

☾

0   5 mi
0   5 km

Isla Taboga

© AVALON TRAVEL

Dam), and **Fuerte San Lorenzo** in a single day. However, it would be a long day, with lots of driving, and it's probably too ambitious for those relying solely on public transportation. Consider striking either Portobelo or Fuerte San Lorenzo off the itinerary; it'd be hard to do both. If at all possible, take the train across the isthmus at least one way. It's the most scenic and pleasant way to make the trip.

The Panama Canal is in the middle of a multi-billion-dollar expansion that will include two new sets of giant locks, one on the Pacific and one on the Caribbean side of the isthmus. It's expected to be completed in 2014, but there's unlikely to be visitor access to the work during the life of this book.

Spending the night somewhere on the Caribbean side is pretty much a must for those who want to add an outdoor activity such as scuba diving, birding, or boating to a visit.

One approach for a longer visit is to stay a night or two on **Isla Grande,** stopping at Portobelo on the way over and visiting San Lorenzo and the canal-area attractions on the way back to Panama City.

Rainfall is far heavier on the Caribbean than the Pacific side of the isthmus. It averages 3.2 meters in Colón, nearly twice as much as in Panama City. For those not metrically inclined, that's more than 10 *feet* of rain a year. The dry season is also not as well-defined on the Caribbean as the Pacific side. In Portobelo, one of the wettest spots in Panama, it rains nearly year-round, as many a miserable Spanish conquistador learned to his dismay as he stood guard against pirates.

THE PANAMA CANAL

The Former Canal Zone

The Pacific side of the former Canal Zone comprises two of the Panama Canal's three sets of locks and the beginning of the approximately nine-mile (14-kilometer) Gaillard Cut through the Continental Divide, the toughest part of the canal to dig and the most dramatic to see. It also contains most of the former zone "townsites," which were home to the civilian employees of the canal and their families. These include Ancón, Balboa, La Boca, and Diablo. It's home also to what were once its most important U.S. military bases, including Howard Air Force Base, Fort Clayton, Fort Amador, Quarry Heights, Albrook Air Force Base, and Rodman Naval Station.

Amador has become a major nightlife and tourism destination. Albrook is now a fairly upscale suburban residential area (and home to Panama City's domestic airport and bus terminal). Parts of Clayton have been converted into something called La Ciudad del Saber (The City of Knowledge), which attracts international academic and research institutions. But much of the former zone has become a series of ghost towns awaiting a development plan, or

are being plowed under to make way for suburban housing, port facilities, highways, and industrial complexes.

SIGHTS

The attractions described here run along the east bank of the canal and are easily accessible from Panama City.

Pacific Side Locks
◖ MIRAFLORES LOCKS

Miraflores Locks, completed in May of 1913, stand at the Pacific entrance to the Panama Canal. They link the Pacific Ocean with the artificially-made Miraflores Lake, raising and lowering ships 54 feet (16.5 meters) in two impressive steps. Of the canal's three sets of locks, these are the easiest to reach from Panama City and the best equipped to handle visitors. Note: Recently, guards have become strict about not letting visitors onto the grounds until the visitors center opens at 9 A.M.

The massive **Centro de Visitantes de Miraflores** (Miraflores Visitors Center, tel. 276-8325, www.pancanal.com, 9 A.M.–5 P.M.

THE PANAMA CANAL

NEW LOCKS FOR A "POST-PANAMAX" WORLD

COURTESY OF THE AUTORIDAD DEL CANAL DE PANAMÁ

Giant locks and new access channels are being added to the canal.

The Panama Canal is in the middle of a multi-billion dollar expansion program due to be completed in 2014. Its centerpiece will be the building of two new sets of locks, one near each ocean, located to the west of the current ones.

The chambers of the existing locks are enormous: each is 1000 by 110 feet (almost 305 by 34 meters). The new ones will be colossal: 1,400 feet long and 180 feet wide (nearly 427 by 55 meters). Each set of the new locks will contain three chambers, beside which will run basins in tiers meant to capture and reuse water used during transits. (The existing locks lose millions of gallons of fresh water to the sea with each lockage; the canal's watershed would have to be greatly expanded to use a similar system for the new locks.) New access channels must also be dug, and existing ones widened and deepened.

Expansion work is well underway, though to date there's little to see but giant holes in the ground.

The project is meant to allow "post-Panamax" ships to transit the canal (Panamax ships are specifically designed to fit through the existing canal). But not everyone is convinced the project will succeed, or even that it's necessary. Of course, the first time around there were plenty of doubters, too.

---

daily, including holidays) is an out-of-place monolith from the outside, but inside it's rather impressive. It contains a four-story museum, an observation deck, a theater that shows documentaries on the canal in English and Spanish, and a restaurant with good views of the locks. Hold on to your ticket to be admitted to the museum and theater. The 1st floor of the museum contains a history of the canal, starting with the failed French effort and continuing through completion by the United States. The 2nd floor is an ecological exhibit that stresses the importance of the Panama Canal watershed and contains displays on the flora and

© KAREN FRIAR

The original locks controls were replaced just a few years ago by a computerized system. The old control boards have been left in place.

fauna found within it. The 3rd floor shows the operation of the canal and includes a full-scale pilot-training simulator and a topographical canal map. The 4th floor is the least interesting, with route maps that stress the importance of the canal to world commerce.

The restaurant has a terrace right on the edge of the locks, making it a great place to come for lunch or dinner. There's also an outdoor snack bar on the ground floor.

Admission to the entire complex is US$8, US$5 for kids ages 5–17, free for children younger than five. Admission just to the ground terrace and shops is US$5, US$3 for kids.

PEDRO MIGUEL LOCKS AND GAILLARD CUT

The Pedro Miguel Locks, about a 10-minute drive farther down Gaillard Highway from Miraflores, raise and lower ships in one 31-foot (9.5-meter) step, linking Miraflores Lake and

Gaillard Cut. These locks are not open to the public, but a little rest stop just beyond them gives a good view of the action. You can also see the beginning of Gaillard Cut (also called Culebra Cut), where the canal was dug right through the Continental Divide. It's a dramatic sight, though the widening of the cut has made it a bit less so by pushing back and lowering the rocky peaks through which the waterway runs. Farther up the road is the Puente Centenario, a dramatic suspension bridge over the canal that was inaugurated in 2004. There are good, if quick, views of the cut from the bridge.

Cerro Ancón
ADMINISTRATION BUILDING

The agency that runs the Panama Canal, now known as the Autoridad del Canal de Panamá (Panama Canal Authority), is headquartered in an imposing building perched on a small hill on the side of Cerro Ancón. Known simply as the Administration Building (Edificio de Administración), it's worth visiting for a couple of reasons.

First, there are dramatic murals inside the building's rotunda that depict the construction of the canal. These were painted by William B. Van Ingen, a New York artist who also created murals for the Library of Congress and the U.S. Mint in Philadelphia. They were installed in January 1915 and underwent a restoration in 1993. The four major panels of the mural show excavation at Gaillard Cut and the construction of Miraflores Locks, the Gatún Dam spillway, and a set of lock gates. They give a sense of what a staggering task the building of the canal was.

Second, there's a sweeping view of part of the former Canal Zone, especially the townsite of Balboa, from the back of the building. Walk through the doors at the back of the rotunda, but note they may lock behind you; in that case just walk around the outside of the building to get back to the front entrance.

In the foreground are what were once Balboa Elementary School (on the left) and Balboa High School (on the right). The marble monolith between them is the Goethals Monument.

THE PANAMA CANAL

THE PANAMA CANAL

COURTESY OF THE PANAMA CANAL COMMISSION

Pedro Miguel Locks, behind which are the Miraflores Locks and the Pacific Ocean

The long, palm-lined promenade is the Prado. Each section of the Prado has the exact dimensions of a lock chamber: 1000 by 110 feet. In the distance is the Bridge of the Americas and Cerro Sosa (Sosa Hill). Those feeling energetic can walk down the long flight of stairs and explore the townsite of Balboa.

Note the large bronze plaque at the foot of the steps. It's dedicated to David D. Gaillard, who led the excavation of Gaillard Cut. The plaque was moved here from the side of a mountain that was leveled during Cut-widening work. It was designed by the sculptor James Earle Fraser, who also designed the Buffalo nickel and is best known for his moving sculpture *End of the Trail*. There's a replica of the plaque at the Miraflores Visitors Center.

Visitors are free to explore the rotunda any time of the day or night, but other parts of the building are off-limits without an appointment. Sign in with the guard at the door.

ADMINISTRATOR'S HOUSE

The Administrator's House, a wooden mansion set in a well-tended garden, is a short drive or an easy, pleasant walk farther up the road from the Administration Building. When the road forks, head left. During construction days this was the home of the canal's chief engineer. It originally sat overlooking what is now Gaillard Cut, allowing the chief engineers (first John F. Stevens, then George W. Goethals) to keep an eye on the excavation even when they were home. In 1914 it was taken apart and moved by train to its present location. It has been the home of the canal's chief executive ever since. Visitors are not allowed in the house, but they can walk around the front entrance. It's also pleasant to walk down Lion Hill Road, the winding, jungle-shrouded road to the right as one faces the house. Unfortunately, the grounds are now enclosed by an ugly green chain-link fence for security. (Pointless personal detail: I lived near the bottom of this road when I was in high school.) The large, nondescript house between this house and the Administration Building is the home of the canal's deputy administrator.

TOP OF CERRO ANCÓN

There's an impressive view from the top of

COURTESY OF JIM GUY

THE PANAMA CANAL

The Administration Building in Cerro Ancón is the headquarters of the Autoridad del Canal de Panamá, which runs the Panama Canal.

Cerro Ancón (Ancón Hill) of Casco Viejo, Panama Bay, and the modern city skyline. Walk behind the communications tower to get a look at the entrance to the Panama Canal, the bridge of the Americas, Miraflores Locks, and the townsite of Balboa. It's also possible to walk up to the giant Panamanian flag, which was one of the first things to go up in the former Canal Zone after the ratification of the treaties that turned the canal over to Panama. This spot has the best view of the Panama City skyline. Historical footnote: The U.S. military dug a tunnel into the heart of the hill, the entrance to which still stands in Quarry Heights, as a secure command post during times of crisis.

The road to the top starts at the entrance to Quarry Heights, once the headquarters of the U.S. Southern Command. Those driving should head up the road that goes past the Administration Building, then take a right when the road forks at the Administrator's House. Go past the guard house (if there's actually a guard there he will probably just wave

you in), then make a left past the headquarters of the environmental nonprofit ANCON. Access from this point on is by a one-way road. Guards at either end of the road tell you when it's safe to go, but honk the horn around curves anyway. The top of Cerro Ancón is two kilometers up from the Quarry Heights gate.

Balboa

Those who want a sense of what life was like in the former Canal Zone should consider spending an hour or two wandering around the townsite of Balboa. The unofficial "capital" of the Canal Zone, it was the most formally planned of the zone communities. Today it's being squeezed between a container port and highway overpasses, and many of the old apartments are either unoccupied or have been converted into offices, but it retains much of its peculiar utilitarian elegance. (Make allowances for some personal bias here, since I spent most of my childhood in Balboa and Balboa Heights and am a graduate of both Balboa Elementary and Balboa High.)

THE "OTHER SIDE"

In the old Canal Zone days, those on the Pacific side of the canal spoke of the area around the Caribbean entrance to the canal as "the Other Side." (Naturally, those "other siders" in turn tended to apply that term to those on the Pacific side.) The Atlantic side felt like another world, even though it was less than 80 kilometers away. There were just two ways to get there by land: by the railroad or by a pothole-riddled "highway" known as the Transístmica. As kids, many Pacific siders, including this one, rarely made what seemed like an epic journey to the Caribbean side: swim meets and the annual football jamboree against our archrival, Cristóbal High School, were about it.

In those days we all thought in terms of the Atlantic rather than the Caribbean side, though the latter is more accurate. Even in a tiny world, the Atlantic side was minuscule, and it got less attention. The canal's headquarters was on the Pacific coast, close to Panama City, and that's where the action was. As a result, the Caribbean communities tended to be tight and socially active. With few diversions, Atlantic siders had to find ways to entertain themselves.

Residents lived in townsites with names such as Cristóbal, Gatún, Coco Solo (birthplace of John McCain), Margarita, and Rainbow City, dotted among which were U.S. military bases, such as Fort Sherman, Fort Gulick, and Fort Davis. Cristóbal was literally across the street from Colón, and partly for that reason the boundaries between the Canal Zone and Panama were especially fluid on this side.

When the gringos left, much of the Canal Zone became a virtual ghost town, and this is especially true of the Caribbean side. Whole townsites have grown silent, and in some places the tropical forest is taking over again.

GOETHALS MONUMENT

This marble monolith at the base of the Administration Building was erected in honor of George W. Goethals, the chief engineer of the canal from 1907 to its completion in 1914. The three tiers of the fountain symbolize the three sets of locks. The monument was controversial when it was erected; some complained it didn't fit into the community's design.

CENTRO DE CAPACITACIÓN ASCANIO AROSEMENA

Along the palm-lined promenade of the **Prado** are what were once **Balboa Elementary School** and **Balboa High School**. Both are now offices used by the Panama Canal Authority. Parts of the old high school, now known as the Centro de Capacitación Ascanio Arosemena (tel. 272-1111, 7 A.M.–4:15 P.M. Mon.–Fri.), are open to visitors. Outside is a breezeway dedicated to the Panamanians who died during the 1964 Flag Riots; their names are inscribed on the pillars. Just inside the building is a display that attempts to walk a delicate line between the still-polarized views on what exactly happened during the riots, the bloodiest and most controversial conflict between the United States and Panama until the 1989 U.S. invasion.

Lining the halls on this floor and the one above is a wealth of rare artifacts from both the French and U.S. canal efforts, including railroad ties and pickaxes, clippings from 19th-century newspapers, bonds sold to finance the disastrous French effort, fascinating black-and-white prints dating from the 1880s, maps, Canal Zone stamps and seals, and historic china and silverware from the Canal Zone governor's house. On the 2nd floor is the **Biblioteca Roberto F. Chiari** (10 A.M.–4 P.M. Mon.–Fri. for "investigators"). This is the library of the Autoridad del Canal de Panamá (Panama Canal Authority), housed in what was once the high-school library. It contains all kinds of technical and historical books and documents on the Panama Canal and Panama. It's not technically open to the general public, but those who fancy themselves "investigators" can certainly stop by and sign in.

STEVENS CIRCLE

Farther down the Prado is Stevens Circle, a rather drab monument to John Stevens, the canal's chief engineer 1905–1907 and its master designer. On the left is the **Balboa post office.** Directly across the main road is what's left of a cafeteria that used to feed canal workers around the clock. Next to it is the **Teatro Balboa,** once a movie theater and now host to occasional concerts and other performances. Across the street from that is the former commissary for canal employees, now offices. Next to the old football stadium is Niko's Café, a decent lunch option.

BALBOA ROAD

Heading down Avenida Arnulfo Arias Madrid (also known as Balboa Road) in the direction of Amador and Panama City you'll see the **Union Church,** an ecumenical church still in use. Just past it is an enormous and rather weird **fountain** built in honor of Arnulfo Arias Madrid, who was elected (and overthrown) president of Panama four times. It was built by Mireya Moscoso, Arias's widow, after she became president in 1999, and depicts Arnulfo flashing a "V for victory" sign at figures representing the Panamanian people, who are struggling to their feet. Shortly after it was erected, some amateur art critics sawed off his index finger, changing the significance of the gesture considerably. The statue was quickly repaired.

◖ Amador Causeway (Calzada de Amador)

This beautiful breakwater extends more than three kilometers into the Pacific, calming the waters at the entrance of the Panama Canal and preventing that entrance from silting up. It was built from spoil dug from the canal and connects three islands: **Naos, Perico,** and **Flamenco.**

The causeway has gorgeous views. On one side the majestic Bridge of the Americas spans the Pacific entrance to the canal, so there's always a parade of ships gliding underneath it or waiting their turn in the anchorage. On

THE PANAMA CANAL

The Amador Causeway is popular with families, especially on the weekend.

the other side is the half moon of Panama Bay, ringed by the ever-growing Panama City skyline.

In the old Canal Zone days, the causeway was a major make-out and hang-out spot for high-school kids. It's seeing more action now than ever before: It's become a nightlife destination for locals, and huge amounts of money are being poured into it in the hopes it will lure international visitors. In the last few years, restaurants, bars, and shopping centers have gone up in this area, as have a hotel, cruise-ship terminal, marina, convention hall, and amphitheater. Most of these have been built on Isla Flamenco on one end of the causeway and in Amador proper on the other. (Amador was formerly a U.S. army base called Fort Amador.)

The causeway itself has gotten an understated and elegant makeover, with new street lights and a renovated walking path that left the palm trees along it intact but added benches for those who need a rest. Near the entrance to the causeway is a row of flags of many countries, though the U.S. one is conspicuously absent; flying the stars and stripes anywhere in Panama, especially at a former gringo army base, would be loaded with controversial symbolism.

Amador and the causeway can get packed with visitors on the weekends, particularly dry-season Sundays. The popularity of the bars and restaurants causes traffic jams on the two-lane road on weekend nights.

For those without cars, the main way to get around here is on foot, though it can be a long walk in the sun from one end of the causeway to another. Fortunately, most of the attractions are clustered at the end of the causeway, on or near Isla Flamenco. There's a bike and scooter rental place at the entrance to the causeway. It may also be possible to flag down a passing taxi or bus for a quick ride up or down the causeway.

Note: Avoid the taxi concession at the Flamenco Shopping Plaza. It's aimed at cruise-ship passengers and their prices are outrageous. (The hourly rate, for instance, is nearly 10 times the norm.)

MUSEO DE LA BIODIVERSIDAD (MUSEUM OF BIODIVERSITY)

Designed by architect Frank O. Gehry, who is married to a Panamanian, this ambitious museum project (www.biomuseopanama. org) is meant to do for Panama what Gehry's Guggenheim did for Bilbao, Spain.

Unfortunately, the museum has been delayed for years by funding shortages. In 2010 the building was finally nearing completion, but finishing and stocking the galleries will be a huge project in its own right. The museum is not expected to open its doors until the end of 2011. Fingers crossed there are no more delays.

In the meantime, the museum now offers talks and a tour of the building site. These are held on Fridays and last about an hour. Tours are free but are in Spanish only.

For safety reasons, children are not allowed, and adults must wear long trousers and closed-toe shoes. Construction and rain can limit the tour to a room that holds scale models of the museum. Those interested can book tours through the museum's website, which also has live webcams showing the work in progress.

EL CENTRO DE EXHIBICIONES MARINAS

There's a long-established little museum, El Centro de Exhibiciones Marinas (Punta Culebra on Naos, tel. 212-8000, ext. 2366, rainy season hours: 1–5 P.M. Tues.–Fri., 10 A.M.–6 P.M. Sat. and Sun.; dry season hours: 10 A.M.–6 P.M. Tues.–Sun., US$2 adults, US$0.50 children), toward the end of the causeway, that's well worth a visit. Try to call ahead of time, as opening and closing hours shift erratically.

This nicely designed marine exhibition center is run by the Panama-based Smithsonian Tropical Research Institute. (Search "Punta Culebra" at www.stri.org for history and current information.) Exhibits set up along a beach-side path explain the extensive natural and human history of the area and touch on that of Panama in general. There's a small outdoor aquarium and an air-conditioned observation building. Free telescopes are set up along the path; check out the ships waiting to transit the canal. At the end of the path are a few hundred square meters of dry forest, once common all along the Pacific coast of Central America, but now mostly wiped out since it's easy to burn. It's amazing what you may find in this little patch of forest. There are lots of iguanas, and the last time I was there I saw a shaggy three-toed sloth walking upside down along a branch just a few meters above my head.

The center is on Punta Culebra toward the end of the causeway. At the public beach on the first island, Naos, make a right when the road forks. There should be large signs.

◖ Panama Canal Transit

A transit of the Panama Canal is unforgettable, and you don't have to buy a cruise to have the experience. These days the most popular way to do it is with **Panama Marine Adventures** (tel. 226-8917, www.pmatours.com) on the *Pacific Queen.* This is an air-conditioned 119-foot vessel equipped with a snack bar, souvenir shop, and television monitors on which cruisers can watch documentaries on the canal when they need a break from the action on deck. Transits take place on Thursdays, Fridays, and Saturdays during the high season (January through March). The rest of the year transits are Saturday only. Transits do not normally go all the way through the canal from ocean to ocean. Instead, they go through two sets of locks, Miraflores and Pedro Miguel, and Gaillard Cut. Transits begin or end at Gamboa, depending on whether it's a northbound or south-bound transit. (Direction of the transit is marked on the company's website calendar.) Customers check in at Isla Flamenco on the Amador Causeway at 9 A.M. The tour includes land transportation between Isla Flamenco and Gamboa. The partial transit takes 4–5 hours and costs US$115 for adults, US$65 for children younger than 12. The price includes pickup at the Flamenco marina on the causeway, lunch and soft drinks, and a bilingual guide.

One Saturday a month the company offers a full transit. This starts at Flamenco at 7:30 A.M. and goes through the entire canal,

ending at Colón, after exiting Gatún Locks. The transit takes 8–9 hours and costs US$165 for adults, US$75 for children younger than 12. It includes all the partial transit services plus a continental breakfast and land transportation back from Colón and Isla Flamenco.

Another group that offers transits is **Canal and Bay Tours** (tel. 209-2009 or 209-2010, www.canalandbaytours.com), with a similar schedule and identical prices (except for the partial-transit kids' fare—it's US$5 cheaper). It uses the 96-foot-long *Isla Morada* and 115-foot-long *Fantasia del Mar,* old ferry boats that made the run to Taboga for many years. The company has spruced them up. They recently introduced a partial Friday-night transit, which gives a very different perspective on the canal. The locks are brightly lit by high-mast lighting, turning night into day, and the rest of the canal is lit well enough to see what's going on.

Note: Transits generally start early in the morning, but it's impossible for either company to promise exact end times. Scheduling is entirely up to the Panama Canal Authority, and since these are smaller vessels they have to make way for larger ships.

◖ Panama Railway

A railway, the descendant of the famed Panama Railroad built for the Forty-Niners during the California gold rush, ran constant daily trips back and forth across the isthmus during the Canal Zone days. It ran along and sometimes over stretches of the Panama Canal, was billed as the world's fastest and cheapest transcontinental journey, and was used as a commuter and cargo train. Panama's military government inherited the railroad and allowed it to fall apart during the 1980s. In 1998 the post-Noriega Panamanian government signed an agreement with two U.S. companies, including Kansas City Southern, a railroad holding company, to create the Panama Canal Railway Company and rebuild the rail link between the Atlantic and Pacific. The result is a 47.5-mile (76.5-kilometer) railway used primarily to move cargo across the isthmus.

However, the train does make one daily

passenger trip, leaving the Pacific side of the isthmus at 7:15 A.M. and returning at 5:15 P.M. It's quite a step up from the utilitarian train of the old Canal Zone days: The cars in this one have dark wood paneling, leather banquettes set around tables, large observation windows, and waitresses in conductors' outfits who serve coffee and muffins. Be sure to step onto the spacious platforms between cars, which offer great views and pleasant breezes. It's also quite a step up in price: The fare is US$22 one-way, half price for those 12 and younger. The passenger train was designed as a commuter service for affluent businesspeople who work in the Colón Free Zone, but it increasingly caters to tourists. Seats are limited and most are set aside for daily commuters, so make reservations if possible (tel. 317-6700, www.panarail.com). If not, show up early. Be sure to ask if there's space in the glass observation car. Sometimes there is only standing room on the between-car platforms available, which is actually quite pleasant since the ride is short.

The train doesn't quite go from ocean to ocean. The new Pacific terminus is at the old Canal Zone townsite of Corozal, about a 15-minute drive away from downtown Panama City. The Caribbean terminus is at Colón. The train is an express and makes no stops en route. The trip lasts about an hour.

Those who take the train from Panama City to Colón can either hire a taxi and spend the day exploring Caribbean-side attractions, such as the nearby Gatún Locks, Fuerte San Lorenzo, and the Colón Free Zone, until it's time for the return train, or else catch a bus back to Panama City at the Terminal de Buses in Colón. However, the logistics of this are a bit dicey. Those who can afford it should instead arrange a tour that includes the train trip and a car that meets your group at the Colón station. It can't be emphasized enough that Colón is a crime-ridden city and not safe for visitors. The immediate area around the train station is safe enough, and there's a guard at the gate. However, typically not many taxis meet the train; beware of phony cabs. Only get into a licensed taxi, which will be painted bright yellow and have a license plate that matches the number painted on its side.

The bus terminal is a five-minute walk straight past the end of the rail line. Do not cross the road into Colón. Be alert at the terminal. It may be possible to find a cab there as well.

ENTERTAINMENT AND EVENTS

Amador Causeway has become a nightlife destination for Panama City dwellers, and on the weekends traffic there can be a nightmare. Panama's biggest concert venue is also in Amador, and there are a few other places to see live music and theater. **Restaurante Pencas** (Amador, tel. 211-3671, www.pencas.com) has *típico* performances on Wednesday nights. During the dry season, a **concert series** is held on the steps of the Panama Canal Administration Building in Balboa on Tuesday and Thursday evenings.

Concerts and Theater

Amador's glitzy **Panama Canal Village** (tel. 314-1414) contains the Figali Convention Center, Panama's largest venue for extravaganzas. It hosts major international rock and pop acts—ones that have gotten local fans revved up in the last few years include Metallica, the Red Hot Chili Peppers, Shakira, Paulina Rubio, and the Jonas Brothers.

Teatro Balboa (tel. 228-0327), an aging former movie house off Stevens Circle in the heart of the former Canal Zone townsite of Balboa, hosts concerts and the occasional play and special event.

The **Theatre Guild of Ancon** (tel. 212-0060, www.anconguild.com) is the only English-language playhouse in the country. It somehow survived the demise of the Canal Zone's once-thriving community-theater scene and still puts on the occasional play. The rickety old wooden playhouse is next to the police station at the base of Cerro Ancón, just off Avenida Frangipani and Manzanillo Place. A bit of Hollywood gossip: Jennifer Aniston's dad, John Aniston, was an actor at the theater in the 1950s.

Bars and Clubs

There are plenty of places to booze and

schmooze in Amador. **Flamenco Shopping Plaza,** the shopping and dining center on Isla Flamenco, has several shoebox-sized bars/ nightclubs on the ground floor at the back of the complex. Each has a different theme— e.g., sports pub, Egyptian, "ciber"—but they're pretty interchangeable. Sometimes people dance a bit, but the clubs are usually too crowded for that. These are mostly places to have a drink and hook up. The common de- nominator in all of them? Deafening music.

Some of the restaurants on the 2nd floor of Flamenco Plaza have live music groups on week- end nights and Sunday afternoons. Chances of hearing "Margaritaville" are good, though the combos I've heard haven't actually been that bad. A folkloric dance group sometimes per- forms in the plaza when a ship is in port.

More ambitious clubs come and go else- where on the causeway and on the "mainland" around the Figali Convention Center, but these rarely last long. Those with their own transpor- tation or a patient taxi should just troll along and follow the crowds.

SHOPPING

Balboa has a couple of good places to buy hand- icrafts. The first is the **Centro de Artesanías Internacional** (behind the YMCA on Avenida Arnulfo Arias Madrid/Balboa Road, 9 A.M.–6 P.M. Mon.–Sat., 10 A.M.–5 P.M. Sun.). It houses many stalls selling handicrafts from all over Panama—including tagua carvings, *molas,* cocobolo figurines, hand-woven baskets, and Panama hats—as well as some from other parts of Latin America.

The tagua carvings, cocobolo figurines, and hand-woven baskets are made by the Emberá and, especially, the Wounaan. They're incred- ibly labor-intensive, so don't expect good-qual- ity ones to come cheap. This is especially true of the baskets, which are internationally fa- mous. A so-so basket about the size of a softball costs US$25. Rainforest Art, a Wounaan-run stall at the very back of the center, is the first place to look for high-quality works.

Those who won't feel satisfied with a visit to Panama unless they buy a "Panama hat" of the kind actually made in Ecuador will find some good-quality ones here. Ask for the stall of Segundo Reyes. His best ones sell for US$100– 200. He also has some coarser ones that start at a tenth of that. All hats come in attractive balsa- wood boxes and make good presents for the geographically challenged. They need blocking and there's a good place in Panama to do it, but it's in such a dangerous part of Panama City I'm not going to tell you where it is. Pay the extra money and have it done at home.

Note: A newer *artesanía* is in the YMCA building itself, and those who work there ag- gressively lure in lost visitors who've heard there's a handicrafts hall nearby. By all means take a look, but don't be confused and miss out on the much bigger and better selection at the main artisans' center.

Farther up Avenida Arnulfo Arias Madrid/ Balboa Road, on the right as one heads toward Avenida de los Mártires, is the **Centro Municipal de Artesanías Panameñas** (8 A.M.–6 P.M. daily). It's run by Kunas and has a wider and better selection of *molas.* You can probably strike a better bargain here, since they see less business. The Kuna women sewing *molas* and wearing *mola* blouses aren't doing it for show. That's re- ally how they dress and what they do.

Most of the original shops at the **Flamenco Shopping Plaza,** at the end of the causeway, closed down in the last couple of years. Little wonder: The shops were hidden behind the plaza's restaurants and many visitors didn't even know they were there. Optimistic new- comers may have taken their place by the time you visit. The small cruise-ship terminal across the parking lot has a few services, including a duty-free shop that's open only to cruise-ship passengers in transit.

SPORTS AND RECREATION
Amador Causeway
The Amador Causeway is a popular place for walking, running, or biking. It's especially pleasant to ramble about in the morning and early evening, when the weather is cool and the light is gorgeous.

A well-run bike-rental place, **Bicicletas**

Moses (tel. 211-2579, 8 A.M.–9 P.M. daily), is at the beginning of the causeway, where the international flags are flown. It's right next to Restaurante Pencas. It rents mountain bikes, tandem bikes, "fun cycles" (they resemble Hot Wheels–style tricycles), and other wheeled transport by the half hour and hour. A one-hour mountain-bike rental is US$2.50. Expect long lines on dry-season weekends. They also rent scooters. Attention parents: They rent baby carriers. There's a nearby ATM if you need cash.

You may see people splashing around in the little beaches along the causeway; don't join them. Way back in high school I participated in a beach cleanup here that netted all kinds of disgusting stuff, including hospital waste, that had washed up from Panama City. No way would I ever set foot in the waters on the Panama Bay side. I'd also avoid the little beach on the canal-facing side.

Panama Bay Cruise

Canal and Bay Tours (tel. 209-2009 or 209-2010, www.canalandbaytours.com) offers Saturday night booze cruises of Panama Bay. The trip departs at 9:30 P.M. from the Amador cruise-ship terminal on Isla Flamenco. The fare is US$25 and features an open bar and blaring disco music.

Marina

The **Flamenco Yacht Club** (Isla Flamenco, tel. 314-0665, www.fuerteamador.com) is a well-equipped marina that offers moorings, repairs, maintenance, and supplies for everything from small pleasure boats to mega-yachts.

Golf

Summit Golf and Resort (tel. 232-4653, www.summitgolfpanama.com), 14 kilometers north of Balboa, is an upscale golf course, hotel, and spa that welcomes nonmembers. It's a 6,626-yard, par-72 course that was given a major makeover a few years back. It has a modern circular clubhouse with pretty views of rolling countryside, as well as a restaurant and bar. Greens fees are US$120 for 18 holes including cart, though they sometimes offer "twilight"

fees for those willing to play as it's getting dark. Club rental is about US$50. Summit is 7.5 kilometers north of Miraflores Locks. The turnoff is on the right 1.5 kilometers before the left turn toward Gamboa.

ACCOMMODATIONS

Hotels and B&Bs are coming at last to the Pacific side of the canal area. There are now a few appealing places, but many travelers still prefer to stay in downtown Panama City, which is quite close by. The ones listed here are listed by town or region, with those closest to Panama City first.

Balboa and Ancón

Simple but pleasant and quiet B&Bs are beginning to pop up in the old Canal Zone towns of Balboa and Ancón. The latter is on the side of Cerro Ancón and now includes the former U.S. Army base of Quarry Heights, formerly the headquarters of the U.S. Southern Command. Evidence of the latter still exists in the form of "The Tunnel," a high-security command post drilled straight into the side of Cerro Ancón that was used for strategic planning in times of crisis.

These areas have the advantage of remaining quiet, tree-shrouded residential neighborhoods that are right next door to the urban chaos of Panama City. Tranquil as this area is, it's important to exercise some caution, especially at night. Streets can be dark and deserted, and the incidence of home break-ins has shot up with the demise of the Canal Zone. Violent crime is unlikely, however. The places listed here all have good security, including locked gates.

US$50-100

The well-established and very popular **La Estancia** (Casa 35, Calle Amelia Denis de Icaza, tel. 314-1581 or 314-1604, www.bedandbreakfastpanama.com, starts at US$82.50 s/d, including continental breakfast) is a 12-room bed-and-breakfast in Quarry Heights, the former headquarters of the U.S. Southern Command, on the side of Cerro Ancón.

Rooms at La Estancia have air-conditioning, telephones, and private bathrooms. Three have their bathrooms down the hall but come with a balcony and hammock to make up for that slight inconvenience. Most rooms have a queen-size bed. There's a common area for guests to relax in, and free wireless Internet. The place is surrounded by trees, and there's a partial view of the Panama Canal and the Bridge of the Americas from some of the balconies. Two of the rooms are actually fair-sized apartments with sitting rooms, kitchenettes, and a small patio. These go for US$109 a night, including breakfast. Guests can use the washer and dryer.

The building was once used as apartments for military personnel and thus is a bit stark and utilitarian, but the owners have made attempts to soften the place and make it cheerful. The owners can arrange tours through their own tour company, Panoramic Panama. To get to La Estancia, take the first left up the hill after passing the guardhouse at the entrance to Quarry Heights. The bed-and-breakfast is 400 meters past the guardhouse. It's house number 35, a peach-colored, three-story building on the right.

Albrook Inn (14 Calle Hazelhurst, tel. 315-1789 or 315-1975, www.albrookinn.com, starts at US$99 s/d, including continental breakfast) is a two-story, 30-unit hotel opened in 2003 in a peaceful middle-class suburban neighborhood next to what had been the Albrook Officers' Club back when Albrook was a U.S. Air Force base. The standard rooms are small and simple with very firm beds, air-conditioning, and cable TV. Larger "junior suites" with a sitting room and sink start at US$110 s/d. There's a restaurant/bar in a backyard *rancho* (thatched-roof hut), a pool with hot tub, and both laundry service and a self-service washer and dryer. This is a good place if you can find a room with beds that aren't slabs of rock; try several.

Opened in 2008, the **◖ Balboa Inn** (2311a Calle Las Cruce. Balboa, tel. 314-1520, www.thebalboainn.com, $80 s, $90 d, including breakfast) is in what had once been a house for Panama Canal employees in the old Canal

Zone days. The area is still a quiet residential neighborhood where you can hear the sounds of chirping birds in the surrounding trees rather than squealing traffic and construction. Security includes a locked gate in the front. Since the inn is near the base of Cerro Ancón, the occasional cute little *ñeque* shows up in the backyard, which really takes me back—I grew up near here, and we always had a family of *ñeques* in our backyard, plus the occasional deer. Nostalgic flashback aside, this is a good option for those who are happy to be somewhere in-between both the canal and the city. It has nine rooms, all with private bath, TV/DVDs, safes, free Wi-Fi, and air-conditioning. Rooms are simple with rather thin mattresses, but each has been decorated with cheerful nature murals, which softens the appearance of the house a bit (old Canal Zone housing tended toward the utilitarian). A couple of the rooms upstairs have windows on two sides that let in lots of light. The friendly and competent staff can help arrange tours and give restaurant advice. Guests are welcome to use the kitchen. Rates drop US$5 after the first night. English, Spanish, and German is spoken here. The Balboa Inn is not easy to find if you don't know the area, and most taxi drivers don't, but there are very thorough, illustrated directions on the inn's website. This is a good find.

◖ Dos Palmitos (532B Guayacan Terrace, Ancón, cell 6581-8132 or 6759-0410, in Europe: 331/7377-7341, Skype: Dos Palmitos, www.dospalmitos.com, US$85 s, US$98 d, including breakfast) is another B&B in former Canal Zone housing. This one is of the older, two-story wooden variety, which has a bit more character. The B&B features four small rooms, all of which are clean and have simple but attractive decor, new bathrooms, comfortable beds, flat-screen TVs, free Wi-Fi, hardwood floors, and air-conditioning.

This is not a posh place; it's clearly a home that's been converted into a simple B&B. But it's immaculate and run well by a hands-on owner and is a good base for independent travelers who want to explore this part of Panama. It's a hidden gem.

The neighborhood is not as well tended as it was in the old Canal Zone days, but this is still a quiet residential area, especially given that the crowded streets of Panama City are just a short walk away. There's a shared kitchen and common area with an Internet computer. Breakfast is served on a back terrace overlooking a walled garden. This is another place where you're more likely to hear birdsong than traffic.

Dos Palmitos is run by Angeline Arnken, a Dutch journalist with an interest in the history of Panama and the canal—be sure to notice the historic photos on the wall, as well as the framed newspapers and stock certificate from the era of the French canal fiasco. She speaks French, Dutch, English, Spanish, and German. She lives on the ground floor of the house, so she's often around. She can arrange tours at very reasonable prices, including day trips to El Valle and Santa Clara (US$40 per person) and Gamboa (US$35). Best of all is a tour that overcomes the problem of taking the Panama Railway across the isthmus. For US$60 per person (not including the US$22 train fare), guests are dropped off at the train in Corozal, picked up in Colón at the end of the ride, taken to Portobelo and Fuerte San Lorenzo, and then driven back to Dos Palmitos. (Presumably guests can request a side trip to visit Gatún Locks, which they should definitely do.) That's a good price for a very full day.

Dos Palmitos is across the street from a large wooden church, Iglesia Plenitud de Cristo; heading towards downtown Panama City, it's the first left after the church, but contact the B&B for detailed directions, as this area is not well known by taxi drivers and there are no good current maps.

Amador

Big hotels have long been planned for Amador and the Amador Causeway (Calzada de Amador). They've been slow to come. The well-established Country Inns and Suites, near the entrance to Amador, is popular with guests who want familiar surroundings close to both Panama City and the Panama Canal. You can't get much closer to the canal: It's literally on the edge of its Pacific entrance.

US$100-150

Country Inn and Suites (Amador, tel. 211-4500, fax 211-4501, www.panamacanal-country.com/amador/, starts at US$127 s/d including breakfast) is on the water just past the entrance to Amador. It's a four-story, 159-unit hotel that resembles the other nondescript members of the chain. Standard rooms include cable TV, telephone, iron and ironing board, coffeemaker, free wireless Internet, and a balcony. It's worth paying the extra US$16.50 to get the view of the Pacific entrance to the canal and the Bridge of the Americas, the proximity to which is the most distinctive thing about this place. The hotel also has 53 suites of various kinds. There's a T.G.I. Friday's, an attractive swimming pool on the edge of the canal, a tennis court, a spa, and a business center. Tours of Panama City, the canal, and other attractions are easy to arrange.

Clayton and Ciudad de Saber (City of Knowledge)

What was formerly known as Fort Clayton, a U.S. Army Base, is now known simply as Clayton. The section of it closest to the canal is the Ciudad de Saber, known in English as the City of Knowledge. This is an ambitious, even admirable, plan to create a kind of research and academic park with institutions from around the world, and it has met with some success.

The rest of Clayton was largely abandoned in the last decade, but now development is coming fast. Expect more lodging, food, and entertainment options in this area soon.

US$25-50

The **Hostel de Clayton** (Building 605 B, tel. 317-1634 or 317-1264, cell 6631-0281 or 6572-5966, www.hostaldeclayton.com, starts at US$13.75 pp, including breakfast) consists of four rooms in old U.S. Army quarters in a particularly deserted part of Clayton. The rooms aren't terribly clean and the mattresses are thin, but the staff is friendly, the area is quiet, and the rates are good. Dorm rooms are US$13.75–17.60. Couples can share a private room for US$39.60. Free Wi-Fi, air-conditioning during the night, a rather barren backyard, and a basic breakfast are included. The hostel is about two kilometers from the main Clayton entrance; see the website for a detailed map. Taxis should charge US$2.50 from Albrook or US$25 from Tocumen.

US$100-150

You are likely to encounter plenty of determined smiles at the newish **Holiday Inn City of Knowledge** (tel. 317-4000, www.holiday-inn.com, US$161 s/d). That's because it was built in conjunction with a hotel-management program, the Panama International Hotel School, at the Ciudad de Saber in Clayton, and its students and graduates run the place. The service can be a bit confused at times, but they definitely try hard. This Holiday Inn is an attractive, seven-story version of the breed, with good-sized rooms that have mini-fridges, free broadband, and modern furnishings. There's a small pool behind the hotel, and a restaurant and bar. But the main attraction of the hotel is that it's literally across the street from the canal and a short drive from Miraflores Locks. Expect to pay a bit more for canal-view rooms, the best of which are on the 6th floor. However, the hotel is not quite close enough to the canal to see much, especially since there are (most welcome) trees partly obscuring the view. The best views are from the stark event rooms on the top floor. The hotel is just off Gaillard Highway, about 10 kilometers from Balboa. It'll be on the right shortly before the main entrance to the City of Knowledge and the turnoff to Miraflores Locks.

West Bank of Canal and Playa Bonita

The area just over the Bridge of the Americas is beginning to see tourist development. This is particularly true of the area that used to be known as Fort Kobbe, a U.S. Army base now known simply as **Kobbe** (sometimes spelled "Koby," which is how it's pronounced), which

hotel developers are trying to recast as Playa Bonita. A big, fancy resort has gone up here, and another one is in the works. Nonguests are not allowed to set foot on the grounds of the current resort. Locals and the backpacking crowd hang out instead in **Veracruz,** right next door, which has a few basic places to eat and drink and not much else.

These are the closest proper beaches to Panama City, and the only ones you might feel safe sticking your toe into without the fear of pollution dissolving it instantly. The shoreline is pretty here, but note that the beaches are rocky and small, so don't expect vast expanses of gorgeous sand.

OVER US$150

The 300-room **⟨ InterContinental Playa Bonita Resort and Spa** (tel. 206-8880 Panama City reservations, tel. 316-1463 at the hotel, www.playabonitapanama.com, US$250 s/d), which opened in 2005, is a fancy resort hotel in a spectacular spot near the Pacific entrance to the canal. It's part of a hotel group that includes the Miramar InterContinental and the Gamboa Rainforest Resort and has others in the pipeline.

This one is on a beach just west of the Bridge of the Americas. Guest rooms are in two five-story buildings designed so each room has a view of the sea, the ships waiting to transit the canal, and the islands of Taboga and Taboguilla in the distance. The beautifully landscaped grounds include a terraced fountain that flows down into five lagoon-shaped swimming pools of various sizes. These end in a small, rocky, half-moon beach. Now called Playa Bonita (formerly Kobbe Beach, when it was on a U.S. military base), the beach is not the greatest, but it's pleasant. This is the closest beach hotel from Panama City. It's an appealing, if pricey, place.

Standard rooms are attractive, with two double beds or one king bed, a safe, minibar, balcony, cable TV, coffeemaker, and wireless Internet access (US$15/day). The resort has three restaurants, including one in a large *rancho* by the beach. Bars are in the lobby and by the pool. A large, modern gym with plate-glass windows facing the ocean is open 24 hours a day. There's also an elegant full-service spa with a Southeast Asian tropical motif.

The resort is a short drive from Panama City, but it's quite secluded and there's nothing much around it. Only guests are allowed through the gatehouse, which is guarded more zealously than Panama's border crossings.

FOOD

Despite all the development in the former Canal Zone, it's far from becoming a culinary destination. Fortunately, downtown Panama City is quite close if the restaurants here aren't appealing.

There are plenty of places to eat on and near the causeway, though I've yet to have a memorable meal at any of them.

The much-lamented **Balboa Yacht Club** (tel. 228-5794) has risen from the ashes (literally, it was burned down some years ago). It's roughly in its old location—despite the name, it's in Amador, above the water near the Country Inn and Suites. At this point it's just an outdoor place serving burgers, buckets of beer, and the like from a wagon, but it's popular with both diehard Zonians and yachties.

Mediocre American chain restaurants (T.G.I. Friday's, Bennigan's, Subway) are also making inroads. Flamenco Plaza on Isla Flamenco and a newer complex on Isla Perico have an impressive number of theme restaurants squeezed into cramped spaces. Oddly, both have been designed so the parking lot is on the best real estate, with a view of Panama Bay and the Panama City skyline, while the restaurants are set so far back they really only have a view of the parking lot. Most are indoor/outdoor places. It's pleasant to sit outside in the evenings and enjoy the tropical breeze. There are also places to eat at the Gran Terminal de Transportes/Albrook Mall.

The food at ◖ **Centro de Visitantes de Miraflores** (Miraflores Locks Visitors Center, tel. 276-8325, noon–11 P.M. daily, US$10–15) is decent. It includes sandwiches, pastas, seafood, salads, and so on. But that's not the

reason to come here. Dining on a terrace just a few meters from the locks of the Panama Canal is, to say the least, a novel experience. Diners can watch ships transiting day or night (high-mast lighting turns night into day at the locks). Come early or reserve a table against the railing, where the view is best. Service charge is included.

Niko's Café (tel. 228-8888, 7 A.M.–11 P.M. daily), at the end of the Prado next to Stevens Circle in Balboa, is one of a small chain of successful cafeterias in Panama City that offer simple, tasty food at rock-bottom prices. This one is in the heart of the old Canal Zone, between what was once the high school football stadium and the employees' commissary, built on the site of a bowling alley. Reflecting its location, the cafeteria has great panoramic black-and-white photos of the Canal Zone, U.S. military bases, and parts of Panama dating from the 1920s and 1930s. Much to the amazement of old Zonians, the seal of the Canal Zone is above the counter. About US$4 will get you heaps of food, which includes traditional Panamanian fare, sandwiches, soups, individual pizzas, and desserts. The café now has wireless Internet access.

Lum's Bar and Grill (tel. 317-6303, 11 A.M.–midnight daily, US$6 or less), just off Gaillard Highway across the tracks from the railroad station in Corozal, is one of the last bastions of meat-and-potatoes Zonian spirit. Turn off the highway at the lovingly preserved Panama Railroad train cars. It's a converted warehouse that features a restaurant in the main room with pastas, salads, sandwiches, and the like. Attached to it is a sports bar with pool tables, ESPN, and, on some nights, live local bands. A favorite is a blues-rock outfit called Bitches Ghost, composed of Panamanians and gringo expats. These include Rod Richards, the original lead guitarist for the late 1960s/early 1970s rock band Rare Earth. Enjoy.

Restaurante Pencas (Amador, tel. 211-3671, www.pencas.com, noon–11 P.M. Mon.–Thurs., 12:30 P.M.–12:30 A.M. Fri.–Sat., noon–10 P.M. Sun.) is just past the Panama Canal Village. It's a large open-air place with tables on a raised deck near the water, and it has a view of the ocean and the Panama City skyline. The menu tends toward American comfort food and includes baby back ribs and other grilled meats, sandwiches, burgers, fajitas, pasta, and seafood. The *filete de canal frances* is a small but tender cut of beef.

Pencas hosts a *típico* music performance Wednesday nights at 8:30 P.M. Other musicians perform Thursday–Saturday nights.

Mi Ranchito (Isla Naos, Amador Causeway, tel. 228-4909, 11:45 A.M.–midnight Mon.–Thurs., 11:45 A.M.–1:30 A.M. Fri.–Sat., 9 A.M.–11:30 P.M. Sun.) is a simple but clean open-air place under a thatched roof on Naos, just past the turnoff to the Centro de Exhibiciones Marinas. It's the most popular place to eat on the Amador Causeway. Instead of adopting a cheesy theme like the others, it serves traditional Panamanian food, with an emphasis on fish and seafood at low prices. It also has—wonder of wonders—a view of the bay. While many people have good experiences here, I've found the food to be just so-so—the corvina is not very flavorful and is drowned in sauce, and the soup is thin. Still, the location is good and a *típico* meal in pleasant surroundings can be had for less than US$10. The *patacones* (fried green plantains) are tasty.

INFORMATION AND SERVICES

The **Smithsonian Tropical Research Institute** (tel. 212-8000, www.stri.org) has its headquarters, the Earl S. Tupper Research and Conference Center, in Ancón. It's a large building on Roosevelt Avenue across Avenida de las Mártires from the Palacio Legislativo. It has a small **research library** (9 A.M.–5 P.M. Mon., Wed.–Fri.; 8 A.M.–5 P.M. Tues.; 9 A.M.–noon Sat.) that contains science periodicals and older research books and a **bookstore** (10 A.M.–4:30 P.M. Mon.–Fri.) with some hard-to-find books on Panama's natural history. Both are worth a visit for detailed information on Panama's flora and fauna. They are open to the public, but visitors must present an ID and sign in to get into the center. The

center also has a cafeteria that serves lunch for US$2–3.

GETTING THERE AND AROUND

Taxis are the most convenient way to get from downtown Panama City to most of the destinations in the former Canal Zone, though they're easy to explore by rental car as well. Many tour operators offer day tours that include stops in Balboa, Miraflores Locks, and the handicrafts market next to the YMCA. Exploring by bus requires a lot of connections.

By Taxi

Taxis from central Panama City to any of these destinations should cost less than US$5. But to explore more than one, it makes more sense to arrange a taxi tour. Agree on a price ahead of time.

By Bus

There are many buses from Panama City to specific canal-area destinations, but trying to explore the whole area by bus is time-consuming, and the fares quickly add up. Taxis are a more practical alternative. Those who want to stick with public transportation can take one of the SACA buses from the Gran Terminal in Albrook.

By Car

The Administration Building is in Altos de Balboa (Balboa Heights), a short drive from downtown Panama City. It's hard to miss. Balboa begins just down the hill from it.

Miraflores Locks are about a 20-minute drive from Panama City, just off Gaillard Highway. The entrance to Miraflores Locks is on the left past Clayton, which is less than 10 kilometers from Balboa. Pedro Miguel Locks are about five kilometers farther on. Just beyond Pedro Miguel is the beginning of Gaillard Cut, now sometimes referred to by its original name, Culebra Cut.

Amador begins near the east end of the Bridge of the Americas. Drivers coming from downtown Panama City can reach Amador by two roads. The older route is to drive through Balboa on Avenida Arnulfo Arias Madrid (also called Balboa Road) and onto the road between the YMCA and the huge statue of Arnulfo Arias. This leads straight to Amador. A faster and more direct route is to take a newer access road that links Avenida de los Mártires directly with Amador near the entrance to the Bridge of the Americas; follow the signs and stay alert— the intersections come up quickly and can be dangerous. Once in Amador, stay straight to get to the causeway.

ISLA TABOGA

Taboga is the most easily accessible island from Panama City. It's just 12 nautical miles away, a trip that takes about an hour by ferry. It's a pretty, quaint little island. If you squint, its whitewashed walls, curving staircases, and flowering trees may remind you of a Greek island.

Taboga is home to a full-time population and attracts many weekend visitors. It's an appealing place that inspires a nostalgic affection somewhat out of proportion to its modern-day charms, especially for those who like deserted, pristine shores. Beaches here are okay, if a bit rocky, but they can get relatively crowded on dry-season weekends, and some trash washes up from Panama City.

Since Taboga's attractions can be explored in a day and there aren't many facilities on the island, you may not want to spend the night. But it is a good place for a day trip.

The ferry ride over is half the fun of a Taboga visit. It leads past the Pacific entrance to the Panama Canal, under the Bridge of the Americas, and along the Causeway. You can occasionally see dolphins on the way over, and if you're very, very lucky you may spot a humpback whale.

An awful lot of history has passed through Taboga since the Spaniards first came calling in the early 16th century. The current town was founded in 1524 and it claims to have the second oldest church in the western hemisphere. Francisco de Pizarro is said to have planned the destruction of the Inca Empire on Taboga. Its visitors have also included pirates, Forty-Niners, and workers on both the French and American canals. Canal workers recovered from their illnesses at a convalescent hospital that has long since disappeared.

A water festival in honor of the Virgen del Carmen is celebrated on Taboga every July 16.

Orientation and Sights

The main beaches are on either side of the floating pier, where the ferries arrive. The more attractive one, **Playa La Restinga,** faces Panama City. A right turn as you leave the pier leads along an ocean path shaded by tamarind trees. Avoid the stretch of beach on the far left as you face the ocean; the smell of sewage will tell you why. At low tide it's possible to walk across a sandbar from Playa La Restinga to the neighboring islet of El Morro. The sandbar disappears at high tide.

The town itself is quite attractive and worth exploring. There are two main roads, a high street and a low street, which are easy to walk on since there are few cars on the island. Both roads are to the left of the pier as you leave the ferry. When the jasmine, oleander, bougainvillea, and hibiscus are in bloom, you'll understand why Taboga is called "the Island of Flowers." Houses tend to be well-maintained and quaint.

When Paul Gauguin first left Europe for the tropics he was so taken with Taboga that he tried to buy land here. However, he was broke and ended up having to help dig the Panama Canal instead, a job he detested. He never could afford Taboga's prices and soon sailed on. He eventually found Tahiti, and the rest is art history. There's a plaque commemorating his stay, from May to July 1887, up the high street by some picturesque Spanish ruins. Don't miss the lovely garden filled with a rainbow of flowering plants.

The quaint, white-washed church in the center of town, **Iglesia San Pedro,** was originally made out of wood, erected after the founding of Taboga in 1524. It's supposedly the second-oldest church in the western hemisphere. Taboga is a hilly island that lends itself to walks past old gravesites, abandoned U.S. military bunkers, and the overgrown remains of Spanish fortifications. The cemetery, on the edge of the ocean toward the end of the road, makes for a picturesque amble.

It's possible to take a moderately strenuous walk to the top of **Cerro de la Cruz,** which, as the name implies, is topped by a cross. There's a good view of the ocean from here. The south side of the island, together with neighboring Isla Urabá, is part of a national wildlife refuge that protects the nesting area of an important brown pelican colony.

Practicalities

Until recently Taboga lacked decent places to spend the night; most people are content with a day trip. There are once again a few options, the most popular of which is **El Cerrito Tropical** (tel. 390-8999, cell 6489-0074, www.cerritotropicalpanama.com, starts at US$77 s/d), which is on a hill about a 10-minute walk from the ferry pier. El Cerrito is a B&B with three "B&B rooms" and three apartments. The apartments range from a one-bedroom for up to two people (US$110) up to a three-bedroom that can sleep six (US$262). The B&B rooms are simple but cheerfully decorated, with airconditioning, private bathrooms, and a shared balcony. These range in price US$77–104.50. Rates include a continental breakfast. Your hosts are Cynthia Mulder, a Canadian, and her husband Hiddo, who is from the "Dutch Caribbean." They can organize a range of tours, including fishing, snorkeling and exploring the island. El Cerrito's website has

good information on the island and how to get around. Also check out www.taboga.panamanow.com.

Food options are still limited; day-trippers may want to pack a lunch. Note that there are no ATMs or banks on the island, so take all the cash you think you'll need.

Ferries to Isla Taboga leave from Isla Naos on the Amador Causeway. A taxi from Panama City to the pier should cost about US$4–5. There is parking near the pier for those who drive.

El Calypso (tel. 314-1730 or 390-2403) uses two ancient ferries—they were already old when I was a kid—the *Calypso Queen* and *Calypso Princess*. The round-trip fare is US$10.

El Calypso ferries make the trip to Taboga at 8:30 A.M. Monday–Friday, with a second ferry at 3 P.M. Monday, Wednesday, and Friday. On weekends and holidays they leave at 8 A.M., 10:30 A.M., and 4 P.M.

Trips back to Amador are at 9:30 A.M. Monday–Friday, with a second ferry at 4:00 P.M. Monday, Wednesday, and Friday. The weekend and holiday schedule is 9 A.M., 3 P.M., and 5 P.M.

Ferry schedules are more theoretical than real; service is erratic. Make a reservation or show up early on dry-season weekends and holidays to be sure of getting a ticket—this is a popular day-trip destination for Panamanians. The ferry requires passengers to arrive at least an hour ahead of time. Also, since there's no assigned seating, board early to claim a spot out of the sun—it's easy to get fried before even reaching the beach.

THE PANAMA CANAL

Gamboa and Vicinity

The townsite of Gamboa, on the banks of the Panama Canal about halfway across the isthmus, is surrounded by extraordinary natural beauty, especially given how close it is to Panama City. It's a gateway to world-famous birding trails, the tropical rainforest of Parque Nacional Soberanía, the powerful Río Chagres, botanical gardens and a zoo, and the huge, artificially-made Lago Gatún. That lake is at the heart of the canal and contains Barro Colorado Island, one of the world's foremost natural laboratories for the study of tropical nature.

Though Emberá and Wounaan people still live up the Río Chagres, Gamboa is the headquarters of the canal's engineering and dredging divisions and has a modern infrastructure.

Gamboa today has few services, accommodations, or places to eat, but Panama City is less than a 45-minute drive away. There are, however, two impressive eco-resorts in the area.

Note: Lago Alajuela (formerly Madden Lake) is a second artificial lake northeast of Gamboa that supplies water for the canal. Some people like to visit its impressive Madden Dam, but because of several instances of tourist muggings, I recommend avoiding it. Those who like dams should visit the even more impressive and easily accessible Gatún Dam, on the Caribbean side of the isthmus.

SIGHTS
Summit Botanical Gardens and Zoo

These gardens (off Gaillard Highway, tel. 232-4854, www.summitpanama.org, 9 A.M.–5 P.M. daily, US$1) are worth a quick side trip on the way to or from Gamboa. They were created by the Panama Canal Company in 1923 for the study of tropical plants and turned over to the Panama government in 1985. The place has deteriorated in recent years, but some efforts are being made to fix it up. At last count there were 4,000 plants representing 366 species still growing in the gardens.

Summit Gardens also has a small zoo that contains tapirs, caimans, jaguars, and other large animals. Many of their cages are tiny and antiquated, which will disturb many visitors.

The harpy eagle compound, Summit's showcase, is more encouraging. The harpy eagle is the world's most powerful bird of prey; it can grow up to a meter long from bill to tail. Sadly, it's also endangered. The bird is indigenous to Panama, and a major purpose of the compound is to try to get the birds to reproduce in captivity. The specimens here are magnificent, with thick plumage, fearsome hooked bills, and steely talons. They look like stoic high chiefs.

Summit Gardens is just off Gaillard Highway, a few kilometers before the town of Gamboa.

◖ Parque Nacional Soberanía

This is a true tropical forest, and it's one of the most accessible in the world. Its 22,000 hectares extend along the east bank of the Panama Canal, ending at Lago Gatún near the town of Limón. The wildlife is amazing, especially considering how close the park is to population centers. Among its inhabitants are 525 species of birds, 105 species of mammals, 55 species of amphibians, and 79 species of reptiles.

All its well-maintained trails are a short drive from Panama City on the Gaillard Highway, making it quite feasible to go for a morning hike during which there's a chance of encountering such tourist-pleasing critters as sloths, coatimundis, toucans, and kinkajous, and then be back in the heart of the city in time for lunch in an air-conditioned restaurant.

A section of the famous **Camino de Cruces (Las Cruces Trail),** which has a history dating to the 16th century, runs through the park. To reach it by car, continue straight when the Gaillard Highway forks just past the railroad overpass with "1929" carved in it. The road, now Madden Road (don't expect a street sign), will pass through a forest, which, sadly, is often strewn with litter. There's a parking area and picnic tables on the left after 6.3 kilometers.

The trailhead is well marked. It's possible to hike this trail for about five or six hours to the Chagres and even camp along it. For just a glimpse of this storied trail, walk at least five minutes along it and you'll come to a section where the ancient paving stones that once lined the trail have been restored. In the dry season, you may have to brush aside dead leaves to find them. (Use your boot to do this, not your hand, as there are still some poisonous snakes in the forest.)

All the other trails are on the road to Gamboa. Back near the "1929" overpass, turn off the Galliard Highway toward Gamboa. The first major trail will be the wide, flat **Plantation Road.** It's a right turn off the highway; follow the Canopy Tower signs. The entrance to the trail is on the left at the base of the road leading to the Canopy Tower.

Farther along the main road is **Sendero El Charco** (literally, "pond trail"), also on the right. This is a very short (844 meters) trail that can easily be skipped. A little waterfall near the entrance sure looked a lot bigger and nicer when I was a kid. A barbecue area on the premises attracts hordes of families on the weekends.

The best trail for viewing birdlife is the famous **Pipeline Road (Camino del Oleoducto).** To get there, cross over the one-lane bridge leading into Gamboa. Continue straight. After about three kilometers the road will fork; take the left fork onto the gravel road. The swampy area to the right, just before Pipeline Road, is worth checking out on the way back from an early-morning birding trip. At around 8–9 A.M., as the forest warms up, there's an excellent chance of spotting capybaras, the world's largest rodents, on the far side of the clearing. A couple of kilometers past this area there's a "Parque Nacional Soberanía" sign indicating you've reached Camino del Oleoducto. Make a right here and park.

For the first six kilometers or so, the forest is mostly secondary growth. You'll see dozens of species of birds if you arrive early. There's a slight chance of finding anteaters, howler monkeys, white-faced capuchins, Geoffroy's tamarin, green iguanas, agoutis, coatimundis, or two- and three-toed sloths. Serious birders will want to continue past this area into old-growth forest, where there's a possibility of seeing such rare specimens as yellow-eared toucanets, crimson-bellied woodpeckers, sirystes, and other gorgeous birds that will impress even those who don't know a russet antshrike from a slaty-winged foliage-gleaner. The unbelievably lucky may see an endangered harpy eagle, but don't count on it. Pipeline Road continues for many kilometers, but the bridges over streams are not well-maintained these days. Bridge collapses can curtail a long hike. Get here by dawn to see this famous birding road in all its feathered glory. It's worth the loss of sleep.

About 1.6 kilometers in from the entrance to Pipeline Road is the **Panama Rainforest Discovery Center** (tel. 264-6266 in Panama City, tel. 314-9386 or 314-9388 in Gamboa, www.pipelineroad.org, 6 A.M.–4 P.M. daily), a new interpretive center and observation tower in the middle of the forest. The tower is a modern steel structure 30 meters high, with rest platforms on the way up and a top platform that's just above the canopy. There is a kilometer of developed trails in the immediate area. The visitor center has restrooms and a gift shop that sells drinks and snacks. Admission to the complex is US$20 for adults and US$4 for kids younger than 12 during the "premium time" of 6–10 A.M., when one is most likely to see wildlife. The price drops to US$15 for adults and US$2 for kids after 10 A.M. But to have the best chance of seeing interesting wildlife, particularly birds, visitors should try to be on site as soon as the tower opens. The center is open daily except for Christmas Day and New Year's Day.

Note that other than the Panama Rainforest Discovery Center, the rest of the Pipeline Road area, and the national park generally, is open to the public at a much more modest fee. Hiking and camping permits are available at the ANAM office at the edge of the park, inconveniently located well before any of the trails. It's on Gaillard Highway at the fork just past the narrow overpass; you can't miss the huge

Parque Nacional Soberanía sign. The office is officially open 8 A.M.–4 P.M. weekdays, but the staff lives in the little house behind the office so there should always be someone there to take your money. Entrance fee is US$5, which gives visitors access to all the trails for the day. The camping fee is another US$5.

Bear in mind there are no developed camping sites in the park (though there are some facilities at Sendero El Charco) and this is a tropical forest. Those planning an early-morning hike can probably pay on the way back without a problem. But otherwise ask about the conditions of the trails, especially Pipeline Road, before venturing out. Note that the Camino de Cruces is quite a hike from the other trails; Gamboa-bound buses take passengers only as far as the fork to Gamboa, after which you'll have to hoof it for six kilometers unless you can flag down a ride. It's much more convenient to take a taxi from Panama City or go with a tour group.

Lago Gatún

Once the largest artificially-made lake in the world, at 422 square kilometers Lago Gatún is still a plenty impressive body of water. It was formed by damming the Río Chagres near its mouth, at Gatún, and is an integral part of the Panama Canal. Transiting ships still follow the submerged riverbed of the Chagres, since it's the deepest part of the lake. It's long been a popular spot with boaters, water-skiers, anglers, and even scuba divers. The diving here is unusual, to say the least. A Belgian locomotive and 8 of its 40 train cars, abandoned during construction days, were recently salvaged from the bottom of the lake, and submerged trees and remnants of old towns are still there. Not surprisingly, however, the water is murky and in some places choked with vegetation. Divers find the experience rather spooky.

However, I advise against diving these days. Caimans have always shared the lake with people, but there are a lot more of them now. An acquaintance whose idea of a fun family outing used to be playing catch-and-release with caimans—we're not talking a wimp here—told

me she would not even go water-skiing in the lake today. "It's infested," she said. The lake now also has crocodiles.

In other words, stay in the boat. The fishing here is terrific—the peacock bass population, accidentally introduced decades ago, is so out of control anglers are actually encouraged to catch them to restore some kind of ecological balance. It's not uncommon for an angler who knows the good spots to catch dozens of fish an hour.

A highlight of a Lago Gatún boat trip is a visit to the **primate sanctuary** scattered among more than a dozen islands in the lake, known collectively as the Islas Tigre and Islas Las Brujas. Here visitors can spot tamarins, spider monkeys, white-faced capuchins, howlers, and night monkeys swinging or peering from trees just a few meters from the boat.

Only visit the sanctuary on a tour led by a responsible naturalist group such as Ancon Expeditions. Do not feed or have any physical contact with the monkeys. All but the night monkeys have been rescued from illegal captivity, and the project is trying to reintroduce them to the wild. The last thing they need is more human contact. Besides, some can be pretty aggressive, so don't get too close. Some boat tours of the area include walks through small, forested islands, some of which have spooky ruins from the old Canal Zone days. Douse yourself with insect repellent before exploring them; the mosquitoes can be voracious.

Barro Colorado Island

BCI, as it's commonly known, is one of the world's most famous biological reserves. Part of what makes it exceptional is that it's been left alone so long: It was declared a protected area in 1923, when such reserves in the neotropics were almost unheard of. Since then its flora and fauna have been more intensely studied than that of any other tropical area of comparable size. The island is administered by the Smithsonian Tropical Research Institute (STRI, tel. 212-8951, fax 212-8026, www.stri.org), which is based in Panama.

Barro Colorado Island was actually a hill

THE PANAMA CANAL

© WILLIAM FRIAR

a white-faced capuchin at the primate sanctuary in Lago Gatún

until 1914, when the damming of the Chagres River to create Lago Gatún made that hill an island. The flooding of the lake left only 15 square kilometers of tropical forest on the island, but they contain 480 species of trees (more than in all of Europe), 70 species of bats, 384 species of birds, 30 species of frogs, 47 species of snakes, and on and on. Just accounting for the insects on the island is an overwhelming task. Take ants, for instance: More than 200 species have been identified so far.

Day visitors, as opposed to research scientists, can walk on only some trails, usually an interpretive loop that takes 2–3 hours to walk at an easy clip. It's fairly flat most of the way, but it does get muddy at times. There's a short side trail off the main loop that's well worth taking. It leads to the aptly named "Big Tree," a kapok *(Ceiba pentandra)* so huge other trees are growing on its branches.

Visitors are not allowed on the trails without an authorized guide. But consider buying *A Day on Barro Colorado Island* (Smithsonian), by Marina Wong and Jorge Ventocilla, anyway. It contains a trail guide and information on the island's flora and fauna that will help you get much more out of your visit. It's sold in a few places in Panama, including the little bookshop at STRI's main office in Panama City. The Gamboa Rainforest Resort may have it as well.

Note: BCI has the kind of wildlife many visitors come to the tropics to see, including tapirs, coatimundis, sloths, ocelots, anteaters, collared peccaries, and three species of monkeys. But as STRI personnel will be the first to tell you, day visitors expecting a jungle crawling with creatures will likely be disappointed. One may see almost no animal life during a short visit to BCI.

The only mammals one is likely to encounter are agoutis and howler monkeys. It's actually hard not to stumble upon howlers. A 1977 census found 65 troops on the island, each with about 19 monkeys. Do the math. Their numbers haven't changed much since.

Access to the island is strictly controlled. Visitors must arrange a tour through STRI or an STRI-approved tour operator, and the few spaces get booked up early. Cancellations are not uncommon, however, so last-minute trips are sometimes possible. Some tour operators offer trips to Barro Colorado Nature Monument, which includes the surrounding mainland as well as the island itself. Make sure the tour actually goes to the island if that's important to you.

The STRI offers **tours** (tel. 212-8951, fax 212-8026, www.stri.org, Tues., Wed. and Fri. at 7:15 A.M.; Sat. and Sun. at 8 A.M.; US$70 pp, US$40 students). The cost includes the launch from Gamboa to BCI, a 2–3-hour hike with a naturalist guide, a tour of the visitors center, and lunch at the field-research station (vegetarian food is available). It may be possible to chat up a research scientist over lunch. Reservations should be made as far ahead of time as possible.

The launch to the island leaves from a pier in Gamboa, about an hour's drive from Panama City (if there's no traffic). It's imperative that visitors arrive early, as the launch to the island leaves on the dot and there's no other way to get there. Visitors are responsible for their own transportation to Gamboa. A taxi from Panama City costs around US$20. The STRI website now has detailed information about the trip and a schematic map explaining how to get to the pier.

Río Chagres

This powerful river supplies most of the water for the Panama Canal and much of the drinking water for Panama City. It once flowed unimpeded across the isthmus, emptying into the Caribbean below the ruins of Fuerte San Lorenzo near the city of Colón. The damming of the river near Gatún Locks created the massive Lago Gatún, and today the river disappears into the lake at Gamboa and doesn't resurface until it approaches the Caribbean. But the upper reaches of the Chagres still wind their way through lovely rainforest. In the dry season, stretches of the river become little more than glorified puddles. In the rainy season, however, the Chagres can rise many meters in a single hour. Flash floods are not unknown.

The Emberá and Wounaan have been relocated from the Darién jungle in recent years to live in communities along the banks of the river surprisingly close to Panama City. The one most visited by tourists is Parara Puru. While these are true Emberá who cling to some of their traditional ways, visitors should note that the "village" is rather touristy and the elaborate traditional costumes the people wear are put on for their benefit. Even the concept of a village is not a traditional part of Emberá culture; historically, families lived in relative isolation from each other.

Still, the trip up the river is beautiful and encounters with Emberá and Wounaan people are always interesting. Visits to the community include dance demonstrations, a walk through a botanical garden, and a chance to buy cocobolo figurines, tagua nut carvings, woven baskets, and other handicrafts. Those inclined can have themselves painted with traditional *jagua* (a kind of vegetable dye) designs, but bear in mind the dye takes many days to fade and can't be washed off. Several tour operators offer trips up the Chagres to Parara Puru. **Aventuras Panama** (tel. 260-0044 or 236-5814, www.aventuraspanama.com) offers an all-day excursion for US$110. The trip includes lunch in the community. River rafting is also possible on the Chagres.

SPORTS AND RECREATION
Canopy Tower

Unless the Canopy Tower (tel. 264-5720, U.S. toll-free tel. 800/930-3397, www.canopytower.com) is packed with guests, it offers day tours to anyone. There's a decent chance of seeing good-sized mammals (other than your fellow visitors) and an excellent chance of spotting lots of birds. Possibilities include an early-morning (6:30–11 A.M.) or lunch (12:30–5 P.M.) visit for US$95 that includes a two-hour guided walk and wildlife viewing from the tower. An evening visit (5:30–9 P.M.), for US$85, includes dinner.

Gamboa Rainforest Resort

You don't have to be a guest at the Gamboa Rainforest Resort (tel. 314-5000, www.

COURTESY OF THE CANOPY TOWER

The Canopy Tower is a unique eco-lodge in Parque Nacional Soberanía.

gamboaresort.com) to use its **activities center** (8 A.M.–6 P.M. daily) or book its tours, which include bird-watching walks and night "safaris" on the lake. The resort rents kayaks, bicycles, and other toys. You can also charter fishing boats here, but expect to pay for it.

The **aerial tram** (9:15–10:30 A.M. and 1:30–3 P.M. Tues.–Sun., US$53 pp) is one of the star attractions of the resort. It's sort of like a ski lift that takes passengers up about 80 meters to a hill, passing through the canopy of a patch of secondary forest along the way. A bilingual naturalist guide travels along in each four- or five-person gondola to spot and describe flora and fauna. Passengers can get off at the top and climb a 30-meter observation tower that offers panoramic views of the canal, the Chagres, and the surrounding forest. The trip takes a little over an hour, not including the stop at the observation platform. Don't get your hopes up about seeing too much wildlife; these canopy trams are a comfortable way to experience tropical forest, but a quick zip through the trees is unlikely to

net many encounters with animals. Particularly since the tram doesn't start running until mid-morning, by then most birds and jungle critters have slipped away. In two visits, my biggest scores have been a glimpse of the tail of a sleepy kinkajou in the crook of a tree, and a roadside encounter with a group of coatimundis on the ride back to the hotel. In my opinion, the rate is excessive for what you get, but if you're lucky enough to glimpse something special, you might feel it's worth it. Contact Gamboa Rainforest Resort for reservations and information.

Before or after a tram ride it's worth wandering around the resort's **flora and fauna exhibits.** They're housed in a series of structures on the road leading up to the tram and include an orchid nursery, a serpentarium with impressive native and nonnative species, a butterfly house, and a small freshwater aquarium that also contains crocodiles, caimans, and turtles. The "model Emberá village" nearby is rather hokey, but it's a chance to meet a few Emberá and buy their tightly woven baskets and other handicrafts.

Fishing, Boating, and Adventure Tours

There's a small **marina** just outside Gamboa, near the one-lane bridge across the Río Chagres, where boatmen offer fishing tours on their basic *pangas.* Stop by at least a day ahead of time to work out a deal. Anglers need to be on the lake just before dawn; by midmorning the peacock bass stop biting. A morning of fishing costs about US$50. The captains can also take visitors on an exploratory cruise around Lago Gatún and/or the Chagres River. The price depends on distance.

A group called **Panama Canal Fishing** (cell 6678-2653, www.panamacanalfishing. com) offers a higher-end, all-inclusive fishing experience on Lago Gatún. Trips are made on a roomy and comfortable *Hurricane Fundeck 201.* Prices are US$395 per boat and include round-trip transfers between Panama City and Gamboa, a fishing guide and captain, picnic lunch and drinks, and all fishing equipment, bait, and lures. Boats can accommodate up to six anglers, at US$20 extra per person after the first two. Prices do not include sales tax (currently 7 percent).

The Panama Canal Fishing company is run by Richard Cahill and his wife, Gaby. Rich has worked for years as an accomplished naturalist guide with Ancon Expeditions, and I highly recommend him. He's guided me around the Darién jungle, not a fishing lake, but he's knowledgeable, reliable, enthusiastic, fun, and an all-around good guy. He's fluent in English and Spanish and can swear colorfully in both. The company also offers tours of the lake's primate sanctuary and the Panama Canal, usually as an add-on to the fishing trip.

Aventuras Panama (tel. 260-0044 or 236-5814, www.aventuraspanama.com) offers rafting trips on the Río Chagres. The rafting is usually quite gentle, with mostly Class II rapids and a few Class IIIs. It's not intended for those who need big white water. However, this is still a long, fairly rigorous trip and the Chagres, like any other powerful river, has seen its share of accidents and needs to be approached with respect. Clients are picked up from their hotel at 5 A.M. and driven into the highlands above Cerro Azul. From there, it's a 1.5-hour hike through the forest to the put-in spot. Rafters spend all day on the river, ending up in Lago Alajuela (also called Madden Lake) in the late afternoon. Clients are dropped back at their hotel around 7 P.M. The trip costs US$165 per person and includes breakfast, lunch, and transfers. Clients must be between the ages of 12 and 70. The company offers many other tours, including rafting trips on the Mamoní and Río Grande and a boat ride up the Chagres to visit the Emberá community of Parara Puru.

ACCOMMODATIONS AND FOOD

To date there are only two hotels in the Gamboa area, but both are impressive, if expensive, places that are destinations in themselves. The only restaurants open to nonguests are at the Gamboa Rainforest Resort, though the Canopy Tower sometimes offers day passes that include a meal. It's also possible to camp in Parque Nacional Soberanía, but there are no facilities and this is a true tropical forest, with all the potential discomfort that implies.

Canopy Tower

I remain impressed by this special place. The Canopy Tower (tel. 264-5720, U.S. toll-free tel. 800/930-3397, www.canopytower.com, high-season Canopy Room packages US$217 pp, including meals and bird tour) is an old U.S. military radar tower that has been cleverly transformed into a 12-room hotel and wildlife observation platform, high above the floor of a protected forest, Parque Nacional Soberanía. Visitors can look out the window of their room right into the forest.

The rooms are simple but cheerful and comfortable, with teak louvered doors and other touches that soften the utilitarian feel of the structure. Each room has two single beds with ceiling fans and a good hot-water bathroom.

Five single rooms have been added on the level below the canopy rooms, about 5.5 meters above the hilltop. Formerly guides' quarters, they are quite small (eight square meters, less than half the size of the canopy rooms), have a single bed, and share a bathroom. The high-season rate is US$150.

The Blue Cotinga Suite (US$245 s/d in high season) is a large room (34 square meters) that can sleep three and has a private balcony with a hammock swing. This is the fanciest place to stay at the tower. The Harpy Eagle Suite, one floor down, is a bit smaller (27 square meters) and plainer, but the rates are the same for one or two people. It can sleep up to four.

The tower is not air-conditioned so as not to scare away wildlife and separate guests from the sound of the forest. However, the elevation is high enough that, with the screened windows open and the ceiling fan on, it's quite comfortable. This is not a place for people who like to sleep in or who want a romantic getaway: The tower is made of metal and sound carries easily.

The rooms, however, are only a small part of a visit to the tower. Stays include all meals and a daily, guided tour into the national park on well-maintained trails. The food here is good, concentrating on simple but tasty local dishes.

One flight up from the canopy rooms are the dining and living room, which offer a near 360-degree view. Guests can continue up to the roof, which is a great place to watch the sun rise and set over the forest, listen to the roar of howler monkeys, and watch for owls and other nocturnal creatures at night.

Rates are lower in the rainy season; the chances of spotting birds and wildlife can plummet during a rain, though they come out to dry afterwards. But the "migration season," which occurs late in the rainy season, can actually be an exciting time to come. This is when literally millions of raptors pass through Panama on their annual migration.

Guests are likely to see more wildlife while lounging in the tower than they would on long hikes in more remote areas. Within five minutes of my first visit I saw a tití monkey (Geoffroy's tamarin) and a host of other creatures. By the end of my second visit, I had seen a kinkajou, a dozen coatimundi moms and babies, a sloth, an unidentified snake, and innumerable birds (short-tailed hawk, three toucans in a single tree, dusky-capped flycatcher, white-whiskered puffbird, white-shouldered tanager, blue-crowned manakin, and on and on). At last count, bird-watchers had identified 283 species of birds just from the tower and Semaphore Hill Road.

The Canopy Tower is 25 kilometers from Panama City, about a half-hour drive. Those driving must take the left fork off Gaillard Highway after the railroad bridge and follow the road toward Gamboa. The well-marked turnoff to the Canopy Tower will be on the right 1.6 kilometers past Summit Botanical Gardens. There's a gate across the entrance to the tower road that you may have to open. Go up the one-lane, well-maintained road 1.7 kilometers to the tower. Note: The tower is not wheelchair-accessible. Access to the top of the tower is by stairs—five dozen of them.

Make reservations, even for day trips, as far in advance as possible; the tower is world-famous and extremely popular.

Gamboa Rainforest Resort

The resort (tel. 314-5000, US toll-free 877/800-1690, www.gamboaresort.com, starts at US$198 s/d, including breakfast), which opened in 2000, is a peculiar mixture of an ecotourism resort, luxury spa, and theme park. Spread over its 137 hectares are a slice of tropical forest with an aerial tram running through the canopy, a full-service spa, a 107-room hotel, an entire neighborhood of one- and two-bedroom "historic apartments" converted from old Canal Zone housing, a huge swimming pool, tennis courts, three restaurants, traditionally dressed Emberá selling handicrafts at a pseudo-"model village," an orchid nursery, a snake house, an amphibian exhibit, several aquariums, a butterfly house, a marina, and on and on.

The location couldn't be better: The resort was built right on the banks of the Chagres, one of Panama's most important rivers, and it is only a stroll away from Lago Gatún, where one can watch ships transiting the Panama Canal. It's bordered by Parque Nacional Soberanía, the major trails of which are just a few kilometers away, as is the Canopy Tower.

There are two basic kinds of accommodations. Those in the main building start at US$275 d for a room with a balcony, air-conditioning, minibar, safe, cable TV, iron and ironing board, coffeemaker, and so on. Room quality is on a par with what one would find at a midlevel business hotel in the United States.

The price for the one-bedroom "historic apartment" is a comparative bargain at US$198 s/d. Whereas the rooms in the hotel are generic, these have character. They consist of renovated wooden buildings dating from the 1930s that actually housed Panama Canal employees and their families in the old Canal Zone days. The renovation was done in simple, cheerful good taste, from the rattan furniture to the historic canal clippings and sketches on the walls. All

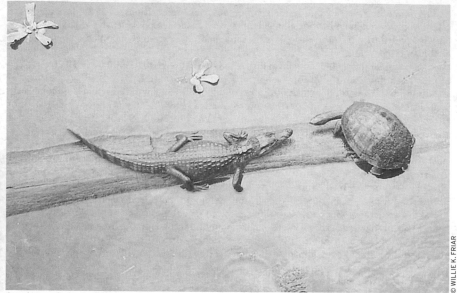

A caiman and a turtle eye each other next to Restaurante Los Lagartos at the Gamboa Rainforest Resort.

have sitting rooms and kitchenettes with microwaves, mini-fridges, and coffeemakers. They don't have a view of the river, but they're surrounded by trees. Why these are the "budget" accommodations is one of those mysteries of life in Panama. However, these old wooden houses are hard to maintain, so be sure yours looks okay.

All kinds of multiday packages are available that combine stays with golfing, bird-watching, spa treatments, ecotours, and so on. The resort's activities center rents mountain bikes, kayaks, pedal boats, and other gear.

The food at the resort is hit or miss. Of the three restaurants, **Restaurante Los Lagartos** (tel. 276-6812, 11:30 A.M.–5 P.M. daily) is the best option because of its terrific location. It's down the hill from the main hotel, built onto an attractive, open-walled wooden terrace that juts into the Río Chagres near where it empties into Lago Gatún. From their tables diners can sometimes see turtles, caimans, and the odd iguana sunbathing on the same log, peacock bass and tilapia nosing about in the shallows,

and little blue herons and jacanas hunting for food among the floating vegetation. Even here the food tends to be mediocre, but the show put on by nature is exceptional.

The **spa** at the Gamboa Rainforest Resort is also open to nonguests and offers a wide assortment of treatments and packages at U.S. prices, varying from manicures and massages to a full day of pampering.

The Gamboa Rainforest Resort is right above the Río Chagres in Gamboa, about a 45-minute drive from downtown Panama City.

GETTING THERE AND AROUND

The end of the road in Gamboa is about a 45-minute drive from Panama City. Taxis charge around US$20 one-way. Buses leave from the SACA bus section of the Gran Terminal de Transportes in Albrook. Gamboa-bound buses take passengers within reasonable walking distance of every attraction in the area except the Camino de Cruces. They're not close to each other, though, so it's not feasible to walk from one attraction to the next. Buses to and from Gamboa stop at designated bus stops along Gaillard Highway about every half hour during daylight hours, but this can be a time-consuming way to visit the various spots. Those who can afford it should consider hiring a taxi for a half-day or full-day tour.

Those driving from Panama City should head west on Gaillard Highway. Just past Pedro Miguel the road summits a small hill and then crosses under a narrow underpass, a railroad bridge with "1929" carved into it. The ANAM office that sells hiking and camping permits is at the fork. Straight leads into Madden Forest, a part of Parque Nacional Soberanía. Here's where you'll find the Camino de Cruces (Las Cruces Trail). A left turn at the fork keeps you on Gaillard Highway and leads to Summit Botanical Gardens, Plantation Road, the Canopy Tower, and Sendero El Charco, in that order. Cross the one-lane bridge (caution—be sure to stop if the red light is on) into the town of Gamboa, where the road ends. An immediate right turn leads up to the Gamboa Rainforest Resort. Staying straight leads to the Isla Barro Colorado launch and Pipeline Road.

Colón and the Costa Abajo

The attractions described in the rest of this chapter are in Colón province, which lies along the central Caribbean coast of Panama. Its capital is Colón, historically Panama's second-most important city. Though this area starts just 80 kilometers north of Panama City, it has long been neglected and has significantly fewer resources and facilities than the Pacific side of the isthmus. A few tour operators, especially dive operators, specialize in the area, but it is still relatively off the beaten track for most tourists. This is slowly changing, with new hotels, cruise-ship departures, and commercial projects in the works. These plans are serious enough to worry environmentalists, who fear especially for the important mangrove forests along the coastline. There is even talk of building a fanciful Dubai-style offshore city stuffed with high-rises next to Colón. For some odd reason, the developers want to build it in the shape of the Panamanian flag.

The coastline west of Colón is known as Costa Abajo (literally, "lower coast"). It is still a lightly developed area with rough roads and few visitors other than avid bird-watchers. But it offers the well-preserved ruins of a Spanish fort and lush tropical forest surrounding the mouth of the storied Río Chagres. These are all on the west side of the canal, across the swing bridge at Gatún Locks that is the only land link between western and eastern Panama on the Caribbean side of the isthmus.

The area is worth adding as a side trip on the way to or from, say, Portobelo or Isla Grande, or for those taking the Panama Railway across the isthmus. As a destination in itself, it's likely to be most appealing to those with an especially keen interest in the Panama Canal or Panama's piratical past.

The area's few main sights—Gatún Locks, Gatún Dam, and Fuerte San Lorenzo—are all clustered close together in a relatively small area southwest of Colón. So are its natural attractions, the mouth of the Río Chagres and the bird-watching spots around Achiote and Escobal.

SAFETY CONSIDERATIONS

Though the city of Colón (pop. 42,133, co-LONE in Spanish and kah-LAWN in English) has a long, colorful history, I urge you to avoid it. For one thing, it has little to offer tourists, and one can see all the region's sights without ever stopping here. But more important, it's just too dangerous. Extreme unemployment and poverty give this crumbling city a terrible reputation as a place where it's a surprise if you *don't* get mugged at knifepoint. Colón loyalists argue these fears are exaggerated, but they tend to follow that up by saying visitors should have

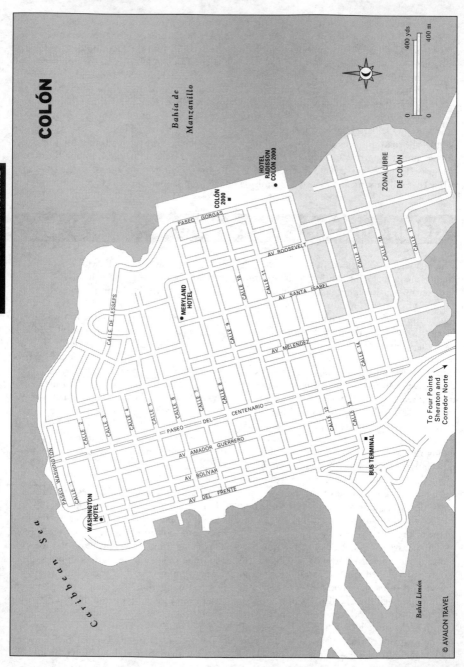

COLÓN

Bahía de Manzanillo

Caribbean Sea

Bahía Limón

HOTEL RADISSON COLON 2000

COLÓN 2000

ZONA LIBRE DE COLÓN

PASEO GORGAS

AV. ROOSEVELT

AV. SANTA ISABEL

MERYLAND HOTEL

AV. MELENDEZ

CALLE DE LESSEPS

CALLE 9

CALLE 10

CALLE 11

CALLE 15

CALLE 16

CALLE 17

CALLE 14

CALLE 12

CALLE 13

CALLE 8

CALLE 7

CALLE 6

CALLE 5

CALLE 4

CALLE 3

CALLE 2

CALLE 1

PASEO WASHINGTON

WASHINGTON HOTEL

PASEO DEL CENTENARIO

AV. AMADOR GUERRERO

AV. BOLIVAR

AV. DEL FRENTE

BUS TERMINAL

To Four Points Sheraton and Corredor Norte

400 yds

400 m

© AVALON TRAVEL

no problem—as long as they take taxis everywhere and never set foot on the streets.

Colón's dangers can be deceptive. On a sunny day, it looks like a colorful, mellow old place with wooden shanties, little different from any number of shabby Caribbean towns. During the week, one can see little schoolgirls in spotless uniforms traipsing alone to school. They're probably safe—but you aren't. You're the one with money.

There's always talk about revitalizing Colón, but little ever seems to change for its poor residents. For the foreseeable future, sadly, visitors should stay well away from the city.

For those who insist on visiting, the hotels and restaurants listed are the best bets. At the very least, do not walk around Colón: Drive or take taxis everywhere. Shopping at the Colón Free Zone and Colón 2000 is reasonably safe.

HISTORY

For most of its history, Colón has been known as a place to avoid. Even the intrepid Columbus decided to steer clear of the area when he and his crew became the first Europeans to see Isla Manzanillo. All they saw was a pestilential swamp filled with mosquitoes, snakes, caimans, and who knows what else.

Throughout the Spanish colonial era, the Colón area was largely ignored. The Spanish built their forts at San Lorenzo to the west and Portobelo and Nombre de Dios to the east.

It wasn't until an American company began work on the Panama Railroad in 1850 that people started living and working on the island and built the foundations of the city of Colón. The railroad had its Caribbean terminus nearby, and a settlement sprang up to house the employees and cater to the Forty-Niners, who gladly paid the then-exorbitant sum of US$25 to take the train to the Pacific side of the isthmus in their dash to the California gold fields.

A nameless boomtown sprang up on Isla Manzanillo, but it was a squalid place notorious as a sink of vice and filth. There was no sewage or drainage system. Everything, including dead animals, was just tossed onto the

AMINTA MELENDÉZ: COLÓN'S FAVORITE DAUGHTER

One special day in Colón's history is November 5. On that day in 1903, separatists in Colón used a young woman, 18-year-old Aminta Melendéz, to smuggle a message to conspirators in Panama City about a plot to disarm Colombian troops that had landed in Colón to put down Panama's incipient revolution. Melendéz was the daughter of Porfirio Melendéz, Colón's police chief and one of the separatists. To do so, she had to walk right past swarms of heavily armed troops, and capture would likely have meant her execution.

The plot was never acted upon, but Aminta's bravery is still celebrated every November 5 as part of Colón's independence celebrations. Throughout her life, it was traditional for the president of Panama to visit her home to pay homage. Oddly, for a country that loves celebrations, this is not a national holiday, something that annoys Colón boosters.

unpaved streets or into the sea. And during the French era, so much wine was consumed in Colón that an entire street, still known by some as Bottle Alley, was paved with inverted wine bottles.

"Searching for the specialty in which [the town] excelled," wrote a disgusted 19th-century historian, H. H. Bancroft, "we found it in her carrion birds, which cannot be surpassed in size or smell. Manzanillo Island may boast of the finest vultures on the planet.... The very ground on which one trod was pregnant with disease, and death was distilled in every breath of air."

The town did not even merit a name until 1852, when it was dubbed Aspinwall in honor of one of the founders of the railroad. Panama was still a part of Colombia at the time, and officials in Bogotá rejected the name, insisting it be called Colón, the Spanish name for

Columbus. A feud over the name erupted between the Panama Railroad Company and Bogotá, resulting in much confusion until 1890, when the Colombian government began rejecting any letters with "Aspinwall" on the envelope. The railroad company finally gave in.

Colón's fortunes declined following the gold rush, but they revived again in the 1880s when the French began their doomed attempt to build a sea-level canal. Colón residents would later reminisce about this as a time when champagne was in far greater supply than the suspect local water. Then Colón burned to the ground in 1885 during the so-called Prestán Uprising and was rebuilt, primarily by the Panama Railroad Company. It wasn't until the French effort collapsed and the U.S. effort began that Colón began to be cleaned up and transformed into a modern city. The gringos installed sewers and plumbing, paved the streets, drained the swamps, and sanitized the whole place.

For the first half of the 20th century, Colón became a rather picturesque little city of three-story wooden buildings with long verandas, and white, neoclassical concrete buildings erected by the Isthmian Canal Commission. Front Street, which faced the railroad tracks and the port of Cristóbal, boasted elegant shops.

As Panama City and the Pacific side of the isthmus grew in importance, Colón again deteriorated. Toward the end of the 20th century, it became dangerous for visitors to wander past Front Street. Now, it's foolish even to venture that far. The fancy shops have long since disappeared.

SIGHTS
Gatún Locks

On the Pacific side of the Panama Canal it takes two sets of locks to raise or lower ships 85 feet (26 meters). Gatún Locks (visiting hours: 9 A.M.–4 P.M. daily), on the Caribbean side west of Colón, do the job by themselves. Each lock chamber is the same size as those on the Pacific—1,000 by 110 feet (almost 305 by 34 meters)—but there are three pairs of them on this side. That makes Gatún Locks absolutely massive, a little less than

© WILLIAM FRIAR

The swing bridge through the Gatún Locks gives a unique perspective on the locks' gates.

a mile (more than 1.5 kilometers) from end to end. It's an impressive sight.

Note: As dramatic as the locks are, most visitors based on the Pacific side of the isthmus are satisfied with seeing Miraflores and perhaps Pedro Miguel without making a special trip just to see these.

An observation platform up a long flight of stairs gives an excellent view of the locks, the Caribbean entrance to the canal, and Lago Gatún. There's another observation spot downstairs. It has a small-scale model of the entire canal. Bathrooms for tourists are in the building behind the model.

The number of tourists visiting the locks is increasing, but free bilingual talks, like the ones offered at Miraflores, are still sporadic here. The best bet to catch a talk is when a cruise ship disgorges its passengers for a tour.

If time and transportation allow, take a quick spin through the townsite of Gatún, next to the locks. The area is still under control of the Panama Canal Authority, and is well maintained—the grass is neatly cut, and the old houses and employee facilities are still in pretty good shape. A visit will give a taste of what life in the old Canal Zone looked like. However, canal expansion is bringing rapid change even to this area. Its days are numbered.

Gatún Dam

The huge (nearly 2.5 kilometers long) earthen Gatún Dam was built to create Lago Gatún (Gatún Lake), a vital part of the Panama Canal. It was the largest such structure in the world when the canal opened in 1914. The dam controls the flow of the mighty Río Chagres, a major obstacle to canal builders, and supplies electricity used at the locks and the surrounding communities. It's an awesome sight when the spillway is opened and the water comes roaring out. A small bridge runs right by the spillway, behind which there's a good view of the canal.

To get to the dam, cross over the swing bridge that spans the north end of Gatún Locks. The wait can be up to half an hour if a ship is transiting, but the bridge provides a fascinating fish's-eye view of the locks, since one actually drives through a lock chamber. Take the first left after the bridge and head up the road for about two kilometers.

Note: There is now a free car ferry across the channel that runs 5 A.M.–9 P.M. daily. But the wait can be as long as an hour, depending on ship traffic, for the three-minute ride. For safety reasons you're not even allowed out of the car. The ferry is meant primarily for heavy equipment and trucks too big for the swing bridge, which is far more interesting and comparatively speedy.

Fuerte San Lorenzo and Área Protegida San Lorenzo

This is one of Panama's newest protected areas. Its 12,000 hectares include a former U.S. military base (Fort Sherman), the impressive ruins of the Spanish fort of San Lorenzo, and four types of forest, including mangroves and freshwater wetlands. The United States left most of this forest standing, and, with the departure of the military, all kinds of wildlife have returned even to formerly populated areas. The big question is what happens next.

Conflicting demands are being made on the area. On the one side are those who want to preserve this vital ecosystem, restricting its use as much as possible to ecotourism and scientific research. This area is a crucial link in the biological corridor that runs the length of Panama, especially since so much of the land to the east and west of it has already been deforested. That also makes it a linchpin in the even more important Mesoamerican Biological Corridor, which runs the entire length of Central America. On the other side are those who see this entire region as prime real estate. Also, slash-and-burn farmers, hunters, and loggers began to invade the area after the departure of the U.S. military.

Still, it seems likely that those pushing for conservation will be at least partly successful. In the short term, only organized groups are being allowed into most of the protected area. That's probably just as well for now, because visitors really wouldn't want to wander around here by themselves. Besides the usual hazards found in a tropical forest, there is unexploded ordnance in the area. The U.S. military conducted jungle-warfare training and had a firing range here. For more information on the protected area, visit www.sanlorenzo.org.pa.

The ruins of Fuerte San Lorenzo (full name: Castillo de San Lorenzo el Real de Chagres) are impressive and surprisingly intact. They sit on the edge of a cliff with a commanding view of the Caribbean coast and the mouth of the Río Chagres, which the Spaniards built the fort to protect. The Welsh buccaneer Henry Morgan won a bloody battle here in 1671, destroying the then-wooden fort before crossing the isthmus to sack Panama City. San Lorenzo was rebuilt as a strong stone fort in 1680, but the British admiral Edward Vernon still managed to destroy it in 1740. It was rebuilt yet again in 1768, with more fortifications added in 1779. These are the ruins visible today. The ruins, along with those at Portobelo, were declared a UNESCO World Heritage Site in 1980. Note: Be careful wandering around the fort. There are few guard rails and it's easy to walk right off a roof or a cliff. Supposedly at least one tourist has.

The entrance to the area is 12 kilometers past Gatún Locks in the former U.S. military base of Fort Sherman; stay straight after crossing over the swing bridge at the locks. Fuerte San Lorenzo is another 11 kilometers up a rough but passable road. It's a left turn past the entrance to Fort Sherman. On the way to Fort Sherman, look for a water-filled channel near the road. This is the French Cut, a remnant of the doomed French effort to build a sea-level canal.

Once-popular Shimmy Beach, to the right as one enters Sherman, is covered in trash washed up from Colón—not the best spot for a swim. The turnoff to San Lorenzo is on the left. It's a 20-minute drive on a sometimes-rough road from here. Those without a four-wheel drive can ask about road conditions at the gate. The guard might possibly know.

From this point on the road is surrounded by beautiful rainforest. It's easy to feel transported back in time and imagine conquistadors and pirates hacking their way through this jungle in their relentless pursuit of treasure. Follow the signs to the fort, which is where the road ends. Road conditions get fairly rough toward the end.

SHOPPING
Zona Libre de Colón

The Zona Libre de Colón (Colón Free Zone, most shops 8 A.M.–5 P.M. Mon.–Fri., a few open on Sat.–Sun.) is the world's second-largest free-trade zone, after Hong Kong. A free zone is an area where goods can be imported and exported free from customs duties. Each year about US$10 billion worth of goods move through its 1,000 companies, which employ an estimated 15,000 permanent workers and thousands more temporary ones. It opened in 1948.

This isn't just some sort of oversized shopping mall: It's a shopping city within a city, one far wealthier and better maintained than the real city that surrounds it. It's huge—400 hectares—and is one of the most important contributors to Panama's GNP. Goods come mainly from Hong Kong, Japan, and the United States and go mainly to Central and South America.

The Zona Libre is primarily aimed at international wholesalers, not consumers. Individuals can shop at some stores there, but getting in and around the place, and getting purchases out, is a hassle. Think twice before going to the trouble: Many goods are just as cheap and far easier to get at airport duty-free stores or even at discount houses back home.

Cruise-ship passengers don't come here often, and stores aren't really set up to deal with them and deliver their purchases to ships. Passengers mostly go to the duty-free shops at Colón 2000, though the Zona Libre's prices are generally better.

Private cars and taxis are not allowed inside the free zone, which is just as well because the streets inside it are permanently gridlocked with trucks. There are parking lots just outside the zone. These are fairly safe, but be alert for muggers.

The main entrance to the Zona Libre is

at the intersection of Avenida Roosevelt and Calle 13. It's a maze inside, and streets are not well marked. Ask for directions to particular stores.

Visitors need a permit to enter the Zona Libre. The office is on the right as one faces the main gate. Have passports and return flight information handy. Be prepared for a long wait in line.

Good values inside the zone include 10-, 14-, and 18-karat gold, jewelry, cosmetics, liquor, high-end handbags, high-end scarves, watches, and stereo equipment. Digital cameras, at least so far, are not a great deal. Gold jewelry is sold by weight depending on the purity.

One store worth checking out is **Motta International** (tel. 431-6000, www.motta-int. com), not far from the main entrance. Motta carries a little bit of a lot of things, including watches, perfume, liquor, electronics, clothing accessories, and crystal. Sample brand names: Cartier, Lalique, Mont Blanc, CK, Fendi, Limoges Castel, Baccarat, and Camusso. The atmosphere is pleasant and the service gracious. Several gold shops are nearby.

Once you've made a purchase, you can't just waltz outside the Zona Libre with it. Remember, this is a free-trade zone and purchases are meant for export only. For those flying out of the country, stores will deliver purchases to the airport for pickup on the day of the flight. Stores tend to charge a minimum of at least US$15 for delivery and need at least two days to deliver the goods.

Here's the drill: Give the store clerk the flight information after making a purchase. He or she produces a receipt. On the day of the flight, arrive at the airport early and take the receipt to the **Equipaje Acompañado** office, which is downstairs and to the right of the main terminal as one faces the airport. Present your passports and tickets. The office is a sketchy-looking place and it'll feel like a minor miracle when someone actually produces the merchandise. There's a daily storage charge, so try not to buy things too far in advance of your departure. Allow plenty of time to transact all this business.

Some unwilling to jump through all these hoops smuggle goods out of the zone. After all, how can anyone tell when and where you bought that gold necklace you're wearing? But note that everyone leaving the zone is subject to search, and anyone caught with *contrabando* can be charged with a crime.

Colón 2000

This cruise port/shopping mall is on the eastern edge of Colón, close to the Free Zone. It opened in (surprise!) 2000 and was supposed to attract fleets of cruise ships to Colón and breathe life into the local economy. This has been slow to happen.   However, since 2007 Royal Caribbean Cruise Lines has been making Colón 2000 a home port, with its *Enchantment of the Seas* offering cruises originating from the port. These cruises are a hit, particularly with Panamanians, Colombians, and other Latin Americans who don't want to fool with the trouble and expense of flying to the U.S. to start a cruise. Some other cruise ships stop at the port as well. A long-planned Radisson hotel has finally opened in the port, catering to cruise passengers and those with business in the Free Zone.

Besides a handful of duty-free shops and some souvenir-trinket stores, most of which are only open during cruise season, the complex includes an enormous Super 99 grocery store, a Western Union branch, Hertz and Budget car rental offices, an ATM, and a couple of places to eat.

During the main cruise season (approximately Oct.–May), folkloric dancers perform for the tourists when a ship is in port. The place is pretty deserted when ships don't show up, and stores are having a rough time holding on.

Note that in spoken Spanish this place is called Colón Dos Mil.

SPORTS AND RECREATION
Bird-Watching

The central Caribbean coast is prime bird-watching country. The Audubon Society once identified 350 species on a single day during its annual Christmas Bird Count. Especially popular spots for birding include what is now the **Área Protegida San Lorenzo** and the **Achiote and Escobal Roads**, in Costa Abajo, west of Colón. The roads to Achiote and Escobal start just past Gatún Dam, though they can be tough to drive, particularly in the rainy season. Bird-watchers should go with an experienced guide.

Tours

Nattur Panama (tel. 442-1340, fax 442-8485, www.natturpanama.com) offers a popular tour, the Conquerors' Path, that includes a boat trip down the lower Río Chagres to Fuerte San Lorenzo, a tour of the fort, and a trip to Gatún Locks. The cost is US$85 per person with a four person minimum. It also offers tours of Portobelo, Gatún Locks, and (gulp) Colón, as well as fishing and birding trips. Consider the birding trip if the owner, Willie Martínez, is leading it; he's widely considered the best birding guide in the country. The group has a new nature lodge in Sabanitas.

ACCOMMODATIONS AND FOOD

Two international chains have recently opened hotels in Colón. There are also two okay local places. Be prepared to be rather isolated, as it is not safe to wander far outside the hotels in and around Colón, and there's nothing much around the more safer but more remote spots. Again, it's generally a better idea to make the Pacific side your base and just make day trips around here.

In Colón

There are several places to stay in or on the outskirts of Colón. The four listed here are the best and safest. Those staying in Colón should eat at their hotel. Otherwise, a reasonably safe dining option away from downtown Colón is **Café Iguana** (in Colón 2000, tel. 447-3570 and 447-3956, 10 A.M.–10 P.M. Mon.–Sat., US$5–12). In the Colón 2000 cruise port/shopping center, the café is upstairs and on the right as one faces the complex. It's a simple but pleasant place

to eat if the air-conditioner is working, with photos from the Panama Canal construction era on the wall and Middle Eastern music on the stereo. People come here for the Lebanese food, but other options include Mexican food, sandwiches, burgers, fish, meats, and pastas. If nothing on the menu looks appealing, there's also a Subway sandwich shop in the Colón 2000 complex, as well as a few other restaurants and cafés.

The **Meryland Hotel** (corner of Calle 7 and Santa Isabel next to Parque Sucre, tel. 441-7055, 441-5309, or 441-7127, www.hotelmeryland.com, US$38.50 s, US$49.50 d). The hotel was built in 2000 in a quiet, sparsely settled part of town. There's a long, narrow park outside and lots of school kids passing by on school days. It definitely feels like the safest place to stay in town. It's a modern, clean place with cheerful neo-Spanish colonial decor, featuring lots of glossy tile and ornate iron fixtures. Amazingly, the paint in the rooms started peeling soon after the hotel opened. All rooms have air-conditioning, cable TV, and phones. The hotel has parking and an Internet café. There's room service from the restaurant (open until 10 P.M. Sun.–Fri., later on Sat.) on the premises. Rooms are dark and the beds need replacing, but this is still a decent value in an okay neighborhood if you need to spend the night in Colón. Some of the houses near the hotel used to be quarters for Panama Canal employees during the Canal Zone days.

The **Washington Hotel** (2nd Street at the northwest end of Colón, tel. 441-7133, www.newwashingtonhotel.com, US$70 s/d) is now officially known as the New Washington Hotel, but no one will ever call it that. Built by the United States in 1913 on the site of a Panama Railroad Company guesthouse erected in 1870, it was once one of Panama's grand hotels. It was built at the order of President William H. Taft, a frequent visitor to Panama during canal construction days, first as Secretary of War and then as president. The hotel has hosted two American presidents (Taft and Warren Harding), a British prime minister (David Lloyd George), Will Rogers, Bob

© WILLIAM FRIAR

The view from the pool at the Washington Hotel is rather unusual.

Hope, Al Jolson, and others. But its decay has mirrored that of Colón itself.

Those glory days are long over. The Spanish-inspired colonial building and common areas are still lovely, if tattered, with brass railings, wrought ironwork, chandeliers, painted wooden beams, and marble stairs. And the hotel is built right on the edge of the sea, with a view of ships at anchor waiting to transit the canal. But the "new" rooms are still drab and musty, with spongy beds. They're large, however, and come with a mini-fridge. They are also significantly better than they were a couple of years ago, and more renovation work took place in 2010. Amenities include a bar, casino, nightclub, and a large pool right next to the seawall; sea spray sometimes splashes close to the pool. It's definitely worth a quick visit for those in the neighborhood, but most would probably prefer staying in the less historic but more comfortable surroundings of the Meryland Hotel, which has comparable rates. Note that even though the hotel feels safely removed from downtown, there have been reports of muggings on its spacious grounds.

The fairly new six-story, 103-room **Hotel Radisson Colón 2000** (Colón 2000, tel. 447-1135, US$120 s/d) is the most upscale place to stay in downtown Colón and the most convenient for those with a cruise to catch. It has good security and is in Colón 2000, which is kind of the city's Green Zone—a relatively safe part of the city. The rooms are pleasant enough, if a bit musty, and there's a restaurant, bar, and small gym and pool, but the whole place gives off a kind of sluggish, sullen Caribbean vibe. Two rooms on the 2nd floor are available, for an extra fee, with a stark balcony that looks out over the pool, but I advise avoiding these: the pool fills up with partiers blasting music, making these potentially the loudest rooms in the hotel. Try for a room that faces away from the pool and the waterfront if peace and quiet are important to you.

The new **❮ Four Points by Sheraton Colón** (Avenida A. Waked, Millennium Plaza, on the outskirts of Colón, tel. 447-1000, www.starwoodhotels.com, starts at US$209) is the fanciest place to stay on the Caribbean side of the canal area. It's a 15-story tower in a gated shopping complex, just off the main road leading into downtown Colón, It's in an industrial area right next to the Free Zone and close to nothing else, but it's certainly the most secure location you could hope for in Colón. The 230 rooms are spacious, attractive, and comfortable, with floor-to-ceiling windows, but not much to look out on (though some of us find it interesting to get a bird's-eye view on the city-within-a-city that is the Colón Free Zone). Service is friendly and attentive. Some of the rooms have a distant view of Limón Bay and the entrance to the canal. There's a restaurant, bar, and a small pool that's right next to the polluted Río Manzanillo.

Outside Colón

◖ **Sierra Llorona Panama Lodge** (tel. 442-8104, cell 6614-8191, www.sierrallorona.com, starts at US$75 s/d, including breakfast) is a lodge south of Colón that's popular with bird-watchers: Approximately 200 species of resident and migratory birds have been spotted in the surrounding forest.

Sierra Llorona means "crying mountain," an apt name for a place that sees rain 286 days a year. Expect predawn rains even in the so-called dry season here. The plus side of all that precipitation is evident in the lushness of the 200 hectares of private primary and secondary rainforest surrounding the lodge. There are four kilometers of well-maintained trails that start about a 10-minute walk from the lodge. Scientists frequent the area to study its flora and fauna, some of which is not found elsewhere. A new species of frog, *Atelopus limosus,* was discovered here in 1995. This is its only known habitat.

The "lodge" is really a sprawling private house with a separate building a short walk down the hill. There are seven rooms of various sizes; none is anything fancy, but they're clean and comfortable. They do not have air-conditioning, TV, or telephones. The lodge sits on a ridge 300 meters above sea level. Even this modest elevation is enough to give the place pleasant breezes in the morning and evening and views of the Caribbean, Limón Bay, and, at night, the lights of Colón.

There is also a campsite in the private reserve

with a *rancho,* outhouse, and rustic camp stove. Campers must bring their own tents. Rates are US$45 during the week, US$75 on the weekend per night for up to five campers. Day-trippers can walk the trails for US$10 per person. Meals at the lodge cost US$12–15.

The lodge offers all-inclusive packages, sightseeing tours, birding trips, and transfers to and from anywhere in Panama, including the airports and Colón train station.

Sierra Llorona is near the small community of Santa Rita Arriba (not to be confused with nearby Santa Rita). If you're coming from Panama City, it's reached by a right turn off the Transístmica a couple of kilometers before Sabanitas.

The **Hotel Meliá Panama Canal** (Avenida de Las Naciones Unidas, tel. 470-1100 or 470-1916, www.meliapanamacanal.com, US$126.50 s, US$148.50 d), a Spanish-owned 258-room resort, is a prime example of Panama's undying faith that if you build it they will come. So far, they haven't. The hotel has a striking location on the forested banks of Lago Gatún near the Área Protegida San Lorenzo in Espinar (formerly Fort Gulick), close to Colón and Gatún Locks. But it's not yet an area that attracts many tourists, and the base itself is still largely a ghost town.

The hotel was built from the remains of the U.S. military's notorious School of the Americas, which had a reputation for training Latin American dictators and torturers. Its parentage notwithstanding, it's quite an attractive hotel, with bright and cheerful Spanish-Mediterranean decor that tosses in a splash of Italian rococo. Rooms are large, with Spanish tile floors, cable TV, tasteful decoration, lots of dark wood, a minibar, and incredibly hard beds. Guests have also complained of wafer-thin walls and musty, poorly maintained rooms. Amenities include an impressive swimming pool, pleasant restaurant, piano bar, casino, business center, and so on. Its restaurant is inconsistent, in my experience.

The hotel also offers tours to Gatún Locks, motorboat and kayak rentals on Lago Gatún, fishing trips, and other activities. Package deals, especially on the weekend and during the rainy season, are often available.

The hotel is not far from Gatún Locks. To get to the locks from Panama City, turn left before the Cuatro Altos overpass outside Colón. Stay straight on this road, which snakes to the right, then back left, for about 1.5 kilometers. Take the second left onto Avenida de Las Naciones Unidas. Look for the Sol Meliá sign.

SERVICES

Colón has banks and a post office and such, but again it's just too dangerous to transact business in this city. The possible exceptions are listed here.

The Colón 2000 cruise port/shopping center has a few facilities of interest to tourists. The **Super 99** supermarket has a Citibank outlet and ATM, a cafeteria, and a pharmacy (10 A.M.–6 P.M. Mon.–Fri., 11 A.M.–3 P.M. Sat.). The store also carries everything from phone cards and cheap mobile phones to camping supplies.

The complex also has a **Western Union office** (tel. 441-7308, 9 A.M.–5 P.M. Mon.–Sat.). The **Colombian consulate** (tel. 441-6170 or 441-0114) is in an upstairs office nearby. **Budget** (tel. 441-7161) and **Hertz** (tel. 441-3272) rental car offices are open approximately 8 A.M.–5 P.M. Monday–Saturday. Duty-free shops (cruise passengers only) and souvenir shops may only be open during cruise-ship season.

There is a newish marina, **Shelter Bay** (tel. 433-3581, www.shelterbaymarina.com), at Fort Sherman, just west of the canal entrance. (The old Panama Canal Yacht Club at Cristobal was torn down suddenly in 2009.) It has a simple restaurant/bar serving burgers and such with nothing more than US$9, a small pool/whirlpool tub, table tennis, and free Wi-Fi, but there's little reason for anyone other than yachties to go all the way out there.

GETTING THERE AND AROUND

A quick and easy trip coast to coast is literally a 500-year-old dream. The dream has finally been realized with the completion of the Corredor Norte from Panama City to Sabanitas, not far from Colón. Depending on Panama City and Colón traffic off the highway, the trip should take no more than 1.5 hours, probably less. Expect it to take nearly twice that long via the old Transístmica. It's not worth it just to avoid the minimal toll.

Most visitors explore the area with a taxi "guide" or a tour operator. Look for tours that include at least a one-way train trip.

By Bus

The **Terminal de Buses de Colón** (on Avenida Bolívar, Colón's major shopping drag, and Calle 13) is a busy place and should be relatively safe, at least during the day, but be alert for pickpockets and backpack thieves. Any bus marked "Costa Abajo" can take you to Gatún Locks and the attractions west of them, including the bird-watching areas around Achiote (fare: US$1). For La Guaira and Nombre de Dios, look for buses that say "Costa Arriba," though be sure to confirm the bus is really going all the way to your destination. Details on a few of the more popular routes:

La Guaira: 9:30 A.M., 11:30 A.M., 1:30 P.M., 3:30 P.M., 4:30 P.M., and 5:30 P.M. The fare is US$2.85. Return buses leave La Guaira every hour or two 5:30 A.M.–1 P.M. The Sunday schedule is different, with buses running at 9:30 A.M., 12:30 P.M., and 3:30 P.M., returning at 10 A.M., 11 A.M., noon, 1 P.M., 2 P.M., and 4 P.M. This schedule changes a lot, so use these times only as general guidelines.

Nombre de Dios: 6 A.M., 9 A.M., 10 A.M., 11 A.M., noon, 1 P.M., 3 P.M., 4 P.M., and 5:45 P.M. Monday–Saturday; 9 A.M., 11 A.M., 1 P.M., 3 P.M., and 5:45 P.M. Sunday. The fare is US$2.75. Return buses run once an hour 4 A.M.–3 P.M.

Panama City: Buses leave every 20 minutes or so 4:30 A.M.–10 P.M. The fare is US$1.80, or US$2.50 for the express bus. Try to get the express, which takes about 1.5 hours. The slower buses can take up to twice as long to cover the same ground when traffic is bad.

Portobelo: 16 buses daily 6:15 A.M.–9 P.M. The fare is US$1.30. Return buses run about every half hour 4:30 A.M.–6 P.M.

By Taxi

A taxi anywhere within Colón should cost about US$1. Take taxis everywhere. A tourist walking in Colón is begging for trouble. To visit area tourist attractions, consider hiring a taxi by the hour. Watch out for fake taxis. Real taxis are yellow, and their license plate numbers match those painted on their doors.

Now that more cruise ships stop at Colón 2000, the taxis have organized into cooperatives and have established standard fares for tours, which they carry around as a laminated sheet. It's easy to find a taxi at Colón 2000 during cruise-ship season, though it may be difficult at other times.

These fares are aimed at cruise-ship passengers and are excessive, but at least there's some semblance of order and security if you go with these guys. And, as one cabbie told me, all rates are negotiable; you can make a deal for less if there are more taxis than passengers around.

Taxi cooperative fares include: US$3 for trips within Colón or to the Free Zone; Colón city tours for US$36 (1–2 people; think twice about this one because of security concerns—people have been mugged doing these); Gatún Locks tour for US$80, or US$160 for Gatún Locks and Portobelo (1–4 people), US$180 for a tour of the Pacific-side attractions, including Miraflores Locks, Casco Viejo, and Old Panama (1–3 people); and transfers to Tocumen International Airport (US$100 for one person, US$120 for two).

By Car

To get to Colón and Costa Abajo from Panama City, take the **Corredor Norte** toll highway to the end of the line. Cars have to finish the journey north on the old **Transístmica** (a.k.a. Transisthmian Highway, a.k.a. the Boyd-Roosevelt Highway).

At the Cuatro Altos (literally, "four stops") intersection, turn west (left) to get to Gatún Locks, Gatún Dam, and the Costa Abajo attractions. Stay straight for Colón. Roads aren't well marked, and highway construction, especially the new overpass at Cuatro Altos, has jumbled things up considerably.

Portobelo and the Costa Arriba

The stretch of coast east of Colón is known as Costa Arriba, which includes Portobelo, Nombre de Dios and its neighboring villages, and La Guaira, the jumping-off point for Isla Grande. For most of the way this is a lovely drive: It's quite striking to zip along the lush, quiet coastline and suddenly come upon the ruins of ancient Spanish forts.

Though the Spanish ruins scattered all over this seaside town hint at its long history, it still may be hard to believe that Portobelo (pop. 3,867) was one of the most important ports in the Spanish empire. Today it's sleepy and impoverished, the decaying houses of its current residents built near or in some cases into the crumbling stone ruins. It truly comes alive only on October 21, for the celebration of the Festival del Cristo Negro (The Black Christ Festival).

The town's poverty can be a bit intimidating, but visitors shouldn't have any problems if they come here during the day and stay alert. Note that Portobelo is one of the wettest spots on the isthmus.

A large swath of this area is part of Parque Nacional Portobelo, whose boundaries extend into the surrounding waters. The park is under increasing development pressure, however, as are the natural treasures that are not even nominally protected. Settlers are rapidly cutting down much of the lush forest in this area, and cookie-cutter suburban housing is going up along the beautiful coastline.

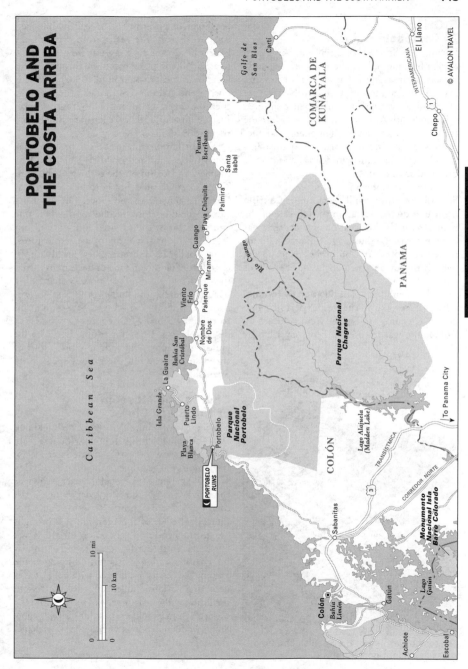

THE PANAMA CANAL

PORTOBELO AND
THE COSTA ARRIBA

Caribbean Sea

Golfo de
San Blas

Cartí

COMARCA DE
KUNA YALA

Punta
Escribano

Santa
Isabel

Playa Chiquita

Palmira

Cuango

Viento
Frío

Miramar

Palenque

Nombre
de Dios

Bahía San
Cristóbal

Río Cuango

PANAMA

La Guaira

Isla Grande

Puerto
Lindo

Playa
Blanca

Parque
Nacional
Portobelo

Portobelo

Parque Nacional
Chagres

PORTOBELO
RUINS

COLÓN

Lago Alajuela
(Madden Lake)

To Panama City

TRANSÍSTMICA

Sabanitas

CORREDOR NORTE

Monumento
Nacional Isla
Barro Colorado

Colón

Bahía
Limón

Gatún

Lago
Gatún

Achiote

Escobal

El Llano

INTERAMERICANA

Chepo

© AVALON TRAVEL

0   10 mi

0   10 km

SIGHTS
◖ Portobelo Ruins

During the Spanish-colonial era, the Costa Arriba became one of the most strategically important areas in the entire Spanish Empire. It was here that most of the incredible treasure of the Incas was brought after being shipped up from South America. All that wealth made the Caribbean coast a target of pirates and buccaneers for hundreds of years. The Spanish fortresses were constantly under siege and were captured several times.

Entering Portobelo from the west, the first Spanish structure you'll encounter is **Castillo Santiago de la Gloria,** on the left side of the road. It's the last incarnation of a fort that was built, destroyed, rebuilt, and tinkered with for more than 150 years and never ended up defending the town particularly well. These ruins date from 1753.

In the town itself is **Castillo San Gerónimo,** which dates from the same period. The nearby Customs House, the **Real Aduana de Portobelo,** was restored in February 1998 by

the Spanish government. If you hadn't seen its state before the restoration, you might have a hard time figuring out what was done to it. Still, the place has been through a lot: Originally built in or around 1630, it was seriously damaged in a 1744 attack, then rebuilt, then damaged again in an 1882 earthquake. Just a couple of walls were left standing before the restoration.

The little museum inside the building has recently been spiffed up with a few modern displays and a film on the history of the area. There's a small model of Portobelo's fortifications just outside the entrance. On the other side of the model is a second room where one can see a bit of the original foundation, but "exhibits" consist mainly of a few old tools, cannonballs, and mortars. There are also replicas of pre-Colombian tools and weapons mixed in with a few pieces of real pottery shards.

Admission to the **museum** (8 A.M.–4 P.M. Mon.–Fri., 8:30 A.M.–3 P.M. Sat.–Sun.) and to the neighboring Museo del Cristo Negro de Portobelo is US$1 for adults, US$0.25 for children. The price includes a guided tour of the displays, though the guides speak only Spanish.

Church and Museum of the Black Christ

The large white church nearby is the **Iglesia de San Felipe,** which is still in use. It dates from 1814, but its tower wasn't completed until 1945. It's famous as the home of the life-sized effigy of the Nazarene of Portobelo, better known as the Black Christ. The effigy, depicting Christ carrying the cross, normally resides on a podium to the left of the altar, but it is brought out to the center of the church for the Black Christ Festival (Festival del Cristo Negro), by far Portobelo's biggest event. The handsome altar of the church is adorned with gold images depicting various emblems of the crucifixion, including nails, instruments of torture, and the dice the Roman soldiers cast for Christ's robe. Small wooden carvings ringing the walls depict the stages of the cross.

Behind this church is the recently renovated

Portobelo was one of the Spanish Empire's most important ports.

© CLEA EFTHIMIADAS

THE PANAMA CANAL

THE BLACK CHRIST FESTIVAL

Every October 21, Portobelo comes back to life at the Festival del Cristo Negro (Festival of the Black Christ). It's quite a spectacle. Thousands throng the Church of San Felipe, home to the life-sized wooden effigy of the Nazarene of Portobelo, otherwise known as the Black Christ. Some come by foot from distant parts of Panama. Others come crawling on their hands and knees, their friends sweeping the ground in front of them free of debris or rocking a small shrine before their faces to keep the pilgrims' eyes on the prize. Still others let their companions pour candle wax on them as they crawl, as a further act of penance.

the Black Christ

What's this all about? There are several legends of the origin of the statue and its festival. One has it that the statue arrived in Portobelo on a ship bound for Cartagena, Colombia. A storm arose each time the ship tried to continue on, and the crew members decided the effigy wanted to stay in Portobelo. Variations on the story have the ship either sinking in the storm and the statue washing up on shore or the crew members throwing the statue overboard in fright. Then, the story goes, on October 21, 1821, Portobelo residents prayed to the Black Christ to be spared from a cholera epidemic sweeping the isthmus; they were.

Each October 21 since, people from all over Panama who have prayed to the Black Christ for help with an illness or other problem give thanks by making a pilgrimage to Portobelo, often performing some act of devotion or penance along the way. Most find just walking here from Sabanitas in the heat and humidity to be sacrifice enough. That's a walk of nearly 40 kilometers; health stations are set up along the way for those who need help. There are no portable toilets anywhere, so you can imagine what Portobelo is like by the end of the night.

Devotees often wear purple robes in emulation of the Christ statue. Those who have asked for a major favor make the pilgrimage for several years. Each year they cut a bit of cloth off the hem of their robes. Some of the robes end up awfully short, presenting the interesting paradox that the most pious also have the most scandalous attire.

The festival is a blend of the sacred and profane in other ways as well. For many, it's an excuse to get very drunk and dance all night. It's not unusual to see a pilgrim in resplendent purple robes making his way to town carrying a beer. The whole vibe is sort of spring-break-with-self-flagellation.

Once in Portobelo, pilgrims crowd into the church to worship before the Black Christ. Many offer necklaces, which are draped around the effigy. Mass is held, and devotees burn hundreds of votive candles and sing songs about the festival and the effigy. Late at night the statue is carried out of the church and paraded through the streets on a litter. The procession takes a long time, as the statue is carried with a peculiar rocking, back-and-forth gait: three steps forward, two steps back.

Those in Panama on October 21 should make an effort to attend the festival. It's a fascinating spectacle. But be forewarned it's also a major mob scene. Be prepared for epic traffic jams and stay alert for pickpockets. Traffic is generally stopped several kilometers outside of Portobelo, forcing even non-pilgrims to walk in. It's best to drive or come with a tour operator. Trying to get a return bus is a nightmare; many pilgrims go back home right after they arrive, so the line for the bus is hours long even in the morning. One strategy is to hire a boat near Portobelo and motor into town, skirting the traffic. Suggest this to your tour guide ahead of time, or call a hotel, restaurant, or dive operator to arrange it. The Coco Plum Eco-Lodge is a good bet.

© KAREN FRIAR

THE PANAMA CANAL

Iglesia de San Juan de Dios, home to the new **Museo del Cristo Negro de Portobelo,** which displays several of the robes donated by Panamanians for the festival, some of which are more than 100 years old. It's well worth a visit. Among the more famous robes is the one donated by the champion boxer Roberto "Manos de Piedra" (literally, "hands of stone") Durán.

The Black Christ figurine's robes are changed twice a year, and each is used just once. The statue is adorned with a red wine–colored robe for the Black Christ Festival held each October 21. This is changed to a purple one for Holy Week. Many of the robes are donated anonymously. Some are simple and others are quite ornate, done up in gold trim and the like, and cost thousands of dollars to make.

If this museum is locked, walk over to the museum at the *aduana* and ask the attendant to open it for you.

Other Forts

If exploring these ruins and buildings doesn't satisfy your historical urges, hire a water taxi

© BONNIE KAY SPINDLER

Pilgrims walk to the Black Christ Festival from all over Panama.

near Castillo Santiago de la Gloria for US$2 per person to take you across the bay to visit what's left of **Castillo San Fernando,** which was designed in the 1750s to replace Castillo San Felipe, demolished in 1739 by Edward Vernon, a British admiral. Unfortunately, American builders used rock from the fort in the construction of the canal, further damaging what little that time, war, and pirates had spared. Also, a short, steep hike above town leads to some fortifications with a good view of the bay; if you're heading east, it'll be on the hill to the right just before town. Drivers can park by the side of the road.

SPORTS AND RECREATION

Portobelo has long been a popular spot for scuba divers and yachties. There are also appealing spots for beach lounging. It's possible to hike in the forests of Parque Nacional Portobelo, but this should be attempted only with an experienced guide.

In 1996, John Collins, the creator of the original Ironman triathlon in Hawaii, visited the Portobelo area on a yacht and decided it would be a perfect place for a triathlon. The first **Portobelo Triathlon** (www.triathlon.org.pa) was held in 1997, and it has become an annual event. It is held the second Sunday of March and increasingly attracts world-class athletes. The event includes an 1,800-meter swim from La Guaira to Isla Grande and back, a 35-kilometer bike ride to Portobelo, and a 10-kilometer off-road run in the Portobelo area.

Diving and Snorkeling

There are 16 dive spots around the Portobelo area, with attractions that vary from coral reefs and 40-meter-deep walls to a small airplane and a cargo ship. The best diving in the area is off the rocky Farallones Islands, a fair boat ride away. There's a chance of seeing nurse sharks, spotted eagle rays, and schools of barracudas there. But any honest dive operator will be the first to admit the diving around Portobelo is for the most part just average: Expect no more than 10 meters of visibility on a typical day. And visibility is quite volatile: up to 30 meters on a great day, and down to 3 when it rains (several rivers empty into the ocean here; the diving is better in the dry season). Portobelo does, however, have two major things going for it: The diving is inexpensive and it is easily accessible.

Portobelo dive operations have been struggling to survive out here since the closing of the American bases at the end of 1999; military personnel and their families constituted much of their business. Most of the operations have disappeared, and the new ones come and go faster than I can keep track of. As always when you dive, bring evidence of certification and ask to see the dive master's credentials.

The one that seems to hang on no matter what is **Scubaportobelo** (tel. 448-2147 in Portobelo or 261-4064 and 261-3841 at the main office in Panama City, www.scubapanama.com). It's five kilometers west of Portobelo. The spot is pleasant, with a wooden mirador built on rocks over the ocean. This is the Portobelo division of Scubapanama, Panama's largest dive operation.

Divers pay for everything separately here. Complete equipment rental is US$20, including one full tank. The second tank costs US$6, and additional tanks US$4.50. Boat transport is about US$7–15, depending on the destination.

Playa Blanca

Playa Blanca is a pretty little beach, by far the nicest in the area, situated on a remote cove at the tip of a forested peninsula 20 minutes by boat from Portobelo. There are no roads leading to it and it is accessible only by sea, which gives it the feel of an island. Day-trippers can hire a water taxi to the beach from the ruins of Castillo Santiago de la Gloria in Portobelo for about US$25 per couple.

Other Activities

Selvaventuras (tel. 442-1042, cell 6680-5309) is a shoestring operation started in 2001 by four eager guys from Colón. They no longer have an office, but they still offer excursions. These include jungle hikes to waterfalls, overnight camping in the forest, horseback riding, fishing trips, and boat transport to nearby beaches. Prices vary depending on the destination and length of trip. For instance, a tour of the closest forts (which you can really do yourself) costs US$2 per person; a half-day hike is around US$20 per person. The guides speak a little English.

There's now a **zipline ride** west of Portobelo in an area called Río Piedras. It's operated by a group called **Panama Outdoor Adventures** (cell 6030-9515, http://panamaoutdooradventures.com), west of Portobelo. This zipline consists of nine cables strung between platforms that are up to 30 meters above the forest floor. The tour lasts about 2.5 hours, including a forest walk. On the way to Portobelo, the group posted signs shortly after the turn-off to María Chiquita and before Río Piedra. Panama Outdoor Adventures offers other adventures, such as river tubing for US$25 and nature walks for US$10.

ACCOMMODATIONS

The best hotel in the region, and one of the best in Panama, is the Coral Lodge, accessible only by plane to Kuna Yala or by a bumpy boat ride from Miramar.

Scubaportobelo (tel. 448-2147, starts at US$52.80 s/d) has cabins meant primarily for divers, but during the frequent slow periods landlubbers can get a room here too. The rooms are basic, small, with low ceilings and crammed with beds. But they have air-conditioning. Up to four people can be squeezed into each room, but you'd better really like each other. There's a basic restaurant on the premises.

The best accommodations around Portobelo are at ⓒ **Coco Plum Eco-Lodge** (tel. 448-2102 or 448-2309, www.cocoplum-panama.com, US$45 s, US$55 d). It's just before Restaurante La Torre on the way to Portobelo. It's a cheerful place, with conch shells ringing the doorframes of the rooms and murals of fish painted on the walls inside. Rooms are clean and pleasant, though a bit dark. There are a dozen rooms, most with air-conditioning.

FOOD

ⓒ **Restaurante Los Cañones** (about six kilometers before Portobelo, tel. 448-2980,

11 A.M.–10 P.M. Mon.–Fri., 8 A.M.–10 P.M. Sat.–Sun., under US$10) is a charming little open-air place on a small bay. Looking out at the Caribbean, it's easy to imagine Sir Francis Drake's ships gliding past on the way to a sneak attack. Seafood is the specialty at this popular place. The food is good. Try the *pulpo en leche de coco* (octopus in coconut milk).

A little farther down the road is **Restaurante Las Anclas** (tel. 448-2102, 10 A.M.–8 P.M. daily, US$8), at the Coco Plum Eco-Lodge. It's a cute place entirely decorated with detritus recovered from the sea, including sewing machines, the wheel of a boat, wheelbarrow parts, gas containers, and so on. Seafood is again the specialty here. The chef is Colombian, so be sure to order the enormous, Colombian-style *patacones* (fried green plantains).

Restaurante La Torre (tel. 448-2039, 10 A.M.–7 P.M. Mon.–Fri., 7:30 A.M.–7 P.M. Sat.–Sun., under US$10) is a cute little open-air restaurant just beyond Restaurante Las Anclas. It's easy to spot because of the stone tower that gives the place its name. Again, seafood is its main thing, though I've had better luck with Los Cañones and Las Anclas. The service is friendly and courteous. There's an illustrated capsule history of Portobelo, in Spanish and English, along one of the wooden walls.

A new open-air Italian restaurant opened in the middle of nowhere about a 10-minute drive east of Portobelo on the road to Nombre de Dios: **Don Quixote Pizzeria** (cell 6682-6103, 8 A.M.–9 P.M. Fri.–Sun.). They were just beginning to bake their fresh bread and pizza when I passed through, and the smells were fantastic. Only open on the weekends, it's almost certainly the best restaurant on the coast.

INFORMATION AND SERVICES

Just as you enter Portobelo there's a large, unmarked wooden building, one of the biggest structures in town, at a fork in the road. This is yet another CEFATI building (tel. 448-2200, 8:30 A.M.–4:30 P.M. Mon.–Fri.), a tourist center run by IPAT, Panama's government tourism institute. It's usually rather barren, but the last

time I was there it had a few devil masks used in the *congos* dances and entries in a competition to design a new bus stop.

Note that the last gas station on this entire stretch of road is at María Chiquita, roughly halfway between Sabanitas and Portobelo.

GETTING THERE
By Bus

Portobelo is about 100 kilometers from Panama City. Those coming by Colón-bound bus from Panama City will have to change buses in Sabanitas. Do not go all the way to Colón, and make sure ahead of time that the bus stops in Sabanitas, which is on the Transístmica 60 kilometers from Panama City. Passengers are let off near the El Rey supermarket. Buses between Sabanitas and Portobelo run only during daylight hours. The fare is US$1.25.

The main bus stop in Portobelo is next to the Iglesia de San Felipe. Colón-bound buses leave Portobelo every half hour 4:30 A.M.–6 P.M. To get from Portobelo to Panama City, take a bus to Sabanitas (Colón-bound buses stop there). Get off at Sabanitas, cross the highway, and take any of the frequent long-distance buses running from Colón back to Panama City.

By Car

Take the Sabanitas exit off the Corredor Norte. The turnoff to Portobelo is at Sabanitas, on the right side of the Transístmica just past the El Rey supermarket as you head north, in the direction of Colón. Stay on this road to Portobelo, about 35 kilometers away.

GETTING AROUND

Portobelo is a small town and easily walkable, though be alert and try not to wander around alone, as in any impoverished town.

A **water taxi** (tel. 448-2266; ask for Carlos) is on the edge of the bay next to Castillo Santiago de la Gloria, the first fort as you enter Portobelo from the west. It's next to the Restaurante Santiago de la Gloria. A trip across the bay to the ruins of Castillo San Fernando is US$2 per person. Prices to area beaches range from US$10 per couple to nearby Playa

Huerta up to US$25 per couple for a trip to Playa Blanca. Prices are likely negotiable if business is slow.

NOMBRE DE DIOS AND VICINITY

Eight tiny towns—villages really—run along the coast east of Isla Grande. Five of these are linked by a road, which is in remarkably good condition. All look pretty dismal and deserted, especially during the day, when their inhabitants are out working in the fields or fishing in the ocean.

The first five—**Nombre de Dios, Viento Frío, Palenque, Miramar,** and **Cuango**—are lined up one after another on a lonesome, 30-kilometer stretch of road that runs along the edge of the sea. The last three—**Playa Chiquita, Palmira,** and **Santa Isabel**—are even more isolated, separated from the others by the Río Cuango. This river is known for gold, and it still attracts wishful-thinking prospectors. The road ends at the river, and those final three towns are accessible only by boat. Santa Isabel is the last town before the Comarca de Kuna Yala (the San Blas Islands). All these towns are so sleepy they're practically comatose.

Frankly, there isn't much reason for tourists to come to this part of Panama, at least these days. Though some entrepreneurs are making noises about opening up Costa Arriba to tourism, little has happened so far and there doesn't seem to be a whole lot of potential. The beaches aren't that great, the area is in the middle of the boonies, and the lovely tropical forest covering its rolling hills is being hacked and burned as quickly as possible to make way for cattle farms.

Historically, this is the home of so-called Afro-Colonials, the descendants of escaped African slaves from the Spanish era. These escaped slaves, known as *cimarrones,* slipped away and established hidden towns called *palenques.* They would emerge from the forest from time to time to raid Spanish mule trains along the Camino Real, more to harass their former captors than for treasure that was useless to them.

It's fun to think that the anglers chatting with you about the tides may very well be descended from *cimarrones* who helped Drake in one of his famous exploits.

In modern times, Costa Arriba has attracted settlers from Los Santos province. They are famous or notorious, depending on your perspective, for their prowess at cutting down trees. Having mostly deforested their own province, they're diligently working on doing the same to this area, which borders a vitally important national park.

Sights

The first, largest, and most famous of the little towns is **Nombre de Dios** (pop. 1,053), about 25 kilometers east of Portobelo. It was the original Caribbean terminus for the Camino Real, the overland route used by the conquistadors to transport plunder from the destruction of the Inca empire. The first European to lay eyes on the area was Rodrigo de Bastidas during his voyage of discovery of the isthmus of Panama in 1501. Columbus rode out a terrible storm here in 1502. Legend has it that Nombre de Dios (name of God) got its name when the unlucky Spanish explorer Diego de Nicuesa ordered his beleaguered and starving crew to take refuge in the harbor, shouting, "Let us stop here, in the name of God!"

Nombre de Dios was a poor, shallow harbor and proved nearly impossible to defend. Sir Francis Drake attacked it in 1572, though a wound forced him to retreat. He returned in 1595 and sacked it. The Spanish abandoned Nombre de Dios and moved the Caribbean end of the Camino Real to the far better and more defensible harbor of Portobelo in 1597. Nombre de Dios quickly faded away.

Today it is a poor, out-of-the-way, oceanside settlement of squat cinderblock buildings connected by dirt roads, as are the other towns along this road. There's nothing to recall its rich past except a modern-era sign that reminds you this humble place is one of the oldest surviving towns in the Americas. The left fork leads to the old part of town, inhabited mainly by anglers. The right fork leads to the "new" side, which is where most of the settlers from Los Santos province live. There's an artificial water channel that runs right through the middle of town; the builders of the Panama Canal scooped up sand from Nombre de Dios to build Gatún Locks after the Kunas turned them away from beaches in the San Blas Islands.

Festivals

These sleepy towns live for festivals, especially Carnaval and their *fiestas patronales,* the saint's day corresponding to the anniversary of the town's founding. These dates are the best bet to catch the colorful, African-derived dances known as *congos.* Some *fiestas patronales* and other local celebrations in the region include April 27 (Nombre de Dios), June 8 (Santa Isabel), June 19 (Playa Chiquita), June 24 (Palmira), July 31 (Viento Frío), September 8 (Palenque), and September 24 (Río Indio). It's not worth making a trip all the way out here just for one of the celebrations, but those who plan to visit anyway should bear those dates in mind.

On October 12, Viento Frío celebrates a big Día de la Raza festival, the Latin American version of Columbus Day. In recent years, of course, attitudes toward that day have become ambivalent throughout the Americas, with some seeing it as a more appropriate time for mourning than celebration. It could be fascinating to attend such an unusual Columbus Day commemoration in an area Columbus actually visited.

Water Activities

Water sports are the main attraction. If you go for a swim, beware of the undertow and rip currents. There is also some scuba diving in the waters off the coast. Wrecks of Spanish ships are still being found out here, including a 500-year-old one discovered in 1998 just off Nombre de Dios that some believe is the *Vizcaína,* one of the four ships used by Columbus on his fourth and final voyage to the Americas. It's well documented that the *Vizcaína* was in fact abandoned in these waters, but studying this wreck and establishing

its identity has been a slow process mired in controversy and red tape. However, the ship appears to date from the early 16th century, which makes it exceptionally rare whoever its captain was. Note that shipwrecks are off-limits to divers, and scavenger-hunting around them is a serious crime.

It's possible to hire local boatmen in these towns for trips to Kuna Yala. However, it's a bad idea. The trip takes a minimum of 1–2 hours in small, open boats on a sea that can quickly turn rough. I've been on quite large boats out here, even a small cruise ship, that bounced around like toys in a bathtub. I would never make the trip in one of the little *pangas* (fishing boats) in this area. Bear in mind that some of the greatest navigators in history have lost ships in these waters.

Skilled, safety-conscious captains with well-maintained boats are in short supply in this area, and it may very well be risky to make the trip. At the very least, go with a captain who has life jackets, or bring your own. Also note that just because a boatman fishes for a living, doesn't make him a good seaman; some around here are notoriously accident-prone.

Practicalities

There are few services of any kind in this remote, neglected part of the country. Most visitors arrange tours from Portobelo or Panama City. There's a pay telephone in each town, but that's about it. There are no banks or ATMs. The best chance of finding official help if one encounters trouble is in Palenque, the administrative headquarters of the district.

There are a few basic places to stay in this area, and as usual camping on the beach is free. This area doesn't get many foreigners, though, so people may wonder what you're up to. It's probably a good idea to let the police and townspeople know you come in peace.

As always, camp only in a tent. *Chitras* (sand flies) are likely to be the least of your troubles. This is cattle country, which means vampire bats, and it's poor and neglected, which means a risk of disease-carrying mosquitoes.

There is a small, open-air seaside restaurant

in Miramar that offers heaps of fried seafood and other simple fare for a couple of dollars.

Getting There

To get to this area by car, first drive through Portobelo, making sure you have a full fuel tank. After about eight kilometers there'll be a crossroads known, logically enough, as El Cruce. Turn right here.

After about 13 kilometers there's a rickety suspension bridge. Grit your teeth and drive over it. The first sizable settlement is Nombre de Dios (15 kilometers from El Cruce, about 25 minutes). The paved road ends a little past Nombre de Dios, turning into a rocky dirt road that's passable in a regular car most of the way. The road continues through Viento Frío (8 kilometers past Nombre Dios), and then through nearby Palenque, Miramar, and Cuango, which are bunched together within a few kilometers

of each other toward the end of the road. The road gets rough beyond Miramar, requiring a four-wheel drive in the rainy season, before coming to a sudden end at the especially run-down Cuango, on the edge of the wide mouth of the Río Cuango.

A small gas station just east of Miramar is the only one in the entire region east of María Chiquita.

Getting to these remote areas by bus can be a hassle, as service is neither frequent nor speedy. Those coming from Panama City can take a Colón-bound bus to Sabanitas and get off at the El Rey supermarket. Look for buses with "Costa Arriba" or the name of the particular destination painted on the windshield. Buses also run between Nombre de Dios and the Colón bus terminal. It's also possible to hire a taxi in Sabanitas or Colón, but the fare will probably be rather steep, depending on the destination.

Isla Grande

This is the closest of the Caribbean islands to the mainland. It's mainly a place for locals who want a quick dose of natural Caribbean beauty and tranquility and don't mind that the hotels and restaurants are generally mediocre and the place a noisy party scene at times. Those planning to go to Bocas del Toro or the San Blas Islands can easily give Isla Grande a miss; those archipelagos have much more to offer. It's quite a humid place; be prepared for some serious afternoon napping.

Isla Grande is not really all that grand—it's about five kilometers long and 1.5 kilometers wide and has around 1,000 inhabitants, most of whom live in the small town that runs along a single waterfront path facing the mainland. It consists mainly of a handful of simple hotels, some run-down houses, and a few tiny stores and open-air restaurants. The island is only a few hundred meters from the mainland.

Though Isla Grande has a couple of small beaches, this is not the place for vast expanses of sand. What the island mostly offers is the

chance to laze about and enjoy some beautiful views of the forested mainland, clear blue ocean, and palm-covered nearby islands.

The beauty of this place has in the past been marred by the trash inhabitants and visitors tossed into the crystal waters. Little wonder the coral nearby is in sad shape. Recently, however, clean-up campaigns have greatly improved the look of the area. Less-disturbed spots are a short boat ride away.

Isla Grande tends to be dead during the week, especially in the rainy season. At these times, there are few dining options, and some of the hotels may be closed. Those who visit during a dry-season weekend, however, will likely find plenty of people having a rowdy good time and blasting music late into the night. Bear that in mind when considering a hotel in town.

SIGHTS

The best, and most popular, stretch of beach on the island is in front of the Hotel Isla

Grande. A better and less crowded beach is on Isla Mamey, a tiny, uninhabited private island with relatively calm, shallow waters. It's possible to snorkel or scuba dive here. This is a popular destination for boat tours. These tours usually include a trip near the mainland through a channel lined with beautiful mangroves. This channel has come to be known locally as the "Tunnel of Love."

West of Isla Cabra is **Bahía Linton,** one of the safest anchorages between Colón and Cartagena, Colombia. (There's another anchorage at **José del Mar,** better known as José Pobre. It's in a cove next to the isolated village of Cacique, between Portobelo and Isla Grande.)

ACCOMMODATIONS AND FOOD

For such a small place, there's quite a range of places to stay on Isla Grande, though no great bargains. Only the lucky or the easy-to-please will think they're getting their money's worth, at any budget. In the hoteliers' defense, it's not cheap to offer big-city amenities in such a remote area. And the cheaper places tend to cater not to foreign couples on a budget but rather to Panamanian weekend partiers who shoehorn as many people as possible into a room.

Most of the hotels are clustered close together along the main strip overlooking the water. Sister Moon is farther along still, on an isolated bluff accessible by a rocky path. Bananas Village Resort is clear on the other side of the island, secluded from everything.

Food on the Caribbean side of the isthmus contains ingredients rarely found elsewhere in Panama. Finding a restaurant on Isla Grande that's both open and serves these dishes can be a challenge, though. Be on the lookout for seafood in coconut sauce and moderately hot red-pepper "congo" sauce.

At meal times, count yourself lucky just to find a place that's open, especially during a rainy-season weekday. The hotels are the best bet for food. Several of the ones along the main drag have simple, open-air restaurants right on the water's edge. What they may lack in quality

they somewhat make up for in rustic island ambience.

Cabañas La Cholita (tel. 448-2962, Panama City tel. 232-4561, US$49.50 s/d), offers 12 rustic rooms in a cheerful garden setting. There's no hot water, but there is air-conditioning and a simple restaurant. This place is often packed on the weekend.

◖ Hotel Sister Moon (tel. 226-9861, cell 6681-6740, www.hotelsistermoon.com, starts at US$35 s, US$70 d, including breakfast) sits by itself on the hills of a palm-covered point overlooking a picture-postcard bay, rolling surf, and the emerald green mainland. The main accommodations consist of a series of thatched-roof cabins on stilts, dotted along the hillside. Each has a double bed. The cabins are rustic but pleasant and tastefully designed. It's like staying in a fancy tree house, and the breeze here is a welcome respite from the island's humidity. There are also eight cabins with bunk beds for backpacker-types. A small, rocky beach with a good surf break is close by. A sun deck juts out right over the surf break, and next to it is a little restaurant and a pub with a billiard table and dartboard. There's also a small, murky swimming pool that's more scenic than inviting. The one odd thing about this place is that it seems to live a perpetual twilight existence. In my many trips to Isla Grande, I've never been there when the place was in full swing. That can be great for those seeking seclusion, but those who make reservations far in advance should confirm before arrival that everything's up and running.

Bananas Village Resort (Panama City reservations tel. 236-8489, cell 6661-6750, resort tel. 448-2252 or 448-2959, www.bananasresort.com, package rates start at US$140 s/d, including breakfast) is the fanciest place on Isla Grande. It's on the north side of the island, tucked away in a lovely, isolated spot facing the ocean. It's accessible only by boat or forest trails. A variety of different, confusing packages are available.

The place, which opened in 1998, is nicely designed, cheerful, and small. The rooms are in eight A-frame cottages on stilts. Each cottage

PRIVATE ISLANDS

On the boat ride over from the mainland to Isla Grande there's a developed island that's largely deforested except for palm trees. This is **Isla Cabra,** a private island. It is not open to visitors, but those with binoculars should keep their eyes open for macaw nests.

At the entrance to **Bahía Linton** is **Isla Linton,** another private island one should not set foot on. However, boat tours of the waters near Isla Linton are popular because of the monkeys that have been introduced here, which boatmen summon by clapping. Be careful: Tourists often feed the monkeys (something you should *not* do), which has made them bold around people. A monkey bit a woman in 2002.

The owners of Isla Linton, Allan and Rosalind Baitel, are conservationists working in conjunction with Florida State University to create a research facility on the island.

The Baitels also run an animal rescue and rehabilitation program behind their home on the mainland (again, this is not open to the public). Here they try to heal animals wounded by hunters or otherwise injured or interfered with, after which they return them to the forest. In some cases, all they can do is give animals a safe home, as is the case with a couple of jaguars that some people kept as "pets" before the couple rescued them. These jaguars would no longer be able to survive in the wild. Unfortunately, Panama has no program for breeding jaguars in captivity, so the Baitels have been trying to find a way to export the jaguars to a country that does have such a program. Ironically, the international CITES treaty, created to protect endangered species, prohibits the export of animals that were not actually bred in captivity, which has proved to be a major obstacle.

has three units: two large rooms below and one very large room above. They're the same price, but the upstairs ones are nicer. All have balconies, hammocks, and air-conditioners. There's a swimming pool, and guests have free access to sea kayaks, snorkeling equipment, beach chairs, and so on. Boat excursions to the surrounding area are extra.

Though the resort is attractive, the service has been bad each of the several times I've stayed here over the years, and the place is not well-maintained. Guests can't count on hot water, for example.

The open-air restaurant is the most expensive on the island, with entrées that reach the double figures. I've had okay meals here, though the food tends to be deep-fried with heavy sauces.

PRACTICALITIES

There is no tourist office on the island. The island also lacks banks, ATMs, or much in the way of services at all. Bring cash. Tours and recreational activities are generally arranged through the hotels.

There is not much to do on Isla Grande at night other than booze it up, and there aren't even many places to do that. Patron saint festivals are held on June 24 and July 16 and involve celebrations on both land and sea.

GETTING THERE AND AROUND

Access to Isla Grande is from the down-at-the-heels village of La Guaira, 120 kilometers from Panama City. La Guaira is 20 kilometers from Portobelo; just drive through town and continue along the same road. The trip from Panama City takes about two hours.

The road is often riddled with potholes. At the entrance to La Guaira look for a sign that reads Isla Grande. Take the left turn indicated. Park by the dock for free, or in the partially fenced-in area on the left, behind Doña Eme's kiosk, for US$2 a day. The fee probably buys nothing but a specious sense of security, but I always go for it anyway. Obviously, don't leave anything valuable in the car. When you come back, one or more teenagers may hit you up for change for "watching" the car. It's up to you whether to give one of them anything, but they can be unpleasant if you don't.

Those coming by bus from Panama City should take a Colón-bound bus and make sure it stops in Sabanitas. Get off at the El Rey supermarket in Sabanitas, which is right on the highway, and switch to a bus bound for La Guaira. The whole ride should cost less than US$5.

Any of the boatmen hanging around the dock at La Guaira will take you to the island (don't expect life jackets). The ride takes about five minutes. The fee is US$1 per person to be dropped off in what passes for downtown Isla Grande. Expect to pay double at night, which you should avoid since few boats in these waters have lights. Boatmen may ask for more if they think you're a clueless gringo. Settle on a price ahead of time, and clarify whether the rate is per person or per group.

Nearly every place on Isla Grande is easily accessible by foot. Those who want to visit Sister Moon or Bananas and don't feel like hoofing it can hire a boatman down by the town waterfront for a couple of dollars. Your hotel can probably arrange for a boat back to the mainland at the end of your trip, but if not it should be easy to find one along the waterfront.

BOCAS DEL TORO

It's hard to leave Bocas del Toro. It's a terribly relaxing place, and at the same time it exudes a funky, romantic charm that has something untamed about it. The place is filled with colorful characters nursing drinks in dilapidated wooden bars or running rustic hotels on remote beaches. It's the kind of Caribbean hideaway one expects to find only in old Bogart films.

And it's just gorgeous. It has emerald islands, pristine beaches, turquoise waters, dense forests, barely explored mountains and rivers, sprawling coral gardens, spooky mangrove channels, and exotic wildlife. Four species of endangered sea turtles still visit the waters of Bocas, coming ashore by the hundreds during nesting season to lay their eggs. Little Swan's Cay, really just a rock in the ocean, is the only Panamanian nesting site of the beautiful red-billed tropicbird. That's just one of more than 350 species of birds attracted to the region. Sloths, caimans, dolphins, neon-colored frogs, and, of course, lots of small tropical fish are easy to spot in the archipelago. No wonder more than a dozen countries have shot their versions of the *Survivor* TV series here.

The people help make Bocas special. More ethnicities and nationalities are represented on the islands than anywhere in the country outside of Panama City. And you are more likely to hear English spoken here than anywhere in the country, period. The islands have long been home to the Ngöbe-Buglé, as well as the descendants of Afro-Caribbean immigrants from the English-speaking islands of Jamaica, San Andrés, and Providencia, many of whom came down to work on the region's enormous banana

COURTESY OF ECLIPSE DE MAR ACQUA LODGE

HIGHLIGHTS

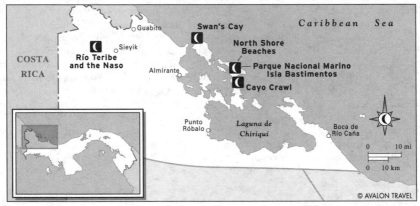

◖ **Swan's Cay:** This picture-postcard islet is one of the last stands of the red-billed tropicbird (page 171).

◖ **Cayo Crawl:** This is the quintessential Bocas scene: rustic restaurants floating just above the surface of a glassy sea and tropical fish swimming just below (page 203).

◖ **North Shore Beaches:** Isla Bastimento's north shore beaches offer pristine sand, monster waves, and brilliant red frogs (page 204).

◖ **Parque Nacional Marino Isla Bastimentos:** The Cayos Zapatillas, which offer cave diving and a pair of undeveloped islands, are the highlight of this marine park (page 207).

◖ **Río Teribe and the Naso:** Explore the beautiful forest world of a little-known indigenous people who are fighting for their survival (page 221).

LOOK FOR ◖ TO FIND RECOMMENDED SIGHTS, ACTIVITIES, DINING, AND LODGING.

plantations. Most of the hotels and restaurants on the islands are owned by Europeans and North Americans. And the mostly young and boho tourists Bocas attracts are coming from all over the world.

For most visitors, Bocas del Toro means the archipelago that stretches about 100 kilometers from Boca del Drago in the west to Isla Escudo de Veraguas in the east. For them the mainland is just a place to fly over or drive through on the way to the islands. But the rest of the province of Bocas del Toro has plenty of spectacular natural beauty, including the Caribbean side of the enormous Parque Internacional La Amistad and the wetlands of San San Pondsack. Lucky hikers, at least those who venture far up into

the mainland forests, may encounter endangered mammals such as Baird's tapirs. All five species of cats found on the isthmus, including jaguars, are hanging in in the most remote reaches of the forest, but the chance of coming across one is slim. The forests are also still home to indigenous peoples trying to hold on to their culture and ancestral lands. This includes the little-known Naso, who welcome visitors to their communities up the Río Teribe.

More than just about anyplace else in Panama, the Bocas archipelago has taken off as a tourist destination. Backpackers spill over from Costa Rica, and more affluent expatriates from the United States and Canada have bought up beachfront property to build their

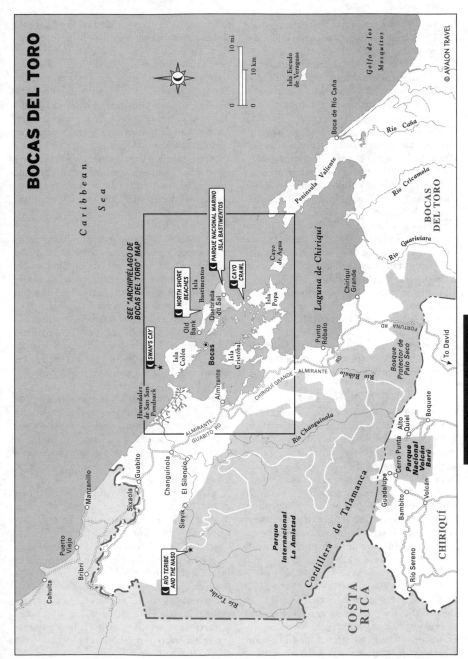

BOCAS DEL TORO

Caribbean Sea

10 mi

10 km

0

0

Isla Escudo de Veraguas

Golfo de los Mosquitos

© AVALON TRAVEL

Boca de Río Caña

Río Caña

BOCAS DEL TORO

Río Cricamola

Peninsula Valiente

Río Guariviara

SEE "ARCHIPIÉLAGO DE BOCAS DEL TORO" MAP

PARQUE NACIONAL MARINO ISLA BASTIMENTOS

Cayo de Agua

Laguna de Chiriquí

Chiriquí Grande

NORTH SHORE BEACHES

Isla Bastimentos

CAYO CRAWL

SWAN'S CAY

Isla Colón

Old Bank

Quebrada de Sal

Isla Popa

Punto Róbalo

Bocas

Isla Cristóbal

CHIRIQUÍ GRANDE — ALMIRANTE

Río

FORTUNA RD.

To David

Humedales de San San Pondsack

Almirante

Río Róbalo

Bosque Protector de Palo Seco

ALMIRANTE

Alto Quiel

Boquete

GUABITO RD.

Río Changuinola

Cerro Punta

Parque Nacional Volcán Barú

Manzanillo

Guabito

Changuinola

El Silencio

Guadalupe

Bambito

Volcán

CHIRIQUÍ

Puerto Viejo

Sixaola

Slevik

Parque Internacional La Amistad

Río Sereno

Bribri

RÍO TERIBE AND THE NASO

Río Teribe

Cordillera de Talamanca

Cahuita

COSTA RICA

BOCAS DEL TORO

fantasy tropical getaways. Everyone is in the real-estate business these days, and condos and big resorts are in the works. But the funk factor is still strong and the islands are not yet a tourist trap. Long-term expats are already grumbling that Bocas isn't what it used to be, but so far the new arrivals have mainly just brought more international flavor and a broader range of lodging, dining, entertainment, and activity possibilities. For now, backpackers and surfers can still find a decent bed for less than US$10 and a full meal for US$3, and those with more money to spend can stay in relatively luxurious surroundings and dine on surprisingly good international cuisine.

Bocas's biggest shortcoming is the rain. It's one of the wettest regions in Panama. The rain never completely stops even in the "dry" season, but even in the rainy season storms usually blow through quickly. Rainfall tends to be heaviest in December and July.

The islands are evolving rapidly from a great backpackers' secret into a more upscale destination. Two bits of advice for those contemplating a visit: 1) Hurry and visit while they still have that quirky, rustic Bocas charm and beauty, and 2) do your part to make sure that charm and beauty survives.

PLANNING YOUR TIME

Given both the area's remoteness and its many attractions, getting anything out of Bocas requires a bare-minimum stay of two nights. Three or four is better. There is enough to keep visitors happy for a full week, especially since the Caribbean heat and pace of life has a tendency to slow even hyperactive types down and make hammock time pretty appealing. Consider staying a bit longer than you think you'll need. Weather is unpredictable in Bocas, and it's not unheard of for it to rain virtually non-stop for three days. It'd be a shame if you had to leave just as the sun finally came out.

The **Archipiélago de Bocas del Toro** is only part of the province of Bocas del Toro, but it's the part that the great majority of visitors come to explore. The islands have far better accommodations, food, and attractions and a more pleasant climate than the mainland towns.

Most visitors stay in **Bocas town** on **Isla Colón.** Nearly everyone has to at least pass through Bocas town, since it has the only airport in the archipelago, and water taxis from the mainland come only here. (It's easy to make day trips from the islands to mainland destinations, though visitors who head up the Río Teribe to visit the Naso or Parque Internacional La Amistad should plan to spend at least one night in the forest.)

Note: Here's where the names start getting confusing. The town, the archipelago, and the province share the same name, often shortened simply to "Bocas." And just to really mess you up, the whole of Isla Colón is sometimes referred to as "Isla Bocas."

Bocas town is getting pretty built up, and its main streets are often congested with an absurd number of cars, taxis, and trucks. This is a big change from just a few years ago, when nearly everyone got around on foot. It's still a fun place, but travelers who come to town expecting a sleepy backwater paradise increasingly complain the town is too busy and overrun with gringos. A closer look reveals it's actually impressively diverse, with people from all over Panama and the wider world. The vibe is still more Euro-bohemian than Florida outpost, and the *Margaritaville* set tends to confine itself to a few watering holes. But those who want a more traditional *bocatoreño* experience will want to spend as little time as possible in Bocas town. Increasingly, the most impressive new places to stay in the archipelago are going up outside Bocas town.

The other commonly visited islands are east of Isla Colón, which is the point of departure to all of them. The services diminish the father east you go. **Isla Carenero** is the second-most developed island, and it's just a few minutes by boat from Isla Colón. The western tip of **Isla Bastimentos** has the second-biggest town in the archipelago, **Old Bank.** Most of the rest of the island, the largest in the archipelago, is sparsely populated, but its natural attractions draw many visitors. **Isla Solarte,** though it starts just 10 minutes by boat from Isla Colón, still mainly draws visitors just to

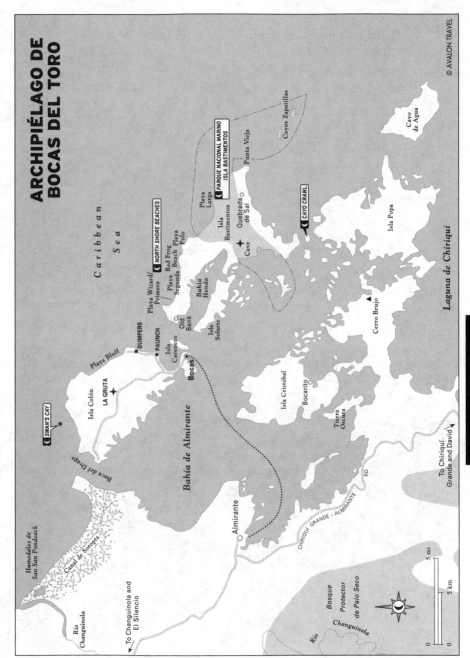

ARCHIPIÉLAGO DE
BOCAS DEL TORO

© AVALON TRAVEL

Caribbean Sea

SWAN'S CAY

Boca del Drago

Isla Colón

LA GRUTA

Playa Bluff

DUMPERS

PAUNCH

Isla
Carenero

Bocas

Humedales de
San San Pondsack

Río
Changuinola

Canal de Soropta

Bahía de Almirante

NORTH SHORE BEACHES

Playa Wizard/
Primera

Playa
Red Frog
Segunda Playa Beach Playa
Polo

Old
Bank

Isla
Solarte

Bahía
Honda

Cave

Playa
Larga

Isla
Bastimentos

PARQUE NACIONAL MARINO
ISLA BASTIMENTOS

Punta Vieja

Cayos Zapatillas

Cayo
de Agua

Quebrada
de Sal

CAYO CRAWL

Isla Popa

Almirante

Isla Cristóbal

Bocarito

Tierra
Oscura

CHIRIQUÍ GRANDE – ALMIRANTE
RD

Cerro Brujo

Laguna de Chiriquí

To Chiriquí
Grande and David

Bosque
Protector
de Palo Seco

Río
Changuinola

To Changuinola and
El Silencio

0   5 mi

0   5 km

BOCAS DEL TORO

Hospital Point, a snorkeling/diving spot at its western tip. The other islands are more remote and still largely undeveloped, though a few secluded little hotels, eco-lodges, and guest-houses are scattered among them, usually in relatively undeveloped spots. So far only Isla Colón has cars.

Those who want to cover a lot of ground or have any kind of nightlife should probably stay in Bocas town or Isla Carenero. Most of the tour operators and interisland water taxis are based in Bocas town. Carenero is so close to Bocas town it's actually easier and quicker to get to and from town from there than it is from other parts of Isla Colón.

Getting back and forth to Bocas town from other parts of Isla Colón and the other islands can easily become time-consuming and expensive, though some hotel packages in the more remote areas include daily trips. Those staying in the remote parts of Bastimentos should plan on spending most of their time in that general area, as Bocas town is a long boat ride away. One strategy is to stay in Bocas town part of the time and spend a night or two in a more distant spot before or afterward.

Afternoons and evenings are the best time to explore Bocas town, which is generally dead during the day; many restaurants are even closed for lunch. The restaurants and few nightspots start to wake up as the sun goes down. It's also easy to arrange a night turtle-watching trip to **Playa Bluff** during nesting season.

Throughout the archipelago, the great beaches and pounding surf tend to be on the north side of the islands, where there's nothing but ocean until Jamaica. Generally the sea is too rough for safe swimming. The water tends to be glassy on the southern side of the islands and in sheltered bays on the eastern sides and that is where the good snorkeling is.

High season on the islands is November or December–April. Prices are higher then and everything is more crowded; some places get booked up. But this traditionally can be the wettest time to visit the islands. Weather in Bocas is usually best during the "mini" dry

© WILLIAM FRIAR

Playa Bluff, Isla Colón

DID YOU HEAR THE ONE ABOUT THE BOA AND THE MONKEY?

When I was last in Bocas, everyone was talking about a rather dramatic episode involving a 2.5-meter boa constrictor and an adult howler monkey. The boa had tried to swallow the howler, but it was too big for him and was slowly choking him to death. Reinier Plooijer, the co-owner of Playa Bluff Lodge, had raised exotic reptiles in his native Holland, so he was the closest to a snake vet around. His solution? He stuck his hand down the boa's throat, extracted the now-deceased monkey, flushed out the boa's digestive tract, then resuscitated it with an air hose. After a few days and a course of antibiotics, the boa was well enough to slip back into the forest, where it has hopefully learned to eat more modest portions.

Don't believe it? The story, with photos, is here, in the local *Bocas Breeze* newspaper: http://bit.ly/greedyboa.

seasons of September–October and February–March. However, in the last couple of years weather in Bocas has been even more unpredictable than usual. It was quite dry in December 2009, for instance, but rained almost non-stop when I visited in the allegedly drier time of late February. Again, try to stay long enough to improve your chances of hitting a dry patch.

Turtles nest on the beaches from about March to October. In other words, if all the planets align correctly, those who visit between September and October may find lower prices, fewer people, dry weather, calm seas, and some busy turtles.

Don't forget to factor in the time needed to get to and from Bocas, which is still quite isolated from the rest of Panama. The quickest way is to fly from Panama City to Isla Colón or, for the few who are more interested

in exploring the mainland than the islands, to Changuinola. The flight takes less than an hour.

Getting to Bocas by land is a much longer affair, though there are now good roads and frequent bus service. A road leads east from the Sixaola-Guabito border crossing with Costa Rica to Changuinola and Almirante, the jumping-off points to the archipelago.

A new road links Almirante with Chiriquí Grande and from there to the rest of Panama. The building of this road has greatly diminished the importance of Chiriquí Grande; there is no longer any water-taxi service from there to the islands, and no reason for travelers to visit it. Outside of Chiriquí Grande, the Fortuna Road heads south over the Continental Divide and to the Interamericana (Interamerican Highway). This is the road link between Bocas and the rest of Panama.

SAFETY CONSIDERATIONS

The archipelago is a friendly, mellow place, and reports of violent crime are rare. But the increase in tourism has brought an increase in petty theft. Don't leave valuables unattended, particularly on the north shore beaches of Bastimentos.

Be alert when using the ATM. Women should also use common sense in dealing with strange men, some of whom can be aggressive in their attentions. Do not tell strangers which hotel you're staying at, for instance.

Booze-fueled brawls are not uncommon. Treat dive bars in the archipelago with as much caution as you would those back home. Be respectful, and certainly don't look for a fight.

Land scams are a problem in Bocas. Be skeptical of great deals on beachfront property or get-rich-quick plantation schemes. Legitimate cheap land in Bocas is a thing of the past. Also, establishing land ownership is tricky in Bocas, Panamanian land-use laws are complicated, and tropical forestry is much harder than many think. Do plenty of research and get legal and technical advice from trustworthy sources. As always, if it seems too good to be true, it is.

Placid seas can turn rough quickly, especially

on the north side of the islands, and the distances between the islands can be deceptively great. Never go on a boat trip of any length without a life jacket. Avoid long night trips since few boats have lights. Traditional *cayucos* (traditional dugout canoes) are fun to paddle, but they're easy to flip, so watch out.

Dengue fever is now a problem in hot climates worldwide, but on my most recent Bocas trip I met a surprising number of people who'd recently contracted this serious illness, including three innkeepers. Many first-time visitors worry about malaria, but the risk is significant only in poor and remote regions of the province. These diseases are spread by mosquitoes, not *chitras* (sand flies). However, *chitras* can carry leishmaniasis. The best defense for all of these diseases is to minimize insect bites.

These warnings aside, most visitors will only have to worry about too much sun and an impulse to stay in Bocas forever.

A FEW (ECO-)FRIENDLY SUGGESTIONS

1. Do not touch coral. Coral is alive and can take years to recover from even minimal contact. Some coral is endangered and protected by international law: To be on the safe side, don't buy coral jewelry.

2. Hire local boatmen and guides. This offers them an alternative to fishing and hunting and gives the local community a stake in preserving their surroundings. Encourage them to take it slow and not toss anchors into coral fields.

3. Stay at small, low-impact places such as the environmentally friendly La Loma Jungle Lodge and Tesoro Escondido.

4. Team up with others for boat tours. It saves money and lessens the disturbance caused by boats that motor through the same popular spots day after day.

5. Do not take "souvenirs" of any kind from the beaches or forests.

6. Stick to established trails.

7. Do not eat sea turtle meat or eggs, or any other endangered species. For one thing, it's illegal. Avoid lobster, which is overfished and locally endangered. There are more decent vegetarian alternatives on the islands than in most parts of Panama.

8. Buy indigenous handicrafts, if possible, directly from the makers.

9. Visit community-development projects such as Proyecto ODESEN, Soposo Rainforest Adventures, and the Ngöbe restaurant in Bahía Honda.

10. Consider volunteering locally, or making a donation to legitimate projects. U.S. residents can make a tax-deductible contribution to the nonprofit Nature Conservancy, which works in Bocas del Toro and elsewhere in Panama. Contributions can be made online (http://nature.org) or by mail (The Nature Conservancy, Attn: Treasury, 4245 N. Fairfax Dr., Suite 100, Arlington, VA 22203, U.S.A., tel. 800/628-6860).

11. Report poaching or signs of environmental destruction to ANAM's hotline (tel. 500-0855, ext. 1111). These *denuncias* can also be made online (www.anam.gob.pa/denuncia_web/default.asp). If enough visitors complain it may have an impact.

12. Don't litter, of course. But also consider picking up and packing out trash left by others.

13. A new group of local businesses called The Bocas Sustainable Tourism Alliance (cell 6086-2231, info@discoverbocasdeltoro.com, www.discoverbocasdeltoro.com) is getting off the ground. They have an office on the ground floor of the building that houses Om Café, on Avenida E between Calle 1 and Calle 2. Contact them for more information and suggestions on how you can help.

Environmental Concerns

Bocas del Toro is one of the loveliest parts of Panama, and it's still relatively unspoiled. The protected areas of the mainland include a large chunk of the enormous Parque Internacional La Amistad and the buffer forest that surrounds it, as well as the wetlands of San San Pondsack. The islands are home to an important national park, Parque Nacional Marino Isla Bastimentos. Bocas is a crucial link in the Mesoamerican Biological Corridor that extends from southern Mexico to eastern Panama.

Even the unprotected parts of the province are still largely undeveloped. Most of the land remains covered with forest, including primary evergreen forests with century-old trees that soar above 30 meters. The hundreds of animal and thousands of plant and insect species here include many that are endangered and some that are found nowhere else on earth.

But Bocas del Toro is under increasing human pressure. For decades the main disrupters of the environment were vast banana plantations. These were created by clearing forests and wetlands and kept alive through the unregulated use of pesticides, fungicides, and fertilizers, to which workers were exposed and which ran off into the rivers and sea.

Now other troubling developments are coming to Bocas, and coming fast. New roads are allowing the incursion of subsistence farmers and cattle ranchers to formerly inaccessible areas. A vivid example of the rapid deforestation that follows can be seen along the new Chiriquí Grande–Almirante Highway, where lush evergreen forests are already disappearing. The waters are also being over-fished, with lobster in particular locally threatened. The national mania for teak farming has spread to Bocas; there have been reports of acres of diverse, species-rich native trees being illegally cut down to plant this nonnative tree, which local wildlife has little use for as a habitat. And there is a strong push to dam the powerful mainland rivers, which have the highest hydroelectric potential in the country but which run through land that is home to both indigenous peoples and important ecosystems.

But on the islands at least, the greatest human impact is caused by tourists and resident expatriates. Seeing tourism come to an area as relatively untouched as Bocas del Toro always provokes mixed feelings. It's so easy to destroy what attracts people to a place like this in the first place. But ecologically sensitive tourism might, with luck, help preserve its natural beauty and maybe even help its people.

It's encouraging to see new tourism operations popping up that try hard not only to be low-impact but to help restore the land and water around them to a healthy state, and who support neighboring indigenous communities. During your stay, please do your part to keep Bocas beautiful and wild for generations to come by seeking these places out and treading as lightly as possible.

HISTORY

When Christopher Columbus sailed into what is now Bahía Almirante in 1502, on his fourth and final voyage, he likely would have found a land long settled by several indigenous peoples. Columbus barely mentions the area, however, and he soon pushed on east with his worm-eaten ships and exhausted, demoralized crew. He was intrigued to find natives wearing large gold discs around their necks, who told him there were rich gold fields on the mainland. Today's indigenous peoples still talk of lost gold mines in the remote highlands.

It's often said that Columbus gave the Bocas islands and other geographical features their names, but there is no evidence of this. It appears they were later named in his honor, such as Isla Colón (i.e., Columbus Island), Isla Cristóbal (Christopher Island), and Bahía Almirante (Admiral's Bay). Columbus does refer to a place called Bastimentos, but this is believed to be the name he gave to Nombre de Dios in eastern Panama.

The earliest evidence of habitation on the coast and along the river valleys dates from 600 B.C. For years the best-known archaeological site was Cerro Brujo on Península Aguacate, an oddly shaped peninsula that juts out between Isla Cristóbal and Isla Popa. It appears to have been a small village whose inhabitants subsisted on farming and fishing, including the hunting of manatees. But in 2002 archaeologists discovered evidence of what appears to have been a large and culturally sophisticated settlement at Boca del Drago on Isla Colón. They believe it was occupied in A.D. 900–1150. Excavation is ongoing and the significance of the site is still being determined.

During the days of Spanish exploration and conquest, the Naso people, also known as the Térraba or Teribe, appear to have been the dominant group, living by the rivers of the mainland, along the coast of Bahía Almirante, and even as far north as Isla Colón. Today they are barely hanging on, with a population of just 3,800 in Panama and a few hundred over the border in Costa Rica. They are now vastly outnumbered by the Ngöbe-Buglé, the largest indigenous group, not just in Bocas but in all of Panama. Tiny populations of Bri Bri and Bokota also remain.

Pressure from the Spanish, tribal warfare, and the introduction of European diseases decimated the indigenous populations. Some, including the Dorasque, were wiped out altogether.

But the Spanish never consolidated their hold on Bocas del Toro. That allowed the incursion of enterprising pirates and traders from England and other countries, the beginning of the international mix the region retains to this day. Early traders dealt in such items as the shell of the hawksbill turtle and coconut, but bananas eventually became the region's most important commodity.

The descendants of English-speaking Afro-Caribbean immigrants are among the longest-established residents of the islands. The earliest of these were brought over as slaves by English traders, but later arrivals came to work for the banana companies. Most trace their ancestry to Jamaica and the Colombian-owned Caribbean islands of San Andrés and Providencia. They are still a dominant cultural force in both Bocas town and, especially, Old Bank on Isla Bastimentos, where Guari-Guari, a Bocas-specific variety of so-called Panamanian Creole English, is still widely spoken.

The banana business began to take off in Bocas toward the end of the 19th century, attracting American and German planters. In 1899 the giant United Fruit Company (now known as Chiquita Brands International; the local division was called the Bocas Fruit Company) took over the whole show. It established its headquarters in Bocas town, which was founded in 1826 but until that point was a sleepy village. The company built a hospital on the tip of Isla Solarte, an isolated area now known as Hospital Point, to quarantine patients with infectious diseases such as yellow fever and malaria. The hospital is long gone, but a headquarters building the company constructed in 1905 became Hotel Bahía, which was recently renovated but retains a few reminders of its history.

The early 20th century was a boom time for Bocas del Toro. Bocas town became a hub for international commerce and one of the most important "cities" in Panama. It was prosperous enough to attract foreign consulates and support three (by some counts five) newspapers.

The islands' prosperity didn't last long, however. A fungus wilt that came to be known as Panama disease decimated the banana plantations on the islands and coastline. The company was forced to shift its operations to the mainland, to the area between the Changuinola and Sixaola Rivers, and over the border into Costa Rica. By 1920 the importance of the islands had declined dramatically. Even the hospital was shut down, as it was too far a trek for company employees on the mainland. The mainland banana plantations continue to thrive, however.

The province saw a few other notable events in the 20th century, including some grim ones. In 1902 it was the scene of a battle in the Thousand Days War, a Colombian civil war fought mostly in Panama (at that time still part of Colombia). And in 1921, Costa Rica occupied Guabito and Almirante as part of a border dispute with Panama. The United States put an end to both these conflicts.

In 1904 a fire in Bocas town, then as now built mostly of wood, destroyed an estimated

160 buildings. Three other major fires followed in the next 25 years.

The province is one of the most seismically active parts of Panama. On April 22, 1991, the border area between Costa Rica and Panama was struck by an earthquake, measuring 7.5 on the Richter scale, that was felt as far away as El Salvador. Costa Rica was hardest hit, but Bocas del Toro suffered greatly. The earthquake killed two dozen people in the province, injured hundreds more, and left thousands homeless. Changuinola and Almirante, on the mainland, sustained most of the damage. There have been other sizable earthquakes since then, but none nearly as damaging.

For most of the 20th century, though, Bocas remained a rather placid place. It has long been seen in Panama as a backwater province, and it still feels culturally and geographically quite separate from the rest of the country. It is now experiencing its second major boom, though this time the lucrative crops are tourists and retirees rather than bananas.

Isla Colón

By far the most developed island in the archipelago is Isla Colón, and by far the most developed part of Isla Colón is the town of Bocas del Toro, at the southeast tip of this large (61 square kilometers) island. Bocas town is nearly an island in its own right; it's connected to the rest of Isla Colón by a slender isthmus.

Almost all the archipelago's hotels, restaurants, tour outfits, and visitor services are in Bocas town. Most of the action is on either side of Calle 3, the broad main street that runs along the water's edge on the east side of town. (It's officially Calle Ephraim S. Alphonse, though no one calls it that.) The busiest section extends from the town plaza, Parque Bolívar, down to the ferry pier. The area west of Calle 3 is mainly residential, as is the section on the northwest waterfront, which is known locally as "Saigon."

Bocas town is laid out in a grid pattern, with numbered streets running more-or-less north to south and lettered avenues running more-or-less west to east. But the streets aren't well marked and there isn't even universal agreement on which road is which: The avenues above Avenida D are called different things on different maps. Fortunately, the town is small enough it's hard to get lost.

A road leads north out of town, past the fairgrounds, where the annual Feria Internacional del Mar is held, and over an isthmus. The road forks north of town. This area is known locally as the *i griega* (literally "Greek i," Spanish for the letter "y," pronounced "ee-gree-EG-a"). The east fork heads up the east coast of the main island, becoming increasingly rough but leading to the island's best beaches. The west fork leads to a road that cuts diagonally across the island. About halfway along the road is La Gruta, a cave popular with those into bats. The road dead-ends at Boca del Drago, a little beach area on the northwest side of the island about 14 kilometers from Bocas town.

SIGHTS

Several of the sights on and around Isla Colón are most easily—or only—accessible by boat. Except for those who bring a car over by ferry, which is rarely worth it, getting around on land usually requires hiring a taxi, renting a bike, or hoofing it, though a bus now makes a few daily trips between Bocas town and Boca del Drago.

Isla Colón has forests and other caves to explore, but don't attempt this without a knowledgeable guide. Night trips to turtle-nesting spots are popular during nesting season, from about March to September. Just wandering around little Bocas town night or day can be a colorful experience in multicultural people-watching. Be sure to venture beyond Calle 3 to get a feel for the non-touristy parts of town.

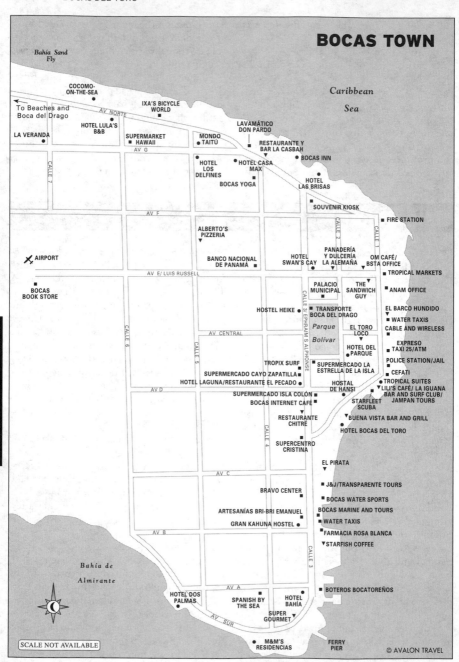

BOCAS TOWN

Bahía Sand Fly

Caribbean Sea

COCOMO-ON-THE-SEA

IXA'S BICYCLE WORLD

To Beaches and Boca del Drago

AV NORTE

HOTEL LULA'S B&B

LA VERANDA

SUPERMARKET HAWAII

AV G

MONDO TAITÚ

LAVAMÁTICO DON PARDO

RESTAURANTE Y BAR LA CASBAH

BOCAS INN

HOTEL LOS DELFINES

HOTEL CASA MAX

BOCAS YOGA

HOTEL LAS BRISAS

CALLE 7

AV F

SOUVENIR KIOSK

FIRE STATION

ALBERTO'S PIZZERIA

AIRPORT

BANCO NACIONAL DE PANAMÁ

HOTEL SWAN'S CAY

PANADERÍA Y DULCERÍA LA ALEMAÑA

CALLE 2

CALLE 1

OM CAFÉ/ BSTA OFFICE

TROPICAL MARKETS

AV E/ LUIS RUSSELL

BOCAS BOOK STORE

PALACIO MUNICIPAL

THE SANDWICH GUY

ANAM OFFICE

CALLE 3/ EPHRAIM S ALPHONSE

HOSTEL HEIKE

TRANSPORTE BOCA DEL DRAGO

EL BARCO HUNDIDO

WATER TAXIS

CALLE 6

AV CENTRAL

Parque Bolívar

EL TORO LOCO

CABLE AND WIRELESS

CALLE 5

HOTEL DEL PARQUE

EXPRESO TAXI 25/ATM

TROPIX SURF

SUPERMERCADO CAYO ZAPATILLA

POLICE STATION/JAIL

SUPERMERCADO LA ESTRELLA DE LA ISLA

CEFATI

HOTEL LAGUNA/RESTAURANTE EL PECADO

TROPICAL SUITES

AV D

HOSTAL DE HANSI

LILI'S CAFÉ/ LA IGUANA BAR AND SURF CLUB/ JAMPAN TOURS

SUPERMERCADO ISLA COLÓN

BOCAS INTERNET CAFÉ

STARFLEET SCUBA

RESTAURANTE CHITRÉ

BUENA VISTA BAR AND GRILL

CALLE 4

HOTEL BOCAS DEL TORO

SUPERCENTRO CRISTINA

EL PIRATA

AV C

J&J/TRANSPARENTE TOURS

BRAVO CENTER

BOCAS WATER SPORTS

ARTESANÍAS BRI-BRI EMANUEL

BOCAS MARINE AND TOURS

GRAN KAHUNA HOSTEL

WATER TAXIS

FARMACIA ROSA BLANCA

AV B

STARFISH COFFEE

CALLE 3

Bahía de Almirante

AV A

BOTEROS BOCATOREÑOS

HOTEL DOS PALMAS

SPANISH BY THE SEA

HOTEL BAHÍA

SUPER GOURMET

AV SUR

M&M'S RESIDENCIAS

FERRY PIER

SCALE NOT AVAILABLE

© AVALON TRAVEL

Playa Bluff

There are no real beaches in Bocas town, and the waterfront is too busy to make wading in the water here much fun. True beaches start north of the isthmus, on the main part of Isla Colón. The best beaches start about a 15-minute drive from town up the east coast. The surf is usually too rough to land boats anywhere along this part of the island. You can bike to the beaches, but the rocky dirt road gets a bit rough in places and it's not an easy ride in the sun.

Those unfamiliar with the island's topography get scandalized at what taxis sometimes ask to make the run up to Playa Bluff. They're not trying to rip you off: Part of the "road" here is really just a path along the beach and through estuaries. The road was better in 2010 than I've seen it in 12 years of visiting, but all it takes is one big storm to wash away big chunks. Sometimes only four-wheel-drive vehicles can make it out there, and even they often have a punishing ride.

Expect to pay about US$8–10 per carload, one way, to get to the beginning of the nice beaches, near La Coralina (an inn with an attractive public restaurant/bar on a ridge). The cost to get to the end of Playa Bluff is US$15–20. Prices go up or down depending on the state of the road. Taxis don't cruise this area looking for rides, but if you have a drink or a meal at La Coralina or Tesoro Escondido (another good option), the staff should be able to call a taxi for you when you're ready to leave.

The difficulty in getting there, and the big waves that pound the beach, mean it's usually possible to have a stretch of beach pretty much to yourself.

The nicest beach is Playa Bluff, about a 25-minute drive from town. It's absolutely gorgeous and often deserted during the week. This is also an important nesting site for endangered sea turtles. The surf can get rough here and is usually too dangerous for swimming, or even for wading above one's knees, though it's a good spot for surfers. Around September–October, however, the winds die down and the water turns to glass; you can even snorkel during this

© WILLIAM FRIAR

Tesoro Escondido has one of the best views on the islands.

calm spell. At least, that's what they tell me— I've never been in Bocas at that time, though I have seen the pictures and it's like a different world during that season.

The road ends just past Playa Bluff, after which the only way farther up the coast is by foot. About an hour hike away is **La Piscina** (the swimming pool), a protected lagoon on the north side of the island. If you go without a guide, ask for directions at Playa Bluff Lodge, on Playa Bluff.

Tropical Research Station

The Smithsonian Tropical Research Institute (STRI) offers a free half-hour tour of its **Bocas del Toro Research Station** (tel. 757-9794, Panama City tel. 212-8564 or 212-8082, www. stri.org) on Thursday and Friday 3–5 P.M. Theoretically, anyway. Call ahead to confirm a time, as drop-ins occasionally get turned away, especially if a school group is touring the facility. The station is on the narrow isthmus that separates Boca town from the rest of Isla Colón and contains laboratories, teaching facilities, and accommodations for researchers and visitors. During the tour, guests can see scientists at work on experiments and some of the specimens they have gathered, including an impressive collection of some of the 70 species of sponge found in the archipelago. There is also an aquarium that contains sea urchins, five types of starfish, sea cucumbers, coral, sea anemones, lobsters, and a green sea turtle. The station is built right in the middle of what the scientists are studying, so the guide can, for instance, point out living examples of red, black, and white mangroves near the dock and the different species of caiman living in the brackish pond in front of the station. The tour is led by a friendly, enthusiastic former boatman who speaks Spanish and okay English. Bring bug spray, as the *chitras* here can be brutal. The research station is a US$0.50–taxi ride from downtown.

Botanical Gardens

Finca Los Monos (tel. 757-9461, cell 6729-9943, US$10 pp) is a 23-acre tropical garden

building a pier, Bocas style

© WILLIAM FRIAR

just north of the isthmus that separates Bocas town from the larger part of the island. Tours of the garden are given 1 P.M. Monday and 8:30 A.M. Friday, or by appointment. It's beautiful, with carefully tended grounds. Howler monkeys, sloths, and lots of birds also like to visit the garden.

The turnoff is on the left between the Smithsonian and the *i-griega* intersection. It's close to town, a short bike ride away. It should be possible to get a taxi from Bocas town for around US$1. Bring binoculars and sturdy footwear.

La Gruta

Halfway across the island on the road to Boca del Drago is La Gruta (literally, "the cavern"), home to zillions of bats. It's at the little settlement of Colonia Santeña, near the Coca-Cola sign. A little store there sells drinks. If your idea of fun is to wade through guano in a claustrophobic cave and inhale disease-carrying particulates, then by all means walk through the thing. The rest of us will be happy with a snapshot of the highly photogenic entrance to the cave, a green grotto with a little statue of the Virgin standing guard. Round-trip taxi fare from Bocas town is US$10. The Boca del Drago bus (Transporte Boca del Drago, cell 6607-7681) can drop you there, but check the return schedule to avoid getting stranded.

Boca del Drago

This is another popular beach area, mainly because it's easily accessible by boat. It lies on the northwest side of the island. Boca del Drago is also the name of the canal separating this part of Isla Colón from the mainland. The water is tranquil, so landing a boat is not a problem; many of the island tours include a stop here. It's also possible to take a scenic drive across the island from Bocas town.

This beach isn't as nice as Bluff, but it's much better for swimming and splashing about. Many people who come here don't realize that beaches continue past the little beach restaurant about a 10-minute walk away. The most popular is Playa Estrella (a.k.a. Star Beach),

named for its abundance of starfish. This is included on many boat tours, so don't expect to have it all to yourself. There are coral gardens close by that extend all along the west side of the island. The snorkeling can be decent, but the coral is not in great shape and visibility isn't always the best.

There's now a biological field station and some cabins for rent, so Boca del Drago is not as isolated as it used to be, but it's still a mellow place.

There's a little thatch-roofed, sand-floored seafood restaurant on the beach called **Restaurante Yarisnori** (no phone, 8 A.M.– 6:30 P.M. Wed.–Mon.). The mixed ceviche is pretty good. Other items include red snapper, shrimp, octopus, lobster, and prawns. Most seafood costs around US$14–19; other dishes average around US$9.

Access to Boca del Drago is by boat, bus, car, or bike. One road extends across the island from Bocas town to Boca del Drago, about 14 kilometers away. A round-trip taxi ride costs US$25 for two people, including a stop at La Gruta for those interested. The bike ride is hilly, and tiring in the heat.

◖ Swan's Cay

A standard boat tour around Isla Colón includes a stop at lovely Swan's Cay, a craggy rock that juts out of the ocean north of the island, about a half hour by motorboat from Bocas. It's so impossibly picturesque that when a friend of mine saw it, he said it looked like it was designed by Disney. Swan's Cay is also called **Isla de los Pájaros** (Bird Island) for reasons that become obvious when you visit it. Most notably, it's the only known nesting grounds in Panama for the red-billed tropicbird, an elegant white bird with tail feathers about a meter long. Do not disturb the birds by walking on the island; you can, however, snorkel around it. The current isn't too strong, but the water can get pretty churned up at times, creating a washing-machine effect that drastically reduces visibility.

The boatman may offer to motor through the narrow cleft in the western crag. It's possible if the boatman times the waves right. It's a fun thing to do—you can see crabs scuttling along the rocky walls centimeters from the boat. Go for it if you trust his boating skills.

Isla Solarte and Hospital Point

Also known as **Nancy's Cay,** Solarte is a seven-kilometer-long island situated two kilometers east of Isla Colón. The boat ride from Bocas town takes about 10 minutes. Its western tip, Hospital Point, is one of the most popular diving and snorkeling spots in the archipelago. There are coral reefs just a few meters from the surface, but there's also a wall that drops about 13 meters. A diving or snorkeling trip to Hospital Point is usually included as part of a tour of the islands.

The point is named for the hospital the United Fruit Company built here in 1900 for its labor force, which was being decimated by malaria, yellow fever, and other tropical diseases. The hospital closed in 1920 after a fungus known as Panama disease wiped out the banana plantations on the islands and surrounding shore, forcing the company to move its operations farther west.

The house on the point is the home of Clyde Stephens, who for 32 years was a banana researcher for United Fruit. He gives lectures on the history of the banana industry, and his books include a history of Hospital Point, which he bought in 1970. His books are available in Bocas town. Try the Bravo Center or Buena Vista Bar and Grill.

Laguna Bocatorito

Otherwise known as **Dolphin Bay,** this lagoon, formed by the east side of Isla Cristóbal and an odd-shaped peninsular blob that juts from the mainland, starts about 10 kilometers south of Isla Colón. A labyrinth of shallow channels formed by mangroves screens its northern entrance, helping to make it a kind of giant natural aquarium, six kilometers across at its widest. Day trips to Laguna Bocatorito are popular because of the possibility of spotting bottle-nosed dolphins close up. The best chance of seeing them is from June to July, when rough seas drive them into the calm waters of the bay. They tend to hang around an unusually long time, which isn't surprising when one considers what a smorgasbord the bay offers them: The mangroves act like a kind of net, drawing fish into the bay.

Sadly, I can no longer recommend this tour. It's become too popular, and groups of boats now swarm around the dolphins, terrifying and sometimes hurting them. If you must do this tour, only do so with a responsible, eco-oriented group like Ancon Expeditions, which will keep a respectful distance. If your captain gets too close, don't hesitate to speak up.

There are also three Ngöbe communities—**Bocatorito, San Cristóbal,** and **Valle Escondido**—on Isla Cristóbal, though as usual they don't have much to see. There are also a couple of rustic places to eat.

Canal de Soropta

If you're looking for a break from the beaches and snorkeling, a boat trip up the Canal de Soropta, on the mainland east of the town of Changuinola, is an interesting off-the-beaten-track jaunt. The 12-kilometer canal was built in 1903 by Michael T. Snyder, a pioneering plantation owner, to shelter his banana barges from the open sea on their way between the mainland and the islands. Sometimes referred to as the Changuinola Canal, it parallels the coastline from the mouth of the Río Changuinola to Almirante Bay.

When the canal was bordered by forest on either side it was a prime birding spot. Unfortunately, slash-and-burn farmers and cattle ranchers have cut away much of the forest in recent years. But it still attracts quite an array of birds. Manatees are occasionally spotted here as well. It makes for a tranquil jungle cruise, though the boats motoring up and down the canal probably don't make the local fauna very happy; at least ask the boatman to take it slow.

It takes about a half hour by boat to reach the entrance to the canal from Bocas town. Heading all the way up to the Río Changuinola takes about 45 minutes at a leisurely pace, but you don't have to go that far to get a good look at the wildlife that's left; there are tons of birds at the very entrance of the canal. Early morning or late afternoon is the best time to go. You may want to include this as part of an Isla Colón tour, since the entrance to the canal is just opposite Boca del Drago. Expect to pay an extra charge, but agree on a price ahead of time.

Sea Turtles

During some months of the year, lucky visitors may get a chance to see sea turtles laying their eggs. Four species of endangered sea turtles find Bocas as attractive as the tourists do: the hawksbill *(Eretmochelys imbricata),* leatherback *(Dermochelys coriacea),* green *(Chelonia mydas),* and loggerhead *(Caretta caretta).* Most lay their eggs on the beaches between March and October.

Night trips to the beach are popular during nesting season. The most accessible site is Playa Bluff on the east side of Isla Colón. Other good places are Playa Larga on Isla Bastimentos and the Cayos Zapatillas. An important spot on the mainland is the strip of coast between the mouth of the Río Changuinola and Peninsula Soropta, just across from Boca del Drago. Sometimes called Playa Changuinola, it's part of the protected wetlands of San San Pondsack.

Female turtles lay eggs several times in a season. The incubation period lasts about 60 days. Only one in 1,000–10,000 baby turtles survives to adulthood.

Only the leatherbacks and hawksbill are easy to find. Few greens nest in Bocas; those that do come from about June to August, their numbers peaking in July. Loggerheads rarely nest anywhere in the tropics. When they're spotted, it's usually as they're swimming by.

Bocas was once the most important nesting ground in the Caribbean for the relatively small hawksbill (about a meter long, up to 80 kilograms), especially on the remote Playa Chiriquí, a vast beach on the mainland east of Peninsula Valiente. They nest from June to October, peaking in August and September. Hawksbills *(carey* in Spanish) are what first drew traders to Bocas. Because they're prized for their meat and shell, their populations are critically endangered worldwide. The majority of hawksbills that come to the islands nest on the Cayos Zapatillas.

The enormous leatherbacks, known locally as the *baula* or *canal,* are the largest of all sea turtles (up to 2.5 meters and 900 kilograms). They nest from March to June, peaking in April and May. Though most numerous on Playa Chiriquí, believed to be the most important leatherback rookery in Central America, they nest on beaches throughout the archipelago and coast.

Turtles are legally protected, but enforcement is lax and they're still poached for their meat, eggs, and shells. Even the leatherback, which lacks a valuable hard shell and palatable meat, is hunted for its eggs. Monitoring teams from the Institute for Tropical Ecology and Conservation, which has a field station in Boca del Drago, have investigated the annual slaughter of 30–40 leatherbacks on the mainland beach near the mouth of the Río Changuinola. Poachers slit off the flippers of the female turtles to make it easier to turn them over, gut them to remove their eggs, and leave them to die slowly on the beach, which is part of a nominally protected area.

Eating turtle eggs and meat is illegal, as is possessing anything made of tortoiseshell. But there are more subtle ways to harm turtles.

Pollution is a threat to turtles. Even a floating plastic bag can choke to death a giant leatherback, which can't distinguish between it and jellyfish, its sole source of food.

Do not use flashlights, take flash photos, or even wear light-colored clothing near nesting spots. This can scare away nesting females or disorient baby turtles trying to make it to the sea.

Stay out of sight while the turtles lay their eggs. Never touch them, which disturbs them and can be dangerous—some have strong jaws and a nasty bite.

Don't handle eggs or disturb the nests. This can introduce bacteria or damage the eggs.

To ensure a responsible visit and support conservation efforts, go with qualified local guides.

ENTERTAINMENT AND EVENTS

Part of the charm of Bocas del Toro is that there's so little to do besides splash around in the water or laze in a hammock. In the daytime, Bocas town is more or less deserted, since most visitors are out snorkeling, boating, surfing, and so on. Things liven up a bit in the evening, though the action is generally confined to the restaurants and bars.

Nightlife

El Barco Hundido (Calle 1 between Avenida Central and Avenida E, near Cable and Wireless, 8 P.M.–12:30 A.M. Sun.–Thurs., 8 P.M.–3 A.M. Fri.–Sat.) is a lively and funky bar whose name, Spanish for "shipwreck," comes from the sunken boat just offshore. Some people call it the Wreck Deck. The bar is an open-sided wooden patio with a view of the *barco hundido,* which is illuminated at night. Semi-competent DJs spin on busy nights, and there's actually dancing. It's no longer the epicenter of Bocas life as it was when it had no competition, but it still gets packed and has become popular with locals.

A popular feature of the place is the *Barco Loco* ("crazy boat"), a party boat onto which the bar scene sometimes spills over for cruises around the islands when the bar's owner is so moved. It now actually resembles a boat—an earlier incarnation of the thing consisted of a deck bolted onto dugout canoes. It looked like part of the bar, and it was not unusual to stand there drinking and suddenly find yourself motoring away from the shore. I've heard tales that this rickety platform was taken absurdly long distances, including as far away as Costa Rica and Isla Escudo de Veraguas, with the party in full swing. It's an insanely dangerous thing to do, but quite believable given the reputation of Benson, the character who owns this bar. Everyone who lives in Bocas seems to have a Benson story.

El Barco Hundido recently added a second bar, **La Gruta,** to its complex. As the name (Spanish for "cave") suggests, it's dark and cozy, with a clubbier atmosphere and DJs who tend to spin electronic music. But on my last visit to Bocas it was always virtually empty no matter how crowded the main bar got.

El Toro Loco (Avenida Central just east of the park, open daily) manages to please both the old gringos and the more urbane European expats, who concede it's a fun place to hang out. Basically a large funky shack with TVs tuned to big games (the Olympic hockey finals seemed to draw every Canadian in western Panama the last time I was there), it's popular with just about everyone. Part of the reason for that is a friendly bar staff that serves some of the cheapest (in both senses) booze in Bocas. It has a dartboard, free Wi-Fi, and serves bar food.

The bamboo-walled bar at **Mondo Taitu** (tel. 757-9425, evenings–12:30 A.M. Sun.–Thurs., later on Fri. and Sat.) is still a popular place for a drink, but the party scene appears to have calmed down from its heyday as *the* place for the young and half-clad to get wasted. It's still a fun place to have a drink, but be warned that if you're older than about 25 you'll feel like a fossil.

La Iguana Bar and Surf Club (Calle 1 next to Tropical Suites, evenings–late daily) has a much lower profile than the "scene" bars, but it's my favorite. It goes for the usual surfer-shack ambience and has a good mix of people—young and older, local and foreign, travelers and residents—and has a fun, boho vibe, without feeling frenetic. Chat and dance by the bar or retreat to one of the quieter tables over the water. Sadly, as of 2010 its future seemed uncertain.

The **Buena Vista Bar and Grill** (Calle 1 between Avenida C and Avenida D, tel. 757-9035, noon–9:30 P.M. Wed.–Mon.) remains a popular hangout, especially for gringos who like to talk real estate and watch U.S. ball games. Older visitors will feel comfortable here.

Festivals

The biggest annual party in Bocas is the **Feria**

Internacional del Mar (International Festival of the Sea), held for about four days in the second half of September (dates vary). It can feature such activities as a beauty contest, boat races, fireworks, volleyball and other games, various cultural events and displays, and, of course, lots of drinking and dancing.

Those planning to be in Bocas on the New Year's holiday should contact Al Natural Resort (tel./fax 757-9004, cell 6496-0776, 6576-8605 or 6640-6935, www.alnaturalresort.com) on Isla Bastimentos for details and reservations for their **New Year's Eve beach party.**

Other celebrations include:

- May 1: **Palo de Mayo.** Maypole dance in Bocas town and Isla Bastimentos.

- July 16: **Día de la Virgen del Carmen.** Parade in honor of the patron saint of Isla Colón. *La Peregrinación a la Gruta,* a pilgrimage to the virgin's shrine at La Gruta, halfway across the island, takes place on the following Sunday.

- October 12: **Columbus Day.** Though the date commemorates Columbus's discovery of America in 1492, Bocas has borrowed it to remember his visit to the archipelago in 1502.

- November 16: **Founding Day** of the province of Bocas del Toro.

SHOPPING

Souvenir kiosks at the north end of Calle 3 have some cheap jewelry, *molas,* and other knick-knacks. Oddly, there are few Ngöbe-Buglé crafts there. Other souvenir stands are around the town park, mostly around Hostel Heike.

Organic chocolate bars made by local companies are sold at a few spots around town, including Super Gourmet and Starfish Coffee. They cost about US$3 for a 100-gram bar. The chocolate is intense, crumbly, and delicious, though more like brownies than a typical chocolate bar. They can make for nice little gifts for folks back home, as long as they don't get too hot and you get home quickly enough; they

have no preservatives, so they only last about a week in transit. Those made by the Caribbean Chocolate Company (www.caribbean-chocolate-company.com) are wrapped in paper and resemble cigars.

Pure Tree Natural Body Products (cell 6607-8962 and 6570-8277, www.upinthehill.com) are made by a couple who use plants and fruit grown on their farm in Bastimentos. (They welcome visitors to their farm/shop, which is called Up in the Hill and is in Isla Bastimentos.) They make all kinds of delicious-smelling oils, balms, salves, and skin-care products in attractive bottles. Three will be of special interest to Bocas visitors at war with the *chitras:* Cococitronella and Fight the Bite to ward them off, and Stop Scratchin' to control the maddening itch. On my latest trip to Bocas, I did an experiment: I coated the left side of my body with Fight the Bite (which has natural ingredients including citronella and lemongrass) and the right side of my body with toxic DEET. It wasn't particularly buggy while I was there, so it wasn't an ideal test, but both seemed to do an equally good job of keeping biting nasties away. Fight the Bite needs to be reapplied regularly, though, since it comes off in the rain or on sweaty skin. From previous experience, I also know that Stop Scratchin' works wonderfully. Again, you have to reapply it from time to time, but it does a great job of soothing my Bocas battle scars. It's easy to find Pure Tree products around Bocas. In Bocas town, try Super Gourmet, Starfish Coffee, and Lili's Café.

Bocas Book Store (Avenida E near the airport, cell 6452-5905 or 6739-0693, 9 A.M.–4 P.M. Mon.–Sat.) is the first true bookstore on the islands. It was just getting started on my most recent visit, so I hope it makes it. It aims to stock thousands of books, mostly used and mostly in English. It's in a house opposite the airport terminal.

Artesanías Bri-Bri Emanuel (Calle 3 between Avenida B and Avenida C, tel. 757-9652, 10 A.M.–8 P.M. Mon.–Sat.), right across the street from Bocas Marine and Tours, seems to carry more Guatemalan souvenirs than Panamanian ones, but it does have a few things, such as devil masks and traditional Ngöbe-Buglé dresses and handbags. It also sells a variety of T-shirts, trinkets, and figurines.

SPORTS AND RECREATION

Few leave the archipelago without taking at least one boat tour, which is by far the most popular outdoor activity. These tours usually include snorkeling, but those not interested in that can just splash around in the water or sun themselves on the boat or the beach during snorkeling stops. Scuba diving and surfing are also popular, and as tourism takes off in Bocas more and more outfitters with more and more toys are showing up. Though of interest to just a minority of visitors, forest hikes and camping are also possible.

Nearly all the guides and outfitters in the archipelago are in Bocas town, and most of these are found along Calle 3.

Diving and Snorkeling

Diving and snorkeling in Bocas can be good, but those with a lot of experience in the Caribbean may not find it as spectacular as other parts of the Caribbean. Several rivers empty into the sea here, so visibility tends to be 15 meters on a good day, 22 meters on an excellent day, and less than 3 meters when I visit. It's a good place for beginning divers and snorkelers because there's so much calm, accessible water and lots to explore at shallow depths.

Bocas has extensive coral and sponge gardens that are easy for even novice snorkelers to explore. There is also more challenging cave, wall, and wreck diving for experienced scuba divers. Popular spots include **Hospital Point,** the **Cayos Zapatillas, Cayo Crawl,** and **Cristóbal Light** (a reef marked by a navigation light on the north side of Isla Cristóbal). A **ferry boat wreck** is off the tip of Bocas town, and nurse sharks can sometimes be spotted there. More ambitious spots include **Cayos Tigre (Tiger Rock),** off the north tip of Peninsula Valiente, more than 40 kilometers southeast of Bocas town, and **Isla Escudo de Veraguas,** which

is more than twice as far away. Dive operators sometimes offer trips to Cayos Tigre, but a trip to Escudo de Veraguas is a major undertaking and the sea is too rough to attempt it much of the year. For other spots, see the dive-site maps on the website of Bocas Water Sports (www.bocaswatersports.com).

The best snorkeling tends to be in the placid, protected waters on the south side of the islands. The north sides are open to the sea and pounding surf. Because of this, the most satisfying spots for snorkelers tend to be Hospital Point and the area near Cayo Crawl, which are quite calm and have lots to see near the surface. There's also some snorkeling between **Boca del Drago** and **Big Bight** on the west side of Isla Colón, but the coral isn't that healthy and the visibility can be poor.

Two well-established groups, plus a new arrival, offer scuba-diving trips and courses. Their basic offerings and prices are similar.

Bocas Water Sports (Calle 3 and Avenida A, near the ferry dock, tel. 757-9541, www.bocaswatersports.com) offers charges US$35 (one tank) or $60 (two tank, half day) for divers, including everything but lunch. Full-day and night dives are also available.

Snorkeling trips leave at 9:30 A.M. and cost $20–30, depending on the destination, and can be either half day or a full day.

The company also offers PADI scuba classes ranging from a half-day Discover Scuba course (US$65) to divemaster certification. Instruction is in English or Spanish.

Dives at **Starfleet Scuba** (Calle 1 next to the Buena Vista Bar and Grill, tel./fax 757-9630, www.starfleetscuba.com) start at US$60 per person for two-tank, two-site dives. Snorkelers pay US$20 per person, including equipment. As with Bocas Water Sports, PADI classes range from a half-day Discover Scuba course (US$75) to divemaster certification. They also offer a PADI Open Water Scuba instructor program.

The Dutch Pirate (Avenida Norte, cell 6567-1812, www.thedutchpirate.com) is a newer place that offers similar dives and courses at similar prices. It has an office on the north end of town, near La Casbah, and in Old Bank on Isla Bastimentos.

Surfing

Bocas del Toro has good surfing, some of the best in the country. Waves are best December–March and least consistent August–October. There are three well-known breaks on Isla Colón, as well as some less-famous ones that local surfers try to keep to themselves. The three main spots, all of which are along the east coast, are listed here, in order of their distance from town.

Paunch breaks left and right. It has long, "rippable" waves that are appropriate for all levels and attract beginners. It's a reef break, so wear booties.

Dumpers (also known as Dumps) is a reef-bottom left break with big tubes and short but dramatic rides. This is a dangerous break that should be attempted only by advanced surfers. Waves can get up to three meters. The reef is sharp, so wear booties. There's also an inner break known, logically enough, as **Inner**

Dumps. It's another left-breaking, reef-bottom wave. It's faster and longer than the outside wave, but not as big.

Playa Bluff is a gorgeous, several-kilometer-long beach at the end of the road. It's a powerful beach break known for destroying surfboards. It features fast-breaking waves and long tubes. Those who know it well say the waves are best when they're no more than about 1–2 meters high. Even when the swell isn't big, the waves are too powerful for beginning surfers and swimmers.

Several places in Bocas rent surfboards, often fairly battered ones. Hostel Heike, Mondo Taitu, and Hostel Gran Kahuna also rent them. Expect to pay about US$10–15 for short boards and US$15–20 for long boards per day.

Surfing lessons are easy to come by. **Bocas Surf School** (office in Hotel Lula's Bed and Breakfast, cell 6482-4166, U.S. tel. 787/823-0610, www.bocassurfschool.com) is run by Dez and Garret Bartelt, retired professional athletes who also own Rincón Surf and Board in Puerto Rico. Classes range from a half-day (US$59)

© WILLIAM FRIAR

sanding a surfboard, Bocas town

or full-day introduction (US$89) to a five-day immersion (US$369), board included.

Tropix Surf (Calle 3 between Avenida D and Avenida Central, near the southwest end of the park, tel. 757-9727, 9 A.M.–noon and 3–7 P.M. daily) sells custom-made surfboards made on the premises.

Kayaking

Bocas Water Sports (Calle 3 and Avenida A, near the ferry dock, tel. 757-9541, www.bocaswatersports.com) rents single kayaks for US$3/hour, US$10/half day, and US$18/full day. Double kayaks are US$5/hour, US$20/half day, or US$35/full day. Note: Kayaking seemed increasingly popular on my most recent visit to Bocas. I saw a number of people in the open ocean with no life jacket—not smart. A glassy sea in Bocas one moment can turn treacherous in seconds when a storm sweeps through. Do not go out on open water without a life jacket.

Hiking

There are undeveloped forest trails on Isla Colón and other islands in the archipelago, but as usual only hike in the forest with a knowledgeable guide. Certainly don't hike alone. Be especially careful on any hike in the forests of Isla Popa, which still has fer-de-lance and other venomous snakes. (Isla Bastimentos enjoys the best reputation among the snake-phobic; a species of nonaggressive coral snake with a mouth too small to be much threat to humans is the only known venomous snake on the island.)

Boat Tours

There is no shortage of boatmen offering tours of the islands and snorkeling spots. Usually these are organized as day trips with fairly standardized itineraries at similar prices. Note that rates are likely to go up because of fast-rising fuel prices.

One tour takes clients around Isla Colón to Swan's Cay for bird-watching and snorkeling, stops for lunch and a swim at Boca del Drago, then stops down the west side of Isla Colón for at least one snorkeling spot, usually the popular

Playa Estrella (a.k.a. Star Beach). Tours sometimes include a side trip up the Soropta Canal.

A cheaper tour goes to Red Frog Beach, the popular snorkeling spot of Hospital Point on Isla Solarte, and the town of Old Bank on Bastimentos.

Expect to pay about US$10 per person for that last trip. Most other tours cost about US$20–25 per person. Note that clients have to pay additional per person entrance fees of US$3 for Red Frog Beach (the surrounding land is private property) and US$10 for the Zapatillas (it's in a national park). Red Frog Beach is the most popular beach on Bastimentos because it's both attractive and accessible.

There are several established tour operators along the water in Bocas town offering sightseeing and snorkeling trips. Tours generally include snorkeling equipment, but it may not be in the best shape, so it's best to bring your own if possible. The most professional operators carry emergency radios, and all should provide life jackets; be sure to check. Trips generally start midmorning and return to Bocas town before dark. Private tours are possible, but expect to pay more if your group has fewer than six people, the minimum for most tours.

Transparente Tours (Calle 3 near Avenida C, tel. 757-9915, transparentetours@hotmail.com, www.bocas.com) has been offering snorkeling and sightseeing boat tours for years now. (It joined forces with the competing J&J Tours a few years back, and it's sometimes listed as J&J Transparente.) Tours start at 9:30 A.M. and return around 4:30–5:30 P.M. They include snorkeling equipment and an ice chest for any drinks/snacks guests bring.

Boteros Bocatoreños (tel. 757-9760, boterosbocas@yahoo.com, www.bocas.com), also called Boatmen United, is a group composed of boatmen who have organized to stay afloat amid growing competition from tour operators.

Bocas Water Sports (Calle 3 and Avenida A, near the ferry dock, tel. 757-9541, www.bocaswatersports.com) and **Starfleet Scuba** (Calle 1 next to the Buena Vista Bar and Grill, tel./fax 757-9630, www.starfleetscuba.com), though primarily scuba outfits, also offer snorkeling trips.

Jampan Tours (Calle 1 just south of the CEFATI, tel. 757-9619) is under new management and introducing new tours, including forest walks, in addition to the usual suspects. It's one of the few places able to offer tours of a small chocolate farm run by a couple of gringo expats who live in the Dolphin Bay area (US$25 per person, plus a US$5 entrance fee). Sadly, the ocelot that adopted this couple has apparently gone to big-kitty heaven.

I feel more confident Jampan's dolphin tour is less likely to terrorize the dolphins, so if you must do this tour, you may want to give these guys a try (though, as always, speak up if you think the boat is getting too close). The owners also have a 50-foot houseboat they can use for big groups.

It's also possible to work out a deal with one of the many freelance boatmen offering "tour guide" services. However, these guys are generally not licensed. I've heard horror stories of drunk, reckless, or otherwise incompetent boatmen, though I've also had good experiences with some of them. Two boatmen I can recommend are Gallardo "Cabrioli" Livingston and Bola Smith. Ask for them at Boteros Bocatoreños. Most boatmen tend to live hand to mouth, so don't be surprised when your tour starts with a run to fill the fuel tank.

Use caution if you go this route. Does the boatman have decent masks, snorkels, and fins? Does he have an emergency radio (unlikely) or at least a cell phone (often useless for distant destinations)? Take a look at the boat before you seal the deal. Does it have life jackets, appear to be in good condition, and have a decent motor? (Some guidelines on horsepower: 75 hp will move you as fast as you're likely to want to go in these little boats, while 15 hp will give you a slow-motion leisure cruise. Time estimates in this chapter are based on a boat equipped with a 75-hp motor unless otherwise stated.)

Yoga

The sun, the surf, and the laidback lifestyle make Bocas a natural magnet for yogis and yoginis, who come to the island on yoga retreats and to teach classes. **Bocas Yoga** (Calle 4 near Avenida G, cell 6658-1355, www.bocasyoga. com, Mon.–Sat.) is a well-established studio run in a large wooden house that is also the home of Laura Kay, a yoga teacher who takes her work seriously, yet seems to have a playful bohemian streak as well. Her studio is modern, spacious, and well designed—it's a nicer space than any of the several yoga studios I've attended in Northern California. It has hardwood floors, air-conditioning, good natural lighting, and new yoga mats and equipment. Because Bocas town can get noisy even on the edge of town, the studio is soundproofed. Laura occasionally hosts guest classes taught by highly respected yoga teachers from Colombia and Costa Rica. Morning group classes are held at 9:15 A.M. Monday–Friday. There are frequent noon, evening, and Saturday classes as well. Group classes are US$5 a session. Private classes are also available, for US$35 for the first person, US$5 more for each additional person.

Day Spa

Spa services come and go in Bocas, but one that seems destined to stick around is **Starfleet Spa** (Calle 1 next to the Buena Vista Bar and Grill, tel./fax 757-9630, www.starfleetscuba.com), upstairs and run by the same couple that owns Starfleet Scuba. It offers massages, facials, waxing, and various skin treatments in pleasant and comfortable treatment rooms, though some street noise inevitably spills over. I had an excellent massage from one of the owners, Georgina, who was trained as a massage therapist in London. Her massages are far better than the ineffectual "fluff and puff" variety one usually gets in Panama. The most expensive is US$65 for 75 minutes. Some of the spa treatments, including reflexology and highlighting, are provided by Donna (cell 6591-3814), a Bocas veteran who also works out of her house in town.

ACCOMMODATIONS

Most of the hotels in the archipelago are in Bocas town, and most of these are built right

BOCAS DEL TORO

on the water. But there are more and more options around Isla Colón and on the other major islands of the archipelago. There's quite a variety of accommodations, ranging from simple but clean hostels to modern midrange hotels to bed-and-breakfasts to rather upscale and exotic bungalows. All have hot water unless otherwise indicated. Rates have climbed faster in Bocas than in other parts of the country. Low-season breaks and other deals are often available. Many of the hotels have websites that are accessible through www.bocas.com. Note, however, that a lot of the lodgings, especially the cheaper ones, are exceedingly lame about keeping their websites up to date or alive at all, and many are bad about answering their email. A phone call is often the best way to go.

Bocas Town
US$10-25

The very popular **Hostel Heike** (Calle 3 just west of the park, tel. 757-9667 or 757-9708, U.S. 925/465-6167, www.hostelheike.com, dorm beds start at US$10 pp, including pancake breakfast) is no longer actually owned by Heike. The current owners are a trio of guys from the San Francisco Bay Area who also own Luna's Castle in Panama City and have a knack for giving the backpacker set exactly what it wants. If you stay here, you'd better like company: Nearly 60 beds are squeezed into dorm rooms with 4–10 bunks. The hostel has shared hot-water bathrooms, free Wi-Fi and Internet computers, lockers, a book exchange, communal kitchen, and other handy hostel extras. Rooms are basic but cheerful—they're brightly painted, designed to let light in, and feature lots of pretty wood. Some have air-conditioning; the others have fans. Private rooms are US$22 (double occupancy) or US$33 (triple occupancy). There's a mirador on the top floor strung with hammocks. Guests can now make online reservations.

Mondo Taitu (north end of Calle 5, tel. 757-9425, www.mondotaitu.com, dorm beds start at US$10 pp) was until recently owned by the three guys who have Hostel Heike; now it's owned by another three guys. It's still a funky,

friendly place with 4–8 person rustic wooden dorms. Rates are US$10 per person in a fancooled dorm, US$12 with air-conditioning. The hostel also has some double rooms for US$22 and a "tree house triple" for US$33. It has a communal kitchen, free loaner bikes (including a couple of tandem bikes), a bar, and a library of free DVDs guests can watch in one of the common areas. Hammocks for napping are strung around the joint; it's hard to find one that's not already occupied. The hostel does not take reservations.

Hostal de Hansi (Avenida D and Calle 1, tel. 757-9085, starts at US$10 s, US$22 d) is a newish two-story wooden place run by Heike, the former owner of Hostel Heike. (That's right: Heike owns Hansi, not Heike. Confused?) Those who've stayed with her before will be unsurprised to find the new place is immaculate and an excellent deal. A small single room is US$11 with a shared bathroom, or US$13 with a private bathroom. If you want a TV (local channels) it's US$1–3 more. A double room with private bath and balcony is US$25 for the first night, US$23 thereafter. All the rooms have ceiling fans and orthopedic mattresses. Guests are welcome to use the communal kitchen and dining area. The bar next door can get loud at night, as Heike herself points out. Heike is German and her English isn't great, but she's a sweet person and a good innkeeper. Note that she doesn't take reservations.

The **Gran Kahuna Hostel** (Calle 3 near Avenida B, tel. 757-9038, www.grankahunabocas.com, US$10 pp) works hard to try to keep their place clean by Panama hostel standards, and it shows. A two-story, bright orange and yellow old-style Bocas house, the Gran Kahuna is hard to miss. Opened in 2008, it features 49 beds with thin foam mattresses and a veranda that looks out over the sea. The hostel also has a little dock right across the street that's just for its guests to hang out. There are lockers, free Wi-Fi, a washer/drier, shared kitchen, cold-water shared bathrooms, and big flat-screen TV in the common areas. It's a mellow, friendly place. Surfboards are US$15 per day and the managers can arrange surf tours and lessons.

© WILLIAM FRIAR

Backpackers have plenty of places to choose from in Bocas.

US$25-50

Hotel Las Brisas (north end of Calle 3, tel. 757-9549, US$27.50 s/d with a/c) is one of the old stalwarts among Bocas hotels, with the accent squarely on "old." It closed down a few years ago, but now it's back and under new management, who seem determined to keep it exactly as it was: with dingy rooms, a cracked toilet tank or two, wonky floors, and a general air of decay. That said, it certainly has character. It's a throwback to pre-tourist-boom Bocas, when Las Brisas was one of the only options for the rare visitor. It's basically a glorified wooden deck built over the sea. Rooms are off a central passageway that opens onto the water and lets in the breeze that gives the place its name. It's not a great first or even second option, but the staff is friendly and the price inviting.

Hotel Dos Palmas (Avenida Sur west of Calle 5, tel. 757-9906, US$30 s/d), at the south end of town, offers nine rooms, all with hot-water bathrooms, air-conditioning, and thin mattresses. It's a clean but basic wooden place run by proudly "100 percent bocatoreños." The furnishings are old-fashioned but serviceable.

The main reason someone would stay here is to live close to the townspeople. It's something of a hangout for those who live in the neighborhood, as this place is slightly removed from the touristy part of Bocas town. The surrounding area is a bit squalid.

Hotel Casa Max (Avenida G near the north end of Calle 4, about a block west of the Bocas Inn, tel. 757-9120, casamax1@hotmail.com, starts at US$35 s/d) is a bright and cheerful Dutch-owned place in a wooden building that's been going strong since the mid-1990s. A recent annex has brought the room total to 14. The original rooms (US$35 s/d) are simple but clean and have private baths, fans, hot water, and firm beds. The new rooms (US$60 s/d) have air-conditioning and TV. The place has a colorful facade that's hard to miss, even at night, when it's lit up prettily. A restaurant on the premises, Rum Runners, serves breakfast and dinner, specializing in Indonesian food.

Hotel del Parque (Calle 2, on the southeast side of the park, tel. 757-9008, delparque35@hotmail.com, US$37.50 s, US$45 d) offers eight rooms—four doubles and four triples—in an attractive wooden house right on the park and surrounded by flowering trees. Rooms are simple but pleasant with okay mattresses, cable TV, air-conditioning, and private hot-water bathrooms. There's a view of the park from the veranda and a nice little garden on the property. Guests are welcome to use the kitchen. This is a friendly place. (They don't seem to check email often; call if you don't hear back in a couple of days.)

La Veranda (Calle H near the corner of Calle 7, tel./fax 757-9211, http://laveranda-panama.tripod.com, US$29–55.50 s/d) is a Caribbean-style wooden house with a wrap-around veranda that gives the place its name. It's at the north edge of town about a block southwest of Cocomo-on-the-Sea. It offers seven pleasant rooms of various quality. The cheapest rooms (US$29 s/d) have shared bathrooms and somewhat thin mattresses. The nicest rooms (US$55.50 s/d) are cheerful and large, with private bathrooms and with air-conditioning. Air-conditioning may not be necessary since this place often gets a nice breeze, though sometimes the neighbors insist on blasting their music. All the rooms have mosquito nets. Guests are welcome to use the kitchen, and there's free wireless Internet. The inn was for sale in 2010.

US$50-100

Hotel Los Delfines (Calle 5 and Avenida G, tel. 757-9963, www.bocasdelfines.com, US$70 s, US$90 d, including breakfast), on the northern outskirts of town, is a clean place built circa 2001 that has 12 pleasant rooms with colorful Peruvian bedspreads, air-conditioning, hot water, cable TV, and wireless Internet. Some of the rooms are quite dark, and the ones on the top floor have low, slanting ceilings. There is a bar/dining area downstairs.

Hotel Lula's Bed and Breakfast (Avenida Norte and Calle 6, tel. 757-9057, cell 6629-0836, information@lulabb.com, www.lulabb.com, starts at US$55 s/d, including breakfast) is a pleasant, clean bed-and-breakfast that features lots of handsome wood and rooms with air-conditioning and attractive bathrooms. The place has two doubles with double beds (US$55 s/d) and four triples with a double bed, single bed, and fold-out-chair bed (US$66 t, another US$11 for a fourth person). The nicest rooms are the two triples that overlook the balcony.

Hotel Bahía (south end of Calle 3, across from the ferry landing, tel. 757-9626, www.hotelbahia.biz, starts at US$80 s, US$88 d) is the grand old lady of Bocas. Built in 1905, it was once the headquarters building for the United Fruit Company. A renovation a few years ago preserved the building's historical character (the fruit company's massive old safe still sits in the office, for instance), while cheering up the place considerably. The 16 rooms are simple, bordering on stark, with air-conditioning, lukewarm-water bathrooms, TV, and lots of attractive wood. However, it is not being terribly well-maintained or cleaned, though another renovation is under way. A basic breakfast is served on the terrace downstairs. The hotel does have tons of character, and the owner, José (Tito) Thomas, is a good guy with a passion for the history of the building and Bocas generally. Be sure to have a chat with him. He tells a funny story, for instance, about that safe in the office: When the last guy who knew the combination died, workers had to drill into the safe to get at its contents. When they cracked it open, they found a piece of paper that had (you guessed it) the safe combination. A new hotel was nearing completion right next door in 2010, looming over its south side.

Cocomo-on-the-Sea (Avenida Norte between Calle 6 and Calle 7, tel./fax 757-9259, www.cocomoonthesea.com, US$88 s/d, including breakfast), now owned by guys from Cincinnati, Ohio, has long been a cozy place to stay in Bocas town. It's right on the water, about a five-minute walk northwest of the town center, and offers four large, cheerful rooms in a wooden building designed with simple comfort in mind. The two rooms in front, Calypso and La Palma, have an ocean view, but all four rooms have access to a comfortable veranda and sundeck, strung with hammocks, that juts into the water. A third person in any room is an additional US$11. Guests have free use of sea kayaks.

Hotel Laguna (Calle 3 about a block south of the park, tel. 757-9091, www.thehotellagunabocas.com, starts at US$85 s/d) offers 22 modern, clean, and air-conditioned rooms in the center of "downtown." Rooms are dark but cheerful with wood paneling and colorful bedspreads. All have hot water, cable TV, firm beds, and telephones. The attractive "deluxe junior suite" (US$160) is simply a larger room with a balcony. Other suites of various size and furnishings are available. The attached indoor/outdoor restaurant is a nice place to watch the passing scene on Calle 3, and it's the new home of El Pecado, long one of the best restaurants in Bocas.

The **Bocas Inn** (north end of Calle 3, Bocas tel./fax 757-9600, Panana City tel. 269-9415 and fax 264-3713, www.anconexpeditions.com, US$99 s/d, including breakfast) is an attractive, two-story wooden lodge set in a lush garden. It's owned by Ancon Expeditions, which has its field office in the building. The place is meant primarily for visitors who've arranged package tours with Ancon Expeditions, but it's also available for those who just want a room. The nicest rooms face the ocean. These open out on a terrace with hammocks (the terrace can be used by all guests). All the rooms are attractive and have air-conditioning and hot-water bathrooms.

On the ground floor is a breezy veranda/pier that has a dining room and bar right on the water and quiet jazz and modern lounge music playing on the stereo. It's a good place to stop for a drink even if you're not staying at the inn.

Guests generally book tours and lodging through Ancon Expeditions' main office in Panama City, though it's also possible to book a room directly through the lodge.

The **Hotel Swan's Cay** (Calle 3 just north of Parque Bolívar, tel. 757-9316 or 757-9090, tel./fax 757-9027, www.swanscayhotel.com, start at US$72 s/US$85 d in the main building) was the first fancy hotel in Bocas, built, oddly enough, smack in the middle of town, instead of on the water. The whole place is thoroughly air-conditioned and features such city-style touches as a carpeted lobby with wood-paneled walls. Rooms have cable TV, telephones, and Italian furniture, but the smaller ones are cramped and the whole place is dark. There are two swimming pools, one of which is a rather uninviting aboveground pool a few minutes' walk from the main hotel. Many find the hotel staid and out of sync with the bohemian ambience of the rest of Bocas. Its formal, air-conditioned restaurant is usually empty.

OVER US$100
Tropical Suites (Calle 1 near Avenida D, tel. 757-9880 or 757-9081, cell 6689-9451, www.tropical-suites.com, starts at US$175 s/d) is a three-story apartment building near the CEFATI office that offers 16 modern, spacious, somewhat stark studio apartments that can be rented by the day, week, or month. Those looking for the funky, Caribbean side of Bocas won't find it here, but it will probably appeal to those who want something more than a hotel room, particularly those who need a long-term place to stay while building their dream home. Each apartment has a queen bed, a double sofa-bed, a balcony, air-conditioning, fully equipped kitchen, DirecTV, bathrooms with two sinks and whirlpool bath, wireless Internet connection, and so on. Utilities and daily maid service are included. Amenities include a coin laundry, security cameras, a marina, and a tiny restaurant nook that's open for breakfast, lunch, and dinner and provides room service. Regular daily rates are US$175 s/d for apartments that look out on the street, or US$225 s/d for a much more appealing sea view. Add US$20 for each additional person. There are significant discounts for weekly and monthly stays. Tropical Suites has the distinction of being the first place in the archipelago with an elevator.

Hotel Bocas del Toro (Calle 1 next to the Buena Vista Bar and Grill, tel. 757-9018 or 757-9771, www.hotelbocasdeltoro.com, starts at US$138.60 s/d) has been my favorite hotel in Bocas town since 2004, when a new owner took over who immediately upgraded the place. She and her staff continue to work hard to make it better all the time. The hotel strikes a good balance between being attractive and comfortable, while retaining traditional Bocas charm. It's easily the best-run hotel in town. Like every other place in Bocas, things can go wrong here, but if they do, the staff immediately sets about fixing it.

The hotel features 11 clean, modern rooms in a Caribbean-style wooden building built right on the water. All the rooms have air-conditioning, TVs, telephones, and in-room safes. The most expensive rooms have balconies that look out on the ocean. It's an attractive place, featuring nine kinds of dark, polished wood. The restaurant needs some work and fortunately it was recently taken over by the hotel management and is gradually improving. It's a good place to go for a traditional Panamanian breakfast of *bistec* (beef), green peppers, onions, and *hojaldre* (fry bread), if you think your heart can take it. Breakfasts run US$3.50–5.

M&M's Residencias (Avenida Sur, past the ferry dock, tel. 757-9004, cell 6596-6076, alnaturalbocas@cwpanama.net, starts at US$120 s/d) is the new project from a couple of the Belgians behind Al Natural on Isla Bastimentos. It's completely different from that bohemian beach paradise, but shows the same creative thinking and feel for what might be termed tropical minimalism. It consists of two rooms available for short-term rentals, above which are two full apartments for longer stays that are often occupied. All four are part of an unusual enclosed complex that includes the Al Natural office and dock. They are built over the water, and everything is made from tropical oak, a handsome, light-colored wood. The two rooms are angled so that their terraces face open water, with the mainland mountains in the distance. You'd never know you were in Bocas town here, and the complex is big enough to muffle much of the sound from the street. The rooms have high ceilings, comfortable beds, and air-conditioning. The "sea-front studio" (US$120 s/d) has a kitchenette with new stainless-steel appliances. The "sea-front one bedroom apartment" (US$150 s/d) has a living area, full kitchen, and larger terrace. There are discounts for longer stays. Those staying at Al Natural also get a discount here, and, for those who can afford it, staying at both places is an easy way to experience both town life in Bocas and its more remote attractions.

Playa Bluff and Environs

My favorite new places to stay on the island are on the northeast coast, on Playa Bluff or just below it. This also happens to be the island's most beautiful beach.

As mentioned elsewhere, taxi transport to this area tends to be pricey because of the distance and road conditions. The going rate for taxis from town is about US$8–10 to get as far as La Coralina, up to US$15 to get to Tesoro Escondido, and US$15–20 to reach the last two places, which are near the end of the road. However, each of the lodgings up here works hard to get their guests free or discounted rides as often as they can, giving them lifts when they can or organizing groups to go together when they can't. It's also possible to ride bikes back and forth into town, but it's a bit of a workout on a hot day.

Guests will probably be happiest if they spend most of their time in this area rather than try to make it into town or to the other islands every day. That's part of the fun of being up there. Because it's still a fairly remote spot, it keeps the crowds down, makes for a real sense of escape, and creates a sense of camaraderie—guests and innkeepers frequently drop by the other inns for a drink or a meal. Tesoro Escondido is the most popular social hub. La Coralina is closer to town, which makes the cross-socializing a bit more difficult but also makes it cheaper and easier to make trips into town.

Places up here are still of the grid, having to supply their own electricity and water, which generally means captured rainwater. Tesoro Escondido, Bluff Beach Retreat, and Playa Bluff Lodge are all on solar power, an eco-friendly solution that also means they don't have air-conditioning. I've not really needed it when I stayed up here, though, as all the places are right next to the ocean and often get a pleasant sea breeze.

US$50-100

(Tesoro Escondido (cell 6749-7435, www.bocastesoroescondido.com, starts at US$38.50 s/d) is Spanish for "hidden treasure," and that's the perfect name for this place, which is between La Coralina and Bluff Beach Retreat. It consists of a wooden house built on a bluff about 10 meters above the surf. The house is built on four levels; from the terrace/dining room/kitchen level there's a spectacular view of the ocean and two beaches, one on either side of the house. Or, rather, a partial view—while I was there, a couple of us urged the owner, Monique, to trim back the lovely trees on the property to open up the view a bit. You'd think we asked her to drown a puppy; that's how much she loves her trees, one of which is home to a sloth that sometimes eavesdrops on guests.

That tells you something about Monique, a Swiss woman who has lived in Bocas since 1995 and manages the neat trick of always seeming relaxed and good-humored but always doing something to make her funky little paradise a little bit better.

Speaking of puppies, you'd better like dogs if you stay at this place: Monique has five, not including the occasional visiting pooch of a guest or worker, nor her cat. They're all good-natured, but watch out when they stampede at once.

Rooms are simple and rustic. In lieu of a mini-fridge, each room has a camping cooler; instead of air-conditioning, there's a clip-on fan over the bed. (There is, however, free Wi-Fi.) But they've all got a bohemian chic feel and are perfectly comfortable. There are whimsical touches everywhere. The tabletops and paving stones are decorated with images of dragonflies, dolphins, and iguanas made from colored glass. The pattern is repeated in colorful glass walls made from salvaged bottles, which are lovely when the sun shines through; birds make nests in these. In fact, whenever possible Monique and her staff have tried to use recycled materials—glass, tile, driftwood, bits of old houses.

There are six rooms in the main house. Rooms 5 and 6 (US$44 s/d) are on the top floor, reached by a spiral staircase made from a tree trunk. They open out onto a balcony with hammocks and feel a bit like a tree-house. They get blazing hot during the day. Rooms 1 and 2 (US$83.50 s/d) are on the level below the dining/bar area, but are perfectly quiet because they're toward the back of the building, which also means only the bathrooms have a view of the sea. All the rooms have access to shared kitchens.

There are also three cabins set in a tropical garden (39 kinds of heliconia!) on the edge of the bluff. The Turtle and Dolphin (US$71 s/d) are next to each other and similar: one-bedroom cabins with private baths, a deck where to watch the sea from a hammock, and a kitchenette. The Dragonfly cabin is a bit further away and a bit bigger, with two decks. It's set back, closer to the road, but it's right above a cove with its own little beach. Monique is building a modern apartment, to be called Casa Verde, next door. My favorite is the Dolphin, because of its stunning view of the waves breaking on the edge of the cove.

Everything is pretty open to nature, so this is not a place for people who are overly skittish about creepy-crawlies. Because of the way the property is positioned and where it is (about seven kilometers from town), guests at Tesoro Escondido are likely to have both beaches to themselves. Off to the right as you face the ocean is La Curva, a lesser-known surf break, which means that surfers can check out the action from the breakfast table and plan their day accordingly.

Tesoro Escondido has a popular French chef, and the lodge arranges various tours and activities, including scuba lessons and trips, boat tours, and horse hire.

(Playa Bluff Lodge (cell 6798-8507, www.playablufflodge.com, US$95 s/d, including breakfast and transportation from town) opened in 2009 near the far end of Playa Bluff and the end of the road. At first glance, it seems to be a modern but unremarkable two-story house—albeit one built right in front of a lovely stretch of beach. But a closer look reveals it to be something quite remarkable indeed. The Dutch owners have turned it into something of a tropical nature preserve. They have built a lush artificial pond in their backyard that attracts reptiles, amphibians, birds, and other jungle creatures. These include incredibly cute red-eyed tree frogs, basilisks, opossums, Amazon parrots, parakeets, and oropendolas. A sloth that was abandoned by its mother now makes its nest in a *rancho* next to the pond (the nest is made from a stuffed sloth doll) and has been kind of adopted by the couple's young daughter. Howler monkeys and white-faced capuchins also stop by from time to time, as does the occasional boa constrictor and green vine snake. Needless to say, this is not a place for those afraid of snakes, though it's worth noting that in five years of living out here, they have never seen a venomous snake. Beyond the pond are 23 hectares of forest with extensive trails that are rather muddy and hilly; one leads to a waterfall.

The owner, Reinier, bred exotic reptiles in the Netherlands, so he really knows what he's doing. The lodge has a terrarium filled with a whole rainbow of Bocas's poison-dart frog, but he keeps them strictly segregated so they don't mix with the naturally occurring varieties in the area.

The lodge runs turtle tours for interested guests from the end of March through the end of June; this usually means camping out on the beach near the house. The lodge can also help arrange other tours and activities, including hiring horses, which is one way to get to the quiet snorkeling spot of La Piscina, about 45 minutes north.

The lodge has four rooms, with two more on the way. Rooms are spacious, modern, and spotlessly clean, with ceiling fans but no air-conditioning; but the rooms are surprisingly cool even in the daytime. Every two rooms share a connecting, hot-water bathroom.

Breakfast is included in stays, and the lodge will pack a sandwich lunch for US$5. For dinner, guests can have a three-course dinner at the lodge (US$15) or, if they prefer, try Tesoro Escondido. Stays also include free use of bikes and use of a local mobile phone. Even though this is the most remote of the Bluff-area hotels, transportation is less of a problem here, at least during the week: The couple's daughter attends school in town, which means that guests can grab a free ride in the morning or afternoon Monday–Friday.

The owners speak English, Spanish, German, and Dutch.

🍸 **La Coralina** (cell 6788-8992 or 6491-8185, www.lacoralina.com, starts at US$55 s, US$66 d, including breakfast) was for many years a neglected old guesthouse in one of the prettiest spots on the island, on a bluff above an isolated cove with pounding surf. The spot is as pretty as ever, and now La Coralina has been given a lovely facelift to match. The main building is a two-story, Spanish-colonial-style building with an airy interior and lots of balconies.

The three rooms in the building have either one queen and one twin bed (US$88 s, US$88 d) or two queen beds (US$110 s, US$121 d), with attractive bathrooms, ceiling fans, and air-conditioning. There are also three less-expensive rooms in a courtyard behind the building. The cheapest one (US$33 s, US$44 d) is tiny, barely big enough for its double bed. The other two have two double beds (US$55 s, US$66 d). All three have ceiling fans but no air-conditioning. The bathrooms are shared, but they're close to the rooms, spotless, attractive, and designed with real flair. All the rooms in the building are simply but cheerfully decorated and painted in bright tropical colors, and the mattresses are good. It's breezy on the top of the hill, which keeps the *chitras* down and air-conditioning easier to do without. Additional guests in a room are US$15 each.

The four large suites (US$143 s, US$154 d; except for the Bamboo Suite, which is US$165 s, US$176 d) next to the main building are luxurious and gorgeous, with loving attention given to the inventive decor, king beds, large showers, air-conditioning, DirecTV, safes, and private patios. The Ocean Suite has a view of the ocean from the patio, and guess what the Garden Suite looks out on? The two new suites are also lovely. The Hammock Suite has a private covered balcony with double hammocks; the Bamboo Suite has an outside tub on the private walled-patio.

The bar and restaurant are housed in an attractive *rancho* on the edge of the bluff with great ocean views and a firepit next door.

Recent additions include a deck with a great view and a swimming pool and whirlpool tub. A day spa, including massages, is also on the way. There's a little gift shop selling good-quality Central American crafts. The restaurant is open 8 A.M.–9 P.M. daily. Last call at the bar is at 10 P.M. Nonguests are welcome. Note the realistic-looking "rock" wall surrounding the base of the bar. It's actually made of foam and was part of a set for the *Miami Vice* movie. The owner brought it down from Florida.

There's plenty to do at the hotel, and the owner is constantly coming up with new ideas. For surfers, Bluff, Dumpers, and Paunch are within easy walking distance. There are 6.5 acres of trails to walk, and horses are available for US$20 for three hours. Bikes and surfboards are also available for rent. There are outdoor movies twice a week, a book exchange, and free wireless Internet.

US$100-150
Bluff Beach Retreat (cell 6677-8867, www. bluffbeachretreat.com, starts at US$145 s/d) consists of a large, lovely "beach house" and two "casitas" set in four acres of tropical garden. The beach house is built from handsome, highly polished dark wood and features a wraparound lanai. The whole place is designed to be as open to its beautiful surroundings as possible without sacrificing comfort. It features three immaculate bedrooms, a large kitchen, and a dining and bar area.

The whole house can accommodate up to nine people for US$425. When I stopped by, though, the rooms were being rented out individually. The house, roomy as it is, doesn't have a whole lot of privacy for people who want to be off by themselves.

The two casitas run US$145–225. La Piña can sleep two guests and Las Palmas can handle four. Both have kitchens and are clean and nicely appointed, There's a three-night minimum stay in any of the rooms.

Yoga retreats are sometimes held here. This place and its grounds are lovely, but it doesn't feel like the bed-and-breakfast it bills itself as, at least when I visited. The owner spends part of the year in Canada, leaving caretakers to run the place. When I stopped by, guests were left pretty much to their own devices, and I was greeted only by the angry barks of a large and rather scary-looking dog; not exactly inviting. On the other hand, later that night I saw the caretaker escorting guests around the area by flashlight and being quite friendly and solicitous of their needs, so I may have gotten the wrong end of the stick. Still, I suspect that families or groups traveling together would love this place, but couples or solo travelers may feel a bit isolated.

Elsewhere Around Isla Colón
There are a few places to stay and eat just north of Bocas town in "Saigon," among the mangroves on the south side of the island, and in and around Boca del Drago.

OVER US$100
The three-story, 118-room **Playa Tortuga** (tel. 302-5424 Panama City reservations, tel. 757-9050 at the hotel, www.hotelplayatortuga.com, starts at $182 s/d, including breakfast) didn't end up as bad as some of us feared. Located just past the *i griega* (the turnoff to Boca del Drago), it's the first large-scale hotel in the archipelago, and when it opened in 2008 it instantly doubled the number of hotel rooms on Isla Colón. Owned by the same group that operates Country Inns and Suites in Panama, it has the feel of a motel and looms over its narrow strip of beach, which isn't wide enough even to lay out a beach towel. Rooms have firm beds, mini-fridges, in-room safes, cable TV, free Wi-Fi, and balconies overlooking the sea. The rooms are clean and new but aging rapidly. The hotel has a pool that's not nearly as

big as it looks on the hotel website, plus a kids' pool, which makes the place popular with some families. The hotel also features two restaurants, a gym, music that's pumped throughout the open common areas, and slow service. The hotel is north of town but the road is good, making it a fairly quick drive. There's a free shuttle service into town three times a day.

The Spanish-owned **Punta Caracol Acqua Lodge** (tel. 6612-1088 or 6676-7186, www.puntacaracol.com, starts at US$400 s, US$460 d, including breakfast, dinner, and transfers) consists of nine bungalows built off the west side of Isla Colón, right on the calm waters of Almirante Bay. Boardwalks link the bungalows to each other and to an attractive open-air restaurant where at night guests dine by the light of kerosene lanterns. That's all that's out there: The little resort feels as though it's floating off by itself in the shallow sea. The place is run on solar power, and there's a septic system (toilet paper must be disposed of in a trash can, not the toilet).

Its five Punta Caracol Suites are cheerful, spacious, two-story wooden bungalows with thatched roofs. Upstairs is a large master bedroom with mosquito nets over a king-sized bed. A window is cut into the thatch to give a view of the water, but it can get stuffy up there at night. Downstairs is a sitting room with a couch that converts into a bed. This leads onto a back terrace with a landing from which guests can go snorkeling or swimming right from their rooms. The clear, shallow sea is your backyard, and there's nothing between you and the mainland mountains in the far distance.

Three newer bungalows, the Luna Suites (US$470 s, US$567 d), are similar to the other bungalows, but have larger terraces and bathing platforms, plus a hammock and hanging chair.

All eight bungalows can sleep up to four people, but the price goes up accordingly. There's also a Master Suite that's twice as big as the Punta Caracol Suites (US$490 s, US$619 d). It can accommodate up to six people, but again, there's a substantial per-person charge.

Rates include breakfast, dinner, transfers to and from the airport, a welcome cocktail, snorkeling gear, and use of kayaks. Food can be delicious here, and a huge breakfast is served in the morning.

As striking as this place is, there are some things that may bother guests, especially given the amount they're paying. The staff is casual, sometimes to the point of near rudeness. Guests have reported wildly different experiences of the food and service. There's a whiff of mangrove stench when the wind blows from shore. Despite the proximity of the mangroves, though, the *chitras* aren't too bad. If you stay here, you really have to be in the mood for isolation without too much entertainment. Expenses accumulate quickly if you want to explore. It's a long boat trip back to town, and the resort charges US$15–30 round-trip to ferry you. Tours of the surrounding area range US$20–60 per person.

This is probably the most photographed hotel in Panama, because it was the first of its kind on the isthmus. That is partly why it can charge some of the steepest rates in Bocas, but similar experiences can now be had elsewhere for less.

FOOD

Bocas town offers a fair range of cuisine, considering its size and location. Some places serve surprisingly good international fare. Pizza is particularly easy to come by, and some of it is quite tasty. A number of fast-food stalls are set around the perimeter of the park. Note that many restaurants are closed for lunch, when the tourists are usually out snorkeling and sunbathing.

Please boycott any restaurant that serves sea turtle meat or eggs or any other endangered species protected by law. It does still happen.

Restaurants and Cafés

The best place to eat in the archipelago is **◖ Restaurante Guari-Guari** (cell 6525-5513 and 6627-1825, 5:30–10 P.M. Thurs.–Tues., US$14). It's a short US$0.50 cab ride north of town, past the Feria del Mar on the

WATER QUALITY AND QUANTITY

Bocas del Toro is one of the few places in Panama that can't depend on safe drinking water coming out of the tap. Bocatoreños cite it as an example of how the central government neglects this remote province, which despite the tourism boom remains one of the poorest in Panama. For more than a decade, protests, sometimes violent ones, have flared up over the need for new waterworks and improved schools, roads, bridges, hospitals, and schools. It doesn't help that the aging infrastructure is occasionally damaged by earthquakes in this seismically active area, and pretty much annually by floods during the rainy season.

Water remains iffy even on the rapidly developing islands. Water is now allegedly safe, but it can still taste funky. Some establishments on the islands filter their water. Consider erring on the side of caution and bring a water purifier or buy bottled water. Local shops sell water for about US$1 a liter. Avoid the temptation to rely on beer as a thirst quencher, as that's a great way to get dehydrated in this hot, sweaty climate.

The islands occasionally experience serious water shortages (and, increasingly, power outages). At the height of tourist season in early 2007, Isla Colón endured a shortage that lasted nearly three months and sometimes forced residents and tourists to get by on a half hour of water daily. The problem abated when the U.S. quietly sent a military ship with a portable desalination plant to the rescue.

Generally, though, there's plenty of water, and after the most recent crisis some businesses installed their own water storage tanks. Ironically, the most remote hotels, which are off the grid, usually have the most dependable water supplies. As for mainland Bocas, many communities are constantly promised better conditions but suffer from a permanent lack of potable water.

isthmus that connects Bocas town with the rest of Isla Colón. (If the cab driver doesn't recognize the restaurant name, tell him to go to "la bomba"—the gas station. The restaurant is near it.)

The restaurant offers a single fixed-price menu each night: six courses for US$19. The food is gourmet and can include delicious takes on fare such as apple and pecan salad, carpaccio with shaved parmesan, a shot of asparagus crème, breaded prawns, and *filete* in red wine sauce. The restaurant is run by a friendly European couple; the chef is Spanish, and her German partner is host and waiter. It's a nicely decorated open-air place within earshot of pounding surf. The bathrooms are spotless. It's the place to go for a special night out.

◖ Restaurante El Pecado (Hotel Laguna, Calle 3 tel. 757-9091, 5–10 P.M. Tues.–Sat., US$10–13) is now in its third home, which lacks the funky charm of its predecessors. But it's on the terrace of the Hotel Laguna, so it's still a pleasant place to sit and watch the passing scene on Calle 3. The food is good and includes French, Thai, Mexican, Lebanese, and Panamanian dishes. The Thai soup is to die for, as is the fried camembert. Starters tend to be big and filling enough to make a meal out of. Guests can also opt for a three-course set dinner starting at around US$17. The French-Canadian owners are colorful characters and at this point practically Bocas institutions. In the last couple of years, the restaurant has gotten on a pizza kick, but even though the plate-sized pies are thick and piled with toppings, they don't have much flavor. Dinner is a safer bet than lunch because the owners are more likely to be on hand and in the kitchen. The sangria is delicious.

Restaurante y Bar La Casbah (near the intersection of Avenida Norte, Avenida G, and Calle 4, no phone, around 5:30–10 P.M. Tues.–Sat., US$10–13) is consistently good, and for several years now has been my top spot in town for great food in a funky atmosphere. Formerly the home of Om Café, the restaurant is shoehorned into the open-air wooden porch of a tiny, ramshackle building (which also houses a hidden, bottom-of-the-barrel hostel). It has a friendly bohemian vibe, and it's a popular hangout for European ex-pat residents. The owner-chef, Christopher, is an excellent cook who makes the best possible use of available ingredients. The French-influenced menu is small but changes daily. Beef filet is especially good here—it's tender, full of flavor, and cooked perfectly. If Christopher has fresh mushrooms, he offers his filets with a cognac and cream sauce that is absolutely delicious. His bacon shrimp rolls may sound odd, but it works and makes for a surprisingly light and fresh appetizer. He also cooks vegetables exactly right; if you don't think you like eggplant, it's only because you haven't had it the way it's prepared here. The bananas flambé is delicious, too.

Alberto's Pizzeria (Calle 5 between Avenida E/Luis Russell and Avenida F, tel. 756-9066, 11 A.M.–3 P.M. and 5–11 P.M. Mon.–Sat., US$6–8) has the best pizza on the island. Ingredients are fresh and the pizzas are lovingly made by the dedicated staff. How dedicated? The last time I ate there, Alberto, the Italian owner, had to tell a client he was out of pepperoni. But a few minutes later, he heard a plane coming in for a landing; realizing his pepperoni was on the plane, he grabbed his bike and pedaled to the airport to pick it up rather than disappoint a customer. A pizza feeds two moderately hungry people. The only drawback of this place at lunchtime is that, even though the dining area is open-sided, it doesn't have fans and can't catch a breeze, so it can be blazingly hot. Fortunately, Alberto's offers fresh lemonade and orange juice. There's also a full bar.

⟨ El Ultimo Refugio (cell 6726-9851 or 6568-8927, 5 P.M.–late Tues.–Sat., US$8–10) is easy to miss because it's at the far south of town, all the way down Calle 3 past the ferry pier. The pier that houses it has hosted several different restaurants over the years, all with tasty food, and this one is no exception. The eclectic menu changes daily, but can include such tempting dishes as shrimp in passion fruit cream sauce, pork tenderloin with balsamic

onion reduction, and chicken and shrimp Asian noodle salad. Starters include homemade chips and bean dip, hummus, and pesto crostini. Everything I've had here has been good. The drinks are strong and well mixed.

Restaurante Chitré (Calle 3 near Avenida D, no phone, 6 A.M.–9 P.M. Mon.–Sat., 10 A.M.–9 P.M. Sun.) is not just the best *fonda* in town, but it also serves some of the tastiest food, period. Meat, rice, and a soda will set you back US$3. Try the *polla en salsa;* it's delicious. The place is a hole in the wall, but it has a front porch that's good for people-watching.

⟨ Om Café (Avenida E/Luis Russell and Calle 3, cell 6624-0898, hours change but generally open for breakfast 8 A.M.–noon, lunch noon–4 P.M., and dinner 6–10 P.M. Thurs.–Tues., US$6–10) is still the hippest restaurant in town. Its current location is far more spacious that its original one, allowing for a bar scene inside and dining alfresco on the 2nd-floor veranda. The boho vibe is completed by good electronic music on the sound system. The owner is Indian-Canadian, and when she runs the kitchen expect delicious Indian home cooking. When she's not around, quality suffers. Try the shrimp tikka, which is great. So are the inventive cocktail concoctions, such as the "Tajmatini," made with vodka, lychee liqueur, and cranberry juice. It's intense. The "Bollywood" (vodka, triple sec, and passion fruit) is refreshing and not too sweet. Cocktails go for around US$5. Breakfast can be had for around US$6 and includes such unusual (for Bocas) items as bagels and yummy chana bhatura, which I haven't had for breakfast since I lived in India.

The Pirate (Calle 3 near Avenida C, no phone, 7 A.M.–11 P.M. daily, US$13–20) is a bar/restaurant on the water next to the downtown water-taxi piers. It serves so-so food, mostly seafood, and is relatively expensive. The best deal is its "executive lunch," a full plate of *típico* food for US$4.95.

A good bet for breakfast is **Lili's Café** (Calle 1 and Avenida D, next to Tropical Suites, tel. 757-9889, cell 6464-0256, www.kodiakbocas. com, 8 A.M.–4 P.M. Mon.–Sat., US$5). It's a

© WILLIAM FRIAR

Bocas town has many colorful dining options.

Bocas favorite as much for Lili's food as for her famous smile. Breakfast is served all day; note that omelets more closely resemble frittatas, but are tasty nonetheless. Other offerings include sandwiches, seafood, salad, lasagna, *gallo pinto* (a rice-and-bean dish), and various daily specials. Be sure to try Lili's own Killin' Me Man hot sauce.

Starfish Coffee (Calle 3 near Avenida B, no phone, 8 A.M.–9 P.M. Mon.–Sat.) is another good bet for breakfast, which it serves 8 A.M.– noon. Most full breakfasts are around US$5. Attention Brits: They don't call it that, but they serve a Bocas version of a full English breakfast here, substituting chipotle for baked beans and adding an extra helping of grease. It's quite tasty. There's a large selection of hot and cold coffee, tea, and chocolate drinks (made with organic Bocas chocolate). Saturday brunch includes such goodies as breakfast burritos, quiche, and an Antillean take on French toast, served with coffee/tea, juice, and a choice of a screwdriver or Bloody Mary. Lunch offerings include sandwiches served on bagels or bread

for US$4.50–7. Tapas (US$3) are served during happy hour, 5–7 P.M. Drinks include wine, beer, cocktails, and smoothies. There's a book exchange and a newsstand that carries new and used magazines to buy or borrow.

"The Sandwich Guy" (Calle 3 between Avenidas F and G, no phone, open evenings until late, US$2–4) is a beloved local fixture known both for his meticulously prepared sandwiches and for a moodiness that has earned him comparisons to the "Soup Nazi" on *Seinfeld*. His sandwiches, which he serves out of a caravan, are a great local favorite. They're easily the best in the islands. The Sandwich Guy is especially famous for his chicken Milanese.

Panadería y Dulcería La Alemaña (Calle 2 near Avenida E/Luis Russell, tel. 757-9436, 7 A.M.–8 P.M. daily), across the street from Om Café, offers so-so fresh bread and tasty buns at cheap prices.

Bocas Blended is an old school bus that's been given a paint job, converted into a smoothie stand, and plopped in the yard in front of Mondo Taitu. The young woman from New York who runs the place makes fresh-fruit smoothies (papaya, banana, melon, etc.) with your choice of milk, soy milk, or water for US$2.50–3. They're refreshing and a rare healthy option for breakfast or a snack on the run.

Markets

In addition to its restaurants and cafés, Bocas town also has an abundance of food stores, though don't come expecting a great selection of food. **Super Gourmet** (Calle 3 near the ferry pier, 9 A.M.–7 P.M. daily) is a godsend for expatriates hungering for something beyond the usual local fare. It has a nice selection of goodies, including fresh bread, cheese, fruit, organic Bocas chocolate, gourmet Boquete coffee, and many items that only in the backwaters of Bocas would be considered "gourmet" (e.g., Old El Paso salsa, ramen noodles, Vienna sausages). It also carries pricey but not necessarily good wine. The best thing about the place is its deli counter, which offers salads

BOCAS DEL TORO

© WILLIAM FRIAR

New places to grab a bite pop up constantly in town.

and sandwiches for around US$6, lasagna, whole roast chickens, pastries, and so on. The sandwiches are only so-so, but they're big. The cookies, many made with Bocas chocolate, are killer.

Tropical Markets (Calle 1 and Avenida E. Luis Russell, 9 A.M.–6 P.M. Mon.–Fri.) is a series of food stalls in an odd two-story building on the east side of town. The stalls carry meat, seafood, produce, wine, and other groceries, with a more upscale selection than is normally found in Bocas stores.

At last count there were a dozen *chinos* (mini-supermarkets) in Bocas town alone. Several are on Calle 3, just north and south of Avenida D. **Supermercado La Estrella de la Isla** (Calle 3, 7 A.M.–midnight daily) is next door to Hotel Laguna. **Supermercado Cayo Zapatilla** (Calle 3) is a similar place across the street. Both have produce stands on the street. The newer Supercentro Cristina is bigger but not really better. **Supermercado Isla Colón** (7:30 A.M.–11 P.M. daily) is on the southeast corner of Calle 3 and Avenida D.

The basic **Supermarket Hawaii** (Calle 6

and Avenida G, 7:30 A.M.–10:30 P.M. daily) is more convenient for those staying north of downtown.

INFORMATION

The Panama government's huge **CEFATI tourist information center** (Calle 1 near Avenida D, tel. 757-9642, 9 A.M.–5 P.M. Mon.–Fri.) is, as usual, heavy on the "center" and light on the "tourist information." The huge, two-story, Caribbean-style complex—situated, oddly enough, next to the town jail—is one of the bigger buildings in the archipelago. Staff in the past have been unfriendly and unhelpful. When I visited in 2010, it was closed and appeared abandoned.

Maps of the town and islands are much better than they used to be, and can be useful in getting one's bearings. The best is made by Rutas de Aventuras and is widely available in Bocas town for US$3.50.

The tiny **ANAM** office (Calle 1, on the water northeast of the park, tel. 757-9244, 8 A.M.–noon and 1–4 P.M. Mon.–Fri.) issues park permits and sometimes has marginally useful maps and brochures of Parque Nacional Marino Isla Bastimentos. Entrance to the marine park is US$10 per person. The fee to camp is another US$5 per tent. The fees can also be paid to the ranger on the Cayos Zapatillas, but those planning to camp there should check in with ANAM in any case to check on current conditions and rules. The office sometimes has information on other natural attractions of the area, including San San Pondsack. It's one block east of Parque Bolívar.

There is useful information about Bocas on the Internet. A good starting place is **www. bocas.com,** which contains links to many of the archipelago's hotels, restaurants, and services as well as dates of special events and holidays, interactive maps, and practical information on visiting the islands. The website for the **Bocas Marine and Tours** (Calle 3, tel./fax 757-9033, www.bocasmarinetours. com) water-taxi service contains nifty interactive maps of Bocas town and the archipelago, though they're no longer kept current. The site also contains useful travel tips and detailed information on getting around. The company's office, on the pier near The Pirate, is a good place to go for transportation information, especially to Costa Rica, during regular weekly business hours.

Farmacia Rosa Blanca (Calle 3 next to Bocas Marine and Tours, tel. 757-9560, 8:30 A.M.–9 P.M. Mon.–Sat., 10 A.M.–noon and 7–9 P.M. Sun.) is a full-service pharmacy and general store.

SERVICES
Nearly all the services in the archipelago are in Bocas town.

Banks
For many years there were just two places to withdraw cash in the entire archipelago. Things have changed now: There's only one. A branch of **Banco Nacional de Panamá** (Avenida E/Luis Russell and Calle 4, 8 A.M.–2 P.M. Mon.–Fri., 9 A.M.–noon Sat.) is in Bocas town on the way to the airport. It has a 24-hour ATM and cashes travelers checks. Even

if the second ATM opens again, both have been known to go on the blink at the same time.

While credit cards are increasingly accepted in Bocas, many transactions are still cash only. This can be a big hassle for those who want to book hotels ahead of time. Some places charge a fee for credit-card use; be sure to ask. Unfortunately, it's usually best to bring all the cash you think you might need during a stay.

Post Office
The post office (8 A.M.–noon and 2–5 P.M. Mon.–Fri., 7 A.M.–noon Sat.) is in the Palacio Municipal.

Internet and International Telephone Services
With the proliferation of free Wi-Fi just about everywhere, those with laptops or smart phones may have little need for Internet cafês, though these are still easy to find. Hostels and some of the hotels also tend to have Internet computers.

Bocas Internet Café (Calle 3 near Avenida D, tel. 757-9390, 7 A.M.–10 P.M. daily) offers Internet access for US$0.50 per 15 minutes, photocopying, snacks including imported chocolate, and service with a frown.

The **Cable and Wireless** office (Calle 1 due east of the park, tel. 882-7817, 8 A.M.–noon and 1–4:30 P.M. Mon.–Fri.) has pay phones and sells telephone cards. A phone card vending machine is outside the building and available 24 hours a day.

Immigration Office
There is an Immigration and Naturalization office, **Migración y Naturalización** (tel./fax 757-9263, 8 A.M.–4 P.M. Mon.–Fri.), in the Palacio Municipal at the north end of the park. But for most immigration concerns, foreigners still have to go to the main office in Changuinola, which is on the mainland, a lengthy bus or taxi trip away, or to David or Panama City.

Launderettes
Launderettes don't last long in Bocas. An exception is **Lavamático Don Pardo** (Avenida

Norte, 8 A.M.–8 P.M. Mon.–Sat.), between Casa Max and Restaurante y Bar La Casbah. It charges US$4.50 to wash and dry.

Marinas

The archipelago, long a haven for yachties, now supports two marinas. **Bocas Yacht Club and Marina** (tel. 757-9800, fax 757-9801, www.bocasmarina.com) is just southwest of Bocas town, across a small bay. It has floating docks that accommodate boats up to 100 feet long. The marina also offers some boat maintenance, laundry, charter, and brokerage services. There's an open-air bar.

Marina Carenero (tel./fax 757-9242, www.careeningcaymarina.com), on the west side of Isla Carenero close to Bocas town, accommodates boats up to 60 feet long. Laundry, boat maintenance, and Internet services are also available. There's a new marina near the entrance to Red Frog Beach, and others are in the works.

Courses

Spanish by the Sea (Calle 4 and Avenida A, tel. 757-9518, cell 6592-0775, www.spanishbythesea.com) is a flexible Spanish-language program run by a friendly staff that operates out of a home in the heart of Bocas town. Prices depend on course length, size of group, and hours per day of instruction. For instance, a five-day group course, with two hours a day of instruction, is US$80 per person. A five-day, six-hour-a-day intensive private course would cost US$430. There are price breaks for longer courses and small groups who enroll together.

Students can spend part of their course at the school's sister facilities, Spanish by the River in Boquete and in Turrialba, Costa Rica. The school can also arrange tours, dance lessons, and cooking lessons for an extra fee. It's also possible to combine courses with volunteer work, including help with a sea-turtle conservation project March–September, for those who want to practice their Spanish in meaningful situations or just help out. (It will connect nonstudents with volunteer work for a US$35 fee.)

Students can stay at the school in very basic rooms with fans and shared bathrooms for US$10 for a shared room or US$15 for a private room. Laundry service (US$5 a load), Internet access (US$1/hour), and breakfast (US$4) are available. Guests are welcome to use the kitchen. The school also arranges homestays with a family in Bocas town for US$15 per person for a private room, including breakfast. Apartments are also available. In 2010, the school acquired a second location closer to the airport and was planning to use this at least until it upgraded its main building.

A Florida-based nonprofit called the **Institute for Tropical Ecology and Conservation (ITEC)** (U.S. tel. 352/367-9128, www.itec-edu.org) has a biological field station in Boca del Drago. It's a private outfit unaffiliated with any university, but it draws its faculty from various U.S. and Latin American universities. It offers three-week winter and four-week summer courses in tropical ecology. Tuition is US$1,650 and US$1,950 respectively. The fee includes room and board—students are housed in the rustic Cabañas Estefani and fed at Restaurante Yarisnori, both of which are next to the station. There is also a two-week "travel session" that takes students around Panama (US$900). ITEC sometimes uses a second research facility on the Soropta Peninsula.

GETTING THERE AND AWAY

Regardless of their final destination in the archipelago, travelers must first get to Bocas town, on Isla Colón. There are two ways to do this—by plane or by land and water taxi/ferry.

By Air

There are several daily flights between Panama City and the archipelago (US$105.19 each way, about 1.25 hours). There is also one flight to and from David during the week (US$58.11 each way, about 20 minutes), as well as two daily flights to and from Changuinola (US$27.90, 10 minutes).

Note: Flight schedules change more frequently for Bocas than other destinations.

Flights can also fill up fast, especially during holidays. Book as far in advance as possible, and double-check departure times a day or two before your flight.

A small Costa Rican airline, Nature Air, flies between Bocas and several destinations in Costa Rica, including San José. Air Panama recently dropped its flights between Costa Rica and Bocas, but it flies between San José, Costa Rica, and David, where it's possible to make air or land connections to Bocas.

The only airport in the archipelago is on Isla Colón, on the edge of Bocas town. Transportation to the other islands is by boat only. The little airport is on the west side of town, along Avenida E. Those without much luggage will probably find it easy to walk to most of the town's hotels, but a taxi or *transporte cooperativa* van to the airport costs US$1 per person.

Note that flights sometimes make an intermediate stop at Changuinola; be sure to get off at the right place. These flight schedules are subject to change, so check with the airlines well ahead of time.

Aeroperlas (reservations tel. 378-6000, David tel. 775-9341, Bocas tel. 757-9341, www.aeroperlas.com) flies between Bocas and Panama City and David.

It offers two daily flights from Panama City to Bocas (6:45 A.M. and 2:55 P.M. daily) and two flights from Bocas to Panama City (9:05 A.M. and 5:20 P.M. daily).

There are three weekly flights from David to Bocas (11:20 A.M. Mon., Wed., and Fri.) and from Bocas to David (12:05 P.M. Mon., Wed., and Fri.). Warning: As this book went to press, flight cancellations on the David–Bocas run due to "maintenance problems" were becoming more frequent. Travelers have been forced to fly the next work day, if space is available. Avoid booking a Friday flight, which if canceled would mean being stranded over the weekend. And consider going by bus instead, at least as a backup plan.

Aeroperlas also has two daily flights for the puddle-jumper hop from Changuinola to Bocas town (8:35 A.M., 4:50 P.M.) and two daily flights from Bocas to Changuinola (8 A.M. and 4:15 P.M.).

Air Panama (tel./fax 316-9000, www.fly-airpanama.com) has two daily flights from Panama City to Bocas (6:45 A.M. and 3:30 P.M. Mon.–Sat., 8 A.M. and 3:30 P.M. Sun.). Its flights from Bocas to Panama City are less frequent these days (4:45 P.M. Mon.–Sat., 9:15 A.M. and 4:45 P.M. Sun.).

The Costa-Rica-based **Nature Air** (Costa Rica tel. 506/2299-6000, U.S./Canada toll-free tel. 800/235-9272, www.natureair.com) offers three (low season) to five (high season) weekly non-stop flights between Bocas and San José, Costa Rica, as well as connecting service to and from other Costa Rican destinations. Contact the airline for prices and schedules.

By Land and Water

The logistics of getting to and from the islands from the mainland aren't that complicated, but they can be confusing to those unfamiliar with the area. It may be helpful to refer to a map when making plans.

Almirante is the mainland port for the Bocas archipelago. The water taxis and the car ferry leave from there. (Water taxis have stopped running from the mainland town of Changuinola, at least for now.)

The closest border crossing with Costa Rica is a bridge over the Río Sixaola that connects the flyspeck town of Guabito (Panama side) with the flyspeck town of Sixaola (Costa Rica side).

International buses run between Costa Rica and the Panamanian town of Changuinola, which is near the border. Buses and taxis run constantly between Changuinola and the Almirante port. There are frequent buses between Almirante and David, and one daily bus between Almirante and Panama City. The Almirante and Changuinola sections have detailed information on buses and taxis.

Warning: The last water taxis of the day leave the mainland at 6:30 P.M. After that, travelers will have to spend the night on the mainland, most likely in Changuinola or Almirante, both of which have a certain backwater-town funkiness but little in the way of charm or

BOCAS DEL TORO

things to do, especially compared with the islands. Changuinola has the broader range of accommodations and services, but it's not the safest place at night. (Though neither is Almirante.)

A better option for those who can afford it is La Escapada, 64 kilometers east of Almirante.

TO AND FROM THE REST OF PANAMA

The land link between the islands and the rest of Panama is the Fortuna Road. It connects Chiriquí, a small Pacific-side town on the Interamerican Highway about 15 kilometers east of David, with Chiriquí Grande, about 100 kilometers away on the Caribbean coast. The route takes travelers over the Continental Divide and the huge Fortuna dam and hydroelectric plant. It's a scenic drive on a good road, but be careful as it averages more than one auto accident a week. Driving the length of the Fortuna Road takes a little under two hours.

The road descends the Caribbean slope quickly and soon reaches the hot and humid flatlands near the coast. Pass the village of Punta Peña. There'll be a crossroads ahead, with a 24-hour gas station and restaurant. Straight leads to the oil-port town of Chiriquí Grande, which has nothing to offer travelers since a ferry service to the islands stopped running years ago.

Instead, turn left at the gas station onto the new road to Almirante. This is a lovely, 70-kilometer drive that takes about an hour. But slash-and-burn farmers and subsistence ranchers have followed the road, and the lush tropical evergreen forest along this entire strip of coast is disappearing fast. Entire hillsides are sliding down into the road, so be careful. It's a disturbing example of how quickly nature can be devastated in the tropics; at this rate, the land here will be of little value to anyone in a few years.

There's a bridge between kilometer markers 8 and 9. This is a good place for a rest stop. Pull over on the right just after the bridge, or turn left and park near the bank of the little river. About five minutes upriver is a massive boulder in the middle of the stream with **petroglyphs** near the top. If the weather is dry, bring a water container to splash river water on the boulder; it's much easier to make out the petroglyphs when they're wet. There are trails on both sides of the river; the petroglyphs are easiest to see from the east side. Cross back over the bridge on foot and follow the path down by the river. When the trail gets very rocky, head uphill, which allows one to look down on the boulder. If you can't find it, and a local is hanging around, ask him or her to show the way. A tip of US$0.25–0.50 for this would be appreciated. The trail on the west side of the river leads into some lovely forest and a waterfall about a half hour away.

TO AND FROM COSTA RICA

To get to the islands from Costa Rica, travelers must go through border formalities at Sixaola-Guabito. From there most take a bus or taxi to Almirante and then a water taxi to the islands.

However, there is now a simpler way to deal with all the logistics. The **Caribe Shuttle** (Taxi 25 pier in Bocas town, tel. 757-7048, www.caribeshuttle.com) is a service that runs travelers between Bocas and hotels in Costa Rica. In Bocas, the service picks up passengers from their hotel and takes them to the Taxi 25 pier, where they are transported to the mainland and taken to the Guabito-Sixaola border crossing and then on to Puerto Viejo in Costa Rica. Pick-up times are 8 A.M. and 2:30 P.M. daily.

For the trip from Costa Rica to Bocas, hotel pick-up in Puerto Viejo takes place between 6:30–7:30 A.M. and 12:30–1:30 P.M. In either direction, the trip costs US$34 one way, US$64 round-trip. Add US$6 each way for pick-up/drop-off for more distant spots in Costa Rica (specifically, Cahuita, Punta Uva, or Manzanillo). Space is limited, so advance reservations are a must. The shuttle is experimenting with transfers between San José and Puerto Viejo for US$67, though those heading to Bocas will have to cool their heels in Puerto Viejo for 3.5 hours before catching the shuttle.

Contact Caribe Shuttle to see if this service is still being offered.

ALMIRANTE-BOCAS TOWN WATER TAXIS

Two water taxi companies run between the mainland town of Almirante and Bocas town on Isla Colón. Water-taxi prices stay pretty stable, but fuel costs occasionally bump them up a bit. Boats sometimes fill to capacity; it's a good idea to book reservations ahead of time, but this can only be done in person. Those with a tight schedule should book their departure from Bocas the night before they intend to leave. Allow extra time, as water taxis schedules are loose.

Bocas Marine and Tours (Almirante tel. 758-4085, Changuinola tel. 758-9033, Bocas town tel./fax 757-9033, www.bocasmarine-tours.com) is the first place you'll come to in Almirante. **Expreso Taxi 25** (Almirante tel. 758-3498, Bocas town tel. 757-9028) is farther down. In Bocas town, the pier for Expreso Taxi 25 is near the police station. The pier for Bocas Marine and Tours is midway down Calle 3, near Transparente Tours and Restaurante Le Pirate. Both have daily departures for Almirante roughly every 30–45 minutes, depending on demand, 6 A.M.–6:30 P.M. The fare is US$4 at either place. The trip takes about 25 minutes.

These days both water-taxi outfits are pretty much the same, so just choose whichever one is ready to go when you arrive. Both recently spruced up their Almirante piers, particularly Taxi 25, which now has a quite decent waiting room.

Those with their own vehicle can park in a guarded parking lot in Almirante for US$3/day at Leiza's, on the road just before the water-taxi piers. There's a sign. Leiza and her family actually live in a house inside the lot, which is surrounded by a tall chain-link fence.

ALMIRANTE-BOCAS TOWN FERRY

Few will want to fool with the painfully slow **Ferry Palanga** (Bocas town tel. 6615-6674, 261-0350, or 229-1742, Almirante tel. 229-1639) that runs between Almirante and Bocas town. It doesn't run often in any case. Only those who insist on bringing a vehicle to Bocas town—something there is very little reason to do—should bother with the ferry. The ferry runs Monday–Saturday, leaving Almirante at 8 A.M. and returning from Isla Colón at 4 P.M. The trip takes 1.5 hours. The fare is US$1.50 for foot passengers, US$1 for kids, US$2 for a bike, US$10 for a motorcycle, US$15 for a car, and US$30 for a four-wheel drive. The ferry pier in Almirante is past the turnoff to the water taxis; look for the Texaco sign. The Bocas town ferry dock is at the southern end of Calle 3, across the street from the Hotel Bahía.

GETTING AROUND
By Water

Many places on Isla Colón are more cheaply and easily reached by boat, which is also the only way to get to the other islands in the archipelago. Fares are standardized to most destinations. Note that rising gas prices may push these rates up.

Freelance boatmen operate a casual water-taxi service between the islands. These boats stop constantly throughout the day at the town piers. Boats operate less frequently at night, and the lack of proper lighting on most boats can make it a riskier prospect; try to travel in daylight. Boats leave when they fill up. Less-common destinations may require hiring the whole boat; it may be more economical and efficient to visit these places as part of a full-fledged boat tour.

A water-taxi collective operates in downtown Bocas town. It's just to the right as you face Bocas Marine and Tours. It focuses on Bocas-Bastimentos transport, but will find you a boat to wherever you want to go.

Another cooperative operates from a landing right next to the Barco Hundido. As you face the bar, the boardwalk to the landing will be on your right. Standard prices are posted, including rates to popular surf spots. There's also a water-taxi landing next to the CEFATI.

The standard per-person fare is US$1 to the nearest point on Isla Carenero, US$3 to Old

Bank and US$5 to Red Frog Beach on Isla Bastimentos, and US$3 to Solarte. Carenero is less than 5 minutes away; it takes about 10 minutes to get to Solarte or Old Bank. Boats can sometimes drop clients on the beaches on the east side of Isla Colón. The surf can sometimes be quite rough, though. Expect to pay more if you're the only one in the boat, or wait until there's at least one other passenger. Rates double to Red Frog Beach and other more distant locations at night, when it's usually not a good idea to be on the water in any case.

Getting to the islands by water taxi often involves fending off *boleteros* (ticket touts) who work for commissions from specific hotels and water-taxi operations. They may offer to carry travelers' luggage to the water-taxi pier for a small tip. Those who want to help local people can find many better ways than handing over spare change to these kids, which is just going to mean more hassle for the next tourist who wanders through.

There have been reports of touts claiming one of the water-taxi services (the one not paying them a commission) is closed. Taxi drivers sometimes steer passengers to a particular water-taxi service or try to overcharge passengers, for instance, by charging as much per person as locals would pay per carload—be sure to clarify the deal before getting in the cab.

Some enterprising characters have set up a kind of tourist shuttle business at the Costa Rican border in which they meet travelers—sometimes before they even cross over to Panama—and offer to usher them all the way to the islands by taxi and water taxi. They charge significantly more for this "service" than you'd pay on your own, and they'll steer you to places that pay them commission.

By Land

There are only two major roads beyond Bocas town: one that extends up the east coast of Isla Colón, dead-ending at Playa Bluff, and a second that cuts diagonally across the island to Boca del Drago. There's no need to ferry a car over, as it's easy to get around the island by taxi, bus, or rented bike or motorcycle.

There is now a mini-bus service, **Transporte Boca del Drago** (cell 6607-7681, US$2) connecting Bocas town and Boca del Drago. It leaves from the northwest end of Parque Bolívar Monday–Friday at 7 A.M., 10 A.M., noon, 3 P.M., and 5 P.M., returning at 8 A.M., 11 A.M., 1 P.M., 4 P.M., and 6 P.M. On the weekend, buses go to Boca del Drago at 10 A.M., noon, 3 P.M., and 5 P.M.; the bus makes the return trip an hour later. This schedule changes from time to time, depending on demand. Riders can save a buck by buying a round-trip ticket, which allegedly guarantees a seat on the return bus (it can get crowded). This is a slow ride, as the bus picks up locals all along the route. It usually takes about an hour.

Sadly, Bocas town is not as pedestrian friendly as it used to be. There are now a ridiculous number of cars, trucks, and motorcycles downtown for such a small place. Be careful on Calle 3.

Taxis troll Calle 3 looking for customers. The fare to or from the airport and anywhere in town, including all the way to the northern waterfront at Saigon, is US$1 per person. Fares within town are US$0.50. The one-way fare to the end of Playa Bluff is US$15–20, depending on the condition of the road and mood of the driver. A round-trip ride to Boca del Drago is US$30 and to La Gruta US$20. *Transporte colectiva* vans operate in town and to the airport, also for US$1 per person. Flag them down just as you would a taxi, and pay when you board.

Bike and scooter rental places come and go, but there are always several to choose from. A place that may be around for a while is **Ixa's Bicycle World** (Avenida Norte between Calle and Calle 6, tel. 757-5379, 8 A.M.–6 P.M.), a bike-repair place near Mondo Taitu that rents bikes starting at US$10 per day and up to US$40 per week. A stand set up in the yard in front of Mondo Taitu rent bikes for US$2 per hour, up to $12 per day. Two-wheel scooters at the same spot are available for US$15 per hour or US$50 per day. To rent scooters from any stand, expect to present a driver's license, passport, and a deposit of US$50 or so.

Isla Carenero

This little island is just a banana's throw across the water from Bocas town. Because it's so close to the busy waterfront and is pretty built up itself, it's not a popular tourist destination. It's more like a suburb of Bocas town. But it's home to a couple of appealing places to stay.

The side of the island facing Isla Colón is rather densely populated, with lots of basic houses squeezed next to each other on the waterfront. The side that faces Bastimentos is more deserted; there's little there except for a couple of small hotels and a bit of beach. The north side of the island has pounding surf, but the coastline is rather rugged and more mud and farmland than beach. Actually, the whole island is ringed by just a narrow band of sandy beach. Visitors have to travel to one of the other islands for big, spectacular beaches. The island is notorious for especially voracious *chitras* (sand flies).

It's possible to walk around the entire perimeter of the island, but be prepared for a bit of an adventure rather than a leisurely walk. It can take up to two hours to walk the whole way around, and there are sections that require scrambling up muddy hills, dropping several feet, slipping through barbed-wire fences, avoiding pounding surf, and negotiating slippery, jagged rocks.

Carenero is popular with **surfers** for a long, barreling reef break off the north side of the island that's considered one of the best waves in Bocas. Called simply Carenero, it's just a five-minute boat ride from Bocas town and thus can get crowded. The reef is shallow; wear booties.

That's about all there is in the way of activities on the island other than splashing and paddling around.

ACCOMMODATIONS AND FOOD

Places to stay on Carenero vary from hostel dorms to fairly upscale little hotels. Most have a restaurant attached. A walking path along the water links all of them. Places here are listed in counterclockwise order, starting from the west side of the island.

The **Careening Cay Resort** (tel. 757-9157, www.careeningcay.com, starts at US$43 s/d) is set in a garden near the water overlooking Isla Colón. It comprises six wooden bungalows and an open-air restaurant, the Cosmic Crab Café, over the water. Three of the bungalows (US$104.50 s/d, US$11 for each additional person) have two rooms, with a queen-size bed, twin-size bunk beds, and a fully equipped kitchenette with gas stove, microwave, and fridge. Note that the room divider doesn't reach the ceiling, limiting privacy. There is also is a one-room bungalow with queen bed (US$82.50 s/d). A new bungalow is twice the size of the two-bedroom ones and sleeps six or more people (US$152.90). All the bungalows have a TV and DVD player and hot-water bathrooms, and all stays include a buffet breakfast. Construction has been taking place for several years on either side of this place, and the area has been attracting trash and rather squalid shacks, presumably housing workers. Careening Cay is insulated from this, on well-tended grounds.

The restaurant attached to the resort is the Cosmic Crab Café (tel. 757-9157, www.careeningcay.com, noon–9 P.M. Tues.–Sun., US$6–10), a friendly place that's especially popular with the gringo crowd. The bar and main dining area is in a large *rancho* over the water, connected by a boardwalk to a line of small private *ranchos*. Offerings include seafood, salads, soups, and burgers. The restaurant is known for its crab cakes, at least when crab is available. At other times they make the cakes with other fish, such as red snapper, which is delicious, as are the conch fritters. This is also a good place to go for hummus and falafel. The wife in the couple that own the place is a mixologist and is always creating new concoctions, which are enormous and cost around US$5–6. Her ginger snap

© WILLIAM FRIAR

Cosmic Crab Café offers good food and a view of the sunset.

martini is refreshing and potent. There's a whole line of ice-cream-based drinks with names like Sex in the Mud (vanilla vodka, Kahlua, crème de cacao, chocolate ice cream, and a frozen banana). There's a sunset dinner three-course special from 4–6 P.M. for US$8, and this is a place you can actually see the sun set.

The **Aqua Lounge Hostel & Bar** (tel. 757-9975, cell 6581-8528, 6734-2550, or 6710-1626, US$10 pp, including breakfast) is, as its owners are fond of pointing out, the only hostel in Bocas that's over the water. That's only one of its attractions. Stays here include breakfast, free wireless Internet, and use of the communal kitchen. The hostel is built onto a dock strung with hammocks, and when it gets too warm guests can roll right into the sea for a swim or a bounce on the water trampoline. The shared bathrooms have hot-water showers. The two dorm rooms have a total of 11 beds, and though they're pleasant enough, some may find them dark and a bit claustrophobic.

But all the extras make this place more like a tropical bohemian playground than a back-packers' crash pad. (Note to Bocas veterans: This place used to be the legendary Bernard's Pargo Rojo.)

Guests need to be comfortable sharing their surroundings with partying hordes, as the attached **Aqua Lounge Bar** (www.bocasaqua-lounge.info) is a popular nightspot. It opens around 10 A.M. and stays open late every night. The big nights here are Saturday (reggae night) and Wednesday (ladies' night—drinks free for the females of the species). The Aqua Lounge is directly across from the Barco Hundido in Bocas town, making it easy to bar hop.

Casa Acuario (tel. 757-9565, casaacuario@ aol.com, www.casaacuario.com, US$77–88 s/d, including breakfast) is a bed-and-breakfast built right over the water that offers four cute, spacious, and sunny wood-paneled rooms with modern bathrooms, air-conditioning, and cable TV. It has its own small stretch of beach. There's a balcony upstairs with a view of the ocean, Isla Colón, and the mountains on the distant shore. Guests are welcome to use the kitchen. A third and fourth person in the room are another US$11 each. The place has a family vibe and not a whole lot of privacy, so pray that your neighbors are *simpático*.

Hotel Tierra Verde (tel. 757-9903, cell 6615-5911, www.hoteltierraverde.com, starts at US$71.50 s/d, including breakfast) is a three-story, surfer-oriented hotel set back from the beach. Built in 2001, it has seven rooms with dark-wood paneling, all with air-conditioning and hot-water bathrooms. A two-bedroom suite (US$165 s/d) was added a couple of years ago. It occupies the 3rd floor and has a private balcony, sitting room, mini-fridge, and cable TV. It's quite attractive. Rates for the other rooms are US$71.50 s/d with a garden view and US$82.50 for an ocean view. Additional guests are US$11 each. Rates are somewhat higher during the holidays. Stays include a continental breakfast, use of kayaks, and wireless Internet access. Guests can also use the Internet computer in the lobby. The hotel arranges a variety of tours.

Doña Mara (tel. 757-9551, donamara10@hotmail.com, www.bocas.com, US$71.50 s/d), on the east side of the island, facing Bastimentos, is a cinderblock building with six simple but pleasant and brightly painted rooms, all with air-conditioning, cable TV, and tile floors. The place is well-maintained. It's on a small beach and has a bar and restaurant that's open 7:30 A.M.–9 P.M. daily.

The **Pickled Parrot** (tel. 757-9093, 11 A.M.–late daily, US$5–6), near the end of the path on the east side of Carenero, consists of a large *rancho* built onto a pier where one can watch waves crashing under one's feet. It serves bar food and big burgers. Mainly, though, it's a relaxing place to drink a beer and meditate on the islands and sea. The kitchen closes at 9 P.M., but the bar stays open until the last customer teeters out. Note that the last water taxi to Isla Colón leaves at around midnight. The joint has a few rooms for rent if you get stranded.

PRACTICALITIES

There are few services of any kind on Carenero, but it's less than five minutes by boat from Bocas town. Water taxis run frequently between Carenero and the two town piers. To get to Bastimentos from Carenero, it's easier to take a boat back to Bocas town and get a Bastimentos-bound boat from there.

However, the island does now have the best gift shop on the islands. **Treasures of the Turquoise Crab** (tel. 757-9157, www.careeningcay.com) at the Careening Cay Resort is an air-conditioned store selling good quality local and imported jewelry and souvenirs. These include tagua carvings, Emberá-Wounaan masks, and so on. The *chaquiras* (Ngöbe-Buglé necklaces) here are among the best I've seen in Panama, with the most elaborate going for about US$50. The owner is a professional jeweler, so there are original creations as well.

BOCAS DEL TORO

Isla Bastimentos

This big, beautiful island (52 square kilometers) has a lot to offer nature lovers. The north shore has pounding surf and miles of gorgeous sandy beaches, some of which attract sea turtles in nesting season. The protected waters on the southeast side of the island, between Cayo Crawl and Punta Vieja, are shallow and glassy, making it easy to explore a large underwater playground of coral and sponges. To the southwest are mangrove islands. And the island itself is home to forest that harbors many exotic and endangered species, including the famous red poison-dart frog *(Oophaga pumilio),* that many come to the island to see. The midsection of the island and some of its surrounding waters are part of a national marine park, Parque Nacional Marino Isla Bastimentos.

Though about 1,350 people live on the island, most are concentrated in the largely Afro-Caribbean town of Old Bank on its western

© WILLIAM FRIAR

commuter, Isla Bastimentos

tip, and in the Ngöbe village of Quebrada de Sal (Salt Creek in English). They're rather ragged places and there isn't much to see, but they're both culturally interesting and worth a visit. The name Bastimentos, by the way, comes from the Spanish word for "supplies" or "provisioning."

Bastimentos is a large, oddly shaped island, and its attractions are spread widely apart. The town of Old Bank, just 10 minutes by boat from Bocas town, is the closest to Isla Colón. Cayo Crawl is at the southern tip, separated by a shallow channel from Isla Popa. The southeast side is sheltered, with glassy water, coral gardens, the Ngöbe village of Quebrada de Sal, and access to the Cayos Zapatillas. Lovely beaches with pounding surf, the famous red frogs, and turtle-nesting spots are on the northern side. Exploring the forested interior, part of which belongs to the marine park, requires a guide to reach caves and a freshwater lake.

SIGHTS
Old Bank

The town of Old Bank, known to many simply as "Bastimentos," is on the west tip of the island, not far from Isla Carenero and Bocas town. Most of its residents live close to each other in crumbling, zinc-roofed homes perched on the waterfront or on the hillside behind it. Its residents are mostly descendants of West Indian immigrants, and the place has a mellow, strongly Caribbean vibe. There's always loud music playing—sometimes live, if you're lucky.

The town is poor, trash-strewn, and has little to see, but it still has lots of local color, and it's the best place in the islands to hear Guari-Guari, a Bocas-specific variety of so-called Panamanian Creole English. It's fascinating to listen to and nearly impossible for the uninitiated to make much sense of, even though it derives primarily from English.

Old Bank is not for everyone, especially as a place to stay. Some people love it, particularly backpackers and surfers who want to experience the "real" Bocas. Others find it dirty and a bit squalid, and the vibe sometimes less than friendly. On my last couple of visits, I've been disturbed to encounter a couple of truly drug-addled characters. But a little friendliness can be warmly reciprocated, and there are some wonderful people among the residents, both local and expat. Roots Bar and Restaurant is a good place to meet friendly folk, beginning with the smiling staff. The town is even a bit cleaner these days, and the sewage problem is allegedly being brought under control.

Two parallel concrete paths extend the length of town. There are several places to stay and a couple of restaurants and bars. A trail to the north-side beaches starts at the east end of town.

Bahía Honda

This mangrove-ringed bay on the south side of Bastimentos has become popular in recent years with travelers interested in exploring the long, mysterious jungle **cave** near its shore. But there's more there than that, including the Ngöbe community of Bahía Honda, which totals about 200 people in 40 families and welcomes visitors. It has a few attractions of possible interest, including a new restaurant. There is also a unique jungle lodge I like a lot.

The Ngöbe's rustic, thatched-roof **Bahía Honda Restaurant** (cell 6726-0968, 6619-5364, or 6592-5162; ask for Rutilio Milton) on the shoreline caters to travelers and supports the local community. The restaurant is open for lunch only, and only with advance notice. Call ahead of time or arrange a visit through your hotel. Lunch is US$6.

There is no real "village" as such and the Ngöbe have lost many of their traditional ways, but Ngöbe women can often be seen making traditional *nagua* dresses, *chakara* woven bags, and *chaquira* beaded necklaces. These are for sale. A child's *nagua* makes a cute present for young girls (US$10; the adult-sized ones are US$30). Visitors can hike surrounding trails or try their luck in a *cayuco* (dugout canoe). Good luck—they're very easy to flip.

The boat trip up the windy creek to the Bahía Honda bat cave is pretty cool, especially if you travel with a boatman who takes it slow and is good at spotting wildlife. Be patient and make sure to douse yourself with insect repellent ahead of time. On my trip, we saw four three-toed sloths, a huge iguana, and a caiman within a couple meters of the boat. The vegetation is striking as well. Black, red, and white mangroves grow on either side, and where the boat ties up there are enormous stands of bamboo and absolutely massive gnarled old trees. The cave is a short walk away, with its bats, stalactites, and water that in places can come up to one's neck.

◖ Cayo Crawl

Boats from Isla Colón that approach Bastimentos from the south pass a series of idyllic mangrove islands, protected as part of the marine park, before coming to Cayo Crawl, a shallow channel between Isla Bastimentos and Isla Popa. In keeping with the Bocas name game, Cayo Crawl is sometimes called Cayo Coral, and in English it's called Crawl Cay or Coral Cay. Got that? It's about a half hour by boat from Bocas town.

The water here is a luminous light green, smooth as glass, and in some places only a meter deep before hitting sandy bottom. The area attracts lots of tropical fish. It's an easy, relaxing place to snorkel or splash around.

Note: Some tour operators, wanting to save on gas, take snorkelers only as far as Cayo Crawl and call it a day. Given that coral gardens don't start until one rounds the point and heads up the southeast coast of Bastimentos—at which point there are kilometers of them—don't agree to this. Find out ahead of time exactly where the boat is heading.

The channel harbors a few rustic thatched-hut restaurants, built on stilts over the water, that are tourist destinations in their own right. Tours to Cayos Zapatillas and around Bastimentos usually include a stop at one of these photogenic spots. These are bare-bones establishments, but at least you know the seafood is fresh. Expect to pay around US$8 for fish, or more than twice that for lobster.

The water is so shallow and clear that diners can watch slender needlefish and brilliant parrotfish, angelfish, snapper, and other aquatic life cavort just off the boardwalk. The fish in the area are so spoiled by free feedings that Restaurante Cayo Crawl attracts a couple of "tame" barracuda.

A good strategy for those who want to eat at any of these places, since service tends to proceed at a languorous Caribbean pace, is to place orders ahead of time and then go snorkeling until the food's ready.

Cayo Crawl to Punta Vieja

The sheltered waters from Cayo Crawl to Punta Vieja, a point about eight kilometers up the southeast coast of Bastimentos, offer some colorful snorkeling. The sea here is so shallow and calm it's like swimming in a tropical aquarium. There's a variety of coral and sponges and lots of small but dazzling fish. However, as elsewhere in the archipelago, the visibility can be disappointing. A few small hotels have been built along the coast, but this is still a remarkably isolated and tranquil spot. Waves are so gentle here that fish swim right up to the narrow strips of sandy beach.

◖ North Shore Beaches

The sea along the north side of Bastimentos is generally much too rough to do more than get one's feet wet. But there are several spectacularly beautiful beaches here. The one most popular with sea turtles is **Playa Larga** in Parque Nacional Marino Isla Bastimentos. Warning: There have been reports of thefts from these beaches, particularly Playa Primera. Do not leave valuables unattended.

The sea is often too choppy to land boats on the beaches. An exception is **Playa Polo,** which is partly protected because waves break on rocks about 100 meters offshore. This means it's easier to go for a swim here, but it also means it's more likely to have visitors than some of the other beaches, and it's far too small to accommodate many people comfortably. There are nicer beaches farther west.

If the sea is rough, the best way to get to these beaches is to walk across the western neck of the island from Old Bank.

The trail to the beach starts toward the eastern edge of town, just past the soccer field and

MOST "RED FROGS" AREN'T RED

What is locally called the red frog is more widely referred to as the strawberry poison-dart frog. But neither name does justice to a species that comes in a jewel box of colors. Though in its best-known form it is red with blue legs, the tiny frog can be green, yellow, purple, orange, black, white, or a combination of these and other colors, with or without spots.

A safer bet is to call it by its scientific name, *Oophaga pumilio.* (It was reclassified in 2006, before which it was known as *Dendobates pumilio.*) It lives along the Caribbean coast from Nicaragua to Panama. Though its common throughout Bocas del Toro, Bastimentos is famous for containing a remarkable number of forms, or morphs, on a single island.

The frogs can be hard to spot because of their small size: just 18-25 millimeters, or less than half as big as a man's thumb. They live in the forests of the islands and mainland but don't mind disturbed areas and are easiest to spot in dry leaf litter or near the forest edge. The males have a surprisingly loud call.

Though its skin produces toxins for defense, *Oophaga pumilio* doesn't pose a threat to humans, particularly those who don't eat one. It's nowhere near as potent as the golden poison-dart frog of Colombia, the aptly named *Phyllobates terribilis.* The skin of a single specimen of these is said to have enough toxin to kill 20,000 mice or a gruesome number of humans. Indigenous hunters of the Colombian rainforest traditionally tipped their blowgun darts with the deadly stuff.

Compared to these formidable creatures, *Oophaga pumilio* is positively cuddly. But their own poison, or pumiliotoxin, is still potent. A group of visiting researchers discovered in 2004 how they get it: from munching a type of small ant.

trash pile. You'll have to walk through towns-people's yards to get to the trail. There are now signs pointing to the start of the trail, but ask for directions to the beach (*playa,* pronounced "PLY-yah") if you can't find the way. It's a very pretty walk over a hill to the beach, with panoramic views from the summit. The walk takes half an hour at a moderate pace. Part of the trail leads through private property, and if the owner is around pay him a US$1 toll to pass through it. The trail can get muddy and slippery near the beach.

The first beach you'll come to is called, logically enough, **Playa Primera (First Beach),** though these days most people know it by its other, more intriguing name, **Playa Wizard**. It's a wide, stunning stretch of sand, big rollers, and, if you're lucky, very few people. Again, beware of the strong surf here. Walk east to get to **Playa Segunda (Second Beach)** and **Red Frog Beach.**

Silverbacks, the biggest surf break in Bocas, is off this stretch of coast and is accessible by boat. It's a huge, barreling reef-bottom right break that is often compared to big Hawaiian waves such as Backdoor. Wave faces can exceed seven meters. It's strictly for expert surfers. There are beach breaks off Wizard/First Beach and Red Frog Beach that are appropriate for intermediate surfers.

Red Frog Beach's namesake is a tiny creature also called the strawberry poison-dart frog *(Oophaga pumilio)* that's easier to spot here than anywhere else in Panama. The toxins in its skin are only a danger to animals who try to eat it. In reality the frog comes in a variety of vibrant colors besides red.

There's a US$3 fee to poke around this area. The beach can be approached by sea only when the water is dead calm. Otherwise, boatmen drop passengers off at one of the beaches to the west and tell them to walk over, or, most commonly, drop them at a trail east of Old Bank that leads over a narrow isthmus to Red Frog Beach. The last is the best option, as the trail is good and it's an easy 10-minute walk to the beach. There are lots of other frogs in the forest here. The noise they make is amazing; it's like a

huge frog convention. There's now also a shuttle service (round-trip included with the US$3 entrance), though there's sometimes a long wait for it. Coolers can be rented for US$5 at the shuttle office. Next door is a yacht marina with a restaurant/bar, Palma de Roca Bar and Grill, that's sometimes open. There's a large, busy open-air restaurant, Kayukos Restaurant and Island Lounge, a five-minute walk up the trail, at the Bocas Bound hostel.

It can be hard to spot red frogs at first, though once you see one, they suddenly seem to be everywhere. Look among the fallen leaves at the end of the trail near the beach. If a resident is around, ask him or her for help in finding the *rana roja* (RAH-na ROH-ha).

In 2008, a major condominium resort and marina planned for Red Frog Beach was shut down, due to a labor dispute and environmental concerns, but a more modest development is going up in its place.

Quebrada de Sal

This village of 450 people is not terribly scenic—it's a bit too simultaneously poor and modernized for that—but it's worth a visit, at least for those already on Bastimentos. It's approached by water on the southeast side of the island, between Cayo Crawl and Punta Vieja. The approach can be one of the best parts of the trip, as the boat has to pass through dense mangrove channels where there's a chance of spotting sloths. The boat docks next to a concrete path that peters out at the edge of the village. Visitors must pay US$1 a head to enter, and sign a registry. There's a meager souvenir shop that has crude, painted wooden figures of animals, some *chácaras* (traditional woven Ngöbe-Buglé handbags) and a few other things, but nothing too memorable.

The center of the community is a spacious field with a cinderblock school house, a dining hall, and a dance hall. A lot of the traditional Ngöbe culture has disappeared from the village, though there are still some thatched-roof houses on stilts and residents who still adhere to their traditional religion. The villagers are courteous if a bit reserved; but if you speak

© WILLIAM FRIAR

the entrance to Quebrada de Sal, a Ngöbe village

some Spanish, you should have little trouble finding someone to chat with.

There isn't much else in the village, but there's a nice forest hike from here that leads to Playa Larga. The trail starts at the far side of the village. It's a good idea to hire a villager for a few dollars to lead the way and point out the flora and fauna. It's also possible to do this hike without a guide, but as always don't head off into the forest alone or in flip-flops. The walk takes about an hour each way and there's a chance of spotting armadillos, *conejos pintado,* and other small creatures.

ENTERTAINMENT AND EVENTS

Entertainment is mostly confined to the bars and restaurants along the waterfront in Old Bank. **Roots Bar and Restaurant** (no phone, 11:30 A.M.–9:30 P.M. Wed.–Mon.) is a friendly place to hang out. **Cantina La Feria** draws partiers, both local and visiting, from all over Bocas for its "Blue Monday" dance parties. This place has all the rough Caribbean character one could want. It's a basic cantina over

the water that serves *seco* (a sugarcane liquor) and beer at locals-friendly prices. The scene can be kind of intimidating at first, especially when the cops come around checking IDs and busting locals for mysterious reasons, but the vibe is generally low-key. Use common sense, go with a group, and be respectful, just as you would at any hard-drinking place back home. And bring earplugs.

Notable annual events, and excuses for a party, in Old Bank include **Palo de Mayo,** a Maypole dance on May 1 that's also held in Bocas town, and **Founding Day** on November 23.

The place to be on New Year's Eve is the Al Natural Resort, which throws an all-night **New Year's Eve beach party.** For a quite reasonable price, the staff provides boat transportation, refreshments, and DJs who are flown down from overseas for the occasion. Everyone eventually crashes wherever he or she likes.

SHOPPING

"Destination shopping" is a novel concept for Bocas, but **Up in the Hill** (cell 6607-8962 and

6570-8277, www.upinthehill.com, 8 A.M.–dark daily) is worth the effort. And the effort is considerable: As its name implies, it's up on the hill above Old Bank, about a 15-minute walk that begins in residents' backyards and junk piles and continues through a secondary-growth forest. You're rewarded at the top by a welcome breeze, lovely views of the ocean and surrounding islands, and a friendly welcome from the young expat couple (he's from Argentina, she's from Scotland) who live on a farm up here with their small child. They're the makers of Pure Tree products, all of which are made from natural ingredients found on the farm. These are available in stores around Bocas, so don't come up here just for that; however, there are lots of pluses. One is a tour of the farm and an explanation of how the plants and fruits are used. With a day's advance notice, they can prepare lunch (US$10/person). There's a rustic but clean cabin (US$70 s/d) with an outside shower, composting toilet, kitchen, and spectacular views on the edge of a cliff; be sure to check out the bird's-eye view of Silverback, Bocas' best surf break. To get there, face the police station (with one's back to the ocean) and take the path that starts to the right of it. Then follow the signs up the hill. The trail continues down to First (a.k.a. Wizard) Beach, making this a nice place to take a break.

SPORTS AND RECREATION

Most people arrange tours through their hotels or back in Bocas town. There are no true tour outfitters on the island and only a few casual ones. **Up in the Hill** (cell 6607-8962 and 6570-8277, www.upinthehill.com) offers surfing lessons for US$40 for two hours, including a longboard. Surf tours are US$100 for a half day and US$150 for a full day. **Hostal Bastimentos** (tel. 757-9053) rents surfboards for US$10 per day. **Pension Tío Tom** (tel. 757-9831, tiotomscabin@gmail.com) sometimes offers tours for around US$20–30 per person, and rents snorkeling gear (US$4 for snorkel, mask, and flippers), boogie boards (US$10), and booties (US$2). **The Dutch Pirate** (Avenida Norte, cell 6567-1812, www.

thedutchpirate.com), over the water on the far eastern edge of town, is a scuba operator that also rents surfboards and other equipment. They also have an office in Bocas town.

◖ Parque Nacional Marino Isla Bastimentos

This 13,226-hectare park is shaped like a bridge, and as its name suggests, most of it is underwater. It starts among the mangrove islands on the southwest side of Bastimentos, arcs across its midsection, and curves down to two lovely little islands.

These islands, the **Cayos Zapatillas,** are the most visited parts of the park thanks to the good snorkeling and diving among the nearby coral gardens and underwater caves, which start about 12 meters down. It's quite dramatic even to snorkel around here; the shallow waters suddenly give way to deep canyons. The coral heads inside the reef are in good shape, and there is a large variety and abundance of fish. Nurse sharks live in this area, as well as two different species of lobsters. Note that it's turbulent around here, which can make visibility cloudy. It's not a good place for snorkelers who aren't fairly strong swimmers. There's an attractive beach on the western island for those who would prefer to lounge, but the *chitras* (sand flies) can get nippy. The Zapatillas are about an hour by fast boat from Isla Colón.

There is an interpretive trail called **El Bosque Detrás del Arrecife** (literally, "the forest behind the reef") on the more easterly of the Zapatillas (farther away from Bastimentos). It starts behind the ranger station. ANAM has put out a glossy booklet, in Spanish only, that describes the trail. Good luck finding a copy. Camping on either island is possible for US$5 more per tent.

Most visitors to Isla Bastimentos come only for the beach, but the **inland forest** is a natural treasure trove, which is why a big swath of it is included in the marine park. For one thing, it is home to 28 species of reptiles and amphibians, more than half of which are threatened or endangered. There's a good chance of spotting sloths, monkeys, and many species of birds in a trip through the forest, especially in the early morning. The **Laguna de Bastimentos,** near the north coast midway across the island, is home to freshwater turtles, caimans, and crocodiles. Do not attempt a hike through the forest without a guide; you will get lost.

Playa Larga, which is part of the park, is an important sea-turtle nesting area, attracting four species of endangered turtles from about April or May through September.

Admission to the park is US$10 per person. Even those just snorkeling or diving in the waters around the Cayos Zapatillas must pay this fee. Ask the tour operator if the fee is included in the price of the tour. There are plans in the works to expand this beautiful park.

Nature Tours

Those staying in Old Bank should consider contacting **Pension Tío Tom** (tel. 757-9831, tiotomscabin@gmail.com) for tours of the island and the surrounding area. Tom Reichelt, half of the laid-back couple that owns the pension, is a landscape gardener and tree expert who is quietly passionate about this beautiful place. He leads tours of the interior of the island and has a special fondness for ones that involve searching for frogs or exploring caves that he says are the largest in Panama. He had gotten a bit burned out on tours when I visited him in 2010, but he was planning on offering them again. Someone sufficiently enthusiastic about frogs can probably talk him into at least doing a frog-spotting trip. Expect to pay around US$10–25/person for tours, depending on the destination. Tom speaks English, German, and some Spanish, and he really knows his stuff.

ACCOMMODATIONS AND FOOD

Most places to stay and eat are in Old Bank, and most of these are budget options. Residents often rent out rooms in their houses to travelers for a few dollars. This is definitely a way to become immersed in the local culture, but these rooms are generally super basic and the surroundings noisy. Residents willing to rent rooms post signs on their houses, making it easy to wander around until something looks appealing. Trust your instincts about whether a place feels safe and comfortable before handing over money.

Cayo Crawl has a couple of restaurants that serve mainly those on boat tours.

The most upscale accommodations are quite a ways away, between Cayo Crawl and Punta Vieja on the southeast side of the island. Out there, boat trips back to civilization are long enough that guests will usually end up eating at or near their lodgings.

Old Bank

All the places to stay and eat in Old Bank (Bastimentos town) are either right along the waterfront or along a concrete path on the hillside above it. The ones included here are listed from right to left as one faces the water. There will likely be several more options when you visit. Many of these are just low-cost rooms in locals' rather dilapidated houses. The adventurous can wander the streets looking for room-for-rent signs and see what looks best.

Pension Tío Tom (tel. 757-9831, tiotomscabin@gmail.com, starts at US$22 s/d) is a fun place to stay for anyone with a bohemian bent. Accommodations are basic and aimed at the backpacking set, but the place is clean and oozes rustic, piratical charm. The pension has three double rooms with shared bath (US$22 d; depending on demand, a single person can sometimes stay in these for US$15) and a large room, the nicest, with a private bath (US$33, for up to four people). Rooms have free wireless Internet access, and there's also an Internet computer guests can use. The pension has a simple restaurant attached that specializes in Asian and Caribbean food and can also do vegetarian fare, with most main dishes around US$5–10. Nonguests can sometimes eat here if it's not too busy.

Tío Tom is built over the water, on a pier that attracts 38 species of colorful fish. Note the tree in the dining area; they've counted 72 species of orchids growing on it. It's now also home to Tom's menagerie of indigenous frogs.

Shortly before my first visit, a couple of guests tied fishing lines to their toes at night, tossed the hooks out their window, and fished while they slept. Fortunately for them, they didn't snag a barracuda. Though Pension Tío Tom has a secluded feel, bear in mind it's in the middle of the town's rather crowded waterfront, and trash along the shore and loud music played by neighbors are part of the local color. The pension is the home of the friendly, easygoing German owners, Tom and Ina Reichelt. They've lived on Bastimentos for more than a decade and know the area well. They sometimes offer nature tours of Bastimentos and the surrounding islands. Tom is especially passionate about frogs and sometimes offers tours to scientists and fellow frog nuts. They speak English, German, and some Spanish.

Hostal Bastimentos (tel. 757-9053, starts at US$20 s/d) offers 28 clean rooms in a sprawling, Caribbean-style yellow wooden building with lots of character. Small, rustic rooms with rotary fans are US$18 s/d. Slightly bigger and nicer rooms are US$20 s/d. The nicest rooms are US$40 s/d with air-conditioning and private bathrooms. The best of these are quite appealing and airy. There are two communal kitchens, lots of balcony space for lazing in hammocks, and Internet access for US$1 per hour. This is an attractive, well-maintained place. It's set back from town on a little hill, giving it a view of the town and ocean.

Roots Bar and Restaurant (no phone, 11:30 A.M.–9:30 P.M. Wed.–Mon., US$3–10) is a pleasant thatched-roof place over the water with a warm Caribbean vibe and smiling proprietors. This is a good place to try traditional Caribbean food with coconut rice and Caribbean sauces (ask for the "secret" Roots sauce). Dishes run toward seafood, including lobster and octopus.

Built in 2004, **Hotel Caribbean View** (tel. 757-9442, hotelcaribbeanview@yahoo.com, starts at US$55 s/d) is in a two-story, Caribbean-style building, white with gold trim, that's right on the water and has 11 rooms with modern hot-water bathrooms, local TV, and telephones. The rooms are small but clean

and in good shape. All have air-conditioning and free Wi-Fi. The nicest are the six rooms upstairs with private balconies. Prices range from US$55 s/d to US$71 s/d for a room with balcony. The outside was in need of a paint job and the front garden was strewn with junk on my most recent visit, but it's still fine inside. There's a small restaurant on the water.

In and Around Bahía Honda

Bahía Honda is a long, deep bay between Isla Bastimentos and Isla Solarte that starts a few minutes by boat east of Old Bank. Some interesting places to stay are popping up in this area. The closest is Eclypse de Mar, near the beginning of the bay and just a two-minute boat ride to Old Bank. Next is a new hostel, Bocas Bound, just above the main trail to Red Frog Beach. The last is La Loma Jungle Lodge, in a much more secluded, forested area on the east side of the bay.

Opened in November 2009, **Bocas Bound** (cell 6949-0330 or 6671-8189, www.bocasbound.com, US$13 pp in dorm) is an increasingly popular hostel about a five-minute walk up the hill from the beginning of the main Red Frog Beach trail, where most boats drop off day-trippers. There are 80 hostel beds and four private rooms. Each dorm has 10 new bunk beds, air-conditioning, tile floors, and lockers. The (cold-water) showers and toilets are in individual stalls with doors, but they are separated from the bedroom only by a doorway draped with a curtain. It feels a bit like bedding down in a dressing room, and it may be a bit awkward to share with strangers. The "private" rooms (US$75 for five people) have exactly the same layout except with double and single beds, rather than bunks. Unless you have the entire room to yourself, these are about as private as an office cubicle. The staff tries to rent these out to families. The private rooms also have air-conditioning, plus water, a minifridge, and a seating area.

Down the hill from the rooms is a huge open-air restaurant/bar/lounge, Kayukos Restaurant and Island Lounge, that is the social hub of the place. Food runs about US$3 for breakfast, US$4 for lunch, and US$6 for dinner. There's table tennis, widescreen TV and DVD player, giant chess board, and free Wi-Fi. Bathrooms are clean and the place is well-run. New surfboards can be rented for US$20 a day, kayaks for US$15 a day, and snorkel gear for US$7 a day. The place is managed by two young guys from Oregon and Georgia, who have lots of ambitious plans for the place, including a zipline tour and swimming pool.

The hostel operates a water-taxi shuttle, the Red Frog Express, to and from Bocas town. This costs US$3 per person and makes the trip at 11 A.M. and 1 P.M., 2 P.M., and 5 P.M.

Note that the hostel is not actually on Red Frog Beach, though it is just a five-minute walk away. It is on a hill and faces south, overlooking a marina, Bahía Honda, and, at least for now, a construction depot with heavy machinery coming and going.

The very cool **(Eclypse de Mar** (cell 6511-4581. www.eclypsedemar.com, starts at US$198 s/d, including breakfast) is one of my favorite newer places in Bocas. Run well by a friendly Argentinean couple, Malena Trevisan and Chango Castro, it shares the same concept as Punta Caracol (bungalows over the water that are linked by boardwalks), but has a very different feel. The bungalows are beautiful, made from dark, polished nispero and cedar. The bungalows have a small glass panel in the floor so guests can watch fish swimming under their feet; lights illuminate the water at night. Bungalows are tastefully designed with modern fixtures, very firm beds, ceiling fans, warm-water bathrooms, and in-room safes. Each has a private deck with a staircase leading right into the water. The four standard bungalows (US$198 s/d, US$264 t, $308 q) are plenty nice, but the two honeymoon suites (US$275 s/d) are even nicer. The bedrooms are bigger and feature king beds, and they have a desk nook and a small living room with a glass-topped coffee table fixed above another opening in the floor. It's fun to have breakfast here while keeping an eye out for curious little fishies. The least expensive accommodations are two rooms in the main lodge. These are small but comfortable, with full beds, in-room safes, private baths, and a balcony strung with hammocks.

Eclypse de Mar is off the grid, powered by solar electricity and with clean, filtered water provided from a spring onshore. There's no air-conditioning, but there are ceiling fans, and it's breezy enough over the water you're unlikely to miss air-conditioning. This is not a first-world setting, so as elegant and lovely as it is, it won't be for everyone. There are lights only when the sun goes down, and toilet paper is deposited in a bin next to the toilet. The vibe here is friendly and familial, so you'll enjoy your stay more if you're at least somewhat social. The staff are warm and make you feel at home. Malena in particular is utterly charming and works hard to keep her guests happy.

The food is the only thing that's still a work in progress. It's tasty and plentiful, but don't expect gourmet. The coconut bread is a nice touch but doesn't have much flavor, and the seafood I've had was overcooked. But they make a delicious pumpkin soup, and food is nicely presented and reasonably priced. There's good wine as well. The restaurant closes one day a week to give the staff a day off. There's free Wi-Fi in the restaurant area and kayaks and basic snorkeling gear are free to guests (visitors can rent kayaks for US$5/hour). The lodge arranges boat tours to all the usual destinations, plus a few that are lesser known.

One nice thing about staying here is you feel secluded without being cut off from everything. Old Bank is a stone's throw away (if the thrower is incredibly strong, anyway), and there's a 2.5-hectare nature preserve onshore, just behind the lodge. This used to be pasture land, but the lodge has replanted it and is trying to restore mangroves that have been cut away and start an iguana-breeding project.

Easy walking trails run through the preserve, the centerpiece of which is a series of ingeniously designed lush artificial "lagoons" on different levels. The water flows slowly from one level to the next, which prevents mosquitoes from breeding, but provides a home to a family of caimans. Some fake Mayan statues, salvaged from one of the many *Survivor* programs filmed here, are dotted around the preserve, which adds a nice Indiana Jones feel to the preserve.

La Loma Jungle Lodge and Chocolate Farm (cell 6619-5364 or 6592-5162, www. thejunglelodge.com, US$104/person, including meals, transportation, and day trips) gives one hope for the future of Bocas. It bucks the trend toward generic, resource-gulping resorts with a unique, low-impact but comfortable little hideaway in harmony with its beautiful surroundings. It's one of my favorite spots in Panama.

A 23-hectare former farm right next to the border of Parque Nacional Marino Isla Bastimentos, La Loma is set back from the mangrove-covered shoreline of Bahía Honda and features secondary-growth forest, a cacao (chocolate) growing and processing operation, and coconut and banana groves. The main lodge has a dining area and an upstairs mirador and is bordered by a creek that ends in a little wading hole and waterfall. The three guest *ranchos* (and a fourth on the way) are on the side of a hill behind the lodge. This may be the most environmentally friendly place to stay in Panama. Visitors are welcome even if they don't spend the night.

Note that beaches are a short boat ride away, but there are no beaches on the property itself. La Loma is sort of the jungle counterpart to the beach retreat of Al Natural Resort. As at Al Natural, accommodations put guests as close to nature as possible without sacrificing comfort. The spacious, immaculate Ngöbe-inspired *ranchos* are "rustic" in the sense of being simple and open-air, but they're quite lovely. Made from handsome wood from fallen trees and sustainably harvested lumber, they are designed to let in evening breezes and look out on the forest and bay. The first *rancho* is close to the main lodge and is best for those who'd have trouble with the rather aerobic climb to the other ones. The second one is a 149-step climb from the lodge, which can be a bit strenuous for those unused to humidity. The third is a bit farther up the hill. (Look carefully at the hill trail;

there were tons of red frogs all around it when I visited.)

The second *rancho* is my favorite because of its panoramic views of the bay, but the third is surrounded by trees that sometimes attract curious white-capuchin and night monkeys. An armadillo sometimes comes sniffing around, too. Each *rancho* has one double and one single bed with mosquito nets, hot-water showers, and flush toilets. They are spaced far apart from each and are quite private. Nights here are wonderfully peaceful, especially with the moon shining on the sea and forest.

A butterfly breeding project was on hiatus in 2010 to allow the lodge to concentrate on its cacao farm and a few other micro-enterprises that guests are welcome to explore.

Among the best things about the place are the owners: Margaret, who's English, and her husband, Henry, a Peruvian-American. They are delightful people who make guests feel like welcome visitors to their home, which is what this place is. They are lively and fun to talk to, but they're also gracious hosts who will leave you alone if that's what you need. Their small staff is warm and friendly.

Stays include round-trip transportation from Bocas town (about 20 minutes away), all meals, day trips to Red Frog Beach, and tours of the garden and butterfly farm. The food is delicious and features produce from the lodge's organic gardens.

Part of the proceeds support community projects among the Ngöbe in Bahía Honda. Other activities are easily arranged for an extra fee, including tours of the Bahía Honda cave, forest hikes with Ngöbe guides, fishing or snorkeling trips, surfboard rental, and so on. The lodge can arrange for guests to participate in or observe a number of activities with members of the nearby Ngöbe community, including cooking lessons, cacao-processing, and craft-making.

Between Cayo Crawl and Punta Vieja

There are three resorts on the nearly 10 kilometers of beautiful curving coastline between

Cayo Crawl and Punta Vieja. Each is quite secluded, both from each other and from everything else. Depending on boat speed, from Isla Colón it can take up to an hour to reach these places.

Tranquilo Bay (tel. 620-4179, U.S. tel. 713/589-6952, www.tranquilobay.com, multiday all-inclusive packages start at US$1,445 s, US$2,230 d for three nights) has the only truly first-world-style accommodations on Bastimentos. Perched on a hill just around the point from Cayo Crawl, it's a small all-inclusive resort that opened in 2004 after several years of construction and planning. Note that the resort isn't on a beach. The hill is set above mangroves, but attractive beaches are a short boat ride away.

The resort is on 100 acres of land that was a banana plantation for 100 years, but which is now being allowed to revert to forest. It offers six large, modern, air-conditioned cabañas, set in a clearing at the top of the breezy hill and linked with each other and the main lodge by a paved path that's shaded by lush tropical vegetation and illuminated at night. The cabañas are attractive and well-appointed, with comfortable beds, a sitting area, and large hot-water bathrooms with handsome granite countertops. There are no phones or TVs, and free wireless Internet is available only in the main lodge. Cabañas look out on either the ocean or the surrounding forest. Each has a front porch with hammocks, Adirondack chairs, and ceiling fans.

The two-story main lodge has a large dining room and bar with a broad deck where one can sit and watch the ocean and colorful oropendolas as they flit back and forth to their hanging nests.

The project is the creation of two enthusiastic and friendly Texan couples, the Kimballs and the Violas, who live at the resort with their small children. They're "can do" people who work with their staff to make sure everything is just right for guests.

Even those who don't need all its creature comforts may be interested in the place for its tours. The resort has the infrastructure, gear,

and staff to offer trips not only to the usual spots but also to more remote parts of the eastern archipelago and mainland not easily accessible to most travelers. Excursions include jungle hikes, kayak trips, scuba and snorkeling, surfing, fishing, and lounging on secluded beaches.

Packages range 3–7 nights, either with or without daily excursions. All packages include transfers, the round-trip domestic flight from Panama City to Bocas, all meals, nonalcoholic and some alcoholic beverages, and water and land activities around the resort. These activities include kayaking, snorkeling, swimming, hikes, and access to Tranquilo Bay's library and video library. Without daily excursions, rates range from US$1,445 s, US$2,230 d for three nights up to US$2,564 s, US$3,920 d for seven nights. Add about US$100 per person per day for packages that include excursions. Excursions can also be booked "à la carte" at the resort.

The semi-rustic but attractive **Casa Cayuco** (no phone, www.casacayuco.com, US$280.50 s, US$335.50 d, all-inclusive) is on the beach between Tranquilo Bay and Al Natural. It consists of a three-story lodge with an open-air dining room, bar, kitchen and sitting area, and three cabins a short walk away, by the water. A fourth cabin is planned. This is another remote spot surrounded by tropical forest and little else. Electricity is supplied by solar power.

Made primarily from nispero wood, the cabins are airy and attractive, with private bathrooms and ceiling fans. The wooden-shuttered windows don't have screens, but the beds have mosquito nets. The two cabins on the beach, Delfin and Tortuga, have one queen and two twin beds. The third one, Coco, is set back from the beach and surrounded by tropical forest. It accommodates up to six guests in two sleeping areas.

Rates for all cabins are US$280.50 s, US$335.50 d. Additional guests are US$104.50 each. There is a three-night minimum stay. Rates include all meals, transfers to and from Bocas, and use of sports equipment, including snorkel gear, kayaks, and surfboards. Rates do not include alcohol or tips.

This is a pleasant, eco-friendly place that caters primarily to groups—yoga, surf, school, and so on—interested in adventure travel and service projects in the neighboring communities. It's owned by an American couple, Tom and Linda Kimbrell, who have considerable experience in this kind of work. Guided excursions range from snorkeling tours of nearby reefs to a boat trip all the way out to the tip of Peninsula Valiente, where there's a secluded beach. Rates for most of these are US$50–75 per person. White-water kayaking on Class I–II mainland rivers is US$125 per person.

C Al Natural Resort (tel./fax 757-9004, cell 6496-0776, 6576-8605 or 6640-6935, www.alnaturalresort.com, starts at US$193.50 s, US$250 d, including all meals, transfers, and use of recreation equipment) has long been one of my favorite places in Panama. It consists of just seven bungalows (the warm and friendly Belgian owners never plan to build more than nine) on a secluded, pristine beach just below Punta Vieja on the southeast side of Isla Bastimentos. The bungalows are based on the traditional Ngöbe-Buglé house design: They're round, thatched-roofed wooden structures on stilts perched on the edge of the clear blue water. Inside, they're remarkably comfortable and well-appointed for such a remote spot. They have private, hot-water showers (a modern flush toilet is in a clean, well-maintained stall just outside each bungalow), good queen- or king-size beds with mosquito netting fine enough to keep out *chitras* (sand flies), and an electrical system powered by solar panels.

The bungalows are designed to put guests as close to the lovely natural surroundings as possible. The entire front of the bungalow is an open deck with gorgeous views of the sea, the Cayos Zapatillas, and the distant mainland. The backs of the bungalows are partly open to the tropical forest behind the resort. But the area is so isolated, and the bungalows so well designed, that each has a great deal of privacy. They also tend to be surprisingly free of creepy-crawlies.

The bungalows are set on nine hectares of land, a former coconut plantation that is reverting to forest. Three species of primates, armadillos, boas, opossums, raccoons, and caiman have been spotted back here. A short, wide trail leads through this patch of secondary-growth forest to a north-shore beach. Guests have free use of sea kayaks, snorkeling gear, and fishing tackle in the calm, protected waters in front of the resort.

The heart of the resort is a large, three-story building—also wooden and thatch-roofed. The bottom floor is the dining/bar area. The 2nd floor houses an open-air games area. There's an observation deck with expansive views on the top floor. Meals are served family-style; the food is simple, but good wine is included with dinners. Some of the food—including bananas, pineapples, and ducks—is grown or raised at the resort. Occasionally a guest chef cooks; when that happens, the quality of the food soars.

This is a great option for couples looking for a romantic spot, for adventurous families, or even for students of ingenious and environmentally appropriate architecture. It's fun to note all the little touches. The showers are lined with pebbles laid out to form traditional Ngöbe-Buglé designs. The bungalows use a great deal of driftwood, with shapes carefully selected to fit into the overall design instead of being cut to fit.

Bungalows have either one or two stories. They come in two basic flavors: Natural House or Superior Natural House. The Natural House has a queen-size bed and 12-volt electrical system. The Superior Natural House is larger, with a king-size bed, one or two single beds, and a 110-volt electrical system, sufficient to run a ceiling fan. It's well worth spending the extra money for a Superior Natural House, which is significantly nicer. The two-story houses can accommodate more people. One of the Natural Houses is hexagonal and has three bedrooms that can be cleverly closed off for privacy.

Given how remote this spot is, it's not surprising maintenance can sometimes be a concern. During one of my stays, for instance, there were glitches with the hot water and one of the boats. These problems were quickly resolved, but anyone who stays here should not expect everything to run like clockwork; it's still a bohemian Caribbean place, even given the exclusive prices.

High-season rates start at US$193.50/US$250 s/d for the first night in a Natural House. Rate drops about US$35 per person on subsequent nights. Rates include transportation to and from Isla Colón in a fast boat, three meals a day including wine with dinner, and free use of snorkeling gear, kayaks, and fishing tackle.

Add about US$25 per person for the Superior Natural House. The larger bungalows are also more expensive but can accommodate more guests. "All-inclusive" packages that add daily half-day tours and all drinks are also available; there's a two-night minimum for these.

Camping

It's possible to camp in **Parque Nacional Marino Isla Bastimentos** for US$5 per tent in addition to the US$10 per-person park entrance fee. Entrance fees for both can be paid at the ANAM office in Bocas town. This entitles you to pitch a tent anywhere in the park. That includes the forest on Bastimentos itself, but as always it's not a great idea to camp in a tropical forest without a qualified guide. Most campers prefer to stay on one of the **Cayos Zapatillas,** which are part of the park, for a romantic, deserted-island experience. It's theoretically possible to buy permits directly from the ranger stationed on the Zapatillas. However, check at the ANAM office in Bocas town about current camping conditions and restrictions before venturing out that far. You'll also need to hire a boatman you can trust to come pick you up when you're ready to return.

PRACTICALITIES

La Loma, Tranquilo Bay, Casa Cayuco, and Al Natural generally arrange all food, transportation, and activities for their guests. Make sure to clarify exactly what is being provided ahead of time, because there's little to buy way out here. Even Old Bank is a significant boat ride

away. In Old Bank there is a *minisuper* (convenience store) near Roots Bar and Restaurant and a police post, health clinic, and phone booth behind Pension Tío Tom. Some of the places to stay have Internet access for guests, but there are no Internet cafés. Isla Colón is a 10-minute water-taxi ride from Old Bank; flag down passing boats. The fare is US$3 per person.

ELSEWHERE IN THE ARCHIPELAGO

New places to stay are beginning to pop up elsewhere in the islands. Some of these are nice and have surprisingly modern infrastructures given their location. They tend to be off by themselves, and the nearest population center or place to eat (besides your lodging) is likely to be a Ngöbe-Buglé village. Note that Popa Paradise Resort, which is right above an attractive beach on Isla Popa, sometimes lets day visitors use its pool, clubhouse, and other facilities for a US$10 entrance fee.

There's a quite appealing place to stay in Laguna Bocatorito (a.k.a. Dolphin Bay), near the village of Bocatorito. **Dolphin Bay Hideaway** (cell 6417 7351 or 6772 9917, www.dolphinbayhideaway.com, starts at US$126.50 s/d, including transfers and breakfast) opened in 2006 with three attractive, cheerful, and spotless rooms in a two-story Caribbean-style house. All have four-poster beds, fans, and stylish modern bathrooms with hot water. None has air-conditioning or TVs: This is a place for people who like to be close to nature. There is free Wi-Fi, however.

Two rooms are downstairs. The smallest room has a queen bed and looks out on the garden (US$126.50 s/d). The corner room is larger, with a king bed and view of the bay (US$154 s/d). It's my favorite. The room upstairs (US$143 s/d) is also quite large and has the most traditional charm, with a queen bed and spacious bathroom. It opens onto the large shared veranda, so it's not as private as the other two rooms. Lunch and candlelit dinners are served on the veranda, which is a pleasant place to hang out on or lounge in hammocks.

Guests need to be comfortable around animals, as the owners have friendly dogs, a restless parrot, chickens, and have been known to get the occasional visits from the odd kinkajou or howler monkey. Note that there's no beach on the property.

The place is run by Erika, a Hungarian who moved to Bocas on a whim (ask for her story—it's really interesting) and her Bocatoreño boyfriend, José.

Stays include free round-trip transport from Bocas, full breakfasts, Internet access, and use of *cayucos* (dugout canoes). They can arrange tours to all the surrounding attractions for an extra fee. Dolphin Bay Hideaway is about 20 minutes by boat from Bocas town.

Popa Paradise Beach Resort (tel. 832-1498, cell 6550-2505, www.popaparadisebeachresort.com, starts at US$132 s/d, including breakfast buffet) is the pioneering lodging on Isla Popa, and it didn't start small. Opened in January 2009, the resort occupies 25 acres of what once was a farm. Only the front five acres have been developed; the rest is being left to return to forest as best it can, helped by the planting of hundreds of trees by the staff. There are eight *casitas* dotted around the property on a ridge above a good-sized crescent beach. The *casitas* are linked by cement paths that lead to the large clubhouse, which has a dining terrace, a small spa, a lounge with a giant-screen TV, and a kidney-shaped infinity-edge pool with a swim-up bar.

The *casitas* are individual bungalows with balconies and attractive Balinese furniture and porches that look out onto the ocean. They either have a four-poster, a queen, or two twin beds, and all are air-conditioned, have satellite TV and DVD players, and hot-water bathrooms.

The *casitas* are either "ocean view," which are set back a ways from the beach (US$352 s/d) or "ocean front," right above the beach (US$385). Ocean-front *casita* number 10 has an extra little cement veranda and is nicest of all.

There are also two "executive suites" (US$440 s/d) on a point above the resort's dock, but in my opinion they don't have as much charm as the *casitas* and were looking a bit worn. They do, however, have kitchenettes and sliding-glass doors that open onto a lovely view. For those who want a truly opulent experience, above these is the penthouse (US$550 s/d), which features 20-foot ceilings, a large bathroom with separate tub (the only room that has one), a full kitchen, a master bedroom, a second bedroom, a stereo, and so on. All three of these have air-conditioning and flat-screen satellite TVs.

There are also five simpler and more economical rooms (US$132 s/d) in the main clubhouse. These lack air-conditioning and TV, but they're still attractive and have porches. Guests in these have access to all the facilities at the resort.

The food is reportedly quite good, cooked by a chef from Seattle. The menu features such interesting-sounding fusion dishes as yuca gnocchi. The fancier main dishes go for around $16–21.

There is free Wi-Fi in the clubhouse, table table, and a resident massage therapist and acupuncturist. There are kayaks and snorkeling gear for guest use. There's a coral reef a few hundred meters offshore, but when the water's not clear the staff can arrange transport to other snorkeling spots. Other boat and walking tours are also available.

Isla Popa is still mostly covered with tropical forest (fortunately) and it does have venomous snakes. Guests should take care if they go on forest hikes, just as they would in a tropical forest on the mainland. However, snakes do not hang out in areas that have been cleared, and all the facilities of the resort are on absolutely manicured lawns. The manager I spoke with told me that in 15 months of living on the island, he has only seen two fer-de-lance, and both were found by gardeners cleaning brush on the edge of the property (who promptly killed them, which is what locals do in Panama).

With all the upscale facilities, and upscale prices, it'd be easy for potential guests to forget they're on a lightly populated, remote tropical island. This is a place for people who like the idea of being far away from everything and, ideally, are into outdoor activities. If it rains, there's not a whole lot to do (though the staff do try to come up with creative ideas during long rainy spells—cooking classes, anyone?). And guests will need at least a slight sense of adventure, especially when making the 40-minute ride over from Bocas town in a small boat.

If the resort isn't too busy, it sometimes allows (well-behaved and sober) day guests to use the pool and other facilities for US$10 per person 9 A.M.–5 P.M.

Those who stay three nights or more get free round-trip transfers between the resort and Bocas town at the beginning and end of their stay. Otherwise, it's US$90 per person round-trip.

Mainland Bocas

Most visitors spend as little time as possible on the mainland of the province. The towns are poor and neglected and have just about nothing that qualifies as a "tourist attraction," but those who haven't experienced the Caribbean boonies may enjoy at least passing through. They have a bit of a rough, frontier feel and should be approached with some caution, at least at night, but, like most places, you can meet kind people here. For most travelers, however, Guabito is just a border crossing, Changuinola and Almirante just transportation hubs on the way to somewhere else, and Chiriquí Grande a name on a map.

Mainland Bocas outside the towns holds more appeal, thanks mainly to the gigantic Parque Internacional La Amistad and increasingly accessible trips up the Río Teribe. Powerful rivers and magnificent evergreen forests lead down from the highlands, where indigenous peoples work to survive both physically and culturally. Important wetlands line the coast, including the—at least nominally—protected San San Pondsack.

ALMIRANTE

You'd have to be bananas (sorry!) to choose to stay in the small, ramshackle banana-port town of Almirante (pop. 12,430) rather than on the islands, but those who miss the last water taxi from town may end up stranded here for the night.

The main street into Almirante leads from the highway and parallels the railroad tracks

as it reaches town. The water-taxi piers are to the right, across the train tracks and not visible from the road. There's a hotel, Hotel San Francisco, and a general store on the left side of the road and a bus terminal to the right. A second road crosses the main street just past the bus terminal. Most of the town's services are on or near this road, including a Banco Nacional de Panamá that doesn't have an ATM.

Accommodations

The best bet for a night's stay is **Hotel San Francisco** (tel. 778-3779, fax 778-3761, starts at US$11 s, US$15.40 d for older rooms with fans, US$19.20 d with a/c). It's close to the railroad tracks, near the bus terminal and water taxi piers. The hotel has 14 rooms, all with TVs and droopy beds. Room quality varies wildly. The cheapest rooms are basic and gloomy, with filthy shared baths.   The most expensive rooms are okay for those without bad backs, and have air-conditioning and private hot-water bathrooms. They go for US$27.50 s and US$38 d/t. These rooms were recently renovated. Room prices may be subject to bargaining depending on demand. The hotel is above a general store that also serves as the hotel reception. There are a few basic places to eat near the hotel. Be careful in Almirante, especially after dark.

Stranded folks who can afford it should consider trying to spend the night at **La Escapada** (cell 6698-9901 or 6618-6106, www.laescapada.net, US$70 s, US$90 d), located about

64 kilometers east of the Costa Rican border on the Almirante–Chiriquí Grande Road. It's between kilometer markers 48 and 49 and is easily the best place to stay along the Bocas coastline.

Run by a couple from Florida, who live on the property with a couple of big, friendly dogs, it consists of four rooms in a wooden building set on a 12.5-acre former cattle ranch that is being allowed to revert to forest. Rooms are simple but clean, modern and air-conditioned, with comfortable beds and screened back porches for those who want to commune with nature while avoiding the *chitras* (sand flies). Four more rooms are in the works. The rooms aren't close enough to the water to have a view, but they are surrounded by trees. A short walk leads down to a dock, at the end of which is the hotel's screened-in terrace bar/restaurant, which appears to float above the glassy water and which has a spectacular view of the ocean and islands. Breakfast, lunch, and dinner are available, with American and Italian main dishes going for around US$10. Electricity is supplied by a generator, at least until the grid finally reaches this remote spot. Kayaks and snorkeling gear are available for guests. This place is popular with those who need to take their vehicles to the island, as it's not too far from the Almirante ferry, which leaves early.

The property is down the hill from the highway and is reached by a long, steep, dirt-and-gravel road that is only accessible by a powerful four-wheel drive or by fairly fit pedestrians with sure footing. Walking up the hill is quite a workout. The owners can probably ferry guests without transportation to and from the highway.

Any bus heading to or from Changuinola and Almirante can drop or pick up passengers at the entrance.

Getting There and Away
BY BUS
Try to arrive well before the last water taxi leaves Almirante at 6:30 P.M. Remember that buses often run late and water taxis can fill up.

Note: Long-haul buses from David, Panama City, and other parts of Panama still do not go into Almirante itself. They drop passengers at the crossroads outside of town and head on to Changuinola. It's a long walk, especially with luggage, from the crossroads to the water-taxi piers. It's worth the US$0.50 per person to take a taxi to the pier area.

There are no direct buses from the Costa Rican border crossing at Guabito-Sixaola to Almirante. To get there, take a bus to the Changuinola bus terminal and switch to an Almirante-bound bus, which drops passengers off at the Almirante bus terminal. They leave about every 25 minutes from about 5:40 A.M.– 7:45 P.M. The trip takes a half hour and costs US$2. The water-taxi services aren't visible from the terminal but are within easy walking distance. Look for the train tracks. Cross over them and head left along the waterfront.

Buses from Almirante to David and Panama City leave from the crossroads at the edge of town. Take a taxi (US$0.50 per person) to get there. There is one direct daily bus to Panama City, leaving Almirante at 8 A.M. A second bus, at 8 P.M., has been added and dropped over the years. The fare is US$23 and the ride takes roughly 10 hours. Passengers are limited to two bags each; additional luggage is charged as cargo. David-bound buses leave every hour or so 5 A.M.–7 P.M. The fare is US$7 and the trip takes about four hours. Buses from Almirante to Changuinola leave from the Almirante bus terminal every 25 minutes from 6 A.M. until late in the evening. The trip takes a half hour and costs US$2.

BY CAR
Those with their own transportation will need 9–10 hours from Panama City or 3.5 hours from David to drive straight through to Almirante. Those coming from Panama City should consider breaking the trip somewhere along the way and spending the night. Finca La Suiza and Lost and Found Eco-Resort are good options in the vicinity of Volcán. Another possibility is Santiago, the provincial capital of Veraguas, on the Interamericana a little under four hours from Panama. It has a range

of services and places to stay but is not exactly a scenic or exciting town.

Coming up the Fortuna Road, continue west on the Chiriqué Grande–Almirante Road for about 60 kilometers. The turnoff to Almirante is on the right and comes up quickly. The main road continues to Changuinola and the Costa Rican border. After the turn, the road will fork. Be sure to take the gravel road to the right. Stay straight, with the train tracks on the right, and turn right just before the bus terminal—it should be the first right after the old Bocas Fruit Company sign. The water-taxi piers are up this road.

You'll probably encounter a *boletero* (ticket tout) eager to show you the way and take you to the water-taxi service he works for. Park at the fenced-in lot at **Leiza's** for US$3 a day. It should be possible to pay when you leave, though you may be asked to pay in advance. I've parked here without problems, as have many other travelers. Leiza is friendly and her house is in the middle of the lot.

CHANGUINOLA

This congested, unlovely provincial town (pop. 39,896) is not exactly what you'd call a tourist destination. It's little more than a single strip of road—Avenida 17 de Abril, commonly known as Calle Central—that's lined with shops offering cheap goods and basic services, plus a few hotels and restaurants. It's not even particularly colorful—it's a hot, humid, nondescript little town surrounded by banana plantations. But it is a commerce and transportation hub.

Those who haven't experienced this part of Panama may be curious to pass by for a quick visit. Primarily, though, it's a crossroads for those traveling between Costa Rica and the islands or heading up into Naso country and the Bocas entrance to Parque Internacional La Amistad. Only those who end up stranded on the way to or from those places will likely want to spend the night.

Central Changuinola is about a kilometer long from north to south, and nearly everything of interest is on or within a block of Avenida 17 de Abril, which runs parallel to the train tracks. Because of that, the town is easily

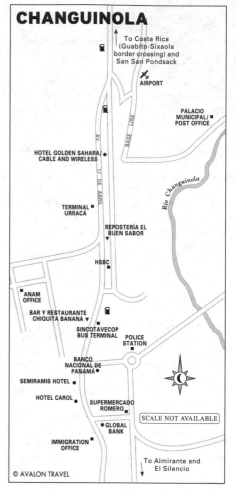

walkable. But Changuinola isn't particularly safe after dark; take taxis instead of walking (US$0.50 or so). The streets are packed with them. Unless otherwise noted, all the places listed are on Avenida 17 de Abril.

Accommodations
US$10-25
Hotel Carol (tel. 758-8731, US$16–23 s/d), near the south end of Avenida 17 de Abril, offers 37 air-conditioned rooms. The rooms

are dark, basic, but okay, with smudged walls and concrete floors. The cheapest rooms are cold-water only and have no TV. The more expensive rooms are nicer, with cable TV, hot water, and tile floors, though they're still not the cleanest. This is the best bet among the cheaper hotels.

Hotel Golden Sahara (tel. 758-7478, 758-7908, or 758-7910, hotelgoldensahara@yahoo.com, US$31.65 s/d), toward the north end of town, has 28 modern rooms with hot water, air-conditioning, and cable TV. Rooms are clean if a bit sterile. The rooms vary quite a bit—some are dark, and others are quite a bit cheerier; try to get one with a window. The hotel is well run, and the staff members are attentive. They're happy to recommend places to eat and give other tips. This place is a good deal.

US$25-50

Semiramis Hotel (tel. 758-6006, 758-6009 or 758-6013, US$30–35 s/d), near the heart of town, across the street from the Banco Nacional de Panamá, has fairly nice, clean rooms with air-conditioning, cable TV, and attractive bathrooms. It has a bar and restaurant that's open 7 A.M.–11 P.M. daily.

Food

Decent food is hard to come by in Changuinola. The two places listed here are the best bets. Some of the hotels have restaurants.

Bar y Restaurante Chiquita Banana (tel. 758-8215, 7 A.M.–11 P.M. daily, US$5 or less) is the best place to eat in town, which isn't saying a whole lot. It serves an extensive menu of Chinese and *criollo* food. The *arroz con pollo* (chicken and rice) is tasty, cheap, and plentiful. There's a daily special—be sure to ask about it, since it's not written down anywhere. Most people eat on the enclosed front patio, which looks out on the busy street, but there's a fancier air-conditioned dining room inside, with a somewhat more upscale menu.

Repostería El Buen Sabor (tel. 758-8422, 8 A.M.–9 P.M. Mon.–Sat., 10 A.M.–9 P.M. Sun.), across the street from the Multi-Credit Bank, is a bakery and pastry shop that offers local specialties such as the *bon de Bastimentos,* which tastes like dry gingerbread, as well as fruit drinks, ice cream, and other goodies.

Information

The local **ANAM office** (tel. 758-6603, 8 A.M.–4 P.M. Mon.–Fri.) may have information on San San Pondsack and Parque Internacional La Amistad, but it's not really set up for travelers, so don't get your hopes up. It's in a residential neighborhood a couple of blocks west of the center of town. Head west on the road that runs past the Hotel El Gran Hong Kong. Turn left after two blocks. The office is a block down this road.

The **police station** is on an unmarked road east of the railroad tracks. It's parallel to and one block east of Avenida 17 de Abril. It's around the corner from the Hotel Alhambra and the Banco Nacional de Panamá.

Services

There are several banks along Avenida 17 de Abril that have 24-hour ATMs in addition to regular banking hours (8 A.M.–3 P.M. Mon.–Fri., 9 A.M.–noon Sat.). **Global Bank** is about a block north of and across the street from the immigration office on the south side of town. The **Banco Nacional de Panamá** is right next to the Hotel Alhambra. **HSBC** is a couple of blocks south of the bus terminal on the east side of the street. The **Multi-Credit Bank** is farther up Avenida 17 de Abril.

The **post office** is in the Palacio Municipal de Changuinola, on an unmarked road east of the airstrip on the north side of town.

Supermercado Romero (8 A.M.–10 P.M. Mon.–Sat., 8 A.M.–6 P.M. Sun.), one block east of the south end of Avenida 17 de Abril, next to the Global Bank, has a pharmacy and ATM.

The local **Cable and Wireless office** (8 A.M.–noon and 1–4 P.M. Mon.–Fri.) is next to the Golden Sahara. It sells telephone cards.

An **immigration office** (tel. 775-4515, 7:30 A.M.–noon and 1–3 P.M. Mon.–Fri.) is at the south end of town.

There are three **gas stations** on Avenida 17 de Abril.

Getting There and Away

Changuinola is a regional transit hub, with two bus terminals and a small airstrip. Sadly, the dilapidated train that used to link Changuinola and Almirante is no more. Those traveling between the Costa Rican border and the islands must pass through this town.

BY AIR

Changuinola has nonstop flights to and from the Bocas del Toro archipelago. Flights to and from Panama City often connect through Bocas town, on the islands. Make sure you get off in the right place. The Changuinola airport is on the north end of town, just east of Avenida 17 de Abril. Taxi fare to and from town is US$0.50.

Aeroperlas (reservations tel. 378-6000, info@aeroperlas.com, www.aeroperlas.com) offers two daily flights from Panama City to Changuinola (6:45 A.M. and 2:55 P.M.) and from Changuinola to Panama City (8:35 A.M. and 4:50 P.M.).

Air Panama (tel./fax 316-9000, www.fly-airpanama.com) offers 1–2 daily flights from Panama City to Changuinola that connect through Bocas town (6:45 A.M. and 3:30 P.M. Mon.–Sat., 3:30 P.M. Sun.) and return flights from Changuinola to Panama City (7:15 A.M. and 4 P.M. Mon.–Sat., 4 P.M. Sun.).

The flight on either airline takes roughly an hour for nonstops or an hour and a half, sometimes more, if there's a stop in Bocas town. The flight costs US$103.50.

BY BUS

Changuinola has two bus terminals. Long-distance buses to Panama City and David leave from Terminal Urracá. Local and regional buses, including those to the Guabito-Sixaola border crossing, leave from the SINCOTAVECOP bus terminal.

Terminal Urracá is on the north end of town between the Hotel Golden Sahara and the Multi-Credit Bank. There is one direct daily bus each way between Panama City and Changuinola. It leaves Changuinola at 7 A.M., arriving in Panama City at least 11 hours later.

The fare is US$24. Two pieces of luggage are allowed; additional luggage is an extra charge. Note this is the same bus that passes by the crossroads at Almirante.

Buses from Changuinola to David leave every half hour 3 A.M.–7 P.M. The trip takes about 4.5 hours and costs US$8.

Local and regional buses leave from the **SINCOTAVECOP bus terminal,** across the street from Bar y Restaurante Chiquita Banana. Destinations include:

Almirante: Every 25 minutes, 5:40 A.M.– 7:45 P.M. The trip takes 30 minutes and costs US$2.

Guabito/Costa Rican border crossing at Sixaola: Every 25 minutes or so, 5:30 A.M.–8 P.M. The trip takes 30 minutes and costs US$1. There's also a *colectivo* taxi that works like a bus and runs between Changuinola and Guabito.

El Silencio: Every 20 minutes, 5:30 A.M.–9 P.M. The trip takes 20 minutes and costs US$0.65.

San José, Costa Rica: There is one direct bus a day from Changuinola to San José, Costa Rica. It leaves at 9:55 A.M. and, depending on road and weather conditions, arrives around 4 P.M. Costa Rica time. The fare is US$12.

Confirm all these schedules before making plans, as routes are subject to change.

BY TAXI AND CAR

It shouldn't be hard to find a taxi on Avenida 17 de Abril. Expect to pay US$0.50 to the airport, US$8 to El Silencio, US$6 to Guabito, and US$20 to Almirante.

To reach Changuinola by car from eastern Panama, stay left on the main road when it forks at Almirante. Changuinola is 21 kilometers farther west, on a scenic and curvy road. Watch out for speeding traffic.

HUMEDALES DE SAN SAN PONDSACK

These wetlands, established as a wildlife refuge in 1994, encompass a strip of coast that extends east and south from the Río Sixaola to the Caribbean. It comprises 16,125 hectares, but only a small part of it is easily accessible. The completely decrepit boardwalk that passes through its heart was being rebuilt when I last visited; if it's actually back in service, it will give visitors a close-up look at this otherworldly place. Animals found in the wetlands include an important population of manatees and leatherback and hawksbill sea turtles, but the manatees are shy and the turtles seasonal, so as usual don't get your hopes up. Birders come here for the 67 known avian species it attracts. The only things visitors are guaranteed to see, however, are mangroves, palms, and eerie, brackish water.

The wetlands can be visited either as part of a boat tour from the islands or by taxi from Changuinola. Arrange for the taxi either to wait or to pick you up for the return trip. To be sure the taxi will show up at the appointed time, don't pay until the return to Changuinola.

Note: There is not yet a consensus on how to spell the wetlands' funky name. You may see it as San San Pondsock, San San Pond Soc, San-San Pond Sak, and so on. It's all the same place, but don't confuse it—easier said than done—with Punta Pondsack, also known as Punta Pond Soc, east of Almirante.

GUABITO

Even by the modest standards of mainland Bocas del Toro, the down-at-the-heels border town of Guabito (pop. 14,360) has little to offer visitors. It's simply a place to pass through on the way to or from Costa Rica. There are no hotels and no appealing places to eat. The nearest place with significant services is Changuinola, about a 20-minute drive away.

The border crossing is on an elevated railway trestle on the edge of the Río Sixaola. The combination immigration, customs, and IPAT office is right on the train tracks next to the bridge that crosses the river.

The border runs right down the middle of the Río Sixaola. Travelers must cross the railroad bridge on foot or in a vehicle. The bridge was built in 1908 and has been deteriorating

ever since. It's a real embarrassment to Panama that the half of the bridge under Costa Rican control is freshly painted, at least superficially well-maintained, and has a protected walkway for pedestrians, while the Panamanian half is rusted, dilapidated, and forces pedestrians to walk right on the tracks. It's not the most inviting way to enter a country, but it makes for a comical photo. The border crossing is quite casual, and anyone who wants to can wander out on the bridge to take a look.

Buses and taxis are available downstairs from customs and immigration.

Access to the Bocas del Toro archipelago is by water taxi from Changuinola or Almirante. There are also flights from Changuinola. Buses to Changuinola run about every 25 minutes, 5:30 A.M.–8 P.M. The trip takes 30 minutes and costs US$1. There are no direct buses from Guabito to Almirante, Panama City, David, or anywhere else you're likely to want to go. Take a bus to the Changuinola bus terminal and change there.

Taxis should charge around US$6 to Changuinola and US$20–25 to Almirante. This is per ride, *not* per person. Taxi drivers and "tour guides" sometimes try to take advantage of clueless new arrivals at the border, so be polite but firm and don't get ripped off.

Buses from Sixaola, on the Costa Rican side, leave for San José, Costa Rica, at 6 A.M., 8 A.M., 10 A.M., and 3 P.M. The ride takes 6.5–8 hours. (Remember that Costa Rica time is one hour earlier than Panama time.) Another option is to take a bus from Sixaola to Puerto Limón and transfer to a San José bus from there.

◖ RÍO TERIBE AND THE NASO

A trip up the Río Teribe is one of the most memorable experiences Bocas del Toro has to offer, and it makes for a nice change of scene for those getting island fever in the archipelago. This is the homeland of the Naso, an indigenous people who live near the river in 11 communities surrounded by beautiful forest. It's a reasonable and accessible trip for those with the slightest sense of adventure, an interest in indigenous cultures, and a desire to explore a bit of tropical forest in rustic but relatively comfortable conditions. The climate is quite different from that on the islands and doesn't fit preconceived notions of a tropical rainforest. It can be rather mild and pleasantly breezy upriver.

About the Naso

The Naso are better known in Panama as the Teribe or Naso-Teribe. Some Naso say that "Teribe" is a mispronunciation of *tjer di*, which means "river of the Grandmother," the ancestral guiding spirit of the people. They are also sometimes known as the Térraba. The Naso are proud to be the last people in the Americas to still have a monarch.

Spanish records suggest that in the 16th century the Naso were already well-established in the region, including Almirante Bay as far north as Isla Colón, and may in fact

NASO TALES

The Naso I've met have been gracious, open, and eager to share their culture with outsiders. They have great folktales, which are especially fun to listen to by candlelight. The Naso I've met don't speak English, but their Spanish tends to be remarkably clear. Visitors who speak a bit of Spanish will probably find it easier to communicate here than they do in, say, Panama City.

Some of the most evocative stories involve the *indios conejos* (rabbit Indians). They were nocturnal, had stripes down their backs, could see well in the dark, and could run superhumanly fast. Sometimes they ran through the forest at night bearing torches. They were also fierce and wild warriors who favored bows and arrows. The Naso say they waged wars with them near Palenque in the time of their grandparents. The only way the Naso could get the upper hand was to attack at daybreak, while their enemy slept.

What makes these tales especially intriguing is that the other indigenous peoples of western Panama have similar stories of going to war with *indios conejos*. Some versions are even more fanciful, describing them as white and just a meter tall, like mutant rabbits. One theory is that these stories are based on real battles with Miskito Indians. Some Naso don't believe the stories, but others are convinced the *indios conejos* did and still do exist, though today they're hidden away in the Chiriquí highlands.

Other tales are of lost cities and gold mines far up the Teribe beyond Palenque. Again, other indigenous people have similar stories.

These may be purely fanciful, of course, but there is evidence the ancient inhabitants of this area had plenty of gold. Columbus was fascinated by the indigenous people he encountered during his brief visit to Bocas del Toro who wore little, mirror-like discs of gold around their necks. And some believe there was once a quite developed civilization in the highlands. A Panamanian guide told me that a park ranger, looking for survivors of a plane crash, once stumbled upon stone houses 40 kilometers upriver from Palenque.

Tales of evil spirits and sinister encounters are also popular with the Naso. One involves Dö (pronounced "DOO"), a spirit that takes the shape of a monkey but has a scorpion's tail. It's said that he abducts people, keeps them in his cave for eight days, and then drowns them in the river. Ask your hosts about this; on the way back down the river, they can point out the mouth of the cave where the spirit lives. The cave is supposedly hugely long, leading between the Sixaola and Changuinola Rivers. The tale gets even better: They say an American found treasure in the cave 50 years ago. He took it, which would have been okay if he'd left something else behind in exchange. He didn't, and he didn't meet a happy end.

Then there's Älu, the spirit of the bongo tree, which takes the form of a monkey without a head. Its eyes are in its armpits, so in order to see it must raise its arms into the air. When Älu appears, blood gushes from around the bongo tree.

Wekso, by the by, is a Naso word that means "the place of bongo trees."

have been the dominant power of the time. The Naso were gradually squeezed out of the area and by the latter half of the 19th century had retreated far up the Río Teribe in the highlands near the Costa Rican border, to communities that came to be known as *palenques* (Spanish for "palisade" or "stockade," the name given by the Spaniards to hidden villages). These villages have long been abandoned and are considered a kind of interim ancestral homeland, a connection with the Naso's ancient past.

By their own account, the Naso have fought just about all the indigenous people in the region at one time or another. By the 17th century their numbers had declined. A tuberculosis epidemic in the early 20th century killed many, including the king.

Today the Naso are among the most beleaguered of Panama's eight surviving indigenous peoples. The cultural identity of the few Naso who remain is being eroded on all sides: by the dominant Latin culture, by missionaries, by intermarriage with other indigenous peoples, and so on.

There are about 3,800 Naso left in Panama. As a Naso man once said to me with a sad smile, *"Estamos en peligro de extinción"* ("We are in danger of extinction").

They are working hard to cling to their traditions and land, however. They still speak their ancestral language, along with Spanish. The men tend to wear nondescript white shirts and black slacks, but many women still wear distinctive dresses. These are cotton-print outfits in a single bright, bold color such as blue or yellow. They have puffy blouses and a tiny floral pattern that from a distance can look like polka dots.

The Naso still do not have *comarca* (reservation) status for their land. This is in stark contrast to their far more populous neighbors, the Ngöbe-Buglé, who now have a *comarca* that covers a huge chunk of western Panama. The Naso continue to tangle with them and others over land ownership, and they are also threatened by a plan to dam the Teribe and a tributary river for a hydroelectric project.

Environmentalists and indigenous-rights activists say the Bonyik dam (sometimes spelled Bonyic) would create a lake that would displace thousands and cause serious environmental damage. A bill to create a 130,000-hectare *comarca* for the Naso has been moving through the Panamanian national assembly at a glacial pace. Meanwhile, as do Panama's other indigenous people, the Naso struggle with widespread poverty.

Wekso

Wekso is about 40 minutes to an hour up the Río Teribe from El Silencio. It has a grim history as the former site of Pana-Jungla, a jungle-warfare/survival school that put elite Panamanian and foreign troops through legendarily difficult training. It was closed in 1990, but spooky remnants of the camp include a cage that once housed a black panther, the ruins of barracks and officers' quarters, and a serpentarium that once held Panama's deadliest snakes. Today, however, it has been transformed into an ecotourist camp currently used by the Naso nonprofit **ODESEN** (cell 6569-3869, www.bocas.com/odesen.htm).

The Wekso camp is on a small hill overlooking the river. The dining area is on the edge of the hillside and has a great view of the river below and the forest beyond. At the back of the camp is a large guest bungalow that resembles an oversized version of a traditional Naso thatched-roof house. It's rustic but perfectly acceptable and tidy, with foam-rubber mattresses, mosquito nets over the beds, and inviting hammocks on the front porch. There's an outhouse with flush toilets. Snakes are not unheard of around the camp; watch your step.

Just below the camp is a ranger station for Parque Internacional La Amistad. This area is not technically in the park but rather in the buffer forest around it. But guests must pay the US$5 park entrance fee anyway.

There is a good chance of spotting a variety of colorful birds in this area, including the white-fronted nunbird, blue-headed parrot, king vultures, long-tailed tyrants, Amazon kingfishers, snowy cotingas, and snowcap and green thorntail hummingbirds. As always, mammals in tropical forests are hard to find, but possibilities include water opossums, white-lipped peccaries, and neotropical river otters. Frogs are generally easy to spot, including red-eyed tree frogs *(Agalychnis callidryas)* and poison-dart frogs *(Oophaga pumilio)*.

A pretty loop trail that starts at the camp takes about two hours to walk at a slow pace. A second trail forks off it about 40 minutes in. The forest alternates between primary and secondary growth. The patches of primary forest contain some huge, impressive trees, including bongo, almond, and ceiba. The trail can be good for birding, including crowd pleasers such as toucans, and there's a chance of spotting sloths. This area is too close to well-settled areas to draw much wildlife, however.

Sieyik

About an hour upriver from Wekso is Sieyik, the Naso "capital." It's a village of about 500 people who live in houses scattered around a lovely hillside overlooking the river.

The center of the village is a clearing that contains the royal residence, a school, and the health post, all of which are made from cinderblocks. The king is assisted by a *consejo* (board of advisers) drawn from the communities. The Naso reserve the right to switch kings if they become unhappy with him. They can vote him out, but the replacement has to come from the royal family. They did just that in 2004 when the then-king, Tito Santana, came out in support of the Bonyik dam. The *consejo* deposed him and named a new king, Valentín Santana. But Tito Santana continues to be supported by some nontraditional Naso. This internal conflict is complicating the struggle to create a Naso *comarca*.

A visit to Sieyik with a tour operator will likely include a walk around the village and a visit to a traditional home, which may include lunch. Traditional Naso homes are built on stilts of one kind of palm *(jira)* and the roofs are thatched with another kind *(palenquilla)*. Residents sleep on the soft bark of a rubber tree. Newer homes use wooden planks for walls

the royal residence and graveyard, Sieyik

and floor, and sometimes have corrugated zinc roofs.

Visits may also include the chance to buy handicrafts, including objects carved from cedar, which are interesting but rarely achieve the level of artistry one sees with Emberá-Wounaan and Kuna works.

Parque Internacional La Amistad

The Río Teribe is the Caribbean gateway of Parque Internacional La Amistad (PILA) and the Palo Seco Buffer Forest that borders it. Far up in the headlands of the Teribe there are still jaguars, harpy eagles, tapirs, and macaws. That's because it's brutally hard to get to this area. The Caribbean side of PILA is far less accessible than the Pacific side, which lies in Chiriquí province and has some developed trails close to population centers. Anyone who wants to enter the park from the Caribbean slope is in for a serious trek and needs a skilled guide and boatmen and considerable supplies. The terrain is steep, there are no trails, and the boat has to fight an increasingly fast and powerful river. Even for the Naso, the upper reaches of the Teribe are becoming a distant memory. Getting to the Naso homeland of Palenque, a long-abandoned village, requires a full day on the river.

Practicalities

Just getting to Naso country is a fun little adventure. In the days of the jungle-warfare school there was a forest road that led as far as the Pana-Jungla, but it has disappeared back into the forest and the ever-shifting river. Today visitors come mainly by boat up the Río Teribe, though some areas can be reached on horseback or on foot on rough, narrow trails.

The departure point for the river journey is El Silencio, a tiny community about 10 kilometers from Changuinola, where the Río Teribe meets the Río Changuinola. River transport is by motorized *piragua* (dugout canoe). It's a beautiful trip. Small rapids ripple the river, and the air feels incredibly fresh and clean after the humidity of the towns and coast. Farm country at the beginning gives way to lush countryside

and a view of the Talamanca Mountains in the distance. The trip downriver is twice as fast. Tour operators sometimes let guests return the old-fashioned way: on "disposable" balsa-wood rafts that follow the current and are abandoned once the destination is reached.

As all this suggests, getting up the Río Teribe and exploring the area requires a fair amount of planning and is usually done through a tour operator or directly through one of two Naso groups, Soposo Rainforest Adventures or ODESEN. Both groups offer single- and multiple-day trips that include transportation, food, accommodations, and guided walks.

Soposo Rainforest Adventures (cell 6631-2222, www.soposo.com) is run by a former Peace Corps worker, Demecia, and her Naso husband, Celestino. Their operation seems professional and well organized. It's based in Soposo, which is on the Río Teribe about five minutes downriver from Wekso. They have built traditional-style huts for guests with double beds, mosquito nets, porches, and hammocks. There is no electricity; lanterns are used at night. Stays include guided hikes and, depending on the length of stay, visits to Sieyik and other communities. Trips include round-trip transportation from Changuinola, accommodations, guided hikes, "cultural activities," and all meals.

A one-night stay is US$130 per person. For those under time pressure, they also offer single-day trips (9 A.M.–4:30 P.M.) to Soposo, for US$90 per person, that feature a traditional lunch and a hike. A two-night stay (US$350 pp) includes a visit to Sieyik and an optional homestay with a Naso family. A five-night stay (US$500 pp) allows time for longer hikes and homestays.

An older ecotourism project is run by a Naso nonprofit called **ODESEN** (cell 6569-3869, www.bocas.com/odesen.htm). It's a Spanish acronym that translates to Organization for Naso Sustainable Ecotourism Development. Assisted by Conservation International, the group uses proceeds from tourist visits to help the community. ODESEN currently houses most guests at the Wekso camp, but this may be changing; contact the group for updates.

Visits can be arranged directly through ODESEN or through tour operators who work with the group. Visitors who book through ODESEN are charged cafeteria-style according to the services they need. A couple should count on paying about US$125 per person for round-trip transportation between El Silencio and Wekso, three meals, lodging, guides, and a hike. No one should come all this way without visiting at least one of the upriver communities, though, so add US$70 per person for a trip upriver to Sieyik, the site of the Naso capital and royal residence.

There is no electricity at any of the facilities used by either ODESEN or Soposo; candles and flashlights provide the only illumination at night. Traditional meals are generally simple and can include such dishes as *palmito* and *plosón* salad. *Palmito* is heart of palm. *Plosón* is a fern that contains a tiny amount of cyanide—it's quite tasty.

Day trips are definitely worthwhile, but it'd be a shame to make this much effort and not spend at least a night; it really deepens the experience.

It rains year-round up the Río Teribe, but less so in January–March and August–October. March is the driest month. Bring rain gear and a light jacket regardless of when you come. It can get cooler and breezy during the "summer" (January–March). It's also a good idea to bring bottled water or water-purification tablets or filters.

CENTRAL PANAMA

The section of Panama that stretches roughly from Altos de Campana in the east to the Fortuna Road in the west contains Panama's most popular beaches, its most accessible highlands, and some of its most important and historic provincial towns.

The Cordillera Central, Panama's central mountain range, forms the backbone of most of this long stretch of land. Its steep, sawtoothed peaks form a fortress-like wall between the Pacific and Caribbean slopes, making it especially easy to discern the Continental Divide here.

The Pacific side contains some of the longest-settled parts of Panama. Significant population centers include the quaint provincial town of Penonomé, the industrial outpost of Aguadulce, and the major transportation hub of Santiago. These and most of the other sizable towns are in the lowlands right on the Interamerican Highway—also known as the Pan-American Highway or, in Spanish, the Interamericana—and most of the beaches are just a couple of kilometers south of it.

These beaches are among the nicest and most accessible in the country, and they're in a part of Panama that sees less rain than average. As a result, the area is booming, with major resorts and condo developments going up at an alarming speed.

Lovely beaches are also found on the Archipiélago de las Perlas, an archipelago of more than 90 Pacific islands that begins just a 15-minute plane ride or hour boat trip from Panama City.

The highlands are all north of the highway,

© WILLIAM FRIAR

HIGHLIGHTS

◖ Farallón: Enjoy the sun at Panama's fastest-growing Pacific beach destination (page 238).

◖ Sunday Market: El Valle's market is a popular weekend destination for Panama City residents in search of crafts, plants, and an excuse to enjoy the cool weather and natural attractions of El Valle (page 248).

◖ Parque Nacional Omar Torrijos H. (El Copé): This little-visited park is an east-

ern outpost of Panama's rugged western highlands, with good facilities for campers (page 260).

◖ Natá de los Caballeros: A little town with a long history, Natá has a 500 year-old church, one of the oldest in the Americas (page 263).

◖ Santa Fé: This peaceful mountain town recalls a pre-boom Boquete (page 270).

LOOK FOR **◖** TO FIND RECOMMENDED SIGHTS, ACTIVITIES, DINING, AND LODGING.

though many of them are easy to get to on good roads. The most popular of these spots is El Valle de Antón. More isolated spots are not much farther away, and their beauty makes it worth the trouble to get there. All are dotted along the Cordillera Central, which means visitors at the higher elevations get to experience both Pacific and Caribbean flora and fauna.

At the Continental Divide, most roads end and the only way forward is on foot through dense tropical forest. Much of the Caribbean slope is less well known and more lightly settled than some remote parts of the Darién. Exploring it requires a serious organized trek through rugged wilderness.

PLANNING YOUR TIME

The destinations in this chapter cover a broad swath of central Panama, and only those with boundless time will be able to cover them all. Which to choose will depend on your taste and where else in Panama you're planning to go.

Those who want a little beach time within easy driving distance of Panama City have lots of options. Plan to spend at least a couple of nights to have time to truly relax.

For big full-service resorts with lots of facilities, go for **Coronado** or the resorts in and around **Santa Clara** and **Farallón.** The resorts at the latter are newer and, though a construction explosion is rapidly transforming it, the area is still not as densely developed

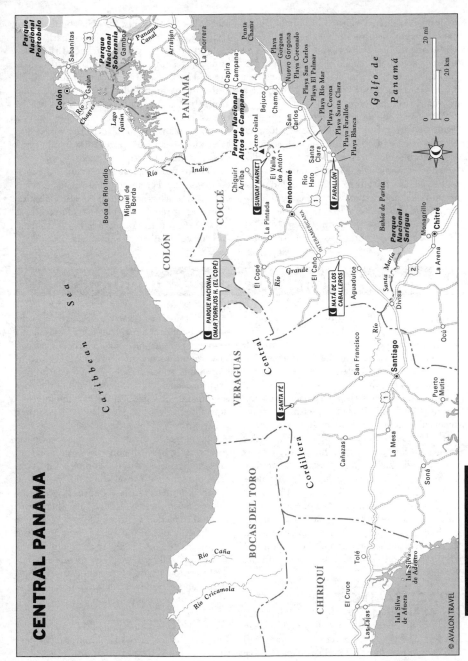

CENTRAL PANAMA

© AVALON TRAVEL

as long-established Coronado. Their white-sand beaches are also among the prettiest on the coast, though the surf can be rough. The other beach spots generally offer cheaper but less attractive places to stay, on beaches that have calmer surf but aren't going to grace a postcard anytime soon.

It's easy to add a day or overnight trip to **El Valle de Antón** from any of these beach spots; Santa Clara and Farallón are especially close to it. If possible, plan to visit El Valle on a Sunday, when its famous little market is bustling.

El Valle has the largest selection of lodgings, restaurants, and activities in the central highlands, and it's the easiest to get to of the mountain spots. **Parque Nacional Omar Torrijos H. (El Copé),** by contrast, is the most remote

and wild of these spots, but it has better visitor facilities than any other national park in the country. It's a good place to spend the night and enjoy some evening and morning hiking and bird-watching. It can get surprisingly chilly in the highlands—take a windbreaker and rain gear at any time of year. As attractive as the central highlands are, those short on time and planning to head to the wilder and even more beautiful western highlands won't miss too much by skipping them.

The **Archipiélago de las Perlas** is the closest major island group to Panama City. It offers beautiful beaches and lots of aquatic activities. However, it tends to get overshadowed these days by the tourist hot spots of Bocas del Toro and the culturally rich Kuna Yala.

Parque Nacional Altos de Campana

Established in 1966, Altos de Campana is Panama's oldest national park. Its 4,817 acres are spread over hillsides that range from 400 meters above sea level to the 850-meter-high Cerro Campana. Birders come up here for a chance to see the gorgeous orange-bellied trogon and other striking species. But the countryside is heavily settled, with only fragments of intact tropical and pre-montane forest left. There's a mirador just up from the park's ranger station, on the left, though the view is plenty dramatic just from the road. That view is the main reason to come up here; this place will appeal to most people more as a highway vista point than as a park to hike and camp in. It offers a breathtaking panorama of the Pacific Ocean, Punta Chame, craggy hills, an estuary that snakes up through the green countryside, and, on a clear day, Isla Taboga in the far distance.

PRACTICALITIES

The **ANAM ranger station** is four kilometers uphill from the turn off the Interamericana, on the left. Pay the US$5 entrance fee here, plus US$5 more to camp. For US$15, you may be able

to rent a bunk in a cabin on a ridge behind the station. It's meant for ANAM staff, but if there's room you're welcome to stay. The cabin has two basic rooms, each with four bunk beds, a common room, and a shared cold-water bathroom. Bring bedding. It's nothing special, but the price is right and you can't beat the location: perched right above a steep, craggy valley, with sweeping views all the way down the hills and out to sea.

The ranger at the station can answer basic questions (in Spanish only) about the area and the single developed trail, **Sendero La Cruz.** Five kilometers up from the ANAM station, or nine kilometers from the turnoff, you'll see a *senderos* sign on the right. Turn there onto a brutal road that requires a four-wheel drive with high clearance and a good warranty. Head up toward the towers as far as possible, then park. The trail leads through mostly secondary forest to a cross 700 meters away and 800 meters above sea level. The hike up and back takes about two hours.

GETTING THERE

The turnoff to Altos de Campana is less than an hour west of Panama City. The

TIPS FOR STAYING SAFE ON PANAMA'S HIGHWAYS

Drivers should take it easy on the windy, hilly stretch of the Interamericana that heads west past Altos de Campana. The curves are deceptively sharp, and many cars lose control. Take the speed signs seriously – they're really not being conservative.

All the mainland areas mentioned in this chapter are well served by buses from Panama City. Try to travel in the morning, when service is more frequent and it's easier to find your way around. It's much tougher to get transportation to more remote areas after dark. For beach and lowland areas, it's not necessary to take a bus that has your destination on the windshield; any bus plying the Interamericana that goes at least as far as your stop will drop you off. Buses to highland destinations are generally less frequent, though it's easy to get a bus to El Valle.

Renting a car is also a reasonable option, especially to get to the beaches. The road from Panama City is good the whole way, if more than a bit dangerous. Speeding is a problem on the Interamericana, so drive defensively. It's possible to get to El Valle, La Pintada, Santa Fé, and San Francisco in a regular car; just about every other highland spot described in this chapter requires a powerful, high-clearance four-wheel-drive vehicle.

Avoid driving through the countryside at night, when visibility is poor and help harder to find if you get into trouble. Note that there's a toll booth about 30 kilometers from Panama City, at the start of the Autopista Arraiján-La Chorrera.

right turn up from the westbound side of the Interamericana, about six kilometers west of Capira, comes up fast, and the road turns bad instantly. Be careful, and approach the turn very slowly. The drive starts steep, on a rough dirt and rock road, and requires a four-wheel drive.

To get to the park from Panama City by public transportation, take a bus that goes at least as far as Capira, which is where you'll switch buses. Buses make the trip from Capira up to Altos de Campana every day 8 A.M.–6:30 P.M. Look for "Capira-Chicá" on the windshield—Altos de Campana is an intermediate stop. Buses make the run every hour or two; service is erratic. Buses head back down to Capira 5 A.M.–4 P.M. The fare is US$1. Taxi fare from Capira is around US$20.

Beach Towns and Resorts

Wide, sandy, and accessible beaches start a little under an hour's drive from Panama City and stretch west for 50 kilometers. This strip of coast is where most people who live in and around Panama City, at least those who can afford it, go for a weekend at the beach. These beaches are great for swimming, body surfing, and lazing about. Some offer decent surfing. Those interested in diving and snorkeling need to head farther west or to the Caribbean side of the isthmus. One spot, Punta Chame, is known for windsurfing and kitesurfing.

The area has undergone major development in the last couple of decades, however, and now the most popular beaches have condo towers looming over them. You sometimes have to contend with weekend personal-watercraft riders, all-terrain-vehicle riders, and boom-box blarers, though some effort has been made to control these nuisances. But it's still quite possible to find clean, secluded spots without another soul on the beach for as far as you can see, especially if you come during the week.

Note: If only pure white sand makes you happy, these beaches may be disappointing. With the exception of the stretch of coast from

Santa Clara to Farallón, which does have light-sand beaches, the sand mostly comes in shades of brown, gray, and even black. But those who can get beyond their postcard preconceptions of a tropical beach will find these quite inviting. They're wide, long, and sandy, and the water is warm.

Many of the places to stay along the beach have restaurants attached. There are lots of other simple places to eat along the side of the road on the way to or from the beaches. But those with their own cars should consider doing what local weekenders do: Pack a cooler. Some of the accommodations have kitchen facilities. The most popular beach areas have small grocery stores with basic supplies. Playa Coronado has a large 24-hour supermarket.

The big resorts cater primarily to package and charter groups from outside Panama, but in the rainy season they sometimes offer special deals for people already in Panama. Keep an eye out for ads online and in Panamanian newspapers. These can be a good deal, but bear in mind that the resorts can get packed with Panamanian partiers blaring music night and day.

There are still (thankfully) few places along the coast to rent boats, ATVs, Jet Skis, and other recreational toys. Those who want a little boat ride can always hire a fisherman and putter around. And *campesinos* (country folk) all along the beaches rent horses, especially on the weekends. If you have trouble finding a likely candidate, ask for help at your hotel. Except at resorts, it shouldn't cost more than a few dollars an hour. Please be considerate about where you ride; horses muck up the beach for sunbathers.

The Pacific coast of Panama is completely different from the Caribbean coast. For one thing, where the Caribbean tides average 30 centimeters, the Pacific's massive tides range about 3.5–5.5 meters. Some of the beaches have strong rip currents and pounding surf, so watch out. The beaches are listed in order of their distance from Panama City, with the closest described first.

PUNTA CHAME

Punta Chame (POON-tah CHA-meh) is at the end of a dry and rather barren peninsula that curves up toward the mainland to the east, forming Bahía de Chame, a long, narrow bay that from shore looks like a quiet strait. Getting here by car from Panama City takes less than 1.5 hours. This is a popular wind-surfing spot.

In the middle of the bay, between the tip of Punta Chame and the mainland, is Isla Taborcillo, which was once owned by John Wayne. It's a rather forlorn spot.

Punta Chame is likely to appeal only to avid sailboarders. The beaches aren't that nice (the best ones are on the side facing the ocean, not the bay) and the village is depressed and nondescript. But the area does offer solitude and lovely views of the sea, islands, and hilly mainland. If you do go, notice the signs around Motel Punta Chame warning not to swim at low tide. That's because of the danger of stepping on a stingray.

A ROADSIDE ATTRACTION

Artesanías Típicas Panameñas (tel. 248-5313, 8 A.M.–6 P.M. daily) on the westbound side of the Interamericana, east of Capira, near kilometer marker 50, has long been a convenient place to stretch one's legs and do a little shopping on the way to and from the beach. It's a large, open building with a moderate selection of fancy hammocks (the most elegant of which are the white ones from Nicaragua, which sell here for about US$150), tooled-leather chairs, traditional Azuero ceramics and devil masks, and other souvenir possibilities. With enough warning, they can make hand-painted ceramic signs with house numbers, family name, or personalized messages. Those with their own transportation can place an order when heading west and pick up the completed sign on the way back east.

Practicalities

Motel Punta Chame (tel. 240-5498, starts at US$55 s/d) was once a shabby, gloomy place, but on my most recent visit it had been renovated in surprisingly good taste and is now rather pleasant. It offers 11 simple but cheerful air-conditioned rooms, the nicest of which run US$88 s/d. The place fills up with windsurfers in November and December. The hotel has a little restaurant/bar (7 A.M.–8 P.M. daily, US$7–8) that serves food in the dry season. During rainy season weekdays, it closes at 4 P.M. It has a large, pleasant *rancho* that overlooks the beach.

Machete Kiteboarding (tel. 227-0806, cell 6674-7772, www.machetekites.com), on the grounds of the Motel Punta Chame, offers beginning (US$300, 6 hrs) and advanced (US$120, 2 hrs) courses during the windsurfing season, mid-November–end of April.

There are few services in Punta Chame itself. The town of Chame, near the Interamericana, has a branch of the Banco Nacional de Panamá and a little store with basic supplies next to a soccer field.

Getting There

The turnoff to Punta Chame is about 70 kilometers west of Panama City. The drive takes a little under an hour. Don't confuse the turnoff to Punta Chame with the town of Chame, which is a few kilometers farther west along the Interamericana. If you see a sign for Chame, you've gone too far. From the Punta Chame turnoff it's another 25 kilometers down to the beach on a potholed road that's unpaved in sections.

To get to Punta Chame from Panama City by public transportation, take a bus that goes at least as far as Bejuco (beh-HOO-coh), about a kilometer past the Punta Chame turnoff. The fare is US$2.15. Get off at Bejuco, which is little more than a way station on the Interamericana, and take either a "bus" (really a pickup truck, US$1) or a taxi (asking US$15, but try bargaining) to Punta Chame. The pickup-buses are by the Texaco station; the taxis are a little farther west, near an underpass. The bus service runs approximately 6 A.M.–7:30 P.M.

PLAYA GORGONA

The next beach area along the coast is Playa Gorgona, about seven kilometers past the Punta Chame turnoff. Gorgona has the feel of a modest weekend beach destination that's past its prime and hovering on the brink of abandonment—which is exactly what it is. There are better hotels and nicer beaches farther west.

The place will be of interest mainly to surfers. **Playa Malibu,** right next to Gorgona, has a reputation for offering the best and most reliable ride along this whole stretch of coast. To get there, take the Gorgona turnoff from the Interamericana and head straight down to the beach. The break is to the left, near the mouth of a river. Those traveling by car should take a four-wheel drive and park it on the beach near the break. Otherwise, there's a good chance someone may break into the car while you're surfing.

Accommodations and Food

Of the handful of places to stay in and near Gorgona, I can only recommend one. There are also two interesting places to eat.

Casa Sin Punto (Calle Los Pescadores, tel 832-6447, cell 6780-5495, www.casasin-punto.com, US$72 s/d, including breakfast) offers three simple but clean and pleasant air-conditioned rooms in a house a few hundred meters from the ocean. There's free wireless Internet, and the friendly German owner can make dinner if requested.

Rincón Catracho (tel. 240-5807, noon–9 P.M. on weekends, call ahead of time during the week) has a friendly sidewalk café ambience in the middle of this down-at-the-heels village. The original chef was a German man who had cooked on cruise ships. He died a couple of years ago, but his Honduran widow learned his recipes and is now the cook. She offers a small menu of international cuisine.

The aptly named **La Ruina** (tel. 240-5126, cell 6527-8462, www.laruinatavern.com, noon–late Thurs.–Sun., under US$10) is a restaurant and bar built into what had been a U.S. military beer hall during World War II

CENTRAL PANAMA

(an anti-aircraft battery was nearby; the U.S. feared a Japanese attack on the Panama Canal). It's the dream project of Frank Marcheski, a retired U.S. Army sergeant from New Jersey, who admired the ruin when he was stationed in Panama in the late 1970s and always wanted to buy it. He and his Panamanian wife, Dilcia, who grew up in a house next to the ruin, now do. It's a large, airy two-story place with two long bars downstairs and staircases that snake about the place to create lots of private nooks upstairs. The fare tends toward burgers, lasagna, seafood, and *arroz con pollo* (chicken and rice). It's a simple place but incredibly atmospheric. Old photos are on the walls and the couple has lots of information on the interesting but little-known history of this area. Frank was a card dealer in Atlantic City, and he's set up a card table upstairs for fun. There's sometimes live music on the weekends.

Getting There

The turnoff to Playa Gorgona is on the Interamericana about seven kilometers west of the turnoff to Punta Chame and four kilometers east of the Coronado turnoff.

La Ruina and Rincón Catracho are in "downtown" Gorgona, which is a right turn before the beach as you head toward Cabaña Playa Gorgona. Follow the prominent signs to La Ruina. Rincón Catracho is right across the street from it. Those without their own wheels will probably have to hoof it from the Interamericana to any of these places. Alternatively, if there are no taxis around, visitors can get off the bus at the Coronado turnoff and get a taxi back to Gorgona from there.

PLAYA CORONADO

Playa Coronado, about 10 kilometers past the Punta Chame turnoff, is the most (over)developed beach in Panama. Because the beach is a long sweep of pure sand, this has long been a favorite place for those living in Panama City to build a weekend beach house. Growth here has exploded in the last couple of decades. It has condo towers, mansions, housing developments, several simple restaurants, and a major

resort hotel. Every centimeter of beachfront property has been built on. However, even here there's a good chance of not having to deal with crowds. Note that the sand is blackish.

Accommodations and Food

A moderate deal in pricey Coronado is **Hotel Gaviota** (Panama City reservations tel. 224-9053 or 224-9056, Coronado tel. 240-4526, http://hotelgaviotapanama.com, US$60.50 s/d). It's about a kilometer past the white condo towers toward the end of Paseo George Smith (also called Paseo Lajas). It offers 10 rooms, most of which are in a motel-style building set back from the beach with no view. The ones in this building are simple, and pleasant. Each has air-conditioning, two good double beds, and attractive warm-water bathrooms. Avoid rooms 1 and 2, which are old and small, set in a separate building. Main dishes in the simple restaurant range in price US$7–15. The restaurant is allegedly open 8 A.M.–5 P.M. daily, but that's likely only the case on dry-season weekends. The place has two swimming pools set in a well-tended, flower-filled garden on a rise overlooking the ocean. Amenities include a bar on the premises and a large new open-air dining room. Warning: Day-trippers from Panama City are shipped in by the busload on dry-season weekends. Day passes that allow use of all facilities except the rooms are US$18. Room prices drop during the week. Packages that include all meals are available.

The small, upscale **Corowalk Inn** (tel. 240-1516 or 240-1517, www.hostalesdelpacifico. com, US$77 s/d), in the shopping complex on the Interamericana, is a 14-room hotel built in 2002. It offers 14 modern, attractive rooms with good beds and air-conditioning. The rooms are small and simple but pleasant. Some rooms have no windows, and others are on a terrace overlooking the El Rey parking lot. The staff is refreshingly friendly. The only real problem with this place is that it's on the highway, not the beach.

Coronado Hotel and Resort (Avenida Punta Prieta, Panama City reservations tel. 264-3164 or 264-2724, U.S. toll-free tel.

866/465-3207, www.coronadoresort.com, starts at US$192.50 s/d), a short drive past the Coronado guard house, is one of the biggest resort hotels outside of Panama City. It has a health spa, 18-hole golf course, four tennis courts, three bars, three restaurants, a large swimming pool, and so on. Its latest addition is a huge equestrian club on a separate property, with its own steakhouse, **Restaurante Estribos de Plata.** Its 76 rooms (they're all suites) are modern and cheerful, ranging in size from large to gigantic. The least expensive are the "standard suites," which have a king-size bed, a sitting room with two sofa beds, minibar, telephone, hot-water bathroom, and TV. Package deals are sometimes available.

One drawback about this place is it's not actually on the beach. A frequent shuttle bus runs between the hotel and its private "beach club" on the water two kilometers away. A nice place to grab a simple lunch at the hotel (hotel guests only) is **La Terraza,** a casual open-air place near the pool. The food is nothing special, but the atmosphere is pleasant.

Guests can rent bicycles, golf carts, ATVs, horses, and more. All kinds of tours are available.

El Rincón del Chef (tel. 240-1941, cell 6676-4834, http://elrincondelchefpanama.com, 8 A.M.–9 P.M. Mon.–Thurs., 8 A.M.–10 P.M. Fri.–Sat., 7 A.M.–9 P.M. Sun., under US$10) is a cute, Spanish-mission–style open-air restaurant offering an ambitious range of dishes, from (rather greasy) corvina wontons to Thai food to imported beef. It's the best bet for a decent meal. They rent coolers (US$7.50/day) and sell ice (US$0.50/bag). It's on the right as you head toward the gatehouse.

Services

There's a modern shopping complex at the turnoff to Coronado that has a huge 24-hour **El Rey** supermarket, whose sign on a tall pole is visible for kilometers. There's a **pharmacy** inside the supermarket.

The complex also includes the Corowalk Inn, a **gas station,** a **Global Bank** (8:30 A.M.–3 P.M. Mon.–Fri., 9 A.M.–2:30 P.M. Sat.), and other stores. Global Bank has an ATM. Two new shopping malls are being built across the street.

Getting There and Around

The turnoff to Coronado is well marked; look for the El Rey supermarket sign. There's a guardhouse at the entrance to the area, and on the weekends access is controlled. Gringos, fair or not, should have little trouble getting past the guard at the gate—if stopped, just say you're going to the Coronado Hotel and Resort or Club Gaviota; you don't have to produce evidence of a reservation. It's a nuisance, especially since all beaches in Panama are open to the public, but it does keep the crowds down.

Buses run constantly between Coronado and Panama City, about 80 kilometers east (US$2.40). From the turnoff you can take a taxi or minibus to the beach or your hotel for a few dollars.

A taxi from the shopping complex on the Interamericana to the beach, three kilometers away, costs US$3. Minibuses make the same run from in front of the hardware store on the road leading into Coronado, across from the shopping complex, for US$0.50.

BETWEEN PLAYA CORONADO AND PLAYA CORONA

The 15 kilometers of beach between Coronado and Corona are relatively undeveloped and have few facilities. The area is most popular with surfers. All beaches are a left turn off the Interamericana, then a couple of kilometers drive or hike to the beach.

The best known spots are **Playa Teta,** about three kilometers west of the Coronado turnoff onto an unmarked dirt road; **Playa El Palmar,** just after the town of San Carlos; and **Playa Río Mar,** two kilometers past San Carlos onto a well-marked road. The sea bottom tends to be rocky in this area, so booties are a must. (Nonsurfers will not find most stretches of these beaches very attractive.) There are 2–3 breaks at each spot. Teta and Río Mar are the most popular.

San Carlos, 11 kilometers west of the

Coronado turnoff, is the only sizable town along the Interamericana between Coronado and Corona. It's about at the midpoint of the surfing beaches along this part of the coast. There's little of interest in town, but there's one decent place to stay. The main significance of San Carlos for tourists is that buses run frequently between it and the highland town of El Valle de Antón. However, these buses pick up and drop off passengers right on the Interamericana, not in the town itself.

Skip the last beach, **Playa Corona.** The beach is rocky with black sand and no appealing places to stay.

Practicalities

The few simple places to stay in this area will likely be of most interest to surfers. Avoid the Bay View Resort, which looks fancy from a distance but is rather rundown. Surf camps and schools come and go in this area. Development all along the coast has claimed some of the long-established places, and it's hard to know what will still be there when you visit. (Note that there are also surf camps in El Palmar, Spain, which can cause Internet surfers some confusion. Make sure you're researching the right country.)

A surf school aimed at beginners is **Panama Surf School** (cell 6673-0820, www.panamasurfschool.com), run by an Argentinean named Flor Villareal. Surf lessons in English or Spanish start at US$40 per adult. Groups and kids get a discount. Experienced surfers can rent short boards for US$15 or long boards for US20 per day. Transportation from Panama City and a variety of land and sea tours are also available.

Villa Sanchez Barry (cell 6667-0808, www.villasanchezbarry.com, starts at US$27.50 s, US$35 d) is on the road to El Valle, not on the beach, but good beaches are a short drive away and it's high enough up in the hills to catch a breeze and offer great views of the coast and ocean. Lodging is in a home that offers a tiny but pleasant and air-conditioned "backpackers' room." An entire apartment in the house with two bedrooms, two bathrooms, a kitchen,

and a solarium is also available (US$66 s/d, three-night minimum). There's also a separate two-bedroom cottage (US$55 s/d, three-night minimum). All accommodations have access to kitchens. You definitely feel like you're living in the owners' house here, so it's a good thing they're a friendly and welcoming Panamanian and American couple. There's an attractive swimming pool. Rates provided are for "bareboat" accommodations. Packages that include meals, transfers, and/or tours are also available.

Getting There

Surfers without their own transportation will probably have to hoof it with their boards at least a kilometer or two from the bus stop on the Interamericana to any of these beaches. Bus fare from Panama City to any of these turnoffs is no more than US$3.

Buses between San Carlos and El Valle run constantly during daylight hours. The fare is US$1. The last bus down from El Valle leaves at 8 P.M. Bus fare between San Carlos and Panama City is US$2.70.

IN AND AROUND SANTA CLARA

The days of Santa Clara as the prettiest area beach with inexplicably little tourism development are rapidly coming to an end. The secret's finally out, and all-inclusive resorts, condos, and golf courses are moving in. Fortunately, a few smaller-scale places are still around. Especially during the week and the rainy season, you probably won't have to deal with crowds, at least not yet. The short road from the highway to the beach has lots of potholes, but is drivable in a regular car if you're careful.

Accommodations and Food

There are a few pleasant places to stay in Santa Clara. None of them is a bargain, however. This is also the best area on this part of the coast for camping. There are still a few places where backpackers can pitch a tent in secure surroundings with good facilities for a few dollars. As usual, you can also just claim any open stretch of beach for free, but keep an eye on your gear.

A new bed-and-breakfast **Villa Botero B&B** (tel. 993-2708 or cell 6616-4991, www.villaboterobb.com, juanpepas2@hotmail.com, US$137.50 s/d, including breakfast) gets good reviews. There are only two guest rooms, both of which face a swimming pool and have minimalist modern decor, flat-screen TVs, in-room safe, air-conditioning, mini-fridge, and free Wi-Fi. Besides the swimming pool, the main house has a barbecue, kitchen, and laundry facilities, which guests are welcome to use. The B&B is a 10-minute walk to the beach. To get to Villa Botero, follow the main road into Santa Clara. Take the unpaved road on the right about 100 meters past the police post. The B&B is the fourth house down, with the large black gate.

Restaurante y Balneario Santa Clara (tel. 993-2123, 11 A.M.–6 P.M. Mon.–Fri., 9 A.M.–7 P.M. Sat.–Sun. in the dry season, under US$8) is a restaurant, bar, and campsite that gets packed on dry-season weekends. During the week, you're likely to have it all to yourself. The restaurant is little more than a large thatch-hut on the beach. The food isn't memorable, but it'll do in a pinch and the location is cool. The place is on the beach near Cabañas Las Sirenas. The restaurant specializes in seafood and pizzas. *Pulpo a ajillo* (octopus in garlic sauce) is chewy but tasty.

Campers can stay here for US$3–5 per person. The rate includes use of a *rancho*—a little open-air thatched-roof hut—and hammock right on the beach, clean bathrooms, and outdoor showers. Day visitors can use these facilities for US$1 each. There's a guard on duty at night. This is by far the best place to camp along this entire stretch of coast.

Restaurante y Balneario Santa also Clara arranges horse rental for about US$6 an hour on the weekends. Motorboat rentals may also be possible.

❰ **Las Sirenas** (Panama City tel. 223-0132, tel. 223-5374, 263-7577, 263-8494, or 263-9478 through Pesantez Tours, Santa

---

BEACH CAMPING

Campers considering sleeping on the beach along this strip of coast should be careful. As usual, sleep in a tent as a precaution against the small but real chance of being bitten by vampire bats, which carry rabies. Locals also warn about *maleantes* (thugs). Given that there are several guarded, inexpensive places with good facilities on or near the beach, you're better off pitching your tent there than on a secluded stretch of beach. The best camping facilities are at Santa Clara.

Clara office (Spanish only) tel. 993-3235, cell 6671-7888 or 6550-2500, www.lasirenas.com, starts at US$143 for one-bedroom cottage) is my favorite place to stay on my favorite Pacific coast beach. It offers the quietest, coziest, and most secluded lodging around. To get there, head down the paved main road from the Santa Clara turnoff and follow the "Las Sirenas" signs, which will lead you onto a dirt road. Both roads are potholed but drivable. Las Sirenas has added cheerful new furnishings, and the place is better than ever. It's not luxurious, but it offers quite comfortable and large beach cottages. The cottages above the beach all have sitting rooms, well-equipped kitchens, barbecue areas, air-conditioned bedrooms, patios with hammocks, in-room safes, TVs, and a view of the ocean. The ones on the beach, numbers 6–10, are similarly equipped. I prefer these because they're more private and the porch looks out on the beach a few steps away. Number 10 is closest to the ocean. The grounds are well cared for, with bougainvillea and other beautiful flowering bushes. The one thing this place lacks is a restaurant. One-bedroom cottages are US$143 and can sleep four. Two-bedroom cottages go for US$198 and can sleep six.

XS Memories (tel. 993-3096, fax 993-3069, www.xsmemories.com, US$60.50 s/d) is a secure and comfortable place to pitch a tent, park the RV, or rent a room. It's run by a friendly couple from Las Vegas who have built a tidy walled compound with a pool, set on well-tended grounds.

The cost to camp is US$2 per person or US$4 per tent. Campers should note, however, that the site is a couple of kilometers from the ocean, on the other side of the Interamericana from the Santa Clara turnoff. Motor homes can hook up here for US$6–10 a day, a price that includes water, electricity, septic service, and access to a small shop for repairs. Campers and RVers are also welcome to use the pool, shower, and all other facilities.

This place is popular with gringos and is well-known among the RV crowd, who stop here on their quest to drive the Interamerican Highway from North America to the end of the road in the Darién. The place gets 100 RVs a year, including some that come down in convoys.

XS Memories also offers three wheelchair-accessible cabins, each with air-conditioning and hot water. One of the cabins has a kitchenette. Rooms are simple but clean, though the mattresses are thin. There's a restaurant and sports bar with a big-screen TV. The restaurant (8 A.M.–8 P.M. Mon.–Thurs., 8 A.M.–10 P.M. Fri.–Sun., US$3–10) concentrates on simple, hearty American fare and bar food, such as hamburgers, chips with guacamole, and a variety of chicken, beef, and pork dishes. There's a tiny zoo on the premises. Bikes can be rented for US$6 a day. XS Memories is on the north side of the Interamericana opposite the turnoff to Santa Clara. The turn is well marked.

Opened in October 2009, the **Breezes Resort** (Panama City tel. 366-9191, U.S. toll-free tel. 877/273-3937, www.breezes. com, starts at US$203 s, US$270 d, including food, drink, and activities) is the first Pacific coast destination for the Breezes all-inclusive chain, which has resorts scattered around the Caribbean. It features 294 rooms, three restaurants, four bars, three swimming pools, a spa, and more. Rooms are in multi-story buildings that surround the pool complex, which cascades in tiers down to the beach like a cross between a series of artificial lagoons and a water

park. Food, booze, activities, and tours are included, but transfers between the airport and resort are US$140. Packages including airfare are also available. For those driving, the turnoff is at kilometer marker 108.

Getting There and Around

The poorly marked turnoff to Playa Santa Clara is 13 kilometers past Corona. It's about a 1.5-hour drive from Panama City, 108 kilometers east. Buses from Panama City make the trip every 20 minutes or so from early morning until mid-evening, though it's best to go during daylight hours. The fare is US$3 and the trip takes around two hours. Any westbound bus heading to Río Hato, Antón, Penonomé, or points farther west can let passengers off here. Buses will often drop passengers off at the beach for an extra US$1; be sure to ask the driver ahead of time. Otherwise passengers will have to walk 1.5 kilometers from the highway to the beach, unless a taxi happens to be hanging around.

The Santa Clara turnoff is about seven kilometers east of the depressed town of Río Hato. Next to that town is a huge old airstrip built by the United States military and the growing beach resort of Farallón. The closest large town is Penonomé, 36 kilometers west.

Those who want to do a bit of exploring under their own steam can rent bikes at XS Memories.

◖ FARALLÓN

The Farallón (far-ah-YONE) area, which starts about three kilometers west of the Santa Clara turnoff, didn't get much attention until the Colombian-owned Decameron hotel chain built a mammoth resort there in late 2000.

Before then, Farallón was just a quiet fishing village with a pretty beach that attracted some weekenders. Next door is a large airstrip built years ago by the U.S. military, since this is one of the driest places in Panama. In the 1980s it was the site of a Panamanian military base that housed some of Noriega's elite troops. U.S. forces wiped out the base during the 1989 "Just Cause" invasion.

Now, suddenly, it's the hot beach destination. The new beach resorts often refer to this area as Playa Blanca, the name of one stretch of beach here, but most everyone in Panama still thinks of the area simply as Farallón. New condominium buildings are sprouting up as far as the eye can see. The days of Farallón and the other sleepy beach villages around here are numbered. Note that the beach resorts are generally not open to day visitors; most of them have gated entrances with security guards.

As with its neighbor, Santa Clara, the beach is lovely and it's a wonder it was neglected for so long. There are a few other simpler and cheaper places to stay and eat in the village of Farallón and around the town of Río Hato, back on the Interamericana, a few kilometers farther west. Río Hato is the nearest semi-urban center, but it's down-at-the-heels and has little to offer other than a few services. The presence of the new resorts hasn't helped it much, a fact the townspeople still grumble about.

Accommodations and Food

The opening of the much-hyped **Nikki Beach Resort and Spa Playa Blanca** (www.nikkibeachpanama.com) has been much-delayed, though one could never tell that from its splashy advertising around Panama and the Internet. A ring wall of large, nondescript towers was erected on the beach, but when I was last in the area it was still a building site. It's about half a kilometer past the Playa Blanca Resort, on the same road. When it's finished it's supposed to include a 220-unit luxury condo hotel, a gated residential community, and spa. Visit their website for updates.

My favorite place to stay along the whole Pacific coast these days is **《 Tógo B&B** (cell 6613-5233, www.togopanama.com, starts at US$121 s/d). Opened in October 2009, it's just down the hill from the Decameron resort, but is light years away from it in scale and style. It reminds me of the beach houses owned by family friends up here, where I would spend many weekends—except that this one has been created with a keen eye for comfort and the budget and taste to do things right.

Named for its owners, Antonio (a Panamanian) and Gordon (from Argentina), Tógo is in a long-established beach neighborhood a two-minute drive west of the Decameron. It is not actually on the beach and doesn't have an ocean view, but it is literally across the road from it. This stretch of beach is just far enough from the resorts that guests, especially during the week and the rainy season, are unlikely to have to compete with hordes of other sunbathers.

Tógo is a beach house that was redesigned as a cozy, comfortable B&B. Everything here has been thought out carefully. Though houses surround Tógo on all sides, a high wall encloses the 2000-square-meter property, creating a quiet compound with rooms that look out on the B&B's lovely garden, which features mature trees, and hammocks from which to admire them. There's even a little artificial "water feature."

You need to be at least somewhat social to stay here, as the owners live in the compound and share their large, open living, dining, and kitchen areas with their guests. Fortunately, Antonio and Gordon are not only relaxed and welcoming hosts, but interesting, sophisticated guys who are fun to chat with. They can offer good tips about what to do and where to go not only in the region but in Panama City as well. The walls are decorated with appealing abstract art painted by Gordon, who is a graphic designer. Antonio is a witty raconteur with fascinating stories about life in Panama over the years. (His family owned the property for decades, with neighbors that ranged from former Panamanian president Arnulfo Arias to deposed dictator Manuel Noriega.)

The house was built in 1976, but was thoroughly renovated and redesigned to be as open to the garden as possible without sacrificing comfort. The decor is an attractive blend of the modern, traditional Miami-style tropical, and even a touch of classic Canal Zone (which is where the handsome wooden beams came from). There are five rooms, four of which have a queen bed and an outside sitting area. The largest is an upstairs room with a queen bed,

© WILLIAM FRIAR

Tógo is a beach house that has been redesigned as a cozy, comfortable B&B.

sofa bed, kitchenette, and private balcony. A third person in any of the rooms is US$27.50 extra. The B&B is adults only.

Rooms are immaculate and spacious, with understated modern furnishings, air-conditioning (which you may not need if the sea breezes are blowing), and attractive bathrooms with high-quality fixtures. A welcome cocktail, breakfast, bike use, and Wi-Fi access are included with stays. Other meals can be arranged for an extra fee. Rates are lower during the week and in the low season. This is an appealing alternative to the mega-resorts. The website has a map and detailed directions to the B&B, which isn't hard to find.

The name of the **Royal Decameron Beach Resort and Villas** (Panama City reservations tel. 214-3535, resort tel. 993-2255, www.decameron.com, all-inclusive packages start at around US$200 s/d, two-night minimum) keeps mutating, but most know it simply as "the Decameron." It's an enormous beach resort—600 rooms set in three-story units above a large, gorgeous stretch of beach. All rooms have the same layout and feature either two full beds or a king-size bed. The rooms are medium-size, cheerful, and modern, if fairly nondescript, and the beds are comfortable. The resort features 10 restaurants and cafés, 11 bars, nine pools, a duty-free shop, and so on. It was built in 2000, which by the standards of this area makes it the grand old hotel of the area. But it remains popular and if anything looks better and better to many locals because it was designed and landscaped to blend in with its surroundings rather than dominate them, as many of the newer places, with their towers and monster pools, are starting to do.

The Decameron is an all-inclusive place that features "unlimited consumption" of food and domestic booze, including taxes and tips. Also included are daily activities, performances, and use of nonmotorized water-sports equipment, such as ocean kayaks and snorkeling gear. Other goodies include a free scuba-diving mini-course and aerobics and dance classes. Tours, fishing trips, use of the 18-hole Mantarraya golf course, and other activities are available for an extra charge. Rates can fluctuate by US$100 a night depending on whether you come during the week (lower), weekend (higher), or rainy season (lowest).

Transportation to and from Panama City is sometimes included in package deals arranged through travel agents. The resort caters mainly to large Canadian, European, and South American groups that are shipped over on charter flights, get a sunburn, and are shipped out a few days later.

The **Playa Blanca Resort and Spa** (Panama City reservations tel. 264-6444, fax 264-3972, hotel tel. 993-2910 or 993-2911, www.playablancaresort.com, US$120 s, US$160 d) is two kilometers farther west down the beach. When it opened in 2003, it offered a smaller-scale alternative to the Decameron. Now, however, it's part of a huge residential development that also includes condo towers, sports and convention centers, and what is billed as the second-largest swimming pool in the world (in reality, a 17-acre artificial seawater lagoon). This area is rapidly turning into another Coronado. To get a sense of what the whole development looks like, check out www.panamaplayablanca.com.

The all-inclusive hotel itself is on the edge of all this, on the beach. It features 222 rooms in seven three- and four-story buildings set around an attractive swimming pool.

The decor is kind of faux-Mediterranean, with the buildings done up in white with blue trim. Facilities include two main restaurants (one seafood, one buffet) plus a sailboat-shaped outdoor restaurant on the beach that's open on the weekends, a spa/beauty parlor, an Internet café, a small open-air theater, gift shops, a nine-hole putting course for golfers, a late-night disco, and so on. An activities center offers personal watercraft, ATV vehicles, kayaks, mountain bikes, sailboarding gear, surfing lessons, fishing trips, sailboats, and tours of El Valle, Panama City, and other sights.

Rates include all meals, domestic liquor, use of nonmotorized aquatic gear (kayaks, pedal boats), and daily activities. The simple but pleasant rooms have one queen-size or two double beds, safes, cable TV, and balconies. Try to get a room in buildings 600 or 700, which are right on the edge of the beach; the others are set around the swimming pools. Day

passes, weekday discounts, and other special offers are sometimes available. There have been some complaints about service and maintenance lately.

The most luxurious beach resort in Panama is the new ◖ **Bristol Buenaventura** (tel. 908-3333, www.thebristol.com, starts at US$434 s/d), which is under the same ownership as the Bristol Hotel in Panama City. This place is something else. Even those who don't go for big resorts are likely to be impressed by the ambition of the place, and the taste with which it has been realized, though only a few will be able to afford what it has to offer.

Opened in February 2009, the resort is in the middle of the new Buenaventura gated development, which starts about 6.5 kilometers from the Interamericana, on the same road as the Playa Blanca and Nikki Beach resorts, but past both of them. As gated communities go, this one is being nicely developed, with plenty of room between individual houses and condos and no towers looming over everything. An 18-hole, par-72 golf course by Nicklaus Design is under way. There's even a small zoo.

The hotel itself is 1.7 kilometers from the gate. It consists of a three-story main building with 114 rooms and a growing number of "villas." The villas are two-story, four-bedroom fully furnished houses that go for US$2,000 a night.

The resort is done up in Spanish-colonial style, with pretty fountains and terraces, an artificial lagoon/canal, and an elegant swimming pool in a garden setting. There's a spa and fitness center, and even a mission-style church for weddings.

Inside, the rooms and common areas are decorated in exquisite modern taste. Even the least-expensive rooms are among the most opulent in Panama. These are large (50 square meters), with hardwood floors, air-conditioning, an iPod docking station, a desk, 42-inch LCD flat screen TVs, marble bathroom with spacious showers and a separate tub, and Egyptian cotton linens. Larger rooms and better views cost more. Only rooms on the 3rd floor have a good view of the ocean, but the view of the

CENTRAL PANAMA

The Bristol Buenaventura is Panama's most beautiful big resort.

artificial lagoon and the grounds of this fantasy mini-city of luxury are eye-pleasing as well. With relatively few guests for such a large, exclusive property, the atmosphere is quiet and serene.

There is one main formal restaurant, as well as three casual cafés and grills, a handsome indoor bar, and a swim-up bar at the pool. A separate clubhouse, El Faro, is named for its lighthouse tower, which overlooks a second long swimming pool that ends in a lovely stretch of beach.

Service at the resort is gracious and attentive. This place is several cuts above the other beach resorts, as one would hope at these prices. This is not an all-inclusive: prices include just the room and taxes. Food, drinks, tours, spa services, etc., are charged separately. Transfers from Panama City to the resort in a Lincoln Town Car are US$250, or more for a fancier car.

The turnoff to the hotel is just before the town of Río Hato. The hotel is three kilometers from the highway, surrounded by new condo developments.

My choice for a good hangout spot in this area is **Pipa's Beach Bar and Restaurant** (tel. 223-0975, 10 A.M.–late Tues.–Sun.), two kilometers past the Decameron. It's a relaxed, friendly place that's open from about 11:30 A.M. daily until the last person passes out. It offers a small menu of seafood and bar food (US$5–15). There's also a volleyball net on the beach. Visitors get there by just walking west along the beach past the Decameron. It's also possible to drive right to the place, but this involves driving through the yards of local fisherfolk who live in the area, so be polite and drive slowly; one reader got hassled by kids going this route. It might be best to park back around the Decameron and walk, but those feeling lazy who have their own transportation can turn right toward the Decameron and keep going straight. After two kilometers the road turns to sand. Keep going. The bar will be up ahead on the left, on the beach. Party down.

If staying on the beach isn't important to you, but saving money is, consider **Hospedaje Las Delicias** (tel. 993-3718, starts at US$12 s/d with fan, US$20 s/d with a/c), just off the north side of the Interamericana on the eastern outskirts of Río Hato. It's set in a yard with flowering trees and has a bright and cheerful facade. Rooms are simple but okay with firm beds. Seven rooms have air-conditioning; five have fans. Note that this place is 7–8 kilometers from the beach at Farallón.

Information and Services

There's an **ATP office** (tel. 993-3241, 8:30 A.M.–4:30 P.M. Mon.–Fri.) on the road that runs past the west side of the airstrip leading from the Interamericana to the Decameron.

Just about anything guests at the Decameron or Playa Blanca Resort could want is provided at the resorts. A couple of the services at the Decameron are also available to nonguests. These include **CB Tours** (tel. 993-2255, ext. 3067, 8 A.M.–6 P.M. daily), in the parking lot of the Decameron. It rents mountain bikes with helmets for US$5 for 1.5 hours or US$20 for a two-hour bike tour. Visitors can also rent ATVs for US$25 for a half hour, US$35 for an hour, US$50 for two hours, and US$70 for three hours. Guided tours by ATV are also available. Near the entrance to the Decameron parking lot is a **Banco Nacional de Panamá** ATM.

There are also a few services in the town of Río Hato, which is divided by the Interamericana, four kilometers west of the Decameron turnoff. **Plaza Río Hato,** in the center of town on the south side of the Interamericana, is a mini-mall with a grocery store, bakery, and, occasionally, an Internet café.

Getting There and Around

To get to this area from the direction of Panama City, continue west past the Santa Clara turnoff for three kilometers. On the far (west) side of the airstrip, turn left. The road runs past an ATP office, then to the Decameron resort on the beach two kilometers from the highway. A right turn at the resort leads to the fishing village of Farallón.

Buses to Farallón from Panama City, about 110 kilometers to the east, cost US$4 and leave every 20 minutes or so, 5:30 A.M.–8 P.M. The trip takes around two hours. Buses drop passengers off at the Decameron or Playa Blanca Resort by request.

A **National Car Rental** (tel. 265-2222, 8 A.M.–1 P.M. and 2–5 P.M. Mon.–Sat., 8 A.M.–4 P.M. Sun.) is in the parking lot of the Decameron.

El Valle de Antón

When the steamy heat of Panama City is too much even for locals, they head to the hills of El Valle de Antón, which everyone simply calls El Valle. It's a pleasant little town nestled in the valley of a huge extinct volcano. The valley floor is about 600 meters above sea level, high enough to make this area significantly cooler and fresher than the lowlands. This is one of the few places in Panama where you'll find houses with fireplaces.

El Valle proper lies along the wide, flat valley floor, and most of the sights are within town or on gentle slopes not far away. That makes it easy to get almost anywhere on foot or by bicycle, a pleasant way to get around given

the mild climate and the flower-lined streets. Watch out for monster potholes.

The first thing you see upon entering El Valle is a *supermercado* (supermarket) with a gas station, to the right. This and the **public market** in the center of town are common landmarks, and most of the directions in this section will use them as starting points. A single main road, sometimes called **Avenida Central** or Calle Central, but not marked in any case, runs through the town from the *supermercado* past the public market, ending in a fork at the west end of town.

Several of El Valle's biggest attractions— the **Chorro El Macho** waterfall, the **Canopy Adventure,** and the petroglyphs of **La Piedra**

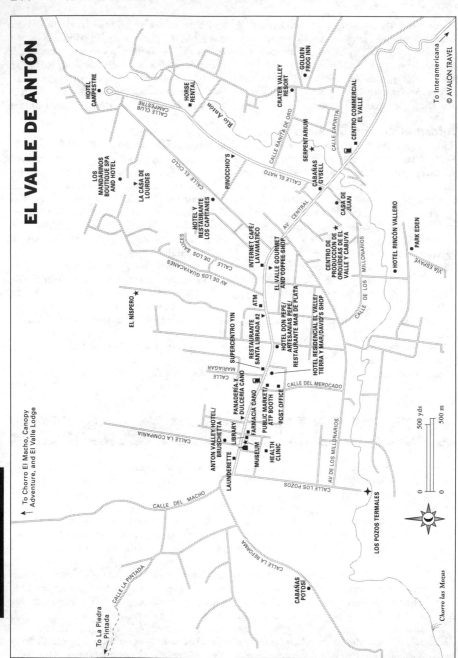

EL VALLE DE ANTÓN

To Interamericana

© AVALON TRAVEL

HOTEL CAMPESTRE

CALLE CLUB CAMPESTRE

HORSE RENTAL

Río Antón

CALLE EL CICLO

GOLDEN FROG INN

CRATER VALLEY RESORT

CENTRO COMMERCIAL EL VALLE

CALLE CAPIRITA

CALLE RANITA DE ORO

SERPENTARIUM

CABAÑAS GYSELL

CALLE EL HATO

PINOCCHIO'S

LOS MANDARINOS BOUTIQUE SPA AND HOTEL

LA CASA DE LOURDES

HOTEL Y RESTAURANTE LOS CAPITANES

CALLE DE LOS SAUCES

AV DE LOS GUAYACANES

INTERNET CAFÉ/ LAVAMÁTICO

AV. CENTRAL

CASA DE JUAN

CENTRO DE PRODUCCIÓN DE ORQUÍDEAS DE EL VALLE Y CABUYA

HOTEL RINCÓN VALLERO

PARK EDEN

VÍA ESPAVÉ

EL VALLE GOURMET AND COFFEE SHOP

CALLE DE LOS MILLONARIOS

EL NÍSPERO

ATM

RESTAURANTE SANTA LIBRADA #2

SUPERCENTRO YIN

HOTEL DON PEPE/ ARTESANÍAS PEPE/ RESTAURANTE MAR DE PLATA

HOTEL RESIDENCIAL EL VALLE/ TIERRA Y MAR/DAVID'S SHOP

CALLE MARIAGAR

CALLE DEL MERCADO

PANADERÍA Y DULCERÍA CANO

PUBLIC MARKET/ ATP BOOTH

POST OFFICE

AV DE LOS MILLONARIOS

FARMACIA CANO

LIBRARY

CALLE LA COMPAÑÍA

ANTON VALLEY HOTEL/ BRUSCHETTA

LAUNDERETTE

MUSEUM

HEALTH CLINIC

CALLE LOS POZOS

LOS POZOS TERMALES

CALLE DEL MACHO

To Chorro El Macho, Canopy Adventure, and El Valle Lodge

CALLE LA PINTADA

To La Piedra Pintada

CALLE LA REFORMA

CABAÑAS POTOSÍ

Chorro las Mozas

0   500 yds

0   500 m

WAVING GOODBYE TO THE GOLDEN FROG?

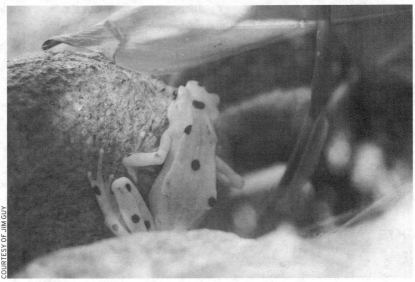

COURTESY OF JIM GUY

golden frog

Panama's famous golden frog, *Atelopus zeteki,* is native to El Valle. Seeing these frogs is supposed to bring good luck, and they have a special place in the heart of Panamanians. They're practically a national symbol, and golden frog *huacas* (ceremonial figurines buried with the dead) are common in pre-Columbian graves.

It's hard to believe something this color can exist in nature. Sadly, it may not. Golden frogs were endangered even before the chytrid fungus, which is devastating amphibian populations throughout Central America, came to El Valle in 2006. The fungus coats the skins of frogs, suffocating them. In 2007,

David Attenborough's BBC series *Life in Cold Blood* came to El Valle to film them and their "semaphoring" behavior – they are believed to communicate by waving one arm. At the end of the shoot, scientists collected the wild specimens for their own protection; Attenborough declared that this would be the last time the frogs would be filmed in nature, as they are believed to be extinct in the wild. Let's hope not. For now, they're being kept alive in zoos and rescue projects. This includes the **El Valle Amphibian Conservation Center,** El Valle's little El Níspero zoo. Hopefully one day they can be returned to the wild to thrive again.

CENTRAL PANAMA

Pintada—are a few minutes' drive past this fork.

You'll hear talk of **La India Dormida** (the sleeping Indian girl) during your stay. This refers to the silhouette some see along a section of the hilltops ringing the valley. Given the correct angle and enough imagination, you may see it too.

El Valle is famous for its nearly extinct **golden frogs** and its square trees. Even though the area is heavily settled there is still wildlife in the protected forests. There's also a small zoo, **El Níspero,** with indigenous and nonnative species.

Those who want to get the old heart pounding should try the **Canopy Adventure** zipline ride. Other popular nature activities in El Valle include hiking, horseback riding, and splashing around under waterfalls. If you come early in the week, especially Monday or Tuesday, you'll likely have El Valle all to yourself. This is nice in some ways, but some may find the place a bit too sleepy. To see the public market in full swing, come on a Sunday morning. Saturday is also a pretty active day, and typically the only busy night. Most visitors leave El Valle by midday Sunday. Note that on holiday weekends in the dry season, every room in El Valle can fill up.

Room prices typically drop during the week, starting Sunday night. It's also possible to do El Valle as a day trip from Panama City, either on your own or through a tour operator. Many of these offer packages that include transportation, a visit to the market, and sometimes the Canopy Adventure.

SIGHTS

El Valle's bare little **museum** (US$0.25, 10 A.M.–2 P.M. Sat.–Sun.) is hardly worth a visit. It contains a few traditional tools of valley life, from a wooden *trapiche* (a press for crushing sugarcane) to a decidedly non-indigenous sewing machine from someone's attic. The museum is right behind the town church, which in turn is just west of the public market.

El Níspero

Though it's usually considered a zoo, El Níspero (no phone, 7 A.M.–5 P.M. daily, US$2 adults, US$1 children) is really more of a plant nursery with caged creatures. Even if you have qualms about animals confined in small places—and some of the cages here are painfully small—consider visiting this one.

For one thing, it's a good place to see Panama's all-but-extinct **golden frogs.** Today they are being cared for by the El Valle Amphibian Conservation Center, a kind of Noah's ark for the little critters and about 40 other critically endangered species. Supported by the Houston Zoo, half of the facility is open to the public and is well worth a visit. For more information, see www.houstonzoo.org/amphibians.

Other indigenous creatures here include the capybara, the world's largest rodent—it can grow up to a meter long and weigh up to 45 kilograms; several species of primates, including Geoffroy's tamarin and the white-faced capuchin; sleepy-looking sloths; a tapir; and two species of felines, the margay and ocelot. Among the decidedly non-indigenous critters here are some emus, of all things.

The zoo also has a greenhouse stuffed with orchids, extensive gardens, and a fish-filled wishing well.

To get to El Níspero, continue west along Avenida Central 1.4 kilometers past the *supermercado* at the entrance to town. Take a right turn at the sign that says El Níspero. Follow the winding road 1.1 kilometers. The road is rough but doesn't require a four-wheel drive. El Níspero is on the left.

There's no guide, but Wednesday–Sunday you can try imposing on one of the caretakers. A small tip would probably be appreciated but is not necessary. The caretakers speak only Spanish.

La Piedra Pintada

El Valle has an impressively large boulder covered with hieroglyphics that is locally known as La Piedra Pintada (literally, "the painted rock"). No one is sure what all the squiggly designs carved (not painted) into the face of this boulder mean, or even who made them, though everyone has a theory. Maybe it's just the doodling of the gods. The boulder is easy to get to and thus worth a visit. It's just a five-minute walk up a trail that follows a pretty little stream.

Drive west on the main road, Avenida Central, past the public market and out of town. Take a left after the bridge. Make the first real right, then follow the road until it ends at a cul-de-sac at a small church. (The whole way is well marked.) Small boys will mysteriously appear, eager to show you the rock—for a fee, of course. Being surrounded by a swarm of tykes can be intimidating, but you shouldn't have a problem. As soon as you choose one the others will back off. He'll probably be pleased with a quarter. By the way, they're not leading you astray if they steer you left rather than straight up, as the misleading sign would have you go.

Square Trees

Behind and to the right of the Hotel Campestre is a trail, often muddy, that runs by a brook and a bit of secondary-growth forest. The trail isn't well marked and has forks, but if you follow your intuition about the "main" trail, you should be okay. After 5–10 minutes, you should see a collapsing bamboo fence on the right. Walk over it into the little clearing. The most convincing specimens are more trapezoidal than square, but at least you can say you've seen El Valle's famous square trees.

The Serpentario

This small serpentarium (cell 6576-6926, 8 A.M.–at least 5 P.M. Mon.–Sat., US$3) is next to a stream north of Avenida Central and east of Calle El Hato. Creepy-crawlies here include a variety of boas (rainbow, constrictor), an eyelash viper, a tarantula, several fer-de-lance,

coral snakes both true and false, and a *patoca* (a.k.a. jumping pit viper). They're kept in glass cages but may still give you the creeps: Come here *after* you've done all your Panama forest hikes. It's the pet project of a respected local biologist, Mario Urriola, who can also provide tour-guide services. The serpentarium stays open an hour or two later on the weekends, depending on demand.

To get there, turn right at the Texaco station near the entrance to town and follow the signs. There's a parking area about 200 meters down a rough road. From there it's about another 100 meters on foot; follow the stream. The serpentarium is not particularly well marked and has moved once, but a new building was half finished when I last visited so presumably this is its permanent home.

Centro de Producción de Orquídeas de El Valle y Cabuya

This small, voluntary conservation association (no phone, 9 A.M.–2 P.M. daily) has about 100 native orchid species on display in greenhouses about 200 meters south of Avenida Central,

El Valle's little zoo, El Níspero, has some striking native species.

near the ANAM office. It's a left turn past Cabañas Gysell, not far from the entrance to town.

SHOPPING
Sunday Market

Some visitors come to El Valle just for the public market, which got a makeover a few years back. Here you'll find crafts from many parts of Panama, in addition to fresh fruit, vegetables, and plants. While the kind and quality of crafts vary week to week, this is usually a good place to buy Panama hats. Note that these are not the elegant, tightly woven hats that most people think of—those "Panama hats" are actually Ecuadorian. The ones here aren't usually even the relatively finely woven ones made in some parts of the Azuero Peninsula. These are more coarsely woven, usually of white and black fibers, and are the most common kind worn in Panama. Prices range about US$10–30. You should expect to pay about US$25 for a decent one. Other items to consider include carved soapstone figures. The limiting factor isn't the price but the weight you have to lug around. The market is quaint and lively, but not big. While a popular weekend destination for lots of Panama City residents and the old Canal Zone crowd, and much-trumpeted by tour outfits, it's unlikely to blow your socks off.

The public market is 1.7 kilometers down the main road as you enter El Valle. You can't miss it—it's smack in the center of town. The market operates on a limited scale during the week, but it's in full swing on Saturdays and especially Sundays. There are also a few souvenir kiosks directly across the street. If you're not in town on Sunday, there are some newer souvenir shops to the east of the market.

Other Craft Shops

David's Shop (tel. 983-6536, 7 A.M.–7 P.M. Sun.–Thurs., 7 A.M.–10 P.M. Fri.–Sat.) has a better selection of crafts than the market itself. There's a little workshop at the back where you can peek in at artisans at work. The shop can also dispense tourist information, arrange horse rentals and trips to the Canopy Adventure, and rent bikes. It's affiliated with Hotel Residencial El Valle upstairs.

Artesanías Pepe (tel. 983-6425, 7 A.M.–7 P.M. daily) next door, below Hotel Don Pepe, is a similar place, though the quality and selection is better at David's Shop.

SPORTS AND RECREATION

El Valle is popular with middle-class and wealthy Panamanians as a weekend getaway. As such, most entertainment takes place inside people's weekend homes. There is almost nothing in the way of nightlife in El Valle. Hiking, horseback riding, and bird-watching are the main things to do around here. These can often be arranged through one's hotel. David's Shop (tel. 983-6536, 7 A.M.–7 P.M. Sun.–Thurs., 7 A.M.–10 P.M. Fri.–Sat.) rents bikes. It's possible to take hikes and horseback trips up into the mountain, but these tend to be on old forest paths used for years as commute routes rather than on developed trails and shouldn't be attempted without a knowledgeable guide. Be sure to bring rain gear, warm clothing, and long-sleeved shirts (to avoid getting cut up by the brush).

Canopy Adventure

The outdoor activity that's gotten the most attention in recent years is the Canopy Adventure (El Valle tel. 983-6547, Panama City tel. 264-5720, http://adventure.panamabirding.com, open approximately 8 A.M.–5 P.M. daily). It's a lot of fun, as long as you're comfortable with heights.

The Canopy Adventure is sort of a cross between a nature hike and a zipline thrill ride. The hike part comes at the beginning, when you head uphill through steamy forest on a trail that's steep and slick at times. The hike takes about 30–45 minutes. You're hiking through protected private land that borders a private forest reserve, so there's a good chance of seeing some wildlife.

Now for the really fun part, the zipline ride. Riders are attached by harness and pulley to four cables strung between trees. Cables are at a gentle downward angle, so you go flying back down to the trailhead in stages. You're about 30 meters above the base of the lovely El Chorro waterfall at the beginning of the ride. Those who've done the ride before should note that the route is slightly different now. A storm knocked a tree down, so some of the platforms were moved and now the ride goes right past the roaring falls instead of above it.

Riders zip through the trees under their own power. The first run is the most dramatic, when you're also the most nervous about slamming into a tree.

The whole ride costs US$50. Clients can also opt to do just the last stage for US$12.50. Those who don't care for heights can opt instead for a four-kilometer guided walk (US$35) or a swim in the pool below the waterfall (US$3.50). For US$125 the Canopy Adventure provides transportation to and from Panama City, lunch, and a tour of El Valle in addition to the ride. Part of the proceeds go to maintaining the nature preserve. The prices do not include sales tax, currently 5 percent.

You will get muddy, but wear long pants to protect your legs. Also, wear sturdy, closed shoes with decent traction. The guides offer water and insect repellent during the hike. Sunday is the busiest day, so show up before 10 A.M. to avoid long lines. Allow two hours for the whole thing.

The Canopy Adventure is three kilometers past the public market (heading west) on the main road. Follow the blue signs reading "El Macho." At the west end of town, the road forks after a bridge. Take the right fork, which is Calle El Macho. The ride's office, a thatched-roof hut, will be on the left.

Horseback Riding

There's a long-established **horse rental** outfit (cell 6646-5813, 8 A.M.–6 P.M. daily, US$8/hour) next to the chapel at the fork in the road. It's one kilometer up Calle El Hato. The price includes a Spanish-speaking guide. You can request a destination or just take the staff's advice; many trails lead up through the wooded hills.

© WILLIAM FRIAR

It's easy to rent horses in El Valle.

Adventure Tours

Nature tours can often be arranged through your hotel. **Hotel y Restaurante Los Capitanes** (tel. 983-6080, cell 6687-8919, www.los-capitanes.com), for instance, offers a variety of hikes guided by local schoolkids for US$2–3, including a two-hour hike to the top of La India Dormida, stopping at three waterfalls along the way.

The **Panama Explorer Tours (PEX)** (Panama City tel. 215-2328, www.crater-valley.com), which operates Crater Valley Resort and Adventure Center, offers a range of outdoor activities in El Valle and the surrounding area. These include hikes, treks, rock climbing, rappelling, ropes courses, rafting, and mountain biking. These are quite reasonably priced, starting at US$7 per person to try the climbing wall and up to US$88 for rafting.

ACCOMMODATIONS

Hotel options used to be quite limited in El Valle, as much of the potential clientele own vacation homes here. But now visitors can choose among simple but pleasant budget accommodations, quaint bed-and-breakfasts, an ecolodge, and resort spas. Rates at some places go down after the high season, which runs approximately November–March.

US$10-25

Backpacker accommodations don't last long in El Valle. One option is **La Casa de Juan** (No. 4, Calle de Los Millonarios, cell 6453-9975, lacasadejuanpanama@hotmail.com, US$10 pp in dorms, US$20–25 s/d). It's in a private home with a cluttered, junk-filled patio and dark, rather dingy rooms. The dormitory has a zinc roof but no fans, so guests may have the rare distinction of feeling hot and stuffy in cool and fresh El Valle. Basic private rooms are US$20 s/d with shared bathroom, US$5 more for private bath. Guests have access to a TV, kitchen, and laundry facilities. This place isn't great, but it may suit those on a tight budget. It's within reasonable walking distance of the market and other downtown attractions. Ironically enough, it's on Calle de Los Millonarios ("the

street of the millionaires"), about 200 meters south of Cabañas Gysell.

US$25-50

Cabañas Gysell (Calle El Hato near Avenida Central, tel. 983-6507, US$25 s, US$35 d) is a cute little place run by friendly folks who've decorated it with lots of love—something that's always a treat in Panama, where so many budget accommodations are functional at best. Rooms are painted blue and white and are decorated with nice touches, such as hand-painted murals on the walls. Its eight rooms are set in a garden with an outdoor kitchen, hammocks, and rocks scattered about with words of wisdom inscribed on them. The rooms are simple but clean and perfectly okay, with good beds and hot-water bathrooms. Some rooms are more attractive than others, so ask to see a few. Rooms are US$5 cheaper in the low season.

Cabañas Potosí (Calle La Reforma, tel. 983-6181 in El Valle, cell 6941-6148, www. vrbo.com/162797, US$43 s/d) offers four cabañas and one room in the family house, all set on two well-tended hectares just west of town. The rooms are plain and very simple, but they have high ceilings and porches with a good view of the hills. It's about one kilometer west of town on the main road. At the end of town, take the first two lefts you come to. The cabañas will be on your right.

The centrally located **Hotel Residencial El Valle** (Avenida Central, tel. 983-6536, cell 6615-9616, www.hotelresidencialelvalle.com, starts at US$49 s/d) is above David's Shop, a souvenir store near the market that's affiliated with the hotel. It offers 17 simple but fine rooms with new beds, hardwood floors, local TV, free wireless Internet, and hot-water bathroom. The rooms have fans and are cheerful, clean, and quite nice. The friendly general manager, Luis Enrique Tiban, worked on the U.S. military bases for 10 years and speaks some English. He can help arrange guides and has a map for guests.

His talented family constructed the building, the beds, even the room mirrors with butterflies and birds painted around their borders.

The place has a spacious terrace with a view of the mountains, including Cerro Gaital and Cerro Cara Iguana, and a good profile of La India Dormida. Laundry service here is US$4 wash/dry. Use of the kitchen is included with your stay. This place is a good value. Next door is the quite similar **Hotel Don Pepe** (tel. 983-6425, tel./fax 983-6835), but the atmosphere is not as warm and laid-back.

US$50-100

The **Hotel Campestre** (tel. 983-6146, US$44 s, US$66 d) underwent a major "renovation" over the last two years that seemed to mostly demolish the most atmospheric parts of the decaying old place, including its massive fireplace, leaving it a rather tattered motel with basic, overpriced rooms that have thin mattresses and are not particularly clean or well-maintained. The makeover is allegedly continuing, so it might be better by the time you visit. It's got one of the best locations in El Valle, on a large expanse of land on a tree-covered hillside, so it'd be a shame if something better doesn't emerge here eventually. There's an open-air restaurant on the grounds.

Hotel y Restaurante Los Capitanes (Calle El Ciclo, tel. 983-6080, www.los-capitanes.com, starts at US$44 s, US$66 d, including breakfast) is set on lovingly-tended grounds in the heart of the valley. There's not much else around it, so you get sweeping views of the mountains ringing the valley. The cheapest rooms are in a long, one-story building next to the main hotel. They're pretty simple and a bit dark. The best rooms are the family suites upstairs in the tower (US$121 for up to three adults). They have lofts and balconies. There's a common lounge area equipped with cable TV. Lately there have been some complaints about maintenance at the hotel.

To get to Los Capitanes, head down the main road into town 0.8 kilometers past the *supermercado*. Turn right at the big anchor. (There should also be a sign.) You'll soon see the hotel on your left. The hotel can arrange pickup and drop-off in Panama City. Prices can go down significantly during the week.

The **Hotel Rincón Vallero** (off Calle Los Millonarios, El Valle tel. 983-6175, Panama City tel. 271-5935, www.hotelrinconvallero.com, starts at US$83 s/d, including breakfast) is surrounded by flowering trees and has an artificial waterfall and fish-filled stream that runs through an enclosed patio that contains the dining room and lobby. All rooms have color TVs, air-conditioning, and hot water. Most of the rooms are in cabins set around a garden with an artificial duck and fish pond. There are 14 rooms. The standard rooms are on the small side and rather dark. The "junior suites" (US$105) are large rooms and there are also full suites (US$138). All these prices are for double occupancy. A third person in any of the rooms costs US$11 more. The hotel is too close to the hills to offer a view.

Directions to the hotel are well marked. As you enter El Valle, make a left turn off the main road 0.2 kilometers past the *supermercado*. Follow the road 0.6 kilometers, then make a left. Follow that road another 0.2 kilometers. The hotel is on the left.

The ◖ **Anton Valley Hotel** (Avenida Central across from the church, tel. 983-6097, cell 6383-5978, http://antonvalleyhotel.com, starts at US$71.50 s/d) is a nine-room inn that, since it opened in 2007, has been getting rave reviews for comfort, cleanliness, service, and location. (It's on the main road, within easy walking distance of the market and most of the available services.) The rooms are the most attractive in "downtown" El Valle. They're simple but cheerful, with queen or two twin beds with orthopedic mattresses, minifridges, ceiling fans, and cable TV. Inviting common areas include a nook with a rock-walled orchid garden where breakfast is served from around 7–9 A.M., with most options around US$5. The popular Bruschetta's restaurant is right next door. The staff can help with everything from arranging tours to renting mobile phones. Significant Internet and seasonal discounts are often available.

US$100-150

The popular **Golden Frog Inn** (tel. 983-

6117, cell 6565-8307, www.goldenfroginn.com, US$86.90–143 s/d) is a pretty bed-and-breakfast set on a hectare of well-tended gardens filled with flowering plants. It's owned by a couple who moved down from Washington State with their two friendly dogs. The B&B, also known as Hostal Rana Dorada, offers six rooms of different size and quality. The two smallest (US$86.90) have a shared bathroom. The largest, Room 3 (US$121 s/d), is also the best value. It has a sitting room and a private veranda with views of the surrounding mountains. Rooms are clean if a bit musty thanks to the damp mountain air, and they're decorated in simple, good taste. There's a clean, well-maintained, and sizable swimming pool. Breakfast is served on the patio of the owners' house, which also has a lending library for guests. The B&B is near Crater Valley Adventure Spa. Upon entering El Valle, turn right at the Texaco station and follow the signs.

(**Park Eden** (Vía Espavé, tel. 983-6167, cell 6695-6190, www.parkeden.com, starts at US$70 s/d, including full breakfast and afternoon tea) is a charming bed-and-breakfast in a lovely garden setting. For 18 years it was the country home of Lionel Alemán Toledano and his wife Moníca, who turned it into a bed-and-breakfast in 2000. Both speak fluent English and Spanish. Staying with them is like visiting your favorite country aunt and uncle: They couldn't be more friendly and attentive.

There are six places to stay, all quite different. Breakfast and afternoon tea are served in a cozy glassed-in porch in the main house, where the couple lives. It has a view of the garden. La Vie en Rose (US$110) is in the front of the main house and has a private terrace and a full and twin bed. As befits its name, it's rose-colored and frilly. La Casita (US$110) is the designated honeymooners' room. The Linda Vista (US$248) is a two-story house with two bedrooms upstairs and a downstairs living room and sunny kitchen. It features big windows that let in a lot of light, a sofa bed, outdoor fountain, and a large terrace with a barbecue grill. Guests usually book the entire house,

but the individual bedrooms are also available by themselves. There are lovely views of the garden and Cerro Gaital and other mountains from the upstairs rooms. Los Limoneros (US$121) has a queen bed, sleeper couch, and small private terrace. Mi Cuartito (US$77) is a room behind the house and has two bunk beds. It's quite small but has its own bathroom.

Most rooms have some combination of TV/VCR, coffeemaker, small fridge, and microwave. All are decorated with quaint and sometimes quirky knickknacks and homey touches.

Crater Valley Adventure Spa (Calle Capirita at the corner of Calle Ranita de Oro, tel. 215-2328, www.crater-valley.com, starts at US$127 s/d, including breakfast) is a spa resort built into an elegant old Spanish-style villa that belonged to a grandmother of one of the current owners. To get there, upon entering El Valle make the first right past the *supermercado* and follow the signs. Pass the two asphalt roads on the right. The spa will be on the left.

Amenities include an attractive swimming pool with tanning deck, a sauna, a large and amazingly turbulent hot tub, spa services, yoga classes, small library, and a souvenir shop. Its large, attractive grounds have a view of Cerro Gaital and are filled with trees, flowering plants, and three fish ponds. There's a bar and dining area.

The spa has eight modern rooms with good beds, hot-water bathrooms, and cable TV. Each of the rooms is completely different. Some are surprisingly plain and others are large and tastefully appointed. Prices range US$127–155 s/d on weekends and holidays. Rates drop by about a third Monday–Thursday.

Over US$150

My new favorite place to stay in El Valle is **(** **Canopy Lodge** (U.S. toll-free tel. 800/930-3397, El Valle tel. 264-5720, www.canopylodge.com and www.canopytower.com, US$217 pp including meals and birding tour), the younger sister to the famed Canopy Tower near Gamboa. Bird-watchers are drawn by the chance of spotting foothill species, such as the rufous-crested coquette, dull-mantled antbird, rufous-vented ground cuckoo, and black-crowned antpitta.

If that list doesn't get your heart racing, you're probably not a birder. But this is still an appealing place to stay by any standard. Opened in 2005, it's set in a lush garden on the Río Guayaco, a rushing river fed by Chorro El Macho. Guests walk through a bower and over a bridge to get to the lodge. The rooms are large, airy, and spotless, with balconies overlooking the river, forest, and Cerro Pajita. Rooms have either one king- or two queen-size comfortable, orthopedic beds. The rooms and bathrooms are modern and deliberately minimalist. There's an observatory on the 3rd floor of the lodge and an outdoor bar/dining area where guests are served simple but tasty meals. The lodge is in a 75-acre private nature reserve owned by the family of the owner, who also owns the Canopy Adventure, 400 meters uphill. Follow the road to El Chorro; the gate and parking lot are on the left.

Prices are set to match those of the "canopy rooms" at the Canopy Tower: US$217 in high season (Dec. 16–April 15), US$146 in the "green season" (April 16–Sept. 15) and US$169 during the migration season (Sept. 16–Dec. 15). Prices include lodging, a daily birding tour, and all meals. Current prices and packages that combine stays at both the Canopy Tower and Canopy Lodge are listed on the Canopy Tower website (www.canopytower.com).

Los Mandarinos Boutique Spa and Hotel (tel. 983-6645, U.S. toll-free 888/281-8413, www.losmandarinos.com, starts at US$176 s/d) is just uphill from La Casa de Lourdes and is owned by members of the same family. It continues the restaurant's semi-Italian aesthetic: It consists of 12 double rooms and four suites set in two-story buildings with stone walls and red-tile roofs. More rooms are on the way. The "executive rooms" (US$176 s/d) are the most economical, with air-conditioning you're unlikely to need, decent beds, cable TV, and large bathrooms with showers. Some of the rooms have stone-walled showers, which are a hit with guests. The suites (US$275 s/d)

are large, with a kitchenette, a sitting/dining room, and a small balcony with a view of the mountains. There's a two-night minimum on the weekends. During national holidays, rates are higher and there's a three-night minimum. The hotel has a full-service spa.

FOOD

El Valle still doesn't have many food options, but the choices are far better than they were just a few years ago. There's a decent option in just about every price range. There's now even a genuinely gourmet restaurant. In addition, there are a bunch of fast-food places around the market, some scarier-looking than others. The few grocery stores are not overflowing with appealing options.

Bruschetta's (Avenida Central at the Anton

ANOTHER ROADSIDE ATTRACTION

Restaurante Los Camisones (tel. 993-3622, 11 A.M. "until the last client leaves" daily, US$8), also known as El Rincón de los Camisones, is a pleasant and popular open-air place that gets absolutely packed on a dry-season Sunday. It's near kilometer marker 104, which is about 7 kilometers west of the turnoff to El Valle and about 10 kilometers east of Santa Clara. The place isn't visible from the road, but the turnoff is marked. As you head west, it's a steep right (north) turn up a narrow road – slow down as you approach the turn, and watch out for cars coming down from the restaurant. It's set back from the road and has no view, but it catches a welcome breeze. It serves a range of typical Panamanian dishes. The food's not bad, but the restaurant's popularity stems more from being part of many families' weekend-getaway ritual than for the quality of its fare. The brave – at least, those carrying pepper spray – can try the *"creeps de la casa"* for dessert.

Valley Hotel, tel. 983-6097, cell 6383-5978, 11:30 A.M.–8 P.M. daily, under US$10) developed a devoted following in the last few years. It serves pasta, seafood, and various meats in a pleasant garden setting.

Restaurante Santa Librada (Avenida Central, tel. 983-6376 or 645-5310, 7 A.M.–9 P.M. daily, under US$8) is a favorite place for simple Panamanian fare at good prices. It's a popular locals' hangout. The decor is nothing fancy, but it's a pleasant open-air place. A full breakfast costs less than US$3. Seafood and grilled meats top out at less than US$8. The big bowl of *sancocho de gallina* (chicken stew, US$2) has a nice flavor but is a little light on the chicken and veggies. The papaya *batido* (shake), however, is killer. The restaurant is on the right as you head into town, down Avenida Central about 1.5 kilometers from the first *supermercado*. The restaurant also rents out a few basic rooms.

Restaurante Mar de Plata (Avenida Central, tel. 641-9472, res_mardeplata@hotmail.com, 7 A.M.–7 P.M. Mon.–Thurs., 7 A.M.–late Fri.–Sat., under US$10), beneath the Hotel Residencial El Valle and next to David's Shop, is a simple eatery that offers some Peruvian food, *comida criolla* (national dishes), seafood, and fruit juices and shakes. The chef told me she once worked in the Hotel El Panamá in Panama City. There's a very similar place with a similar menu next door, below Hotel Don Pepe (7 A.M.–10 P.M. daily).

Pinocchio's (Calle El Hato, Avenida Central, tel. 983-6715, noon–9 P.M. Mon.–Sat., noon–8 P.M. Sun.) serves quite tasty if somewhat greasy thin-crust pizzas. Individual pizzas cost around US$6 and are actually big enough to feed two reasonably hungry people. The English-speaking owner is friendly and takes a justifiable pride in his cooking. Other items on the menu include chicken, pork chops, burgers, tacos, shakes, and fruit juices. It moved recently from its old home on Avenida Central and is now in a more attractive building about 500 meters down from the horse rentals.

El Valle Gourmet and Coffee Shop is across Avenida Central from the Internet café on the way into town, but it's only open on the weekends.

Stop by **Rincón Vallero** (off Calle Los Millonarios, tel. 983-6175, 7 A.M.–9 P.M. Mon.–Thurs., 7 A.M.–11 P.M. Fri.–Sun., under US$15) for a meal even if you're not staying there. It's pleasant to eat on its enclosed patio, which has an artificial waterfall and a fish stream running through it. It's a cute place, and the decor is attractive. Fortunately, the food is good, too. You can make a meal just on the appetizers. Try the *plato típico,* which consists of favorite Panamanian finger food: *patacones, carimañolas,* chorizos, and *bollas*—all basically fried death, but tasty and worth experiencing at least once if you haven't been served the stuff a zillion times already. Also go for the fried ceviche, which is a rarity in Panama and quite delicious. Main dishes run the range of meat, chicken, fish, and seafood.

La Casa de Lourdes (off Calle El Ciclo, tel. 983-6450, noon–11 P.M. daily, depending on reservations) is El Valle's first gourmet restaurant. It's the latest project of Lourdes de Ward, the celebrated owner-chef of one of Panama City's favorite upscale restaurants, the now-closed Golosinas. The menu is small and changes seasonally. It features French- and Asian-influenced Panamanian nouvelle cuisine such as blackened fish in tamarind sauce and yuca croquettes. Food here can be quite good and service warm and attentive; though others have complained about downright awful meals.

However, it's still one of the loveliest-looking places to eat in the country—it somewhat resembles a salmon-colored Italian villa, with a colonnade that leads to a terrace with a fireplace, reflecting pool, and hillside garden.

La Casa de Lourdes sits by itself in a relatively undeveloped area north of the town center. Head north on Calle El Ciclo, pass Hotel y Restaurante Los Capitanes, and make a left at the next major intersection. Make another left and wind your way down to the restaurant. Note that the last few hundred meters are on a rough gravel and dirt road. This is a small place, so it's a good idea to make reservations; if no one is around, they sometimes close early.

Panadería y Dulcería Cano (Avenida Central, no phone, 7:30 A.M.–8 P.M. daily, more or less) is a bakery and pastry shop across the street from the church.

INFORMATION AND SERVICES

There's an **ATP kiosk** at the west end of the public market, though it quite likely won't be staffed. If it is, don't expect the staff to speak any English or have much information.

Farmacia Cano (tel. 983-6940) next to the museum has no fixed hours. If you need something and it's closed, just call the number. Someone should come by to open up and serve you.

There are no banks in El Valle, but there is a **Banco Nacional de Panamá** ATM near Restaurante Santa Librada on Avenida Central.

The **post office** (9 A.M.–2:45 P.M. Mon.–Fri., 7 A.M.–noon Sat.) is behind the public market, off Calle del Mercado.

A new **public library** (no phone, 8:30 A.M.–4:30 P.M. Mon.–Fri., 8:30 A.M.–1:30 P.M. Sat.) with Internet computers has gone up right next to the church and across the street from the Anton Valley Hotel. It charges US$1 per hour. There's another **Internet place** (tel. 983-6688, 8 A.M.–noon and 1:30–6 P.M. Mon.–Fri., 8 A.M.–5 P.M. Sat., 11 A.M.–3 P.M. Sun.) on the north side of Avenida Central, one block west of Calle El Ciclo, the street that leads up to Hotel y Restaurante Los Capitanes.

In the same building is a *lavamático* (8 A.M.–5 P.M. Mon.–Sat., 8 A.M.–1 P.M. Sun.) that charges US$0.75 to wash and US$1 to dry a load.

Supercentro Yin (7 A.M.–7 P.M. daily) is a basic grocery store across the street from Hotel Residencial El Valle. There's a similar store next to the gas station at the entrance to El Valle.

Both **Los Mandarinos Boutique Spa and Hotel** (tel. 983-6645, U.S. toll-free 888/281-8413, www.losmandarinos.com) and the

Crater Valley Adventure Spa (Calle Capirita at the corner of Calle Ranita de Oro, tel. 215-2328, www.crater-valley.com) have spa services that include massages, facials, manicures/pedicures, saunas, hot tubs, and so on, at prices comparable to similar facilities in the United States. You do not have to be staying at either place to use the spas.

GETTING THERE AND AROUND

El Valle is 120 kilometers from Panama City, a drive that takes a little under two hours. If you're driving, head west on the Interamerican Highway for 95 kilometers, which takes about an hour and a quarter. The turnoff to El Valle will be on the right. It's better marked than it used to be, but keep an eye open. If you're coming from Panama City and you get to Playa Corona, you've gone too far. Double back at the first turnoff.

Turn off the Interamericana and head north up the winding two-lane road over the hills and into the valley. The road leads straight into El Valle, about 25 kilometers from the highway. It's a lovely drive, with a craggy ring of lush, forested hills before you and a good view of the Pacific behind. This road used to have more craters than the moon but is now in great shape, though it floods in heavy rains. Watch out for tire-eating roads in the town itself.

Buses to El Valle from Panama City leave every half hour or so, 7 A.M.–7 P.M. every day except Sunday, when they run 6:45 A.M.–9 P.M. The fare is US$3.50. The ride takes about 2.5 hours.

Taxis are near the public market, or you can ask your hotel to track one down; less than US$2 should get you just about anywhere, though you'll usually find it just as easy to walk around the central part of the town.

To get to other parts of Panama (besides Panama City) by bus, you'll probably have to take a bus to San Carlos and transfer there. Buses between San Carlos and El Valle run constantly during daylight hours. The fare is US$1.

Penonomé and Vicinity

PENONOMÉ

There isn't much to see in Penonomé (pop. 15,840), the capital of the province of Coclé. Most of it is not even very pretty, but somehow it remains one of Panama's quainter towns. It has given way to modern industrial bustle without entirely giving up its quiet Spanish colonial charm, at least in the heart of town.

Penonomé is in the middle of wide expanses of flat, humid lowland, with the Interamericana curving north to meet it before dropping back down south on its way west. Visible off to the distant north are the tantalizingly lush highlands.

One interesting thing about the town is its long-standing appeal among immigrant merchants—including Turks, Chinese, and Arabs—who are so woven into the life of the town you probably won't even notice them.

Sights

In the evenings it's pleasant to wander around the town plaza, which sometimes attracts a surprisingly cool breeze and, more often, the neighborhood skater kids. The plaza has a gazebo and (miraculously) a few shade trees. It faces the **Catedral de Penonomé,** whose most distinctive features are its small, modern stained-glass windows, which look pretty when the sun is right. To the side is the **Casa de Gobierno,** the municipal government offices, which has some fine wrought-iron grillwork on the outside. This is all ringed by a few old, sloping red tile–roofed buildings, some of which feature bright green doors that somehow fit into the scene. There is also a small museum, **El Museo de Penonomé** (Calle San Antonio near Parque Ruben Dario Carles, tel. 997-8490, 9 A.M.–4 P.M. Mon.–Sat., 9 A.M.– noon Sun., US$1 adults, US$0.25 children) several blocks from the plaza in the direction of the Interamericana. Though hours are listed, it's always closed whenever I try to visit.

That's about it for the historic charms of Penonomé, which can be exhausted in about an hour.

Shopping

Penonomé has two main commercial drags: Avenida Juan Demóstenes Arosemena, which leads up to the Interamericana a kilometer or so away, and about three kilometers of the Interamericana itself that skirts the edge of town. The first is mainly a busy shopping street for cheap goods. The latter strip has the better hotels and restaurants, plus street vendors selling (real) Panama hats. Those interested should find a good selection of hats outside the Restaurante Universal, which is near Hotel and Suites Guacamaya.

Mercado de Artesanías Coclé (Interamericana, 9 A.M.–4 P.M. Mon.–Fri.) is about a half kilometer east of the Hotel Dos Continentes. It's hard to miss since the building is in the shape of a Panama hat. It has a decent, though hardly exceptional, selection of Ngöbe-Buglé bags, assorted ceramics, and small souvenirs.

Accommodations

There are several places to stay in and around town, but most are pretty grim. Here are the two best places.

Hotel y Suites Guacamaya (Interamericana, tel. 991-0117, US$33.50–36.50 s/d), on the Interamericana just east of the entrance to town, is a modern 40-room hotel built in 2001. Rooms are simple but pleasant and have air-conditioning and cable TV. When I stayed here the bed in my room was so saggy it was like sleeping in a soft ditch, but I've since been assured from a regular that I drew the short straw and most beds are better.

On the western outskirts of town is the modern **Hotel La Pradera** (Interamericana, tel. 991-0106, www.hotelpradera.com, US$34.40 s/d). Built in 2001, it has 30 clean rooms with air-conditioning, hot water, cable TV, and good beds. Half the rooms have one double bed, and the other half have two double beds. There's a restaurant and bar and a small pool set in a back yard. It's the best hotel in Penonomé.

Food

A Peace Corps volunteer in the area wrote to tell me about **El Portal Café** (tel. 997-9935, 10 A.M.–9 P.M. Mon.–Sat., under US$5), which he called Penonomé's "hidden gem." He was right on both counts. First, it sure is hidden; I chatted with someone who was born and raised in town and had never heard of the place. Second, it truly is a gem—it offers the best subway sandwiches I've had in Panama: tasty meats and salads in toasted bread that actually tastes like bread. There are a couple of tables outside in a little strip of garden with a tiny fountain; this is what passes for dining al fresco in Penonomé, but it's actually a pleasant oasis in this busy town. A 12-inch sub and soda combo goes for less than US$5. Pastas, salads, juices, shakes, and wraps are also available. To get there head down the main shopping street, Avenida Juan Demóstenes. When you reach a store called Casa Peter, look on the right side of the street for a doorway framed by wrought-iron fencing. El Portal is down this passageway. It's right next to a building called Edificio Don Bosco.

Panadería y Refresquería Romellini (Avenida Juan Demóstenes Arosemena, 7 A.M.–10 P.M. daily), just down from Hotel Dos Continentes on the way toward downtown Penonomé, offers sandwiches for a couple of bucks and delicious smells for free.

Formerly Parrillada El Giagante, **Restaurante Steak Mar** (Interamericana, tel. 997-1864, 10 A.M.–9 P.M. daily), on the north side of the Interamericana just west of Hotel Dos Continentes, is what passes for an upscale place in these parts, but don't get your hopes up. I haven't been back since it changed its name and started specializing in seafood.

There are five outlets of the local **Gallo Pinto** chain (6 A.M.–9 P.M. Mon.–Sat., 6 A.M.–2 P.M. Sun.) in the area. Each serves basic *comida corriente* (fast food) in an equally basic atmosphere. Full meals here cost a couple of dollars.

The ones likely to be most convenient are Gallo Pinto #1, on Calle Nicanor Rosas near the center of town, and Gallo Pinto #2, on Avenida Juan Demóstenes Arosemena near its intersection with the Interamericana.

Restaurante Las Tinajas (Interamericana, tel. 997-9606, 7 A.M.–10 P.M. daily, US$2–3) is a cafeteria with a quaint thatch-roofed dining area with traditional Panamanian designs on the walls.

There's a **public market** between Calle Damian Carles and Avenida Juan Demóstenes Arosemena near the town plaza. A large Super 99 grocery store is on the Interamericana just west of Penonomé.

Services

Super Farmacia Coclé (Avenida Juan Demóstenes Arosemena near its intersection with the Interamericana, tel. 997-9849, 8:30 A.M.–7:30 P.M. Mon.–Sat., 8:30 A.M.–12:30 P.M. Sun.) is a pharmacy just down from the Hotel Dos Continentes. There's a supermarket, **Supercentro Coclé,** next door.

There are several banks with ATMs down Avenida Juan Demóstenes Arosemena on the way into town. **HSBC bank** (8 A.M.–3:30 P.M. Mon.–Fri., 9 A.M.–noon Sat.) is just a bit farther down on the way into town. There are also a couple of Internet places that charge about US$0.50 per hour. **Hobby Chat Internet Café** (9 A.M.–10 P.M. daily) is upstairs from the Delta gas station.

The **post office** (Calle Damian Carles, 7 A.M.–5:45 P.M. Mon.–Fri., 7 A.M.–4:45 P.M. Sat.) is about a block south of the town plaza.

Getting There and Around

Penonomé is 143 kilometers west of Panama City, a drive that takes about two hours.

Buses leave from different places in Penonomé depending on the destination. Buses to Panama City leave from the large building with the "Utrapep Terminal de Transporte de Penonomé" sign emblazoned on the front. It's across the Interamericana from the Hotel Dos Continentes. They depart every 20–30 minutes, 4 A.M.–7 P.M. Fare is US$4.35.

CENTRAL PANAMA

Regional buses (such as to Santiago, Chitré, and Las Tablas) stop at the Restaurante Universal, near Hotel y Suites Guacamaya on the Interamericana. Buses to David have to be flagged down at bus stops on the Interamericana.

Most of the local area buses leave from a loosely defined terminal area near the public market between Calle Damian Carles and Avenida Juan Demóstenes Arosemena just south of the public market. Destinations of possible interest include La Pintada, Chiguirí Arriba, El Copé, and Aguadulce.

LA PINTADA

Because it's so close to Penonomé, those in the area should consider a half-day trip to La Pintada (pop. 3,700), in the foothills northwest of town. It's a pleasant, mellow town ringed by hills, including some big ones by Panamanian standards. The most storied of these is Cerro Orarí, a low, jagged-toothed peak that has inspired Panamanian poets and musicians but would go unnoticed by those from a truly mountainous country.

It's a pleasant, quiet town with some nearby petroglyphs, a pretty little river, and a cigar factory. The hat makers in this district are famous for a variety of Panama hat called a *sombrero pintado* (painted hat), named for the rings of black fibers woven into it.

Sights

The artisans' market, *mercado de artesanías* (7 A.M.–3 P.M. Mon.–Fri.), has a decent selection of hats of different weaves made in the surrounding area. The best ones cost US$90 and up. A pretty decent one can be had for around US$25. A few pieces of pottery and some bric-a-brac are also on sale. It may be possible to hire a guide there for a few dollars.

There are now signs pointing the way to the *piedras pintadas* (petroglyphs). They are on private land, so you may be asked to pay a small fee to visit them. Getting to them involves a short walk and a little scrambling over rocks. The closest are across a *quebrada* (brook) that only has water in the rainy season. They consist

of a few dim figures of some kind of animals, though they're too abstract to identify. The second set is farther upstream. These are clearer, seemingly depicting two reptiles. The third set, a little farther up, is just a bunch of squiggles. The one next to it has a couple of figures. The most interesting thing about all of these is trying to guess what they might have once signified to the pre-Colombian indigenous people who carved them. Are they maps? Messages? Simple artistic expression? No one knows.

The **Río Coclé del Sur** is a pretty little river that runs by the edge of town. To get there, make a right turn past the church as you head into town and look for the *balneario* sign. You can hire a little painted boat and captain to paddle you around for US$0.50 at Balneario J. Los Algarrobos, the river's popular little water hole.

Those interested in seeing how Panamanian cigars get made can visit **Cigarros Joyas de Panamá** (tel. 692-2582 or 634-4437), a small factory right before town on the way up from Penonomé. To get there, look for a sign on the outskirts of town. Make a hard left turn, which will double back onto a side road in the direction from which you just came. Stay right at the fork. The cigar factory is a couple hundred meters down on the right.

Popular **festivities** in La Pintada include the district's famous El Topón procession, a Christmas-day parade featuring effigies of Mary and the baby Jesus; Carnavalito, a mini-Carnaval celebration held the month before the actual Carnaval; and October 19, the anniversary of the town's founding.

Practicalities

There are no places to stay and just a few simple places to eat in La Pintada, but there is a lot of construction going on and plans for a gated community catering to gringos. This place will likely be utterly transformed in a few years, so visit it now while it still has its small-town charm.

Getting There

To get to La Pintada by car, take the road

Culecos, in which partiers are doused with water, are a daily ritual during Carnaval.

leading west from the plaza in downtown Penonomé and stay straight for 13 kilometers. The road ends at La Pintada. The road to the petroglyphs is two kilometers before town, on the left.

Buses from Penonomé to La Pintada leave from near the town market every 20 minutes, 6:20 A.M.–8 P.M. The fare is US$0.70, and the trip takes 15 minutes.

CERRO LA VIEJA

Posada Ecológica del Cerro la Vieja (Panama City tel. 263-4278, lodge tel. 983-8905, www.posadalavieja.com, starts at US$82.50 s, US$98, including breakfast) is a pleasant surprise. It's a combination mountain inn and off-the-beaten-path spa resort in a spot you wouldn't expect to find either. Those with limited time who are heading up to the western highlands can give it a miss, but it has several things to recommend it. (Note: This place likes to change its name; for a while it was known as Trinidad Spa and Lodge.)

For one thing, it's perched atop a 470-meter ridge with a terrific view of a huge forested valley and the green peak of the 520-meter-high Cerro La Vieja (literally, "old lady mountain"), which looks close enough to touch. The breezes here blow strong and cool, but when they stop it can be as hot and humid as the lowlands. The surrounding land is heavily settled by farmers—the drive up will give a real flavor of Panamanian country life—but the lodge is attempting to bring back native vegetation on its 250 hectares.

The lodge's owner, Alfonso Jaén C., also owns the tourist restaurant Las Tinajas in Panama City. He takes understandable pride in this place. Spa services are available at reasonable rates. A 50-minute massage, for instance, is US$50.

There are 22 rooms, all with hot water, and some are definitely nicer than others. The best are in the pair of modern two-story cabañas perched right on the edge of the ridge. Rooms on the top floor are best of all, but all have balconies and hammocks.

The lodge offers many different excursions for its guests, most of which cost US$15–25 per person.

The food is simple but tasty, and the restaurant has a spectacular view of the valley and Cerro La Vieja.

Getting There

The lodge is 28 kilometers northeast of Penonomé on the Chiguirí Arriba road. Those driving from Panama City should turn right off the Interamericana at the Hotel Dos Continentes. Look for a sign reading "Caimito" and turn right. Continue straight up into the hills. The paved road ends at the town of Caimito. Continue straight on the dirt road to the lodge. At the time I visited, the upper stretch was impassable except by four-wheel-drive vehicle, though it's supposedly in better shape these days. The drive takes about 45 minutes. Buses leave from the public market in Penonomé every 60–90 minutes during daylight hours (US$1.50). Look for the "Chiguirí Arriba" bus. You can also come by taxi from Penonomé, which will cost you US$25–30 depending on the condition of the road and the driver's mood.

◖ PARQUE NACIONAL OMAR TORRIJOS H. (EL COPÉ)

This somewhat hard-to-reach park consists of more than 25,000 hectares of forested highlands stretching down the Pacific and Caribbean sides of the Continental Divide. Its full name is Parque Nacional General de División Omar Torrijos Herrera, but most people know it simply as El Copé, and that's how it'll be referred to here.

The park was created to honor the late military dictator Omar Torrijos, who died in a mysterious plane crash in these mountains on July 31, 1981. Supposedly some charred remains of the plane are still intact on Cerro Marta, a peak you'll see to the right as you enter the park, but you'd have to be a major bushwhacking mountain climber to prove it.

Because this park is hard to get to, it's filled with thousands of acres of primary forest you'll likely have to yourself. It's a beautiful place with sweeping vistas, as long as it's not too foggy. Even when it is, the morning mist rising off the mountains is quite dramatic.

El Copé is about as far east as the birds of the western highlands venture. If you're not an experienced bird-watcher or guided by one, however, you may not spot many species. El Copé is well known as a place to see hummingbirds, especially the snowcap and green thorntail. The rare bare-necked umbrellabird—which looks as though it's wearing a thatch roof—has been spotted here in the last few years. Its call sounds like the roar of a bull.

All the feline species of Panama are still found in the park, but chances are slim you'll bump into any. Ditto for Baird's tapirs, white-lipped peccaries, and collared peccaries.

Yes, there are venomous snakes, but you're unlikely to see one. That said, in the interest of full disclosure you should know that acquaintances have come across a bushmaster, an eyelash palm pit viper, and coral snakes here, all of which are deadly. Watch where you step and sleep. And let someone else go first.

Note: This area gets rain and fog year-round and is quite a bit cooler than the lowlands, so bring warm, waterproof clothes.

Trails

Several good, wide trails start from the entrance to the park. Facing into the park, with the visitor shelter and park sign to your right, you'll see two trails. The one to the left heads straight up to the top of a mountain with views of both oceans (about a half-hour's walk). The one to the right heads down toward the Caribbean slope (endless). The latter trail is rocky and rutted, and you'll have to cross several streams. Be prepared for ankle-deep mud. An hour into it there's a far more rugged, strenuous trail that leads back to the shelter. The umbrellabird has been spotted here (as have venomous snakes). Do not take this trail without a guide: You will get lost. It takes about an hour to get back to the shelter. There is also a half-kilometer interpretive trail that starts behind the shelter. There's a rudimentary trail map posted on a signboard. The ranger may be available to guide you; as always, a small tip is appreciated.

Practicalities

The **ranger station** is on the left just as you come to the official entrance to the park at the crest of the hill. The park entrance fee is US$5, another US$5 to camp in a tent, and US$20 for up to four people in the modern cabin. There's also an **ANAM administrative station** in the small town of El Copé, below the park, that's theoretically open 8 A.M.–3 P.M. Monday–Friday.

In 2002 the glorified tool shed that served as a visitors shelter was replaced with what may be the nicest cabin in the entire Panama national parks system. It's simple but pleasant and has a bathroom with running water.

Just 128 paces behind the shelter is an attractive **visitors center** that's allegedly open 8 A.M.–5 P.M. daily. It's on a ridge with an awe-inspiring view of mountains, the valley, and the Caribbean.

Since my last visit to the park, several community-run projects have gotten off the ground in the area, with some help from volunteers. **Alberque Navas** (tel. 983-9130, around US$30/night pp, including meals) is run by the local Navas family in Barrigón. Their house is on the right as one heads up toward El Copé; this is where the road usually turns rough: Look for the small "Navas" sign on the front of their house. For years they have allowed visitors to park here and provided a shuttle service up to the park. This has become less necessary as the road has improved. They host overnight visitors in their house and offer visits to their forest cabin in a remote area called La Rica, where those who don't mind roughing it a bit can hike, bird-watch, and splash about in a waterfall. They speak only Spanish, but they are experienced in making themselves understood to monolingual gringos. Detailed information on this and other community projects in the area can be found here: http://bit.ly/elcope.

A new project is **La MICA Biological Station** (cell 6707-8900, la.mica@yahoo.com, www.lamica.org), directed by Julie Ray, a gringa biologist who did her PhD research up here and then stuck around to make the natural attractions of the area more accessible to visitors and other researchers, and to give the local community new sources of income.

It is located in Santa Marta, a remote village of subsistence farmers with a population of about 700 and no electricity. It's accessible by four-wheel-drive or a two-hour hike from El Copé. The project has a cabin and a dormitory that sleeps up to 25 people for US$12/person. Campers can pitch a tent for US$5.

I have not yet had a chance to visit the project, but it's at the top of the list for my next trip. It opens the door to a beautiful part of Panama still little known even to most Panamanians. They offer logistical support at quite reasonable prices, putting isolated communities and wild nature within reach of even the most ill-equipped visitor. The project can supply transportation from and to Panama City (US$90 each way), Santa Clara (US$75 round-trip), Penonomé (US$35 round-trip), and Aguadulce (US$40 round-trip). Rates are for up to four people, except for Panama City, which is an additional US$10/person after the first passenger. La Mica can also supply meals (US$13/day), porters (US$10/day), equipment rental, and guided tours of the park and other attractions, such as Chorro Las Yayas, a waterfall in Barrigón that is also maintained as a community project. The Las Yayas project, by the way, offers a thatched-roof cabin for visitors for those interested in spending the night (US$10–15 per person).

Getting There

The turnoff to El Copé is 20 kilometers west of Penonomé. The turnoff wasn't marked on my last visit. If you're coming from the direction of Penonomé, turn right just before the pedestrian bridge that spans the Interamericana. From here it's a 33-kilometer drive into the mountains. The last seven kilometers are on a dirt road that used to be horrendous. It's now much improved, but it's still a rough, bumpy drive that requires a four-wheel drive. The trip can take more than an hour from Penonomé even with a powerful vehicle, depending on road conditions.

Direct buses from Panama City to El Copé run once or twice an hour 6 A.M.–7 P.M. The trip takes about three hours and costs US$5.50. If you're coming from Penonomé, you can take an El Copé bus (US$1.50) from there as well. In either case, switch at the little town of El Copé to the Barrigón bus (US$0.40). From Barrigón hike uphill into the park, a rocky four kilometers that takes about an hour. You can also ask someone in Barrigón for a ride; this is a common practice, and the fee should be less than US$10 if the road isn't too bad.

Aguadulce and Vicinity

AGUADULCE
The industrial town of Aguadulce (pop. 7,700), 53 kilometers east of Santiago in Coclé province, lies on a vast, dusty, sun-blasted plain that may remind Californians of the wasteland around Bakersfield. It has just about as much charm and can easily be skipped. None of the few sights, restaurants, or hotels here are anything special. The area is known for producing salt, shrimp, and sugar, and there's a big dairy on the edge of town.

Sights
Museo de la Sal y el Azúcar (Avenida Sebastián Sucre, tel. 997-4280, 8:30 A.M.–noon and 1–4 P.M. Tues.–Fri., 8:30 A.M.–12:30 P.M. Sat., US$1 adults, US$0.25 children) is a tiny museum housed in a turn-of-the-20th-century building that was once the town post office. It's on the plaza, facing the cathedral. An earnest, Spanish-speaking guide will explain the simple displays and tell you more than you're likely to want to know about how salt and sugar are produced in the area. One interesting note is that salt has been harvested in the province since pre-Colombian times using much the same method: Seawater is diverted into artificially-made channels near the shore and allowed to evaporate. The current elaborate, mazelike channel system has been used for more than 100 years. The best thing about this museum is how hard the staff tries to make do with such very limited resources.

Las Piscinas is one of those surreal, only-in-Panama projects. Because the "beach" around here is really gooey mudflats, the community has seen fit to build four tile swimming pools, the largest of which is about 15 meters long, smack in the middle of a rocky part of those flats. At low tide the pools drain out. At high tide during the dry season, local folks splash around in them. Others come here to check out the plentiful shorebirds.

To get to the pools, take the unmarked road to the left of the church in Aguadulce. The road runs past some shrimp farms. Park two kilometers farther on at Kiosco Piscinas del Mar. Mangroves will be on the left. Walk about 200 meters until the path turns rocky. The pools are up ahead on the right. A taxi here costs about US$5 each way.

Accommodations and Food
There isn't enough in Aguadulce to warrant spending the night, but if you do, the best place in town is the **Hotel Carisabel** (Calle Eduardo Pedreshi, tel. 997-3800, US$32.50 s/d). It's a 21-room motel with air-conditioning, TV, and a bathtub-sized swimming pool. It's a modern but spartan place and the walls are a bit smudged. Some of the beds are good, some aren't—shop around. The restaurant right next door looked promising but was closed when I visited.

Pannito's Café (Avenida Abelardo Herrera, tel. 997-5555, 6:30 A.M.–10:30 P.M. Mon.–Sat., 7:30 A.M.–10:30 P.M. Sun.) is a popular and friendly cafeteria next to the church (take the street on the right as you face the church). Offerings include traditional Panamanian breakfasts, whole grilled chickens, sandwiches, pizzas, and baked goods, and nearly everything costs less than US$5. It may close for a few hours in the late afternoon.

Information and Services

There are no tourist offices in Aguadulce. The best bet for general information is to ask a staffer at the Museo de la Sal y el Azúcar.

Aguadulce has several banks with ATMs, all on Avenida Rodolfo Chiari, the main road that leads to the cathedral. The closest to the church is HSBC. INAC, Panama's ministry of culture, has opened a surprisingly big cultural center, **Centro Cultural Anel Omar Rodríguez Barrera** (tel. 997-4389) that sometimes hosts concerts, art shows, and other high-toned happenings. It's right across the street from Hotel Carisabel.

Getting There and Away

It's a couple of kilometers from the Interamericana to the center of town, an awfully long walk in the hot sun. If you get dropped off by the highway, consider a cab into town. It costs less than a dollar.

Regional buses leave from the town plaza. Buses to Panama City, David, and other distant spots don't come into the city; go to the Interamericana to catch one of these.

Buses to El Copé leave from the side of the museum every 45 minutes, 6 A.M.–6 P.M. The fare is US$1.50.

Minibuses to Santiago leave every 15 minutes, 5:45 A.M.–7 P.M. from the town plaza. Large, David-bound buses stop at Santiago, but these must be caught on the Interamericana.

A taxi to Natá should cost about US$4. A trip all the way to Penonomé is around US$20.

AROUND AGUADULCE
◖ Natá de los Caballeros

The Spanish founded Natá on May 20, 1522, which makes it the oldest surviving town in Panama and one of the oldest in the Americas. Its origins are older than that, however—it was the center of an important indigenous chiefdom. Its last leader was named Natá; the Spanish took his name for their new town, then used the town as a base from which to conquer the native peoples of western Panama. Legend has it that it got its full name, Natá

de los Caballeros, when the king of Spain sent 100 *caballeros* (knights) to help in these wars. The town remained an important regional center of Spanish power throughout the colonial period.

Natá's past is far more interesting than its present, however. Today it's a sleepy village of onion and tomato farmers. Pretty much the only attraction left is its famous, ancient church, the **Basílica Menor Santiago Apostól de Natá.** Though built over several decades after the founding of the town, it lays claim to being the oldest church along the entire Pacific littoral of the Americas. While of interest to historians, it's actually a rather simple if attractive stucco church with a plain wooden ceiling and red-tile roof. Its most notable features are its elaborate carved wooden altars. It was renovated in 1998. Every July 25, a statue of Santiago Apostól, the patron saint of Natá, is paraded through the streets of the town for the faithful. The nearby chapel, **Capilla de San Juan de Dios,** is supposed to be renovated eventually.

The church is in the heart of town, less than a kilometer from the Interamericana. If it's closed, ask for help at the *alcaldía* (mayor's office), next to the church.

El Caño

This little town nine kilometers northeast of Natá has an important archaeological dig (9 A.M.–noon and 12:30–4 P.M. Tues.–Sat., 9 A.M.–1 P.M. Sun., US$1 adults, US$0.25 children) that's open to visitors, but there isn't much to see today. Its centerpiece was a ring of carved stone columns, about six meters high, in the shape of human and animal figures. In the 1920s a North American adventurer, A. Hyatt Verrill, removed nearly all of them, 150 in total, and shipped them to museums in the United States along with gold and ceramics found at the site. Only the stone pedestals from which the figures were cut remain in the field today. Nearby is an excavated cemetery where five exposed skeletons can still be seen at the bottom of a four-meter-deep pit. The site dates approximately A.D. 800–1100.

© WILLIAM FRIAR

A 1920s American adventurer cut archaeologically important stone figures off their pedestals at El Caño.

There's a small museum on the site in the quaint house with the red-tile roof. It's worth a quick visit. While most of the few pieces not taken out of the country aren't displayed here, for security reasons, there are a few small stone statues and ceramics, photos of statues that were removed, a crude model of the site, and some pieces that date from the Spanish era.

The complex is three kilometers from the Interamericana and is accessible by a dirt road that runs by the left side of El Caño's church, Iglesia San Lorenzo, as one faces it. Keep left at the fork. The site is kind of isolated. Those without their own transport are probably best off hiring a taxi in Natá.

Note that in the rainy season the site is a swamp swarming with ferocious mosquitoes. If possible, wear rubber boots and douse yourself with gallons of insect repellent.

Getting There

Both Natá and El Caño are just off the Interamericana on the way to Penonomé and can be visited as a side trip from either of those large towns in a couple of hours. Rather than fool with buses, those without their own transportation should consider hiring a cab in Aguadulce (or Penonomé—it's just 21 kilometers east of Natá). However, any bus running between Aguadulce and Natá can drop visitors off along the Interamericana at the edge of these towns.

Santiago

Though it's one of Panama's main cities and the provincial capital of Veraguas, most people treat Santiago (pop. 32,480) as a place to break their journey to somewhere else. Usually that somewhere else is David or Panama City, since Santiago falls just about midway between the two. It's about a 3.5–4-hour drive to either city.

Santiago is a homely commercial and transportation hub on the Interamerican Highway with little to offer tourists. But it does have the facilities and bus connections one would expect of a growing Panamanian town with such a strategic location. And it has a real town life, some decent places to stay and eat, and even some entertainment possibilities. It's a good place to stop for the night on cross-country trips.

The Interamericana forks at the eastern outskirts of town. Taking the left fork off the Interamericana leads into town via Avenida Central, also known as Avenida Hector A. Santacoloma, though few call it that. The road leads through a busy commercial stretch before splintering by the town church, the Catedral Santiago Apóstol. Roads from here lead down to the surfing beaches of Playa Santa Catalina and to Puerto Mutis, a launching point for trips to Parque Nacional Coiba.

Most of the hotels, restaurants, shops, and services of interest to visitors are not in Santiago proper but rather on the Interamericana. Instead of turning in to Santiago at the fork, stay right; facilities are on either side of the Interamericana.

A little farther west, the Interamericana is intersected by Calle 10A Norte, also called Calle Polidoro Pinzón. This cuts southwest into Santiago (a left turn, if coming from the direction of Panama City) and is where the main bus terminal and a few other facilities for visitors can be found.

Celebrations in Santiago include the religious festivals of Jesús de la Misericordia on April 8 and the Virgen del Carmen on July 16; the Patronales de Santiago Apóstol

© WILLIAM FRIAR

Santiago's teachers' college, La Escuela Normal Superior Juan Demóstenes Arosemena, is noted for its ornate architecture and murals painted by Roberto Lewis.

(patron saint's day) on July 25; and the Grito de Separación de Panamá de Colombia (the town's call for independence from Colombia) on November 9.

SIGHTS

A self-guided walking tour of Santiago's few sights shouldn't last longer than a couple of hours, including people-watching.

The **Catedral Santiago Apóstol,** on the west end of Avenida Central, contains the remains of General José de Fábrega, a key figure in Panama's decision to declare independence from Spain and become a part of Gran Colombia in 1821. As always, it's interesting to see how lively churches in Panama can get on a given day, but it's unadorned by Catholic standards and isn't worth a special trip.

La Escuela Normal Superior Juan

Demóstenes Arosemena (Avenida 5A Norte between Calle 6B Norte/Calle Domingo García and Calle 8A Norte/Calle Eduardo Santo, tel. 998-4295) is an imposing teachers' college and pretty much the proud symbol of Santiago. It's worth a quick look if you're in the neighborhood, which is several blocks northeast of the cathedral.

It's a bulky structure with a red-tile roof, but what will grab your attention is the flamboyantly ornate entrance, which features nudes frolicking up the columns and across the arch. Visitors are welcome to peek inside, where there are more ornate columns and, across the hall, a theater with murals painted by Roberto Lewis, the famous Panamanian artist who also painted the ceiling of the Teatro Nacional in Panama City. They're not in great condition and, frankly, aren't terribly impressive, but you've got to admire the ambition: The murals depict key moments from pretty much the whole span of human history, from the discovery of fire to the Code of Hammurabi to the crucifixion of Christ to Copernicus. He tossed in the Spanish enslavement of Native American peoples for good measure.

SPORTS AND RECREATION

Santiago's de facto port, **Puerto Mutis** (MOOtees) is a jumping-off point for boats to Coiba and other fishing and diving spots.

Some sportfishing and diving operations still operate out of here, though Santa Catalina is supplanting it as the port of choice. It's also possible to work out cheap trips to Coiba with local fishermen, but it's a risky proposition and I do not recommend it. These are small, open boats on seas that can quickly turn rough. The boats are unlikely to have a backup motor, life jackets, or a radio, let alone sportfishing gear. One of these boats goes adrift on the ocean every other month.

Puerto Mutis is 24 kilometers southwest of Santiago on a good road and is easily accessible from Santiago by bus or taxi. The "town" is just a few houses, hole-in-the-wall restaurants, gas stations, and shops lining the road, which ends at a pier on an estuary.

Right at the end of the road is **Montijo's Bay Restaurante, Bar, y Gasolinera** (tel. 999-8174), where you can dine right across from a huge gasoline tank. It's a surprisingly pleasant, modern, open-air place on stilts that looks out on a pretty view of the estuary.

The road to Puerto Mutis is not well marked. To get there by car, follow Avenida Central (Avenida Hector A. Santacoloma) toward the cathedral and take the left fork once you reach it. Turn left behind the church onto Calle 2 Norte. The Hotel Santiago will be on the left. Take the second right (it's Avenida 5B Sur, but it's not marked) and then stay straight all the way to Puerto Mutis.

ACCOMMODATIONS

Santiago has quite a range of accommodations, most of which are on the Interamericana just outside of town. The places listed here are the best options, but there are several others.

US$10-25

Santiago now has its very own hostel, **Hostal Veraguas** (tel. 958-9021, cell 6669-6126, http://svbackpackers.tripod.com, dorm bed for US$8–9, private rooms start at US$14, with breakfast). The hostel is in a small private house in a nondescript suburb, Barriada San Martín, north of the Interamericana. Rooms are bare but clean, and stays include free Internet use and continental breakfast. Common areas include the home's living room and a little *rancho* in a garden that also has a small aboveground swimming pool. There's a book exchange, laundry facilities, free Wi-Fi, and a kitchen for guests. Your host is Lidia Jaramillo, a Santiago native who speaks decent English and some French. Opened in 2006, the hostel is still taking shape and new features are added from time to time. Spanish lessons cost US$6 per hour or US$60 for a week of 10 classes. Campers can pitch a tent for US$5. Everything is flexible here, so price breaks and even free stays may be possible for longer stays or help around the hostel.

The hostel is a bit hard to find. Starting at the Centro Los Tucanes on the Interamericana, turn north at the overpass onto the road that leads to San Francisco and Santa Fé. (If you're starting from the main Santiago bus terminal, you're already on this road; just head north.) Turn right at the gas station two blocks down. Make an immediate left. The Universidad de Panamá branch should be on the left and Instituto Urracá on the right. Go three blocks and turn right. The hostel is on the right five blocks down. You may have to call or ask for "la casa de Lidia Jaramillo." For those on foot, it's about 2 kilometers from Centro Los Tucanes and 2.5 kilometers from Centro Pyramidal. Note that this hostel is sometimes referred to as Hostel Santiago or Hostel Backpackers.

Hotel Gran David (Interamericana, tel. 998-4510, 998-2622, or 998-2622, tel./fax 998-1866, US$20 s, US$25 d), easily confused with the nearby Hotel Plaza Gran David, is on the north side of the Interamericana, just past the turnoff to Santiago as you head toward David. It offers simple but pleasant rooms with firm beds set in a maze of hallways. The rooms are a little older and more worn than those at the Hotel Galeria, but they're fine and, amazingly, are designed to let light in rather than keep it out. All the rooms have air-conditioning and TV. There's a small pool on the premises. This is a popular place and often fills up; reservations are a good idea.

US$50-100

Hotel Galeria (Interamericana, tel. 958-7950 or 958-7951, http://hotelgaleria.net, US$49.50 s, US$55 d) is on the north side of the Interamericana, just east of the Hotel Gran David. It's next to a small mall and offers 40 rooms, a bar, and a restaurant. It's not a fancy place, but it's long been popular with business travelers and tourists who can afford it because it offers clean and modern rooms with comfortable beds, hot showers, air-conditioning, and cable TV. There's even a weight room. The restaurant is open for breakfast, lunch, and dinner.

The [**Hotel La Hacienda** (Interamericana, tel. 958-8580 or 958-5477, fax 958-8579, US$70 s, US$85d) is the best hotel in the whole region. On the Interamericana less than three kilometers west of town, it offers 42 bright and cheerful rooms carefully decorated with furnishings that seem imported directly from Puebla, Mexico. There's a small gym, a small but attractive swimming pool, laundry facilities, a restaurant and bar, and an Internet café. Rooms come with double, queen, or king beds, and suites are moderately priced. All rooms have air-conditioning, free Wi-Fi, and cable TV. There's no hot water in the bathroom sink but there is in the shower. There's (awful) live music in the bar on Tuesday nights. Day passes and special deals are often available.

About eight kilometers west of Hotel La Hacienda is the **Hotel Vista Lago Ecoresort** (tel. 954-9916, Panama City office tel. 393-9405, www.hotelvistalago.net, starts at US$60 s/d), which opened in mid-2009. "Eco-resort" here apparently just means "hotel plopped down in a barren, overgrazed field next to a small artificial lake." It's a pretty odd place. It has 24 unadorned rooms with cable TV, free Wi-Fi, and a view of the water. It's in the middle of absolutely nothing, so the only reason to stay here is to get a bed as far as possible from town. However, the common areas are open and cheerful, and there's an attractive L-shaped pool. Day passes (US$5 adults, US$3 children) to use the pool and other facilities are available from 9 A.M.–6 P.M. The hotel is less than 10 minutes by cab from Santiago, so a day trip might be worth it on a hot day with nothing else to do. It's also an okay place to take a break during a long road trip. There's a restaurant.

FOOD

The restaurant at the **Hotel Gran David** (Interamericana, tel. 998-4510 or 998-2622) is basic and dingy, and the waiters are harried and overworked, but it's a good place to go with a big appetite and small budget. It's best for breakfast. A plate of delicious, nongreasy tortillas and white cheese with a cup of coffee costs a couple of bucks. It's open for breakfast, lunch, and dinner.

Restaurante Tropicalismo (Avenida Hector A. Santacoloma and Avenida 14A Sur near the ATP office, tel. 998-3661, 9 A.M.–11 P.M. daily) is a simple but clean indoor/outdoor place that's a decent option for a budget meal. It specializes in Cuban food and also offers an assortment of pastas, sandwiches, seafood, meats, fresh juices, and so on. Breakfast is a couple of bucks, as is the daily lunch special of meat, chicken, or fish with side dishes. The Cuban sandwich tastes *auténtico*.

(La Cocina del Abuelo (tel. 958-9334, noon–midnight daily, US$8–10) recently relocated to the Hotel Plaza Gran David, which is on the north side of the Interamericana, 1.5 kilometers east of Santiago. It's a bit hard to spot from the road. (Don't confuse this with the Hotel Gran David, which is farther west.) The food is mainly Panamanian and Spanish, but the menus also include pizzas, sandwiches, salads, and such. The *sancocho* (traditional meat-and-yam soup) is flavorful, as are the grilled meats. A handful of old guys sometimes shows up to sing and play guitar. They're quite talented—they harmonize beautifully—and content to sit in a corner and enjoy themselves, rather than pester clients for tips. The restaurant also offers free wireless Internet. Service is friendly. The name of the place, by the way, translates to "granddad's kitchen." There's a bar next door.

The restaurant at **Hotel Galería** (Interamericana, tel. 958-7950 or 958-7951, under US$10) has an ambitious menu of meats, seafood, and pasta, but this is a place to keep things simple. The food is okay, but nothing special by any means. It's open for breakfast, lunch, and dinner.

Restaurante Puerto Perú (across the Interamericana from the Centro Pyramidal, tel. 998-6455, noon–3 P.M. and 6–11 P.M. Mon.–Sat., 1–9 P.M. Sun., under US$15), formerly Restaurante Delicias del Mar, specializes in Peruvian seafood, of all things, and offers a range of other ambitious fish and meat dishes. I haven't been here since the recent name change, but this used to be a surprisingly good place

Restaurante Los Tucanes (Interamericana, tel. 998-6490, 11:30 A.M.–10:30 P.M. daily, US$7), is in a gas-station plaza on the Interamericana just west of the Hotel Gran David. It's a quiet, pleasant air-conditioned place with tablecloths that takes a stab at both international cuisine and local food. Offerings include meat, pasta, chow mein, conch, and rice every which way. The *filete a la plancha en salsa chimi-churry* is a chewy but tasty piece of grilled steak in a brown sauce, served with green peas. The service is gracious.

The food at the **Hotel La Hacienda** (Interamericana, tel. 958-8580, 6 A.M.–10 P.M. daily, US$6) is passable but no great shakes. It features Mexican and Peruvian dishes as well as the usual meat and seafood offerings. The guacamole is bland, though the chips are homemade. The enchiladas are the best bet among the Mexican offerings. Don't order anything too ambitious here. The restaurant itself is attractive.

PRACTICALITIES

The **ATP office** (Avenida Central, also called Hector A. Santacoloma, tel. 998-3929, fax 998-0929, 8:30 A.M.–4:30 P.M. Mon.–Fri.) is in Plaza Palermo, a small strip mall across and down the street from Restaurante Tropicalismo. The staff here is friendly, understands a couple of words of English, and may have a little more marginally useful printed material than usual.

There are late-night pharmacies at the transportation centers on the Interamericana (Los Tucanes and Pyramidal). The Galeria has a 24-hour one.

Los Tucanes and Pyramidal have ATMs. There's a **Banco Nacional de Panamá** (9:30 A.M.–5:30 P.M. Mon.–Fri., 9 A.M.–noon Sat.) across the street from Los Tucanes that has a drive-through ATM. A few banks with ATMs are clustered along Avenida Central in the blocks leading up to the cathedral, starting with **Global Bank** (Calle Rogelio Girón R., 8 A.M.–3 P.M. Mon.–Fri., 9 A.M.–noon Sat.). There are plenty of grocery stores in Santiago, including a 24-hour Super 99; look for the high signpost.

Internet cafés that stay up late are all over

the place, but they disappear too quickly to keep track of. There will almost certainly be several near the main bus terminal and on Avenida Central.

There are several launderettes near the cathedral. **Lavamático El Sol** (Avenida Central, 8 A.M.–10 P.M. daily), a short walk behind the cathedral on Avenida Central, is a self-service place that charges US$0.50 to wash (US$0.75 for hot water) and US$0.75 to dry a load. The little store next door sells detergent.

The Galeria on the Interamericana resembles any small strip mall in the United States, complete with American fast food and American blockbusters playing at the little multiplex, Cines Moderno. There's also a 24-hour pharmacy and ATM.

Day passes to use the pool and other facilities at Hotel La Hacienda and Hotel Vista Lago Ecoresort are often available.

GETTING THERE AND AROUND

Because Santiago is about midway between Panama City and David, it's an important transportation hub with excellent, frequent connections to many destinations. The Interamericana is four lanes of divided highway from Panama City all the way to Santiago. West of Santiago it narrows to two lanes of somewhat rougher road until David, though in mid-2010 it was in better shape than ever before and there are now occasional passing lines. It takes about 3.5 hours to drive the 250 kilometers between Panama City and Santiago at a safe clip, and, depending on road conditions, about 3–4 hours to drive from Santiago to David. Those heading west should note there are few gas stations west of Santiago. Fill up here.

By Bus

Santiago has three bus depots: the main terminal, in Santiago itself, and the Centro Pyramidal and Centro Los Tucanes, on the Interamericana near the east and west entrances to town, respectively.

The two *centros* on the Interamericana are where large, long-haul buses (Padafront,

Terminales David-Panama) bound to and from Panama City and David stop. International buses take a break there as well.

Terminales David-Panama (tel. 998-4006, 6:30 A.M.–9:30 P.M. Mon.–Sat., 7 A.M.–8 P.M. Sun.), the larger long-haul carrier, has an office on the west end of the Pyramidal complex. It sells tickets and (grudgingly) dispenses information.

Its buses to David leave every hour or so, 8:30 A.M.–11:30 P.M. There are also three express buses, at 2 A.M., 3 A.M., and 8 A.M. Fare is US$7.50.

Its buses to Panama City leave approximately every hour or 1.5 hours 6 A.M.–11 P.M. There are also two express buses, at 2 A.M. and 3 A.M. The fare is US$7.50. Local buses to Panama City leave more frequently from the Santiago bus terminal, but some of them are smaller and less comfortable minibuses, and there's less metal between you and the dangers of the road.

The Pyramidal also has a hotel, air-conditioned restaurant, outdoor cafeteria, ATM, gas station, pharmacy (8 A.M.–midnight daily), call center (9 A.M.–10 P.M.) and gas station.

The main city bus terminal, the **Terminal de Transporte de Veraguas,** is on Calle 10A Norte, also called Calle Polidoro Pinzón. It has a small bakery and pharmacy and a left-luggage place (starting around US$1 per day, more for bigger and more valuable items). There's a little 24-hour grocery store and Internet cafés across the street.

Those heading to Playa Santa Catalina should note that there are no direct buses from Santiago. Take the bus to Soná and transfer to a Santa Catalina bus there. Note that there are only three daily buses from Soná to Santa Catalina, at 5 A.M., noon, and 4 P.M. (US$3.85).

The following are some popular routes:

Chitré: Every 30 minutes, 5:30 A.M.–8 P.M.; US$2.50. The trip takes about 1.5 hours.

Ocú: Every 20–30 minutes, during daylight hours; US$1.70. The trip takes a little less than an hour.

Panama City: Every 30 minutes, 24 hours a day; US$7.50. The trip takes 3.5 hours. (Some of these are now big buses versus the old mini-buses that usually run from here. However, the David-Panama City long-haul bus companies don't stop here; go to the Centro Pyramidal or Centro Los Tucanes on the Interamericana.)

Puerto Mutis: Every 15–20 minutes, 7 A.M.–10 P.M. Monday–Friday. The last bus on Saturday is at 8 P.M., on Sunday at 6:45 P.M.; US$1.10. The trip takes a little less than an hour.

Santa Fé: Every 30 minutes, 5 A.M.–6:30 or 7 P.M., returning 4:40 A.M.–6 P.M.; US$2.40.

The trip takes about an hour. The bus stops by San Francisco on the way.

Soná: Every 20 minutes, 5:30 A.M.–9:15 P.M.; US$1.75. The last bus leaves at 8 P.M. on weekends. The trip takes a little less than an hour.

By Taxi

Those who want to take a taxi to Playa Santa Catalina should be prepared to pay US$50, but this may be negotiable—this isn't a common trip, and taxi drivers don't have a fixed idea of the price. Taxis to Puerto Mutis are US$12–15 each way. Taxis within town should cost less than US$1 for most destinations.

Santa Fé and San Francisco

◖ SANTA FÉ

I owe Santa Fé an apology. I lived in Panama for years without knowing anything about it, and when I finally visited a few years ago I could take it or leave it, and said as much in these pages. My only excuse is the weather was grim when I visited, and the places to stay and eat even grimmer.

I've since been back when the sun was shining, and I can see now what should have been obvious then. It's a bit like Boquete before the gringo invasion: a humble little highland town with its own simple charm, beautiful surroundings, and almost no tourists.

When that all changes thanks to people like me, I'll owe Santa Fé another apology.

A road down to the Caribbean coast, the first for this entire region, is coming, and it will undoubtedly lead to more deforestation and settlement. But for now it's an appealing destination for those who want to experience a peaceful country town from another time, as long as they don't mind simple accommodations and know how to make their own entertainment.

Santa Fé (pop. 2,800) is 54 kilometers north of Santiago. Founded around 1557, it and the surrounding hills were the scene of fierce battles between the Spanish and indigenous peoples

under the command of Urracá, an especially skilled warrior who managed to beat back the conquistadors for a time and today is commemorated on Panama's one *centavo* coin.

Santa Fé is 470 meters above sea level, which is high enough to get some cool breezes and fog.

Santa Fé itself scores low on the quaintness scale: It's a sprawl of nondescript houses and little else. The charm is to be found in the slower, simpler pace of life of its inhabitants.

But the countryside is pretty, and the drive up is stunning. There are sweeping vistas of rolling hills and pasturelands, and in the distance the mountains of the Continental Divide, still green with dense forests (for now) as they spill down toward the Caribbean slope.

The main road up from the south forks just as it enters town. Staying straight leads into the heart of town, where there are a couple of markets, the town church and plaza, a couple of places to eat, and not much else. The left (west) fork leads up to the trail head to Alto de Piedra.

Tours

Hostal La Qhia (tel. 954-0903, www.panama-mountainhouse.com) and Delight Café are the best sources for tourist information.

Hostal La Qhia works with local cooperatives and indigenous people to offer a variety of tours and hikes, including half day and full day **forest hikes** to area waterfalls, waterholes, and river areas. The best-known spot is Alto de Piedra, but there are several other options. Night hikes and tours that use horses or vehicles are also possible.

With a day's notice, the hostel can arrange **coffee tours** (US$15 for the first person, US$5 for each additional person) of the cooperative's farms and processing plant for its guests. The processing plant is just uphill from the hostel, and the delicious smell of roasting coffee sometimes wafts down. A tour of a local farm noted for its huge collection of **orchids** (US$5 pp) is also available. It's a 45-minute walk from the hostel, but the hostel can arrange transport for those who want it. Lunch at the farm is another US$2 per person for those interested.

Hostal La Qhia also offers all-day trips over the Continental Divide to Río Piedra, in the **Ngöbe-Buglé comarca** (reservation). This costs US$30 per person, two-person minimum, and is best attempted by fit people who speak at least some Spanish. The visits support the local community. For the hardcore hiker, the hostel may be able to arrange a four-day hike over the Continental Divide down to the Caribbean coast. This is a difficult trek and costs several hundred dollars. Don't attempt it unless you're in excellent shape and are prepared to supply all the necessary camping gear.

Cesar Miranda (cell 6792-0571, http://aventurascesamo.blogspot.com) offers horse tours and birding and is known for running a pretty professional operation. Horseback riding trips are around US$20 per person.

If tubing down a river is more your style, Hostal La Qhia or Delight Café can also hook you up with a Panamanian guy named William, by the Río Mulaba, who rents inner tubes and life jackets for US$5. You can also try calling him at cell 6583-5944.

Santa Fé is known for its orchids, and the person most responsible for that is **Berta de Castrellón** (tel. 954-0910), an orchid grower who lives in town. She's the head of the Asociación de Orquideología de Veraguas, which puts on a three-day **orchid festival** here in mid-August. She and her brother, Mariano Gonzalez, are also birding guides. Berta lets visitors tour the huge collection of orchids at her house, but she's often away these days.

Accommodations and Food

Santa Fé sees so few visitors that until recently it only had one basic place to stay and very limited food options. Now it has a great hostel and one inviting place to eat, though restaurant possibilities are still severely limited. There are no real grocery stores and the "restaurants" are none-too-clean *fondas* (cafeterias). If you plan to spend any length of time up here, bring food.

◖ **Delight Café** (cell 6011-4180, noon–9 P.M. Wed.–Mon., under US$4), opened in late 2009, is run by the warm and friendly Elizabeth Gallardo, a former U.S. Peace Corps worker, and her husband, Geiner. It's on the right just as one comes into town. It offers pizza, nachos (including nachos made from *patacones*, twice-fried green plantains), burgers, sandwiches, salads, and shakes. It's easily the most appealing place to eat in Santa Fé, even though it more resembles a warehouse than a restaurant. Elizabeth is a great resource for things to do and see in the area.

◖ **Hostal La Qhia** (tel. 954-0903, www.panamamountainhouse.com, US$11 dorm beds, private rooms start at US$27.50) is the most attractive hostel in the country. It's set in a garden at the end of town, just up from the bus "station," and has a breathtaking view of the mountains. The hostel itself is a pretty, wide-open house with stone walls and floors and a bohemian-chic vibe. The dorms are now in a separate building with eight beds and attractive tilework. Private rooms are upstairs in the main house. The walls are made of lacquered cane, so splintered sunlight streams in and pleasant mountain breezes blow through. There's also a long balcony for those who want to hang out and enjoy the view. Private rooms are US$27.50 s/d with shared bathroom, US$33 s/d with private bathroom. All the beds have mosquito nets. Downstairs is a bar/dining

© WILLIAM FRIAR

Hostal La Qhia is the prettiest hostel in the country.

area that opens onto a large terrace strung with hammocks. Breakfast is around US$3. You're on your own for lunch, but the Belgian (Stefanie) and Argentine (Horacio) couple who own the hostel offer a small, international dinner menu that changes daily. There's a book exchange and communal kitchen. The owners speak English, Spanish, and French and happily share tourist information and arrange guided tours to all the area's natural attractions. Guests have access to detailed hike descriptions and maps. This place is great.

The **Hotel El Sol de Santa Fé** (tel. 954-0941, www.hotelsolsantafe.com, starting at US$23 s/d), a 20-room motel 500 meters south of the town entrance, has the only other decent guest accommodations in the area. It's right off the main road, but it's a little tough to spot. Clean, cold-water rooms are set in a breezy yard with a lovely view of the surrounding hills. Tiny spartan rooms without TV, air-conditioning, or fans are US$13 s, US$15–18 d. Larger rooms with air-conditioning and cable TV are US$25 s/d. Note that you may not need air-conditioning or fans here. The

rooms are basic and this is an okay place. There's an uninviting-looking bar/restaurant on the premises.

Mercado Agricola y Artesanal Santa Fé (in the center of town, on the east side near the church, no phone, 7:30 A.M.–6:30 P.M. daily) is an open-air market with some fruits and vegetables for sale, as well as a few handicrafts, mostly Ngöbe-Buglé.

The **Centro de Mercadeo de Productos Agropecuario, Orgánico, y Artesanal** (no phone, 6 A.M.–8 P.M. daily, closed during lunchtime) has a name bigger than its building. It's a cooperative that sells a few veggies and beans, straw hats, Ngöbe-Buglé handicrafts, and the local coffee. To get there, keep right at the fork as the road leads into town. Continue up to the northern edge of town, then turn right onto the dirt road. The cooperative is on the right, next to the bus station. The restaurant (no phone, 5:30 A.M.–9 P.M. daily) below it is pleasant and breezy, and the food is basic and cheap. A substantial lunch here costs less than US$2.

A *minisuper* in the bus station sells basic groceries.

SAN FRANCISCO

The small town of San Francisco (pop. 2,220) is on the road to Santa Fé about 20 kilometers north of Santiago. It's not very scenic, but its unusual church makes it worth a stop on the way to or from Santa Fé.

The church, **Iglesia San Francisco de la Montaña,** dates from 1727, more than 100 years after the town was founded. It's one of the most charming churches in Panama. It's noted mainly for its nine baroque cedar altars, painted in rich reds and golds, which in their carvings depict unusual syncretisms, fusing European and indigenous images and traditions. The outside is brick at the bottom, with a more modern whitewashed tower planted incongruously on top. A glacier-paced renovation of the church has restored the whole outside to a semblance of its former glory.

To get to the church, make a right turn off the main road to Santa Fé at the police station.

Make another right upon entering town. The church will be straight ahead.

Refresquería y Quesería El Mirador (tel. 954-2128, 9 A.M.–8 P.M. daily) is a snack bar and cheese shop by the side of the road two kilometers north of San Francisco. It makes decent flavored yogurt and cheese (think cream and cottage cheese, not fancy *fromage*) on the premises and sells it at the counter. The menu also includes burgers and such, to be consumed on a large terrace with views of the surrounding valley and hills. It's a good place to stop on the way to or from Santa Fé.

GETTING THERE AND AWAY

The road is good all the way from Santiago to Santa Fé. The same bus passes by San Francisco and can drop passengers off; just tell the driver ahead of time. After visiting the church, catch another bus the rest of the way to Santa Fé or back down to Santiago.

To get to San Francisco and Santa Fé by car,

San Francisco's church, which dates from 1727, is noted for its unusual fusion of European and indigenous images and traditions.

© WILLIAM FRIAR

CENTRAL PANAMA

turn north off the Interamericana at the crossroads just west of Santiago. The turn is right before the overpass, but may not be marked. Turn north and head up into the hills for 17 kilometers and turn right at the police station to get to San Francisco. Stay straight on the main road for another 37 kilometers to get to Santa Fé. The road has now been paved all the way to Alto de Piedra, the most popular area for hikes. It's five kilometers up from Santa Fé and the route is well signposted. After that the road is still mud and requires a four-wheel drive.

Archipiélago de las Perlas

Ninety named islands and more than 130 unnamed islets make up this archipelago, which begins just 15 minutes by plane or a couple of hours by fast boat from Panama City. *Perlas* is Spanish for pearls, and pearls are what first brought these beautiful islands international fame. When Vasco Nuñez de Balboa crossed the Darién looking for the "South Sea," one of his motives was to find and conquer the islands he had heard were overflowing with the precious little oyster byproducts. The conquistadors did just that. In the process, they wiped out the islands' indigenous population.

The archipelago has a way of periodically achieving brief international notoriety. In 1983, the island of Contadora was the site of the first meeting of the Contadora Group, formed by the leaders of several Latin American countries to try to promote democracy in Central America and influence U.S. foreign policy in El Salvador, Nicaragua, and Guatemala, which were being torn apart by bloody military conflicts. In 1979, the same island briefly played host to the exiled shah of Iran. In more recent years, the archipelago has hosted wave after wave of *Survivor,* the reality-TV series, and its spinoffs and imitators.

There are lush forests on the islands, lovely sandy beaches on their shores, and healthy coral reefs a short swim away. The latter attract a wealth of brilliant small fish and impressive larger creatures, including sea turtles, manta rays, white-tipped reef sharks, and moray eels. The Perlas are considered one of the better spots in the country for divers in search of big fish.

Note that none of the islands in the archipelago, including Contadora, have ATMs or banks. Bring all the cash you may need with you.

CONTADORA

By far the most developed and visited of the islands is Contadora, named for its role as the

ARCHIPIÉLAGO
DE LAS PERLAS

Isla Pacheca
Saboga
Isla Saboga
Isla Contadora
Isla Chapera
Isla Mogo Mogo
0   5 mi
0   5 km
Isla Bayoneta
Isla Casaya
Isla Viveros
San Miguel
Isla Pedro González
Isla del Rey
Bahía del Rey
Bahía San Telmo
Isla San Telmo
Isla San José
Isla Galera
Golfo de Panamá
© AVALON TRAVEL

counting-house island for the Spanish pearl trade. Wealthy Panamanians have beach homes here, and it has nearly all the accommodations, places to eat, and tour operations in the archipelago. It's a small island—just 1.2 square kilometers. It's easy to explore just about all of it on foot in a couple of hours, or scoot around it in a four-wheeler, which can be rented near the airstrip.

The setting is beautiful, but potential visitors should note that the island is pricey, even though many of its facilities have seen better days. Contadora was Panama's first true resort island; it had its heyday in the 1980s and went into decline when the tourist trade moved on. However, things are in flux there and the island seems to be on a bit of an upswing at the moment.

Sports and Recreation

Contadora has several nice beaches, including one, **Playa de las Suecas** (translated "Swedish women's beach"), where you can sunbathe nude. My favorite, **Playa Cacique,** is a pretty, secluded beach behind Villa Romántica and away from the crowds. Contadora's largest and busiest beach, the aptly named **Playa Larga,** is somewhat rocky at low tide. **Snorkeling** is possible just off Playa de las Suecas, Playa Galeón, Playa Ejecutiva, and Playa Larga. There's very little else to do on the island, though Hotel Contadora has a nine-hole golf course and tennis courts for those so inclined.

Boat tours of Contadora and the surrounding islands are a popular activity, as are snorkeling, diving, and deep-sea fishing. Those on a budget can negotiate for a tour with a boatman (try Playa Larga or Playa Galeón), but don't expect life jackets or well-maintained boats.

Dive operators can take guests to nearly two dozen **scuba-diving** spots within a 45-minute boat ride from Contadora. Most are only 10 minutes away. The diving in the Perlas can be impressive, especially for those fond of big fish: There's quite a good chance of spotting white-tipped reef sharks, manta rays, and moray eels. Among the many other critters you may come across are angelfish, parrotfish, grunts,

snappers, amberjack, sergeant majors, and triggerfish. Personal-watercraft rental is also available for those who feel the need to shatter the peace of the fish and fellow visitors.

Dive shops come and go on Contadora. **Coral Dreams** (cell 6536-1776, www.coraldreams.com) has been around for a while now, however. It offers snorkeling and diving tours, as well as courses ranging from Discover Scuba to divemaster. It's right next to the Contadora airstrip. Look for the "Dive Center" sign.

Accommodations

Lodging options are severely limited on Contadora. Fortunately, there's one place just about everyone loves. **Contadora Island Inn Bed and Breakfast** (cell 6699-4614, www.contadoraislandinn.com, starts at US$88 s/d, including breakfast and transfers to and from the airstrip) consists of two vacation homes that were converted into a friendly bed-and-breakfast. It's in a residential area on the west side of the island. Neither house is actually on the beach, but several beaches are a short walk away.

Each house features large decks, a spacious living room with TV/DVD player and stereo, and a full kitchen guests are welcome to use. The original inn sleeps up to 12 people in five bedrooms. The Hibiscus House, added in 2007, sleeps up to nine in five bedrooms. All the rooms are different and priced accordingly; prices are per room, not per guest. The most expensive is the two-room Hibiscus Suite, one with a king bed, the other with a twin, for US$154. All rooms have air-conditioning, ceiling fans, hot-water bathrooms, orthopedic mattresses, in-room safes, and outdoor sitting areas. Entire houses can also be reserved. Full Panamanian breakfasts are included with stays. The innkeepers are retired teachers from Florida who are happy to help arrange tours. Prices go up during the holidays and down during the rainy season.

Villa Romántica (tel. 250-4067, www.villa-romantica.com, starts at US$125.40 s/d in the main house, US$105.60 s/d in the old annex) is a quirky place that has to be approached with the right attitude to be enjoyed. It's on the south side of the island right above beautiful Playa Cacique and offers 12 air-conditioned rooms in two houses. Two of the rather glitzy rooms in the main house have waterbeds. Potential guests should look at the photos on Villa Romántica's website before deciding to book here; the hedonistic-1970s vibe is not for everyone.

Rooms in the main house are nicer and closer to the beach than those in the separate "guest house," which in turn has a bit more privacy.

The owner is going for a romantic getaway vibe, as the name of the place suggests. That atmosphere is helped by the large veranda and open-air restaurant, Restaurante Romántico, that looks right out on the secluded beach. But it's diminished by the clutter and air of cheerful chaos about the place. The Austrian owner is an enthusiastic, effusive, and friendly character named Charley who offers boat tours.

Punta Galeón Resort and Spa (tel. 250-4234 or 250-4221, www.hotelpuntagaleon. com, starts at US$135.30 s/d) has a lovely location on a low, rocky point above Playa Galeón, as its name suggests. Rooms are in a series of white-washed one-story buildings and perched on the edge of the point. Rooms are simple but cheerful and attractive. All are air-conditioned and have TVs and in-room safes. It's gone through rocky times in the past, with complaints about service, maintenance, and, especially food. However, it appears to be on the rise again and may be worth taking the plunge. Even if the hotel disappoints, the location is great. It's above an attractive but often crowded beach.

Food

Contadora is not known for good restaurants. What's worse, diners have to pay quite a bit even for mediocre food, since everything has to be brought over from the mainland. Expect to pay US$20 or more for an entrée that costs half that in Panama City. Gerald's and Restaurante Romántico are the best bets for getting a decent meal, but they're both expensive. There are

grocery stores near the airstrip. I've never had good food or service at either Hotel Contadora or Punta Galeón. This is a good place to arrive with lots of snacks stashed in the luggage.

Formerly known as El Suizo, **Gerald's** (no phone, noon–3 P.M. and 6–11 P.M. or so daily), in a large, attractive *rancho* on a hill just above the airstrip, is known for its seafood and steaks. It's a pleasant place to hang out in the evenings.

Restaurante Romántico (tel. 250-4067, roughly 8 A.M.–3 P.M. and 6–10 P.M. daily), the restaurant attached to Villa Romántica, offers expensive food in a good location: It's an open-air place right above a pretty beach that's likely to be deserted when you visit. It's known for its "hot rock" shtick, in which you're given a piece of meat and a hot plate to grill it on. This is allegedly romantic, which may be why you're expected to pay upwards of US$20 for a meal you cook yourself. Other offerings include prawns, shrimp, fondue, and various meat and fish dishes. The seafood is good, but fare here tends to be a little heavy and rich. This place is a bit of a hike from the main hotels.

Fonda Sagitario (6:30 A.M.–8:30 P.M. daily), near the police station, is a basic but clean locals' hangout that serves simple food at cheap prices. Fisherfolk take note: This place will cook your catch for a few dollars.

Getting There and Away

Most come to Contadora by small plane. The flight lasts about 20 minutes and costs US$62 each way.

Aeroperlas (tel. 775-7779, www.aeroperlas. com) flies between Panama City and Contadora at 9:15 A.M. and 5 P.M. daily. Return flights are at 9:45 A.M. and 5:30 P.M. except on Sunday, when they're at 4:30 and 5:30 P.M. There's an extra round-trip on Saturday, leaving Panama City at 1 P.M., returning 1:30 P.M.

Air Panama (tel. 316-9000, www.flyair-panama.com) flies to Contadora at 9:30 A.M. Monday–Saturday and 4:30 P.M. daily. Return flights are a half hour later.

Ferry services from Panama City to Contadora have been started and abandoned many times over the years. After a couple of false starts, a new service, **Sea Las Perlas** (cell 6780-8000, tel. 263-5044, http://sealasperlas.com) had finally started up as this edition went to print.

The ultimate ambition is to make it a daily service, which would be a first for the islands, which in the past have not had enough visitors during the week, particularly during the rainy season, to sustain a daily operation. For now, at least, the service runs Thursday–Sunday. The "ferry" (actually a 54-foot catamaran) leaves at 8 A.M. from the Amador Causeway near Panama City, dropping passengers off on Contadora by the Punta Galeón Resort and Spa. It makes the return trip to the mainland at 3 P.M. The ride takes about an hour and 45 minutes, and the fare is US$38/person. Day excursion packages to nearby Saboga and other islands may also be available.

I have not yet had a chance to try the service, so I can't vouch for its reliability or safety. Make sure there are enough lifejackets and a working marine radio before boarding, as the trip to Contadora is on open ocean. The mainland ferry dock is next to the Brisas de Amador development on Isla Perico, which is toward the end of the Amador Causeway.

ISLA SAN JOSÉ

This remote, 44-square-kilometer private island, the second-largest in the archipelago, saw few visitors before the opening of the 17-cabaña **Hacienda del Mar** (Panama tel. 269-6634 or 269-6613, U.S. toll-free tel. 866/433-5627, www.haciendadelmar.net, starts at US$412.50 for up to four people, including breakfast). It's easily the most exclusive place to stay in the archipelago.

The cabañas look rather rustic from the outside, with their cane walls and red zinc roofs. But inside they're quite modern and feature air-conditioning, hot-water bathrooms, in-room safes, ceiling fans, and balconies. The resort's "clubhouse" has a sports bar with satellite TV, pool table, sauna, and so on. It leads out to an attractive swimming pool. All this is on the southeast side of the island, perched above a sandy beach.

Hacienda del Mar offers 14 beachfront cabañas and three rooms. The 10 standard cabañas have two double beds and sleep up to four people (US$412.50 in the high season). The most expensive accommodations are in the main building, where the two-bedroom Almiral Suite goes for US$770.

Possible activities at Hacienda del Mar include hikes or ATV tours through the island's forests, snorkeling and scuba diving, mountain biking, and deep-sea fishing. All these activities are extra, as are lunch and dinner. There's an extensive trail system through the island's forests, which are home to white brocket deer, peccaries, iguanas, anteaters, and other wildlife.

Most guests arrive by plane from Panama City, 90 kilometers away. The flight takes about 20 minutes. The resort handles the plane reservations. The round-trip fare is US$128 per person.

Beautiful as Isla San José is, it has a less than peaceful history. During and immediately after World War II, the United States, with support from Canada and Great Britain, dropped or detonated thousands of chemical weapons on the island to test their use in tropical warfare, according to a 2002 article in *Bulletin of the Atomic Scientists.*

A 2001 inspection team found several unexploded chemical bombs on the island. The Panamanian government temporarily placed the island in quarantine, but a more thorough inspection to search for other weapons has not taken place. A conflict between the United States and Panama over who should pay for the inspection and possible cleanup has dragged on for years and has yet to be resolved.

Resort management says all these weapons tests took place many kilometers from Hacienda del Mar. I have heard no reports of guests being harmed in any way.

OTHER ISLANDS

The islands listed here are just a sampling of what else the archipelago has to offer. However, most of the islands are not easily accessible. There's no commercial air or ferry service among the islands (except for the ferry between Contadora and Saboga). Most visitors use Contadora or San José as a base to explore the nearest islands on a boat tour.

Saboga is just a few minutes west of Contadora by boat. There is little on it, but a major residential and tourism project is in the works that, if it happens, would develop its entire coastline.

Pacheca, immediately north of Contadora, is also known as Isla de Los Pájaros (Bird Island) because it's a sanctuary for magnificent frigate birds, brown pelicans, and cormorants, among other seabirds.

Mogo Mogo, less than five kilometers south of Contadora, is a picturesque island with nice beaches. The one time I snorkeled here there wasn't much to see, but supposedly there are extensive coral fields off a part of the island I didn't visit.

Casaya, about three kilometers farther south, still has a small village of pearl divers. One can shop for pearls here, but don't expect any great treasures; those days are long over.

Isla del Rey is, at nearly 240 square kilometers, the giant of the islands. To its south is **San Telmo,** a private nature reserve owned by the nonprofit environmental group ANCON. It's home to a large brown pelican colony as well as to boobies, cormorants, magnificent frigate birds, and endangered moist premontane forest.

WESTERN HIGHLANDS AND BEACHES

Western Panama offers some of Panama's most spectacular, and diverse, attractions.

On the one hand, there are the verdant highlands, home to the country's tallest mountain and the picturesque town of Boquete, which now rivals Bocas del Toro as Panama's hottest destination for foreign tourists and retirees. On the other, there are the remote Pacific islands and beaches of the Golfo de Chiriquí, which is so large and species-rich some consider it a small sea, as well as those of the Golfo de Montijo further east.

The region also includes Panama's second-largest city, David, near the coast not far from the Costa Rican border. Most visitors simply pass through David on the way to somewhere else, usually the highlands, but it has all the services you would expect of a busy, modern provincial capital. There are a few large

beaches within a couple hours' drive of David, the most popular of which are Playa Barqueta and Playa Las Lajas. The coastline and islands around the fishing village of Boca Chica are beautiful and beginning to take off as a tourist destination, though getting to them can be a bit of an adventure. Farther east, remote Playa Santa Catalina is internationally famous as one of the best surfing spots in Latin America.

Those who visit the western highlands after a trip to the beaches and islands may feel they have entered a different world, a world filled with powerful rivers, gigantic waterfalls, imposing mountains, secluded hot springs, and green forests bursting with life. The highlands are also home to Volcán Barú, a dormant volcano that, at 3,475 meters, is Panama's biggest and most dramatic mountain.

COURTESY OF THE COFFEE ESTATE INN

HIGHLIGHTS

☾ **Finca Lérida:** This highland coffee farm is one of the best places anywhere to see the resplendent quetzal (page 305).

☾ **Parque Nacional Volcán Barú:** Panama's tallest mountain is visible from everywhere in the western highlands, and on a clear day adventurous hikers can see both oceans from its summit. Don't miss Sendero Los Quetzales – the most popular hike in the highlands – while you're here (page 314).

☾ **Parque Internacional La Amistad:** A gigantic international park, PILA has some of the most diverse flora and fauna in Panama (page 331).

☾ **Cañon Macho de Monte:** This impressive and accessible canyon appeals both to birdwatchers and inner-tube rafters (page 340).

☾ **Parque Nacional Marino Golfo de Chiriquí:** A remote and still little-known tropical paradise, this marine park is lightly peppered with deserted islands, bohemian hangouts, and exclusive resorts (page 350).

☾ **Playa Santa Catalina:** Panama's top spot for surfers, remote Catalina has one of the most consistently awesome breaks in all of Latin America (page 358).

☾ **Parque Nacional Coiba:** Panama's answer to the Galapagos, Coiba is the crown jewel of the country's islands, with virgin forest covering it, rich sea life surrounding it, and a Devil's Island mystique about it (page 369).

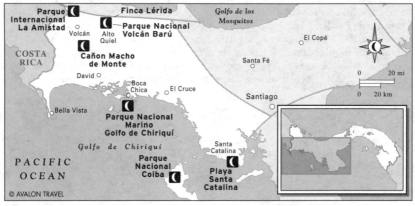

LOOK FOR ☾ TO FIND RECOMMENDED SIGHTS, ACTIVITIES, DINING, AND LODGING.

There's plenty to keep outdoorsy types busy, including hiking, horseback riding, biking, the country's best white-water rafting, kayaking, even rock climbing and rappelling. The western highlands are popular with bird-watchers, since the forests attract hundreds of species, including many spectacular ones.

Most of the highland sights are clustered on the west and east sides of Volcán Barú. While the west side of Barú is a bit cooler and more dramatic looking, the east side has both great beauty and something its western neighbor lacks: a charming little town called Boquete.

Boquete is booming. As a result, there are more options for lodging, food, outfitters, and guided tours on this side of the mountain. The west side of Barú is quieter, less densely populated, and more rugged. It also has easily

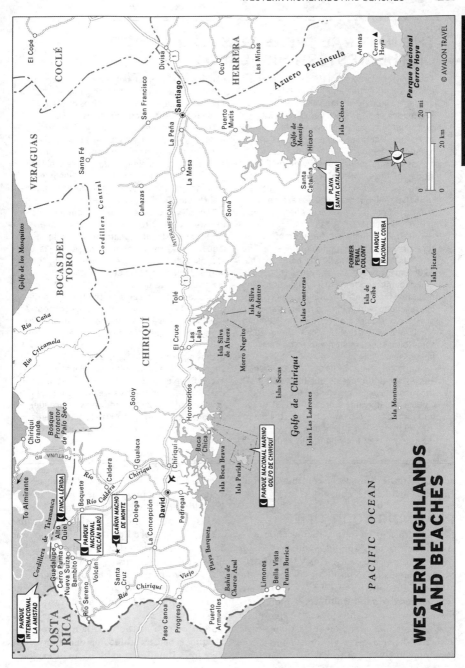

WESTERN HIGHLANDS
AND BEACHES

THE NATURAL TREASURES OF THE WESTERN HIGHLANDS

The western highlands of Panama start at the Costa Rican border and head east for hundreds of kilometers along the Cordillera de Talamanca and the Cordillera Central. Much of Parque Internacional La Amistad and all of Parque Nacional Volcán Barú are in the highlands.

This chapter deals mainly with the Pacific slopes of the Continental Divide, since the parks and other sights are more accessible from that side. But the highlands extend north into Bocas del Toro province, where they descend toward the Caribbean.

The western highlands harbor more virgin forest than any other region of Panama. The area's huge national parks are home to a bewildering array of plant- and animal life, much of it endemic and some of it endangered. The mountain forests are threatened by encroaching farmland, which in turn is threatened by erosion. But there's a growing sense among highland dwellers that they're surrounded by something special that needs to be carefully preserved.

Spend any time up here and you'll soon know how cloud forests got their name. At the highest elevations you are literally in the clouds, and it's quite a dramatic sight to see puffy white billows blowing through the moss-draped trees in the afternoons.

Some parts of the woods may remind you of a temperate forest, but don't be fooled; you are still in the tropics. The forest has many of the same dangers and attractions as the lowland jungles, including venomous snakes.

This is one of the best places in the Americas to see the resplendent quetzal, an absolutely stunning bird. In the dry season, visitors often see several on a single outing. You're likely to see several species of jewel-toned hummingbirds among the hundreds of other bird species that make their home here.

Though you'd be very lucky to spot one, the forests are home to all five species of endangered felines found in Panama, including the jaguar. They are also home to one of the last stands of the endangered Baird's tapir, the largest land mammal in Central America.

Boquete is famous for its coffee and oranges, and the streams on the west side of Barú are filled with human-introduced trout. Flowers, strawberries, race horses, and dairy cows are also raised in the highlands.

It's refreshingly cool in the highlands, with temperatures that dip down to 7°C and sometimes lower. And it's wet: Rainfall can exceed five meters. Even in the dry season, the mountains and valleys are often shrouded in what's affectionately known as *bajareque*, a foggy drizzle that can create photogenic rainbows. No matter when you come, bring rain gear.

accessible trails through the enormous Parque Internacional La Amistad.

PLANNING YOUR TIME

Most visitors to western Panama choose to spend their time in the highlands, either on the west side or the east side of **Volcán Barú.** To truly do justice to both sides of the mountain would require up to a week. The eastern side, centered around **Boquete,** is more popular. Allow at least three days to explore the town, go for a hike, and do at least one of the activities the area is known for, such as a coffee tour, white-water rafting trip, or search for quetzals. The highlights of the western side, including a long hike, can be covered in two days. Physically fit visitors who want to see both sides of the mountain should consider hiking the **Sendero Los Quetzales** from one side to another when they're ready to relocate; allow a full day for this.

It's fun to combine a trip to the highlands with a visit to the beaches and islands of the Golfo de Chiriquí. It's quite a contrast. Those who just want a little beach time can spend a night or two at the mainland beaches of **Barqueta** or **Las Lajas,** or make day trips there from **David.** David itself can be explored in half a day, and most people give it even less time than that. Getting just about anywhere else in the Golfo de Chiriquí takes time and planning, especially for those of us who don't own private yachts.

Parque Nacional Coiba is about two hours by boat from the nearest mainland ports; only private planes can fly there, and only then with special permission. Reaching **Playa Santa Catalina** or **Parque Marino Golfo de Chiriquí** usually means a fair amount of driving, but the roads to both places have recently been paved and are now much more accessible. They are both beginning to take off as tourist destinations. Most guests arrive at the **Islas Secas Resort** by private plane arranged by the resort.

Few will have the time or inclination to visit both marine parks. Coiba and its surrounding waters and islands are stunning, at the top of most visitors' wish lists. The most accessible

parts of **Parque Marino Golfo de Chiriquí** are not as uniquely impressive as Coiba, but it has plenty of small, deserted islands to explore, and it's easier and cheaper to get to.

Most people get to the islands of the gulf through a tour, dive, surf, or fishing operator, though some areas close to shore can be reached by taking a taxi, bus, or private vehicle to the coast, where fishing boats can generally be hired. Even Coiba can be reached this way, though it's not the safest and certainly not the fastest way to go. Plan to spend at least two nights on the islands to enjoy the surroundings and recover from the hassle of getting there.

Exploring the **Fortuna Road area** makes most sense for travelers who are going to or from Bocas del Toro by land. Otherwise, combining it with a visit to the Volcán Barú or Golfo de Chiriquí area means more traveling time than most are likely to want.

David

Depending on where one draws the boundaries, David (dah-VEED), the provincial capital of Chiriquí province, is the second- or third-largest city in Panama (pop. 140,000). It's the lowland hub for visits to the highlands and other parts of western Panama and has the largest concentration of visitor services in the region.

David is a bustling, congested commerce and transportation center for Chiriquí province, which has the most productive farmland in the country. Every year the city hosts the Feria Internacional de David, an enormous agriculture and livestock fair that draws participants from around Latin America, Europe, and even Asia.

Few foreign visitors who aren't into farming or business spend much time in the city. Though David was settled by the Spanish in 1602 and has a history of indigenous inhabitation far older than that, few traces of all that rich history remain, and most of the contemporary buildings and byways are utilitarian at best. Its lowland location close, but not close enough, to the coast can also make it wiltingly hot and humid.

© WILLIAM FRIAR

The national flag and the Chiriquí provincial flag; *chiricanos* have a strong regional identity.

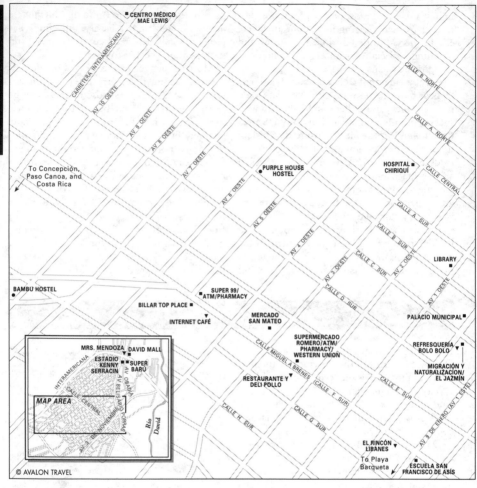

© AVALON TRAVEL

Those who spend much time on this side of the country, though, will likely have to spend at least one night here. Fortunately it has decent places to stay and eat, and even a few city-style diversions. It can offer a good change of pace after time spent in the boonies.

Although there has been local concern in the last couple of years about a rise in youth gangs, David is a pretty safe and mellow town. I've walked all over the place at all hours of the day and night and never felt threatened. Davideños are generally easygoing and cordial, and there just isn't enough tourism here for scams and rip-offs to be a serious concern. But David is a growing city, and visitors should keep their city smarts about them, particularly women traveling alone. Also, streets beyond the center of town are poorly lit and deserted at night.

SIGHTS
Parque Cervantes

David is not a pretty town, and it has little that qualifies as a true sight. The best way to get a feel for the place and its people is to wander around,

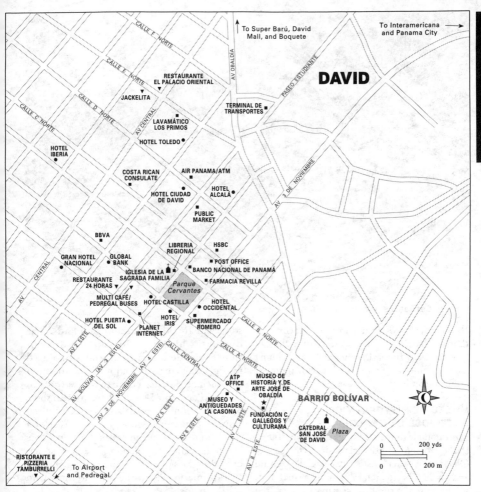

↑ To Super Barú, David Mall, and Boquete

To Interamericana and Panama City →

DAVID

especially near Parque Cervantes, the plaza at the center of town. As one might expect, it's the symbolic heart of the city. The park recently got a facelift that I have mixed feelings about. Some of the huge, lovely old trees have been cut down, robbing the park of shade. The street vendors have been kicked out (some can be found on Calle A Norte east of the park), making it less colorful and interesting. And in the center is a weird, diamond-shaped metal fountain that's just plain ugly. On the other hand, the park does feel more spacious and inviting than it used to.

The church on the northwest side of the plaza, **Iglesia de la Sagrada Familia,** dates from the 19th century, but the current interior is newish and generic and has all the ambience of an income-tax office.

Barrio Bolívar

There are some colonial-era buildings on the southeast side of town in an area of a few square blocks known as Barrio Bolívar. This area is also sometimes known as **El Peligro** (The Danger). There are different theories

© WILLIAM FRIAR

Parque Cervantes, David

about how it got that name. My favorite is that the barrio is in the vicinity of a church, a cemetery, a funeral home, and a jail. Don't let the name put you off: It's worth roaming around a bit here.

MUSEO DE HISTORIA Y DE ARTE JOSÉ DE OBALDÍA

Most notable of the buildings in Barrio Bolívar is the Museo de Historia y de Arte José de Obaldía (Avenida 8 Este between Calle Central and Calle A Norte, tel. 775-7839), a small museum housed in the 19th-century wooden, red tile–roofed home of José de Obaldía (1806–1889). Note: The museum has been closed for restoration for years now. Call before venturing out to see it. An important figure in 19th century Panamanian history, Obaldía was instrumental in the founding of Chiriquí province in 1849. Among his other notable accomplishments was a stint as acting president of New Granada, which encompassed Panama and Colombia, 1854–1855.

This "history and art" museum is an extremely modest place, though not unusually

so by Panamanian museum standards. The displays, which have virtually no descriptions, include a metate (a flat stone used for grinding corn) and a broken statue from the ancient Barriles culture, whose roots in Chiriquí date to 734 B.C. There are also some Spanish colonial swords and wooden church figures. Some mementos from the War of a Thousand Days are upstairs. Several items in the museum's collection have been stolen over the years. The attendant can give a little information about the place to those who speak Spanish.

FUNDACIÓN C. GALLEGOS Y CULTURAMA

Next to the Obaldía museum is Fundación C. Gallegos y Culturama (Avenida 8 Este and Calle Central, tel. 774-0536, 8 A.M.–noon and 1–5 P.M. Mon.–Fri., 8 A.M.–5 P.M. Sat.). It's a nonprofit foundation and cultural center that's recording the history, including oral histories, of as much of Chiriquí as it can. This is all too rare in Panama, and the commitment of the participants is inspiring. The place is of possible interest to visitors because it's another 19th-century building with character, it contains historic photos of David and its leading residents, and it has a substantial library of historic books and documents. Visitors are welcome, and the friendly, enthusiastic members have interesting information to share on the history of the area (at least with those who speak Spanish).

The street that runs past the front of the museum and the foundation, Avenida 8 Este, was once David's main street. If you squint, you can get a sense of what the city must have looked like a hundred years ago.

CATEDRAL SAN JOSÉ DE DAVID

Near Avenida 10 Este and Calle A Norte is the crumbling tower of the Catedral San José de David, which was consecrated in 1891. The cathedral was built on the site of a shrine that first appears in the historical record in 1722. Repeated "restorations" over the years have destroyed the cathedral itself. It now looks like a warehouse, though it's still a hub of civic activity; worshippers often gather in the evening while families play with their children in the neighboring park. The tower is the only part of the cathedral that's more or less intact, though it looks fragile and still bears the scars from bullets that struck it during the War of a Thousand Days. The cathedral bell hasn't rung since Panama's centennial celebration in 2003, but the local *padre* says that has nothing to do with fear the tower might collapse.

MUSEO Y ANTIGUEDADES LA CASONA

Be sure to stop by the Museo y Antiguedades La Casona (Calle Central between Avenida 6 Este and Avenida 7 Este, tel. 775-2239, 9 A.M.–noon and 3–6 P.M. Mon.–Fri., 9 A.M.–1 P.M. Sat., free). The museum contains a curious mixture of antique furniture, religious artifacts, and displays illustrating traditional *chiricano* life, all housed in a private home that dates from the 19th century. The museum has a more interesting collection of historic pieces than many of the country's public museums.

ENTERTAINMENT AND EVENTS
Nightlife

I've given up listing dance places in David; they open and close so quickly recommendations are useless. It's impossible even to point partiers to a nightlife neighborhood, as there isn't one. My best guess for a place to try would be Calle Miguel A. Brenes/F Sur, which is a booming commercial corridor. Also check out Avenida Obaldía, the main entrance into the city. Live dance-music shows are sometimes held in venues on or near the Interamericana. Taxi drivers will know the current hot spots (but be sure to ask for a "disco" rather than a "nightclub"—the latter is usually a euphemism for strip clubs and brothels). Or try the technique Andrea at the Purple House Hostel uses when her guests want to go clubbing: She sticks her head out the window, listens for the loudest music, and points them in that direction. It works.

Pool players can knock balls around at **Billar Top Place** (Calle Miguel A. Brenes/F Sur and Avenida 5 Oeste), next to Restaurante Jenny #19, for US$1.50 an hour.

The best bets for movies are the **Gran Hotel Nacional** (Calle Central between Avenida Central and Avenida 9 de Enero/1 Este, tel. 775-2221 or 775-2222, http://hotelnacionalpanama.com) and the **Chiriquí Mall** (Interamericana, west of David), both of which have six-screen multiplexes. Movies cost US$2.50, or US$1.80 for matinees. **Fundación C. Gallegos y Culturama** (Avenida 8 Este and Calle Central, tel. 774-0536) screens alternatives to Hollywood blockbusters on Wednesday nights.

Festivals

The **Feria Internacional de San José de David** (www.feriadedavid.com), usually shortened to Feria Internacional de David or simply Feria de David, is a huge trade fair that draws thousands of attendees from all over the country and abroad for 10 days in mid-March. It's essentially a giant agriculture, livestock, and commerce convention, though it does make room for folkloric crafts and dances. The fairgrounds take up 12 hectares on the western outskirts of town near Avenida 9 de Enero/1 Este, the road that leads to Playa Barqueta. In recent years it's drawn 500 exhibitors from around Panama, Latin America, and beyond, including some from Europe and Asia, as well as 600 prize livestock specimens. It's said to draw a staggering 300,000 attendees a year, though that's hard to believe. One suspects a few of these get counted more than once over the 10 days.

David's Barrio Bolívar celebrates the **Festival del Tambor** at the end of November, around the time of Panama's celebration of its independence from Spain on November 28. This is a traditional festival that features *tambores* (drums), *tunas* (marching bands), folkloric dances in colorful local costumes, and traditional *chiricano* food.

David and its surrounding communities celebrate **Carnaval** along with the rest of the country. A particularly popular place to go for the celebration is Dolega, a small town about midway between David and Boquete. It's less than 20 kilometers up the David–Boquete road. It's a more mellow affair than Carnaval in Las Tablas and Panama City.

March 19 is the *fiesta patronal de San José,* David's patron saint's day.

SHOPPING

Avenida 3 de Noviembre (Avenida 4 Este), which runs past Parque Cervantes northeast toward Avenida Obaldía, is a crowded commercial street with many shops hawking inexpensive clothes and household goods and such. There is an ever-expanding **mall** on the Interamericana at the crossroads with the road to Boquete. A slightly older shopping center, **Chiriquí Mall,** is a few kilometers west of David on the Interamericana. It's never really taken off, but it has a multiplex, a branch of **El Hombre de la Mancha bookstore** (tel. 774-1174, 10 A.M.–7 P.M. daily), fast-food stalls, clothing stores, and so on.

Those who'd like to take back some good-quality Chiriquí highland coffee without going to the Chiriquí highlands can buy gourmet-roast Café Ruiz coffee, one of the finest in Panama, at the **Super Barú** supermarket (Interamericana and Avenida Obaldía, 7 A.M.–midnight Mon.–Sat., 8 A.M.–10 P.M. Sun.). It's one of the few stores in Panama that carry the gourmet roast. Other kinds of Café Ruiz are more widely available.

SPORTS AND RECREATION

Regional and youth baseball games are held in **Estadio Kenny Serracín,** a stadium two blocks south of the Interamericana between Avenida Obaldía and Avenida Belisarrio Porras. **Béisbol** games are held only in the dry season, from January to around early May. Tickets should be no more than US$5 and can be bought at the gate. Schedules are not well publicized, but some information is available from the official Chiriquí province baseball website, http://chiriquibeis.com/. Their telephone number is 260-69816.

The most popular beach within easy driving distance of David is **Playa Barqueta,** a wide, black-sand beach with pounding surf that's usually far too rough for swimming. Think seriously before going into these waters above your calves. I grew up body surfing in fairly big surf on Panama's Pacific beaches, and I wouldn't dare go for a splash in what I've seen at Barqueta.

To get to Playa Barqueta by public transit, take the Guarumal bus from the David bus terminal.

For those driving, the main turnoff from David to Playa Barqueta is at the Escuela San Francisco de Asís, a large school at the corner of Calle Miguel A. Brenes/F Sur and Avenida 9 de Enero/1 Este. There's no name on it, so look for the statue of St. Francis in front. Head southwest on Avenida 9 de Enero and keep on going. The trip is about 30 kilometers long and takes about half an hour.

ACCOMMODATIONS

The range of lodging in David has much improved in recent years, with good options both for budget travelers and those with a bit more to spend. Accommodations tend to be clustered around Parque Cervantes, in the heart of town.

Note: There's a high-profile hotel, Las Olas Resort, on Playa Barqueta not far from David. It's not included here for a couple of reasons. First, it's a rather generic place that started life as an all-inclusive hotel on an isolated stretch of beach with huge, pounding waves that don't lend themselves to safe or comfortable swimming. More recently, construction at the hotel and an associated condominium development has generated a great deal of controversy for allegedly causing serious environmental damage.

Under US$25

Opened in 2002, the **Purple House Hostel** (Calle C Sur and Avenida 6 Oeste, 774-4059, www.purplehousehostel.com, starts at US$7.70 pp) is a true hostel in a—you guessed it—purple house. Though it's 10 hot blocks from the heart of the city, it's within easy walking distance of a commercial district with all kinds of services and good transportation connections. The hostel offers 21 spaces in a configuration that's constantly changing. The house is simple but clean and comfortable and totally geared toward the budget traveler. There is a backyard garden with beach chairs and sprinklers when guests need to cool off. Its owner, Andrea, a former U.S. Peace Corps volunteer from New York, is a great source of useful area information and travelers' tips. Staying here gives guests access to lots of extras, including a book exchange, lockers, use of the kitchen, luggage storage, free wireless Internet access and use of a computer terminal, all the fresh orange juice you can squeeze (in season), free coffee and tea, and discounts on some area services, restaurants, and transportation. Note that all these amenities are available only to guests. English and Spanish are spoken. There's no curfew, but quiet time starts around 11:30 P.M. This is not a wild-party kind of place. The house is in a residential neighborhood, and hostelers are guests in Andrea's home.

Rates are US$7.70 per person in a fan-cooled four-bunk or six-bunk dorm room. A private room with fan and orthopedic mattresses is US$20 s/d. Air-conditioners are available in the private rooms for US$5 at night or US$10 all day. Hot water and laundry service are available for an extra fee. Note that availability is limited in October; call ahead if you plan to be in David at that time. Guests can use the pool at the nearby Plaza Mirage Hotel and Casino for US$2 a day.

With advance notice, Andrea will try to arrange dance (salsa, merengue, and *típico*) and Spanish language lessons for guests. The Purple House also sometimes offers a free or discounted bed in exchange for volunteering at the hostel. Andrea can sometimes arrange transfers to Boca Chica if there's enough guest interest.

Bambu Hostel (Calle de La Virgencita, San Mateo Abajo, tel. 730-2961, www.bambuhostel.com, starts at US$8.80 pp), which opened in 2008, is in a rather bare house with a big backyard close to the Interamericana. It offers 8-bed and 12-bed dorms with thin mattresses and floor fans as well as four private rooms with air-conditioning (US$27.50 s/d). Some rooms have private bathrooms. The best thing about this place is the swimming pool in the backyard, which measures about 4 by 6 meters. There's free Wi-Fi, Internet computers for guest use, a shared kitchen, and a barbecue in the backyard. Camping is available in the backyard for US$5 a night.

The management is new to the area and Panama in general, so local information and insider tips are sparse, though this may change in time. Guests seem to be largely left to their own devices here, which may suit some people just fine. The hostel is a little tricky to find. It's close to the Santa Rosa sugar factory.

US$25-50

Hotel Toledo (Avenida 9 de Enero/1 Este between Calle D Norte and Calle E Norte, tel. 774-6732, 774-6733, 775-0694, or 775-2446, starts at US$25 s, US$27.50 d) has 39 old but well-maintained rooms, some with good beds. Try the mattresses in several rooms. All rooms have air-conditioning, a phone, and cable TV. There's a restaurant/bar attached.

The **Hotel Iris** (Calle A Norte between Avenida Bolívar/3 Este and Avenida 3 de Noviembre/4 Este, tel. 775-2251, hotel_iris-panama@hotmail.com, US$20 s/d with fan, US$30 with air-conditioning) was renovated a few years back and now has decent rooms with okay beds, telephones, and slightly grungy but passable bathrooms. The best thing about it is its location right on Parque Cervantes, with balconies from which to people-watch. Rooms 223, 245, 346, and 266 overlook the park, but they're also likely to be the loudest rooms in the place. Since the balcony is shared and the bar/restaurant also has a balcony, it might be better to go for a room at the back of the hotel and sit outside when the spirit moves you. Rooms are fairly small, but there are bigger ones for a few dollars more. This is a good value for budget travelers, especially if you can do without air-conditioning, which is tough in David.

Hotel Occidental (Avenida 3 de Noviembre/4 Este between Calle A Norte and Calle B Norte, tel. 775-4068, 775-4695 or 775-8340, fax 775-7424, US$20.90 s, US$26.40 d), on the southeast side of Parque Cervantes, seems older than its 20 years, but offers 61 well-maintained and clean rooms with air-conditioning and phones. One nice feature is the spacious balcony that overlooks the plaza. There's an authentically retro vibe about the place that gives it character.

Hotel Alcalá (Avenida 3 Este/Bolívar between Avenida Obaldía and Calle D Norte, tel. 774-9018, 774-9019, or 774-9020, fax 774-9021, http://hotelalcalapanama.com, US$25 s, 27.50 d) is a newish, modern hotel that offers 55 pleasant rooms with air-conditioning, cable TV, and phones. Surprisingly, the mattresses aren't very comfortable. The hotel is close to the public market and has a restaurant that's open until around 10:30 P.M. daily.

Hotel Iberia (Calle B Norte and Avenida 1 Oeste, tel. 777-2002 or 775-7395, fax 774-1950, hoteliberia@hotmail.com, US$31.90 s/d) opened in 2002 with 34 spare but modern, comfortable, and clean rooms with air-conditioning, cable TV, and telephones. The hotel has a computer with free Internet access and a bar and restaurant. This place is a good value.

❰ Hotel Castilla (Calle A Norte between Avenida 2 Este and Avenida 3 Este/Bolívar, tel. 774-5236, 774-5260, 774-5261, or 774-5262, fax 774-5262, www.hotelcastillapanama.com, US$44 s/d) remains popular with business travelers and is the best option for those who want a quiet, comfortable place in the heart of town (it's across the street from Parque Cervantes). The Castilla offers 68 pleasant, clean rooms with air-conditioning, phones, and cable TV. It's my favorite place to stay in David. It stays comfortingly the same: spotless, well-maintained, and a good deal. (In practice, rates are often less than those listed, especially for singles.) My only gripe is that the "hot water" is never more than lukewarm, though that doesn't matter too much in a sweltering place like David. A few rooms have balconies. The hotel has an underground, gated car park, which is a plus for those driving these busy streets. The restaurant here is decent but nothing special. Dollar-fed Internet computers are in the lobby. This place fills up, so make reservations at least a day ahead of time if possible.

US$50-100

The **Gran Hotel Nacional** (Calle Central between Avenida Central and Avenida 9 de Enero/1 Este, tel. 775-2221 or 775-2222, fax 775-7729, http://hotelnacionalpanama.com, starts at US$74.80 s, US$85.80 d) was for decades the fanciest place in town, with 75 rooms and suites, a swimming pool, a casino, a poolside barbecue restaurant, a cafeteria, a pizzeria, and a six-screen theater that shows first-run movies. It's designed to vaguely resemble a Spanish-colonial hacienda, with red-tile roofs, white-washed walls, and breezy corridors.

This place inspires strong opinions. Some hate it, usually because they've encountered rude service. The hotel is an institution that for decades could rest on its laurels as *the* place to stay in western Panama, which has given some of the staff the people skills of grumpy government bureaucrats. Others rave about it, though one suspects they're unaware of the other lodging options in David these days.

Rooms are large but rather spare, with cheap furniture and beds that can feel like padded planks. Try the mattresses before committing to a room.

The Gran Hotel Nacional is definitely more *gran* than most of the competition, but it's overpriced and needs a makeover. Everything but the swimming pool is open to the public, so there's no reason to stay here just for the movie theaters and so forth. There are more comfortable places to stay for almost half the price.

Hotel Best Western David (Calle 3 between Avenida A and Avenida B Sur, tel. 777-0000, bestwesterndavid@email.com, www.bestwestern.com,, starts at US$88 s/d, including breakfast) is an eight-story, 108-room hotel in what for several years was the derelict Hotel El Rey. It's been thoroughly refurbished and reopened in November 2009. Rooms are simple but pleasant and modern, with flat-screen TVs and expansive views of the not terribly photogenic David downtown, with a glimpse of the mountains in the distance. An extra US$11 buys a "suite," which is a somewhat bigger room with a bathtub. There's an Italian restaurant, a wine bar, a business center, and a gym. The hotel is managed by an English-speaking couple from Florida.

Over US$100

The most luxurious place in town is the new ◖ **Hotel Ciudad de David** (Calle D Norte between Avenida 9 de Enero/1 Este and Avenida 2 Este, tel. 774-3333, www.hotelciudaddedavid.com, starts at US$137.50 s/d), a six-storied, twin-towered, mirrored-glass business hotel with 103 rooms. Opened in late 2009, it's a quiet, air-conditioned oasis in the middle of busy, muggy David. The service from the staff, clearly proud to work at the best hotel in town, is formal but cordial. Rooms are modern, attractive, and tastefully decorated, with flat-screen TVs, mini-bars, in-room safes, and free Wi-Fi. Security is good here: a card key is needed to operate the elevators, and rooms

---

HIDDEN FAVORITE

Though it's not conveniently located close to anything, especially for those without their own transportation, **Marisquería Nueva Sol de Mar** (tel. 770-6841, 11:30 A.M.-midnight or later daily US$5-10) is a great place for well-prepared but reasonably priced seafood. It's an open-air place on the north side of the Interamericana just west of Concepción and almost exactly midway between David and the Costa Rican border (about 23 kilometers from either). The *langostinos* (prawns) are delicious. It's a rather cozy place with a large bar area in the back.

---

are equipped with smoke detectors and sprinklers. One of the rooms is equipped with disability aids.

A good-sized, attractive pool nestles between the towers on the 3rd floor. Other amenities include a business center, a ritzy-looking restaurant and bar, and a small gym, complete with a sauna for those who can't be bothered to get a natural sauna by merely stepping outdoors.

FOOD
Restaurants and Cafés

Dining options are slowly getting better in David. But there's still only one place where you might describe the food as "cuisine" without snickering. The best you can hope for at most places is to fill up with cheap, inoffensive fare. There are also lots of gringo and local fast-food outlets. Most are located along Calle Miguel A. Brenes, which is quite a hike from downtown. Closer to Parque Cervantes, in central David, most dining options are in the hotels.

The casinos serve a full lunch, including drink, for about US$3.30. These are popular with budget travelers. The Fiesta Casino, across the street from the Gran Hotel Nacional, is centrally located.

The best place to eat in David is, bizarrely

enough, at the airport. **Bernard's** (tel. 6674-5913, 6 A.M.–5 P.M. Mon.–Sat., under US$10) is a simple but attractive international café, the latest creation of Bernard Bahary, an Iranian expat who for many years was the chef/owner of one of the best restaurants in Bocas. He's gambling that David's airport is really going to take off as an international hub.

The menu is eclectic, ranging from Thai and Middle Eastern cuisine to pasta, burgers, Panamanian food, and daily specials. The prices are a bargain for the quality of the food offered. Breakfast with a bottomless cup of coffee or tea is served all day. Breakfast offerings are equally wide-ranging, from waffles with fresh fruit to a hearty Panamanian country breakfast. Everything I've ever had at one of Bernard's restaurants has been excellent. Bernard himself is reason enough to stop by—he's an interesting and sophisticated character, with the emphasis on "character."

Because the restaurant has to close when the airport does, it's not a place for dinner (unless you dine before 5 P.M.). Call ahead of time if possible, as the restaurant's actual opening hours seem to depend on Bernard's mercurial moods.

Restaurante El Palacio Oriental (Calle E Norte and Avenida Central, tel. 777-2410, 10 A.M.–11 P.M. daily, US$2.50–6) is a longtime favorite for Chinese food, served in a bustling atmosphere. The menu is huge.

The no-frills **Restaurante 24 Horas** (Avenida 2 Este between Calle Central and Calle A Norte, tel. 774-0412, open 24 hours daily), formerly Churrasco's Place, is around the corner from the Hotel Castilla. It's popular for its cheap, simple *criolla* (local) food. You can stuff yourself silly with tasty but greasy food for around US$2. Prices top out around US$6. This is a good place to have *arroz con pollo* (chicken and rice). It's also an authentic place to sample traditional Panamanian breakfast fare, including *hojaldres* (a sort of fried bread) and *tortillas de maiz* (thick fried corn tortillas). This is a good place to mingle with the locals, but it's not particularly clean and you'll have to put up with desultory service.

There are three dining options at the **Gran Hotel Nacional** (Calle Central between Avenida Central and Avenida 9 de Enero/1 Este, tel. 775-2221 or 775-2222). The cafeteria (6:30 A.M.–11 P.M. daily, under US$10) offers pizza, pasta, and fancier than usual meats and fish. On Monday–Saturday noon–2 P.M., the cafeteria offers a great deal: an all-you-can-eat buffet of pretty good food and a glass of wine for US$7.50. The buffet includes several salads, a variety of meat and fish dishes, some veggies, and several desserts. On Sunday noon–2:30 P.M., there's a popular brunch buffet with a glass of champagne for US$8.50. The hotel's pizzeria is open 11:30 A.M.–10:30 P.M. daily. At night there's a pleasant open-air barbecue (5–11 P.M. daily, around US$15) under a *rancho* by the pool, with a variety of grilled meats. Save room for the delicious strawberry ice cream.

The restaurant at the **Hotel Castilla** (Calle A Norte between Avenida 2 Este and Avenida 3 Este/Bolívar, tel. 774-5236 or 774-5260, 7 A.M.–10 P.M. Mon.–Sat., 7 A.M.–3 P.M. Sun., US$5–10) is pleasant enough and the food is decent. It's worth eating here just for the fascinating "English" translations of the dishes. You can feast on such mysterious delicacies as "beef steak in the horse," "rice with sailor," or "filet of fish in the white lady." Yum. Breakfasts are big and plentiful, but the coffee is awful.

El Rincón Libanes (Calle Miguel A Brenes, Calle F Sur, and Avenida 9 de Enero/Avenida 1 Este, tel. 774-2700, 11 A.M.–midnight daily) offers a reasonable approximation of Lebanese food in a pleasant and lovingly decorated, air-conditioned setting. It's not uncommon to see a table of Middle Eastern immigrants discussing business and sucking on hookahs at the table next to you. Full Lebanese meals go for around US$8, and a variety of pita-bread sandwiches are available for about US$5. My main gripe about this place is that the breads are reheated in the microwave, which turns them into leather as they cool.

Lots of cheap rotisserie chicken and snack places come and go along this same busy corridor, near El Rincón Libanes. A popular option is **Restaurante y Deli Pollo** (tel. 777-4108, noon–midnight daily), which offers a roasted half-chicken with *patacones* or *yuca* for US$4.30.

€ Jackelita (Calle E Norte between Avenida 1 Oeste and Avenida Central, tel. 774-6574, 7:30 A.M.–10 P.M. Sun.–Fri., 4–10:30 P.M. Sat.) is a simple open-air drive-in near Restaurante El Palacio Oriental that's locally famous for its homemade ice cream, yogurt, and juices. They're all made with fresh fruit, including *zarzamora* (blackberry), *guanábana* (usually called "soursop" in English, if that helps), *piña* (pineapple), mango, *fresa* (strawberry), and both *pipa* and *coco* (fresh and dry coconut). The yogurt isn't on the menu, oddly enough, but the place has got tons of it. This is a great place on a hot day (i.e., every day). Try the *yogurt de fresa*—it's delicious. It also carries *duros,* a kind of fruit popsicle in a cup I have fond memories of from my childhood in Panama. Jackelita also makes cheap breakfasts and fast food, including burgers and chicken. Nearly everything on the menu is less than US$2.

Ristorante e Pizzeria Tamburrelli (Avenida 3 de Noviembre/4 Este and Calle E Sur, tel. 774-4951, 11:30 A.M.–11 P.M. Sun.–Thurs., 11:30 A.M.–midnight Fri.–Sat.) is a popular Italian fast-food place with an air-conditioned interior and a few outside tables overlooking a busy street. The food is comparable to that at a U.S. pizza-chain outlet. The pizza isn't great—it's greasy and somewhat sweet—but it's tasty enough for the price if you need gringo comfort food. Pastas, seafood, meats, and desserts are also available. Prices are around US$4 for an individual-size pizza, around US$6 for pasta. This place delivers locally.

An outlet of the Mexican chain **Mrs. Mendoza** (Interamericana, tel. 730-4999, 11 A.M.–11:30 P.M. daily) is on the Interamericana, a short drive west of the David Mall. It's a fast-food joint, but it has tastier Mexican food than most of the other places around here, plus it has free Wi-Fi. A taco or burrito platter is around US$6–7, but if you like chips you'd better order extra because they're pretty stingy with them.

The brave can try the "Chicago-style burrito," whatever the heck that is. The mind reels. They deliver locally.

The Hare Krishna-run **Refresquería Bolo Bolo** (Avenida Central between Calle C Sur and Calle D Sur, tel. 730-4568, noon–9 P.M. Tues.–Sat., US$5) is a vegetarian place offering veggie burgers, falafel, fruit salad, shakes, smoothies, and so on at reasonable prices. Nothing about the veggie burger and fries I had here looked homemade, but they were tasty nonetheless and the buns, salad, and cooking oil were all fresh. Smoothies are also good. This is a pleasant, clean, air-conditioned little café, and a welcome addition to David. The only real problem with this place is the monotonous devotional music the owners insist on playing on the stereo. It becomes unbelievably irritating after the first minute.

Markets and Supermarkets
The two city markets downtown closed in 2010, scattering vendors around the city, at least temporarily. Until they find a permanent home, the vendors can be found in makeshift stalls around the Terminal de Transportes and the Palacio Municipal.

However, **Mercado San Mateo** (Calle Miguel A. Brenes/Calle F Sur between Avenida 3 Oeste and Avenida 4 Oeste, 5 A.M.–9 P.M. daily) has a brand-new building right behind its old home. It's a fresh fruit and vegetable market within walking distance of the Purple House Hostel. At night vendors set up huge vats of oil and cook fried-death snacks until 5 the next morning.

Super Barú (Interamericana and Avenida Obaldía, 7 A.M.–midnight Mon.–Sat., 8 A.M.–10 P.M. Sun.) is a large grocery store with a bakery, gringo-oriented packaged foods, and good veggies. It also has a pharmacy and a bank with an ATM.

There's a 24-hour **El Rey** supermarket with a pharmacy across the Interamericana from Super Barú.

Super 99 (Calle Miguel A. Brenes/F Sur near Avenida 5 Oeste, 24 hours daily) is a large grocery store with a pharmacy and ATM.

Supermercado Romero (a half block northeast of Calle Miguel A. Brenes/F Sur between Avenida 2 Oeste and Avenida 3 Oeste, 24 hours daily) is a grocery and dry goods store behind the McDonald's on Calle Miguel A. Brenes. It has a bakery, pharmacy, and ATM. It cashes travelers checks.

There's another **Romero** (Calle A Norte and Avenida 3 de Noviembre/Avenida 4 Este, 8 A.M.–midnight Mon.–Sat., 9 A.M.–6 P.M. Sun.) at the south end of Parque Cervantes. It's mainly a department store, but it has an attached grocery and pharmacy.

The **Do-It Center** (Interamericana, tel. 775-3648, 9 A.M.–8 P.M. daily), a DIY store next to the El Rey on the Interamericana, carries outdoor gear such as rain ponchos, lightweight sleeping bags, rather flimsy life jackets, and cheap (in both senses) tents.

INFORMATION AND SERVICES
Tourist Information

The local **ATP office** (Avenida Central and Calle 6 Este, tel. 775-4120, 8:30 A.M.–4:30 P.M. Mon.–Fri.) is in the Barrio Bolívar, near the Museo de Historia y de Arte José de Obaldía, but don't expect much from it. There's also an ATP booth at the airport.

The regional office for **ANAM** (tel. 775-2055 or 775-3163, 8 A.M.–4 P.M. Mon.–Fri.) is on the road to the airport. Heading into town from the airport it'll be on the right. Hikers can get permits to visit Parque Internacional La Amistad and Parque Nacional Volcán Barú here (US$5 to enter, another US$5 to camp), but it usually makes more sense to get them at the ranger stations in the highlands.

Medical Services

There's a huge **Farmacia Arrocha** (7 A.M.–9:45 P.M. daily) on the Interamericana next to the Do-It Center and El Rey (a supermarket that also has a pharmacy, which is open 24 hours a day).

Farmacia Revilla (Calle B Norte between Avenida 3 Este/Bolívar and Avenida 3 de Noviembre/4 Este, tel. 775-3711, 7 A.M.–11 P.M.

Mon.–Sat., 8 A.M.–10 P.M. Sun.) is a large pharmacy on the northeast side of Parque Cervantes that sells lots of general goods as well.

Hospital Chiriquí (Calle Central and Avenida 3 Oeste, tel. 774-0128 or 775-8999, fax 774-0144, hchiriqui@pananet.com) is a modern hospital with a 24-hour pharmacy. A comparable option is **Centro Médico Mae Lewis** (Interamericana near Calle B Sur, tel. 775-4616).

Receiving and Sending Money

There are now ATMs pretty much everywhere in David, as well as tons of banks. A branch of **HSBC** (8 A.M.–3:30 P.M. Mon.–Fri., 9 A.M.–noon Sat.) is across the street from the post office. It has an ATM.

A **Banco Nacional de Panamá** (Calle B Norte between Avenida 3 Este/Bolívar and Avenida 3 de Noviembre/4 Este, 8 A.M.–3 P.M. Mon.–Fri., 9 A.M.–noon Sat.) with an ATM is at the northeast side of Parque Cervantes.

Global Bank (Calle A Norte between Avenida 9 de Enero/1 Este and Avenida 2 Este, 9 A.M.–3 P.M. Mon.–Fri., 9 A.M.–noon Sat.; ATM booth 10 A.M.–5 P.M. Mon.–Fri., 9 A.M.–2 P.M. Sat.) is near the Hotel Castilla.

Post Office

The post office (Avenida 3 de Noviembre/4 Este and Calle C Norte, 7 A.M.–5:30 P.M. Mon.–Fri., 7 A.M.–4:30 P.M. Sat.) is one block northeast of the plaza.

Internet Services

Internet places open and close all the time in David. Most charge US$0.50–0.75 an hour. Two popular 24-hour places are **Planet Internet** (Avenida Bolívar/3 Este and Calle Central/E. Pérez Ballardares, 24 hours daily), across the street from the Hotel Puerta del Sol, and **Pars Computer Technology** (Calle Miguel A. Brenes/F Sur near Avenida 5 Oeste, tel. 774-7510, 24 hours daily), next to Restaurante Jenny #19. If they go out of business, there are plenty of others nearby. Many hotels also have Internet computers, and, increasingly, free Wi-Fi.

Immigration Office and Costa Rican Consulate

Those who need their visa extended can apply at the **Migración y Naturalización office** (Calle C Sur and Avenida Central, tel. 775-4515 or 794-1332, fax 775-6823, 8 A.M.–3 P.M. Mon.–Fri.). It's in a residential area southwest of downtown. It's worth calling or visiting the office to get the latest requirements before starting on the laborious process since the particulars seem to change depending on the government in power, the immigration office, and the mood of the bureaucrat dealing with you.

Come first thing in the morning, bring a snack and something to read, and be prepared to spend at least half the day there. If you need anything laminated, several places in David can do it, but the easiest to find is probably **Librería Regional** (Avenida Bolívar/3 Este, on Parque Cervantes next to the church, 8 A.M.–6 P.M. Mon.–Sat.). Lamination costs about US$1 at the store's upstairs copy center.

El Jazmín (tel. 775-1084 and 774-6514, 7:30 A.M.–6 P.M. Mon.–Fri., 7:30 A.M.–1 P.M. Sat.), right next door to the immigration office, takes visa-sized carnet photos for US$2 for two, US$3 for four. The store also sells water and soft drinks, which will most likely be welcome while you wait (and wait) at the immigration office.

The **Costa Rican consulate** (Consulado de Costa Rica in Spanish, Calle C Norte and Avenida 9 de Enero/1 Este) has moved from the suburbs to the 2nd floor of a three-story office building downtown. It's now across the street from the *policlínica*.

Launderettes

There are few launderettes in the center of David, but it's worth checking the prices at your hotel to see if it'd be better just to let them do it. There are, however, several launderettes near the Hotel Toledo, not too far from the bus station. **Lavamático Los Primos** (Calle E Norte between Avenida Central and Avenida 9 de Enero/1 Este, no phone, 7 A.M.–8 P.M. Mon.–Sat., 9 A.M.–8 P.M. Sun.) washes and dries clothes for US$2.50.

GETTING THERE AND AWAY

David is the transportation hub for all of western Panama, with good connections to the highlands around Volcán Barú, Bocas del Toro, the Costa Rican border, and Panama City. It has a large bus terminal, a small but growing international airport, and outlets for major rental car agencies.

By Air

David's **airport** (off Avenida 3 de Noviembre/Avenida 4 Este, on the way to Pedregal), formally known as Aeropuerto Internacional de David "Enrique Malek," is less than five kilometers south of downtown. The airstrip is being lengthened with the idea of making the airport a true international hub. If all goes as planned, flights between David and the United States may be offered by the time you visit. This may affect the schedule of regional flights listed below as well; be sure to check ahead of time.

The only domestic service is between David and Bocas del Toro (Isla Colón, about 20 minutes, US$60) and Panama City (about one hour, US$106). Those who want to fly between David and Changuinola now must catch a connecting flight on Isla Colón. For all other destinations within Panama, passengers must go through Panama City. Air Panama offers three weekly flights to and from San José, Costa Rica (US$106, 10:30 A.M. Mon., Wed., and Fri.).

Aeroperlas (tel. 775-7779, www.aeroperlas. com) flies from David to Panama City and to Bocas del Toro (Isla Colón).

Aeroperlas/TACA has offices at the airport and around the corner from Hotel Puerta del Sol (Calle Central between Avenida 2 Este and Avenida 3 Este/Bolívar, 8 A.M.–5 P.M. Mon.–Fri., 8 A.M.–3 P.M. Sat., closed Sun.).

Aeroperlas flies to Panama City (7:55 A.M., 1:25 P.M., and 6:25 P.M. Mon.–Sat. and 1:25 P.M. and 6:55 P.M. Sun.) and to Bocas del Toro (Isla Colón, 11:50 A.M. Mon., Wed., and Fri.).

Air Panama (tel. 316-9000, www.flyairpanama.com) flies to Panama City (7:45 A.M., 1:15 P.M., and 5:15 P.M. Mon.–Fri.; 10:30 A.M.

and 5:15 P.M. Sat.; and 9:45 A.M. and 5:15 P.M. Sun.) and to San José, Costa Rica (10:30 A.M. Mon., Wed., and Fri.).

Several rental car companies—Thrifty, Hertz, Alamo, Dollar, Avis, Budget, and Hilary—have desks at the airport. Café Kotowa, a gourmet coffee producer based in the Chiriquí highlands, has a coffee bar at the airport with Starbucks-style drinks and prices. There is also an ATM.

By Bus

David's busy Terminal de Transportes is east of downtown on Avenida Estudiante, which begins near the corner of Avenida 2 Este and Avenida Obaldía. Buses for destinations throughout Chiriquí province and the rest of the country leave from here.

There's a left-luggage facility (6 A.M.–8 P.M. daily) near the Caldera bus stall. Travelers can leave backpacks here for US$0.50, US$1 for larger suitcases.

There's a stark Internet café (7 A.M.–6 P.M. Mon.–Fri., 7 A.M.–4 P.M. Sat.) in the bus terminal that offers Internet access for US$0.50 a hour. Those in need of visa-sized photos can have them taken here for US$1 for a half-dozen prints.

The following are some of the more popular routes:

Almirante (Bocas del Toro): Almirante is a port town, the jumping-off point for water taxis to the archipelago of Bocas del Toro. Buses run every 30 minutes, 3 A.M.–7 P.M., but to catch the last water taxi to Bocas (they run only during daylight hours) take the 2 P.M. bus at the very latest. Even that is cutting it close; to be safe, take an earlier bus. Those who miss the last water taxi will have to spend the night in or around Almirante, which has severely limited accommodations and appeal. The trip takes about four hours and costs US$7. Note that the bus stops at the crossroads outside of Almirante, and it's a long walk to the water-taxi pier. A taxi from the crossroads costs US$0.50 per person and is well worth it. Passengers crossing the Costa Rican border at Guabito-Sixaola can continue on to Changuinola for another US$1.

© WILLIAM FRIAR

Ngöbe-Buglé coffee pickers fill the David bus terminal the Sunday before the new school year starts.

Boquete: Buses run every 20–25 minutes, 5:50 A.M.–9:45 P.M., though slightly less frequently in the evenings. The trip takes 45 minutes and costs US$1.45.

Changuinola: Those crossing into Costa Rica at the Guabito-Sixaola crossing must first get to Changuinola. Buses run every 30 minutes, 4 A.M.–7 P.M. The trip takes about 4.5 hours and costs US$8. (Same schedule on the way back.)

Las Lajas (town): Buses leave at 11:45 A.M., 12:45 P.M., 4:25 P.M., and 5:20 P.M. and return at 2:15 P.M. and 3:15 P.M. The trip takes 1.5 hours and costs US$2.25. Note that the town is eight kilometers from the beach, which means you'll have to take a taxi, if you can find one. The bus timing doesn't work well for beachgoers, especially those who don't plan to spend the night. A better option is to take a San Felix or Tolé bus to El Cruce de San Felix (US$2.25), the crossroads that leads into Las Lajas, and then take a taxi (US$4) to the beach from there. San Felix and Tolé buses leave about every hour, 7 A.M.–6:50 P.M., but their schedules are staggered so there's a departure every 30 minutes most of the day. Buses are somewhat more frequent on the weekend.

Panama City: Two companies run large air-conditioned buses between David and Panama City. The fare on either is US$12.60 one way, or US$15 for an express bus. The trip is supposed to take about 6.5 hours, but buses often run late. The bus makes stops at provincial towns along the Interamericana, most notably Aguadulce, Penonomé, and Santiago. Other stops are made by request. In Santiago, buses generally take a half-hour break at the Hotel Pyramidal or Centros Los Tucanes complex, each of which has a cafeteria, restaurant, bathrooms, pharmacy, ATM, and other services.

Especially on the expresses, those heading somewhere short of Panama City should ask the ticket seller—and double-check with the driver—that the bus will, in fact, stop at that destination.

Note that these companies frequently shift their schedules, so call ahead if you want to

ensure getting the bus you need. However, there's almost always a bus to Panama City within the hour, especially during the day.

Terminales David-Panama (tel. 775-7074 or 775-2974, tel. 775-2923 for cargo, terminal@cwpanama.net) is a large bus company and the main way those without their own wheels travel between David and Panama City. It has its own air-conditioned waiting room at the bus terminal. Its schedule changes slightly from time to time, but it generally departs every 1–1.5 hours, 3 A.M.–midnight. The 3 A.M., 10:45 P.M., and midnight buses are expresses.

Padafront (tel. 774-9205) has departures every 1–2 hours, 7:15 A.M.–midnight. The 11 P.M. and midnight buses are expresses.

Paso Canoa: This is the main border crossing with Costa Rica, and buses have *frontera* (border) written on the front. They run continuously 6 A.M.–8 or 9 P.M. daily. The trip takes about 75 minutes and costs US$1.75. The Padafront buses from Panama City also continue from David to the border.

Puerto Armuelles: Those heading to Punta Burica must first get to this port town. Buses run every 15–30 minutes, 4 A.M.–10 P.M. The trip takes about 2.5 hours and costs US$3.

Playa Barqueta: Take a Guarumal bus at 7 A.M., 8:20 A.M., 11:20 A.M., 1:20 P.M., 3:20 P.M., or 6:20 P.M. Check with driver about return times, as these vary during the year.

Río Sereno: This little-used border crossing with Costa Rica is in the Chiriquí highlands. Take this bus to get to Finca Hartmann (about 2.5 hours into the trip, US$3.65). The trip all the way to Río Sereno takes a little under three hours and costs US$4.25.

San José, Costa Rica: Agencia Tracopa (David tel. 775-7269 or 775-0585, Paso Canoa tel. 727-6581, San José, Costa Rica tel. 506/222-2666) has one bus departure to San José daily, at 8:30 A.M. The trip takes about eight hours and costs US$15. The bus lets passengers off at the Coca-Cola bus terminal in San José. Be careful on arrival in San José, as the area around the terminal is considered unsafe. Also note that Costa Rican time is always one hour behind Panama time. Tracopa has an office at the David bus terminal (7:30 A.M.–noon and 1–4 P.M. Mon.–Fri., 7:30 A.M.–2 P.M. Sat., and 7:30 A.M.–noon Sun.).

Volcán, Bambito, Cerro Punta, and Guadalupe: Look for the minibuses with "Cerro Punta" on the windshield. These make all the highland stops on the west side of Volcán Barú. Buses generally continue past Cerro Punta all the way up to Guadalupe, but ask to be sure. Fares are US$2.50 to Volcán, US$2.75 to Bambito, and US$2.90 to Cerro Punta/Guadalupe. The trip all the way up takes about two hours. Buses run every 15 minutes, 5 A.M.–8 P.M. daily.

By Car

David is just south of the Interamericana. Depending on road conditions, it takes about 7–8 hours to drive the nearly 450 kilometers between David and Panama City at a reasonable clip with few stops. It takes a little over an hour to drive between David and the Costa Rican border crossing at Paso Canoa.

The road is a mostly well-maintained divided highway from Panama City to Santiago. From Santiago to David, it's mostly a two-lane road, though it's recently been repaired and now features the occasional passing lane.

The drive between David and Santiago is through lovely countryside, with little but farmland, blue sky, and, close to David, rolling hills that lead to fog-shrouded mountain ranges in the distance. Passengers should keep their eyes open for the occasional mammoth waterfall pouring down from those mountains. Drivers should keep their eyes on the road.

Consider stopping for a break east of David at the Ngöbe-Buglé artisan stands set up along the Interamericana near the town of Tolé.

There are few gas stations between Santiago and David; fill up before driving anywhere in western Panama.

RENTAL CARS

It's easy to rent a car in David. Those wanting a four-wheel drive should book a reservation as far ahead of time as possible, as these are popular and can be in limited supply. Rental cars cannot be taken across the Costa Rican border. The companies listed have outlets both in town and at the airport.

- **Avis:** tel. 774-7075 or 774-7076, airport tel. 771-0844, fax 774-7250, www.avis.com.pa

ROAD SAFETY

Many of the highland roads are newly resurfaced and in great shape. Ironically, that can make them even more dangerous than usual. New roads are oily, and the lack of potholes encourages drivers to see how fast they can take those hairpin turns. If you drive, be extremely careful. Honk the horn at blind curves. Drive with low beams and hazard lights even in the daytime. (Don't forget to turn them off when you park.) If you're visiting in the rainy season, try to drive in the morning, when you're less likely to be hit by torrential rains. If at all possible, stay off the roads at night or when it's foggy.

If you take a taxi, don't be shy about asking your driver to slow the heck down. Remember, you're paying. A firm *"Despacio, por favor"* (des-PAW-see-o, por-fah-VOR) should get results. If you take a bus, just shut your eyes and hope for the best.

Gringo paranoia? Nope. One road in the highlands – fortunately, not one you're likely to take – is nicknamed La Carretera de la Muerte (Death Highway). Another one has a sign tallying the dozens of annual fatalities along a single stretch of road. I learned to drive on Panamanian roads and have the local survival skills, yet on a trip to Cerro Punta a few years back my car was totaled by a speeding, hydroplaning truck coming down the mountain. The 3.5-hour wait for the cops on a dark, rainy night gave ample time to wonder what would have happened if someone had been hurt, which luckily no one was.

- **Budget Rent A Car:** tel. 775-5597 or 775-1667, airport tel. 721-0845, fax 775-1667, www.budgetpanama.com

- **Dollar:** tel. 721-1103, www.dollarpanama.com

- **Hertz:** tel. 775-8471, www.rentacarpanama.com

- **Hilary Rent A Car:** tel. 775-5459 (no website)

- **National Car Rental:** tel. 721-0974, www.nationalpanama.com

- **Thrifty Car Rental:** tel. 721-2477, airport tel. 721-2478, www.thrifty.com

GETTING AROUND

Downtown David is concentrated in a small, congested area, so walking is the most practical way to get around. The rest of the town is sprawling, however, and those who walk for any distance in the daytime can get broiled quickly. The best way to get around is by taxis, which are everywhere. A ride most places in town costs US$1–1.25 for one person. Additional passengers are an extra US$0.25 per person. Drivers are also allowed to add a US$0.25 surcharge for night trips. The fare from the town center to the airport is US$2 per person. A trip to Pedregal, David's entryway to the Pacific Ocean, is US$3.

The only area bus one may want to fool with goes to the riverside port of Pedregal. Buses leave outside the Multi Café near the town center, at Calle A Norte and Avenida 2 Este. They run constantly 6 A.M.–11 P.M. The fare is US$0.30.

WEST OF DAVID

There are a few notable places between David and the Costa Rican border, though they are not high on most people's list of tourist attractions. The industrial port of Puerto Armuelles is important in the shipment of bananas and oil, Paso Canoa is the major border crossing with Costa Rica, and Punta Burica is an extraordinarily remote spot for surfers who truly want to get away from absolutely everything.

Paso Canoa

This grim little frontier outpost has nothing to interest visitors, no places to stay, and sketchy-looking greasy spoons that will appeal only to the brave or starving. But many tourists are forced to visit it every day, as it is the main border crossing with Costa Rica. They spend as little time here as possible. It's become even uglier in recent years with an influx of stores selling cheap (in both senses of the word) goods to Costa Rican day-trippers.

As with the two other border crossings in western Panama, it's hard to tell where Costa Rica ends and Panama begins. A barren stretch of road is the only thing separating the two.

Immigration, customs, and an ATP government tourism office are housed in a cement monolith at the border. The main function of the **ATP office** (tel. 727-6524, 7 A.M.–11 P.M. daily) is to sell tourist cards for those entering from Costa Rica. As usual, it has little tourist information to offer.

There are two banks, a pharmacy, and a few places to eat down the road leading to Puerto Armuelles. As one faces Costa Rica, the road is on the left at the intersection just before the border crossing. Everything of interest is within a few hundred meters of the intersection. The **Banco Nacional de Panamá** (8 A.M.–3 P.M. Mon.–Fri., 9 A.M.–noon Sat.) is across the street from the Zona Libre Mall. Farther down the same street is a branch of **Banco Universal** (9 A.M.–5 P.M. Mon.–Fri., 9 A.M.–2 P.M. Sat.). Both banks have ATMs, but neither exchanges money.

Farmacia Tiffany #3 (no phone, 7:30 A.M.–10 P.M. daily) is up the street from Banco Nacional de Panamá.

GETTING THERE

There's a bus and taxi stand on the Panama side just east of the immigration/customs building. A taxi between Paso Canoa and David costs about US$25, but, if business is slow, haggling may be possible. However, bus service to downtown David is frequent and fairly quick. Buses run continuously 6 A.M.–8 or 9 P.M. The trip takes about 1.25 hours and costs US$1.75.

Padafront (Paso Canoa tel. 727-7230, David tel. 774-9205) has multiple buses to Panama City, with intermediate stops along the Interamericana. The trip takes 8–9 hours, somewhat less for an express. The fare is US$14, or US$17 for an express. Alternatively, travelers can take any bus to David and board a bus to Panama City there.

There's a small **Tracopa bus office** (7–11:30 A.M. and 12:30–4 P.M. Mon.–Sat., 7–11 A.M. Sun. and holidays) on the north side of the street between the Costa Rican and Panamanian immigration offices. It sells tickets to San José, Costa Rica, for US$10–11.80 (depending on number of stops). Buses leave at 4 A.M., 7:30 A.M., 9 A.M., and 4:30 P.M. Costa Rica time (one hour earlier than Panama time). But this office is mainly of interest to travelers looking to meet the "proof of onward travel" requirement to enter Panama. Tracopa offers a refundable US$12.50 open ticket that's good for three months. Some travelers simply buy the ticket, show it at the border, and cash it in at the Tracopa office at the David bus terminal. Note: Immigration officials are wise to this ruse and are beginning to crack down on it. If you try this, there's a chance of being turned away at the border or at least being forced to go back and buy a bus ticket with a firm date.

For those heading to Costa Rica who need *colones* (Costa Rican currency), next to the Tracopa office is a branch of **Banco de Costa Rica** (8 A.M.–5 P.M. Mon.–Sat., 8 A.M.–noon Sun.). It has an ATM. Other ATMs are nearby.

Those with their own transportation can just head straight on the Interamericana to get to David and points east.

Note: Panamanian police routinely stop cars on the highway between the Costa Rican border and David to check for smugglers, illegal immigrants, and, more prosaically, drunk or unlicensed drivers. This happens throughout the country but is more common west of Santiago. These checks are normal and no cause for alarm. Just make sure your papers are in order.

Punta Burica and Puerto Armuelles

The Burica Peninsula is a finger of land that separates Panama's Pacific coast from Costa Rica's. Most of the peninsula falls on the Panamanian side. At its very tip is Punta Burica, which consists of a stretch of sandy beach broken by occasional wide slabs of striated rock that reach out to sea. The shoreline is fringed by palm trees and the occasional fisherman's house. That's about it.

The beach itself isn't all that great. The only draw for visitors—other than the area's extreme isolation and the adventure of getting there—is the **surf.** This is still a spot little known to all but a few pioneering surf dudes and dudettes. Long, tubing waves break left along the tip of the point. I've been told there's usually something to ride, but the one time I visited the tip the sea was like glass, and at least one ex-pat who lived out there for years says the quality of the surf is overhyped. Have some kind of backup entertainment planned (picnic, games, cooler of liquid refreshment) in case the surf's not happening, as there is absolutely nothing else out there but sand and sea.

GETTING THERE

Access to Punta Burica is through Puerto Armuelles, a surprisingly tidy little town considering the especially rough times this sleepy little place has been through in recent years. It holds little of interest for visitors, though it has been the center of quite a bit of international economic activity as a port town fueled by the banana business and a nearby oil pipeline.

Note: This area is near the border, so remember to have all your papers in order, as there are frequent checkpoints along the Interamericana.

Buses to Puerto Armuelles leave from the David bus terminal every 15 minutes, 4 A.M.–10 P.M. (US$3, 2.5 hours). Buses makes the return trip to David 4 A.M.–9:30 P.M. Those driving should head west toward the border. At Paso Canoa, about 50 kilometers from David, make a left. Puerto Armuelles is another 40 kilometers south.

From Puerto Armuelles there are two ways to get to Punta Burica: by boat and by car. At the waterfront in Puerto Armuelles, it should be possible to hire a fisherman and his boat to go down to Punta Burica. Expect to pay about US$40 each way, just to get to the point. The trip takes about 1.5 hours.

It's also possible to get to Punta Burica by land, but this is even more of an adventure than a boat trip. A road is gradually being extended toward Punta Burica, but chances are good at least part of the trip will still involve driving on the beach itself.

There's a big old Ford pickup "bus" that makes the trip between Puerto Armuelles and Punta Burica at low tide. In central Puerto Armuelles, ask around for *el carro de la costa.* The fare is US$1.50.

It's also possible to drive oneself, but until and unless the road is completed the whole way, this requires some tricky off-road maneuvering. Only attempt it in a high-clearance four-wheel drive with a powerful engine. Don't go alone. For one thing, you'll need a second person to scout out the route at some points.

Drive west from Puerto Armuelles through the Petroterminal complex. The road ends at the beach. Drive on the damp sand, which is more solid and holds traction better. To make the trip the whole way, the tide has to be quite far out. Otherwise, you'll round a bend and find your way blocked by the sea. This is a hairy drive at times. There are some wide stretches of slippery, jagged, volcanic rock that have to be navigated. Here's where the scout comes in; have him or her hop out and plot a course.

Some of the worst bits toward the end can be avoided by taking a detour up a dirt loop road between the microscopic villages of Limones and Puerto Balsa. Ask anyone you see to point out the road, which can be hard to spot from

the beach. The road is rough and steep, leading through some desolate fields, but it's better than the rock obstacle course. Be sure to park well above the high-tide line.

Punta Burica itself is the tip of the peninsula. Costa Rica begins on the western side of the tip. This is a rather pretty spot, and it's certainly away from it all, but there's just about nothing here except a palm-lined beach and the sea. It may be possible to hire a fisherman at Puerto Balsa to run you out to Isla Burica for another US$30–40, if you're so inclined.

There are two places to stay way out here. The first is a simple nature reserve called **Mono Feliz,** run by a gringo character named John Garvey, better known locally as "Juancho." It seems to be living a twilight existence these days. Try emailing Juancho at juancho_3@hotmail.com or mono_feliz@hotmail.com, or just show up and take your chances.

A newer place is **Tigre Salvaje** (davidteichmann@yahoo.com, vielkateichmann@hotmail.com, www.tigresalvaje.com, US$50/person, including meals), a wildlife reserve and rehabilitation project at the end of Punta Burica. Talk about remote: After driving along the beach to the village of Bella Vista, it's a 45-minute hike or horseback ride to the reserve. I have not yet made it out to Tigre Salvaje, but it looks like a pretty cool project, with surprisingly modern guest facilities. Its aim is to help endangered species, particularly sea turtles and the red-backed squirrel monkey. The couple who run it are only able to check their email every couple of weeks; they say they will accommodate anyone who shows up unannounced, which is the spirit of adventure and flexibility you'll need to visit this remote spot.

Those planning just to camp on the beach should bring a tent, food, water, and supplies. There are no stores or restaurants of any kind in the area.

Boquete

The main attraction on the east side of Volcán Barú is Boquete (pop. 3,833 in central Boquete, 16,943 in the district), a cute little town and one of Panama's top tourist draws.

Boquete has long been famous in Panama for its coffee and oranges, and for a flower festival that each year draws thousands of visitors from around the country. As with Bocas del Toro, it was finally discovered in the late 1990s by foreign backpackers and other adventurous travelers, who were soon followed by older North Americans looking for a pleasant place to retire—and by developers and land speculators. In recent years, real-estate madness had reached such a pitch that some land in downtown Boquete was going for the same price as prime real estate in San Francisco, California. A woman who works as a maid for an acquaintance turned down a US$10 million offer for farmland owned by her campesino (peasant farmer) family. Her

father had worked hard to get that land, she explained, and he had made her vow never to sell it.

The gold-rush atmosphere has calmed down a bit, and some of the more disturbing housing developments have been stopped or slowed. Boquete is still booming and its few streets are now busy with too many cars in a hurry, but it stubbornly retains its charm. It's a peculiar kind of charm, as most of the buildings jumbled together downtown are not attractive and "urban planning" is as much an oxymoron here as anywhere else in Panama. But the setting makes it beautiful. It's in the middle of a picturesque valley surrounded by forested mountains and bordered on the east by the churning waters of the Río Caldera.

On a clear day, the Barú volcano dominates the landscape to the northwest. And those who venture beyond Boquete's main streets will discover the town itself is still laid-back, a relaxing

Boquete is one of the most popular spots in Panama for tourists and retirees.

© WILLIAM FRIAR

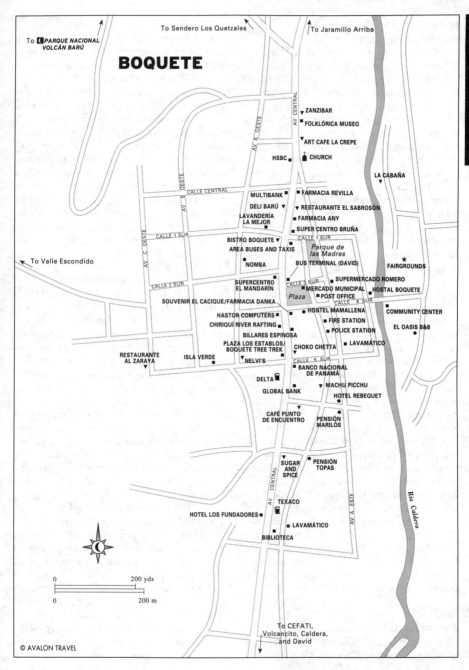

BOQUETE

To **☾** *PARQUE NACIONAL VOLCÁN BARÚ*

To Sendero Los Quetzales

To Jaramillo Arriba

ZANZIBAR

FOLKLÓRICA MUSEO

ART CAFE LA CREPE

HSBC

CHURCH

LA CABAÑA

CALLE CENTRAL

MULTIBANK

FARMACIA REVILLA

DELI BARÚ

RESTAURANTE EL SABROSÓN

LAVANDERÍA LA MEJOR

FARMACIA ANY

SUPER CENTRO BRUÑA

BISTRO BOQUETE

CALLE 1 SUR

AREA BUSES AND TAXIS

Parque de las Madres

To Valle Escondido

NOMBA

BUS TERMINAL (DAVID)

FAIRGROUNDS

CALLE 2 SUR

SUPERCENTRO EL MANDARÍN

SUPERMERCADO ROMERO

CALLE 3 SUR

MERCADO MUNICIPAL

HOSTAL BOQUETE

SOUVENIR EL CACIQUE/FARMACIA DANKA

Plaza

POST OFFICE

CALLE 4 SUR

COMMUNITY CENTER

HASTOR COMPUTERS

HOSTEL MAMALLENA

CHIRIQUÍ RIVER RAFTING

FIRE STATION

EL OASIS B&B

BILLARES ESPINOSA

POLICE STATION

PLAZA LOS ESTABLOS/ BOQUETE TREE TREK

CHOKO CHETTA

LAVAMÁTICO

RESTAURANTE AL ZARAYA

ISLA VERDE

NELVI'S

CALLE 5 SUR

BANCO NACIONAL DE PANAMA

DELTA

GLOBAL BANK

MACHU PICCHU

HOTEL REBEQUET

CAFÉ PUNTO DE ENCUENTRO

PENSIÓN MARILÓS

SUGAR AND SPICE

PENSIÓN TOPAS

AV CENTRAL

AV A ESTE

Río Caldera

TEXACO

HOTEL LOS FUNDADORES

LAVAMÁTICO

BIBLIOTECA

0 200 yds

0 200 m

To CEFATI, Volcancito, Caldera, and David

© AVALON TRAVEL

place to hang out and plan day trips to the many attractions nearby.

At a little over a kilometer above sea level, it doesn't get quite as chilly here as it does in the higher mountain towns on the west side of Barú, but it's still pleasantly cool compared to most of Panama, and it can sometimes get surprisingly cold. Expect the foggy drizzle known as *bajareque* year-round, which can be quite refreshing and produce stunning rainbows. Again, bring warm, waterproof clothes.

What most people think of as Boquete is officially **Bajo Boquete** (Lower Boquete). Its main drag is **Avenida Central,** which descends from Alto Boquete (Upper Boquete), runs north through town, and continues past a small church to the hills beyond. The plaza midway through town, on the east side of Avenida Central, is the town hub. Just east of it is a little square, **Parque de Las Madres,** with a statue depicting a mother with two small children who appear to be squirming in agony. Just south of it is another square with a cute fountain and a railroad car from the old train that used to run to the highlands.

A coffee tour, a stroll through Boquete's surreal gardens, a hike along a mountain trail, and a quest for quetzals are all worthwhile ways to spend time in this area. Try to find time to do them all. The most popular activities for outdoorsy types are white-water rafting, hiking the **Sendero Los Quetzales,** and climbing **Volcán Barú.** Areas near Boquete of possible interest to visitors include **Bajo Mono,** northwest of Bajo Boquete, which has a lovely loop road and the trailhead for Sendero Los Quetzales; **Caldera,** which is southeast of Boquete and has good hot springs, some petroglyphs, and a bunch of little waterfalls; and the road to **Volcancito,** which starts near the CEFATI building in Alto Boquete and has a couple of attractions, most notably **Paradise Gardens,** a lovely little wildlife refuge.

SIGHTS
Paradise Gardens
This wildlife sanctuary (cell 6615-6618, http://paradisegardensboquete.com, 10 A.M.–4 P.M.

Tues.–Sun., minimum donation of US$5 requested for adults, children free) is a must-see for anyone with any interest in Panama's flora and fauna. Located on the Volcancito road about 700 meters from the CEFATI in Alto Boquete, Paradise Gardens features a menagerie that could include Geoffrey's tamarins, howler monkeys, white-faced capuchins, a margay, parrots, a striking variety of macaws, kinkajous, (Australian) cockatoos, many butterflies, and other critters both domestic and imported. The mix changes because this is a wildlife rescue project filled with abandoned "pets" and the offspring of animals killed by hunters. It's run by volunteers. Taxis from downtown Boquete cost US$1. Look for the sign on the right past Fresas Mary.

El Explorador
This peculiar private garden (tel. 720-1989, cell 6627-6908, 9 A.M.–6 P.M. Fri.–Sun., US$3) in the hills above town is worth a visit if approached with a sense of humor. A winding path leads through two hectares of terraced land with orange and lemon trees, a rose garden, stands of papyrus, a bonsai nursery, and much more. But the human touches are what's most striking about this place. All kinds of junk—shoes, bottles, shopping carts, TVs—has been turned into planters. Cartoon eyes peer out from trees and topiary shrubs. Classical music is pumped throughout the place. And dotted around the garden are wise sayings and encouraging words in Spanish. One sign leads the way to the "greatest miracle in the world." When you get there, you find—what else?—a mirror. What starts off seeming kitschy ends up making you feel rather, well, loved. This is a good place to recharge your batteries. If you see gardeners, thank them: They take great pride in the place. There's a great view of the valley from the rose garden.

El Explorador is about three kilometers northeast of town, near La Montaña y el Valle: The Coffee Estate Inn. Head north through Boquete on Avenida Central, pass the church, and then take the right fork toward the Panamonte Inn and Spa. Look for the signs.

The road gets rocky toward the end, but a four-wheel drive isn't necessary if you're careful. It's also possible to walk from town, but it's uphill most of the way, steep at times. On days when the garden is officially closed, it may be possible to get in by appointment. There's a small food stand on the premises.

Mi Jardín Es Su Jardín

There must be something about the Boquete air that makes folks' dream gardens come out a little wacky. Mi Jardín Es Su Jardín (9 A.M.–5 P.M. daily, free)—My Garden Is Your Garden—is a formal garden as it might have been conceived by the designer of a miniature golf course. We're talking a topiary dinosaur, brightly painted cow statues, a toy windmill, and so on, set on a sloping lawn crisscrossed by fountains and artificial streams. There's an impressive view of the valley and surrounding mountains from the observation tower. It's a toss-up whether this garden or El Explorador is quirkier. The garden is on private land, but it's open to the public, no reservations necessary. From the plaza, head north on Avenida Central past the church, keeping left at the fork. You'll soon see the entrance on the right. Drivers must park outside.

◖ Finca Lérida

This is one of the more famous birding spots in Panama. Though a working coffee plantation that produces some of the finest coffee in Panama, the Finca Lérida (tel./fax 720-2285,

---

COFFEE 101: MADE IN THE SHADE

Boquete is coffee country, but as you look around you may wonder where they're hiding the farms. Scanning the hillsides, all you see are shady trees, particularly orange trees. Look closer: If it's a coffee farm, you'll see tall shrubs below the trees. In the picking season, these will have ripe, cherry-red berries. The seeds are coffee beans.

Most of the coffee here is shade-grown, a traditional method in which coffee bushes grow in the shade of a forest or among trees planted by farmers. Farther west, especially around Río Sereno near the Costa Rican border, coffee is grown in open fields. This method produces a greater yield, but conservationists say it's a poor trade-off.

They argue that trees protect the crop from pests, produce natural mulch, preserve the chemical balance of the soil, and prevent erosion. Shade-grown coffee therefore requires less pesticide and fertilizer and is less disruptive to the environment. The money saved on fertilizer helps offset the lower productivity of shade-grown coffee. Also, the trees provide a habitat for mammals and hundreds of bird species, particularly migratory birds. This habitat becomes ever more important as forests are cleared in coffee-producing countries. It's a pretty efficient

system. The pulp of the berry that surrounds the bean is even used as compost, and the dried husk encasing the bean is used as fuel.

In Boquete, orange trees are commonly planted along with coffee and provide an extra source of income for the farmers. This also helps make up for the lower productivity of the shade-grown method. You can almost always find good oranges in Boquete. Navel oranges grow eight or nine months out of the year. Valencias take over February–March.

But even eco-friendly coffee processing has its limitations. Processing uses a great deal of water, which is then flushed into the rivers. The runoff is filled with pulp and sugar compounds that upset the biological balance of the rivers and streams. In 2006, Panama enacted a law requiring the local coffee industry to purify their runoff before dumping it.

It's also hard to grow coffee completely organically. Few farms in Boquete use herbicides, but the orange trees attract Mediterranean fruit flies, which farmers do fight with pesticides. Still, the main enemy in the highlands is fungal disease, not insects. Because it's so wet up here, farmers plant coffee so that air flows through the rows of bushes, keeping everything a bit drier.

© WILLIAM FRIAR

There's something magical about Finca Lérida.

cell 6450-3848, www.fincalerida.com) contains 650 acres of primary and secondary forest that is home to hundreds of species of birds, as well as howler monkeys, peccaries, deer, and other mammals. There's a good chance of seeing resplendent quetzals here January–August. The *finca* (country house) is up in the hills of Alto Quiel northwest of town, in a setting so picturesquely alpine you may find yourself humming the theme from *The Sound of Music*. That's part of the secret of the coffee's success: It's grown at elevations of up to 1,600 meters, on the highest plantations in Panama.

Birding tours lead to a part of Lérida above the main estate, along a brutal road that leads through coffee and vegetable plantations that give way to dense, beautiful secondary cloud forest. The road ends at an even more gorgeous grove of primary forest, where you're likely to encounter quetzals, howler monkeys, and nasty mosquitoes.

Because Finca Lérida is private property and visitors must go with an authorized guide, this entry does not contain directions on how to get to the bird-watching spots at the *finca*. These are usually arranged through tour guides. Visitors can also book a tour directly through the *finca* that includes bird-watching, a nature walk, a tour of the coffee facilities, and lunch. Visitors can also hike a five-kilometer trail system (using a trail map) on the *finca*. The chances of spotting quetzals without a good guide, however, are not great.

Finca Lérida now has an ecolodge, B&B, and restaurant.

Coffee Tours

A tour of one of Boquete's many coffee operations is a pleasant way to spend a few hours, and it'll deepen your appreciation of the area and its people, not to mention the incredible amount of work that goes into that morning caffeine buzz. It's not necessary to be a coffee addict to enjoy one of these tours, but it does help.

The tour of **Café Ruiz** (just north of town on Avenida Central, tel. 720-1000, cell 6672-3786 and 6642-3786, www.caferuiz-boquete. com and www.caferuiz.com), Panama's largest producer of gourmet coffee, is best for those

THE BEST COFFEE IN THE WORLD?

© WILLIAM FRIAR

coffee beans drying the old-fashioned way: in the sun

Three years in a row, 2005-2007, a Panama coffee was voted the best in the world by the Specialty Coffee Association of America, the industry's largest trade association.

The marketplace has taken notice: The price of the coffee, La Esmeralda Especial, keeps setting records. In 2007, 10 132-pound bags of the coffee sold at auction for an astonishing US$130 a pound. By comparison, the coffee voted second best went for US$11.80 a pound. The coffee has become so popular the grower decided to put its entire 2008 harvest up for auction, even though La Esmeralda slipped to second best in the world that year. Today, it remains among the most sought-after coffee in the world.

Why all the fuss? La Esmeralda Especial is grown by the Peterson family, longtime Boquete residents whose Hacienda Esmeralda is one of Panama's finest coffee producers. Several years ago the family discovered it could brew an unusual-tasting cup of coffee from an arabica variety called geisha that had been growing neglected on one of its farms. Origi-nally from Ethiopia, geisha was introduced to Central America in the 1950s because it is disease resistant, but it never caught on be-cause the plants are low yielding. But in the age of the coffee aficionado, there is a market for this coffee.

Those who've tasted geisha coffee say it has a floral, citrusy taste that is strikingly different from that of other coffees. Hacienda Esmeralda currently produces about 200 132-pound bags of the Especial a year. Two other growers in Boquete, Garrido and Don Pachi, produce a small amount of geisha, but the total world supply is tiny at the moment. A few months after the 2007 auction, a coffee house in New York was selling La Esmeralda Especial for US$18 a cup. Not surprisingly, other Boquete growers are now planting their own geisha.

Prices are so high it's hard to find geisha in Panama; nearly all of it gets exported. If none is available in Boquete, visit www.haciendaes-meralda.com for a list of current retailers of La Esmeralda Especial.

who want a real nuts-and-bolts look at the whole coffee-production process.

The full tour (three hours, US$25 pp, 9 A.M. and 1 P.M. Mon.–Sat. or by special arrangement) takes visitors to one of Ruiz's coffee farms; through its impressive mill in Palmira, near Alto Boquete; and ends up at its roasting facility/coffee shop, where visitors can taste two of its coffees and see how the coffee is roasted, ground, and packaged. An alternative (90 minutes, US$20–25, 8 A.M. Mon.–Sat.) is a visit to the roasting facility that includes a brief lesson in how to recognize different kinds of coffee, followed by a "cupping" (coffee version of a wine-tasting). Reservations should be made in advance. Clients can also opt just for a 45-minute tour (US$7) of the roasting facility without the lesson and cupping. Prices for all tours include pickup and transportation. Sign up at the Ruiz coffee house or call for a reservation.

Café Kotowa (tel. 720-1430, www.kotowacoffee.com) offers a tour that is on a smaller scale but more charming and scenic.

COFFEE 101: IT'S ALL IN THE TIMING

Coffee in Boquete is normally harvested from October to February. The beans of the best coffee are sun dried, a process that takes 8-12 days. The beans are then stored for at least three months to cure them. The whole process is delicate; any misstep from bush to roaster can degrade the quality of the coffee.

Coffee is ready to sell in late March or early April. That's when the buyers come and the "cupping," the coffee equivalent of wine-tasting, begins. The different farms compete to see who will have the highest-rated crop that year.

April to June is the best time to come to Boquete if you want to taste ultra-fresh coffee. Even then, you should aim for coffee that's been roasted within the last two weeks, if possible. If you grind the beans, you've got two days to taste it at its best.

Its small mill is up in Palo Alto, a few kilometers north of Boquete. It faces a breathtaking view of Barú across rolling pasture. Behind the mill, coffee farms run far up the steep slopes of emerald hills until they're lost in the clouds. This is cloud-forest country, and it gets quite wet up here.

Kotowa is the Ngöbe word for "mountain," and the company is named in recognition of the indigenous people who work the farms. It's widely considered to make some of the finest coffee in Panama. The operation is owned by Ricardo Koyner MacIntyre, the grandson of a Scot who moved here from Canada after reading a newspaper article about Boquete in 1918. The original wooden coffee mill, powered by water and brought all the way over from Scotland, has been lovingly preserved and is part of the tour, as is the modern-day mill.

The tour concludes at an espresso bar in the wooden mill. **Coffee Adventures** (tel. 720-3852, cell 6634-4698, http://coffee-adventures.net) is the official tour operator for Café Kotowa. The excellent coffee tours are given by a Dutch couple, Hans van der Vooren and Terry van Niekerk. I've taken the tour with Hans, and his enthusiasm and good humor make learning about coffee beans a surprisingly entertaining experience. Tours last three hours and cost US$28.50 per person, two-person minimum, and include transportation from and to hotels and a coffee cupping at the end. Contact Coffee Adventures for reservations.

Finca Lérida (tel./fax 720-2285, cell 6450-3848, www.fincalerida.com) also offers tours of its coffee facilities, which consist of several quaint wooden buildings that house the coffee mill, the family, and a new hotel and B&B set in pretty countryside. It's a highly photogenic place.

Los Pozos de Caldera

These hot springs are a fair haul southeast of Boquete near the town of Caldera, famous in Panama as a home of cowboys and witches. Those who love hot springs will enjoy the Pozos

© WILLIAM FRIAR

petroglyphs near Caldera

de Caldera. Those who can take them or leave them will find the trip here a bit of a hassle for the payoff. That said, the springs are attractive, situated in a secluded stretch of forest near the bank of the roaring Río Chiriquí.

Unlike hot springs that belch forth a sulfurous stench, these barely smell at all. There are four pools. The first one is the warmest, supposedly 42°C (108°F). There's one closer to the river that's hard to spot but quite nice. It's not as warm as the first one, but it's surrounded by trees and is less developed (the others are lined with large, flat rocks).

Not far from the springs is a tributary to the Río Chiriquí that, if you don't mind quite a bit of scrambling over slippery rocks and muddy banks, you can follow upriver to five waterfalls, each more picturesque than the one before. This hike is best done with a guide. At the very least, as with any other forest hike in Panama, don't go alone. A dip in the hot springs is especially pleasant after splashing about in these brisk waters. Note: A hydroelectric dam is being planned for this area, though the builders say it won't affect the hot springs.

But ask any area resident if the springs are still there before venturing out this far.

To get to the *pozos* from Boquete, head south out of town on Avenida Central. After about 12 kilometers look for a blue sign that says Caldera. Turn left here and continue past the town of Caldera. Another blue sign indicates a right onto a gravel road. Those with a four-wheel drive can follow this road to within a 15-minute walk of the springs. Otherwise, park and hike the rest of the way, about a 40-minute walk. Do not leave anything of value in the car; cars get broken into around here. After crossing the cable-and-plank bridge, make a left turn uphill (there should be a sign). Make the first left at the barbed-wire gate, which is easy to miss because there's no sign. From here the springs are about 15 minutes straight down the trail. Admission is US$1, which goes to keeping the area clean. The caretaker will most likely find you. Warning: I've heard reports of an unscrupulous guy posing as the caretaker and collecting the admission, meaning that people have had to pay twice. If this happens to you, report it to the police and to the ATP staff at the CEFATI in Alto Boquete.

On the way to the hot springs, it's worth stopping to check out the **Piedra Pintada.** This is yet another huge, riverside boulder etched with mysterious squiggles by a pre-Colombian people about which little is known. Just before "downtown" Caldera, look for a "Piedra Pintada" sign on the right side of the road. Pull over and park. Duck under the barbed wire and bamboo fence behind the beer garden and walk across a pasture toward the water. Head in the direction of a metal post with the number 80 painted on it. On the left as you face the river is a three-meter-high boulder just above the river that is covered with crude faces and figures (and some modern-day idiots' graffiti).

Buses and taxis between Boquete and Caldera cost US$1.50 per person each way. Buses leave Boquete at 7 A.M., 10:45 A.M., 1 P.M., and 5 P.M., returning 8:30 A.M., 1:30 P.M., and 4 P.M.

ENTERTAINMENT AND EVENTS
Nightlife
Boquete is hurtin' for real nightlife. One hot spot is **Zanzibar** (Avenida Central, no phone, 5 P.M.–midnight or later daily), at the north end of Avenida Central. It's a cute and cozy place with an African safari theme. They have a Facebook page (http://bit.ly/zanzibarboquete) but no phone or website. Regular entertainment includes belly-dancing on Wednesdays, house music DJs on Fridays, and live music on Saturdays.

A newer place is **La Cabaña** (no phone), on the east side of the Caldera just north of the fairgrounds. It has a faux log-cabin look and keeps erratic hours. It's usually open on weekends starting at 9 P.M. and going all night long, much to the chagrin of everyone trying to sleep on that side of the river. Its Facebook page is here: http://bit.ly/cabanaboquete.

The nicest watering hole in town is the bar at the **Panamonte Inn and Spa** (tel. 720-1324, noon–11P.M. daily), which is now both cozy

and sleek. It's quite relaxing to sit with a drink at either of its two stone fireplaces (one indoors, one out). Be sure to check out all the antiques. The only unwelcome addition is a big-screen TV. **Bar Mr. George,** next to the bus station office on the north side of the plaza, is a blue-collar dive with zero atmosphere but a friendly, drunken vibe. A pool hall, **Billares Espinosa** (Avenida Central, no phone, 3 P.M.–midnight Mon.–Fri., 10 A.M.–midnight Sat.–Sun.) is on Avenida Central just south of the plaza.

Valle Escondido
This gated community (tel. 720-2454, www.valleescondido.biz) in a valley close to central Boquete attracts expatriate retirees from North America eager for insulated first-world living at prices made possible by a third-world setting. The valley itself is lovely, even though it now hosts a large housing development, a nine-hole golf course, a hotel, a gymnasium and spa, an amphitheater, a mini-mall, a couple of restaurants, a bar, etc., all built in a pseudo-Spanish mission style.

Some of the facilities are open to visitors, though the rules on this change from time to time. The community is a short drive west of Boquete. Heading north on Avenida Central, turn left on Calle 5a Sur, just before downtown, toward Isla Verde. Continue past the cabañas and follow the signs to the security checkpoint.

Fairs and Festivals
The **Feria de las Flores y El Café** is Boquete's showplace event. The Fair of Flowers and Coffee draws tens of thousands of people from all over Panama to view the stunning flowers that carpet Boquete's fairgrounds on the east side of the Río Caldera. The fair has its roots in a celebration first held in 1950. Though gardens all over Boquete are spruced up for the event, the fairgrounds are the epicenter, transformed each year into a floral playground with fanciful landscaping. The festival also includes concerts, folkloric dancers, handicraft exhibits, and a chance to sip gourmet coffee and chug vast amounts of other liquids. It's held for 10

days in the middle of January. Check with ATP (CEFATI, tel. 720-4060) for exact dates, which change annually.

Note: Friends who have lived in Boquete for years tell me the quality and abundance of the flowers at the fair have declined in the last couple of years, which has coincided with or perhaps caused a drop in attendance. In the past, the beauty of the fair has compensated for the blaring music, crowds, full hotels, and heavy public drinking. Unless the fair returns to its former glory, it may be best to avoid Boquete at this time.

The **Boquete Jazz Festival** (http://boquetejazzfestival.com) was held for the first time in 2007 and has become an annual event, bringing Panamanian and international jazz musicians to town for three days of performances in February.

After the Feria de las Flores y El Café in January, the fairgrounds remain open until late March or early April, when a smaller festival, the **Feria de las Orquídeas** (Orchid Festival) closes out the season with a four-day celebration. Again, check with ATP (CEFATI, tel. 720-4060) for exact dates.

The entire country celebrates Panama's independence from Spain on November 28, but Boquete's celebration is the biggest, presided over by the president of Panama and drawing people from far beyond the highlands for a huge party. No one's yet explained to me why Boquete's **Día de la Independencia** celebration is so grand. My favorite theory came from a tour guide who explained that was the date Boquete got its very own team of firefighters; he neglected to mention Spain at all.

SHOPPING

New stores have followed the influx of foreigners, but there still isn't much worth buying. The only noteworthy "souvenir" item in these parts is coffee.

Los Establos Plaza, on the left at the entrance to downtown Boquete, is a mini-mall with a few shops selling handicrafts, jewelry, souvenirs, and the like.

Packages of good coffee are easy to come by in Boquete, as you might imagine, in an overwhelming variety of roasts, qualities, and flavors. You can choose either whole bean or ground coffee, though whole beans preserve the coffee's flavor longer. Attractive souvenir packs are often available, which make for nice gifts. Finca Lérida, Café Ruiz, and Café Kotowa are safe bets for excellent coffee.

Panama's most widely available boutique coffee is **Café Ruiz** (tel. 720-1392, www.caferuiz. com, 7 A.M.–6 P.M. Mon.–Sat., 10 A.M.–6 P.M. Sun.). The best-quality Ruiz is the gourmet, which is a lighter roast and is sold in gold bags. Ruiz coffee is increasingly easy to come by throughout Panama, but its gourmet coffee is sold only at its Boquete shop (just north of town on Avenida Central), its shop in Panama City, and a few gourmet stores and upscale supermarkets, including Super Barú in David. La Berlina Estate is arguably the best of the gourmet varieties. To get to Café Ruiz, keep left at the fork past the church. It's the white complex on the right, near Mi Jardín Es Su Jardín.

Café Kotowa (tel. 720-1430, www.kotowacoffee.com, 7 A.M.–7 P.M. daily) is becoming the mini-Starbucks of Panama, except that Kotowa's brew actually tastes like coffee. Kotowa café-cum-store outlets and bags of coffee are popping up around the country. Kotowa has two outlets in Boquete, one at the CEFATI and one at Los Establos Plaza.

Some companies will ship coffee overseas. Several have also made their coffee available for online sale, either directly through their websites (e.g., Kotowa and Ruiz) or through international distributors (e.g., Finca Lérida). However, prices are considerably higher than in Boquete, and shipping costs can exceed the cost of the coffee itself.

The **Folklórica Museo** (Avenida Central, tel. 720-2368, 10 A.M.–6 P.M. Wed.–Mon.) is really more like a rather pricey antique/junk store than a museum, but it's worth a quick stop. Items of possible interest include a small collection of vintage postcards from around the country, cocobolo statues, and paintings of Ngöbe-Buglé children. It's north of the church on Avenida Central.

Souvenir El Cacique (tel. 720-2217, 10 A.M.–7 P.M. Mon.–Sat., 10 A.M.–2 P.M. Sun.) sells Ngöbe-Buglé necklaces, *molas* (hand-crafted blouses), cocobolo statues, and other crafts from Panama, as well as a few things from Guatemala and Peru. The staff speaks English here. It's on the south side of the town plaza.

The Bookmark (tel. 776-1688, dembook@ yahoo.com, 9 A.M.–5 P.M. Tues.–Sun.) is in Dolega, a small town about midway between David and Boquete. Though not a large place, it has the largest collection of English-language books in the country. It has a little bit of everything, mostly used: bestsellers, true crime, science fiction, nonfiction, history, romance, and so on. There are some rare, out-of-print books on Panama, including some from the old Canal Zone library, and a small Spanish-language section. This is a good place to sell or swap that tattered beach book. It's worth stopping by even if the place seems closed. It's run by a friendly American, Hal De Mun, who lives in the back of the house, and he might be around when you stop by. As you head up toward Boquete, look for it on the left 17 kilometers after the turnoff from the Interamericana.

SPORTS AND RECREATION

There are plenty of options for outdoor activities around Boquete. The most popular and impressive of these are a zipline ride, white-water rafting, hiking the Sendero Los Quetzales, and climbing Volcán Barú.

The zipline company, **Boquete Tree Trek** (tel. 720-1635, www.aventurist.com), also rents **mountain bikes** (US$15 a day) and offers tours and outings, including **mountain-biking trips** (US$35 pp), **horseback rides** (US$35 pp), and **rock climbing** at Los Ladrillos (US$40 pp), an unusual rock wall north of town on the Bajo Mono loop. These all last roughly 3.5 hours.

A couple of local outfitters offer boating, fishing, and sea-kayaking packages off the Pacific coast, about an hour away. Those primarily interested in sea-kayaking should contact **Chiriquí River Rafting** (tel./fax 720-1505 or 720-1506, cell 6618-0846, www.panama-rafting.com) and **Boquete Outdoor Adventures** (cell 6474-0274, www.boquete-outdooradventures.com).

Zipline Ride

Zipline rides are beginning to pop up all around Panama, but **Boquete Tree Trek** (tel. 720-1635, www.aventurist.com, US$60 pp) is the longest and most impressive. On a zipline, riders wear harnesses connected to pulleys that are then attached to a series of cables stretched between trees at a slight downward angle. Riders shoot along the cable, braking manually to keep from smacking into the approaching tree.

The Boquete Tree Trek features 12 stages and 14 platforms spread over three kilometers and passing over two waterfalls. The longest run is 360 meters, during which you can reach speeds of up to 18 kilometers an hour. One stretch of the ride is about 90 meters above the forest floor. It's an exhilarating, scenic experience that is over much too quickly. I was impressed both by the natural beauty—the zipline is in a cloud forest right below the Continental Divide, and on a clear day there's a view of Volcán Barú—and by the guides. Without exception they are friendly, enthusiastic, and highly professional. All are bilingual. There's an attractive lodge (with bathrooms) that serves food and drinks before and after the ride. Four modern log cabins are being built and should provide a picturesque, if isolated, lodging option for outdoor types, as there are lots of hiking possibilities in the area.

Note: This ride requires somewhat more upper-body strength than other ones in Panama, particularly if the lines are wet. Riders must be able to apply enough pressure with their gloved hands to slow down, and be able to pull themselves along if they stop short of a platform.

The ride starts at an elevation of nearly 1,900 meters, in an area up the mountain from the Café Kotowa mill in Palo Alto, but the guides pick guests up from the Boquete Tree Trek office, which is in Los Establos Plaza in downtown Boquete.

Pickup times are 8 A.M., 10 A.M., and noon

daily. The whole thing, including transportation from downtown, lasts about four hours. The ride itself lasts about 1.25 hours.

White-Water Rafting

Western Panama has fantastic white-water, some of it truly world class. The main commercially run rivers are the powerful **Río Chiriquí** (east of Boquete) and **Río Chiriquí Viejo** (west of Boquete, near the Costa Rican border). Even experienced rafters will likely find the runs here thrilling. They feature very long wave trains, relentless runs, hair-raising moments, and lots of variety. There are also much more peaceful sections of the river where timid beginners can get their feet wet.

One of the great things about rafting on these rivers is the sense of solitude. Yours may be the only raft on the river, and you may not see a soul along the banks. Other than the occasional cow, all rafters are likely to encounter are forest, gorges, tributaries, and huge, beautiful birds. And, of course, big water.

COURTESY OF CHIRIQUÍ RIVER RAFTING

The western highlands offer world-class river rafting.

Gentler rides, featuring Class II and III rapids, are available on the nearby Río Gariché, Río Dolega, and Río Majagua.

Part of the Río Chiriquí has been dammed, and the sections that remain wild can only be run between June and November, when there's enough rain to keep the river flowing. The Panamanian government is authorizing dams all over western Panama, and other wild rivers are endangered, including the Chiriquí Viejo, one of Central America's most spectacular white-water rivers. If you have an opinion about this, send an email to ANCON, Panama's largest environmental non-profit (ancon@ancon.org). The Habla Ya website has detailed information on the endangered rivers and other suggestions about how to make your voice heard: www.hablayapanama.com/ecotourism/rivers/.

Chiriquí River Rafting (tel./fax 720-1505 or 720-1506, cell 6618-0846, rafting@panama-rafting.com, www.panama-rafting.com), is the oldest white-water outfit in Panama. The company is run by Hector Sanchez, who was for years in charge of recreational services for the U.S. military bases in the old Canal Zone. He's fully bilingual, as are some of the guides and other staff members. The rest speak enough basic English to get you through the rapids.

The company offers different day trips on these two rivers, with rapids varying from Class II and III to solid Class IV. The most hard-core, and expensive, of these is the Palon section of the Chiriquí Viejo, a four-hour blast through deep canyons. It costs US$105 per person. The cheapest is a gentle, 45-minute ride through Class II rapids suitable for families with children as young as five. The price is US$85 per person.

Some of the rivers can only be run during the height of the rainy season, approximately June–November. The water level is too low at other times. There's always water in the Chiriquí Viejo, but during times of heavy rainfall it can be too rough to run.

Prices include transportation, equipment, and a picnic lunch by the river. Five-day packages that include rafting, hiking, a boat trip around Parque Nacional Marino Golfo de Chiriquí, and other outdoor activities are also available.

Contact the company as far ahead of time as possible. Many trips require a minimum of 3–4 people, so advance warning helps the company coordinate groups of sufficient size.

A newer operation is **Boquete Outdoor Adventures** (cell 6474-0274, www.boquete-outdooradventures.com). It offers full-day rafting trips for US$90 per person and overnight trips for US$150 per person (four-person minimum). A kayak "sampler" trip on gentle rapids is US$80 per person, two-person minimum.

The company also offers guided overnight hikes to the summit of Barú, multiday whitewater and sea-kayaking trips, deep-sea fishing excursions, and other outdoor adventures.

☾ PARQUE NACIONAL VOLCÁN BARÚ

The most popular activities in this national park are hiking the gorgeous Sendero Los Quetzales, which skirts the north side of Barú and links Boquete with Cerro Punta, and climbing Volcán Barú.

Hiking Sendero Los Quetzales

Note that Cerro Punta is nearly a kilometer higher in elevation than Boquete, so you'll be walking uphill most of the way. Because of that, most people choose to hike in the other direction.

However, some reckon the uphill hike, though strenuous, is actually easier than hiking downhill since the steep descent is rough on the knees and can set you up for a case of the "wobbles," which is no fun when you still have hours of downhill hiking ahead of you. And some of those who regularly hike the trail claim there's a better chance of outrunning the rain hiking uphill, since it often rains in the morning on the Cerro Punta side and in the afternoon on the Boquete side. Besides not getting wet, you'll have a much better chance of seeing birds.

It's best to go with a guide when hiking the trail up to Cerro Punta, as there are a couple of places where it's easy to miss a turn. Get an early start.

Hiking uphill also takes longer than hiking downhill. Allow six hours just to hike between the two ANAM ranger stations—Alto Chiquero (Boquete side) and El Respingo (Cerro Punta side). And bear in mind the stations are a long way from any town. It's possible to camp or stay in a dorm room at the stations.

Access to the Boquete entrance is from the scenic Bajo Mono loop road; the turnoff onto the road leading to the trailhead is marked but can be confusing. Take the road that's bordered by the pipeline. Note that from this turnoff it's a three-kilometer uphill walk to the Alto Chiquero ranger station, a walk that will add at least 1.5 hours to the hike. Pay the park admission fee (US$5) at the station. The trail officially starts here. Some guides drive all the way to the ranger station; when hiring a guide, be sure to ask where the tour begins and ends. The road was recently paved and is in excellent shape. Those with their own vehicles can park at the station. Don't leave any valuables in the car. There's a US$1 parking fee.

From the station, hike down the dirt road for about 45 minutes. The Los Quetzales trailhead is on the left. There may be a sign marking it, but you can't count on that; keep your eyes open, as it's possible to miss the turnoff and walk too far on the dirt road.

The trail gets far steeper about 2.5 hours into the hike. After another hour, there's a campsite with vista points but few facilities. This is a good place to take a break and eat lunch.

Once at El Respingo, it's another 1.5-hour hike downhill to the road linking Cerro Punta and Guadalupe. From here you may be able to flag down a bus or taxi. If this doesn't sound like a fun way to end a hike, consider arranging for a taxi to meet you at El Respingo station. Because the road is so rough, the fare to Cerro Punta will be about US$30.

Those who choose to hike from the Bajo Mono turnoff all the way to the Cerro Punta–Guadalupe road should plan on a nine-hour hike.

Arrange transportation back to Boquete ahead of time or plan to spend the night in the Cerro Punta area. The trip by bus takes at least three hours, not including waiting time in David, where travelers must change buses. One-way trippers: Consider shipping luggage ahead to meet you. Hire a taxi to do so, or make arrangements through your hotel or guide. Those who choose one of the latter options should find out how the luggage will be sent and when it will arrive. There have been cases of tourists getting stuck waiting for bags that had been sent by courier services that make the trip only once a day. No fun.

Climbing Volcán Barú

The summit of the dormant volcano that gives the park its name is, at 3,475 meters, the highest point in Panama. Those wanting to climb to the top of Barú will find the Boquete summit trail easier to manage than the one on the west side of Barú. When the road is in slightly less horrendous shape than normal, which means the dry season, it may even be possible to drive to the summit from this side. Even then, however, this requires a good four-wheel drive with a winch. The "road" more closely resembles a steep riverbed. It's an absolutely brutal drive.

If you hike instead, allow at least 4–5 hours up and 3–4 hours back down. The hike is strenuous but not technically difficult. Remember, there's a risk of hypothermia, especially for those who get stranded on the mountain, so be sure to bring warm, waterproof clothing.

Unless you're looking for a marathon hike, drive or hire a taxi (US$10) to the ranger station at the trailhead. A four-wheel drive is needed even to get this far. From Boquete, head north through town and take the second left past the church (look for the blue "Volcán Barú" sign). Continue straight past the first intersection, then take the right fork uphill. There's a fork after 6.7 kilometers. Take the

COURTESY OF THE COFFEE ESTATE INN

Climbing Volcán Barú is a popular challenge.

right fork. The road forks again in about 800 meters. Take the left fork. After another 600 meters, take the right fork up the very steep gravel road.

Entrance is US$5, payable at the little ranger station at the entrance to the park, which is in an area called Camiseta. There's an outhouse at the station. It's another US$5 to camp in the park, but there are no facilities. From the station (elevation 1,840 meters) it's another 13.5 kilometers to the top. The trail is fairly steep and very rocky. Those determined to start their trek in downtown Boquete should add another nine kilometers to the total.

More Hiking

A less-ambitious hike is along a stretch of the **Bajo Mono loop,** a scenic, 20-kilometer paved road. It features lush forest, dramatic volcanic cliffs, and a valley with a pretty river flowing through it. It's easy to flag down a bus if you get tired. Be careful—many of the truckers plying these roads seem to have a death wish. Take food and water, as there's no place to buy them during this hike. The Bajo Mono loop starts north of Boquete. Follow Avenida Central and keep left at the fork past the church. The loop is well marked. It's also possible to bike or drive the road.

Nature Tours

A guide is a good idea for more ambitious hikes, such as summiting Volcán Barú or hiking the Sendero Los Quetzales. A knowledgeable birding guide also greatly increases the chance of spotting quetzals. Many guides have access to four-wheel-drive vehicles, a plus for those without their own transportation. Several of the hotels, especially the more upscale ones, can arrange tours for their guests. So can Boquete Tree Trek (tel. 720-1635, www. aventurist.com).

Please note: Though most of the guides in Boquete are good, safe, and reliable people, there have been some complaints about dangerous practices as well as inappropriate behavior toward women. This is likely a function of the relatively thriving tourism business in Boquete versus other parts of the country—there are just more people trying to break into the business, not all of them competent or professional. If possible, try not to take guided tours alone.

Some also let the desire for business overcome common sense. No matter what a tour guide might tell you, for example, a hike to the top of Volcán Barú or the length of Sendero Los Quetzales is too much for young children and adults who aren't in reasonably good shape. All the guides listed here have good reputations.

Coffee Adventures (tel. 720-3852, cell 6634-4698, http://coffeeadventures.net) is a guide outfit that consists of Terry van Niekerk and Hans van der Vooren, the warm and eminently dependable Dutch couple who own Tinamou Cottage. They offer an excellent, well-organized guided hike along Sendero Los Quetzales (US$129 pp). The tour includes snacks, but breakfast and/or a picnic lunch are available for another US$10–17 per person. The cost includes transportation to and from the trail. Discounts are available for groups of three or more. They also offer a half-day birding trip to Sendero Los Quetzales (US$39 pp).

They offer other full-day and half-day hiking and birding trips, both in the Boquete area and as far away as the Fortuna Road. In addition, they can combine a birding trip or visit to a Ngöbe settlement with ground transportation to or from Almirante (Bocas del Toro). Some of these tours are not at all strenuous. Tours start at US$35 per person, minimum two people, and include transportation and snacks. The birding tours are usually led by Terry, an accomplished birder who speaks English, Dutch, and Spanish. Terry and Hans take a first-aid kit and cell phone along on all their hikes. As the name Coffee Adventures suggests, they also offer excellent tours of coffee facilities.

Santiago "Chago" Caballero (cell 6626-2200) has been guiding people in the highlands for 18 years and is often employed by top guide outfits. He is generally acknowledged as the best quetzal spotter around; if your main aim is to see a quetzal, he's your guy. He's a kind, gentle man and can be depended on to show up on time.

He's got his own four-wheel drive and is a careful driver. His bird-watching tours cost US$120 for 1–2 people, US$150 for 3–4 people.

Chago also takes guests on Sendero Los Quetzales (US$170 for 1–2 people, US$60 pp for 3–5 people). Other offerings include tours of the Cerro Punta side of the mountain, including either Parque Internacional La Amistad or Cañon Macho de Monte and the Lagunas de Volcán (both US$140 1–2 people, US$50 pp for 3–5 people). All tours include a box lunch and transportation. Chago also offers transfers to David (US$30), Cerro Punta (US$70), and Almirante (US$180), which is the jumping-off point for Bocas del Toro.

ACCOMMODATIONS

Lodging is in or near downtown Boquete unless otherwise specified. There are some good options in the outlying area, but those without their own transportation may find getting around inconvenient. Hostels and other backpacker-friendly places are more plentiful than they used to be, and there are quite a few pleasant, economical options for those on a modest budget. Private homes are increasingly posting room-for-rent signs in front of their houses. These tend to be pretty basic. A number of the more upscale places periodically offer great rates for those who book through their websites; be sure to check. Hotel rooms can get booked up in Boquete, particularly during major festivals. Make reservations well in advance if possible.

Under US$10

◖ Pensión Marilós (Avenida E Este, tel. 720-1380, www.pension-marilos.com, US$6.95 s, US$9.90 d with shared bath; US$9.90 s, US$15.95 d with private bath) remains one of the best deals in all of Panama. Marilós offers seven simple but clean and tidy rooms at bargain prices. It's two blocks south of the plaza, on Avenida E Este, which is parallel to and two blocks east of Avenida Central. Guests can use the kitchen and dining room. The prices here haven't gone up in years. Amazing.

US$10-25

Nomba (Ave. A Oeste, cell 6920-4169 or 6497-5672, ryan@miradoradventures.com, www.nombapanama.com, dorm rooms US$8–9 pp, private rooms US$15 s, US$22 d, including breakfast and good local coffee) is a friendly hostel in a residential area just west of downtown Boquete.

Rooms are clean and range in size from 2–6 beds. There are no private bathrooms, but the three shared bathrooms have hot water. There are two shared kitchens, a hammock lounge, laundry facilities, a foosball table, and other extras.

It's run by a warm couple (he's from Colorado; she's from Boquete) who offer their guests much more than a bed for the night. It's an especially good option for those interested in outdoor adventures. The hostel is literally attached to Mirador Adventures, and has good-quality outdoor equipment for rent, ranging from tents and sleeping bags to warm socks. You don't have to stay at the hostel to rent the equipment, and they'll stash your luggage for free while you use it. The owners also lead free hikes twice a week. This is the best place for backpackers interested in climbing Barú, as they can equip and prepare guests and give them good advice on how to tackle it.

The hostel is one block west of Avenida Central. If you're heading uphill from the town plaza, turn left at Supercentro El Mandarín and make the next right. The hostel is the third house on the right and is painted bright green.

The German-run **Pensión Topas** (Avenida Belisario Porras, tel./fax 720-1005, schoeb@cwpanama.net, starts at US$8.80 s, US$11 d) is three blocks south of the plaza on Avenida Belisario Porras, which is parallel to and one block east of Avenida Central. This is a cheerful place with eight rooms set in a garden filled with flowering trees. A simple breakfast (8–11 A.M.) on the terrace is US$2.50; fancier fare is US$6–7. The owner, Axel Shöb, speaks English and is helpful on advice about where to go and what to see. There's a volleyball net and small swimming pool on the premises. The pension can also help arrange tours. The least expensive rooms are very simple and small with a shared bath. Rooms with private bath range from US$22–42. Allow 10 days for an answer to email; Axel hates computers.

El Bajareque Lodge (tel./fax 720-1505 or 720-1506, www.panama-rafting.com, US$13 pp) is tucked away among the coffee plantations in Palmira, a short drive from Alto Boquete. It's run by the Sanchez family, the folks who run Chiriquí River Rafting, and is in fact on their farm, right next to their quite attractive, modern home. The hostel-style rooms are simple but comfortable, with bunk beds, plenty of blankets, and private, hot-water bathrooms. The place caters mainly to kayakers, who can stash their kayaks in a secure shed on the property, but rooms are available to anyone. Guests can use the kitchen for free or arrange meals. All-you-can-eat breakfasts are US$5, dinners are US$10, and you're on your own for lunch. The turnoff to the lodge is near the Café Ruiz *beneficio* (processing mill); call for directions. The last stretch of road is rough, but a regular car can make it. Taxis from Boquete cost about US$3; ask the driver to take you to *"Hector Sánchez en Palmira."*

US$25-50

Hostal Boquete (Calle 4a Sur, tel. 720-2573, US$33–38 s/d), near the west bank of the Río Caldera and just north of the bridge spanning it, offers 15 basic but cheerful rooms with private bath and cable TV. The place is under new management and was renovated recently. It has a picturesque location on the banks of the Río Caldera, with a view of the fairgrounds on the east bank. Note that even if you could get a room here during a festival, you probably wouldn't want to—the music blasting across the river from the fairgrounds would render you deaf in seconds. There's a riverside deck with a small restaurant (most items around US$5). This place is popular with gringo travelers on a budget.

The 40-room **Hotel Los Fundadores** (Avenida Central, tel. 720-1298, starts at US$27.50 s/d) is a Boquete stalwart. It's on the left side of Avenida Central just before downtown; its faux Arthurian-castle facade is hard to miss. Rooms here are small, drab, and well past their prime, but a babbling creek runs right through the middle of the building, which makes up for a lot. Rates are US$27.50 s/d for a room with two single beds, US$33 s/d for a queen-sized bed, and US$55 s/d for a king.

Hostel Mamallena (tel. 720-1260, www. mamallena.com, starts at US$11 pp dorm rooms, US$33 s/d private rooms, including pancake breakfast) is the sister of the hostel of the same name in Panama City. This one is in a two-story wooden building that dates from the 1950s and has tons of charm. It's right on the south side of the town plaza. It offers 23 dormitory beds with new and clean shared bathrooms, of different sizes and shapes. There's free Wi-Fi and computers for guest use. It's managed by friendly people who speak Spanish and English and have voluminous amounts of local information to share and can set up a number of low-price tours, including a popular visit to a small local coffee farm. Advice and access to a thick binder is available to anyone who passes by. This is a great addition to the local backpacker scene, and it should get even better once the hostel gains control of the rather noisy bar next door and turns the volume down.

US$50-100

The best thing about **El Oasis B&B** (tel. 720-1586 and 720-1827, cell 6615-3769, www.oasisboquete.com, US$82 s/d) is its location. It's in a residential area right on the east bank of the Río Caldera, set in a garden just south of the grounds of the Feria de las Flores y El Café. A recent extension adds a few apartments upstairs. It's a clean and tidy place with firm beds, a shared terrace strung with hammocks, and free wireless Internet. There's also an Internet-connected computer in the common room that guests are welcome to use. Rooms are simple but newish. Note that the cheaper rooms are dark and have no view. Try to get a room away from the common areas, which can get noisy.

Villa Marita (tel. 720-2165, www.villamarita.com, US$88 s/d for cabins) is about four kilometers northeast of downtown Boquete in an area called El Santuario. It offers six attractive, hardwood-paneled cabins set on a 1,200-meter-high plateau with a panoramic view of Barú and the surrounding hills and valleys. The cabins have sitting rooms and firm beds, and two of them have fireplaces. All have cable TV, fridges, and free wireless Internet access. The owners have added three more basic rooms in a single building (US$55 s/d) and a family cabin with two bedrooms and a full kitchen (US$143 s/d), but these are set back on the property and lack that great view.

To get to Villa Marita, head north up Avenida Central past the church, bearing left when the road forks. The road will fork again two kilometers past the church, and you'll see a sign pointing left to Los Naranjos and right to Arco Iris. Take the right fork. Cross the bridge and head up the hill. After one kilometer there's a sign pointing right off the main road toward Villa Marita. Take that right and follow the signs. The lodge is less than a kilometer uphill.

(Boquete Garden Inn (tel. 720-2376, www.boquetegardeninn.com, starts at US$97.90 s/d), consists of 10 units in five peach-colored, two-story hexagonal cabañas in a pleasant garden setting along the Río Palo Alto. There's a *rancho* bar right by the river. The place is under new management and rooms have been thoroughly spruced up, with attractive furnishings, good mattresses, kitchenettes, cable TV, stylish bathrooms (with hot water in the shower, though not in the sink), free Wi-Fi, and the sound of the rushing river. Stays include a continental breakfast and an evening drink in the *rancho* by the river. This place has a friendly vibe. The hotel is about 2.5 kilometers northwest of downtown. Cross over the bridge near the Panamonte Inn and Spa and make a left. Stay on this road, heading

© WILLIAM FRIAR

Boquete Garden Inn consists of five two-story hexagonal cabañas in a pleasant garden setting along the Río Palo Alto.

north toward Palo Alto, for 1.5 kilometers. The hotel is on the left past the Palo Alto Riverside Restaurant. They speak English and Spanish here.

◖ Tinamou Cottage (tel. 720-3852, cell 6634-4698, www.coffeeadventures.net, starts at US$99 s/d) actually consists of three cottages on a coffee farm, Finca Habbus de Kwie. It's southeast of Boquete in Jaramillo Abajo, a little more than five minutes by car or a hefty hike from downtown. It belongs to Hans van der Vooren and Terry van Niekerk, a charming and friendly Dutch couple who also are among the best tour guides in Boquete.

Of the 8.5-hectare *finca* (country house), a little under half of it still grows coffee. The rest has been allowed to revert to nature, and the couple has built 1.5–2 hours of trails through the secondary growth, through which run several creeks and little waterfalls. There's some good birding here.

Little Tinamou is cozy and cheerful, offering two comfy single beds that can be pushed together, a sitting area, and a kitchenette with fridge, oven, and sink. The owners' home is just next door, as are their three good-natured dogs. The other two cottages, Highland Tinamou (US$154 s/d) and Great Tinamou (US$159.50 s/d) are more secluded, situated deeper into the plantation and surrounded by forest. They each have two bedrooms, an open kitchen/living room, and a porch looking out on the view. These cottages can sleep 4–5 people. All cottages have cable TV. The rate for additional guests in any of the cottages is US$15 per person. They offer a discount to those who book directly through their web page.

An extensive, Dutch-style breakfast is available for US$7 per person. Hans and Terry will pick up arriving guests from downtown Boquete for free. If guests prefer, they can call for directions on how to hike to the farm. It takes about an hour from downtown. They can arrange hikes to any of the area's attractions, some of which they lead themselves. They speak Dutch, English, Spanish, and some German.

Isla Verde (Calle 5a Sur, tel. 720-2533, fax 720-2751, http://islaverdepanama.com, starts at US$88 s/d), two blocks west of Avenida Central on the south end of town, is an unusual place. Its most notable features are the six hexagonal "roundhouses" set in a garden and connected by paths. Each roundhouse has a comfortable bed downstairs, another one up in a loft in the center of the cabin, and a kitchenette. Three of the roundhouses sleep a maximum of four people; the other three sleep six, have a more extensive kitchen area, and are wheelchair-accessible. The decor in all is bright and cheerful. Two newer suites, in a rectangular two-story building, have kitchenettes and balconies. All accommodations have cable TV and free wireless Internet. Rates are US$88 s/d in the smaller cabañas and lower suites and US$110 s/d in the larger ones and upper suites. Additional people are US$10 each. Breakfasts to order (US$1.75–7) are served in an open-sided geodesic dome in the middle of the "village." The owners speak English, Spanish, and German. If you're heading into Boquete from the south, Isla Verde is a left turn off Avenida Central onto Calle 5a Sur just as you enter downtown. Look for it on the right after two blocks.

◖ Panamonte Inn and Spa (tel. 720-1327 or 720-1324, fax 720-2055, www.panamonte. com, starts at US$93.50 s/d) is a Boquete institution—it dates from the early 20th century and has been owned by the Collins family since 1946—that has lots of Old World charm. In the past it's had a bit of a musty, shabby-chic air, but it benefited from a renovation a few years back that spruced things up considerably. Famous guests have included Charles Lindbergh and Admiral Richard Byrd, who wrote an article about his Arctic exploits for *National Geographic* while relaxing here. The hotel's charming, semiformal restaurant makes it worth a visit even for those who don't stay here. The spa is lovely, too.

The Panamonte's 16 rooms are quaint and clean. The least expensive ones are on the small side, but there are also four spacious garden cabañas (US$152.80 s/d) and an especially appealing three-bedroom apartment (US$264, sleeps six), El Fresal, with a wraparound porch across the street from the main hotel. There's a Honeymoon Suite (US$126.50 s/d) on the 2nd floor that once hosted Ingrid Bergman. All rooms have a safe, cable TV, telephone, air conditioner(!), and other amenities. The Panamonte Inn and Spa is about 0.7 kilometers north of the town center. Follow Avenida Central past the church and head right when you come to a fork. It's the blue wooden building on the left.

Finca Lérida Ecolodge (tel./fax 720-2285, cell 6450-3848, www.fincalerida.com, US$90–99 s/d) is a nice addition to the Boquete lodging scene. The *finca* (country house) has long been famous for bird-watching and gourmet coffee, and even those not particularly interested in either will likely find there's something magical about the place and its natural beauty. Now overnight guests have a chance to soak up the scenery.

There are actually two lodging options at the *finca*. The ecolodge itself consists of 11 rooms in a single building up on a hill with a view of the gardens, coffee plantation, and surrounding mountains. The rooms are attractive, with hardwood floors, firm beds, and plate-glass windows that look out on the view. All the rooms are on the ground floor and have a front patio with a bench. There's a large common room with a fireplace.

The Collins family, the owners of the *finca,* have also turned the old board-and-batten family homestead into a B&B. There are a half dozen rooms here, all different. Only two rooms are in the house itself; the other four are in a neighboring building. Rooms are more rustic than those in the ecolodge, but they have a lot of old-country character. There's less privacy in the rooms in the house, which the family still uses, except when a group rents the whole building. The home was built in 1917 by Tollef B. Mönniche, a Norwegian engineer who was an important figure in the construction of the Panama Canal. It's very cool to see the Norwegian-style stone fireplace he built in one of the common rooms, and to thumb through the books in his personal library. In the last couple of years, quetzals have been spotted in the backyard of the house mid-January–end of February, but there is of course no guarantee you'll see one.

The Coffee House Restaurant (7 A.M.–8 P.M., US$6–8) is between the ecolodge and the B&B. It serves salads, sandwiches, and other simple fare. The spectacular view of the Boquete valley is the draw here.

All this is located in a single compound in the community of Alto Quiel, about a 10-minute drive above Boquete. To get there, drive north on Avenida Central and continue straight past Café Ruiz and the stadium. At the next intersection, follow the road leading to Callejon Seco. Follow the steep, winding road up into the mountains for about another five kilometers. Look for a "Finca Lérida" sign on the right.

US$100-150

Hotel Ladera (tel. 730-9000, www.hotel-ladera.com, US$142 s/d) is essentially a business hotel in a country-resort location. It's just across the bridge from the Panamonte, on the east bank of the Río Caldera and offers formal service and rooms that have firm beds, terraces, TVs, and a vaguely Japanese-minimalist air. The restaurant/bar is handsome in an austere 1970s-bachelor-pad kind of way (split-level, double-sided fireplace).

Just up the street from Pensión Marilós is **Hotel Rebequet** (tel. 720-1365, US$96.80 s, US$121 d), a modern place with nine large, clean, pleasant rooms set around an interior courtyard. All have small TVs and refrigerators. Prices for this place have doubled since the last edition of this book, so it's not the great deal it once was. Boquete hotels in this price range generally offer more. But the Rebequet is a consistently solid option, and it's worth calling to see if deals are available.

Hotel Los Establos (tel. 720-2685, www.losestablos.net, US$143 s/d, US$253 for suites) was originally part of the Valle Escondido empire, with similar Spanish-mission decor, but is now under new management. It's 0.7

kilometers farther up the hill from La Montaña y El Valle: The Coffee Estate Inn. As its name suggests, it was originally meant to be a horse stables but became a hotel instead. Its pastoral setting is stunning: It has a panoramic view of Volcán Barú and the surrounding countryside. On its four hectares, a spacious bar area with pool table looks out on a large garden, at the far edge of which is a new restaurant (7 A.M.–9 P.M. daily) with terrific views of Boquete valley and Barú.

There are just four rooms downstairs and two suites upstairs in the main building. Two new rooms have been added in a separate building. The suites consist of a small bedroom attached to a small sitting room, though the latter is glass-enclosed and gets a lot of light.

Each of the downstairs rooms has a tiny terrace, but, oddly enough, only one of them looks out on the volcano. All the rooms have cable TV and a DVD player; guests need to bring their own DVDs (they can be rented in downtown Boquete).

The **Riverside Inn** (tel. 720-1076, www.riversideinnboquete.com, starts at US$137.50 s/d, including breakfast), consists of six opulent rooms in a lovely wooden house by the Río Palo Alto. The best of the bunch (and, naturally, the most expensive) is the Orchidea, which features a handsome, king-size four-poster bed and a large bathroom with a whirlpool tub, both of which look out on the Río Palo Alto. All rooms have free wireless Internet access and televisions with cable TV and DVD players. The common areas feature a cozy sitting room with stone fireplace and a TV room/solarium. The hotel is under the same management as the Rock Restaurant, which is just next door.

Over US$150

Some innkeepers have hospitality wired into their genetic code. Meet Jane Walker and Barry Robbins, Canadian expatriates who have turned their 2.5 hectares of forested land above Boquete valley into one of the most appealing places to stay in the country. They call it (■ **La Montaña y El Valle: The Coffee**

Estate Inn (tel./fax 720-2211, www.coffeeestateinn.com, US$159.50 s/d). You get a sense of the couple's obsessive attention to detail as soon as you make a reservation. (And it's a popular place, so advance reservations are a must.) They immediately send out a fat information package with solid advice on what to do and how to get around in Boquete and other parts of Panama.

The inn consists of three large, modern, immaculate bungalows set on a hillside just northeast of Boquete. They're essentially small apartments, and they're tastefully decorated. Each has a balcony, sitting room, kitchenette, flat-screen TV with cable TV and DVD player, safe, wireless Internet access, and a terrific view of Barú and the valley. (The estate is at 1,300 meters.)

Barry and Jane are always finding ways to make a great place even better. Guests can enjoy Barry's homemade breads and scones for breakfast, and twice a week those who are interested can dine by candlelight in their bungalows (US$19–25 for main dishes). Offerings include rack of lamb, braised halibut, five-spice roasted duck, and so on. This is incredibly romantic for couples and a treat for anyone else, as the staff festoons the whole bungalow with candles and artful flower arrangements. Appetizers and simpler suppers are available every other night of the week. Options include a smoked salmon platter, vegetarian moussaka, and cannelloni stuffed with spinach and beef (US$10–12 pp).

The property is a working coffee farm that produces more than 2,000 kilos of coffee a year. The coffee grows in the shade of a pretty, well-tended little forest that attracts more than 100 species of birds and lots of other highland critters. More than 50 indigenous trees have been identified so far. As usual, though, orange trees are especially well-represented. They produce thousands of oranges a year, so help yourself to as many as you like.

Stays include a free, optional tour of the owners' coffee operation from soil to cup. The (free) coffee you drink here has never been out of the roaster more than two days. You can buy souvenir packs to take home. They have also concocted a delicious coffee liqueur, called Barubica, which is also for sale.

Barry and Jane are a great source of information on the area's attractions. Guests are invited to walk through the couple's lovely gardens and more than a kilometer of trails on the property and use their extensive library, which also has a computer with free Internet access.

Note to those who like things funky: Barry and Jane run a tight, gleaming ship. The inn has more in common with a modern first-world country getaway than some bohemian third-world tree house. But this is a great place to pamper yourself, which can be especially fun if you've been roughing it for a while. Stay here a couple of days and you may find yourself thinking of Jane and Barry as Mom and Dad. Still, if you want to be left completely alone, they'll respect your privacy. This is a popular place with honeymooners.

To get there, take Avenida Central north past the church and follow the signs. The entrance gate is past El Explorador. The last stretch of road is rough and rocky but doesn't require a four-wheel drive if driven carefully. A third person in the room is another US$55. Children must be 14 or older.

Valle Escondido Resort Golf and Spa (tel. 240-2454, http://resort.valleescondido.biz, starts at US$154 s/d), also known as Hotel Escondido, is part of the Valle Escondido gated community. Accommodations include rooms in the hotel, bungalows dotted about the complex, and, for longer stays, condominiums. The rooms are pleasant and feature patios, flat-screen TVs with cable TV and DVD players, and free wireless Internet. If you stay here, try to get a room that looks out on the lovely river. Guests are welcome to use Valle Escondido's pools and fitness center. Golfers must pay to use the nine-hole golf course. There's a formal restaurant, Sabor Escondido, on the grounds, and a café that features a riverside deck shaded by a banyan tree. I've found food at both places inconsistent, depending on the quality of the ingredients available. Note that Valle Escondido is close to but feels quite separate from the rest of Boquete.

As the name suggests, **Rancho de Caldera** (tel. 772-8040, toll-free U.S./Canada tel. 877/810-0898, cell 6612-2147, gina@ranchocaldera.com, www.ranchocaldera.com, standard rooms US$176 s/d) is in Caldera, about a 25-minute drive from Boquete. This is one of the nicest places to stay in western Panama, but prospective guests should know it has a very different feel from Boquete proper: There's no *bajareque*, no view of the volcano, and no cool mountain air. "It's swimming-pool weather," as the owner puts it, who thoughtfully has supplied a lovely pool and deck next to the restaurant, with a view of the surrounding hills.

The main accommodations consist of three sets of three rooms set along a rise with a view of the 20-hectare former cattle and horse ranch as well as the hills in the distance. Rooms are very large, cheerful, and decorated simply. The east-facing wall of each is a six-meter-wide sliding-glass door that opens onto a private porch; guests can watch the sun rise over the hills in the morning if they can manage to wake up early in such comfortable surroundings.

The standard rooms (US$176 s/d) have a king or two queen beds, a well-stocked modern kitchenette, flat-screen satellite TV, air-conditioning, and an iPod docking station. Some rooms have bathtubs; see the ranch's website, which lists each room's features in detail. The junior suites (US$198 s/d) add a full kitchen, dining/living area, and massage chair. Prices are a bit higher for rooms closer to the pool and restaurant. Free Wi-Fi is available throughout the property.

For those on a tighter budget, there are also two far smaller and more modest rooms in the main house. They have no TV, no air-conditioning, and share a bathroom, and the owner's home is on the floor above, but they are perfectly nice and a fantastic deal at US$66 s/d, especially since all the ranch's public facilities are available to guests in these rooms.

There are still some horses at the ranch. These can be hired for US$20 pp for about 90 minutes, or US$35 pp for a trip to and from the Caldera hot springs. The owner sometimes invites guests up to watch a movie in her lovely home, which has a large movie screen that lowers from the ceiling.

It's not easy to get to the ranch by public transportation, so those without a car should either be prepared to walk the last couple of kilometers to the ranch or willing to pay around US$25 for a taxi to or from Boquete. Heading south from Boquete, make a left at the Caldera turnoff and continue straight towards Caldera for 10 kilometers. Note: Do not confuse Rancho de Caldera with Montañas de Caldera, a gated residential community between the rancho and Boquete. As you reach Caldera you'll see a church and soccer field on the left. Turn left here and head uphill for two kilometers. The last 700 meters is on a one-lane track, so drive cautiously. A couple of large, friendly dogs greet new arrivals.

Another incentive to make the trip: The restaurant serves some of the finest food in Panama (no joke). It's open to the public and offers some great deals.

Camping

Though it's not as cold around Boquete as it is in the higher elevations on the west side of Barú, it can still get plenty chilly. As always in the highlands, campers should bring plenty of warm, waterproof clothing and a waterproof tent if planning to camp. Expect drizzle even in the dry season.

Camping is possible in **Parque Nacional Volcán Barú,** but those who pitch their tents high up should be prepared for weather that can approach freezing. Also, the elevation is high enough that altitude sickness is a possibility. If you feel nauseated or get a bad headache, head down the mountain immediately. It will only get worse. Be sure also to bring plenty of water; there are no facilities in the park itself. Campers can get a camping permit from the ranger station at the start of the Volcán Barú summit trail. Camping permits are US$5, plus the US$5 park entrance fee. It's also possible to camp at the **ANAM ranger station** at Alto Chiquero, the Boquete-side end of the Sendero Los Quetzales. The station has two dorm rooms upstairs, each of which has four bunk beds and lockers for storing gear. There's also a kitchenette. The cost is US$5 per bed. Parking is US$1.

FOOD
Restaurants

The restaurant at the ◖ **Panamonte Inn and Spa** (off Avenida Central, north of town center, tel. 720-1327 or 720-1324, www.panamonte. com, 6–10 A.M., noon–3 P.M., and 6–9 P.M. Mon.–Fri.; 7:30–11 A.M., noon–3 P.M., and 6–9 P.M. Sat.–Sun., US$8–12) is the fanciest in town, with tablecloths, fresh flowers, candles, fine china, and lots of fascinating antiques. It's got an almost dollhouse charm, and the waitresses serve guests in frilly old-country uniforms. When everything comes together, this is the best restaurant in Boquete. However, it suffers from the usual Boquete problem of inconsistency, which has been a problem recently since its celebrated chef, Charlie Collins, has been focusing his attentions on a new cooking school. The food tends toward continental cuisine. There are also vegetarian options and a budget menu of burgers and sandwiches. The soups can be delicious—try the spicy pumpkin soup if it's available—and this is a good place to sample the highland trout. Save room for dessert, as it tends to be done well. The rum cake is excellent, as is the Chocolate Decadence, and I've heard good things about the key lime and apple pies.

◖ **Machu Picchu** (tel. 720-1502, noon–11 P.M. Mon.–Sat., noon–9 P.M. Sun.) is the sister of the popular Machu Picchu in Panama City, and some reckon this is actually the better of the two. I've enjoyed the seafood here. Tip: At least one regular recommends sticking with the chef's specialties. The teak furniture, blue tablecloths, and Peruvian music on the stereo contribute to the pleasant atmosphere, as does the friendly service. Save room for dessert: The lemon pie is tasty. The restaurant is at the south end of downtown, one block east of Avenida Central and half a block south of Calle 5 Sur.

Bistro Boquete (Avenida Central, tel. 720-

1017, 6 A.M.–10 or 11 P.M. daily) is a popular gringo hangout and one of Boquete's better dining options. An airy, high-ceilinged place with large windows that open right onto Avenida Central, it offers a wide selection of bar-food items such as chicken wings, quesadillas, and burgers, as well as a few fancier dishes. The curry chicken salad is tasty. Prices range from about US$3 for burgers to US$10–12 for filet mignon and such.

☾ Ristorante y Pizzeria Il Pianista (tel. 720-2728, noon–10 P.M. Tues.–Sun.) is just insanely cute. It's a stone-walled little place with a handful of tables that look out on a gushing waterfall just a few feet beyond the windows. The waterfall is lighted at night. This is easily the best place in Boquete for Italian food, and one of the best restaurants, period. The (Italian) chef makes his own pastas and uses the best and freshest ingredients he can find, and it shows. Offerings include pizzas, calzones, and bruschettas, all served by the chef's friendly *bocatoreña* wife. The restaurant is about four kilometers north of downtown on the Palo Alto road. Head toward the Boquete Garden Inn and continue straight for another 1.6 kilometers. The restaurant is on the right, on the ground floor of the owners' house. Parking is a bit tricky, and the restaurant is near a somewhat sketchy coffee workers' barracks. If you drive, lock the doors and don't leave valuables in the car.

Madre Tierra (cell 6604-9028, www.ranchocaldera.com, lunch noon–3 P.M., and dinner from 6:30 P.M. Thurs.–Mon.) is at Rancho de Caldera, an appealing inn a 25-minute drive from Boquete. It's worth making the drive, or gathering a group to share the US$25 cab ride, for a meal at this place.

For one thing, the food is outstanding. The chef, Craig Miller, insists he plans to stick around, which is probably a good thing for the famous names in Panama City's fancy restaurants, as he would immediately outshine most of them. Whenever possible he uses local ingredients, and he combines them in innovative ways. The menu changes constantly, but keep an eye out for the watermelon salad with kalamata olives, feta, red onion, mint, and harissa dressing, as well as for the Thai pulled pork sandwich with green papaya slaw and some of the best fries I've ever had.

For another, the setting is gorgeous: It's a simple but attractive place that opens onto a pool deck and has a view of the surrounding mountains.

Finally, there are good deals to be had. For US$15, diners not staying at the ranch can have lunch and all-day access to the pool. This makes it a reasonable indulgence even for those on tight budgets, particularly if they're willing to take a bus from Boquete to Caldera and hoof it for the last two kilometers up to the ranch.

No alcohol or soft drinks are served. Instead, Craig makes innovative drinks such as a Thai Citrus Sparkler (fresh orange and lime juice, honey, a pinch of cayenne and sparkling water), or the fresh Basil and Lime Fizz.

In the evenings, a fixed-price menu for US$23 is served at 6:30 P.M.. Reservations are required. These are themed (e.g., Mexican, Indian, Italian, Thai, etc.) and change nightly.

When I ate at Madre Tierra, all the other guests were speaking French—the word is starting to get out. It's well worth making a special trip, or stopping there on the way to or from the Caldera hot springs.

Heading south from Boquete, make a left at the Caldera turnoff and continue straight towards Caldera for 10 kilometers. You'll pass the Montañas de Caldera gated community along the way; continue straight past it. As you reach Caldera proper you'll see a church and soccer field on the left. Look for the sign for Rancho de Caldera. Turn left here and head uphill for two kilometers. The last 700 meters is on a one-lane track, so drive carefully.

If you have an irresistible craving for pizza and don't want to go all the way up to Ristorante y Pizzeria Il Pianista, **Pizzeria La Volcánica** (12:30–10 P.M. Tues.–Sun.) serves the best in Boquete proper, which isn't saying much. (Avoid Ristorante Salvatore, on the outskirts of town; both the pizza and service are bad.) Fairly tasty but greasy pizzas with thin cracker crusts range in size from *chica* to *gigante*. A *chica* will feed two moderately hungry adults and starts at US$4.25. You can also get sandwiches, or half a roast chicken for US$5.50. It's one block before the park on the main road.

Restaurante El Sabrosón (Avenida Central, tel. 720-2147, 6:30 A.M.–10 P.M. Mon.–Fri., 6:30 A.M.–midnight Sat.–Sun., under US$4) is a popular place with low-budget diners. It's on the east side of Avenida Central at the north end of town, just down from where the road forks at the church. Its steam-table offerings include the usual, plus some Chinese dishes. It's best known for its fresh trout, which the cook will prepare however you like. It's good.

Nelvi's (cell 6578-6528, 7:30 A.M.–3:30 P.M. daily, under US$2) is a newer *comida corriente* (fast food) place that has quickly become a favorite among locals looking for cheap decent food. It's my hole-in-the-wall of choice in Boquete. It's behind Los Establos Plaza on the road to Valle Escondido. Daily offerings may include various preparations of chicken, pork, spaghetti, mystery meat, and, happily enough, salads. The fried chicken is decent; the rice with *guandu* (a legume) is not. A full meal here runs less than US$2. (Pay after you eat.) They'll pack food to go if you like. A second, much-more attractive branch recently opened in Alto Boquete (cell 6414-1393, 7 A.M.–7 P.M. daily).

The **Coffee House Restaurant** (tel. 720-2285, www.fincalerida.com, 7 A.M.–8 P.M., US$6–8) is on the grounds of Finca Lérida. It's a rather unadorned place serving salads, sandwiches, and other simple fare. The spectacular view of the Boquete valley is the draw here, so even those not staying at the *finca* (country house) should consider making their way up for breakfast or lunch. Call ahead of time to make sure it's open.

Sugar and Spice (Avenida Central, 8 A.M.–6 A.M. Thurs.–Tues.) offers good fresh bread, cakes, and cookies. It's on the right side of town as you drive into town, a block and a half past the Texaco station.

Cafés

◖ **Art Cafe La Crepe** (Avenida Central next to Zanzibar, tel. 720-1821, 11 A.M.–9 P.M. Tues.–Sat., 9 A.M.–9 P.M. Sun., closed Mon.) is on everyone's list of favorite places to eat in Boquete these days. It offers excellent savory and sweet crepes, as well as a range of salads, seafood, and meat dishes. Most crepes are around US$6.50. A daily three-course set menu is US$12. There's a popular Sunday brunch (9 A.M.–noon). Service is gracious and the atmosphere is cheerful, with vibrantly painted café furnishings.

Café Kotowa (tel. 720-1430, www.kotowacoffee.com, 7 A.M.–7 P.M. daily) has two coffee shops in Boquete. The one in Los Establos Plaza shares space with Boquete Tree Trek. The other is in the CEFATI building in Alto Boquete. Both offer a full range of espresso drinks and a handful of snacks. Brightly colored, gift-worthy packages of coffee are sold in both shops.

The gourmet coffee company ◖ **Café Ruiz** (Avenida Central, tel. 720-1392, www.caferuiz.com, 7 A.M.–6 P.M. Mon.–Sat., 10 A.M.–6 P.M. Sun.) has a coffee shop that serves espresso drinks, cakes, snacks, and other goodies at its roasting and packaging plant just north of town on Avenida Central. Keep left at the fork past the church. It's the white complex on the right, near Mi Jardín Es Su Jardín. The espresso here is among the best I've ever tasted—strong but not bitter. You can also buy a wide range of packaged coffees fresh from the plant. They come whole bean *(grano)* or ground *(molido)*, sealed in plain packaging or a variety of gift packs. You can book tours of the entire Ruiz operation.

Café Punto de Encuentro (7 A.M.–noon daily, US$2.50–5.50), one block west of Pensiçn Marilós, is a cute little outdoor breakfast café attached to a home. Also known as Olga's, in honor of its proprietor, it serves pancakes, French toast, well-stuffed omelets, and other breakfast goodies. It's a simple, friendly place.

Choko Chetta (Avenida Central and Calle 5 Sur, tel. 720-1997, 10:30 A.M.–9:30 P.M. daily,

COFFEE 101: DON'T BURN THE BEANS

Like many a would-be coffee snob, I'd always preferred hearty dark-roast coffee over the bitter stuff Americans traditionally consumed or the scorched water they now drink at Starbucks. As true coffee connoisseurs in Boquete will point out, though, dark roasts are often used to mask low-quality coffee. Gourmet coffees tend to get a lighter roast, allowing you, in the catchphrase of one Boquete grower, to "taste the coffee, not the roast." If you like your coffee strong, just brew more beans per cup. Those with sensitive stomachs should also note that dark roasts are more acidic. Another tip: Coffee made from somewhat coarse grounds often tastes better than finely ground stuff.

US$3–9), across from Plaza Los Establos, gets its peculiar name from its dessert-on-a-stick shtick: It offers goodies such as strawberries and marshmallows on a brochette, usually drowned in chocolate and ice cream. Dessert purists can go for the brownie with ice cream, which is delicious. Other offerings range from salads and sandwiches to full meals. The mod decor—all glass and steel—is something new for Boquete. A plus here is they'll deliver to your hotel.

Anyone can come for breakfast on the terrace at **Pensión Topas** (Avenida Belisario Porras, tel./fax 720-1005, 8–11 A.M. daily, US$2.50–7), but guests staying at the pension get priority. The pension does not serve other meals.

Pastelería Alemana Marianne's Café (approximately 12:30–8 P.M. Thurs.–Mon., usually closed Tues. and Wed.), a little German pastry shop on the main road through Alto Boquete, is a popular place to stop for a sugar fix on the way to or from downtown Boquete. Its pies, cakes, and other sweets are delicious,

and the prices are good—about US$1.25 for a slice, or US$5 for an entire pie. Try the lemon meringue pie, the pineapple pie, the choco-vanilla cake, or the chocolate chip cookies. It's about a kilometer south of the CEFATI building. The café is closed in June.

 Fresas Mary (tel. 720-3394, 10 A.M.–7 P.M. daily, US$2.25 or less) is an attractive snack kiosk built into the front of a house just a half kilometer down the Volcancito road from the turnoff at the CEFATI building. It'll be on the left as you head toward Volcancito. The strawberry *batidos* (milkshakes) here are so good and fresh they'll make your knees buckle. The other nine flavors of *helados caseros* (homemade ice cream) include papaya, banana, *zarzamora* (blackberry), and *guanábana* (a tropical fruit sometimes known in English as soursop). Hamburgers and other hot bites, coffee, and sweets are also available. There's a comfortable indoor sitting area if it's raining.

Markets

A produce and meat market, the **Mercado Municipal** (also known as the Mercado Público, 6:30 A.M.–6 P.M. daily), is on the northeast corner of the plaza. Note that there are two entrances, one on the south side and one on the east side of the building. It's worth exploring the whole complex to see who's got the best stuff that day.

There are several supermarkets within a couple of blocks of the plaza. Besides groceries, **Supercentro El Mandarín** (Avenida Central at the Calle 2a Sur) carries a range of toiletries, hardware, and other dry goods. The 24-hour **Supermercado Romero,** behind the post office, has a bakery and pharmacy. They also sell used books in English.

Deli Barú (8 A.M.–8 P.M. daily) offers a modest selection of imported cheese, chocolate, and other goodies that are normally hard to find up here.

INFORMATION AND SERVICES
Tourist Information and Maps
ATP's **Centro de Facilidades Turísticas**

e Interpretación Volcán Barú-Boquete (CEFATI, tel. 720-4060, 8:30 A.M.–4:30 P.M. Mon.–Fri., 9:30 A.M.–5:30 P.M. Sat.–Sun.) is in Alto Boquete on the main road just before it heads downhill into the town of Boquete. The place, almost as imposing as its name, was a costly undertaking for a glorified information booth, especially since the information it offers is negligible. Three good things about it: It has bathrooms, there's a great view of the Boquete valley and Río Caldera behind the building, and there's a Café Kotowa shop (7 A.M.–7 P.M. daily) next door. A decent museum display upstairs contains some background on the region's culture, history, and coffee industry.

Boquete Tree Trek (Los Establos Plaza, tel. 720-1635, cell 6615-3300, www.aventurist.com) is a better source of local tourist information, even for those who don't book one of their tours.

Boquete maps come and go. If the CEFATI doesn't have a decent one, try Boquete Tree Trek, Café Ruiz, or one of the Café Kotowa outlets.

Banks
Banco Nacional de Panamá and **Banco General** are on Avenida Central at the entrance to downtown (both open 8 A.M.–3 P.M. Mon.–Fri., 9 A.M.–noon Sat.). **HSBC** (8:30 A.M.–3:30 P.M. Mon.–Fri., 9 A.M.–noon Sat.) is at the north end of town, across Avenida Central from the church.

Communications
The **post office** (tel. 720-1265, 7 A.M.–5 P.M. Mon.–Fri., 7 A.M.–noon Sat.) is on the east side of the plaza.

Hastor Computers (tel. 720-2855, 8 A.M.–10:45 P.M. Mon.–Sat., 10 A.M.–10:45 P.M. Sun.), next to the Chiriquí River Rafting office, charges US$0.75 an hour for Internet access. Travelers can also make international calls here, with rates starting at US$0.08 a minute.

Mailboxes Etc. (Avenida Central, tel. 720-2684, 8:30 A.M.–6 P.M. Mon.–Fri., 8:30 A.M.–12:30 P.M. Sat.), across from La Reina, offers a variety of communication services, including

sending and receiving faxes. Internet access is US$1 an hour.

Pharmacies
A branch of **Farmacia Revilla** (tel. 720-2995, 7 A.M.–9 P.M. Mon.–Sat., 8 A.M.–6 P.M. Sun.) is at the north end of town near the church.

Farmacia Danka (Calle 3 Sur, tel. 775-1788, 8 A.M.–8:30 P.M. Mon.–Sat., 8:30 A.M.–6:30 P.M. Sun.) is a pharmacy next to Pension Doña Cata. **Farmacia Any** (Avenida Central, tel. 720-1296, 8 A.M.–9 P.M. daily) is just north of Super Centro Bruña on the east side of Avenida Central. It has a Moneygram outlet.

Launderettes
Lavandería La Mejor (Calle 1 Sur, tel. 720-1280, 8 A.M.–5 P.M. Mon.–Sat., 9 A.M.–1 P.M. Sun.) charges US$2 to wash and US$2 to dry. It's a half block west of Avenida Central on Calle 1 Sur.

Spanish Courses
The **Habla Ya Language School** (Los Establos Plaza, tel. 720-1294, cell 6480-4506, www.hablayapanama.com, 8 A.M.–8 P.M. Mon.–Fri., 9 A.M.–2 P.M. Sat.) offers a flexible menu of Spanish courses that includes an ultra-compressed "Spanish for travelers" package (10–20 hours over 2–5 days), beginner crash courses, and longer-term, total-immersion packages that can include homestays with local families. Prices are per hour, starting at US$105.95 (group class) or US$150 (private lessons) for 10 hours. Special offers are sometimes available. Free extras at the school include a café with wireless Internet, Wednesday-night Spanish-language movies, conversation sessions, and Saturday afternoon salsa and *merengue* lessons. The school also arranges lodging, field trips, and outdoor adventures.

Spanish by the River (tel. 720-3456, cell 6759-5753, spanishbytheriverboquete@gmail.com, www.spanishatlocations.com) is actually by a road, not the river. Specifically, it's in Alto Boquete just off the main road, on the turnoff that leads to Palmira.

However, it's a pleasant spot, and it's a quick bus ride or $0.50 shared cab ride to downtown. Instruction is given in open-air "classrooms" in the school's spacious and surprisingly quiet backyard.

Prices depend on course length, size of group, and hours per day of instruction. For instance, a five-day group course, with two hours a day of instruction, is US$80 per person. A five-day, six-hour-a-day intensive private course would cost US$430. There are price breaks for longer courses and small groups who enroll together.

Students can spend part of their course at the school's sister facilities, Spanish by the Sea in Bocas del Toro and in Turrialba, Costa Rica. The school can also arrange tours, horseback riding trips, and volunteer work.

The staff can arrange home stays, and there are also four small, spotless rooms with good beds at the school itself. These go for US$17 s, US$25 d. Priority is given to students, but anyone can stay here when there's no demand. Most people don't realize this, so it's possible to find a room here even when more expensive and less appealing accommodations are full in downtown Boquete.

Massages and Spa Treatments

Those who would like some pampering have several options. A quite opulent spa called **The Haven** (tel. 730-9345, www.boquetespa.com) was nearing completion on a hill near the entrance to Bajo Boquete as this book went to press. I got a tour of the facilities before it was completed, and it was shaping up to be quite a place—the first place in Boquete one might consider a "destination spa." It was going to offer a full range of massage therapies, clinical treatments including acupuncture, facials, and the like, all at or below what you'd expect to pay in the United States. It also has state-of-the-art exercise equipment. It was also going to offer five small but well-appointed guest rooms.

The **Panamonte Inn and Spa** (off Avenida Central, north of town center, tel. 720-1324, 8 A.M.–7 P.M. daily) has a quaint and airy day spa where you can relax to the tune of the Río Caldera rushing by. It offers massages (average price US$75 for 55 minutes), facials, mud therapy, and the like.

GETTING THERE AND AWAY

The city of David, in the lowlands, is less than 40 kilometers from Boquete and is the transportation hub for buses and planes to and from other parts of the country, most notably Bocas del Toro and Panama City. Some hotels and guides offer transportation to David, the west side of Barú, the Costa Rican border, and Almirante, the port of entry for the archipelago of Bocas del Toro. Fees for this service generally range US$20–30 for David–Boquete up to US$150–200 for Boquete–Almirante.

Boquete is 45 minutes by car from David, seven hours from Panama City. Those driving west from Panama City should turn right at the first major intersection upon entering David. Follow the road all the way into Boquete, which is less than 40 kilometers north of David.

Boquete-bound buses leave the David bus terminal about every 15–30 minutes, 5:15 A.M.–9 P.M., with a final bus at 9:45 P.M. David-bound buses leave Boquete approximately every 25–30 minutes, 4:15 A.M.–7 P.M. Catch the bus to David in front of the Hostal Palacio on the northwest side of the plaza. The trip costs US$1.45 each way and takes about 45 minutes. The Oficina de Transporte Boquete-David, a fancy name for a tiny office on the north side of the plaza, has the latest bus schedule and may even have a staff member who speaks English.

Boquete Tree Trek (tel. 720-1635, www. aventurist.com) offers a shuttle service between David or David's airport (US$10). It can also help arrange car rentals and plane tickets. Some hotels offer pickup and drop-off service, usually for an extra fee.

Taxis between Boquete and David cost US$25 (downtown or bus station) and US$30 (airport). Expect to pay US$40–60 for trips to Cerro Punta or the Costa Rican border. A trip to the Respingo entrance to Sendero Los Quetzales, on the Cerro Punta side of Barú, costs US$80. It's also possible to arrange a taxi between Boquete and Almirante, the jumping-off point for the islands of Bocas del Toro. Expect to pay anywhere from US$135–180.

GETTING AROUND

You probably won't need transportation in town since it's easy to walk from one end of Boquete to another in just a few minutes. Buses and taxis to surrounding areas are plentiful and cheap. Note that taxis can be hard to come by at night.

Drivers should be careful at night. The streets outside of town are dark and have no sidewalks. Pedestrians, including some very drunk ones, often walk down the middle of the streets at night.

Urbana minibuses that roam around the nearby hills leave from Avenida Central just north of the plaza. Their destinations are written on their windows. (Note that El Bajo refers to Bajo Boquete.) Sample bus fares include US$1.50 to the Bajo Mono loop and US$1.50 to Caldera.

Since taxis here are reasonable you may want to try them first for nearby destinations. It's easy to catch one along Avenida Central. Taxis within town shouldn't cost more than US$1.50. Taxis to places just outside of Boquete, such as El Explorador and Mi Jardín Es Su Jardín,

shouldn't cost more than US$3. The drive to the ranger station *caseta* for the climb up Volcán Barú is US$10 and should be made in a pickup taxi.

The fare is also at least US$10 to the Alto Chiquero ranger station, near the Boquete-side trailhead for Sendero Los Quetzales. Expect to pay US$15 to get within walking distance of the Pozos de Caldera.

Daniel Higgins (cell 6617-0570) is a fully bilingual Panamanian taxi driver with an excellent reputation. He drove me from Almirante to Boquete and David on a recent trip and I found him punctual, good-natured, friendly, interesting to talk to, and, most important, a safe and skilled driver. He'll drive you around in his late-model four-wheel drive for US$20 an hour, which includes a commentary on the history of the area. Longer trips include Cerro Punta (US$65) and Almirante (US$150), the jumping-off point for the islands of Bocas del Toro.

I've also heard good things about **Juan Carlos Contreras** (cell 6709-5369, tel. 720-1140—ask the dispatcher for Juan Carlos), who doesn't speak English but understands a fair amount. He charges US$15 an hour.

Both Higgins and Contreras also offer regular taxi service to the surrounding areas for the going rates.

Cerro Punta and Vicinity

The west side of Volcán Barú looks like a pastoral paradise. As the road winds its way up the foggy mountains, it passes one tranquil dairy farm after another. Soon there are neat quilts of green-and-brown farmland clinging at impossible angles to mountain slopes. Down in the valleys, race horses romp in vast pastures. It's all so picturesque it's easy to overlook the fact that intensive farming is damaging this beautiful area. Erosion and pesticide overuse are serious problems. The developed land also borders two of Panama's most spectacular parks, and in some cases encroaches on them. Illegal logging, farming, and even cattle ranching still take place in them.

Environmentalists have made some difference here, though, including stopping an ill-conceived plan a few years back to build a road right through the heart of one of the parks. Hikes through these parks are thus still among the great attractions of the area. Cerro Punta has the most accessible entry into Parque Internacional La Amistad, a park so important UNESCO declared it a World Heritage Site in 1990.

All the towns and tourist sights on the west side of Barú are linked by a single road that starts in the lowland town of Concepción and ends at Guadalupe, elevation 2,130 meters.

The first town is Volcán, officially known as Hato de Volcán, which has most of the visitor services, but little else.

The road forks here. Straight leads to a little-used Costa Rican border crossing at Río Sereno. A right turn leads farther up the mountain toward Bambito, Cerro Punta, and Guadalupe. Bambito has hotels and a few places to eat, but the "town" itself is really just a few roadside stands. The vistas open up at little Cerro Punta and tiny Guadalupe just beyond it. You're up in the clouds here, and you may feel you've found Shangri-la.

The town of Cerro Punta consists of little more than a small commercial strip in the middle of a heavily developed agricultural area. There are gas stations, a couple of dreary bars and pool halls, a few greasy-spoon restaurants, small grocery stores, and a launderette.

SIGHTS

Natural beauty is the major draw of this area, particularly for those looking to hike in the mammoth Parque Internacional La Amistad or along the popular Sendero Los Quetzales. Visitors will get more out of the hikes with the help of a naturalist guide; it also greatly improves the chances of spotting quetzals. Those with extra time should consider a visit to the impressive Finca Dracula orchid farm. The horse, strawberry, and flower farms are also worth a quick visit.

◖ Parque Internacional La Amistad

The enormous and magnificent Parque Internacional La Amistad (PILA), which lies along the Talamanca mountain range, was established in September 1988 and declared a UNESCO World Heritage Site in 1990. It's "international" in that a little less than half of it is in Costa Rica. That leaves 207,000 hectares on the Panama side. Nearly all of this land is in the province of Bocas del Toro, but the 3 percent of it that pokes into Chiriquí province is far more accessible.

The park's plant and animal life are among the most diverse in Panama. The forests vary from lowland tropical to subalpine, and much of the vegetation is virgin. Five of the six species of Central American felines—the jaguar, puma, ocelot, jaguarundi, and margay—are still hanging on here, as is the also-endangered Baird's tapir. Among the nearly 600 types of birds identified in the area are such spectacular species as the resplendent quetzal, the three-wattled bellbird, and the rarely seen bare-necked umbrellabird.

All that said, you may not see much wildlife other than birds on a day hike near Cerro Punta. But the park is well worth a visit even if you're not a birding fanatic. The forests are dense and varied and there are several kilometers of well-maintained trails near town.

The main entrance to the park is at Las Nubes, about seven kilometers west of Cerro Punta. Heading up to Cerro Punta from the south, look for the sign indicating a left turn off the main road just before one enters "downtown." Make another left at the Las Nubes sign. The road from this point on can sometimes be brutal. Ask about the current state of the road before venturing here without a four-wheel drive. Round-trip taxi fare from Cerro Punta is US$5–7.

There's an **ANAM ranger station** (regional office tel. 775-3163 or 775-2055; there's a radio but no phone at the station itself; 8 or 8:30 A.M.–4 P.M. daily, US$5) on the right at the end of the road, where the trails start. Pay the entrance fee here and get trail maps from the friendly staff. There's a small display on the park and its flora and fauna. There's also a *comida corriente* (fast food) restaurant next door.

Finca Dracula

Don't worry, you don't need to bring garlic. Finca Dracula (tel. 771-2070, www.fincadracula.com) is named for the 30 varieties of the *Telipogon vampirus* that are among the more than 2,000 species of orchids found in this famous botanical garden. It has one of the most important collections in Latin America—it claims to be one of the 10 largest in the world—and is known for its experiments in propagating endangered species. The lovely landscaped grounds, which are crisscrossed with streams and ponds, make for a pleasant walk.

The collections at the *finca* (country house) are contained in three areas, separated according to climate, from those that thrive at the local temperature of 14–20°C up to those that need a temperature of 25°C or higher.

Even if you're not a flower freak, you're likely to find this collection worth a visit. Specimens include carnivorous orchids, orchids the size of a nail head, orchids that disguise themselves as bees, orchids with a delicious fragrance, and orchids that bloom for only one day.

Finca Dracula is in Guadalupe, about a 20-minute walk or very short car ride past Los Quetzales Lodge and Spa. When the road splits past the hotel, take the right fork and then turn left onto the gravel road. You'll need a four-wheel drive if you're driving. You'll see a sign across the gate of the *finca* on the left, at the turnoff to the entrance to the dirt road that leads to the Los Quetzales cabañas.

© WILLIAM FRIAR

one of the more than 2,000 species of orchids at Finca Dracula

Contact Finca Dracula to arrange a tour, or just drop by. Guides speak little English. Minimum tour length is half an hour, but it can go quite a bit longer depending on the level of detail you're interested in. Tours are available 8 A.M.–5:30 P.M. daily. The cost is US$10 per person.

Farms

Those who want to get a closer look at some of the crops the rich volcanic soil and mild weather of this region produce may be interested in paying a quick visit to the flower and strawberry farms. They're more photogenic and interesting than you might think. Several of them are located along the road that links Guadalupe and the turnoff to Parque Internacional La Amistad. There's no need to make an appointment. Just stop by during regular business hours and ask if you can poke around. They might think you're a little strange, but they'll probably let you.

Haras Cerro Punta (tel. 227-3371, www.harascerropunta.com) breeds some of Panama's best racehorses in one of Panama's prettiest spots. The *haras* (stud farm) comprises wide-open pasture land ringed by mountains. Visitors are welcome to tour the farm with advance notice. The main entrance is just before Guadalupe on the Cerro Punta–Guadalupe road.

SPORTS AND RECREATION

Hiking and looking for quetzals in the national parks are the big activities here, but there are a few other outdoor possibilities. White-water companies are headquartered in Boquete, on the other side of Barú, but they can usually pick clients up here for trips on either side of the mountain. Cerro Punta produces the finest horses in the country. Visitors can arrange rides on much more modest steeds for around US$5–6 an hour. **Los Quetzales Lodge and Spa** (tel. 771-2182 or 771-2291, fax 771-2226, www.losquetzales.com) charges US$8 an hour, with an extra US$5 for a guide. The hotel also rents mountain bikes for US$5 an hour.

Genover Santamaria is a friendly, reliable

local guide who works with Los Quetzales Lodge and Spa. He specializes in long hikes, including ones to the summit of Volcán Barú (US$80 for two people) and Sendero Los Quetzales to Boquete (US$40 for two people). He's also available for multiday treks. Ask for him at the hotel.

A good guide is essential on wilderness trails, particularly up Volcán Barú. But for nearby, less rugged destinations, it's simpler to make arrangements on your own than go through a guide. This is especially true of visits to Finca Dracula, which supplies its own tour guides for a fraction of what third-party outfits charge.

Hiking in Parque Internacional La Amistad

Three main trails start from the ANAM ranger station at Parque Internacional La Amistad. **Sendero La Cascada** is a 3.4-kilometer, two-hour round-trip hike that leads to a picture-perfect 55-meter waterfall. The trail is wide and well maintained. It's a 1.7-kilometer uphill hike to the falls, with the elevation climbing from 2,180 to about 2,500 meters. There are three *miradors* (observation platforms) along the trail with sweeping views of the mountains and valleys. However, if it's a foggy day you won't see a thing from them.

The first *mirador* is unmarked, but it's on the right as the trail levels off and comes out of the woods. Mirador La Nevera is on the left a little farther on. The trail forks at Mirador El Barranco. To get to the falls, head down the steep wooden staircase to the right. (Warning: Some of the stairs are loose and slippery. Watch your step.) Those in the mood for more exercise can take the left fork. If it's a clear day, a two-hour hike from here offers a view of the Caribbean.

Sendero El Retoño, a two-kilometer loop trail, is much less strenuous but even more beautiful. The trail is mostly level and remarkably varied. It leads through lush green forest, over bridges spanning rushing streams, and into a tunnel formed from leaning stands of bamboo. The hike takes about an hour at a very leisurely pace.

There are a few forks along the trail: To stay on the main trail, just take every left fork. For a longer hike, there's a loop within the loop that starts halfway down the trail at a marked fork to the right. It ends near the exit to the main trail.

A newer trail, **Vereda La Montaña,** leads up the side of Cerro Picacho. According to the rangers, this rustic trail (*vereda* is Spanish for footpath) is four kilometers long and a quite strenuous uphill trek, though there's a wooden cabin with a kitchen and bathroom at the top. Ask the rangers about it before attempting this hike. Allow six hours for the trip up and back.

For those who just want to take a little stroll, **Sendero Panamá Verde** is a 400-meter walk near the ranger station that takes about 15 minutes to walk.

Do not attempt any of the longer hikes without a good guide. The forest here is rugged wilderness, and it's very easy to get lost. Those who speak Spanish can ask the forest ranger at Las Nubes for guidance. It's possible to camp in the park or stay in a dormitory at the ANAM station.

Serious trekkers may be interested to know there's an unmarked eight-hour hike through the forest to some hot springs, though this should not be attempted without an experienced guide. That's one-way; you'd have to camp out by the springs.

For the truly hard-core, there's also the possibility of multiday treks over the cordillera toward the Caribbean coast. Los Quetzales Lodge and Spa may be able to help arrange an eight-day trek for those feeling brave. Be warned this is an extremely hard-core trip through mountainous wilderness and deep mud. You'll spend the last two days traveling in *cayucos* (dugout canoes) through Naso (also called Teribe) territory. For food and shelter you'll mostly rely on lonely, friendly folk living in huts in the woods. Trekkers must have their own tents, sleeping bags, and all other equipment. Los Quetzales has booked this trip only once. Even the Naso who live in this forest will probably think you're nuts.

Sendero Los Quetzales

This popular trail through Parque Nacional Volcán Barú curves around the north side of Barú, linking Cerro Punta with Boquete to the east. Hiking it in either direction is far less challenging than a climb to the top of Barú, but it's still a serious hike.

It's not essential to have a guide, at least in this direction, but do not attempt it alone. Bring a first-aid kit. Do not hike the trail in shorts; it's cool in the forest, and if it rains it gets downright cold. A walking stick can come in handy.

The Sendero Los Quetzales gives a taste of real wilderness, but is well-defined enough it's not technically difficult to walk. And, because of the rapid change in elevation, it offers a vivid lesson in life zones, starting with mossy cloud forest dotted with towering oaks and picture-postcard streams that quickly give way to palms, bamboo, and serpentine lianas and vines. You'll encounter some forest giants, but most of the forest is secondary growth. Despite its name, this trail is not the best place to see quetzals.

It's a developed trail, with bridges and steps and the like, but it's not being well maintained, so watch your step. There are lots of signs along the trail, though whoever put them up has a fanciful sense of distance; don't pay much attention to them.

About a third of the way down, there's a designated campsite with few facilities other than an open-sided wooden shelter and some rotting benches. The ground slopes at a pretty steep angle; campers who want to pitch a tent here are best off doing it in the relatively level shelter. A short walk behind this campsite leads to a couple of *miradors* (observation platforms), the second of which has a beautiful, expansive view down toward Boquete. The red-roofed building off in the distance is the little ranger station at the Boquete entrance to the trail.

It's less grueling to hike the trail from Cerro Punta to Boquete than vice versa since it's downhill most of the way, descending nearly a kilometer in altitude (though there is an uphill stretch at the end, just when you think you're literally out of the woods).

The hike requires some planning since hikers end up far away from Cerro Punta, on the other side of the mountain. The bus ride back takes at least three hours, not including waiting time in David, where you have to switch buses. The best strategy is to leave early in the morning and either have someone meet you with a car at the end of the trail or plan to spend the night in Boquete. Some who choose the latter option arrange to have their luggage shipped ahead to Boquete, usually through their hotel or guide, but be sure to nail down exactly when the luggage will arrive. Some tourists have had their luggage sent by couriers who only make the trip once a day, leaving them stranded without their belongings, waiting for their luggage to catch up with them.

So how long will the hike down take? This question trips up a lot of hikers, who end up with a much longer outing than they bargained for. It takes an average of five hours to get from El Respingo ranger station (near Cerro Punta) to the Alto Chiquero ranger station (near Boquete, sometimes known as La Roca), but that doesn't take into account getting to and from the ranger stations.

El Respingo station is at the end of 5.5 kilometers of uphill road that branches off the main road that links Cerro Punta and Guadalupe. The turnoff is halfway between Cerro Punta and Guadalupe, or about 1.5 kilometers past the Hotel Cerro Punta. As you head toward Guadalupe, there's a huge trail sign on the right just after a little bridge. Turn here and follow the road toward the Bajo Grande area. Note that the road soon turns brutal and drivers must have a four-wheel drive with high clearance.

If you want to walk to the station from the turnoff, add about two hours to the hiking estimate. You may want to opt instead for a taxi, which, unless the horribly rough road has been paved by the time you visit, will cost about US$30 from Cerro Punta to the station. Guests at Los Quetzales Lodge and Spa can get a ride to or from the El Respingo station for the same price, in a van that can carry up to 10 people. An alternative is to hire a taxi to take you to the end of the paved road (US$3) and then hike the rest of the way to the station, which cuts the two-hour walk in half.

Those with a vehicle can park near the station. Don't leave anything of value in the car. Park entrance is US$5, US$1 to park, and US$5 more to either camp or use a bunk in the quite nice ranger station.

From the Alto Chiquero ranger station at the Boquete end it's another 1.5-hour hike to get to the Bajo Mono loop road. From there you can catch one of the frequent buses to downtown Boquete for US$1.

Note: **Finca Fernández,** on the road to Sendero Los Quetzales, has long been famous as a prime place to see quetzals. Sadly, there have been so many reports of thefts from tourists' cars here I can no longer recommend the *finca* as a safe place to visit. There are plenty of other places to see quetzals and plenty of other guides to find them for you.

ACCOMMODATIONS

There are only a few, widely scattered places to stay around Cerro Punta. Fortunately, these include a couple of appealing possibilities.

US$25-50

Hotel Cerro Punta (tel. 771-2020, US$45 s/d) is on the left just as one approaches downtown Cerro Punta. It offers 10 decent rooms with okay beds. Six of the rooms are in an annex facing a gorgeous view of the mountains. Perversely, the windows are in the back, looking out on nothing. The rooms in the main building are nicer, and two have a good view for no extra charge. The service here is friendly.

US$50-100

Easily the best-run place to stay on the entire west side of the mountain is ◖ **Hostal Cielito Sur Bed and Breakfast** (tel./fax 771-2038, cell 6602-3008 www.cielitosur.com, starts at US$99 s/d, closed in Oct.). Along with Los Quetzales Lodge and Spa, it is also the coziest

and most pleasant. Actually 4 kilometers south of Cerro Punta and 10 kilometers north of Volcán in a postage stamp–sized "community" called Nueva Suiza, Cielito Sur sits by itself on 2.5 hectares of land just off the main road, but within easy driving distance of most of the area's attractions. It consists of four modern, spacious rooms, each with decor inspired by one of Panama's indigenous peoples—the Kuna and Teribe rooms (US$99 s/d), and the larger Ngöbe-Buglé and Wounaan-Emberá rooms (US$110 s/d, add US$40 for a third person), which also have a minifridge and microwave. Even if you don't stay in the Wounaan-Emberá room, you should ask to check out the especially beautiful specimens of their woven baskets mounted on the wall.

Everything here is done just right. The back patio of the bed-and-breakfast overlooks a spring-fed stream that runs through a carefully tended garden that attracts 10 species of hummingbirds. A stay includes an enormous breakfast in a sunny dining room and use of a private, enclosed hot tub. There's a common lounge with a fireplace, CD player and CDs, library, and Internet-connected computer (free).

Your hosts are Janet and Glenn Lee, a Panamanian-American couple who speak fluent English and Spanish and are a good source of information on just about anything you'd like to know about the whole area. They can arrange transfers to or from David for US$35 each way, and ground transportation to or from just about anywhere else in western Panama, including Bocas and the Costa Rican border, as well as make domestic plane reservations and ground-transfer arrangements to or from Panama City. Rates depend on the destination.

◖ **Los Quetzales Lodge and Spa** (tel. 771-2182 or 771-2291, fax 771-2226, www. losquetzales.com, starts at US$75 s/d/t, including breakfast) is really a destination in itself. Mostly this is because some of the accommodations are in a 350-acre private cloud-forest reserve that's inside both a national park (Parque Nacional Volcán Barú) and an international one (Parque International La Amistad). The owner bought land here in 1968, before the parks were founded. Los Quetzales was one of Panama's first ecotourism operations and remains among its most committed.

As the name suggests, there are actually two Los Quetzales: a hotel in the little town of Guadalupe, three kilometers past Cerro Punta, and five "chalets" (large cabins, really) in a forest farther uphill. The hotel is an attractive place with lots of handsome woodwork, on the edge of a fast-flowing river. It features 10 rooms next to the main building and five large suites and dorm rooms in a nearby annex. The main building resembles a comfy ski lodge, and the smells wafting up from the bakery/ pizzeria on the 1st floor add to the cozy feel. There's an Internet café (free to guests, US$1/ hour for others), bar, restaurant, and rec room on the 2nd floor. The paintings everywhere, some of them rather spooky, are by Brooke "Cookie" Alfaro, your host's brother and one of Panama's most famous artists.

Small rooms have one queen and one single bed and a shower. Larger, considerably nicer and brighter rooms with terraces are US$85 s/d/t. Suites go for US$95–110 and sleep up to four people. These are quite large and have fireplaces, sitting rooms, and balconies. One of the suites is wheelchair accessible. All the rooms have orthopedic beds and phones that can be used for local and international calls.

There are also three dorm rooms crowded with bunk beds, featuring the same warm wood as the private rooms. Each has a shared toilet and shower. The smallest dorm room has lockers. Dorm beds are US$18, or US$5 more with continental breakfast.

A health spa right next to the river helps guests recover from a grueling hike with a massage, sauna, or dip in an outdoor hot tub. Guests get 30 percent off spa services including massages and facials. They also get free use of the sauna, hot tubs, small gym, horses, and mountain bikes.

My favorite cabins in the park, Chalet 2 and Chalet 3, are slightly rustic in the mountain-cabin sense, but they're very comfortable and nicely designed. None of the cabins have electricity, but all have wood-burning stoves or fireplaces, hot water, and a kitchen. Ten kinds of colorful hummingbirds are among the more than 100 species of birds identified near here. You'll see them buzzing around like mosquitoes.

Chalets 2 and 3 are large, wooden, two-story structures built at more than 2,020 meters above sea level, right in the middle of a stunning cloud forest. The Chiriquí Viejo River runs through the property. There's a hot tub outside Chalet 3, but it's not always working.

Prices for the cabins are the same regardless of group size, so larger groups can get a great deal. Rates are US$105–160, sleeping between five and eight people. A newer place, Cabin Bajo Grande, is outside the park. Chalet 2 at Bajo Grande sleeps up to 10 people for US$175, while Chalet 1 is US$100. All chalets offer enough privacy that friendly acquaintances can share them to save money. Daily guided hikes are included.

Eight trails originate from the area around the chalets. Foggy mountains, trees draped in moss, waterfalls, orchids, the lovely songs of countless birds—it's like a fairy kingdom up there. Daily tours, led by Ngöbe-Buglé guides who speak only Spanish, are available. Los Quetzales can supply boots, rain jackets, and horses. There's a very good chance of seeing quetzals here January–May.

The park chalets are only 2.5 kilometers from the main hotel in Guadalupe, but the road is so ferociously bad it takes about 25 minutes to get there by four-wheel-drive vehicle. (Transportation is included with cabin rental.) Among other things, vehicles must ford a shallow river. That's something to bear in mind if you decide to hike in. Even if you go by four-wheel drive, it's a short but steep walk up to Chalets 2 and 3.

Camping

It's possible to camp in **Parque Internacional La Amistad** for US$5, but as usual with Panamanian parks don't expect developed campsites. There's also a surprisingly pleasant dormitory at the **ANAM station** at the main entrance to the park for the same price. It offers bunk beds in shared rooms, a large fireplace, and a kitchen. Bring your own bedding. For more information, ask at the station, or call the ANAM regional office in David (tel. 775-3163; there's a radio but no phone at the station itself). This place is a great deal.

There's a similar setup at **El Respingo ranger station** at the trailhead for Sendero Los Quetzales. It'll cost US$5 either to camp or to use a bunk in the quite decent ranger station, which is on a hill surrounded by nicely landscaped grounds. The view from here is stunning, and it's a great place to pitch a tent. The bunks are in a small, dark wooden room that's quite okay and has lockers.

FOOD

There are few dining options this far up the mountain. More possibilities are farther down, around Bambito and Volcán. Many small kiosks also offer fruit shakes and burgers and the like for US$1–2 along the road from Volcán all the way to Guadalupe. Most of them are between Bambito and Cerro Punta. There are also some fruit and vegetable stands for those who want to stock up on fresh produce.

Los Quetzales Lodge and Spa (tel. 771-2182 or 771-2291, 7:30 A.M.–8 P.M. daily, US$6–9) has a new chef who makes good use of local fresh ingredients. The hotel features trout from its own pond, produce from its own garden, and tasty pizza from its own pizzeria.

The decor is plain in the dining room of the **Hotel Cerro Punta** (on the left as you approach downtown Cerro Punta, tel. 771-2020, US$5–9), but the food is surprisingly tasty and the service is refreshingly warm and friendly. The veggie rice dish (*arroz jardinero*) is a godsend for those tired of meat and deep-fried starches. There's also the usual assortment of meats and fish. The fresh-fruit shakes (*batidos*) are pretty good.

INFORMATION AND SERVICES

Services are limited on this side of the mountain and become sparser the higher up you go.

Cerro Punta has some basic necessities, but for many things (such as an ATM) visitors have to go down at least as far as Volcán. There's an **Internet café** (tel. 771-2182 or 771-2291, US$1/hour) at Los Quetzales Lodge and Spa, and there's usually at least one operating in town as well.

Lavandería Cerro Punta (8 A.M.–8 P.M. Sun.–Fri.) is on the left as one drives through Cerro Punta on the way to Guadalupe. It charges US$2.50 to wash and dry a load.

GETTING THERE

The lowland city of David is the bus and airline hub for the western highlands. It takes 6–7 hours by car to get from Panama City to David. From there it's about a two-hour drive to Cerro Punta. If you're driving from David, take the Interamericana west to Concepción, 26 kilometers away. Turn right and head uphill. After another 34 kilometers you'll come to Volcán. Turn right at the fork to get to Bambito, Cerro Punta, and Guadalupe. There may be no sign at the intersection except one pointing toward Hotel Bambito. Follow it. Bambito is the first place you'll come to, about six kilometers north of Volcán. Cerro Punta is about another eight winding kilometers further up the mountain.

In all, Cerro Punta is about 74 kilometers from David, a distance that takes a little over two hours to cover by bus and a bit less by car. The village of Guadalupe is three kilometers farther uphill.

Bus fare from David is US$3 to Cerro Punta and Guadalupe. Look for the bus with "Cerro Punta" painted on the windshield; it stops at all the towns along the way. The Cerro Punta bus should go all the way to Guadalupe, but ask to make sure. If not, taxi fare from Cerro Punta to Guadalupe is US$1. Buses bound for Cerro Punta leave David 5 A.M.–8 P.M.; David-bound buses leave Cerro Punta 4:45 A.M.–6:45 P.M. Buses run every 15 minutes. Those coming from Costa Rica can also catch the Cerro Punta bus at Concepción rather than go all the way to the David bus terminal. Taxis between David and Cerro Punta charge around US$35 one way.

GETTING AROUND

This is a pleasant place to go for a walk, though attractions, hotels, and restaurants tend to be rather spread out. You can flag down any long-distance minibus running along the main road, since they all make stops between Cerro Punta/Guadalupe and Volcán on their way to or from David. For destinations off the main road, taxis are the best way to go. Sample fares include US$1 between Cerro Punta and Guadalupe, around US$5–7 between Cerro Punta and the Las Nubes entrance to PILA, and US$30 from Cerro Punta up the brutal road to El Respingo, the trailhead for Sendero Los Quetzales.

Volcán and Vicinity

Volcán is what passes for an urban center on the west side of Barú. It's really little more than a homely crossroads, but there are several sights and an entrance to Parque Nacional Volcán Barú nearby. It also has the only banks and ATMs for many kilometers, as well as most of the dining options.

There are a couple of decent places to stay between Volcán and Bambito, but for the most part the choice is between lousy "budget" hotels that charge too much and overpriced "luxury" hotels that aren't that luxurious. Unless you plan to explore the area extensively, you may want to head up toward Cerro Punta, 14 kilometers up the mountain, where the lodging and scenery are more attractive.

SIGHTS
Parque Nacional Volcán Barú

Though only a fraction the size of its imposing neighbor, La Amistad, this park is still plenty impressive. Its centerpiece is the dormant volcano that gives the park its name and whose summit, at 3,475 meters, is the highest point in Panama. The park was founded in 1976.

This is a good place for long hikes, camping, and bird-watching. Because of the change in elevation, the park has quite a range of life zones for its size (14,000 hectares). You'll pass through several different kinds of forests before reaching its barren and rocky summit. In the bushes near the top you can spot the rather plain-looking volcano junco. This is its only Panamanian habitat. Other birds you might encounter at the higher elevations before the forest ends include the timberline wren, black-and-yellow silky-flycatcher, and large-footed finch.

Lagunas de Volcán

These picturesque lakes are part of a protected area comprising Panama's highest wetlands (the elevation is 1,200 meters). They're famous for good bird-watching. On the lakes there's a chance of seeing masked ducks and northern jacanas. Look for pale-billed woodpeckers, flycatchers, antbirds, and the rare rose-throated becard in the woods.

To get to the *lagunas*, turn left off the main road toward Río Sereno at the sign for the Oasis Place Hotel. Pass the hotel and go straight for 0.9 kilometers. Turn right at Mini Super Casa Elsa and continue straight for 1.7 kilometers on the severely potholed road until you get to the old airstrip. Here you have two choices. You can cross the airstrip and continue straight, but the road is awful. You'll need a powerful four-wheel drive with high clearance. A better option is to head over to La Torcaza Estate and ask to use the shortcut on a better road that runs behind the facility. Ask nicely, because someone has to unlock a gate for you. It might help your cause if you buy some coffee and take their coffee tour.

The *lagunas* are a 15-minute drive from "downtown" Volcán, more if the road's in bad shape (which it usually is), and you need a four-wheel drive in the rainy season. Note: Vehicles have been broken into here. If you drive, keep an eye on the car. Admission is free and there are no facilities.

La Torcaza Estate

This mill and farm (tel. 771-4306, www.estate-cafe.com, tours: 8:30 A.M.–noon, 1–5:30 P.M. Mon.–Sat., open Sun. by arrangement only, free), near Volcán's decaying and more-or-less abandoned airstrip, offers free tours of its facilities, in English or Spanish. It's run by the Janson family and is still known to some as Janson Family Coffee. There's also an espresso bar/shop on the premises where one can sip a cup and watch the beans roast. You can buy souvenir packages of coffee here or, if you want to avoid schlepping kilos of coffee around the country, you can wait until you get home and buy it (for a heftier price) through the Internet. To get to the mill, turn left off the main road toward Río Sereno about 300 meters past the crossroads, at the sign for the Oasis Place Hotel. Pass the hotel and go straight for 0.9 kilometers. Turn right at Mini Super Casa Elsa and continue straight for 1.7 kilometers on the torn-up road until you get to the old airstrip. Turn right onto the airstrip and drive for another kilometer. Look for a gate marked "Janson's Coffee House," which leads to a large building off in the distance to the right. That's your destination. A taxi from central Volcán costs about US$2.50 each way.

Sitio Barriles

This field, on Finca Landau near central Volcán, is one of Panama's most important archaeological sites, but as usual the site (no phone, 7 A.M.–6:30 P.M. daily, free) itself has little to offer visitors but a view of some holes in the ground. Most of the items recovered here are now in Panama City's anthropology museum, which makes for a better visit. Still, those with an archaeological bent may want to take a quick look to help them connect the pieces with their place of origin.

The Barriles culture is intriguing, mostly because so little is known about it. It's believed to have been an agrarian, warrior-dominated society with roots extending back to 734 B.C.

It consisted of about four dozen human settlements that extended from this area to the north and east as far as Cerro Punta. The highland settlements are the most ancient. The relatively lowland Barriles site is much more recent, dating from around 60 B.C. It was the ceremonial center of the Barriles society.

The pieces found here are mysterious. The most numerous are odd stone statues depicting a proud figure wearing a conical hat who is being carried on the shoulders of a stockier man. Because these pieces were discovered in 1947–1948 through *huaquería* (grave robbing) rather than professional excavation, nearly all their historic context has been lost. But later research has helped to date the site and its treasures. An authorized archaeology dig in 2001 uncovered more pieces.

Barú's last major eruption, in A.D. 600, scattered the Barriles culture, though the Barriles site itself was far enough away from the volcano that it may have remained populated until A.D. 800. There's some evidence it was recolonized in A.D. 1200.

Just about the only remnants of all that history are some petroglyphs near the home of the Landau family, which owns the *finca* (country house) the site is on. They're trying to make it a tourist attraction—including neatly embedding some pottery into the walls of a hole in an attempt to simulate what a dig might look like. If you're pressed for time, and even if you're not, you can easily skip the place. They do have some tasty homemade cheese and jams to sell, though.

To get to the site from Volcán, head toward Río Sereno for one kilometer past the crossroads. (If you get to Hotel Don Tavo, you've gone too far.) You should see a sign on the left; make a left turn onto that road. The site is just down the road; look for the sign. A taxi from "downtown" Volcán costs US$3.

Los Pozos Termales de Tisingal

These undeveloped hot springs are set among countryside within easy driving distance of Volcán. The road is in surprisingly good shape the whole way, though there are mud traps and steep sections that require a four-wheel drive. A creek runs right across the road near the hot springs, and in the rainy season it can rise high enough to be impassable. If the creek's not too high, park on the near side and wade across, hiking the rest of the way.

The turnoff to the hot springs is 10 kilometers from the Volcán crossroads on the road to Río Sereno. Look for a sign on the right as you crest a hill. Turn right and follow the winding road until you come to the springs.

☾ Cañon Macho de Monte

This dramatic canyon, which features sheer faces, waterfalls, and the boulder-choked Río Macho de Monte at the bottom, is a prime bird-watching area. You have a decent chance of spotting orange-collared manakins, riverside wrens, fiery-billed aracaris, and orange-bellied trogons. The turnoff to Macho de Monte is about 12 kilometers south of Volcán at the tiny community of Cuesta del Piedra. If you're heading downhill, the unmarked turn will be on the left. Look for Restaurante El Porvenir and Mini Super Meinor; the road to the canyon is between them. Head down this road for less than three kilometers, past the guardhouse for the hydroelectric plant. You'll cross two bridges. Park by the tin-roofed *rancho* on the right. For a spectacular vista, walk down the slippery path, climb over the barbed wire fence (there to keep cattle in, not hard to climb over), and scramble over a few boulders until you come to a vertiginous drop-off. Needless to say, watch your step. A path near the guardhouse leads down to the river. Ask the guard to point it out.

Truchas de Bambito

If shooting fish in a barrel sounds too challenging, Truchas de Bambito (north of Volcán, tel. 771-4373 or 771-4374, www.hotelbambito. com, 7 A.M.–4 P.M. daily) is for you. This is the Hotel Bambito's trout farm (*trucha* is Spanish for trout). Tons of the big guys swim about in a series of concrete tanks, and you're welcome to fish one out or ask the workers to catch one for you. Note: Catch and release is not allowed.

The trout farm is on the left 0.4 kilometers past Hotel Bambito as you head uphill. Fishing poles are available for rent, and you have to pay for what you catch.

SPORTS AND RECREATION

The tourist infrastructure on this side of the mountain is far less developed than it is around Boquete. Guiding operations are more casual, and several of the guides I've recommended in the past are no longer in the area. The safest bet is to make arrangements through your hotel, particularly if you're staying at Los Quetzales Lodge and Spa or Hostal Cielito Sur in Cerro Punta; these two places should know the best available guides. Another option is to arrange a package with an outside tour operator that employs naturalist guides, such as Ancon Expeditions.

Summiting Volcán Barú is the big physical challenge around here, but there are plenty of other high-adrenaline possibilities, as well as gentler options. Hostal Cielito Sur (tel./fax 771-2038, cell 6602-3008, www.cielitosur. com) in Cerro Punta rents mountain bikes for US$5 an hour or US$20 a day. Hotel Bambito (tel. 771-4373 or 771-4374, www.hotelbambito.com) rents mountain bikes for US$5 an hour and horses for US$8 an hour.

Hiking

There are three major trails in **Parque Nacional Volcán Barú.** One of these is Sendero Los Quetzales. The other two lead to the summit of Barú from either side of the mountain. On a clear day (ha!) you can see both oceans from the summit.

From either of these last two trails reaching the summit takes about five or six hours up and four or five hours down. It's a strenuous climb, but not technically difficult. A very rough road serves as a trail on the east side of the mountain. Neither trail is suitable for children.

Do not attempt the summit trail on this side of the mountain without a safety-conscious and knowledgeable guide. There are lots of forks and it's easy to get lost, especially when the fog rolls in. It's also essential that you plan well. The average temperature at the higher elevations is 7.2°C (45°F) and it can get down to freezing; hypothermia is a real possibility. And, like every place else in the highlands, it's often incredibly wet. Plan either to start very early or else camp out on the mountain. As an incentive, the best chance of a clear view is to be at the top close to dawn.

Dress warmly in waterproof clothes, and if you plan to camp bring a good tent and a second set of clothes. Bring plenty of water, as there are no facilities anywhere near the summit. Also, bear in mind that the elevation is high enough for altitude sickness to be a possibility. If you feel nauseated or get a bad headache, head down the mountain immediately.

One bummer about this hike is that people have scrawled graffiti all over the rocks near the summit. Try to ignore it; concentrate on the view and your sense of smugness for having made it to the top.

If you have a cell phone that works in this part of Panama, bring it. There's a communication tower at the summit, so it might be possible to make a call if you get into trouble.

For the hike to the summit of Barú, drive to the trailhead, unless you're up for a marathon trek. The trailhead is at the end of 7.4 kilometers of dirt and gravel road, half of it horrible, that heads east across the plains from the main road between Volcán and Bambito. The road is not marked but your guide will know the way.

Admission to the park is theoretically US$5, US$5 more to camp, but there are usually no rangers around to collect it. This is yet another reason to exercise caution in climbing the mountain; don't expect the Mounties to come to the rescue if you get in trouble. Make sure there's someone back in town who knows where you are and is prepared to call for some sort of help if you don't return at a specified time. Again, a summit climb is absolutely not appropriate for young children.

Birding Tours

Los Quetzales Lodge and Spa (tel. 771-2182 or 771-2291, cell 671-2182, www.losquetzales. com) arranges birding tours, including a vehicle with driver and guide, for US$60 for a half day, US$90 for a full day. **Hostal Cielito Sur** (tel./fax 771-2038, cell 6602-3008, www.cielitosur. com) arranges birding tours for US$40–60 for

a half day, US$70–100 for a full day, not including transportation.

Other Activities

A number of hotels and guides offer **whitewater rafting trips**. Note that all of them contract out to rafting companies in Boquete, on the east side of Barú, so find out if the tour planner is charging you a premium just to book the trip for you. You might do better to contact the company directly. The companies can usually pick rafters up and take them to rivers on either side of the mountain. Organized guide services and outfitters have been slow to take hold on this side of the mountain. Going through your hotel is the best bet for now.

ACCOMMODATIONS

Lodging around Volcán is generally unsatisfying. Consider heading farther up the mountain to the area around Cerro Punta. There are a couple of places worth checking out, however.

US$25-50

Hotel y Restaurante Don Tavo (tel./fax 771-5144, www.hoteldontavo.com, starts at US$28.88 s, US$38.12 d) is on the right just past downtown. It's set around a pretty courtyard and offers 16 simple but clean rooms with TV. It's by far the best moderately priced place to stay in the area, and the best value overall.

US$50-100

Hotel Dos Ríos (tel. 771-5555, www.dosrios. com.pa, starts at $77 s/d, including a minimal continental breakfast), on the outskirts of the Volcán area, 2.7 kilometers from the crossroads on the road to Río Sereno, was renovated in 2000 by its former owner, the Spanish Barceló chain. It's an attractive place consisting of 14 rooms, two suites, and two *casitas* (here meaning tiny bungalows with bunk beds) set in a garden with a creek flowing by. Rooms are dark but have cheerful touches, especially the painted vines and startled-looking toucans that adorn the walls. Windows can't be opened, so forget about ventilation, and the rooms were already showing signs of wear shortly after the renovations thanks to a casual attitude toward maintenance and cleaning. Rooms have TVs that get fuzzy local channels. All the polished wood everywhere is a mixed blessing. It looks nice, but it makes the place resonate like the sound box of a guitar, ensuring that anyone who walks by sounds like an army of storm troopers. Try to get a room on the 2nd floor.

You can choose from 19 quaint cottages at **Cabañas Kucikas** (Bambito tel./fax 771-4245, www.kucikas.com, starts at US$72 s/d), 0.7 kilometers up from Hotel Bambito, just past the trout farm. It's on the left, but there's no sign so it's easy to miss the turn. The cottages are on forested grounds snug up against the mountains. It's a pleasant, if aging, place. All the cottages are different, with some more cheerful and well appointed than others. There's no restaurant on the premises, but all the cottages have full kitchens. This place is a good deal for larger groups. There's a fancy Honeymoon Cottage for US$72. Rates for the other cottages, which are intended for groups, run US$81–181 for 6–10 people.

US$100-150

Hotel Bambito Resort (tel. 771-4373 or 771-4374, www.hotelbambito.com, starts at US$99 s, US$110 d, including breakfast), about six kilometers north of Volcán, is an aging luxury hotel that's pretty imposing, but which you may find out of keeping with the natural beauty of the surroundings. It was built in 1981 and almost nothing about it has been changed since then, including the Last Days of Disco decor. It offers surprisingly plain standard rooms and several varieties of large suites. The place has seen better days. There are tennis courts, an indoor/outdoor swimming pool, sauna, hot tub, and a few pieces of gym equipment. Note that rates can be as low as US$77 during low-season weekdays or during promotions, which occur frequently. Check the hotel's website and ads in national newspapers.

Camping

Be sure to bring plenty of warm clothing and a good tent if you camp out. It can get quite cold and drizzly even in the dry season.

It's possible to camp in **Parque Nacional Volcán Barú,** which you may want to do if you hike to the summit. The fee is US$5, but good luck finding someone to pay it to. If you want to do things by the book you can buy a permit ahead of time at the ANAM office in David or Panama City.

FOOD

On my last visit to Volcán, several of the better dining options had opened or relocated away from the center of town, which is a bit of a nuisance for those without transportation. But any place not within walking distance shouldn't be more than a US$1 cab ride away.

Café Cerro Brujo (cell 6660-9196, noon–9 P.M. daily, US$12.50–14) is now located down a bumpy dirt about one kilometer north of "downtown." It's amazing this place is still around, as it has stylish, relatively haute cuisine aspirations that you wouldn't expect out here, at big-city prices. It has a limited menu that changes daily but might include unexpected dishes like chicken in a Thai curry sauce and bananas foster for dessert. Soup and salads tend to be quite good and are probably the safest bet. To get there, turn north off the main drag at the American Shop. The road forks after one kilometer. Turn right. The restaurant is on the right, in a house that's been converted into a simple but pleasant-looking café with a back patio.

Café Restaurante Acropolis (tel. 771-5184, cell 6624-9687, US$2.50–7.50) is now located in a house on the main road 1.4 kilometers from the crossroads on the way to Río Sereno. It serves a variety of Greek food, though don't be surprised if not everything on the menu is available. The *tzatziki* yogurt dip and the hummus, both served with fresh, hot pita bread, make good appetizers. The moussaka is tasty if oily. The restaurant also serves the usual meats, plus pastas, burgers, and fresh shakes and juices.

Some think **Ristorante Il Forno** (tel. 771-5731, noon–9 P.M. Thurs.–Sun.) is one of the better Italian restaurants in Panama. Pizza is baked in a brick oven (though one fired by gas, not wood.) Il Forno is in a house just down a side street near the crossroads. As you head in the direction of Río Sereno, it's a left turn just past the Banco Nacional de Panamá.

The restaurant at **Hotel Dos Ríos** (on the outskirts of the Volcán area 2.7 km from the crossroads on the road to Río Sereno, tel. 771-5555, US$5.50–11.50) is the fanciest in town, which isn't saying a whole lot. It's pleasant to sit out on the patio, but the food is so-so at best. My dinner there was memorable for overcooked and chewy beef complemented by undercooked rice. Options include steaks, pasta, and pizzas. The brave can opt for *la sorpresa de la casa* (house surprise). Yikes.

Restaurante Las Truchas (in the Hotel Bambito, tel. 771-4265, US$10–15) features plate-glass windows that look out on the artificial terraced pond in front of the hotel and the side of a mountain right across the street. The house specialty, as the name of the restaurant implies, is trout from its own trout farm up the street, prepared any way you can think of.

There's a 24-hour **Supermercado Romero** (tel. 771-4524) at the crossroads. It has a pharmacy, and the pharmacist can be called day or night in an emergency.

SERVICES

Farmacia Don Bosco (tel. 771-4317, 8 A.M.–8 P.M. daily) is near HSBC. **Farmacia Volcán** (tel. 771-4651, 7:30 A.M.–10 P.M. Sun.–Thurs., 7:30 A.M.–6 P.M. Fri., 6–10 P.M. Sat.) is on the left, one kilometer from the crossroads on the way to Río Sereno.

The only banks on the west side of Barú are in the town of Volcán. As you head up from the lowlands, **HSBC** (8 A.M.–3:30 P.M. Mon.–Fri., 9 A.M.–noon Sat.) is on the right shortly before the road forks. A branch of the **Banco Nacional de Panamá** (8 A.M.–3 P.M. Mon.–Fri., 9 A.M.–noon Sat.) is on the left, straight past the fork on the road to Río Sereno. Both

banks have ATMs and will cash travelers checks.

The local outlet of **Western Union** (tel. 771-4258, 8 A.M.–9 P.M. daily) is next to Hotel y Restaurante Don Tavo (on the right, just past downtown, tel./fax 771-5144, www.hoteldontavo.com). The door is always locked; ask at the restaurant for service.

A 24-hour **Internet café** (tel. 771-4461 or 771-4055) is attached to the Hotel y Restaurante Don Tavo.

GETTING THERE

Buses between Cerro Punta and David all stop in Volcán (US$2.50) and Bambito (US$2.75). Look for the bus with "Cerro Punta" painted on the windshield. David-bound buses leave Cerro Punta 4:45 A.M.–6:45 P.M.; buses run every 15 minutes. Those coming from Costa Rica can catch the Cerro Punta bus at Concepción, rather than going all the way to the David bus terminal.

Buses run between Volcán and Río Sereno about once an hour, 5 A.M.–5 P.M. daily. The fare is US$2.65. The bus stops at Finca Hartmann by request.

Taxi fare from David to Volcán is about US$25, a bit more to go farther up the mountain. Some of the highland hotels will arrange pickup at the airport or bus terminal, for a fee. Check with your hotel. Taxi fare from Volcán to Finca Hartmann is US$15, US$20 to Río Sereno.

GETTING AROUND

It's easy to walk around central Volcán, but those staying at a hotel on the road to Río Sereno without their own transportation will probably have to rely on taxis. There's a taxi stand at the crossroads, next to Supermercado Romero. Taxis anywhere within the vicinity of Volcán are US$0.75. Between Volcán and Cerro Punta the fare is US$5, US$3 more to get to Las Nubes entrance to PILA. Other fares include Sitio Barriles (US$4), Lagunas de Volcán (US$5), and Los Pozos Termales de Tisingal (US$15). Catch the Cerro Punta–David bus if you want to take a bus between Volcán and the Bambito area.

WEST OF VOLCÁN

If you stay straight on the road through Volcán rather than turning right toward Cerro Punta, you'll head west and eventually end up in **Río Sereno,** a tiny town (pop. 3,289) with nothing to offer visitors but a little-used border crossing with Costa Rica that is not always open to foreign travelers. The main reason to come this way is to visit Finca Hartmann, a combination gourmet coffee farm and private forest reserve with a couple of cabins for birders and other nature lovers. It's 27 kilometers west of Volcán, 15 kilometers east of Río Sereno.

The road to Río Sereno is one of the prettiest in Panama. Bright, tiny flowers dot the shoulders. The road crosses over rivers and winds past splashing waterfalls, forested hills, coffee plantations, tall stands of evergreens, and plump cows grazing in fields.

But the road also features blind curves and trucks that barrel down the hills without a thought for what might lie around the bend. Count on landslides and washouts in the rainy season, though the road was re-paved recently and should be in good shape. Be careful.

Though the countryside is attractive, Río Sereno itself isn't. It consists of a couple of basic stores (the best bet for food), a central plaza, a bank, the border crossing, and little else. There's an open-air market by the plaza with modest offerings, catering to Costa Rican day-trippers. Given the limited services here, and the fact that even the immigration officials don't quite know what to make of tourists, visitors should enter or exit Panama through the far less attractive but much more convenient crossing at Paso Canoa.

Finca Hartmann

This family-owned coffee farm (tel./fax 775-5223, cell 6450-1833, www.fincahartmann.com) is a great favorite with birders—more than 280 species have been identified—but even if that's not your thing you may want to consider visiting for its away-from-it-all natural beauty, for a tour of its coffee operation, or just for a cup of coffee with some friendly folks. The Hartmanns have two remote cabins, one of them surprisingly comfortable, for guests who want to stay overnight. The *finca* (country house) is in the community of Santa Clara, 27 kilometers from Volcán on the road to Río Sereno.

The Hartmanns offer tours of their small coffee mill. The coffee here, not surprisingly, is excellent, and there's a small coffee shop with an attractive wooden *rancho* where you can buy a cup or pick up some souvenir packs to take home. A tour of the coffee operation and access to the grounds for birding or hiking is US$15 per person.

The patriarch of the clan is the friendly and gregarious Ratibor "Chicho" Hartmann, now in his 80s but in fantastic shape. He's an entomology enthusiast who worked for years in the Canal Zone at Gorgas Hospital, an important center for tropical medicine. Ask him about it; he's got interesting stories. Research scientists have been studying the farm's rich flora and fauna for years. Their gratitude has included naming two new beetles species and a new species of cloud-forest bee after Hartmann.

Reflecting his hobby, he has built a tiny museum in the compound that contains an impressive insect collection from the area and around the world. There's an incredible array of bizarre specimens. There's also a small collection of pre-Columbian pottery and stone figures, mostly from Chiriquí.

The real treasure of the place is the fragmented primary cloud forest 3.7 kilometers up from the main *finca* on a brutal road that requires a four-wheel drive with high clearance. It's called **Ojo de Agua** (eye of water) for the spring that runs between the two cabins in a clearing at the end of the road. Besides the incredible array of birds, the lucky might encounter a few of the 62 species of mammals that have so far been identified on the *finca,* including red brocket (a kind of deer), peccaries, armadillos, porcupines, opossums, and close to 20 species of mice, as well as white-faced capuchin, red spider, and howler monkeys.

Ojo de Agua borders Parque Internacional

La Amistad (PILA). To the west one can see clear to Costa Rica. Five trails start from near the cabin: a one-kilometer uphill one that connects with the road, a three-kilometer trail that leads up a hill and that skirts PILA, another three-kilometer one that leads to a small river, a 350-meter walk to a 50-meter waterfall, and a 500-meter trail that leads to an enormous ficus tree.

The two cabins are quite different. The larger one is a two-story building that's been used as a research station, so creature comforts have not been a main concern. It's a basic place with a concrete floor, kitchen with gas stove, dining/sitting area, fireplace, and five bedrooms. There's no electricity, just kerosene lamps, but it does have hot-water showers. The smaller cabin is quite a bit nicer. It's still rustic, but it features finished wood, a snug bedroom, a kitchenette, and hot-water bathroom. Electricity is on the way; expect prices to go up when it arrives.

Rates run from US$20–35 for a bunk bed to US$70 for a cabaña for two. Optional food service is available. If you need transportation from the *finca* to the cabins, the Hartmanns will take you there for US$20 round-trip.

Río Sereno Practicalities

The **Posada Los Andes** (no phone, US$20 s/d) is the only option for those stranded in Río Sereno on the way to someplace more interesting. It's in the building that looks like a factory looming over the plaza; rooms are upstairs from the shops. Don't expect the Ritz. Finca Hartmann is a better, but more remote, alternative.

A branch of **Banco Nacional de Panamá** (8 A.M.–3 P.M. Mon.–Fri., 9 A.M.–noon Sat.) is next to the plaza in the center of Río Sereno.

Getting There and Around

To drive to Finca Hartmann from Volcán, continue straight at the crossroads rather than turning right toward Cerro Punta. The drive takes about a half hour. You'll see a sign on the left side of the road; make a quick right onto the gravel road. The 42 kilometers from

Volcán all the way to Río Sereno takes about 45 minutes by car. Just stay straight on the main road.

Buses run between Volcán and Río Sereno about once an hour, 5 A.M.–5 P.M. daily. The fare is US$2.65. The bus will stop at Finca Hartmann if requested. Taxi fare from Volcán is US$15–20 to either place.

Buses between David and Río Sereno run every 45 minutes, 5 A.M.–5 P.M. The trip takes nearly three hours and costs US$4. Tell the driver if you want to get off at Finca Hartmann (about 2.5 hours, US$3.65).

Río Sereno is tiny. You can walk from one end of "downtown" to the other in five minutes. You can also wander right over to Costa Rica for a minute, if you want that weird little thrill of crossing a border. The crossing is wide open and not even marked; you'll only know which country you're in from the flags flying at the tiny *migración* offices.

ALONG THE FORTUNA ROAD

The area around the Fortuna reservoir, farther east along the cordillera, is known for its sweeping vistas and great bird-watching, but so far it doesn't see many visitors or even have that many residents.

Because the Fortuna Dam generates more than 30 percent of Panama's electricity, there's an economic incentive to keep its watershed well protected. That's good news for nature lovers, as the forests here are overflowing with life. It can get cool at the higher elevations, down to about 14°C (57°F), but it's significantly warmer than the area around Volcán Barú.

The reservoir, just south of the Continental Divide, is surrounded by the **Reserva Forestal Fortuna** (Fortuna Forest Reserve, 19,500 hectares), which in turn is bordered by the enormous **Bosque Protector de Palo Seco** (Palo Seco Buffer Forest, 244,000 hectares) to the northwest. The Continental Divide marks the border between the provinces of Chiriquí and Bocas del Toro.

A good, though dangerous, road—often referred to as the Fortuna Road—cuts north across the mountains from the town of

Chiriquí on the Interamericana to the oil port of Chiriquí Grande on the Caribbean coast, less than 100 kilometers away. A fairly new road links Chiriquí Grande with Almirante, the jumping-off point for water taxis and ferries to the archipelago of Bocas del Toro. Along the way there are rugged access roads into the forest, making it relatively easy to explore the area.

More than 1,000 plant species have been identified just in the Fortuna Forest Reserve, which is also home to 40 mammal and 70 amphibian and reptile species. Endangered mammals here include the white-lipped peccary and Baird's tapir. The area has some of the best bird-watching in Panama. Besides the ever-popular resplendent quetzal, there's a chance of seeing such spectacular specimens as the bare-necked umbrellabird, azure-hooded jay, black-bellied hummingbird, lattice-tailed trogon, and yellow-eared toucanet, to name just a few. Some of these are rare and nearly impossible to spot, so you'll get a lot more out of a hike if you go with a good guide.

Sights

Finca La Suiza is on the right about 40 kilometers up the Fortuna Road from Chiriquí. Those with time to spare should consider taking a hike in its private reserve; the trails are good and well marked.

The **Continental Divide** is at kilometer marker 60; flora and fauna quickly change as one heads down the Caribbean slope. The road also leads over the impressive **Represa Fortuna** (Fortuna Dam), whose hydroelectric plant supplies more than 30 percent of Panama's power. The road goes across the top and offers lovely views of the reservoir and the hills that ring it.

For a break, pull off the road at the bridge near kilometer marker 67. On the west side just past the bridge is a gorge. Walk down the little trail by the side of the road; it's not marked, but it's near a sign that says "Celestine." Do not open this gate and go up the steps; that's private property. The trail is to the left of it, starting at the guard rail. The trail leads down

to a little *quebrada* (brook) with a **swimming hole and waterfall,** El Suspiro, in a narrow box canyon. The waterfall is at least 30 meters high and is absolutely stunning and pristine. Those so inclined can slip behind the waterfall. Even though this is close to the road, as usual travelers shouldn't wander around solo. Even at low water you'll get wet; wear swim trunks and reef sandals, and bring plastic bags for the cameras. There's not a scrap of trash anywhere; please keep it that way. This is probably not the safest place to be during a heavy rainstorm.

Sports and Recreation

You do not have to stay there to hike the **Finca La Suiza trails.** These trails are among my favorites in all of Panama, both because of their beauty and because they are so well marked and maintained. For much of the main trail you're in the thick of the forest, then suddenly you come upon spectacular waterfalls or sweeping valley views. The forest is alive with sights and sounds. On my first visit I had hiked in only a few hundred meters when a group of white-nosed coatis scampered through the trees right above my head. There are big cats in the forests here, but it's very unlikely you'll have the good fortune to see them. However, on rare occasions there are reports of one attacking cattle.

Be advised that this is a somewhat strenuous hike that goes from an elevation of 1,150 to 1,700 meters. It's relentlessly uphill for the first half, and the trail "down" has lots of uphill parts. It crosses several streams, which can be tricky in the rainy season when the water is high and the trail is slippery. As with any forest trail in Panama, do not hike alone. If you get lost, the rescue fee is US$100. Officially it takes six hours to hike the trail, but that's being conservative. Going at a reasonable clip shaves at least an hour off that estimate. There is also an easier three-hour loop. Warning: Don't eat the things that look like blueberries growing along the side of the trail. They're poisonous.

The trail fee is US$8. Guests at the *finca* pay only once no matter how many times they hike. If you're just planning to hike the trail, pay the fee to one of the Ngöbe-Buglé women in the house just up the hill and get a map of the trail from her. You must start the trail between 7 and 10 A.M. This is for your own protection, as you don't want to be stuck out there at night. The trailhead is a steep, seven-minute walk up the dirt road. The trailhead is to the left.

There's a newer trail at the *finca* that starts from an area called **Alta Vista** and heads up through a cloud forest, past a huge waterfall to the top of **Cerro Hornito.** It is an extremely tough trail and it would be hard to retrieve a hiker if there's an accident. Unlike the rest of the trails, the Cerro Hornito is true wilderness. If you get lost, you're finished. This can only be hiked with a guide from the *finca;* you will get lost on your own. The fee for this is US$72 for 1–4 people, US$18 for each additional person. It takes about six hours to get to the top. The elevation changes from about 1,700 meters at Alta Vista to 2,100 at Cerro Hornito (the lodge is at 1,220 meters).

Finca La Suiza has a total of 20 hours of trails, so those who want to hike them all should plan to stay in the area three nights.

Accommodations

Two appealing places to stay are aimed at ecotourists and are essentially nature sights in themselves. (A third one, Rancho Ecológico Willie Mazu, was badly damaged in a terrible storm and is temporarily closed. The owners plan to rebuild it eventually. For its status, contact Nattur Panama, tel. 442-1430, info@ natturpanama.com, http://natturpanama. com.) They are also good bases for exploring the area.

Sort of a cross between a mountain guesthouse and a nature reserve, **⬛ Finca La Suiza** (tel. 6615-3774, www.panama.net.tc, US$44 s, US$55 d, two-night minimum) is well worth a visit. It consists of 205 hectares of mountainous primary and secondary forest through part of which the friendly Swiss owners have built terrific trails. Those owners, Herbert Brullmann and Monika Kohler, rent out three large and cheerful bedrooms with private bath in their small house,

which is set on a ridge 1,220 meters above sea level. The views are spectacular. On a clear day, you can see lovely valleys, Pacific islands, Volcán Barú, and even a slice of Costa Rica.

The food here is gourmet and includes such unexpected treats as pesto, gnocchi, watercress and endive salad, and blackberry parfait. The produce is from the organic garden on the *finca* (country house). Three-course dinners cost US$14.50. A big breakfast featuring homemade jams is US$5. They can also fix sandwiches for a lunchtime hiking stop.

Note: The lodge and trails are closed in June and September 1–November 15. Reservations can be made by email, but note that Herbert and Monika can only check email once a week. Phone reservations should be made at least three days ahead of time. The best time to call is 7–9 P.M.

Finca La Suiza is 55 kilometers from David on the road to Chiriquí Grande, just past Los Planes and the one gas station on the road. A sign for the *finca* is on the right. The lodge is not visible from the gate. Try not to arrive after sundown. The gate is always closed at 6:30 P.M.

Only those with a four-wheel drive that has high clearance can drive up to the lodge. Otherwise park just inside the fence, watching out for muddy stretches, and walk up the steep dirt road. You'll pass the trailhead on the left. *Finca* guests can continue straight to get to the house. If you don't have a four-wheel drive, leave the luggage in the car or at the house up the hill. The owners will help you retrieve it. Do not venture onto the property without permission; large dogs patrol the premises when the owners are out.

Lost and Found Eco-Resort (cell 6462-8182 or 6920-3036, www.lostandfoundlodge. com, US$12 dorm beds, US$30 s/d private room) is, depending on your perspective, either an ecolodge for the backpacking set or a hostel for nature lovers. Opened in 2007 by a couple of Canadians named Andrew and Patrick, it's got a great location on 30 acres of hilly, forested land just south of the Continental Divide at 1,255 meters above sea level. Lost

WESTERN HIGHLANDS

© WILLIAM FRIAR

The Lost and Found Eco-Resort is a forest hostel near the Continental Divide.

and Found is aptly named, as it's not visible from the Fortuna Road. Getting there requires a 10-minute climb up steep stairs carved into the side of a hill; those lugging a heavy backpack will get their day's exercise.

The hostel consists of a series of terraced platforms that hold an open-air kitchen/dining area, a dorm, private rooms, a "chill-out" room, and outhouses with clean, hot-water showers and flush toilets. The wooden dorm has multiple tiers of bunk beds with double mattresses. A bed costs US$12; every third night is free. There are also three bare but perfectly adequate private rooms for US$30 s/d. Two of these have a view of Volcán Barú. Guests are welcome to use the communal kitchen (and provisions are sold onsite) or pay US$4–7 for a prepared meal.

The hostel is a pleasant, friendly, and well-equipped place, especially given its isolation, but the surroundings are the star attraction. Guests can watch the sun set behind Volcán Barú and go for day and night hikes on the network of trails, which connect with trails used by the Smithsonian Tropical Research Institute. Hikers can sometimes glimpse the Pacific from the trails, which climb as high as 1,800 meters above sea level. There's a one-time US$3 fee to use the trails. A guided hike is US$7 per person or US$24 for groups. Guests don't always have to go hiking to spot wildlife. Kinkajous and sloths sometimes come to the hostel looking for food, and white-faced capuchins are occasionally spotted on the property as well.

The hostel offers a variety of tours, including a coffee tour (US$23), an overnight jungle safari tour (US$40), a trip to a hot spring (US$10), beach excursions (US $20–$25), a guided jungle hike (US$15), and horseback riding (US$35). Panama-wide tours are also available. Those in need of transport to their next destination can also opt for the hostel's "transportation tours," which combine a visit to local attractions with a drop-off in Boquete (US$20), Las Lajas (US$20), or Boca Brava (US$25). All prices are per person. Lost and Found can also pick up arriving guests in David for US$30. For the more sedentary, the chill-out room has a foosball table, book exchange, karaoke machine, and a TV and DVD player with 200 movies available to rent.

Lost and Found is just beyond kilometer marker 42 on the Fortuna Road. It's north of the weigh station and the sign for Valle de la Mina. Look for the sign that reads, "You have found the Lost Paradise." Those coming by bus (US$2.50 from David, US$5 from Almirante) can ask the bus driver to stop at the *"casa amarilla"* on the Fortuna Road. Those with their own transportation can park at a neighbor's house for US$2.

Information and Services

This is a remote area with few services of any kind and certainly no tourist information booths. The best bet for information and guides are Finca La Suiza and Rancho Ecológico Willie Mazu. Don't attempt a hike into the forest without a guide.

Getting There

The Fortuna Road begins at the town of Chiriquí, 15 kilometers east of David on the Interamericana. Turn north off the highway at Chiriquí and head straight past town. Keep left when you come to the fork at Gualaca. The two-lane route, unofficially known as the Fortuna Road, soon starts winding through the highlands and the views become spectacular. Beware of landslides and washouts and sudden dips and bumps in the road caused by soil erosion below it. Returning to the Interamericana on the way back down can be a bit confusing. At Gualaca, be sure to turn left at the crossroads, following the signs that say "CPA" (apparently for Carretera Pan-Americana, i.e., the Interamericana).

Any bus running between David and Chiriquí Grande or Almirante uses this road and can drop off and pick up passengers anywhere along it. The trip from David to Finca La Suiza takes about an hour and costs US$2.50. To return to David or Almirante you'll have to flag down a bus by the side of the road.

Note to those driving to or from Boquete: A road links Caldera and the Fortuna Road that can potentially shorten the trip considerably since it spares you from having to drive all the way down to the Interamericana. It was recently paved most of the way and should be in good shape. However, it's prone to landslides and washouts, so ask locals about conditions before attempting. The road is about 38 kilometers long. It's a pretty drive.

In and Around the Golfo de Chiriquí

The Golfo de Chiriquí extends from Punta Burica at the western edge of Panama toward the Azuero Peninsula to the east, encompassing the entire coast of Chiriquí province and much of the Pacific coast of Veraguas. It's a region of superlatives. It contains the richest mangrove forests in Central America, the largest island in Panama, and one of the largest coral reefs in the Pacific. It offers truly world-class diving, surfing, and sportfishing.

Conservation organizations have targeted this area as one of the most ecologically important in Central America. This area has seen less development than other parts of Panama, but human pressures are mounting. Panama has reacted by establishing protected areas, most notably two huge marine parks: Parque Nacional Marino Golfo de Chiriquí and, more recently, Parque Nacional Coiba.

Because the Golfo de Chiriquí is still relatively remote and untouched, it's only now beginning to take off as a tourist destination. When I first started writing about this area in 1999, there was really only one (rather rustic) place to stay in the entire Parque Nacional Marino Golfo de Chiriquí that was worth writing about, and it stayed that way for years. There are now half a dozen good options, plus decent places to eat and reliable tour operators. More are on the way. Playa Santa Catalina is also growing fast, both because it's the best surfing spot in Panama and because it's a convenient jumping-off point for Parque Nacional Coiba. All these places are much more accessible than ever before.

◖ PARQUE NACIONAL MARINO GOLFO DE CHIRIQUÍ

Parque Nacional Marino Golfo de Chiriquí is a 14,740-hectare marine park that encompasses two dozen islands and their surrounding waters. The park is a refuge for all kinds of wildlife, including howler monkeys, leatherback and hawksbill turtles, and tiger-herons. Humpback whales come here to calve between September and November. This area was for years the well-kept secret of backpackers and deep-sea fisherfolk, but in just the last couple of years it's begun to take off as a more mainstream tourist destination.

As this region becomes better known, the shorthand to refer to it is shaping up to be either **"Boca Chica,"** which technically is just the fishing village and anchorage that are the gateway to the islands, or **"Boca Brava,"** which is actually just one of the islands.

It's still a bit of an adventure to get to the islands that start just off the coast east of David; that's half the fun of visiting this area. You get the sense of being in the middle of nowhere without actually being that far from civilization or having to spend a lot of money to get there. The only population center nearby is the little fishing village of Boca Chica, which is more than an hour by road or sea from David. Accommodations and places to eat are near Boca Chica and out on the islands a short boat ride away.

If all this sounds more like fun than hassle, you have the right attitude to visit this place. The islands and ocean here are beautiful and still feel like an undiscovered paradise.

Another plus about this whole region: Dry season tends to start earlier than in other parts of Panama, around November, and ends at about the same time, in April.

Nearby Islands and Coast

There is an endless maze of mangroves to explore in the estuaries of several rivers that empty into the sea near Boca Chica. But most come here to enjoy the islands.

Isla Boca Brava is the closest to Boca Chica. The island is 14 kilometers long, six kilometers wide, and overflowing with wildlife. It's right on the edge of the park.

Because of the rivers on the mainland, the water gets clearer the farther away one gets from shore. The closest uninhabited islands are **Linarte, Saino,** and **Las Ventanas** (*ventana* means window; the name refers to the caverns that run straight through their rocky sides).

But the best islands are farther out. The snorkeling is decent around **Isla San José,** a short boat trip away, but it's definitely worthwhile to head out even farther. **Isla Bolaños** is 13 kilometers from Boca Brava, about 45 minutes by small boat equipped with a decent outboard motor. This is a lovely little deserted island with a couple of sandy beaches, lots of coconut palms, and snorkeling when the tide's low. This is one of the best places to see humpback whales and their young between August or September and November. Twenty minutes from Bolaños is **Isla Gámez** (sometimes spelled "Gámes"), also lovely and even smaller. This one, however, tends to attract yachts and the weekend personal watercraft crowd, while Bolaños is rarely visited. (Sadly, though, even Bolaños has its share of trash.) Both these islands are tended by the nonprofit environmental group ANCON. **Isla Parida,** just across from Gámez, is a big, inhabited island with lots of trash and can easily be skipped. There's an ANAM station on Parida next to a bunch of ramshackle huts and a dirty beach. You can spend the night at the station, but it's hard to see why you'd want to.

Remote Islands

The scuba diving is said to be terrific around **Islas Las Ladrones** and **Islas Secas,** where the water is clearest and the sealife the richest. The diving visibility can be up to 30 meters at Las Ladrones. The islands are very far away: Las Ladrones islands are 40 kilometers southwest and the Islas Secas 30 kilometers southeast

© WILLIAM FRIAR

the dock at Boca Chica

of Boca Brava. Do not attempt to go this far on the open sea without something more substantial than the little *pangas* common around here. If you do find a way to get there, the snorkeling should be good, too. There is now a high-end resort on the Islas Secas. Though it's expensive, staying there is by far the easiest way to get to and explore the islands.

Sports and Recreation

Even with the sudden growth, this area is not exactly crawling with tour operators and recreational facilities. That may change soon; for one thing, there are plans to build a full-service marina. Guests generally arrange excursions through their hotels, some of which offer tours for nonguests as well. There is one dive operator based in the area. Note that there's a US$5 per-person fee to enter the marine park, usually collected by the tour operator.

The best bet for an economical boat tour is **Hotel Boca Brava** (tel. 851-0017, fax 700-0250 or 676-3244, www.hotelbocabrava.com), which offers a wide variety of tours to all the attractions in the area. Round-trip

excursions to the nearest islands, for instance, are US$4–7 a person. A half-day snorkeling and hiking trip to Isla San José costs US$35 total for up to four people. The hotel has a more substantial excursion boat it can use for day trips to distant destinations, such as Islas Secas (US$280 for up to six people, including snorkeling gear and lunch). The hotel also rents snorkels and masks for US$2. Single sea kayaks are US$3 an hour or US$15 a day; two-person kayaks are US$4.50 an hour or US$22.50 a day.

Diving in the region is best during the dry season, December–April. Divers should try to make it all the way out to Islas Secas or Islas Ladrones.

Boca Brava Divers (tel. 775-3185, cell 6600-6191, www.scubadiving-panama.com) is run by Carlos Spragge, who runs a highly professional operation. A full day of diving costs US$150 per diver, including boat, divemaster, tanks, weights, and a picnic lunch. Trips are limited to 4–8 divers.

Carlos converted a 46-foot commercial vessel into a somewhat spartan live-aboard, *Miss*

Bessy, that he uses for day trips to Islas Secas and Islas Ladrones, as well as for "cruises" that last up to seven days. Per-person prices are US$150 for the first day and US$250 for each additional day, including a berth, three daily meals, dive-master, tanks, and weights. Overnight trips are limited to 4–5 people.

Accommodations and Food

The area suddenly has a surprisingly diverse range of accommodations, catering to those on budgets ranging from starvation to luxury. Prices here tend to be significantly cheaper in the low season, but if this place really takes off, be prepared for the rapidly rising prices Boquete and Bocas del Toro experienced.

Chitras (sand flies) and occasionally mosquitoes can be a nuisance all around here in the evenings, but much less so during the breezy dry season. That's the price of having healthy mangroves.

This place is changing fast and the few places to stay and eat in or near Boca Chica may change, too: At the time of writing, Wahoo Willy's had closed down, leaving just two places on the mainland. In order of distance from the village, they are Gone Fishing Panama Resort and Seagull Cove Lodge.

Other places are accessible only by boat, though in the case of Restaurante y Cabañas Boca Brava and Panama Big Game Fishing Club, the boat ride is a stone's throw across the harbor and costs US$1 by fishing boat. They are next to each other on the inland side of Isla Boca Brava. Cala Mia is significantly farther away, on the ocean-facing side about a 20-minute, US$25 *panga* ride from Boca Chica on open seas. Pacific Bay Resort is perched on the tip of Punta Bejuco, which is on the mainland but is accessible only by sea. The trip from Boca Chica by *panga* takes about 25 minutes and costs around US$20 one way.

There's also an ANAM ranger station on distant Isla Parida that can provide lodging for a small fee, but the island is inhabited and quite junked up. There's no reason to stay here when you can sleep in a hammock at Hotel

Boca Brava for the same price, or camp on a deserted island with a little planning.

Boca Chica and Horconcitos have a couple of rock-bottom places to eat, but most people dine where they stay. The restaurants at Seagull Cove Lodge, and Hotel Boca Brava are easily accessible and open to the public.

Hotel Boca Brava (tel. 851-0017, fax 700-0250, hotelbocabrava@hotmail.com, www.hotelbocabrava.com, US$7 pp in a hammock, rooms start at US$17.50 s, US$33 d) was for several years the only hotel in the whole region. It's a cool place to stay or visit and I have a soft spot for it, but it's definitely not for everyone. It's certainly not for those skittish about creepy-crawlies. I hadn't been there an hour on my first visit, back in 1999, when a snake dropped from the rafters of the hotel's open-air bar. The owner instantly started slashing at it with a machete; fortunately or not, it got away. An armadillo on the island has been known to race across the dance floor in the evenings.

The cabins and restaurant are on a cliff 20 meters and a long flight of stairs above the ocean on the eastern edge of the island, giving it striking views of the Pacific and the surrounding islands.

The place is a good deal as long as you don't mind some rusticity and living close to nature. Since my most recent visit, Frank Köhler, the mercurial German character who pioneered guest lodging in this area, has finally sold up and moved away. The hotel is now run by a couple, Lupita and Esteban, who have worked in tourism in Mexico and the U.S. and seem to be bringing a more service-oriented orientation to the operation.

There are more than 10 kilometers of trails that lead into the forest and down to the island's beaches. The forest is home to monkeys, anteaters, coatimundis, all kinds of birds, and a wealth of trees and plants. The previous owner proudly maintained that the island has "no poisonous spiders, but every kind of poisonous snake." He always insisted they're mellow, but don't go for a forest hike without good boots. And watch your step. This is also one of the most economical places to book a tour of the surrounding islands and other natural attractions.

In recent years some (relatively) upscale rooms have been added. The "fanciest" are still pretty basic but have air-conditioning, hot water, a terrace, tile floors, cable TV, loft beds with double mattresses, and a table with chairs (US$55 s/d). The midrange accommodations (US$44 s/d) all have private baths, electricity, and fans. There is also a *casita* (US$49.50) with a TV and terrace. These are very simple midrange rooms—mattresses lie on raised platforms on the floor—and far from immaculate but perfectly fine.

A step down in quality and price are two rustic rooms (US$17.50 s, US$33 d) with shared shower and toilet. Those on a tight budget can also rent a hammock (US$7) or mattress (US$10) in an open-sided hut. The price includes access to the showers and toilet. Only the air-conditioned rooms can be reserved; the rest are first-come, first-served. This place has become well known on the backpackers' circuit and sometimes fills up. Call for reservations.

The restaurant and bar is an open-air affair on the edge of the cliff. It used to be all groovy and wooden, but the wood rotted away and was replaced with much less boho-looking cement. The panoramic view is still terrific, however, and Frank added a second floor. The food here isn't fancy, but it's fine. *Cambute,* a kind of conch, is the house specialty. (If you're into that kind of thing, you can row out with Frank to the underwater net where the live critters are kept and help him extract them from their shells—definitely not for the squeamish.) The average price of a meal is US$4. Vegetarian meals can be arranged with notice. The piña coladas here are amazing, and the homemade papaya liquor is refreshingly sweet but deadly.

There's a boat to and from Boca Chica (US$1) at around 9 A.M. and 1 P.M. daily, though you may be able to flag down passing boats at other times. The Köhlers can also arrange transportation to or from David for US$30.

It's a tough call, but **⬤ Pacific Bay Resort** (cell 6695-1651, U.S. tel. 617/782-3228, www.pacificbayresort.net, $88 s/d, including all meals) arguably has the best scenery in the region. It certainly has the most: It extends over 65 hilly hectares, fewer than 10 of which are developed. The rest is covered with tropical forest that runs down to three long, brown-sand beaches. South Beach, as it's come to be known, is especially lovely, a crescent-shaped expanse of sand with an islet just offshore that keeps the surf tranquil. It's backed by shallow, vine-draped caves. Very *Treasure Island.* The photos on the website do not do this place justice.

The presence of the resort has discouraged hunters and encouraged wildlife to return, including howler monkeys, white-faced capuchins, hawks, deer, ocelots, white-nosed coatis, iguanas, anteaters, and sloths. The usual caveat applies, though: During any visit, don't be disappointed if you only see birds and hear howlers in the distance.

The owner, Frank (not to be confused with Frank on Boca Brava), was born in Panama but grew up in Boston: His nifty Panamanian-Boston accent is a first for me. He's a friendly, easygoing guy who seems to genuinely love this place and be more interested in sharing it with like-minded visitors than making a fast buck.

Facilities are more basic than at the higher-end places in this area. There are nine cabins on the property, five of which are intended for guests. The cabins are borderline rustic, though the cement floors were covered with wood veneers, which should cheer things up. Each cabin has a queen and full-size bed, fan and screened windows, bathrooms with showers, and a small patio with hammock. All of them have a view of the ocean. Cabins are set in gardens and spaced far enough apart for privacy, so long as there's no one in the room next door (the cabins are duplexes).

Each cabin is named for a province of Panama, arranged to roughly correspond to the geographic position and, even more roughly, the characteristics of the province. My favorites are Veraguas and Chiriquí, which are set on hilly terrain that leads down to the beach, not unlike their namesakes.

An open-air restaurant/bar is on the edge of a cliff with sweeping views of the ocean and coast. With advance notice, Frank can arrange a sunset barbecue out on nearby Turtle Point, named for the large sea turtles that sometimes make an appearance. The US$88 price includes a cabin and three daily meals for two people. Note that the price does not include transportation, which the resort can arrange. Fishermen in Boca Chica charge US$20 each way. Each cabin can accommodate two more people for an additional US$33 each, including meals. In other words, this is probably the most economical eco-resort in the country.

Activities available include kayaking, horseback riding, and boat trips to the islands. Telephone communications way out here are unreliable, and email is the best way to make reservations. The U.S. telephone number reaches a college bar Frank owns in Boston, which can result in some baffling conversations. Bring shoes with good traction, as the paths are paved and can get slippery.

Gone Fishing Panama Resort (cell 6573-0151, www.gonefishingpanama.com, $110–137.50 s/d), opened in 2006, is on the mainland between the Boca Chica pier and Seagull Cove. It offers four rooms, two in the home of the owners, a retired Florida couple, and two in a cabaña next door. The cabaña rooms are considerably smaller but more private. The ones in the house are quite large and feature sliding-glass doors with an ocean view and televisions with DVD players. All the rooms are air-conditioned, with queen beds, terraces, and private bathrooms, and all are hand-painted with tropical scenes.

There's a decent-sized infinity-edge swimming pool in the backyard, but the social hub of the place is the terrace bar, which opens at 7 A.M. and closes when the last guest staggers to bed. Meals are available for about US$5–15; guests are not allowed to use the kitchen. As the name suggests, Gone Fishing is aimed at deep-sea fishers, but offers a range of other land and sea excursions, including trips to Coiba. This place tends to attract gringos and Canadians. Smokers and small children are welcome. The owners are planning to add 16 condo units to the property.

(**Seagull Cove Lodge** (tel. 700-0236, U.S. tel. 786/735-1475, www.seagullcovelodge.com, $137.50 s/d), also opened in 2006, offers a little bit of everything: It's supremely comfortable, it has striking views, it's accessible, it's run by service-oriented people, and you don't have to take out a second mortgage to stay here. It's on the mainland just a few minutes uphill from the village of Boca Chica.

Seagull Cove features six roomy, red-tile-roof bungalows staggered on a hillside and linked by a steep staircase that leads to a pier and small beach. Four of the bungalows have queen-size beds and two have two double beds each. They are otherwise identical, with modern furnishings, air-conditioning, sliding-glass doors, a terrace, firm mattresses, cable TV, safe, walk-in closet, and large, attractive bathrooms. The 7,500-square-meter property is steep but narrow, which means guests must close their curtains to have privacy from their neighbors and those passing by on the stairs. The *chitras* and mosquitoes are less of a nuisance here, thanks to the air-conditioned bungalows.

Five of the bungalows have great views of the tranquil anchorage, ocean, and surrounding islands. The sixth is at the top of the hill closest to the restaurant, and it looks out mainly on forest. But it's also the most secluded of the bungalows, and the trees around it are filled with oropendola nests. (Oropendolas are large, flamboyant birds known for their hanging nests.)

Seagull Cove is the latest creation of Pilar Ibañez and Flavio Nobili, a Spanish-Italian couple who also made their mark in Bocas del Toro, where they ran one of its best restaurants, El Ultimo Refugio, and in Boquete, where they had a hotel, La Vía Lactea (now Boquete Garden Inn). Both places are now under new management. They are warm and friendly hosts.

The lodge's restaurant is a large, comfortable, Italian-style terrace at the top of the hill with a terrific ocean view. Breakfast is for guests only, but the restaurant is open to the public for lunch and dinner. Flavio, the chef, does his best with the available ingredients. Highlights of the menu include beef scaloppini, shrimp piro piro, and, for breakfast, fluffy and delicate banana pancakes. There's a small plunge pool next to the terrace that's a nice spot to wallow in and watch the ocean on a hot day. (Hotel guests only.)

Opened in 2006, **(Cala Mia** (tel. 700-0259 or 700-0025, cell 6747-0111 or 6617-5352, starts at US$198 s/d, including breakfast) is one of the loveliest places to stay in Panama. It consists of 11 modern, elegant bungalows on a narrow, rocky spit of land on the far side of Boca Brava, about 15 minutes by boat from Boca Chica. It's flanked by two deserted beaches, a short stroll down the hill from the bungalows. The beaches aren't the loveliest in the area, but gorgeous ones are a short boat ride away. Behind the beaches is tropical forest, home to howler monkeys and plenty of other small critters, which guests are free to explore. (A one-hour trail leads over the island to Restaurante y Cabañas Boca Brava.)

The bungalows are large and comfortable, with plate-glass sliding doors that look out on a private, thatch-roofed terrace and a view of the ocean and surrounding islands. The well-appointed bathrooms feature circular glass-block showers. The bungalows do not have air-conditioning, and it can get a bit warm in there, but they do have ceiling fans and screened windows. At the tip of the little peninsula is an artfully decorated bar and dining room; a circular staircase leads to a *mirador* (observation platform) with 360-degree views. Outside is a small but appealing infinity-edge swimming pool, and across a rope bridge is an islet with a tiny crow's nest of a spa that seems to float above the sea. The whole place has an air of bohemian elegance, and everything is done so tastefully it's hard to believe the Italian-Dutch couple who own the place designed it without any background in architecture.

Stays include free use of kayaks, snorkeling equipment, and sailboards. Half-day and full-day trips to the islands are possible, including

as far away as Islas Secas (US$180 for up to four people). Scuba and snorkeling packages are also available, as are deep-sea fishing trips to the waters near Isla Coiba. Horseback riding in the forest is US$30 an hour. The spa offers massages, manicures/pedicures, and exfoliation treatments. Yoga packages are also sometimes available.

Note that *chitras* (sand flies) can be a nuisance out here, though much less so in the dry season, when the breezes keep them at bay. One impressive thing about this place is that the owner states flat out in the promotional literature that they know their very presence in such a pristine area causes harm. It certainly causes a lot less than most hotels, and they try to minimize the damage not only by eco-friendly practices such as using solar power, but by doing something for the community—they say that 5 percent of their proceeds go to community-service projects in the area.

The **Panama Big Game Fishing Club** (tel. 6674-4824, U.S. toll-free tel. 866/281-1225, www.panamabiggamefishingclub.com) shares the same general idea as Restaurante y Cabañas Boca Brava—cabins and a restaurant/bar perched high up on the edge of Isla Boca Brava—but the result couldn't be more different. The Big Game Fishing Club is an upscale, all-inclusive sportfishing lodge.

The four modern, cheerful cottages are similar except for the bright, hand-painted murals. Each cottage is 600 square feet, big enough for two queen-size beds in different wings of the cottage. The beds are separated from each other by a partial partition (but not doors). The cottages are air-conditioned and have huge, glass block–walled showers. Each cottage can sleep up to six people.

At the top of the hill is an attractive, semicircular bar and restaurant with plate-glass windows overlooking the sea, nearby islands, and the forested mainland. Above the restaurant, a ladder leads to an observation tower with an even more sweeping view.

The club offers fishing packages that last 3–6 days for US$2,461–5,980, not including taxes and tips. Packages include in-country transport and all meals and drinks. Off-season rates are cheaper.

Getting There and Away

Some of the hotels will help arrange transport from David. Transfers are included with stays at Panama Big Game Fishing Club. Cala Mia offers a scenic, hour-long boat transfer from Pedregal (David's port) to Boca Brava for US$250 (up to four people; US$10 more per extra passenger). The Purple House Hostel in David sometimes arranges transport for its guests.

BY BUS

Any bus plying the Interamericana, including the long-distance ones that run between David and Panama City, can drop passengers off at the Horconcitos turnoff so long as the bus runs past that point. From David, these include a few buses with Horconcitos as the final destination, as well as the Tolé, San Felix, Las Lajas, and Remedios buses. The fare from David is US$1.25. Get off at the crossroads leading into Horconcitos, not Horconcitos itself, and hope there's a taxi hanging about. Expect to pay about US$15–20 per ride, perhaps less. Show up early to improve chances of getting a ride. However you plan to get there, be sure to make return arrangements at the same time.

BY TAXI

Taxi prices from David to Boca Chica are hard to predict, as the road keeps getting better but gas prices keep going up. Expect to pay US$30–40 for one or two people, a bit more for additional passengers.

DRIVING TO BOCA CHICA

For those coming on their own, the easiest access to the islands is through the little town of Horconcitos, the turnoff to which is about 40 kilometers east of David on the Interamericana. The turnoff is poorly marked; if you're coming from David it'll be on the right—look for signs advertising hotels and water sports. Horconcitos itself is five kilometers from the Interamericana on a good road. Then it's a

16-kilometer drive south to the fishing village of Boca Chica. This road used to be horrendous, but the last 16 kilometers were finally paved in 2008, turning what used to be a brutal trek of an hour to a spectacularly scenic drive of around 20 minutes on a good day. About 10 kilometers from Horconcitos, the road forks. The left fork leads to a beach, Playa Hermosa. Straight continues to Boca Chica. The road dead-ends at a pier. Parking by the pier is US$1 a night, though there wasn't anyone to pay the last time I was there.

FROM BOCA CHICA TO THE HOTELS

Gone Fishing and Seagull Cove Lodge are just up the hill from the pier. Those heading to the islands from Boca Chica usually hire fishermen to make the trip unless a hotel or tour operator has arranged to meet them. Rates are US$1 per person for nearby destinations, US$20–25 or more for more distant ones. There's a pay phone at the pier in case you get stranded and need to call for assistance.

ISLAS SECAS

The ☾ **Islas Secas Resort** (U.S. tel. 805/729-2737, www.islassecas.com, starts at US$1,089 d, all-inclusive) is the most exclusive place to stay in all of Panama. It consists of 16 small private islands far away from just about everything. The resort itself is on Isla Cavada, where there are six *casitas* (little houses) for guests, a dining/lounging area, and a spa. There are generally no more than 14 guests at a time. The *casitas* are on a cove facing the ocean and are circular, yurt-style buildings that provide a panoramic view of the surroundings. Each has a queen-size bed, minibar, and bathroom. The largest, the Casa Grande, has a full kitchen.

While it's possible to do nothing but relax on a deserted beach, the resort's location is spectacular and lends itself to lots of nature activities. Possibilities include scuba diving or snorkeling, surfing near Morro Negrito, ocean kayaking, deep-sea and inshore fishing, and hiking on the islands. Diving and fishing in this region are outstanding.

There's a two-person and four-night

minimum per *casita*. This includes room, all meals, and excursions. These excursions include scuba-diving, snorkeling, surfing, fishing, and boat trips to surrounding islands. Sportfishing and spa services are extra, as are transfers to and from the island.

There is an airstrip on Isla Cavada. While boat transportation from David (about 1.5 hours) is sometimes available, nearly all guests arrive by private plane from Panama City (1 hour, US$850 pp round-trip). Charter flights from other airports can sometimes be arranged.

LAS LAJAS

The most popular mainland beach in the region is at Las Lajas, the turnoff to which is about 75 kilometers east of David (or 35 kilometers east of Horconcitos) on the Interamericana. It's a long, wide, gray-sand beach with few facilities. It's not all that pretty or otherwise special, but it's the most accessible large expanse of sand around and it's big enough to offer seclusion even on busy dry-season weekends.

The crossroads of the Interamericana and the road leading down to Las Lajas is known as **El Cruce de San Felix.** El Cruce is a common pit stop for buses and private cars making the long haul across the country. It has a gas station, but skip the hole-in-the-wall greasy spoon and hotel, and don't take your eyes off your stuff for a second. In fact, avoid spending time in El Cruce altogether. Once, a scammer drove a nail into one of my car's tires when I wasn't looking. When I started to leave, he kindly pointed it out to me—he couldn't have seen the tire from where he was standing—and offered to fix it. I drove on instead and had the tire repaired down the road. Beware.

The beach is a 13-kilometer drive south down a paved but pitted road from El Cruce, a drive that leads through the town of Las Lajas itself. Curve right when the road forks at a small yellow building; if the road turns to dirt, you've missed the turn. The road ends at the beach.

Accommodations and Food

The road to the beach ends in a T-intersection. A few rustic places to stay and eat are scattered along the dirt roads to the left and right of this intersection. You'll probably need a four-wheel drive to get down these roads in the rainy season. This is a good place to come with your own bedding and a full cooler.

There are plans to build more upscale accommodations and facilities on the beach—there was even talk of a golf course—but there is no evidence of construction. The land under the short-lived Las 3 Palmeras hostel, which attracted a boho party crowd, was sold and the place shut down, but the owner was planning to open its successor, simply called **La Palmera** (cell 6516-6788, lapalmerapanama@gmail.com), closer to the T-intersection. The only thing there when I visited was a dilapidated work site and a couple of uninhabited tents, but the operation is planning to start off with six tents with double mattresses for US$6 a night. Those with their own tents can crash there for US$3. Slightly less rustic accommodations may follow.

A good option for backpackers is **Cabañas Panamá** (cell 6561-9470, starts at US$20/cabin), in a secluded spot about 700 meters down the dirt road to the right as you face the beach. (Confusion alert: This place has had a variety of names over the years, and you may just see a sign for "cabañas"). It's a fenced-off

---

ANOTHER HIDDEN FAVORITE

The town of **Tolé,** about 25 kilometers east of El Cruce de San Felix, is worth a visit if you're in the area. During the day, Ngöbe-Buglé vendors set up roadside stands along the Interamericana just east of town. This is a good place to buy their crafts, including popular hand-woven *chácaras* (bags), traditional dresses, and *chaquiras* (necklaces made from bright beads). The best of the necklaces are suitable for framing.

property with nine cabins—bamboo huts, really—right on a long, wide, peaceful beach. Each has foam mattresses, cement floors, a loft for sleeping bags, and a picnic table outside. They're super-rustic but adequate for a no-frills stay. They don't have bathrooms; a separate building houses basic shared toilets and showers. There are also six rooms in a building set back from the beach. These do have cold-water bathrooms but zero charm: They're basically four concrete walls, bunk beds, and a cement floor. A restaurant and bar on the premises prepares meals when there are enough guests, which usually means the dry season. At other times, dinner is whatever you bring yourself.

Rates are per accommodation, not per person. High-season rates are US$20 for the cabins and US$40 for the rooms back from the beach. Prices are halved in the rainy season. If you stuff more than a car's worth of people into either, though, they'll charge another US$5 for the second car. That buys a 24-hour stay. Camping on the property is US$10 per group (US$5 in the rainy season). Day use of the facilities is US$5; the fee is waived for overnight guests. Again, a "group" is defined as a carload. The caretaker, Abdiel, is a friendly and reasonable guy.

There are five relatively "upscale" two-story **A-frame cabins** (cell 6574-4986, 6539-6969, or 6611-6579, starts at US$15 s, US$30 d) that haven't been named yet. The cabins aren't fancy by any means, but they have mosquito netting and cold-water bathrooms. A friendly Colombian man recently took over management and started to renovate the place, so the cabins may be nicer when you visit. Electricity could be on the way. The larger ones sleep up to four people for a flat US$38.50; smaller cabins are US$15 per person. The odd thing here is that the cabins were just plopped down in the car park and don't really have a view of the beach, which is a 10-second walk away. A large *rancho* on the beach houses a bar/restaurant. As you face the beach at the T-intersection, this place is 700 meters down the dirt road to the left.

Getting There and Around

Buses to the town of Las Lajas leave the David bus terminal at 11:45 A.M., 12:45 P.M., 4:25 P.M., and 5:20 P.M. and return at 2:15 P.M. and 3:15 P.M. The trip takes 1.5 hours and costs US$2.25. Note that the beach is eight kilometers from the town, however, and taxis may be hard to find. A better option is to take any bus running along the Interamericana that goes as far as El Cruce de San Felix (US$2.25), the Las Lajas crossroads. Get off there and take a taxi (US$4) to the beach, which is 13 kilometers away. Good bets from David include the San Felix and Tolé buses, which run about every 20 minutes. Getting back to El Cruce can be tricky during the week and in the rainy season. Consider arranging a pickup time with the taxi driver, or at least ask for his phone number.

◖ PLAYA SANTA CATALINA

Santa Catalina is the best surfing spot in Panama, with one of the most consistent breaks in Central or South America. There's something to ride here every month of the year.

While Santa Catalina is of great interest only to serious surfers, it's a pretty place even for those who just want to watch the rollers from a distance, and it's becoming the prime jumping-off spot for trips to Coiba. However, much of the beach is strewn with rocks and boulders, and it's a remote and isolated spot west of the Azuero Peninsula, at the tip of sparsely settled farmland. It's definitely a get-away-from-it-all kind of place. Most lodging and dining options are basic, though options are improving rapidly. Those who just want some beach time have many better, more accessible options elsewhere.

The best time for really big waves is February–August, when wave faces get as high as 6–9 meters. At other times the average is 2–3 meters. There are several other breaks, some within walking distance, some requiring a boat ride to reach, that can get even bigger.

National and international surf competitions are sometimes held in Santa Catalina, during which the place gets packed and advance reservations are a must. Those not participating

© WILLIAM FRIAR

Playa Santa Catalina

may want to avoid the area during these times. Check www.santacatalinabeach.com or local hotels to see if a contest is scheduled during your proposed visit.

The nearest sizable settlement on the drive down to the beach is Soná, an unattractive crossroads town with little to offer travelers. You can get some provisions there, but you're better off stocking up back in Santiago, on the Interamericana, a two-hour drive from the beach.

The road ends right at the beach. Along the road are several places to stay, two dive operators and a new kayak operation, a few houses, and a couple of bars. This is part fishing village, part surfers' hangout. A left turn up a steep, rough road leads to most of the surf camps and restaurants. That's about all there is to Santa Catalina other than the amazing surf.

Surfing

The internationally famous surf break at Santa Catalina has been described as a "perfect" point break with long, powerful hollow waves that break left and right. The sea bottom is volcanic rock, so bring booties. This place is strictly for experienced surfers; it's all too easy to bust a board or a head on those rocks. There's also a **sand beach break** next to town with hollow lefts and rights that are somewhat smaller than waves at the point.

Several other breaks in the area are less well known. **Punta Brava,** about a half-hour walk southeast of Santa Catalina point, is a hollow left-hand, rock-bottom which can get twice as big as those at Santa Catalina. **Punta Roca,** about a half-hour walk northeast of Catalina, is another left-hand point break, about the same size as Catalina. Except for the Santa Catalina point break, which can be surfed at medium or high tide, experienced surfers say these other waves can be ridden only at medium to low tide.

Isla Cebaco, which is accessible only by boat, is an island with a beach break and point break, with left- and right-breaking waves that tend to be somewhat bigger than Catalina point. The truly ambitious can opt for a trip to **Isla Montuosa,** 3–4 hours west of Coiba. The waves here have five-meter faces and are

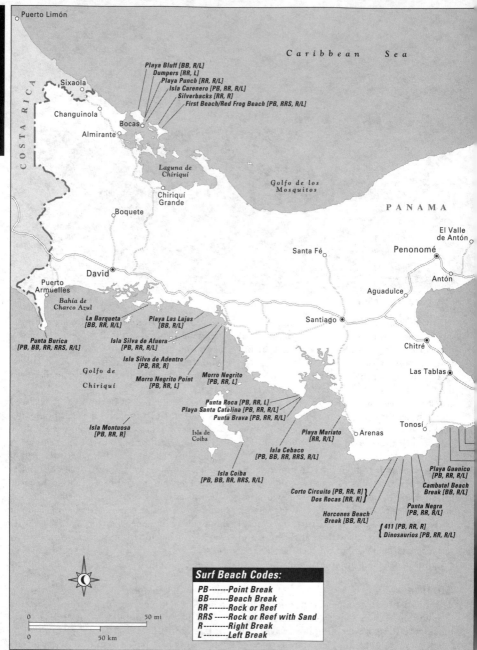

Puerto Limón

C a r i b b e a n   S e a

Playa Bluff [BB, R/L]
Dumpers [RR, L]
Playa Punch [RR, R/L]
Isla Carenero [PB, RR, R/L]
Silverbacks [RR, R]
First Beach/Red Frog Beach [PB, RRS, R/L]

Sixaola

Changuinola

Bocas

Almirante

C O S T A   R I C A

Laguna de Chiriquí

Golfo de los Mosquitos

Chiriquí Grande

P A N A M A

Boquete

El Valle de Antón

Santa Fé

Penonomé

David

Antón

Puerto Armuelles

Aguadulce

Bahía de Charco Azul

Santiago

La Barqueta [BB, RR, R/L]

Playa Las Lajas [BB, R/L]

Chitré

Punta Burica [PB, BB, RR, RRS, R/L]

Isla Silva de Afuera [PB, RR, R/L]

Las Tablas

Isla Silva de Adentro [PB, RR, R]

Golfo de Chiriquí

Morro Negrito Point [PB, RR, L]

Morro Negrito [PB, RR, L]

Punta Roca [PB, RR, L]
Playa Santa Catalina [PB, RR, R/L]
Punta Brava [PB, RR, R/L]

Tonosí

Isla Montuosa [PB, RR, R]

Isla de Coiba

Playa Mariato [RR, R/L]

Arenas

Isla Cebaco [PB, BB, RR, RRS, R/L]

Playa Guanico [PB, RR, R/L]

Isla Coiba [PB, BB, RR, RRS, R/L]

Cambutal Beach Break [BB, R/L]

Corto Circuito [PB, RR, R]
Dos Rocas [RR, R]

Punta Negra [PB, RR, R/L]

Horcones Beach Break [BB, R/L]

{ 411 [PB, RR, R]
Dinosaurios [PB, RR, R/L]

0 ——— 50 mi

0 ——— 50 km

Surf Beach Codes:

PB -------Point Break
BB -------Beach Break
RR -------Rock or Reef
RRS -----Rock or Reef with Sand
R ---------Right Break
L ---------Left Break

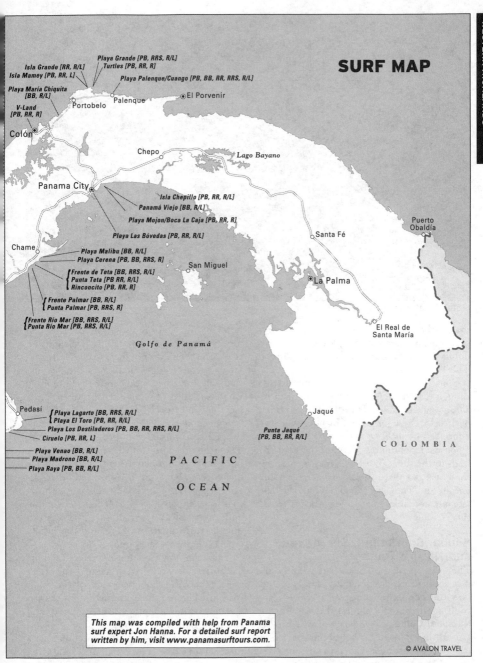

SURF MAP

Isla Grande [RR, R/L]
Isla Mamey [PB, RR, L]
Playa María Chiquita [BB, R/L]
V-Land [PB, RR, R]
Colón
Portobelo
Playa Grande [PB, RRS, R/L]
Turtles [PB, RR, R]
Playa Palenque/Cuango [PB, BB, RR, RRS, R/L]
Palenque
El Porvenir

Chepo
Lago Bayano

Panama City
Isla Chepillo [PB, RR, R/L]
Panamá Viejo [BB, R/L]
Playa Mojon/Boca La Caja [PB, RR, R]
Playa Las Bóvedas [PB, RR, R/L]

Santa Fé
Puerto Obaldía

Chame
Playa Malibu [BB, R/L]
Playa Cerena [PB, BB, RRS, R]
Frente de Teta [BB, RRS, R/L]
Punta Teta [PB RR, R/L]
Rinconcito [PB, RR, R]
Frente Palmar [BB, R/L]
Punta Palmar [PB, RRS, R]
Frente Rio Mar [BB, RRS, R/L]
Punta Río Mar [PB, RRS, R/L]

San Miguel
La Palma

Golfo de Panamá

El Real de Santa María

Pedasí
Playa Lagarto [BB, RRS, R/L]
Playa El Toro [PB, RR, R/L]
Playa Los Destiladeros [PB, BB, RR, RRS, R/L]
Ciruelo [PB, RR, L]
Playa Venao [BB, R/L]
Playa Madrono [BB, R/L]
Playa Raya [PB, BB, R/L]

Jaqué
Punta Jaqué [PB, BB, RR, R/L]

COLOMBIA

PACIFIC

OCEAN

This map was compiled with help from Panama surf expert Jon Hanna. For a detailed surf report written by him, visit www.panamasurftours.com.

© AVALON TRAVEL

© WILLIAM FRIAR

Main Street, Playa Santa Catalina

shallow, hollow, and powerful. Do not attempt to surf them unless you really know what you're doing. This is far, far away from any hospital. This is a two-day trip.

Some of the surf camps rent surfboards, though expect these to be pretty banged up. The going daily rate is US$10 for a short board or US$15 for a long board. There's a **surf shop** (cell 6451-9939, 6 A.M.–9 P.M. daily) in a house a few minutes' walk up the road that leads to the surf camps. The managers live in the house, so there should usually be someone around. Half-day rentals, at half the daily rate, are available, as are boogie-board rentals (US$7.50/day).

Scuba, Snorkeling, Sea Kayak, and Nature Tours

There are plenty of beautiful islands and dive spots to explore. Nearby islands include **Isla Cebaco,** known for clear waters and good coral. But the biggest draw is **Parque Nacional Coiba,** at the heart of which is the astonishing **Isla de Coiba,** about a 1.5-hour trip away by fast boat. Given the distance and

how amazing Coiba is, those with the time and money should consider staying overnight on the island. You may not have to go nearly that far to encounter spectacular sea life. On my first visit, I watched as an enormous humpback whale surfaced near my boat between Santa Catalina and Isla Cebaco.

Some of the hotels and surf camps offer trips to the islands, usually on pretty basic *pangas.* These should be fine for trips to nearby islands, but I don't recommend them for trips on the open ocean. For trips to Coiba and other distant destinations, stick with substantial boats that have life preservers, an emergency radio, and, preferably, a spare motor. The seas can quickly turn rough out here, and the ride to Coiba is bumpy year-round.

There are now two dive operators in Santa Catalina. They're virtually across the street from each other, near the end of the main road just before the beach, making it easy to do comparison-shopping. Both seem good and run professional operations.

Both offer dives on 25-foot boats at a number of spots close to Santa Catalina

© WILLIAM FRIAR

Playa Santa Catalina is the best jumping-off point for Isla de Coiba.

and around Parque Nacional Coiba, which is about a 90-minute boat ride away. The cheapest scuba trips at either place are a two-tank dive at nearby spots (US$55 pp). A two-tank trip to Parque Nacional Coiba starts at US$95. Rates include guide, tanks, and weights. Add US$15 to the prices to rent full diving gear.

Both dive operators also accommodate snorkelers and those interested in exploring Isla Coiba by land. Be sure to ask for the itinerary of these trips, as the area around the ranger station is a popular first stop, but only a taste of what the island and its waters have to offer. A good introduction to the area would also include a visit to the Bahía Damas area, on the east side of the island.

Note that the entrance fee for Parque Nacional Coiba is US$20 per person, payable at the ranger station on Isla Coiba.

Besides Coiba and the local area, **Coiba Dive Center** (tel. 938-0007 or 202-9214, www.coibadivecenter.com or www.scuba-charters.com) makes trips all over the Golfo de Chiriquí, including Islas Secas, Islas Ladrones, and Isla Montuosa. There's a two-diver minimum on all dive trips.

A full-day Coiba snorkeling trip costs US$50 per person, but consider the US$60 per person Coiba tour, which includes a half day of snorkeling and a half day on the island, including a tour of what's left of the penal colony. All prices include gear and transportation. PADI certification courses start at US$130 for a one-day, one-dive Discover Scuba course. Other courses range from a scuba refresher up to PADI Advanced Open Water.

Scuba Coiba (tel. 202-2172, www.scubacoiba.com) was the first land-based scuba operation in Santa Catalina, having opened in 2003. They speak English, Spanish, and German here. Besides its day trips to local spots and Parque Nacional Coiba, it also offers multiday Coiba trips, with overnight stays on Isla Coiba.

There's a two-diver minimum on most of the trips, but singles can arrange a two-tank dive close to Santa Catalina for US$75. PADI certification courses start with a one-day, one-tank Discover Scuba courses around

Santa Catalina (US$70) or Coiba (US$110). Other courses range from a scuba "tune up" to Advanced Open Water.

Fluid Adventures (cell phone 6560-6558, http://fluidadventurespanama.com) offers a whole range of water-based adventures. These include sea-kayak trips around Santa Catalina (US$40–50 pp) and Isla Coiba (US$105 pp, four-person minimum, including boat transport to Coiba but not the park entrance fee). Overnight and multiday kayak trips are available. Single (US$35/day) and double (US$55/day) kayaks are available to rent, as are surfboards. They also offer surf and yoga classes. Their office is toward the end of the main road, next to Scuba Coiba.

Accommodations

More comfortable accommodations are slowly coming to Santa Catalina. The relatively "upscale" places are primarily along the main road that leads into the village. Most of the surf camps (and restaurants) are off the dirt road that intersects the main street. The sea view gets better and better the farther along the road you go.

Those without their own transportation should note that it's a considerable walk between most of the surf camps and town. It takes about 20 minutes at a good clip to get from the last one, Oasis Surf camp, to the town's main road. Carry a flashlight, as there are no lights along the road and without a moon you'll literally be stumbling about in the dark.

Those with their own transport should note that the road to the surf camp often requires a four-wheel drive. As you drive into town, it'll be the steep, rocky road to the left. It quickly levels off, but beware of car-eating mud-holes—it's not unusual to get stuck up there. The surf camps are at the ends of private roads that veer off the main road toward the water. Every place is either right above or a short walk away from the main point break.

US$10-25

It's been fun to watch the evolution of

Cabañas Rolo (cell 6598-9925, tel. 998-8600, http://rolocabins.net, cabinasrolo@yahoo.com, most rooms US$10 pp). Other surfers' hangouts come and go, but Rolo just keeps getting bigger, better, and more popular. Most of the rooms are in two motel-style rows near the end of the main road and just up from the beach. They're simple but cheerful and clean, cooled only with rotary floor fans and equipped with hammocks to lounge in on the front terrace. There are shared toilets and showers next door. There's a communal kitchen and a little restaurant that's open from the morning to 9 P.M.

In 2007 Rolo added a two-story hacienda-style building with two fancier air-conditioned rooms, one on each floor. They both have a double and single bed with okay mattresses, and a front terrace with table. These start at US$40 s/d, US$5 more for a third person. The upstairs room is a "suite" with a terrace for US$50 d. Keep an eye on the papaya tree next to the terrace. One time when Rolo was showing me around, we stood there and watched an opossum eating a big hole in a ripe papaya that was still hanging from the tree. The critter looked a bit sheepish when we caught him in the act. Note: The landline telephone number reaches the town's public phone, so if you call that, let it ring a reeeeally long time and ask whoever answers for "Rolo." Email is the best way to reach him until phone service finally arrives.

The Blue Zone Surf and Dive Hostel (www.bluezonepanama.com, US$13 s, US$26 d) consists of a hive of rooms in a long, funky adobe-style building near the edge of a bluff just above the rocky beach and surf break. Its five fan-cooled rooms are rustic, a bit snug, and have foam beds, but are pleasant enough for the price. The walls are made from cinderblocks and don't have screens, but the beds have mosquito nets. There are three shared bathrooms, a shared kitchen and dining room, and laundry facilities. It's located just past and on the same road as Pizzeria Jamming.

The new **Boarder's Haven** (cell 6572-0664, starts at US$10 pp) is a tiny surf hostel with three rooms next to and managed by La Buena Vida on the main road. The mattresses are decent and there are hot-water shared bathrooms. The roof is corrugated zinc, so it can get boiling hot in this little place during the day. The best thing about it are the doorways, which are shaped like surfboards. Note that this place is a fair walk to the nearest surf break.

Hotel Costa America (tel. 998-8600, US$22.50 s/d) looks out of place here. It's a pink, 10-room hotel at the intersection of the main road and the dirt road that leads to the surf camps. It offers air-conditioned rooms with double beds, cold-water bathrooms, and no charm. But the management is nice enough and the rooms are fine if all you want is a bed near the beach. There's a restaurant and *minisuper* (convenience store) on the ground floor, both of which are open 7 A.M.–9 P.M. daily.

US$25-50

At the end of the dirt road that runs past the other surf camps is 【 **Oasis Surf Camp** (tel. 202-1022, cell 6588-7077, www.oasissurfcamp.com, US$38.50 s/d with fan). It's past the end of the road, on Playa El Estero, a beach at the estuary of a small river. It's actually nicer than the "surf camp" name suggests, but the best thing about this place, which opened in 2002, is that it's right on a wide, black-sand beach rather than on a hill looking down on rocks. It's the nicest spot for those who just want to sunbathe or splash about, and the surf here is much better for beginners, thanks to gentler waves and sand bottoms. Oasis Surf Camp rents boards (US$10–25/day) and offers lessons (US$20 including board). Airport transfers and boat excursions are sometimes available.

Oasis offers six somewhat rustic but pleasant rooms, three with double beds and three with two single beds, in cabañas on the edge of the beach. Each can sleep up to three people and has a cold-water bathroom, fan, and front patio with hammock facing the beach. Air-conditioning is available for US$11 more. A larger *casa* can sleep six. The place is owned by an Italian family from Rome and is run by the younger members of the family: Silvia and David.

Breakfast, lunch, and dinner are available (US$3–5). Dinner is the highlight, with David and Silvia cooking authentic Italian food. A new bar/restaurant in a *rancho* behind the cabins is in the works. Note that Oasis Surf Camp is on the far side of the estuary from town. A four-wheel drive can ford it in the dry season, but those with regular cars will have to park and splash across year-round.

Surfer's Paradise (cell phone 6895-3236, surfcatalina@hotmail.com, US$25 s, US$33 d) is a popular surf camp that offers bunk beds with foam mattresses in windowless rooms with air-conditioning and cold-water bathrooms. The rooms upstairs have been under "renovation" for ages now and offer barebones accommodations for considerably less than the downstairs rooms. The place is owned by the Salgados, a surfing family that has lived in the area for years. (Italo Salgado, the dad, was a champion surfer in his native Brazil; his son Diego is one of Panama's top surfers.) Breakfast and lunch are on offer for a few bucks. This place is still pretty basic, but there's a pleasant deck and a *rancho* strung with hammocks that looks down on the rocky surf and a great view of the ocean. Unlike some other camps in the area, it has a friendly vibe.

Cabañas Sol y Mar (tel. 202-9214, cell 6681-8299, www.solymarpanama.com, US$44 s/d) is what passes for luxury accommodations in Santa Catalina, at least until big developers start to arrive. Opened in 2005, Sol y Mar sits on a steep hill on the main road leading into Santa Catalina, just a few minutes' walk from the ocean, but a fair distance from the surf breaks. There are six rooms in three duplex corrugated-roof cabins on the hillside; a fourth cottage is nearing completion. Each room has two okay double beds and a sitting area with two foam-rubber fold-out futons. A third and fourth person in each room is US$11 each. The rooms are fairly bare and a bit musty, but they have cable TV, a minifridge, hot water, air-conditioning, and a front porch with hammock. Wireless Internet is available for US$5 a day. The place is managed by Luis Manuel Marques de Silva, a capable Portuguese guy who one suspects will continue to upgrade the place as finances allow. He can arrange Santa Catalina transfers for US$50 each way.

The newly renovated **Rancho Estero** (cell 6562-9747, www.ranchoestero.com, starts at US$40 pp) consists of cane-walled, thatched-roof cabins on a rise just above the estuary, towards the end of the surf-camp road. The grounds are well tended and the cabins are pleasant, but the asking price is excessive for this area. Prices may drop as things shake out. There are plans for larger cabins with air-conditioning and a bar/restaurant in a **rancho** on the edge of the hill.

US$50-100

⟨ La Buena Vida (cell 6572-0664, www.labuenavida.biz, US$55 s/d, US$11 more for each additional person, US$5 children under 18) opened in 2007 with just three cabañas, but the owners are planning to build more eventually. A good thing, too, as the accommodations are the nicest in Santa Catalina. It's just down the street from Cabañas Sol y Mar, and like it, is just a few minutes' walk from the ocean, but a bit of a hike to the nearest surf break. It's a cute little complex that includes a gift shop selling local handicrafts and a terrace café/restaurant that's a pleasant spot for a meal or a drink. The place is owned and operated by Mike and Michelle, a friendly young couple from Alaska. Michelle is also a massage therapist who offers massages for US$60 an hour.

The cabañas have different designs, but are equally pleasant. The split-level Bird Room sleeps four and has two double beds and a desk upstairs. The Butterfly Room accommodates up to five; its most memorable feature is the outdoor (but private) shower. The newest when I visited was the Gecko Villa, which is the most whimsical and charming yet. Geckos feature throughout, from a giant tile gecko along the shower to another one right above the bed; its eyes are reading lights. All are spacious and have air-conditioning, a ceiling fan, screened windows, a fridge, and a private terrace and

© WILLIAM FRIAR

The Gecko Villa is the most whimsical and charming of the cabañas at La Buena Vida.

hammocks. Guests also have access to a binder stuffed with local tips about anything you could possibly ask. There are loving touches throughout the complex, such as pretty mosaic-tile designs and tree branches that have been left alone to grow in and around the buildings.

NEAR PLAYA SANTA CATALINA

There is one place to stay on the way to Santa Catalina worth considering, especially for nature lovers who don't need to be on a sandy beach with crashing breakers. **Hibiscus Garden** (US$45 s/d) is run by two friendly German couples from Munich who offer four large, simple cabins along a stretch of beach on the Golfo de Montijo. The rooms are a bit bare, but have air-conditioning, hot-water bathrooms, and bed frames and bathroom sinks made from polished driftwood. The place is near the mouth of the Río Lagatero, and the beach ends in mudflats that stretch out 600 meters before meeting the sea at low tide. The tide here is six meters, so twice a day it comes rushing right up to the property line in half an hour. This is an isolated spot so those who come here should be looking for peace and quiet.

Breakfast, lunch, and dinner are served in a *rancho* nearby, with most items US$5–10. A pizza oven is new and a swimming pool is in the works. They also make German bread (!) here, but sadly there was none to sample when I visited.

Daily surfboard rentals are US$10 for short boards or US$15 for long boards, but surf breaks are a boat or car ride away. The owners offer a shuttle service to Playa Catalina (US$3 pp), which is about 11 kilometers away.

Things to do here include horseback riding (US$15 for three hours) and bird-watching (especially shorebirds). Snorkeling and fishing trips to Isla Cebaco (US$45 pp for a half-day trip) include lunch. Trips to nearby mangroves to go caiman-spotting are also possible.

There's a communal kitchen on the property. Those coming by bus will be dropped off along the main road at the flyspeck village of Lagatero. From there it's a kilometer walk along a cattle path; those driving need a four-wheel drive, particularly in the rainy season. The turnoff is three kilometers before Hicaco on the way to Santa Catalina.

CAMPING

Camping is best done in the dry season, as it can get awfully wet and mucky around here in the rainy season. The nicest and safest place to camp is **Oasis Surf Camp** (tel. 202-1022, cell 6588-7077, www.oasissurfcamp.com, US$5 pp) on Playa Estero. Campers can also pitch a tent for free on the beach, but I'd suggest working out a deal at one of the surfing camps or with a farmer to camp on their land. Maybe it's just me, but it doesn't always feel safe to camp on this beach, at least near the village itself. Some of the characters who hang out around there give off bad vibes. Part of it is just the usual surf territorialism, but there's also a hint of a real *maleante* (rough translation: hooligan) air about some of them.

Food

Like the accommodations, dining options are improving in Santa Catalina. It's still a good place to come with a cooler and supplies, if possible, especially since the nearest grocery store of any size is back in Soná, about 70 kilometers away. (A small general store and a fruit and vegetable stand are along the main road, however.) Also, few places are open for lunch and even fewer for breakfast. Most restaurants open around 6:30 P.M. for dinner. Nearly all of them are located along the dirt road about a 10–15-minute walk from town, and there are no street lights; take a flashlight. In addition to the places listed, **Oasis Surf Camp** (tel. 202-1022, cell 6588-7077, www.oasissurfcamp.com) will prepare Italian dinners for nonguests whenever it has guests.

La Buena Vida (cell 6572-0664, 7 A.M.–2 P.M., US$6–7.50) is a cute open-air spot on the main road, and the food sure sounds appetizing. Breakfast is US$2.50–5 and includes fruit salad, pancakes, homemade granola, breakfast burritos, fresh-fruit smoothies, and a Greek scramble. Lunch includes salads, Mexican tacos, and sandwiches. A more exotic daily lunch special might include Thai, Indian, Mexican, or Italian fare. They can also make a "to-go" lunch for those going on excursions if the order is placed the night before. La Buena Vida has options for vegetarians, a rarity in the region.

The popular **Restaurante Donde Viancka** (cell 666-6426, 3–10 P.M. daily, under US$7) is a cute little open-air place a few minutes' walk down the dirt road leading to the surf camps. The menu changes daily depending on what's fresh, but includes seafood, pasta, and Panamanian fare. It looks out on a field rather than the ocean, but there's a breezy upstairs balcony where groups can sit and catch a glimpse of the sea. The best thing about the restaurant is Viancka herself. Panama's 2001 surfing champion, she's a warm and friendly hostess who goes out of her way to make her clients happy.

Some say ◖ **Pizzeria Jamming** (no phone, 6:30 P.M.–whenever Tues.–Sun., US$6 for a pizza) has the best pizza in Panama. That's hyperbole, and the competition's not that stiff in any case, but the place does serve real Italian pizza baked in a real wood-burning brick oven by real Italians (from Florence, to be exact). It's an open-air place near the edge of a bluff leading down to the surf break. It's possible to climb up there from the beach, but it's hard to find the trail in the evening and it's a bit jungly. It's better to go down the dirt road leading to the surf camps and follow the signs. There's a bar scene, and one end of the pizzeria is strung with hammocks where battered surfers can recover from their battles with monster waves. It's a cozy, relaxing spot to hang out in the evening.

Those with a meat craving should stop by the Argentinean-owned **Los Pibes** (no phone, 6:30 P.M.–until guests leave daily, US$6.50–8), which has great burgers. It's a friendly, open-air place about a 15-minute walk from town, down the dirt road in the surf-camp area. To get there, head past Restaurante Donde Viancka and turn right at the sign. Another plus here is if you show up with a freshly caught fish they'll cook it for you in their outdoor oven for free. The owners speak English, Spanish, and French.

The aptly named **Dive** (no phone, 4–10 P.M. daily), at the end of the main road just before the town beach, serves Mexican food, but it's mainly known as a great local boozer. The gringo owner, Schmoo, makes regular trips to Panama City to forage for bottled beer, and as a result he's got probably the best selection in the country. There were about 22 kinds when I visited, including a number of premium European varieties.

A nameless **bakery** (no phone, 5–9 A.M. and 1–9 P.M. or so daily) has just started up. It's across the main road from La Buena Vida and offers delicious smells and warm smiles. As usual in Panama, the actual baked goods are rather bland, but they're fresh and cheap.

Information and Services

There are few services of any kind in Santa Catalina. For anything more than the basics, most people have to go to Soná or Santiago.

Even basic communications have been slow to come to Santa Catalina. There is no home telephone service, and because of that there are also no ATMs (the nearest is in Soná). The dive shops now accept credit cards, but most other businesses are cash only. The area finally has mobile-phone reception, but it can still be pretty spotty. This is a place to come with enough cash to cover your stay and activities. There is one pay phone, on the main street near the beach.

A good website, **www.santacatalinabeach. com,** provides all kinds of useful information, and maps, on Santa Catalina and its accommodations, restaurants, and attractions. A giant area map is also signposted on the main road near the beach, but is not kept current.

Wi-Fi is gradually coming to Santa Catalina, which is a good thing because the only Internet café these days is inconveniently located one kilometer before town, along the main road. It's called **Los Tecales** (8 A.M.–9 P.M. daily, US$2/half-hour, US$3/hour). It also has a simple restaurant.

Getting There and Away

Rumor has it that Santa Catalina may get an airstrip someday, but for the foreseeable future getting here means a long road trip, except for those few who come by private boat.

BY BUS

There are no direct bus connections to Playa Santa Catalina from major towns or cities. Travelers must first get to Soná, usually by way of Santiago, then take a bus or taxi to Santa Catalina, about 50 kilometers away.

Buses from Panama City to Soná (US$6, about 4.5 hours) leave at 8:20 A.M., 10:20 A.M., 12:45 A.M., 4:20 P.M., and 5:45 P.M. from the Gran Terminal Nacional de Transportes. An alternative is to go first to Santiago and take a Soná-bound bus from there. Buses to Santiago run constantly from Panama City, David, and other major cities. Any bus going at least as far as Santiago will drop passengers at the Santiago bus terminal. Best bets are the long-haul buses between David and Panama City. Buses from Sonáto Panama City leave at 1:30 A.M., 4 A.M., 8:30 A.M., 10:30 A.M., 1:30 P.M., and 4 P.M.

Buses from Santiago to Soná leave from Santiago's Terminal de Transportes (every 20 minutes, 5:30 A.M.–9:15 P.M. Mon.–Fri., 6 A.M.–8 P.M. Sat.–Sun., US$1.75, a little under an hour).

Buses from Soná to Santa Catalina (US$3.75) leave at 6 A.M., noon, and 4 P.M., returning at 7 A.M., 8 A.M., and 2 P.M.

BY TAXI

Travelers who decide to take a taxi from Santiago to Santa Catalina should expect to pay up to US$50, but the price may be negotiable—this is not a common trip, so there aren't really established prices. Taxis between Santa Catalina and Sonáare US$25. There are no resident taxis in Santa Catalina.

DRIVING TO SANTA CATALINA

Those coming by car must pass through Santiago, the provincial capital of Veraguas. It's on the Interamericana between Panama City (250 km, about 3.5 hours) and David (190 km, about 4 hours). As you drive west, the highway forks just before Santiago. Take the left fork and drive into Santiago. This road forks at the church. Drive past the right side of the church and make the first right. Continue past the Museo Regional de Veraguas. Make a left at the first four-way intersection. You should see a communications tower on the left. Continue straight to Soná, which is 50 kilometers southwest of Santiago on a scenic road that was recently repaved and has new bridges. (The fact that the current president is from Soná is surely just a coincidence.)

To continue to Santa Catalina, make a left at the gas station just before Soná; the turn is marked. Make a note of the mileage here. Continue on this okay, but pothole-riddled, road another 48 kilometers, then make another left. The turnoff may not be signposted, so keep an eye on the odometer. The road from here to Santa Catalina used to be brutal but was paved a few years ago and is in excellent shape.

The village of Hicaco is nine kilometers

down this road. Make a right at the Hicaco police station. The road ends at Playa Santa Catalina, eight kilometers away. Driving straight through, the entire trip from either Panama City or David takes about five hours.

◖ PARQUE NACIONAL COIBA

Everything about Parque Nacional Coiba is big. It's one of the largest marine parks in the world. The island at the center of the park, **Coiba** (pronounced "COY-bah"), is Panama's largest—a massive 493 square kilometers. It has the second-largest coral reef in the eastern Pacific Ocean. And the waters are filled with big fish—very big fish, as in orcas, dolphins, humpback whales, whale sharks, manta rays, barracudas, amberjack, big snappers, three kinds of marlin, moray eels, and white-tip, hammerhead, and tiger sharks. A total of 760 species of fish and 33 species of shark have been recorded. Sharks and mantas are plentiful, and there's a decent chance of coming face to face with a sea turtle. Visibility can be unpredictable, but even on "bad" days one is likely to see some impressive creatures. The diving here has been described as a cross between diving off the Galapagos Islands in Ecuador and diving off the Cocos Islands in Costa Rica.

The park became even larger in 2004 when Panama enacted a law that raised its status and nearly doubled its area, to 430,821 hectares. Besides Coiba, the park includes the comparatively tiny (242-hectare) island of **Coibita** just off its northeast tip, the 20-square-kilometer island of **Jicarón,** the **Islas Contreras,** and 35 other islands and their surrounding waters, mangroves, and coral reefs. UNESCO declared it a World Heritage Site in 2005.

Coiba itself is still mainly covered in virgin forest—it's reportedly 85 percent intact—though there has been some deforestation and forest disruption. Rare moist tropical forest is the most common vegetation. As on most islands, there isn't a huge diversity of animal species on Coiba itself, but there are at least 36 species of mammals, including howler monkeys, and dozens of amphibians and reptiles, including the deadly fer-de-lance snake.

You're much more likely to come across beautiful birds, however, of which there are about 150 known species. Coiba is just about the last stand in Panama of the gorgeous scarlet macaw, which are concentrated in an area called **Barco Quebrado.** Other impressive birds common on Coiba include the bicolored hawk and the enormous king vulture. Coiba also has several endemic species, including the Coiba spinetail (a bird—*Cranioleuca dissita*), Coiba agouti *(Dasyprocta coibensi),* and a local variety of howler monkey *(Alouatta palliata coibensis).*

Coiba attracts visitors largely on the strength of its world-class diving and deep-sea fishing. But the impact of human pressures, including the appearance of commercial fishing vessels that trawl these waters illegally, is beginning to mount.

Two things have so far kept nature more or less intact on and around Coiba: It's quite remote and hard to get to, and from 1919 to 2004 it was the home of a Devil's Island–style penal colony with convicted murderers, rapists, and other serious criminals. Prisoners were confined to a series of colonies around the massive island, but they were not locked in. Instead, guards locked themselves in their quarters with their guns at night. The island jungle and shark-filled ocean kept prisoners from straying too far.

Naturally, a place such as this inspires endless stories, some of which may even be true. There's a legend, for instance, about the "mud man," a runaway prisoner who roamed the island, covered in mud. He was said to steal up on other prisoners and strangle them to death, a "mercy killing" accompanied by whispered apologies.

The prison camp, along with its legacy of horror and misery, has been slowly phased out in recent years. Officially, the last 25 prisoners were removed from the island in 2004, but as late as 2008 a few guards and model prisoners were reportedly left behind to maintain the area.

For years there has been talk of building "low-impact" tourist developments in the park, but little has happened so far. Conservationists and subsistence fishermen continue to combat attempts to allow commercial fishing and other exploitation of the park's resources. And there is still concern that commercial tuna boats are illegally using massive nets to fish the waters within the park limits, damaging fragile ecosystems. One hopes that common sense and long-term self-interest will prevail. Losing this Garden of Eden would be a tragedy for Panama and the world.

The island of Coiba is still relatively little known even by scientists. It's hilly in the center and crisscrossed by many rivers, including the 20-kilometer Río Negro. But because of the penal colony, access to the island itself is only now loosening up. Most visitors only come ashore in the area around an ANAM field station on the northeast tip of the island, which still has the only guest accommodations. The guest cabins are rustic but okay, and the station is on a sandy cove. However, tour operators are increasingly venturing to **Bahía Damas,** on the east side of the island, to visit the spooky ruins of the penal colony and dive among spectacular coral reefs.

There is a landing strip on Coiba, but only charter flights make the trip. Otherwise, access to the island is a long haul by land and sea. The logistical hassles in getting to Coiba almost force travelers to go with some kind of tour operator. This can get expensive, but you'll see a lot more and have a far more comfortable—and safe—trip than if you tried to get there on your own.

Sports and Recreation

Dry season is the best time to see monkeys and other animals on shore. **Diving** can be good year-round, though visibility can vary dramatically day to day.

The waters off **Bahía Damas,** a bay on the east side of the island, have the largest coral reef in Central America (135 hectares) and the second-largest in the eastern Pacific. That and the density and diversity of large sea creatures have made the park famous among scuba divers. The sea life in some spots is what a nature guide friend calls "aggressive—everyone in town comes by," including turtles, orcas, and sharks that zip right past divers. Because of the fragility of the environment here, and the necessity of knowing these waters well, diving trips should be arranged through reputable professionals. As my friend put it, anyone found tossing an anchor onto the reef will likely get an anchor tossed at his head.

A good and accessible spot for **snorkeling** is **Granito de Oro,** a lovely islet a short boat ride from the ANAM field station. There are coral fields, including brain and fan coral, and schools of pretty little tropical fish just off the islet's sandy beach. The current becomes very strong just beyond the rocky cove—even strong swimmers should be careful not to swim out too far.

There are two trails—short walks, really—around the ANAM ranger station. The **Sendero del Observatorio** (Observatory Trail) is a 15-minute walk at a very slow pace that leads to an elevated bird-watching station. It's not a particularly good place to watch birds, but the view is nice. The trail starts behind cabin 6. Note the sign that says the trail is "approximately" 527.81 meters long. Another brief walk behind the kitchen leads up to a second lookout point on a small hill. It has a lovely view of the sea and Isla Coibita.

The **Sendero de Los Monos** (Monkey Trail) is not accessible from the ranger station. It requires a boat ride to the area near the Granito de Oro islet. It takes about an hour to walk and curves inland from one beach to another. There are howlers and white-faced capuchins along the trail, but you'd be lucky to spot them; best bet is in the dry season. Other flora and fauna found along the trail include fiddler and hermit crabs, coconut trees, the guinea pig–like ñeque de Coiba *(Dasyprocta coibae),* boa constrictors, and fer-de-lance snakes.

Sportfishing within the park limits is catch-and-release only and requires a permit, and the government has finally begun to enforce this law. **Hannibal Bank,** between Isla de Coiba and Isla Montuosa, is an especially famous fishing spot.

Tour Operators

Diving and snorkeling trips are offered by **Boca Brava Divers** (tel. 775-3185, cell 6600-6191, www.scubadiving-panama.com) in Boca Chica and by **Coiba Dive Center** (tel. 938-0007 or 202-9214, www.coibadivecenter.com or www.scuba-charters.com) and **Scuba Coiba** (tel. 202-2172, www.scubacoiba.com) in Playa Santa Catalina. The Santa Catalina operators also offer nature tours of Isla Coiba. Guests at Islas Secas Resort can arrange chartered flights to the island.

Several operators offer multiday deep-sea fishing trips to the waters around Coiba. It's worth doing some research before settling on a package, as they tend to be quite expensive and some of the operations are not well run and either use dilapidated boats or go out of business overnight. Operations tend to be run out of either Puerto Mutis, a port 24 kilometers southwest of Santiago, or Pedregal, David's port.

A fishing group that enjoys a good reputation is **Coiba Adventure Sportfishing** (Panama tel. 998-8108, U.S. toll-free tel. 800/800-0907, www.coibadventure.com). The operation is run by Tom Yust, who has been running fishing trips to Coiba since 1991 and was the skipper on the original *Coiba Explorer* mother-ship. His current operation doesn't use a mother-ship, but rather a 31-foot Bertram and a 21-foot Mako. He also has a 14-foot inflatable and two sit-on-top sea kayaks.

The outfit offers four- to six-day fishing trips. Rates are US$3,625–7,375 depending on the trip length, number of anglers, and choice of boats. Prices include a round-trip charter flight between Panama City and Coiba, all meals, and a room at the ranger station.

The **Panama Big Game Fishing Club** (tel. 6674-4824, U.S. toll-free tel. 866/281-1225, www.panamabiggamefishingclub.com) offers several fishing packages. Their boats run out of Pedregal, and guests stay at their high-end cabins on Isla Boca Brava.

Another group to consider is **Pesca Panama** (U.S. toll-free tel. 800/946-3474, www.pescapanama.com). This fishing operation is run out of Pedregal and uses a cozy 70-foot barge as a mother-ship. It sleeps up to 16 in four air-conditioned guest cabins. Fishing is from 27-foot Ocean Masters. The standard package consists of six days of fishing. Per-person rates are US$2,995–3,895 depending on the number of anglers per boat. The package includes two nights in a luxury hotel in Panama City and food and accommodation during the five nights on the barge. Transportation and food in Panama City and transfers to David are not included in the rate.

Practicalities

The most commonly visited part of the island has an **ANAM field station** on a pretty, sandy cove backed by hills. Even day visitors must register here and pay a US$20-per-person national park entrance fee. The complex includes a boat anchorage, guest cabins, a kitchen and dining area, and a small museum. The museum contains the skeleton of a humpback whale and specimens of other critters recovered from the park, including pickled fer-de-lance and coral snakes.

Each of the six cabins for guests has two rooms with separate entrances. The cabins are quite basic and bare-bones, but they're perfectly fine, especially given the extreme isolation of this place. They're even air-conditioned. Rates are US$10 per person, plus the one-time US$20-per-person park entrance fee.

It is much less of a hassle to arrange a visit through a tour operator that frequents the island. To set up a visit on your own, contact ANAM in Santiago (tel. 998-4271). You can also try calling the field station on the island (tel. 999-8103). Note: Management of the park is scheduled to change, and contact numbers may change with it. ANAM should be able to provide updated information if this happens.

The station supplies diesel for electricity 6 P.M.–midnight. Those who want air-conditioning through the night have to bring their own diesel supply. About 15 gallons of diesel per cabin should last through two nights.

Independent travelers should also note the need to bring not only food but also the gas to prepare it (stoves are provided). Meals are eaten in an open-air *rancho*. Be prepared for mosquitoes and *chitras* (sand flies), which are fierce around here. There's nothing to do in the evenings but enjoy the tranquility.

Though this place is paradise, it's easy to see that life here could get a bit tedious. No wonder the rangers have befriended some of the local wildlife. The most impressive is Tito, a three-meter crocodile (*Crocodylus acutus*) that emerges from the water when called to dinner. Another is Pancho, a Geoffroy's tamarin. Sara is a fat and lazy deer—not surprising, since her diet now includes junk food.

Getting There

There's a landing strip on Coiba, but only charter flights make the trip. Nearly everyone comes by boat.

Playa Santa Catalina is emerging as the primary gateway to Parque Nacional Coiba. It takes about 90 minutes by fast boat to get to the island from there. Some folks come out from Puerto Mutis, Santiago's port, which is much closer to Panama City but a longer boat ride: 2–3 hours, depending on the boat. Other trips originate from Pedregal.

Wherever the starting point, be careful whom you travel with. The trip is on open ocean that can quickly turn rough. I don't advise striking a bargain deal with a local fisherman for this trip, as you'll be riding in a small boat that probably won't have a backup motor, life jackets, or a radio. One of these boats goes adrift at sea every month. Even if you make it, you won't be able to do much more than snorkel (with your own gear) from these boats. It's better to go with an experienced, safety-conscious tour operator with a substantial boat and good equipment.

MORRO NEGRITO SURF CAMP

Started in June 1998, Morro Negrito Surf Camp (www.surferparadise.com) is on two islands in the Gulf of Chiriquí, due north of Isla de Coiba. It's just off the opposite (northwest) side of the same little peninsula where you'll find Playa Santa Catalina, and it's even more remote. The actual surf camp, Morro

Negrito, is on an island that the locals call **Ensenada.** The camp has rustic cabañas, running water, and a dining area. Electricity is generated in the evenings. The waves here are smaller than on the second island, with faces that range 1.5–2.5 meters on average. The other island is **Isla Silva de Afuera,** a half hour away by boat. This is the main surfing island, with wave faces that average 3.5–5.5 meters. There are both left and right breaks on both islands. Ten breaks have been discovered so far. The best time to find big waves is April–October. For nonsurfers there's a long beach, ocean kayaking, horseback riding, snorkeling, and fishing (bring your own gear for the last two). It's also possible to hike to a 15-meter waterfall.

Only weeklong package deals are offered. Packages cost US$650 per person and include airport pickup and drop-off, a night in a Panama City hotel, transportation to the camp (a five-hour drive from the city), all food, and daily boat trips to surf spots. The package runs from Saturday to Saturday.

THE AZUERO PENINSULA

The Azuero Peninsula is a paradoxical place. It's a heavily settled, terribly deforested land where wilderness has largely been supplanted by farms. In some places erosion has transformed forest into wasteland. Yet it still feels isolated from modern Panama, frozen in an idyllic past, and there's lots of charm and natural beauty left. It's a land both much beloved and much abused.

The Azuero is inevitably called Panama's "heartland," a designation that overlooks the country's widely scattered indigenous populations, not to mention, for instance, those of African descent.

Still, the peninsula occupies an important, almost mythological, place in the Panamanian psyche. It is the wellspring of Panama's favorite folkloric traditions, many of which originated in Spain but have taken on a uniquely Panamanian form—often thanks, ironically enough, to borrowings from the above-mentioned indigenous and African peoples.

Beautiful traditional clothing, such as the stunning *pollera* (hand-embroidered dress), and handicrafts, such as ceramics based on pre-Colombian designs, originated and are still made on the Azuero. The same is true of some important musical and literary traditions. Even Panama's national drink, the sugarcane liquor known as *seco,* is made here. Traces of Spanish-colonial Panama—rows of houses with red-tile roofs and ornate ironwork, centuries-old churches overlooking quiet plazas—are easy to find, especially in well-preserved little towns such as Parita and Pedasí.

HIGHLIGHTS

◖ **La Catedral de San Juan Bautista:** Chitré's cathedral, at the heart of this cozy provincial town, has an understated elegance that's rare in Panama (page 381).

◖ **La Arena:** This entire town is devoted to making pottery, with pre-Colombian designs, that is eternally popular around the country (page 381).

◖ **Parita:** Visiting this immaculately pre-served Spanish-colonial town is like stepping through a time portal to the Azuero of a hundred years ago (page 382).

◖ **Carnaval in Las Tablas:** Here you'll find the biggest pre-Lent party north of Rio de Janeiro (page 396).

◖ **Pedasí:** This Spanish-colonial Azuero town is on the verge of becoming a hot beach destination (page 400).

LOOK FOR ◖ TO FIND RECOMMENDED SIGHTS, ACTIVITIES, DINING, AND LODGING.

Most of all, the Azuero is known for its festivals. It has the biggest and best in the country, from all-night bacchanals to sober religious rituals. At the top of the heap is Carnaval, held during the four days leading up to Ash Wednesday. No Latin American country outside of Brazil is more passionate about Carnaval than Panama, and no part of Panama is more passionate about it than the Azuero. But there are plenty of others to visit throughout the year. It's rare for a single week to go by without some festival, fair, holy day, or other excuse for a major party somewhere on the peninsula.

For all the affection the Azuero inspires among Panamanians, most who live outside the peninsula know it only as a place to come for festivals. It flies below the radar of most foreign visitors altogether. But those who want a taste of an older, more stately Panama should consider a visit. In some places, it's as though the 20th century never happened.

The Azuero is large enough to be shared by three provinces. The nearly landlocked Herrera province, Panama's smallest, is to the north; Los Santos to the southeast has an extensive coastline ringing the eastern and southern sides of the peninsula; and huge Veraguas, the only province with a Caribbean and a Pacific coast, dips into the Azuero on its western side.

The Azuero is a region of farmers, cattle ranchers, and, on the coast, fishermen. Slash-and-burn agriculture and logging have been more extensive in the Azuero than in any other part of Panama, and the inevitable result has

THE AZUERO PENINSULA

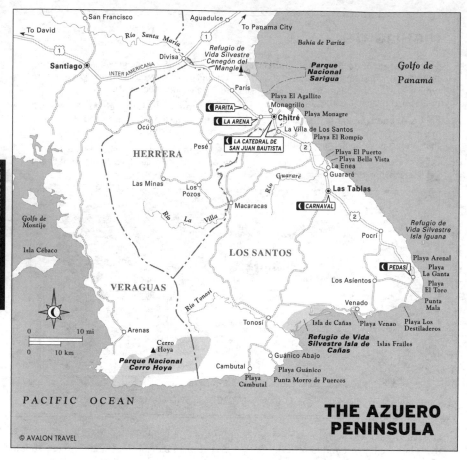

THE AZUERO PENINSULA

© AVALON TRAVEL

been both dramatic and sad. Deforestation has turned some parts of this region into barren desert, and most of the rest of it is pastureland.

Residents of Los Santos province are especially well-known for their tree-chopping prowess. Having cut down most of the trees in their own province, *santeño* farmers and cattle ranchers have spread out to deforest other parts of the country, including, most sadly of all, the forests of the Darién.

The hilly southwestern tip of the Azuero is the least developed, with a few patches of unspoiled wilderness left. These are extremely

hard to get to, which is why they're still lovely. The accessible lowland areas are now mostly farm country.

The east coast of the Azuero, as well as a strip of coast in Coclé province to the north, is known as the *arco seco* (dry arc), because of its lack of rainfall. While good news for sunbathers, that scarcity is bad news for the environment, showing the effects of creeping desertification.

The east-coast beaches resemble those within a couple of hours of Panama City, minus 30 years of development. They're easy to get to, yet for dozens of kilometers at a stretch there's little sign of human habitation. However, tourism is beginning to come to this area, especially Pedasí, Playa Venao, and, most recently, Cambutal. Some of the lodgings and tour operations are appealing. Others seem to exist primarily to create a market for real-estate sales. Buyer beware.

Don't expect pure white sand. But those who don't mind brown, gray, and in some cases black sand will have no trouble finding a deserted seaside paradise. The beaches are wide and long, often backed by rugged cliffs and facing rolling surf. Their waters are filled with big fish and, in some places, extensive coral. Isla Cañas, off the south coast of the Azuero, is the most important nesting spot for sea turtles on Panama's Pacific coast: Tens of thousands lay their eggs there each year.

The interior of the peninsula is taken up mostly by farmland, cattle pasture, and towns. There are few facilities for visitors there, but visiting this heart of the "heartland" is like stepping back in time.

The people of the Azuero are among the friendliest in Panama, and the percentage of smiles per capita seems to go up the farther south you head. People seem not just content but genuinely happy. It'll probably rub off on you.

PLANNING YOUR TIME

It's possible to explore the biggest towns of the Azuero—**Chitré** and **Las Tablas**—and their surrounding attractions in a couple of days. It's a straight shot, for instance, to pull off the road for a quick look at **Parita,** shop for pottery in **La Arena,** visit **La Catedral de San Juan Bautista** and **El Museo de Herrera** in Chitré, then pop by La Villa de Los Santos before ending up in Las Tablas for the night. Those who have their own transportation can do all that in a day. Those relying on buses and taxis, however, should plan on spending at least two days in the area, probably making Chitré home base for excursions to the surrounding area. And those who arrive during festival times should plan to stay longer than that, as many of the festivals are several days

long. The biggest **Carnaval** celebration is in Las Tablas; Chitré runs a close second. Bear in mind that just about everything shuts down during big celebrations. Add at least one more day to visit more remote destinations, especially along the coast, where you'll want time to enjoy the beach.

Nearly the entire Azuero is well served by buses. Bus service between the peninsula and other parts of Panama is also good. Buses run constantly, for instance, to and from Panama City and Chitré and Las Tablas.

Las Tablas and Chitré are the major transportation hubs on the Azuero. They can be used as bases for exploring the east coast of the peninsula, but those looking for good beaches should head all the way down to **Pedasí,** near the southeast tip of the Azuero.

To drive to the Azuero Peninsula from Panama City, head west on the Interamericana until Divisa, which is little more than a crossroads. Divisa is about 215 kilometers from Panama City, a drive that takes around three hours. There's a new overpass across the highway there. Head south (left) here. Straight leads to Santiago and from there to western Panama.

Most of the notable towns in the Azuero are on a single main road, an ambitiously named *carretera nacional* (national highway) that runs down the east coast of the peninsula. The stretch of road from Divisa all the way to Pedasí is about 100 kilometers long and takes a little under two hours to drive. The stretch between Chitré and Las Tablas was widened to a divided four-lane road in 2010.

As is so often the case in Panama, it's easy to drive right by a town that time forgot without noticing it. That's because the part of the town abutting the main road is often quite ugly and industrial. It's worth pulling off the highway or hopping off the bus from time to time to explore the older parts of the towns, which are set back from the road. The best bet for finding a slice of colonial quaintness is to head for the town church and check out the buildings set around its plaza.

The interior of the peninsula has a confusing

network of roads of various quality. But a closer look reveals reasonably well-maintained loops that link up the towns of most interest to travelers. These are also served by buses. The largest of the loops connects Chitré, Las Tablas, Pedasí, Tonosí, and Macaracas (a tiny town whose sole claim to national fame is its Epiphany Festival, held around January 6, during which it stages a reenactment of the gift of the Magis to the baby Jesus). The loop ends back at Chitré.

FESTIVALS

Carnaval is celebrated throughout the country, but those who can get away try to come to the Azuero during those four days of partying. The Carnaval celebration held in the town of Las Tablas, in southeastern Azuero, is the most famous in the country. For those who don't mind a madhouse, this is the place to be. Smaller but no less enthusiastic Carnaval celebrations are held in other towns and villages throughout the peninsula.

Another big event is the Festival de Corpus Christi, which takes over the tiny town of La Villa de Los Santos for two weeks between May and July every year. Ostensibly an allegory about the triumph of Christ over evil, it's most notable for its myriad dances, especially those featuring revelers in fiendishly elaborate devil costumes. Then there's the Festival Nacional de la Mejorana, Panama's largest folkloric festival, which takes over the sleepy town of Guararé each September. It draws performers and spectators from around the country.

That's just for starters. Los Santos alone has more religious festivals than any other province in the country.

Dates for some of these festivals change yearly. ATP, Panama's ministry of tourism, publishes updated lists of festival dates and details each year. Stop by any of the several ATP (ministry of tourism) offices scattered throughout the Azuero. This is one part of the country ATP does a decent job of covering, especially when it comes to the parties.

It sometimes feels as though the entire peninsula is dedicated to preserving the past, at least symbolically. This includes maintaining the charming but definitely antiquated custom of the *junta de embarre* (rough translation: "the mudding meeting"), in which neighbors gather to build a rustic mud home, called a *casa de quincha,* for newlyweds. Miniature versions of these are sometimes made during folkloric events. Some tradition-minded music festivals go so far as to ban, by town decree, the use of newfangled instruments—such as the six-string classical guitar.

HISTORY

The Azuero Peninsula has an incredibly ancient history. Evidence of an 11,000-year-old fishing settlement, the earliest sign of human habitation in all of Panama, has been found in what is now Parque Nacional Sarigua. Ceramics found around Monagrillo date to at least 2800 B.C., possibly much earlier. It's the oldest known pottery in all of Latin America.

Excavations taking place right now at Cerro Juan Díaz, near La Villa de Los Santos, indicate the site was used as a burial and ceremonial ground off and on for 1,800 years, from 200 B.C. until the arrival of the Spanish brought a bloody end to the indigenous civilizations.

Just how complete that victory was can be seen in the modern-day residents of the Azuero. They are by and large the most Spanish-looking people in Panama, with lighter skin and eyes than residents of most other parts of the country.

The Azuero has continued to play an important role in the history of the country into the modern era. On November 10, 1821, for instance, residents of the little town of La Villa de Los Santos wrote a letter to Simón Bolívar asking to join in his revolution against the Spanish. This Primer Grito de la Independencia (First Cry for Independence) is still commemorated today. It was the first step in Panama's independence from Spain and union with Colombia.

Chitré

The provincial capital of Herrera province, Chitré (pop. 7,756 in town, 42,467 in district; pronounced sort of like chee-TRAY) is one of the largest towns on the peninsula. The other is Las Tablas, which usually gets more attention but can't compete with Chitré in charm. By Panamanian scale, both qualify as "cities."

This is a mellow place that's clinging to its Spanish-colonial past. The high-curbed streets are still lined with row houses that have red-tile roofs and ornate iron window screens. Each house is tiny and melds seamlessly with its neighbors. Life is lived and observed in the front rooms and porches of these modest homes, which overlook the streets.

Many men wear traditional straw hats, without affectation, as they go about their daily business. On dry-season evenings, people still gather in the town plazas to sit and enjoy the breeze.

The town was founded October 19, 1848, though according to some historians it was first settled by the conquistadors in 1558, which would make it one of the oldest surviving towns on the isthmus.

There isn't much to see in Chitré beyond its attractive cathedral and small museum. But it's a pleasant place for people-watching and to get a sense of life on the Azuero. It's also a good base for exploring the surrounding area, including the well-preserved Spanish-colonial town of Parita, the pottery shops of neighboring La Arena, and three unusual natural attractions. Villa de Los Santos is just four kilometers south, which makes this a convenient place to stay during that town's Festival de Corpus Christi and other big events.

For those coming from the north, the main road into Chitré starts at the little town of La Arena, about two kilometers west of Chitré. The road forks here.

To get to downtown Chitré, keep going straight. The road will lead through La Arena into Chitré, where it becomes Paseo Enrique Geenzier, the main west–east promenade, before morphing into Calle Manuel María Correa near the cathedral downtown.

The right fork circumvents downtown and heads toward Los Santos province. This is the more direct route to Chitré's ATP information center, Hotel Guayacanes, the bus terminal, and DKDA's Restaurante. They are all on Calle 19 de Octubre (also called Avenida Roberto Ramírez de Diego and Vía Circunvalación) before the road links up again with the main road leading south toward Villa de Los Santos and Las Tablas.

The cathedral is at the heart of downtown Chitré, and most of the town's hotels, restaurants, and services are within a few blocks of it.

Avenida Herrera cuts across town from north to south. It starts near the ocean, at Playa El Agallito, then runs down past the airport and the east side of Chitré's cathedral. Several of the cheaper places to stay are on this avenue, near the cathedral.

SIGHTS

Sightseers can take in Chitré's few landmarks in a couple of hours. The best way to do this is on foot, if the heat's bearable. Soaking up the street life on the way is at least as interesting as seeing the landmarks.

To get a quick overview of Chitré, start at the cathedral, then head west past Parque Unión (the church plaza) on Calle Melitón Martín. Turn right on Avenida Julio Arjona and walk north one block, to the Museo de Herrera. After visiting the museum, head east down Calle Manuel María Correa, a busy shopping street. Finish the tour by wandering up and down Avenida Herrera, another shopping street. There may be a vendor or two selling Panama hats here. The tour ends back at the cathedral. That's pretty much downtown Chitré.

The ceramic shops of La Arena, the historic towns of Monagrillo and Parita, and the natural attractions of Playa El Agallito, Parque

THE AZUERO PENINSULA

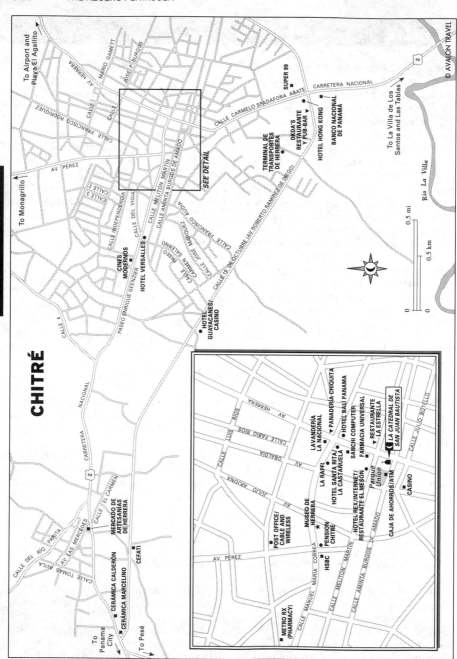

© AVALON TRAVEL

CHITRÉ

To Airport and
Playa El Agalito

To Monagrillo

To Panama City

To Pesé

CARRETERA NACIONAL

To La Villa de Los
Santos and Las Tablas

Río La Villa

To Pará

Map labels (main map):

- AV MARIO GAMETT
- JOSÉ E BURGOS
- AV HERRERA
- CALLE FRANCISCO RODRIGUEZ
- AV PÉREZ
- CALLE CARMELO SPADAFORA ABATE
- SUPER 99
- CARRETERA NACIONAL
- BANCO NACIONAL DE PANAMÁ
- HOTEL HONG KONG
- DKOA'S RESTAURANTE Y PUB-BAR
- TERMINAL DE TRANSPORTES DE HERRERA
- SEE DETAIL
- CALLE MELITÓN MARTÍN
- CALLE AMINTA BURGOS DE AMADO
- CALLE DEL VIGÍA
- CALLE INDEPENDENCIA
- CALLE 3
- CALLE 2
- CALLE FRANCISCO AGÍA
- CALLE 19 DE OCTUBRE/AV ROBERTO RAMÍREZ DE DIEGO
- CINES MODERNOS
- HOTEL VERSALLES
- PASEO ENRIQUE GEENZIER
- CALLE JOSÉ MARQUEZ
- CALLE CARMEN SALERNO
- CALLE PASEO
- HOTEL GUAYACANES/CASINO
- CALLE 4
- CARRETERA NACIONAL
- MERCADO DE ARTESANÍAS DE HERRERA
- CEFATI
- CALLE EL CARMEN
- AV LAS MERCEDES
- CERÁMICA MARCELINO
- CERÁMICA CALDERÓN
- CALLE DEL RÍO PARITA
- CALLE TOMÁS AVILA
- 0.5 mi
- 0.5 km

Detail inset map labels:

- METRO RX (PHARMACY)
- POST OFFICE/CABLE AND WIRELESS
- MUSEO DE HERRERA
- HSBC
- PENSIÓN CHITRÉ
- LA RAFFI
- HOTEL SANTA RITA/LA CASTAÑUELA
- HOTEL REX/INTERNET/RESTAURANTE EL MESÓN
- PANADERÍA CHIQUITA
- LAVANDERÍA LA NACIONAL
- HOTEL BALÍ PANAMA
- SANCHI COMPUTER
- FARMACIA UNIVERSAL
- RESTAURANTE LA ESTRELLA
- LA CATEDRAL DE SAN JUAN BAUTISTA
- Parque Unión
- CAJA DE AHORROS/ATM
- CASINO
- AV HERRERA
- CALLE FABIO RIOS
- CALLE LUIS RIOS
- AV OBALDÍA
- AV JULIO ARJONA
- AV PÉREZ
- CALLE MANUEL MARÍA CORREA
- CALLE MELITÓN MARTÍN
- CALLE AMINTA BURGOS DE AMADO
- CALLE JULIO BOTELLO

Nacional Sarigua, and the Refugio de Vida Silvestre Cenegón del Mangle are all outside of Chitré. They're accessible by car or bus.

La Catedral de San Juan Bautista

Chitré's cathedral was built between 1896 and 1910 on the site of an earlier church (on the east end of Parque Unión). With its tall twin towers, it's an easily spotted landmark. Inside, it's most notable for what it lacks: over-wrought decorations. Instead, it makes taste-ful, restrained use of dark woods, gold trim, attractive frescos, and stained glass. An arched ceiling made from thick beams, some of them hand-hewn, gives the cathedral a cozy feel.

It recently underwent a tasteful restoration that, among other things, exposed the hand-some stone walls of the exterior. The cathedral looks especially attractive at night, when it's illuminated.

Museo de Herrera

Chitré's museum (Calle Manuel María Correa and Avenida Julio Arjona, tel. 996-0077, 8 A.M.–noon and 1–4 P.M. Tues.–Sat., 8–11 A.M. Sun., US$1 adults, US$0.25 children) is housed in a lovingly preserved Spanish colonial building. The collection downstairs is devoted to archaeological finds from all around the central provinces, including stone tools from Monagrillo dating 2400–1000 B.C. Be sure to check out the collection of ancient ceramics. Local artisans are still inspired by the same designs the indigenous peoples used more than 1,500 years ago. In the middle of the ground floor is a re-creation of the burial site of a *cacique* (tribal chief) found by the Spanish in 1517, including exact replicas of beautifully wrought gold jewelry, made by the Reprosa jewelry company in Panama City.

The displays upstairs are devoted to the his-tory of Herrera province, from Spanish times to the modern era, represented by a signed baseball and Chicago White Sox cap donated by major-leaguer Olmedo Sáenz, who is from Chitré. Other exhibits include devil masks, *polleras* (hand-embroidered dresses), and

© BONNIE KAY SPINDLER

THE AZUERO PENINSULA

Chitré's little Museo de Herrera is one of the country's better museums.

traditional musical instruments from the area. A diorama outside depicts a traditional local kitchen garden and sugarcane press. As small and simple as this museum is, it's one of the better ones in the country.

La Arena

This town, two kilometers west of Chitré, could be renamed Ceramics City. All along the main street that passes through the little town (pop. 6,429), which is practically a suburb of Chitré, are small shops selling the pottery this area is famous for throughout Panama. These include pots, mugs, ashtrays, plates, vases, pitchers, and even entire tableware.

The pottery is based on designs created thousands of years ago by the indigenous residents of this area. The most traditional piece is the *tinaja* (pot) that was once used to store household water. These are used as decorative items all over Panama. One of the country's most famous painters, Sheila Lichacz, made a career out of her pastel images of and montages using these *tinajas,* which fascinate her. She was born in nearby Monagrillo. When she was a child she'd swim in the river on her family's ranch and accidentally kick up shards from broken pots that dated back 500 years or more.

The oldest designs made in La Arena are based on pre-Colombian patterns, mostly abstract, painted in earth tones on the reddish-brown piece. More modern designs incorporate bright colors, glazes, and representational images, and these have become popular in recent years. It can now be difficult to find more traditional pieces. The factories are constantly experimenting. After a little comparison shopping it's easy to spot the distinctive style of each *taller* (workshop/factory).

La Arena is also known for its bread, though remember that what's called good bread in Panama is called "hot dog buns" in other countries.

Monagrillo

One of the most ancient inhabited spots on the isthmus can be reached from Chitré by heading north on Avenida Pérez two kilometers from where it intersects Paseo Enrique Geenzier. Avenida Pérez runs past the Cable and Wireless office; look for the tall communications towers. Ceramics found in this area date from at least 2500 B.C., the oldest found in Central America and among the oldest anywhere in the Americas. There are no archaeological displays or other traces of that ancient history, but those with spare time who just like the idea of being near that much history should consider a quick drive-through. The town (pop. 9,549) does have a quaint little church with some well-preserved old homes with red-tile roofs. It's similar to Parita, though not quite as scenic. The taxi ride from Chitré will cost about US$1. Buses also make the run between Monagrillo and Chitré, and if it's not too hot you can even walk it.

◖ Parita

This amazingly well-preserved Spanish colonial town is 10 kilometers northwest of Chitré. As you drive up from Chitré, the turnoff is on the left at a gas station. Those without their own transportation can visit the town by bus on the way to or from Chitré. Any bus heading between Chitré and the Interamericana can stop there. The fare is US$0.50 from Chitré's bus terminal.

There's nothing much to do here but walk around and take photos, but Parita hints at what towns in the Azuero must have been like in olden days. It's also home to a nationally famous devil-mask maker.

Parita was founded in 1556 as Santa Elena and was later renamed. Work began on the town church, **Iglesia Santo Domingo de Guzmán,** a century later. It's a simple but attractive church filled with ornately carved woodwork. It's worth a quick visit. A little museum in the back that houses silver ceremonial pieces and other artifacts from the Spanish era has been closed for renovation every time I've visited.

The townspeople live next to each other in narrow, block-long buildings with red-tile roofs set around the plaza and church. The pride residents take in the place is evident in the spotless streets and the riot of flowering plants that cover the whole front of some buildings. It's a supremely mellow place, and so removed from the flow of modern life that many Panamanians don't know it exists.

Parque Nacional Sarigua

This 8,000-hectare national park (tel. 996-7679 in Chitré, no local phone, 8 A.M.–4 P.M. daily, US$5) stretches east toward the coast and out to sea. It's 10 kilometers northwest of Chitré, near Parita.

Sarigua was the site of a fishing settlement an astonishing 11,000 years ago. That's the oldest trace of human habitation on the entire isthmus. It was also home to the country's oldest known farming community, which tilled the land here up until about 1,500 years ago.

That long history makes it all the sadder to realize what modern humans have done to this area in just a few decades in the 20th century. Sometimes tourist officials try to bill this place as a desert. That misses the point entirely. It's not a desert: It's a wasteland. It's a vivid, horrifying example of just what deforestation in the tropics can look like. This area used to be covered by species-rich mangroves and dry coastal forest. They were chopped and burned away. Strong winds blow here in the dry season; without the buffer of the mangroves, the wind blew sand inland, hastening the deforestation.

The average temperature now is around 36°C (97°F), far above the norm for the surrounding areas that still have vegetation, and it can get even hotter. The area gets less than a meter of rain yearly, a fraction of the precipitation in other parts of the Pacific coast. Note the garbage sticking out of the mounds around the ranger station; Parita used the area as a dump before 1980.

There's a *mirador* (observation platform) near the station that visitors can climb to get a good view of the sweeping nothingness. The ranger will probably come up and give a little lecture and may speak a little English.

It's possible to drive around here even when the ranger station is closed, but it's not a good idea to come by in the late afternoon in any case. It's too hot. Visitors can drive only about two kilometers into the park. After that there's a private shrimp farm that's not open to the public.

To get to the park from Chitré, head northwest on the main road toward Parita for about 10 kilometers. Turn right before Parita at the large park sign. After about three kilometers, turn left onto the dirt road and follow some more signs into the park.

Refugio de Vida Silvestre Cenegón del Mangle

Cenegón del Mangle is a 776-hectare wildlife refuge that's worth a quick visit on the way to or from Chitré or Las Tablas. There's no admission fee or set opening hours. It's best to go in a four-wheel-drive vehicle.

The part that's accessible to visitors consists of a half-kilometer-long boardwalk that loops through tall black mangroves near the shore. It makes for a short, scenic walk that's halfway between spooky and pretty, since it's easy to imagine all kinds of creatures in the mangroves and the murky marsh below one's feet.

This is a major heron hangout. In fact, some of the herons that grace the fountain in the Palacio de las Garzas (Palace of the Herons), the presidential palace in Panama City, are captured here. The area attracts what birders call "mixed colonies" of herons, including the great egret, tricolored heron, and cattle egret.

It's also easy to spot caimans here, especially when some of the herons nest, June–September. The toothy critters wait patiently under the nests, like dogs by the dinner table, in hopes the odd egg will fall from a nest and into the marsh. Yum. Also be on the lookout for iguanas and the occasional crocodile. Herons can be spotted year-round.

Access to the refuge is from the village of **París,** the turnoff to which is at a gas station seven kilometers north of Parita. If you're heading up from Chitré, which is 17 kilometers southeast of París, the turnoff is to the right. There's no sign marking the turn from this direction. París is one kilometer down this road.

Once in París, which won't remind you of the one in France, take the right fork when the road splits at the church. Then make a right turn 0.3 kilometers past this fork onto a road that quickly turns to dirt. Go six kilometers, until the road forks at the none-too-scenic garbage dump.

The left fork leads to the mangroves. Park just past the dump. There's a dirt trail on the left. Follow this to the boardwalk, about a five-minute walk away. This area is parched in the dry season, but even then there are plenty of marshy areas as one gets closer to the shore.

If you have trouble finding all this, ask around back in París. A local kid will probably hop in your car and show the way for a quarter or two.

The right fork back at the dump, by the way, leads to some so-called thermal pools said to have medicinal properties. These consist of shallow, foot-wide puddles with nasty-looking stagnant water. They look like boils on the face of a sunbaked patch of earth. To say this is easily skipped is a wild understatement.

It takes about 45 minutes to drive to the refuge from Chitré.

THE AZUERO PENINSULA

Playa El Agallito

This is not a bathing beach, though Chitré has made a half-hearted attempt to dress it up as one. Rather, it consists of mudflats that lead into mangroves. This becomes obvious at low tide, when the muck stretches nearly two kilometers out into the distance. The tide varies by six meters from high to low. You can literally see it coming in and going out.

The beach, such as it is, is artificial. It dates from 1967, when the residents of Chitré decided they wanted a town beach and cut down mangroves to create one. The main reason to come out here is to watch the impressive bird life. Playa El Agallito attracts 35 species of shorebirds, including sandpipers, black-bellied plovers, willets, whimbrels, American oystercatchers, yellowlegs, ospreys, and warblers. Most of all, it attracts *Calidris mauri,* the western sandpiper. According to Franciso Delgado, a dedicated local ornithologist, about 10,000 of these shorebirds come to the beach each year. They start showing up in late October and leave in early March.

To get to Playa El Agallito from downtown Chitré, head north on Avenida Herrera for six kilometers past the cathedral. The road ends in the beach. A taxi ride should cost around US$2–3.

ENTERTAINMENT AND EVENTS
Festivals

The **Carnaval** celebration in Chitré is the biggest in the Azuero after Las Tablas. As always, it takes place in the four days leading up to Ash Wednesday. The festivities are similar to those in Carnaval at Las Tablas.

The town celebrates two events tied to its origins. The first is **October 19,** the day on which the district of Chitré was founded in 1848. This is cause for a big parade and festivities. The other event commemorates the town's patron saint, **San Juan Bautista** (John the Baptist), on June 24. This latter celebration also dates from the 19th century, when an image of St. John was brought to town.

The **Festival de Corpus Christi** is held in neighboring La Villa de Los Santos sometime between May and July. The dates change yearly.

Nightlife

Nightlife when no festival takes over the town is normally very limited, consisting mainly of some grimy bars. There's a large **casino** (Calle 19 de Octubre, tel. 996-9758 or 996-8093, www.losguayacanes.com) at the Hotel Guayacanes and another one two blocks south of the cathedral.

La Castañuela (corner of Calle Manuel María Correa and Avenida Herrera, tel. 996-8719, 9 A.M.–11 P.M. Mon.–Sat., 10 A.M.–6 P.M. Sun.), next to Hotel Santa Rita, is a bar with a few slot machines and occasional live music.

The **Cines Modernos** (tel. 996-6121, Paseo Enrique Geenzier) is a gringo-style multiplex complete with Hollywood blockbusters and the mall rats they attract. It's west of and across the street from Hotel Versalles.

SHOPPING

The best place in La Arena to get a sampling of the range of available ceramics is at the **Mercado de Artesanías de Herrera** (8:30 A.M.–4:30 P.M. daily), the white two-story building at the fork in the middle of town. It sells pieces from a variety of *talleres* (workshops). The prices are highly reasonable; a small pot costs US$2 or less.

It's also possible to stop by the workshops themselves during work hours, and this is where you can find the best pieces. The most garish pieces are displayed outside. Don't be dissuaded by this; go in and poke around. Visitors are welcome to step back into the workshop to see the wood-burning ovens, the drying rooms, the painting workshops, and so on. **Cerámica Marcelino** (tel. 974-4801, 7:30 A.M.–6 P.M. daily) is at the west end of La Arena, where the road from Chitré meets the road from Los Santos. I especially like the work at **Cerámica Calderón** (tel. 974-4946 or 974-4157, early morning–late evening daily), a few houses closer to Chitré on the main road. Pieces here are well made, with clean designs

Panama hats for sale on the streets of Chitré

and striking patterns. Those with the time can design their own pieces and have them made here. Proprietor and lead designer Angel Calderón and his son, also called Angel, pull out books of photos and sketches of actual pre-Colombian ceramics, some of them museum pieces, and let you pick and choose designs you like. It's possible to order a full, custom-made 12-piece dinner set for around US$250. They deliver to Panama City, but you may have to make your own arrangements to ship the pieces out of the country. Sadly, I can't recommend any shipping company. Someone I know used a highly regarded one and ended up with nothing but shards. If possible, pack it carefully and take it with you. Making a set takes several weeks.

Those interested in Panama-style Panama hats can find a street vendor with a good selection on Avenida Herrera near the cathedral.

While in Parita, pay a visit to the home workshop of **Darío López** (tel. 974-2015, 7 A.M.–5 P.M. daily). He's nationally famous for his fearsome *diablicos* (devil masks), which are worn by dancers during the Corpus Christi

Festival in nearby Villa de Los Santos. He's been making them for 40 years, helped out in recent years by his nine children.

The large masks cost US$25 and take two days to make. Don't expect to find them in stock close to Corpus Christi or other festivals, when they're much in demand, but smaller models—including ones barely big enough to mask a finger—are usually on sale for significantly less.

López's house, which is also his workshop, is on the highway, across the street from and north of the Shell station, near Calle José Angel Bosquez B. His home is next to Kiosco Chely. Look for devil masks hanging on the front of the house.

ACCOMMODATIONS

Chitré has the biggest array of accommodations on the Azuero. These include a number of budget hotels and *hospedajes,* as well as a few relatively upscale choices. Those planning to visit during Carnaval, the Corpus Christi festival, or other big events should book several months in advance and expect to pay premium prices. At other times, there should be plenty of options available.

US$10-25

Pension Chitré (Paseo Enrique Geenzier and Avenida Perez, next to the Museo de Herrera, tel. 996-1856, US$8 s, US$12 d) is a basic six-room place with cold-water bathrooms. Rates more than double during festivals.

The 18-room **Hotel Santa Rita** (Calle Manuel María Correa near Avenida Herrera, tel. 996-4610, fax 996-2404, US$11 s, US$15.40 d with fan; US$15.40 s, US$19.80 d with a/c) is a clean, neat, old-fashioned place with character. Rooms are dark and offer thin mattresses, tiny TVs, and cold-water bathrooms that must be shared with the room next door. That aside, the rooms are pleasant enough. Some have balconies overlooking the loud, busy commercial street below. Rates during festivals are higher (US$23.10 s/d with fan; US$30.80 s/d with a/c).

US$25-50

The popular and centrally located **◖ Hotel Rex** (just north of the cathedral on Calle Melitón Martín, tel. 996-4310 or 996-2408, US$33 s, US$44 d, including breakfast) has 37 bright, simple rooms with hot-water bathrooms, cable TV, and air-conditioning. The rooms on the top floor are the cheeriest. A pleasant terrace upstairs overlooks the cathedral plaza. There's a restaurant and Internet café on the premises. Though the Rex is not as fancy as the Hotel Guayacanes or Hotel Versalles, its location right in the heart of Chitré will appeal to those who want to soak up the local atmosphere. This is the best of the budget hotels.

Hotel Hong Kong (Calle Carmelo Spadafora A., tel. 996-4483 or 996-9180, www.hotel-hongkongpanama.com, starts at US$26.50 s, US$48 d), on the southern outskirts of town, once offered two kinds of rooms: old and older. But recently it was given a facelift that improved things considerably. It's still a tad gloomy and the beds are on the soft side, but it's one of the better options in town. There are

32 rooms in all, all with air-conditioning, cable TV, and telephones. There's a 24-hour Internet café, a bar, and a Chinese restaurant. The decor is vaguely Chinese. The hotel has a somewhat surreal mini aquatic park—a water slide and three small pools, dominated by a Buddha statue—that's extremely popular with kids.

Hotel Balí Panama (Avenida Herrera, tel. 996-4620, www.hotelbalipanama.com, US$30 s, US$35 d), formerly Hotel Prado, is a simple 27-room hotel saved by a generally pleasant and friendly atmosphere. (Some of the photos on its website are, shall we say, more aspirational than realistic.) Ask for the corporate rates, which are half the normal ones. Rooms have thin mattresses, cable TV, and hot-water bathrooms. Some have safes. The place is moderately clean and has a spacious open-air lobby/restaurant/sitting area overlooking a busy street. The attached restaurant serves breakfast, lunch, and dinner.

◖ Hotel Versalles (Paseo Enrique Geenzier, tel. 996-4422, 996-3133, or 996-4563, www.hotelversalles.com, starts at US$27 s, US$49 d) is a clean and fairly cheerful place with 80 rather institutional, mustard-yellow rooms, featuring good mattresses, cable TV, Wi-Fi, and air-conditioning. Corporate rates are at least US$5 cheaper. There's a small pool and an attractive lobby, bar, and restaurant. This place fills up; make reservations as far ahead of time as possible. Reservations for Carnaval should be made by October. The hotel's one real drawback is its isolated location on the west end of Paseo Enrique Geenzier, the main avenue that heads east into town.

US$50-100

Hotel Guayacanes (Calle 19 de Octubre, tel. 996-9758 or 996-8093, www.losguayacanes.com, US$88 s, US$99 d, including welcome cocktail and full breakfast) is the fanciest place to stay in town. Until recently it was a member of the Spanish Barceló chain. Built in 2001, it's kind of an odd place. Rooms are in several two-story buildings set around an artificial duck pond with an artificial waterfall. The hotel has a pool that's popular with day groups, plus a restaurant, bar, large casino, and little garden in back. It started having problems, such as perpetual shortages of hot water, within its first year of opening. During my last visit, the duck pond was turning into a swamp, the infrastructure was already crumbling, and the room I stayed in was invaded by tiny ants. In spite of all that, it was still an okay place to stay. The hotel is in a sparsely populated area a short drive from downtown Chitré. It's quite insulated from its surroundings, which will not appeal to those who come to the Azuero to mix with the locals. Prices have doubled in the last few years and it is now distinctly overpriced.

FOOD

Restaurants are generally mediocre at best in Chitré. There are grocery stores on Paseo Enrique Geenzier and a large Super 99 supermarket across the Carretera Nacional from Hotel Hong Kong if none of the following appeal to you.

The restaurant in the Hotel Guayacanes, **Restaurante Las Brisas** (Calle 19 de Octubre, tel. 996-9758, 7 A.M.–11 P.M. Sun.–Thurs., 7 A.M.–midnight Fri.–Sat.), has an outdoor dining room covered by a large wooden roof held up by massive wooden pillars. There's also a fancier, air-conditioned dining room, but no one ever seems to use it. During my last visit, a souvenir shop had been built along one side of the outdoor area, blocking what had been the restaurant's best feature: a strong, pleasant breeze that gave the restaurant its name. The menu is limited—pastas in addition to the usual assortment of meats—and the dishes are hit or miss. The spaghetti marinara and spaghetti bolognese, for instance, are fairly good, while the *hongos al ajillo* (garlic mushrooms) are vulcanized rubber.

The restaurant at **Hotel Versalles** (Paseo Enrique Geenzier, tel. 996-4422 or 996-3133, 6:30 A.M.–10 P.M. daily, US$10) is pricey by Chitré standards, but the food is decent. The grilled chicken and the *patacones* (twice-fried green plantains) are good.

Panadería Chiquita (two blocks north of the cathedral on Avenida Herrera, tel. 996-2411,

5 A.M.–10 P.M. daily) serves pastries, coffee, and juices as well as fast-food options that include sandwiches, chicken, burgers, and pizza. The most expensive thing on the menu is US$6.25.

DKDA's Restaurante y Pub-Bar (Calle 19 de Octubre, tel. 996-3339, 9 A.M.–11 P.M. Mon.–Thurs., noon–midnight Fri.–Sat., noon–11 P.M. Sun., US$5–7), pronounced deh-ca-DAHS, is a pleasant enough outdoor place despite the mounted TVs playing shows at full volume. It serves all the usuals—meat, fish, seafood, and poultry. The filet mignon is big and edible. Avoid the wine.

 Restaurante El Mesón (just north of the cathedral on Calle Melitón Martín, tel. 996-4310, 7 A.M.–11 P.M. daily, under US$7), on the ground floor of the Hotel Rex, has an extensive menu that varies from burritos and tacos to lasagna and pastas to seafood, meats, and salads. It also offers two dozen sandwiches. Patrons can sit outside on a front deck overlooking the church or in the nicely air-conditioned dining room. The food's pretty good, definitely one of the better fancy dining options in town. I always go for the tacos, which actually taste like tacos. They're not spicy, but they're pretty yummy. The daily lunch special goes for US$3 and is an especially good deal. Sample menu: grilled chicken, rice, beans, and salad.

Restaurante La Estrella (Avenida Herrera and Calle Melitón Martín, no phone, 6 A.M.–10 P.M. daily) is a *comida corriente* (fast food) place in an attractive building that dates from 1913. It's across the street from the northeast corner of the cathedral. It offers cafeteria items, pizzas, and sandwiches for a couple of bucks. Come early before the food gets too old and scary-looking. There are a couple of similar options around the cathedral.

La Raffi (Calle Manuel María Correa near Avenida Herrera, no phone, 8 A.M.–9 P.M. daily) is a clean new pastry place. Pickings are slim—pizza and cake and little else—but it's pleasant. It's next door to Hotel Santa Rita.

INFORMATION

The attractive **CEFATI tourist information center** (Calle 19 de Octubre, tel. 974-4532,

8:30 A.M.–4:30 P.M. daily, including holidays) actually has some tourist information. The staff is friendly and eager to help.

Displays in the building give some information on the history and culture of the Azuero in Spanish and something that bears a faint resemblance to English. Sample: "The rival 'tunes' are very meticulous in that their Queen and the cars leaves in everyone an unforgettable experience." No doubt.

The CEFATI is one kilometer east of the Los Santos/Chitré fork at La Arena. Take the right fork toward Los Santos. The CEFATI is off the road to the right. It's a two-story building with a red-tile roof.

SERVICES
Banks
HSBC (Paseo Enrique Geenzier, 8 A.M.–3:30 P.M. Mon.–Fri., 9 A.M.–noon Sat.) is across the street from Pension Chitré, near the museum. The **Caja de Ahorros,** just east of the cathedral across Avenida Herrera, has a 24-hour ATM. There are plenty of other banks on Paseo Enrique Geenzier or downtown.

Communications
The **post office** (Avenida Perez, tel. 996-4974, 7 A.M.–6 P.M. Mon.–Fri., 7 A.M.–5 P.M. Sat.) is a long block north of the museum. It's around the corner from, but in the same building as, the main **Cable and Wireless** office.

Sanchi Computer (Avenida Herrera, tel. 996-2134, 8 A.M.–midnight daily) offers Internet access for US$0.60 an hour. It's across the street from Pension Central, close to the cathedral. The Internet café at the **Hotel Rex** (just north of the cathedral on Calle Melitón Martín, tel. 996-4310 or 996-2408) charges US$0.50 an hour.

Launderette
Lavandería La Nacional (Avenida Herrera, 7 A.M.–5:30 P.M. Mon.–Sat.) charges US$2.50–4 to wash and dry a load. It's across the street and down from Panadería Chiquita as one walks away from the cathedral.

Pharmacies
Farmacia Universal (Calle Melitón Martín and Avenida Herrera, tel. 996-4608, 8 A.M.–8 P.M. Mon.–Sat., 8 A.M.–noon Sun.) is a drugstore across the street from the north end of the cathedral. **Metro RX** (Paseo Enrique Geenzier, tel. 996-7119, 7 A.M.–10 P.M. Mon.–Sat., 8 A.M.–10:20 P.M. Sun.) is a pharmacy between Hotel Versalles and downtown.

GETTING THERE AND AROUND
By Bus
The **Terminal de Transportes de Herrera** is a large regional bus terminal two kilometers south of downtown on Calle 19 de Octubre (also called Avenida Roberto Ramírez de Diego), the street that runs past Hotel Guayacanes. It has a 24-hour greasy spoon and a few little shops selling snacks, pharmaceuticals, and knickknacks.

Some of the more common destinations include:

Las Minas: Every 30 minutes, 6 A.M.–6:15 P.M. The trip takes an hour and costs US$1.50.

Las Tablas: Every 10 minutes, 6 A.M.–9 P.M. Monday–Friday, until 8 P.M. Saturday–Sunday. The trip takes about 45 minutes and costs US$1. The bus also stops in **Guararé** (US$0.80). Those heading to **Pedasí** have to take a bus to Las Tablas and catch a Pedasí-bound bus there.

Los Pozos: Every 25 minutes, 6 A.M.–7:25 P.M. Monday–Friday and 6:40 A.M.–7:25 P.M. Saturday–Sunday. The trip takes 45 minutes and costs US$1.50.

Ocú: Every 30 minutes, 6:30 A.M.–7 P.M. The trip takes an hour and costs US$1.75.

Panama City: The Tuasa bus company (tel. 996-8652) has a departure every 45 minutes in the morning and every hour in the afternoon, 1:30 A.M.–6 P.M. The trip takes 3.5 hours and costs US$7.50. Look for the ticket booth with the *boletería* sign.

Pesé: Every 15 minutes, 6:40 A.M.–6:45 P.M. The trip takes 30 minutes and costs US$0.90.

ROADSIDE FAST FOOD, AZUERO STYLE

Toward the weekend, a rustic but fun place to eat on the road between Chitré and Las Tablas is **Fonda El Ciruelo** (tel. 966-7910, 6 A.M.-8 P.M. Thurs.-Sun.). It's 4.5 kilometers southeast of La Villa on the road to Las Tablas; look to the left for a large, open-air shed with a corrugated zinc roof. Food is cooked in an old-fashioned wood oven fueled by a mountain of wood stacked at the back of the place. Everything on the menu is US$2 or less. The *sancocho* (a classic Panamanian chicken stew) is disappointingly bland, but that's not why people come here. They come instead for the delicious tamales, which go for US$0.50 each. Bet you can't eat just one.

The place has a lot of character. Chickens wander through the "restaurant," waiting for their turn to end up in the pot. It's easy to imagine food being prepared the same way at the same spot a hundred years ago.

Santiago: Every 30 minutes, 5 A.M.–6:30 P.M. The trip takes about 1.25 hours and costs US$2.50. Those going to David can change buses in Santiago; they leave constantly. The alternative is to take a bus to Divisa (US$1.25). It lets passengers out near the Interamericana, where it's easy to catch a west-bound bus to Santiago or David.

Tonosí: Every 1.5 hours, 6 A.M.–7 P.M. The trip takes two hours and costs US$4.

By Air

The airport is three kilometers north of downtown on Avenida Herrera, the avenue running by the east side of the church. **Aeroperlas** (Chitré tel. 996-4021, Panama City tel. 315-7500, fax 315-7580, www.aeroperlas.com) flies from Panama City to Chitré at 7:40 A.M. and 3:30 P.M. Monday–Saturday and 3:30 P.M. Sunday. The return flight to Panama City is at 8:25 A.M. and 4:15 P.M. Monday–Saturday and 4:15 P.M. Sunday. The trip takes about 35 minutes and costs US$36.75 one way, US$73.50 round-trip.

Getting Around

A taxi ride between the bus terminal and anywhere in town costs US$1.15 for one person or US$1.40 for two. Other destinations include the airport (US$2), Villa de Los Santos (US$1.50), Parque Nacional Sarigua (US$8), Playa Monagre (US$8), and Las Tablas (US$12).

Buses between Chitré and Villa de Los Santos, four kilometers away, run constantly. The fare is US$0.30.

La Villa de Los Santos

Four kilometers south of Chitré lies La Villa de Los Santos, which, as the name suggests, is in Los Santos province. Río La Villa, which the road crosses just northwest of town, marks the border between Los Santos and Herrera provinces.

La Villa de Los Santos is commonly known simply as La Villa. It's also sometimes called Los Santos, which makes it easy to confuse with the whole province.

This tiny town has played a big role in Panama's history through the years. Founded by the conquistadors, its moment of glory came on November 10, 1821. On that date a group of La Villa residents wrote a letter to Simón Bolívar, who had recently defeated the Spanish and won independence for Gran Colombia. In it, they complained of exploitation by the Spanish governor and voiced their wish to sign on to Bolívar's revolution.

This Primer Grito de la Independencia (First Cry for Independence) was followed just 18 days later by Panama's actual declaration of independence from Spain and union with Gran Colombia, decided at a meeting in Panama City.

The house in which this letter was signed is now a museum, where each year La Villa commemorates the *primer grito,* also known as La Grita de La Villa (The Cry of La Villa) with a solemn ceremony attended by dignitaries, often including the president of Panama.

The area's history goes much deeper than that, though. Indigenous peoples used nearby Cerro Juan Díaz, a hill at the edge of the Río La Villa, both as a village and as a burial and ceremonial ground off and on for 1,800 years, from 200 B.C. until the arrival of the Spanish. There's an archaeological dig at the site, but it's not set up for tourists. Ornaments made from gold, shells, pearls, and the like have been excavated, along with a more grisly find: human jawbones from which the teeth were pried (postmortem, thankfully). Because teeth with holes drilled in them have been found at other sites, it's believed the missing teeth were used to make grim necklaces.

The main town of La Villa de Los Santos consists of just a few blocks of homes and businesses, some quite old and well-preserved, on the northeast side of the Chitré–Las Tablas road. Places to stay and eat are in the newer suburban area directly across from town, on the southeast side of the road. Any of the many buses plying the road between Chitré and Las Tablas can drop passengers off in La Villa. The fare from Chitré is US$0.30.

SIGHTS

Most of La Villa's few sights surround Parque Simón Bolívar, the town plaza. Unless a festival has taken over the town, which happens pretty frequently, visitors can see La Villa's attractions in about an hour.

Iglesia de San Atanasio

La Villa's church, sometimes spelled Iglesia de San Atanacio, was declared a national monument in 1938, though what's inside is more impressive than the building itself. It has a huge main altar, an ornate wooden affair in gold and blue that was erected in 1733. That makes it older than the current church, whose beginnings date from 1773. The altar and other fixtures recently underwent a major restoration. (The decaying church building itself has not.) Among the church's other features is a tall, fantastically ornate archway, also erected in 1733, that is covered with gold arabesques and splashes of reds and blues. It looks almost Chinese. The church is in the center of town, next to the plaza.

El Museo de la Nacionalidad

This little museum (tel. 966-8192, 8:30 A.M.–4 P.M. Tues.–Sat., 9 A.M.–noon Sun.) is on the northwest side of the church plaza. As is so often the case with Panama's museums, its name (The Museum of Nationality) is far grander than its offerings. Ostensibly tracing the history of the area from its earliest days to its role as the first town in Panama to call for independence from Spain, it makes the most it can out of a few scraps of history and little explanation of their significance.

The museum is installed in the house where the town leaders signed their famous letter to Bolívar, declaring they wanted in on his revolutionary movement. The centerpiece of the museum is a display commemorating La Grita de La Villa. It attempts to replicate the room where the letter was signed, using furniture from the period. Other than that, the displays consist mainly of a few pieces of pre-Columbian pottery, some random 18th-century religious objects, rusty conquistador swords, and the like.

Centro de Estudios Superiores de Folklore Dora Pérez de Zárate

This school for students of folklore is run by the Instituto Nacional de Cultura (INAC). While not set up to receive tourists, it's housed in a pretty, old blue and white building that's worth a quick peek. Lucky visitors might hear, through the upstairs balcony doors, the strains of students practicing traditional music. It's a couple of blocks southwest of the plaza, toward the highway.

ENTERTAINMENT AND EVENTS

La Villa lives for its festivals. At other times, there's little in the way of entertainment in this sleepy little town. The main party is the Festival de Corpus Christi. La Grita de La Villa, the town's other nationally known event, is a more serious affair.

Festival de Corpus Christi

This is the biggest celebration in La Villa, drawing revelers from all over Panama. Though it's celebrated elsewhere, no place can compete with La Villa. The festival lasts nearly two weeks and is quite a production.

Pope Urban IV sanctioned the Corpus Christi (Body of Christ) festival in A.D. 1264, though its origins go back even further. It is still celebrated throughout the Catholic world, with lots of local variation.

The festival officially commemorates the Eucharist, but in La Villa it is far more elaborate and far-reaching than that. By incorporating "pagan" dances into the celebration, Spanish colonial priests in Panama used the celebration both as a colorful way to attract

© WILLIAM FRIAR

Fearsome devil masks made on the Azuero Peninsula are used in the Festival de Corpus Christi.

converts and as a graphic lesson in the church's views on good versus evil.

These dances are at the heart of the festival and have evolved through the years. Keeping them alive is practically the main industry of La Villa. The dances include **El Gran Diablo, El Torito, Los Diablícos Sucios, La Montezuma Española, La Montezuma Cabezona, El Zacarundé,** and several others.

Many of these seemingly have little or nothing to do with the Eucharist, the sacrament in which Catholics consume the body and blood of Christ. El Zacarundé, for instance, remembers the African slaves who escaped from the Spanish in the Darién. La Montezuma Española is about the conquest of Mexico. El Torito involves a predawn search for a bull effigy whose significance I, for one, have never quite gotten a handle on.

The main story line that holds the two-week celebration together is the battle between the forces of evil, led by the Gran Diablo, against the forces of good, led by the Archangel Michael. The diabolical side of the struggle tends to get most attention and energy. Artisans compete to outdo each other in making the most frightening and horrendous devil masks for the dancers.

The two-week celebration always kicks off at noon on the first day with huge explosions and music and the appearance of a band of devils. They have a plot to terrorize the world and carve up the cosmos into four pieces they will then divvy up among themselves. Eventually, of course, the forces of good prevail.

The whole thing involves more than 100 dancers, actors, and musicians. The festivities take place up and down the streets of La Villa, in people's homes, and inside the town church. At one point, the devils ask and receive permission from the Archangel Michael to enter the church, something that fascinates scholars.

By tradition, only men are allowed to perform. Though, in a mild concession to the excluded, there's a *día de la mujer* (woman's day) tacked on to the end of the celebration during which women are allowed to dance. In recent years a *día del turismo* (tourism day) has also

THE AZUERO PENINSULA

been added to the end of the festivities. It compresses the highlights into a single day for those unable to get away for two weeks of partying.

The dates of the celebration vary considerably from year to year, since they're based on several Catholic holy days. Generally it's held sometime between late May and early July. Check with ATP for dates. The **CEFATI** tourist information center in Chitré (Calle 19 de Octubre, tel. 974-4532, 8:30 A.M.–4:30 P.M. daily, including holidays)should also be able to provide information.

La Grita de La Villa

Every November 10 local and national dignitaries, often including the president of Panama, gather to reenact La Grita de La Villa, the town's call for independence from Spain on November 10, 1821. This date is a national holiday. The ceremony starts in the morning at El Museo de La Nacionalidad, the house in La Villa where the historic letter was signed. It's a pretty solemn occasion, but a parade and music performances have been added to the event through the years. Santeños love to party.

ACCOMMODATIONS AND FOOD

La Villa is so close to Chitré that visitors can easily stay in either town. In fact, those who like to party but want to get away from the action when it's time to sleep should consider staying in Chitré for the big La Villa events,

such as the Corpus Christi festival, and staying in La Villa for the big Chitré festivals, such as Carnaval. On festival days, of course, visitors may feel lucky to get a room anywhere.

(Hotel La Villa (tel. 966-9321, fax 966-8201, www.hotellavillapanama.com, starts at US$16.50 s, US$20 d) has 38 rooms with air-conditioning and cable TV in a quite pleasant garden setting. There's also an attractive restaurant attached that serves breakfast, lunch, and dinner daily.

The place is clean, the beds are firm, and this is generally one of the better lodging options in the whole area. The place is decorated with love. The owner is high on folkloric art, particularly *tinajas* (the earthenware pots this part of the Azuero is famous for). They're everywhere: in the lobby, hanging from the rafters, used as planters, on the tables, and so on. It's no surprise to see a poster in the lobby signed by Sheila Lichacz, the local artist internationally famous for her depictions of *tinajas*.

Price start low for the most basic rooms and can be twice that for the nicer ones. Add a few dollars for weekend visits and take off a few for longer stays. You can probably haggle here. The newer rooms are significantly more pleasant than older ones, which have tired furniture and dreary fake-wood paneling.

The hotel is at the end of a quiet cul-de-sac 700 meters southwest of the main road. To get there from Chitré, look for the signs as you enter La Villa; it's a right turn off the road.

Loop Road: Pesé to Ocú

Those who want to truly immerse themselves in the culture and rhythms of the Azuero Peninsula should consider exploring the loop road that circles through the heart of the peninsula. Even though the wilderness long ago surrendered to cattle pasture, farms, and teak plantations, the drive is still scenic and the rolling countryside quite pretty. The road is in good shape most of the way, and new stretches continue to be paved.

One festival or another always seems to be happening in one of these towns. A few are discussed, but, since many of them change yearly, check with ATP (the main office is near the start of the road, on the outskirts of Chitré) for a current calendar of the major events. Without some sort of festival taking place, the towns themselves don't hold much interest.

The loop starts at Pesé, about 25 kilometers southwest of Chitré. To get to Pesé, turn west off the main road just north of La Arena (north of where the main road forks at Cerámica Marcelino). The turn is marked.

From Pesé traveling clockwise, the road leads through the towns of Los Pozos, Las Minas, and Ocú. Note that these are also names of districts, of which the towns are the *cabecera,* sort of the Panama equivalent of a county seat. The loop can also be driven counterclockwise. Those without wheels can explore this area by bus. They run frequently between each of the towns and Chitré.

The clock itself seems to turn back with every kilometer along the road. Towns here— really rural villages—probably don't look much different than they did 100 years ago. This is the real heartland of the heartland. Be prepared for curious stares. Not many foreigners make it this far into the interior.

Distances below assume driving the loop counterclockwise. Even though the distances aren't great, allow a half day just to drive the loop, or a full day to stop and explore what the towns have to offer. Each has some claim to fame.

PESÉ

The cutest of the towns is Pesé (pop. 2,547), 19 kilometers from the turnoff. It has a quaint little church surrounded by red-roofed buildings half-hidden behind flowering trees. Horse carts are still used to haul goods around here.

In the odd juxtaposition one sometimes sees in small Panamanian towns, across the street from the church is a Seco Herrerano factory. *Seco* is sugarcane liquor, and Panama's national drink. There are no official tours of the factory, but curious visitors who show up on a normal workday, which also includes Saturday before noon, can probably convince someone to let them poke around.

Given this cozy combination of the sacred and profane, it's only fitting that Pesé is noted for a live reenactment of the suffering and final days of Jesus Christ during Semana Santa (Holy Week), the week leading up to Easter. This may sound pretty somber, but in recent years the Catholic Church has chided the town

for, essentially, having too much fun during what is supposed to be a religious observance.

LOS POZOS AND LAS MINAS

There's really not much to see in Los Pozos (pop. 2,268), the next significant town. It's 19 kilometers south of Pesé. Las Minas (pop. 2,209), 13 kilometers west of Los Pozos or 51 kilometers from the start of the loop, is kind of cute, though not as cute as Pesé. At this point, the road has turned hillier and the surrounding countryside greener and more lush. The big party in Las Minas is on December 4, in honor of the village's patron saint, Santa Barbara.

OCÚ

Ocú (pop. 8,150), 21 kilometers farther north on a potholed road, is not quaint. The houses and church are made from cinderblocks, for instance. But the town works hard to preserve the old ways, and it's often considered the folkloric center of Herrera province. The town and its namesake district are known for producing lovely *polleras* (hand-embroidered dresses) that are quite unlike those made in Los Santos province. The area is also known for producing distinctive white hats with a black band that more closely resemble the famous "Panamas" made in Ecuador than do other traditional Panamanian hats. A national folkloric festival, the **Festival del Manito,** is held here annually on the second weekend in August. A highlight of the festival is the chance to see a traditional country wedding, with the bride on horseback in a beautiful white *pollera,* her proud groom mounted behind her, protecting her from the sun with an umbrella. The town's other big multiday celebration is the **Feria de San Sebastián,** a country fair that takes place in the week leading up to and including January 20, the town's patron saint day.

BACK TO CHITRÉ

The fastest way back to Chitré is to finish the loop to Pesé, 30 kilometers away. From there it's a 19-kilometer drive to the main road leading into Chitré. Getting back to Pesé from Ocú can be a bit tricky. Don't be shy about asking for directions if you get lost; the people are friendly, and they know roads get confusing out here.

The road to Pesé starts past a supermarket to the east of downtown. The road was recently paved and should be in good shape. After 13 kilometers, make a right. This will lead south into Pesé. From there just continue east to Chitré.

Note: This also means that those wanting to go straight from Chitré to Ocú can take this more direct route rather than drive the whole loop. Those not already on the Azuero Peninsula can also drive directly to Ocú from the Interamericana. The turnoff is west of Divisa.

Guararé

This small, not particularly scenic town (pop. 3,883) is famous throughout Panama for the Festival Nacional de la Mejorana, a huge folkloric festival held annually in September. There's little reason to visit the town between festivals.

Guararé is right on the main highway linking Chitré, 25 kilometers to the north, and Las Tablas, 5 kilometers to the south. The main town is just east of the highway. It boasts a tiny folkloric museum, a couple of fireworks factories that are probably worth staying well clear of on a hot day, and an elaborate open-air stage on the church plaza that was built for the Mejorana.

A quite decent hotel is on the west side of the highway and a quite basic *hospedaje* is on the east side. The hotel is the best bet for food, though there are some other basic eateries in town.

La Enea (pop. 1,128), sometimes called La Enea de Guararé, is an even tinier town tucked away just north of Guararé, toward the coast. It's sort of a suburb of Guararé and is famous for producing beautiful *polleras* (hand-embroidered dresses). Beyond it are a couple of mediocre beaches, Playa Bella Vista and Playa El Puerto, that aren't worth a special trip. That's just about it.

SIGHTS

This backwater town holds a few surprises even when no festival has invaded the place. While there's not enough to justify an overnight stay between festivals, those with a spare hour or two should consider exploring the town's modest attractions. At the top of the list is the chance to see a master *pollera* (hand-embroidered dress) maker at work.

Casa-Museo Manuel F. Zárate

Two blocks past the church as you head into Guararé from the highway, a small folkloric museum (tel. 994-5644, 8 A.M.–4 P.M. Mon.–Sat., 8 A.M.–noon Sun., US$0.75 adults, US$0.25 children) was installed in the home of the late Manuel F. Zárate. He was a chemistry professor who, along with his wife, Dora Pérez de Zárate, and a few colleagues founded the Mejorana Festival in 1949. He is nationally known for his work to revive and preserve Panama's folkloric traditions.

The museum's offerings are, as usual, meager. Displays consist mainly of folkloric costumes, including some old but not especially fine *polleras,* as well as photos of traditional homes, a few impressive devil masks, and so on. It's worth a very quick visit.

The Art of the *Pollera*

One of Panama's most famous *pollera* makers, **Ildaura S. de Espino** (tel. 994-5527), lives in La Enea, the teeny town between Guararé and the beaches. It takes her six months to make a *pollera,* Panama's heavily embroidered national dress, and each sells for US$1,500–2,000. She takes orders, but be prepared for a long wait. Those just curious to see an artist at work are welcome to stop by for a visit.

La Enea is about two kilometers past Guararé on the way to Playa El Puerto. Look for the church steeple in the distance on the right. That's where the town square is.

Once in La Enea, look for the house with a green-tile front right on the town square, near the statue of the Virgin Mary. Don't be shy about asking for directions—everyone knows Ildaura and will probably point her out without prompting; she's the main reason out-of-towners stop by. She's gracious and happy to show visitors her work. She's now in a wheelchair and looking a bit frail, but she still spends her days making beautiful costumes.

Another area famous for its *polleras,* by the way, is San José, a tiny town near Pocrí. If you find craftswomen the world needs to know about, please let me know. Happy hunting.

ENTERTAINMENT AND EVENTS

Guararé is synonymous with the Mejorana Festival, which is just about the only reason visitors come to this remote town. There's little in the way of entertainment at nonfestival times.

Every September, Guararé hosts **La Festival Nacional de la Mejorana,** Panama's biggest and most important folkloric festival. The weeklong festival was started in 1949 by a small group of local folklore preservationists, and through the years it has ballooned into one major party.

The festival is named in honor of a Panamanian song form called the *mejorana,* which is played on a small, five-string guitar called a *mejoranera.* Just to make things confusing, the instrument itself is sometimes called a *mejorana,* as is a traditional dance that it accompanies.

The festival's celebrants are so determined to preserve tradition that the town banned by law all modern or foreign music and dance during the festival. Even playing a six-string guitar is forbidden.

However, the festival does attract hundreds of folkloric dancers and musicians whose styles diverge from the *mejorana* tradition. They come from far beyond the Azuero heartland, varying from performers from Bocas del Toro in western Panama to the African-inspired *congos* dancers of Colón in eastern Panama.

Competitions are held for the best performer

in all kinds of categories, including competitions for both the best spoken-word and song-form *décima,* a traditional Spanish poem consisting of 10 eight-syllable lines, and a *saloma* competition for the best Panamanian-style yodeler.

A queen is chosen each year. She wears a pointed crown and presides over the festivities from her throne when not dancing with different groups in her gorgeous *pollera.*

Other attractions include bullfights, a parade of super-elaborate floats pulled by oxcarts, fireworks, strolling musicians, and handicraft booths. Each day an *abandadero* (standard-bearer) is chosen to lead that day's events.

Probably the wackiest part of the festival is **La Atolladera,** which very loosely translates to "Day of the Mud Fight." It's a day to sling mud at your friends. The queen and her court show up in pure white outfits just so winging mud balls at them is all the more satisfying. Good times.

The festival is a big deal and attracts Panamanian tourists from all over the country. Give up all hope of finding lodging in Guararé without a reservation made months in advance. Las Tablas is the nearest town, but it may be necessary to look for a place in Chitré, 25 kilometers away, or maybe even farther afield.

The Mejorana Festival is always held in September, though the dates and length of the festival vary yearly. It's always pegged to the town's commemoration of its patron saint, La Virgen de las Mercedes, which lasts for nine days, climaxing on September 23–24. The Mejorana generally dovetails with the end of that religious observance and lasts about a week. Check with ATP for exact dates and a schedule of events.

ACCOMMODATIONS AND FOOD

The red tile–roofed **Hotel La Mejorana** (tel. 994-5794, fax 994-5796, US$12.10 s, US$14.30 d small rooms; US$22 s/d larger rooms) is lovingly decorated with Guararé's role as a folkloric center in mind. The walls of the common areas are adorned with devil masks, sketches of women in *polleras,* paintings of sugarcane presses—all the traditional touchstones. Its 22 rooms are much simpler and dark, with tiny windows, but they're clean and pleasant enough, with pretty good beds, hot-water bathrooms, air-conditioning, local

TV, and telephones. Reserve 2–3 months in advance for all festivals.

The cheerful open-air restaurant at the hotel serves most of the usuals, but it also offers a surprisingly extensive seafood selection. Most main dishes are US$10 or less.

Las Tablas

Las Tablas (pop. 7,980 in town, 24,298 in the district) has more sprawl and less charm than Chitré, its sister town 30 kilometers north in Herrera province. It feels more like a city in miniature, sacrificing coziness for a somewhat more urban atmosphere. However, the *tableños* are just as mellow and easygoing as the people you'd find in smaller towns.

Most visitors come here for exactly one reason: Carnaval. Las Tablas hosts Panama's biggest, wildest celebration, which is saying a lot for a country known for the fervor of its Carnaval spirit.

Las Tablas is built up around an L formed by two roads. The first is the stretch of highway that runs north to south from Chitré to Las Tablas. It intersects in downtown Las Tablas with Avenida Belisario Porras, which runs east through town and turns back into highway outside the town limits.

Most of the restaurants, hotels, and services are along these two streets or within a block or two of them. At the base of the L is the town church, plaza, and a museum dedicated to favorite son Belisario Porras, a three-time president of Panama. A stroll from the plaza east down Avenida Belisario Porras is a good way to get a sense of town life.

As is true of every town in Panama, most streets have multiple names, none of which may appear on a road sign or be known even by those who live on the street. The only street that people may know by name is Avenida Belisario Porras, which is basically the town's main drag.

SIGHTS

Though Las Tablas is an important provincial "city," it has very little in the way of sights. After taking in the museum and church around Parque

Porras in downtown Las Tablas, there's little left to do but wander around and people-watch. A good place to start is along Avenida Belisario Porras, which begins at Parque Porras and heads east.

Museo Belisario Porras

The town museum (Avenida Belisario Porras and Calle 8 de Noviembre, tel. 994-6326, 8:30 A.M.–5 P.M. Mon.–Fri., 9:30 A.M.–5 P.M. Sat.–Sun., US$0.50 adults, US$0.25 children), on the south side of the church plaza, contains personal effects, important documents, and memorabilia from the life of Porras, a national hero who is considered one of Panama's founding fathers and was its president three times. He was born in Las Tablas in 1856 and died in 1942. The displays have been damaged in recent years, according to preservationists, through neglect and smoke from Carnaval fireworks.

Parque Porras and Iglesia Santa Librada

The name of the town plaza is Parque Porras, though it contains more *cemento* than *parque.* It's at the heart of Las Tablas, where the north–south highway into town intersects Avenida Belisario Porras, which runs west–east. This is ground zero during Carnaval.

The town church, Iglesia Santa Librada, on the west side of the plaza, is more notable for the constant devotion of the worshipers inside than for the building itself. The centerpiece is a large altar covered with gold leaf.

◖ CARNAVAL

To say that the Carnaval celebration in Las Tablas is its biggest annual party is putting it

far too mildly. It's one of the biggest parties in the entire country. Other major Carnaval locations on the Azuero include Chitré, Parita, Ocú, and Villa de Los Santos, but none can compete with Las Tablas.

Carnaval officially lasts from the Saturday before Ash Wednesday until what we gringos call Fat Tuesday, the last hurrah before the 40 abstemious days of Lent.

In Las Tablas, though, things get started on Friday, with the coronation of the town's two Carnaval queens. Las Tablas's first Carnaval queen was crowned in 1937, but since 1950 the town has had two rival queens and their attendant courts, or *tunas:* that of Calle Arriba (high street) and Calle Abajo (low street).

Throughout Carnaval, the two retinues try to outdo each other in the beauty, opulence, splendor, and ingenuity of their costumes and floats *(carros alegóricos)*. It's easy to imagine more resources go into creating these than the entire town produces in a year. They also compose songs, called *tonadas,* that, among other things, praise the beauty and grace of their chosen queen and mock the supposed ugliness and witchiness of the rival one. These *puyas* (taunts) are part of the fun and usually taken in stride, but the *tonadas* are approved ahead of time by a censorship board to make sure they don't get too nasty and personal.

Both *tunas* take to the streets every day for a huge parade, with different jaw-dropping floats and costumes each day. These are usually incredibly flamboyant and elaborate, reminiscent of those found at Rio de Janeiro's Carnaval.

Neither costumes nor behavior tend to get as risqué as that at Rio's Carnaval or even New Orleans's Mardi Gras. Carnaval everywhere in Panama, while it certainly has a lot of booze and steaminess, is still considered a family affair. In fact, when some revelers acted lewd and showed too much skin during the Carnaval celebration in Chitré in 2002, their "immoral" and "pornographic" behavior caused a public outcry and lots of official tsk-tsking.

Still, this is a decidedly secular celebration with deep pagan roots. The reigning deity is Momo, also known as Momus, the Greek god of laughter and mockery. This is a huge party, the goal of which seems to be to make sure everyone has something to atone for come Lent.

Though masks were featured in Panama's early Carnaval celebrations, which were officially recognized nationwide in 1910, they quickly faded out and are rarely seen during Panama's Carnaval today. One Panamanian addition is for the queens to include stunning *polleras*—Panama's flowing, embroidered national dress—among their many costumes.

Another important part of the Carnaval celebration, in Las Tablas and throughout the country, is the *culecos*. Each morning of Carnaval, to the cry of *¡agua, agua!,* large water trucks with hoses spray revelers with thousands of gallons of water, cooling them off as they dance in the heat. Some participants also flirtatiously squirt each other with water guns. The tradition is somewhere between a mild version of a wet T-shirt contest and the ritual opening of fire hydrants during a summer heat wave in a U.S. city.

The *culecos* are such a beloved part of the celebration they're officially sanctioned even during water shortages, though officials urge residents to conserve water in the days leading up to the celebration.

Music played at maximum volume is an important part of the proceedings, as it is at every Panamanian festivity. Temporary discos sprout up, and *murgas* (strolling musicians) march in the processions. At night, fireworks light the skies—and maybe houses and partiers, too, given the drunken knuckleheads that sometimes fire off rockets in the middle of downtown.

The celebration climaxes on Tuesday night. Or rather, it climaxes at dawn on Ash Wednesday, since the final party goes all night long.

There's a saying in Panama, kept alive by its own citizens, that the only thing Panamanians take seriously is Carnaval. In that sense *tableños* are the most serious people in the country.

No sooner is Carnaval over than plans begin to select the following year's queens. These are introduced on **New Year's Eve,** another huge party that resembles the last night of Carnaval. The two new queens are greeted and the two retiring queens seen off with fireworks and a parade.

ACCOMMODATIONS

For a place that attracts what seems like the entire country for Carnaval, Las Tablas has few hotel rooms. Most visiting Carnavalites stay with friends or family, or else rent houses during the nearly weeklong celebration. At that time, residents looking to make some quick bucks rent out even the most modest homes to eager revelers. The hotels I used to like have gone bad or out of business. There's only one place I feel comfortable suggesting. Unless things improve, it's best to spend the night elsewhere. Hotel La Mejorana in nearby Guararé is much nicer than any option in Las Tablas.

Just south of the town center is **Hotel Sol del Pacífico** (Calle Agustin Cano Castillero, tel. 994-1280, US$30 s/d); it has 13 rooms and three apartments, with 18 more rooms on the way. Rooms are spartan but okay, with air-conditioning, local TV, and private baths. The hotel is on Calle Agustin Cano Castillero, which runs west–east at the southern end of downtown Las Tablas. It's two blocks south of Belisario Porras and about two blocks southeast of the town plaza. Note: For some reason, this place is also sometimes referred to as Hotel Costa del Pacífico.

FOOD

Dining options are severely limited in Las Tablas. The following are the best bets.

◖ Restaurante y Bar Jorón Moravel (Avenida Rogelio Gáez, tel. 994-7250, 7 A.M.– 11 P.M. daily, US$8), two blocks southwest of the bus terminal, is a cute little place that, with its thatched roof, resembles a giant *rancho*. Lunch offerings include lasagna, chicken, spaghetti, and *sancocho* (stew). The lasagna is pretty good. It also does seafood, meat, Chinese fried rice, pizza, and sandwiches. Breakfast costs just a couple of bucks. The place does a thriving takeout business.

Housed in an old home in the center of town, **Restaurante Los Portales** (Avenida Belisario Porras, 6 A.M.–10 P.M. Mon.–Sat., 6 A.M.–3 P.M. Sun., US$8 or less) has a certain rustic charm. It features high ceilings, arched doorways, a sloping red-tile roof, and tables set around a porch right on Avenida Belisario Porras. It's a basic place but offers a wide range of food, including prawns, calamari, octopus, corvina, spaghetti, and various meats. The *bistec picado* comes in a kind of sweet-and-sour sauce and is surprisingly tasty.

Restaurante El Caserón (Avenida Moises Espino, tel. 994-6066, 7 A.M.–11 P.M. daily, US$10 or less) is a pleasant-enough open-air place known for its heaps of meat. The *parrillada mixta* (mixed grilled meat) offers a pile of chicken, pork, beef, and local sausage. It's reasonably tasty, especially the sausage, though it's a good way to use up a whole year's quota of grease and cholesterol. The restaurant also serves pizza, seafood, chow mein, pasta, and more meat. The restaurant is on Avenida Moises Espino, which is parallel and one block north of Avenida Belisario Porras. It's about two blocks northeast of Hotel y Restaurante Manolo.

SERVICES

Farmacia Miriam (Calle Bolívar, tel. 994-0735, 7:30 A.M.–10:30 P.M. Mon.–Sat.,

8 A.M.–8 P.M. Sun.) is on the northwest corner of the town plaza.

Most banks are set around or close to the town plaza. Other services are spread out around the downtown area.

A branch of **Banco Nacional de Panamá** (Avenida Carlos L. Lopez, 8 A.M.–3 P.M. Mon.– Fri., 9 A.M.–noon Sat.) is next to the bus terminal on the main street running south into downtown. **HSBC** (Avenida Belisario Porras and Calle 8 de Noviembre, 7:30 A.M.–3:30 P.M. Mon.–Fri., 9 A.M.–noon Sat.) is at the intersection of Las Tablas's two main streets. It has an ATM.

The main **post office** (Calle Ramón Mora, tel. 994-6611, 7 A.M.–6 P.M. Mon.–Fri., 7 A.M.–5 P.M. Sat.) is a block and a half west of the bus terminal.

Cyberworld (Calle 8 de Noviembre, tel. 994-1319, 8 A.M.–10 P.M. daily, US$0.75/hour) is an Internet café across the street from the southeast corner of the town plaza.

There's a self-service **launderette** (Calle 3 de Noviembre, 7 A.M.–6 P.M. Mon.–Sat., 8 A.M.–noon Sun.) a block north and east of Hotel Sol de Pacífico.

GETTING THERE AND AWAY

Taxis are easy to find in Las Tablas, and there are taxi stands all over. The **taxi stand** (tel. 994-8532 or 994-8533) near the launderette on Calle 3 de Noviembre is open 24 hours a day. Buses within town should cost around US$1 or less. A bus as far as Pedasí will probably cost at least US$20. For those who can't afford the cab fare, buses to Guararé leave from downtown every 10 minutes (US$0.30) from early morning to evening. They can be flagged down on Avenida Carlos L. Lopez, the main road heading north out of Las Tablas.

Buses to more distant locations leave from the town bus terminal at the north end of town, shortly after the national highway morphs into Avenida Carlos L. Lopez. The cross street is Avenida Emilio Castro. There's a taxi stand at the bus terminal. Though it's just a half kilometer to the center of town, it can feel like a major hike in the heat when you're toting luggage. Avoid the misery and cough up the US$1 cab fare.

There is no direct service to Santiago or David. A few of the most important routes are:

Panama City: The first bus leaves at 6 A.M. every day. After that, buses leave every hour on the half hour, 7:30 A.M.–4:30 P.M. There are two additional early departures at 2 A.M. and 4 A.M. Monday–Friday. On Friday and Sunday there's a final departure at 5:30 P.M. Got all that? Never mind—all times are more theoretical than real in any case. The fare is US$8 and the trip takes 4.5 hours.

Pedasí: Buses run every 45 minutes, 6 A.M.–7 P.M. The trip takes 45 minutes and costs US$2. These buses also stop along Avenida Belisario Porras in the heart of town.

Tonosí: The first buses to Tonosí leave Las Tablas at 8 A.M., 10 A.M., and 11 A.M. Monday–Saturday and 8:30 A.M. and 10 A.M. on Sunday. They then run about every hour, 12:30–5:30 P.M. The trip takes about an hour and 20 minutes and costs US$3. Note that this is an inland route and does not lead down the coast near Pedasí, Playa Venao, or Isla Cañas.

Pedasí and Vicinity

◖ PEDASÍ

Driving into Pedasí (pop. 1,830) this time, I was dismayed to see all the billboards lining the road on the way to town. That's it, I thought, Pedasí is done. But somehow, the charm of Pedasí continues to resist efforts to make it nothing but a tourist trap and beach-head for real-estate developers.   Pedasí was until recently a Spanish-colonial town that time forgot, with the same kind of architecture and the same civic pride in keeping the place clean and quaint as in Parita. But it has finally been discovered.

There are new hotels and places to eat in the area, including some you would never expect to find way out here. And a huge, French-owned real-estate project being built by the beach just south of town may, as one developer jokingly put it, turn Pedasí into "the San Tropez of Panama."

The is the hometown of Mireya Moscoso, Panama's president 1999–2004. A cynic might believe Pedasí benefited a few years back from the presidential connection. The road is perfect between Pedasí and Las Tablas, 43 kilometers north; it turns bad a few kilometers south of town. Commercial flights now land at its new airstrip. A large, modern branch of Banco Nacional de Panamá now gleams at the north entrance to town. It looks bigger than

the town itself. Money has come to Pedasí, and the houses are being spruced up.

But the charm of this friendly little town is still intact, and it doesn't yet look like a museum exhibit. Townspeople still live in town, and most of the restaurants are still *fondas* (taverns) whose backbone clientele are the local laborers. It's main road is busier now, but Pedasí is still a haven of tranquility surrounded by natural beauty. I can't think of a more pleasant place to discover heartland Panama.

Most of Pedasí is on either side of a one-kilometer stretch of two-lane road that runs north–south through the town. The ocean is just a couple of kilometers to the east. The town church and plaza are on the southeast side of town.

Visitors can take in the town itself in less than an hour. The main attractions are its nearby beaches; a couple of unusual islands, Isla Iguana and Isla de Cañas, that aren't too hard to get to; and a surfing spot, Playa El Venao, about 30 kilometers south of town that's great for beginners. The waters off Pedasí offer good diving and fishing, and Pedasí now has an outfitter to take advantage of that fact. Humpback whales can be spotted offshore from around August to October or November.

November 25 is the celebration of Pedasí's patron saint, Santa Catalina. The town also

© WILLIAM FRIAR

There are still lots of Spanish-colonial touches in Pedasí and other Azuero towns.

has its own elaborate Carnaval celebration. This would be a more sane place than most to celebrate Carnaval on the Azuero. Pedasí has a big *desfile de carreta* (parade with floats) in November; dates vary.

Sports and Recreation

Pedasí still feels as though it has more beaches than tourists, which is one of its charms. It's also a good base for planning trips to nearby diving, snorkeling, and surfing spots.

NEARBY BEACHES

Pedasí is only a couple of kilometers from the ocean, and its beaches are easily accessible. Here's a sampling of the better options.

Playa Arenal is three kilometers east of town on a good road. To get there, follow the road behind the gas station that leads past the CEFATI. Arenal is absolutely massive. You have to take a short hike across the sand just to get to the water, and it stretches along the coast farther than the eye can see. Fisherfolk anchor their boats here, but there's more than enough beach and surf to go around.

My favorite beach in the area is **Playa Los Destiladeros,** 10 kilometers south of town. Head south down the main road through town until you get to Limón, three kilometers away. The turn will be on the left.

When that road forks, take the right fork. The road dead-ends at Los Destiladeros, seven kilometers away. It's a wide brown beach with a great view. Locals don't tend to come here since there are no facilities or shade, but it's shaping up to be the main tourist beach. There are a couple of little beach hotels, and major construction on the French-owned real-estate development. A trip to Los Destiladeros should run US$5.

DIVING AND SPORTFISHING

The main dive destinations are the waters around **Isla Iguana** and the **Islas Frailes.**

Isla Iguana has extensive coral fields, though human pressures and El Niños have damaged them. The Islas Frailes, considerably farther out, off the southeast tip of the Azuero, are a pair of rock outcroppings that offer good open-water diving. There is no beach on either of the Frailes; all diving is from the boat. There are also two wrecks south of Punta Mala, in 20-meter-deep waters: a U.S. Navy ammunition ship that dates from before World War II and a shrimper.

Diving is best during the rainy season, April–December. In December–mid-March, dry-season winds stir up the sea and limit visibility. Wetsuits are necessary in January as protection from the cold waters of the Humboldt Current. They also fend off the stings of tiny jellyfish.

There's more demand for sportfishing than diving around here. This area has been nicknamed the "Tuna Coast," and there's even a major international tuna research facility, Laboratorio Achotines, on the coast 30 kilometers south of Pedasí. Other big fish found in these waters include sailfish, wahoo, and black, blue, and striped marlin.

It's possible to hire a local fisherman to take you sportfishing, but this will be in a fairly small *panga*, you'll probably need to bring your own fishing gear, and there's a decent chance your captain may be drunk even in the early morning. Only go this route if you get a local recommendation from someone you trust; the recommended hotels should be good sources. Expect to pay US$150–200 for this adventure.

Sportfishing trips with a professional operation that has a well-equipped boat and good gear are increasingly easy to come by, but expect to pay upwards of US$700 for a day out. **Buzos de Azuero** (tel. 995-2405 or 995-2894, www.dive-n-fishpanama.com) is the only diving and deep-sea fishing operator in town. It's also known as Dive-N-Fish Pedasí. It offers weeklong packages that include four nights in a Pedasí hotel, two nights in Panama City, transfers, gear, and breakfasts. Packages that include three days of sportfishing or diving are US$795 per person, two-person minimum. It also offers tours of area attractions including horseback riding, snorkeling at Isla Iguana, whale-watching, a visit to Laboratorio Achotines, and turtle-watching at Isla de Cañas for US$45 per person, two-person minimum.

It's located between the Accel gas station and the abandoned CEFATI building at the north end of town. It recently built the Pedasí Sports Club (www.pedasisportsclub.com).

Accommodations

Try to call ahead for hotel reservations in the rainy season. The risk is not so much that places will fill up as that business may be so slow the manager may not even be around to check guests in. Most of the places listed here are in town, but there are a few others either on or near the beach. Three of the nicest accommodations are near Playa Destiladeros, south of town.

US$10-25

Hotel Residencial Pedasí (tel. 995 2490, www.residencialpedasi.com, US$20 s, US$25 d), on the main road at the north end of town, offers 14 clean, spartan rooms with air-conditioning, Wi-Fi, and computers for rent. The beds are a bit saggy and the rooms tend to be somewhat dark. But the spot is nice and quiet. There's an open-air restaurant that opens when the hotel has guests.

US$25-50

Dim's Hostel (tel. 995-2303, cell 6664-1900, mirely@iname.com, US$27 s, US$33 d, including breakfast) is on the west side of the main road about midway through town. It's actually a simple bed-and-breakfast, not a hostel. Accommodations consist of eight air-conditioned rooms with private baths in the aging home of the owner, Mirna Batista. Rooms are basic, but they have character and were recently renovated. None of the rooms has hot water but most have cable TV. Guests are served full breakfasts out of on an attractive thatch-roofed patio area with a massive mango tree as the centerpiece. Guests can bring their own food for lunch and dinner and use the backyard kitchen to prepare it. Out back there's a traditional *casa de quincha*—an adobe house built during community festivals. Mirna now lives out there. The guesthouse has an Internet computer (first half hour free, then US$1/hour).

Mirna is an energetic, attentive, and helpful host who speaks pretty good English. She's very friendly and will cheerfully take guests under her wing if they want her to. She's the go-to person for help setting up a trip to Isla de Cañas and other area attractions. Expect to pay US$30 for transportation and US$15 for a guide. This place is popular, so make reservations as far in advance as possible, especially during the dry season and holidays.

Rosa de Vientos (US$40–45 s/d) does not offer air-conditioning or even electricity. (The latter, at least, is allegedly working its way to the property.) What it does offer are three clean, simple rooms with firm beds and high ceilings, 700 meters from the coast. It's run by a Swiss woman who has lived in Pedasí since 2005. It's about two kilometers from downtown Pedasí on the road to Playa Toro, which is popular with locals.

Breakfast is available for US$4. This place is a good value.

US$50-100

The popular **Casita Margarita** (tel. 995-2898, www.pedasihotel.com, US$99 s/d, including buffet breakfast) is in a two-story yellow building on the south end of town, on the main road and the corner of Calle José A. Carrasquilla. It offers five clean, spacious rooms with air-conditioning, flat-screen TVs, good beds, and Wi-Fi. Flowering vines sheleter a front terrace, and a second, glassed-in terrace is strung with hammocks for guests who'd like a snooze. The inn is run by a family from Pennsylvania and has a friendly, relaxed atmosphere. The small restaurant is open to the public on Friday and Saturday nights, but private dinners can be arranged for guests staying at the inn on other nights. Tours are available, including boat trips to Isla Iguana (US$25–40 pp, depending on group size) and a variety of fishing packages. Prices are significantly higher during major holidays but drop by about US$10 in the low season. There is a two-night minimum for weekend stays.

Posada Los Destiladeros (cell 6673-9262 or tel. 6676-5571, fax 6676-5572, www.

panamabambu.net, starts at US$75 s/d, including breakfast) is south of Pedasí on a ridge just above Playa Destiladeros. It consists of 12 attractive bungalows in a garden compound with a swimming pool, sundecks, and comfortable common areas including a large dining room and a breakfast *rancho*. Each bungalow is different, ranging from little cabañas to split-level A-frame affairs. Some have thatched roofs, and others resemble traditional adobe Azuero houses with red-tile roofs. They're fairly rustic but comfortable, with a "Swiss Family Robinson" bohemian vibe (e.g., four-poster beds made of bamboo or driftwood).

The whole place has a certain funky elegance about it. The cheapest bungalows, Sophie and Julie (US$75 s/d), are set back from the beach but still have a view of the ocean. My favorites, especially for a romantic getaway, are the small but cozy Virginia and Bouboulina (US$150 s/d), the red-tile-roofed cottages right above the beach. Each has a ceiling fan, air-conditioning, double beds, bathrooms, and a porch where one can sit and watch the sea. Breakfast is included with stays, and dinner is available for US$20.

OVER US$100

The new ◖ **Casa de Campo Pedasí** (tel. 995-2733, cell 6780-5280, www.casacampopedasi.com, starts at US$94.50 s/d) is a special place. The owners, Ovidin, who is from Pedasí, and his wife, Koby, who is from Guararé, have taken their spacious family home and transformed it into a chic B&B. It's the loveliest place of its kind I've yet encountered in my travels around the country.

The property is right on the main road leading into town, but it's a quiet, peaceful spot because it's in a 7,000-square-meter compound, much of which is given over to trees and a burgeoning organic garden.

The design was the work of the same Moroccan designer behind Villa Camilla and shares a similar aesthetic: modern, eclectic, and luxurious, and as open as possible. The ceilings are high and the common areas all flow into each other and into an interior courtyard with half-century-old trees, including a particularly massive mango tree.

Four rooms sit apart from the rest of the house around a fairly large and lovely swimming pool. Another two "family rooms" (US$137.50, including breakfast) are available in the main house when needed. The cabañas (US$94.50 s/d) are the smallest, with two single beds, but these two have high ceilings, plus a view of the pool. The Junior Suite Irene (US$110 s/d) is quite spacious, and the Master Suite Marina (US$137.50) has two bathroom sinks, a shower, and separate stone bathtub. All the rooms are decorated in good taste with elegant bathroom fixtures, free Wi-Fi, and comfortable beds. The entire B&B can be rented out for a week (six nights) for US$2,500 in high season or US$2,000 in low season. Expect all the rates to go up as this place is discovered.

The only thing that still needs some improvement is the food, which is authentically local but not as gourmet as its elegant surroundings demand. The owners are working on that.

The staff can arrange tours and a range of outdoor activities, including boat trips for around US$50 and whale-watching (in season) for US$125.

There are lots of nice touches here—meals on the terrace, a retro-mod bar by the pool, *ranchos* for snoozing or socializing—but best of all are the hosts themselves. They make guests feel at home and care deeply both about the history and folkloric traditions of the Azuero. They are constantly trying to make their place even better. Take time to chat with them, especially if you speak Spanish (Ovidin's English is quite good; Koby is a bit shy about hers). They are good hosts, and Koby in particular is utterly charming. I love this place.

◖ **Hotel Villa Romana** (tel. 843-3002 or 995-2922, U.S. tel. 786/264-1387, www.villapedasi.com, starts at US$109 s/d), which opened in April 2009, is on a rocky bluff in Puerto Escondido, which is on the western edge of Playa Destiladeros (the side farther from town). As the hotel's name suggests, it

As the name suggests, Hotel Villa Romana resembles a lovely Roman villa.

resembles a lovely Roman villa. Formerly the home of the Italian owner (who speaks fluent English) and his Colombian wife, the place has proved so popular they no longer actually live there, though they still manage the place and give it a warm, friendly, familial vibe.

It had six rooms when I visited, but four more were nearing completion in 2010 and should be done by the time you visit. A swimming pool is in the works, to supplement the bathtub-sized kids' pool already there.

All the rooms are attractive and have air-conditioning, stocked mini-bars, well-appointed bathrooms, comfortable beds, TVs, and ocean views. Accommodations range from the small but pleasant junior suites (US$109 s/d) with two single beds, up to spacious master suites (US$219) for up to four people. The latter have a queen bed, a single, and a sofa bed. My favorite among these is Master Suite 1, a split-level room in a separate building with a wraparound terrace, though Master Suite 2 is slightly larger.

There is a restaurant and bar in the main,

two-story building, which is on the edge of the bluff and has great views, especially from the upstairs terrace. (Check out the house on the distant point to the right: It's owned by a member of Lichtenstein's royal family.)

The restaurant is open to the public (6–10 P.M. Mon.–Sat.) but reservations are a must to make sure there's enough food and the chef is definitely around (if there are no guests at the hotel, the restaurant is closed Sunday and Monday). Dinners consist of a set three-course dinner for US$20.

The hotel is above a boulder-strewn stretch of coast, but beaches are a short walk away. The *chitras* (sand flies) get a bit nippy around here when the breeze dies down.

Hotel Villa Romana is south of Pedasí, 7.5 kilometers from the turnoff to Playa Destiladeros. Getting there requires driving through the Azueros housing development, which is still under construction. The road can get rough and trucks use this road, so drive carefully. It's best attempted with a four-wheel drive, particularly in the rainy season. There are signs pointing the way, but it's still possible to get lost at night. However, the rough road conditions help keep the crowds away. This place is a great find and often books up.

◖ Villa Camilla (tel. 232-6721, www.azueros.com, US$300–450 s/d) is the most beautiful little hotel in all of Panama. It consists of just seven rooms: all different, all exquisitely designed and decorated. Little wonder: It was created by Gilles Saint-Gilles, a celebrated French architect, as a guesthouse for visitors to his incredibly ambitious Azueros project: up to 300 homes on a 357-hectare property surrounding Playa Destiladeros. Quite a few houses had been built, and the developers are renting out split-level lofts in addition to rooms at the villa.

Unhappy with the level of local construction available, Saint-Gilles created his own construction company and trained plumbers, builders, electricians, and craftspeople to work on the project and this boutique hotel. Most of the furnishings were created on-site, though a few items were brought from China, in keeping with the aesthetic of the place, which blends formal Chinese and casual Mediterranean elements to create an eminently comfortable place to stay that harmonizes well with its environment.

Every room at the villa is gorgeous, and each has unique elements: one has a bathroom sink carved out of a single block of polished cocobolo (redwood); another has an enormous, two-headed shower. Of the smaller rooms, Saffron (US$300 s/d) is my favorite because it's next to a breezy rooftop terrace and sundeck and has a good view of the ocean. It's also the brightest room at the villa; the one quibble about this place is that most of the rooms seem designed to keep light out, which keeps things cool but is not ideal for a beach villa. Common areas blend seamlessly into a breezy terrace where delicious meals are served. A three-meal plan is US$50 per person per day. Meals can also be bought separately. The dinner, at US$25, is well worth it; the breakfast, when presumably the French chef is not in the kitchen, is not. An infinity-edge pool sits on the edge of a hill that rolls down to the sea in the distance. Villa Camilla is about a 10-minute walk from the beach, not on the beach itself.

Food

Pedasí is not the place for fine dining. In fact, sometimes it's not the place for any kind of dining. Despite their alleged opening hours, it's quite possible to find every eatery in town closed at meal times. This is a good place to bring a well-stocked cooler.

However, things are gradually changing, with Italian, Spanish, and other international dishes on offer, though most of these are only open for dinner. **Hotel Villa Romana** (tel. 843-3002 or 995-2922, U.S. tel. 786/264-1387, www.villapedasi.com) serves dinner to outside guests who are willing to drive or cab it to Puerto Escondido. **Casita Margarita** (on the main road and the corner of Calle José A. Carrasquilla, tel. 995-2898, www.pedasihotel.com) serves dinner to the public on Friday and Saturday.

There are also several *fondas,* holes-in-the-wall that cater to workers who get an early start and are willing to eat whatever's on hand, served at rock-bottom prices. The best bet for breakfast is to show up no later than 8 A.M. Most restaurants start shutting down shortly after nightfall.

Restaurante Angela (tel. 999-2207, 7 A.M.–9 P.M. Mon. and Wed.–Sat., 3–9 P.M. Sun.), right next to Dim's Hostel, was once a barebones *fonda,* but has been remade into a cute and cheerful little open-air place with a covered terrace on the main street. It's still quite simple and cheap. Breakfast is US$2.25 or less, and a full lunch or dinner is US$4.50 or less.

El Gringo Ducek (tel. 995-2869, noon–9 P.M. Mon.–Sat., under US$10) serves seafood and Panamanian dishes in the house of a gringo named Ducek. It's on the main road between Dim's Hostal and Casa de Campo Pedasí.

Pasta e Vino (6:30–10:30 P.M. Wed.–Sun., US$5) is a new Italian place that serves (you guessed it) pasta and wine in a house on the road to Playa Toro. It was closed when I was last in town, but I'm told (by an Italian, no less) that both the pasta and the wine are good. To get there, walk or drive down the road to Playa Toro, turning right about two blocks past the *Centro de Salud* (health center).

Tiesto (8 A.M.–10 P.M. Wed.–Mon., 8 A.M.–4 P.M. Tues.), on the town plaza, is a pleasant little coffee house. Offerings include full breakfasts, sandwiches, pastries, and fresh *chichas* (fruit juices). An individual pizza is around US$2.

Refresquería y Dulcería Yely (9 A.M.–8 P.M. daily, and maybe open until 9 P.M. on Sat.), across the street from and south of Residencial Moscoso, is a clean sweets shop locally famous for its cakes. Slices are just US$0.25–0.50. The *nueces* (nut) cake is good; the rum one is just so-so. Other temptations include flan and *tres leches.* It also offers sandwiches, empanadas, and other snacks. Only the hungriest will spend more than US$2 here.

There's a minimally stocked **supermercado** on the town plaza next to Restaurante Brisas de Pedasí. The **minisuper** near the Texaco station is the only store open late at night.

Information and Services

With the abandonment of the government tourism office in Pedasí, the best sources of information are the hotels. Dim's Hostel, Casita Margarita, and Casa de Campo Pedasí are good sources. Casita Margarita has a notice board with useful information in its reception area.

The mammoth **Banco Nacional de Panamá** (8 A.M.–3 P.M. Mon.–Fri., 9 A.M.–noon Sat.) is hard to miss at the north end of town.

Refresquería y Dulcería Yely (across the street from and south of Residencial Moscoso, 9 A.M.–8 P.M. daily, and maybe open until 9 P.M. on Sat.) has Internet computers for US$1 an hour. So does the **public library** (town plaza, 9 A.M.–noon and 1–5 P.M. Mon.–Fri., 8 A.M.–1 P.M. Sat.). While there, check out the historic photos of Pedasí.

Centro Commercial Pedasí, a basic grocery store across the street from Dim's Hostel, has a small pharmacy.

The **post office** (tel. 995-2221, 7 A.M.–6 P.M. Mon.–Fri., 7 A.M.–5 P.M. Sat.) is behind the ambitiously named Palacio Municipal, across the street from Restaurante Angela.

The café part of the **Surf Shop and Café** (tel. 995-2926, www.manosurf.com) is on indefinite hiatus, but anyone is welcome to sit on their terrace and use their free Wi-Fi. Surfboard rentals are US$10–15 and surf lessons are sometimes available.

Lavamático Esy (tel. 995-2203) is a self-service launderette a block east of the main street near the south end of town, near the ANAM office. It charges US$0.75 to wash and US$1 to dry.

Getting There and Around

Las Tablas has direct buses to Pedasí. They leave every 45 minutes, 6 A.M.–7 P.M. The trip takes 45 minutes and costs US$2. Catch the return bus on Pedasí's main street, 6 A.M.–5 P.M. There is no longer bus service between Pedasí and Tonosí, though a bus goes as far as Cañas, the jumping-off point for Isla de Cañas, at 8 A.M. and 4 P.M. The fare is US$2.25. The bus stop in Pedasí is opposite Restaurante Angela.

There are now commercial flights to Pedasí. Air Panama flies there at 1:15 P.M. on Wednesday and 3 P.M. Friday and Sunday. Return flights are at 2:25 P.M. and 4 P.M. Friday and Sunday. The flight takes about 35 minutes and costs US$77 each way.

The town is easily walkable; the main street is just a kilometer long. There's a taxi stand (tel. 995-2275) on that street just north of Residencial Moscoso for longer trips. One-way fares are less than US$5 to nearby beaches, US$18 to Playa Venao and Las Tablas, US$30 to Tonosí, and US$40 to Cambutal. Those on a tight budget can also hike to Playa Arenal, Playa Toro, or Playa Garita without much trouble. They're about three kilometers from the center of town.

A **motor scooter rental place** (tel. 995-2822, 9:30 A.M.–5:30 P.M. Thurs.–Tues.) on the main street near the south end of town rents motor scooters for US$25 an hour or US$100 a day. Multiday packages are available. They also hire horses for US$20 an hour or US$100 a day, with price breaks for multiple horses.

REFUGIO DE VIDA SILVESTRE ISLA IGUANA

Isla Iguana is a small, narrow island that, along with its surrounding waters, was declared a wildlife sanctuary in 1981. It's accessible by boat from Playa El Arenal in Pedasí. The island is a popular spot for snorkeling since it has the biggest (15 hectares) and oldest (500 years) coral reef in the Gulf of Panama, and it's the only one that's nominally protected. It contains more than a dozen species of coral and attracts about 200 species of reef fish.

Among the dozens of bird species drawn to the island, the most important is a colony of 5,000 magnificent frigate birds, the largest colony in the eastern Azuero.

Sadly, the island and its waters are far from pristine. The current brings garbage from as far away as Panama City, as do some thoughtless visitors who junk up the beach, drop anchors on the coral, and take back souvenirs.

Also, the U.S. military used this island for target practice during World War II, as evidenced by the craters in the middle of the island. More than half a dozen bombs have been found and detonated on the island since then; there may be more that haven't been discovered, so don't wander off the trail.

Still, there's lots of natural beauty left that humans and coral-damaging El Niños haven't yet destroyed.

Snorkeling is best off the west side of the island, where the longest beach is. Known as **Playa El Cirial** or simply La Playa, it's a pretty, long, light-sand beach, as long as you ignore the motor-oil bottles, tires, plastic buckets, and so on that can wash up and spoil the scene. Swimmers should not venture out past the reef, as the water quickly turns rough.

Divers may be able to find moray eels off the north end of the island, octopus and large jewfish around the rocky outcroppings on the southern end, and big schools of fish among the mushroom coral fields off the southeast side. Note that the waters around the island can get quite turbulent.

The boat ride takes about 20 minutes from Playa El Arenal, 30 minutes if the water is choppy. Be prepared for one hell of a bouncy adventure on a windy dry-season morning; it feels more like a watery roller-coaster ride than a boat trip. On those days, the return trip can be much faster, as the wind and waves practically blast the boat back to shore.

Since Isla Iguana is a government wildlife refuge, there's a US$10 charge to visit, collected on the island.

Fishermen charge about US$40 round-trip for the boat ride to Isla Iguana from Arenal. **Iguana Tours** (tel. 226-8738, www.nvmundo.com/iguanatours/index.htm), specializes in trips to the island from Panama City and may be able to tell you about current reef conditions.

PLAYA VENAO

Also called Playa Venado, this beach, 34 kilometers southwest of Pedasí, is popular with surfers, and it's easy to see why. The beach describes a huge, easy arc, and the surf offers an

THE AZUERO PENINSULA

exceptionally long and gentle ride that breaks left and right. It's a good place for beginners.

Practicalities

Heading south, Playa Venao is a left turn 1.4 kilometers south of La Playita Resort turn-off. The road is good and it's possible to drive right up to the beach. A taxi here costs about US$12–15 one way from Pedasí.

Facilities improved vastly in this area in the last few years, though some of these look better from a distance than close up. The new places are overcharging for what they offer, but this may shake out as the tourism market becomes established in this up-and-coming area.

El Sitio (tel. 832-1010, elsitiopv@gmail. com, US$140 s/d) is a new beach hotel with a restaurant/bar in an attractive *rancho* right on the beach. The hotel is a two-story affair with a red-tile roof and modern-looking rooms with air-conditioning, TVs, and beds with foam mattresses (the kind you would normally expect to find in a hostel). For this and a view of the ocean, the hotel charges US$140 a night. That's very high for this area and will probably go down once things shake out. The surf shop at the hotel charges US$25 to rent a surfboard or take a surf lesson, which is nearly twice the going rate at other surf spots throughout Panama.

On the opposite side of the beach is **Bar y Restaurante Playa Venao,** which popped up in 2010 on the site of what was for many years a very basic beach beer garden with a few rustic sheds for surfers. The new place is a major improvement, with wooden lounge chairs on an attractive deck. It offers reasonably priced drinks and bar food. A-frame cabins are being built. Surfboard rentals here are US$5 an hour, maxing out at US$15 for the day. Surf lessons are allegedly in the works.

There are public toilets at both El Sitio and Bay y Restaurante Playa Venao. Campers are allowed to pitch a tent on the grounds of both places, but I suspect this won't last. Remember that anyone can pitch a tent on the beach for free; report anyone who says otherwise to the police.

Eco Venao (tel. 202-0530, cell 6507-0726, www.ecovenao.com, US$12 for dorm bed, US$27.50 s/d for private room) is a friendly surf camp on a hill above Playa Venao. It's on a 135-hectare reforestation project, which makes this a quiet and secluded place to crash. The main building is on the edge of a bluff and catches the breeze. Accommodations consist of a dorm with eight bunk beds and good mattresses, and two small private rooms with fans and double beds. The rooms are rustic but pleasant, and guests have access to a full kitchen, a volleyball court, and lots of hammocks that are strung about the place. There are also three houses for rent and a campsite (between December and May). The place is run by an Englishman named Nicholas and a Panamanian caretaker named Pablo. The place offers surf lessons (US$10/hour), board rentals (US$20/day), and horseback riding (US$15/tour). Eco Venao is about one kilometer from Playa Venao by road.

Villa Marina (tel. 263-6555, www.villamarinapanama.com, $165 s/d, including continental breakfast) is on the beach about a kilometer north of the turnoff to the surf break. It offers nine simple but pleasant rooms with air-conditioning, hot water, cable TV, and wireless Internet. There's an attractive stone-lined swimming pool and the beach is just a few paces away. This is a private spot, so this stretch of beach is essentially secluded. There's a restaurant and bar. However, the place is rather pricey for what it offers and if you're not sportfishing you may feel out of place here. The hotel offers five-hour fishing trips on *pangas* for US$150. Horses can be had for US$8 an hour.

REFUGIO DE VIDA SILVESTRE ISLA DE CAÑAS

Isla de Cañas is the most important nesting site for sea turtles on Panama's Pacific coast. Five species come here. By far the most numerous is the olive ridley *(Lepidochelys olivacea),* the smallest of the turtles that come to Panama, weighing in at about 35–45 kilograms and with a shell about 70 centimeters long. The second-most frequent visitor is the Pacific green *(Chelonia mydas)*, followed, in very limited numbers, by the loggerhead *(Caretta caretta)*, leatherback *(Dermochelys coriacea)*, and hawksbill *(Eretmochelys imbricata)*.

To make things confusing, the green turtle is known colloquially in Panama as the *tortuga negra* (black turtle) and the olive ridley as the *tortuga mulata* (mulatto turtle).

Every year 20,000–30,000 turtles show up to lay their eggs in successive waves, which makes for a spectacular sight if you time a visit right. That's not necessarily an easy thing to do, since no one seems to agree on the best time to come. Visitors should be able to see the best action between September and November, though nesting season can begin as early as April or May, and islanders say that massive inundations of turtles have occurred as late as the end of December. Very few turtles nest during the dry-season months of January–March.

Getting to the island is kind of complicated, but the trip is fun. From Pedasí, head south on the main road to the town of Cañas, about 40 kilometers away, or 11 kilometers south of Playa Venao. The turnoff is on the left, and it's easy to miss because the sign faces the northbound traffic. Head down the rocky but okay road until it dead-ends at the shore, 2.5 kilometers away. Isla de Cañas is a long, narrow barrier island parallel to and quite close to shore. It's an unusual island: Its ocean-facing beach is 13 kilometers long, but the island is just 175 meters wide at its narrowest point.

From the landing it's a five-minute boat ride through mangroves to the island (US$0.50 pp each way). Go at high tide if you don't want to slop around in muck. If there's no boat waiting, call the island's one phone (tel. 995-8002); it's a pay phone. Ask for Neyla or for a *lancha* or *bote*. The closest pay phone to make the call is back in Cañas.

The biggest pain in all this is getting to the flyspeck village of Cañas, on the mainland. The area is not well served by buses, especially since a route running between Pedasí and Tonosí was dropped in recent years. Only two buses make the trip from Pedasí, at 8 A.M. and 4 P.M. The fare is US$2.25. Taxis from Pedasí are about US$20 each way; make sure to arrange a pickup time, try not to pay until the return trip, and hope for the best.

Given the logistical hassles involved in getting here, many will find it worthwhile to arrange a guided trip. Most of these will have to be arranged with a tour operator back in Panama City, but those near Pedasí should contact Mirna Batista at Dim's Hostel (tel. 995-2303, cell 6664-1900, mirely@iname.com), who if she has time may be able to arrange a trip for a quite reasonable fee, probably no more than the cost of a taxi. She knows the area well.

The island is a colorful place with a population of about 900, most of whom live in cane houses. The community has been here since the 1920s, drawn from mainland towns and the surrounding countryside. They protect the turtles and their eggs, in exchange for which they're legally allowed to harvest some eggs (but not the turtles).

There are a few ultra-basic, no-name huts for rent near the beach for US$10–15 per night, but those who want to hang out here are better off pitching a tent on the beach for free. A local sugarcane farmer, Señor Fernando, will take visitors for a ride on his cane cart for US$8 per group, but the beach where the turtles do their thing is just a five-minute walk across the island.

Sea turtles lay their eggs only late at night, but trying to get to the island alone after dark can be tricky, not to mention spooky. Camping on the beach is probably the best bet for those not traveling with a guide. Do not use flashlights or wear light-colored clothing at night; the turtles are easily disoriented and scared off by anything brighter than moonlight.

Those visiting the island without a guide should still hire a villager to guide them to the turtles. It likely will cost less than US$10 per group (arrange the price ahead of time), and the tourism dollars help ensure the turtles are left in peace to procreate rather than end up on someone's dinner plate.

THE AZUERO PENINSULA

Southwest Azuero

The road stays in fairly good shape south and west of Playa Venao, but until recently there was little reason for most people to come all this way. The only sizable town is the backwater of Tonosí, and the two main beaches, Playa Guánico and Playa Cambutal, have mainly been of interest to adventurous surfers. There is a national park, and Parque Nacional Cerro Hoya, but it's accessible only by boat on seas that are often rough. There is no road to the park and no facilities of any kind.

However, Playa Cambutal suddenly seems on the verge of taking off. When I first visited the area circa 1998, the area saw few visitors and the coastal "road" was a riverbed that could only be traversed in the dry season.

Now, however, it's got a few quite nice places to stay and is just waiting to be discovered. It's still mainly of interest to surfers and deepsea fishers, but with beaches as attractive as Playa Venao and not much farther to drive, it should also appeal to those who think surf is just meant to be looked at. It's more attractive than Playa Guánico, which has black sand and probably will appeal only to surfers.

TONOSÍ

Really little more than a glorified crossroads, Tonosí (pop. 2,272) will be of interest mainly to those going to or coming from nearby Playa Guánico and Playa Cambutal. It's not a pretty town, though it does have some facilities, including one surprisingly decent place to stay, as well as a couple of more basic but cheaper options. Other services include a post office and a few gas stations and pharmacies.

Most everything in town is built around a Y-shaped intersection. The northeast road forks six kilometers east of town. Its right fork heads north to Isla de Cañas, Playa Venao, and Pedasí, and continues from there to Las Tablas. The left fork is a more direct route to Las Tablas that cuts out the intermediate stops.

Only one thing passes for a sight in Tonosí. One kilometer south of town on the road to the beaches, make a quick stop at the overpass over the Río Tonosí. Look left down at the pond: It's absolutely crawling with caimans. Locals sometimes feed them bread as though they were ducks. Those who have trouble spotting the pond should ask in town where to find the *lagartos*.

Practicalities

Pensión Boamy (tel. 995-8142, US$18–25 s/d), a pleasant surprise on the road to Playa Cambutal, has 11 rooms with air-conditioning, TVs, and hot-water bathrooms. It's a clean, perfectly fine place by a church on the edge of town. It also has a cheerful little restaurant. It's the best place in town.

Banco Nacional de Panamá (8 A.M.–3 P.M. Mon.–Fri., 9 A.M.–noon Sat.), near the center of town, does not have an ATM.

Getting There and Away

Buses to Las Tablas leave from the center of town every hour and a half or so (6 A.M.–4 P.M. Mon.–Sat. and 7:30 A.M.–4:30 P.M. Sun.). The trip costs US$3 and takes an hour and 20 minutes. Buses no longer run between Tonosí and Pedasí, oddly enough.

Buses to and from Las Tablas use the road that leads northwest out of Tonosí and winds through the still relatively unspoiled southwest tip of the Azuero. It starts out hilly, with sweeping views of deforested but still scenic hills, passes through the town of Macaracas, and ends up in the flatlands as it gets close to Chitré, about 100 kilometers away. This is a somewhat faster road than the coastal route. Those who drive this way should watch out for tire-eating potholes and one-way bridges.

PLAYA CAMBUTAL AND VICINITY

Those who make it all the way down here will find accommodations ranging from a basic surf camp to a quite appealing boutique hotel. This is definitely a place to come with a cooler,

© WILLIAM FRIAR

fisherman mending a net, Playa Cambutal

though, as there are few places to eat outside of the handful of lodgings.

All the places to stay are on a 1.5-kilometer stretch of beach just beyond the town of Cambutal.

Practicalities

The "town" of Cambutal has virtually nothing but a phone booth and a real-estate office that lets visitors piggyback on its wireless signal. The lodgings here are listed in order of their distance from town, with the closest first. They begin about 1.5 kilometers from town.

Hotel Playa Cambutal (tel. 832-0948, Skype: Hotel Playa Cambutal, www.hotelplayacambutal.com, starts at US$135 s/d, including breakfast) is a modern, two-story boutique hotel that opened in January 2010. The 10 rooms face the ocean and have a balcony, simple but tasteful decor, air-conditioning, good beds, and handsome hot-water showers. It's one of the most attractive hotels in the Azuero. Kayak, surfing, fishing, and horseback-riding tours are available. The hotel has a restaurant and bar.

Next door is **Boom Shiva** (tel. 832-0443, boomshiva@gmail.com, US$100 s/d) which consists of three attractive teak bungalows on the beach. Each has a loft bedroom, warm-water bathrooms, a mini-fridge, and seating area. Air-conditioning was about to be installed when I visited, which is a good thing because these things are hot boxes during the day. Pleasant though this spot is, it has the feel of a place that won't be around long. The owners are in the real-estate business, and the on-site manager seemed more like a caretaker than someone who could meet guests' needs.

About 1300 meters beyond these is **Los Buzos Resort** (tel. 994-1547, www.losbuzos. net, starts at US$65 s/d), which offers six rooms in a one-story building across the road from the beach. The property looks nice, with two large, attractive *ranchos* to house a bar grill and a reception area. The rooms have air-conditioning and private bathrooms. Other vacation rental "villas" are available, with prices ranging from US$110–200 a night. The restaurant serves a buffet breakfast, lunch, and dinner for US$10–15. The main focus of this project seems to be real-estate development and sportfishing.

On the beach directly opposite Los Buzos is a little place called **Gonzales Surf Camp** (no phone), run by champion Panamanian surfer Gonzalo Gonzales and his extremely proud mother. This is a casual and friendly spot. When asked how much she charges for campers, Doña Gonzales shrugged and said whatever donation felt right. US$5 a tent should do it. Surf lessons are sometimes available; again, make an offer. A breakfast, lunch, or dinner of whatever's on her stove goes for a buck or two and is served in a cute little *rancho* on the beach. This is not a pristine spot—there's junk in the yard and horse droppings on the beach—but the price is certainly right. It's safer than just pitching a tent at a remote spot on the beach.

Getting There and Away

The nearest sizable town with regular transportation connections is Tonosí, about 11 kilometers north.

There is no regular public transportation between Pedasí and this area. Playa Guánico is about 75 kilometers from Pedasí, or around an hour by car. Playa Cambutal is a little under 100 kilometers from Pedasí, which takes around 1.5 hours by car. There is no bus service to either place. The closest bus stop is Tonosí, from where it's possible to get a taxi. There is one direct bus to Tonosí from Panama City, leaving daily at 7:30 A.M.

To get to either beach by car from Tonosí, head south out of town. After about 15 kilometers there'll be a marked left turn into the town of Guánico, for those who want to visit that beach. Otherwise, take the left fork that appears 5 kilometers past the Guánico turnoff. (The right fork leads to the nearly inaccessible Parque Nacional Cerro Hoya.) The town of Cambutal is 10 kilometers past the turnoff. Drive through it to get to the beach and lodgings.

When I first visited the area over 10 years ago, only adventurous surfers went all the way down here, and the coastal "road" was not passable in the rainy season. Now, however, the road remains in pretty good shape until Gonzales Surf Camp, after which only four-wheel drives can continue.

KUNA YALA

Welcome to paradise. Cartoonists who draw tropical islands as small discs of soft sand with a coconut palm or two could have gotten the idea from Kuna Yala, otherwise known as the San Blas Islands. That image fits countless idyllic spots in this archipelago of nearly 400 islands off the eastern Caribbean coast of Panama. When the sun hits the sea you'll think of emeralds and sapphires.

The islands are just part of the Comarca de Kuna Yala, a semiautonomous homeland of the Kuna people. Kuna territory also encompasses a mountainous strip of mostly virgin forest on the mainland, along the Caribbean slope of the Darién. It runs the length of the archipelago, ending at the Colombian border.

Most visitors prefer to hang out on the islands. Nearly all the estimated 40,000 Kuna who live in the *comarca* (reservation) inhabit just 40 of the islands, none of which is very large. As one might imagine, things get pretty crowded: On many islands, the thatch roofs of the Kunas' cane huts almost touch, making walking around a bit of a challenge. Visitors generally spend as much time as possible on the uninhabited islands, but be sure to visit a village. The chance to meet the Kuna, who have one of the most vibrant indigenous cultures in Latin America, is reason enough to visit.

A word of warning: If you're looking for an island resort, Kuna Yala is emphatically not for you. Even the most "exclusive" accommodations are quite simple, and there's little to do on the islands except swim, snorkel, laze in hammocks, and visit villages. The food on the islands is generally poor, bland, and basic.

© WILLIAM FRIAR

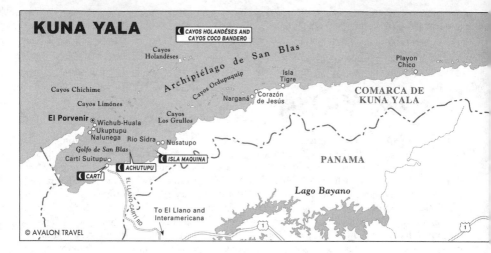

Coral Lodge is the only place out here with a first-world infrastructure, and it's not actually in the archipelago.

More disturbing, any lingering romantic notions one has about indigenous people's harmonious relationship with nature gets a jolt upon realizing how severely the Kuna are overfishing their own waters, or seeing the garbage and sewage they routinely dump into pristine blue waters.

On the other hand, there are still plenty of lovely, uninhabited islands in the archipelago, more than anyone could possibly see during a visit. A big part of the charm of these islands is their very simplicity: no timeshare condos or tacky T-shirt shops here. Nodding off in a hammock slung between coconut palms, watching a Kuna woman sewing a *mola* (handcrafted blouse), and showering by the light of a kerosene lantern can soon seem like a pretty good way to spend the day.

PLANNING YOUR TIME

The Comarca de Kuna Yala consists of a strip of mountainous coast and a nearby archipelago that stretch 226 kilometers down the eastern Caribbean side of the isthmus to the Colombian border. Nearly all the islands are within five kilometers of the mainland. Only a handful of the inhabited ones have much in

the way of visitor facilities. Few tourists visit the coast, which is home primarily to Kuna farms and dense tropical forest.

The islands most popular with and accessible to visitors are organized into five clusters in this chapter. It's possible to visit more than one of these island clusters during a visit. However, distances are too great and the sea sometimes too rough to make a day trip from one cluster to another practical by the chief means of transportation: small wooden boats powered by outboard motors. Unless you have access to a large powerboat or yacht, choose just one area to explore. If

KUNA PHOTOS

It's tempting to take photos of the Kuna, especially the colorfully dressed women. But always ask first, and expect to pay for the privilege. If the Kuna are going to be treated as curiosities, they figure the least tourists can do is compensate them for it. Note that the going rate is US$1 per subject, *not* per photo, as some try to claim. A Kuna woman you've just bought something from is more likely to let you snap her photo, and she may not even charge you. Photos of village scenes that don't focus on an individual are free.

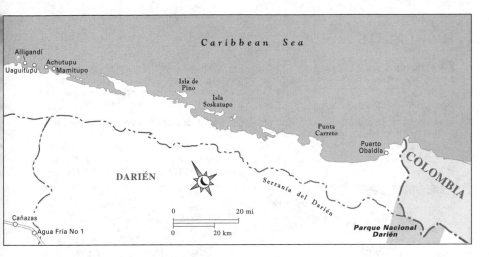

your schedule allows, you can also fly to a second area and spend one or more nights there, but that will increase the logistical hassles significantly; interisland flights are tricky to arrange.

Visitors will get the most out of their visit if they take time both to explore Kuna villages and to escape to one of the uninhabited islands for snorkeling or sunbathing. Most island groups offer an attractive combination of both. Those who stay around the busy hubs of **El Porvenir** and **Cartí,** for instance, have easy access to the uninhabited island of **Achutupu** and other pristine spots. Those who stay on the tranquil hotel islands around **Río Sidra,** on the other hand, can take a day trip to explore the nearby village islands, including traditional and picturesque **Isla Maquina.**

Try to stay a bare minimum of two nights on the islands. That allows enough time to explore a Kuna village, go snorkeling, shop for *molas* (handcrafted blouses), and lounge in a hammock. A three-night or longer stay gives visitors a better sense of the rhythms and beauty of life on the islands. Time will go much faster than you expect.

WHEN TO GO

Late in the dry season, late February–March, is generally reckoned to be the best time to visit the islands. The winds are calmer,

improving snorkeling visibility. This calmer weather can last until mid-April. There are strong trade winds December–February, which creates lots of chop in the sea. It also tends to be cloudy then, which drops snorkeling visibility even more.

There's less wind in the rainy season, which begins around mid-April and lasts until the end of the year. This calms the water, but underwater visibility near land can be poor because of runoff from the rivers. The lack of wind can also make it quite hot and humid. On the other hand, the seas are calm enough to go exploring by boat outside the reef that protects the western half of the archipelago from the open ocean. The fishing is also better then, and there are fewer tourists. The high season for tourists is December–March. According to experienced sailors, if there are hurricanes out in the Caribbean (Panama is beyond the hurricane belt), the weather in the Kuna Yala tends to be good.

Holidays in Kuna Yala include the anniversary of the Revolución Tule (the Kuna war against Panama in 1925) on February 21, which is celebrated throughout the archipelago, and a celebration in honor of Charles Robinson, an important figure in the revolution, which is celebrated only on his native island of Narganá.

HIGHLIGHTS

◖ **Achutupu:** You'll find easy and accessible snorkeling in crystalline waters by this island (page 423).

◖ **Cartí:** Though one of the most touristed areas in Kuna Yala, this cluster of islands near El Porvenir has an interesting blend of traditional and modern Kuna life, as well as a museum that offers insight into that life (page 423).

◖ **Isla Maquina:** The vibrant Kuna culture is going strong on Isla Maquina, one of the most traditional, charming, and attractive inhabited islands in the archipelago (page 428).

◖ **Cayos Holandéses and Cayos Coco Bandero:** These cays are among the archipelago's most remote and stunning string of sparsely inhabited islands, with clear water and spectacular coral (page 435 and 436).

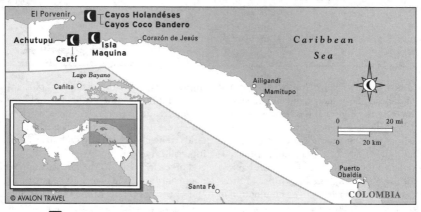

LOOK FOR ◖ TO FIND RECOMMENDED SIGHTS, ACTIVITIES, DINING, AND LODGING.

Kuna Yala Islands

The island clusters of the *comarca* (reservation) are covered in geographical order in this chapter, starting with the westernmost one and heading southeast down the archipelago. This is followed by a description of the most popular of the lovely, remote, and sparsely inhabited outer cays.

Farther down the archipelago, east of Corazón de Jesús, the reef ends and the islands are subject to higher seas. This area sees few tourists.

Island names are confusing. Some have both Spanish and Kuna names, and there is rarely agreement on how to spell them in either

language. Different islands sometimes have the same name. The most common names and their alternatives are used in this chapter.

SPORTS AND RECREATION
Water Activities

Underwater visibility in these crystalline waters can be better than 30 meters on a good day. The best **snorkeling** is found among the sparsely inhabited outer cays at the western end of the archipelago, where the coral is extensive and indescribably beautiful. The most popular of these are the **Cayos Holandéses.**

A visit to a traditional Kuna community is fascinating.

The hotels typically have snorkeling equipment to rent or borrow, but it's usually not in good shape. Bring your own if possible. The Kunas have banned scuba diving in their waters.

Several groups now offer **kayak** adventures, which can be a great way to explore the islands. When conditions are right, you can see many meters down, and, if you're lucky, dolphins will swim along the kayak. Groups to consider include Aventuras Panama (tel. 260-0044, info@ aventuraspanama.com, www.aventuraspanama. com), Mountain Travel Sobek (U.S. toll-free tel. 888-831-7526, info@mtsobek.com, www.mt-sobek.com), and Expediciones Tropicales (tel. 317-1279, info@xtrop.com, www.xtrop.com).

Don't swim around inhabited islands, as human and animal waste is allowed to flow out to sea; try even to avoid sea-spray during boat rides near them.

Hiking Tours

Some hotels now offer tours of the rainforest near the coast for an extra fee. These usually go to a waterfall or Kuna cemetery. The more ambitious of these can be hikes through true jungle. Come prepared, and do not attempt to explore the forests without a Kuna guide.

ACCOMMODATIONS AND FOOD

Most of the phone numbers listed for lodgings are in Panama City, where nearly all the hotels have offices. Typical hotel packages include room, meals, pickup and drop-off at the airstrip, and one or two daily boat tours to a snorkeling spot or Kuna village. Some will also arrange plane reservations.

Some hotels allow guests to opt out of the full package and fend for themselves for meals and transport. However, unless you have your own boat you'll probably find it cheaper, and certainly simpler, to go with a package deal. Remember that nearly all accommodations out here vary from fairly rustic to very rustic. Also, there are no true restaurants in Kuna Yala. Most visitors eat all their meals in their hotel's simple dining area.

The food is usually mediocre at best. Bring snacks. Once you've had your third straight meal of tasteless fried fish and rice, your hotel's offer of lobster might be tempting. Bear in mind that lobster, once a subsistence food for the Kuna, has been so commercially over-exploited it's in danger of local extinction. At the very least, do not eat lobster during the mating season, which runs March–July. Also, even those with a package deal will probably pay extra for lobster, something you may not realize until you're presented the bill.

It's probably also wise to avoid squid. Kuna fishermen typically chase squid out of aquatic caves by squeezing bleach into the cave entrance. It's bad for the environment and bad for you.

Beer and sodas are widely available on the islands; wine and spirits are not.

Kuna hotels have unpredictable life spans. Make sure your hotel of choice still exists before making too many plans.

Do not camp on a "deserted" island without permission from the island's owner—every

KUNA YALA

PARADISE UNDER PRESSURE

The spectacularly clear water around the islands makes the underwater flora and fauna of the *comarca* (reservation) the big draw for most visitors. For starters, consider the coral reefs that can make navigating these waters so treacherous: According to the Smithsonian Tropical Research Institution, which until recently had a research facility on the islands, Kuna Yala has more coral species than just about anywhere else in the Caribbean. It's easy to spot colorful staghorn, brain, fan, and leaf coral, among many others. Nearly 60 species of marine sponges grow on the western side of the *comarca*.

Sadly, however, over-fishing and reef destruction have decimated marine life. Five types of lobster are found here, but they are in danger of local extinction because Kuna divers catch them to sell to outside commercial interests. The same thing is happening with other marine creatures, including sea turtles and, beginning in the early 1990s, even small tropical fish, which are ending up in household aquariums in the United States. Marine life in the region, while still impressive, is not what it was even a decade ago.

The Kuna also lost nearly 80 percent of their remaining coral in the last three decades of the 20th century, according to a study conducted in 2003, due mainly to "coral mining" to build seawalls and landfill to expand islands, as well as some natural causes.

About 90 percent of the territory of the *comarca* on the mainland is still covered with forest. Though these forests are under pressure, animals found in them include the collared and white-lipped peccary, Baird's tapir, red brocket deer, and iguana.

island belongs to a person or community. Even then, don't camp except with an organized group. Smugglers, including drug traffickers, run these waters. You really wouldn't want them to stumble upon you in the middle of the night.

INFORMATION AND SERVICES

There are few modern services of any kind on the islands. Bring just about anything you'll need during your stay, as only the most basic supplies are sold anywhere.

Bring enough cash to cover any expenses you expect to incur on the islands. Bring lots of small bills (US$1 and US$5); anything larger than a US$10 is hard to break. There's only one bank in the archipelago, on Narganá, and it doesn't have an ATM.

The inhabited islands usually have telephone booths that accept calling cards, and mobile phone signals now reach some of the inhabited islands. But expect to be more or less cut off from the rest of the world during your stay.

One of the most maddening things about visiting the islands is trying to get in touch with people. Even the longest-established

hotels and services are perpetually changing their phone numbers, names, and email addresses. I list as many as possible in the hope that at least one of them will still work by the time you read this.

More places now have websites, but how long they'll stick around is anyone's guess, and most give a far more idealized image of what they offer than what they actually deliver. Again, don't come expecting a resort, or even a Motel 6. Think Robinson Crusoe and you might be pleasantly surprised, or at least not too disappointed.

GETTING THERE AND AROUND

The islands' isolation is what help keeps them relatively unspoiled and the Kuna culture more or less intact. Most visitors arrive by small plane from Panama City. The affluent or adventurous arrive by boat. And a newly paved road means that increasing numbers of intrepid travelers are coming by land.

By Sea
The best way to explore the islands is by

© BONNIE KAY SPINDLER

Kuna trading vessels run up and down the archipelago.

yacht. I have found **San Blas Sailing** (tel. 314-1800 or 314-1288, www.sanblassailing. com) to be a good way to go for those who can afford it. It charters a range of yachts with competent, experienced captains. However, some captains speak no English. This has proved a hindrance to those who don't speak at least some Spanish; bring a phrasebook just in case. Trips are custom-designed depending on the interests and time of the passengers, but typically in Kuna Yala they're made on comfortable 34- to 42-foot catamarans and monohulls and include all meals, wine, visits to villages, and use of snorkeling gear. Most yachts have a two-person kayak, and all have a dinghy with outboard motor. Rates depend on the yacht chosen, the length of trip and the number of clients. A 41-foot monohull with two double berths runs about US$175/ person per day with four clients or US$225/ person for a couple who want the yacht to themselves. These rates are for a minimum of three days; there's a discount after the seventh day. The company can do quick trips, but it recommends at least a four-day cruise,

which in my opinion is the minimum to truly unwind and enjoy all that the islands have to offer when visited by boat. You'd be amazed how quickly a week slips by out here. The longest trip is a 21-day voyage to Cartagena, Colombia.

The catamarans have a very shallow draft, allowing them to explore a wide variety of remote and beautiful spots. If they want, clients can explore Kuna villages by day and then come back to the yacht at night, which generally anchors well away from population centers. Weeklong cruises include a forest hike. Airfare from Panama City to the islands is not included, but it can be arranged by the company, as can hotel stays and a day tour in Panama City.

The second best way to explore the islands is by small, adventure-type cruise ship. These cruises can be very pricey, but they often feature academic and naturalist guides who can deepen the experience of visiting the islands. And they're certainly a comfortable way to go. Among the outfits that regularly include Kuna Yala in their itineraries are **Tauck World**

THE KUNA PEOPLE

Some still refer to the Kuna as the San Blas, because of the Spanish name for the archipelago where most Kuna live. But Kuna is the preferred term, and the archipelago is increasingly known by its official name, Kuna Yala (Land of the Kuna). To confuse matters, the Kuna call themselves the Tule, though they refer to themselves as Kuna when dealing with uagas (outsiders).

No one knows for sure where the Kuna originally came from, but surprisingly enough they have only been on the islands a few hundred years. Before that they lived in the Darién forest. Wars with the Spanish, the Emberá-Wounaan, and descendants of escaped African slaves gradually pushed them toward the Caribbean coast and islands. Some Darién rivers that are now part of Emberá and Wounaan territory still bear Kuna names.

Some Kuna remain in the mainland forests, mostly in two other comarcas (reservations), Madungandí and Wargandí. The mainland Kuna were historically known as the Kuna Bravo (fierce Kuna, for their warriorlike ways). The most remote of these see few visitors, cling especially tightly to their traditional ways, and tend to exclude outsiders, whom they view with considerable suspicion. A distinction is still made between the more open and adaptable "island Kuna" and the traditional "mainland Kuna."

Most of the inhabitants of the Comarca de Kuna Yala are island Kuna, but even they travel by cayuco (dugout canoe) to the mainland to farm, hunt, and bury their dead. About 40,000 of the estimated 61,700 Kuna live on the islands. The rest live in the mainland forests, in Panama City, and scattered around the country.

The Kuna have done a remarkable job over the centuries of keeping invaders out and holding onto their rich culture. They even fought and won a revolt against the Republic of Panama in 1925, which eventually earned them their semiautonomous status. Today, no foreigner is allowed to own land in Kuna territory.

Kunas have gained a greater voice in Panamanian government in recent years. In 1999 a Kuna, Enrique Garrido, became the head of Panama's general assembly.

Visitors are inevitably struck by the beautiful traditional dress of the Kuna women, which is not worn to impress tourists. The Kuna

---

Discovery (U.S. toll-free tel. 800/788-7885, www.tauck.com), **Cruise West** (U.S. toll-free tel. 888/851-8133, www.cruisewest.com), and **Star Clippers** (U.S. toll-free tel. 800/442-0551, www.starclippers.com). Several of the huge cruise ships that transit the Panama Canal also stop in the islands. Tourists can outnumber Kunas during these brief visits, which are hardly the ideal way to experience the islands or Kuna culture.

Note: Some tourists are under the misapprehension it's easy to buy passage on a boat from El Porvenir to Colombia. This is not true. Though I don't recommend hitching a ride in these waters, which are known drug-trafficking routes, it's far easier to do so from Colón or Isla Grande. Tourists have been known to get stranded on Porvenir for days waiting for a ride, if they get one at all. It may be possible to buy passage down the archipelago, or trade a ride for work, on a private yacht, a Colombian trader, or a 75-foot-long Kuna supply boat. The latter two options are quite rustic, slow, and most likely unsafe. It's also possible to arrange boat transportation from the area around Nombre de Dios, but this is generally on small motorized fishing boats and is a quite risky way to get to the islands. A less risky and far more comfortable option is to book a berth on a private yacht that's going to or from Cartagena, Colombia; these stop over in the islands. This is an informal arrangement and can be quite affordable, but it is not without its dangers. There is no approved commercial boat transport to and from the islands.

themselves cite the preservation of women's traditional clothing and ornamentation as vital to maintaining their culture.

The most famous part of this dress are the panels of intricately worked cloth that decorate the front and back of the woman's blouse. Known as *molas* (*mola* is Kuna for blouse), these panels are prized by collectors around the world. Older women in particular also wear gold rings through the bottoms of their noses and tight strings of beads around their forearms and lower legs.

The Kuna are physically striking in other ways. For one thing, by European standards they are short, growing to about 150 centimeters (five feet), but have what to outsiders seem to be disproportionately large heads and limbs. In spite of their short stature, basketball is the most popular sport on the islands. Kunas also have the highest rate of albinism in the world for reasons that are still not well understood. Known as "moon children," albinos are treated as special people but, sadly, have a shortened life expectancy because of their susceptibility to skin cancer. Why a people so close to the equator should have such a high rate of albinism has fascinated scientists for years.

The Kuna have always been wary of outsiders, and that's a major reason they still exist. One can have a relatively inexpensive stay in the San Blas Islands, but nothing is free; even taking a photo of a Kuna usually costs a dollar. The Kunas' reticence, and a belief that visitors should pay for the privilege of visiting their homeland, can be off-putting to those who come with stereotyped notions of fun-loving, generous people. It's not hard to see the Kunas' point of view, though. Outsiders have been trying to take their home away from them for centuries, and even visitors with more benign intentions often treat them as colorful parts of the scenery. One Kuna official I chatted with a few years back angrily recounted instances in which he felt Kunas were treated, at best, as so much travel-brochure fodder, concluding: *No somos animales* ("We are not animals").

Try to bear that in mind during your stay. At the very least, never take a photo of a Kuna without asking permission first. You'll probably find that if you're willing to accept the Kuna on their own terms, you'll get a glimpse of a fascinating world.

By Air

Most visitors come by small plane from Panama City, though the greatly improved road to Kuna Yala is taking away a lot of business from the flights to the westernmost islands. Flying on these tiny, sometimes aged-looking contraptions can be an adventure in itself, especially while crossing the coastal range. But on a clear day the views are breathtaking, and the flights are mercifully short.

Panama's two domestic airlines, **Aeroperlas** (tel. 315-7500, www.aeroperlas.com) and **Air Panama** (tel. 316-9000, www.flyairpanama.com), fly from Panama City to islands and coastal airstrips in the *comarca* (reservation). Each generally offers one daily, early-morning flight to and from the major island groups. The planes usually make several stops, so be careful to get off at the right place—on my last visit, a couple got off at the wrong place and spoiled their entire yacht trip. Nonstop flights to most destinations are around 30–45 minutes, but with stops they can last longer than an hour, not including delays.

For those staying at one of the island hotels, transportation by small boat between the closest airstrip and the hotel is included with a stay. There are no true airline offices in the archipelago, but hotels can sometimes make or change reservations for guests. However, it's best to come to the islands with a round-trip ticket and stick to the itinerary.

Airfare is the same on both airlines and is quite reasonable. However, rising fuel prices are making airfares go up faster than in the past. As this book went to press, the longest and most expensive flight cost about US$80 one way and took an hour of nonstop flying. That was to Puerto Obaldía, near the Colombian border. Only Air Panama currently makes that trip, and only on Tuesdays and Thursdays. The only travelers who go there are attempting to cross over into Colombia. (Warning: The conflict in Colombia has made Puerto Obaldía a dicey place, and visitors are being advised to stay well away from it.) Shorter flights cost proportionately less. The round-trip fare to all destinations is double the one-way fare.

By Land

Shortly before Lago Bayano is the **El Llano-Cartí Road,** which heads north over the Continental Divide and down into the Comarca de Kuna Yala. It is the only land access to the islands, and most of its 30-kilometer length was recently paved. However, as one approaches the Caribbean coast, vehicles must still ford a river and there can be washouts, particularly during the rainy season. There are also hairpin turns with sheer drops. Do not attempt this trip without a good four-wheel-drive vehicle with high clearance and, preferably, a winch.

I do not advise travelers to drive themselves. It is far better, and probably cheaper, to go with a Kuna transport service. These are informal affairs—usually just a guy with a four-wheel drive and a mobile phone—but they have experience on this road, will know its condition, and will be able to help with the logistics of getting into and around Kuna territory. They all charge US$25 per person each way from Panama City, which is a good deal. They typically pick up clients from their lodgings before dawn, usually around 4 or 5 A.M. The trip takes about three hours, including brief stops to admire the spectacular views.

I recommend booking transport through one of the Kuna hotels, a reputable hostel, or tour operator, as they send clients out all the time and will have the latest information on road conditions and reliable drivers. But travelers can also book directly with the Kuna family that does the lion's share of these trips. For information, call Alexis (cell 6528-5862) or Judy (cell 6706-2810).

Once you arrive at the shore, the Kuna "taxes" begin. Expect to pay at least US$6 "tourist tax" and US$2 "port tax" (the rate fluctuates), plus boat fare to whichever island you're going to if you're not being met by a boat from your hotel. Boat transport to the Islas Robinson, the most common backpacker destinations, is US$7.50 each way. In other words, total round-trip transportation costs per person from Panama City to the islands will cost at least US$75 per person; still cheaper than flying, but not as much as many initially think.

One advantage of going by road is you're not limited by the strict baggage-weight allowance of the small planes. Consider bringing a medium-sized cooler stocked with ice, food, snacks, and drinks—though concentrate on things that are safe and pleasant to consume at room temperature, because you won't find any ice on the islands. (The last real stores you're likely to encounter on the road are at 24 de Diciembre, on the eastern outskirts of Panama City, and they may not be open by the time you pass through in the morning.) Also, bring large jugs of water to limit having to buy bottled water on the islands.

For those who want—or need—to break their land journey, there is an appealing eco-lodge, **Burbayar Lodge,** (tel. 393-7340, cell 6674-2964, www.burbayar.com) up in the mountains along the El Llano–Cartí Road.

Tours

No formal tour operators are based on the islands. Visitors usually arrange tours and boat trips through their hotels, which offer a daily excursion in their standard packages. It's also easy to hire Kuna boatmen and guides, but almost none of them speak English, and some don't even speak much Spanish. Agree on a price and itinerary ahead of time.

Note that the prices listed here may rise, as the cost of tours is mainly driven by the cost of boat fuel. That also goes for lodging packages that include daily boat tours, which most do.

You may find it simpler to arrange a trip to the islands through a tour operator in Panama City, who will book the flights or land transport, make room reservations, and make sure a boatman's there to meet the plane.

El Porvenir and Vicinity

EL PORVENIR

The small island of El Porvenir is the western point of entry for the archipelago. It has a landing strip, a couple of government offices, and a basic hotel. There's also an **artisans' cooperative** that sells *molas* (handcrafted blouses) and other arts and crafts. The two-story yellow building housing the newish **Museo de la Nación Kuna** (Museum of the Kuna Nation) is on the far side of the island. I've yet to find it open, but it's supposed to have displays on Kuna art, history, and culture. There's little else on the island, but because it's isolated from the densely populated islands nearby, El Porvenir's little beach is clean and pleasant. For most people, though, this island is just a transit point.

◖ ACHUTUPU

Also known as **Isla de Los Perros** (Dog Island), Achutupu is a private island a short boat ride to the east that is inhabited only by a family of caretakers. Visitors must pay them a US$2 entrance fee. (Note: Don't confuse this Achutupu with the large, crowded island of the same name much farther east.) Everything about this pristine speck of sand and palm trees is straight out of a postcard. The water is calm and crystalline, with great snorkeling visibility. There's an old shipwreck in shallow water just off the south side of the island. It's overgrown with brilliant coral and has become a playground for a variety of small and medium-sized tropical fish.

Achutupu is surrounded by other lovely islands, with rustic Kuna sailboats and the occasional sleek foreign yacht gliding around them. If Achutupu isn't perfect enough, ask the boatman to do some more exploring.

◖ CARTÍ

South of the Porvenir area, about a 40-minute motorized boat ride away, is a cluster of islands and a bit of coast known collectively as Cartí (Gardi). There's a large, vibrant village on **Cartí Suitupu** (Gardi Sugdup), which makes it a popular cruise-ship destination. This place sees more foreigners than any other part of the archipelago, so it's perhaps not surprising it has an estimated two dozen bars/soda stands. There's an ultra-basic dormitory and three private rooms, **Cartí Homestay** (cell 6734-3454 Germain, in Panama City; or 6517-9850 Eulogio, in Cartí; US$35 pp, including meals and a boat trip), formerly known as Hostal Cartí, for those who get stranded going to or from the islands by the El Llano–Cartí Road or want to stay on a busy inhabited island with a relatively modern infrastructure. There is generator-powered electricity 6 P.M.–midnight. This place is growing in ambition with the influx of tourists coming by road. They can arrange road transportation to and from Pamama City (US$25 pp) and trips to Puerto Obaldía by cargo boat ($150 pp, but as I've stressed repeatedly, this is not a good idea for many reasons, mostly having to do with safety).

Especially noteworthy is a small **Kuna museum** (tel. 299-9002 or 299-9074, 8 A.M.–4 P.M. daily, US$2) housed in a thatch-roofed hut. It has its own dock, so small boats can go there directly. The displays are modest but include an interesting mix of traditional implements, exhibits on the Kuna puberty ritual (only girls go through this, and it's a huge, drunken party for the whole village), vintage *molas* (handcrafted blouses), and so on. It gives a glimpse into the mythology, history, rituals, and daily life of the Kuna. A Kuna man named José Davis, who established the museum along with his father, gives guided tours of the exhibits in English and Spanish, with lots of intricate and sometimes hard-to-follow explanations of Kuna history and religion. One of the more interesting tidbits is a description of Kuna burials. (The cemeteries are on the mainland, where the Kunas dig underground rooms and string them with hammocks into which the deceased are placed.)

Visitors are welcome to stop by the other

KUNA YALA

KUNA YALA IN COMFORT

© WILLIAM FRIAR

Coral Lodge, just outside the borders of Kuna Yala, offers the most comfortable accommodations in the region.

The best place to stay in Kuna Yala is not actually in Kuna Yala. **Coral Lodge** (tel. 232-0200, cell 6681-2360, lodge tel. 832-0795, www. corallodge.com, high-season rates US$295 s, US$430 d, including all meals and daily activity), which opened in 2006, is on a lovely cove on Escribano Point, right about where the province of Colón stops and Kuna Yala begins. It's accessible only by sea – in a powerful motorboat. It's about a 45-minute ride from El Porvenir or a half hour from Miramar, in Costa Arriba.

Accommodations consist of six "water villas" – spacious and comfortable modern bungalows over the water – that are linked by a boardwalk to a small half-moon beach. A larger beach is a short walk away. The bungalows have tall thatched ceilings, air-conditioning,

islands in the group as well, which are not quite as modernized or heavily touristed as Cartí Suitupu.

OTHER ISLANDS

Clustered just to the south of El Porvenir are Wichub-Huala (WITCH-ub WAH-la), Ukuptupu (ook-oop-TOO-puu), Nalunega (nah-loo-NEH-gah), and Isla Corbisky. All but Ukuptupu have villages. All have generator-powered electricity 6 P.M.–midnight, and it's much easier to find English speakers here than elsewhere in the archipelago. They are just a couple of minutes from each other by motorized boat.

Ukuptupu is entirely covered with a sprawling wooden complex connected by boardwalks that was the home of a Smithsonian Tropical Research Institute facility for 21 years. The Kuna, ever suspicious of foreigners in their *comarca* (reservation), finally kicked the researchers out of Kuna Yala in 1998. The research facility is now a rustic hotel. **Nalunega** is home to the Hotel San Blas, the oldest hotel in the archipelago. **Wichub-Huala** has the attractive Hotel Kuna Niskua, a health center, ceiling fans, excellent beds, simple but tasteful teak and rattan furnishings, and small sundecks. Spa bathtubs are in the bedroom right next to windows that look out on the ocean; showers are in the attached bathroom. All the bungalows are angled for maximum privacy, but number 6, at the end of the boardwalk, has the best unobstructed view – there's nothing in front of it but sea. (This may change if the planned two-bedroom suite is built at the end of the boardwalk.)

On the beach is a large swimming pool that's illuminated at night. Meals are served next door in a large modern dining room with a thatched roof, 20 meters above the tile floors. The lodge also has a couple of Internet computers and a little game room with a TV and DVD player. There's an open-air bar over the water. The chef is Peruvian.

Most guests fly into El Porvenir and travel to the lodge by boat. At the end of the trip, they go by boat to Miramar and return to Panama City by road. Factor in considerable extra expense for this. The lodge can provide some or all of the transfers, and this is the most seamless way to go. Transfers include a tour and snorkeling trip around El Porvenir on the way over and a visit to Portobelo on the way back, which is a good way to cover a lot of sightseeing ground.

Kayaks, snorkeling gear, and daily guided activities are included with stays. Possible activities range from forest hikes or horseback riding on the mainland to overnight stays in Kuna Yala. Scuba diving is extra. The Kunas do not allow diving in the *comarca* (reservation) itself, but there's a dive master at the lodge who can take guests to little-visited spots just outside Kuna territory. The Escribano reef, for instance, is just two kilometers away.

The American-Peruvian owner, who owns two well-regarded hotels in Peru, plans eventually to add 12 lower-cost accommodations on the beach for divers on a budget.

This is one of my favorite places in all of Panama, but it is not for everyone. The accommodations are luxurious enough to convince potential guests they're coming to a first-world resort where everything works perfectly. That's impossible out here; this is a remote spot surrounded by nothing but sea and tropical forest. The boat ride to and from the lodge can be bumpy when the wind picks up, and diving and fishing conditions can change without warning. The diving and fishing are best Easter–October, which is also the rainy season. And the *chitras* (sand flies) can be voracious when the wind dies, since there's a healthy mangrove system near the lodge. To be happy out here you have to be easy-going and have at least a slight sense of adventure. This is a great spot even during a thunderstorm; the view is gorgeous and the sound of rain falling on the thatch can induce blissful afternoon naps.

and a small community. A kiosk near the pier sells beer, water, soda, and other basic goods.

Isla Corbisky, sometimes spelled "Corbiski," offers a chance for visitors to live with a Kuna family.

ACCOMMODATIONS AND FOOD

Nearly all visitors fly into El Porvenir and stay at one of the basic hotels on the surrounding islands. Hotel stays generally include all meals, transfers to and from the airstrip on El Porvenir, and daily boat trips. These trips are generally to Achutupu or Cartí, but jungle hikes on the mainland or boat rides to the Cayos Limónes, Cayos Grullos, or the remote Cayos Holandéses are sometimes possible for an extra fee. Expect to pay at least US$150 per boat for a trip to the Holandéses.

The **Hotel San Blas** (cell 6538-1141 Karina I. Burgos, in Panama City; tel. 257-3310 or 257-3311; hotelsanblas@hotmail.com, US$50 pp, including all meals and a daily boat trip), on Nalunega, is the old stalwart among the archipelago's hotels. Sometimes known as Cabañas San Blas, it consists of 30 rooms

KUNA YALA

with shared bathrooms on the southern side of Nalunega. There are several kinds of accommodations here. The four huts right on the beach have sand floors and offer slightly more privacy, as they are a few centimeters away from their neighbors. If a breeze is more important than privacy, for the same price one can get a room in the large two-story building behind the huts. Be warned, though, that this is essentially a dormitory with cane dividers that don't reach all the way to the very tall thatch roof.

Meals are served in a large, unadorned cement-block dining room. A few more rooms are upstairs. The ones by the terrace have a view of the sea. Avoid the one right above the kitchen.

The hotel was started decades ago by Luis Burgos, a laid-back Kuna who speaks English and Spanish, and is still owned by the Burgos family.

The rest of the island is taken up by a village of about 450 inhabitants. One of the charms of this place is staying in such close proximity to the Kuna. There's a general store with basic supplies and several kiosks that sell sodas, cookies, beer, and such.

As with other Kuna villages, this one is none too clean, but the hotel staff rakes the sand around the hotel every day, ensuring its little patch is tidy (but not free of outhouses over the water). Rats are a fact of life on the islands, and they tend to make an appearance here more often than at some other Kuna hotels. I've never heard of anyone being bitten, but the rustling critters have been known to upset a good night's sleep.

[C] Hotel Kuna Niskua (tel. 259-3471 or 259-9136, cell 6709-4484 or 6537-3071, http://kuna-niskua.com, US$55 pp, based on double occupancy, including all meals and a daily boat tour, US$10 supplement for those traveling alone), on Wichub-Huala, is the most attractive of the simple hotels. It's still quite basic, but it's a tidy, well-cared-for place. The main building is concrete, but softened by intricately woven cane walls. More rooms are on the 2nd floor of a second building, which also

has a terrace strung with hammocks. There are 10 rooms with private bathrooms and 3 with shared ones. There's no difference in price. Per person rates are US$5 less with three people in a room, US$5 more for solo travelers. The rooms in the second building (also with shared bath) are darker and offer less privacy. Most have just a single window, so try to get the corner room overlooking the water; it has more windows.

Kuna Niskua recently completed a new place, **Kuna Niskua Isla Wailidup** (contact Kuna Niskua, bungalows start at US$125 pp first night, US$95 after first night, including all meals and a daily boat tour), a short boat ride to the east of Wichub-Huala. Also known as Waily Lodge, it's on pretty, uninhabited Wailydup (pronounced WHY-lee-doop), a sandy island just a few hundred meters long. It offers two rustic wood-floored, thatched-roofed cabins, each with a good double bed, private shower and flush toilet, and a little back porch overlooking the sea and nearby islands. There's electricity at night. The snorkeling around here is good. A sand-floored dining hall is nearby, and four more cabins are in the works. There's nothing else on the island. The one problem with this place is the abundance of *chitras* (sand flies): When I was there, a nice breeze was blowing and they weren't a problem, but I'm told that when the wind dies, they're ferocious.

Though the location is great, prices are steep for such a simple place. The owners plan to offer packages that combine stays here and at Kuna Niskua; they might be more economical. Those not staying here can visit for US$10 per person.

There are two reasons to stay at **Hotel Corbiski** (cell 6708-5254, 6703-8378, or 6682-0625, tel. 257-7189, Panama City tel. 257-7189, eliasperezmartinez@yahoo.com, www.corbiski.com, $55 pp, including all meals and a daily boat trip). The first is the owner, Elías Pérez. He's a warm, friendly guy who speaks Spanish and quite a bit of English and has a great deal of experience as a tour guide. (He works with Ancon Expeditions in the dry season; he's the island's schoolteacher the rest of the year.) He can sometimes offer special trips for an extra fee, including kayak expeditions and forest hikes on the mainland. The second is the chance to live close to a Kuna family in the heart of a Kuna community. When I last visited, the rooms were basic, even by the standard of Kuna accommodations, but new cane-walled rooms over the water have been built that at least have some charm and a bit more privacy, even if they are still quite rustic. There are now a total of 12 rooms. The proximity to a Kuna village is not for everyone. Other houses are crammed nearby, as are outhouses that empty into the sea. Elías works with the guys who run Cartí Homestay, so if you have trouble reaching them or want to stay at both places, get in touch with him. Elías can also arrange land transportation to and from Panama City. This place is also sometimes known as Hospedaje Corbiski, and as with the island, is sometimes spelled "Corbisky."

Note that, while this is a thriving Kuna community (a puberty ceremony was underway right next to the hotel when I visited), it's a fairly modern one; expect cinderblock buildings and electricity at night.

Cabañas Ukuptupu (cell 6746-5088 or 6744-7511, tel. 293-7893, 293-8709, or 299-9011, www.ukuptupu.com, US$55 pp, including all meals and a daily boat trip) is the only thing on the rocky island of Ukuptupu, nestled between Wichub-Huala and Nalunega. The hotel, which until 1998 was a Smithsonian research facility, consists of 15 basic, but spacious, cane-and-wood rooms over shallow water, connected to each other by boardwalks. Because it's very easy to walk off the boardwalks into the ocean, this is not a place to bring small children. The hotel completely covers the tiny island, so it's more private and isolated than the other hotels in this region, without the pros and cons of sharing an island with a Kuna village. Service was pretty disorganized when I last visited. Beds consist of foam mattresses in a wooden frame. Bathrooms are shared but have flush toilets. Guests take bucket baths from barrels filled with rainwater. There's an open-air bar and a little library with battered books.

The hotel has good views of the ocean and the surrounding inhabited islands. Hammocks are strung up around the place, which tends to get a nice breeze. An underwater rock corral houses the lobsters, crab, and other sea creatures guests may be offered for dinner. The elderly owner, Juan García, worked in a U.S. military mess hall for five years and speaks fluent English.

The **Hotel Kikirdub** (tel. 396-1223, cell 6048-3358 or 6673-8767, www.hotelkikirdub.com, US$100 pp, including all meals and daily boat trip), on a tiny islet between El Porvenir and nearby Wichub-Huala, is the first lodging in the archipelago with truly modern infrastructure. It can sleep up to 10 people in four rooms, with more on the way. Some of the rooms are in the house, but the nicest and most private one has a separate entrance with a hammock-strung terrace. All the rooms have dark wood floors and paneling, modern bathrooms, and thin mattresses. There's electricity 6 P.M.–6 A.M.

This is the home of Enrique Garrido, formerly the president, and still a member, of Panama's general assembly. He flies home on the weekends. Though the house is modern, traditional Kuna ways are much in evidence: When I visited, a Kuna granny was on the back porch, snoozing in a hammock. There is no beach on the island, which is not much bigger than the house itself, and the only other things on it are a thatched-roofed kitchen and bar and an artificial pond with turtles and other wild creatures. The staff is friendly. The hotel also offers day trips from Panama City, including all land and boat transport, for US$120, minimum six people, though why anyone would want to make such a long trip without staying at least one night is a mystery to me.

If all accommodations are full, the 13-room **Hotel El Porvenir** (cell 6692-3542 or 6718-2826, Panama City tel. 221-1397, 262-9922, or 292-4543, http://hotelporvenir.com, US$50 pp, including all meals and a daily boat tour) may have to do. Rooms here are drab, dark, and run-down, and they have worn mattresses and zero charm. The staff is friendly, though, and there are toilets and showers in

KUNA YALA

the rooms, though they're not especially clean. As the name suggests, the hotel is on the island of El Porvenir, which is also home to the area's airstrip and some small government offices. There's nothing else on the island, which means you'll have plenty of peace and quiet—at least until an airplane lands, since the hotel is almost on the airstrip. The little beach here is pleasant, and the water seems much cleaner than that surrounding the crowded islands nearby. But you'll likely feel quite isolated.

GETTING THERE

The "traditional" way to get to this area is to fly into El Porvenir and transfer to the surrounding islands. Flights from Panama City to El Porvenir cost US$59 each way. Air Panama has a daily flight that leaves from Albrook around 6 A.M. Sunday, Monday, Wednesday, and Friday. Return flights leave El Porvenir at 6:55 A.M. Monday, Wednesday, and Friday. Flights often stop on Cartí on the way over or back. The flight takes as little as 25 minutes or as much as an hour, depending on the number of stops. Aeroperlas does not currently list El Porvenir flights, which suggests that the El Llano–Cartí Road is hurting business. This is the easiest and most economical part of the archipelago to get to by the land route.

Río Sidra and Vicinity

RÍO SIDRA

Río Sidra is a densely packed island of about 2,000 inhabitants that has seen more and more visitors in recent years thanks to a growing range of accommodations in the area.

Río Sidra actually comprises two communities, **Mamartupo** and **Urgandí,** that have distinctive identities. The school is the unofficial dividing line between the two. Mamartupo faces the sea; Urgandí faces the land. It's quite crowded, with huts packed tightly together over the entire surface of the island. Some of the inhabitants sport modern clothing; it's jarring to see a teenage Kuna kid in gangsta-inspired street wear.

KUANIDUP

Kuanidup is a gorgeous private island a half hour away by motorized boat from Río Sidra. Actually, there are two Kuanidups. The first is Kuanidup Grande, which is home just to Cabañas Kuanidup, a sandy beach, a sand volleyball court, and hammocks strung between coconut palms. About the same size as tiny Isla Robinson, it's *"grande"* only in comparison to its little sister, Kuanidup Chico. There's nothing but a single hut, sand, and palm trees on Kuanidup Chico, which is an easy swim away (maybe 300 meters) for a moderately fit swimmer. The hotel staff on Kuanidup Grande can also ferry guests over. Nonguests should ask permission to visit either island; expect to pay a fee.

There's pretty good snorkeling around the islands. It's fun to circumnavigate Kuanidup Chico and explore the coral shelf that rings the island; it has surprisingly diverse coral species. Take it slow and really check things out: There are lots of small, hidden natural treasures. Watch out for sea urchins, fire coral, and sudden shallows. Visibility plummets after a rain because of the proximity to mainland rivers.

◖ ISLA MAQUINA

One island well worth a visit is Isla Maquina (**Mormarketupo** in Kuna), about a 10-minute boat ride from Río Sidra. It's the quietest and most purely traditional of the islands in the region and one of the most traditional in the archipelago. It's known for its *mola* (hand-crafted blouse) makers. Huts aren't as squashed together, and it's quite tidy and significantly cleaner than other islands. It has a school and an aqueduct, but very little else in the way of facilities—no hotel, no health center. It's pleasant to wander around the narrow paths lined with cane fences that border homes. There are a few places to buy sodas and snacks.

THE ART OF THE *MOLA*

Mola sales are an important source of income for the Kuna.

Molas (handcrafted blouses) are made from several layers of brightly colored cotton cloth. Kuna women create these works of art using a technique of cutting and sewing sometimes referred to as reverse appliqué. The way the cloth is cut reveals the layers beneath, which all go into creating the overall design. Designs can be abstract or representational. The best designs are such works of art that *mola*-making has been described as painting with a needle.

What should you look for in a *mola*? Anthropologist Mari Lyn Salvador conducted a study in which she asked Kuna women themselves that question. A few of her findings:

- The design should be balanced and all the spaces filled.

- The lines should be thin and evenly spaced, with smooth edges.

- Stitches should be small, even, and nearly invisible.

- The design should stand out and be easy to see, which is largely a matter of the proper use of contrast and color.

For more information on Kuna arts and culture, see *The Art of Being Kuna: Layers of Meaning Among the Kuna of Panama* (UCLA Fowler Museum of Cultural History), edited by Mari Lyn Salvador.

OTHER ISLANDS

Other islands in the area include **Nusatupo (Isla Ratón),** a populated island next to Río Sidra, and the small, private **Islas Robinson,** between Río Sidra and Kuanidup.

ACCOMMODATIONS AND FOOD

There are a few basic places to stay on and around Río Sidra, but the most appealing options are on uninhabited islands farther out to sea. As usual, hotel stays generally include all meals and daily boat tours, though room-only options are available. Typical tours go to Achutupu (the uninhabited one with the shipwreck, not the one farther down the archipelago) or Río Sidra. With at least one day's notice and permission from local authorities, it's possible to visit a mainland cemetery. This requires a guide, which will probably be an extra fee. Visitors are not allowed to take photos at the cemetery.

Thanks to the El Llano–Cartí Road, the cheaper accommodations in this area are surging in popularity with backpackers and more-adventurous Panamanians. They are scattered among a few small private islands known collectively as the **Islas Robinson**—piggybacking on the success of the pioneering backpacker cabins that went by that name. Names, contact information, quality, and lifespan of accommodations are more in flux here than anywhere else in the islands, and it's likely to be a while before everything shakes out.

Visitors can normally expect to pay around US$25 for private rooms, meals, and one boat tour. Dorm rooms usually go for around US$5 less and may not include the tour. Camping is sometimes available for around US$15, including meals. Typical accommodations are cane-walled, thatched-roof huts with hammocks and sand floors on an island with an outhouse over the water, a communal outdoor shower, a common sitting/dining area, spectacular views, and nothing else. These are places for those who don't need much more than a rustic shelter from the elements.

If all this sounds appealing, the best way to ensure a decent place to stay is to go through a

KUNA YALA

Panama City hostel. (I've given up listing contact numbers; they always change by the time the book is out.) Usually this service is only available to guests, but **Luna's Castle** (Calle 9 Este and Avenida Eloy Alfaro, Panama City, tel. 262-1540, http://lunascastle.com) may be willing to book the land transfer and trip to the islands for nonguests: Go by or give them a call. They also try hard to keep current with what the islands are offering, and they get reports back from the many guests they send out there. Try not to go during national holidays in Panama, as these places can fill up. In fact, if possible you might want to try to keep your plans loose; the lodgings are close enough together that for a few dollars you can survey several and choose the one that looks most appealing when you arrive, or perhaps transfer to after the first night. Expect to pay at least US7.50 each way for the boat trip from Cartí to these islands, or twice that for boats to or from the El Porvenir airstrip.

The best place to stay in the region, ◖ **Cabañas Kuanidup** (cell 6635-6737 or 6656-4673, http://kuanidup.8k.com, US$95 pp, including meals and daily boat tour) is a good bet for those who want the beauty of a remote island without spending a fortune for the privilege of living simply. The location is gorgeous. Because the nearest sizable settlement is a half-hour boat ride away, the sea here is clean and the beaches free of trash. There are 10 cabañas with foam mattresses, sand floors, and the usual thatched roofs and cane walls. They are spaced a few feet away from each other to offer a bit of privacy. Accommodations vary from a small cabaña with a double bed to a couple of large ones with four single beds. The cabañas are rustic but comfortable. There are shared toilets and showers with very weak water pressure in a separate hut and a small open-sided dining room on the opposite end of the island. Guests can buy beer, wine, water, and *seco* at a little bar area. Lights in the dining room are powered by solar panels, but the cabañas are lit only by kerosene lanterns. The standard package includes daily boat trips to tour Río Sidra or snorkel and laze around Achutupu. The only other entertainment will be looking at the blue ocean, the occasional small fishing boat, and the islands off in the distance. You have to be truly in the mood to get away from everything to come here.

GETTING THERE

Río Sidra is about an hour from the Porvenir/Cartí area by motorized boat. Río Sidra has a well-established airstrip, but neither domestic airline is currently listing flights there. The El Llano–Cartí Road appears to be to blame, as most tourist traffic consists of backpackers heading to the Islas Robinson, and most of these are taking the land route to Cartí and then going by boat to their island of choice. The airlines frequently add and drop routes, however, and it's always worth giving them a call because planes will sometimes make unscheduled stops if there is enough demand. Note that the Río Sidra airstrip is actually on the mainland coast rather than the island itself.

Corazón de Jesús and Narganá

Another hub of island life lies about 40 kilometers east of El Porvenir, centered around the inhabited islands of Corazón de Jesús and Narganá (pop. 12,685), which are linked by a footbridge. These are the least traditional islands in the archipelago. There are more concrete buildings than thatch-roofed huts, and most younger women do not wear traditional clothing. There's electricity around the clock, and at night residents gather in the homes and stores of those with TVs to watch shows, with great enthusiasm.

These islands are unlikely to interest most travelers. Since the closing a few years back of the Kwadule Eco-Lodge, once the archipelago's most upscale hotel, there is no appealing place to stay here. Only those who've spent a great deal of time on the more traditional islands are likely to find these more modern and less colorful ones of great interest, and only then for the contrast they provide.

The more southerly island, Narganá, has the archipelago's one true bank, a small branch of the Banco Nacional de Panamá. The central square has a statue of Charles Robinson, a pivotal figure in Kuna Yala's 1925 war against Panama. Public phones are at the side of the square, and a hospital, school, church, and police station are nearby. It also has the best place to eat and the only hotel. With quite a bit of humor, residents have named the "barrios" of this small island after those in Panama City—the vicinity of the lone bank thus becomes the *area bancaria* (banking area), the posher homes are in "Paitilla," the poorer ones are in "Chorrillo," the main walkway is "Avenida Central," and so on.

Corazón de Jesús is across a short footbridge (watch for loose planks) on the seaward-facing side of the island. It has the airstrip, a simple restaurant, a pool hall, and little else.

Isla Tigre, also called Río Tigre, is a few kilometers east. A visit to the traditional Kuna community here is the most common day trip for visitors.

PRACTICALITIES

The only hotel on either island is **Hotel Noris** (public phones tel. 299-9009 or 299-9090, US$10 s, US$15 d with fan; US$15 s, US$20 d with a/c), a pink, two-story concrete building facing the mainland that has seven spartan but okay rooms. Some have air-conditioning and private toilets and showers; the rest are more basic, with fans and shared baths. Room 1 is the nicest. The location isn't very nice, however—it's right on a somewhat swampy shore that smells of sewage. Boat rides to a nearby beach are US$5 per person; trips to Isla Tigre are US$15. Meals can also be arranged. Laundry is US$3 a load. Call one of the public phones and ask for Paco, the half-Kuna, half-Spanish owner of the place.

Restaurante Nali's Café (6:30 A.M.–10:30 P.M. daily) is the nicest place to eat on either island. A full seafood meal costs no more than US$4, and the food is both good and nicely presented. More basic dinners cost US$2.50. Breakfast offerings include eggs, ham, and sausage. Diners, if they want, can rent a film at the café and watch it on the TV inside. But most will probably prefer to sit in the open-air area, which is right on the beach overlooking the channel between Narganá and Corazón de Jesús.

A couple of *minisupers* in town carry basic supplies. There's a pleasant-looking *fonda* (tavern) just after the bridge over on Corazón de Jesús. It's next to the pool hall, **Billar Akuanusa**, which can look intimidating from the outside but is actually a friendly place to have a beer and knock balls around.

Narganá has a small branch of the **Banco Nacional de Panamá** (8 A.M.–2 P.M. Mon.–Fri., 9 A.M.–noon Sat.). It has no ATM, but it does cash travelers checks.

It takes about 2.5 hours by motorized *cayuco* (dugout canoe) to reach these islands from El Porvenir. Unless you've got a yacht, it's much more practical to come by plane. The airstrip is on Corazón de Jesús. Air Panama has daily flights that leave Panama City at 6 A.M. on Monday, Wednesday, and Friday. The return flight leaves around 6:45 A.M. Airfare is US$61 each way. The flight takes about 35 minutes if it's nonstop and can last longer than an hour if not.

Playon Chico and Vicinity

PLAYON CHICO

Playon Chico (Ukupseni in Kuna) is a fairly large, somewhat bedraggled village island of about 3,000 inhabitants. It's a relatively modern community with a two-story health center, the churches and missionaries of a half dozen religions, some houses made of concrete, and even a group of allegedly drug-dealing teens who hang out in a graffiti-covered "youth hall." But there are still lots of traditional huts and traditional ways. Though none too tidy, Playon Chico is full of life, and it's fascinating to walk down the main drag and watch kids romping, a father playing a flute for his children, local dancers practicing for a festival, women sewing *molas* (handcrafted blouses) and old men playing dominoes. A concrete footbridge connects the island with an airstrip on the mainland.

ISLA IGUANA

Isla Iguana (Arridup) is a private island 20 minutes by boat from the hotel island Sapibenega. It's cared for by the hotel, whose staff rakes the sand and clears debris and trash to make it appealing for guests. It's a nice place to hang out on the beach by a coconut palm and look at the sea or the forest-covered mountains, but the snorkeling isn't good. The coral has been decimated, the water is often turbulent and cloudy, especially after a rain, and the fish are scarce.

OTHER ISLANDS

There are two hotel islands, **Sapibenega** and **Yandup,** a few minutes' boat ride away from Playon Chico.

There are other islands nearby, both uninhabited and with traditional villages, that can be visited with guides. Trips to the nearby cemetery or a waterfall on the mainland can also be arranged, as can more ambitious forest hikes.

ACCOMMODATIONS AND FOOD

There are few facilities, no hotels, and no appealing places to eat on Playon Chico. Visitors generally stay on one of the two hotel islands.

《 Yandup (tel. 394-1408 or 394-1409, cell 6579-2911, www.yandupisland.com, starts at US$100 pp, including meals and daily tour), a small island about five minutes by boat from Playon Chico, offers five bungalows over the water with wooden floors, bamboo walls, decent mattresses, private bathroom, mosquito nets, and wraparound porches overlooking the sea. There are two other bungalows on the edge of the water with private bathrooms, and one smaller cabin with a shared bathroom. There's an open-air dining room. This place was significantly upgraded a few years ago and now features some of the most spacious and comfortable accommodations on the islands (though, as always, they're still quite simple). The main problem is it's near a mangrove forest, and the *chitras* (sand flies) can be a serious nuisance. Over-the-water bungalows cost US$5 more per person, and it's worth it. There's also a one-time payment of US$10 per person "community tax" just to set foot on the island.

《 Sapibenega: The Kuna Lodge (tel. 215-1406 or 215-3724, Skype: sapibenega.s.a, www.sapibenega.com, US$254 s, US$336 d, US$394 t, two-night minimum, including all meals and two daily boat tours; there are discounts for children), just a few minutes by boat from Playon Chico, has some of the best accommodations and service in Kuna Yala. Formerly known as Iskardup, it's a small island with nothing much on it but guest cabins, each of which has two units. Most have double beds, but some can accommodate three or four people in each unit. The cabins are spacious, with wooden floors, cane walls, comfortable beds, flush toilets, ceiling fans, and tiled showers with hot water and good water pressure. All look out on the sea, and hammocks are strung up just outside the back doors, on the edge of the water. Like everyplace else in Kuna Yala, though, accommodations are still rustic and close to nature. Don't be surprised to find small crabs in the shower or geckos hiding in the soap dish.

Sapibenega has an attractive dining room, a bar, and a lounge area with rough-hewn furniture inside a large thatched-roof building with high ceilings and open sides. Another bar is in a little *rancho* set on pilings above the water, connected by a walkway with the island. There is electricity 24 hours a day, supplied by solar cells and a generator. Food here can be good, and tiki torches are set up on the grounds at night so guests can dine under the stars. The island is within hailing distance of the shore, but far enough away from everything to feel remote and tranquil.

However, Sapibenega seems to be on a downswing these days. Some clients have complained of poor service, lack of water, mediocre food and small portions, and of being "nickeled and dimed" for extras. It's difficult to maintain a high standard in Kuna Yala, but at these prices clients have a right to expect it.

GETTING THERE AND AWAY

Playon Chico is far down the archipelago, and most people arrive and leave by airplane. The airstrip is on the mainland, connected by a footbridge with Playon Chico. Air Panama and Aeroperlas have daily flights that leave Panama City at 6 A.M. and 6:35 A.M., respectively. They return from Playon Chico around 7 A.M. (Air Panama) and 7:15 A.M. (Aeroperlas). The fare is US$66 each way. The flight takes about 45 minutes nonstop, or nearly 90 minutes with lots of puddle-jumping.

Mamitupu, Achutupu, and Vicinity

Quite a bit farther south and east down the archipelago, less than 100 kilometers from the Colombian border, is yet another island cluster with several inhabited, fairly traditional islands and a number of small, uninhabited private islands. The former include Mamitupu, Achutupu, and, farther away, Ailigandí.

Don't confuse the Achutupu here with the little snorkeling spot near El Porvenir. This one is a densely inhabited island, in the middle of which is a huge gathering house. These long thatch-roofed buildings are the center of community life in Kuna villages. If you're lucky, a puberty ceremony or community meeting will be taking place on the island during your stay. If you're very lucky, you'll be allowed to observe some of it.

Immediately to the east of Achutupu, about a minute away by boat, is **Uaguitupu,** also known as Dolphin Island. About half the island is taken up by Kuna huts, while the other half is home to the long-established Dolphin Island Lodge, also known as Uaguinega. The island is pretty and offers tranquil views. However, it doesn't offer much in the way of a beach. This is primarily a place to collapse in a hammock for hours on end, and for that it's just about perfect. There are two newer places to stay in the area, Akwadup Lodge and Dad Ibe Lodge, adding to the sense of this area as a center for relatively upscale lodging. Each is

KUNA YALA

© BONNIE KAY SPINDLER

hanging on the dock at Mamitupu

on a private island a short boat ride away from the mainland.

About 20 minutes north of these islands are a series of coral heads. If the sea is calm and the visibility good, the snorkeling here is okay. Sadly, though, intensive fishing in the area makes it unlikely you'll see much besides tiny fish. In fact, I've found the snorkeling in this densely populated part of the archipelago to be disappointing in general. The area's charm comes from the beauty and peace of the surroundings and the proximity to more-or-less traditional inhabited islands.

Other tour possibilities include trips to the nearby inhabited islands of **Ailigandí** or **Mamitupu,** forest hikes, and a tour of a Kuna cemetery. Several tours to more distant locations are available for an extra fee.

ACCOMMODATIONS AND FOOD

Uaguinega Ecoresort, also known as ◖ **Dolphin Island Lodge** (tel. 263-7780 or 263-1500, www. uaguinega.com, starts at US$180 s, US$280 d, US$375 t, including all meals and a daily boat trip), is in some ways a good blend of the other accommodations in the archipelago. It offers seclusion and comfortable accommodations, yet there's an interesting Kuna village just minutes away on Achutupu. The only thing on Uaguitupu (Dolphin Island, pronounced "wah-ghee-TOO-poo") is the lodge and quarters for the staff. The lodge's name, Uaguinega (WAH-ghee-NEH-guh), literally means "dolphin house." It consists of large, attractive, and comfortable bungalows and a common dining area. The bungalows have hardwood floors, cold-water showers, sinks, and toilets. Most have a back porch right on the water, where you can lie in a hammock or write postcards at a little table. Uaguinega has the distinction of being the first hotel in the archipelago to offer its guests satellite Internet access. Some may hope this experiment fails, as one of the delights of Kuna Yala is feeling entirely cut off from the rest of the world.

The open-air dining room is on the northern edge of the island, looking out on open sea.

The lodge is owned and run by a Kuna family

called the de la Ossas, and service is personal and friendly. One of the sons, Horacio, learned English during a three-month visit to the hippie enclave of Bolinas in Northern California, which he found a fascinating anthropological experience. (He thought it was *muy interesante* that there are 60-year-old North American women who smoke marijuana.)

The owners of Uaguinega have opened a somewhat more upscale sister hotel, **Akwadup Lodge** (tel. 396-4805 or 396-4806, cell 6105-9441, www.uaguinega.com, US$199 s, US$350 d, US$450 t, including meals and daily boat tour). It's on the small island of Akwadup (OCK-wah-doop), about a 10-minute boat ride away from Achutupu. This one consists of half a dozen thatched-roof, wooden-floored cabins on pilings right over the ocean. Each has mosquito netting, a ceiling fan, a terrace with hammocks, private bathrooms, and 24-hour electricity. There is also a bar/dining room. Rates drop around US$25 per person after the first night, depending on group size.

The newish **Dad Ibe Lodge** (cell 612205448 or 6784-5978, www.dadibelodge.com, US$110 s, US$180 d, US$240 t, including all meals and a daily boat tour; there's a one-time charge of US$10 for first night) consists of three substantial cane-walled, thatched-roof cabins on a small private island about 10 minutes by boat from Ailigandí. Dad Ibe (dodd-EE-bay) appears similar to the other "upscale" accommodations in the archipelago: relatively comfortable but still basic cabins on a small private island. Cabins are over the water, with balconies and private bathrooms with flush toilets. There's an open-air dining room above the water. Those enticed to the place by promises of such things as "decorator-appointed luxury beachfront cabins" will likely be disappointed; some have been. Tour possibilities include two nearby uninhabited islands with beaches and a visit to the village on Ailigandí or the mangroves around it.

GETTING THERE AND AWAY

This section of the archipelago is quite a hike from more commonly visited areas, and distances are much too great to take a small boat from any of them. There are airstrips at both Mamitupu and Achutupu; if your hotel is meeting you, be sure to agree which airstrip you should use. Aeroperlas flies to Mamitupu (sometimes spelled Mamitupo) on Monday, Wednesday, and Friday and to Achutupu on Tuesday, Thursday, Saturday, and Sunday. Flights leave Panama City around 6 A.M. to either destination and return at about 7:55 A.M. Air Panama flies to Mamitupu on Tuesday, Thursday, and Friday. Flights leave Panama City around 6 A.M. and return at about 6:55 A.M. Air Panama does not currently have scheduled flights to Achutupu. The flight takes around an hour and airfare is US$68.27 each way to either place. Destinations are confusing down here; make sure you get off at the right place.

The Uninhabited Cays

The loveliest and most unspoiled islands in the archipelago are fairly remote, and they can be difficult to visit unless one has access to a yacht. There are no accommodations on these remote cays.

◖ CAYOS HOLANDÉSES

The Cayos Holandéses are the best known of the many gorgeous uninhabited and lightly populated islands toward the western end of the archipelago. They are 15 kilometers north of the mainland, farther offshore than any others in the archipelago. Yachts like to hang out here, as do snorkelers. The coral in some areas is beautiful, though even out here the waters have been overfished and the coral damaged.

To the west of the Holandéses, and closer

THE SPIRIT OF THE UAGA

All things come from Mother Earth. Nothing exists that is more necessary than she is. Without her, life is not possible. Our ancestors fought for her because they recognized her value. "I am nothing without the earth. I would be poor without her," so they said....

We always left medicinal plants in the fields when we cleared and cut trees. The elders give us advice about how to take care of useful plants. Therefore, in Kuna Yala we still have forests. The foreigners don't do this. They thoughtlessly destroy nature for their livestock.

The jungle and the forests provide us with meat, as well as wines, poles, and medicinal plants. In them lie our history and our culture. We know that Europeans don't have the same resources because their scientists come to the comarca (reservation) to see what is in our forests. I want it to stay this way, but I'm afraid that one of them will arrive with a chainsaw.

The lobster traders are responsible for the deterioration of our main resources – only for the money. Even if we want to control the fishing of lobsters, we won't succeed, because the young people who are involved in this activity are making their living from it.

Our tradition of working together no longer exists. Once, when a decision was made to address a problem, everyone complied unanimously. Now they follow money. We are acquiring the spirit of the uaga (foreigner, outsider).

Once everything is evaluated in terms of money, it changes one's way of being, it makes one selfish. So said our forefathers. Thus we are beginning to deceive our forefathers. That's what I think.

From "The Spirit of the Uaga" by Cacique General Carlos López, recorded by Valerio Núñez from Plants and Animals in the Life of the Kuna, *by Jorge Ventocilla, Heraclio Herrera, Valerio Núñez, edited by Hans Roeder, translated by Elisabeth King, 1995. Courtesy of the University of Texas Press.*

to the Porvenir area, are the also lovely **Cayos Chichime,** the **Cayos Limónes,** and, farther south, the **Cayos Los Grullos.**

◖ CAYOS COCO BANDERO

About 40 minutes east of the Holandéses by large motorboat (the smallest thing one should be in this far out) are the Cayos Coco Bandero (**Ordupuquip** in Kuna). It's a pristine group of more than a half dozen islets that's rarely visited by anyone other than yachties. It's stunningly beautiful out here. A Spanish galleon supposedly sank around this area, but neither the ship nor the gold have ever been found. There's also a modern-day wreck, a cargo ship, that's lodged upright on the nearby reef. It makes for quite a haunting sight. The waters are calm, protected by the same reef that snagged the ship, making it an appealing spot for snorkelers.

GETTING THERE AND AROUND

The Cayos Holandéses are accessible by boat from the Porvenir, Río Sidra, and the Corazón de Jesús/Narganá areas, but it's quite a haul on open sea that can turn rough. Coco Bandero is much closer to Corazón de Jesús/Narganá. No hotels offer a visit to the more distant of these island groups as part of their standard packages, but they may be able to arrange a trip for an extra fee. Do not attempt the trip without a life jacket. Most visitors will be content with exploring islands closer to where they're staying.

The cost of a boat trip obviously depends on where you're coming from and how many islands you want to explore. From El Porvenir, for instance, the trip to the Cayos Holandéses is several hundred dollars. For those who can afford it, a far better way to explore this area is by private yacht.

THE DARIÉN

The Darién: It's a name filled with magic.

In many people's minds the magic is of a dark and sinister kind. The Darién has historically been seen as a foreboding, dangerous place, a Conradian wilderness into which explorers venture, never to return. But the Darién is magical in many more positive ways as well. It is one of planet Earth's last great bastions of pristine tropical nature. Its biodiversity is so incredible it's been named both a World Biosphere Reserve and a Natural World Heritage Site by UNESCO.

The province of Darién is, at 16,671 square kilometers, by far the largest in Panama. It's extremely sparsely inhabited; only 40,000 people live in the entire province. Parque Nacional Darién alone is enormous, covering 579,000 hectares of wilderness that sprawl across the isthmus near the Colombian border. It contains the most extensive lowland tropical forest left along Central America's Pacific coast. Balboa stepped out of this forest in 1513 and became the first European to set eyes on the "South Sea."

The great attraction of the Darién is its magnificent forests and the incredible biodiversity they contain. Hiking, trekking, and bird-watching are what draw most nature tourists. But there are a couple of places along the coast of the Darién with accessible beaches and coral reefs. And the waters off Piñas Bay offer world-class deep-sea fishing.

What's commonly thought of as "the Darién" extends beyond Darién province itself. It encompasses all of eastern Panama except the islands of Kuna Yala.

The part of the Darién of most interest to

© WILLIAM FRIAR

HIGHLIGHTS

◖ **Santa Cruz de Cana:** Cana is the most remote part of Panama, and one of the most beautiful, with extensive trails through pristine foothills, up to a cool cloud forest, and around the jungle-choked remains of an old mining camp. It's also one of the world's top birding destinations (page 458).

◖ **Pirre Station:** This is a relatively accessible entrance to the fabled Parque Nacional Darién, Central America's grandest tropical forest (page 460).

◖ **Punta Patiño Nature Reserve:** Patiño

is the largest private nature reserve in the country, and the most comfortable place from which to visit the coast and rivers bordering the Golfo de San Miguel (page 462).

◖ **Mogue:** This is the best bet for those who'd like to spend the night in an Emberá village (page 467).

◖ **Bahía de Piñas:** Considered by many the best deep-sea fishing destination on the planet, the Piñas area also has stunning forests, colorful villages, and the only luxury hotel in the Darién (page 469).

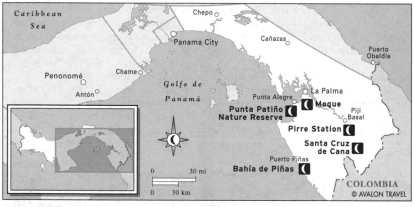

LOOK FOR ◖ TO FIND RECOMMENDED SIGHTS, ACTIVITIES, DINING, AND LODGING.

visitors lies toward the southeast section of the province, where there are no roads. The only way to get around here is by plane, boat, and foot. This contains the most accessible entry points into Parque Nacional Darién.

Two of the best spots in the park are Cana, on the east side of 1,615-meter-high Cerro Pirre, and Pirre Station, on its west side. These are right in the middle of barely inhabited tropical forest. Cana, the most remote point in Panama, is especially impressive.

The most popular coastal areas are Punta Patiño, on the Golfo de San Miguel, and the Bahía de Piñas, farther down the coast near

the Colombian border. Those looking for a trip up a Darién river usually find themselves on the Sambú, Mogue, Balsas, Pirre, or Tuira, though innumerable others crisscross this part of the Darién.

For every tree in the forest there's a saying about the Darién. My favorite, and one likely to resonate with any visitor, is this: Though many have come before you, you'll feel as though you're the first to enter the Darién.

HISTORY

The earliest known inhabitants of the Darién were the Cuevas, who were wiped out by the

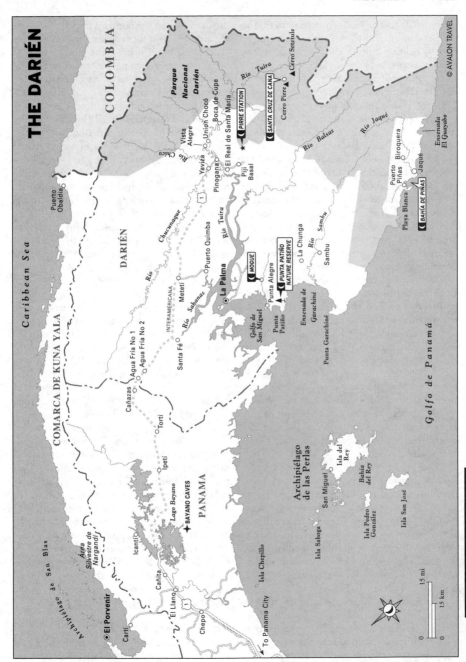

THE DARIÉN

Caribbean Sea

COLOMBIA

ARCHIPIÉLAGO de San Blas

COMARCA DE KUNA YALA

Área Silvestre de Nargandí

Puerto Obaldía

Parque Nacional Darién

DARIÉN

Río Chico

Río Tuira

Cerro Setetule

Río Tuira

Boca de Cupe

Unión Chocó

Vista Alegre

El Real de Santa María

★ PIRRE STATION

SANTA CRUZ DE CANA

Cerro Pirre

Yaviza

Pinogana

Piji Basal

Río Balsas

Río Jaqué

Ensenada El Guayabo

Puerto Piñas

Biroquera

Jaqué

BAHÍA DE PIÑAS

Playa Blanca

Río Chucunaque

Puerto Quimba

Río Tuira

Río

INTERAMERICANA

Río Sabanas

Meteti

MOGUE

La Palma

Punta Alegre

PUNTA PATIÑO NATURE RESERVE

Punta Patiño

Golfo de San Miguel

La Chunga

Río Sambu

Sambu

Ensenada de Garachiné

Punta Garachiné

Santa Fé

Agua Fría No 1

Agua Fría No 2

Cañazas

Torti

Ipeti

Icanti

Cañita

El Llano

Chepo

BAYANO CAVES

Lago Bayano

PANAMA

Archipiélago de las Perlas

Isla Chepillo

Isla Saboga

San Miguel

Isla del Rey

Bahía del Rey

Isla Pedro González

Isla San José

Golfo de Panamá

To Panama City

El Porvenir

Carti

15 mi

15 km

0

0

© AVALON TRAVEL

THE DARIÉN

conquistadors. The Kunas moved in to fill the void and managed to resist the Spanish, in part by helping English and French pirates in their constant raids against the Spanish forts, towns, and gold mines. Many of the rivers in the Darién still bear Kuna names.

In the 18th century, a new group of indigenous peoples, traditional enemies of the Kuna, moved into the region. Once known collectively as the Chocó, because they came from the Chocó region of Colombia, they were actually two linguistically distinct but culturally similar peoples, the Emberá and the Wounaan. They spoke the same language an estimated 3,000 years ago and a third of their vocabulary still overlaps. But their languages have grown so far apart that today the Emberá and Wounaan speak Spanish when they want to communicate with each other.

Centuries of conflict with the Spanish, Emberá-Wounaan, and so-called "Afro-Colonials" pushed the Kuna north toward the Caribbean coasts and islands, though some traditional-minded Kuna still live in the Darién. The Emberá-Wounaan triumphed in their wars, some believe, because of superior war technology: They, unlike the Kuna, knew how to use blowgun darts tipped with the toxin from the tiny golden poison frog *(Phyllobates terribilis)*. It's the most lethal poison of any known land animal; the toxin on the skin of a single frog is said to be powerful enough to kill 100 adult humans.

There are an estimated 22,000 Emberá and 7,000 Wounaan in Panama, though some place their numbers at just half that. Most still live in the Darién, generally along rivers that flow into the Golfo de San Miguel. Other villages are inhabited by Afro-Colonials, the descendants of African slaves who escaped from the Spanish. They are also known as *darienitas* or *costeños.* The Emberá-Wounaan have integrated into some of these villages.

The Emberá-Wounaan tend to live in thatched-roof, open-sided huts on stilts. The stairway leading up to the living quarters is a log with steps chopped into the side. If the log is inverted, with the notched steps pointing down, it's a sign the family wants privacy. The log is pulled up at night to keep out unwelcome visitors, both two-legged and four-legged. As befits the climate, the people traditionally wear very few clothes, but the influx of "civilization" has eroded this practice.

Village life is a relatively new thing for the Emberá and Wounaan. Traditionally, families set up house in relative isolation from others along a river. The patriarch of a clan would live upriver, with his children in homes some distance away downriver. They lived a seminomadic existence, settling into an area and practicing slash-and-burn agriculture and hunting, then moving away to fresh territory, allowing the depleted area to recover. This worked as long as the human pressures on the land were small. This mobile way of life changed in the 20th century, when the Panamanian government pressured the Emberá-Wounaan to form villages.

The Emberá-Wounaan continue to have land conflicts with loggers, cattle ranchers, poachers, and small farmers from outside the Darién who followed the building of the Interamericana and devastated the rainforest in western Darién from Chepo to Yaviza. The subsistence ranchers and farmers are known as *colonos,* many of whom moved to the Darién from heavily deforested Los Santos province.

The Panamanian government established about 25 percent of the Darién as Emberá-Wounaan *comarcas,* semiautonomous reservations, giving them much greater control over their land and lives. The issues of land stewardship are complex. Parts of the *comarcas* as well as other areas the Emberá-Wounaan have traditionally seen as theirs overlap with the boundaries of the Parque Nacional Darién, where they are no longer legally allowed to hunt, farm, or extract timber. Poor Emberá-Wounaan increasingly log their own land and sell the timber, helping them survive in the short run but endangering their future.

FLORA AND FAUNA

From rainforests to sandy beaches to cloud forests to mangroves, the Darién has a greater variety of ecosystems than any other place in tropical America. Lush doesn't even begin to cover it. Flying over the Darién opens up an endless expanse of forest, broken only by an occasional snaking river or a lone flowering tree trying to add a splash of bright red, orange, or yellow to the sea of green.

The wildlife is spectacular. Mammals alone include jaguars, ocelots, pumas, margays, jaguarundi, giant anteaters, capybaras, white-lipped and collared peccaries, howler monkeys, white-faced capuchins, spider monkeys, Geoffroy's tamarins, two- and three-toed sloths, and Baird's tapirs. And unlike so many other places in the neotropics, there's a fair chance of spotting at least a couple of these.

However, don't get your hopes up too much. Most creatures in a tropical forest evolve to stay hidden. A hiker could be standing right next to a jaguar and never know it's there.

On the other hand, the Darién is one of the best places in the world to spot birds. More than 400 species have been identified, including plenty to impress those who don't give a hoot about birds. In some places it's actually hard not to see flocks of flamboyant blue-and-yellow, red-and-green, great green, and chestnut-fronted macaws. The rare harpy eagle, the world's most powerful bird of prey, lives here, as does the lovely golden-headed quetzal.

Reptiles and amphibians abound as well, including caimans, crocodiles, and jewel-like poison-arrow frogs. And yes, there are lots of snakes, including some very venomous ones. The wisdom is it's rare to spot them, and those who do should count themselves lucky. My experience is that if you do any amount of serious hiking in the tropics, you will eventually come across at least one, probably several. Most are not aggressive, and if you leave them alone they won't bother you.

The most common venomous snake in the Darién is also one of the most lethal: the fer-de-lance, a tan pit viper with a diamond pattern on its skin. They are everywhere in the Darién, though again you probably won't see one. If you do, don't play with it.

PLANNING YOUR TIME

Where you go and how long you choose to stay in the Darién depends on how deeply you want to enter into this formidable world. It may help to think in terms of three Dariéns: the coast,

© WILLIAM FRIAR

Coastal Darién is a different world from the forests of the interior.

the rivers, and the foothills and highlands of Parque Nacional Darién. Ecosystems, accommodations, and the overall experience are quite different in each.

Those with the time and ability for serious trekking should consider an organized trip that touches on all three Dariéns. This requires at least a week and perhaps two and involves all-day hikes in rugged, hot, and humid conditions. These trips are really mini-expeditions and do not come cheap. The best way to arrange one is through a good tour operator that can provide qualified guides, keep trekkers safe, and handle the considerable logistics.

Visiting just one part of the Darién can be done in as little as two or three days, particularly if you fly. Given the time and expense involved in getting around this part of the country, visitors will not get much out of the experience if they attempt a stay shorter than that. Visitors to Tropic Star Lodge, the only true resort in the entire Darién, generally stay for a week, though half-week packages are sometimes available.

The only parts of the Darién you can consider visiting without a guide are the towns along the Interamericana or those that can be reached by air, which also happen to be among the least appealing and least attractive places in the Darién. No one should set foot in the forest or venture far on a river without experienced guides.

The coast is the most accessible part of the Darién, and the least rugged. The most comfortable accommodations are found here. This area includes the **Bahía de Piñas, Jaqué,** and **Punta Patiño,** as well as the town of **La Palma,** the provincial capital of the Darién. Most people fly in or come by ocean-going vessel.

The rivers are the main means of transportation in the interior of the Darién, and most visitors spend at least a little time on them. It can be a pleasant way to get around, and it's certainly scenic, but boat travel can also be hot, humid, and wet. Most transport is by long dugout canoes called *piraguas,* which can get uncomfortable after an hour or two. Getting any distance by boat can take a long time, depending on conditions: The crew may need to clear tree falls or drag the *piragua* through shallow stretches of some rivers.

Rivers worth considering include the **Río Sambú, Río Balsas, Río Mogue,** and **Río Marea,** all of which have Emberá-Wounaan villages along their banks.

The **Río Pirre** is far less densely settled and quite beautiful. The **Río Tuira** is wide and lightly populated between La Palma and El Real, then narrows and is lined by villages as it flows farther east. For their own safety, visitors are not allowed to travel up the Tuira past the village of **Boca de Cupe,** and sometimes not even that far. The same goes for the **Río Jaqué** (near the Bahía de Piñas) past the village of **Biroquera.** Those who want to spend a night on the river will camp in a village with few facilities. Only **Mogue** and the Río Sambú area have true visitors' accommodations; staying in any other village requires negotiating for a spot in someone's hut or a place to pitch one's tent. The town of **El Real,** on the Río Tuira near the Río Pirre, also has guest accommodations and a couple of basic places to eat and drink.

The foothills and highlands of Parque Nacional Darién are among the wildest and most beautiful parts of the country. Most visitors go to the area around **Cerro Pirre,** usually making their base at **Rancho Frío,** in the lowlands just northwest of the mountain, or **Cana,** on its eastern slope. Hikers can stay at **Pirre Station** (the ranger station at Rancho Frío) or the rustic lodge at Cana. This area is particularly treasured by bird-watchers, but the magnificent primary and secondary forests will impress anyone.

Cana has more trails and facilities, it's more comfortable, and it has a nifty cloud-forest camp. Conditions at Pirre Station are more rustic, but a trip there can be arranged far more cheaply. Those on a moderate budget will find Pirre Station the most accessible part of the national park. (Pirre Station and Cana are only about 20 kilometers apart, but no trails connect them.)

The average temperature in the Darién is 26°C (79°F), but as usual in the tropics that average sounds milder than it feels. The Darién lowlands are hot and humid year-round. Be prepared to feel wet and sticky even in the dry season, and don't expect ever to get completely dry in the rainy season. The Pacific and central parts of the Darién can see as much as 2.5 meters of rain a year. The Caribbean side gets up to 3.5 meters a year. Trekkers on long expeditions often take just two sets of clothing, which after the first day can be categorized as "wet" and "wetter." Sleep in the former; hike in the latter.

The highlands, however, can get surprisingly cool at night. You'll probably need a light jacket or windbreaker, for instance, at Cana's cloud-forest camp.

With few exceptions, transactions are cash only in the Darién, and there are no ATMs anywhere east of Metetí. Those traveling independently should calculate a rough budget ahead of time and bring a stash of cash with them, including lots of small bills.

SAFETY CONCERNS

Unlike other chapters, this one is written with the idea you will travel to the Darién only with experienced, respected nature guides. I strongly urge you to do so.

Those who don't speak Spanish and know the area will find it hard to get logistics set up for a Darién trek. A naturalist guide can spot and describe animals and plants the uninitiated will miss. Most important, those who venture off by themselves have a great chance of getting lost and dying. Seriously. The Darién is a fantastic place and definitely worth visiting. But it must be treated with respect.

There are human hazards as well. Colombia's civil war has spilled over the border into the Darién, and there are guerrillas and paramilitaries working in some areas. Gun battles between guerrillas and Panamanian police in 2010 raised tensions in the border areas. Drug traffickers and bandits also hide out in the forest. All these baddies have done unwitting good for conservation:

AREAS TO AVOID IN THE DARIÉN

There's a general rule of thumb here. Look at a map of the Darién and picture an imaginary line drawn from Punta Carreto (west of Puerto Obaldía in the Comarca de Kuna Yala, on the Caribbean coast) through the town of Yaviza in the heart of the Darién, down to Punta Piñas on the Pacific coast. Travel east of this imaginary line is usually considered dangerous.

This was roughly accurate in 2010, with some caveats. El Real and the area around Pirre Station and Cana in Parque Nacional Darién were not considered high-risk spots by those who know the area well.

Travel up the Río Tuira beyond Boca de Cupe is dangerous and off-limits. Boca de Cupe itself has a police post, but that doesn't necessarily make it safe. In early 2010, Panamanian police on a patrol in the area encountered FARC guerrillas and a firefight that left three guerrillas dead.

As this book went to press, the U.S. State De-partment's travel advisory warned visitors to avoid basically any part of the province that's not on the Interamericana: "While the number of actual incidents remains low, U.S. citizens, other foreign nationals and Panamanian citizens are potentially at risk of violent crime, kidnapping, and murder in this general area."

Violence between Panamanian police and alleged drug traffickers near the village of Jaquí was a problem in mid-2010. Avoid this area.

Travel to Puerto Obaldía is also considered unsafe. The situation in the Darién is fluid, and a quiet spot today can be an area of concern tomorrow, and vice versa.

Those who know the Darién well feel the risk of coming across warring Colombian factions is exaggerated. They point out that combatants use the forests on the Panamanian side of the border as a place to hide out and rest. The last thing they want is to draw attention to themselves by provoking conflict.

DARIÉN SURVIVAL TIPS

Those going on a multi-day trek in the Darién, versus staying in a lodge with screens, should start taking antimalarial medication in advance of the trip.

There are three hospitals in the Darién: in Yaviza, La Palma, and El Real. There are also six *centros de salud* (health centers), in Boca de Cupe, Metetí, Santa Fé, Garachiné, Jaqué, and Sambú, plus a subcenter on the Río Balsas. All should have antivenin for venomous snakes. The El Real hospital sees 12–15 snakebites a year, mostly fer-de-lance. The hospitals are reasonably well stocked, but serious cases are stabilized and flown to Panama City.

Be careful in the forest during and after a rain. Tropical trees have shallow roots and fall all the time. You can hear them crashing all around you.

Keep your passport with you at all times. There are police checkpoints throughout the Darién and you'll be asked repeatedly to present your papers. As always in Panama, be respectful toward the police. To keep the passport dry, double-bag it in Ziploc plastic bags.

The Darién is one of the few places in Panama where water can be unsafe. Bring a good water purifier or water purification tablets.

Campers should always sleep in tents. Always. Among the dangers of sleeping in the open are malaria, which is endemic to the Darién, and rabies from vampire bat bites. There is no cure for rabies, and only one person in history has survived it (though taking a series of vaccinations after exposure can usually prevent infection). On one trek, an experienced Darién guide got so hot he ignored his own advice and unzipped his tent a speck. He woke up the next morning with congealed blood in his hair and little bite marks on his scalp – a vampire bat had feasted on him. Back in Panama City a doctor gave him his shots and told him the only thing else he could do was wait. For what? To see whether he died. He didn't, but he'll never leave his tent open again.

Some cell phone networks reach only as far as Chepo. Others carry as far as Punta Patiño. None penetrates deep into the forest. But even some remote villages have a pay phone. Buy a prepaid local phone card in Panama City, as these phones get choked with change.

Even hunters with guns are afraid to enter some areas.

Knowing which regions are unsafe is tricky. Again, experienced guides can be helpful, since it's in their interest to know the dangerous spots. Border police and park rangers are also sources of information. Be sure to check the U.S. State Department's travel warnings and Consular Information Sheet at www.travel.state.gov. However, these advisories are not always accurate or up to date.

GETTING THERE AND AWAY

Traditionally, the Darién starts at the town of Chepo, just 50 kilometers east of Panama City, though the city has expanded so much it's hard to believe this area was pure wilderness less than three decades ago. It's possible to drive into the Darién as far as the town of Yaviza, but it's not pleasant. Though the road was recently much improved, the drive still takes a solid day, and all one encounters along the way are vast expanses of deforested land.

By Air

For most travelers, flying into the Darién is the only reasonable option. Except to places served only by charter planes, such as Cana, flights are reasonably priced and flying is a much faster and less tiring way to get to the most interesting parts of the Darién. Planes often run late out here, sometimes by many hours. But arrive at the airstrip at least an hour early on the way back. If by some miracle the plane shows up early, it'll leave early, with or without you. The carriers are **Aeroperlas** (tel. 315-7500, www.aeroperlas.com) and **Air Panama** (tel. 316-9000, www.flyairpanama.com).

Flight times in the Darién are rough approximations at best. Be ready to leave an hour early but prepared to wait as long as it takes, which can be many hours.

By Land

The Interamericana (Interamerican Highway) extends east from Panama City to Yaviza, about 270 kilometers away. Here the "highway"—really a two-lane road nearly all the way from Panama City—comes to an abrupt end about 50 kilometers from the Colombian border, and the famous Darién Gap begins.

Going into the Darién by four-wheel drive or bus is becoming increasingly common. The road was mostly paved all the way to Yaviza in 2010, but is still a long, tiring trip through unlovely countryside. Anywhere the road has been extended, deforestation has followed, and the view out the windows is of sad little towns, villages, farms, and cattle pasture, not the majestic rainforest most come to the Darién to see. Roads deteriorate quickly out here, and when it's in sad shape you can expect an all-day, vehicle-punishing journey. It can take up to eight hours by four-wheel drive, including stops for breakfast and lunch, to cover the approximately 270 kilometers from Panama City to Yaviza in the dry season, which gives some sense of the road conditions.

However, traveling by bus is the cheapest way to get into the Darién. There are frequent daily buses from Panama City that go at least as far as Metetí and make interim stops at all the towns and villages along the highway.

Budget travelers can take a bus from Panama City to Metetí, switch buses to the nearby river port of Puerto Quimba, and then cross the wide mouth of the Río Tuira to La Palma, the capital of Darién province. From there it's possible to arrange expeditions to explore the Emberá-Wounaan and Afro-Colonial villages and the coasts and lowland forests of southwestern Darién province. It's also possible to hire a boat to go far up the Río Tuira toward Parque Nacional Darién.

Alternatively, when road conditions allow, those on a budget can continue all the way to Yaviza, take a motorized *piragua* (long dugout canoe) to the nearby town of El Real, and

---

GOD'S HANDS

Cuando entres al Darién, encomiéndate a María. En tu mano está la entrada; en la de Dios la salida.

An anonymous bit of verse, said to have been carved into the walls of a Spanish fort at the edge of the Darién. It reads: "When you enter the Darién, commend your soul to the Virgin Mary. In your hands lies the way in; in God's, the way out."

---

from there plan trips to visit villages up the Río Tuira or to Pirre Station, the most accessible part of Parque Nacional Darién.

Once you get off the bus, however, expenses mount quickly. Expect to pay US$200 round-trip per small group for transportation for any significant distance upriver to forest destinations. That doesn't include the cost of food, guides, park fees, and so on. And a competent, knowledgeable guide is a must even for the most independent-minded traveler.

By River

Because there are (thankfully) still few roads in the Darién, most travel within the province is done the old-fashioned way: on the river. Spend much time in the Darién and you'll become intimately familiar with *piraguas,* 30- to 45-foot-long dugout canoes that are still the best way to get around on the rivers. Their shallow drafts and tough bottoms allow them to skim over water that's just a few centimeters deep or be dragged across rocky bottoms without springing a leak. The only concession to modernity is the outboard motor, to make upriver trips much easier. Making a *piragua* is a long, labor-intensive job, which is why they can sell for as much as US$1,500.

The indigenous people also use *cayucos*—small, paddled dugout canoes—for shorter trips and rafts made from lightweight balsa wood. The rafts are one-way, makeshift affairs used to travel downriver with the current, after which they're abandoned.

Travel by *piragua* is nothing fancy. You sit on a wooden plank along the bottom, often in a puddle of water. They're completely exposed to the elements, which means it can be broiling hot and humid in the sun and startlingly chilly in the rain. Some sort of cushion to sit on and, in the rainy season, a poncho with hood will make long *piragua* trips more comfortable. Consider bringing a life jacket; flashfloods are possible on some rivers. Don't forget to wear sunscreen on the open river. And stay alert: Tree falls and other obstacles can suddenly appear on a fast-flowing river, requiring a quick limbo to avoid getting knocked out of the boat.

It's possible to arrange a river trip on your own, but it will entail a great deal of planning and hassle, particularly for those who don't speak decent Spanish. Life will be a lot easier and safer if you go with a qualified guide who knows the good boatmen and can make all the arrangements.

If you do decide to go it alone, the main points of entry for the rivers discussed here are El Real, La Palma, Punta Patiño, and the area around Sambú.

How much a river trip costs depends primarily on how far you want to go, as the main expense is fuel. Expect to pay at least US$100 one-way per group for a solid couple of hours of motoring, which will take you pretty far, probably as far as you'd like to go in a day. Note that this just covers the cost of the boat, fuel, and crew. The crew will consist of at least a captain and a poleman. The latter stands up front with a long pole, on the lookout for snags and shallows. Food, supplies, guides, porters, and tips are all extra, as is lodging for those who plan to spend the night.

The best "cultural" rivers, which give a taste of Emberá-Wounaan village life, are the Río Sambú and the Río Balsas. The farther upriver you go, the more traditional the villages are. Other possibilities are the Río Mogue and Río Marea. The sparsely inhabited Río Pirre is a good bet for sheer natural beauty; those venturing up to Pirre Station in Parque Nacional Darién can take the river most of the way to the station in the rainy season.

Rivers to avoid because of Colombian guerrilla and paramilitary activity include the upper reaches of the Río Jaqué and the stretch of the Río Tuira upriver from Boca de Cupe. As with all travel in the Darién, the closer one gets to the Colombian border, the greater the risk of coming across a dangerous situation.

Because the Río Balsas starts so far from any population center—it's between La Palma and El Real—a trip up the Balsas is considerably more expensive than on many of the other rivers. Normally, visitors fly into La Palma and then travel by boat up the Río Balsas to the Balsas ranger station, about 4–5 hours upriver.

Those traveling between La Palma and El Real might consider a trip along the Río Tuira as an alternative to flying, though a longer and more expensive one. It takes about two hours and can cost up to US$200 per group to hire a boat, though it may be possible to hitch a ride for considerably less. It's a different kind of river experience, as the Tuira is quite wide for most of the way, especially the closer you get to La Palma. Being out on open water near the ocean is incredibly refreshing after the heat and humidity of the forests and towns.

The Tuira is the longest river in Panama (with the possible exception, depending on who ask, of the unbelievably tortuous Chucunaque) and carries the greatest volume of water. It's easy to imagine you're on the Amazon on this stretch of the river. The water is brown with sediment and the river too wide to see much wildlife, though when I took this trip we spotted a four-meter-long American crocodile sunning itself on a sandbar.

That may suggest this is not a place to go for a swim (few rivers in the Darién are in any case, especially those near human settlements, because of the risk of disease). Because the wide mouth of the Tuira opens into the Golfo de San Miguel, saltwater animals including hammerhead sharks also venture pretty far up the river. Tides affect the river as far east as El Real.

Note: Be sure any boat you take on the Tuira between El Real and La Palma has an extra outboard motor. There is virtually nothing and no one on this part of the river, so it's not a great place to get stranded.

Western and Central Darién

The western Darién is fairly accessible by road from Panama City. The Lago Bayano area is particularly easy to get to, and it's now also possible to drive north across the western Darién all the way to Kuna Yala. Most people heading farther east than that prefer to fly. However, travelers with more time than money can get to La Palma, El Real, and parts of Parque Nacional Darién by road and boat.

LAGO BAYANO

Even those who'll pass on a drive all the way into the Darién might be interested in going at least as far as the Bayano Dam area, where there are a couple of places to check out. It's about 90 kilometers east of Panama City. Note that there's an active police checkpoint at Bayano, and your papers will definitely be scrutinized here.

Lago Bayano is an artificial lake, created when the Río Bayano was dammed in 1976. It flooded 350 square kilometers of tropical forest and displaced thousands of Kuna and Emberá. It is the second-largest source of power in the country, after the Fortuna Dam in western Panama.

Bayano, by the way, was the name of a famous leader of the *cimarrones* (rebel African slaves), who held the conquistadors at bay for two years before he was finally captured.

The 10 Kuna communities in this area banded together and in 1996 gained *comarca* (semiautonomous reservation) status. Called the **Comarca Kuna de Madungandí,** its government office is right at the checkpoint, along with a little stand selling (rather poorly made) *molas* (handcrafted blouses). Sometimes the name is spelled Madugandí. They have clashed in recent years with the Panama government over compensation for land lost decades ago with the building of the dam.

Bayano Caves

Some caves on the south side of the lake make for a pretty cool day trip for the adventurous.

Exploring the caves of Lago Bayano makes for an exciting day trip.

© WILLIAM FRIAR

On my most recent visit, this trip was being offered by some Panama City hostels and was catching on with the backpacking set. The caves are best explored with a good guide, but it's possible to arrange a trip on your own.

There's a boat-launching ramp to the right of the Bayano bridge and usually a few boatmen hanging around. Ask near the checkpoint for Mateo Cortéz, who probably knows the caves as well as anyone. The trip across the lake takes about half an hour in his 30-foot boat and costs about US$50 for a single person or small group. If Mateo isn't there, ask around for someone willing to go to *la cueva.*

There are actually three caves, though nearly everyone just explores the first one. The second one requires crawling through narrow passages on hands and knees—pretty intense. Even Mateo hadn't yet explored the third. He's been trying to find someone crazy enough to go with him.

THE DARIÉN

are minimized by the fast-flowing river that washes out the cave.

Flashlights are a must; it's utterly dark in some sections. After a couple of minutes you'll hear a roar of water and the squeaking of thousands of wings. Shine the flashlight straight ahead and you'll likely see a solid wall of agitated bats. This is what a guide friend of mine likes to call "a high-adrenaline moment." Some may have second thoughts at this point, and probably with reason. Those who continue shouldn't be bothered by the bats—they'll flit right by—and will be rewarded by a large open area, with shafts of light streaming down from high above. Impossibly long tree roots hang through the cracks overhead, and otherworldly mounds formed by calcium deposits cling to the walls. It's all very *Indiana Jones*.

The cave is about two kilometers long, though the water is usually too deep to go the whole way except at the height of the dry season.

It's a spooky but beautiful place. No wonder the locals have stories about troll-like creatures that live in the cave and a human skeleton somewhere in the forest above it. Real, live creatures may be enough to keep the cautious (sane?) out, though: After coming back out of the cave, my little group spotted the head of either an unusually large caiman or a rather small crocodile lurking about the entrance. It could easily have come inside to swim with us.

Practicalities

Those coming on their own can drive or take any Darién-bound bus to Lago Bayano, getting off at the checkpoint just before the bridge, Puente Bayano. Buses from Panama City that go only as far as Lago Bayano leave from the Gran Terminal in Albrook daily every 40 or so minutes, 3:20 A.M.–6 P.M. The fare is US$3 and the trip takes about 2.5 hours.

Cañita (pop. 2,140), a little over 20 kilometers east of the Chepo turnoff, is a good place to stop for a break on the way to or from the Darién. It has a few basic restaurants and stores and a couple of rustic places to spend the night.

El Descanso, a pleasant open-air restaurant

SPENDING THE NIGHT IN A VILLAGE

It's generally possible to spend the night in an Emberá-Wounaan village, though I don't recommend it. Malaria is endemic and you'll probably be sleeping in an open-sided hut without screens. If you do stay in a village, sleep in a tent, no matter how hot it gets, stay indoors in the evenings (or as close to indoors as feasible), and douse yourself with insect repellent. Also, plan to start taking antimalarial medicine well before a visit; it takes several weeks to kick in. You must ask permission to stay in a village, and you'll probably have to pay. Ask to speak to the *dirigente* (leader, pronounced dir-ee-HEN-tay); US$10 per night for a couple should do it.

The first has a river flowing through it, the Río Seco, which is fed by creeks and underground springs. At the height of the rainy season, it's possible to steer the boat a fair distance inside the cave. At other times visitors have to get out of the boat and wade in through chest-high water—make sure valuables are sealed in plastic bags and be prepared to carry them over your head, or else leave them behind. Carrying a camera is a pain, and it's hard to get good photos in here; it's dark, and the humidity fogs up the lenses.

This trip requires lots of scrambling over slippery rocks, and it's remarkably easy to break an ankle or crack your head. Scuba or surfing booties work well here. Second-best are sneakers with good traction. There are some aggressive fish with sharp, pointy teeth swimming around in the dark; I saw one actually capture and eat a large frog. It's probably best not to wear open-toed shoes.

Wear a bandanna or T-shirt over your nose and mouth. There are lots of bats in this cave, and there's always a chance of contracting something unpleasant from the droppings, such as histoplasmosis, a potentially serious or even fatal infection. Chances of this on the north side of the road, is a popular place to eat. It's owned by immigrants from Los Santos province and is known for its soups, such as *sancocho* (stew) and *sopa de carne* (beef soup). A breakfast of steak, tortilla, juice, and coffee costs about US$3. The old ocelot, jaguar, and peccary pelts hanging from the rafters are disturbing reminders of the toll humans have taken on nature in this area, and the endangered turtle eggs that may be for sale proves it's not a thing of the past. Please don't buy them; for one thing, it's against the law. In fact, if they're being sold you can boycott the place and tell the management why you're doing so. If you do stop for a bite, be careful the house sparrows don't poop in your food.

THE EL LLANO-CARTÍ ROAD

Shortly before reaching Lago Bayano there's a turnoff to a road that leads all the way down to the Comaraca Kuna Yala. This is the 30-kilometer long El Llano–Cartí Road, which heads north over the Continental Divide to the Caribbean coast, ending at the Kuna town of Cartí. It is the only land access to the islands. This road has finally been paved. There are still some rough spots and it shouldn't be attempted without a high-clearance four-wheel-drive vehicle and a competent driver. But the road has opened up the islands to a whole new group of travelers who either couldn't afford or were too scared of the plane journey to Kuna Yala. (Enterprising Kunas have set up a low-cost transportation service from Panama City to Kuna Yala via this road.)

The road has encouraged squatters, cattle ranchers, and poachers to invade Kuna land. To try to stop this encroachment, the Kuna established a nearly 100,000-hectare forest reserve in this area called the **Área Silvestre de Narganá**. With funding from international organizations, they built a rustic lodge along the Continental Divide in an area called Nusagandí, hoping to attract ecotourism. The Kuna ecotourism project never quite got off the ground and the lodge is pretty much abandoned.

However there is another ecolodge, **Burbayar Lodge,** along the road that attracts birders and other nature lovers.

The lodge is used by hikers walking the length of the road or exploring the forests along it. This area is popular because it offers a true taste of the Darién surprisingly close to Panama City, and the lodge and road make a visit relatively affordable, accessible, and comfortable.

Practicalities

The unmarked turnoff to the El Llano–Cartí road is about 15 kilometers east of Chepo, just before the flyspeck town of El Llano (pop. 2,839). There's a rice field on the right. Turn left onto the unpaved road. It's possible to pick up some provisions in El Llano, but Cañita, eight kilometers farther east, is better stocked.

There is one appealing place to stay along the road. **Burbayar Lodge** (tel. 393-7340, cell 6674-2964, www.burbayar.com, US$190 pp for the first night, including all meals, transportation from and to Panama City, and a guided hike; US$155 pp for subsequent nights) lies along the San Blas mountain range 14.5 kilometers north of the Interamericana and 22 kilometers south of the Caribbean coast. An experienced naturalist guide who has made many Darién expeditions calls it his favorite rustic nature lodge in the country. It's at 375 meters above sea level, high enough for cooler temperatures, pleasant breezes, and, apparently, no mosquitoes. There is electricity and running water, and the accommodations are simple but comfortable. The lodge can accommodate just 14 people at a time, in shared rooms. Meals are served family-style on a terrace in the main lodge. The lodge appears to be making a genuine effort to be as eco-friendly as possible.

The lodge borders the Narganá forest reserve and offers six forest trails of varying degrees of difficulty. The lodge also offers tour packages. These include visits to Lago Bayano and the Bayano caves as well as a tough all-day hike to Cartí, in Kuna Yala. Once there, hikers can spend the night in a Kuna hotel on one of the islands. Tour packages generally include transportation to and from Panama City, boat transportation, a local guide, and meals.

This area has the finest birding in eastern Panama after Cana and Pirre Station. This is the best place in Panama, for instance, to see the speckled antshrike, black-headed antthrush, and black-crowned antpitta. An estimated 400 bird species pass through the area, of which birders at Burbayar have so far counted about 300. The dry season is the best time for birding.

Those who choose not to stay at the lodge can also do some exploring along the road on a day trip. The view from even a few kilometers above the Interamericana is sweeping and lovely, though the sight of hill after deforested hill now covered with teak plantations on the Pacific side shows just what the Kuna are so worried about.

It's also possible to trek from the highway all the way to Cartí, but this means two long days of hiking. Hikers can arrange to spend the night either at Burbayar or strike a deal with local Kuna to crash at what's left of the Nusagandí lodge. Plan to arrive at Cartí, on the Caribbean shore, early in the morning; after the morning planes come and go; there probably won't be anyone around to take hikers to the islands until the next day. It's possible to do this hike without a guide, but it's not a good idea. In any case, the usual mantra applies: Do not hike alone. Only truly fit people should attempt this one.

ON THE ROAD TO YAVIZA

With the exception of the El Llano–Cartí Road and the area around Lago Bayano, there's little to interest travelers on the road to Yaviza. Most people will not choose to spend the night in any of the towns along the highway unless stranded on the way to somewhere else. Leave Panama City as early in the morning as possible to improve the chances of getting to your destination the same day. Breakdowns and missed connections on the road are common.

Attempt the drive only in a four-wheel drive with high clearance, a couple of spare tires, a winch, and plenty of fuel. The road is tough or impossible to navigate the whole length in the

---

ENTERING THE DARIÉN GAP IS SUICIDAL

Even Darién experts who have made many coast-to-coast treks through the forest say it is crazy to hike through the Darién Gap into Colombia. Despite or perhaps because of all the warnings, some still insist on trying it. It's an extraordinarily dangerous thing to do.

A few years ago an English orchid-hunter, Tom Hart Dyke, and his friend, Paul Winder, were captured by Colombian guerrillas while trying to cross the Gap. Anyone who thinks trying this is an exciting lark should read their account of their horrific ordeal, *The Cloud Garden*.

They were held for nine months, during which time they had nothing to do but learn enough Spanish to understand their captors' arguments, which mainly concerned whether to kill them or not.

In January 2003 Robert Young Pelton, an adventure-travel writer, and two 22-year-old American backpackers were kidnapped by a right-wing paramilitary group near the Kuna village of Paya, close to the Colombian border. They were held for nearly a week before being released unharmed. Less fortunate were four Kuna village leaders in Paya and Púcuru, who were tortured and murdered during this attack. A fifth Kuna was reported missing, and hundreds of refugees from the villages poured into the police-patrolled village of Boca de Cupe. Panama and Colombia pledged to beef up security around the border in the wake of these tragedies.

After his release, Pelton, the author of *The World's Most Dangerous Places* and *Come Back Alive,* called the Darién Gap "probably the most dangerous place in the western hemisphere."

rainy season, and even in the dry season there can be rough patches. Still, there are tire-repair stands at regular intervals along the road, which may very well come in handy. Note also that, while there are police checkpoints all along the highway, these are at widely spaced intervals. Those who get stranded or have an accident are in for a long, long wait before help arrives. There is exactly one transit police station along the entire 200 kilometers between Chepo and Yaviza, and it doesn't even have a phone. It's in the tiny town of Zapallal, just east of Santa Fé, about 80 kilometers from the end of the road.

From Panama City, take the Corredor Sur toward Tocumen until it peters out, then follow the signs east to Chepo and the Darién. If you forget something, stop at the town of 24 de Diciembre, at the turnoff to Cerro Azul. There's a mall here with a supermarket, gas station, and the last McDonald's until Colombia (talk about entering the wilderness…).

The highway passes through or close to all the towns listed, though few travelers will be inclined to stop unless stranded for some reason. There are several other small towns and Kuna, Emberá, and Wounaan villages along the way, some of which have *minisupers* (convenience stores), pay phones, dirty and rustic places to stay, and little else. Any bus going at least as far as Metetí stops by them all.

Chepo

Though actually in eastern Panama province, Chepo (pop. 12,734) has traditionally been thought of as the starting point for the Darién. This view persists today, despite the fact that Panama City has grown so far east and this area has been so heavily settled Chepo now seems more like a suburb of the city. It's a big, sprawling town with a hospital, filling station, ATM, and stores where travelers can stock up on provisions.

The first police checkpoint on the road is just before the turnoff to town. Chepo itself is five kilometers south of the Interamericana. It's not a scenic place, however, and because it's just 50 kilometers from Panama City, there's little

reason to stop here on the way to or from the Darién. It's locally popular during Carnaval, though.

The **Río Mamoní** crosses the Interamericana just east of Chepo. At the beginning of the 1970s, it marked the beginning of the Darién Gap. There was solid rainforest from this point east, pure wilderness. It's sobering how quickly and completely all that has vanished.

Darién province actually starts about 85 kilometers east of the Bayano Dam, at **Agua Fría No. 1.** The only things there are a couple of houses, an agriculture checkpoint, some transit police, and an ANAM office.

Santa Fé

Santa Fé (pop. 5,764), about 200 kilometers east of Panama City, is a surprisingly large and lively town, though not a scenic one. There's little trace of it today, but the town has a long history thanks to its accessibility: It's possible to navigate from the Pacific all the way to Santa Fé by river.

Though the place can draw an interesting mix of people from neighboring areas during a festival, there isn't much reason to visit it. It does, however, have a hospital and other services you would expect to find in a remote provincial town. All buses going at least as far as Metetí pass by it. There are a few basic places to stay for stranded visitors.

Metetí

The last real town before Yaviza is Metetí (pop. 6,244). Most residents are colonists from the province of Chiriquí, of all places—it's clear on the other side of Panama, on the Costa Rican border.

Metetí is mainly of interest to travelers as the crossroads for travel to Puerto Quimba on the Río Tuira. From there it's possible to take a water taxi to La Palma or, with more difficulty, arrange boat trips to El Real and Yaviza. Along with other services, there are several hole-in-the-wall restaurants and places to stay.

Hotel Felicidad (tel. 299-6544 or 264-9985, hotel_felicidad@yahoo.com. US$20 s/d), the most substantial and best-run hotel in

THE END OF THE ROAD – AT LEAST FOR NOW

No road has ever penetrated all the way through the Darién, and many hope none ever will. The Interamericana (Interamerican Highway) comes to a complete stop in Yaviza, and from there the road doesn't pick up again for another 100 kilometers, well inside Colombia. The Darién Gap is the only missing piece in a system of roads that links North and South America from Alaska to Patagonia.

The completion of the highway was long stalled by fears that hoof-and-mouth disease would spread from South America to Central and North America. Those fears have abated, but environmental ones have grown.

Wherever there is a road, massive deforestation has followed. Logging, ranching, farming, and hunting have decimated enormous tracts of the Darién. If the Interamericana is completed, it is all but certain the days of the Darién as a magical place will be numbered.

So far, building those last 100 kilometers of road continues to be put on hold, due to conservation concerns, the war in Colombia, and worries about giving drug traffickers yet another route to the north.

But even without the road, the Darién is under enormous pressure. How well protected the Darién, and particularly Parque Nacional Darién, is depends on the whim of the particular government in power. The consensus among environmentalists is that in the first few years of the 21st century, the Darién has been sadly neglected at best.

Even in better times, Parque Nacional Darién never had more than about a dozen rangers to protect an area the size of some countries. Now there are only two ranger stations being staffed in the entire park, Pirre Station and Balsas Station. The Cruce de Mono Station (a.k.a. Cruzamono Station) was abandoned and poachers have moved in. There have been reports of hunters almost all the way to Cana, which is among the most remote and pristine areas in the entire country. Wild peccary meat is being sold everywhere, illegally.

For now, however, the Darién remains a fantastic nature destination. Try to get there if you possibly can.

---

the region, offers air-conditioned rooms. It's on the Interamericana just before the crossroads. There are a couple of other, more rustic places to stay at the crossroads.

There's a branch of **Banco Nacional de Panamá** (tel. 299-6052 or 299-6054, 8 A.M.–3 P.M. Mon.–Fri., 9 A.M.–noon Sat.) at the Metetí crossroads. It has an ATM and can supposedly cash American Express travelers checks. There's also a large police post and checkpoint, filling station, and pay phones. There's an ANAM station a right turn off the road before the crossroads as one heads toward Yaviza. You'll likely find the staff absolutely useless.

Most services are at the crossroads outside Metetí rather than in the town itself. To get to the town, turn south off the Interamericana. The road continues to Puerto Quimba.

Puerto Quimba (KEEM-buh) is Metetí's

"port." It's sometimes spelled Puerto Kimba or even Kimball. Pickup "buses" link Puerto Quimba and Metetí.

A water taxi runs from Puerto Quimba to La Palma, 7:30 A.M.–6:30 P.M., and from La Palma to Puerto Quimba, 5:30 A.M.–5 P.M. Theoretically it runs every 60–75 minutes, but after the first trip of the day, the boat leaves when it gets a full load. It's US$3 one-way and takes about 30–45 minutes.

Those who need a boat up the Río Tuira to El Real, Yaviza, or Parque Nacional Darién may find someone willing to make the trip at Puerto Quimba, but the chances are better in La Palma. How much this will cost depends on the number of passengers and whether the boat was already going that way. It may be possible to hitch a ride for about US$5 per person, but expect to pay US$100 or more to hire your own boat.

YAVIZA

Welcome to the end of the road. And not just any road: Yaviza (yaw-VEE-sa, pop. 3,177) marks the abrupt end of the Interamericana, which those in a less environmentally aware time once dreamed would link North and South America. Fortunately, sanity has so far prevailed and the road has been indefinitely halted, which is at least delaying the ecological destruction that would inevitably follow. The famous Darién Gap begins here. Depending on how one measures it, the gap consists of about 100 kilometers of unbroken wilderness near the borders of Panama and Colombia, through which no road has ever been built.

Just paving the existing stretch of road between the Lago Bayano area and Yaviza, which might possibly be completed in the next few years, will likely bring dramatic change to this backwater.

Only a true optimist would be confident those changes will be for the better. On the other hand, it's hard to imagine Yaviza getting much sketchier. It's got the vaguely menacing, unpredictable vibe one expects from a frontier town in the middle of nowhere. It's also hot and humid, the very essence of jungle rot.

When the first vehicles ever to make it to Yaviza emerged from the jungle in 1960, on a brutal expedition to study the feasibility of a road through the Darién Gap, some towns-people were so frightened by these mechanical beasts they jumped into the river. Not a whole lot has changed since then. Yaviza still looks like a backwater Panamanian town from 100 years ago.

Yaviza is certainly colorful, and it's an interesting place to spend an hour or so on the way to somewhere better. That's all the time needed to get the flavor of this tiny town. Those who need to spend the night in the area are better off in the nearby (and much friendlier) town of El Real, or in Metetí, back west along the Interamericana. That said, if you get stuck here there is one semi-okay place to stay.

Yaviza has a long history. A Spanish fort, **Fuerte San Jerónimo de Yaviza,** was built by the Spanish in the 18th century to prevent pirates from raiding the gold mines of Cana by river. What's left of the fort's crumbling walls can still be seen perched on the edge of the Río Chucunaque. Erosion is wearing away the riverbanks, and this haunting bit of history is slowly tumbling into the murky waters, with no attempt to preserve it. It's the only real sight in town and is worth a quick visit. It's a short walk toward the water from the Hotel Tres Americas. It's easy to find, but if you have trouble ask anyone where the *fuerte* is.

The Chucunaque snakes around the edge of Yaviza, making for a natural boundary. There's a **boat landing,** on the right at the entrance to town, where 45-foot-long *piraguas* (dugout canoes) loaded with *plétanos* (plantains) and *ñames* (yams) from riverside plantations unload their cargo onto trucks, which carry them to Panama City. These same boats are the main source of transportation for those venturing deeper into the Darién.

Watching the *piraguas* in "port" is just about the only other entertainment in town. The wiry stevedores who do the unloading are impressive guys. They carry huge, hand-woven baskets on their backs up a slippery incline to the trucks. There the baskets are weighed on a mechanical scale, and the weight is shouted to a supervisor sitting comfortably in the shade, who makes a note in his ledger. Each basket-ful weighs 60–90 kilos. It hurts just watching them.

Party days in Yaviza include the Festival de San Francisco Javier, the town's patron saint, on March 12, and the Festival de la Virgen del Carmen, usually celebrated throughout the province and the country on July 16, though sometimes it comes earlier here.

Practicalities

The town consists mainly of dilapidated two-story wooden buildings, incongruously well-paved streets, and a large, fenced-in police station. Ask for the *cuartel* (police station). Travelers should register their passport information and intended destination at the station as soon as they arrive. It's the law, and it's an excellent idea in any case. Those who go missing out here—and, sadly, it does happen—have a better chance of being found if there's a record of where they were last spotted. Travelers will need to register at every town, village, or checkpoint they pass through from this point on. Drivers can park their vehicles at the police station, where it should be safe.

Hotel Tres Americas (no phone, US$15 s/d with fan, US$20 s/d with a/c) is the only real option for those who get stuck in Yaviza, and it's not a great one. It's by the basketball courts in the plaza at the center of town and offers rooms with fan. A couple of the rooms are okay; the others aren't. The shared bathroom is icky. Air-conditioned rooms are in a separate building behind the main hotel. These are actually grimmer and literally stink. The hotel also has a basic bar and restaurant. The bar can get raucous at night—don't expect to get much sleep on the weekends or holidays.

Those who forgot something in Panama City can find all kinds of basic provisions at hole-in-the-wall stores in Yaviza: food, equipment, machetes, rope, ammo—everything one needs for a Darién expedition. Yaviza also has a small hospital.

Getting There and Away

If the road is especially bad, which is likelier in the rainy season, buses make it only as far as Metetí. In that case, getting to Yaviza from there means traveling up the Río Tuira.

It takes about eight hours by four-wheel drive, including stops for breakfast and lunch, to cover the approximately 270 kilometers from Panama City to Yaviza in the dry season.

If you're able to convince a taxi driver with a four-wheel drive to make the trip to the end of the road, expect to pay at least US$200 one-way from Panama City, depending on the condition of the road and fuel prices.

There are only two ways to venture farther into the Darién from Yaviza: by foot or by river. Continuing east toward the Colombian border is highly dangerous. Those foolish enough to try run a real risk of meeting Colombian guerrillas, paramilitaries, or plain old bandits. The far better option is to head southwest by boat,

first on the Chucunaque and then onto the mighty Río Tuira, to El Real. It's a good base for reaching the national park and other parts of the Darién. The closest airport in this whole region is in El Real.

Cargo-carrying *piraguas* (long dugout canoes) charge about US$5 a head to El Real, a trip that takes less than an hour with a 30-horsepower motor. Those attempting this trip on their own should note that *piraguas* aren't always available, and even when they are it can take hours to unload the thousands of kilos of produce before the boatmen are ready to head back out.

EL REAL DE SANTA MARÍA

Known by everyone simply as El Real, this sleepy town (pop. 1,185) sits on the edge of the Río Tuira and is mainly of interest to travelers as the staging ground for trips into Parque Nacional Darién or up and down the enormous Río Tuira. The town is friendlier and more laid-back than nearby Yaviza. Still, few visitors use El Real as anything other than a stepping-stone to someplace else.

The Spanish founded El Real in the early 17th century. Today it boasts little more than an airstrip, a small hospital, a couple of places to stay, three utterly basic restaurants, a few bars, and one billion roosters, all of which are eager to rouse exhausted travelers insanely early.

A big party day around here is August 15, the festival of La Virgen Santa María la Antigua. It's a good excuse for cockfighting and drinking.

Practicalities

El Real's ramshackle houses are connected by a short network of streets and footpaths. It takes maybe 10 minutes to see the whole place. All the places listed here are within shouting distance of each other. If any are closed when you arrive, ask around: The owner is probably nearby and would be happy to open up for a potential customer.

Cana Blanca (no phone) is the most attractive and interesting of the town's bars. It's a

60-year-old cantina with a thatched roof and cane walls, a local institution that's a popular place to begin or end an expedition.

Hotel El Nazareno (tel. 299-6567 or 299-6548, US$10 s, US$12 d) is an old wooden tinderbox of a place on what passes for the main street in what passes for downtown. If you stay here, don't light a match, and pray no one else does, either. It's rustic and the plumbing doesn't work well—one flushes the toilets by dumping a bucket of water down them. Rooms are equipped with fans, and some have private baths. The "best" rooms are on the balcony facing the street. Reception is at the small general store next door.

A better, though not more attractive, lodging option is the very basic rooms rented out by **Narciso "Chicho" Bristán** (tel. 299-6566, US$8 pp). However, these are generally only available to those using Chicho's expert boatman services. Rooms have foam mattresses, plywood walls that don't extend all the way to the ceiling, fans, and that's about it. Showers and toilets are down the hall. This is basically a rustic barracks, but it's about as good as it gets in this part of the Darién.

The most appealing of the three hole-in-the-wall eateries in town, **Fonda Maná** (no phone) consists of a few tables in what is essentially someone's living room. The food is pretty good, considering, and as in all *fondas* (taverns) consists of whatever's on hand that day. Nothing costs more than a buck or two.

The general store next to Hotel El Nazareno and a similar store just up the street carry the bare necessities for a Darién adventure, from machetes to dry noodles.

Those heading into the national park, including Pirre Station, must pay the US$5 park entrance fee at the **ANAM office** (tel. 299-6965, 8 A.M.–4 P.M. Mon.–Fri.) in town. A bed in the dormitory at Pirre Station costs US$10 per person per night. Make that US$5 if you just want to pitch a tent on the grounds. It may be possible to hire an ANAM forest guard to guide you for about US$10 each way.

There's an office of the **Servicio Nacional** **para la Eradicación de Malaria** (SNEM, tel. 299-6299) in town. It can supply antimalaria pills for free if you're running low.

Getting There and Around

Thanks to the improvement of the road from Panama City to Yaviza, there are no longer flights to El Real, at least by now. Most visitors now travel by four-wheel-drive or bus to Yaviza and then travel by boat to El Real.

El Real is the closest transportation hub to Pirre Station, an ANAM ranger station in the most accessible part of Parque Nacional Darién. There are two ways to get to Pirre Station from El Real: by boat up the Río Pirre and on foot along a forest trail.

Most transportation around here is by river. It shouldn't be tough to hitch a ride on a *piragua* (long dugout canoe) to or from Yaviza, where the Interamericana begins (or ends, depending on one's perspective). The fare is US$5 a head.

Longer river trips require more planning and considerable expense. Fuel costs a lot in the Darién, shallow waters take a toll on motors, and the rivers are often blocked by logjams that have to be cut through with chainsaws.

Narciso "Chicho" Bristán (tel. 299-6566) has a well-deserved reputation as the most able boatman in the Darién. He's a sharp, serious guy who shows up on time and hires a top crew. He lives in El Real; everyone knows him. Chicho charges US$75 each way for a trip up the Río Pirre to Piji Basal, the closest village to Pirre Station. A day trip up the Río Tuira to visit the villages along the river costs US$160 round-trip to go as far as Union Chocó. A voyage down the Río Tuira to La Palma, the provincial capital of Darién province, costs at least US$200 one-way (expensive because he has to go back to El Real at the end of the trip). All prices are for up to five people and do not include tips (a good guide will advise whom to tip, and how much; at the very least, tip the hardworking poleman).

Caution: The steps leading down to El Real's "port" are incredibly slippery.

THE ART OF THE *JAGUA*

Emberá-Wounaan men, women, and children sometimes decorate themselves with a black dye drawn from the *jagua* fruit *(Genipa americana),* creating a kind of temporary tattoo. The fruit is pulped, and the liquid from the pulp is painted onto the face and body. The liquid appears clear at first, but as it dries it gradually turns black and the pattern emerges. Traditionally this consists of a geometric pattern across the body up to the lower jaw.

These days Emberá-Wounaan typically only go in for *jagua* decoration at festivals or special occasions. But they've discovered that offering to paint tourists is a good way to entertain them when they visit.

One little catch, though: The dye doesn't wash off. It wears off gradually, usually in a week to 10 days. Sheepish-looking tourists heading home with their faces tattooed-up like Maori warriors can be an amusing sight at the airport. One wonders what the immigration officials make of them back home.

Maybe the Emberá-Wounaan actually came up with a way to entertain *themselves,* not the tourists.

If you decide to get painted, think about where you have to go and what you have to do in the next two weeks. At the very least, you might want to skip the face.

UP THE RÍO TUIRA TOWARD BOCA DE CUPE

Those with a morning to kill and an interest in the flavor of village life in the Darién should consider a trip up the Río Tuira from El Real. The riverbanks are dotted with small communities of Emberá and Wounaan and *darienitas* (descendants of African slaves).

These villages have far too much contact with the modern world to be particularly "traditional." Their narrow streets tend to be paved, for instance, and the Emberá and Wounaan do not traditionally live in villages, period. Those who want to immerse themselves in an older era of indigenous life should consider an expedition far up the Río Sambú or Río Balsas.

This stretch of river is certainly colorful and interesting, but it's too densely populated to be particularly pretty. The river is brown with silt, which is probably a good thing since everything gets dumped in the river. It's not clogged with trash, but it's disheartening to see bottles and foam cups floating by in what used to be Eden. I once even saw a cooler bobbing along. Villagers bathe in the river, which is not something you'll want to try.

Still, green forest lines the banks, unbroken except for the occasional little rice and plantain field. Towering cuipo trees and bizarre-looking kapoks, which can have a crown broader than the tree is tall, jut up from time to time, and majestic neotropical cormorants and other water birds fish along the banks.

Boats are welcome to put in at any community. Villages here tend to be laid-back to the point of torpor, and visitors will likely be looked upon with mild curiosity but little enthusiasm. As always, be respectful and courteous. Do not, for instance, take a photo of anyone without asking permission.

Travelers must register at every police outpost along the river. This means regularly scrambling up muddy banks to present passports and answer a few questions. This is not meant as harassment but rather as a way to tightly monitor all movement in the area. Any boatman with any sense will automatically pull in at every post. Trying to slip by without stopping would be a very, very bad idea.

Officially these guys are police, but a stranger might be forgiven for thinking they were soldiers in a combat zone. They're big dudes with black T-shirts, khaki fatigues, and aging AK-47s, and they spend their days fighting boredom inside semicamouflaged compounds lined with sandbags.

Heading up the Tuira means getting closer and closer to the frontier with Colombia and thus to areas frequented by guerrillas, paramilitary troops, and other characters you won't want to meet. Traveling east past **Boca de Cupe** (pop. 902), about four hours upriver from El Real, is dangerous. Boca de Cupe, sometimes known as Boca de Cupé, has the last police post on the river, and thus the last semblance of law and order. The village itself saw some serious ugliness on November 15, 1997, when a group of unidentified gunmen—some say Colombian guerrillas, others say bandits masquerading as guerrillas, no one knows for sure—attacked the police post and killed one of three officers manning it. The area has seen more recent violence as well: In early 2010, Panamanian police on a patrol in the area came across FARC guerrillas and the ensuing firefight left three guerrillas dead.

The main reason visitors come here is to hike into or out of Cana, a two-day trek southwest. Boca de Cupe was once the supply town for the gold-mining camp in Cana, and though it's hard to believe today, a railroad once linked the two areas.

At the height of the dry season, the river level can drop so low that boat transportation all the way to Boca de Cupe is impossible. Most daytrippers will probably be satisfied with touring the river and the villages closer to El Real.

It's easy to distinguish Emberá and Wounaan villages from Afro-Colonial ones. The houses of the former, made either of planks or (more traditionally) of cane, are built on stilts. The latter are built right on the ground. There are representative examples of each well before Boca de Cupe.

Pinoganá, an Afro-Colonial village about a half hour upriver from El Real by motorized *piragua* (long dugout canoe), is the first village. Though it has a population of only about 350, that's apparently big enough to support three cockfighting rings, which offers pretty much the only entertainment option in town unless you arrive on a festival day. The Fiesta de la Virgen de la Candelaria, held around the end of January and beginning of February, is a big one. There's a tiny place to eat and no official place to sleep. It's kind of a sad little town. There's a police checkpoint.

Vista Alegre, about an hour farther upriver, is a Wounaan village that has another police checkpoint. This is a good place to buy one of the Wounaan's world-famous hand-woven baskets, since every girl in the village age 12 and older makes them. Expect to pay US$60–70 for one the size of a bowling ball. Before haggling too much, look around at how poor this place is and bear in mind it takes two months to weave a basket that size. Baskets are about all the place has to offer.

Union Chocó, less than half an hour farther up, is most notable for the sizable police station in the heart of the village.

All these villages have pay telephones. Remember to bring calling cards in case of an emergency; phones tend to fill up with coins.

The trip back downriver is much faster, thanks to the current. A *piragua* with a 30-horsepower motor can cut trip time in half on the way back down.

Parque Nacional Darién

█ SANTA CRUZ DE CANA

Those who can possibly spare the time and money should make a trip to Santa Cruz de Cana, in the heart of Parque Nacional Darién. More commonly known simply as Cana, it's the most remote spot in all of Panama: The nearest human settlement, Boca de Cupe, is 2–3 days away by foot, and there are no roads. Cana is a truly amazing place that offers genuine wilderness amid relative comfort, a rare combination. It's my favorite spot in the Darién.

Cana sits in a forested valley up against the eastern slope of the 1,615-meter-high Cerro Pirre. Given its extremely isolated location in the middle of dense, uninhabited forest, it's hard to believe Cana has been a major player in the history of the isthmus for at least 500 years. Even more astonishing is that at various times in that period it has hosted large, important settlements. During the Spanish colonial era it grew to be a town of 20,000. Later, it became the first place in all of Panama to have electricity, not to mention an ice plant.

The reason for all this attention was gold. The early conquistadors founded a settlement here and named it Santa Cruz de Cana, but it wasn't until 1665 that they discovered the area's fabulous gold deposits. "The richest gold mines ever yet found in America," the buccaneer historian William Dampier called them in 1684. You can almost hear him drooling.

The Spaniards forced slaves to work the mines, which came to be known as Las Minas del Espíritu Santo de Cana. At their height, they produced 100,000 troy ounces of gold a year. But repeated attacks by English pirates, rebellions, and disease forced the Spanish to abandon the mines in 1727.

They were lost to the jungle for many years before they were reopened in the 19th century. Their most productive period was 1887–1912, when they were run by an Anglo-French outfit called the Darien Gold Mining Company. During this era there was a railroad linking Cana with Boca de Cupe, and from there to the outside world.

The mines were abandoned once again, and once again the jungle swallowed up most traces of human habitation. But in 1962 the last survivor of the Anglo-French operation, a hearty 73-year-old named Medardo Murillo, guided an expedition to the mines. He had started working as a mule driver in 1904, when he was 15, and he still remembered the way. The whole place was overgrown, naturally, but they did find one house still completely intact and still stocked with viable dynamite.

Though mining was revived once again for a spell starting in the 1960s, today Cana is treasured for different kinds of natural riches: amazingly diverse and abundant flora and fauna. Two of Murillo's grandsons now work at an ecological field station at Cana, which, except for a tiny border-police post, is the only inhabited facility of any kind in the entire region. Though in the middle of Parque Nacional Darién, Cana is operated by ANCON, a nonprofit environmental organization, and the tourist concession is operated by Ancon Expeditions, its for-profit tour-operator sister. Other tour operators can use the facilities, but arrangements have to be made through Ancon Expeditions. The imposing abandoned mines (do not try to explore them; for one thing, it's the perfect lair for jaguars and other beasties) and rusted mining equipment overwhelmed by vegetation give the place a slightly spooky *Heart of Darkness* feel. But for the most part it's an open, airy, and inviting spot that doesn't square with stereotypes that the uninitiated may harbor about the forbidding jungle.

Flora and Fauna

The wildlife here is breathtaking. As usual, the only things you're guaranteed to see are some of the most gorgeous birds in the world. But, there's a better chance here of coming across impressive land animals than in most parts of

Panama. Spider monkeys are likely, and it's a near certainty you'll be surrounded by the uncanny bark of howler monkeys. It's not uncommon to come across fresh jaguar prints. Jaguars have been known to take a leisurely stroll down Cana's landing strip, but you'd be extremely lucky to spot one during a brief visit.

Herds of literally hundreds of white-lipped peccaries sometimes descend on the station and tear up the turf, rooting for food. When this happens, everyone locks themselves in the lodge. Peccaries, the only creature I've seen Darién guides get nervous about, can be aggressive; they have sharp teeth, and they run faster than you do. Don't make the mistake of thinking they're just cute little pigs.

The very lucky few might also come across a Baird's tapir, the largest land mammal in Central America. At the cloud-forest camp above Cana, a tapir once sat on a guide's tent while the guide was sleeping in it, much to the surprise of both of them.

Cana has been called one of the 10 greatest bird-watching spots on the planet. Even those with only the slightest interest in feathered creatures will likely be bowled over. Blue-and-yellow, red-and-green, great green, and chestnut-fronted macaws streak across the valley all day long. Keel-billed toucans, looking as if they just flew off a Froot Loops box, peer down at visitors from the trees.

The lodge is a barely converted mining-camp building that dates from the 1960s. It's a rustic wooden structure containing six basic rooms with little in them besides a bed and a few shelves. Fresh linens are supplied and there are screens on the windows. There are shared bathrooms and showers with running water. A generator provides electricity 7–9 P.M., after which everyone switches to candles and flashlights. A plan to upgrade the facilities is on indefinite hold because there are not yet enough visitors to justify the cost.

Trails

Since Cana's elevation is nearly 500 meters, the forest here is premontane, and it's neither as hot nor as buggy as one might expect. The valley offers beautiful views of the surrounding hills, which are covered with lush virgin forest. There's also a cloud-forest camp on the mountain itself, at 1,280 meters, where it can get cool in the evenings.

Five main trails originate from Cana, not counting a short trail near the station that follows railroad tracks to an abandoned locomotive. The **Boca de Cupe Trail** is the longest. It continues for a solid two days, all the way to the village of Boca de Cupe. Hiking in for at least a few kilometers is well worthwhile. It's a mostly flat trail offering spectacular birding and the chance of seeing larger wildlife. The **Machinery Garden Trail** is a lovely and exotic two-kilometer loop that features both nature and the rusting remains of the 19th-century mining operation. The **Seteganti Trail** leads down to the Río Seteganti. Visitors can easily explore all these trails during a brief visit.

The Pirre Mountain Trail is a somewhat strenuous nine-kilometer hike that leads three-quarters of the way up Cerro Pirre to the cloud-forest camp. The hike takes 4–5 hours at a reasonable clip. The hike down takes about three hours.

It's absolutely worth the effort. The trail itself leads through beautiful primary forest alive with animals. On a single trip I encountered large groups of spider monkeys crashing through the trees, a fer-de-lance snake, and, of course, dozens upon dozens of flamboyant birds.

The cloud-forest camp itself is a pretty impressive operation. A full field kitchen is set up in one large thatch-roofed hut, and tents with pads are set up in another. The camp can accommodate about two dozen guests. It's relatively cushy for its location. Generally all you have to take is a day pack; the cook and staff bring the food and water and set up the tents. (Tips are much appreciated; the guides can suggest amounts.) The view of nearby Cerro Setetule and the forested valley is breathtaking, and the nights are a riot of forest sounds. Big animals have been known to wander through camp at night.

The truly dedicated can continue a bit

farther up the mountain on the **Cloudforest Trail,** but the summit can't be reached from this side of the mountain. There's a slim chance of spotting the rare golden-headed quetzal on this trail.

Guides lead all these hikes. Do not attempt to venture out anywhere alone.

It's hard to exaggerate just how special the Cana area is. It's an enormous expanse of nearly pristine tropical forest, an overwhelming oasis of biodiversity. It's not cheap to get there and the trip is a bit of an adventure, but nature lovers will likely find it the highlight of their trip to Panama.

Getting There

The easiest, though by far the most expensive, way to visit Cana is by airplane, since only small chartered planes make the trip. Visits are generally arranged through tour operators, who offer package deals that include airfare. The trip over takes about 1.25 hours. The view is incredible. Planes land on a grass landing strip that ends in the mountain, which makes take-offs and landings adventures in themselves.

Ancon Expeditions (tel. 269-9414 or 269-9415, fax 264-3713, www.anconexpeditions. com) offers a five-day all-inclusive package to Cana, "The Ultimate Darién Experience," for US$1,495 per person. Larger groups pay significantly lower per-person rates. Prices do not include sales tax, currently 5 percent. A visit to Cana is sometimes included as part of other packages.

A far cheaper, though far more strenuous, way to visit is on foot. It's a two- to three-day trek from Boca de Cupe, following the route of the old railroad. Most get to Boca de Cupe by river from El Real or Yaviza. This is a popular leg of many multiday Darién treks and definitely something to be tried only with well-equipped, knowledgeable guides.

◖ PIRRE STATION

The area around Pirre Station, an ANAM ranger station in Parque Nacional Darién, offers an experience similar to Cana at a fraction of the cost. While Pirre is in the lowlands and

Cana is in the foothills, they are on opposite sides of Cerro Pirre and share many of the same birds and other wildlife. Both have good trails, including ones that lead up onto Cerro Pirre.

Pirre Station is just within the boundaries of Parque Nacional Darién, in an area known as **Rancho Frío.** The forest here is lush and primeval; it has never been cut. The birding is excellent. Specialties include such beauties as lemon-spectacled and scarlet-browed tanagers, white-fronted nunbirds, and crimson-bellied woodpeckers. Those who wouldn't know a white-fronted nunbird from a nun should keep their eyes and ears open for flocks of macaws, an impressive sight by anyone's standards. Mammals include sloths, spider and howler monkeys, white-faced capuchins, and Geoffroy's tamarins. A 150-kilogram jaguar has been seen in the area, but as usual the chances of spotting it are extremely slim.

The station is surrounded by primary forest and little else. Facilities are minimal, consisting of a dormitory, an outhouse with flush toilets and showers, a field kitchen, and a couple of picnic tables. The dormitory is basic, to say the least. It consists of two bedrooms and a bare common area with concrete floors. Visitors sleep on bunk beds that are nothing more than foam mattresses on wooden frames. The rangers sleep in the second bedroom. There is no electricity at the station.

The site itself, however, is beautiful. The crystal waters of the Río Peresenico run by the camp, which sits in a clearing ringed by verdant forest.

Trails

Two main trails originate from the station. One is an easy two-kilometer **loop trail** that leads to a series of waterfalls just 15 minutes away from the station. It's a real *Blue Lagoon* scene. The first waterfall is about five meters tall and pours into a deep pool filled with cold, clear water and surrounded by deep green vegetation.

Those feeling adventurous or foolish or both can climb the sheer, slippery face of the first waterfall and follow the river to two more falls.

Be aware that there are several ways to get seriously hurt doing this, and it's a long, long way to a hospital from here.

Hernan Araúz, probably the top Darién guide in the country, nearly bit it not once but twice here. The first time he scrambled to the top of the waterfall only to come face to face with an annoyed fer-de-lance snake. He had to dive back down the waterfall and was lucky not to break his neck. The second time he slid down the face of the waterfall in a more measured way, only to get pushed underwater by the fast-flowing current; his companion had to dive in and pull him out.

So don't attempt to clamber around without a good, strong guide to help you. Throw rocks into the brush at the side of the falls to scare away venomous snakes. Watch your step at the higher falls; it's easy to step out into space and fall into a chasm. Be prepared to swim hard when you slide back down the first waterfall, especially if wearing lots of jungle gear. And make sure someone's always nearby in case of an emergency.

The trails around Cerro Pirre offer some of the best bird-watching in the world.

A fork in the middle of the loop trail leads up to a clearing that has a communications tower, but it's a tough, two-hour climb up a steep incline, and clouds usually obscure the view.

The **Cerro Pirre trail** leads up the mountain, starting in the forest and coming out onto an exposed ridge that skirts the mountain, rather than climbing to its summit. It's a fairly steep hike, very steep at times, with lots of ups and downs. Expect the trail to be muddy and slippery. It's a moderately strenuous trail and only reasonably fit hikers should attempt it.

It takes about two hours at a rapid clip to get to **Rancho Plástico,** which, despite its name, is only a reference point and has no facilities. It offers a view of the Río Balsas. Theoretically one could continue along the ridge for two days before turning back. Note that this trail does not link up with Cana's Cloudforest Trail on the other side of the mountain.

It's possible to camp along the ridge, but there are no facilities.

It's especially important to have a guide on this hike. The trail is not well defined and is not being maintained. It's easy to get lost, and tree falls sometimes completely block the way. If you're alone and get lost or hurt, there's a real chance you won't make it out.

Practicalities

Pirre Station is too far from El Real, or anywhere else, for a day trip. Plan to spend at least one night here, two if possible.

Visitors must bring their own towels and will probably want to bring sheets, though the latter can be rented at the station for US$3. Because there is no electricity, or even kerosene lanterns, bringing lots of extra flashlight batteries is a good idea. Bring a good water purifier or purification tablets unless you don't mind toting water all the way from El Real.

The rangers keep the grounds of the station well groomed and clear of debris. But within about 100 meters of the station the forest is literally crawling with venomous fer-de-lance snakes. You're unlikely to come upon one, but never wear sandals and shorts outside the

© WILLIAM FRIAR

THE DARIÉN

immediate station area. In the Darién, I generally wear boots and long pants even in camp, especially at night.

Visitors should pay the national park fees ahead of time at the **ANAM office** (tel. 299-6965, 8 A.M.–4 P.M. Mon.–Fri.) in El Real.

Travelers must bring their own food, usually from El Real. The rangers will cook and wash dishes for a small tip. Around US$5 a day for a small group is about right. It'd be a nice gesture to bring enough food for the rangers, too. Remember that these are forest guards, not hotel staff. They're your hosts, and you'll have a more enjoyable time if you've won their goodwill. If you arrive without a guide, consider hiring a ranger to take you on the trails, though their wilderness skills and knowledge of the area vary. Again, do not venture far on a trail without a competent guide.

Getting There

Unlike many places in the Darién, it's possible to visit Pirre Station on your own without tremendous hassle or expense. However, I recommend going with a good tour operator, as you're likely to have a safer, more enlightening trip and won't have to deal with making all the considerable arrangements.

Getting to Pirre Station can be an adventure. The usual point of entry is El Real. There are two ways to get to Pirre Station from El Real: by boat up the Río Pirre and on foot along a forest trail.

The trail leads directly to Pirre Station. Do not hike it without a knowledgeable guide. Hiking in takes about 2.5 hours in the dry season, when it is generally the only option because the Río Pirre drops to an unnavigable trickle. In the rainy season, though, the trail to Pirre Station turns into a boot-sucking ribbon of mud and the hike becomes a miserable four-hour slog.

When it's runnable, the river is definitely the way to go for those who can afford it. **Narciso "Chicho" Bristán** (tel. 299-6566) in El Real is an excellent boatman and the obvious first choice. The trip costs US$75 for up to five people each way and takes travelers up the Río Pirre to the poor little Emberá village of Piji Basal. This leg of the journey can take up to three hours if the river is choked with fallen trees, which it frequently is. Watching a boatman chainsawing a massive trunk in the middle of a fast-flowing river suddenly makes the fare seem quite reasonable.

It takes about 90 minutes to hike the trail from Piji Basal to Pirre Station, a little less if you take an overgrown shortcut for the first part of it. Again, go with a knowledgeable guide. It's good politics (and karma) to hire a porter in Piji Basal. It'll cost about US$5 up to Pirre. Don't count on the porter knowing the way, oddly enough.

The trip back down the Río Pirre is much faster. Stay alert throughout the lovely ride. It's remarkably easy to get your head taken off by treefalls if you're dozing.

Coastal and Upriver Darién

◖ PUNTA PATIÑO NATURE RESERVE

Punta Patiño is, at 30,000 hectares, the largest private reserve in the country. It's owned by ANCON, a Panamanian environmental nonprofit, and operated by its for-profit sister organization, Ancon Expeditions. It's a great place to come to get a taste of "coastal Darién," which has a much different feel from the interior. Punta Patiño offers quite a range of vegetation and wildlife, and it's the most comfortable place to stay in the Darién outside of the Tropic Star Lodge. It's on the Golfo de San Miguel, a little under an hour by boat from La Palma.

Large swaths of Patiño, about a third of the reserve, were used for a cattle, coconut, and lumber operation before it became a protected area. The coconut plantation is still standing, but nothing is being done with it. Nature is making a surprisingly strong recovery in the disturbed areas. A large reforestation project is under way, and ANCON is also working to preserve red and black mangroves here.

Punta means "point." The point is off to the left as you face the beach, where the lighthouse is. The closest settlements from here are the small Afro-Colonial town of Punta Alegre, between Punta Patiño and La Palma, and an Emberá village up the Río Mogue.

Flora and Fauna

The forest around the lodge is secondary growth, but primary forest isn't far away.

Notable trees include the massive cuipo, whose blossoms burst into bright red or orange at the end of the dry season, and the spiny cedar, which has sharp spikes covering its trunk.

There's a decent chance of seeing at least one kind of exotic critter that doesn't have wings here. You're almost guaranteed to see capybara, the world's largest rodent (picture a giant guinea pig), and gray foxes at night toward the end of the rainy season (late December–January). Sightings drop off thereafter. Other largish mammals include *tayras* (a lanky weasel with a long, bushy tail), Geoffroy's tamarins, night monkeys, and collared peccaries.

PANAMA'S MAGNIFICENT NATIONAL BIRD: THE HARPY EAGLE

COURTESY OF JIM GUY

Luigi, a harpy eagle at the Peregrine Fund's conservation program at Clayton

The Darién is one of the last Panamanian homes of the harpy eagle *(Harpia harpyja),* the world's most powerful bird of prey. It is Panama's national bird. Deforestation has endangered this magnificent creature, which inhabits lowland tropical forests from southeastern Mexico to parts of Argentina and

Brazil. So has hunting, especially since harpy eagles don't generally fear humans. It doesn't help that they produce at most one chick for every nesting attempt, and that they nest only once every three years. This is the longest known breeding period for any raptor.

Conservation programs are underway in Panama, including a breeding program to re-introduce harpy eagles into wilderness areas where they've disappeared. The first harpy eagle bred in captivity in Panama, or anywhere else in Central America, was born in January 2002 at the Peregrine Fund's Neotropical Raptor Center near Panama City.

The eagle can grow to over a meter long from fierce hooked bill to tail, more than half the height of a tall man. Its wingspan can reach 2.1 meters, as wide as a basketball player is tall. Its talons are the size of a grizzly bear's claws. Adults have a distinctive two-pronged crest, making them easy to distinguish from other eagles.

You'd be extremely lucky to spot a harpy eagle even in the Darién, as they rarely soar above the treetops. They hunt within the canopy with remarkable agility given their great size. They favor monkeys, sloths, and other hefty mammals, which they scoop up in their powerful talons at speeds of up to 80 kilometers per hour.

THE DARIÉN

Caimans lurk in the swampier areas, and there are also lots of iguanas. Pilot and humpback whales and bottle-nosed dolphins can sometimes be spotted in the Golfo de San Miguel. Bird specialties at Patiño include black-tailed trogons, boat-billed herons, and night herons. A jaguar has been known to hunt capybara in the area, but don't expect to see it.

Sports and Recreation

There are several well-developed trails—in some cases they lead to old roads—leading into a variety of ecosystems.

The **Sendero Piedra de Candela (Flintstone Trail)** is named for the reddish quartzes along this stretch; striking them with a machete sets off sparks. It's a loop trail that takes about an hour to walk. It goes through secondary-growth coastal forest where birders can hunt for mannakins, common black hawks, woodpeckers, and tanagers. It's also a good place to spot Geoffroy's tamarin and, at night, red-eyed tree frogs. It's a flat, easy trail. After 2.5 kilometers it meets a coastal road that eventually leads to the Afro-Colonial town of Punta Alegre in one direction and back to the lodge in the other.

A trail that starts behind Cabin 10 merges with a road leading to the back part of the reserve, which consists of primary lowland forest. There's also a road/trail that leads through the coconut plantation into some wetlands, and another short one leading onto the airstrip.

While walking the trails is the main activity here, don't forget the beach just down the hill from the lodge. It's black sand, but pleasant, and you'll have it all to yourself. There's a second beach a 10-minute boat ride away.

Accommodations

Guests stay in **ANCON's lodge,** high on a hill behind a long, deserted beach. It's a steep walk, but the reserve has a "tractor taxi," a tractor with a wagon hitched to it, to transport guests and luggage. The lodge has a dining hall with a wrap-around balcony fitted with strategically placed hammocks. There's a *mirador* (observation platform) upstairs. The balcony and *mirador* have gorgeous views of the Golfo de San Miguel and the point where historians believe Balboa stepped out of the forest and became the first European to see the Pacific. On the left there's a sweeping view of the old coconut plantation. Sunsets can be spectacular here, especially during the dry season. The lodge is high enough to watch mangrove black-hawks sail by at eye level. It's an incredibly tranquil spot, especially when it's breezy.

The 10 simple but pleasant cabins are behind the lodge. They're surrounded by flowering trees, and all are air-conditioned and have a view out over the coconut plantation from their balconies. Each has two beds, high ceilings, and a private cold-water shower and toilet. Towels and soap are provided. A generator supplies electricity in the lodge and cabins 6 P.M.–6 A.M.

The place is well managed and guest-oriented. Thoughtful touches include being greeted with a *pipa* (fresh coconut), finding fresh-cut flowers in the cabin, and discovering that a staff member has fired up the air-conditioner in the cabin before you turn in for the night. Lime trees are everywhere, so there's always plenty of fresh limeade to cool you off.

However, because Patiño is surrounded by mangroves, it's much buggier than places such as Pirre Station and especially Cana. The mosquitoes are intense in the late rainy season, and insect repellent just seems to make them thirstier. As annoying as this is, Patiño has so many charms that it's worth a little crazed scratching and a welt or two.

This place is a good compromise for those who'd like a taste of the Darién, but don't want to rough it too much.

Getting There and Around

There is a private airstrip at Punta Patiño, but only chartered aircraft land there. The nearest commercial airstrip is in La Palma. From La Palma it's about an hour down to Patiño by boat, which will be arranged for those who go with a tour operator. **Ancon Expeditions** (tel. 269-9414 or 269-9415, fax 264-3713, www.anconexpeditions.com) offers a four-day, three-night package to Patiño for US$625 per person. The price includes lodging, airfare, guided hikes in the forest, tours of the Emberá village on the Río Mogue, and meals. For another US$70 per person, guests can stay another day to search for harpy eagles and spend the night in the *tambo* (traditional Emberá open-sided thatched-roof hut) in Mogue.

Sales tax, currently 7 percent, is not included. The company also includes a visit to Punta Patiño as part of other trips.

LA PALMA

La Palma (pop. 3,884) is the provincial capital of the Darién, with the accent squarely on "provincial." Branches of the major government offices are here, including ANAM (the environmental regulatory agency), a police headquarters, a grim jail, and even an outpost of the national lottery.

La Palma's location is striking. It's at the wide mouth of the Río Tuira, just where it races into the Golfo de San Miguel. Balboa became the first European to discover the Pacific near here. The ruins of Spanish fortifications are on craggy islets topped with emerald vegetation a few minutes' boat ride away. It's a natural launching point for trips by water into the heart of the Darién.

Look away from the water, though, and the view becomes less appealing. La Palma is a hot, humid town where garbage piles up on the side of the road or is just chucked into the fast-flowing river. It consists of a strip of road wedged between an unbroken chain of hole-in-the-wall restaurants, bars, stores, and hotels perched above the river mouth on one side and a steep hill crowded with shanties on the other side. A remarkable number of minibuses ply this single road, which leads to the village of Setegantí, about 20 kilometers south of the airstrip. Walking the length of "downtown," from the airstrip at one end to the Cable and Wireless office at the other, takes about 10 minutes at a slow pace. The town does not have a friendly vibe. Be prepared for lots of poker-faced stares.

As with Yaviza and El Real, most visitors use La Palma as a way station and provisioning post on the way to somewhere else. Still, town life in La Palma can be fascinating for an hour or two: a drunk staggering around at 10 in the morning, a surly Colombian shop owner grumbling about being ostracized by the locals, a tailor working his foot-pedaled Singer on the street, kids setting off to school in neat blue-and-white uniforms.

An important festival day here is the Fiesta de San José, held on March 19.

Sights

Other than the town itself, the only thing in the area that constitutes a sight is **El Fuerte de San Carlos de Boca Chica,** the ruins of which are five minutes by motorboat from La Palma on the island of Boca Chica. It should be easy to find a boatman willing to make the trip. Ask down by the boat ramps about *el fuerte de Boca Chica.* About US$10 for a small group should do it.

Note there's a small battery on a neighboring islet, but the main fortifications are on Boca Chica. The Spanish built El Fuerte de San Carlos de Boca Chica in the mid-18th century as part of their network of defenses for the Espiritu Santo gold mines in Cana. It's not a big fort and the jungle has devoured much of it—a strangler fig has practically melded with what's left. But it's an impressive, photogenic sight, and it brings history vividly to life. It doesn't take much imagination to picture a poor, homesick Spanish soldier on lookout here, sweating in the jungle and keeping an eye out for pirates. The fort is a couple of minutes uphill from shore and so shrouded by forest it's no longer easy to see from the water.

There are two Afro-Colonial towns a few minutes by boat from La Palma: Punta Alegre on the Golfo de San Miguel to the southwest and Chepigana near the mouth of the Río Tuira to the southeast, though they're little more than collections of zinc-roofed shanties on the water's edge.

Accommodations and Food

Hotel Biaquirú Bagará (tel. 299-6224,

the Darién version of takeaway food

© WILLIAM FRIAR

US$10 s, US$15 d for a room with fan and shared bath; US$20 s, US$30d with a/c and private bath), near the end of town heading away from the airstrip, is by far the best place to stay in La Palma. The place is a local institution and has been the home base of many expeditions. It offers 13 tidy little rooms, some of which are surprisingly cheerful. A few have balconies. The two best rooms have air-conditioning and private bathrooms. Amenities include satellite TV, a pay phone, and free drinking water. It's by no means a fancy place, but after spending time in the jungle, it'll feel like the Ritz. There's a lovely view of the river from the balcony. Meals can be arranged at the hotel with notice. Price depends on what you want.

A couple of other somewhat grim places in town will do in a pinch.

All the "restaurants" in La Palma are *fondas,* little holes-in-the-wall that serve whatever they happen to have on hand that day for a buck or two. Sometimes this includes peccary (usually called *puerco de monte,* mountain pig). Hunting and eating peccaries and other wild animals is illegal and punishable by jail time. Do not order it.

Services

All the services in town are squeezed together one after another on La Palma's main road. The exception is the hospital, which is now in a new structure on the hill at the far side of the town's airstrip, outside of town. Every bus running between La Palma and Seteganti drives near the place.

La Palma carries just about anything you'd need for a Darién expedition. It's also one of the few places in the Darién with fresh produce. There are a couple of general stores, offering provisions ranging from sodas to machetes.

Banco Nacional de Panamá (8 A.M.–3 P.M. Mon.–Fri., 9 A.M.–noon Sat.), near the airstrip, cashes American Express travelers checks.

The **Cable and Wireless office** (8:30 A.M.–4:30 P.M. Mon.–Fri.), at the far end of town from the airstrip, sells Telechip phone cards.

Getting There and Around

The crumbling "airport" at the edge of town

doesn't inspire much confidence, but most visitors come and leave by air.

Aeroperlas (tel. 315-7500, www.aeroperlas.com) flies between La Palma and Panama City on Monday, Wednesday, and Friday. Flights leave Panama City around 10:25 A.M. and return around 11:15 A.M. **Air Panama** (tel. 316-9000, www.flyairpanama.com) flies on Monday and Friday, leaving around 10:45 A.M., returning to Panama City around 11:35 A.M. Sometimes there are intermediate stops in El Real and Sambú. The flight is around an hour, depending on stops. Tickets cost US$72 each way.

These times are approximate at best. One time the flight back to Panama City was so late I could have gotten back faster by boat and bus.

A water taxi runs from Puerto Quimba to La Palma, 7:30 A.M.–6:30 P.M., and from La Palma to Puerto Quimba, 5:30 A.M.–5 P.M. The water taxi to La Palma theoretically runs every 60–75 minutes, but in reality only the first one of the day is reliable. After that, the boat leaves when it gets a full load. The trip costs US$3 one-way and takes about 30–45 minutes.

MOGUE

The Emberá village of Mogue (MOE-gay), up the river that gives it its name, welcomes visitors and in fact has become a tourist destination for the area. It's about midway between Punta Patiño and La Palma.

It takes about a half hour by boat from either Patiño or La Palma to get to the mouth of the Río Mogue. It's a potentially bumpy boat ride on the ocean. The Mogue is a beautiful river, in a slightly spooky, Conradian sense. It's swampy, still, and serpentine, with towering black mangroves on either side.

Boats have to take it slow up this murky river to avoid damaging the engine. It's about a 25-minute cruise from the mouth of the river to Mogue village. On the river and the trails around the village, birders might spot white ibises, willets, whimbrels, mangrove black-hawks, roseate spoonbills, red-throated caracaras, laughing falcons, black oropendolas, orange-crowned orioles, and other gorgeous birds.

You'll know the village is near when the mangroves give way to plantain fields. It's a 15-minute walk from where the boat puts in to Paraíso Mogue (Mogue Paradise), as a welcome sign in the village puts it.

The Emberá established Mogue in the late 1960s. It's a relatively pretty little village that caters to tourists, putting on traditional dances and opening handicraft stalls when tour groups arrive. But it feels relatively "traditional," given that the Emberá do not traditionally live in villages at all.

It's possible to spend the night in Mogue in relative comfort. There's a huge version of a *tambo*, a traditional Emberá open-sided thatched-roof hut raised on stilts about 15 feet off the ground, where visitors can pitch tents and relax in hammocks. It's breezy up there and has an eavesdropper's view of the surrounding village, as well as a vista of the forest-covered hills in the distance. If you stay here, drown yourself in insect repellent and be prepared to be awakened early by roosters and crying babies.

Primary forest starts 15 minutes from the village. An hour hike from here leads to a harpy eagle nest. An hour hike in the opposite direction leads to the nest of a crested eagle. You'll need a guide to show the way in either case.

A big festival in these parts is held on November 14, the anniversary of the building of the local school.

Practicalities

Because of Mogue's proximity to Punta Patiño, most visitors come here with **Ancon Expeditions** (tel. 269-9414 or 269-9415, fax 264-3713, www.anconexpeditions.com) as part of a stay at Patiño. Ancon Expeditions brings in food, which the villagers cook. Depending on the itinerary, visitors either spend the night or just pay a short day visit.

Mogue has showers for tourists that may actually work, and a rather scary-looking latrine.

UP THE RÍO SAMBÚ

The Río Sambú makes for a memorable boat ride. Its wide, muddy mouth opens into the Ensenada de Garachiné, a cove that in turn opens into the Pacific Ocean. The mouth is about midway between Punta Garachiné to the south and Punta Patiño to the north. The river is bordered by an intricate tangle of mangroves, behind which rise lush green towering trees. It's a beautiful sight. Even though there are settlements along the banks and many small fishing boats plying the waters, there's no doubt you're in Mother Nature's living room here.

It's easy to spot birds sailing overhead or hanging by the water as you motor upriver, particularly such water-loving fowl as herons, egrets, frigate birds, pelicans, and cormorants. You'll probably see at least a couple of hawks perched high atop the tallest trees. Toucans and parrots are a bit harder to spot, but they're around. And the occasional splash and burble in the river will set your mind wondering exactly what is lurking in there.

La Chunga and Sambú

The touristy Emberá village of La Chunga (la CHOON-guh) is about an hour upriver. It's along the banks of the Río Chunga, a sluggish but no less scenic little river that empties into the Sambú. A *chunga* is a kind of black palm with sharp spines, used by the Emberá-Wounaan to make decorative baskets. Ask a villager to point one out. The village is about a 20-minute walk down a wide, flat path from where the boat lands.

You may have mixed feelings about visiting La Chunga. The village, which has a population of about 300 people, has obviously been shaped with tourists in mind. Most of the tourists come from small cruise ships that offer a taste of the Darién as part of a transcanal itinerary. Those who slip into the village ahead of a tour group may see women taking off their blouses and bras and men kicking off their jeans to look appropriately native for their visitors. Decked out in little more than short skirts or loin coverings, they dance around as tourists snap photos. The whole thing looks as uncomfortable for the villagers as it will probably feel to you.

When a tour group is expected, Emberá and Wounaan come from nearby settlements to join the villagers in selling handicrafts at tables set up around the village. It's possible to get some well-made souvenirs at good prices, and the money is going right to the needy source. Popular items include cocobolo (rosewood) figurines, tightly woven baskets and bowls, and tagua nuts (also known as ivory nuts) carved in the shape of forest animals.

The airstrip for the area is in the tiny, ramshackle town of Sambú, whose residents are a mixture of Afro-Colonials, Emberá, and Wounaan. There are a couple of new guesthouses in town.

Accommodations

The residents of La Chunga managed to turn their village into one of the more comfortable places to stay in the Darién. "Comfort" is a relative term where the Darién is concerned, but amazingly enough this place has real flush toilets and running water. Four solid thatch-roofed, bamboo-sided cabins on stilts are rented out to visitors. The rooms, officially known as the **Hotel Emberá,** are a short walk from the village proper, set in a little clearing where medicinal plants are grown for the edification of visitors. The cabins have two rooms, each equipped just with two wooden beds topped by foam mattresses and mosquito nets. One of the cabins has double beds; the rest are singles. Showers are in a neighboring hut and consist of a cold-water spigot. Rates are US$150 for one person, US$60 for each additional person. This includes lodging, meals, and tours, but not airfare to Sambú.

Your host is Ricardo Cabrera, *cacique* (chief) of La Chunga and 11 other villages. Ricardo is a friendly guy who speaks English well. (He's the only one in the village who speaks more than a word or two.) It's startling to hear American slang from him until you learn he spent six months in Southern California helping a missionary document the Emberá language. He can arrange guided hikes on which you might see all kinds of critters, including crocodiles in a nearby lake, golden-headed quetzals, peccaries, and, of course, snakes. Ricardo has recently opened a second, three-room guesthouse, **Villa Siesta,** in the tiny town of Sambú itself. Rates are US$20 for the room alone. He's also working on a third place farther up the river.

To stay at Hotel Emberá or Villa Siesta, get in touch with Ricardo Cabrera. Getting in touch with him can be tricky. Start by calling Ricardo's sister in Panama City (tel. 234-8281). Ricardo has a mobile phone (cell 6687-2271), but he's often out of range. There is one public telephone in the village (tel. 299-6083); ask for Ricardo. However, be advised that the phone is often out of order. If all else fails, send a telegram from a post office to: Ricardo Cabrera, La Chunga, Darién, Zona 4. List your contact information, proposed date of arrival, number in the party, and how long you want to stay. If Ricardo knows you're coming, he'll arrange to meet you at the airstrip, but don't be surprised if you have to wait around for a while.

Another new place in Sambú is **Sambú Hause** (tel. 268-6905, cell 6627-2135 or 6766-5102, http://sambuhausedarienpanama.com, US$125 s/d, including meals) consists of four rooms in a simple wooden house about 500 meters from the airstrip. One of the rooms has a private bathroom; the rest share bathrooms. The house has electricity, mosquito screening, modern fixtures, a TV/DVD player, a deck and front porch, an outdoor barbecue, and a fully equipped kitchen. It is by no means a luxurious place, but these things alone mean it offers by far the best-equipped village accommodations in the Darién.

This place is the creation of Michael Harrington, an American married to a *darienita*. It is managed by his sister-in-law, María Asprilla and her daughter, Mabel. It is still a work in progress: Everything must be brought in by boat or plane, so construction is slow and expensive. But it appears to be a good midrange option for those who want a bit of comfort during a Darién trip, but have an adventurous spirit, are comfortable with rustic surroundings, and like the idea of staying in the heart of a hand-to-mouth Darién community.

Sambú Hause can arrange guided forest hikes (about US$15/hour) and river trips on motorized *piraguas* (about US$35/hour). As at La Chunga, the local indigenous people perform Emberá-Wounaan dances (no charge, but a US$20 tip is expected and appreciated) and sell baskets, tagua carvings, and other handicrafts.

Sambú Hause offers adventurous overnight treks, arranged through a man named Juancito, who can also come up with cheaper, more rustic accommodations for those who can't afford Sambú Hause.

Getting There and Away

With the exception of those who come by boat from Punta Patiño or elsewhere, most visitors fly to Sambú. From there they can hire a boat to La Chunga if they haven't arranged for someone to meet them. **Air Panama** (tel. 316-9000, www.flyairpanama.com) makes one flight on Monday, Wednesday, and Friday. The cost is US$69.33 each way. Aeroperlas does not fly here these days.

Air Panama flies over at around 10:30 A.M. The return flight is around 11:25 A.M. The flight takes about 45 minutes nonstop but can last about 90 minutes with stops.

◖ BAHÍA DE PIÑAS

The Bahía de Piñas (Piñas Bay) is far down the Pacific coast of Panama, southeast of the Golfo de San Miguel and just 56 kilometers from the Colombian border. It is world-famous for deep-sea fishing, but the area is so extraordinarily beautiful that even those who don't want to go near a fish will likely enjoy a visit. It's also a culturally interesting area.

Approximately 200 deep-sea fishing world records have been set in this area, more than anywhere else on the planet. Most of these are for black, blue, or striped marlin and Pacific sailfish.

What accounts for this? It has a lot to do with **Zane Grey Reef,** a dramatic seamount

THE DARIÉN

(underwater mountain) that rises from the 100-meter-deep sea bottom in three peaks, two of which top out within 45 meters of the surface. The current sweeps plankton around the reef, which feeds huge amounts of baitfish, which in turn attract large predators. The area is a giant natural aquarium filled with, among other things, sharks, rays, jacks, snappers, dorado, tuna, and, of course, billfish. The reef is particularly renowned among anglers for black marlin. The area is carefully protected: Panama enforces a 32-kilometer exclusion zone around the bay, into which commercial fishing vessels with their huge nets are not allowed. Panama's marine authority keeps a small ship stationed in the area that investigates any suspected infractions; violators are fined and can lose their fishing licenses.

The Bahía de Piñas itself is a small, narrow bay formed by two fingers of land that jut out to sea. Between are the landscaped grounds of Tropic Star Lodge. Close to 6,000 hectares of the surrounding land is owned by Tropic Star, and nearly all of this has been left undeveloped and pristine. It is heart-stopping gorgeous: Emerald forests filled with massive trees spill down the hilly countryside to the very edge of the coast, which ends in sheer, rocky cliffs broken by the occasional waterfall. Dolphins like to romp around inside the bay, and humpback whales are sometimes spotted outside it. Indigenous people still pan for, and sometimes find, gold nuggets on the Río Piñas.

Playa Blanca, a small but gorgeous white-sand beach just north of the bay, offers clear blue water and snorkeling near a coral reef just offshore. It's on property owned by Tropic Star Lodge, but as with all beaches in Panama it's open to the public. However, only guests of the lodge may hike into the forest.

Nearby are two small coastal towns, **Puerto Piñas** and **Jaqué,** which have a mixed population of Afro-Colonial and Emberá inhabitants. Several indigenous villages are up the Río Jaqué, one of which, the Wounaan village of **Biroquera,** is open to day visitors.

Puerto Piñas

To the southeast of the lodge, about 10 minutes by boat, is the small fishing village of Puerto Piñas (pop. 819). It's a dilapidated place, but the people are friendly and laid-back and it's right on a gray sandy beach. A little more than half its residents are estimated to be Emberá and the rest Afro-Colonial. Dwellings consist of modest cinderblock houses next to traditional cane or plank thatch-roofed huts. There is also a good airstrip, a police bunker, an ultrabasic place to stay, a couple of equally basic places to eat and drink, an Aeroperlas "office," a primary school, a tiny general store, several churches, a volleyball court, a sand soccer field, and a whole lot else. An odd little factoid: The town and its environs have a dog population of about 400, one for every two residents.

Past the soccer field, on the far end of the village, is an enormous open-sided thatched-roof hut used for village meetings and Emberá dances presented to tourists. About half of the adult residents of the village work at Tropic Star during the fishing season. Otherwise, they sustain themselves through fishing and subsistence agriculture, especially bananas, plantains, and rice.

The area surrounding Puerto Piñas has been turned into farmland. It and the neighboring village of Jaqué are both at the edge of swampy plains backed by hills; the flatlands have largely been deforested, but the hills are mostly intact.

Jaqué

The area around the town of Jaqué (pop. 2,244) is even more deforested. They actually graze cattle here—thankfully the only place along this stretch of coast that does. They mainly fish and grow crops that include rice, plantains, yuca, and yams. It's considerably larger and relatively more affluent-looking than Puerto Piñas, with some fairly substantial houses, but it's still a place where people live pretty close to the bone. There's an airstrip, a hospital, two *hospedajes,* a soccer field, and a handful of basic places to get a bite or a drink. A police bunker is at the edge of town near the mouth of the Río Jaqué, and there's a camouflage netting–covered main *cuartel* (police station) in the center of town. In 2000, the Colombian civil war pushed hundreds of refugees from the Colombian town of Juradó over the border into Jaqué and its surroundings. Stories appeared in the Panamanian press at that time saying that some of these refugees had been placed on Colombian death lists, and there was concern the war might spill over the border into this area. This didn't happen, and a beefed-up police presence in town and up the Río Jaqué kept the situation under control for several years. However, in June 2010, two Panamanian policemen were maimed by anti-personnel mines near the village of Jaqué, on the Bahía de Piñas. This is the first time anti-personnel mines have ever appeared in Panama. These were allegedly planted by drug traffickers. Yet more police have poured into the area, and the president of Panama, Ricardo Martinelli, has begun making tough speeches against the traffickers and Colombian guerrillas. The situation appeared volatile as this book went to press. Until local conditions change, I strongly advise visitors to avoid Jaqué and the surrounding area (though Tropic Star

Lodge still appears to be largely insulated from the conflict).

All that said, when left on its own the town is mellow and the people are friendly to strangers. Those who come to Jaqué, when it's safe to do so, by boat must get from open sea to the mouth of the Río Jaqué, and doing so often means riding waves that can be three meters high or even bigger. Managing this requires an experienced captain with a feel for surfing, and no one should attempt it without life jackets. This wave actually can be surfed, though few have made it all the way down here with their boards.

Near Jaqué

Warning: Before heading upriver, check in with the police station in town to make sure it's safe to do so. There are four indigenous villages on the Río Jaqué within about 20 kilometers of the town of Jaqué: Biroquera, Lucas, El Coco, and El Mamey. There are police posts in each village, but the upper reaches of the Río Jaqué beyond El Mamey are not patrolled and are supposedly used as a rest spot by combatants

© WILLIAM FRIAR

The indigenous villages up the Río Jaqué welcome visitors.

THE DARIÉN

in the Colombian civil war. All the villages are Emberá except the first one, Biroquera, which is Wounaan. It's about 15 minutes by fast boat from Jaqué and is the only village Panamanian authorities are allowing foreign travelers to visit. For your own safety, do not attempt to travel farther upriver. Note also that getting to the Río Jaqué by sea can be rough.

Biroquera is a fairly tidy and spacious village built right on the edge of the river. It's worth a quick visit. Houses are a mixture of traditional white cane–walled huts on stilts and more "modern" huts with walls made of wooden planks. A concrete path winds through the village, which is lit for a couple of hours in the evening by a small generator. The Wounaan are renowned for their crafts and it should be possible to buy directly from the craft-makers here. Hiring a boat from Jaqué to Biroquera should cost about US$40 for a small group.

About 20 kilometers southeast of Jaqué there's a small bay, **Ensenada El Guayabo,** that has a white sand beach that's said to be even prettier than Playa Blanca. All that's there is a handful of indigenous huts. It makes for an easy day trip from Jaqué or Piñas. Visitors can trade fishing hooks and sodas with the residents for fresh coconut milk. It's probably not a good idea to head much farther down toward the Colombian border.

Tropic Star Lodge

Most foreign visitors to this area stay at the Tropic Star Lodge (U.S. toll-free tel. 800/682-3424, U.S. tel. 407/843-0125, www.tropicstar.com), a four-decades-old institution that looms large over the area and has made the Bahía de Piñas world-famous in fishing circles.

An exclusive fishing resort that can accommodate no more than 36 guests at a time, the lodge is set on lovely, landscaped land right above the bay. There's a small beach in front, flowering trees all around, a swimming pool with a bar, and a river that cuts across the grounds.

It's the kind of place pop stars, screen idols, and famous athletes frequent—notable guests have ranged from John Wayne to Walter Peyton to George Strait. Ask about the time Lee Marvin was kicked out for throwing a chair through the restaurant window. It's entertaining to thumb through the old guest books looking for familiar names.

This was originally the vacation home of a Texas oil millionaire named Ray Smith, who turned it into a fishing lodge in 1965. It has been owned by the Kittredge family since 1976. The current owners are Terri Kittredge Andrews and her husband, Mike Andrews.

Accommodations are, as one might expect, quite comfortable, though this is definitely a fishing lodge and not an ultraposh hotel. Given the lodge's remote location, however, it is remarkably well maintained and filled with creature comforts. It's easy to forget the nearest road is more than 100 kilometers away.

Most rooms are in two-unit cabins with wraparound wooden porches or in a single long building near the beach. The rooms are spacious, with air-conditioning, twin beds, and large private bathrooms/dressing rooms. All have a view of the bay. Up the hill is El Palacio, a three-bedroom house with a sunken living room that was the original owner's home. It can accommodate up to six guests. It's reachable by climbing 122 stairs or taking the more popular cable car.

The food is delicious, with multicourse candlelit dinners served at night in the circular, air-conditioned restaurant/bar or out on the veranda. There are no telephones, fax machines, or televisions at the lodge, so guests can have a true sense of getting away from it all. Expect pampering: A staff of 80 serves the 36 guests.

The lodge still has a 1960s vibe about it, though a 2004 updating of the facilities has meant some welcome changes—such as replacing wall-to-wall carpet in the cabins with tile—while retaining the vintage feel of the place.

Daily fishing trips are made on 31-foot Bertrams, of which the lodge owns 14. The prime black marlin season runs mid-December–April. Pacific sailfish are caught year-round, with April–July especially good months. The lodge is open December–September.

Guests have free use of kayaks to explore the bay or travel up the Río Piñas.

Several kilometers of trails wind through primary and secondary forest. These are well worth walking, especially in the early morning when there's the best chance of spotting wildlife. I came across a group of curious coatimundis during a hike shortly after dawn. Don't expect to see many animals, as hunters from surrounding villages have taken their toll through the years. But pumas, three-toed sloths, and foxes have been spotted near the lodge, and the staff has found jaguar prints on the beach.

The staff can also arrange a trip up the Río Jaqué to visit the Wounaan village of Biroquera.

None of this comes cheap, of course. The basic fishing package in the high season starts at about US$5,150 per person, including seven nights of lodging, six days of fishing, and three meals a day, but not tips or transport from Panama City. Rates vary depending on the season, length of stay, and number of people in the boat. Nonfishing packages are sometimes available. Charter airfare to and from Panama City is US$500 per person. The lodge is small and popular, with lots of repeat business. Reservations must often be made a year or two in advance.

Practicalities

Again, until conflicts in this area die down again, I do not advise staying in or around Jaqué. Tropic Star Lodge is quite separate from the area on a large stretch of private land, so presumably it will remain relatively insulated from the conflict. However, you should contact the lodge for current conditions before visiting (it's in their interest to make sure their guests remain safe and happy, and they have years of experience in doing so).

There are two basic *hospedajes* (lodgings) in Jaqué and an ultrabasic one in Puerto Piñas. Enterprising souls can probably strike a bargain to rent a room in someone's house upon arrival. The only places to eat are rustic to say the least; this is a good place to come with one's own food supply.

Aventuras Anamar (tel. 233—5976 or 221-7423; ask for Señor Herman Torres or Señora Praxedes Torres, US$10 s/d) in Jaqué offers the best rooms in either town. The *hospedaje* is a two-story building on a rather attractive stretch of beach past the east edge of town. It's completely basic but surprisingly okay, with three rooms that look out on a porch facing the ocean and four darker ones behind them. Room 1 is the nicest. It's a corner room with lots of glass windows and a partial view of the ocean. Bathrooms are shared. Management here is friendly and animated and should be able to arrange food.

Food and booze are available at a handful of nondescript kiosks, *fondas* (taverns), and cantinas in Jaqué. Near the river is a tiny general store with an airless little bar next door.

Getting There and Away

Commercial flights from Panama City often stop at both Jaqué and Puerto Piñas (sometimes known to the airlines as Bahía Piña), though the order of arrival varies. The two airstrips are about two minutes' flight time away.

Aeroperlas makes the trip on Tuesday and Thursday at 10:38 A.M. The return flight supposedly leaves around 12:12 P.M. from Piñas and 12:40 P.M. from Jaqué.

Air Panama flies to Bahía Piñas and Jaqué at 10 A.M. Monday and Friday. The return flights leave Piñas at 11:35 A.M. and Jaqué around 11:55 A.M.

The flights take about an hour. Make sure to get off at the right airstrip. All these departure times are optimistic estimates. The fare is US$78.97 each way to Piñas; it's about US$2 cheaper each way to Jaqué.

The new concrete airstrip at Piñas is in great shape. The Jaqué airstrip is not, and it gets quite muddy in the rainy season—an acquaintance compared landing here to an off-road adventure in a four-wheel drive.

BACKGROUND

The Land

The Republic of Panama covers 75,517 square kilometers, which makes it slightly bigger than Ireland and slightly smaller than South Carolina. Panama is young in geological terms. It emerged from the sea just 2.5 million years ago, dividing the Atlantic from the Pacific and forming a natural bridge that connects the North and South American continents. The bridge has allowed North and South American species to intermingle. Known as the Great American Interchange, this mingling had a profound effect on the ecology of South America.

Panama's peculiar shape—like the letter "S" turned on its side—causes confusion for many visitors. It takes a while to get used to the notion that the Caribbean Sea is to the north and the Pacific Ocean to the south. Many also find it strange to be able to watch the sun rising over the Pacific and setting in the Caribbean, or to realize that when a ship transits the Panama Canal from the Pacific to the Caribbean it actually ends up slightly west of where it started.

Panama is at the eastern end of Central America, bordered to the west by Costa Rica and to the east by Colombia. It's far longer than it is wide. The oceans are just 80 kilometers apart at the Panama Canal, near the middle of the country, and that isn't even the

COURTESY OF THE AUTORIDAD DE CANAL DE PANAMA

narrowest spot on the isthmus. But the country stretches surprisingly far to the east and west; Panama has nearly 3,000 kilometers of coastline along its Caribbean and Pacific flanks.

People often wonder which body of water is the "higher" of the two. The reality is that there's no difference in elevation—sea level is sea level. A locks canal was necessary in Panama not to keep the oceans from spilling into each other, but to carry ships over the landmass of the isthmus. But there is a dramatic difference between the tides on each side. The Caribbean tide averages less than half a meter; Pacific tides can be more than five meters high.

Many visitors are surprised to discover how mountainous Panama is. The most impressive mountain range is the Cordillera Central, which bisects the western half of the country, extending from the Costa Rican border east toward the canal. It contains Panama's highest mountain, Volcán Barú, a dormant volcano that is 3,475 meters high. Another impressive range runs along Panama's eastern Caribbean coast, starting at the Comarca de Kuna Yala and ending at the Colombian border. It officially comprises the Serranía de San Blas to the west and the Serranía del Darién to the east, where it enters Darién province.

Most parts of Panama experience few significant earthquakes, which is one of the reasons it was chosen as the site of an interoceanic canal. However, western Panama, particularly Bocas del Toro and Chiriquí, is far more seismically active. In 1991, an earthquake measuring 7.5 on the Richter scale struck along the Costa Rica–Panama border, leaving two dozen people dead in Bocas del Toro and thousands homeless.

Besides the humid tropical forests that people expect to find, which compose a third of Panama's remaining forests, Panama has a great variety of other ecosystems, ranging from cloud forests to an artificially-made "desert." Extensive mangroves, coral reefs, and hundreds of islands can be found on both the Pacific and Caribbean sides of the isthmus. Panama also has at least 500 rivers.

CLIMATE

Panama lies between 7 and 10 degrees north of the equator. The climate is mainly tropical, and days and nights are almost equally long throughout the year. Sunrise and sunset vary by only about half an hour during the year: The sun rises approximately 6–6:30 A.M. and sets approximately 6–6:30 P.M.

Temperatures in Panama are fairly constant year-round. In the lowlands, these range from about 32°C (90°F) in the day down to 21°C (70°F) in the evening. It never gets cold in the lowlands, and dry-season breezes are very pleasant there in the evenings. It gets considerably cooler in the highlands. At the top of Volcán Barú temperatures can dip below freezing. Humidity tends to be quite high year-round, but especially so in the rainy season, when it approaches 100 percent.

Most of Panama has two seasons, the rainy and the dry. The dry season, also known as summer *(verano)*, lasts from about mid-December to mid-April. Rain stops completely in many parts then, especially on the Pacific side. Flowering trees burst into bloom around the country at the start of this season. Toward the end, vegetation turns brown or dies, and smoke from slash-and-burn agriculture and the burning of sugarcane fields can make the skies hazy.

The rainy season, also known as winter *(invierno)*, generally lasts from about mid-April to mid-December. The rains tend to be heaviest and longest at the end of the season, as though the heavens were wringing out every last drop of moisture. October, November, and the beginning of December are especially heavy. Thunderstorms are a near daily occurrence during the rainy season.

Some parts of Panama, including Bocas del Toro and the western highlands, have microclimates that differ from this general dry season/rainy season pattern.

Yearly rainfall averages around three meters. It's far wetter on the Caribbean side than the Pacific side. The rains in most parts of Panama tend to come in powerful bursts in the afternoon or early evening. Mornings are usually dry on the Pacific side.

Dirt roads and trails can become impassable

in the interior during the rainy season, and paved roads and bridges are often washed out by mudslides and rising rivers. Flooding is a serious problem in parts of the interior, such as Bocas del Toro and Chiriquí.

The rain never stops completely along the Caribbean coast, in the western highlands, and on the islands of Bocas del Toro. Rainfall patterns in Bocas are quite different from other parts of Panama. It has no true dry season, but generally little rain falls September–October and February–March.

Panama is south of the hurricane zone, so it's spared those terrible storms.

Flora and Fauna

Panama's shape and location—at the southernmost range of many North American species and the northernmost range of many South American species—makes it home to a particularly rich variety of plant and animal life. Sadly, the future of this abundant life is by no means secure: The World Conservation Monitoring Centre's Red List of threatened animals includes 112 species found in Panama.

A total of 972 species of birds have been identified so far, more than are found in the United States and Canada combined. The country is also home to well over 200 mammal and 200 reptile species, close to 200 amphibian species, and more than 10,000 species of plants. Some of these are found nowhere else on earth.

TREES AND PLANTS

Panama's plant life is among the most diverse in the world. The country contains 12 of the planet's 30 Holdridge life zones. By far the most common is humid tropical forest, which accounts for about a third of Panama's remaining forest cover. All of these zones but one, humid premontane forest, are represented in a system of protected areas. Of Panama's estimated 10,000 species of plants, about 1,500 of them are found nowhere else on the planet. Panama also has extensive wetlands, mangroves, and coral reefs.

Panamanian environmentalists like to point out that, per square kilometer, Panama has 21 times the plant diversity of Brazil. Trying to identify the plants even in a small patch of rainforest is daunting. There are 480 species of trees just on the 15 square kilometers of Isla Barro Colorado, more than are found in all of Europe.

The Panama tree (*Sterculia apetala*) is widely thought of as the national tree, and some maintain it gave the country its name. It has a straight trunk that can grow up to 35 meters tall, with vertical buttresses around its base.

The ceiba or kapok (*Ceiba pentandra*) can reach 60 meters and often juts above other trees in the forest. One kapok specimen on Isla Barro Colorado is so huge other trees grow on its branches.

The *espavé* or wild cashew (*Anacardium excelsum*) has a trunk so straight and tall that indigenous peoples use it to make dugout canoes. One explanation of its name is that *espavé* is a contraction of *es para ver* ("it's for seeing"), meaning it's a good tree to climb to see what's off in the distance.

The *mata palo* or strangler fig (*Ficus obtusifolia*) starts as a seedling on a host tree that eventually surrounds and engulfs. The mature strangler fig can be hollow inside, its original host completely decomposed. It's easy to spot because of its enormously thick strangler roots, which can also engulf boulders and the ruins of buildings.

The massively thick trunk of the abundant cuipo (*Cavanillesia platanifolia*) also makes it easy to identify it in the forest.

In the dry season, flowering trees burst into bloom around the isthmus, dotting the green canopy with brilliant colors.

Panama has more than 1,000 species of orchids, many of them endemic. The delicate white *espíritu santo* (holy ghost) orchid, also known as the dove orchid, is considered Panama's national flower.

BIRDS

Panama is especially well known for its incredible number and diversity of bird species. Besides its vast local populations, more than 120 species are migrants that regularly cross the isthmus on the way to and from their winter homes.

The famous (among birders) "raptor migration" of broad-winged hawks, Swainson's hawks, and turkey vultures is absolutely spectacular. During the fall and spring, particularly October–mid-November and March–early April, they pass overhead in flocks that can number in the many thousands. It's an unbelievable sight. The first comprehensive study of the migration was conducted in fall 2004, when researchers tallied more than 2.7 million raptors. One researcher counted 92,000 in a single day. They are easiest to spot around the

COURTESY OF CATHY DOIG AND LARRY WILKINSON

Baltimore Oriole overshadowing a thrush, Boquete

former Canal Zone. Good places to see them include Cerro Ancón, the Canopy Tower, and the top of the aerial tram at the Gamboa Rainforest Resort.

Other species likely to impress nonbirders include five species of macaws (blue-and-yellow, chestnut-fronted, great green, red-and-green, and the rare scarlet); several species of toucans and toucanets; the harpy eagle, the world's most powerful bird of prey; and the resplendent quetzal, which has been called the most beautiful bird on the planet.

LAND MAMMALS

The country's national parks are filled with animals that thrill foreign visitors, though many are hard to spot. There are five species of big cats on the isthmus—jaguars, jaguarundis, pumas, margays, and ocelots—but finding one in the wild is exceedingly hard. The forests harbor every species of nonhuman primate found in Central America: western night monkeys, mantled howler monkeys, white-faced capuchins, several types of spider monkeys, and Geoffroy's tamarins. Howlers are generally the easiest to spot (or at least hear) in the wild, but a few years ago a wildlife rescue project introduced four species of primates to islands in Lago Gatún, where the night monkey still occurs naturally. It's easy to spot several species during a boat tour of the lake.

Many visitors find white-nosed coatis (a.k.a. coatimundis) and kinkajous, with their long tails and furry bodies, terribly cute. They're reasonably easy to find, especially around Gamboa.

Capybaras are the world's largest rodents, but they more closely resemble giant guinea pigs than rats. They can grow up to a meter long and weigh up to 45 kilograms. They're shy, but they're pretty easy to spot in Gamboa and Punta Patiño.

Far smaller but equally cute are Central American agoutis, known locally as *ñeques*. They're generally less than half a meter long and weigh just 3–4 kilograms. They're covered in fur and have a rather large rump. They're among the easiest mammals to spot in Panama;

COURTESY OF PAUL SABAN

A cacomistle has a late-night dinner.

they're diurnal and found just about anywhere there's forest. Agoutis are sometimes confused with pacas because of the latter's scientific name, *Agouti paca*. But pacas are quite a bit larger, and their brown fur is marked with rows of white spots, giving rise to their local name, *conejo pintado* (painted rabbit).

Small red brocket and white-tailed deer are common. Isla San José is the only place in Central America where gray brockets are found. Other notable land mammals include giant anteaters, white-lipped and collared peccaries, two- and three-toed sloths, and Baird's tapirs, the largest land mammal in Central America. The last can weigh up to 300 kilograms and are rather odd-looking creatures with a trunklike nose.

SEA LIFE

Five species of sea turtles can be found in Panama's waters, and four of them lay their eggs on its islands and coasts. They are the hawksbill, leatherback, loggerhead, olive ridley, and green.

Sea turtles are easiest to find in mating season on the islands and coasts of Bocas del Toro

in the Caribbean (roughly March–October, with most activity in the later months) and on Isla Cañas in the Pacific (most numerous September–November). Nesting season varies by species, location, and the mood of the turtles, but dry season is generally the worst time to see them.

The hawksbill and leatherback are the most abundant in Bocas. All five species make their way to Isla Cañas, but by far the most numerous are the olive ridley. Many thousands make their way to the long island every year, making for a dramatic spectacle at night. The loggerhead rarely, if ever, lays eggs in Panama. (It's a subject of some debate.)

The West Indian manatee can be found in the Panama Canal, most easily seen around the Gatún Yacht Club and, to a lesser extent, the rivers and channels of Bocas del Toro.

The seas are filled with brilliant tropical fish as well as impressive large specimens, including orcas, several species of dolphins, humpback whales, marlins, manta rays, jewfish, moray eels, barracudas, big snappers, and white-tip, hammerhead, tiger, and whale sharks. The biggest creatures are found in the Pacific, especially around the Islas Perlas, the Golfo de Chiriquí, and the Bahía de Piñas, where dozens of deep-sea fishing records have been set. Small, radiant tropical fish are easiest to find among the coral gardens in the clear waters off the Caribbean islands.

AMPHIBIANS

Of the nearly 200 species of amphibians in Panama, the best loved and studied are the frogs and toads. Bocas del Toro is especially well known for its many different morphs, or forms, of strawberry poison-dart frogs (*Oophaga pumilio,* though until recently classified as *Dendrobates pumilio*). In addition to the distinctive red morphs that give the species its common name, these tiny frogs come in green, yellow, purple, orange, black, white, and multicolor forms, sometimes within a surprisingly small area. Panama is also known for its nearly extinct golden frogs (*Atelopus zeteki),* which are easiest to find in El Valle.

REPTILES

The country's many reptile species contain several that make visitors most nervous about the tropics: venomous snakes. It's unlikely you'll encounter any snakes at all during a hike, and highly unlikely any will bother you if you don't bother them.

That said, one of the country's most venomous snakes is also one of the most prolific: the fer-de-lance *(Bothrops asper)*, a pit viper more commonly known in Panama as an *equis* ("X," for the diamond or X-pattern on its brown skin) or a *terciopelo* (which means "velvet"). A full-grown adult can be more than 2 meters long. The females give birth to up to 50 young at a time, which are born venomous and can actually be more deadly than an adult because they have not learned to regulate their venom. Fer-de-lance can be aggressive, especially during mating season.

Another forbidding creature is the bushmaster *(Lachesis acrochorda, Lachesis muta,* and *Lachesis stenophrys)*, the world's largest viper and the largest venomous snake in the western hemisphere. Known locally as a *verrugosa* ("the warty one"),

it can grow up to three meters long, but is much more rarely encountered. That's a good thing, since its bite has a high fatality rate. The eyelash palm pit viper *(Bothriechis schlegelli)* comes in an assortment of brilliant colors. It's quite beautiful and sinister-looking at the same time (a snake fancier in Panama once described its visage as "unmasked malice in pure form"). Panama also has several species of coral snake. Assume any coral snake you encounter is dangerous—the rhymes used to distinguish venomous from nonvenomous corals in the United States do not work in Panama. Other notable venomous snakes include jumping pit vipers *(Atropoides nummifer* and *Atropoides picadori),* known locally as *mano de piedra* ("hand of stone") and *patoca.* The yellow-bellied sea snake *(Pelamus platorus)* is commonly known as the Pacific sea snake since they only occur in the Pacific and Indian Oceans (the risk of it spreading to the Atlantic was an argument against building a sea-level canal). Its venom is deadly, but it is not aggressive and is rarely encountered—in all my years in Panama, I've come across just one, and it had washed up on the beach, dead.

Iguanas are officially protected in Panama.

Nonvenomous but potentially dangerous snakes include the boa constrictor, which averages a little under two meters long and can bite if provoked. There are also plenty of harmless snakes, including a variety of vine snakes.

Caimans *(Caiman crocodilus)* are, despite their scientific name, a kind of alligator found in great abundance in some of Panama's rivers. They're easy to spot in Gamboa. They are generally small and rather placid, though some can grow to be about 2.5 meters long. There have been reports of the far larger American crocodile *(Crocodylus acutus)* in the waters of the Panama Canal, especially around Gamboa, though this endangered species can be hard to find. It spends most of its time in estuaries on the Pacific side of the isthmus. On a recent trip to the Darién, I encountered an enormous one on a sandbank on the Río Tuira.

Green iguanas are a protected species in Panama, but they are sometimes still hunted as food. Efforts are being made to reintroduce iguanas in various parts of the country.

INSECTS, ARACHNIDS, AND OTHER SMALL CREATURES

Visitors will most certainly have some encounters with insects, but many parts of Panama are not nearly as buggy as one might think. The mosquito population, for instance, is strictly controlled because of the risk of disease.

But the variety of insects found on the isthmus is staggering. It's estimated there are at least 10,000 species of beetles alone.

Most visitors would just as soon not encounter some of these insects, such as chiggers, bullet and army ants, giant cockroaches, Africanized bees, and stinging centipedes, not to mention the vast array of impressive arachnids, which include such creepy-crawlies as scorpions, tarantulas, and the stunning golden orb spider. But Panama is home to plenty of less-intimidating little creatures, such as 16,000 species of butterflies. One of the most spectacular of these is the huge and luminous blue morpho, which can often be seen floating slowly through the forest canopy.

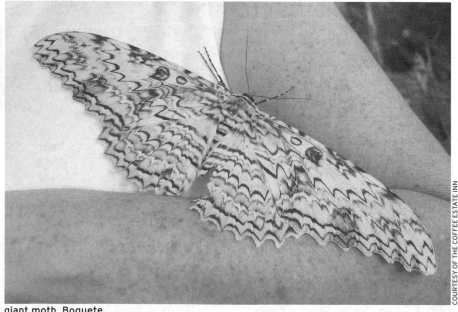

giant moth, Boquete

Environmental Issues

Environmental destruction in the tropics is a terrible, disheartening thing to witness—and there's plenty of it going on in Panama. Panama and its friends woke up to the problem toward the end of the 20th century and took several encouraging steps, including the creation of new protected areas, the introduction of environmental protection laws, and the establishment of environmental nonprofits. On my most recent tours of the country, however, I have been dismayed to see greed and the march of "progress" starting to undo some of what was accomplished. New roads, real-estate developments, mining operations, and the usual ranches and farms are pushing ever farther into pristine countryside.

Government and nonprofit environmental watchdog agencies are often either toothless or end up accused of rubber-stamping destructive projects. However, while it's still far too common to see citizens trash their own country, there are also people out there cleaning up the mess—or at least refusing to add to it. It may have limited resources and often lacks the power to create real, lasting change, but there is now a fledgling environmental movement in Panama, a claim that would have been hard to make 20 years ago.

DEFORESTATION

About 40 percent of the Republic of Panama was still covered by primary forest at the beginning of the 21st century. That's the good news.

The bad news is that 50 years ago, the figure was 70 percent. In other words, in the last half of the 20th century Panama lost nearly half its remaining primary forests—about 2.2 million hectares (5.4 million acres) of wild, species-rich nature wiped out.

Even more disturbing, the trend continues in an era of increased environmental awareness. Though estimates vary, deforestation is believed to claim up to 50,000 hectares (123,500 acres) of forest a year. That's a loss of more than 1 percent each year.

These forests have mostly been converted into farms and cattle ranches or paved over to make way for cities and towns. There is intense pressure on the remaining forests from subsistence farmers, ranchers, and large commercial interests. They have almost completely deforested the heartland provinces of Los Santos and Herrera on the Azuero Peninsula, as well as the Pacific slopes of western and central Panama. Eventually this land becomes useless and barren—there is even an artificially-made "desert" on the Azuero Peninsula. This has driven people north to the Caribbean slopes and east and west to forests that were once nearly inaccessible.

Whenever a road enters a forest, the forest begins to disappear. So-called *colonos* (colonists)—slash-and-burn farmers in need of new land—follow the road. So do timber interests in search of magnificent old-growth giants. Once the forest cover is gone, the soil erodes easily under Panama's incredible downpours. This is worsened by the fact that nearly 78 percent of Panama's land is mountainous, with a high potential for erosion. The soil is generally of poor quality in any case—nearly all the nutrients in a tropical forest are contained in the trees themselves, not the soil—and is quickly overexploited, leading to the need for more land and thus more deforestation. Within just a few years the soil is exhausted and ranchers bring in cattle to graze on what is now sparse pastureland. The farmers, loggers, and ranchers move farther into the forest, and the cycle continues.

Deforestation is proceeding at a particularly alarming rate in the Darién, Bocas del Toro, Colón province, and the new Ngöbe-Buglé *comarca* (reservation), all of which are rich in biodiversity and primary forests. Even the Kuna, who traditionally have been successful in keeping invaders off their land, have in recent years protested the incursion of *colonos* onto their mainland reservations in the Darién.

While much of the deforestation is driven by

the needs of impoverished subsistence farmers, Panamanian and multinational commercial interests have also done substantial damage to the environment. Banana, coffee, and sugarcane plantations, for instance, wiped out forests and contaminated rivers with pesticides and other kinds of chemical runoff. The government continues to grant gold- and copper-mining concessions to corporations in the heart of important ecosystems. And large hydroelectric dams that flood forests, disrupt rivers, and displace indigenous people are being built.

To cite just one example, a few years back Panama granted concessions for four large hydroelectric dams—three on the Río Changuinola and one on the Río Bonyic, a tributary to the Río Teribe—in the buffer zone for Parque Internacional La Amistad (PILA) in western Panama. PILA is a World Heritage Site and one of the most important protected areas in the Americas. If these dams are built, the destructive impact on the park's biodiversity and watershed, and the indigenous peoples who live near the park, will be profound. It is likely to threaten the very existence of the Naso people.

Some efforts have been made in the last two decades to reforest parts of Panama where the soil has not become too degraded. Tax incentives have helped turn tree planting into a popular get-rich-quick scheme throughout the country.

Critics, including Panama's own environmental protection agency, point out that the policy has several flaws. The one most frequently cited is that about two-thirds of the trees planted so far are teak, a nonnative species that Panama's birds, animals, and other flora and fauna seem to have little use for. Teak is most often grown in plantations instead of being planted alongside native species, creating monocultures that do little for the local environment and, according to some, actually degrade it further. There have even been reports of species-rich native forest being illegally cleared to make way for teak plantations.

By the beginning of the 21st century, a total of 46,000 hectares (114,000 acres) of land had been reforested, less than is lost every year through deforestation.

The difference between the still-intact Caribbean and heavily deforested Pacific slopes is startling, especially when seen from the air. But deforestation is creeping toward the Caribbean as well. New roads and even open-pit mines are being built right in the heart of it. The loss or fragmentation of these last forests, which some see as all but inevitable unless immediate steps are taken, will have profound, far-reaching effects. Panama is a vital part of the Mesoamerican Biological Corridor that links the ecosystems of North and South America. Consider birds alone: 122 migratory bird species regularly pass through Panama. What happens to them if the biological corridor disappears?

WATER RESOURCES

Water pollution and the shrinking of Panama's watersheds are also serious problems. Raw sewage and industrial waste are dumped directly into the Bahía de Panamá (Panama Bay), for instance, turning parts of what was once a tremendously vital body of water into toxic zones. Some older folks still remember swimming in Panama Bay right across the street from bustling Panama City. Now doing so is a serious health risk. Fishing in the bay has long been banned. At low tide, the smell wafting off the bay can be overpowering. After decades of discussion, a plan to treat sewage and clean up the bay was finally approved in 2006. The project is expected to cost at least US$350 million, and will take years.

The most remote, untouched islands and beaches of Panama sometimes have a ring of trash on the shores, carried there by currents that pass near cities and towns where garbage is dumped indiscriminately. Pollution and deliberate destruction are also decimating coral reefs, and over-fishing is doing even more damage to the biodiversity of the seas.

Mangroves are a vital and fragile component of marine ecosystems, and they help prevent coastal erosion. Panama has the most extensive mangrove forests in Central America.

But in the last three decades, Panama lost well over half its mangroves, which were cut down to make way for construction projects, resorts, cattle ranches, shrimp farms, and the like. Mangroves have also been lost through pollution.

The Panama Canal watershed is the most important in Panama. It supplies the water needed to run the Panama Canal and provides drinking water to the greater metropolitan areas of Panama City and Colón, where most of the country's people live. Slash-and-burn agriculture, urbanization, and pollution have done considerable damage to the watershed, diminishing the quantity and quality of its fresh water.

The purity of Panama's drinking water, a legacy of the Panama Canal Company's strict hygiene standards, has long been a source of pride. One can turn on a tap almost anywhere in the country and be sure the water is safe to drink. However, studies have concluded that if immediate steps aren't taken to curtail pollution, city dwellers may soon find themselves forced to drink bottled water.

sea turtle eggs being sold illegally near Chitré

AIR QUALITY

Those who've traveled extensively in the developing world will not be overwhelmed by air pollution even in Panama's most congested urban areas. But this problem is growing, particularly as more and more cars clog Panama's roads. Parts of Panama City register well above acceptable limits for airborne toxins. In the past, strong winds kept Panama City's air relatively fresh. In recent years, however, a brown haze hangs over the city more and more often.

PARKS AND PROTECTED AREAS

Panama has set aside 76 protected areas covering nearly two million hectares (close to five million acres) of land, or about 25 percent of Panama's total area, and a substantial portion of its territorial waters. Most of these protected areas are part of an extensive system of 13 national parks and marine parks

and one international park, the giant Parque Internacional La Amistad (PILA) that extends over the border into Costa Rica. There are numerous wildlife refuges, buffer forests, protected wetlands, and so on. There are also laws on the books to protect endangered or threatened animals.

The protected areas are a relatively new phenomenon. The first national park, Parque Nacional Altos de Campana, was set aside in 1966, and all the others have been created just in the last 25 years. The parks and other protected areas are managed by the Autoridad Nacional del Ambiente (ANAM), which translates as National Environmental Authority.

As anyone who travels extensively in Panama's national parks will soon discover, just being named a protected area does not confer much protection. Illegal hunting, fishing, logging, and even farming continue in many of the protected areas.

All the parks have at least rudimentary ranger stations, but few have much in the way of visitors' facilities or developed trails. Large sections of some parks, notably the Caribbean slope of PILA and almost all of Parque Nacional Cerro Hoya, are almost inaccessible, which is the main reason they're still intact.

ANAM has only a couple hundred workers spread throughout the entire system of protected areas; there's an average of about one employee for every 7,000 hectares. Sometimes they're spread far more thinly than that: There are only a handful of rangers at two rustic ranger stations to guard the entire 579,000 hectares of Parque Nacional Darién. A third of the protected areas do not have a single ranger assigned to them.

Anyone who witnesses poaching, the sale or captivity of endangered species, habitat destruction, or other kinds of illegal environmental damage can report it to ANAM's hotline (tel. 500-0855, ext. 1111). These *denuncias* can also be made online (www.anam.gob.pa/denuncia_web/default.asp).

CONSERVATION GROUPS

Panama's largest conservation group is the nonprofit **Asociación Nacional para la Conservación de la Naturaleza** (National Association for the Conservation of Nature, tel. 314-0052, www.ancon.org), or ANCON. Since its founding in 1985 it has played an important role in Panama's attempts to protect its environment by taking on such basic but critical projects as demarcating park boundaries and training park rangers. ANCON does have its critics, who sometimes accuse it of giving a seal of approval to big development projects that are destructive to the environment.

ANCON owns the country's largest private nature reserve, the 65,000-hectare Punta Patiño Reserve on the Darién coast. Its other holdings include Isla San Telmo, in the Archipiélago de las Perlas, which protects endangered moist premontane forest and is a sanctuary for brown pelicans and other animals. It also owns several nature lodges around the country that are managed by Ancon Expeditions, a private for-profit organization that spun off as a separate entity. ANCON welcomes foreign volunteers to its projects.

The U.S.-based Nature Conservancy works with local organizations on several projects in Panama. For more information contact the **Nature Conservancy** (4245 N. Fairfax Dr.,

Sign in Santa Fé: "What you do to the earth, you do to yourself."

© WILLIAM FRIAR

Arlington, VA 22203-1606, tel. 800/628-6860, http://nature.org).

The prestigious **Smithsonian Tropical Research Institute** (STRI, www.stri.org) is based in Panama. STRI is one of the leading centers for the study of tropical animals, plants, marine life, evolution, conservation, and much more.

The **Sociedad Audubon de Panamá** (Panama Audubon Society, tel. 232-5977, www.panamaaudubon.org) hosts regular bird-watching tours, and nonmembers are invited to come along. The society is also a good source of information on nature hikes and backcountry places to stay, and some of its members are freelance guides.

History

There is hardly another place in the world, as a Panama historian once pointed out, where so much has happened yet left so little trace behind. The jungle swallowed up whole civilizations, and grave-robbers made away with the crumbs.

But some of the earliest evidence of human habitation in the Americas has been found in Panama. Remarkably advanced cultures flourished millennia after that. And since Spanish explorers discovered the isthmus, it has played an important role in determining the shape of the modern world. Over the last 500 years, Panama helped establish Spain and the United States as great world powers, nearly bankrupted France, and forced Scotland to give up its sovereignty and become part of the United Kingdom.

ANCIENT HISTORY

Archaeologists estimate that humans have lived on the isthmus of Panama for 12,000 years, possibly longer. No massive structures, such as the pyramids found elsewhere in the Americas, have been discovered, and knowledge of the ancient inhabitants of Panama is sketchy. Many of the archaeological sites that have been uncovered have been damaged by the elements, looters, and amateur excavations. But the surviving indigenous peoples of western Panama still tell intriguing if fanciful tales of lost cities in little-known and nearly inaccessible mountain forests—so who knows what may turn up one day? Archaeology in Panama is still in many ways in its infancy.

The earliest evidence of human habitation found to date is Clovis-type arrowheads found near what is now Lago Alajuela (Madden Lake) in the Panama Canal. Archaeologists dated them to about 9000 B.C. Agriculture appears on the Pacific coast of central Panama at around 5000 B.C. Ceramics appear around 3000 B.C. A particularly rich site was Monagrillo, on the Azuero Peninsula, where archaeologists uncovered large numbers of decorated ceramics dating from at least 2500 B.C., the oldest in Central America and among the oldest known in the Americas.

Most of the archaeological treasures dug up in Panama are far more recent. The roots of the Barriles culture of western Panama are believed to go back to at least 700 B.C., but the culture reached its zenith between about A.D. 400 and A.D. 600, when the eruption of Volcán Barú dispersed it. Intriguing, mysterious stone sculptures have been dug up that depict what appear to be chiefs or priests being carried piggyback by other men, as well as an elaborate and oversized metate (stone used to grind corn) that may have been used for sacrifices. Some of these are on display at Panama City's anthropology museum, Museo Antropológico Reina Torres de Araúz.

But the bulk of the evidence of advanced civilizations, at least so far, is found in Central Panama. One of the most famous pre-Colombian archaeological sites in the Americas, Sitio Conte, was found between the Río Grande and Río Coclé near the town of Penonomé.

The site was a cemetery used for hundreds

COURTESY OF THE PANAMA CANAL COMMISSION

There may have been as many as two million indigenous Panamanians when the Spanish arrived.

of years, approximately A.D. 750–950. It was discovered when the Río Grande changed its course in the early 20th century and washed gold ornaments and pottery from the riverbanks. Excavated by scientists from Harvard in the 1930s, most of its treasures are scattered among museums in the United States and Europe. It's considered the richest pre-Colombian site ever discovered in Central America. About 60 graves, more than 1,000 gold ornaments, and literally tons of pottery and carved stone were dug up there. One tomb, apparently that of a great leader buried around A.D. 750, contained about half the gold found at the site, as well as the remains of 22 followers. Nothing remains at the site today, which is on a private farm and cattle ranch and is not open to the public.

Another important archaeological site that raises more questions than it answers is Parque Arqueológico del Caño, on the outskirts of the town of Natá, not far from Sitio Conte. It contained a cemetery and a large circular field marked off by carved stone columns in the shape of animal and human figures. Some of these statues are six meters high, and they may have been used to demarcate a ceremonial ground or playing field. Unfortunately, nearly all these figures were removed in the 1920s by an American adventurer and taken to museums in the United States. Only their pedestals remain. The site dates from about A.D. 800–1100.

Mysterious petroglyphs carved into boulders have been found near streams and rivers at dozens of sites around the country, including remote forests and islands. They consist mainly of abstract designs, especially spirals and squiggles, as well as crude animal and human figures. No one knows their purpose or when they were carved, but archaeologists have speculated they could be anything from ceremonial or sacrificial sites to "no trespassing" warnings. Wishful thinkers speculate they're maps to buried treasure awaiting someone clever enough to crack the code.

THE SPANISH CONQUEST

The arrival of the Spanish in 1501 spelled the end of the indigenous peoples' dominion over the isthmus and the beginning of the European conquest. The first arrival was an explorer named Rodrigo de Bastidas, who sailed along the Caribbean coast from the Darién at least as far west as Nombre de Dios. His crew included a seaman by the name of Vasco Núñez de Balboa; 12 years later Balboa would become the first European to hack his way through the Darién and lay eyes on the "Southern Sea," the Pacific Ocean.

Christopher Columbus came to the isthmus during his fourth and final voyage to the New World, which left Spain on May 11, 1502. His most glorious days behind him, Columbus had the use of four dilapidated ships to explore the Caribbean coastline that Bastidas had not seen, from Bocas del Toro in the far west of the isthmus to Nombre de Dios in the east. In Bocas he came across indigenous people wearing gold jewelry, a discovery that excited his crew far more than the quest for a passage to Asia.

During the voyage, Columbus's ships anchored near the mouth of the Río Belén, on the border between the modern-day provinces of Colón and Veraguas. It was here, on Epiphany, January 6, 1503, that Columbus established the first European settlement on the isthmus, Santa María de Belén. Almost immediately, however, battles with the indigenous population, led by a chief known to history only as "the Quibián," brought this first Spanish foothold in Panama to a bloody end. Columbus sailed back to Jamaica with two barely seaworthy ships, having been forced to abandon the other two: the *Gallega* at the mouth of the Belén and the *Vizcaína* somewhere near Portobelo.

Balboa and the Discovery of the Pacific

Balboa's career as a great explorer began inauspiciously. Though he was among the first Europeans to explore Panama, when he was a crew member on Bastidas' voyage of discovery in 1501, he spent the next eight years in Hispaniola (modern-day Haiti and the Dominican Republic) getting into financial trouble. Determined to change his fortunes, he stowed away on a ship bound for the isthmus, slipping past his creditors by hiding in a cask that was loaded onto the ship. When he was discovered, the angry captain almost left him marooned on a desert island, but he soon made himself indispensable because of his knowledge of the isthmus.

When the early settlements began to fall apart, Balboa suggested a new colony be founded at a place in the Darién he remembered from his early days with Bastidas. This became Santa María de la Antigua del Darién, or Antigua, the first lasting European settlement. It was established in 1510 and eventually became the first capital of Castilla del Oro.

Balboa proved to be popular with the men and quickly moved into a position of power. He became the administrative head of Antigua and acting governor of Castilla del Oro, subjugating any indigenous peoples who opposed him. Though his methods were vicious, Balboa became known for his strategy of making peace with the indigenous peoples who submitted to him. By the standards of his day, he was considered fair and merciful, particularly compared to his murderous contemporaries and successors.

Told by native allies of a sea to the south along whose coast were cities of gold, Balboa set out from Antigua on September 1, 1513, with 190 of his men, an estimated (and probably exaggerated) 1,000 indigenous peoples, and a pack of dogs. Among his men was Francisco Pizarro. Along the way they had to fight both the hardships of the jungle and indigenous peoples on whose land they were trespassing. At 10 A.M. on September 25, Balboa told the 67 of his men who had survived the brutal trek to wait while he climbed one last hill and became the first European to lay eyes on the "Southern Sea"—the Pacific Ocean. When he finally made it down to the shore four days later, he found himself on the edge of a large gulf off the Pacific coast of the Darién that he named the Golfo de San Miguel. He waded out into the water in full armor and promptly claimed the entire sea and all the lands touching it for the Spanish crown, no doubt the biggest land grab in history.

The Founding of Panama City

Meanwhile, King Ferdinand of Spain had appointed a new governor of the isthmus, Pedro Arias de Ávila, better known as Pedrarias. On the isthmus, he had an even more fitting designation: Furor Domini (the wrath of God). He saw the popular and resourceful Balboa as a rival and had him beheaded for treason in January 1519 at Aclá, a settlement on the Caribbean coast of the Darién.

Pedrarias decided to move the capital from Antigua to the site of a fishing village called Panama, on the central Pacific coast of the isthmus. He founded Panama City, the first European settlement on the Pacific coast of the Americas, on August 15, 1519. He also proceeded to slaughter the indigenous inhabitants of the isthmus.

His men met fierce resistance and sometimes suffered losses at the hands of warriors led by rulers impressive enough to have made it into Spanish records, such as París and Urracá. It was, of course, just a matter of time before the Spanish prevailed. París, for instance, died of natural causes, but he was hounded even in death: The Spaniards looted his grave of its gold. Urracá made peace with the Spaniards, but his people have long since vanished and his only lasting legacy is his profile on Panama's one-centavo coin.

Panama was home to large, diverse populations of indigenous peoples when the Spanish arrived at the turn of the 16th century. Some put the population of the isthmus at that time at two million or even higher, two-thirds of the modern-day population. The Spanish decimated these original inhabitants through war and disease. Today only eight groups of indigenous peoples remain, and three of these are barely hanging on.

COLONIAL ERA

During the colonial period, Panama's great importance to Spain was as a transshipment point for the silver, gold, pearls, and other treasures plundered from South America once the conquest spread to include the Inca Empire. These riches were taken to Panama City, and then had to be carried over to the Caribbean coast, where Spanish ships transported them to Europe. They were carried across the isthmus by two main routes, both of which had their Pacific terminus at Panama City and were established by the Spanish in the early 16th century.

The Camino Real and the Camino de Cruces

The first route was the Camino Real, an overland route that linked Panama City with Nombre de Dios (and with Portobelo, when Nombre de Dios was abandoned in 1597). Its name, which translates to "royal road," was rather regal for what was essentially a mule trail, only part of which was paved. It was brutal and muddy, and where it crossed over the foothills it grew so steep that travelers had to climb through the muck on their hands and knees.

The second was the Camino de Cruces, known in English as Las Cruces Trail. This was an overland route from Panama City to Venta de Cruces, a village on the Río Chagres about a third of the way across the isthmus. The trail was wider than a man is tall during the Spanish Colonial era, and it was paved with flat stones. From Venta de Cruces, it became a water route, with cargo moved by boat or barge up and down the Chagres, which flows into the Caribbean. Fuerte San Lorenzo was built at the mouth of the Chagres to defend it. Because this route was considerably farther west than the Camino Real, goods had to be transported by sea between the mouth of the Chagres and Nombre de Dios or Portobelo to the east. The whole trip took 1–2 weeks each way.

Though an easier and cheaper route, especially for shipping heavy loads, the Camino de Cruces was more vulnerable to pirate attack than the Camino Real, which had the natural protection of the jungle for much of its length.

The Spanish established the Camino de Cruces in 1527, and it was still being used up until the mid-19th century. The Forty-niners used it in their own hunt for treasure, as they rushed to the gold fields of California. It was finally abandoned with the building of the Panama Railroad in the 1850s. The village of Venta de Cruces is now at the bottom of the Panama Canal, but part of the Camino de Cruces is still intact and can be walked. The Camino Real was abandoned in 1826.

Gold gets all the attention in romantic tales of Caribbean pirates and Spanish galleons, but silver made up the bulk of the riches Spain looted from South America, mostly from the mines of Peru. By the end of the 17th century, Spain had tripled the amount of silver in circulation throughout the world. An estimated 60 percent of it came through Portobelo alone.

Trade Fairs

This silver, and other treasures from the New World, were traded at massive fairs held at Nombre de Dios and Portobelo. Spanish merchants from Europe and South America converged at the fairs for several weeks each year, more or less, during which they exchanged treasure for European finished goods, which included everything from nails to fine cloth. Merchant ships heading across the Atlantic to and from Spain were escorted by the Spanish navy.

The first organized fair was held in 1537. At their peak, the fairs surpassed those held anywhere else in the world. Bars of silver were stacked high in the streets, but the presence of the heavily armed Spanish fleet kept pirates away.

Not so between fairs. Despite its great importance to the Spanish Empire, the isthmus was neglected and never adequately defended against pirates. Panama was always treated as a notch below, say, Peru, a wealthy and powerful viceroyalty. Panama had the lower administrative rank of *audencia* and was governed by a president.

The trade fairs and treasure shipments marked the first time Panama became a crucial link in world commerce, a role it has continued to play over the years—as a route for the Forty-niners, as the site of the Panama Canal, and as an international banking capital. One can even see the Colón Free Zone, along the coast where the ruins of the Spanish fortifications still stand, as a kind of descendant of the Spanish trade fairs.

After 1628, these fairs diminished in importance along with the declining fortunes of the Spanish Empire. They were finally abandoned in 1739.

Elizabethan Pirates and Privateers

Lack of funds, poor planning, and procrastination have been blamed for the fact that Panama was constantly sacked and looted throughout the Spanish era.

Nombre de Dios was always a bad choice for a port—the harbor was shallow and exposed, and it would have been hard to defend even if it had had better fortifications. Sir Francis Drake attacked it in 1572 and would likely have sacked it then if he had not been wounded during the conflict. Still, he and his men went on to ambush a mule train on the Camino Real loaded down with so many tons of silver they couldn't carry it away. They buried it instead and made off with some gold. The Spanish dug up the silver before Drake could return for it.

Drake's many exploits on the isthmus as a young adventurer during this period read like something straight out of *Treasure Island*. As historians have pointed out, one gets a sense he had an enormously good time tweaking the Spanish. He had help in his adventures from *cimarrones*, escaped African slaves who lived in hidden towns in the jungle and also delighted in harrying their former Spanish masters.

Drake returned to the isthmus years later for more adventures, but he fell sick and died on January 28, 1596, and was buried at sea in a lead-lined coffin near Portobelo. Expeditions have searched for that coffin, but it has never been found.

The Spanish abandoned Nombre de Dios and moved west to Portobelo in 1597, before the fortifications were even completed. Portobelo was a far better location for an important port town. The harbor was long and narrow, surrounded by hills. The Spanish fortified it heavily, but the design was poor from the beginning and constant redesigns over the years didn't seem to help matters much.

Portobelo was barely completed by the time the English pirate William Parker attacked and looted it in 1601. It was sacked and rebuilt several times over the next 200 years.

Morgan and the Sacking of Panama City

The Welsh buccaneer Henry Morgan took Portobelo and held it for ransom in 1668. He did so by landing his troops at night some distance from Portobelo and attacking the fortifications by land. The defenders' cannons, pointing out to sea, were useless. Still, it was a vicious battle. At one point, Morgan's men used Spanish priests and nuns as human shields, forcing them to erect scaling ladders against the fort walls. The Spanish governor ordered the poor hostages shot down. When Morgan captured the city, he tortured its inhabitants if they refused to reveal where they

Henry Morgan sacked Panama City in 1671.

had hidden their goods. The Spanish finally paid him a ransom of 100,000 pieces of eight to get him to leave.

As this tale suggests, the buccaneers of the 17th century earned a reputation as a far crueler, bloodier, and less dashing lot than the Elizabethan privateers of the previous century.

Morgan was determined to sack and loot Panama City, and he knew where to start his raid. There was another Caribbean fort, Castillo de San Lorenzo el Real, better known today as Fuerte San Lorenzo. It was built near the mouth of the Río Chagres. An imposing cliff there overlooks the river mouth and the sea, the perfect place for a fortress. Oddly, however, the fort was made of wood and its buildings had thatched roofs. As bizarre as it sounds, even the fort's gunpowder was stored in a thatched hut. When Morgan invaded the isthmus, he was able to sack and destroy San Lorenzo, even though the Spanish knew he was coming, by shooting flaming arrows over the walls. He then proceeded up the Chagres by canoe and sacked Panama City. The city was burned to the ground—whether by Morgan or the Spanish is still a matter of debate—and later rebuilt at a more defensible location eight kilometers farther west. This second Panama City still stands, as a historical part of modern-day Panama City known as Casco Viejo or Casco Antiguo.

The Scottish Colony

One of the stranger and more tragic episodes during this period was the doomed Scottish colony of New Edinburgh. It was the dream of an entrepreneur named William Paterson, who convinced the Company of Scotland, an overseas trading company created by the Scottish parliament, to invest hundreds of thousands of pounds in his scheme to establish a colony on the Caribbean coast of the Darién. He argued the colony would be ideally situated to become a trading center between Europe and Asia and would help transform Scotland's struggling economy. In July of 1698, Paterson and 1,200 colonists set sail for the Darién.

Those who survived the crossing arrived in the Darién on November 2. They built a fort, Fort Saint Andrew, on a long, narrow bay they named Calidonia, a name it retains to this day. The colonists were completely unprepared for life in the tropical rainforest, and the colony was a debacle. The first attempt at settlement was abandoned in less than a year, and only a third of the colonists made it back to Scotland. Attempts were made to reestablish the colony, but incompetence, in-fighting, battles with the Spanish, opposition from the English, shipwrecks, and disease brought an end to New Edinburgh by 1700. Scotland, deeply in debt, was forced in 1707 to give up dreams of independence and empire, and joined England to form Great Britain.

THE TUMULTUOUS 19TH CENTURY

With the decline of the Spanish Empire and the drying up of the treasures of the Inca Empire, Panama became a colonial backwater. When independence movements swept through Latin America, Panama eventually got caught up in the tide.

Independence from Spain

On November 10, 1821, residents of the little town of La Villa de Los Santos on the Azuero Peninsula wrote a letter to Simón Bolívar complaining of mistreatment by the Spanish governor and asking for his help. This Primer Grito de la Independencia (First Cry for Independence) is commemorated as a national holiday in Panama.

This was followed 18 days later by a meeting in Panama City in which Panama broke away from Spain and joined Colombia in an uneasy union that for a while included Venezuela and Ecuador. November 28 is celebrated in Panama today as the first of several steps toward independence.

In 1826, Bolívar called a congress, held in what is now the Casco Viejo section of Panama City, in an attempt to create a union of Latin American republics. The Congress of Panama took place June 22–July 15. Though Bolívar

himself did not attend and the talks ended in failure, the attempt is still considered an important moment in Latin American history.

The isthmus of Panama was in turmoil through much of the 19th century. It attempted three times between 1831 and 1841 to break away from Colombia, but each time it failed.

The Prestán Uprising

One of the bloodiest incidents of the 19th century in Panama was the so-called Prestán Uprising of 1885. Depending on whom one chooses to believe, Pedro Prestán was either a revolutionary martyred in the cause of freedom or a rabble-rousing mulatto with an irrational hatred of foreigners, especially white ones. When a former president of the department of Panama, Rafael Aizpuru, tried to seize power in Panama City, Colombian troops were dispatched to the city from the Caribbean side of the isthmus, leaving the city of Colón largely undefended. Prestán took advantage of this, reportedly leading a band of machete-wielding men in a looting spree along Front Street. He then took hostages, whom he threatened to kill if the U.S. warship *Galena,* at port in Colón, landed troops. He also demanded he be given a shipment of arms that had been smuggled by ship and were waiting for him in the harbor.

The commander of the *Galena* had been ordered not to interfere in Panama's domestic affairs unless the Panama Railroad was threatened, which so far it hadn't. The American consul, one of Prestán's hostages, promised to turn over the weapons. Prestán released the hostages, but the *Galena* towed the steamer with the cargo of guns away from shore before Prestán could get access to them.

On March 31, Colombian troops returned from Panama City and battled Prestán's men at Monkey Hill, just outside the city. Routed, Prestán allegedly set fire to Colón as his men retreated. The city, which was built almost entirely of wood, burned to the ground, leaving at least 18 dead and thousands homeless. The Colombian troops rounded up dozens of Prestán's men and executed them. Prestán himself was tried and hanged in Colón, above the railroad tracks. Aizpuru, whose own failed rebellion in Panama City left dozens dead, was sentenced to 10 years in exile.

The War of a Thousand Days

The isthmus was also the scene of major battles in the War of a Thousand Days (1899–1902), a Colombian civil war fought between the Liberal and Conservative parties.

One of the most important of these was the battle of La Vieja Negra, fought outside the city of David in western Panama on March 31, 1900. Liberals who had taken refuge in Nicaragua from the ruling Conservative party invaded Panama from the west, captured David, and defeated better-trained and -equipped Conservative forces at La Vieja Negra, after which they marched on Panama City and were defeated. A peace treaty was signed on July 26, 1900, but was quickly broken. Bloody battles continued to flare up around the isthmus. Colombia called on the United States to intervene, and the war finally came to an end with the signing of a peace treaty aboard the warship U.S.S. *Wisconsin* on November 19, 1902.

Though the Liberals lost the war, Panama considers the leaders of the Liberal forces to be heroes and founding fathers of the country. These include Belisario Porras, the civilian head of the isthmian forces, and Victoriano Lorenzo, who commanded an army of his fellow *cholos* (people of indigenous descent but Latino culture) that played a key role in many of the battles. Porras would later serve as president three times when Panama finally became an independent country. Although the peace treaty was supposed to grant the combatants amnesty, Lorenzo was executed by firing squad on May 15, 1903, which Panama remembers as one of the darker days in its history.

GOLD RUSH DAYS

The California gold rush brought Panama back onto the world stage in another quest for treasure. The fastest way to get to the gold fields was to cross at Panama, but it was hardly the easiest. Thousands made their way by foot or mule across the 50 miles of the isthmus by way of the muddy, brutal Camino de Cruces, the same trail used by the Spanish during their own bout of gold fever. Untold others died attempting it, of cholera, dysentery, yellow fever, malaria, and the other dangers that made the Panama route notorious.

If a railway could be built across the isthmus, it would make the crossing faster and far safer for the Forty-niners who, not incidentally, would be willing to pay a small fortune for the privilege. A forward-thinking U.S. merchant named William Henry Aspinwall negotiated a treaty with Nueva Granada to build just such a railway shortly before the California gold rush began.

Though only 47.5 miles long, the railroad was an incredibly costly undertaking, both in dollars and lives. It was said that every railroad tie represented one worker dead from disease. That's a wild exaggeration, but thousands did die building the little railroad through the jungle. In 1852, a cholera epidemic struck so quickly that workers died on the tracks, to be eaten by ants and land crabs. So many died that the Panama Railroad Company started a lucrative side business shipping cadavers preserved in barrels to medical schools and hospitals around the world. Engineers had to contend with the powerful Río Chagres, which could rise 40 feet overnight, and with obstacles such as the seemingly bottomless Black Swamp. When the railroad was completed in 1855, it included 304 bridges and culverts. The company was able to charge US$25 in gold for a one-way trip, a huge sum for the day.

The massive influx of foreigners on the isthmus, some of them rather rough characters, caused some conflicts. The worst incident occurred in April of 1856, when an allegedly drunk train passenger who had just arrived in Panama City grabbed a slice of watermelon from a black vendor and refused to pay for it. This sparked the so-called Watermelon War, a day of rioting that had racial, anti-American, and class overtones. It left at least 16 dead, almost all North Americans, and caused extensive damage to railroad property.

THE PANAMA CANAL AND INDEPENDENCE FROM COLOMBIA

For hundreds of years, visionaries had dreamed of building a canal across the isthmus. Even the early Spanish colonists toyed with the idea until King Philip II allegedly declared that if God had wanted a canal joining the oceans, God would have put one there himself.

The French Canal

The French were the first to undertake the challenge, in 1882. The moving force behind the effort was Ferdinand de Lesseps, a charismatic diplomat with no engineering background who was basking in the glory of leading the successful effort to build the Suez Canal. He insisted that building a sea-level canal at Panama would be far easier. After all, Suez was twice as long.

But this was Panama, and a sea-level canal here meant digging through mountains, not sand, and contending with its tropical diseases, fierce heat, torrential rains, and forbidding terrain.

The French failed disastrously. It has been estimated that 20,000 workers died, mostly of disease, during the seven-year French effort. The French canal company ran out of money in 1889, and the ensuing financial crisis nearly bankrupted France.

The U.S. Canal

The United States had long toyed with building its own canal. It bought out the French concession, but clashed with the government of Nueva Granada (i.e., Colombia) over payments and the granting of rights over the proposed waterway. When negotiations stalled, the United States, under President Theodore Roosevelt, decided to support a small independence movement in Panama spearheaded by a few prominent Panamanians and Panama Railroad officials. In a display of literal "gunboat diplomacy," America sent a warship to Panama to intimidate the Colombian forces on the isthmus. On November 3, 1903, Panama declared its independence from Nueva Granada.

COURTESY OF THE PANAMA CANAL COMMISSION

testing Gatún Locks, June 11, 1914

It was a remarkably peaceful civil war. Bloodshed was likely averted by a fast-thinking Panama Railroad official. He convinced a Colombian general who had just landed with his troops in Colón that it was only fitting that he and his officers should ride in a special train car ahead of his men, who were left stranded in Colón. When the officers arrived in Panama City, Panama-based Colombian soldiers who had been bought off by the revolutionaries took them prisoner. The only casualty during the whole conflict was a Chinese shopkeeper, asleep in his bed, who was killed by an errant shell from a Colombian gunboat. A second shell killed a donkey in a slaughterhouse. By November 6, the revolution was over.

The United States immediately signed the controversial Hay–Bunau-Varilla Treaty with the new Panamanian government, which gave America the right to build a canal in Panama. It would become a source of contention for decades to come that no Panamanian signed the treaty. The official signatory for Panama was a Frenchman, Philippe Bunau-Varilla, the former director of and major shareholder in the French canal effort. The revolutionaries had reluctantly agreed to let him negotiate with Washington on their behalf as an "envoy extraordinary." He signed the treaty in New York before the Panamanian delegation even arrived.

The treaty granted the United States control "in perpetuity" over the canal and a 50-by-10-mile strip of land surrounding it. The United States paid the new country of Panama US$10 million, plus an annual payment of US$250,000. The French canal company received US$40 million for all the equipment, infrastructure, and excavation it left behind, much of which proved useful to the Americans.

The American effort was quite different from the French one. Instead of a sea-level ditch, the U.S. plan called for a lock canal that would lift ships over the isthmian landmass. The plan was designed by John Stevens, a brilliant railway engineer, and seen to completion by his successor as chief engineer, George W. Goethals. All work on the canal had to be halted, however, until disease could be controlled. Under the leadership of a forward-looking sanitary officer named Dr. William Gorgas, the Americans eliminated yellow fever from Panama, brought malaria and other deadly diseases under control, and introduced clean water and modern sanitation to the isthmus.

The canal was a colossal task. It required an excavation three times as massive as that at Suez. And among other challenges, the builders had to cut right through nine miles of mountains at the Continental Divide, a job overseen by David Gaillard, for whom the resulting Gaillard Cut is named. The lock chambers were among the largest structures ever made by humans. The mighty Río Chagres was contained by the largest earthen dam in history, forming the largest artificially-made lake in the world. The canal is still considered one of the most extraordinary engineering feats of all time.

The U.S. canal effort cost US$352 million

Colonel and Mrs. David D. Gaillard having tea at their home on the banks of Culebra Cut

COURTESY OF THE PANAMA CANAL COMMISSION

and took 5,600 lives, most of them West Indians who made up the bulk of the labor force. But the canal opened for business on August 15, 1914, under budget and ahead of schedule.

THE NEW NATION

The first president of the new Republic of Panama was Dr. Manuel Amador Guerrero, an elderly, well-respected medical doctor from a prominent Panamanian family and the leader of the little band of revolutionaries. Panama was a kind of democracy, but leaders inevitably came from the wealthiest, whitest families.

One of the biggest challenges to the new republic was an independence movement among the Kunas of the San Blas Islands. The Kuna declared their independence from Panama in February of 1925 and announced the creation of their own country, the Republic of Tule. A brief war ensued that left about two dozen dead. The United States intervened and presided over a peace treaty between Panama and the Kunas that gave the latter the semi-autonomous status they retain to this day. The other indigenous peoples of Panama have slowly gained similar control over their ancestral lands over the years through the establishment of *comarcas* (reservations). Some are still fighting for *comarca* status.

Arnulfo Arias

A figure who loomed large in Panamanian politics through much of the 20th century was Arnulfo Arias Madrid, a Harvard Medical School graduate from a family of provincial farmers. Along with his brother, Harmodio Arias Madrid, he was a leading figure in a group called Acción Comunal that overthrew the president, Florencio Harmodio Arosemena, in a bloody assault on the presidential palace in 1931. (Note: Many of the major figures in Panamanian politics have similar names, including many who are not remotely related.) Arosemena was replaced by Ricardo J. Alfaro, a choice acceptable to Acción Comunal. The following year, Arnulfo's brother was elected president. The United States decided not to intervene in any of this. It was the country's first successful coup.

But it was hardly the last. Arnulfo Arias himself, ironically enough, endured them incessantly. He was elected president of Panama at least four times (voter fraud makes the official outcome in two elections hard to confirm) between 1940 and 1984. Each time he was either deposed or forbidden to take office by the Policía Nacional (National Police) or its successor, the Guardia Nacional (National Guard).

Arnulfo, as he is known in Panama, was a charismatic populist who espoused a vehement brand of nationalism known as *panameñismo*. He was also a fascist sympathizer during World War II who was determined not only to rid the isthmus of North Americans but also of fellow citizens he deemed undesirables. Nevertheless, he was beloved by many of Panama's poor and disenfranchised, who saw him as a counterweight to the power of the oligarchy.

In 1941, at the beginning of his first aborted administration, he introduced a new constitution that replaced the one instituted in 1904. Among other things, it increased the presidential term of office to six years. But it's most notorious for blatantly racist provisions that forbade the immigration of blacks from non-Spanish-speaking countries, as well as Chinese, Indians, and Arabs. It also stripped those already in the country of their citizenship. It was replaced with yet another constitution five years later, after he was overthrown the first time. But Arias is also credited with establishing many of Panama's most important institutions, such as the social security system, and expanding the rights of some of its citizens.

The Rise of the National Guard

The commander of the National Police, José Antonio Remón Cantera, militarized and increased the power of the force and served as kingmaker (and breaker) for several Panamanian presidents before running for president himself. In a strange series of events, he first opposed and then installed Arnulfo Arias as president in 1949, declaring, without presenting evidence, that the election of the year before should have found Arias the victor. Arias's second attempt at wielding power deteriorated rapidly, and demonstrations against him turned so violent he was forced to hole up in the presidential palace with his most loyal supporters. Two officers of the National Police were shot dead on the steps of the palace under mysterious circumstances. The murders were to prove emblematic of the enmity that would exist for the rest of the century between the *arnulfistas* and the National Police, later the National Guard. Arias was removed from power a second time.

Remón decided it was time to become president himself. He was elected in 1952 and began a campaign of social and economic reforms that was cut short in 1955 when he was machinegunned to death at a horse-racing track on the outskirts of Panama City. All kinds of conspiracy theories have been put forth about who was behind the assassination. One even points the finger at the American mobster "Lucky" Luciano. Panama City's racetrack was renamed in Remón's honor.

EMERGING NATIONALISM

Tensions between Panama and the United States flared up repeatedly through much of the 20th century. Again and again, especially in the early days of the republic, the United States intervened in the domestic affairs of the country. Because of the strategic and economic importance of first the Panama Railroad and then the Panama Canal, the United States insisted on reserving the right to play a hand in the destiny of the isthmus in treaty after treaty.

Tensions occasionally erupted in violence. When the Panamanian national legislature met in 1947 to consider a treaty that would allow the United States to continue to use military bases outside the Canal Zone, 10,000 protesters took to the streets and clashed with Panama's National Police, with deaths on both sides. The legislature rejected the treaty unanimously. Violent anti-U.S. demonstrations flared up again in 1958 and 1959.

The Flag Riots

The most infamous incident, though, was termed the Flag Riots of 1964. The United States had agreed to fly the Panamanian flag alongside the U.S. one in a few places in the Canal Zone, even though some feared (and others hoped) this would throw U.S. sovereignty over the zone into doubt. In an attempt to avoid controversy, the governor of the Canal Zone decided to take down some flagpoles in the zone altogether. One of these spots was Balboa High School. A group of high school students objected to this, and before the pole could be removed, they raised a U.S. flag themselves. When a group of Panamanian college students heard of this, they organized a march to the high school and attempted to lower the U.S. and raise the Panamanian one. A scuffle broke out, during which the Panamanian students claimed their flag had been torn.

What happened after that will probably forever be a source of passionate debate, depending on one's sympathies and prejudices. What everyone can agree on is that rioting, looting, and destruction followed, mostly along Fourth of July Avenue, which separated Panama City from the Canal Zone. In the end, two dozen people were killed and millions of dollars of property destroyed. The Panamanians who died are officially considered martyrs in Panama, and January 9 is still a national day of mourning in their honor. Fourth of July Avenue was renamed Avenida de los Mártires.

In the wake of this terrible clash, President Lyndon B. Johnson announced that the United States would undertake negotiations with Panama on an entirely new canal treaty.

A NEW TREATY

In 1968 Arnulfo Arias was again elected president. He took office on October 1 and immediately called for the turnover of the canal to Panama and attempted to take control of the National Guard. The second move was a mistake. A military junta deposed him on October 11, and, ironically enough, he fled to the Canal Zone for protection. He had served 11 days in office, his shortest term yet.

Omar Torrijos

After a period of chaos and demonstrations, a National Guard colonel named Omar Torrijos Herrera assumed power. He was himself the subject of an attempted coup by three rival colonels when he took a trip to Mexico early in his rule. When he learned of this, he returned to Panama, rallied supporters in the western city of David, and marched on the capital. He regained power and sent the colonels into exile.

Torrijos had himself promoted to general and became a remarkably popular figure. Though a military dictator, he was also a populist who flirted with socialist ideas—he had a friendly relationship with Fidel Castro—and instituted sweeping social reforms. Though he installed a figurehead president, Demétrios Lakas, everyone knew who was really in charge. In 1972 he introduced yet another new constitution that confirmed him as head of a powerful central government and curtailed civil rights. He ordered the redistribution of land to the campesinos (country people, farmers), greatly expanded public health programs, reformed the school system, built roads and bridges in rural areas, and laid the groundwork for Panama's emergence as an international banking center. Some of these changes came at the expense of the oligarchy.

For all these accomplishments, however, corruption and nepotism blossomed under Torrijos, and the bodies of his political enemies are still being dug up around the country.

One of the things that helped ensure Torrijos's popularity was his focus on a new treaty that would turn control of the canal over to Panama. Negotiations began with the Nixon and Ford administrations, but progress was slow until Jimmy Carter took office in 1977. On September 7 of that year, Torrijos met Carter in Washington, D.C., to sign two new Panama Canal treaties. The first called for a gradual turnover of the canal to Panamanian control, to allow the small country time to absorb the massive undertaking. Panama gained complete jurisdiction over the canal and former Canal Zone at noon on December 31, 1999. The second one, the Neutrality Treaty, bound the United States and Panama to guarantee the canal's neutrality in peace or war and allow unimpeded transit of the ships of all nations. The United States reserved the right to act against any perceived threat to the canal, but not otherwise intervene in the domestic affairs of Panama. This second treaty was open-ended and is still in effect, and it continues to be a source of discontent in Panama from time to time. Two-thirds of the Panamanian people voted in favor of the new treaties, a weaker show of support than expected.

To gain support in Washington for the treaties, Torrijos had agreed to begin a process of democratization. He stepped down as the official head of government but retained ultimate authority by retaining his position as head of the National Guard. He allowed Arnulfo Arias to return to Panama and start rebuilding his political support. The constitution was amended in October 1978 to weaken the power of the executive branch somewhat and increase that of the Asamblea Legislativa, the national legislature. The legislature voted in Aristides Royo, a candidate backed by Torrijos, as president.

The first political party granted official recognition was the Partido Revolucionario Democrático (Democratic Revolutionary Party) or PRD, which was controlled by Torrijos and his supporters and would come to be known as the National Guard's party. National elections were held in 1980. Opposition parties gained some representation in the national legislature, but Torrijos ensured that most seats were reserved for the PRD.

Noriega Takes Power

On July 31, 1981, Torrijos died in a small plane that crashed in the mountains above El Copé in central Panama. The area has since been turned into a national park named in his honor. Rumors that the crash was arranged by one of his political rivals circulated immediately. A period of turmoil followed, with a parade of military figures succeeding each other in power.

By 1983, General Manuel Antonio Noriega

had firm control of the National Guard, which he soon renamed the Fuerzas de Defensa de Panamá (Panama Defense Forces), and the country as a whole. Torrijos had spotted Noriega's potential early in his own military career, and when he became dictator he had put Noriega in charge of military intelligence. Despite this long association, some speculated that Noriega was behind the death of Torrijos. The contrast between the two dictators could not have been more stark. Torrijos was a handsome, charismatic man who inspired loyalty among his supporters and enacted many popular programs. Noriega's pockmarked face earned him the nickname *cara de piña* (pineapple face), and he ruled through fear.

In the 1984 elections, the Noriega-controlled PRD nominated Nicolás Ardito Barletta Vallarino, a former World Bank vice president with a degree in economics from the University of Chicago. Opposing him was the indefatigable Arnulfo Arias. Barletta was elected president in what was widely agreed to be a fraudulent vote count. The United States decided to recognize him anyway.

But in September 1985 a horrific event occurred that began Noriega's spectacular fall from power. Dr. Hugo Spadafora, a colorful and charismatic Noriega opponent who had been a guerrilla fighter in Africa and a protégé of Torrijos, decided to return to Panama by bus to challenge Noriega's hold on power. He claimed to have information on Noriega's illegal dealings throughout Latin America that would force him from power. He took a bus from the Costa Rican border toward Panama City on September 13, but he was stopped near the town of Concepción and forced off the bus. He was subsequently tortured and beheaded, his decapitated body later found in a river across the border in Costa Rica. Suspicion immediately fell on Noriega.

The following year, the Pulitzer Prize–winning investigative reporter Seymour Hersh began breaking stories in *The New York Times* that detailed a laundry list of shady dealings by Noriega: that he had long been a CIA asset, that he was deeply involved in drug dealing and money laundering, that he'd rigged the 1984 election, that he did intelligence work for Cuba, that he was implicated in the murder of Spadafora. When the Iran-Contra scandal broke, Noriega emerged as a vital player who was said to have a cozy relationship with Oliver North, CIA director William Casey, and other Iran-Contra figures. He was accused of helping the Contras with everything from shipping arms to planning sabotage operations in Nicaragua. Noriega was proving an increasing embarrassment, first to President Ronald Reagan and then President George H. W. Bush, whom Noriega had known since Bush's days as CIA director in the 1970s.

Operation Just Cause

A new election was held on May 7, 1989, with a Noriega-backed candidate named Carlos Duque running against Guillermo Endara, a lawyer and protégé of Arnulfo Arias, whose long political career had finally ended the year before, when he died at age 86. Panama always elects two vice presidents, and Endara's running mates were Guillermo "Billy" Ford and Ricardo Arias Calderón.

The election was a sham: votes were bought; eligible voters were turned away from the polls; ballots were destroyed. Jimmy Carter, who had flown to Panama as an election observer, held a press conference at a Panama City hotel and declared, "The government is taking the election by fraud." He said the opposition had won by a margin of three to one.

Endara and his two running mates led a protest march three days later that was attacked by Panama Defense Forces troops and Noriega goons. Demonstrators were blasted with buckshot and tear gas. Endara was knocked unconscious by an attacker wielding a steel pipe, and Arias Calderón and Ford were beaten and shot at. Images of the bloodied candidates were beamed around the world.

By now, some officers of the Panama Defense Forces were becoming nervous at what seemed to be Noriega's increasingly erratic behavior. Major Moises Giroldi decided to mount a coup, with tentative support from a suspicious Washington. On October 3, 1989, Giroldi and his supporters took Noriega hostage at his headquarters, the Comandancia, but hesitation and confusion allowed Noriega time to phone his most loyal troops, who surrounded the Comandancia and engaged in a firefight with the rebels. Noriega prevailed and the coup plotters were tortured and executed. The Bush administration denied having any involvement with the coup attempt, despite considerable evidence it had encouraged the coup, then declined to give it support at the vital moment.

Periodic violent clashes between the Panama Defense Forces and U.S. military personnel traveling outside the Canal Zone reached a low point when a U.S. Marine Corps lieutenant, Robert Paz, was shot dead in Panama City on December 17. Three days later, on December 20, 1989, President Bush ordered an invasion of Panama, dubbed Operation Just Cause. It left somewhere between 200 and 4,000 civilians dead. The true number may never be known, as it was in the interest of the United States and the subsequent Panamanian government to downplay the number, and of those with other political agendas to inflate it. The hardest-hit area was El Chorrillo, an impoverished neighborhood of wooden tenements and anti-Noriega sentiment that lay right next to the Comandancia. It was swept by a fire that left an untold number dead and thousands homeless.

Noriega escaped and sought asylum at the residence of the papal nuncio, the representative of the Vatican in Panama, on Christmas Eve. U.S. troops surrounded the house and "psychological operations" personnel blasted loud rock music to keep him from getting any rest. He surrendered on January 3, 1990, and was flown to Florida. On July 2, 1992, he was sentenced to 40 years in a Miami prison on drug and racketeering charges. The sentence was later reduced.

With time off for good behavior, Noriega completed his sentence on September 9, 2007, having served 17 years in prison. He remained in custody in Florida until 2010, however, while he fought extradition to France, where he faced charges of laundering drug money. He was finally extradited, and in July 2010 was tried and sentenced to seven years in a French prison.

The Panamanian government has called for his extradition to Panama, where he was convicted in absentia of a number of crimes, including murdering the leaders of the 1989 coup attempt. What would actually happen to Noriega if he is ever returned to Panama is unclear. He is now in his 70s, and under a new law convicts older than 70 can serve their sentences under house arrest.

A NEW DEMOCRACY

Guillermo Endara, who had been robbed by Noriega of the presidency in 1989 and brutally beaten along with his vice-presidential candidates in the protests that followed, was finally sworn in as president during the invasion. His term was a period of instability, as Panama worked to recover from the devastation of the invasion and the U.S. economic sanctions that preceded it. A final military coup was attempted and failed. The Panama Defense Forces were disbanded, and today Panama no longer has a military. But crime increased in Panama while order was restored and a new civilian police force organized.

Endara—a figure of some fun in Panama because of his obesity, lack of political experience, and infatuation with his young, attractive wife—managed to serve out his term, and democracy took hold in Panama.

Endara was succeeded in 1994 by Ernesto Pérez Balladares, a member of the PRD, the party of Noriega and Torrijos. He won with 33 percent of the vote in an election that also featured Mireya Moscoso, the widow of Arnulfo Arias, and Rubén Blades, the famous salsa singer and actor. The election was considered fair.

The PRD attempted to distance itself from the Noriega years, but during the Balladares administration it continued to face accusations of drug trafficking, money laundering, and corruption. Balladares, popularly known as El Toro (The Bull), enacted free-market reforms that sparked protest in Panama and caused his popularity to suffer. He attempted to change the constitution to allow him to run for a second term, but Panamanian voters defeated the proposal by a two-to-one margin.

In 1999, Moscoso ran again for the presidency on the ticket of the Partido Arnulfista (PA) or Arnulfista Party. This time her main opponent was Martín Torrijos, the young son of the late dictator, who represented the PRD. Moscoso won and became Panama's first female president. A peaceful democracy proved to be well established as full control of the Panama Canal was turned over to Panama at noon on December 31, 1999.

The new millennium began with things looking pretty bright for Panama. The Panama Canal was in the middle of a billion-dollar expansion and was increasingly being run as a business, its raised tolls making a major contribution to the economy. New construction was transforming the Panama City skyline, and thanks to Balladares, the road system throughout the country was greatly improved.

But a downturn in the world economy hit Panama's services sector hard. Moscoso also generated a great deal of animosity, and not just from her political rivals. Her administration, like the one before it, was plagued by accusations of corruption. She did little to endear herself to the poor people among her supporters when, early in her administration, she presented each of the 72 members of the national legislature with a Cartier watch as a "Christmas present."

Environmentalists also complained that her policies were wreaking immeasurable damage for short-term gain. Her support for a road linking Cerro Punta and Boquete, for instance, sparked public outrage. Her critics maintained that a rough road already existed farther down the mountain and, if improved, would help many impoverished communities along the route with minimal harm to the environment. Moscoso favored building a new road right through the heart of Parque Nacional Volcán Barú; public protests and a negative environmental impact study halted the plan.

Some of Moscoso's actions were applauded, however. In 2001 her administration established a Comisión de la Verdad (Truth Commission) to investigate the disappearance of 110 people under the Torrijos and Noriega dictatorships. Forensic anthropologists dug up human remains all over the country, and in its final report the commission concluded that at least 70 of the cases it investigated were murders.

Throughout her term in office, Moscoso and her government continued to be hounded by impassioned accusations of corruption and incompetence that were striking for Panama, which traditionally has had a cynical attitude toward the actions of those in power. A widely quoted poll of Latin American countries, conducted toward the end of her time in office, put her approval rating among Panamanians at 15 percent, the second-lowest for a Central American leader at the time.

Moscoso's term ended in 2004. Martín Torrijos ran a second time for the presidency and this time was elected. He took office on September 1, 2004—as always, to a single, five-year term.

Torrijos's term had its share of troubles. A 2005 overhaul of the Caja de Seguro Social, Panama's ailing social security system, led to sometimes-violent protests, including a month-long strike. Under the new law, workers' required contributions were increased, and the retirement age was raised by five years. It also faced repeated protests from Suntracs (Sindicato Único de Trabajadores de la Construcción y Similares), Panama's powerful construction workers' union, over pay, benefits, and safety.

In 2006, the government was widely criticized for a public-health crisis that led to the deaths of at least 115 patients poisoned by cough syrup. Panamanian public-health officials made the syrup using what they believed to be glycerin, but which was actually diethylene glycol, an industrial solvent used in antifreeze. The counterfeit glycerin was supplied by a Chinese company that did not have a license to sell drug ingredients. Chinese companies have been blamed for similar cases around the world. Investigations into the tragedy, including how the chemical ended up in the public-hospital system, continue. Officials doubt the true number of those killed or injured by the tainted medicine will ever be known. Victims' families have slammed the government for not being aggressive enough in its investigation.

But many things also went well during Torrijos's watch. Most notably, Panama's economy boomed. That may help account for his relatively high approval rating, which remained above 50 percent throughout most of his term. On the other hand, rival politicians and some among the public complained that the Torrijos administration deferred tough decisions and spent too much time and money on public relations. Polls suggested that Panamanians were increasingly worried about issues they feel are not receiving enough attention, such as a perceived rise in violent crime, the increasing cost of living, and inadequate public transportation in congested Panama City.

If nothing else, Torrijos will be remembered for his support of the third-locks project at the Panama Canal, which was approved in a national referendum on October 22, 2006. Work on the project officially began on September 3, 2007, and is expected to be finished by 2014. Officials expect the project to cost US$5.3 billion, to be funded largely through increased tolls. Critics, however, believe the final figure could be twice as high, and they worry about where all that money will end up coming from. In any case, if and when the project is finally completed it should greatly expand the canal's capacity.

On May 3, 2009, Ricardo Martinelli, the leader of the *Cambio Democrático* (Democratic Change), was elected president of Panama in a landslide. He received 60 percent of the vote, far ahead of his closest rival, Balbina Herrera of the PRD, who received about 36 percent.

The wealthy owner of a supermarket chain, Martinelli immediately set about cracking down on corruption, investigating former leaders, firing public workers who were not performing, and launching a plan to bring a modern transportation system to Panama City. For a while, he was the most popular leader in Latin America. His approval ratings had begun to slip, however, with some complaining that he was trying to accumulate too much power.

Government and Economy

Panama is a constitutional democracy. The chief executive is the president, traditionally assisted by two vice presidents, all of whom are elected to a single five-year term. A change to the constitution in 2004 reduced the number of vice presidents to one, starting with the 2009 election. The popularly elected Asamblea Nacional, formerly the Asamblea Legislativa, is the national legislature. It's a unicameral (one house) body. The number of legislators has fluctuated in the past, but the constitutional reforms of 2004 fixed the number at 71, starting with the 2009 election. Legislators serve five-year terms that run concurrently with the presidential term. There is also a supreme court consisting of nine justices who serve 10-year terms, along with several superior courts and courts of appeal.

For much of Panama's history, however, the government was essentially controlled by the oligarchy, the military, or both. Especially during the military dictatorship that lasted from the 1968 coup to the 1989 U.S. invasion that removed Noriega from power, the president was often a figurehead, and neither the legislature nor the courts held much independent power.

Every election from 1994 on has been widely considered free and fair, with less controversy surrounding them than, for instance, recent U.S. elections. Though corruption and influence peddling are still acknowledged to be

A sustained surge in highrise construction in Panama City has given Panama's economy a major boost.

problems, Panama's democracy appears healthier and more firmly entrenched than ever before. Suffrage is "universal and compulsory"—that is, everyone 18 years and older is required to vote in all national elections.

Panama either adopted a new constitution or amended an existing one several times during its first 100 years, usually motivated by expanding or contracting the government's power and citizens' rights or realigning its relationship with the United States, particularly concerning U.S. intervention in Panama's affairs and its rights in the Canal Zone. In 2004, it amended the constitution again, making a total of 67 changes. Significant changes included approving the expansion of the Panama Canal.

The central government loosened its control over large sections of the country through the creation of *comarcas,* or semiautonomous reservations for the country's indigenous peoples.

Panama's nominal gross domestic product (GDP) in 2009 was US$24.75 billion. Unlike its Central American neighbors, Panama's economy depends mainly on an extensive services sector, not agriculture. About three-quarters of its GDP comes from the Colón Free Zone, international banking, the Panama Canal, ports, ship registry, tourism, and related services. Agriculture comprises less than 7 percent of GDP. The main agricultural exports are bananas, rice, coffee, sugarcane, and shrimp. Panama's largest trading partner, by far, is the United States.

Panama has always been a "dollarized" economy, meaning its currency is tied to the U.S. dollar. In fact, Panama's paper currency, officially known as the balboa, *is* the dollar.

The economy took a major hit toward the end of the 1990s with the departure of U.S. military personnel and their dependents (and dollars), but Panama Canal profits have helped soften the blow since 2000. Canal revenues in fiscal year 2009 were US$1.96 billion.

Panama has experienced impressive economic growth in recent years, driven in large part by a boom in construction. This in turn has been fueled in part by an influx of foreigners, especially North American retirees, tourists, and affluent Colombians and Venezuelans fleeing instability and social upheaval in their home countries.

Panama has had one the fastest-growing economies in the Americas in recent years, for several years posting GDP growth greater than 7 percent and sometimes in the double figures. In 2009, GDP growth dropped to 2.4 percent as a result of the worldwide recession, which Panama was weathering better than most Latin American economies thanks to a stable and cautious financial sector that did not take the same risks as some of its neighbors, coupled with a construction boom that just kept on booming.

A healthy economy has also cut the unemployment rate in recent years. The official rate was estimated at 7.1 percent in 2009. Canal construction is expected to create thousands of new jobs.

Panama historically has had quite low inflation, estimated at 2.9 percent in 2009. It fluctuated a bit more in recent years, but remains lower than most other Latin American countries.

Though one of the region's most affluent countries, Panama has one of the most unequal distributions of wealth in the world. Despite the strong economy, nearly 40 percent of the population still live in poverty. Half of these people live in extreme poverty, trying to get by on less than US$1 a day. At the other extreme, a widely quoted study claimed in 2004 that just 80 individuals accounted for half of Panama's total GDP.

People and Culture

Panama's 1911 census, the country's first, estimated its population at just 336,742. By the 2010 census it had grown to 3,322,576. The population today is believed to be close to 3.3 million.

Panama is a young country: Nearly one-third of the population is 14 years or younger, and just 6 percent are older than 64.

Despite widespread poverty and high unemployment, Panamanians remain prosperous by Latin American standards. A primary-school education is compulsory, and more than 93 percent of the population aged 10 and older can read and write. Average life expectancy at birth is 75 years, about the same as in Poland. Women outlive men by nearly five years.

Panamanians often identify themselves by their family's province of origin, each of which has regional stereotypes associated with it. There are nine provinces: Bocas del Toro, Chiriquí, Veraguas, Herrera, Los Santos, Coclé, Panamá, Colón, and Darién. There are also a number of *comarcas* (indigenous reservations) and in recent years the national legislature has been adding more by carving out territory from existing provinces.

More than two-thirds of Panama's people live in urban areas. The most densely inhabited part of the country borders the Panama Canal, an area that encompasses Panama City and Colón and the most developed parts of the provinces (Panamá and Colón) that contain them.

Most of the rest of Panama's population is concentrated on the Pacific hills and lowlands of the isthmus, particularly in the so-called central provinces of Coclé, Herrera, Los Santos, and Veraguas. This area, particularly the Azuero Peninsula, is considered by many Panamanians to be their heartland because of its preservation of traditional folklore and crafts, the Spanish Colonial architecture that can still be found in its provincial cities and towns, and its long agricultural history. It occupies in the Panamanian imagination a place somewhere between that occupied by the Old West and the Great Plains in the gringo one. Not surprisingly, given its early settlement, it's also the most severely deforested part of Panama.

The province of Chiriquí contains the fertile mountains of western Panama and the country's second largest city, David (pop. 77,734 in the central city, 124,280 in the entire district), in its humid lowlands. Chiricanos have a strong regional identity and are proud of their beautiful homeland. It's sometimes said that they consider themselves Chiricanos first and Panamanians second. Stickers depicting the provincial flag adorn the windows of many homes and the bumpers of many cars, and fake Chiriquí "passports" are sometimes sold as novelties in stores. The area around Volcán Barú, Panama's highest mountain, has been experiencing a tourist boom in recent years, particularly the cozy town of Boquete.

Bocas del Toro also feels somehow separate from the rest of Panama, but here it takes the form of neglect. Bocatoreños often complain of their region being treated as a backwater province. It is one of the few places in Panama that still cannot rely on a steady supply of clean water, which is one of the grievances that spark occasional demonstrations. Paradoxically, the islands of Bocas del Toro are developing rapidly thanks to a tourism explosion.

The Darién (which traditionally includes both Darién province and the eastern side of Panama province) to the east and the Caribbean slope to the north are still mostly forested and lightly populated, though that's changing rapidly.

INDIGENOUS PEOPLES

While pockets of the indigenous peoples of the isthmus can be found all over the country, either clinging to vestiges of their way of life or assimilating fully into the Panamanian mainstream, most still live on their ancestral lands. *Comarcas* (semiautonomous reservations) are still being established.

Most Kuna (pop. 62,000) live in one of three *comarcas*. The largest of these is Kuna Yala, or the San Blas Archipelago, which includes a strip of mainland and a string of nearly 400 coral islands that extends down the eastern Caribbean coast from Colón province to the Colombian border. The other two Kuna *comarcas*, Madungandí and Wargandí, are on the Caribbean slope of the Darién rainforest.

The Ngöbe-Buglé are the largest indigenous group in Panama.

COURTESY OF PAUL SABAN

The Kunas refer to themselves as Tule, though they recognize the name Kuna as well. The name is sometimes spelled "Cuna," but that's now considered anachronistic.

The Emberá (pop. 22,000) and Wounaan (pop. 7,000) live in *comarcas* on both the Caribbean and Pacific slopes of the Darién. They are culturally similar, but speak different languages. In the past they have been known collectively as the Chocos, but the name is seldom used today. Emberá-Wounaan is preferred when speaking of them as a group.

The Ngöbe (pop. 170,000) and Buglé (pop. 18,000) have traditionally been known as the Guaymi, but the name is increasingly falling out of favor. Ngöbe-Buglé (pronounced NO-bay BOO-glay) is preferred when speaking of them collectively. Like the Emberá and Wounaan, they are culturally similar but speak different languages. They are by far the largest indigenous group in Panama. Most live in the mountains of western Panama. In 1997, they gained their own, enormous *comarca,* carved out of the provinces of Chiriquí, Bocas del Toro, and Veraguas.

The remaining recognized indigenous people are the Naso, also known as the Teribe (pop. 3,800), who live along the rivers on the mainland of Bocas del Toro and are trying to gain *comarca* status; the Bri Bri (pop. 2,500), who also live in Bocas del Toro; and the Bokota (pop. 993), whose few surviving members live in eastern Bocas del Toro and northwest Veraguas.

Most indigenous people make a living through subsistence farming, fishing, and hunting. The Kuna and Emberá-Wounaan are also able to bring in some cash through the sale of their handicrafts, which are prized by collectors around the world. Many Ngöbe-Buglé work on coffee plantations in the Chiriquí highlands. Indigenous peoples are increasingly experimenting with tourism, especially ecotourism, to improve their economic conditions. By far the most experienced at this are the Kuna, who have allowed foreign tourists on their islands for decades.

Unemployment, poverty, illiteracy, and poor health are consistently highest among the indigenous people. An estimated 95 percent live in poverty, most in extreme poverty, defined as trying to get by on less than US$1 a day. Poorest of all are the Ngöbe-Buglé.

ETHNIC MAKEUP

Panama is a remarkably diverse country by Central American standards, thanks to its surviving indigenous peoples and its status as an important transit point for international commerce for more than 500 years. While most of the arrivals during that time came from Spain and sub-Saharan Africa, Panama also has a substantial population of immigrants from around the world, especially China, India, the Middle East, Central Europe, and North America.

Of these, the longest-established group is the Chinese, who first came over to build the Panama Railroad in the 19th century. Many stayed to open shops and restaurants, and today they are in all walks of life. The traditional community is cohesive enough in Panama City to support three newspapers, three temples, a small Chinatown, a cultural center, and a radio station. People of Chinese descent also can be found throughout the country. Some estimates put their number as high as 150,000, or 5 percent of the total population.

People of African origin have lived on the isthmus since the 16th century. In Panama, a distinction is made between Afro-Colonials, the descendants of Spanish slaves, and Afro-Antillanos, who came later from the Caribbean islands. The latter are generally referred to as West Indians by English-speakers on the isthmus.

Afro-Colonials who escaped from their Spanish masters were known as *cimarrones,* and they built secluded villages, or *palenques,* along the eastern Caribbean coast and the Darién jungle. Some of these still exist today.

The Afro-Antillanos include Jamaicans brought over to dig the French Canal, banana-plantation workers from Jamaica and the Colombian islands of San Andrés and Providencia who settled in Bocas del Toro, and workers from around the West Indies who supplied most of the labor for the Panama Canal. Most of this last group, which numbered 20,000 in all, came from Barbados.

Race and Class

The ethnic breakdown of Panama is generally thought of as being about 65–70 percent mestizo (mixed Amerindian and Caucasian) and 8–10 percent Amerindian, with the bulk of the remaining population consisting of those of African and/or European descent. These estimates are quite rough and have recently been called into question, with one local DNA study concluding that 75 percent of Panama's "common gene pool" is of African and Amerindian origin and just 25 percent from Europe. Estimates of the number of smaller minorities, such as those of Chinese, Indian, and Middle Eastern ancestry, are even more unreliable.

Race relations on the isthmus are complex. Most Panamanians, whether officially mestizo or not, are the product of a mixture of different ethnicities, and the country is increasingly proud of being a *crisol de razas* (racial melting pot). Some of the country's legendary national heroes are of African and Amerindian descent.

But a racial pecking order lingers in Panama, tied closely to socioeconomic class. The country has traditionally been ruled by an oligarchy drawn from the elite families, many of whom have light skin and European features and can trace their ancestry back to Spain. They still wield a great deal of power in Panama and tend to marry within other elite families. They are known disparagingly by other Panamanians as *rabiblancos* (white tails).

The indigenous peoples and those of African descent are among the nation's poorest, and they still find it difficult to move up in society. As late as 2002, Panama found it necessary to pass a law forbidding discrimination against minorities in commercial establishments, sparked by repeated incidents of blacks being turned away at the door of bars, discos, and restaurants.

In 1941 the national legislature passed a new constitution that stripped English-speaking blacks (meaning the Afro-Antillanos or West Indians) and other non-Latino minorities of their Panamanian citizenship. It also outlawed the immigration of new arrivals from the English-speaking West Indies, as well as China, India, and the Middle East. The constitution was overturned in 1946.

Afro-Antillanos in particular had an uneasy existence on the isthmus during much of the 20th century. They faced discrimination both in the Canal Zone and Panama, but had largely lost their ties to the Caribbean islands from which they came. As the years have gone by, most have adopted Spanish as their first language and assimilated more fully into mainstream Panamanian society. The process sped up with the decline and disappearance of the U.S. Canal Zone, where many families had lived and worked since canal construction days.

The military dictatorship that took power in 1968 was the most serious challenge to the rule of the oligarchy, opening up opportunities for those of different ethnicities and lower socioeconomic classes to rise to positions of power. A relatively large middle class began to emerge. In modern times especially, academic achievement, professional success, and other new sources of societal clout can sometimes overcome the traditional obstacles of race and family connections.

CULTURE

In part because of the long U.S. presence in Panama and in part because of its even longer role in world commerce, Panama has been quicker to "internationalize" than many of its Latin American neighbors. Siestas, for instance, are not really a part of daily life, and in many ways Panama City today has more in common with Miami than it does with, say, Madrid.

But for all Panama's diversity, the country's dominant culture does derive directly from Spain. The extended family is by far the most important social unit. Taking care of one's family comes first, and family-oriented occasions such as baptisms, Mother's Day, and birthdays are treated as important celebrations. Most hotels, especially outside Panama City, are still oriented to accommodate fairly large Panamanian families that share the same room for a weekend or holiday retreat, rather than foreign couples or singles exploring the country. Panama is also a quite child-friendly country, all the more so since such a high percentage of the population is younger than 14.

There is a strong feeling of national pride in Panama. Panamanians often express a sense that their country is somehow different from others in the region, in part because of Panama's unique geographical position and unusually rich history for such a small place. Many, for instance, don't really consider Panama a part of Central America, whatever a map might say. The sense of Panama as someplace special is best summed up in the popular phrase that is in essence Panama's national motto: *puente del mundo, corazón del universo* (bridge of the world, heart of the universe).

Family and Society

Home is sacrosanct, and it's quite possible to

© THOMAS GORISSEN, WWW.THOMASGORISSEN.COM

The entire country celebrates at Carnaval.

be friends with a Panamanian for years without setting foot in his or her home. Dining with the middle and upper classes of Panama City usually means meeting at a restaurant. To be invited to someone's house or weekend country home is something special and can mean you're considered family. Outside Panama City, especially among the campesinos (country people, farmers), entertaining at home is more typical.

Whom one is related to is still extremely important in determining status in Panamanian society. Panama is a small enough country that the names of the prominent families are widely known. Even in non-elite circles, the names of one's father and mother can help one get ahead or hold one back.

Men and Women

Machismo is a fact of life in Panama. But it's not as pronounced as in some other Latin American countries, and stereotypical sex roles have begun to break down in modern times. Women are now in more positions of power outside the home; in 1999, Panama even elected its first female president (albeit one best known for being the widow of a popular male politician). Still, boys tend to be given more freedom during their upbringing, in rural areas men work in the fields and women in the home, and the tradition of married men having a mistress and even an entirely separate family has not died out; women are still expected to dress and act in "feminine" ways, and men on the street think nothing of openly ogling any attractive woman who passes by.

Manners and Mores

Foreigners often comment on how laid-back and peaceful Panamanians are—except behind the wheel. One word any visitor is likely to hear often is *tranquilo* (calm, peaceful, easy-going), used both as an injunction (as in, "take it easy") and as an expression of praise (as in, "what a peaceful place"). It says a lot about what's valued in Panama.

But boisterous celebrations are also extremely popular. Panamanians take time off seriously,

first day of school, Playa Santa Catalina

© WILLIAM FRIAR

and the calendar is filled with national holidays, religious observances, and other excuses to party. The entire country comes to a halt for big celebrations, such as Carnaval. Parties often last all night and feature music played at ear-shattering volumes. Those who can afford it have cottages at the beach or in the mountains, or *fincas* (literally farms, but often just a country home) that they use for weekend getaways or extended holidays.

Another important word to know is *dignidad* (dignity). Treating others with politeness and respect is extremely important in Panama, and slights are taken seriously.

On the other hand, Panama is also quite a tolerant place, and a laissez-faire attitude prevails. While, just as in any other country, there is racism and discrimination, people of different nationalities, religions, and lifestyles have generally been left in peace. Open homosexuality is still a thing of the future, but gays have begun to assert their rights, and gay bars and clubs aren't subject to raids and official harassment. While abortion is officially illegal in this Catholic country (punishable by up to three years in jail for the woman and up to six years for the practitioner), it's surreptitiously available at some clinics. Birth control is practiced by a majority of the sexually active. Prostitution is legal and regulated by the government.

Perceptions of Time

Among the hardest things for visitors to adjust to, especially those from North America and northern Europe, are local attitudes toward time. As in many other Latin American countries, showing up later than an agreed-upon time is normal, even expected. It's not unusual for guests at a sit-down dinner party to show up an hour or two after the appointed hour.

There's also ample opportunity for culture clashes concerning appointments. As in other Latin American countries, foreigners trying to do business in Panama often complain of the *mañana* syndrome: putting off for a vague future time what would seem possible to do right now. Miscommunications are common. What a visitor may interpret as a commitment to call or show up somewhere without fail may actually have been intended only as a polite expression of intent to help out if nothing more urgent comes up.

Panama and the United States

Not surprisingly, the United States generates a range of feelings in Panama. The United States has intervened in the affairs of the isthmus constantly since its own early days as a republic. It often has used the isthmus to further its own strategic and commercial interests, and for most of the 20th century had military bases and a largely foreign community planted in a 500-square-mile zone that bisected the country and over which Panama had little control.

Students, politicians, activists, and nationalistic citizens regularly denounced the U.S. presence on the isthmus as imperialistic and paternalistic, quite often with good cause, though sometimes Panama's leaders used the U.S. presence as a bogeyman to deflect attention from domestic problems.

Though some in Panama were violently opposed to the U.S. presence, others had largely positive attitudes toward it. Many others were ambivalent, seeing the United States as instrumental in helping Panama gain independence but selfishly robbing it of true self-determination, in spurring great improvements in health and welfare on the isthmus but keeping most of the spoils for itself, and in propping up but finally removing the military dictatorships that ruled the country for decades.

What most can now agree on is that the end of the Canal Zone and the closing of the U.S. military bases have made possible a healthier and more equal relationship between the two nations. There's a widespread sentiment in Panama that the country did not gain full sovereignty until December 31, 1999, when it gained full control of the Panama Canal. *Soberanía* (sovereignty) is still a word one hears often in Panama, and its importance to many is undeniable. When the Panamanian government created a new national park through a swath of the Panama Canal's watershed, it named it Parque Nacional Soberanía. Evidence of the U.S. presence in the former Canal Zone has been steadily eroded, with streets renamed and English-language signs removed.

Panama and the United States generally enjoy good relations these days. A free-trade agreement between the two countries was awaiting U.S. Congressional approval in 2010. However, Congress was delaying approval of the pact over the most serious and bizarre diplomatic clash between the two countries in many years: In September 2007, Pedro Miguel González Pinzón, who is wanted in the U.S. on murder charges, was elected president of Panama's national assembly. González is accused of killing U.S. Army Sergeant Zak Hernández and wounding another soldier in 1992 before a visit by President George H. W. Bush. González, under pressure from the Panama business community, among others, announced that he would not seek reelection when his term as assembly president expired in September 2008.

American pop culture took hold long ago, apparent in everything from the Hollywood movies playing at the multiplexes to the popularity of American fast-food franchises, to the clothing and music tastes of young people. Baseball, basketball, and, to a more limited extent, American football have long been popular in Panama. European football (soccer) has only come into its own in recent years. For wealthier Panamanians, Florida is a popular shopping destination, and U.S.-style malls sprouted up in and around the major cities. Middle- and upper-class students often go to the United States for college and graduate school.

SPORTS

Panama has produced a considerable number of outstanding world athletes and a few bona fide legends. Many of them have come from the ranks of Panama's poorest families.

Panama is known for producing great boxers, the best known of whom is Roberto Durán. Nicknamed Manos de Piedra (Hands of Stone), he held world titles in four weight categories: lightweight, welterweight, junior middleweight, and middleweight. He earned the welterweight title in a famous match against "Sugar" Ray Leonard in June 1980. But his career took a sharp downward turn during a rematch with Leonard in November of that same year. Durán, after being taunted repeatedly by a fast-moving Leonard, told the referee during the eighth round that he wanted to stop the fight. The two words he spoke to end the match, *no más* (no more), would haunt the rest of his career and cause an uproar back home. The words are better remembered today than the fact Durán went on to win two more world titles. His best days behind him, a car accident finally forced him to retire in 2002 at the age of 51. He is considered one of the best boxers in history, with 104 wins in 120 fights, 69 of them knockouts.

Panama has also produced champion horse-racing jockeys, by far the most famous of whom is Laffit Pincay Jr. In 1999, Pincay broke Willie Shoemaker's record for career wins. He rode until April 2003, when a fall during a race left him with a broken neck and forced him to retire at the age of 56. By then, he had racked up an astonishing 9,530 victories.

But in sheer volume of great athletes, Panama's biggest contribution to world sports has been the disproportionate number of major-league baseball players. These include Hall-of-Fame first baseman Rod Carew, who retired in 1986 with 3,053 career hits. He was born on a train going from Colón to Panama City and was named Rodney after the doctor who delivered him. Stars include New York Yankees relief pitcher Mariano Rivera and Houston Astros left fielder Carlos Lee.

Panama's greatest international football (soccer) star to date is forward Julio César Dely Valdés, who earned the nickname "Panagol" for his prowess as a striker while playing for Nacional de Montevideo in Uruguay. He spent much of his career playing in Spain and Uruguay before retiring in 2004 at the age of 37. He's considered one of the best football players to come out of Central America.

Panama has also had some track and field stars. Long-jumper Irving Saladino won a gold medal at the 2008 Olympic Games, Panama's first.

THE ARTS

Panama takes great pains to preserve its traditional music forms, dances, costumes, crafts, and customs. It also has a vibrant contemporary arts and entertainment scene with roots in its unique history.

While music and dance are extremely popular, one often hears complaints in Panama that the fine arts and literature play far too small a role in daily life.

A number of painters have received at least some international recognition, though Panama's most widely known artistic creations are the work of anonymous indigenous artists, especially the Kuna with their *molas* (hand-crafted blouses) and the Emberá-Wounaan with their tagua and cocobolo carvings and woven baskets.

Music and Dance

Given its geographical location, it's not surprising that a wide variety of music is popular in Panama. Dance clubs may spin a salsa, cumbia, merengue, or reggae number, then follow it up with a Latin pop music hit, a bit of electronic dance music, or a rock song in English or Spanish. What may be more surprising is how strong a hold Panamanian folkloric music still has on the country, both in purist and modernized forms.

Important instruments in folkloric music include the accordion, *los tambores* (wooden drums with the top covered by cowhide), *la caja* (a small wooden drum with both sides covered with hide), *la mejoranera* (a small, five-stringed guitar), *la bocona* or *socabón* (a four-stringed guitar), *la guáchara* or *churuca* (a gourd-shaped instrument played by scraping an implement across notches carved into it), maracas, and violins. Folkloric music can be instrumental or feature singing, the most distinctive element of which is the *saloma*, a Panamanian form of yodeling. The music is an acquired taste for those who didn't grow up listening to it.

Folkloric music is often accompanied by traditional dances, the most famous of which is the drum-based *el tamborito*. This is Panama's national dance, with many regional variations, and is usually what is performed for visitors or on other special occasions when there is a folkloric dance performance. Women dress in beautiful hand-embroidered *polleras* (formal hand-embroidered dresses) and the men in either long-sleeved white *camisillas* (shirts) and black pants or a colorful embroidered shirt and pants cut off below the knees. In either case, the man wears some variety of traditional Panama hat, often the *sombrero pintado* (painted hat). All of these hats are quite different from the so-called Panama hats that are made in Ecuador.

Other important dance-music forms include the *mejorana*, a type of song accompanied by the *mejoranera*, and the festive dance music performed by *murgas* (strolling bands of musicians) during Carnaval.

All these folkloric traditions come from Panama's central provinces, particularly the Azuero Peninsula. Other traditional dance forms include the *congos*, derived from Africa and still performed occasionally by descendants of African slaves, and the *balsería*, which is really something between a festival and an extreme sport performed by the indigenous Ngöbe-Buglé peoples; it involves throwing balsa poles at the legs of participants, often with painful results.

Music rooted in Panama's folkloric traditions has changed with the times and evolved into what is known as *música típica* or simply *típico*, a dance-music form that features traditional elements such as accordion and yodeling, but has a livelier beat, modern lyrics, and an almost pop sensibility. It's enormously popular in Panama. Its biggest stars include the accordionists Osvaldo Ayala and Ulpiano Vergara and the brother-sister duo Samy and Sandra Sandoval.

Panama's most famous musician outside its own borders is the salsa star, actor, and politician Rubén Blades. He first gained fame for his work with salsa legend Willie Colón before launching a solo career notable for both his politically conscious lyrics and musical innovation. He ran an unsuccessful campaign for the presidency of Panama in 1994. He is currently the director minister of tourism.

Another international music star is Danilo Pérez, an innovative jazz pianist noted for blending Latin, African, and other influences with established jazz forms. Both he and Blades spend a great deal of their performance time abroad, and concerts in Panama are special events.

El General (born Edgardo A. Franco) had some reggae-influenced, Spanish-language dance hits in parts of the United States and Latin America in the early 1990s. He is now considered one of the forefathers of reggaeton, a hugely popular blend of rap, reggae, rock, dancehall, and calypso that has become hugely popular in the last few years. Nando Boom, a Panamanian reggae star, is also considered an early influence.

Reggaeton is usually characterized by a driving, syncopated snare-drum rhythm that's come to be known as "Dem Bow." It's a notoriously controversial genre, both because non-fans tend to find the music irritating at best and because the lyrics of many songs are deemed misogynistic, violent, pornographic (often through innuendo), racist, or all the above. Perhaps fortunately, many don't have a clue what the lyrics are, since they tend to be delivered in heavily accented Spanish, English, or patois. Despite or because of all this, it has a large audience around the Spanish-speaking world.

Many trace reggaeton's roots to Panama, though most of the genre's stars are Puerto Rican. The biggest Panamanian star is El Roockie (sometimes spelled El Rookie), who has so much street cred he once made a video that featured rival street gangs. Félix Danilo Gómez, who records under the name Nigga, had a major hit in Mexico in 2007–2008. He plans to record under the less controversial name Flex to try to crack the U.S. market. Nearly all reggaeton's hitmakers so far are male. But Panama's Lorna (Lorna Zarina Aponte) had an international hit a couple years back with "Papi Chulo," which was many European club goers' first exposure to reggaeton.

Panama has a sizable rock scene, with a number of bands of varying skill performing original songs and covers in Spanish and English. The veteran band Los Rabanes has met with the greatest success outside of Panama, with tours in Latin America and the United States. Cage9, which records in both English and Spanish, plays modern hard rock and seems poised to gain an international audience as well. Other popular bands include Son Miserables, Os' Almirantes, Señor Loop, the long-established Los 33, newcomer Filtro Medusa, and the band formerly known as Big Fat Hen, which in 2003 wisely changed its name to Polyphase.

Jazz and classical music draw urban sophisticates to occasional performances at concert halls and restaurants in Panama City. Panama has also been trying to establish regular music festivals, including an annual Panama Jazz Festival, held in Panama City during the dry season.

High-toned cultural events—such as performances by the 60-person national symphony orchestra, the national ballet, and visiting arts groups—are generally held in the Teatro Nacional or Teatro Balboa. Smaller groups sometimes perform in the intimate Teatro Anita Villalaz. These kinds of performances are rare outside of Panama City.

Fine Arts

Panama has a number of notable artists. An important early figure is the painter and sculptor Roberto Lewis (1874–1949), known for his paintings of Isla Taboga and his sweeping murals, which depict romantic scenes drawn from history and mythology. The latter still adorn the Teatro Nacional, the presidential palace, and the Escuela Normal Juan Demóstenes Arosemena in the provincial city of Santiago.

Alfredo Sinclair (b. 1915) and Guillermo Trujillo (b. 1927) are widely considered to be two of Panama's great master painters. Their work has been displayed around the world. Other major figures include Manuel Chong Neto (b. 1927), whose paintings often feature fleshy women with birds, and Juan Manuel Cedeño (1914–1997), a disciple of Lewis. Important younger artists include Isabel de Obaldía (b. 1957), noted for her paintings as well as her glass art, and Brooke Alfaro (b. 1949), whose subjects include the marginalized of Panamanian society and who now works mainly in video.

Making generalizations about any diverse group of artists is difficult, but it's striking how many of Panama's best-known painters make use of warm, vivid colors and dreamlike or primitive elements in their work.

Other popular and widely collected artists include Sheila Lichacz (b. 1942), whose main subjects are the *tinajas* (clay pots) that date from pre-Colombian days and are folkloric icons throughout Panama. She is relatively well known outside of Panama, but some art aficionados in her home country were surprised in 2003 when her work was exhibited at the Smithsonian in Washington, D.C. Al Sprague (b. 1938), a Panama-born American who was an art teacher at Balboa High School in the former Canal Zone, is popular locally and among former zone residents for his paintings, drawings, and prints of the Panama Canal, the Canal Zone, and daily life in Panama.

Some of Panama's finest art is made by its indigenous people, though these works are usually made anonymously and sold as souvenirs. The carved tagua nuts, cocobolo statues, and woven baskets of the Emberá-Wounaan have begun to receive the international fame long accorded the *molas* of the Kuna people. A few Emberá, Wounaan, and Kuna artists now sign their work.

Literature

Panamanian literature has made a small splash beyond the country's borders, in part, perhaps, because much of it has been inward-looking, drawing inspiration from distinctly Panamanian themes of national identity and history, the country's natural beauty, and daily life on the isthmus. Even in Panama it can be hard to find books by Panamanian authors, whose works are often printed cheaply in modest, limited editions. Panama's literary output leans heavily toward poetry and short stories, followed by novels and essays and, to a far lesser extent, plays. Nearly all of it is in Spanish.

Ricardo Miró (1883–1940) is the country's most revered poet, often referred to as "El Poeta de Panamá" and for whom the country's most prestigious literary awards are named. His most famous poem is "Patria," an ode to his beloved country. He also produced short stories and novels. Other notable early poets include María Olimpia de Obaldía (1891–1985), whose main theme was family life, and Amelia Denis de Icaza (1836–1911), most famous for her patriotic "Al Cerro Ancón."

One of the country's most important literary figures in the 20th century was Rogelio Sinán (1902–1994), the pen name of Bernardo Domínguez Alba. Sinán is remembered for the breadth and quality of his work, which included short stories (particularly "A la Orilla de Las Estatuas Maduras"), novels (most notably *Penilunio*), poetry, and even a children's play, *La Cucarachita Mandinga*. Other major figures of the period included the poets Ricardo J. Bemúdez (1914–2000), Demetrio Korsí (1899–1957), Demetrio Herrera Sevillano (1902–1950), and Stella Sierra (1917–1997).

Novelists and short-story writers have come to the forefront in the modern era. Prominent contemporary authors include Ernesto Endara (b. 1932), known especially for his short stories and plays; Rosa María Britton (b. 1936), a physician whose novels include *El Señor de las Lluvias y el Viento* (1984) and *Todas Íbamos a Ser Reinas* (1997); and the prolific Enrique Jaramillo Levi (b. 1944), whose works include the short-story collection *Duplicaciones* (1990) and many other short stories, poems, and essays. He is also a scholar and cultural promoter who has probably done more than any other living person to draw attention to Panamanian literature. He is the editor of *Maga,* a Panamanian literary review.

The historical novels of Jorge Thomas, the pen name of the lawyer Juan David Morgan (b. 1942), are relatively easy to find in Panama, especially *Con Ardientes Fulgores de Gloria* (1999).

El Caballo de Oro (2005), about the building of the Panama Railroad, is his first novel published under his real name.

In 2006, Cristina Henríquez, whose father is Panamanian, published *Come Together, Fall Apart,* a collection of short stories about life in Panama. It met with glowing reviews in U.S. newspapers and found a fan in Isabel Allende. In 2010 she published her first novel, *The World in Half.* Both are easy to find internationally.

Panama City has an active theater scene, and works by Panamanian and foreign playwrights are staged frequently. Plays range from hoary classics to experimental pieces. One playhouse, the aging Teatro Guild de Ancón in the former Canal Zone, still offers works in English.

RELIGION

An estimated 85 percent of Panamanians are Roman Catholic. Various sects of Protestantism have made inroads over the years, accounting for most of Panama's other followers of organized religion.

Catholicism is taught in public schools unless parents request that their children be exempted. Catholic holidays, festivals, and rites are widely observed. However, many Panamanian Catholics take a "cafeteria" approach to church doctrine. Birth control, for instance, is widely available and practiced throughout the country. And Panama has a long history of religious freedom and tolerance.

Judaism and Islam have significant minority followings and a long history in Panama, particularly in the cities. Islam is believed to have first come to the isthmus with African slaves in the 16th century. The first Jewish congregation in Panama, Kol Shearith, was founded in 1876. Panama City has one of the world's seven Baha'i Houses of Worship, as well as a prominent Hindu temple. The Greek Orthodox Metropolitanate of Central America is based in Panama. Many of Panama's indigenous peoples still practice their traditional religions to some degree.

LANGUAGE

The official language of Panama is Spanish. English is the major second language, but it's not as widely spoken as one might think given the long U.S. presence in the country and Panama's role in world commerce and finance. In fact, even in Panama City it seems harder to find someone fluent in English than it was 25 years ago.

A nationalistic emphasis on Spanish, combined with the exodus of U.S. civilians and military personnel when the Canal Zone disappeared, has led to a steady erosion in English on the isthmus. Even the large English-speaking West Indian immigrant populations, which learned Spanish as a second language when they came to the isthmus, are gradually losing their English skills as they become fully assimilated into the Panamanian mainstream.

The role of English in Panamanian life is still a touchy subject. A major controversy erupted in 2002 when a proposal to make English an official second language of business was floated in the national legislature, with many denouncing it as unconstitutional and impractical.

But the greatly diminished U.S. presence on the isthmus has helped make English less of a political hot potato. There's a growing belief in Panama that English skills are crucial to the survival of its services-oriented economy. The point was driven home in 2002 when the HSBC Bank tried to open a 600-person call center in Panama. Of the 1,600 applicants, only 41 were fully bilingual in English and Spanish. The bank set up the call center in Malaysia instead. That same year, a Panamanian official estimated that only about 2 percent of government employees speak English well.

In 2003 the Panamanian government passed a law requiring the teaching of English in all primary and secondary schools. Private schools of English have sprung up all over the country. Suddenly, everyone wants to learn English, but progress has been slow.

All that said, English-speaking visitors usually have little trouble getting around even if they don't speak Spanish. It's not hard to find someone who speaks at least some English, especially in the fancier hotels and restaurants.

Outside of Panama City, English is mostly widely spoken along the Caribbean coast, particularly in Bocas del Toro. There are few English speakers in the rural areas and *comarcas* (semiautonomous reservations). In some of the *comarcas*, even Spanish is not universally spoken.

Panama's indigenous people still speak their traditional languages to varying degrees. Ngöbere (spoken by the Ngöbe) and Kuna (spoken by the Kuna) are probably the least endangered, mostly because of the sheer number of speakers.

Those who speak neither Spanish nor English will have a harder time getting around, as no other European languages are widely spoken on the isthmus, let alone languages from other parts of the world. Panama City, Bocas town on Bocas del Toro, and, to a lesser extent, Boquete have the greatest mix of international residents and visitors.

Some descendants of Chinese immigrants in Panama City and larger towns in the interior still speak their ancestral languages, especially Hakka and Yue (Cantonese). Arabic and Hebrew are among the other languages with a foothold in cosmopolitan Panama City.

So-called Panamanian Creole English (PCE) is still spoken among the descendants of immigrants from Jamaica, Barbados, San Andrés, Providencia, and other West Indian islands. Most speakers live in Colón, the former canal area, Panama City, and Bocas del Toro, whose distinctive regional variation of PCE is called Guari-Guari. It's almost impossible for uninitiated speakers of standard English to understand PCE.

ESSENTIALS

Getting There and Away

Most visitors come to Panama by air, and it's rarely a bargain. Except for occasional promotions, such as an airline inaugurating a new route, standard fares don't change much.

The cheapest way to get to Panama from North and Central America is by bus, so long as one has lots of time and doesn't mind a bit of adventure and discomfort. Driving from North America to Panama, even all the way to the Darién Gap, is a popular adventure for intrepid road warriors that requires considerable planning and resourcefulness. There are no roads between Colombia and Panama, and no ferry service. The only safe way to travel between Panama and South America is by air. Panama has no international rail service.

Make reservations far in advance for travel around holidays and festivals, particularly Christmas and Carnaval. Planes and buses are generally more crowded during the dry season, which is high season for both in-country and foreign tourists and summer vacation for Panamanian students. November is filled with national holidays, which can make travel logistics trickier. There are typically fewer flights and buses on Sundays. Important note: Domestic and regional airlines typically revert to a Sunday schedule for holidays, sometimes without notice. On my most recent visit, a couple had to cancel their visit from San José, Costa Rica, to Panama because they held a

© WILLIAM FRIAR

ticket for a weekday flight that turned out not to exist—the date fell on a national holiday. The airline didn't notice the problem when it booked their reservation and sold them the ticket for the imaginary flight.

Remember that visitors to Panama must be able to show proof of onward travel. This is enforced more often than it used to be, and visitors without proof can be turned away at the border.

The departure tax to leave the country is US$40. It is now included in the price of air tickets.

CHARTER FLIGHTS AND PACKAGE DEALS

All-inclusive packages, sometimes including charter flights, are popular, especially with Canadians, Europeans, and Latin Americans. They can be a good deal for those who don't mind traveling with the herd and like having accommodations, meals, and activities concentrated in one place.

The all-inclusive resorts generally offer tours of the surrounding attractions for an extra fee, but visitors should expect to spend most of their time at or near the hotel.

BY AIR

Panama has good air connections with destinations throughout the Americas and parts of the Caribbean and Western Europe.

Travel to and from anywhere farther east, including Australia and Asia, is more complicated and will probably require at least one change of plane and/or airline. Generally, few European and no Asian, African, Middle Eastern, or Australian airlines offer passenger service to Panama.

Note: The information in this section is particularly subject to change. Carriers add and drop service to Panama frequently. However, routes dropped by one airline are generally picked up by another.

In mid-2004, Panama regained its "Category 1" International Civil Aviation Organization (ICAO) rating following an inspection by the U.S. Federal Aviation Administration. This means Panama's civil aviation authority again meets all international safety standards (its ratings slipped in 2001), which paved the way for new flights to the United States.

Carriers serving Panama include:

- U.S. airlines: American, Continental, and Delta

- European airlines: Iberia and KLM

- Central American and Caribbean airlines: Copa, TACA, LACSA, and Cubana

- South American airlines: Avianca, Aero República, and Aires

Most of the airlines have so-called "code share" agreements with other carriers, meaning flights booked on one airline may actually be operated by a partner airline that's supposed

THE WORLD HAS TWO PANAMA CITIES

When booking a flight, make sure it's for Panama City in the Republic of Panama, and not Panama City, Florida. I've heard more than one tale of visitors from the United States and United Kingdom ending up in that Florida beach town. They were – briefly – pleasantly surprised at how short the flight from Miami was, though they wondered why the plane was so small. When making a reservation, be sure to verify the correct destination. And when the ticket or e-ticket arrives, double-check that it has the airport code for Tucumen International in Panama City, Republic of Panama: PTY.

Those who use the Internet to search for flights should also note that pull-down menus on airline websites, especially those in Spanish, sometimes list Panama under "Ciudad de Panamá," "Tocumen," "Aeropuerto Omar Torrijos Herrera" (the international airport's erstwhile name), and so on.

to meet similar standards of quality and safety. For instance, Copa, Panama's national airline, has code share agreements with several airlines, including a well-established alliance with Continental Airlines and a new one with KLM. Copa's own fleet, fairly large by Latin American standards, flies to 40 destinations in 21 countries. It's a growing airline with a good reputation.

Grupo TACA, a consortium of major Central American airlines that includes El Salvador's TACA and Costa Rica's LACSA, has code share agreements with a number of carriers, including United Airlines, Air France, Iberia, Lufthansa, and Avianca. Grupo TACA also has an alliance with Panama's largest domestic airline, Aeroperlas.

International Airports

Panama's main international airport is **Aeropuerto Internacional de Tocumen** (tel. 238-2761, www.tocumenpanama.aero). Its airport code is PTY. Commonly referred to simply as Tocumen (toe-KOO-men), it's about 25 kilometers east of downtown Panama City. A multimillion-dollar expansion and modernization in 2006 improved it considerably. A second expansion is underway.

The airport has a branch of the Banco Nacional de Panamá (tel. 238-4161 or 238-4178, 7 A.M.–11 P.M. daily). It's one of just two places in the country that exchange a number of currencies. The commission charged varies by currency. Panacambios in Panama City carries a wider variety of currencies. There is also an ATM in the arrivals lounge.

There are ATP information booths between the *aduana* (customs) area and in the arrivals lounge that may or may not be staffed. They carry a few hotel fliers but little else. There are also a couple of airport information booths in the terminal.

There's a Cable and Wireless office (7 A.M.–7 P.M. daily) near the ticket counters upstairs that sells phone cards and has fax, Internet, and long-distance calling services.

Those who made purchases at the Colón Free Zone can pick them up at the Equipaje

© BONNIE KAY SPINDLER

"airport" in Kuna Yala

Acompañado office, which is downstairs and to the right of the main terminal as one faces the main terminal, next to the police office.

A number of duty-free and other shops are in the departure lounge. They carry electronics, liquor, clothing, some souvenirs, and so on. There are two new coffeehouses, one in the terminal and one in the departure lounge. They are the only sit-down restaurants. The branch in the terminal is larger and more pleasant.

David, in western Panama, is expanding its runway in the hopes of attracting international flights, which to date have not really taken off there (pardon the pun). Officially known as Aeropuerto Internacional de David "Enrique Malek," its airport code is DAV.

There are also a few flights between Costa Rica and the small airport on Isla Colón in Bocas del Toro. Its airport code is BOC.

Airport Transportation

Though Panama City is just a 25-kilometer drive from Tocumen, there's no satisfactory public transportation to or from it.

To be sure of getting a licensed taxi driver, book through the taxi-cooperative booth in the arrivals lounge (ground floor). The fare to Panama City is US$25 for one or two persons. There's an extra charge of US$2.40 to pay for the toll road, but it's well worth the savings in time. Most destinations in the former Canal Zone—including Amador, Albrook, Clayton, and "Kobby" (Kobbe Beach, home to Playa Bonita Resort and Spa)—run US$30–35 for one or two people. Other fares available at the booth include Gamboa (US$45) and Colón (US$65) for up to four people. Those passing through Panama who have a long layover can get a tour of the Panama Canal for US$60. More ambitious tours are also offered. Add US$10 to most of these fares for a third person. Pay at the booth and take the receipt. Your driver will be pointed out to you, most likely a neatly dressed man with a clean, late-model car. It's not customary to tip taxi drivers in Panama. Panama City taxis should charge about US$20–25 for the trip back to the airport, but settle on the price before getting in the cab.

It may be possible to save a few dollars by negotiating with other taxi drivers, licensed or otherwise, who hang around the terminal, but there's a risk of getting ripped off or worse by an unscrupulous character. These guys often try to take tourists to hotels that pay them commissions.

A few hotels in Panama City offer airport pickup and drop-off for less than the cost of a taxi; ask when making room reservations.

It's possible to take a bus into the city, but it's a hassle and should only be attempted by those on a tight budget. Buses do not stop at the terminal. To catch one requires hauling your luggage outside the grounds of the airport. There's a bus shelter on the roundabout a hot and humid half-kilometer away on the main road. The fare is US$0.25 for a more-frequent non-air-conditioned bus, but it's well worth coughing up extra change for an air-conditioned bus if one passes by. The final stop is at Plaza Cinco de Mayo in downtown Panama City, a trip that can take 1.5 hours in traffic. Buses that travel along the Corredor Sur are far quicker; look for a sign that says *corredor* painted on the bus. Buses run frequently but erratically. There is no luggage storage compartment; you'll have to squeeze on with all your gear. I don't recommend attempting all this at night, which is quite likely when your plane will arrive.

On the return trip, Tocumen-bound buses can be caught in front of the artisans' stands on Plaza Cinco de Mayo. Tocumen-bound buses also stop along Calle 50; there's a stop next to Panafoto (Calle 50 and Calle 49A Este). Buses to and from Tocumen also stop at the Gran Terminal de Autobuses in Albrook, which is a safer option for those arriving or leaving at night. Be sure the bus stops near the airport. Passengers are dropped off with their luggage at the roundabout outside the airport.

Rental cars are available at the airport. All the major companies have offices there. Only those planning road trips outside Panama City should fool with them, though, because driving and parking in the city is a hassle.

The quickest route between Tocumen and Panama City is by way of the Corredor Sur, a toll highway to the airport that starts on the eastern outskirts of the city, rather than on the congested surface streets. The toll is US$2.40 to the end of the line. The Corredor Sur section of the drive takes only a few minutes, but heavy traffic in Panama City can slow getting to or from the highway. Allow at least an hour to drive between Tocumen and most parts of the city, more during the height of morning and evening rush hours.

From the United States and Canada

Panama's gateway cities in the United States are Atlanta, Houston, Dallas/Fort Worth, Los Angeles, Miami, Newark, New York City (JFK), Orlando, and Washington, D.C. There are nonstop flights between all of them and Panama City. Those coming from other U.S. cities will have to make one stop en route, and in some cases more.

Allow at least two hours to connect through any U.S. airport when returning from Panama City; clearing U.S. customs and immigrations can take a long time.

The busiest route is Miami–Panama City, with several daily nonstop flights each way. The flight takes a little less than three hours. Copa is the only airline that flies nonstop to Orlando, with 11 weekly flights.

The major carriers offering nonstop service from U.S. gateway cities are American (from Miami and Dallas/Fort Worth), Continental (Houston and Newark), Copa (Miami, New York City, Washington-Dulles, Los Angeles, and Orlando), and Delta (Atlanta and New York). The discount airline Spirit Air introduced daily flights between Fort Lauderdale and Panama City in 2008.

Many visitors from the West Coast of the United States are surprised to discover they have to fly not just south but considerably east to get to Panama—Panama City is actually slightly east of Miami. Those traveling from the San Francisco Bay Area, for instance, most often take connecting flights through Houston, Atlanta, or Miami.

Airfares between the United States and Panama fluctuate, though bargain fares and packages are not as easy to come by as they are in, for instance, tourist-saturated parts of the Caribbean. Expect to pay around US$400–700 round-trip from most U.S. cities. Flights out of Miami and Houston tend to be on the cheaper end of the scale. The least expensive West Coast flights usually originate in Los Angeles, though the difference is generally not great enough to make it worthwhile for those outside of Southern California to route their trip through Los Angeles International Airport (LAX).

Except for charters, there are no direct flights from Canada to Panama. Those flying to or from Canada will most likely have a stop in the United States or Mexico. Advance-purchase fares hover around C$1,000. Flights out of Toronto are generally cheaper than from other cities. Canadians are a major market for package deals that often include charter airfare. These can be very good value for those who like all-inclusive resorts. Check with a travel agent or contact any resort hotel listed in this book for current offers.

From Mexico

The U.S. carriers that fly into Panama City also fly into Mexico City, but that doesn't mean they fly *between* Panama City and Mexico City. At least, not directly: American's Mexico-Panama flights require a circuitous stop in Miami or Dallas, for instance. It makes more sense to fly with the Latin American carriers. Expect to pay US$400–600 round-trip; nonstops are more expensive.

Copa offers two daily nonstops between Panama City and Mexico City, as well as 10 weekly nonstops to and from Cancún, and five weekly nonstops to and from Guadalajara. Copa also has a code share agreement with Aeroméxico. Mexicana has two daily flights to and from Mexico City. The airlines of Grupo TACA also fly out of Mexico City, usually with at least one Central American stop en route.

From Central America and the Caribbean

Getting to Panama by air from most Central

American capitals generally means taking the "milk run" down the Central American isthmus; expect to make at least one stop en route, possibly more. The exceptions are Costa Rica and El Salvador, both of which have regular nonstop flights to and from Panama City.

The major carriers for flights within Central America are Grupo TACA and Copa. Both airlines fly between most Central American capitals and Panama City. Advance-purchase round-trip fares to and from most places are around US$500–700, though prices vary quite a bit and deals are often available through the airlines' websites.

FROM COSTA RICA

There are plenty of nonstop flights between Panama City and San José, Costa Rica. For such a nearby destination and popular route, prices can be steep. Advance-purchase fares are about US$350–500 round-trip, with the cheaper fares available through website deals and other promotions. The flight takes about an hour, or closer to two on a small plane. Note that Costa Rican time is always an hour behind Panama time.

Copa has the most flights between the two capitals—five daily each way. Air Panama, which is primarily a domestic airline, flies three times a week between Panama City and San José.

There are also several flights between San José and David, in western Panama. Air Panama flies three times a week. Grupo TACA makes the trip four times a week. More flights may be coming.

There are also a few flights between Costa Rica and Bocas del Toro. Air Panama and the Costa Rica–based Nature Air offer this service.

FROM THE CARIBBEAN

Copa flies between Panama City and Cuba, Jamaica, Puerto Rico, Haiti, the Dominican Republic, and Trinidad and Tobago. TACA flies to Cuba. Cubana, Cuba's national airline, has daily flights between Panama City. Travel to and from other parts of the Caribbean generally requires flying through Miami or doing some island-hopping by small plane after arriving at one of the gateway islands.

A visit to Cuba is a popular add-on for travelers to Panama. Standard round-trip air fare from Panama starts at around US$550, but package deals that include airfare, three nights' accommodation, some meals, airport transfers, and tours are widely available and popular. European and Canadian visitors sometimes route their trips to Panama to include a visit to Cuba on the way over or back. There are severe restrictions on visits to Cuba by U.S. citizens.

Air Caraïbes flies to the French-speaking islands of the Caribbean. It's possible to fly to Aruba or Curaçao on Avianca, but this requires going through the airline's hub in Bogotá, Colombia.

From South America

Panama has good connections with much of South America, particularly Colombia. Flights will most likely be on a Central American or South American airline. Few other carriers fly directly between South America and Panama, but tickets can be booked through an airline's code share partners. American Airlines has an especially extensive network of South American flights operated either by itself or its partners.

Copa flies between Panama City and Colombia (Bogotá, Barranquilla, Cali, Cartagena, and San Andrés), Argentina, Venezuela, Peru, Chile, Brazil, and Ecuador (Quito and Guayaquil). Other airlines that fly between Panama and South America include Avianca, Grupo TACA, and Aero República.

Colombia and Ecuador are less than two hours from Panama City, and standard round-trip, advance-purchase fares to these and other relatively close destinations run about US$500–800. Promotional deals can cut fares in half, especially for popular routes. Nonstop flights to or from the most distant locations, such as Argentina and Brazil, take at least seven hours and can cost well over US$1,000 for advance-purchase fares.

From Europe and the United Kingdom

KLM and Iberia are the only European airlines offering direct service to Panama. KLM offers three weekly nonstops from its hub in Amsterdam. Iberia flies between its hub in Madrid and Panama City, usually connecting through Miami or San José, Costa Rica.

The best deals are sometimes available through carriers that don't fly directly between Europe and Central America. Often this requires no more than one stop. U.S. carriers that fly to both Europe and Panama offer connecting flights through their East Coast hubs in the United States. British Airways, Virgin Atlantic, and Air France offer flights in conjunction with code share partners.

Expect to pay around €800–950 for round-trip tickets between most European countries and Panama. Lower fares may start to appear if Panama becomes a hot tourist destination, as many are gambling it will. Consider buying an air pass if you plan to travel elsewhere in the Americas.

A good way to compare all current routes and fares is through an Internet travel search service such as www.kayak.co.uk or www.expedia.co.uk. Those in the United Kingdom should also check out **Journey Latin America** (tel. 020/8747-3108, www.journeylatinamerica.co.uk), a knowledgeable, London-based tour operator and travel agency that books flights to Panama, sells several kinds of air passes, and offers a few adventure-oriented Panama tours. Its website has lots of current information.

From Elsewhere in the World

There is currently no direct service between Panama and Asia, Australia, Africa, and the Pacific. However, Asian carriers attempt Panama routes from time to time, so this may well change. Getting to Panama from points east of Europe generally means flying to San Francisco, Los Angeles, or Mexico City and connecting there with Panama-bound flights. It's usually a quite expensive proposition. Try to find a good travel agent or be prepared to do a fair amount of independent research to find reasonable fares. Round-the-world tickets or travel using an air pass may prove to be the most economical way to go.

BY LAND

There are three border crossings between Panama and Costa Rica: at Paso Canoa on the Pacific side of the isthmus, at Río Sereno in the highlands, and at Guabito-Sixaola on the Caribbean coast. Paso Canoa, which is on the Interamericana (Interamerican Highway), is by far the most traveled. The Guabito-Sixaola crossing is used mainly by those traveling to and from Bocas del Toro. The Río Sereno crossing is rarely used and is not always open to foreign visitors.

The Interamericana comes to an end at the town of Yaviza in eastern Panama, where the famous Darién Gap begins. There are no roads linking Panama with Colombia and the rest of South America, and no car-ferry services. Travelers generally must fly from Panama to Colombia and continue their journey from there.

By Private Vehicle

It's possible to drive the entire length of the Interamericana (often referred to as the Pan-American Highway outside of Central America) from North America to Panama, but this is a long, serious trek and there's always some risk of encountering bandits, brutal roads, and dyspeptic border guards. Making the trip requires serious planning and a well-equipped vehicle. Allow about three weeks from the Mexican border to Panama at a reasonable pace. Bear in mind that North American auto insurance policies don't apply south of the border.

Cars rented in Costa Rica cannot be driven in Panama, and vice versa. Even trying to drive cars registered in one of the countries across the border into the other is a nuisance and a source of continuing squabbles. It's not worth the hassle for a short trip; take the bus instead.

RV convoys occasionally make pilgrimages down the Interamericana. The only true RV park in Panama is **XS Memories** (tel. 993-3096, fax 993-3069, www.xsmemories.com)

IF THE CHICKEN CROSSES THE ROAD

Among the many road obstacles intrepid drivers are likely to encounter on the back roads of Panama are suicidal chickens. Chickens are definitely free range in the countryside, and they have a way of blundering out into the road with no notice. If you hit one, you are expected to find the owner and pay him or her for the pummeled poultry. Seriously. Make the effort to do the right thing, since for many people chickens are an important means of subsistence. The going rate is US$5 per befouled fowl. You are, of course, then welcome to take the roadkill with you, if you have a means of preparing it. More likely you'll turn the deceased over to the grieving farmer. Also be on the lookout for dogs — an alarming number of them have only three legs due to tangles with traffic.

in Santa Clara, about a two-hour drive west of Panama City. It has 22 hookups for campers and mobile homes and can provide current information for those interested in shipping vehicles to South America.

By Bus

Inexpensive, relatively comfortable buses make daily trips from southern Mexico, Guatemala, Honduras, El Salvador, Nicaragua, and Costa Rica to Panama. This is, obviously, quite a long haul—nearly four solid days from the Mexico-Guatemala border, including two overnight stays in El Salvador and Nicaragua. Few take buses the whole way. Buses between San José, Costa Rica, and Panama City are popular, however.

Two bus companies, Tica Bus and Panaline, make one daily trip between Panama City and San José, Costa Rica. Both leave from the Gran Terminal de Transportes, Panama City's main bus terminal in Albrook. Try to make reservations at least a month ahead of time

during the dry season and on holidays. At other times, booking about four days ahead of time should be fine. Reservations can be made by phone or email, but they must be bought in person at the Albrook bus terminal, with cash. Travelers can check two pieces of luggage and take one carry-on at no extra charge.

Transport is by large, long-haul air-conditioned buses with toilets and reclining seats. The trip costs US$35.10/US$70.10 one-way/round-trip on either line and takes about 16 hours, which usually includes a lengthy stop at the Paso Canoa border crossing to go through immigration and customs, as well as a half-hour or so break in Santiago, about halfway across Panama, where travelers have access to a cafeteria, restaurant, pharmacy, ATM, and other services.

Note: Costa Rica time is always one hour behind Panama time. Times listed here are all local.

Tica Bus (Panama City tel. 314-6385, San José tel. 506/222-8680, www.ticabus.com) leaves from the Albrook bus terminal at 11 A.M. daily, arriving on Paseo Colón in San José around 4 A.M. the next day.

The bus from San José to Panama City leaves at noon daily, arriving at Panama City's Gran Terminal de Transportes at 4 A.M. the next day.

Panaline (Panama City tel. 314-6383, San José tel. 506/256-8721, www.panalinecr.com) leaves from the Albrook bus terminal at 10 P.M. daily, arriving in San José around 3:30 P.M. the next day. The bus drops off passengers in San José, 200 meters north of Hospital San Juan de Dios, near Terminal Coca Cola. Note that this is a rough part of San José.

Buses from San José leave from the same spot at 1 P.M. daily and arrive around 5 A.M. the next morning at the Albrook bus terminal.

A third bus company, **Agencia Tracopa** (David tel. 775-7269 or 775-0585, Paso Canoa tel. 727-6581, San José tel. 506/222-2666), has one bus departure from David to San José daily, at 8:30 A.M. The trip takes about eight hours and costs US$12.50.

Tica Bus also links Panama with Nicaragua,

Honduras, Guatemala, and Tapachula, Mexico, which is near the Guatemalan border. Connections are pretty good between Panama and Nicaragua. Theoretically, one could make the trip to or from Managua in a brutal 30 hours or so either way, including a layover of just an hour or two in San José if timed right. Trips to or from El Salvador, however, require an overnight stay in Nicaragua, and trips starting or ending anyplace farther north require overnight stays in both Nicaragua and El Salvador. Travelers must find their own accommodations, so consider booking rooms ahead of time. Passengers are free to break their travel anywhere and catch a bus on another day, but they must book reservations ahead of time for the onward journey. The longest trip, between Mexico and Panama, costs around US$120 one way.

BY SEA
Cruise Ships
The Panama Canal is one of the top cruising destinations in the world, though "destination" is not really the right word. More than 150,000 people transit the canal each year, but most never set foot in Panama itself. Panama has been trying to change that. It now has two cruise-ship ports on the Caribbean side of the isthmus near Colón. A cruise-ship terminal and other facilities have been completed at Amador on the Pacific side, though ships must bring passengers ashore by tender boats.

Royal Caribbean Cruise Line was the first major cruise line to make Panama a home port, meaning it offers cruises that originate in Panama. It offers one-week cruises on its massive *Enchantment of the Seas,* departing from the Colón 2000 port.

The main Panama Canal cruise season begins in October, when ships end their Alaska cruises. They head down south and transit the canal to position themselves for their Caribbean and Panama Canal cruises. The main season lasts until the end of the dry season, around mid-April. A canal transit takes 8–10 hours. Ships sometimes visit Panama's islands, especially those of Kuna Yala.

A REAL LIFESAVER

If you know ahead of time you'll be making trips on open ocean or even fast-flowing rivers, bring a life jacket with you to be on the safe side. Few boats are equipped with them, and even the larger ferry services don't always have enough for all passengers. These are light and easy to carry in your luggage, and during safe stretches of water they make a convenient cushion over the hard wooden planks that serve as seats. At the end of the trip, donate the jacket to the boatman; hopefully someone else will use it to make their own trip safer. This leaves extra room in your luggage for souvenirs on the way back home. Those who forget to bring one down to Panama should be able to find them in a sporting goods, home-supply, or department store in the larger cities. Try Novey or a Do It Center in Panama City.

By Yacht and Cargo Boat
Panama has long been a haven for yachties, who come to transit the canal and explore the islands and beaches. It may come as a surprise, then, that facilities for yachts are still quite limited. Slips are scarce and haul-out facilities can be quite crude. However, this is beginning to change. Marinas near the canal include the Panama Canal Yacht Club, at Cristóbal near the Caribbean entrance to the canal, and the Balboa Yacht Club and Flamenco Yacht Club, at Amador near the Pacific entrance to the canal. The famous and funky wooden clubhouse at the Balboa Yacht Club, alas, burned down a while back. Today it consists of little more than moorings, a dock, and a burger stand. The newish Isla Flamenco Yacht Club has extensive, modern facilities, but they're expensive. A new marina, Shelter Bay, recently opened on the site of the old Fort Sherman, near the Caribbean entrance to the canal.

Long-established ports and anchorages include Pedregal, Boca Brava, Puerto Mutis, and Isla Taboga on the Pacific side of the isthmus and Bocas del Toro, Portobelo, Isla Linton, and José del Mar (a.k.a. José Pobre) on the Caribbean side. Yachts also frequent the Islas Perlas and several islands in the Golfo de Chiriquí, but with the exception of Contadora and a few other islands, most of these spots are uninhabited and lack even rudimentary marinas.

Facilities vary dramatically outside the canal area. The two marinas in Bocas del Toro can accommodate large yachts and perform limited maintenance work, and both are right in the middle of all the Bocas action. José del Mar and Boca Brava, on the other hand, are remote though lovely spots offering little more than a place to anchor and get a bite and a beer. A new marina has been proposed for Boca Brava, however, as have others around the country. How many of these actually materialize remains to be seen, but there may be more options by the time you read this.

The San Blas Islands (Kuna Yala) are a popular yachting destination, but yachties should be prepared to pay a small fee when anchoring off islands in the archipelago. The waters out there can be treacherous; this is a place for skilled, experienced sailors. Transiting the canal by yacht is a complex and time-consuming process. An increase in tolls has made transiting a quite expensive proposition. The minimum cost is US$600 for yachts up to 50 feet. Many yachts need to take on additional crew at the canal to help handle lines.

Joining a Crew

Landlubbers looking for a free canal transit can sometimes join a yacht as a line handler. This is not a pleasure cruise, however. Don't consider this unless you're fairly strong, respond quickly to orders, and are prepared to get a little training. Yachties sometimes pay for the service, but not if there are enough volunteers around. Yachts are sometimes required to stop in the middle of the canal, sometimes for the night, so be prepared for the possibility of sleeping onboard. The transit is a one-way trip; so if you need to get back, figure out ahead of time how you're going to do it. The yacht owner sometimes coughs up the bus (US$2) or cab fare (about US$40).

The best places to look for needy yachts are the Balboa Yacht Club or the Flamenco Yacht Club, on the Pacific side of the isthmus, and the Panama Canal Yacht Club or Shelter Bay, on the Caribbean side. Ask around. Note: The Panama Canal Yacht club is right next to Colón. It's dangerous to wander anywhere outside the grounds of the club.

Panama City hostels may be able to help connect line handlers and yachts.

It may also be possible to sign on as a crew member on a yacht for a longer trip, but this is not common, especially for those who aren't experienced sailors. Ask around at any of the yacht clubs. The dock master will likely know who's going where and/or is in need of new crew members. It's also sometimes possible to pay for passage. Local authorities are keeping a wary eye on this practice, however, out of concern people are slipping illegally in and out of the country. Travelers with recreational drugs—which they should definitely not have in Panama anyway, as it can land them in jail for years—should get rid of them before boarding a boat. If the yacht is stopped and any drugs are found aboard, both the traveler and the yacht owner are going to be in big trouble. It's foolish, and grossly unfair to the owner.

To Colombia by Sea

There is no commercial ferry service between Panama and Colombia, but the adventurous occasionally book passage on yachts to or from Cartagena. Some yachts make this trip often enough that it's become a commercial service for them, albeit an informal one. Most yachts charge US$400–500 per person, including meals. The trip takes 4–5 days, most of which is spent sailing among the uninhabited islands of Kuna Yala. Yachts typically anchor near the beautiful, remote islands of Chichime, Coco Bandero, or Cayos Holandéses. An itinerary like this would normally cost many times what these yachts charge, though of course this is not a luxury cruise.

Warning: Think carefully before making this trip, as there are many risks to consider. The seas around Kuna Yala can turn rough very quickly. They are also notoriously dangerous because of shallow reefs that lurk like depth charges throughout the archipelago. There are lots of shipwrecks there to prove it, and at least two lives have been lost from yachts out there in the last few years. The winds blow so strongly in the dry season that many boats won't even make the trip.

Also, Panama is a popular transshipment point for drugs coming up from South America. If you're unlucky enough to be aboard a vessel intercepted with a few tons of cocaine in the hold, you'll have some tricky explaining to do. Boats are also sometimes caught with less-sinister but no-less-illegal contraband.

A few horror stories I heard on my most recent visit: passengers stranded because their perpetually drunk captain was thrown into a Kuna jail for fighting; passengers arrested in Panama when their captain didn't handle immigration formalities properly; unbelievably filthy boats; a yacht that ran aground in Cartagena.

Those not put off by all that can check with Panama City hostels to see what's available.

Zuly's Independent Backpackers or Luna's Castle are good possibilities.

The truly adventurous sometimes strike a deal for passage on a cargo boat, such as the Colombian trading vessels that ply the waters of Kuna Yala or the Kuna-owned boats that travel the same route. I strongly advise against this. For one thing, some of these boats are barely seaworthy rust buckets. Those who insist on hitching a ride should know it's tough to join a boat in Kuna Yala. Many a tourist ends up stranded in El Porvenir because they've heard that's the place to hop on a boat. It's much easier to arrange from Colón. Even here, I've heard tales of passengers having to wait 10 days for their boat to get even as far as Isla Grande, which is less than 50 kilometers east of Colón. Those still interested should start by asking around at Panama City hostels.

Finally, some people fly from Panama City to the border town of Puerto Obaldía, on the Caribbean coast, and take a launch to Colombia from there.

However you go, don't board any boat that doesn't have life jackets, well-equipped lifeboats, communication equipment, and a captain who inspires confidence.

Getting Around

It's easy to get almost anywhere in Panama by bus or small plane. Commercial boat service, ironically for a country that owes so much to its waterways, is harder to come by.

The main roads in Panama are generally in good shape, and they've been much improved in recent years. The nation's major artery is the Interamerican Highway, or Interamericana, which in Panama stretches from the Costa Rican border along the Pacific slope of the isthmus all the way to the town of Yaviza in the Darién, where all roads stop.

The Interamericana is a divided highway in mostly good shape from just west of Panama City to around Santiago, halfway across the isthmus. From there to the city of David there are poorly maintained, two-lane sections with monster potholes, detours, and washouts. However, work is proceeding on extending the divided highway all the way to David. The easternmost section of the highway to the Darién is not paved all the way. It is drivable all the way to Yaviza only in the dry season, and then only with great effort and a good four-wheel drive or bus. At other times it's almost impossible to get much beyond Meteti.

Buses offer the cheapest way to explore most parts of Panama and are the best option for many travelers. Rental cars are a viable option for those who can afford it, are in a hurry, plan to travel extensively beyond the cities, and are up for the many hazards of driving in Panama. Panama's domestic airlines offer the fastest way to get from point A to point B in many parts of Panama, and for some remote spots they're the only reasonable option.

BY AIR

Panama is dotted with airstrips served by a network of small commercial prop planes and jets. The longest flights take a little over an hour (not including interim stops). There are several flights a day along some popular routes.

Note that the planes are essentially air taxis that often make several stops, and not always in the order you expect. Planes to Kuna Yala often go island-hopping down the archipelago, landing at several airstrips. Make sure to get off in the right place.

Panama City has the country's main domestic airport, Aeropuerto Marcos A. Gelabert, in the Albrook neighborhood a short drive from downtown. Most taxi drivers won't know it by name: Ask to go to the **Aeropuerto de Albrook.** (Note: Some old maps still show the domestic airport in Punta Paitilla, but the airport was moved to its current location in 1999.)

Most flights originate from and end at this airport, though Bocas del Toro and David have a couple of flights to other destinations, and it's occasionally possible to fly between islands in Kuna Yala (San Blas Islands). There are few other point-to-point flights; travelers nearly always have to go through Albrook on the way to somewhere else. Panama's domestic carriers are not really set up for complicated itineraries. It's usually best to think of Panama City as your flight hub and plan trips that begin and end there. Also, beware of flying on holidays. Flight schedules automatically revert to a Sunday schedule on these days, but this is not always accounted for in the airline's reservation system. Passengers have actually arrived at the airport to learn they hold a ticket to a flight that doesn't exist. If you fly on a holiday be sure to confirm with a live person that your flight isn't fictitious. To be ultra safe,

don't book a holiday flight that isn't also listed for a Sunday.

There are two regular domestic carriers: Aeroperlas and Air Panama. The latter is the current incarnation of an airline that has gone by other names in the past.

Aeroperlas (tel. 315-7500, www.aeroperlas.com) is the older and somewhat larger of the airlines.

Air Panama (tel. 316-9000, www.flyairpanama.com) flies to most of the same destinations as Aeroperlas, plus Chitré and San José, Costa Rica. Frequent fliers grumble that its flights often run late. On the other hand, I've had all-day waits for Aeroperlas flights, too.

Aeroperlas has been around since 1970. According to the Aviation Safety Network, one of its planes crashed on the way to Puerto Obaldía in 2000, killing the 10 people onboard. Another plane overshot a runway that year, damaging the plane; there were no fatalities. In 2004, an Aeroperlas plane was forced to make an emergency landing; again, no fatalities. That same year Aeroperlas became affiliated with TACA, an international airline. It is now part of TACA Regional, a network of Central American domestic airlines, and the Aviation Safety Network has recorded no incidents on Aeroperlas since 2004.

According to the same source, an Air Panama plane overshot the airstrip in Bocas del Toro in 2006. The plane sustained substantial damage but there were no fatalities. In 2007 one of its flights "sank" on takeoff from Albrook and hit the runway; again, there was substantial damage but no fatalities.

In other words, flying within Panama is hardly risk-free. Passengers have traditionally complained about questionable maintenance, aging aircraft, deteriorating runways, and a casual attitude toward air safety. I've had white-knuckle flights on a variety of domestic flights over the years, and friends have had some truly terrifying rides. On the other hand, the views are spectacular and the flights don't last long. Also, these pilots fly constantly and, at least from my lay perspective, often have impressive skills. Flying is quite likely the safest way to get around, given the hazards of traveling by road and sea. Given a choice, I prefer to fly Aeroperlas, but this is purely a gut feeling.

Weight Limits

The baggage weight limit on domestic flights is 25 pounds (about 12 kilograms). Note that this is total weight, including both checked luggage and carry-ons. Do not try to slip by with more; planes are sometimes dangerously overloaded. Passengers are sometimes also asked to report their own body weight. If anything, err on the side of exaggerating your weight.

Fares

Domestic airline fares are regulated by the government. Standard fares are the same regardless of airline or season. They tend to go up only very slowly from year to year, though the recent rise in fuel prices is exerting unusual upward pressure. But in 2010, the most expensive one-way domestic fare was still just over US$100. The round-trip fare is always double the one-way fare. There are usually discounts

for young children. Try to make reservations at least several days in advance, and reconfirm the reservation 72 hours before the flight. Be at the airport at least an hour before the scheduled departure time.

BY BUS

Panama's buses are the backbone of its transportation system. Except for the relatively few able to afford cars, Panamanians rely on buses to get just about everywhere. They're cheap, run frequently, and are generally fast—sometimes too fast. The only ones not worth fooling with, except for those on a starvation budget, are buses within Panama City. They crawl across the city's congested streets, and anyone who can afford it takes the inexpensive taxis instead.

Many buses, especially in rural areas, run from dawn to dusk. There are few night buses except in the cities and along a few major long-distance routes. Few buses are expresses. Generally you can take any bus that goes at least as far as your destination. For instance,

local Panama City buses

to get from Panama City to Penonomé, you can take a bus with a final destination of, say, Aguadulce or Santiago, both of which pass by Penonomé.

Panama's biggest bus terminal, not surprisingly, is in Panama City: the Gran Terminal de Transportes, in the Albrook neighborhood not far from downtown. Buses leave from there to every part of the republic, often without any changes.

The other major hubs are Santiago and David. The hubs on the Azuero Peninsula are in Chitré and Las Tablas.

Reservations are seldom necessary (and not always possible). On most popular routes, if a bus fills up there's usually another one shortly thereafter. However, a reservation or at least an early arrival at the station is a good idea if you need to make specific connections. In Bocas del Toro, for instance, travelers need to arrive in time to get a water taxi to the islands.

BY BOAT

Organized ferry and water-taxi service is available between Panama City and Isla Taboga and sometimes Contadora, and between the mainland and Isla Colón in Bocas del Toro province. Other than these services, boat transportation for travelers is generally more casual and arranged ad hoc.

Boats are the main means of regional transportation within the archipelagos of Bocas del Toro and Kuna Yala (San Blas Islands). They are also the main way to get around the densely forested parts of the Darién and mainland Bocas close to rivers, especially in the rainy season when the rivers are more easily navigable.

The Bocas archipelago is the only place with anything resembling scheduled, cheap, commercial boat transportation among the islands. Boat transportation everyplace else is usually a matter of tracking down a fisherman or enterprising local boat owner and negotiating a price for a tour or extended trip. This can get expensive quickly. Tours are generally charged by the hour per group; the price for longer trips is based on distance; with gasoline the biggest expense. The price always includes the boat, a

Dugout canoes are the most common vehicle in the Darién.

captain (and crew, if needed), and fuel. As always, agree on a price ahead of time.

Transportation is generally in exceptionally long wooden dugouts called *piraguas,* though fiberglass boats *(botes)* are also used in some places. Both come equipped with outboard motors. For long trips especially, check the horsepower of the motor, and ask if there's a backup motor and life jackets *(salvavidas). Piraguas* are actually the preferred form of transportation on the river. Long dugouts used on the ocean are similar, but they have higher sides and an angled prow to break the waves. Short dugouts called *cayucos* are powered by a single wooden paddle and are all too easy for inexperienced paddlers to flip; it's unlikely you'll find yourself in one except for a very short trip.

Chartered sailboats, fishing or diving trips, and other outdoor activities on more substantial boats are easy to come by, but they tend to be quite expensive.

It's possible to take a partial or complete transit of the Panama Canal every Saturday via small vessel.

BY RAIL

The only passenger rail service in the country is on the recently rebuilt Panama Canal Railway, which runs between Corozal, a few minutes' drive north of downtown Panama City, and Colón. Some Panamanian businesspeople use it as a commuter service, but for most travelers it's a day excursion, and getting there is all the fun.

BY TAXI

Taxis are everywhere in Panama, especially Panama City. They're clearly marked and nearly always small Japanese cars. By law, taxis must be painted bright yellow. Fares are based either on a series of zones established by law or on long-established prices for particular routes. There are no metered taxis in Panama.

Taxis are cheap, and drivers do not expect a tip. Always ask for the price ahead of time, and clarify whether the price quoted is per person or the total amount. Fares are typically based on a single person in a taxi, with a small surcharge added for each additional passenger. Taxis are often allowed to charge a bit more late at night, on Sunday, or during holidays.

It's rare to pay more than US$2 or US$3 even for long rides in Panama City. Fares within other cities generally top out at US$1. Rides outside the cities are more negotiable and more expensive, though it's rare to pay more than US$20 even for a long trip on bad roads. Most shouldn't cost more than US$5–10.

In rural areas, the taxis are sometimes pickup trucks, occasionally converted into a kind of homemade minibus. These *cooperativos* are especially useful for travel on dirt or badly maintained roads. Some taxis running specific routes, especially the converted pickups, operate more like buses than taxis and charge by the head.

Taxis can be hired by the hour for tours, though few taxi drivers speak much English. This can be a good option for those who want to cover a lot of ground in a short amount of time and would like the driver to wait between stops. There are no set prices for this service, but expect to pay about US$7 an hour within Panama City, or considerably more for long trips. Again, agree on a price ahead of time and don't pay until the end of the tour.

Taxi drivers throughout the country are usually honest, decent, hardworking folks. However, the chance of encountering an unscrupulous character goes up somewhat in the more touristy parts of town and around the posher hotels. I try to walk away from these areas before hailing a taxi.

In Panama City, so-called "tourist taxis" (they have "SET" license plates) hover around the more expensive hotels. These are larger, air-conditioned cars that are authorized to charge several times the going rate. It's a pricey way to go, but may be of interest to those who want a more comfortable ride and the security of a lot more metal around them on the capital's chaotic streets. Those who want the cheaper ride can just walk down to a main street and hail a cab.

Taxi drivers tend to drive fast and aggressively, and their cars have the dents to prove it. Buckle in and hope for the best. If a driver is making you uncomfortable, a firm but polite *"despacio, por favor"* ("slow, please") should help a bit. If it doesn't, demand to be let out and get another taxi.

It's usually easy to find a cab night or day, and the international hailing sign of the raised arm works just fine. There are so many taxis eager for business that they often tap their horn at pedestrians to get their attention. This can get to be a little annoying if you're just out for a walk, but it's just an advertisement for business, not harassment.

At night, it can be worth calling for a radio taxi rather than waiting on the street. Many hotels, restaurants, and bars will be happy to call one for you.

RENTAL CARS AND DRIVING LAWS

Do not bother with rental cars for travel within Panama City or any other urban area. It's far easier, cheaper, and more convenient to take taxis. But renting a car is a reasonable option for longer trips. Note there is a standard charge of US$180 to drop a car off in a different city from the one you rented it in.

Visitors can drive in Panama for 90 days with a driver's license from their home country; there's no need to get an international or Panamanian driver's license or permit. Be prepared to present both your driver's license and passport if stopped by the transit police for any reason.

Two kinds of insurance are obligatory when driving a rental car in Panama. Different rental companies call them by different names, but they're essentially collision and robbery insurance (called something like *cobertura de colisión y robo* and comparable to collision damage waiver—CDW—in the United States) and insurance against liability for harm to third parties (called something like *cobertura de daños a terceros o responsabilidad civil* or *suplemento de seguro de responsabilidad contra terceros*). Other kinds of insurance are optional. Your credit card, home auto insurance, or travelers' insurance may include some car-rental protection, but be sure to check ahead of time that it covers driving in Panama. When I have to rent a vehicle in Panama, I err on the side of too much rather than too little insurance.

Drivers and passengers are required by law to wear seatbelts. Cars are not yet required to have airbags, so ask if your car has them.

It's against the law to drive while talking on a cell phone. If you need to make a call, pull over. It's also illegal to drive without a shirt—seriously, you'll get ticketed for this.

Rental car agencies in Panama do not allow customers to take cars out of the country. Visitors are allowed to drive foreign-registered vehicles within Panama for up to 90 days.

Panama's streets are increasingly choked with enormous SUVs, so consider that when contemplating renting a subcompact car. For some more remote, rugged areas, a four-wheel-drive vehicle with high clearance is a must to navigate rough, rocky dirt roads and small streams. In the rainy reason, some roads will be impassable no matter what you're driving. Four-wheel drives are popular, so be sure to make a reservation for these well ahead of time. If you're unused to driving these vehicles, bear in mind many have a high center of gravity and it's disturbingly easy to flip them over on sharp turns or when dodging road obstacles, both of which pop up often on Panama's roads. Four-wheel drives are known in Panama as *cuatro por cuartos* (four by fours), *vehículos con doble*

Panama City's streets are perpetually jammed.

© WILLIAM FRIAR

Traffic accidents are all too common in Panama.

traccion (vehicle with double traction), or simply *dobles*.

Rental cars are most widely available in Panama City, but they can also be found in David and a few other places. In Panama City, the highest concentration of offices is in the Vía España area, though there are branches dotted around the city and at the international airport. Rates are about the same and sometimes cheaper than they are in the United States, and promotions are often available, including packages that combine a car rental with domestic flights and/or hotel stays. These can be great deals.

The major companies are Hertz, Avis, Thrifty, Dollar, Alamo, National, and Budget. Which company is best changes so rapidly, depending on current local management, it's impossible to recommend one over another. Vehicles rented in Panama City should be reasonably well maintained. Outside the capital things are dicier. I once rented a car in David from a major U.S. agency and was presented with a muddy old clunker.

Toll Roads

Panama has three toll highways: the Corredor Norte, the Corredor Sur, and the Autopista Arraiján–La Chorrera. The Corredor Sur links Tocumen International Airport and central Panama City. The Corredor Norte extends north from Panama City across the isthmus toward Colón. Both of these latter highways were begun in the 1990s and are still works in progress to some degree. The Corredor Norte is being extended to Sabanitas, not far from Colón.

Tolls on the *corredores* are based on distance driven, the amount collected in increments at toll plazas along the way. Payments are made in cash or through an electronic debit system that only regular commuters bother with. Most tolls are around US$1 or less.

The Autopista Arraiján–La Chorrera, completed in 1981, is Panama's oldest toll road. It's on the Interamericana west of Panama City. The toll plaza is about 30 kilometers west of Panama City. The toll for a passenger car is US$0.50.

Tolls on all three highways are collected in either direction. Take the receipt the attendant hands you and hold onto it until you exit the highway. Tolls are higher for larger vehicles.

BY BICYCLE

Panama is not a bicycle-friendly country. There are no bike lanes, few places to rent bikes, and only a handful of areas where it's even marginally safe to venture out on a bike. A trailblazing friend is determined to build a bike trail through Parque Natural Metropolitano in Panama City, and it may actually exist by the time you visit.

If not, the best bet for a reasonably safe workout are the hilly loop roads above Boquete, though even here it's important to keep a sharp eye out for speeding trucks and cars. The Calzada de Amador is a good place for a flat, leisurely ride with great views. Isla Colón in Bocas del Toro is pretty much the only place that lends itself to biking as a sightseeing activity.

There are few bike shops and rental places in the country. The main place in Panama City to rent bikes is **Bicicletas Moses** (tel.

211-2579, 8 A.M.–9 P.M. daily) on the Calzada de Amador, which not coincidentally is pretty much the only place in Panama City where it's safe to ride them. Bikes can also be rented in Gamboa, Santa Clara, Farallón, El Valle, Boquete, Bambito, and Bocas del Toro. Do not expect high-quality bicycles at any of these locations. Rentals tend to be basic mountain bikes or clunky old road bikes. Bike rentals are usually around US$2–5 an hour.

Some true adventurers (masochists?) have biked all the way from North America to the Darién Gap.

HIKING

Panama is a great place for hikes, both casual day trips and major backcountry treks. There are very few developed campsites in the country, however, and few rangers to help out stranded hikers. Trails are often rugged and rudimentary.

Never, ever hike in the forest alone. Go with a qualified naturalist guide. It's surprisingly easy to get lost, and in some parts of Panama—such as the Darién—getting lost can be fatal. Also, rainforest trails can be very slippery, and you don't want to be stuck alone in the forest with even a twisted ankle. I'm embarrassed to admit how many times I've wiped out on what looked like an easy trail or gentle stream crossing.

Appropriate gear is key to a safe, enjoyable hike in the tropics. Always camp in a tent, even on the beach, to prevent insect and possible vampire-bat bites. Treat even small scratches with antibiotics; wounds quickly become infected in the tropics.

HITCHHIKING

Hitchhiking is not common in Panama, and it's just as dangerous here as it is in your own country.

ORGANIZED TOURS

Panama has many tour operators and guides, of wildly different quality. Companies appear and disappear constantly, and I've encountered many a "guide" who hasn't a clue what he or she is talking about. Even the more established companies can be hit or miss.

The ones included here are among the most prominent and well established, and I have indicated the ones I recommend highly. In addition to arranging tours, many operators can also make hotel and travel arrangements. Those especially interested in nature travel should be sure to sign up with a group that uses qualified naturalist guides; ask about credentials.

In addition to the guides and services described here, a couple of other individuals are worth mentioning. A naturalist guide and environmental activist named Guido Berguido works with a guide outfit called **Advantage Tours** (tel. 232-6944, www.advantagepanama. com). They typically offer 10-day birding trips, but other tours are offered. They have a field station in Gamboa and can take groups to two sites in the Darién.

Iann Sanchez (kayakinn@hotmail.com), the son of Hector Sanchez of Chiriquí River Rafting fame, also has a good reputation. He's worked as a U.S. park ranger and a rafting guide in the United States and Panama, and he is known for being knowledgeable and safety-conscious. He offers some unusual trips, including kayaking tours around Lago Gatún. He is completely bilingual.

Ancon Expeditions

Ancon Expeditions (P.O. Box 0832-1509 WTC, Panama City, Republic of Panama, tel. 269-9414 or 269-9415, fax 264-3713, www. anconexpeditions.com) is Panama's top nature-tour company. It's known for employing some of Panama's best naturalist guides, particularly in the Darién.

These include Hernan Araúz (www.hernanarauz.com), Rich Cahill (www.richardjcahill.com), Iván Hoyos (ivan@panamensis. com), and Rick Morales (morales.rick@gmail. com), all of whom I've traveled with and can recommend. They're all fluent in both English and Spanish. Hernan (one of Panama's top birding guides and Darién experts) and Rich are particularly experienced, with multiple

© WILLIAM FRIAR

tourists photographing tourists, Casco Viejo

trans-Darién treks and many shorter adventures to their credit. They're a blast to travel with: filled with a sense of fun and adventure, but always responsible and safety-conscious. I've learned a lot from both. Ancon Expeditions also runs some unique ecolodges, including ones in Cana, Punta Patiño, and Bocas del Toro. Tours range from easy day trips to ambitious, multiday treks through the forest. The company occasionally organizes ocean-to-ocean adventures through the heart of the Darién. It also offers a weeklong trip that includes a multiday hike along what remains of the historic Camino Real, which once stretched from Panamá La Vieja across the isthmus to Portobelo.

Boquete Outdoor Adventures

This is a fairly new operation led by John Miller (cell 6474-0274, www.boqueteoutdooradventures.com), who worked for 10 years at the Nantahala Outdoor Center as a rafting guide and kayak instructor. It offers a variety of trips but specializes in weeklong white-water kayaking adventures in western Panama.

Chiriquí River Rafting

Chiriquí River Rafting (tel. 720-1505 or 720-1506, cell 6618-0846, www.panama-rafting.com) is a safety-conscious, highly professional operation that I've had great experiences with. It primarily runs white-water rivers in the western highlands, but it also offers tamer river trips.

Ecocircuitos

This company (tel./fax 314-1586, www.ecocircuitos.com), based at the Country Inn and Suites in Amador, offers a wide range of short and multiday tours around the country. It hires friendly and accommodating guides who speak English and Spanish.

Exotics Adventures

This group (tel. 223-9283, www.panamaexoticsadventures.com) is led by a Frenchman named Michel Peuch who comes highly recommended. Unusual offerings include a fast and arduous ocean-to-ocean Darién trek and a kayak trip in Bocas del Toro. His Darién trips focus on the western end, relatively close to Panama City and far from the dangers of the

Darién Gap. These include hikes along the El Llano–Carti Road to Kuna Yala. Other offerings include a day hike along a part of the Camino de Cruces.

Gold Coast Expeditions

This operation (tel. 441-4339, cell 6635-2292, http://goldcoastpanama.homestead.com) is run by Skipper and Jill Berger, longtime residents of the Caribbean side of the former Canal Zone. They offer a variety of snorkeling/diving, sailing, and sightseeing trips around Panama, with the Caribbean side of the canal area their specialty. Popular trips include kayaking excursions around Portobelo and the lower Río Chagres.

Iguana Tours

Iguana Tours (tel. 226-8738, 226-1667, or 226-4516, fax 226-4736, www.nvmundo.com/iguanatours) specializes in trips to Isla Iguana off the Azuero Peninsula, but it offers a range of tours all over the country.

José Saenz

José (based in Panama City, cell 6614-7811, tel./fax 399-4003 or 251-0698, www.goldenfrog.net) is a taxi driver, but if you spend any amount of time in Panama you'll realize he's an important part of the tourist infrastructure. I highly recommend him. He's punctual, responsible, polite, dependable—and a safe driver. These are qualities to prize among Panama taxi drivers. He charges US$25 for transfers to and from Tocumen International Airport. Transfers to or from most Panama City hotels to the domestic airport at Albrook is US$5. With enough notice, he can make hotel and domestic airline reservations. He charges US$12 an hour for Panama City tours. These prices are for one or two people. José also offers tours all over Panama, including Chiriquí, the Azuero Peninsula (his specialty; that's where he's from), and Bocas del Toro. Rates for this vary. Besides his air-conditioned cab, he has access to a minibus and pickup truck. He speaks pretty good English.

Nattur Panama

This group (tel. 442-1340, fax 442-8485, www.natturpanama.com) is headed by Willie Martinez, who is recognized as one of the best birding guides in Panama. The company offers a range of nature tours throughout the country. Its unique offerings include stays at Martinez's own ecological retreat, Willie Mazu, in the species-rich Fortuna area. The group recently opened a similar retreat near Colón. It also offers a popular boat tour on the Río Chagres near the Caribbean entrance to the Panama Canal.

Panama Travel Experts

Many offerings from Panama Travel Experts (tel. 265-5323, fax 265-5324, U.S. tel. 877/836-5300 or 707/226-2640, www.panamatravelexperts.com) are higher-end multiday packages that include stays at luxury hotels, but the group also offers less expensive day tours.

Pesantez Tours

Pesantez (tel. 223-5374 or 263-7577, www.pesantez-tours.com) is a long-established company that enjoys a solid reputation. It specializes in tours of Panama City and cultural tours, rather than nature trips.

San Blas Sailing

This outfit (tel. 314-1800 or 314-1288, www.sanblassailing.com) arranges memorable multiday yacht tours of Kuna Yala (San Blas Islands). Though not cheap, these trips are not as expensive as one might expect and offer good value. For those who don't have yachts of their own, it's the best way to explore and enjoy the islands.

Scubapanama

Scubapanama (tel. 261-3841 or 261-4064, www.scubapanama.com) is Panama's biggest dive operator. Common offerings include diving around Portobelo, a dive in both oceans in a single day, and diving in the Panama Canal.

Visas and Officialdom

Tourist-entry requirements for Panama are a muddle. Rules are in flux, and government officials often seem the last people you can count on for accurate information. It's possible to call a half dozen consulates and get a half dozen contradictory answers to basic questions. Things got immeasurably worse in 2007 with the introduction of a new tourist-entry law that confused everyone. In 2010, the confusion got worse when Panama eliminated *tarjetas de turismo* (tourist cards), which those from the United States, Canada, Australia, and a few other countries had to buy from their airline or at the border. Now tourists from these countries are allowed to enter with just their passports, but Panama officialdom has not yet updated its websites and documentation accordingly; some forms issued by the Panama government still had the old rules printed on them.

The website of Panama's immigration and naturalization office (http://migracion.gob.pa/) is the best place to go for current information if it's ever working properly, but even it is not the final word. All that ultimately matters is what the immigration official who greets you in Panama says the rules are.

That said, it's not hard for most people to enter Panama as tourists, especially by air. With all the changes, two things have remained constant: Tourists can normally stay in Panama at least 30 days, and U.S. citizens need only their passport to enter.

All foreign nationals need to present a passport that is valid for at least six months from their date of entry. Tourists must also be able to show proof of having at least US$500 (a credit card or travelers checks are usually good enough) and a return or onward travel ticket out of Panama. In practice, this rule will probably not be enforced, especially for clean, neatly dressed North Americans and Western Europeans. Bedraggled backpackers may get more attention. Bus passengers arriving at Paso Canoa without proof of onward travel are usually required to buy a bus ticket back to Costa Rica, whether they intend to use it or not.

VISAS

Panama divides foreign tourists into two categories, depending on nationality: those who need a tourist visa; and those who don't need anything but a passport to enter Panama. Tourist visas are further broken down into "stamped visas" and the more restrictive "authorized visas."

Countries whose citizens need only a passport to enter Panama include: Argentina, Australia, Austria, Belgium, Canada, Chile, Columbia, Costa Rica, Cyprus, the Czech Republic, Denmark, Estonia, Finland, France, Germany, Great Britain, Greece, Hungary, Iceland, Ireland, Israel, Italy, Japan, Luxembourg, Mexico, the Netherlands, New Zealand, Norway, Poland, Portugal, Slovakia, South Korea, Spain, Sweden, Switzerland, Singapore, Taiwan, and the United States. Note: This list changes often; check with the consulate or embassy in your country for current requirements.

Stamped Visa

Panama issues a so-called "stamped visa," a kind of tourist visa that lets some travelers enter the country multiple times over the course of a year. It is available only through a Panamanian consulate or embassy, and as the name implies it consists of a stamp placed in the traveler's passport. Length of stay is at the discretion of the Panamanian authorities, but is generally 30 days for each visit.

Anyone eligible to travel to Panama on a tourist card can choose to apply for a stamped visa instead, if they want. Citizens of some countries are required to get a stamped visa.

Countries whose citizens must have a stamped visa to travel to Panama include the Dominican Republic, Ecuador, Georgia, Peru, Russia, Ukraine, Vietnam, and Zimbabwe. Remember, these lists are subject to change.

Authorized Visa

Citizens of some countries need a so-called

visa autorizada (authorized visa). This is the most restrictive kind of tourist visa. It is available only through a Panamanian consulate or embassy, which decides whether to approve the visa application and determines the length of stay. Most countries on this list are in Africa, the Middle East, Eastern Europe, and Asia.

Confusingly, stated requirements can vary by consulate, so double-check with the nearest one before beginning the process to make sure to have all the required documents in order. But even the loosest interpretation of the rules makes applying a lengthy hassle, and they sure aren't designed to make the applicant feel welcomed with open arms. Begin the process at least 30 days before the start of travel.

Applicants will probably need to present:

1. A completed one-page application form

2. A valid passport

3. A copy of the passport including pages showing entry and exit stamps

4. A letter from a local "sponsor" in Panama, as well as a recent bank statement and utility bill from the sponsor. (It may be worth arranging at least one tour with a Panamanian guide company or tour operator and have them supply this letter for you—again, start this process well in advance, as getting this letter may be a nuisance. Don't pay for the tour until the letter's supplied.)

5. A copy of your most recent Panama visa (if applicable)

6. A copy of your "residence or identification card" from your home country

7. Two passport-size photographs

Some consulates require proof of a round-trip. If so, make sure the ticket's refundable in case the application is turned down.

Not surprisingly, many prefer to apply for this visa through a lawyer or visa service.

Countries whose citizens can travel to Panama only with an authorized visa include: Bangladesh, Cuba, Haiti, India, Pakistan, the People's Republic of China, and South Africa. Again, this list changes frequently.

Extended Stays

How long can one stay in Panama as a tourist? Excellent question. It's a major source of confusion these days. Sadly, I can't give a definitive answer, and even if I could the law might well change by the time I finish this sentence.

Everyone agrees that tourists can generally stay for at least 30 days. The upper limit for most tourist stays is 90 days, but this is discretionary. When a tourist enters the country, the immigration official now asks for length of intended stay and, if he or she agrees, writes that number on the entry stamp in your passport. If you think you may stay longer than 30 days, say so and hope the official approves.

Tourists who want to extend their stay beyond that authorized when they entered the country must apply for a *prórroga de turista* (tourist extension) at an immigration office. Just who's eligible for a *prórroga* these days is a matter of debate.

Getting a *prórroga* is a serious nuisance. Gather all the materials needed and start the application process about four working days before the visa or tourist card expires. Wear your nicest clothes and be unfailingly polite.

Applicants must submit:

1. Their passport and tourist card or visa

2. A photocopy of the passport pages that show the applicant's photo, personal details, and latest entry stamp for Panama

3. A photocopy of the tourist card or visa

4. A sponsorship letter from a Panamanian or foreign resident, along with a photocopy of the sponsor's *cédula* (national identity card) and a photocopy of his or her latest telephone or utilities bill

5. A photocopy of a return or onward-travel ticket that's valid for a year

6. Proof of one's own financial solvency (e.g., travelers checks, credit cards, or US$500 in cash)

7. Two passport-size photos

8. A payment of US$1 to open a file and US$15 to make the *carnet de prórroga* (ID card)

Applicants need to fill out a simple Spanish form (those who don't speak Spanish may want to bring a phrasebook). The whole procedure can sometimes be completed in a day but can take longer. Applicants are required to leave their passport (be sure to make an extra photocopy or two for yourself).

Tourists can get up to 60 more days in Panama through this process. Note that getting the full extension is not guaranteed. The number of days granted is at the discretion of immigration authorities.

After the extension expires, tourists have a two-day grace period to leave the country. The penalty for staying beyond that, interestingly, is not that bad. Tourists whose stay has expired are required to pay a *multa* (fine) before leaving the country. The fine is US$25 for overstaying a month, and it goes up slowly from there, topping out at US$300 for a year or more. Still, it's not a good idea to get enmeshed in the cogs of the Panamanian bureaucracy by overstaying your official welcome.

The main immigration office is in Panama City. It's formally known as the **Ministerio de Gobierno y Justicia, Dirección de Migración y Naturalización** (Avenida Cuba and Calle 29 Este, tel. 207-1800, 777-7777, or 227-1077, tel./fax 227-1227, 8 A.M.–3 P.M. Mon.–Fri.). The influx of foreigners has made this place a jammed-packed nightmare. It's so crowded the line to get in forms at 6 A.M. The first thing one needs to do is take a number: This being Panama, enterprising locals show up early, take the numbers, and sell them to foreigners who chose to sleep in. If you can't get to the office by about 10 A.M., you might as well not bother; go the next day.

A street kiosk next to the office, Kiosca Yolanda, makes photocopies for US$0.10. Just up the street is an Internet café (8 A.M.–10 P.M. Mon.–Fri., 10 A.M.–1 P.M. Sat.–Sun.) that also makes photocopies.

There are other immigration offices around the country, including one in David, one in Chitré, and two in Bocas del Toro. On my most recent visit to Panama, I got my extension in David; the official running the place these days is strict, but the little office is not a madhouse like the one in Panama City.

LIVING AND WORKING IN PANAMA

It's tough to get a permit to work in Panama. The country has high unemployment and the government wants jobs to go to Panamanians, not foreigners. However, foreign investors, entrepreneurs, and retirees are welcome to make their home in Panama if they meet certain conditions.

Coming to Panama as anything other than a tourist requires considerable paperwork, the services of a Panamanian lawyer, and certification by a Panamanian consulate. The process is time-consuming. Allow several months for the paperwork to make its way through the system, and try to get a lawyer who specializes in immigration law.

The biggest and most established law firms include: Morgan and Morgan; Galindo, Arias, and López; Arias, Fábrega, and Fábrega (ARIFA); and Icaza, González-Ruiz, y Alemán (IGRA).

A useful book for those planning a move to Panama is *Living in Panama,* by Sandra Snyder. It covers the daily realities of life in Panama, particularly Panama City, and includes tips on everything from registering a car to choosing a school to how to pay the phone bill. It's widely available in Panama or can be ordered online; visit www.livinginpanama.net. (Full disclosure: Sandra is a family friend, but her knowledge is solid. She has lived for years in Panama and is so plugged into the local scene some Panamanians turn to her for tips.)

Residency for Foreign Retirees

Foreign retirees who want to make their home in Panama must get a *visa de turista pensionado* (pensioned tourist visa). Retirees are required to hire a lawyer to handle the process.

Fortunately, Panama wants relatively affluent retirees, so the requirements are not nearly as onerous as in some other countries. These include a recent medical evaluation certifying the applicant is in good health, an HIV test, proof of retiree status, and a monthly pension of at least US$500, plus US$100 for each dependent the retiree wants to bring along. The dependents also need a clean bill of health. The applicant must also show proof of not having a police record back home. The lawyer will explain the kind of documentation needed, as well as the photos, passport photocopies, and other bureaucratic fodder that must be supplied.

Benefits of *turista pensionado* status, besides the right to live in Panama, include the right to import up to US$10,000 worth of possessions for personal use duty-free, as well as the duty-free import of a vehicle every two years. A huge plus for retirees, both foreign and domestic, is discounts at restaurants and hotels, for transportation and many medical services, and for some financial dealings. These can range from 10 percent to 50 percent.

Retirees are allowed to invest in Panama, but are not allowed to work except under certain special circumstances.

Work Permits, Temporary Visitor Visas, and Immigrant Visas

Work permits are generally only granted if a Panamanian company has offered the applicant a job, and even then only if it can be proved no Panamanian could do that job. The permits are issued by Panama's labor ministry, El Ministerio de Trabajo y Desarrollo Laboral, and getting one requires a good Panamanian attorney. The applicant must then apply for a temporary visitor visa, again with legal help. Executives who want to work in the Zona Libre de Colón, technical and scientific experts, and qualified candidates interested in working at one of the Ciudad del Saber (City of Knowledge) projects have the best chance of being approved.

Investors who want to live and do business in Panama must meet several other conditions, not the least of which is a commitment to invest at least US$40,000 in capital and hire at least three Panamanian employees.

Anyone with assets of at least US$200,000

regulations for water-taxi drivers, Bocas del Toro

in a Panamanian bank account can apply for an immigrant visa, even without job prospects.

EMBASSIES AND CONSULATES

Panama City is home to the embassies and consulates of quite a number of countries. But some major nations are missing: Australia, for instance, advises its citizens to contact the Australian embassy in Mexico if they need help. A few countries with embassies or consulates in Panama City include:

- **Canada:** World Trade Center, Calle 53 Este in Marbella, tel. 264-9731, fax 263-8083, www.dfait-maeci.gc.ca/panama/menu-en.asp

- **Colombia:** World Trade Center, Calle 53 Este in Marbella, tel. 264-9513 or 264-9266 (embassy), tel. 223-3535 (consul general), fax 223-1134, www.embajadadecolombia.org.pa/

- **Costa Rica:** Avenida 2 Sur/Samuel Lewis, tel. 264-2980 or 758-9128 (consulate), fax 264-6348 (Costa Rica also has a consulate in David: Calle C Sur and Avenida 2 Este Avenida, tel. 774-1923.)

- **Cuba:** Avenida Cuba and Ecuador, tel. 227-5277 or 227-0359, fax 225-6681

- **El Salvador:** Calle 58 and Avenida Samuel Lewis, tel. 223-3020

- **France:** Plaza de Francia in Casco Viejo, tel. 211-6200, fax 211-6235

- **Germany:** World Trade Center, Calle 53 Este in Marbella, tel. 263-7733, fax 223-6664, www.panama.diplo.de

- **Great Britain:** MMG Tower, Calle 53 Este in Marbella, tel. 269-0866, fax 223-0730, www.britishembassy.gov.uk/panama

- **Guatemala:** Vía Argentina, tel. 269-3406, fax 223-1922

- **Mexico:** ADR Tower, Calle 58 and Avenida Samuel Lewis, tel. 263-4900 or 263-2159, www.sre.gob.mx/panama

- **Nicaragua:** Vía España y Calle Elvira Mendez, Edificio Torre Delta, tel. 269-6721 or 264-6431, consulnicpa@cableonda.net

- **Spain:** Calle 33 and Avenida Perú, tel. 227-5122, fax 227-6284, emb.panama@mae.es

- **United States:** The U.S. embassy recently moved from central Panama City to an enormous, fortress-like compound in Clayton, in the former Canal Zone. The American Citizens Service Unit (Building 520, Clayton, tel. 207-7030, fax 207-7303, http://panama.usembassy.gov, 8 A.M.–noon Mon.–Fri.) is closed on the last Wednesday of every month and on all U.S. and Panamanian holidays. The main embassy phone number is 207-7000.

BORDER CROSSINGS

There are three border crossings between Panama and Costa Rica: at Paso Canoa on the Pacific side of the isthmus, at Río Sereno in the highlands, and at Sixaola-Guabito on the Caribbean coast. Paso Canoa, which is on the Interamericana, is by far the most traveled. The Sixaola-Guabito crossing is used mainly by those traveling to and from Bocas del Toro. The Río Sereno crossing is rarely used, and foreign travelers are not always allowed across.

The Interamericana comes to an end at the town of Yaviza in eastern Panama, where the famous Darién Gap begins. There are no roads linking Panama with Colombia and the rest of South America. There is a border crossing at Puerto Obaldía, at the very eastern tip of the Caribbean coast, but the civil war in Colombia sometimes makes crossing here too dangerous to attempt even when it's actually open. Flying is the safest way to travel between Colombia and Panama.

General Considerations

Panama is trying, not always successfully, to strike a balance between retaining control over its borders and encouraging tourists and potential investors to visit. This includes cracking down on foreign nationals who are living in Panama without changing their tourist status;

they merely pop across the border for 72 hours, then come back.

On arrival at any border crossing, be prepared to present immigration officials with an onward ticket out of Panama and evidence of having US$500. Except at Paso Canoa these aren't often asked for, but officials have the right to refuse entry to anyone without them. Arriving at the border looking clean and neatly dressed in long pants and good shoes (e.g., no sneakers, flip-flops, sandals, etc.) increases one's chances of being waved through without incident.

Try to arrive at border crossings during regular business hours to avoid a lengthy wait at the border for immigrations and customs officials to show up. Borders are open every day.

Paso Canoa

The border crossing at the decaying town of Paso Canoa (sometimes also know as Paso Canoas) is on the Interamericana and is the route taken by the great majority of visitors coming from or going to Costa Rica by land. It's about an hour by bus or car west of David, the provincial capital of Chiriquí province. It tends to be the strictest border crossing.

Going through formalities on both sides can be surprisingly quick or painfully slow, especially when a bus arrives. Count on an hour or two for the whole process and hope for the best. Panama time is always one hour ahead of Costa Rican time.

Caution: I've had credible reports that Panama-bound tourists without proof of onward travel are being solicited for US$10 bribes.

Panama immigration, customs, and an ATP government tourism office are housed in a new cement monolith at the border. The **ATP office** (tel. 727-6524, 7 a.m.–11 p.m. daily) has very little to offer tourists. Don't expect much tourist information.

Those arriving by bus tend to encounter the most inconvenience. Passengers are generally expected to hand-carry their luggage across the border for inspection on either side. Also, processing a busload of visitors takes time, especially if the bus arrives early in the morning.

It's impossible to get lost crossing over, but the offices aren't well marked. Streetwise little boys may offer to help navigate for a small tip. This may be worthwhile if the procedures are baffling or if you just want to stop the other kids from bugging you. About US$0.25–0.50 should make your assistant happy.

Men wearing money pouches hang around the immigration office offering to buy or sell Costa Rican colones. If changing money on the streets of a grungy border town doesn't sound like a smart thing to do, exchange money before arriving at the border. There are ATMs between the two borders that dispense both colones and dollars.

There are plenty of buses and taxis about 50 meters past immigration/customs.

Sixaola-Guabito

This border crossing is used primarily by those traveling between Costa Rica and Bocas del Toro. Sixaola is the border town on the Costa Rican side; Guabito is on the Panamanian side. The border itself runs down the middle of the Río Sixaola. Travelers must cross over a short, rickety railroad bridge, either by foot or in a vehicle. Pedestrians should look out for traffic, missing handrails, and gaps in the planking.

Travelers usually find border formalities here quick and laid-back. The Panamanian border post is on an elevated railway trestle on the edge of the Río Sixaola. The **immigration office** (tel. 759-7019, 8 a.m.–noon and 12:30 p.m. to 6 p.m. daily) is right on the train tracks next to the bridge that crosses the river. Travelers can enter and leave Panama only when the office is open. An IPAT representative at the post sells tourist cards to those eligible. Remember that Panama time is always one hour ahead of Costa Rican time.

There are no hotels, no appealing places to eat, and almost no services in Guabito. The nearest place with significant services is Changuinola, about a 20-minute drive away.

Those entering Panama without onward transportation should walk down from the railroad tracks to get a bus or taxi after clearing customs and immigration. Taxi drivers and unofficial "tour guides" sometimes try to overcharge new arrivals or take them to hotels that pay them a commission, so be cautious.

Río Sereno

This little-used border crossing is a possible alternative to Paso Canoa for those coming from or going to the western highlands of Panama. However, it's rarely used and is not always open to foreigners. There's nothing much of interest for tourists there, and you're likely to be the only foreigner in town. It's a far prettier spot than Paso Canoa, but it's not really set up to deal well with foreign visitors, it's out of the way for any destination but the area around Volcán, and the road leading east into Panama is dangerous. It's a better idea all around to cross over at Paso Canoa.

The Panamanian **immigration/customs office** (tel. 722-8054, 7 A.M.–7 P.M. daily) in Río Sereno is on a hill above the town plaza. It's near the radio tower and shares a building with the police station.

The nearest major junction for onward travel in Panama is at Volcán, 42 kilometers east of the border. The drive, on a beautiful but dangerous road, takes nearly two hours. The pickup-taxi ride costs about US$20, and you'll be sharing the ride. Buses from Río Sereno run 5 A.M.–5 P.M. every 45 minutes to Volcán and David.

There is one basic but okay place to stay for those unlucky enough to get stranded at the border: Posada Los Andes (next to the plaza, no phone, US$20 s/d).

Puerto Obaldía

The only marginally safe way to cross the Colombia-Panama border by land is to go through the grim border town of Puerto Obaldía, on the Caribbean coast. Because of the civil war in Colombia, even this border crossing is not always open or safe.

Even at the best of times, this route is only for the adventurous. I do not recommend it. Traveling by boat and bus through western Colombia can be dangerous, and the trip can take days. It's the cheapest way to go, but the modest savings aren't worth the effort and risk.

Aeroperlas is the only airline flying between Panama City and Puerto Obaldía, and only Wednesday–Sunday. Flights fill up, so make reservations as far in advance as possible. The flight costs US$85 one-way and takes at least an hour, depending on stops. From there, travelers must hire a launch to Capurganá, a beach resort on the Colombian side. The fare is US$10 per person, but there's a minimum; single travelers may have to pay as much as US$30 if no one else is going. The trip takes about an hour and is a bumpy ride, especially in the dry season. Expect to get wet. The boat does have life jackets, though. A boat between Capurganá and Turbo takes about two hours and costs about US$20. Again, this tends to be a wet, wild ride. Turbo has bus connections with other parts of Colombia, notably Cartagena and Medellín. *Warning:* Turbo has historically been a hotbed of paramilitary activity. Be careful, and travel only in the daytime.

Travelers must seek out the immigration officials in Puerto Obaldía and Capurganá to get their exit/entry clearance. Expect also to be interviewed and possibly searched by border police. Exchange currency ahead of time, as it can be tough to do so near the border. Those entering Panama via this route must have an onward ticket out of Panama. Proof of a yellow fever vaccination is no longer officially required but is probably still a good idea, just in case the officials out here in the boonies haven't yet gotten the memo. Those flying from Puerto Obaldía to Panama City will probably have to go through a second grilling upon arrival at Albrook to make sure they're not drug traffickers, Colombian fighters, or illegal aliens.

Getting through all this in a single day requires plane reservations, documents in perfect order, and luck, particularly with connections. It's not unusual to get stuck on either side of the border for at least a night. Capurganá is a popular beach resort and has a wide range of accommodations. Puerto Obaldía, however, is a backwater, though rock-bottom rooms are available for about US$5.

CORRUPTION, BRIBES, AND SCAMS

Nepotism, corruption, *amiguismo* (crony-ism), and conflicts of interest have been serious problems in Panama throughout its history. In 2002, Panama's then-president, Mireya Moscoso, repeatedly defended nepotism as a long-established tradition in Panama. Panamanians place little faith in their legal system or political parties. Panama has also long been notorious as a transshipment point for drugs and a haven for money launderers.

There have been attempts in recent years to address these problems through new anticorruption commissions, press exposés, stricter banking laws to crack down on money laundering, transparency laws designed to stop illegal deals, subjecting once-secret government and business negotiations to public scrutiny, and removing from the public payroll so-called *botellas* (literally, "bottles"—well-connected appointees without the skill or inclination to do their assigned jobs).

Many of these efforts have been dismissed as cynical or halfhearted. Reformers in Panama maintain that an attitude of *juega vivo* (roughly, "live game" or "the game of life") is still firmly rooted in daily life. *Juega vivo* refers to a belief that one should grab any opportunity life presents, even if ethically or legally shaky.

Corruption does remain a fact of life in Panama. But societal attitudes seem to be shifting. It's much more common these days to hear people assert that putting the interests of family and self first can hurt society as a whole, and that Panama cannot be a modern, successful country without trustworthy public institutions.

It's unlikely most tourists will find themselves in a situation where a bribe is expected. The possible exception is being stopped by a police officer, usually for a traffic violation, and being encouraged to pay the "fine" on the spot instead of going to the trouble of paying it at the courthouse. How to handle this is a judgment call. Some adamantly refuse to pay a bribe out of principle. Sometimes the officer will lose interest and let the violator go; other times this leads to a time-wasting visit to the local courthouse. Paying or offering a bribe is illegal, and theoretically it can get a visitor in far more serious trouble. Others find paying a few dollars the easiest way to deal with the nuisance.

In recent years, there have been reports of travelers being stopped by police repeatedly while driving in western Panama. This occurs between Divisa and David on the Interamericana. They are accused, rightly or not, of speeding or not staying within the lane and then told to pay a "fine" of US$20. Some have refused to pay and are let go; others pay, only to be stopped again farther down the road. The police reportedly spot likely looking tourists as they drive by and radio ahead to their confederates to stop them. Those driving in western Panama should obey the speed limit and all other traffic rules and try as much as possible not to look too touristy.

More recently, there have been reports of bribe demands at the Paso Canoa bordering crossing with Costa Rica.

Those interested in Panama real estate should proceed carefully. Land scams are a problem, especially since the start of the tourist and retiree boom in Bocas del Toro and Boquete. Be especially cautious with timber plantations and other get-rich-quick schemes. If it looks too good to be true, it is. A great deal of land in Panama is untitled, which makes buying it tricky and in some cases legally precarious—don't "buy" a piece of land from someone who doesn't actually own it. Some people have been buying into Panama sight unseen, which is nuts. Besides the danger of getting ripped off, Panama is not a place everyone would want to live or invest in. To avoid disappointment, get to know the country first.

Scams against regular tourists are still not much of a problem, though touts and taxi drivers sometimes steer visitors to hotels and services that pay them a commission. Most visitors are more likely to be ripped off by a fellow foreigner than by a Panamanian. But stay alert and be cautious with overly friendly strangers.

POLICE

Panama's police force is a lot less intimidating now than in the days of the military dictatorship. Law-abiding visitors are unlikely to have any bad dealings with the police. In fact, Panama is so eager to protect tourists and give them a positive impression of the country there's a whole detachment of police officers, known as the policía de turismo (tourist police), dedicated to watching out for them in Panama City. They're generally bicycle cops, easy to spot in their khaki uniforms with short pants. They're most visible in the Casco Viejo section of the city, where the force is headquartered.

Transit police sometimes crack down on certain offenses on busy stretches of road. They're usually on the lookout for speeders, those making illegal turns, drivers talking on cell phones, and so on. Drivers signal that the transit police are staking out an area by flashing headlights at each other. I sometimes flash lights to slow down reckless drivers even when no cops are around.

The police sometimes set up roadblocks to check drivers' licenses and registrations. This is normal and no cause for alarm. If a police officer stops you, be unfailingly polite and friendly. Be prepared to hand over your passport and driver's license. Police officers rarely speak English, which some use to their advantage when stopped for a traffic violation, feigning an inability to speak Spanish in the hopes the officer will lose patience and just wave the driver on instead of handing out a ticket.

Conduct and Customs

Despite Panama's undeserved reputation among those who've never been there as a dangerous country, you'll likely find it a remarkably mellow and low-key place to travel. It's extremely rare to encounter hostility or belligerence. Courtesy is considered quite important, however. Panamanians may take offense if they feel they're not being treated with proper dignity and respect.

Foreigners sometimes complain that the Panamanians they encounter in stores and offices seem unfriendly or sullen. This complaint is most often made about Panama City; in the countryside, visitors are frequently overwhelmed by the warmth and friendliness they encounter. If you feel you're being treated rudely, do not raise your voice or snap at the offending party—this will get you absolutely nowhere. Be patient and polite, and take your business elsewhere next time. Similarly, the less you expect punctuality and speediness the happier you will be.

As in other Latin American countries, machismo is a fact of life in Panama. Women may find they have to deal with unwanted male attention.

DRESS AND APPEARANCE

It's tempting to wear skimpy, sloppy clothes in the Panamanian heat. Resist the temptation. Panama is not Margaritaville; it is in some ways a rather formal and conservative country. Neat dress, good grooming, and cleanliness are expected.

The influx of foreign tourists and retirees has led to a proliferation of Hawaiian shirts, T-shirts, shorts, baseball caps, tank tops, sneakers, sandals, and the like on city streets and even in fancy restaurants. This is a no-no in Panama. Many businesses will look the other way, out of politeness or a desire for dollars. But it's considered disrespectful and inappropriate to dress like this anywhere other than the beach. Even the poorest Panamanians dress neatly and cleanly; imagine how rude it must seem that far more affluent foreigners, who don't have to work in the fields and can afford nice clothes, won't make the same effort.

If offending local sentiments is not enough of a disincentive, bear in mind that people are judged by their appearance to a greater extent in Panama than in more casual countries. Well-groomed, well-dressed people get better, more courteous service. And just wearing shorts or a Hawaiian shirt on the streets instantly marks you as a clueless foreigner for the unscrupulous to take advantage of, or worse. Few longtime expatriates dress like that, and not coincidentally they are far less likely to be hassled in dodgy parts of town. Overly casual dress also limits where you can go. Those wearing sneakers, sandals, or shorts are not allowed in nightclubs or government offices, and they can be turned away from churches.

It's actually against the law to drive or walk down a city street without a shirt; violators are subject to fines. What constitutes a "city" street is broadly defined: Shirtless travelers have been ticketed for walking down the main street in Bocas town, a place that hardly qualifies as an urban setting in most people's minds.

Neat clothing made from cotton, linen, and other lightweight fabrics can be quite comfortable, and it provides better protection from the sun and bugs than beachwear does.

Suits have largely replaced guayabera shirts as business and semiformal wear for middle- and upper-class Panamanian men, made practical by the widespread use of air-conditioning in the cities. Women tend to dress as elegantly as their budget will allow, and two-piece suits or conservative dresses are the norm for professional women.

One funny side effect of the recent influx of gringos and other tourists is that it's now more common to see Ecuadorian-style "Panama hats" on the streets. They were popular during the Gold Rush and canal-construction days, but they've never been made in Panama and haven't been seen on Panama streets in many decades. When tourists arrived and demanded to buy what they thought of as Panama hats, the market responded, just as it did more than a century ago.

Children wear uniforms to school, and, though spiky modern hairstyles and casual clothes have made some inroads in recent years, it's rare to see even teenagers take their fashion sense too far. (Chances are excellent that the Spanish-speaking dude you see in shorts and a baseball cap is actually not Panamanian but rather a visitor from another Latin American country.) But long-haired kids are no longer hauled off by the police for a haircut, as they were during the military dictatorship of the 1970s.

Mochileros (backpackers) sometimes get a bad rap in Panama as an unkempt and disreputable lot that add little to the economy. There's little animosity, but one occasionally senses a mild distrust. To this day, most tourism efforts are pitched at the affluent, and some shudder at the thought of Panama being overrun with foreign backpackers, as they believe Costa Rica has been. This attitude has softened somewhat as real backpackers proved to be less scary than feared. Still, those traveling on a frugal budget will feel more welcome if they do their best to look especially neat and respectable, and if they stash the backpack in a safe place when possible.

ETIQUETTE

Formality extends to etiquette as well. Titles are taken seriously (such as *doctor* for a physician, *licenciado* for an attorney or even someone who holds a bachelor's degree, *profesor* or *maestro* for a teacher, *ingeniero* for an engineer, etc.). If known, they should be used in introductions and correspondence. Courtesies in writing and speech tend to be more elaborate in Panama than in English-speaking countries. Some allowances are made for foreigners, but try to make up for any gaps in eloquence with cordial body language.

Women often greet each other and men with air kisses. Unlike in some other Latin American countries, men rarely greet each other with an *abrazo* (hug) unless they are on quite friendly terms. Handshakes are the norm, but these tend to be far lighter (some say limper) than in other countries. A crushing handshake is considered aggressive.

It's not typical in Panama to greet someone with an *hola* (hello). This is considered quite casual and, especially if the person is unknown to you, not very polite. The main greetings are *buenos días* (good morning), *buenas tardes* (good afternoon), and *buenas noches* (good evening). In casual situations this is often shortened to a simple *buenas,* which conveys a tone somewhere between "hey" and "howdy." It's become fashionable in recent years, for some reason, to say *"ciao"* when parting.

Courtesy may be less elaborate among the poor working classes of the city and the country, but being polite is just as important. Even more so, in some ways. It's considered extremely insulting to address someone of perceived lesser status as though they're inferior. When in doubt, use formal terms of address

(such as *usted* instead of *tú*) with strangers, and be especially sensitive about not lapsing into casual forms with someone who's performing a service for you.

Many Panamanians are proud of their country and do not take kindly to criticism of Panama and things Panamanian. Complaints they may make to each other are one thing, complaints from a foreigner are quite another. This is especially true when it comes from U.S. citizens, not surprising given the long and complicated relationship between the two countries.

Food

Traditional Panamanian food relies heavily on starches and red meat, chicken, and pork. Green vegetables do not grow well in the tropics, so outside of better restaurants in the cities don't be surprised if fried plantain is as close as you'll come to a veggie side dish. Vegetarians will have a tough time finding a balanced meal

even in cosmopolitan Panama City. Their best bet is usually Chinese restaurants, which are found throughout the country.

Fish is excellent in Panama. The most common on the menu is also one of the most delicious: corvina, a delicately flavored saltwater fish. Restaurants often prepare it a dozen

Mexican food is catching on in Panama.

different ways, but usually simplest is best. Prepared well, *corvina a la plancha* (grilled corvina) is hard to beat. *Guabina* is similar to corvina; it tends to be found at the fancier restaurants.

Other seafood includes shrimp *(camarones)*, prawns *(langostinos)*, squid *(calamares)*, octopus *(pulpo)*, crab *(cangrejo)*, red snapper *(pargo rojo)*, and lobster *(langosta)*. Think twice about eating lobster in Panama since it's terribly overfished.

Ceviche in Panama is delicious. Traditionally it consists of raw corvina marinated in lime juice, peppers, and onions, which chemically "cook" the fish. It's increasingly common to find shrimp or octopus ceviche, or ceviche made from a combination of all three.

A staple of the Panamanian diet is yuca or manioc. (Don't confuse yuca with yucca, the desert plant.) It's a root vegetable prepared in a variety of ways. Most common is deep-fried yuca, which when done right is crispy and golden brown on the outside and chewy on the inside. *Carimañolas* are a kind of roll made from ground and boiled yuca that is generally stuffed with meat then deep fried.

Plantains *(plátanos)*, which are similar to bananas, are even more common. By the end of your trip you will probably have had more than your fill of *patacones,* which are green plantains cut crossways into discs, fried, pressed, and then fried again. These can be tasty when hot; they turn into concrete when cold. Ripe plantains are typically sliced lengthwise and then either fried or sprinkled with cinnamon and baked, or broiled with butter. Fried plantains are called *tajadas;* the baked or broiled plantain dish is known as *plátanos maduros* or *plátanos en tentación.*

Other typical treats include *empanadas,* a kind of turnover made with flour or corn pastry that is stuffed with spiced ground meat and fried; tamales, which are made from boiled ground corn stuffed with chicken or pork and spices, then wrapped in banana leaves and boiled; and tortillas, which in Panama are thick, fried corncakes often served with breakfast in the countryside.

Panama Beer

The Panamanian palate doesn't tend to favor lots of spices, and you may find some of your meals rather bland. But done well, even the simplest country fare can be delicious. Try *sancocho,* a thick and hearty soup usually made with chicken, yuca, and whatever vegetables are around. *Ropa vieja* ("old clothes") is also good; it consists of spiced shredded beef served over rice. *Arroz con pollo* (rice with chicken) is also a common dish. Food is spicier in parts of Caribbean Panama, where hot sauce and dishes made with coconut milk are sometimes available.

Outside of Panama City, the menu can get monotonous. Main dishes will typically involve beef (usually referred to as *"carne,"* though literally this just means "meat"), chicken *(pollo)*, and pork *(puerco)*. A good strategy to keep from getting jaded is to take advantage of the very good international restaurants in Panama City and save traditional fare for trips into the hinterland.

Panamanians tend to like hot lunches. Lunchtime traffic in Panama City can be almost as bad as rush hour, as the streets get jammed with drivers eager to go home or out to a restaurant for a hot meal. Even workers (and travelers) on a tight budget partake when they can, filling hole-in-the-wall restaurants called *fondas*, which serve big plates of *comida corriente*. This is the traditional Panamanian equivalent of fast food, generally consisting of a variety of local dishes *(comida criolla)* served from steam tables in a cafeteria setting. It's easy to fill up for less than US$2 at these places, which are often open for breakfast and dinner as well.

Tips for Travelers

WHAT TO TAKE

Plan to travel light, especially if travel plans call for domestic flights, where there's a severe **weight restriction on luggage.** Launderettes aren't hard to come by once clean clothes are exhausted.

Most parts of Panama are hot and humid year-round. Bring lots of **thin cotton or breathable, moisture-wicking synthetic clothing.** Keep in mind that dress in Panama is conservative.

It can cool off significantly in some regions of Panama, and air-conditioning can raise goose bumps in the lowland cities. A **light sweater or fleece** along with a **waterproof windbreaker or parka** is a useful combination. Consider taking along a **small umbrella** for use in town.

If you think you'll spend much time island-hopping, consider bringing a **life jacket.** These are often not standard equipment.

Consider bringing a **bedroll or light sleeping bag** even if you're not planning on doing serious camping. It can come in handy if you have to spend a night in a place without decent linens. And don't forget the **binoculars.**

OPPORTUNITIES FOR STUDY

The easiest way to study in Panama is through an exchange program through one's university back home. With the possible exception of casual, short-term programs, visiting students must travel with a special visa. Student visas are a kind of temporary visitor visa, with many of the same requirements as other visas (HIV test, criminal record report, medical certificate of good health, letter of sponsorship, etc.). Applicants must also show proof of acceptance into the academic program and evidence of "economic solvency." The process generally requires a lawyer, but presumably the academic institution will help with the process.

For several decades **Florida State University** has had a satellite program in Panama (tel. 314-0367, http://panama.fsu. edu/) that draws students from Latin America, the United States, and Canada. Instruction is in English. Students can enroll in bachelor's and associate's degree programs in environmental studies, international affairs, Latin American and Caribbean studies, computer science, information studies, and the social sciences, offered in collaboration with the **Ciudad del Saber** (City of Knowledge) at Clayton. FSU Panama now occupies what was once the campus of Canal Zone College, a community college at the foot of the Bridge of the Americas near the Pacific entrance to the Panama Canal. Note: Don't confuse this program with the FSU campus in Panama City, Florida.

The **Smithsonian Tropical Research Institute** (STRI) coordinates a variety of short-term and long-term fellowships for undergraduate, graduate, and postdoctoral students that are offered either through STRI itself or by the Smithsonian Institution. Information on STRI fellowships is available through the Smithsonian Tropical Research Institute, Office of Education (www.stri.org). For information on Smithsonian Institution fellowships in Panama, contact the Smithsonian Institution's Office of Research Training and Services in Washington, D.C. (www.si.edu).

The **Ciudad del Saber** (City of Knowledge, www.cdspanama.org) in Clayton hosts a variety of academic programs in a number of disciplines.

Panama has several universities, the most prominent of which is the **Universidad de Panamá** (tel. 523-5000, www.up.ac.pa), opened in 1935, which offers a wide array of degree programs. Through its main campus in Panama City and extension programs around the country, it has about 74,000 students. Instruction is in Spanish. Foreigners interested in attending must apply through the university's Secretario General three months before the start of term.

A Florida-based nonprofit called the **Institute for Tropical Ecology and Conservation** (ITEC, U.S. tel. 352/367-9128, www.itec-edu.org) has a biological field station in Bocas del Toro.

VOLUNTEER OPPORTUNITIES

Those interested in doing volunteer work in Panama will most likely have to come up with a scheme of their own. Few formal volunteer programs exist as of yet. The best way to start is to find a place or a cause one is interested in and then pitch a volunteer plan to the director, highlighting your skills. Many will be happy for the free labor.

The **Canopy Tower** (tel. 264-5720, U.S. toll-free tel. 800/930-3397, www.canopy-tower.com) accepts volunteers willing to work at the tower in exchange for room, board, and a stipend of about US$400 a month. Volunteers are expected to take on a full range

---

TIPS FOR RESPONSIBLE TRAVEL

An overseas trip is supposed to be fun, not an exercise in political consciousness. But visitors will get more out of Panama, and help keep it an enjoyable destination for others, if they make at least some effort to get to know the place and how their actions may affect it.

Start by reading up on the fascinating history of Panama, which for hundreds of years has earned its reputation as the "crossroads of the world," and by learning a bit about its flora and fauna.

SOUVENIRS

It would be nice to think it goes without saying that buying souvenirs made from the body parts of endangered animals – jaguar teeth, tortoiseshell jewelry – is a big no-no. If not, remember that possessing these products is a serious crime in Panama, punishable by fines and jail time. Trafficking in *vida silvestre* (wildlife) is punishable by six months to two years in jail. Note this includes *all* animals found in the wild, not just endangered species. The same thing goes for possession of pre-Columbian pottery and other historic artifacts. Collecting these is known as *huaquería* (roughly, "grave robbing") and is illegal. Obviously, it's also ille-gal to eat endangered animals; do not partake of tortoise eggs or the like. Do not buy jewelry made from coral, which is being severely damaged in Panama. Leave intact shells on the beach; they're potential homes for a variety of sea creatures.

FOOD

Think about what you eat in Panama. Lobster, for instance, has been terribly over-harvested in the San Blas Islands (Kuna Yala). You'll be tempted to try one on the islands, but bear in mind that what was once a subsistence food for the Kuna is now in danger of extinction, which would have serious consequences for the Kuna and their environment. And it's not just in the San Blas you should consider this: Poor lobster divers sell their catch to fancy restaurants in Panama City. If nothing else, avoid lobster during the mating season, which runs March–July. Consider that a female lobster carries thousands of eggs, but divers scoop up the expectant moms right along with the other lobsters. It'd be a shame if your dinner meant the end of a whole generation of baby lobsters.

Among the many other reasons not to eat

of responsibilities at the tower. Management prefers volunteers willing to stay at least three months. Those interested should send an email to the tower's owner, Raúl Arias de Para, at birding@canopytower.com. He speaks fluent English.

Los Quetzales Lodge and Spa (tel. 771-2182 or 771-2291, fax 771-2226, www.losquetzales.com) sometimes uses volunteers to help run the hotel. Panama City hostels and the **Purple House Hostel** (Calle C Sur and Avenida 6 Oeste, 774-4059, www.purplehousehostel.com) in David are other possibilities. Those interested can also try one of the universities or research institutes.

The environmental nonprofit **ANCON** (tel. 314-0052, www.ancon.org) sometimes takes volunteers as well. The best approach is to send

ANCON a letter or email detailing skills and saying when you'd like to come down and how long you'd like to stay. Try to be as specific as possible about what you can contribute.

The **Spanish by the Sea** (tel. 757-9518, www.spanishbythesea.com) program in Bocas del Toro can sometimes organize volunteer work. Possibilities include a sea-turtle conservation project.

WOMEN TRAVELING ALONE

This is a tough one. Women who travel alone in Panama are likely to be safer than in many other countries, but it's still not the safest way to go. On the one hand, it's unusual for any traveler to face serious harassment in Panama. It's an easygoing, live-and-let-live kind of place. On the other hand, it is a macho country, and

---

beef is the fact that cattle ranching is not at all sustainable in Panama. It has led to massive deforestation and the destruction of entire habitats. Carnivores should cut down in Panama.

"ECO" ACTIVITIES AND RESORTS

Personal recreational watercraft (Jet Skis and the like) panic marine life, shatter the tranquility of other beachgoers, and pollute the environment. Resist the temptation to go for a spin.

Be skeptical of tour operators and hotels that advertise themselves as eco-conscious. Ask them exactly what they mean by that, and what kind of environmentally conscious services they offer.

Because hotels and tour operators know that "eco" can spell money for them, they have an incentive to exaggerate just how ecologically conscious their operations are. This has begun to happen in Panama, with just about any place that has a view labeling itself an "eco-resort" no matter how many resources it gobbles. To help readers make informed decisions about who to go with, this book attempts to highlight the features of a place or an operation likely

to appeal to a low-impact tourist (e.g., small-scale, locally-owned hotels that tread lightly on their surroundings) as well as those features that may be off-putting (e.g., a private zoo on the property).

Environmentally sensitive tourism is so new to Panama it's hard for tourists to be entirely pure about where they stay and how they travel. Probably the most useful thing to do is to seek out those that are on the right track, and through our own actions to encourage those qualities we like and discourage those we don't. Most of the best operations are owned and run by intelligent businesspeople who take great pride in what they're trying to accomplish. Don't be afraid to give them feedback, including criticisms. They're all still trying to figure out just what it is low-impact tourists want, and they'll likely be eager to hear your comments.

Nature tourists to Panama in the next few years may well play a critical role in shaping the future of Panamanian tourism. If entrepreneurs see a demand for responsible, low-impact nature travel, and they are shown that it can pay, in a few years there may be more simple eco-lodges and fewer sprawling five-star resorts.

women are subject to lots of cat-calling, honking horns, smooching noises, and other obnoxious behavior from dudes on the street. Generally, that's as aggressive at it gets, but it can certainly make women who travel alone feel unsafe, sometimes with good reason.

Women are most likely to encounter this nonsense in Panama City. Some women have also reported unwanted attention in Bocas del Toro and Boquete, where a sudden influx of foreign tourists has collided with provincial attitudes. A woman friend was practically stalked in Bocas by a few eager guys a couple years back, so much so she cut her visit short. More recently, there have been reports of attempted rapes in Bocas. In one case, a woman woke up to find men she'd met earlier had gotten into her room; screams scared them off. Rape is punishable by 1–5 years in jail, but convictions are rare.

Common sense can reduce the risk of ugly encounters. Never tell a casual acquaintance the name of your hotel, and certainly not your room number. Women who travel alone should be especially alert in Bocas and Panama City. The Calidonia and Casco Viejo neighborhoods of Panama City are not the best places for women traveling on their own.

Panamanian women who get bothered on the street tend to ignore the culprits completely. That's probably the best tack to try at first. Try not to lose your cool. Knowing at least some Spanish and appearing confident and at home can also help diffuse unpleasant encounters. Befriend fellow visitors and travel in groups if possible. Cabs are probably safer than walking at night, but avoid taking them alone. Women who go to bars and discos alone are often assumed to be looking for sex, and there will be no shortage of guys eager to help them find it. Especially outside sophisticated circles in Panama City, the same goes for a woman who agrees to visit a man's home or allows him into her room late at night.

GAY AND LESBIAN TRAVELERS

Panama is a quite tolerant and open-minded place for a predominantly Roman Catholic Latin American country. I've yet to hear a story, for instance, about a police raid on a gay club. However, gays and lesbians are still for the most part closeted. Same-sex affection on the streets would cause a sensation at best, an ugly encounter at worst. Homosexuality is not illegal in Panama, but neither is it legally protected.

Foreigner status helps protect gay and lesbian travelers from harassment. Gay and lesbian acquaintances in Panama say they've never felt threatened, but it's hard to know how much of this is just the natural immunity that comes from having power in a society that's sharply divided between the haves and have-nots. Poorer gays do sometimes get beaten and harassed, and they have little protection or legal recourse.

In 2001, after a three-year battle, Panama gave legal recognition to its first gay and lesbian organization, **La Asociación de Hombres y Mujeres Nuevos de Panamá** (AHMNP, The Association of New Men and Women of Panama, tel. 264-2670, www.ahmnpanama. org). AHMNP advocates the rights of "sexual minorities," including gays, lesbians, bisexuals, and transgendered people. It also aims to provide education about preventing sexually transmitted diseases and support for those infected with HIV.

In 2007, activists from 14 countries in the Americas met in Panama for a conference that ran parallel to a meeting of the general assembly of the Organization of American States (OAS). The meeting was meant to encourage greater participation of gays, lesbians, and other sexual minorities in the OAS. Among the speakers was Aristides Royo, a former president of Panama and the country's chief representative to the OAS.

The visibility of gays and lesbians in popular culture is also increasing. Local soap operas, enormously popular in Panama, have introduced gay characters who are portrayed in a positive light, and a few years back one of the hosts of a popular TV chat program, *La Cocoa,* was an openly gay man. Gays have also been allowed to enter floats in Panama's Carnaval celebration in recent years, complete with a Carnaval queen in drag. However, Panama was not quite ready for this: Cross-dressing in Carnaval parades has now been banned throughout the country on "moral grounds." In 2008, gay groups withdrew from the parades in protest.

For more information on international gay rights issues, check out the International Gay and Lesbian Human Rights Commission (www.iglhrc.org), the International Lesbian and Gay Association (www.ilga.org), and http://gaynewswatch.com. Information on gay-run and gay-friendly accommodations can be found at www.purpleroofs.com. None of these groups has much information on Panama, however.

Information on parties, clubs, and events in Panama aimed at the GLBT crowd is available at www.farraurbana.com.

ACCESSIBILITY FOR TRAVELERS WITH DISABILITIES

Travelers with disabilities will not find Panama an easy country to maneuver around. Accessibility and rights for people with disabilities are new concepts in Panama.

In 1999, Panama passed Ley 42 (Law 42), which guarantees equal opportunity for and makes it illegal to discriminate against people with disabilities in employment, education, services, transportation, health services, and so on. That same year, Panama signed the Organization of American States' Inter-American Convention on the Elimination of all Forms of Discrimination Against Persons with Disabilities.

However, Panama has been slow to enforce compliance with either agreement and other disability-rights laws on the books.

Even in the fanciest hotels and restaurants it's still unusual to encounter ramps, handrails, and other accommodations for people with disabilities. Ley 42 requires making both public and private buildings accessible, but advocacy groups estimate that to date only about 5 percent of public buildings meet the requirements.

Awareness of disability issues, at least, improved under the Martín Torrijos administration (2004–2009). He and his wife, Vivian Fernández de Torrijos, have a daughter with disabilities. The first lady made the rights of people with disabilities one of her priorities.

In recent years the government has installed ramps and "mainstreamed" some kids in public schools, but facilities are still inadequate. By law, at least 2 percent of a company's employees must be people with disabilities, but the actual number is nowhere near that, and those with disabilities tend to get paid less than nondisabled people doing the same job. The organization responsible for placing workers with disabilities held a job fair in 2007; 100 companies were invited, but only 8 showed up.

That same year, the government gave greater autonomy and a separate budget to the agency responsible for protecting the rights of people with disabilities, La Secretaría Nacional para la Integración de las Personas con Discapacidad (SENADIS, The National Secretariat for the Integration of People with Disabilities). Funding for disability programs has increased, but it is still modest compared with the need.

The modern infrastructure of Panama City makes it perhaps the easiest place for visitors with disabilities to get around. The abundant elevators and taxis help, though almost all taxis are rather cramped and there are no taxi services geared toward those with wheelchairs. Conditions quickly become difficult in the countryside, particularly in the Darién or any of the island groups, where paved roads disappear, transportation is often by small boat, and it can be somewhat challenging for just about anyone to get around.

Some information on accessible travel worldwide is available at www.access-able.com, though there are no Panama-specific tips.

SENIORS

Seniors are treated with deference and respect in Panama, where the old-fashioned honorifics *don* and *doña* are sometimes still used for venerable older people. Panamanian seniors and foreign residents are entitled to discounts as high as 50 percent on a whole range of services, but these are not available to visitors.

TRAVELING WITH CHILDREN

Panama is a child-friendly country. There are many young families in the country, so lodgings often include little playgrounds, child-oriented activities, and guest rooms with multiple beds.

Vaccination recommendations and other preventative-care measures are often different for small children than for adults. Visit the U.S. Centers for Disease Control's website (www.cdc.gov/travel) or ask your doctor for information.

Panama's warm weather and abundance of outdoor-recreation possibilities make the country a great place for kids. But parents need to be especially alert when traveling around Panama given the comparatively fewer safeguards for children than in more developed countries (missing handrails, sudden drop-offs, chaotic traffic, etc.).

Kids are welcome just about everywhere; only a few hotels and other establishments do not allow or at least discourage bringing children. These are usually ecolodges that don't want the wildlife disturbed or are concerned about children falling off boardwalks into the water. I do not recommend taking small children to most parts of the Darién or to Kuna Yala (San Blas Islands) because of the rugged conditions and possible dangers from wildlife. Rats, for instance, are a fact of life in the San Blas Islands, and while the risk of a bite is small, rustling in the rafters has been known to shatter more than one worried parent's rest.

Since 1995 Panama City has had a nighttime curfew for those under age 18. Unattended minors are supposed to be off the streets 8 P.M.–6 A.M. Sunday–Thursday and 11 P.M.–6 A.M. Friday–Saturday. Exceptions are made for students and young workers, but only with proper documentation. The curfew is aimed at residents, but theoretically foreign minors could be stopped by the police if unaccompanied by a parent or legal guardian. Violators are taken to a police station until picked up by their parents, who are subject to a fine.

TRAVELING WITH PETS

Bringing a pet to Panama is a bad idea unless one is planning a lengthy or permanent stay. Dogs and cats must be quarantined for 30 days, though a recent law allows for home quarantine in lieu of a stay in a kennel. Travelers on the road will obviously not be able to provide a home in which to quarantine the pets, so kenneling at the quarantine office may be the only option. There is also considerable paperwork involved that may require the help of a lawyer or at least a relocation-service agent. (José Saenz—based in Panama City, cell 6614-7811, tel./fax 399-4003 or 251-0698, www.goldenfrog.net— provides such a service.) The process can't be started any sooner than 10 days before the pets are shipped, because all documents must be as up-to-date as possible. Leaving the country with a pet requires a whole other round of permissions. Requirements are more stringent for birds and other animals. Contact a Panamanian consulate for current requirements.

Health and Safety

It's extremely unlikely you'll contract a serious disease in Panama. Health conditions are generally good, especially for a developing nation. For instance, the country has not had a single report of polio since 1972, yellow fever since 1974, diphtheria since 1981, or cholera since 1993. Panama City and the former Canal Zone are particularly safe.

However, those planning to spend a considerable amount of time in rural areas, especially if camping, can do several things to stay healthy.

The most important of these is to avoid insect bites as much as possible. Always use insect repellent in the countryside, particularly in the evenings and early mornings. Sleep in screened-in rooms or use mosquito netting. Wearing long-sleeved shirts and long pants will also reduce insect bites. If you're only planning to spend a few days in these areas and know you'll be sleeping under mosquito nets or in screened-in rooms, you may not want to fool with malaria prophylaxis.

For current information on health conditions in Panama, contact the Centers for Disease Control in Atlanta, Georgia (U.S. tel. 877/394-8747, www.cdc.gov/travel).

BEFORE YOU GO

Make preparations for any needed vaccinations or antimalarial medication as far ahead of time as possible. Some vaccinations can't be administered at the same time, and some antimalaria meds need to be started a week or two before traveling.

The information that follows is meant to give travelers general guidelines on staying healthy in Panama. It's drawn from a number of public-health sources, but it's not intended as medical advice and is certainly no substitute for profession medical care in case of emergency. Do not attempt to diagnose or treat yourself for any illness.

Vaccinations and Other Prophylaxis

Note that many physicians unfamiliar with Panama except for a vague and dated notion

that the place is synonymous with "tropical disease" go overboard in prescribing all kinds of unneeded preventative measures. Many a visitor who plans only to visit Panama City and the Panama Canal area comes loaded with expensive antimalaria medications that serve no purpose other than to amuse their fellow travelers and hosts. Some travelers also worry about official warnings they see about disease risk in Bocas del Toro and Kuna Yala. These warnings are generally based on remote areas of the mainland, not the islands that tourists visit.

What kind of precautions to take depends largely on where travelers plan to go and what they plan to do. Those who will spend most of their time in Panama City and the Panama Canal area probably do not need more than minimal protection. Those planning a trek across the Darién may want every defense against disease they can find.

Health conditions and vaccination recommendations can change quickly, so check current requirements and advisories through the CDC (www.cdc.gov/travel) or your doctor.

All visitors should make sure their routine immunizations are up to date, especially against measles-mumps-rubella and tetanus-diphtheria. The incidence of these diseases in Panama is low to nonexistent, but the CDC recommends everyone stay current on their immunizations against them, including nontravelers.

The CDC also recommends that travelers to Central America be vaccinated against hepatitis A and, in some cases, hepatitis B. A rabies vaccination is recommended for those who expect to spend a lot of time outdoors, particularly in rural areas. The CDC suggests typhoid fever vaccinations for those traveling in Central America, though the chance of contracting it in Panama seems remote.

Those planning to travel to rural parts of Panama, especially near the Costa Rican or Colombian border, should probably be vaccinated against yellow fever and may want to consider antimalaria medication.

There is a far greater risk of someone bringing yellow fever to Panama than of catching it there (the last known case in Panama was in 1974). Until recently, Panama required proof of a current yellow-fever vaccinations from travelers entering the country from anyplace where yellow fever is endemic. This regulation comes and goes, so it's probably a good idea to have the vaccination if coming from an endemic area, just in case. This means tropical South America, including Colombia, and most of sub-Saharan Africa. Check the CDC website for current information and for a list of U.S. clinics that administer the vaccinations.

Beware: Panamanian authorities have been known to vaccinate those arriving from infected countries at the airport if the traveler cannot present a yellow-fever certificate. Better to take care of this before leaving home. Be sure to bring a properly stamped and signed international yellow-fever certificate, which the person administering the vaccine should give you.

There is no vaccine for malaria, but there are several kinds of antimalarial drugs meant to be taken daily or weekly before, during, and after travel to an endemic area.

Visitors to most parts of Panama should not need to take them. However, outside of Panama City and the area around the former Canal Zone there is a slight risk of contracting malaria. The risk is greatest in the Darién and the Comarca de Kuna Yala (San Blas Islands and mainland). The highest-risk areas west of the Panama Canal are the rural parts of Bocas del Toro and Veraguas provinces.

Many travelers even to these areas don't take antimalarial medication unless they plan to spend a fair amount of time in remote villages or sleep somewhere that doesn't have screened-in rooms. The true risk is almost impossible to measure, so think about the kind of traveling you want to do and discuss options with your physician.

There is a chloroquine-resistant strain of malaria in the Darién and Kuna Yala. Mefloquine, doxycycline, or atovaquone/proguanil is recommended for those planning to spend a significant amount of time in these regions. Chloroquine is considered effective against any strains found west of the Panama Canal.

These medications go by an assortment of brand names, which can cause confusion. Some antimalarial medications have serious side effects and are not recommended for everyone (pregnant or breast-feeding women should avoid them). They can also make one more susceptible to sunburn. Some of the contraindications are unusual—mefloquine, for instance, is not recommended for those with a history of depression—so do some research and quiz your doctor carefully. To be effective, travelers must continue to take the medications anywhere from a week to a month after returning home.

INSECTS AND ARACHNIDS

Insects generally come second (after snakes) in the list of creatures tropical neophytes worry about. But most parts of Panama are not nearly as buggy as one might think, and certainly can't compare to, say, the mosquito swarms of an Alaskan summer.

Mosquito populations are kept down around populated areas because of the potential risk of mosquito-borne diseases. Still, mosquitoes can be a nuisance in certain places, especially in the rainy season. Dusk and dawn tend to be active times. Insect repellent and long-sleeved shirts and pants are effective at keeping mosquitoes at bay. Sleep in tents or screened-in rooms to avoid bites at night.

Sand flies (a.k.a. sand fleas or no-see-ums) are locally known as *chitras* and can be a real irritation. They love to bite feet and ankles and can cause itching for hours. To avoid infection, try not to scratch. Mosquito repellent helps. They tend to like beach spots without breezes, especially near mangroves, and dine in force in the early evenings. They can be a nuisance in Boca Brava, parts of Bocas del Toro (there's actually a Sand Fly Bay off Isla Colón), and Kuna Yala. They're worse during the rainy season; dry-season breezes keep them at bay.

Some claim *chitras* like pale skin, so consider working on a leg tan. Keeping feet covered with shoes and socks provides some protection. Anti-inflammatory and itch-relieving creams, such as hydrocortisone, can help with the irritation after bites. Eurax is locally popular for the itching, as is coconut oil. I've found the Pure Tree Natural Body Products (cell 6607-8962 and 6570-8277, www.upinthehill.com) made in Bocas del Toro effective in controlling the itching. They also make a *chitra* repellent, but I haven't tried it yet. *Chitras* can spread leishmaniasis, so it's a good idea to minimize exposure as much as possible.

Chiggers are a type of parasitic mite that hikers can pick up wandering through a field or grassy area. They often climb up the hikers' legs and like to burrow into the skin around the elastic bands of underwear or pants. Once they latch on, they stay attached for days and cause their hosts to itch like crazy. Insect repellent on the clothes, especially around the legs and feet, can offer some protection. Experienced hikers often tuck their pants into their boots and seal them off with masking tape to keep the things out. Some also sprinkle powdered sulfur into their boots to ward them off.

In general, be careful where you put your hands and feet when hiking. Many plants have sharp spines and the like and may harbor aggressive ants, poisonous caterpillars, and other nasties.

There's a reasonable chance of coming across a scorpion, especially in rural and semirural areas. Except for small children the sting is rarely life-threatening, but it's quite painful. Ditto for some spider bites. To be on the safe side, shake out your shoes and clothes before putting them on. When I'm traveling in the countryside, I stuff my socks into my shoes before going to bed at night and shake them out in the morning. In the canal construction days, workers slept with their boots under their pillows. Tarantulas and other large spiders sometimes make an appearance, which is more startling than dangerous; if you leave them alone, they'll do likewise.

Panama has Africanized bees—the so-called "killer bees"—which can be aggressive and dangerous. Keep well away from any bees you come across. If you disturb them and they start chasing you, try to run through dense brush. They will have a hard time following. Do not jump into a body of water to escape them; they will wait for you to surface.

Stay out of the way of ants. Some, such as the bullet ant, have ferocious stings, and less-nasty ones can still swarm over an unsuspecting hiker remarkably quickly.

INSECT-BORNE DISEASES
Dengue Fever

Dengue fever is a viral infection that gets little press but is becoming an increasingly serious public health threat around the world, including the Americas. It's spread through a bite from infected mosquitoes, and so far the only way to prevent it is to keep mosquito populations down and avoid mosquito bites as much as possible. There is no vaccine against the disease and no specific medications to treat it, but anyone who suspects an infection should get medical attention immediately. It's a serious illness, and in some cases can be fatal if untreated.

The main carrier is the *Aedes aegypti,* the same mosquito responsible for yellow fever, but it is also carried by the *Aedes albopictus,* a resilient, adaptable mosquito colloquially known as the Asian tiger mosquito because of its coloration: black with white stripes.

Aedes aegypti is endemic to Panama, but *Aedes albopictus* originated in Asia and has only recently spread to other parts of the world, including the United States. It was not discovered in Panama until 2002.

The disease comes in two forms. Classic dengue fever is characterized by high fever, nausea, vomiting, headache, and pain in the back, joints, and eyes. Pain can be intense, which is how the disease earned the ominous nickname "breakbone fever." Symptoms are often milder for younger children. Recommended treatment includes pain medications, rest, and drinking lots of fluids under a doctor's care while the virus runs its course.

Dengue hemorrhagic fever (DHF) is a far more serious form of the disease. It can be fatal if not properly recognized and treated. With good medical care, however, the mortality rate is generally less than 1 percent. Symptoms include a fever that lasts 2–7 days, accompanied by symptoms that are easily confused with those of other illnesses, such as nausea, vomiting, headache, and stomach pain. This stage is followed by signs of hemorrhage, including a tendency to bruise easily, bleeding nose or gums, and sometimes internal bleeding. Without treatment, this stage can be followed by circulatory failure, shock, and death.

Both dengue fever and DHF are caused by four distinct but closely related viruses. All four now exist in Panama. Infection by one type provides no immunity against later infection by another type.

Dengue epidemics are becoming increasingly common in the Americas. In 1993 Panama had its first reported case of dengue in nearly 50 years. In 2007, there were more than 1,000 dengue cases, and 2 cases of DHF. (By way of comparison, Costa Rica reported more than 25,000 cases of dengue and 300 of DHF in 2007. The population of Costa Rica is about 4.1 million vs. 3.3 million for Panama.)

Dengue thrives in poorer urban areas, and by far the largest concentration of cases has occurred in the sprawling San Miguelito district on the outskirts of Panama City. But dengue is a risk anywhere mosquitoes are found. I was surprised during my last visit at the number of people in comfortable (though usually rural) surroundings I met who'd had a bout of dengue. Mosquito populations are kept down through removing or covering standing pools of water and through fumigation. Panamanian officials have been lax about this in recent years, but they have ramped up their sanitation and fumigation efforts recently. Anyone with uncovered water containers on their property can be fined.

Yellow Fever

Yellow fever was the most dreaded disease in Panama until a massive sanitation and public health program eliminated it from the isthmus in 1906. While it has never had a serious resurgence in Panama (the most recent known case was in 1974), the country has to be constantly on guard against the possibility. Panama provides a perfect home for the disease and its local vector, the *Aedes aegypti* mosquito. Relaxed sanitation standards helped the mosquito reestablish itself on the isthmus in 1985, which sparked a new public-health push to control it. So far, the mosquito has brought with it dengue fever but not yellow fever.

The biggest concern is that the disease will be brought to the country by foreign visitors from a neighboring country that still has the disease, such as Colombia, which experienced a yellow-fever outbreak in 2004 that killed several people.

Yellow fever symptoms typically come in two phases. The first is characterized by fever, intense muscle pain, nausea, headache, chills, and vomiting. For about 15 percent of sufferers, there is a drop-off in symptoms that is followed in a few days by a return of the fever, and sometimes jaundice (hence the name "yellow fever"), stomach cramps, vomiting, and hemorrhaging. About half of these latter patients die within 10–14 days after the onset of the first symptoms. There is no cure, but most people do survive a yellow-fever attack. Those who do are immune to the disease thereafter, which is a mild consolation. Seek medical help immediately at the first sign of symptoms.

Malaria

Malaria is a tenacious disease that has not been entirely eradicated either in Panama or most of the rest of the world where it's endemic. But it was drastically reduced during Panama Canal construction days as a result of the same sanitation program that eradicated yellow fever. It's been kept at bay ever since.

Chloroquine-resistant strains of the disease exist in eastern Panama, but any strain found west of the Panama Canal is not believed to have acquired immunity to this medication.

Symptoms of malaria usually do not appear

until at least a week after infection from the bite of an *Anopheles* mosquito. Flu-like symptoms such as fever, chills, headache, muscle pain, and fatigue are common. Malaria can also cause anemia and jaundice. Symptoms can be intense or quite mild. Those infected may not realize it for some time, which is dangerous. Malaria is a serious disease and potentially fatal if not treated quickly. The U.S. Centers for Disease Control urge any traveler to an endemic area to get medical care immediately at the first sign of fever or flu-like symptoms for a full year after returning home. Be sure to tell the doctor where you've been.

Leishmaniasis

Leishmaniasis is a parasitic disease spread by bites from infected sand flies. The type most commonly found in Latin America is known as cutaneous leishmaniasis, which is characterized by skin sores and is far less serious than visceral leishmaniasis, which attacks the internal organs but is found primarily in Brazil, Africa, and southern Asia.

There is no vaccine for leishmaniasis; the best way to avoid the small chance of contracting it in Panama is to reduce contact with sand flies as much as possible. The only travelers likely to be at risk in Panama are adventurous types who travel far off the beaten track.

Sores develop weeks or even months after the victim is bitten by an infected sand fly. The sores may be painless, and they may or may not scab over. Untreated sores can last from weeks to years and develop into prominent craters on the skin. Anyone who suspects an infection should see a tropical-medicine specialist for diagnosis and treatment.

American Trypanosomiasis (Chagas' Disease)

Chagas' disease is a parasitic infection carried by triatomine bugs (blood-sucking insects sometimes known as the assassin, cone nose, or kissing bug). The parasite, *Trypanosoma cruzi,* often produces a small sore at the point where it enters the body. If this happens around the eye, the eyelid may become swollen. Other symptoms can include a fever and swollen lymph nodes, but infection can be asymptomatic. There is no vaccine against the disease. Those who suspect they might be infected should see a tropical-medicine specialist for diagnosis and treatment. Chronic infections can cause damage to the heart and intestines and even death.

It's rare for travelers to contract Chagas' disease, in Panama or anywhere else. The bugs tend to infest ramshackle buildings made of palm thatch, mud, or adobe, especially those with lots of nooks and crannies in the walls and roof. The disease can also be spread through transfusions of blood that has not been screened for the parasite.

Panama has found about 500 cases of Chagas' disease in the entire country in the last 25 years, and the Pan American Health Organization has noted a marked decline in the presence of the disease since 1993. Central Panama seems more vulnerable to the disease than other parts of the country.

RABIES

The chance of catching rabies is remote, but the consequences of doing so are extreme. There is no cure for rabies, and it's fatal. Only one person in history has ever recovered from a full-blown case of rabies: a girl who was bitten by a bat in the rural United States in late 2004 and treated with a bold experimental technique that could easily have killed her.

Rabies is almost always transmitted by an animal bite. Any mammal can be a carrier, but in Central America one should be particularly wary of vampire bats, feral or aggressive dogs and cats, and monkeys.

In Panama, most cases of rabies in humans are caused by bat bites. In 2002, a 69-year-old woman and her daughter, residents of the community of San Juan Demóstenes Arosemena in Colón province, died from rabies after being bitten by a vampire bat. The last confirmed rabies cases before that occurred in 1995, again from bat bites.

The CDC recommends rabies vaccines

for travelers to Latin America who expect to spend considerable time outdoors in rural areas at night or in the evening, even if the trip is brief. This is especially true for those who like to explore caves.

Anyone bitten or scratched by an animal should immediately wash the wound with plenty of soap and water and iodine, if available. Don't panic: Most suspect mammals, even violent ones, do *not* have rabies. The animal should be captured—if possible to do so without risking further attacks—and taken to a medical center for testing. Those potentially exposed to rabies need a series of shots, usually given over the course of a month. This is true even if the victim has had a pre-exposure rabies vaccine. The recommended injections these days are no more painful than flu shots. Prompt treatment after exposure can nearly always prevent rabies infection.

Most people bitten by vampire bats do not realize it at the time. The bat usually approaches its victims at night, while they're sleeping (yes, just like in all those B movies). It lands next to the victim and waddles over to a vulnerable spot. The bat drools onto the site before biting it. The saliva contains an anesthetic and an anticoagulant that lets the bat bite its victim without waking it and lap up the blood that trickles steadily out. Human victims generally don't discover they've been bitten until the next morning, when they find a clump of dried blood near the wound site.

Disgusting? You bet. That's why I recommend travelers sleep only in a tent or screened-in room in rural areas, including beaches and forests. This is especially true around cattle, a favorite blood supply for vampire bats.

"Endemic zones" for rabies in Panama include Chilibre, eastern Panama province, La Chorrera, the Darién, the district of David in western Panama, and various spots along the Interamericana.

Symptoms of rabies include paralysis, spasms of the swallowing muscles in the presence of water (hydrophobia), delirium, and convulsions, followed by coma and death.

STOMACH AILMENTS

Gastrointestinal complaints such as dysentery, giardia, E. coli infections, and even so-called "traveler's diarrhea" are far less common among travelers to Panama than in most parts of Latin America.

It's safe to drink water out of the tap almost everywhere in the country. The destination chapters alert you to the few places where that still isn't a good idea, such as some parts of the Darién and Bocas del Toro. Never drink untreated water from a stream or lake, no matter how pristine it looks.

Hygiene standards in restaurants tend to be fairly high, particularly in Panama City. You're unlikely to get so much as a stomachache. But if a place looks dirty or unpopular, you're probably better off going elsewhere. Street-vendor fare is somewhat riskier. Make sure whatever you munch has just been fried at high temperature. It's not a good idea to eat ice cream and other milk- or water-based sweets sold by street vendors.

The CDC warns that certain fish and shellfish served in tropical countries can contain biotoxins even when well cooked. Barracuda has the highest level of these toxins and should always be avoided. Other possibilities include red snapper and sea bass. I've never heard of anyone in Panama being poisoned by these delicious fish, but if you experience stomach distress accompanied by a sudden change of temperature, weakness, or other unusual symptoms after eating fish, get medical help.

Mild traveler's diarrhea doesn't usually need to be treated with anything more than fluids, rest, and a modest diet of bland foods. Anything more serious, such as bacterial or amoebic dysentery, needs to be treated with drugs and requires a visit to the doctor.

HANTAVIRUS

There was an outbreak of hantavirus pulmonary syndrome in Las Tablas and Guararé in Los Santos province in late 1999 and early 2000 that infected a dozen people and left three dead. It forced the cancellation of the Carnaval celebration in Las Tablas that year. Panama's biggest Carnaval is held in Las

Tablas, and the cancellation was a major blow to the local economy.

Hantavirus is an infectious disease most often spread through the inhalation of particles from the feces, urine, or saliva of infected rodents. However, person-to-person infection is also possible. The disease is characterized by fever, headache, and muscle pain followed by hypotension, shock, difficulty breathing, and pulmonary edema (fluid in the lungs). It's a serious disease and the fatality rate can be above 50 percent. There is no treatment, cure, or vaccine. However, getting health care immediately, especially oxygen therapy, greatly increases one's chance of recovery. Anyone who has been around rodents and experiences shortness of breath and fever should tell a doctor immediately.

Hantavirus was first discovered in the Four Corners region of the western United States in 1993, and before the Las Tablas outbreak it had not been diagnosed in Central America. A major public-health push, in coordination with the U.S. Centers for Disease Control, appears to have largely contained the disease so far, though officials remain vigilant about the possibility of a major flare-up, especially around Carnaval time. There have been a handful of cases both on and outside the Azuero in the years since the initial outbreak. In 2007, five people nationwide were diagnosed with the virus, two of whom died.

The chance of contracting hantavirus is exceedingly low, especially for those who avoid contact with rodents. Mice and rats infest some lodgings in the Panamanian countryside, especially the cheaper places. It's probably worth splurging for better digs in Los Santos province, since that's where the disease erupted in Panama. Rats are a fact of life in Kuna Yala, unfortunately, and it's not unusual to hear them rustling in the rafters of tourist huts or running along the beach at night. Clean up messes and keep all food packed away at night.

SEXUALLY TRANSMITTED DISEASES

Estimates of the number of people living with HIV in Panama range from 17,000 to more than 30,000. Given the country's small population, that makes it the third-highest rate in Central America. HIV in Panama is more often transmitted through heterosexual than homosexual sex. According to a United Nations agency in Panama, HIV rates have skyrocketed in recent years.

The sexually adventurous should also remember that other STDs are serious and not necessarily easily treatable. An antibiotic-resistant strain of gonorrhea, for instance, is on the rise around the world. Be sure to get a hepatitis B vaccination and always use condoms and other safer-sex methods.

OTHER DISEASES

Panama has seen flare-ups of viral meningitis, pertussis (whooping cough), and tuberculosis in recent years, but travelers are at little risk of contracting them.

SUN

Remember that Panama is just 8 degrees north of the equator, and it's easy to get sunburned amazingly fast. Pale northerners have been known to get a nasty sunburn after just a half hour out in the noonday sun. Try to stay in the shade noon–3 P.M. Don't be fooled by mild or cloudy days. Even if you don't feel hot, ultraviolet rays are frying you. Always wear sunscreen. Be especially careful when out on the water, which reflects sun rays like a mirror. (Ever had a chin burn?) Sunglasses and a hat are also a good idea. Drink lots of water to avoid dehydration even when it feels humid.

OCEAN DANGERS

A rip current, sometimes erroneously referred to as an "undertow," is created when surf gets trapped on its way back out to sea, often by a sandbar. Pressure builds up until a concentrated stream of water rips a hole in the sandbar and water surges back out in a narrow channel, sometimes at impressive speed. It's similar in effect to pulling the plug on a bathroom drain.

Be on the lookout for patches of muddy,

dark, or disturbed water, which can indicate a rip. If you feel yourself being pulled out to sea, don't panic and don't try to fight against the current—it's stronger than you are. Instead, swim with the current but try to veer off at a 45-degree angle to it. Contrary to popular belief, rip currents don't drag swimmers under or sweep them out to sea. They are typically short and narrow and swimmers should be able to swim out of the channel fairly quickly. Tired or poor swimmers should just float with the current until it weakens, then swim parallel to shore to escape it. Stay calm and conserve your strength. Once you escape the rip current, swim back to shore.

Panamanians often prefer to bathe along stretches of beach with muddy sand and little surf, knowing from experience how powerful those majestic, rolling waves on the picture postcard beaches can be. Waves can get enormous on some of Panama's beaches and give swimmers a real pounding. Use common sense and don't wade in past your shins when the surf is high, and look out for hidden rocks and reefs.

Shark attacks are highly unlikely, particularly in the Caribbean. The Pacific sea snake is one of the most toxic creatures in the world, but the chances of coming across one are slim—I've only ever seen one in all my years of swimming in Panama, and it was dead, washed up on the shore. Barracudas may be scary-looking, but they're not generally aggressive toward humans. However, do not wear shiny jewelry while swimming or diving. The flash of the sun off jewelry looks to a barracuda like the scales of a fish, and they may dart in the direction of it.

Look out for sea urchins and fire coral, and never touch any other kind of coral; it'll scrape you up and cause serious damage to the coral. Shuffle your feet on entering or exiting the water to avoid stepping on a hidden ray.

HYPOTHERMIA

The chance of contracting hypothermia in a tropical country such as Panama may seem slim, but it can get quite chilly in the highlands, even in the Darién, something not all travelers are prepared for. Do not go hiking in the highlands, particularly around Volcán Barú, in just shorts and a t-shirt. It can get down to freezing at the top of Barú even when it's sweltering hot far down the volcano. Bring warm, waterproof clothing to change into if it gets wet and chilly, which it often does.

Hypothermia is caused by a drop in the body's core temperature, so it's possible to become hypothermic even in milder conditions. To avoid hypothermia, stay dry, dress warmly, avoid alcohol and rapid changes of temperature, and drink lots of water.

Early warning signs of hypothermia include loss of coordination, inability to concentrate, and involuntary shivering. If the afflicted person continues to shiver even when bundled up, the hypothermia is more serious.

WILD ANIMALS

Almost every hiker new to the tropics worries about snakes. As has been mentioned several times throughout the book, it's rare to come across a snake while hiking and extremely rare to be bothered by one. The chances of coming across one near any population center are even smaller, partly because Panamanians are aggressive about exterminating snakes in their midst. However, be cautious around leaf and trash piles even in the cities, just in case.

There are several things hikers can do to make it even less likely they'll be bothered by a slithering critter.

First, be careful stepping over tree falls, which attract snakes (not to mention stinging insects). Also be careful around piles of dried leaves. Before gathering any to start a fire, shuffle boot-clad feet through them.

This should go without saying, but don't play with snakes in the tropics. Some people seem irresistibly drawn to disturbing the creatures, which usually just want to be left alone. A European tourist I was hiking with in the Darién once tried to use his walking stick to prod a baby fer-de-lance we came across. The fer-de-lance is a deadly pit viper, and even the babies can be lethal. They can also be extremely aggressive and quick when disturbed. The guide and I managed to save the guy from his foolish, possibly suicidal, curiosity.

In the extremely unlikely event of being bitten, try not to panic. All that accomplishes is to increase one's heart rate and pump any injected venom faster through one's system. Poisonous snakes don't always inject venom when they strike. Obviously, get to the nearest hospital as soon as possible. If possible without risking further bites, kill the snake and take it with you to be identified. Do not try slashing at the wound and sucking out the poison, as usually this is ineffective and can actually make things worse. Keep the site of the wound below the heart and head if possible.

Do not feed, tease, or get too close to monkeys. Some can be aggressive if they feel threatened and will fling feces, bite, or otherwise attack. If bitten by a monkey, get medical help immediately. They can carry rabies and other nasty diseases.

Peccaries, a kind of wild pig, are a concern in the more remote forests, particularly in the Darién. Because their natural predator, the jaguar, has been hunted to near extinction, peccary populations have exploded in some areas. They sometimes descend on a spot by the hundreds and tear everything up. They can run surprisingly fast and have fearsomely sharp teeth. Those unlucky enough to get in the path of a herd should climb the nearest tall tree and stay there until they move on.

TRAFFIC ACCIDENTS

Traffic accidents pose by far the greatest hazard for visitors to Panama. Traffic in Panama tends to be chaotic, road conditions poor, and enforcement of driving laws lax. About one person a day is killed on the roads, which is a lot for a country of 3.3 million people, many of whom don't have cars. Be alert at all times on the road, and if you're a passenger don't be shy about asking a speeding driver to slow down.

If you're involved in an accident, do not move the cars—it's against the law. Stay on the scene until the *tránsito* (transit police) arrive. If someone is injured or it's otherwise an emergency, call the police emergency number (104) or the fire department (103). Panama has been gradually rolling out an ambulance dispatch service (911) in urban areas. Once the *tránsito* arrive they'll fill out a report that will include your description of the accident. Be fully cooperative and polite. Contact your insurance company or the car-rental agency as soon as possible.

Panamanian attitudes toward safety in general tend to be far more relaxed than those in, say, Northern Europe and North America. Accidents, including traffic accidents, are the second leading cause of death in Panama, after cancer.

LOCAL DOCTORS, CLINICS, AND HOSPITALS

Panama has world-class medical facilities and doctors, many of whom were trained in the United States and speak English. Even those without medical insurance can receive good care for far less than it would cost them in the United States. It's possible to get a checkup from, say, a specialist trained at Johns Hopkins for about US$35.

The best medical facilities are in Panama City. The hospitals in David also have a good reputation.

Note: U.S. Medicare does not cover medical care outside the United States.

Condoms and other nonprescription means of birth control are available at pharmacies. To avoid a visit to a local doctor, those taking birth-control pills should bring a sufficient supply to last while visiting Panama.

Centros de salud (health centers) and small rural hospitals are scattered throughout the country, though they can be poorly staffed and equipped. Serious medical problems should be treated in Panama City if at all possible. Those planning adventurous travel in remote spots may want to consider buying travel insurance that includes emergency evacuation provisions. I strongly advise all travelers to buy at least basic travel insurance.

ILLEGAL DRUGS

Panama is famous for its marijuana (the "Panama Red" of hippie anthems) and notorious as a transshipment point for cocaine. Don't let that fool you into thinking the consumption of illegal drugs is treated casually in Panama. If you're caught you could very well find yourself spending years in a squalid, overcrowded prison.

Simple possession of even a small amount of marijuana or any other drug is punishable by a minimum of one year in prison. Those caught with more than a tiny bit of a drug are assumed to be trafficking in it, and punishment is correspondingly harsh. Anyone caught buying or selling drugs is looking at 5–10 years behind bars.

Dealers have been known to set up gullible tourists for a bust, sometimes in the hope of sharing a bribe with a corrupt cop. Resist all temptations to sample the local products. It's an extremely foolish risk to take.

CRIME

Panama is by and large a peaceful, mellow place despite its undeserved reputation as some sort of danger zone. You'll likely be safer in Panama City than you would in any city of comparable size back home. Violent crime against tourists and affluent Panamanians is still so unusual that when it does happen it's huge news and causes lots of local hand-wringing about the decline of Panamanian society.

Property theft and other kinds of nonviolent crime are the main concern for the haves, and even this is mainly a problem for those who live in the cities, not travelers.

However, violent crime is on the rise. Most of this is gang-on-gang or drug-related violence in areas few travelers visit. Extreme unemployment and poverty make Colón, historically Panama's second most important city, unsafe for any outsider. There's an excellent chance of getting mugged if you wander around here. Avoid that city altogether for the foreseeable future.

Even in Panama City, avoid the poorest neighborhoods, such as El Chorrillo and Curundu, and be alert in transitional ones, such as the historic Casco Viejo area.

Because of reports of robberies at the secluded Madden Dam (on Lago Alajuela), I do not recommend that travelers visit it even in groups. I have also heard the occasional unconfirmed report of robberies in the national parks around Panama City, but this does not yet appear to be a major problem. Just do not hike alone, which is never a good idea anyway.

Rural areas are generally quite safe, but do not leave valuables even in a locked car when going for a hike in remote spots.

As tourism increases, it's probably inevitable that scams and crimes against tourists will increase as well. More tourists are complaining of thefts from their rooms at both budget and luxury hotels, particularly in Panama City. In the last few years, hotels around the country have added in-room safes; use them. There are also reports of thefts from beaches while tourists are swimming or surfing. These generally occur at the more popular surfing spots, such as the north side of Bastimentos in Bocas del Toro. Again, this is not a major problem, at least not yet. Even the "scams" usually amount to being overcharged for a taxi ride or taken to a hotel one is not interested in. Be alert and use common sense when traveling in the relatively more touristed parts of Panama.

Money

Panama's currency is the balboa. The balboa's rate of exchange has always been tied to the dollar, with one dollar equal to one balboa. In fact, Panama does not print paper money, so the U.S. dollar is legal tender in Panama. Panamanian coins (1-, 5-, 10-, 25-, and 50-cent pieces) are the same size, weight, and color as the U.S. ones and are used interchangeably with them. The only difference is what is printed on the faces; except for the one-centavo coin and special-edition coins, heads is always a portrait of Balboa and tails is always the shield of Panama. The one-centavo coin has Urracá, a fierce indigenous chief who won many battles against the conquistadors. You may see prices quoted with either a "B/" or "$" before them. Both mean the same thing.

Despite Panama's status as a world banking capital, it's tough to exchange foreign currencies almost everywhere in Panama. Try to bring only dollars to Panama.

CHANGING MONEY

Those who can't avoid changing money in Panama have only a few options, and most are in Panama City. Changing money at the border is difficult to impossible except at Tocumen International Airport and Paso Canoa, on the Costa Rican border. Even there options are limited.

BANKS

Banks are generally open 8 A.M.–2 or 3 P.M. Monday–Friday and 9 A.M.–noon Saturday. ATMs are located throughout Panama and are by far the easiest way to access cash; look for red signs that read Sistema Clave. Some find service at the state-run Banco Nacional de Panamá (BNP) to be slower and more bureaucratic than at private banks, but BNP is sometimes the only option in more remote areas.

FINANCIAL SERVICES

Panama's extensive financial services sector is focused on offshore banking, not serving short-term visitors. Try not to get involved with bank transfers and such during your stay, as it'll most likely be an expensive exercise in bureaucratic frustration. For those who must wire money to or from Panama, the best option is to use Western Union or Moneygram, which have many outlets throughout the country.

TRAVELERS CHECKS

Travelers checks are difficult to cash in Panama. Merchants are reluctant to accept them since banks treat them as foreign checks and put a 45-day hold on them before the merchants' accounts get credited. Travelers checks are generally more nuisance than they are worth. Often banks are the only place to cash them, and some banks have begun to refuse them. Trying to cash anything other than American Express checks is even more difficult. Given the ubiquity of ATMs, it's better to rely on cash cards than travelers checks in Panama. It's still a good idea, however, to bring some travelers checks as a backup, or as way to prove economic solvency when crossing borders.

CREDIT CARDS

Credit cards are widely accepted in the cities, especially in the more upscale hotels and restaurants and most stores of any size. Visa and Mastercard are the most widely accepted. Other cards can generally only be used in the most cosmopolitan establishments, such as five-star hotels. Simpler hotels and restaurants are often cash only, as are most personal services (taxis, tour guides, small outfitters, etc). The farther away one gets from an urban center, the less likely it is credit cards will be accepted. Bring lots of small bills to more remote parts of Panama, such as the Comarca de Kuna Yala (San Blas Islands), where credit cards are not accepted and larger denominations are hard to break. Casinos can be a good place to break larger bills. Some businesses in Bocas del Toro still impose a surcharge on credit-card purchases; ask ahead of time.

TAXES AND TIPPING

A 10 percent tourism tax is added to hotel room bills. Room prices quoted in this book include the tax unless specified. Panama sales tax is 7 percent. The airport departure tax for those leaving the country is US$40; it is now generally included in the price of the air ticket.

It's customary to tip 10 percent in restaurants. Bellhops, porters, and others who perform special services should be tipped. How much to tip depends on the service and the discretion of the tipper. Anywhere from US$0.25 to US$1 should do it for minor services. Porters at the international airport expect a buck a bag. Taxi drivers do not expect a tip.

In rural areas, park rangers and other workers sometimes provide guide services, cook food, tote luggage, etc., for campers and hikers. It's good karma to tip at least US$5 a day for these services on top of the camping or transportation fees.

BARGAINING AND DISCOUNTS

Haggling is not the norm in Panama. It's sometimes possible to get a slight break on major purchases, such as expensive electronics, or on handicrafts, such as *molas* (blouses), but don't expect much. Crafts sellers will sometimes start out with an inflated price but they quickly come down to a firm offer and are unlikely to budge. It's always worth asking if there's some kind of *descuento* (discount), though. There may be a price break for buying more than one item; those willing to buy two or more *molas,* for instance, can sometimes get a break.

Senior and student discounts are generally only available to Panamanians and resident expatriates, not visitors. In fact, in some places, such as the national parks, there is a two-tier system of fees, with foreigners expected to pay more than residents. It may be possible to get a student or senior discount at museums and the like, though the entrance fee is usually so small to begin with it's probably not worth bothering with.

Maps and Tourist Information

MAPS

Tourist maps of Panama and Panama City are getting better, but even the best ones are instantly out of date. New roads, bridges, and buildings just go up too fast. The maps recommended here are widely available online, especially through online bookstores such as Amazon.com.

National Geographic's **Panama Adventure Map** (http://shop.nationalgeographic.com), part of its "adventureMAP" series, is the best map of the entire country. It's especially useful for outdoorsy types, as it shows elevations clearly and marks all the protected areas.

A map entitled **Panamá: Mapa Guía,** put out by Distribudora Lewis in Panama, has easy-to-read street maps of Panama City, with insets of the areas of most interest to visitors, including Panamá la Vieja. There are also inset maps of David, Santiago, Chitré, and the Panama Canal. There's a decent country map

that highlights beaches, main roads, protected areas, and major towns. It's quite useful and will meet the needs of most travelers.

International Travel Maps and Books (ITMB) has made good Panama maps in the past, but they are not updated frequently.

Every issue of the freebie tourist magazine **Focus Panama** contains fold-out maps of the country, Panama City, Colón, and David. The city maps aren't terribly detailed, but they can be useful. The magazine is widely distributed to hotels, restaurants, and shops frequented by tourists.

Other maps of various quality are available in Panama, especially Panama City. Best bets in Panama City include Exedra Books, Librería Argosy, and El Hombre de la Mancha bookstores, Farmacia Arrocha drugstores, or Gran Morrison department-store outlets.

The **Instituto Geográfico Nacional Tommy Guardia** (Vía Simon Bolívar/Transístmica, tel.

236-2444 or 236-1844, fax 235-1841, www. mop.gob.pa, 8 A.M.–3:30 P.M. Mon.–Fri.) in Panama City sells a wide variety of physical, political, and topographical maps of the country, including a nine-sheet 1:12,500 scale map just of Panama City. The prices are low, but most of its maps are too large and detailed to be of use to most visitors. Many of the more popular maps, including ones of central Panama City, are frequently unavailable. The place is affectionately known as "Tommy Guardia" and most taxi drivers should know it. It's on the north side of the Transístmica directly across the street from the Universidad de Panamá. The **Islamorada Internacional** (Bldg. 808, Avenida Arnulfo Arias Madrid/Balboa Road, tel. 228-4348 or 228-6069, www.islamorada. com, 8 A.M.–5 P.M. Mon.–Fri.) store in Balboa is an excellent resource for those who need nautical charts.

TOURIST INFORMATION

Large-scale tourism is still a new concept for Panama, and getting good, accurate, and current tourist information in the country is not always easy. Take everything you read and hear with a grain of salt, as much of the material out there is more interested in promoting tourism and selling real estate than giving balanced information.

The best way to get current information on Panama before a trip is through the Internet. A good place to start is **www.panamainfo. com,** an enthusiastically pro-Panama-tourism site that consistently has the most up-to-date information of any of the overview sites. It's written in both English and Spanish. Panama's government tourism sites are **www. visitpanama.com** and **www.atp.gob.pa.** They contain some useful information, such as an updated schedule of festivals and holidays.

The Panamanian newspaper with the best and most extensive coverage of tourist destinations and promotional deals is ***La Prensa,*** a daily widely available throughout the country. It has a good website that gives free access to most of its content, including its archives: www.prensa.com.

Panama's government tourism agency, the **Instituto Panameño de Turismo** (Panamanian Tourism Institute, international toll-free numbers listed on website, www.visit-panama.com), widely known as IPAT (EE-pat), provides little actual information to tourists. Each change of government brings new optimism that IPAT will be galvanized into action, usually with mixed results at best.

IPAT has both small information booths and massive tourist-information complexes known as CEFATIs (Centros de Facilidades Turísticas e Interpretación, which roughly translates to tourist and interpretative centers) dotted around the country. These sometimes have minimally informative printed information, but the attendants often know surprisingly little about the area's attractions and rarely speak anything other than Spanish. CEFATIs are sometimes worth a visit for their displays on the history and culture of the given area.

Film and Photography

EQUIPMENT

Good-quality cameras are widely available around Panama, particularly Panama City. Don't expect great deals, though—the equipment is probably at least as expensive as it is back home. Good places to shop for photo equipment in Panama City are the walking section of Avenida Central, along Vía España, and at the huge Panafoto store on Calle 50. The latter is also a good bet for photo processing for you nondigital types. It's not worth shopping for photo equipment in the Colón Free Zone unless you're in the market for a dozen cameras or so. Film is easy to come by; try any of the pharmacy chains, such as the omnipresent Farmacia Arrocha.

Disposable cameras are widely available, waterproof disposable cameras less so. Bring a disposable underwater camera or a waterproof case from home if you expect to spend much time snorkeling or diving; the photo possibilities can be spectacular.

TIPS

Bring a couple of large, sturdy plastic bags to wrap the camera in to protect it from Panama's sudden torrential downpours and sloshing from boat trips, as well as sand and salt near the ocean. The country's heat and humidity are hard on cameras, film, and memory sticks; try to keep them in as cool a place as possible. Also,

allow time for the camera to adjust from the air-conditioned indoors to the steamy outdoors.

The light is usually best in the early morning and late afternoon, but the sun rises and sets fast near the equator, so work quickly. The scenery can get washed out by the sun around midday.

PHOTO ETIQUETTE

Always ask permission before taking someone's picture. Snapping away at a "colorful local" is a good way to offend someone's dignity. Do not take photos of police or sensitive government installations. In a Kuna village, always ask first and expect to pay for the privilege of taking someone's photo. The going rate is US$1 per subject.

Communications and Media

Panama has a relatively free and aggressive press, certainly in comparison with the days of the military dictatorship, which controlled and censored the press either directly or through intimidation and violence. But Panama continues to be widely criticized for restrictive and antiquated laws that, for instance, make it a criminal offense for a journalist to "insult" public officials, even if the criticism is factually accurate. Newspaper reporters, TV journalists, and editorial cartoonists continue to be arrested and fined for these and other "offenses." While journalists are usually released quickly, international press-freedom organizations have denounced the laws and worry about the chilling effect it has on the media. Physical attacks, threats, and harassment of journalists sometimes occur as well. Despite new transparency laws, it remains difficult for journalists to get access to many government documents and records that are publicly available in other countries.

As in the United States and elsewhere, there is also concern about concentration of media ownership in the hands of a powerful few, including those with their own political agendas.

NEWSPAPERS

Panama has an abundance of Spanish-language daily newspapers, all headquartered in Panama City, but most are widely available throughout the country. Panama's various news outlets tend to have allegiances to parties, political stances, and families, which can color what they cover and how they cover it.

The best of the bunch is *La Prensa,* which is comparable to a major U.S. daily. It has a bewildering array of weekly supplements, on everything from fashion to health, and does the best job of any paper in covering tourism and other topics likely to be of interest to visitors. *El Panamá América* and *La Estrella de Panamá* are fallbacks if *La Prensa* is sold out. Panama also has popular tabloids, notably *La Crítica* and *El Siglo,* which specialize in gory, sensationalist crime stories and inflammatory political topics.

Panama no longer has a major daily English-language paper. In 2007, *La Estrella* introduced an English-language supplement, the *Panama Star,* in all but its Sunday editions. The best sources for English-language news are online, particularly www.panama-guide.com. Bocas del Toro (the *Bocas Breeze*) and Boquete (the *Bajarque Times*) now have small, local newspapers in English.

There are also three well-established Chinese-language newspapers that cater to the large Chinese immigrant population.

TELEVISION AND RADIO

For years Panama had just two television stations: RPC (channel 4) and TVN (channel 2), as well as the U.S. armed forces station (SCN, channel 8 on the Pacific side of the isthmus and channel 11 on the Caribbean side). The armed forces stations disappeared with the closing of the American bases, but several other networks, including Telemetro (channel 13, which is owned by the company that owns RPC) have popped up in recent years. The entire country is increasingly plugging into "cable" television—actually satellite TV—through DirecTV and the plethora of Spanish- and English-language stations it offers.

The country's airwaves are crammed with the sounds of radio stations, most offering *típico,* Latin pop, and mainstream American rock. English-language talk shows, usually aimed at older expatriate residents, are beginning to appear. Radio Metropolis (93.5 FM) has a Sunday night show 6–10 P.M. that can also be heard online at www.pbcpanama.com. Ultra Stereo (98.9 FM) has a morning talk and music show 8–10 A.M. Monday–Friday.

TELEPHONE SERVICES

The country code for Panama is 507. Do not dial 507 when making calls within the country. Cellular phone numbers begin with the number "6" and have eight digits compared with seven for landlines. These can be more expensive to call, but they're often the best way to contact someone.

The emergency number for the **police** *(policía nacional)* is 104. The emergency number for the **fire department** *(bomberos)* is 103. In smaller communities, these numbers don't always work; you have to dial a local number instead. Ask a resident or call directory assistance for help. **Directory assistance** *(asistencia al directorio)* is 102. The **national operator** can be reached at 101. To reach the **international operator,** dial 106.

Panama is finally rolling out an official emergency medical response service, starting with the major urban areas. Dial 911 to call an ambulance (note that this is only for medical help; dial 104 for the police). This service, *Sistema Único de Manejo de Emergencias* (translation: Unified System for the Management of Emergencies, http://www.sume911.pa/) is new, and how well it works will take time to ascertain. If an ambulance doesn't come fast, your best bet may be to grab a taxi and get to the closest hospital.

Pay phones pop up in the most unlikely places, including dirt-poor villages and islands in the middle of nowhere. Long-distance calls within the country generally cost no more than US$0.15 per minute. Instructions on using modern pay phones are in English and several other languages, but finding one that actually works can sometimes be a problem. Also, many of these phones accept only prepaid calling cards.

Those with an unlocked cell phone should consider buying a local SIM card. They're available from outlets of Panama's main telephone service provider, Cable and Wireless (C&W), and from a competing company, Movistar. They cost about US$1 and usually include a usage credit. They're used in conjunction with C&W's prepaid Móvil phone cards in denominations up to US$50. These disposable cards contain a code that the user enters into the phone, which is then credited for the amount (instructions are in Spanish and English). Calling rates are quite reasonable, so don't buy a larger denomination than you're likely to need. The Móvil cards are easy to find, as they're sold in stores and vending machines around the country. However, low-denomination credits expire more quickly.

Some Internet cafés offer international calling and fax services. Calls can be quite reasonable (e.g., US$0.15 per minute to the United States), but check carefully before sending or receiving a fax. International fax service isn't that common at most of these places, and the charges can be steep, especially to send. It's not unusual to be charged US$1 a page to receive and up to US$5 a page to send, plus international dialing charges. The high-end hotels tend to have business centers with computer and phone services.

The international access code for placing direct calls from Panama is "00" followed by the country code. The country code for the continental United States or Canada is 1, the United Kingdom is 44, Spain is 34, Germany is 49, France is 33, Australia is 61, Costa Rica is 506, Nicaragua is 505, Colombia is 57, and Mexico is 52. Check a local phone book or call the international operator (106) for other access codes and for help making a call.

MAIL SERVICE

Mail between Panama and other countries is not too speedy. A postcard sent from Panama takes at least 5–10 days to reach the United States, and longer to more distant destinations. Postcards to the United States cost US$0.25. Airmail letters weighing up to 20 grams (0.7 ounce) cost US$0.35. Add US$0.05 to postcards and airmail letters for Canada addresses, US$0.10 for European ones, and US$0.15 for addresses in Asia, Africa, and Oceania. Some of the more expensive hotels sell stamps. Note that bulky packages sent to or from Panama sometimes get "lost" in the mail.

Do not put tape (Scotch tape, etc.) on an envelope; the post office may refuse to accept it or return international mail that has tape on it. One explanation I've heard for this strange rule is that it discourages thieves from opening mail and then resealing the envelope to hide the crime.

Post office hours are generally 7 A.M.–6 P.M. Monday–Friday, 7 A.M.–5 P.M. Saturday. Post offices are closed on Sunday.

Another oddity about mail in Panama is there is no home delivery; even in modern Panama City, everyone must have mail sent to an *apartado postal* (post-office box). Frustration with slow and sometimes unreliable postal service has driven many who can afford it to subscribe to private mail and courier services, some of which are only slightly more satisfying.

There are a number of international mailing and shipping stores in Panama City. Mail Boxes Etc. has outlets around the city, including one at Vía España and Calle 61 and one in the Albrook Mall next to the Gran Terminal de Transportes. They also have fax services.

INTERNET ACCESS

Internet cafés are everywhere in Panama. You will have little trouble finding one in the cities, and they're beginning to pop up in fairly remote areas as well. Charges are rarely more than a dollar or two an hour, often less. Most of these cafés use Windows-based machines. Free Wi-Fi is proliferating all over the country, particularly in mid-price hotels and businesses that cater to tourists. Macintoshes are sometimes available as well.

Panamanian websites are rarely designed to work with any browser but Internet Explorer.

Weights and Measures

Panama uses the metric system, though auto fuel is sold by the gallon, and pounds, inches, and feet are still sometimes used interchangeably with their metric equivalents.

ELECTRICITY

Panama's voltage is almost universally the same as it is in the United States: 110 volts. Sockets are two-pronged, and U.S. appliances don't need an adapter. There are still a few remote places that use 220 volts, however, so if there's any doubt, ask before plugging in. Note that short blackouts and power surges are common in Panama. Those traveling with sensitive equipment, such as a laptop computer, may want to bring a surge suppresser.

TIME ZONE

Panama is on eastern standard time. There is no daylight savings time in Panama, so the time difference with U.S. destinations changes by an hour during daylight savings time in the United States. Put another way, Panama time is five hours behind Greenwich Mean Time. Panama is always one hour ahead of Costa Rica, something to remember when crossing the border.

Holidays

If you are in Panama around Christmas, New Year's, Carnaval, Semana Santa (the week leading up to Easter), or the November independence holidays, be prepared for celebrations and business closures even on days that are not officially listed as holidays. Also note that when holidays fall on a weekday they are often celebrated on a Monday to create a long weekend. In October–November every city, town, and tiny village has a drum corps and marching band that practices incessantly. Some will find the incessant drumming colorful. Others will find it maddening. Check with IPAT (www.visitpanama.com) for exact dates of holidays that change yearly, and for a current list of the many other festivals, fairs, religious observances, and regional celebrations that take place somewhere in the country just about every week. The major national holidays are:

- January 1: Año Nuevo (New Year's Day)
- January 9: Día de los Mártires (Martyrs' Day)
- The four days leading up to Ash Wednesday: Los Carnavales (Carnival Week)
- Friday before Easter Sunday: Viernes Santo (Good Friday)
- May 1: Día del Trabajo (Worker's Day)
- November 3: Separación de Panamá de Colombia (Independence from Colombia)
- November 4: Día Nacional de la Bandera (Flag Day)
- November 10: Primer Grito de Independencia de España (First Call for Independence from Spain)
- November 28: Independencia de Panamá de España (Independence from Spain)
- December 8: Día de Las Madres (Mothers' Day)
- December 25: Navidad (Christmas)

RESOURCES

Glossary

abrazo a hug

Afro-Antillano Panamanian of African descent from the West Indies

Afro-Colonial Panamanian of African descent from the Spanish-Colonial era

águila eagle

apartado postal post office box, often abbreviated to *apartado*

aparthotel apartment-style hotel designed for long-term stays

ardilla squirrel

arnulfista supporter of the Partido Arnulfista, a political party started by Arnulfo Arias

arrecife reef

artesanías handicraft

baina thing (colloquial)

banco bank

barco ship

batido milk and/or fruit shake

biblioteca library

bicicleta bicycle

bienes raices real estate

bohío a thatched-roof, open-sided hut; also called a *rancho*

bombero firefighter

bote boat

botero boatman

brisa breeze

bucero diver

buho owl

caballero gentleman

cacique chief

campesino country person, farmer

cangrejo crab

canoa canoe

caracol shell

carimañola a kind of roll made from ground and boiled yuca that is generally stuffed with meat and then deep fried

carro car

cascada waterfall (also *chorro*)

catedral cathedral

cayo cay, small island

cayuco small dugout canoe

chakara handwoven bag made by the Ngöbe-Buglé

chaquira necklaces made by the Ngöbe-Buglé

chicha fresh juice, usually made from fruit or corn; sometimes alcoholic

chitra sandflea, sand fly, no-see-um

chiva small, often makeshift bus

churro tube-shaped, doughnut-like fried snack

cimarron escaped African slave during Spanish-Colonial era

colectívo shared taxi or van

colono settler, often used in Panama to refer to farmers and ranchers on recently deforested land

comarca in Panama, a semiautonomous reservation for indigenous people

comida corriente fast food

conejo rabbit

conejo pintado agouti paca (literally, "painted rabbit")

congos traditional dances performed by Afro-Colonials on special occasions

criollo native, local

crucero cruise ship

culebra snake

delfin dolphin

desfile parade

dueño owner
equis fer-de-lance snake (literally, "x")
estrella star
extranjero foreigner
finca farm; also, country house
fonda basic restaurant serving comida corriente
fuerte fort
gato cat
gato solo coatimundi, white-nosed coati (literally, "lone cat")
gavilán hawk
gerente manager
guandu a small, pea-like legume
gucamayo macaw
hojaldre fry-bread; a breakfast dish
hospedaje guesthouse; often a low-cost one
hostal a hostel, but can refer to more upscale inns as well
huaca ceremonial treasures buried with the dead; in Panama, usually refers to pre-Colombian gold figurines or modern replicas
iglesia church
joven young person
kiosco kiosk, usually a food or grocery stand
lagarto alligator, usually refers to caiman
lago lake
lancha (boat) launch
lavamático launderette
lavandería a cleaners, especially dry cleaners
librería bookstore
loro parrot
macho de monte Baird's tapir (literally, "man of the mountain")
maleantes thugs, troublemakers, thieves
malpache raccoon
manigordo ocelot
minisuper convenience store
mola Kuna blouse, but generally refers to front panel of mola blouse, which is sold as handicraft made from layers of brightly colored cloth
mono monkey
mono araña spider monkey
mono aullador howler monkey
mono cariblanco white-faced capuchin (monkey)
mono tití Geoffroy's tamarin (monkey)

moto motor scooter
museo museum
naturaleza nature
oso perezoso sloth (literally, "lazy bear")
panadería bakery
panga boat, usually a fiberglass boat with an electric motor
parque park
patacones twice-fried green plantains
patoca jumping pit viper; also mano de piedra (literally, "hand of stone")
perro dog
pesca fishing
pescado fish
piedra pintada boulder with hieroglyphics (literally, "painted stone")
piragua large dugout canoe
piscina swimming pool
pollera formal, embroidered dress
puerta door
puerto port
pushboton a hotel designed for private sexual encounters; also called a push (from the english word "pushbutton," so-called because patrons have little contact with management)
quebrada brook, ravine
rabiblanco pejorative term for Panama's white ruling elite (literally, "white tail")
rana frog
rancho thatched roof, open-sided hut; also called a bohío
refresquería snack or refreshment bar
reggaeton music form that blends reggae, rap, and dancehall
residencial low-cost accommodations, similar to hospedaje
restaurante restaurant
saíno peccary; also called puerco de monte (literally, "mountain pork")
saludos greetings; usually used in letters
salvavidas life jacket or lifeguard
sapo toad
seco dry; also the name of a popular Panamanian alcohol made from sugarcane
sendero trail
serpente serpent
tagua ivory nut
taller workshop

tigre tiger, but often used in Panama to refer to jaguar

típico literally "typical," but in Panama also refers to *música típica,* a dance-music form that features traditional elements such as accordion and yodeling

tortuga turtle

vegetariano vegetarian

velero sailboat

verrugosa bushmaster snake

viento wind

COMMONLY USED ABBREVIATIONS

ANAM Autoridad Nacional del Ambiente; Panama's national environmental authority

ATP Autoidad de Turismo de Panameño; Panama's government tourism institute, formerly known as IPAT

CEFATI Centro de Facilidades Turísticas e Interpretación; large tourist-information centers run by ATP (roughly, "tourist and interpretative center")

INAC Instituto National de Cultura (Panama's national institute of culture); government agency that runs the country's museums and other cultural institutions and events

PA Partido Arnulfista; a political party

PILA Parque Internacional La Amistad; an international park shared by Panama and Costa Rica

PRD Partido Revolucionario Democrático; a political party

STRI Smithsonian Tropical Research Institute

Suntracs Sindicato Único de Trabjadores de la Construcción y Similares; a construction workers' union

Spanish Phrasebook

Your Panamanian adventure will be more fun if you use a little Spanish. Panamanian folks, although they may smile at your funny accent, will appreciate your halting efforts to break the ice and transform yourself from a foreigner to a potential friend.

Spanish commonly uses 30 letters – the familiar English 26, plus four straightforward additions: ch, ll, ñ, and rr, which are explained in *Consonants.*

PRONUNCIATION GUIDE

Once you learn them, Spanish pronunciation rules – in contrast to English – don't change. Spanish vowels generally sound softer than in English. (Note: The capitalized syllables receive stronger accents.)

Vowels

a like ah, as in "hah": *agua* AH-gooah (water), *pan* PAHN (bread), and *casa* CAH-sah (house)

e like ay, as in "may:" *mesa* MAY-sah (table), *tela* TAY-lah (cloth), and *de* DAY (of, from)

i like ee, as in "need": *diez* dee-AYZ (ten), *comida* ko-MEE-dah (meal), and *fin* FEEN (end)

o like oh, as in "go": *peso* PAY-soh (weight), *ocho* OH-choh (eight), and *poco* POH-koh (a bit)

u like oo, as in "cool": *uno* OO-noh (one), *cuarto* KOOAHR-toh (room), and *usted* oos-TAYD (you); when it follows a "q" the **u** is silent; when it follows an "h" or has an umlaut, it's pronounced like "w."

Consonants

b, d, f, k, l, m, n, p, q, s, t, v, w, x, y, z, and ch
pronounced almost as in English; **h** occurs, but is silent – not pronounced at all.

c like k as in "keep": *cuarto* KOOAR-toh (room), Tepic tay-PEEK (capital of Nayarit state); when it precedes "e" or "i," pronounce **c** like s, as in "sit": *cerveza* sayr-VAY-sah (beer), *encima* ayn-SEE-mah (atop).

g like g as in "gift" when it precedes "a," "o," "u," or a consonant: *gato* GAH-toh (cat), *hago* AH-goh (I do, make); otherwise, pronounce **g** like h as in "hat": *giro* HEE-roh (money order), *gente* HAYN-tay (people).

j like h, as in "has": *Jueves* HOOAY-vays (Thursday), *mejor* may-HOR (better)

ll like y, as in "yes": *toalla* toh-AH-yah (towel), *ellos* AY-yohs (they, them)

ñ like ny, as in "canyon": *año* AH-nyo (year), *señor* SAY-nyor (Mr., sir)

r is lightly trilled, with tongue at the roof of your mouth like a very light English d, as in "ready": *pero* PAY-doh (but), *tres* TDAYS (three), *cuatro* KOOAH-tdoh (four).

rr like a Spanish r, but with much more emphasis and trill. Let your tongue flap. Practice with *burro* (donkey), *carretera* (highway), and Carrillo (proper name), then really let go with *ferrocarril* (railroad).

Note: The single small but common exception to all of the above is the pronunciation of Spanish **y** when it's being used as the Spanish word for "and," as in "Ron y Kathy." In such case, pronounce it like the English ee, as in "keep": Ron "ee" Kathy (Ron and Kathy).

Accent

The rule for accent, the relative stress given to syllables within a given word, is straightforward. If a word ends in a vowel, an n, or an s, accent the next-to-last syllable; if not, accent the last syllable.

Pronounce *gracias* GRAH-seeahs (thank you), *orden* OHR-dayn (order), and *carretera* kah-ray-TAY-rah (highway) with stress on the next-to-last syllable.

Otherwise, accent the last syllable: *venir* vay-NEER (to come), *ferrocarril* fay-roh-cah-REEL (railroad), and *edad* ay-DAHD (age).

Exceptions to the accent rule are always marked with an accent sign: (á, é, í, ó, or ú), such as *teléfono* tay-LAY-foh-noh (telephone), *jabón* hah-BON (soap), and *rápido* RAH-pee-doh (rapid).

BASIC AND COURTEOUS EXPRESSIONS

Most Spanish-speaking people consider formalities important. Whenever approaching anyone for information or some other reason, do not forget the appropriate salutation – good morning, good evening, etc. Standing alone, the greeting *hola* (hello) can sound brusque.

Hello. *Hola.* But in Panama, *buenas* is more commonly used in informal greetings.

Good morning. *Buenos días.*

Good afternoon. *Buenas tardes.*

Good evening. *Buenas noches.*

How are you? *¿Cómo está usted?*

Very well, thank you. *Muy bien, gracias.*

Okay; good. *Bien.*

Not okay; bad. *Mal* or *feo.*

So-so. *Más o menos.*

And you? *¿Y usted?*

Thank you. *Gracias.*

Thank you very much. *Muchas gracias.*

You're very kind. *Muy amable.*

You're welcome. *De nada.*

Goodbye. *Adios.*

See you later. *Hasta luego.*

please *por favor*

yes *sí*

no *no*

I don't know. *No sé.*

Just a moment, please. *Momentito, por favor.*

Excuse me, please (when you're trying to get attention). *Disculpe* or *Con permiso.*

Excuse me (when you've made a boo-boo). *Lo siento.*

Pleased to meet you. *Mucho gusto.*

Closed *Cerrado*

Open *Abierto*

What is your name? *¿Cómo se llama usted?*

My name is . . . *Me llamo . . .*

How do you say...in Spanish? *¿Cómo se dice...en español?*

Do you speak English? *¿Habla usted inglés?*

Is English spoken here? (Does anyone here speak English?) *¿Se habla inglés?*

I don't speak Spanish well. *No hablo bien el español.*

I don't understand. *No entiendo.*

Would you like . . . *¿Quisiera usted . . .*

Let's go to . . . *Vamos a . . .*

TERMS OF ADDRESS

When in doubt, use the formal *usted* (you) as a form of address.

I *yo*
you (formal) *usted*
you (familiar) *tú*
he/him *él*
she/her *ella*
we/us *nosotros*
you (plural) *ustedes*
they/them *ellos* (all males or mixed gender); *ellas* (all females)
Mr., sir *señor*
Mrs., madam *señora*
miss, young lady *señorita*
wife *esposa*
husband *esposo*
friend *amigo* (male); *amiga* (female)
sweetheart *novio* (male); *novia* (female)
son; daughter *hijo; hija*
brother; sister *hermano; hermana*
father; mother *padre; madre*
grandfather; grandmother *abuelo; abuela*

TRANSPORTATION

Where is . . .? *¿Dónde está . . .?*
How far is it to . . .? *¿A cuánto está . . .?*
from...to . . . *de...a . . .*
How many blocks? *¿Cuántas cuadras?*
Where (Which) is the way to . . .? *¿Dónde está el camino a . . .?*
the bus station *la terminal de autobuses*
the bus stop *la parada de autobuses*
Where is this bus going? *¿Adónde va este autobús?*
the ship *el barco*
the taxi stand *la parada de taxis*
the train station *la estación de ferrocarril*
the airport *el aeropuerto*
I'd like a ticket to . . . *Quisiera un boleto a . . .*
first (second) class *primera (segunda) clase*
round-trip *ida y vuelta*
reservation *reservación*
baggage *equipaje*
Stop here, please. *Pare aquí, por favor.*
the entrance *la entrada*
the exit *la salida*

the ticket office *la oficina de boletos*
(very) near; far *(muy) cerca; lejos*
to; toward *a*
by; through *por*
from *de*
the right *la derecha*
the left *la izquierda*
straight ahead *derecho; directo*
in front *en frente*
beside *al lado*
behind *atrás*
the corner *la esquina*
the stoplight *la semáforo*
a turn *una vuelta*
right here *aquí*
somewhere around here *por acá*
right there *allí*
somewhere around there *por allá*
avenue *avenida*
road *camino*
street *calle*
highway *carretera*
toll road *autopista, corredor* (in Panama)
bridge; toll *puente; cuota*
address *dirección*
north; south *norte; sur*
east; west *este; oeste*

ACCOMMODATIONS

hotel *hotel*
room *habitación, cuarto*
standard room *habitación estandar*
Is there a room? *¿Hay habitación?*
May I (may we) see it? *¿Puedo (podemos) verlo?*
What is the rate? *¿Cuál es el precio?*
Is that your best rate? *¿Es su mejor precio?*
Is there something cheaper? *¿Hay algo más económico?*
a single room *una habitación sencilla*
a double room *una habitación doble*
double bed *cama matrimonial*
twin beds *camas gemelas*
with private bath *con baño*
hot water *agua caliente*
luxury *lujo*
shower *ducha*
towels *toallas*

soap *jabón*
toilet paper *papel higiénico*
blanket *frazada; manta*
sheets *sábanas*
air-conditioned *aire acondicionado*
fan *abanico*
key *llave*
manager *gerente*

FOOD

I'm hungry *Tengo hambre.*
I'm thirsty. *Tengo sed.*
menu *lista; menú*
order *orden*
glass *vaso*
fork *tenedor*
knife *cuchillo*
plate *plato*
spoon *cuchara*
kitchen *cocina*
spicy *picante* (*caliente* is used only for hot in temperature, not "hot" with chilis)
napkin *servilleta*
soft drink *refresco*
coffee *café*
tea *té*
drinking water *agua pura; agua potable*
bottled carbonated water *agua mineral*
bottled uncarbonated water *agua sin gas*
beer *cerveza*
wine *vino*
milk *leche*
juice *jugo*
cream *crema*
sugar *azúcar*
cheese *queso*
breakfast *desayuno*
lunch *almuerzo*
dinner *cena*
the check *la cuenta*
eggs *huevos*
bread *pan*
salad *ensalada*
fruit *fruta*
apple *manzana*
banana *plátano; banana*
blackberry *zarzamora*
guava *guayaba*

lemon *limón*
lime *lima*
mango *mango*
orange *naranja*
papaya *papaya*
passion fruit *maracuya*
soursop *guanábana*
strawberry *fresa*
watermelon *sandía*
fish *pescado*
mero *grouper*
shellfish *mariscos*
red snapper *pargo rojo*
shrimp *camarones*
trout *trucha*
meat (without) *(sin) carne*
chicken *pollo*
pork *puerco*
beef; steak *res; bistec*
bacon; ham *tocino; jamón*
fried *frito*
roasted *asada*
grilled *a la parilla*
barbecue; barbecued *barbacoa; al carbón*

SHOPPING

money *dinero*
money-exchange bureau *casa de cambio*
I would like to exchange travelers checks. *Quisiera cambiar cheques de viajero.*
What is the exchange rate? *¿Cuál es el tipo de cambio?*
How much is the commission? *¿Cuánto cuesta la comisión?*
Do you accept credit cards? *¿Aceptan tarjetas de crédito?*
money order *giro*
How much does it cost? *¿Cuánto cuesta?*
What is your final price? *¿Cuál es su último precio?*
expensive *caro*
cheap *barato; económico*
more *más*
less *menos*
a little *un poco*
too much *demasiado*
clothing *ropa*
jewelry *joyas*

HEALTH

Help me please. *Ayúdeme por favor.*
I am ill. *Estoy enfermo.*
Call a doctor. *Llame un doctor.*
Take me to . . . *Lléveme a . . .*
hospital *hospital*
drugstore *farmacia*
pain *dolor*
fever *fiebre*
headache *dolor de cabeza*
stomachache *dolor de estómago*
burn *quemadura*
cramp *calambre*
nausea *náusea*
vomiting *vomitar*
medicine *medicina*
antibiotic *antibiótico*
pill; tablet *pastilla*
aspirin *aspirina*
ointment; cream *pomada; crema*
bandage *venda*
cotton *algodón*
sanitary napkins use brand name; e.g., Kotex
birth control pills *pastillas anticonceptivas*
contraceptive foam *espuma anticonceptiva*
condoms *preservativos; condones*
toothbrush *cepilla dental*
dental floss *hilo dental*
toothpaste *crema dental*
dentist *dentista*
toothache *dolor de muelas*

POST OFFICE AND COMMUNICATIONS

long-distance telephone *teléfono larga distancia*
I would like to call . . . *Quisiera llamar a . . .*
collect *por cobrar*
station to station *a quien contesta*
person to person *persona a persona*
credit card *tarjeta de crédito*
post office *correo*
general delivery *entrega general*
letter *carta*
stamp *estampilla, timbre*
postcard *tarjeta*
aerogram *aerograma*

air mail *correo aereo*
registered *registrado*
money order *giro*
package; box *paquete; caja*
string; tape *cuerda; cinta*

AT THE BORDER

border *frontera*
customs *aduana*
immigration *migración*
tourist card *tarjeta de turista*
inspection *inspección; revisión*
passport *pasaporte*
profession *profesión*
marital status *estado civil*
single *soltero*
married; divorced *casado; divorciado*
widowed *viudado*
insurance *seguros*
title *título*
driver's license *licencia de manejar*

AT THE GAS STATION

gas station *gasolinera*
gasoline *gasolina*
unleaded *sin plomo*
full, please *lleno, por favor*
tire *llanta*
tire repair *reparación de llantas*
air *aire*
water *agua*
oil (change) *aceite (cambio)*
grease *grasa*
My...doesn't work. *Mi...no sirve.*
battery *batería*
radiator *radiador*
alternator *alternador*
generator *generador*
repair shop *taller mecánico*

VERBS

Verbs are the key to getting along in Spanish. They employ mostly predictable forms and come in three classes, which end in *ar, er,* and *ir,* respectively:

to buy *comprar*
I buy, you (he, she, it) buys *compro, compra*

we buy, you (they) buy *compramos, compran*
to eat *comer*
I eat, you (he, she, it) eats *como, come*
we eat, you (they) eat *comemos, comen*
to climb *subir*
I climb, you (he, she, it) climbs *subo, sube*
we climb, you (they) climb *subimos, suben*
Got the idea? Here are more (with irregularities marked in **bold**).
to do or make *hacer*
I do or make, you (he she, it) does or makes *hago, hace*
we do or make, you (they) do or make *hacemos, hacen*
to go *ir*
I go, you (he, she, it) goes *voy, va*
we go, you (they) go *vamos, van*
to go (walk) *andar*
to love *amar*
to work *trabajar*
to want *desear, querer*
to need *necesitar*
to read *leer*
to write *escribir*
to repair *reparar*
to stop *parar*
to get off (the bus) *bajar*
to arrive *llegar*
to stay (remain) *quedar*
to stay (lodge) *hospedar*
to leave *salir* (regular except for **salgo,** I leave)
to look at *mirar*
to look for *buscar*
to give *dar* (regular except for **doy,** I give)
to carry *llevar*
to have *tener* (irregular but important: **tengo, tiene,** *tenemos,* **tienen**)
to come *venir* (similarly irregular: **vengo, viene,** *venimos,* **vienen**)

Spanish has two forms of "to be." Use *estar* when speaking of location or a temporary state of being: "I am at home." ***"Estoy** en casa."* "I'm sick." ***"Estoy** enfermo."* Use *ser* for a permanent state of being: "I am a doctor." ***"Soy** doctora."*
Estar is regular except for **estoy,** I am. Ser is very irregular:

to be *ser*
I am, you (he, she, it) is *soy, es*
we are, you (they) are *somos, son*

NUMBERS

0 *cero*
1 *uno*
2 *dos*
3 *tres*
4 *cuatro*
5 *cinco*
6 *seis*
7 *siete*
8 *ocho*
9 *nueve*
10 *diez*
11 *once*
12 *doce*
13 *trece*
14 *catorce*
15 *quince*
16 *dieciseis*
17 *diecisiete*
18 *dieciocho*
19 *diecinueve*
20 *veinte*
21 *veinte y uno* or *veintiuno*
30 *treinta*
40 *cuarenta*
50 *cincuenta*
60 *sesenta*
70 *setenta*
80 *ochenta*
90 *noventa*
100 *ciento*
101 *ciento y uno* or *cientiuno*
200 *doscientos*
500 *quinientos*
1,000 *mil*
10,000 *diez mil*
100,000 *cien mil*
1,000,000 *millón*
one-half *medio*
one-third *un tercio*
one-fourth *un cuarto*

TIME
What time is it? *¿Qué hora es?*

It's one o'clock. *Es la una.*
It's three in the afternoon. *Son las tres de la tarde.*
It's 4 A.M. *Son las cuatro de la mañana.*
six-thirty *seis y media*
a quarter till eleven *un cuarto para las once*
a quarter past five *las cinco y cuarto*
an hour *una hora*

DAYS AND MONTHS
Monday *lunes*
Tuesday *martes*
Wednesday *miércoles*
Thursday *jueves*
Friday *viernes*
Saturday *sábado*
Sunday *domingo*
today *hoy*
tomorrow *mañana*

yesterday *ayer*
January *enero*
February *febrero*
March *marzo*
April *abril*
May *mayo*
June *junio*
July *julio*
August *agosto*
September *septiembre*
October *octubre*
November *noviembre*
December *diciembre*
a week *una semana*
a month *un mes*
after *después*
before *antes*

– Adapted from *Moon Pacific Mexico.*
Courtesy of Bruce Whipperman.

Suggested Reading

Some of the books listed are out of print or most readily available in Panama, but even these can generally be special-ordered through bookstores or the Internet.

GENERAL INFORMATION
Espriella III, Ricardo de la. *Panamá: Resumen Histórico Illustrado del Istmo, 1501–1994.* Colombia: Antigua Films, 1994. A slender coffee-table book with historic photos and brief summaries of major events in Panama's history. In Spanish.

Friar, William. *Portrait of the Panama Canal: From Construction to the Twenty-First Century.* Portland, Oregon: Graphic Arts Center Publishing, 2003. A photo-essay book by the author of this travel guide.

Navarro Q., Juan Carlos. *Panama National Parks.* Panama: Ediciones Balboa. A beautiful coffee-table book depicting Panama's national parks. In English and Spanish.

Salvador, Mari Lyn (ed.). *The Art of Being Kuna: Layers of Meaning Among the Kuna of Panama.* University of Washington Press: October 1997. A hefty coffee-table book with fascinating photos and scholarly essays on Kuna life, culture, art, beliefs, and history. The best introduction to the Kunas and their *molas* (blouses).

HISTORY, POLITICS, AND CURRENT EVENTS
Anderson, Dr. C. L. G. *Old Panama and Castilla del Oro.* New York: North River Press, 1911. A fascinating, in-depth account of the Spanish conquest and pirate history of Panama, written by a medical doctor who worked for the Panama Canal during its construction.

Buckley, Kevin. *Panama: The Whole Story.* New York: Simon and Schuster, 1991. Solidly reported and well written, this is the most reliable account of the U.S. invasion that removed Noriega from power in 1989.

Díaz Espino, Ovidio. *How Wall Street Created a Nation: J. P. Morgan, Teddy Roosevelt, and the Panama Canal.* New York: Four Walls Eight Windows, 2001. An impassioned polemic about behind-the-scenes dealings leading to Panama's separation from Colombia and the 1903 Panama Canal treaties.

Dyke, Tom Hart, and Paul Winder. *The Cloud Garden: A True Story of Adventure, Survival, and Extreme Horticulture.* Guilford, Connecticut: Lyons Press, 2004. An alternately funny and horrifying account of two backpackers kidnapped by guerrillas in the Darién jungle in 2000.

Howarth, David. *The Golden Isthmus.* London: Collins, 1966. Also published as *Panama: Four Hundred Years of Dreams and Cruelty.* Contains fascinating tidbits on the exploits of Spanish conquistadors, Elizabethan adventurers, and bloody buccaneers. Becomes unreliable as it enters the modern era.

Howe, James. *A People Who Would Not Kneel: Panama, the United States, and the San Blas Kuna.* Washington: Smithsonian, 1998. Gives interesting insights into the history and culture of the Kuna.

Lindsay-Poland, John. *Emperors in the Jungle: The Hidden History of the U.S. in Panama.* Durham, North Carolina: Duke University Press, 2003. Investigative journalism examining the history of U.S. military involvement in Panama.

McCullough, David. *The Path Between the Seas: The Creation of the Panama Canal, 1870–1914.* New York: Simon and Schuster, 1977. The definitive history of the Panama Canal. An astonishing book that reads like a thriller.

Prebble, John. *The Darien Disaster: A Scots Colony in the New World, 1698–1700.* New York: Holt, Rinehart, and Winston, 1968. A readable account of the doomed Scottish attempt to establish a colony in the Darién jungle.

PANAMA CITY HISTORY

Spanish-speakers interested in learning more about Panama City's history will have their best chance of finding locally written books at local bookstores. However, these generally are academic works produced on a minimal budget and containing far more minute detail than the average reader will have much use for.

Castillero Reyes, Ernesto J. *Leyendas e Historias de Panamá la Vieja.* Panama City: Producciones Erlizca, 2nd edition 1998. The history and legends of Old Panama from its founding to its sacking by Henry Morgan, with crude illustrations and a blurry map of the city during its heyday.

Díaz Szmirnov, Damaris. *Génesis de la Ciudad Republicana.* Panama City: Agenda del Centenario, 2001. A detailed account of the emergence of modern Panama City in the late 19th and early 20th centuries. Though likely to be of most interest to residents, it fills in many gaps in Panama's recent history, something that has not been well documented, especially from a Panamanian perspective. It contains some small but interesting historical photos.

de La Espriella III, Ricardo. *Panamá: Resumen Histórico Ilustrado del Istmo, 1501–1994.* Bogotá: Antigua Films, 1994. A slender coffee-table book with historic photos and brief summaries of major events in Panama's history.

NATURE AND WILDLIFE

Forsyth, Adrian, and Ken Miyata. *Tropical Nature: Life and Death in the Rain Forests of Central and South America.* New York: Simon and Schuster, 1995. An introduction to tropical ecology.

Kircher, John. *A Neotropical Companion: An Introduction to the Animals, Plants, & Ecosystems of the New World Tropics.* Princeton, New Jersey: Princeton University Press, 1999. A detailed explanation of just about anything you'd like to know about the New

World tropics. Reading it will deepen hikers' experience of the forest.

Ventocilla, Jorge, Heraclio Herrera, and Valerio Nunez. Elisabeth King, trans. *Plants & Animals in the Life of the Kuna*. Austin, Texas: University of Texas, 1995. This book is notable for describing flora and fauna, forest life, and environmental destruction in Kuna Yala from the point of view of the Kuna themselves, often in their own words.

Wong, Marina and Ventocilla, Jorge. *A Day on Barro Colorado Island*. Panama: Smithsonian, 1995. A slim volume that contains an overview of the flora and fauna of the island and a detailed trail map.

FIELD GUIDES

Reid, Fiona A. *A Field Guide to the Mammals of Central America and Southeast Mexico*. New York: Oxford University Press, 1998. Comprehensive illustrated guide to mammals found in Panama, including aquatic ones. Includes range maps, descriptions, habitats, and habits. The English and Spanish names, nicknames, and regional names of species are included, which is a nice touch.

Ridgely, Robert S., and John A. Gwynne Jr. *A Guide to the Birds of Panama*. Princeton, New Jersey: Princeton University Press, 1989. Though overdue for an update, this is still the bible of Panama bird-watching. Also contains information on birds found in Costa Rica, Nicaragua, and Honduras.

TRAVEL GUIDES

Pritchard, Raymond, and Audrey Pritchard. *Driving the Pan-American Highway to Mexico and Central America*. Costa Rica: Costa Rica Books, 1997. Quite out of date, but at the time of writing the only guidebook on driving to Panama from North America.

Zydler, Nancy Schwalbe, and Tom Zydler. *The Panama Guide: A Cruising Guide to the Isthmus of Panama*. Port Washington, Wisconsin: Seaworthy Publications, 2001. A guide to yachting destinations along both sides of the isthmus, with detailed tips and 187 charts.

LIFE IN PANAMA

Henderson, Malcolm. *Don't Kill the Cow Too Quick: An Englishman's Adventures Homesteading in Panama*. Lincoln, Nebraska: iUniverse, 2004. Homespun account of an expatriate couple's adventures building their retirement dream in Bocas del Toro.

Henríquez, Cristina. *Come Together, Fall Apart: A Novella and Stories*. New York: Riverhead Books, 2006. Though fiction, this well-written and widely praised collection of short stories will give English-language readers some insight into modern Panamanian life. Henríquez, who has a Panamanian father and gringa mother, grew up in the United States. The best stories explore how it feels to be an expat Panamanian trying to reconnect with one's roots. But some basic facts and flavors of Panamanian life are slightly off.

Knapp, Herbert, and Mary Knapp. *Red, White, and Blue Paradise: The American Canal Zone in Panama*. New York: Harcourt Brace Jovanovich, 1984. An account of life in the old Canal Zone from a couple who lived it.

Snyder, Sandra. *Living in Panama*. Panama: Tantoes, S.A., 2007 (2nd ed.). A thorough guide for expatriates moving to Panama, covering everything from dinner-party etiquette to registering cars. Widely available in Panama or through www.livinginpanam.net.

Internet Resources

There is at last a fair amount of useful information about Panama on the web. However, most websites are badly designed, rarely get updated, and don't work well with any browser other than Internet Explorer. Be especially wary of booking through websites, as their forms often don't work well. There are also plenty of easy-to-find community forums on the Web by and for tourists and resident expatriates.

TRAVEL
Bocas del Toro
www.bocas.com
This visitor-information site for Bocas del Toro contains listings for many hotels, restaurants, and services as well as some background information on Bocas.

Bocas Marine & Tours, S.A.
www.bocasmarinetours.com
Bocas Marine & Tours is a Bocas del Toro water-taxi service, but its site also contains useful, updated maps of the Bocas archipelago and mainland, transportation schedules, and facts about Bocas. However, it is no longer regularly updated.

Boomers Abroad
www.boomersabroad.com/panama.html
This is an overview site for those interested in retiring or investing in Panama. It takes a more measured approach than similar sites, which can be aggressive about hyping Panama.

Journey Latin America
www.journeylatinamerica.co.uk
Journey Latin America is a London-based tour operator and travel agency that's a good place to start for those going to Panama from Europe and points east.

LegalInfo Panamá
www.legalinfo-panama.com
This site contains detailed legal information

for those interested in moving to or doing business in Panama, as well as listings of lawyers and law firms. It's in Spanish with some English content.

Panama
www.visitpanama.com
The official site of Panama's government tourism institute, IPAT. It's in English and Spanish. IPAT also has another, Spanish-only website: www.ipat.gob.pa.

Panamainfo
www.panamainfo.com
Panamainfo is a frequently updated Panama-promotion site that accentuates the positive; it's not the place to go for critical reviews of places or services. Its visitor information is geared primarily toward traveling on a moderate-to-high budget, but it also contains general information for various regions of Panama.

TransPanamá
www.transpanama.org
This is the website for a very cool volunteer-run project to build a trail across Panama from Costa Rica to Colombia. It is also creating a GPS map of the route, which hopefully it will eventually put on this site, which is in English and Spanish. The project welcomes volunteers.

U.S. Department of State
http://travel.state.gov
The website of the U.S. State Department contains general entry requirements and travel warnings for U.S. citizens traveling abroad, listed by country.

The Visitor
www.thevisitorpanama.com
The Visitor/El Visitante is a bilingual tourist newspaper published every two weeks and widely available at tourist haunts in Panama City. Contents include information on

upcoming festivals and events, features on destinations, and reviews of restaurants, primarily in Panama City. Current and back issues are on its website.

ECOTOURISM
Almanaque Azul
www.almanaqueazul.org
The "blue almanac" is a wiki-style guide to the beaches and coasts of Panama meant to raise awareness of conservation issues while providing useful practical information for visiting even the most remote beaches. Anyone can add to the almanac. In Spanish only.

ANCON
www.ancon.org
ANCON is Panama's largest environmental organization. The site contains some information on the country's national parks and a list of endangered species. In Spanish only.

Panama Audubon Society
www.panamaaudubon.org
The Panama Audubon Society organizes frequent bird-watching trips that are open to foreign visitors and listed on its site, which is in Spanish and English.

Planeta
www.planeta.com
Long-established, thoughtful website on ecotourism issues, with practical advice on low-impact travel. It contains some Panama-specific information.

Smithsonian Tropical Research Institute
www.stri.org
The website of the Smithsonian Tropical Research Institute (STRI) contains information on its projects and installations, including Barro Colorado Island. It also shows live video from user-controllable webcams set up on Barro Colorado and Parque Natural Metropolitano.

NEWS SITES
Bajareque Times
www.boquete-bajareque-times.com
Similar to the *Bocas Breeze*, but covering Boquete and the surrounding area.

The Bocas Breeze
www.thebocasbreeze.com
A print and online newspaper run by resident expatriates living in Bocas del Toro. It covers tourism and environmental issues likely to interest visitors. Stories are in English and Spanish. The print edition appears monthly.

Panama-Guide
www.panama-guide.com
The best and most balanced online source for news articles in English, including articles translated from Spanish-language Panamanian newspapers. It's the place to start for information on Panama that is neither promotional nor overly cynical. Though it grinds its share of axes and engages in occasional online feuds, it does a good job of separating news and opinion.

La Prensa
www.prensa.com
Panama's best Spanish-language newspaper. Free registration allows access to its extensive archives.

Rob Rivera
www.rob-rivera.com
Interesting and articulate English-language blog by an up-and-coming Panamanian writer. Rivera offers rare insight into Panamanian life from the perspective of a well-educated young guy who speaks perfect English. Or, as his blog's tagline puts it, "This is where first-world mentality meets a third-world country."

GOVERNMENT
Dirrección Nacional de Migración y Naturalización
http://migracion.gob.pa
The official website of Panama's immigration and naturalization service contains useful

information (in English!) on visa laws and procedures. Note: The pulldown menus for which country's citizens need which visa are "sticky" and don't update properly, sometimes producing misleading results.

Panama Canal Authority
www.pancanal.com
The website for the Panama Canal Authority contains news and history about the Panama Canal, and tide tables for Balboa and Cristóbal. But its coolest features are the live video feeds from the webcams set up at Miraflores Locks, Gatún Locks, and the Centennial Bridge over Gaillard Cut.

República de Panamá
www.pa
General Panamanian government site with telephone listings and links to government ministries and organizations, including the tourism and culture institutes. In Spanish.

MISCELLANEOUS INFORMATION
Centers for Disease Control and Prevention
wwwn.cdc.gov/travel
The U.S. Centers for Disease Control lists comprehensive immunization information and health advisories for destinations around the world.

Central Intelligence Agency
www.cia.gov/library/publications/the-world-factbook
The U.S. Central Intelligence Agency lists statistics and background information on Panama here.

CZBrats and the Lost Paradise
www.czbrats.com, http://lostparadise.com
Nostalgia sites for Zonians, containing photos, stories, and memorabilia from the former Canal Zone.

Paginas Amarillas
www.paginasamarillas.com
Online telephone book for Panama and other Latin American countries.

Index

List of Maps

Acknowledgments

For Karen

Writing a guidebook restores your faith in humanity; you meet so many people who are generous with their time, knowledge, and hospitality. The following are just a few of the many people who made this new edition possible.

I am fortunate to have in my family one of the foremost experts on the Panama Canal: my mother, Willie K. Friar. Her expertise and support—not to mention her networking prowess—were invaluable as always. I don't know how I could ever keep up with the lightning changes in Panama City without help from Mary Coffey, Sandra Snyder, and David Wilson year after year. And trying to do so would be much more difficult and far less pleasant without Clotilde O. de la Guerra and Tony Barrios.

The list of people to thank around the country is now too long for this small space, but I am especially indebted once again to Jane Walker and Barry Robbins in Boquete, Andrea Aster in David, and Carla Rankin in Bocas. Paul Saban and Jim Guy were kind enough to donate terrific photos to the cause. I also am grateful for the many readers who took the time to contact me with tips, updates, and kind remarks.

My colleagues at Avalon once again had to be as patient with me as they are professional. Those who made sure this edition finally saw print include Tiffany Watson, Brice Ticen, and Darren Alessi.

Most of all, I need to thank my wife, Karen, who not only kept the home fires burning during this endless project but also cut and hauled the firewood. I couldn't have done it without her kind heart, patience, wisdom, and loving support.

www.moon.com

MOON.COM is ready to help plan your next trip! Filled with fresh trip ideas and strategies, author interviews, informative travel blogs, a detailed map library, and descriptions of all the Moon guidebooks, Moon.com is all you need to get out and explore the world—or even places in your own backyard. While at Moon.com, sign up for our monthly e-newsletter for updates on new releases, travel tips, and expert advice from our on-the-go Moon authors. As always, when you travel with Moon, expect an experience that is uncommon and truly unique.

MOON IS ON FACEBOOK—BECOME A FAN!
JOIN THE MOON PHOTO GROUP ON FLICKR

MAP SYMBOLS

▭ Expressway		⚓ Highlight		✗ Airfield		⚓ Golf Course
▭ Primary Road		○ City/Town		✈ Airport		🅿 Parking Area
▭ Secondary Road		◉ State Capital		▲ Mountain		Archaeological Site
▭ Unpaved Road		✺ National Capital		✛ Unique Natural Feature		⚲ Church
▭ Trail		★ Point of Interest				⛽ Gas Station
▭ Ferry		• Accommodation		ᔭ Waterfall		Glacier
▭ Railroad		▼ Restaurant/Bar		⚑ Park		Mangrove
▭ Pedestrian Walkway		■ Other Location		⯐ Trailhead		Reef
▭ Stairs		⟁ Campground		⛷ Skiing Area		Swamp

CONVERSION TABLES

°C = (°F - 32) / 1.8
°F = (°C x 1.8) + 32
1 inch = 2.54 centimeters (cm)
1 foot = 0.304 meters (m)
1 yard = 0.914 meters
1 mile = 1.6093 kilometers (km)
1 km = 0.6214 miles
1 fathom = 1.8288 m
1 chain = 20.1168 m
1 furlong = 201.168 m
1 acre = 0.4047 hectares
1 sq km = 100 hectares
1 sq mile = 2.59 square km
1 ounce = 28.35 grams
1 pound = 0.4536 kilograms
1 short ton = 0.90718 metric ton
1 short ton = 2,000 pounds
1 long ton = 1.016 metric tons
1 long ton = 2,240 pounds
1 metric ton = 1,000 kilograms
1 quart = 0.94635 liters
1 US gallon = 3.7854 liters
1 Imperial gallon = 4.5459 liters
1 nautical mile = 1.852 km

MOON PANAMA

Avalon Travel
a member of the Perseus Books Group
1700 Fourth Street
Berkeley, CA 94710, USA
www.moon.com

Editor: Tiffany Watson
Series Manager: Kathryn Ettinger
Copy Editor: Naomi Adler-Dancis
Graphics Coordinator: Darren Alessi
Production Coordinator: Darren Alessi
Cover Designer: Darren Alessi
Map Editor: Brice Ticen
Cartographers: Kat Bennett, Allison Rawley,
  and Chris Henrick
Proofreader: Nikki Ioakimedes
Indexer: Judy Hunt

ISBN-13: 978-1-59880-647-2
ISSN: 1555-9459

Printing History
1st Edition – 2005
3rd Edition – November 2010
5 4 3 2 1

Front cover photo: © Art Wolfe / Artwolfe.Com
Title page: © William Friar
Interior color photos: pages 4-5 Courtesy of Tranquilo
Bay; page 6 (inset) Courtesy of the Panama Canal
Commssion, (bottom) © Brian Gratwicke; page
7 (top left) © William Friar, (top right) Courtesy of
Eclypse de Mar Acqua Lodge, (bottom left) © Thomas
Gorissen, www.thomasgorissen.com, (bottom right)
Courtesy of the Coffee Estate Inn; page 8 Thomas
Gorissen, www.thomasgorissen.com; page 10 (top)
Courtesy of the Coffee Estate Inn, (bottom) ©
William Friar; page 11 (top) Courtesy of Eclypse de
Mar Acqua Lodge, (bottom) © William Friar; page 12
courtesy of the Autoridad del Canal de Panamá; page
13 © William Friar; page 14 © William Friar; page 15
Courtesy of Eclypse de Mar Acqua Lodge; page 16
Courtesy of Paul Saban; page 17 © Karen Friar; page
19 (top) © William Friar, (bottom) Courtesy of the
Coffee Estate Inn

Printed in Canada by Friesens

KEEPING CURRENT

If you have a favorite gem you'd like to see included in the next edition, or see anything
that needs updating, clarification, or correction, please drop us a line. Send your
comments via email to feedback@moon.com, or use the address above.